PSYCHOLOGY

A STUDENT'S HANDBOOK

PSYCHOLOGY

A STUDENT'S HANDBOOK

Michael W. Eysenck

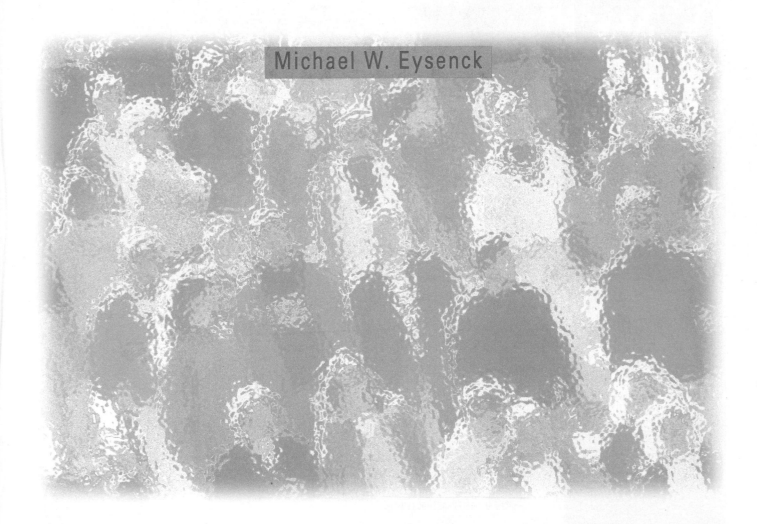

Psychology Press
a member of the Taylor & Francis group

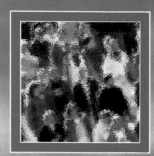

Psychology Press Ltd, Publishers
27 Church Road
Hove
East Sussex, BN3 2FA
UK

British Library Cataloguing in Publication Data

A catalogue record for this book is available from the British Library

ISBN 0-86377-474-1 (Hbk) 21485321
ISBN 0-86377-475-X (Pbk)

Printed in Hong Kong by Midas Printing Limited

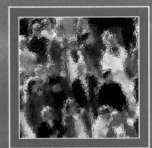

*To William with love
(and also to those other great guitarists
Eric Clapton and Jimi Hendrix)*

*The art of being wise is the art
of knowing what to overlook*

—WILLIAM JAMES

Contents

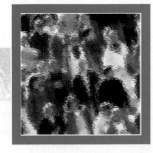

About the Author

Michael W. Eysenck is one of the best-known British psychologists. He is Professor of Psychology and head of the psychology department at Royal Holloway University of London, which is one of the leading departments in the United Kingdom. His academic interests lie mainly in cognitive psychology, with much of his research focusing on the role of cognitive factors in anxiety in normal and clinical populations. He supports Crystal Palace and Wimbledon football clubs, which he feels is probably not a very wise thing to do.

He is an author of many titles, and his previous textbooks published by Psychology Press include *Simply Psychology* (1996), *Cognitive Psychology: A Student's Handbook* (1995, with Mark Keane), *Perspectives on Psychology* (1994), *Individual Differences: Normal and Abnormal* (1994) and *Principles of Cognitive Psychology* (1993). He has also written the research monographs *Anxiety and Cognition: A Unified Theory* (1997) and *Anxiety: The Cognitive Perspective* (1992), along with the popular title *Happiness: Facts and Myths* (1990).

Acknowledgements

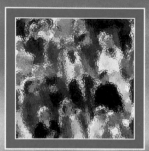

Consultants:	Evie Bentley (Chapters 7, 8, 9 and 10)
	Sara Berman (Chapter 19)
	Anne Brazier (Chapter 11)
	Roz Brody (Chapter 21)
	Eleanor Brown (Chapters 29, 31 and 32)
	Mike Dobson (Chapters 3 and 18)
	Perry Hinton (Chapter 32)
	Judith Lee (Chapters 12, 13 and 15)
	Diana Pilcher (Chapters 14, 23, 24, 26 and 28)
	Emma Robson (Chapters 5, 6, 20 and 22)
	Julie Shearing (Chapters 2, 4, 16, 17, 25, 27 and 30)
Revision questions:	Paul Humphreys
Copy editor:	Jenny Millington
Proof reader:	Michael Wright
Cold reader:	Liz Farrant
Desk editor:	Mark Fisher
Author index:	Ingrid Lock
Subject index:	Christine Boylan
Editorial administrator:	Sarah Webb
Managing editor:	Paul Dukes
Project manager:	Tanya Sagoo
Page design and typesetting:	John Stevens, Facing Pages, Southwick
Drawings and cartoons:	Sean Longcroft, Foghorn Studio, Brighton
Line figures:	Ray Hollidge and Mike O'Malley, Chartwell Illustrators, Croydon
Commissioned photography:	Bipinchandra Mistry, Brighton
Cover design:	Leigh Hurlock, Hurlock Design, Lewes
Printer:	Midas Printing (UK) Limited, London

Preface

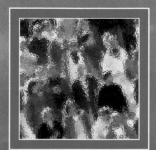

One of the rewards of writing a book is that you learn a lot in the process. For example, I now know there is an athletic event called an ultra marathon, in which the runners have to cover a total of 57 miles. As you might imagine, those who take part in an ultra marathon are absolutely exhausted afterwards, and sleep much longer than usual for the next two nights. I mention all of this because the experience of producing some 450,000 words for this book must be the mental equivalent of running an ultra marathon every week for two years. Hopefully, the task of reading this book will be much less exhausting than writing it has been!

Something else that impressed itself on me when writing this book is that today's student of psychology needs to have a broad *and* a deep understanding of all the main areas of psychology. Refreshingly, there is also a growing emphasis on the importance of cultural differences. It is refreshing because for too long it has been assumed that the behaviour of American college students is representative of the behaviour of people of all ages living in amazingly diverse cultures! This assumption has been convincingly disproved numerous times.

I would like to express my great thanks to those who so kindly agreed to read a first draft of the manuscript or parts of it. They include my wife Christine (who teaches A level psychology at Surbiton High School and Tiffin's Girls School in Kingston), Sarah Buckle (who teaches A level psychology at Tiffin's Girls School), Roz Brody, John Gammon, Simon Green, Mike Stanley, and Paul Humphreys, the Chief Examiner for A level. In addition, John Valentine, Steve Anderson, and Marco Cinnirella of the psychology department at Royal Holloway University of London all provided useful guidance. Their comments have helped considerably to improve the final manuscript by correcting some of my errors and by identifying important omissions. As authors always feel duty-bound to say (but it is absolutely true in my case), any errors or omissions that remain are entirely my responsibility. I would also like to express my thanks to Mike Forster, who is in charge of *Psychology Press*. He has an uncanny knack of coming up with an endless stream of good ideas for books that I might write. More importantly, he has been very supportive of my bookwriting activities for about 15 years so far, and this has encouraged me to keep going.

Finally, I want to thank my family for their total support throughout the writing of this book. Without that support, my life would be poorer and this book would have remained unwritten. The book is dedicated to my dear son, William, who is as yet more interested in playing the guitar than finding out what psychology is all about!

Michael W. Eysenck
ACAPULCO, MEXICO

1

What Is Psychology?

We will start by considering what is meant by psychology. The most common definition of psychology is that it is the scientific study of behaviour. Most psychologists accept that it is very important to observe and to measure behaviour, but it is too limiting to regard psychology simply as the study of behaviour. The reason is that the main interest of psychologists is usually in trying to understand *why* people or members of other species behave in certain ways. In order to achieve that understanding, it is necessary to consider internal processes and motives. We thus arrive at the following definition of psychology: psychology is the science that makes use of behavioural and other evidence to understand the internal processes leading people and members of other species to behave in the ways they do.

Diversity of Psychology

As you read this book, you may be bewildered by the large number of different approaches that psychologists have adopted in their attempts to understand human behaviour. The main reason for the existence of numerous approaches is because our behaviour is jointly determined by several very different factors, such as the following:

- The specific stimuli presented to us.
- Our genetic endowment.
- Our physiological system.
- Our cognitive system (our perceptions, thoughts, and memories).
- The social environment.
- The cultural environment.
- Our previous life experiences (including those of childhood).
- Our personal characteristics (including intelligence, personality, and mental health).

The notion that there are various levels of explanation can be seen if we consider a concrete example. Suppose that a man attacks another man in a very aggressive way by punching him repeatedly on the head and body. How can we understand this behaviour? It may depend in part on the genes that the attacker has inherited from his parents. It may also depend on his childhood experiences, for example, the presence of violence within the family. It may depend in part on the man's clinical history. For example, he may have a history of psychopathic or anti-social behaviour. It may depend on his thoughts and feelings (e.g. he has been frustrated or upset by the other person). It may depend on social factors. For example, the man behaving aggressively may believe that the other man has insulted members of his family. It

Social psychology looks at our relationships with other people and society.

may depend on the physiological state of the man behaving aggressively: his internal bodily state may be highly aroused and agitated. Finally, it may depend on cultural factors, in that expressing one's aggression by punching is regarded as more acceptable (or less unacceptable) in some cultures than others.

The key point of this example is that there is no single "correct" interpretation of the aggressive man's behaviour. Almost certainly, most of the factors just discussed contributed to his behaviour. Thus, the scope of psychology is very broad, because it needs to be if we are to understand human behaviour. Eysenck (1994b, p.15) argued that psychology is a multi-disciplinary science, pointing out that "psychology has been enriched by physiologists, neurologists, sociologists, zoologists, anthropologists, biologists, and others."

Some of the main areas within psychology are as follows: social psychology; comparative psychology; biopsychology; abnormal psychology; cognitive psychology; and developmental psychology. We will now consider very briefly *what* each area is concerned with, and *why* that area is important.

Social psychology

Social psychology serves the valuable function of examining how we relate to other people and to the society in which we live. It is based on the fact that we are social animals. We continually interact with other people, and our behaviour is much influenced by the presence of others. Even when we are alone, we use our social knowledge to make sense of our lives, and we reflect on social events in which we have been involved.

Comparative psychology

Comparative psychology involves studying various non-human species in order to understand the biological and other processes underlying their behaviour. A crucial issue within comparative psychology concerns the extent to which the findings from other species can be generalised to humans. One of the advantages of approaching human psychology

How much can the study of chimpanzee behaviour tell us about the relationship between human mothers and their children?

in this indirect way is that certain important experiments can only be carried out on other species than our own, for ethical reasons.

Biopsychology

Biopsychology is concerned with the attempt to understand human behaviour from the biological perspective. It involves studying physiological processes within the body, the detailed functioning of the brain, and so on. As the processes studied by biopsychologists are involved in all human behaviour, it is clear that the biopsychological perspective is of major importance.

Abnormal psychology

Abnormal psychology is concerned with understanding the causes of mental disorders and with the treatment of those disorders. The notion that such disorders can be understood from a psychological rather than a medical perspective owes most to the influence of Sigmund Freud. The strongest evidence for the importance of abnormal psychology comes from the increased success of therapy, and the reduction in misery thus produced.

Cognitive psychology

Cognitive psychology is concerned with internal processes such as attention, perception, thinking, reasoning, language, and memory. At one time, these processes were mostly studied by means of laboratory tasks. However, it has become increasingly clear that the cognitive approach is of value in understanding developmental issues, social functioning, and the development and treatment of many mental disorders.

Developmental psychology

Developmental psychology is concerned mainly with the changes that occur during the course of childhood, and with the impact of childhood experiences on adult behaviour. Recently, there has been increased emphasis on life-span developmental psychology, which is based on the assumption that individuals change and develop throughout their lives. It is generally agreed that the developmental perspective has proved valuable in shedding light on adult behaviour, as well as revealing patterns of development.

The experiences we have during childhood have a great impact on our adult lives.

Methods in Psychology

As we have seen, psychologists have used several different approaches in order to arrive at a detailed understanding of human behaviour. They also differ among themselves as to the best method or methods to use to achieve that understanding. Many argue that psychology is like other sciences, in that understanding is most likely to result from detailed and well-controlled laboratory studies. In contrast, other psychologists argue that laboratory studies are usually very artificial, and that it is preferable to use a range of non-experimental methods to understand human behaviour. For example, people can be observed going about their everyday lives, they can be interviewed, or they can be studied over time in great detail by means of a case study. Thus, there is a very wide range of techniques available to psychologists.

What is the best way of studying people? There is no clear answer to that question. Each method has its own strengths and limitations, and each method is more appropriately used in some situations than in others (this issue is discussed more fully in Chapter 30). The hope is that by combining information from all methods we will finally achieve the goals of psychology. However, as you will find out when you read this book, we are still a considerable distance away from reaching those goals!

"Psychology Is Just Common Sense"

One of the unusual features of psychology is the way in which everyone is to some extent a psychologist. We all observe the behaviour of other people and of ourselves, and everyone has access to their own conscious thoughts and feelings. One of the main tasks of psychologists is to predict behaviour, and the prediction of behaviour is important in everyday life. The better we are able to anticipate how people will react in any given situation, the more contented and rewarding our social interactions are likely to be.

The fact that everyone is a psychologist has led many people to underestimate the achievements of scientific psychology. If the findings of scientific psychology are in line with common sense, then it can be argued that they tell us nothing we did not already know. On the other hand, if the findings do not accord with common sense, then people often respond "I don't believe it!"

There are various problems with the view that psychology is no better than common sense. It is misleading to assume that common sense forms a coherent set of assumptions about behaviour. This can be seen if we regard proverbs as providers of common-sense views. A girl parted from her lover may be saddened if she thinks of the proverb "Out of sight, out of mind". However, she will be cheered up if she tells herself that "Absence makes the heart grow fonder".

"Look before you leap" vs "He who hesitates is lost".

There are several other pairs of proverbs that express opposite meanings. For example, "Look before you leap" can be contrasted with "He who hesitates is lost", and "Many hands make light work" is the opposite of "Too many cooks spoil the broth". As common sense involves such inconsistent views of human behaviour, it cannot be used as the basis for explaining that behaviour.

The notion that psychology is just common sense can also be disproved by considering psychological studies in which the findings were very different from those most people would have expected. A famous example is the work of Stanley Milgram (1974), which is discussed more fully in Chapter 21. The experimenter divided his participants into pairs to play the roles of teacher and pupil in a simple learning task. The "teacher" was asked to give electric shocks to the "pupil" every time the wrong answer was given, and to increase the shock intensity each time. At 180 volts, the "pupil" yelled "I can't stand the pain", and by 270 volts the response had become an agonised scream. If the "teacher" showed a reluctance to give the shocks, the experimenter (a professor of psychology) urged him or her to continue. (In fact, the "pupil" was a confederate of Milgram, and no electric shocks were really given at all, although the "teachers" did not know this at the time.)

Do you think you would be willing to give the maximum (and potentially deadly) 450-volt shock in this experiment? What percentage of people do you think would be willing to do it? Milgram (1974) found that everyone denied that they personally would do any such thing. Psychiatrists at a leading medical school predicted that only one person in a thousand would go on to the 450-volt stage. In fact, about 60% of Milgram's participants gave the maximum shock. This is 600 times as many people as the expert psychiatrists had predicted! In other words, people are much more conformist and obedient to authority than they realise. There is a strong tendency to go along with the decisions of someone (such as a professor of psychology) who seems to be a competent authority figure.

In sum, we can see that common sense is of little use in understanding and predicting human behaviour. According to most psychologists, the best way of achieving these goals is by means of the experimental and other methods available to the psychological researcher. These methods are discussed in Chapter 31.

Hindsight bias

We have seen that it is wrong to assume that the findings in psychology merely confirm common sense. Why is it, then, that so many people claim that most psychological findings are not surprising and contain nothing new? In other words, why do they argue, "I knew it all along?" An important part of the answer was found by Baruch Fischhoff and his colleagues in some research discussed next.

Fischhoff's studies

Fischhoff and Beyth (1975) asked American students to estimate the probability of various possible outcomes on the eve of President Nixon's trips to China and Russia. After the trips were over, the students were asked to do the same task, but without taking into account their knowledge of what had actually happened. In spite of these instructions, participants with the benefit of hindsight gave events that had actually happened a much higher probability than had the same participants before the events had occurred. The participants had added their knowledge of what had happened to what they already knew in such a way that they could not remember how uncertain things had looked before the trips. This tendency to be wise after the event is known as **hindsight bias**.

Slovic and Fischhoff (1977) carried out a similar study involving predictions about the results of a series of scientific experiments. Some of the participants were told what had happened in the first experiment of the series, but they were told not to use this information when making their predictions. However, participants thought a given outcome was much more likely to occur in future experiments if it had already been obtained. This is another example of hindsight bias.

Hindsight bias seems to be very strong, and is hard to eliminate. In another study, Fischhoff (1977) told his participants about hindsight bias, and encouraged them to avoid it. However, this had little or no effect on the size of the hindsight bias. Hindsight bias poses a problem for teachers of psychology, because it produces students who are unimpressed by almost everything in psychology!

Discussion points

1. Can you think of any ways in which we could try to eliminate hindsight bias?
2. When you think about the views you used to have about psychology, is it possible that you have shown hindsight bias?

Studying Psychology

This book is designed to provide a detailed (but easy-to-read) account of psychology. As a result, it should be of value to *all* those students who are starting to study psychology, and who want a readable introduction to the subject. In order to study psychology successfully, you will need to develop a good level of knowledge and understanding of psychological theories, studies, methods, and concepts. In addition, you will need to be able to analyse and interpret your knowledge in an effective and coherent way.

The structure of the book is designed to help you to achieve these goals. The chapters are clustered together in broad topic groups, namely: Chapters 1–2, introduction; Chapters 3–6, biopsychology; Chapters 7–10, comparative psychology; Chapters 11–14, cognitive psychology; Chapters 15–18, developmental psychology; Chapters 19–22, social psychology; Chapters 23–26, clinical psychology; and Chapters 27–32, testing and issues. I have used what I call the **TEE approach** throughout the book. My discussion of most topics starts with theory (T), moves on to evidence (E), and then concludes with evaluation (E). Evaluation mostly involves considering the various strengths and limitations of the theories or ideas that have been discussed.

KEY TERMS
Hindsight bias: the tendency to be wise after the event, using the benefit of hindsight.
TEE approach: an approach to learning based on the three aspects of theory (T), evidence (E), and evaluation (E).

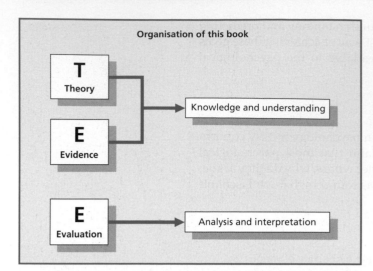

Organisation of this book

T Theory

E Evidence

→ Knowledge and understanding

E Evaluation

→ Analysis and interpretation

Special features

There are several special features running through this book. They have been included to facilitate your task of understanding what psychology is all about. They have also been included in the hope and expectation that they will make it easier for you to become actively involved in the learning process.

Each chapter contains the following: introduction, detailing key topics; key studies with evaluation and discussion points; research activities; key terms; case studies; self-assessment questions; cross-cultural and ethical issues; revision questions; further reading; chapter summaries; and personal reflections. Most of these features are self-explanatory, with the possible exception of personal reflections.

The sections on personal reflections contain some of my personal thoughts, and should be treated as such. You may (or may not!) agree with my personal views, but these sections should provide useful bases for discussion.

Key skills

There is growing emphasis within education on the development and subsequent demonstration of age-related key skills. The most relevant key skills at all stages of school education include the following: communication; application of number; information technology; improving own learning; and working with others. As part of this attempt to cover key skills, you will find tinted areas in each chapter containing descriptions of key research. Each of these also contains discussion points that may be useful to you in developing and expanding your key skills.

Study skills

Students of psychology should find it easier than other students (at least in theory!) to develop good study skills. This is because psychological principles are at the heart of study skills. For example, study skills are designed to promote effective learning and remembering, and learning and memory are key areas within psychology. Study skills are also concerned with motivation and developing good work habits, and these also fall very much within psychology. Most of what is involved in study skills is fairly obvious. As a result, I will focus on detailed pieces of advice rather than on vague generalities (e.g. "Work hard"; "Get focused").

Motivation

Most people find it hard to maintain a high level of motivation over long periods of time, such as an A-level or degree course. What can you do to make yourself as well motivated as possible? As is discussed in Chapter 6, there is good support for the notion that much of human motivation depends on how we think about the future, and about the kinds of goals we set ourselves. Edwin Locke (1968) put forward a goal-setting theory that has proved very influential. According to the original version of this theory, our level of work performance depends mainly on goal difficulty: the harder the goals we set ourselves, the better our performance is likely to be. Wood, Mento, and Locke (1987) reviewed 192 studies that had examined this hypothesis, and concluded that it was supported in 175 of them.

As you might imagine, motivation involves more than goal difficulty. For example, it also involves goal commitment. There is little point in setting yourself the goal of obtaining an excellent examination result in psychology if you do not fully commit and dedicate yourself to the achievement of that goal. Research on goal-setting theory (reviewed by Locke & Latham, 1990) indicates that goal setting is most effective in the following seven circumstances:

1. You must set yourself a goal that is hard but achievable.
2. You need to commit yourself as fully as possible to attaining the goal, perhaps by telling other people about your goal.
3. You should focus on goals that can be achieved within a reasonable period of time (e.g. no more than a few weeks). A long-term goal (e.g. obtaining an Upper Second class degree in psychology) needs to be broken down into a series of short-term goals (e.g. obtaining an excellent mark on your next essay).
4. You should set yourself clear goals, and avoid very vague goals such as simply doing well.
5. You should do your best to obtain feedback on how well you are moving towards your goal (e.g. checking your progress with a teacher or friend).
6. You should feel pleased whenever you achieve a goal, and then proceed to set slightly harder goals in future.
7. You should try to learn from failure by being very honest about the reasons why you failed: was it really "just bad luck"?

Your attempts to motivate yourself are only likely to be successful if you make use of all seven points. If you set yourself a very clear, medium-term goal, and obtain feedback, but the goal is impossible to achieve, then you are more likely to *reduce* rather than *increase* your level of motivation.

Most people going into further education aspire to graduate in their chosen subject as a long-term goal, but the day-to-day studying involves a series of smaller goals, such as getting a good mark for an essay.

Reading skills

You probably spend a fair amount of time reading psychology books, and it is obviously important to read in as effective a way as possible. Morris (1979) described the SQ3R approach, which has proved to be very useful. SQ3R stands for Survey, Question, Read, Recite, Review, and these represent the five stages in effective reading. We will consider these five stages with respect to the task of reading a chapter.

Survey. The Survey stage involves getting an overall view of the way in which the information in the chapter is organised. If there is a chapter summary, this will probably be the easiest way to achieve that goal. Otherwise, you could look through the chapter to find out what topics are discussed and how they are linked to each other.

Question. The Question stage should be applied to fairly short sections of the chapter of no more than 3000 words or so. The essence of this stage is that you should think of relevant questions to which you expect this section to provide answers.

Read. The Read stage involves reading through each section identified at the Question stage. There are two main goals at this stage. First, you should try to answer the questions that you thought of during the previous stage. Second, you should try to integrate the information provided in the section of the chapter with your pre-existing knowledge of the topic.

Recite. The Recite stage involves you in trying to remember all the key ideas that were contained in the section of the chapter you have been reading. If you cannot remember some of them, then you should go back to the Read stage.

Reading effectively: SQ3R

| **S**urvey | Take an overall view of the entire chapter |

| **Q**uestion | Set yourself questions you expect to be answered from short sections within the chapter |

| **R**ead | Read the short sections, keeping your questions in mind. Think about how to integrate what you discover with what you already know |

| **R**ecite | Try to remember all the key ideas in the section you have just read. If you can't, go back to the Read stage |

| **R**eview | When you have read the whole chapter, try to combine information from different sections into a coherent structure. If you can't remember or relate ideas and concepts, go back to the Read stage |

Review. The Review stage occurs when you have read the entire chapter. If all has gone well, you should remember the key ideas from the chapter, and you should be able to combine information from different sections into a coherent structure. If you cannot do these things, then go back to earlier stages in the reading process.

The most important reason why the SQ3R approach works so well is because it ensures that you do not simply read in a passive and mindless way. Instead, it encourages you to engage with the reading material in a very *active* and *proactive* way. As Eysenck (1998) pointed out, there is another important reason why the SQ3R approach is effective. If you read a chapter in a book in a passive way, you may convince yourself that all is well when the material in it seems familiar. However, there is a big difference between *recognising* information as familiar and being able to produce it at will during an anxiety-inducing examination. In order to succeed in examinations, you must be able to *recall* the information you need. The Recite and Review stages of the SQ3R approach are designed to achieve precisely that.

Time management

What do you do with the 100 or so hours a week during which you are awake? Probably the honest answer is that you only have a vague idea where most of the time goes. As time is such a valuable commodity, it is a good idea to make the most efficient use of it. Here are some suggestions on how to achieve that goal:

WEEKLY ACTIVITIES:

	Sleeping	Washing/ Dressing/ Eating	Travelling	Studying at school	Part-time employment	Free time Social life/ Private study	Total
Monday							24
Tuesday							24
Wednesday							24
Thursday							24
Friday							24
Saturday							24
Sunday							24
Total							168
Average	56	16	6	25	5	60*	168

* 60 hours' free time a week allows plenty of time for private study and school work.

- Create a timetable of the time that is available over, say, a whole week. Indicate on it also times that are *not* available. You will probably be surprised at how much time there is, and how much you tend to waste. Now indicate on your timetable those subjects that are going to be given study time on different days, and how much time within each day you are going to spend on any subject.
- Decide what is, for you, a reasonable span of attention (possibly 30–40 minutes). Set aside a number of periods of time during the week for study. Make a commitment to yourself to use these periods for study.
- Note that the more of a habit studying becomes, the less effortful it will be, and the less resistant you will be to making a start.
- No-one has limitless concentration. After initially high levels of concentration, the level decreases until the end is in sight. Regular breaks are needed to bring you to a fresh peak of concentration. So make sure that the time you commit to studying is realistic. You can probably improve your level of concentration by including short (10-minute) rest periods. Remember to avoid distractions like the television in your study area.
- During these study times, there will be a tendency to find other things to do (e.g. watch the end of a television programme; have a drink). This is where the hard part begins. You must try to be firm and say to yourself that this is time you have committed to studying, and that is what you are going to do. However, you will have time available later for other things. It is hard to do on the first occasion, but it gets easier.

Planning fallacy

We are nearly all familiar with the planning fallacy, even though we may never have heard it called that. It was first systematically studied by Kahneman and Tversky (1979). They defined the **planning fallacy** as "a tendency to hold a confident belief that one's own project will proceed as planned, even while knowing that the vast majority of similar projects have run late."

Why are we subject to the planning fallacy? Kahneman and Tversky distinguished between singular information (focusing on the current task) and distributional information (focusing on similar tasks completed in the past). When we are deciding how long a current work task will take to finish, we typically make use of singular information but ignore distributional information. According to Kahneman and Tversky, it is this failure to take account of our previous failures to keep to schedule that produces the planning fallacy.

Buehler, Griffin, and Ross (1994) also found evidence for the planning fallacy. On average, students submitted a major piece of work 22 days later than they had predicted. The tendency to underestimate the time to completion was just as great among those students who were specifically told that the purpose of the study was to examine the accuracy of people's predictions. They found that students were much more accurate at predicting completion times for other students than for themselves. The reason for this is that they were more likely to use distributional information when making predictions about other students.

Discussion points

1. Why do people continue to show the planning fallacy even when they have underestimated the time to complete numerous assignments in the past?

2. Can you avoid the planning fallacy? Some of my thoughts on that question are given later.

It is important for you to avoid the planning fallacy. There are three main ways of doing this. First, simply being aware of the existence of the planning fallacy may make you more accurate in predicting completion times. Second, make use of information about the length of time taken to complete previous essays or assignments. Third, focus on the kinds of difficulties that might occur during the preparation of a piece of work: problems in finding the right books; problems in organising your essay; minor illnesses; and so on. Such a focus should correct the tendency to underestimate completion times.

> **KEY TERM**
> **Planning fallacy**: the tendency to underestimate how long a work task will take to complete in spite of evidence from similar tasks completed in the past.

How to succeed at psychology

- Set yourself hard, clear, short- and medium-term goals, and commit yourself to them.
- Be an active participant in the learning process: have clear aims in mind when you read a textbook, and avoid being passive and uninvolved.
- Follow the TEE strategy: make sure you know the key theories and ideas, the relevant evidence, and that you know how to evaluate them.
- Remember to focus on both breadth and depth in your answers.
- Remember that every theory and study in psychology is limited in some ways: do not be afraid to point this out!
- Try to master the key skills.
- Avoid the planning fallacy.

PERSONAL REFLECTIONS

- It is usually assumed that psychology is the meeting place for several other scientific and non-scientific disciplines. I sometimes wonder whether that is too optimistic a view. The alternative view is that psychology is fragmented, and is not really a single, unified science at all. If that is the case, psychology as a subject may not exist in 50 years time!

SUMMARY

Diversity of psychology?

Psychology is the science that makes use of behavioural and other evidence to understand the internal processes underlying behaviour.

Methods in psychology

This task is complex, and so psychologists have devised a wide range of experimental and non-experimental methods to shed light on human behaviour.

The SQ3R approach—an active and focused approach to reading effectively.

It is misleading to assume that common sense forms a coherent set of assumptions about behaviour, as can be seen from a study of proverbs. Many psychological findings (e.g. those of Milgram) are very different from what most people would have predicted. In spite of this, hindsight bias leads many people to underestimate the achievements of psychology.

"Psychology is just common sense"

To succeed at psychology, you need to acquire detailed knowledge of theory and research in psychology. As importantly, you need to be able to evaluate this knowledge, and criticise it effectively. This book uses the TEE approach, in which theory, evidence, and evaluation are clearly identified. Numerous features of the book (e.g. text questions; research activities; discussion points; personal reflections; ethical issues) are designed to facilitate the task of acquiring the skills you will need to master psychology. For maximal motivation, you should set yourself hard, clear, medium-term goals to which you are committed. You should obtain feedback, praise yourself for success, and analyse failure honestly. Effective reading involves the five stages of Survey, Question, Read, Recite, and Review (SQ3R). This is an active and focused approach. Effective time-management involves setting and keeping to a timetable, allowing short breaks when studying, and avoiding the planning fallacy.

Studying psychology

FURTHER READING

A useful book on developing effective study skills is P. McBride (1994), *Study skills for success*, Cambridge: Hobsons Publishing. Alternatively, another good source of information on study skills is M. Coles and C. White (1985), *Strategies for studying*, London: Collins Educational.

- **The psychodynamic approach**
  A theory of human emotional and
  sexual development.

  *Freud's theories of the structure and
  functioning of the mind*
  Psychosexual development
  Personality theory
  Psychoanalysis as a form of therapy

- **The behaviourist approach**
  Understanding behaviour used only
  objective evidence, not internal factors
  such as thoughts and feelings.

  Watson's behaviourism
  Pavlov's work on classical conditioning
  Skinner and operant conditioning
  Behaviour therapy

- **The humanist approach**
  The importance of subjective
  experience, personal growth, and
  fulfilment.

  Maslow and self-actualisation
  Rogers' Q-sort method
  Client-centred therapy

- **The cognitive approach**
  The internal processes involved in, for
  example, problem solving or learning
  language.

  Computer analogies
  *Broadbent's views on perception and
  communication*
  Top-down and bottom-up processing

- **Free will vs. determinism**
  Is our behaviour determined by
  internal and external forces in life, or
  are we free to choose how to behave?

  The role of science
  William James and soft determinism
  Free will and the self

- **Reductionism**
  Should we always try to reduce
  complex phenomena to simple
  principles and laws?

  A hierarchy of sciences
  Psychology and physiology
  The eclectic approach

2

Approaches to Psychology

As was pointed out in Chapter 1, psychology is related to several other disciplines, including physiology, neurology, biology, sociology, biochemistry, medicine, and anthropology. This helps to explain the complexity and the richness of contemporary psychology, and it sheds light on the ways in which psychology has developed over the past century or so. However, the development of psychology has also been powerfully influenced by a small number of theoretical approaches or "schools" of psychology. One of these, the physiological approach, is important but it is not considered in this chapter. The physiological approach is dealt with in detail in Chapters 3–6.

The following four major approaches are considered in detail in this chapter: psychodynamic approach; behaviourism; humanism; and cognitive psychology. They are considered in that order because it corresponds to the historical order in which the approaches were developed. The psychodynamic approach was developed by Sigmund Freud in Vienna at the turn of the century. It was mainly based on a form of clinical therapy known as psychoanalysis. However, Freud extended the psychodynamic approach to account for normal childhood development and the development of personality. The behaviourist approach was developed by John Watson and others in the United States from about 1912 onwards. This approach had its origins in animal research, and was mainly concerned with understanding the processes of learning under highly controlled conditions.

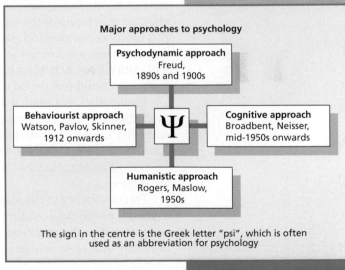

Major approaches to psychology

Psychodynamic approach
Freud,
1890s and 1900s

Behaviourist approach
Watson, Pavlov, Skinner,
1912 onwards

Ψ

Cognitive approach
Broadbent, Neisser,
mid-1950s onwards

Humanistic approach
Rogers, Maslow,
1950s

The sign in the centre is the Greek letter "psi", which is often used as an abbreviation for psychology

Humanism is sometimes known as the "third force" in psychology, with the psychodynamic and behaviourist approaches being the other two forces. It was developed in the United States in the 1950s, and had its origins in philosophy. The humanist approach shared with the psychodynamic approach a major focus on therapy. Finally, there is the cognitive approach, which was developed in the United States and the United Kingdom. This approach gradually became more and more influential from about the middle of the 1950s onwards. Cognitive psychology had some of its origins in the behaviourist approach, with its emphasis on controlled observation of behaviour. However, the cognitive approach is distinctively different from behaviourism, in that it considers a wide range of cognitive processes (e.g. attention; perception; reasoning; problem solving; memory) in addition to learning.

This chapter is also concerned with some of key issues within psychology. More specifically, we will be

■ Research activity: What are your views on free will vs. determinism? Do we choose how to behave, or is our behaviour determined? Make some notes now, then look back after reading this chapter to see if your opinion has changed, and how you have been influenced by the various approaches to psychology described here.

considering whether people are free to choose how to behave or whether our behaviour is determined by environmental and other factors. This is known as the debate between free will and determinism. The other key issue is that of reductionism, and whether psychology can at some point in the future be reduced to more basic sciences such as physiology or biochemistry.

The Psychodynamic Approach

The psychodynamic approach was started by Sigmund Freud (1856–1939). He has had an enormous impact on psychology, and even now his work is referred to in the psychological literature more often than that of any other psychologist. His fame rests mainly on his position as the creator of **psychoanalysis**, which consists of two main strands:

1. A complex set of theories about human emotional development and personality formation.
2. A form of treatment based in part on those theoretical ideas.

Assumptions

At the theoretical level, Freud assumed that the mind is divided into three parts. First, there is the **id**. This contains the sexual and aggressive instincts, and is located in the unconscious mind. The sexual instinct is known as libido. The id works in accord with the pleasure principle, with the emphasis being on immediate satisfaction. Second, there is the **ego**. This is the conscious, rational mind, and it develops during the first two years of life. It works on the reality principle, taking account of what is going on in the environment. Third, there is the **superego**. This develops at about the age of 5 when the child adopts many of the values of the same-sexed parent (the process of identification). It is partly conscious and partly unconscious. It consists of the conscience and ego-ideal. The conscience is formed as a result of the child being punished, and it makes the child feel guilty after behaving badly. The ego-ideal is formed through the use of reward. It makes the child feel proud after behaving well.

Freud also assumed that there were three levels of the mind: the conscious; the preconscious; and the unconscious. The conscious consists of those thoughts that are currently the focus of attention. The preconscious consists of information and ideas that could be retrieved easily from memory and brought into consciousness. The unconscious consists of information that is either very hard or almost impossible to bring into conscious awareness.

Freud's theory of the mind represents a theory of motivation, a cognitive theory, and a social psychological theory. The id contains basic motivational forces, the ego corresponds to the cognitive system, and the superego or conscience internalises the values of family and of society generally. However, Freud did not really develop the social and cognitive aspects, and it would be misleading to regard him as a social or cognitive theorist.

Defence mechanisms

An important part of Freud's theory was the notion that there are frequent *conflicts* among the id, ego, and superego. Conflicts are perhaps most common between the id and the superego, because the id's demands for instant gratification clash with the superego's moral standards. Conflicts cause the individual to experience anxiety, and this leads the ego to devote much time to trying to resolve these conflicts. The ego defends itself by using a number of **defence mechanisms**, which are strategies designed to reduce anxiety. Some of the main defence mechanisms are as follows:

1. Repression: according to Freud (1915, p.86), "The essence of repression lies simply in the function of rejecting and keeping something out of consciousness."
   However, Freud sometimes extended the term "repression" to include conscious

Sigmund Freud, 1856–1939.

awareness of threatening thoughts in the absence of an emotional reaction.

2. Displacement: this involves the unconscious moving of impulses away from a threatening object and towards a less threatening object. For example, somone who has been made angry by their boss may go home and kick the cat.

3. Projection: this involves individuals attributing their undesirable characteristics to others. For example, someone who is very unfriendly may accuse other people of being unfriendly.

4. Denial: this involves simply refusing to accept the existence or reality of a threatening event. For example, patients suffering from life-threatening diseases often deny that these diseases are affecting their lives (Eysenck, 1998).

5. Intellectualisation: this involves thinking about threatening events in ways that remove the emotion from them. An example would be responding to the sinking of a car ferry with considerable loss of life by thinking about ways of improving the design of ferries.

Ego defence mechanisms

- **Intellectualisation** — Thinking about threats in ways that allow emotion to be eliminated
- **Repression** — Keeping troublesome emotions out of conscious awareness
- **EGO**
- **Denial** — Refusing to accept the existence of a threat
- **Displacement** — Unconsciously transferring impulses from a threatening object to a less threatening one
- **Projection** — Attributing undesirable impulses or characteristics to others

Psychosexual development

One of Freud's key assumptions was that adult personality depends very much on childhood experiences. In his theory of psychosexual development, he assumed that all children go through five stages as follows:

1. Oral stage: this lasts for about the first 18 months of life; during this stage, the infant obtains satisfaction from eating, sucking, and other activities using the mouth.

2. Anal stage: this lasts between about 18 and 36 months of age; toilet training occurs during this stage, which helps to explain why the anal region becomes a source of satisfaction.

3. Phallic stage: this lasts between 3 and 6 years of age; the genitals become a key source of satisfaction during this stage. At about the age of 5, boys acquire the **Oedipus complex**, in which they have sexual desires for their mother and consequent fear of their father. This complex is resolved by identification with their father, involving adopting many of their father's attitudes. A similar process operates in girls based on the **Electra complex**, in which they desire their fathers.

4. Latency stage: this lasts from 6 years of age until the onset of puberty; during this stage, boys and girls spend very little time together.

5. Genital stage: this starts from the onset of puberty and continues throughout adult life; during this stage, the main source of sexual pleasure is the genitals.

What kinds of experiences might be so upsetting that they are kept out of conscious awareness? What other everyday examples are there of things that could be explained in terms of the defence mechanisms?

Useful mnemonic

To help you remember Freud's stages of psychosexual development, the following mnemonic is made from the initial letter of each stage: Old Age Pensioners Love Greens!

FREUD'S STAGES OF PSYCHOSEXUAL DEVELOPMENT

Stage	Approximate age	Summary
Oral	0–18 months	Satisfaction from eating, sucking, etc.
Anal	18–36 months	Interest in and satisfaction from anal region
Phallic	3–6 years	Genitals become source of satisfaction
Latency	6 years old–puberty	Boys and girls spend little time together
Genital	From onset of puberty	Genitals main source of sexual pleasure

KEY TERMS
Oedipus complex: in Freudian theory, this involves boys having sexual desire for their mothers at about the age of 5.
Electra complex: in Freudian theory, this involves girls desiring their fathers at about the age of 5.

Personality theory

Freud coupled the theory of psychosexual development with a theory of personality. If a child experiences severe problems or excessive pleasure at any stage of development, this leads to **fixation**, in which basic energy or libido becomes attached to that stage for many years. Later in life, adults who experience very stressful conditions are likely to show **regression**, in which their behaviour becomes less mature and like that displayed during a psychosexual stage at which they fixated as children. According to Freud, these processes of fixation and regression play important roles in determining adult personality. Here are some personality types with descriptions and the stage of psychosexual development at which fixation may have occurred:

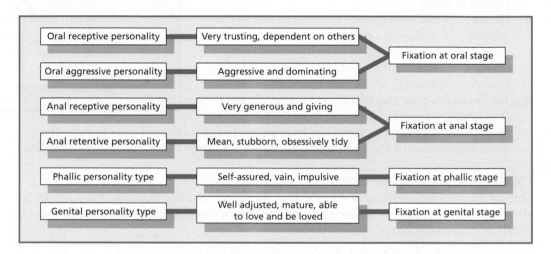

Oral receptive personality	Very trusting, dependent on others	
		Fixation at oral stage
Oral aggressive personality	Aggressive and dominating	
Anal receptive personality	Very generous and giving	
		Fixation at anal stage
Anal retentive personality	Mean, stubborn, obsessively tidy	
Phallic personality type	Self-assured, vain, impulsive	Fixation at phallic stage
Genital personality type	Well adjusted, mature, able to love and be loved	Fixation at genital stage

Psychoanalysis as therapy

We turn now to psychoanalysis as a form of treatment (discussed more fully in Chapter 26). Freud assumed that many forms of mental illness could be treated successfully by psychological rather than medical means. He also assumed that the unconscious mind could have a powerful influence on the development of, and subsequent recovery from, mental illness. More specifically, Freud argued that most neuroses (e.g. anxiety disorders) stem from unresolved conflicts and traumas (powerful shocks) going back to childhood. Anxiety-laden information about these conflicts is stored in the unconscious mind, and is not usually accessible to the conscious mind. This information is in the unconscious because of repression, which as we have seen is the process of forcing very threatening thoughts and memories out of the conscious mind.

How can neurotic patients be helped? Freud assumed that the best way was to allow them to gain access to their repressed ideas and conflicts, and to face up to whatever emerged from the unconscious. Freud used the term **insight** to refer to this process of

KEY TERMS
Fixation: in Freud's theory, spending a long time at a given stage of development because of problems or excessive gratification.
Regression: returning to earlier stages of development when severely stressed.
Insight: in Freudian theory, access to and understanding of emotional memories emerging from the unconscious; the goal of therapy.

Repressed ideas are more likely to appear in dreams.

accessing and coming to terms with repressed memories. Various methods can be used to uncover repressed ideas, including dream analysis, free association, and hypnosis (see Chapter 26).

So far as dream analysis is concerned, Freud assumed that there is a censor inside the mind which keeps repressed material out of conscious awareness. However, this censor is less vigilant when we are asleep (it nods off?), and so repressed ideas are more likely to appear in dreams. These ideas usually emerge in disguised form because of their unacceptable nature (see Chapter 5).

Contributions

Development

Freud's theory of psychosexual development was a major contribution in various ways. It is generally accepted now that the study of childhood can help us to understand adult thinking and behaviour. However, this view had not been put forward in a systematic way before Freud. In addition, the notion that childhood consists of a series of developmental stages was not commonly held before Freud's time. For these reasons, Freud has some claim to be regarded as the founder of developmental psychology.

Personality

Freud's theory of psychosexual development can also be regarded as one of the first systematic theories of personality. Most contemporary theorists would accept that childhood experiences influence adult personality, even if they disagree with the details of Freud's theory. Freud assumed in his theory of psychosexual development that certain personality characteristics tend to be found together. For example, orderliness, meanness, and obstinacy are all aspects of the anal retentive character, and there is evidence that these three personality characteristics do cluster together (Pollack, 1979). There is also evidence for clusters of personality characteristics resembling those of the oral receptive character and the oral aggressive character (Kline & Storey, 1977).

The unconscious mind

Freud also made a major contribution with his theoretical account of the unconscious mind. The notion of the unconscious was not original to Freud, but he developed it far beyond any previous theorists. One of the implications of Freud's approach was that the conscious mind is less important than is generally assumed. For example, the ego's use of defence mechanisms serves the purpose of keeping conflicting thoughts out of conscious awareness.

Convincing evidence for unconscious processes has been obtained by cognitive psychologists in recent years. For example, consider what happens when pictures of snakes are presented so rapidly to snake phobics that they cannot be seen at the conscious level. The snake phobics nevertheless experience some anxiety, but are unable to indicate the reason for it (Ohman, 1986).

In spite of the similarities, there are some important differences between Freud's views and those of contemporary cognitive psychologists. Freud regarded the unconscious as a complex part of the mind, whereas cognitive psychologists regard it as consisting of relatively simple and automatic processes. For example, individuals who are able to touch-type have automatic processes that allow them to find all the letters on the keyboard without any conscious thought. It is a long way from such simple unconscious processes to the major conflicts that Freud believed occurred in the unconscious mind.

Defence mechanisms

Freud's notion that individuals make use of various defence mechanisms to protect the ego from anxiety is a valuable one. There is evidence for the existence of repression (see Chapter 13), and some support for other defence mechanisms. For example, Speisman et al. (1964) showed an emotion-provoking film, and measured their participants' emotional reactions in terms of physiological responses and self-reported anxiety. These emotional reactions were reduced when the participants were told to use denial or intellectualisation while viewing the film. Some of the biases and errors in attributional processes studied by social psychologists support the view that people often think in distorted ways to protect their self-esteem (see Chapter 19).

Therapy

Psychoanalysis as a form of therapy was a tremendously important contribution, because it was the first systematic psychological treatment for anxiety and depression. Psychoanalysis led directly to neo-Freudian therapy, and indirectly to client-centred therapy and cognitive-behaviour therapy (discussed later in the chapter).

Play therapy

Play therapy is an example of a style of therapy that is modified and extended from Freud's original ideas. Axline (1971) describes how a small boy named "Dibs" was able to express his unconscious wishes and fears during play therapy, which was carried out in a play group where he felt safe. Dibs was able to act as he chose without fear of interruption or disapproval. A little at a time, Dibs came to terms with his own feelings and apparently acquired some "insight". Eventually he was able to cope with the hostile feelings he had towards other members of his family. Through play therapy Dibs learned to understand and cope with his feelings.

We might expect that more recent forms of treatment would be more effective than psychoanalysis, which Freud began to develop about 100 years ago. However, Smith, Glass, and Miller (1980) found in a large-scale review of the evidence that all of the major forms of therapy are about equally effective, and some recent reviews have reached the same conclusion (e.g. Wampold et al., 1997; see page 722). That may no longer be the case, because some very effective forms of cognitive behaviour therapy have been developed in the last few years. However, it is still a staggering achievement on Freud's part to have put together a form of treatment that was hardly improved upon for over 80 years.

One of the key assumptions underlying psychoanalytic therapy is that adult neuroses have their origins in the conflicts and problems of childhood. George Brown obtained evidence supporting this claim in a study of 400 women in Islington, an area near the centre of London (see Eysenck, 1994b). Childhood adversity (e.g. parental indifference or abuse) had been suffered by 64% of the women with panic disorder and by 39% of those with depression. These percentages are much higher than the figure of 17% for women free from disorder.

Wider horizons

Finally, it could be argued that Freud's greatest contribution was that he enormously increased the scope of psychology. Before his time, philosophers and psychologists had studied limited aspects of human thinking and behaviour such as associations of ideas, learning and memory, and reaction time. In contrast, Freud argued that psychology could shed light on personality, abnormal behaviour, human sexuality, dreaming, the unconscious mind, and almost everything else.

Evaluation

Someone once said to me, "Freud is the best psychologist, but he is also the worst psychologist." In other words, Freud had great strengths and great weaknesses. His strengths were dealt with in the previous section, so we will focus on his weaknesses here.

Falsifiability

The greatest problem with the psychodynamic approach at the theoretical level is that the *unscientific* approach adopted by Freud makes it very hard to test most of his theories. As is discussed on page 772, Popper (1969, 1972) argued that the crucial feature of a scientific theory was *falsifiability*: it should be possible to imagine some evidence that could disprove it. Many of Freud's theories lack falsifiability. For example, consider his notion that the mind is divided into three parts: id, ego, and superego. What evidence (of any kind) could possibly disprove that notion? As Crews (1996, p.67) pointed out:

The vagueness of the theory is such that it can withstand almost any number of surprises and be endlessly revised according to the theorist's whim, without reference to data.

What about Freud's theory of defence mechanisms? It is hard to test this theory, because it is ethically unacceptable to create experimentally the high levels of anxiety that are needed before individuals develop defence mechanisms. However, there is support for the defence mechanism of repression (see Chapter 13). As Eysenck (1998, p.435) pointed out:

> the greatest weakness of Freud's account ... is that we cannot predict ahead of time which defence mechanism will be used by a given individual. According to Freud, someone who is exposed to an extremely anxiety-provoking situation is likely to resort to a defence mechanism, but it is impossible to predict whether that defence mechanism will be repression, displacement, denial, intellectualisation, projection or reaction formation. This greatly reduces the scientific usefulness of the theory.

Lack of information

What about Freud's theory of psychosexual development? It is usually only possible, 20 or 30 years afterwards, to obtain very limited and distorted information about an individual's experiences when being fed or toilet trained. In addition, the main evidence for the theory consists of *correlations* between certain childhood experiences and type of adult personality. Correlations cannot prove causes, and so these correlations cannot show that adult personality has been caused by childhood experiences.

Those parts of the theory of psychosexual development that can be tested have been mostly found to be incorrect. Freud argued that fear plays an important part in the development of identification in boys. It follows that boys whose fathers are threatening and hostile should show more identification than boys whose fathers are supportive. In fact, however, the evidence indicates that what happens is exactly the opposite (Mussen & Rutherford, 1963). There is also very little evidence for the existence of the Oedipus complex or the Electra complex (Kline, 1981).

Considering that Freud was working within a strict Victorian society, why was sexual behaviour so strongly emphasised in his theory of development?

Reliance on untested observations

Freud never carried out any experiments to test his ideas. He relied on the observations that he made of his patients over the years. This approach is problematic in two ways. First, these observations were made in an unsystematic (and probably biased) way, and so cannot be regarded as convincing evidence. Second, Freud's approach involved a very non-representative sample of the population. Most of Freud's patients were middle-class women from Vienna. Any notions about human behaviour based on such a sample are likely to be very limited.

A key weakness with psychoanalysis as a form of therapy is that it developed largely from Freud's interactions with his patients in the therapeutic situation. We have

Freud's work was largely with middle-class women in Vienna in the 1890s and 1900s. How relevant do you think his ideas are to other cultures, particularly given the social changes during the twentieth century?

surprisingly little information about these interactions, because Freud only reported on about 12 case studies in his published work. The evidence obtained from patients is suspect, because there are grave dangers of contamination. This can happen in at least two ways:

1. What the patient says may be influenced by what the therapist has said previously, and thus be contaminated by the therapist's theoretical views.
2. The therapist may use his or her theoretical preconceptions to interpret what the patient says in ways that distort what has been said.

As a result of these sources of contamination, we do not really know *why* psychoanalysis is effective.

Emphasis on the past

Psychoanalysis as a form of therapy is limited in its approach. Freud believed that sexual problems going back to the years of childhood were generally at the root of mental illness. This belief was disputed by the neo-Freudians such as Alfred Adler (1870–1937), Erich Fromm (1900–1980), Karen Horney (1885–1952), and Harry Stack Sullivan (1892–1949). According to them, social factors such as interpersonal relationships typically play a larger part than sexual problems in producing mental illness. They also argued that therapists should address the patient's current concerns rather than focusing mainly on the past. This emphasis on current concerns is also found in behaviour therapy and cognitive behaviour therapy.

PSYCHODYNAMIC APPROACH: A SUMMARY

Key assumptions	Strengths	Weaknesses
Defence mechanisms	Evidence from other research suggests that people do think in distorted ways to reduce their emotional response and protect their self-esteem	Theory is hard to test and cannot be proved or disproved
Psychosexual development	One of the first theories of development related to personality	Theory based on retrospective personal accounts from childhood which may be distorted. Based on correlations that cannot prove causality
Personality theory	Other researchers' evidence suggests clusters of personality characteristics that resemble those described by Freud	Very little evidence in support of the Oedipus and Electra complexes
Psychoanalysis	Has been considered to be as effective as other forms of therapy. Freud's original ideas have been modified and extended in successful forms of therapy	Success has been challenged by more effective cognitive behaviour therapy

The Behaviourist Approach

Assumptions

Watson

The behaviourist approach to psychology started in the United States in the early years of the twentieth century. The key figure in this new approach was John Watson (1878–1958). According to Watson (1913):

> *Psychology as the behaviourist views it is a purely objective, experimental branch of natural science. Its theoretical goal is the prediction and control of behaviour. Introspection forms no essential part of its method.*

Note that Watson believed that a major goal of psychology is to control behaviour. This helps to explain the emphasis that the behaviourists placed on the study of learning rather than on other aspects of psychological functioning. If you want to change someone's behaviour, then the relevant learning experience needs to be provided.

The behaviourists initially focused on attacking the approaches that were current in psychology at that time. For example, as we have seen, Watson argued that psychologists should not rely on **introspection**, which involves the observation and reporting of one's own mental processes. After a while, the behaviourists began to develop a system based on positive assumptions. Some of their major assumptions were as follows:

John Watson, 1878–1958.

Why do you think the behaviourists rejected introspection as a valid part of psychological method?

S–R is a commonly used abbreviation for "stimulus–response".

- Psychology should be the study of behaviour, because behaviour is objective and observable.
- The unit of analysis in psychology should be the simple stimulus–response association; complex behaviour consists of numerous stimulus–response associations.
- Behaviour is determined by environmental factors rather than by heredity; according to Watson (1924), "There is no such thing as an inheritance of capacity, talent, temperament, mental constitution and characteristics. These things depend on training that goes on mainly in the cradle."
- Learning can be understood in terms of conditioning principles such as those put forward by Pavlov; these principles apply to most species.
- The brain is not of central importance: "Though the brain remains a connecting station, it is for the behaviourist no more intelligible to say that we think with the brain than to say that we walk with the spinal cord" (Murphy & Kovach, 1972).

As can be seen from these assumptions, behaviourism was concerned in part with the methods that should be used in psychology. Of particular importance is the emphasis on behaviour (which is observable and relatively objective) rather than on introspection (which is unobservable and subjective). Behaviourism was also concerned with the attempt to put forward a theory of behaviour. This theory was based on the principles of conditioning, on simple stimulus–response associations, and on environmental determinants of behaviour.

Pavlov

Watson and the other early behaviourists were greatly influenced by the work of Ivan Pavlov (1849–1936) on classical conditioning in dogs (see Chapter 10). Dogs salivate when food is put in their mouths, and Pavlov found that they could be trained to salivate to a neutral stimulus such as a tone. This tone was presented just before food on several occasions, so that the tone signalled the imminent arrival of food to the dog. Finally, Pavlov presented the tone on its own without any food, and found that this led to the dog salivating. This association between tone and salivation is known as a conditioned reflex, and it illustrates **classical conditioning**.

Why was Watson so impressed by Pavlov's work? First, Pavlov focused on observable stimuli and responses, and so his research seemed to be scientific. For example, learning could be assessed by measuring the amount of salivation produced by the tone. Second, Pavlov's work suggested that learning involves the formation of an association between a stimulus (e.g. a tone) and a response (e.g. salivation). Watson assumed that most (or all) learning was of this type.

Ivan Pavlov, 1849–1936.

Skinner

B.F. Skinner (1904–1990) was the most influential behaviourist. His main assumption was that nearly all behaviour is under the control of reward or reinforcement. Responses that are followed by reward will increase in frequency, whereas those not followed by reward will decrease in frequency. This is known as **operant conditioning**. The responses studied by Skinner were very simple (e.g. lever pressing; pecking), and it is unlikely that operant conditioning explains more complex forms of learning.

> **KEY TERMS**
> **Introspection**: examination and observation of one's own mental processes.
> **Classical conditioning**: a basic form of learning in which simple responses are associated with new stimuli.
> **Operant conditioning**: a form of learning in which behaviour is controlled by the giving of reward or reinforcement.

B.F. Skinner, 1904–1990.

Skinner seems to have favoured the notion of **equipotentiality**, according to which virtually any response can be conditioned in any stimulus situation. A very different approach was taken by Seligman (1970). He put forward the notion of **preparedness**. According to this notion, each species finds some kinds of learning much easier than others because of their biological make-up. For example, it is natural for pigeons to peck for food. As a result, it is easy to train pigeons to peck at coloured discs for a food reward.

The behaviourists emphasised the importance of external or environmental determinants of behaviour. According to Skinner (1971), "The environment not only prods or lashes, it selects ... Behaviour is shaped and maintained by its consequences." The behaviourists tended to ignore the significance of internal factors such as cognition, physiology, and inherited characteristics. In the words of Skinner (1980), "A science of behaviour has its own facts ... No physiological fact has told us anything about behaviour that we did not know already."

Contributions

Behaviour therapy

The greatest long-term contribution of behaviourism is **behaviour therapy**, which is based on the assumptions that abnormal behaviour develops through conditioning, and that it is through the use of conditioning principles that recovery can be achieved. There are numerous forms of behaviour therapy, including exposure or flooding; systematic desensitisation; aversion therapy; and token economies (see Chapter 26). According to a large-scale review of treatment studies by Smith et al. (1980), behaviour therapy is an effective type of therapy that is of comparable effectiveness to other types of therapy (e.g. psychoanalysis).

Operant conditioning has been used in numerous ways and types of situations, two of which we will consider here: organisational behaviour modification and programmed learning.

Organisational behaviour modification

Organisational behaviour modification involves the use of reinforcement principles in organisational settings to improve work performance. One of the most influential approaches to organisational behaviour modification was the five-step procedure put forward by Luthans and Kreitner (1975):

1. Identify the critical behaviour required for satisfactory work performance.
2. Measure the frequency with which the critical or desired work behaviour occurs.
3. Carry out a functional analysis of the worker's current behaviour in order to understand how reward and/or avoidance of punishment is maintaining it.
4. Develop an intervention strategy designed to modify the worker's behaviour in the desired direction, using reinforcement or reward to achieve this goal; the rewards can be very varied (e.g. money; compliments; use of the executive washroom).
5. Evaluate the success of the intervention strategy in terms of its effectiveness in changing work behaviour.

An example of the usefulness of this approach was given by Arnold, Cooper, and Robertson (1995). A company called SJR Foods had a problem with absenteeism, which was running at about 15% per day. The production manager, Radha El-Bakry, decided to introduce a lottery scheme. Each worker received one free lottery ticket every day they turned up for work, plus two extra tickets if they were at work throughout the week. There was a draw with prizes every Friday evening. The introduction of the lottery led to the absenteeism rate dropping to only 2–3% of the workers.

Discussion points

1. Do you think that organisational behaviour modification would work better in some organisations than others?
2. Might organisational behaviour modification have more effect on some workers (e.g. those who are not naturally highly motivated) than on others?
3. Do you think that organisational behaviour modification might be useful in allowing you to study more effectively?

KEY TERMS
Equipotentiality: the view that essentially any response can be conditioned to any stimulus.
Preparedness: the notion that each species finds some forms of learning more "natural" and easier than others.
Behaviour therapy: forms of clinical therapy based on the learning principles associated with classical and operant conditioning.
Organisational behaviour modification: the use of reinforcement principles in organisational settings to improve work performance.

Programmed learning

Skinner argued that the principles of operant conditioning could be used to develop new methods of learning for students. This led to **programmed learning**, which typically involves the following features:

- The learning material is presented in a series of small steps; this can be done via special books, teaching machines, or a computer.
- The student is asked questions at each step to ensure that he or she has understood the material.
- The student is provided with almost immediate feedback, indicating whether each answer is correct or incorrect.
- Learning programmes are either linear or branching. Linear programmes work through the material in a single, unchanging order; branching programmes are more flexible, allowing more able students to proceed more rapidly.

The use of small steps in programmed learning means that most students make very few errors as they work their way through the material. Thus, they receive much positive reinforcement (being told they are correct), which should improve learning. Furthermore, this reinforcement is provided shortly after the students have responded, which should also improve learning.

Programmed learning suits some topics better than others: which subjects would use the method to its full potential, and which would not?

Evaluation

Scientific status

Behaviourism has proved to be of lasting importance because of its insistence that psychology should be a genuine scientific discipline. Psychologists in Germany (e.g. Weber; Fechner; Ebbinghaus) had carried out scientific experiments before the start of behaviourism. However, the behaviourists spelled out more systematically than had been done before exactly how psychology could achieve scientific status. In particular, the behaviourists argued that the careful observation of behaviour in controlled settings is of fundamental importance to psychology.

On the negative side, the insistence on a high level of control of the experimental situation carries with it the danger of artificiality. For example, the dogs taking part in Pavlov's studies were usually put in a restraining harness. It can be argued that little can be learned about dogs' normal behaviour in such artificial and restricted conditions.

External vs. internal factors

At a theoretical level, the most general problem with behaviourism is that the impact of environmental stimuli on behaviour was exaggerated, whereas the influence of internal factors (e.g. past knowledge and experience) was largely ignored. Bandura (1977) expressed this point very neatly: "If actions were determined solely by external rewards and punishments, people would behave like weather vanes, constantly shifting in radically different directions to conform to the whims of others." In fact, much of our behaviour is relatively consistent, because it is under the control of various internal goals.

Some of the other major assumptions made by the behaviourists have been shown to be incorrect. For example, they assumed that individual differences in behaviour depend on different learning and conditioning experiences rather than on genetic differences. However, there is convincing evidence (mainly from twin studies) that genetic factors are of importance in determining individual differences in intelligence and personality (see Chapters 23 and 27).

Inter-species differences

The behaviourists assumed that conditioning principles apply in very similar ways in different species. In so doing, they drastically underestimated the differences between species. For example, the fact that humans possess language transforms our learning ability. Rats who have learned to press a lever for a food reward will keep pressing for a long time after food has stopped being provided. In contrast, most people will stop immediately if they are told that no more rewards will be given.

Performing or learning?

The behaviourists assumed that reward or reinforcement has a major impact on learning. In fact, however, reinforcement typically has more effect on performance than on learning. For example, suppose you were offered £1 every time you said, "The earth is flat." This might lead you to say it several hundred times. However, although the reward would have influenced your performance or behaviour, it would not have affected your knowledge or learning to the extent that you started to believe the earth was actually flat.

Oversimplification

Many of the early behaviourist theories were very oversimplified. For example, Watson argued that thinking is merely sub-vocal speech. This led the philosopher Herbert Feigl to remark wittily that Watson "made up his windpipe that he had no mind." Watson's position was disproved in a dangerous study (Smith et al., 1947). Smith was given a drug that paralysed his entire musculature, and he had to be kept alive by a respirator. He was unable to engage in sub-vocal speech or any other bodily movement, and so, according to Watson's argument, he should have been unable to observe what was going on around him, to understand what people were saying, and to think about these events while in the paralysed state. In fact, Smith reported that he was able to do all of these things, indicating that thinking is possible in the absence of sub-vocal speech.

Therapy and behaviour modification

What about the contributions of behaviourism to behaviour therapy, organisational behaviour modification, and programmed learning? We will consider these contributions in turn. As was mentioned earlier, behaviour therapy has been shown to be effective for the treatment of a wide range of clinical conditions. However, the success of behaviour therapy does not depend solely on conditioning principles. Patients who undergo behaviour therapy probably recover mainly because of cognitive changes (e.g. to their expectations and knowledge).

Cognitive factors

The importance of cognitive factors was shown by Lick (1975) in a study on systematic desensitisation. This is a form of therapy in which patients with a phobia (extreme fear) of some object or situation (e.g. spiders) learn to respond in a relaxed fashion while progressively more frightening stimuli relating to their phobia are presented to them. Behaviour therapists argue that this form of treatment works because relaxation responses incompatible with the fear response are linked to the phobic or fear-related stimuli. Lick told his patients that he would present phobic stimuli so rapidly that they could not be seen consciously, and they were presented with physiological feedback apparently indicating that they were becoming more successful in remaining relaxed when presented with these stimuli. In fact, no stimuli were presented, and the physiological feedback was fake.

As Lick's procedure differed so much from the one advocated by behaviourists, they would expect this "make-believe" treatment to be ineffective. In fact, it worked well, presumably because it produced cognitive changes (e.g. the patients believed they could control their fear of phobic stimuli).

> **KEY STUDY EVALUATION — Lick**
>
> Lick's study involved a certain amount of deception, which is ethically questionable in psychological research (see Chapter 29). The physiological feedback given to the participants, who were phobia sufferers, was fake, and no phobic stimuli were actually presented to them. However, the patients reported that the treatment helped to lessen their phobic symptoms. Do the ends justify the means in studies like this?

Discussion points

1. Why do the findings of Lick pose problems for the behaviourist approach to therapy?
2. Can you think of ways of measuring the cognitive changes that this "make-believe" treatment created?

Organisational behaviour modification has been used successfully in many companies. However, it has various limitations. First, this approach works best in highly controlled situations where appropriate work behaviour is easy to observe. It works much less well when the work performance of individual workers depends importantly on the efforts and support of fellow workers. Second, organisational behaviour modification has rarely been used among managerial or professional workers, so that little is known of its potential usefulness at the higher levels within companies. Third, there are ethical concerns about the use of techniques that involve the systematic manipulation and control of workers.

■ Research activity: Choose one of the major contributions of behaviourism (behaviour therapy, organisational behaviour modification, programmed learning) and create a table like the one below to summarise its strengths and weaknesses.

Contribution	Description	Evaluation
		Strengths: (1)
		(2)
		Weaknesses: (1)
		(2)

Programmed learning has been found to be about as effective as other forms of learning (e.g. lectures), but it is generally not superior. Programmed learning is most useful for teaching specific knowledge or skills, and it is less successful when used to teach more general or complex knowledge (Taylor, 1964). Examples of specific knowledge include learning the meanings of concepts (e.g. "Operant conditioning is a form of learning in which behaviour is controlled by the giving of reward or reinforcement") and the steps involved in using a statical test (e.g. "The first step is to take the sum of the scores in each condition"). General or complex knowledge is involved when you learn how to evaluate theories and research in psychology.

In sum, behaviourism as a theory and as an approach based on conditioning cannot be regarded as generally adequate. As Hearnshaw (1987, p.219) concluded in his discussion of Skinner's contribution: "It is ... an intensely limited psychology that he has proposed, however powerful within the strict limits of its validity."

The Humanist Approach

The humanistic approach to psychology was developed mainly by Carl Rogers and Abraham Maslow in the United States during the 1950s. According to Cartwright (1979, pp.5–6), humanistic psychology

is concerned with topics that are meaningful to human beings, focusing especially upon subjective experience and the unique, unpredictable events in individual human lives.

Humanistic psychologists have tended to focus on personal responsibility, free will, and the individual's striving towards personal growth and fulfilment. Of particular importance, the humanistic psychologists strongly favoured a reliance on **phenomenology**, which involves reporting pure experience with no attempt to interpret it.

Attempts have been made to apply research into conditioning to behaviour at work, in order to improve productivity.

Assumptions

The assumption by the humanistic psychologists that we should try to understand human behaviour by relying on phenomenology made the humanistic approach very different from the behaviourist approach that preceded it. There are doubts as to whether the humanistic approach can be regarded as scientific in any meaningful sense, although what is meant by science is a complex and difficult issue (see Chapter 28). How did the humanistic psychologists respond to this criticism? According to Maslow (1968, p.13), "The uniqueness of the individual does not fit into what we know of science. Then so much the worse for that conception of science. It, too, will have to endure re-creation." Rogers (1959) was also unconcerned that the humanistic approach could be regarded as anti-scientific. According to him, the phenomenological approach based on self-reports of conscious experience allows us to understand more about the meaning of people's experiences than does the traditional scientific approach favoured by the behaviourists.

Why do you think the degree of "science" involved in any psychological approach is seen by some as so crucial?

KEY TERM
Phenomenology: an approach focusing on the reporting of pure experience; favoured by humanistic psychologists.

Abraham Maslow

Maslow (1970) pointed out that theories of motivation had focused mainly on basic physiological needs, or on our needs to reduce anxiety and to avoid pain. He

Maslow characterised Abraham Lincoln as a famous individual who demonstrated "self-actualisation" —including characteristics such as self-acceptance, resistance to cultural influences, empathy and creativeness.

assumed that human motivation is actually much broader than that. He proposed a **hierarchy of needs** consisting of seven levels (see Chapter 6). Physiological needs (such as those for food and water) are at the bottom of the hierarchy. Next come security and safety needs, followed by needs for love and belongingness. Moving further up the hierarchy, we come to esteem needs, then cognitive needs (such as curiosity and the need for understanding) and aesthetic (artistic) needs. Finally, there is the need for **self-actualisation**, which involves fulfilling one's potential in the broadest sense.

Self-actualised individuals are characterised by an acceptance of themselves, spontaneity, the need for privacy, resistance to cultural influences, empathy, profound interpersonal relationships, a democratic character structure, creativeness, and a philosophical sense of humour. Maslow (1954) identified Abraham Lincoln and Albert Einstein as famous people who were self-actualised.

How can we measure self-actualisation? Maslow (1962) focused on **peak experiences**, in which the world is accepted totally for what it is, and there are feelings of euphoria, wonder, and awe. Peak experiences happen most often during sexual intercourse or when listening to music, and sometimes when doing both at the same time. Maslow (1962) found that self-actualised individuals reported more peak experiences than other people. It is also possible to assess self-actualisation by means of self-report questionnaires (e.g. the Index of Self-Actualisation).

Carl Rogers

Carl Rogers (1902–1987) devoted himself to the search for improved methods of treating clinical patients. This search also led to an interest in personality. Rogers (1951, 1959) assumed that the concept of "self" is of great importance to an understanding of human personality. An individual's self-concept is mainly conscious. It consists of his or her thoughts and feelings about himself or herself as an individual and in relation to others.

According to Rogers (1951), there is an important distinction between the **self-concept** and the **ideal self**. The self-concept is the self as it is currently experienced, whereas the ideal self is the self-concept that an individual would most like to have. Happy people tend to have a much smaller gap between their self-concept and their ideal self than do those who are unhappy.

Q-sort method. One way of assessing the self-concept and the ideal self is to use the Q-sort method:

1. An individual is presented with a pile of cards, each of which contains a personal statement (e.g. "I am a friendly person"; "I am tense most of the time").
2. The individual decides which statements best describe his or her own self, which statements are the next best, and so on, right down to those statements that are the least descriptive.
3. The same procedure is followed with respect to the ideal self.
4. The experimenter works out the size of the gap between the statements selected as descriptive of the self-concept and the ideal self.

There are three problems with using the Q-sort method or any similar method to assess the self-concept and the ideal self. First, such methods cannot shed any light on those aspects of the self about which there is no conscious awareness. Second, there are obvious possibilities of deliberate distortion. For example, it is more desirable to be a friendly rather than an unfriendly person, and so many unfriendly people may pretend to be friendly for the purposes of the test. Third, people may possess a number of self-concepts, but the Q-sort method is designed to assess a single self-concept.

KEY TERMS

Hierarchy of needs: in Maslow's theory, a range of needs from physiological ones at the bottom of the hierarchy to self-actualisation at the top.

Self-actualisation: fulfilling one's potential in the broadest sense.

Peak experiences: heightened experiences associated with feelings of joy and wonder.

Self-concept: the self as it is currently experienced.

Ideal self: the self-concept that one would most like to have.

Client-centred therapy. Carl Rogers is probably best known for his development of client-centred therapy. This is discussed in detail in Chapter 26, so a brief account will be given here. There are two central assumptions underlying client-centred therapy:

> ■ Research activity: Write a brief description of how you see yourself (call this "A"). Then write a brief description of the person you would like to be (call this "B"). How different are A and B? Remember that our "ideal selves" are often different from our perceived selves.

1. Incongruence (in which some experiences are not incorporated into the self-concept) plays a major role in the development of mental illness.
2. Therapists should try to reduce their clients' level of incongruence.

What are the processes underlying incongruence? One process is rationalisation, in which an individual distorts the interpretation of his or her own behaviour to make it consistent with his or her self-concept (e.g. "My behaviour looked bad, but it wasn't really my fault"). Another example is fantasy: an individual may fantasise about himself or herself (e.g. "I am Napoleon"), but then deny or refuse to accept those experiences that disprove the fantasy (e.g. "I can't speak French").

Rogers argued that the best way to reduce a client's incongruence is to provide a supportive environment in which he or she feels able to be open to experience. As a result, those therapists who are most effective tend to be:

1. Unconditional in positive regard.
2. Genuine.
3. Empathic (i.e. understanding another person's feelings).

There is some evidence that these characteristics are valuable in therapists. Truax and Mitchell (1971) reviewed several studies, and concluded that the most successful therapists tended to possess these three characteristics. However, other evidence indicates that being unconditional in positive regard, genuine, and empathic are less important than was claimed by Rogers (e.g. Beutler, Cargo, & Arizmendi, 1986).

Contributions

The humanistic approach has made several contributions to psychology. First, humanistic psychologists addressed issues of fundamental importance to human beings. They focused on the self-concept, on our most profound motivating forces, on our attempts to realise our potential as individuals, and so on. These issues are more central to our lives than are most of those that have occupied more experimentally minded psychologists.

The humanistic approach, with its emphasis on the self, was developed in a Western culture. Would it be so acceptable in a collectivistic non-Western culture?

Second, the humanistic approach provides a more comprehensive account of human motivation than is available in most other approaches. The fact that there are millions of people in Western society who feel very depressed and unfulfilled in spite of having all their basic physiological needs catered for suggests the importance of growth needs.

Third, humanistic forms of therapy (e.g. client-centred therapy; encounter groups) have proved to be fairly effective. The value of client-centred therapy was assessed by Davison and Neale (1986, p.489):

> *As a way to help unhappy but not severely disturbed people understand themselves better ... client-centred therapy may very well be appropriate and effective ... Rogerian therapy may not, however, be appropriate for a severe psychological disorder, as Rogers himself has warned.*

Fourth, humanistic psychology has forced many psychologists to question some of their basic beliefs. Humanistic psychologists differ from most other psychologists in focusing on conscious experience rather than on behaviour; on free will rather than on determinism; and on discussion of experience rather than on use of the experimental method. Whether or not the views of humanistic psychologists are valid, they have certainly succeeded in injecting a breath of fresh air into psychology.

Evaluation

In spite of the various contributions of the humanistic approach, there are several criticisms that can be made of it. First, phenomenology is concerned only with those thoughts of which we have conscious awareness. As a result, it ignores all the important processes going on below the level of conscious awareness. Another problem with reliance on an individual's conscious experiences is that his or her report of those experiences may be systematically distorted (e.g. to create a good impression).

Can you name any cultures in which self-actualisation may not be possible due to external factors?

Second, the assumption that everyone is born with the potential to become a self-actualiser provided their basic needs are met is dubious at best. The fact that a small percentage of people are self-actualised does not show that everyone could be. The main explanation for self-actualisation may simply be that self-actualised people tend to be more intelligent, talented, well educated, and motivated than the rest of us.

Third, the notion that self-actualised people are creative, self-accepting, and have excellent interpersonal relations ignores the fact that many people possess only some of those characteristics. For example, the artist van Gogh was outstandingly creative, but he was so lacking in self-acceptance that he committed suicide. There are numerous examples of very creative individuals whose personal and emotional lives were disaster areas—should they be regarded as self-actualised or not?

Fourth, humanistic psychologists argue that self-actualisation occurs mainly because of needs within the individual rather than because of the beneficial impact of the environment. However, the environment often helps the process of self-actualisation. For example, most Western societies provide their citizens with many years of schooling, training opportunities for those with special skills, part-time courses, and so on. It is probable that self-actualisation depends on external (environmental) as well as internal (need) factors.

■ Research activity: Create a table like the one below to describe and evaluate the two main theories in humanistic psychology.

	Main concepts	Strengths	Weaknesses
Rogers			
Maslow			

Fifth, the humanistic rejection of the scientific approach involves some clear costs. Science tends to make progress over time, even if the rate may seem slow at times, and even though some scientific approaches end up in a cul-de-sac. In contrast, there is much less sense of progress with the humanistic approach. Its validity is not much clearer now than it was 40 years ago.

The Cognitive Approach

One of the main reasons why the cognitive approach developed in the 1950s was a growing dissatisfaction with the behaviourist approach. Suppose that we wish to understand cognitive abilities, such as our mastery of language or the processes involved in problem solving. It is very hard to do this from the behaviourist perspective, with its emphasis on observable behaviour. What is needed is a focus on internal processes, and this is what cognitive psychologists tried to do.

Another reason for the emergence of the cognitive approach was the arrival of the "computer revolution". Psychologists have often tried to understand the complexities of human cognition by comparing it with something simpler and better understood. For example, catapults and telephone exchanges are among the many comparisons or analogies that have been used. Cognitive psychologists argued that the computer analogy provides a better basis for understanding human cognition. Computers share some of the complexities of the human brain, and they resemble our brains in having inputs and outputs, memory stores, and active processing systems.

There were several key figures in the development of cognitive psychology during the 1950s and 1960s, including Herb Simon, George Miller, Jerome Bruner, and Ulric Neisser. However, Donald Broadbent's (1958) book, *Perception and Communication*, is regarded by many psychologists as the most important single contribution to the development of cognitive psychology. Before Broadbent, psychologists had studied attention, or short-term memory, or perception, or some other aspect of cognition in isolation from other aspects. Broadbent's great achievement was to put forward a theory that indicated how some of these aspects relate to each other. For example, he argued that selective attention determines what information goes into short-term memory. Participants presented with 2 8 6 in one ear at the same time as 9 3 4 in the other ear can select one ear and rehearse only the digits presented to that ear (e.g. 2 8 6) in short-term memory. In the terms used by cognitive psychologists, Broadbent (1958) proposed an information-processing system.

> Whereas the behaviourists reduced psychology to stimulus and response (S–R), cognitive psychologists have added an extra dimension. Instead of dismissing the internal cognitive processes and the issue of how the stimulus provokes the response, they have focused on this middle, internal stage (stimulus–information processing–response).

Assumptions

What are the key assumptions of the cognitive approach? The fundamental assumption is that human cognition depends on an information-processing system, although that system is usually thought of as being more complex than the one proposed by Broadbent (1958). Various other assumptions follow from the fundamental one:

*   Information made available by the environment is processed by a series of processing systems (e.g. attention; perception; short-term memory). For example, we *attend* to what a friend is saying, you *perceive* the meaning of what she is saying, and you keep an updated record of what she has said in *short-term memory*.
*   These processing systems transform or alter the information in various ways (e.g. five connected lines are presented to our eyes, but we see a pyramid).
*   The aim of research is to specify the processes and structures (e.g. long-term memory) that underlie cognitive performance. For example, there is evidence that knowledge about how to ride a bicycle or play the piano is stored in a different part of the brain from knowledge about our personal experiences (see Chapter 13).
*   Information processing in people resembles that in computers, in that both can be regarded as having information-processing systems.
*   There is **bottom-up processing**, which is determined by external stimuli; there is also **top-down processing**, which is affected by an individual's knowledge and expectations rather than by external stimuli. For example, suppose you are waiting for a friend in a busy part of town. The fact that you fully expect to see your friend may make you think you have spotted her when someone else resembling her walks by.

Contributions

Cognitive psychologists have made numerous contributions to our understanding of the processes and structures involved in perception (Chapter 11), attention and performance (Chapter 12), memory (Chapter 13), and language and thought (Chapter 14). These contributions have taken various forms, leading Eysenck and Keane (1995) to identify three main strands in cognitive psychology (I have added a fourth):

> **KEY TERMS**
> **Bottom-up processing**: processing that is determined by external stimuli.
> **Top-down processing**: processing that is affected by an individual's knowledge and expectations rather than directly by external stimuli.

1. Experimental cognitive psychology: this approach relies largely on laboratory-based studies of cognition in normal individuals.
2. Cognitive science: this approach involves producing computer programs to mimic the processes and outputs of the human brain; it is a very precise approach, because full details of how a cognitive task is performed need to be spelled out in the program.
3. Cognitive neuropsychology: this approach involves studying cognitive processes in brain-damaged patients to understand the workings of the cognitive system (see Chapter 4). For example, the fact that some brain-damaged patients can *understand*

> **Cognitive science**
> The precision of detail needed to mimic human thought processes using computers is demonstrated by a story that may or may not be an account of a real experiment. A group of cognitive scientists wanted to see if a computer-controlled robot could be programmed to mimic a human being building a pile of wooden bricks. However, the first few attempts failed because someone forgot to include the effects of gravity in the computer program, and the robot tried to begin the pile at the top! No human being would make such a mistake; we all understand about gravity from a very early age, but remembering to include every single item of such knowledge in a computer program is a huge task.

The Evolved Octopod—a robot whose artificial "brain" allows it to move by itself.

language but cannot *speak* or *write* coherently suggests strongly that different language functions are based in different parts of the brain.

4. Cognitive neuroscience: this approach involves using advanced techniques such as PET scans, MRI scans, single-unit recording, and squid magnetometry (see Chapter 4) to study the brain in action.

One of the most notable developments has been the way in which the cognitive approach has been applied successfully to other areas such as developmental psychology and social psychology. Children's cognitive processes develop enormously during the years of childhood, and there is much interest in understanding what is happening during cognitive development (see Chapter 16). In social psychology, there is more and more focus on social cognition (see Chapter 19). It is assumed that how we behave in social situations depends on the cognitions that we have about ourselves and about others.

Evaluation

The greatest strength of cognitive psychology is the fact that it makes use of experimental research, studies on brain-damaged patients, computer simulations, and advanced techniques for studying the brain. In general terms, looking at human cognition from four different angles is likely to increase our understanding much more rapidly than looking at it from only one angle. In addition, it is reassuring to discover that many key assumptions of cognitive psychology (e.g. the distinction between short-term memory and long-term memory) have been confirmed by all four approaches. However, there are some problems with each of these approaches, as is discussed next.

The greatest limitation of experimental cognitive psychology is that it is often rather artificial. This occurs because most experiments are carried out under highly controlled conditions in a laboratory (see Chapter 30). As a result, such experiments often lack **ecological validity**, meaning that they cannot be applied to everyday settings.

Problems of ecological validity also apply to cognitive neuropsychology, because experiments on brain-damaged patients are normally carried out under controlled laboratory conditions. So far, cognitive neuropsychology has not told us much about general cognitive processes such as thinking and reasoning. In order for cognitive neuropsychology to be of most value, we would need to find patients who have very limited brain damage that affects only one type of cognitive function (e.g. speech comprehension). In fact, however, brain damage is often much more extensive than that.

There is much controversy about the value of the computer analogy used by cognitive scientists. There are usually several different processes going on in the human brain at any given time, and human thinking tends to be *imprecise* because we find it hard to bear in mind a number of different pieces of information at once. In contrast, until fairly recently, most computer programs permitted only *one* process to occur at a time, and computer functioning is typically very *precise*. There also seem to be some fundamental differences between computers and humans. As the philosopher A.J. Ayer pointed out, it is hard to "allow machines an inner life, to credit them with feeling and emotion, to treat them as moral agents."

Cognitive neuroscientists make use of an impressive range of techniques based on technological advances. However, most of these techniques do not provide detailed information of what is happening in the brain on a moment-by-moment basis (see Chapter 4). As a result, cognitive neuroscience has tended to confirm what had already been discovered previously in other ways rather than producing breakthroughs in our knowledge.

KEY TERM
Ecological validity: the extent to which the findings of laboratory studies are applicable to everyday settings.

Free Will Versus Determinism

The issue of **free will** versus **determinism** has occupied philosophers and psychologists for centuries. According to those who believe in determinism, people's actions are totally determined by the external and internal forces operating on them. Those who believe in free will argue that matters are more complicated. Most of them accept that external and internal forces are important. However, they argue that people have free will because each individual is nevertheless able to choose his or her own behaviour.

The distinction between free will and determinism can be seen if we consider the following question: "Could an individual's behaviour in a given situation have been different if he or she had willed it?" Believers in free will answer that question "Yes". In contrast, advocates of determinism respond "No". Some of the main arguments for and against each of these positions are discussed next.

How might the notions of free will and determinism be important in a situation where doctors need to decide if a criminal is responsible for his or her own actions?

Determinism

Determinists argue that a proper science of human behaviour is only possible if psychologists adopt a deterministic account, according to which everything that happens has a definite cause. Free will by definition does not have a definite cause. If free will is taken into account, it becomes impossible to predict human behaviour with any precision. According to determinists, it is often possible with other sciences to make very accurate predictions from a deterministic position (e.g. forecasting planetary motion). If determinism is regarded as not applicable to psychology, then it is either a very different science to physics, chemistry, and so on, or it is not really a science at all.

These arguments were greatly weakened by the progress of science during the twentieth century. Precise prediction based on an understanding of the causal factors involved is the exception rather than the rule even in physics and chemistry. For example, according to the principle of indeterminacy, it is impossible to determine the position and the movement of an electron at the same time.

Behaviourist and Freudian approaches

More psychologists believe in determinism than in free will. The behaviourists believed especially strongly in determinism. Skinner argued that virtually all of our behaviour is determined by environmental factors. He proposed that we repeat behaviour that is rewarded, and we do not repeat behaviour that is not rewarded. Other behaviourists argued that we can predict how someone will respond given knowledge of the current stimulus situation and that individual's previous conditioning history.

Freud was also a strong believer in determinism. He even argued that trivial phenomena, such as missing an appointment, calling someone by the wrong name, or humming a particular tune had definite causes within the individual's motivational system. For example, Freud (1971, p.157) suggested that in cases of failure to meet others as agreed, "the motive is an unusually large amount of contempt for other people."

Think of a time when you have called someone by the wrong name. Can you think of any underlying reason why you may have made this mistake?

Soft determinism

Many psychologists favour a position that was labelled **soft determinism** by William James. According to this position, there is a valid distinction between behaviour that is highly constrained by the situation (and so appears involuntary) and behaviour that is only modestly constrained by the situation (and so appears voluntary). For example, a child may apologise for swearing because he or she will be punished if an apology is not forthcoming (highly constrained behaviour) or because he or she is genuinely upset at causing offence (modestly constrained behaviour). Behaviour is determined in both cases. However, the underlying causes are more obvious when it is highly constrained by situational forces.

Evidence consistent with the views of William James was reported by Westcott (1982). Canadian students indicated how free they felt in various situations. They felt most free in situations involving an absence of responsibility or release from unpleasant stimulation (e.g. a nagging headache). In contrast, they felt least free in situations in which they had to recognise that there were limits on their behaviour (e.g. when they had to curtail their desires to fit their abilities).

Testability

The major problem with determinism (whether soft or not) is that it is not really possible to submit it to a proper test. If it were, then the issue of free will versus determinism would have been settled, and so would no longer exist as an issue! If all behaviour is determined by internal and external forces, then in principle it should be possible to predict behaviour from a knowledge of these causal factors. In fact, we usually only have very limited knowledge of the internal and external forces that might be influencing an individual's behaviour. As a result, it remains no more than an article of faith that eventually we will be able to predict human behaviour accurately.

The issue of free will versus determinism was considered in detail by Valentine (1992). In spite of the various criticisms of the deterministic position, she came to the following conclusion: "Determinism seems to have the edge in this difficult debate."

Free will

Most people feel that they possess free will, in the sense that they can freely choose what to do from a number of options. As Dr Samuel Johnson (1709–1784) said to Boswell, "We know our will is free, and there's an end on't." Most people also have feelings of personal responsibility, presumably because they feel that they are in at least partial control of their behaviour.

Humanistic approach

Humanistic psychologists such as Carl Rogers and Abraham Maslow are among those who believe in free will. They argued that people exercise choice in their behaviour, and they denied that people's behaviour is at the mercy of outside forces. Rogers' client-centred therapy is based on the assumption that the client has free will. The therapist is called a "facilitator" precisely because his or her role is to make it easier for the client to exercise free will in such a way as to maximise the rewardingness of the client's life. As we saw earlier in the chapter, humanistic psychologists argued that regarding human behaviour as being determined by external forces is "de-humanising" and incorrect.

Causality

Those who believe in free will have to confront two major problems. First, it is hard to provide a precise account of what is meant by free will. Determinism is based on the assumption that all behaviour has one or more causes, and it could be argued that free will implies that behaviour is random and has no cause. However, very few people would want to argue for such an extreme position. Anyone whose behaviour seemed to be random would probably be classified as mentally ill or very stupid. If free will does not imply that behaviour has no cause, then we need to know how free will plays a part in causing behaviour.

Determinism vs. Free will	
Determinism	**Free will**
Behaviourism	Humanistic approach
Freudian psychodynamics	
Do you think the cognitive psychologists fit into one or other of these lists? Can you explain your answer?	

Second, most successful sciences are based on the assumption of determinism. It is possible that determinism applies to the natural world but does not apply to humans. If that is the case, then there are enormous implications for psychology which have hardly been addressed as yet.

Conclusions

The issue of free will versus determinism has created more heat than light for various reasons. First, it is not clear that it makes much sense to talk about "free will", because this assumes there is an agent (i.e. the will) that may or may not operate in an unrestrained way. As the philosopher John Locke (1632–1704) pointed out, "We may as properly say that the singing faculty sings and the dancing faculty dances as that the will chooses."

Second, the issue is philosophical rather than scientific, as it is impossible to design an experiment to decide whether or not free will influences human behaviour. As William James (1890, p.323) put it, "the fact is that the question of free will is insoluble on strictly psychological grounds." In other words, we can never know whether an individual's behaviour in a given situation could have been different if he or she had so willed it.

Third, although those who believe in determinism or free will often seem to have radically different views, there is more common ground between them than is generally realised. Regardless of their position on the issue of free will versus determinism, most psychologists accept that heredity, past experience, and the present environment all influence our behaviour. Although some of these factors (such as the environment) are external to the individual, others are internal. Most of these internal factors (such as character or personality) are the results of causal sequences stretching back into the past. The dispute then narrows to the issue of whether a solitary internal factor (variously called free will or self) is somehow immune from the influence of the past.

Fourth, and most important, we can go a step further and argue that there is no real incompatibility between determinism and free will at all. According to determinists, it is possible in principle to show that an individual's actions are caused by a sequence of physical activities in the brain. If free will (e.g. conscious thinking and decision making) forms part of that sequence, it is possible to believe in free will and human responsibility at the same time as holding to a deterministic position. This would not be the case if free will is regarded as an intruder forcing its way into the sequence of physical activities in the brain, but there are no good grounds for adopting this position. In other words, the entire controversy between determinism and free will may be artificial and of less concern to psychologists than has generally been supposed.

> ■ Research activity: In small groups, think of some important decisions you have made or will probably make in the future. Discuss the extent to which they are made using free will. It might be useful to think of them on a scale from 1 to 10, where 1 is free choice and 10 is fully predetermined.

Reductionism

According to the *Concise Oxford Dictionary*, **reductionism** means "the analysis of complex things into simple constituents". Within the context of psychology, the term has been used to refer to two rather different theoretical approaches. First, there is the belief that the phenomena of psychology can potentially be accounted for within the framework of more basic sciences or disciplines (such as physiology). Second, there is the assumption that complex forms of behaviour can be explained in terms of simple principles. For example, the behaviourists argued that complex forms of behaviour could be regarded as consisting of a set of simple stimulus–response associations.

> **KEY TERM**
> **Reductionism**: the notion that psychology can ultimately be reduced to more basic sciences such as physiology or biochemistry.

Reductionism across scientific disciplines

Psychology is related to several other scientific disciplines. It involves trying to understand people's behaviour, and this is influenced in part by basic internal processes of interest

Reductionism: the analysis of complex things into simple constituents.

to physiologists and biochemists. As people are social animals, their behaviour is also affected by various social processes (e.g. conformity; the desire to impress others). The multi-disciplinary nature of psychology has led many psychologists to focus on the ways in which it is related to other sciences.

Scientific disciplines can be regarded as being organised in a hierarchical way, with the less precise and more general sciences at the top, and the more precise and narrowly focused sciences at the bottom. One could construct a hierarchy including psychology looking like this:

- Sociology: the science of groups and societies.
- Psychology: the science of human and animal behaviour.
- Physiology: the science of the functional working of the healthy body.
- Biochemistry: the science of the chemistry of the living organism.

Physiological and psychological explanations

Neurology and biochemistry underlie all behaviour. What happens when a person sees a sunset? The physiological explanation would be that light reflected from the landscape forms an image on the retina, which is converted into a neural signal and transmitted to the brain, and so on. No-one disputes that this is true, and the process is absolutely essential, but does it give a full and adequate explanation of what is going on? A psychological explanation would probably include the personal and social relevance of the experience, which many would argue are of equal value.

Reductionists argue that the sciences towards the top of the hierarchy will at some point be replaced by those towards the bottom. In the case of psychology, this implies that it should ultimately be possible to explain psychological phenomena in physiological or biochemical terms. However, it should be noted that other hierarchical orderings are possible. For example, Putnam (1973) favoured the following ordering: social groups; multi-cellular living things; cells; molecules; atoms; and elementary particles.

Advantages of reductionism

The reductionist approach has an immediate appeal. Biochemistry, physiology, psychology, and sociology are all concerned with human functioning, so there is some overlap in their subject matter. As a result, it would seem that much could be gained from research co-operation among these disciplines. There might be an increased understanding of psychology resulting from taking full account of the relevant contributions of other sciences. Over time, this might lead to a *theoretical unification* in which the theories put forward by psychologists, physiologists, and biochemists become increasingly similar.

Biochemistry and physiology can be regarded as more developed and "scientific" than psychology or sociology. For example, it is probably true that there are more well-established facts and theories in biochemistry and physiology than in psychology or sociology. These arguments provide grounds for preferring biochemical or physiological explanations of behaviour to those offered by psychology, and thus for making use of a reductionist approach.

Even those who are not fully convinced of the benefits of reductionism generally accept that psychological theories should be consistent or *compatible* with physiological findings. For example, research by Zeki (1993) has shown that in brain studies of visual perception, different processes take place in different areas of the brain (see Chapter 4). Future theories of visual perception put forward by psychologists will need to take those findings into account.

Disadvantages of reductionism

In spite of its attractions, there are strong arguments against reductionism. Much human behaviour cannot be understood solely in terms of basic biological and physiological processes. As Putnam (1973, p.141) pointed out:

> *Psychology is as under-determined by biology as it is by elementary particle physics, and ... people's psychology is partly a reflection of deeply entrenched societal beliefs.*

Putnam's position can be illustrated by considering a simple example. Suppose a psychologist wants to predict how a group of people will vote in a forthcoming election. No-one in their right mind would argue that a detailed biochemical and physiological examination of their brains would be of much value! Voting behaviour is determined by social attitudes, group pressures, and so on, rather than directly by underlying biochemical and physiological processes. However, it is reasonable to assume that some issues within psychology do lend themselves to the reductionist perspective. Thus, the usefulness of the reductionist approach may depend very much on the specific questions we are asking.

Further problems for the reductionist approach can be seen if we consider the relationship between psychology and physiology. As Valentine (1992) pointed out, psychology typically describes the *processes* involved in performing some activity (e.g. visual perception), whereas physiology focuses more on the *structures* that are involved. In other words, psychologists tend to be interested in *how* questions, whereas physiologists are interested in *where* questions. These differences pose formidable obstacles to any attempt to reduce psychology to physiology.

Another obvious problem with reductionism is that it has not worked very well in practice. It is hard to think of many examples of psychological phenomena that have been explained completely in physiological or biochemical terms. This suggests that the psychodynamic, behaviourist, and humanistic psychologists were well advised to avoid the assumption that psychology could be reduced to physiology or biochemistry.

A final problem with reductionism is that lower-level explanations (such as those provided by physiologists) often contain many irrelevant details from the perspective of psychology. This can make it very hard to distinguish between what is relevant and what is irrelevant in a physiological account. This problem may have struck you if you have ever looked through a textbook of physiological psychology.

Simplifying complex issues

Reductionism in a different sense is involved when theorists try to reduce complex phenomena to separate simple parts. This approach often involves ignoring the findings from other sciences when developing theories. The behaviourists were reductionists in this sense. As was mentioned earlier, they argued that the simple stimulus–response association was the appropriate unit of analysis in psychology. According to the behaviourists, we can explain complex forms of behaviour (e.g. use of language; problem solving; reasoning) by assuming that they involve the use of numerous stimulus–response units, and by assigning key importance to reward or reinforcement. The behaviourists tended not to be interested in physiological processes, arguing that what was important was to focus on observable stimuli and responses.

An example of the ways in which the behaviourists tried to simplify matters was Skinner's (1957) attempt to explain the complexities of language acquisition. He argued that children produce words and sentences that are rewarded or reinforced (see Chapter 14). However, language acquisition cannot be accounted for in such simple terms (Chomsky, 1959).

Some of the problems of this type of reductionist position can be seen if we consider the chemistry of water (H_2O). It is possible to reduce water to hydrogen (H) and oxygen (O). Hydrogen burns and oxygen is necessary for burning, but water lacks both of those attributes. Here is a case where a reductionist approach confuses rather than clarifies.

Most phenomena in psychology are usually better explained in terms of various factors operating at different levels of complexity than in terms of a range of simple factors. For example, a full account of the ways in which children acquire language requires the combined expertise of developmental, social, and cognitive psychologists, as well as that of psycholinguists.

The limitations of the reductionistic approach used by the behaviourists can also be seen if we consider theoretical developments within cognitive psychology (see Chapters 11–14). For example, many theorists focus on **schemas**, which are organised

Can you suggest some issues within psychology that might lend themselves to a reductionist approach?

KEY TERM
Schemas: organised packets of information stored in long-term memory.

packets of information stored in long-term memory. Schema theories have proved very useful, but it makes no sense to regard schemas as consisting of stimulus–response units.

The reductionist position of the behaviourists is also rather limited in terms of its application to behaviour therapy as a form of treatment for mental disorders (see Chapter 26). According to the behaviourist approach, patients have learned certain symptoms or responses through faulty learning, and therapy should involve changing those responses into more useful ones. Some of the limitations of this approach can be seen if we consider panic disorder, a condition in which patients experience numerous panic attacks (see pages 685–686). It proved hard to devise forms of behaviour therapy for panic disorder patients, in part because their problems cannot be regarded simply as faulty responses. In essence, panic patients exaggerate the threateningness of their own bodily symptoms, and it is this, rather than their actual physiological activity, that is the problem needing treatment.

In sum, reductionism is not a detailed theory in the sense of producing testable hypotheses. What it does is to provide a set of assumptions that can be used to guide theory and research. As such, it is hard to know whether or not reductionism will prove of value in the future. However, the evidence available so far does not really support the reductionist emphasis on simplicity.

Alternatives to reductionism

The humanistic approach discussed earlier in the chapter provides one alternative to reductionism. As we have seen, humanistic psychologists such as Maslow and Rogers attached great importance to the self-concept, and to the efforts by humans to realise their potential by means of self-actualisation. Within this approach, there is no systematic attempt to divide the self up into smaller units, or to identify the physiological processes associated with the self-concept.

Many psychologists argue that the humanistic approach to reductionism is too limited. The refusal of humanistic psychologists to consider any kind of reductionism suggests that they do not regard physiological and biological factors as having any real significance. It may be true that each individual's conscious experience is of importance in understanding his or her behaviour. However, it is likely that other factors need to be taken into account.

Another alternative to reductionism is what could be called the **eclectic approach**, in which relevant information is gathered together from various sources and disciplines. Consider, for example, research on the causes of schizophrenia (a serious condition involving hallucinations and loss of contact with reality). There is evidence that genetic factors are involved. At the biochemical level, some studies have suggested that schizophrenics tend to be unduly sensitive to the neurotransmitter dopamine (see Davison & Neale, 1990). Other evidence reviewed by Davison and Neale indicates that poor social relationships and adverse life events also play a part in producing schizophrenia (see Chapter 25).

Reductionists might be tempted to produce a biochemical theory of schizophrenia. However, such an approach would involve ignoring environmental factors such as life events. According to the eclectic approach, a full understanding of schizophrenia involves considering all the relevant factors and the ways in which they combine.

The main problem with the eclectic approach is that it is very hard to combine information from different disciplines into a single theory. For example, it is not very clear how the concepts of biochemistry can be combined with those of life-event research. However, psychology should not ignore potentially valuable information from other disciplines. This can be seen clearly in recent studies on the brain by cognitive neuroscientists (see Chapter 4). Observation of physiological processes in the brain by means of MRI and PET scans is increasing our knowledge of human cognition.

KEY TERM
Eclectic approach: an approach to psychology in which relevant information from other sciences (e.g. physiology; biochemistry) is incorporated into psychological theories.

PERSONAL REFLECTIONS

• In the early days of psychology, most psychologists identified themselves as belonging to a school of psychology (e.g. behaviourism; psychoanalysis). As a result, the various major approaches have considerable historical importance. Nowadays, however, the impact of these approaches is fairly indirect. For example, I regard myself as a cognitive psychologist, but some of the ideas put forward by behaviourists, humanistic psychologists, and psychodynamic psychologists have greatly influenced my thinking.

SUMMARY

The psychodynamic approach was started by Freud, who put forward a complex set of theories about human development and proposed a form of treatment known as psychoanalysis. He argued that the mind is divided into the id, ego, and superego, and that it has conscious, preconscious, and unconscious levels. There were five stages in his theory of psychosexual development: oral stage; anal stage; phallic stage; latency stage; and genital stage. Fixation at any of these stages influences adult personality. Freud founded developmental psychology, proposed one of the first systematic theories of personality, and devised a form of therapy that was unsurpassed for over 80 years. However, his approach was basically unscientific, making many of his ideas untestable. Most of his testable ideas have been disproved. Psychoanalysis is an effective form of treatment, but little is known of why it is effective.

Psychodynamic approach

The behaviourists argued that psychology should be the study of behaviour, with the unit of analysis being the stimulus–response association. Learning is of key importance, and can be understood in terms of conditioning principles. Behaviour depends on environmental rather than genetic factors. Among the numerous contributions of behaviourism are behaviour therapy, organisational behaviour modification, and programmed learning. Behaviourism has had enormous influence through its emphasis on behaviour rather than introspection, and its insistence on studying behaviour in controlled conditions. However, the theory of behaviour put forward by the behaviourists has been rejected by most psychologists. The notion that any response can be conditioned in any stimulus situation is incorrect, and the behaviourists de-emphasised the influence

Behaviourist approach

Although behaviourist ideas have influenced theories of learning, organisational behaviour, and therapy, much of the work has relied on highly controlled laboratory experiments.

of internal factors such as motivation and knowledge. In many ways, the behaviourists put forward a theory of performance rather than of learning.

Humanist approach

Humanistic psychologists focused on personal responsibility, free will, and the individual's striving towards personal growth and fulfilment. They relied heavily on phenomenology as a technique for understanding behaviour. Maslow argued in his hierarchy of needs that human motivation includes physiological needs, security and safety needs, needs for love and belongingness, esteem needs, cognitive needs, and the need for self-actualisation. Rogers assumed that the concept of self is of great importance; he distinguished between the self-concept and the ideal self. He developed client-centred therapy, in which the therapist is unconditional in positive regard and is genuine and empathic. Humanistic psychology is a comprehensive approach, and client-centred therapy is moderately effective. However, humanistic psychology suffers from being unscientific, focusing too much on conscious awareness, and minimising the impact of the environment on the individual.

Cognitive approach

Cognitive psychologists assume that there is an information-processing system in which information is altered or transformed. The goal of research is to specify the structures and processes (bottom-up and top-down) underlying cognitive performance. There are four main strands in cognitive psychology: experimental cognitive psychology; cognitive science; cognitive neuropsychology; and cognitive neuroscience. The findings from these approaches often agree, but each approach has its own limitations

Free will versus determinism

Determinists argue that all human behaviour has a definite cause. The behaviourists and psychoanalysts are determinists. According to those who favour soft determinism, some behaviour is highly constrained by the situation, whereas other behaviour is only modestly constrained. The major problem with determinism is that it is not possible to submit it to a proper experimental test. Most people feel that they possess free will, and so are able to choose freely what to do in many situations. Humanistic psychologists believe in free will. If free will does not imply that behaviour has no cause (and thus is random), then we need to know how free will helps to cause behaviour. In fact, most psychologists accept that heredity, past experience, and the present environment all influence behaviour, and so the key issue is whether there is an internal factor known as free will which also influences behaviour.

The study of psychological processes can be likened to being at a crossroads with different approaches pointing you in different directions.

Sciences can be seen as organised in a hierarchy, with the more general sciences at the top and the more precise and narrowly focused ones at the bottom. Reductionism has potential advantages: different sciences have overlapping interests; lower-level sciences are more developed than higher-level ones; theoretical unification could increase the explanatory power of psychology. Reductionism has several disadvantages: many psychological phenomena cannot be reduced to physiological or biological terms; psychology is concerned with processes, whereas physiology is concerned with structure; reductionism has not worked very well in practice. Reductionism also refers to attempts to reduce complex phenomena to separate simple parts. In fact, most phenomena in psychology are best explained in terms of factors operating at different levels of complexity. According to the eclectic approach, psychologists should gather relevant information together from various sources and disciplines.

Reductionism

FURTHER READING

All of the topics discussed in this chapter are covered in M.W. Eysenck (1994), *Perspectives on psychology*, Hove, UK: Psychology Press. Another book covering all the topics is A.E. Wadeley, A. Birch, and A. Malim (1997), *Perspectives in psychology (2nd Edn.)*, Basingstoke: MacMillan.

REVISION QUESTIONS

1   Compare and contrast the behaviourist and psychodynamic approaches to psychology.   (24 marks)
2a Explain what is meant by reductionism.   (6 marks)
2b Discuss examples of reductionism in psychology.   (18 marks)
3   Critically consider contributions made by psychology to the free will versus determinism debate.   (24 marks)

- **Central and peripheral nervous systems**
  Brain, spinal cord, and nerve cells: what they are and how they work.

  The three main regions of the brain and their functions
  The five divisions into which the regions can be subdivided
  The structure of the spinal cord
  The somatic and autonomic nervous systems

- **Endocrine system**
  The endocrine glands and the hormones they produce.

  The hypothalamus and its functions
  Hormone-producing glands: pituitary, gonads, adrenals, thyroid, and pancreas

- **Influences of the three systems**
  How the systems interact to affect our feelings and behaviour.

  Studies by Magoun et al. and by Andersson et al. on homeostasis

- **Neural and synaptic activity**
  Neurons are the basic units of the nervous system. How do they work?

  Pinel's descriptions of electrical activity in and around neurons: resting and action potentials
  Synapses and neurotransmitter release
  The five classes of neurotransmitters
  Pinel's seven stages of neurotransmitter action
  Effects of drugs on neural activity

- **Drugs and behaviour**
  How drugs, both legal and illegal, can affect our bodies and our behaviour.

  Addiction: physical or psychological dependence?
  Depressants, including alcohol and its effects
  Opiates, including morphine and heroin
  Stimulants, including cocaine and amphetamine
  Hallucinogens and cannabis

3

The Nervous System

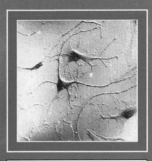

Mature human brain cells grown in a laboratory culture.

This chapter, and the three following ones, are all concerned with **biopsychology**. It can be defined as "the scientific study of the biology of behaviour" (Pinel, 1997, p.3). In other words, biopsychology involves using a biological approach to study psychology and to obtain an understanding of human and animal behaviour.

Any serious application of a biological approach to psychology must involve a systematic focus on the brain and how it works. That is a central concern of this chapter and the next. In this chapter, our starting point is the nervous system. Some of the nervous system (the central nervous system) is located within the brain and the spinal cord, with the rest of it (the peripheral nervous system) being located outside those parts of the body. We will deal with the processes involved in the transmission of neural impulses within the nervous system. We will also discuss the relationships between the nervous system and hormonal processes in the endocrine system.

The final part of this chapter is devoted to the effects of drugs on behaviour. Why is this of relevance in a chapter on basic neural and hormonal processes? The answer is that drugs have their effects on behaviour because they influence basic neural processes. Indeed, it is as a result of our enhanced understanding of neural transmission that drug companies have been able to develop increasingly sophisticated drugs having fairly precise effects on behaviour.

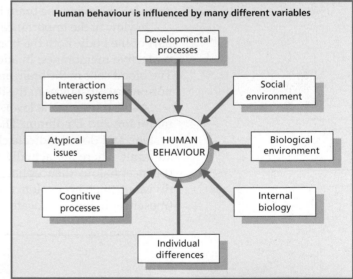

Human behaviour is influenced by many different variables

- Developmental processes
- Interaction between systems
- Social environment
- Atypical issues
- HUMAN BEHAVIOUR
- Biological environment
- Cognitive processes
- Internal biology
- Individual differences

Nervous System

The nervous system contains all of the nerve cells in the body. It is made up of between 15 and 20 billion neurons. **Neurons** are cells that are specialised to conduct electrical impulses, and they form the basic units of the nervous system. There are various kinds of neurons, but they all possess certain key features:

- A cell body or **soma** which contains a nucleus.
- At one end of the cell body are **dendrites**, which conduct nerve impulses towards the soma.
- At the other end of the cell body is the **axon**, which conducts nerve impulses away from the soma and towards the terminal buttons.

KEY TERMS
Biopsychology: a biological approach to the study of psychology.
Neurons: cells that are specialised to conduct electrical impulses.
Soma: a cell body containing a nucleus.
Dendrites: parts of the neuron that conduct nerve impulses towards the soma or cell body.
Axon: a part of the neuron that conducts nerve impulses away from the cell body or soma.

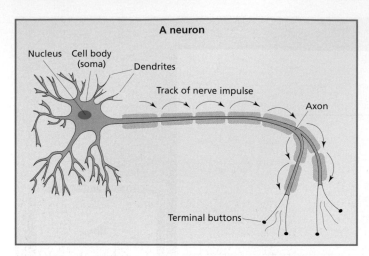

A neuron

Nucleus   Cell body (soma)   Dendrites

Track of nerve impulse

Axon

Terminal buttons

Why are "involuntary" muscle movements so important?

- There is an outer layer or cell membrane, which allows electrically charged particles or **ions** to enter or to leave the neuron.
- Receptors, which are cells that respond to specific types of stimuli.

The nervous system is divided into two main sub-systems:

- Central nervous system: this consists of the brain and the spinal cord; it is protected by bone and by fluid circulating around it.
- Peripheral nervous system: this consists of all the other nerve cells in the body. It is divided into the somatic nervous system, which is concerned with voluntary movements of skeletal muscles (those attached to our bones), and the autonomic nervous system, which is concerned with involuntary movements of non-skeletal muscles (e.g. those of the heart).

Central nervous system

We will start our coverage of the central nervous system with the brain, and then consider the spinal cord. The first point that needs to be made about the brain is its complexity. In order to understand the brain, we must learn about its structure and about the functions of the various parts. It has proved rather easier to study structure than function. Only recently have technological advances allowed us to identify the functions of different brain areas by observing the brain in action (see Chapter 4).

In view of the importance of the brain, it is not surprising that it is the most protected part of the body. Both the brain and the spinal cord are encased in bone and covered by protective membranes. In addition, there is what is known as the **blood–brain barrier**. The blood cells in the brain are designed in such a way that they prevent several toxic or poisonous substances in the blood from gaining access to the brain.

At the most general level, the brain can be divided into three main regions: forebrain; midbrain; and hindbrain. These terms refer to their locations in the embryo's nervous system, and do *not* indicate clearly the relative position of the different brain regions in an adult. There are actually five major divisions of the brain. Two of these divisions (telencephalon; diencephalon) are contained within the forebrain, and two other divisions (metencephalon; myencephalon) are in the hindbrain. The remaining division (mesencephalon) is located in the midbrain. The four divisions apart from the

KEY TERMS
Ions: particles that are either positively or negatively charged.
Blood–brain barrier: the system of blood cells in the brain that provides a defence against poisonous substances in the blood entering and damaging the brain.

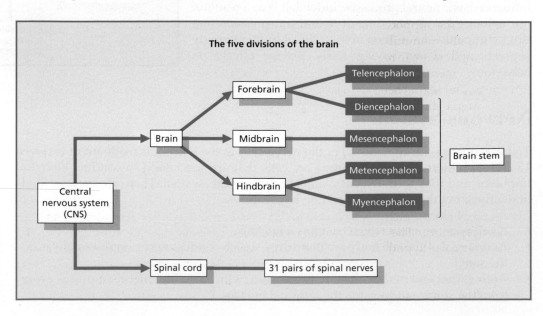

The five divisions of the brain

Central nervous system (CNS) → Brain → Forebrain → Telencephalon, Diencephalon

Brain → Midbrain → Mesencephalon

Brain → Hindbrain → Metencephalon, Myencephalon

Diencephalon, Mesencephalon, Metencephalon, Myencephalon → Brain stem

Central nervous system (CNS) → Spinal cord → 31 pairs of spinal nerves

telencephalon are sometimes described as the brain stem. We will consider all five divisions of the brain in turn.

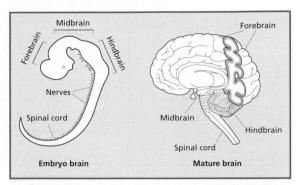

Embryo brain   **Mature brain**

Telencephalon

This is easily the largest and the most important division of the human brain. It plays a crucial role in thinking, the use of language, perception, and numerous other cognitive abilities. The two cerebral hemispheres are covered by a layer of tissue known as the cerebral cortex. The cerebral cortex is deeply furrowed or grooved. The ridges between these furrows are known as gyri. By far the largest furrow is the longitudinal fissure that runs between the cerebral hemispheres. The two hemispheres are almost separate from each other, but are connected by the corpus callosum and a few other structures.

Two of the most obvious features of each hemisphere are the central fissure or furrow and the lateral fissure. These fissures help to define the four lobes or areas of each hemisphere. The frontal lobes are at the front of each hemisphere, and their boundary is formed by the central and lateral fissures. The precentral gyri, which contain the motor cortex, are located in the frontal lobes. Behind the frontal lobe at the top of each hemisphere is the parietal lobe. The parietal lobes contain the postcentral gyri, which in turn contain the somatosensory cortex concerned with bodily sensations.

The other two lobes are the temporal lobe and the occipital lobe. The temporal lobes are behind the frontal lobes and underneath the parietal lobes. The superior temporal gyri, which contain the auditory cortex, are located in the temporal lobes. The occipital lobes are at the back of the cortex, and they are involved in visual processing.

About 90% of the human cerebral cortex is neocortex (literally new cortex), which consists of six layers. The neurons in the neocortex are mainly linked to other neurons within the same layer or within an adjacent layer. As a result, neocortex is organised in columns, with each column running vertically through the six layers. One part of the cortex that is not neocortex is the hippocampus, which is located in the temporal lobes. According to Pinel (1997, p.374), it "is involved in the consolidation of long-term memories for spatial location, not their storage."

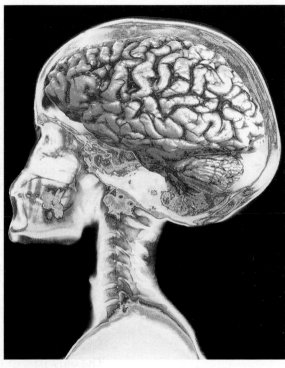

A computer enhanced illustration of the human brain in situ.

Some parts of the telencephalon are located mostly or entirely in subcortical areas; they include the limbic system and the basal ganglia motor system. The limbic system consists of a number of structures including the amygdala, the septum, the hippocampus, the cingulate cortex, the fornix, and the mammillary body. The main functions of the limbic system are to regulate several kinds of motivated behaviour, including eating, aggression, avoidance behaviour, and sexual behaviour, and associated emotions such as anger and anxiety (see Chapter 6). The basal ganglia consist of the striatum, globus pallidus, and the amygdala (which is often regarded as part of this system as well as the limbic system). One of the key functions of the basal ganglia is to assist in the production of voluntary motor responses (see Chapter 4).

> It is interesting to note that the "newer" areas of the brain (in evolutionary terms) contain centres for the mediation of relatively "new" skills (again in evolutionary terms). What are these "new" skills, and what mediation centres could we find in "old" parts of the brain? Can you link some of these activities with "old" parts of the brain—in evolutionary terms?

Diencephalon

The diencephalon, which is the other major division of the forebrain, is much smaller than the telencephalon. The two most important structures in the diencephalon are the thalamus and the hypothalamus. The hypothalamus is much smaller than the thalamus. It is situated below the thalamus. The hypothalamus is involved in the control of several functions such as body temperature, hunger, and thirst. It is also involved in the control of sexual behaviour. Finally, the hypothalamus plays an important role in the control of

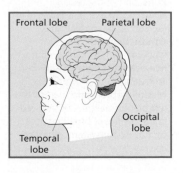

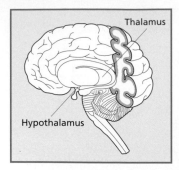

the endocrine (hormonal) system. For example, the hypothalamus is directly connected to the anterior pituitary gland, which has been described as the body's "master gland".

What about the thalamus? One of its main functions is to act as a relay station passing signals on to higher brain centres. For example, the medial geniculate nucleus receives signals from the inner ear and sends them to the primary auditory cortex. In similar fashion, the lateral geniculate nucleus receives information from the eye and sends it to the primary visual cortex, and the ventral posterior nucleus receives somatosensory (bodily sensation) information and sends it to the primary somatosensory cortex.

Mesencephalon

The mesencephalon or midbrain has two major parts: the tectum and the tegmentum. In general terms, the mesencephalon plays a much less central role in human behaviour than does the forebrain. However, it has various important functions. The tectum forms part of both the visual and auditory systems. The tegmentum contains part of the **reticular formation**, which is concerned with arousal and other functions (see later). It contains the substantia nigra and the red nucleus, both of which are important parts of the motor system. It also contains the periaqueductal grey matter. This is involved in controlling movements and in producing the pain-reducing effects of opiates.

Metencephalon

This is one of the two divisions of the hindbrain. The two main parts of the metencephalon are the **pons** and the **cerebellum**. The pons contains part of the reticular formation concerned with consciousness, and the cerebellum is concerned with precise control of movements.

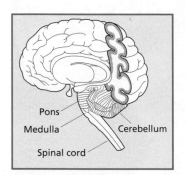

Myencephalon

The myencephalon is the other division of the hindbrain. It contains one important structure known as the medulla. Parts of the reticular formation are located in the **medulla oblongata**, and are involved in the control of respiration and regulation of the cardiovascular system. Most of the myencephalon is devoted to the function of relaying signals between the other divisions of the brain and the body.

Spinal cord

The only part of the central nervous system we have not discussed is the spinal cord. It is a thin structure going from the base of the brain all the way down to the coccyx bone at the lower end of the back. The spinal cord is protected by 24 vertebrae or bony segments running from the neck to the lower back regions. There are holes in these vertebrae, and the spinal cord passes through these holes.

The spinal cord consists of an inner area of grey matter and an outer area of white matter. White matter consists mainly of myelinated or sheathed axons, whereas grey matter consists of cell bodies and unmyelinated axons. The spinal cord contains 31 pairs of spinal nerves, with each nerve dividing into two roots as it approaches the spinal cord. The dorsal root, which is at the back, contains sensory neurons that assist in the transmission of sensory signals to the brain. The ventral root, which is at the front, contains motor neurons. These neurons are involved in the transmission of motor signals to skeletal muscles and to the internal organs (e.g. stomach; heart).

Peripheral nervous system

The peripheral nervous system comprises all the nerve cells in the body that are not contained within the central nervous system. It consists of two parts: the somatic nervous system and the autonomic nervous system. The somatic nervous system is concerned with interactions with the external environment, whereas the autonomic nervous system is concerned with the body's internal environment.

The first issue to be discussed is the relationship between the peripheral nervous system and the central nervous system. Most of the nerves of the peripheral nervous system project from the spinal cord. Some spinal nerves are involved in receiving signals

KEY TERMS
Reticular formation: a part of the cortex concerned with arousal, the regulation of sleep, the control of respiration, and regulation of the cardiovascular system.
Pons: part of the reticular activating system; it is involved in the control of consciousness.
Cerebellum: part of the hindbrain; it is involved in the fine control of balance and co-ordination.
Medulla oblongata: part of the reticular formation; it is involved in the control of breathing, the cardiovascular system, digestion, and swallowing.

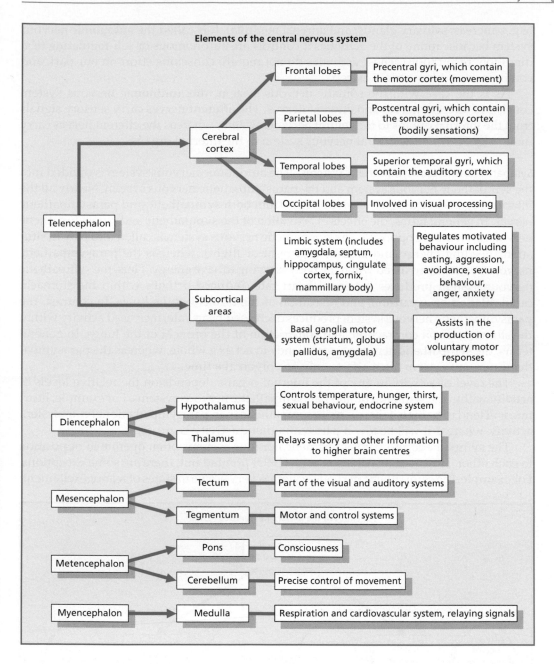

Elements of the central nervous system

Telencephalon

Cerebral cortex
- Frontal lobes → Precentral gyri, which contain the motor cortex (movement)
- Parietal lobes → Postcentral gyri, which contain the somatosensory cortex (bodily sensations)
- Temporal lobes → Superior temporal gyri, which contain the auditory cortex
- Occipital lobes → Involved in visual processing

Subcortical areas
- Limbic system (includes amygdala, septum, hippocampus, cingulate cortex, fornix, mammillary body) → Regulates motivated behaviour including eating, aggression, avoidance, sexual behaviour, anger, anxiety
- Basal ganglia motor system (striatum, globus pallidus, amygdala) → Assists in the production of voluntary motor responses

Diencephalon
- Hypothalamus → Controls temperature, hunger, thirst, sexual behaviour, endocrine system
- Thalamus → Relays sensory and other information to higher brain centres

Mesencephalon
- Tectum → Part of the visual and auditory systems
- Tegmentum → Motor and control systems

Metencephalon
- Pons → Consciousness
- Cerebellum → Precise control of movement

Myencephalon
- Medulla → Respiration and cardiovascular system, relaying signals

from (and sending them to) skeletal muscles within the somatic nervous system, whereas others receive signals from (and send them to) the internal organs within the autonomic nervous system. In addition, there are connections between the central nervous system and the peripheral nervous system via 12 pairs of cranial nerves. Most of them contain both sensory and motor fibres, and nearly all transmit signals to and from the head or neck. The major exception is the tenth or vagus nerve, which regulates the functioning of the abdominal and thoracic organs.

Somatic nervous system
The somatic nervous system consists of afferent nerves that carry signals from the eyes, ears, skeletal muscles, and the skin to the central nervous system, and efferent nerves that carry signals that have come from the central nervous system to the skeletal muscles, skin, and so on.

Autonomic nervous system
The autonomic nervous system is concerned with regulating the functioning of the internal environment, including the heart, stomach, lungs, intestines, and various glands

Can you think of situations where long-term practice could alter the sensitivity of somatic afferent/efferent pathways? Example: a chef may become accustomed to a hot atmosphere.

(e.g. pancreas; salivary glands; and adrenal medulla). It is called the autonomic nervous system because many of the activities it controls are autonomous or self-regulating (e.g. digestion; respiration). These activities do not require conscious effort on our part, and continue even when we are asleep.

As is the case with the somatic nervous system, the autonomic nervous system consists of afferent nerves and efferent nerves. The afferent nerves carry sensory signals from the internal organs to the central nervous system, whereas the efferent nerves carry motor signals from the central nervous system to the internal organs.

Sympathetic and parasympathetic systems.   The autonomic nervous system is divided into the sympathetic nervous system and the parasympathetic nervous system. Nearly all the internal organs of the body receive signals from both sympathetic and parasympathetic nerves. In general terms, the effects of activation of the sympathetic and parasympathetic nervous systems are opposite. The sympathetic nervous system is called into play in situations needing energy and arousal (e.g. fight or flight), whereas the parasympathetic nervous system is involved when the body is trying to save energy. Thus, the sympathetic nervous system produces increased heart rate, reduced activity within the stomach, pupil dilation or expansion, and relaxation of the bronchi of the lungs. In contrast, the parasympathetic nervous system produces decreased heart rate, increased activity within the stomach, pupil contraction, and constriction of the bronchi of the lungs. In general terms, the sympathetic nervous system tends to act as a whole, whereas the parasympathetic nervous system often affects only one organ at a time.

The level of activity in any of the internal organs depends on the relative levels of activity within the sympathetic and parasympathetic nervous systems. For example, heart rate will tend to be high if there is more sympathetic than parasympathetic nervous system activity, whereas it will be low if parasympathetic activity is greater.

The sympathetic and parasympathetic nervous systems often operate in opposition to each other. However, as Atkinson et al. (1993) pointed out, there are some exceptions. For example, the sympathetic nervous system is very active in states of fear or excitement,

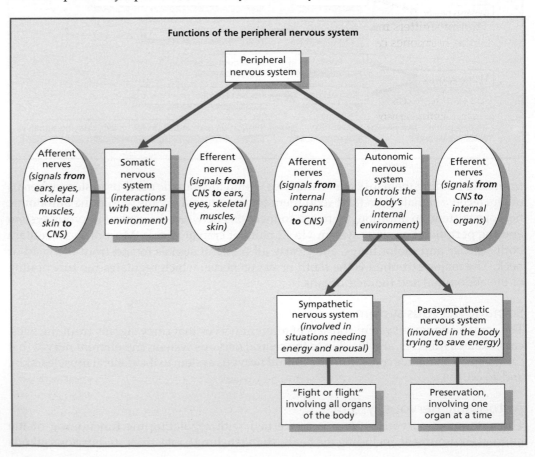

and yet parasympathetic activity can cause people who are fearful or excited to have an involuntary discharge of their bladder or bowels. Another example is sex in the male. Parasympathetic activity is required to obtain an erection, whereas sympathetic activity is needed for ejaculation.

Endocrine System

The endocrine system consists of a number of glands, including the following: the pituitary gland; the thyroid gland; the parathyroid gland; the adrenal gland; the pancreas; and the gonads. The endocrine system is not part of the nervous system, but there are numerous interactions between the endocrine system and the peripheral nervous system. More specifically, the endocrine glands secrete **hormones**, which are chemical substances released into the bloodstream. They are so important that they have sometimes been described as "the messengers of life".

Hormones can have dramatic effects on our feelings and behaviour. However, they take some time to produce their effects because they are transmitted fairly slowly by the bloodstream. Endocrine glands are ductless glands. They can be contrasted with glands having ducts or passages along which substances such as sweat or tears travel to the surface of the body.

Can you think of a good example of a system in the human body that shows an interaction between the endocrine and nervous systems?

What are the main differences between the endocrine system and the nervous system? Some of the key ones are as follows:

- The nervous system generally acts rapidly, whereas the endocrine system acts fairly slowly.
- The nervous system controls the activities of the body *directly* by activating muscles and glands, whereas the endocrine system exerts control *indirectly* via hormones circulating in the bloodstream.
- Neurotransmitters (chemicals, see later) in the nervous system have specific and highly localised effects, whereas hormones typically spread around the body.
- Neurotransmitters in the nervous system generally have short-lived effects, whereas hormones can remain in the bloodstream for long periods of time.

Nervous system	Endocrine system
• Consists of nerve cells	• Consists of ductless glands
• Acts by transmitting nerve impulses	• Acts by release of hormones
• Acts rapidly	• Acts slowly
• Direct control	• Indirect control
• Specific localised effects of neurotransmitters	• Hormones spread around the body
• Short-lived effects	• Hormones remain in the blood for some time

Westen (1996, p.85) summarised the differences between the two systems in a neat way. He argued that

the difference between the communication that takes place through the two systems is analogous to the difference between word of mouth [nervous system] and mass media [endocrine system] (which can communicate information to hundreds of millions of people at once).

Hypothalamus

The parts of the endocrine system are distributed in various parts of the body. However, most of the endocrine system is controlled by the hypothalamus, which is a small structure at the base of the brain in the diencephalon. There are direct connections between the hypothalamus and the anterior pituitary gland. What happens is that hypothalamic hormones (e.g. corticotropin-release factor or CRF) stimulate the anterior pituitary gland

KEY TERM
Hormones: chemical substances released into the bloodstream by the endocrine glands.

to secrete its hormones. After that, the hormones secreted by the anterior pituitary gland control the functioning of the other endocrine glands. However, what happens is not simply that the hypothalamus controls the anterior pituitary gland, and the anterior pituitary gland controls the other endocrine glands. In addition, hormones released by the endocrine glands often influence the hypothalamus and the anterior pituitary gland.

Pituitary gland

In view of its importance, the pituitary gland, anterior and posterior, is often referred to as the "master gland" of the body. The anterior pituitary gland releases several hormones, including the following: somatotrophic hormone, which stimulates the pancreas; adrenocorticotrophic hormone (ACTH), which stimulates the adrenal cortex; gonadotrophic hormones, which stimulate the sex glands; and thyrotrophic hormone, which stimulates the thyroid gland. The posterior pituitary gland is an outgrowth of the hypothalamus, and releases the following hormones: antidiuretic hormone, which stimulates the kidneys to retain water in the body; and oxytocin hormone, which produces contractions of the smooth tissues of the uterus during labour.

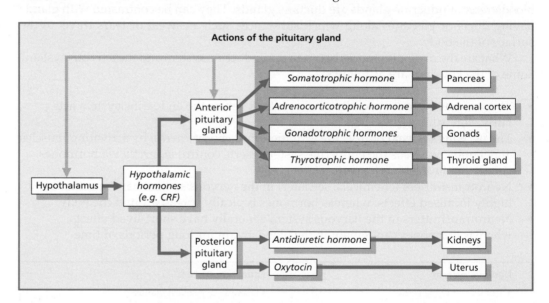

Gonads

The gonads are the sexual glands of the body. The male gonads are known as testes and the females gonads as ovaries. Activity in the gonads is stimulated by luteinising hormone from the anterior pituitary gland. The male gonads produce sperm, and the female gonads produce ova or eggs. The gonads also secrete various hormones:

- Androgens: these are male sex steroid hormones, and are found in greater quantities in male gonads; the main androgen is testosterone, which affects sex drive.
- Estrogens: a range of sex hormones produced mainly in the ovaries, the main one being estradiol; they influence the growth of breasts, the development of the female genitals, and may affect sex drive.
- Gestagens: a range of hormones produced by the ovaries; these hormones (of which progesterone is the main one) help to facilitate and to maintain pregnancy.

Female primates have a reproductive cycle known as the menstrual cycle, whereas the females of other mammalian species have estrous cycles. Both kinds of reproductive cycle start with the anterior pituitary gland secreting gonadotrophic hormones. These hormones stimulate the growth of ovarian follicles which surround the ovum or egg. Estradiol is secreted as the ovarian follicles develop, producing growth in the lining of the uterus.

Do you think there is a connection between prolonged exposure to stress and changes in the human body due to hormonal imbalances?

After that, luteinising hormone is secreted by the anterior pituitary gland, and this causes ovulation.

Adrenal glands

There are two adrenal glands, which are located just above the kidneys. Each gland consists of a central part known as the adrenal medulla, and an outer covering known as the adrenal cortex. When the adrenal glands are stimulated by ACTH from the anterior pituitary gland, they secrete various corticosteroids. The corticosteroids released by the adrenal medulla include adrenaline and noradrenaline, both of which produce increased arousal (e.g. increased heart rate and blood pressure). Their effects resemble those of the sympathetic nervous system. Indeed, according to Green (1994, p.107), adrenaline and noradrenaline "can almost be seen as part of the ANS [autonomic nervous system]."

> Doctors prescribe steroids for some medical conditions, e.g. arthritis. Some athletes take steroids illegally to build muscle size and power. What are the advantages and disadvantages of each of these situations? What safeguards would you propose to try to make use of steroids safer (consider the immune system)?

What could be the consequences of suppressing the immune system?

The adrenal cortex releases the glucocorticoids including cortisone, hydrocortisone, and corticosterone. The glucocorticoids help to convert stored protein and fat into more usable forms of energy. They also serve to suppress the immune system.

Thyroid and parathyroid glands

The thyroid gland is situated just underneath the larynx, which contains the vocal cords. The thyroid gland produces the hormone thyroxin, which increases the body's metabolic rate. Someone whose thyroid gland produces too much thyroxin suffers weight loss and insomnia, whereas under-production of that hormone causes obesity and general sluggishness.

The parathyroid gland is close to the thyroid gland. It has rather limited functions. It releases the hormone calcitonin. This hormone reduces the release of calcium from the skeleton, and by so doing prevents the level of calcium in the blood from becoming too high.

Pancreas

The pancreas is in the middle of the body close to the adrenal glands and the stomach. It secretes two important hormones: insulin and glucagon. Insulin controls the concentration of glucose in the blood, whereas glucagon stimulates the release of glucose into the blood. If insufficient insulin is produced, this leads to high blood-sugar levels and to a condition called diabetes mellitus. This condition is potentially dangerous, but it can be kept under control by means of insulin injections. If too much insulin is produced, this leads to low blood-sugar levels, and to a condition characterised by extreme tiredness and dizziness.

Influences of the Three Systems

We have discussed the central nervous system, the peripheral nervous system, and the endocrine system as if they were largely independent in their functioning. In fact, nothing could be further from the truth. As we have already seen, there are strong connections between the central nervous system and the peripheral nervous system via the spinal cord and the cranial nerves. In addition, there are neuronal pathways from the hypothalamus in the central nervous system to parts of the autonomic nervous system within the brain stem. The hypothalamus also plays a central role in determining activity within the endocrine system.

Do you think there are any systems in the human body, or any psychological processes, that can be considered to be independent in their functioning?

It is probably correct to say that all three systems are nearly always involved in determining our behaviour. The involvement of all three systems is especially clear with respect to motivation, emotion, and stress, all of which are discussed in Chapter 6. In this chapter, we will consider combined influences of the three systems in connection with the important phenomenon of **homeostasis**. This refers to the body's tendency to maintain a fairly constant internal state that permits cells to function and to live.

Homeostasis

The French physiologist Claude Bernard noticed that the body's internal environment generally remains almost constant in spite of large changes in the external environment. This observation led to much work into the phenomenon of homeostasis. One of the most obvious examples of homeostasis is body temperature, which in humans is normally very close to 98.6°F or 37°C. This is the case in spite of the fact that the external temperature in the United Kingdom can vary by as much as about 54°F or 30°C between winter and summer.

There are numerous other forms of homeostasis, including regulation of the body's water supply, its oxygen concentration, and its concentration of nutrient substances such as glucose. The concentration of glucose in the bloodstream needs to be between 60 and 90 milligrams per 100 cubic centimetres of blood. If it falls below this range, then coma and death can result. If it consistently exceeds this range, then diabetes or some other disease is likely to follow. In similar fashion, death can occur if our body temperature remains considerably above or below its normal level for several hours, or if we are totally deprived of water for four or five days.

As Carlson (1994) pointed out, the regulatory mechanisms within the body that allow homeostasis to occur all involve four key features:

1. A system variable: this is the characteristic (e.g. temperature) that needs to be regulated.
2. A set point: the ideal or most appropriate value of the system variable.
3. A detector: the actual or current value of the system variable needs to be assessed.
4. A correctional mechanism: this serves to reduce or eliminate the discrepancy between the actual value and the ideal value.

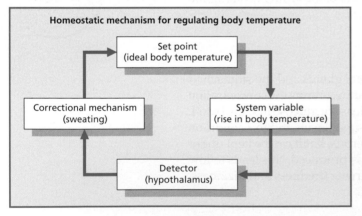

Homeostatic mechanism for regulating body temperature

All these regulatory mechanisms are present in central heating systems, which are designed to regulate temperature. The thermostat is set to the chosen temperature, and it detects deviations between the actual and chosen temperatures. When the temperature falls too low, the boiler of the central heating system is activated to restore the chosen temperature.

The regulatory mechanisms involved in the control of eating and drinking behaviour are discussed at length in Chapter 6. Here we will focus mainly on the ways in which regulatory mechanisms produce homeostasis for body temperature. This is achieved in different ways in different species, and we will focus mainly on warm-blooded animals including the human species. Parts of the hypothalamus (which is in the central nervous system) seem to be involved in detecting the current value of blood temperature, which is usually closely related to body temperature. The hypothalamus is also involved in initiating corrective action.

Body temperature

How does the hypothalamus regulate body temperature? It contains receptor cells responding to the temperature of the fluids surrounding the brain. Evidence for this was obtained by Magoun et al. (1938). Cats whose anterior hypothalamus was heated artificially reacted as if they were too hot by panting and by vasodilation (widening of the skin's capillaries), even though the rest of their bodies were below normal temperature.

Detailed research suggests that the anterior hypothalamus plays a role in cooling the body down, whereas the posterior hypothalmaus is involved in heating the body up. For example, Andersson, Grant, and Larsson (1956) found in goats that electrical stimulation of the anterior hypothalamus caused vasodilation and panting. In contrast, destruction of that area caused death by overheating.

The hypothalamus influences the autonomic nervous system in the regulation of body temperature. The parasympathetic nervous system is activated when the body temperature is too high. It is involved in producing sweating or panting which causes heat loss by evaporation. It also produces vasodilation, which sends warm blood to the skin and causes heat loss by radiation. The sympathetic nervous system is activated when the body temperature is too low. There is vasoconstriction, in which there is a narrowing of the skin's capillaries. This conserves heat by removing blood from the cold periphery of the body. The sympathetic nervous system is also involved in producing shivering. In some species, it also causes the fur to stand out and so create additional protection against the cold. The goose pimples we experience in cold weather are the human equivalent, but are of no use to us because members of the human species are no longer covered in fur!

Regulation of body temperature can include deciding to take various actions, and this involves parts of the central nervous system within the telencephalon. If we are too cold, we often put on extra clothes such as a sweater or coat, or we become more active. On the other hand, if we are too hot, we may take off some of our clothes, have a cold drink, or go for a swim.

Ethical issues

You will have noticed that the studies by Magoun et al. and Andersson et al. were carried out some time ago—in 1938 and 1956—when ethical considerations were regarded somewhat differently from today. It would be very difficult, if not impossible, to get permission to carry out this kind of research today. However, the results of studies like these have provided vital insights into the way the brain works and the functions of its different areas, which have improved human life in many ways. The arguments for and against the use of animals in research are many and often fully justified, but there are only certain studies that can safely be carried out on fully informed human volunteers.

Discussion points

1. Consider some of the limitations of the regulation of body temperature that occur when the weather is either very hot or very cold.
2. How would our lives be different if we were not reasonably efficient at regulating our body temperature?

There are similarities between the regulatory mechanisms for body temperature and those that apply to other examples of homeostasis. In particular, the two parts of the autonomic nervous system (the sympathetic and parasympathetic nervous systems) often play a central role in correctional mechanisms. More specifically, the sympathetic nervous system increases activity levels when they are too low, and the parasympathetic nervous system decreases activity levels when they are too high.

Sweating is part of the **parasympathetic** nervous system's response to high body temperature. The evaporation of sweat from the skin helps to cool the body down.

Sleep

There has been a fair amount of controversy about the functions of sleep (see Chapter 5). However, several theorists such as Oswald (1980) and Horne (1988) have argued that sleep serves various homeostatic functions. According to their recovery or restoration theories, sleep permits energy conservation, and it also allows for the repair of tissues. Some aspects of homeostasis are disrupted during the hours we are awake, and are restored during the hours we are asleep.

Some evidence supports these theories. For example, it has been found that species having a high metabolic rate generally have more deep or short-wave sleep than species with a low metabolic rate (Allison & Cicchetti, 1976). This is only correlational evidence, but it suggests that those species with the greatest need to conserve energy have the most short-wave sleep.

Oswald (1980) argued that deep or slow-wave sleep is of particular importance. The reason is that during this stage of sleep, growth hormone is released, and this helps in the repair of tissues. There is evidence that short-wave sleep is of special importance to humans. People who had run an ultra marathon showed a more marked increase in slow-wave sleep than in other stages of sleep during the following night (Shapiro et al., 1981).

Neural and Synaptic Activity

As was mentioned earlier, neurons are cells that are specialised to conduct electrical impulses. The average neuron transmits signals to about 1000 other neurons. There are three kinds of neurons: sensory neurons, motor neurons, and interneurons. Sensory or afferent neurons transmit signals from receptors that detect events inside or outside the body. Motor or efferent neurons transmit signals from the brain to the body's musculature or glands. Finally, interneurons connect neurons with each other. Most interneurons are located in the central nervous system.

Membrane potentials

In order to understand how neurons work, we will start by considering the membrane potential, which is the difference in electrical charge between the inside and the outside of a neuron. The membrane potential can be assessed by inserting one electrode inside a neuron and a second electrode in the extracellular fluid. The **resting potential** is about –70mV (millivolts). In other words, the potential inside the neuron is 70mV less than outside it.

Both inside and outside the neuron are ions. These are particles, some of which are positively charged and the remainder of which are negatively charged. The fact that a neuron's resting potential is –70mV is due to a higher proportion of negative ions inside the neuron compared to outside it. There are complex reasons why this should be so. Part of what is involved is the sodium–potassium pump, which pumps potassium ions into the neuron and sodium ions out.

Synapses are the very small gaps that exist between adjacent neurons. When neurons fire, they release chemicals or **neurotransmitters** which cross the synapses and affect the receptors on the adjacent neurons. These neurotransmitters either increase or decrease the membrane potential of the adjacent neurons. If they increase the membrane potential, they reduce the likelihood of the receptive neuron firing.

So far we have been talking as if the receptor area of each neuron only has a single synapse. In fact, there are generally thousands of synapses associated with the receptor area of each neuron. What determines whether or not any given neuron fires? According to Pinel (1997, p.86) it depends "on the balance between the excitatory and inhibitory signals reaching its axon hillock—the conical [cone-shaped] structure at the junction between the cell body and the axon." If the membrane potential is reduced to –65mV or less, then the neuron fires. This consists of an **action potential** which is generated at the axon hillock. It is a brief electrical and chemical event, and it is always the same size and duration. More specifically, an action potential lasts for about 1 millisecond, and it reverses the membrane potential from about –65mV to about +50mV.

Pinel (1997) compared the firing of a neuron to the firing of a gun. In both cases, there is a threshold that has to be reached: sufficient stimulation by other neurons or sufficient pressure on the trigger. In both cases, exceeding the threshold does not increase the size of the effect. If the action potential is always the same, how can we tell the difference between a strong and a weak stimulus? When a strong stimulus is presented, far more neurons fire, and they fire more frequently, than is the case when a weak stimulus is presented.

We will now discuss in a little more detail some of the processes that occur during an action potential. What happens initially is that the sodium and potassium ion channels open. This causes sodium ions to enter the neuron, followed very shortly by potassium ions being driven out of the neuron. After about 1 millisecond, the sodium ion channels close, followed by the potassium channels. The closure of these channels causes the action potential to come to an end. However, there is a period of 1 or 2 milliseconds after the start of an action potential before a neuron can fire again; this is known as the **absolute refractory period**.

Many neurons in the nervous system have axons that are covered in a fatty sheath known as myelin, whereas other neurons do not. In addition, there are numerous

An action potential recorded from the giant axon of a squid

ACTION POTENTIAL

RESTING POTENTIAL

Inside voltage (mV)

+40

0

–70

0 1 2 3 4 5 6 7

Time (msec)

neurons that do not have axons and so do not produce action potentials. Myelinated axons have gaps in the myelin sheath known as the nodes of Ranvier, and action potentials jump from node to node along the axon. Action potentials travel much faster along myelinated axons than along unmyelinated axons, with respective speeds of 80–100 metres per second versus only 2 or 3 metres per second.

Synaptic transmission

Most synapses are directed synapses, meaning that the site of neurotransmitter release from one neuron is very close to the site of neurotransmitter reception at another neuron. Neurotransmitters initiate reactions in the postsynaptic neuron by binding to its receptors. Most neurotransmitters are able to bind to various types of receptors, but the nature of the receptor response varies from one type to another. It is possible to think of neurotransmitters as keys and of receptors as locks: there has to be a fit between the two for anything to happen.

There are two basic types of receptor (Pinel, 1997):

1. Ion-channel linked receptors: neurotransmitters often have the effect of opening sodium channels (producing excitatory postsynaptic potentials) or of opening potassium or chloride channels (producing inhibitory postsynaptic potentials); other neurotransmitters close ion channels.
2. G-protein linked receptors: the effects of neurotransmitters on these receptors (compared to ion-channel linked receptors) are "slower to develop, longer-lasting, more diffuse, and more varied" (Pinel, 1997, p.95). In some G-protein linked receptors, neurotransmitters produce excitatory or inhibitory postsynaptic potentials. In others, they produce a chemical known as a second messenger that can affect the postsynaptic neuron in various ways.

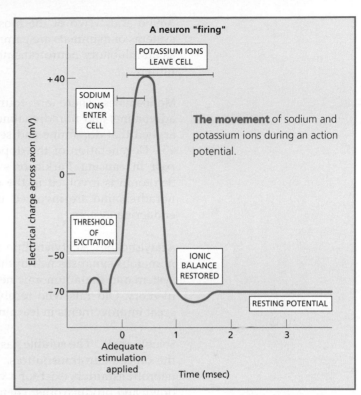

The movement of sodium and potassium ions during an action potential.

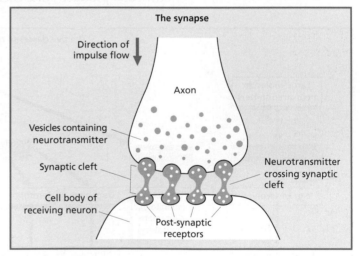

There are two mechanisms that prevent a neurotransmitter from having a long-lasting effect on synapses. First, there is re-uptake, in which neurotransmitters are drawn back into the presynaptic neuron. Second, there is enzymatic degradation. What happens here is that the neurotransmitter is degraded or broken apart in the synapse by the action of chemicals known as enzymes.

Neurotransmitters

There are five classes of neurotransmitters, one of which is large-molecule and four of which are small-molecule. The class of large-molecule transmitters consists of neuropeptides. Some neuropeptides are neuromodulators, meaning that they affect the sensitivity of neurons to signals but do not themselves send signals to other neurons. Endorphins are among the most important neuropeptides. They play a significant role in activating the systems involved in pain suppression and in pleasure. Drugs such as heroin, morphine, and opium affect the same receptors as the endorphins.

The four classes of small-molecule neurotransmitters are as follows: the amino acids; the monoamines; acetylcholine; and the soluble gases.

Amino acids. Two of the most commonly found amino acids in the central nervous systems of mammals are gamma-aminobutyric acid (GABA) and glutamate. GABA acts as an inhibitory neurotransmitter, whereas glutamate acts as an excitatory neurotransmitter.

Monoamines. There are four monoamine neurotransmitters: dopamine; serotonin; adrenaline; and noradrenaline. All these neurotransmitters are important. It has been argued that dopamine and serotonin are both involved in schizophrenia (see Chapter 25). Degeneration of the dopamine-releasing neurons in the substantia nigra plays a part in causing Parkinson's disease, a disorder involving poor muscular control. Serotonin is involved in the regulation of arousal, sleep, and mood. Adrenaline and noradrenaline are involved in emotion (see Chapter 6) and in the workings of the endocrine system.

Acetylcholine. Acetylcholine is the only neurotransmitter in its class. It is found at numerous synapses within the nervous system, including those in the central nervous system and the autonomic nervous system. Acetylcholine is involved in learning and memory. Old rats who received neural transplants containing acetylcholine showed great improvements in learning ability (Bjorklund & Lindvall, 1986).

Soluble gases. The soluble gas transmitters were discovered more recently than most of the other neurotransmitters. They include carbon monoxide and nitric oxide. These neurotransmitters exist for a very short period of time, because they are rapidly broken down and produce other chemicals or second messengers.

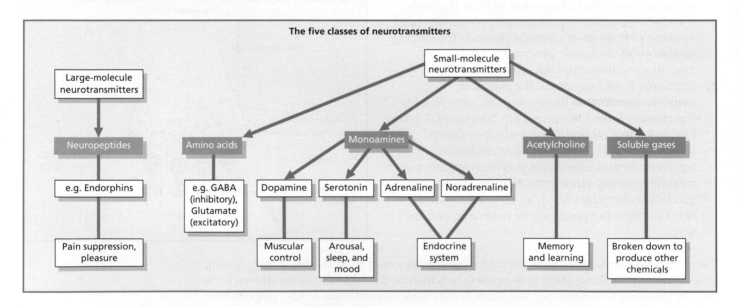

Practical applications

What are the practical applications of discovering the detailed processes involved in synaptic transmission? Probably the greatest benefit has come from the development of drugs designed to have certain effects on synaptic transmission. Here, we will consider some of the various ways in which drugs affect synaptic transmission. Their effects on behaviour are discussed in the following section.

Drugs affect synaptic transmission by changing the effects of neurotransmitters. Some drugs (which are known as **agonists**) increase the effects of a given neurotransmitter on synaptic transmission. In contrast, other drugs (known as **antagonists** or blockers) reduce the effects of a neurotransmitter. Agonists and antagonists can be divided into those that act directly and those that act indirectly. Drugs that act directly are typically very similar in chemical structure to the neurotransmitter, and like the neurotransmitter they affect synaptic receptors. Direct-acting agonists stimulate synaptic receptors, whereas direct-acting antagonists prevent the neurotransmitter from stimulating synaptic receptors. Heroin is an example of a direct-acting agonist, and the depressant drug chlorpromazine is an example of a direct-acting antagonist (Cardwell et al., 1996).

Indirect-acting drugs also change the effects of neurotransmitters, but they do not do so by affecting synaptic receptors. Cardwell et al. give examples of indirect-acting drugs. The stimulant drug amphetamine is an indirect-acting agonist that increases the release of neurotransmitter substance from the presynaptic terminal. Parachlorophenylalanine (PCPA) is an indirect antagonist. It produces a large reduction in the production of the neurotransmitter serotonin by inhibiting one of the enzymes needed to synthesise serotonin.

The effects of neurotransmitters and of drugs on synaptic transmission are much more complex in some ways than has been indicated so far. Pinel (1997) argued that neurotransmitter action often involves seven distinct stages or processes (some of which we have discussed already):

1. Neurotransmitter molecules are synthesised under enzymal control.
2. Neurotransmitter molecules are stored in vesicles (cavities).
3. Any molecules that leak from vesicles are destroyed by enzymes.
4. Action potentials cause vesicles to release the neurotransmitter molecules into the synapse.
5. Neurotransmitter molecules bind with presynaptic receptors and inhibit additional neurotransmitter release.
6. Neurotransmitter molecules bind to postsynaptic receptors.
7. Neurotransmitter molecules cease to affect postsynaptic receptors via re-uptake or enzymatic degradation.

As you can imagine, the fact that several processes are involved in neurotransmitter action means that there are several ways in which drugs can change neurotransmitter action. Pinel (1997) identified six mechanisms of agonistic drug action and five mechanisms of antagonistic drug action. Some agonists increase the synthesis of neurotransmitter molecules (Stage 1), whereas others destroy degrading enzymes (Stage 3), or block the inhibition of neurotransmitter release (Stage 5), or block the processes of re-uptake or enzymatic degradation (Stage 7). Some antagonists destroy synthesising enzymes (Stage 1), and others increase the leakage of neurotransmitter molecules from vesicles or cavities (Stage 3), or increase the inhibition of neurotransmitter release (Stage 5), or block the binding of neurotransmitter molecules to postsynaptic receptors (Stage 6).

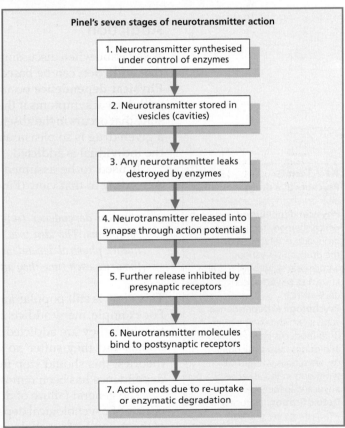

Pinel's seven stages of neurotransmitter action

1. Neurotransmitter synthesised under control of enzymes
2. Neurotransmitter stored in vesicles (cavities)
3. Any neurotransmitter leaks destroyed by enzymes
4. Neurotransmitter released into synapse through action potentials
5. Further release inhibited by presynaptic receptors
6. Neurotransmitter molecules bind to postsynaptic receptors
7. Action ends due to re-uptake or enzymatic degradation

Drugs and Behaviour

There are hundreds (or possibly thousands) of different drugs. The media have tended to focus on drugs that are illegal such as ecstasy, heroin, and cocaine. However, there are numerous legal drugs that are taken every day by millions of people. These include alcohol, nicotine, and caffeine (which is found in tea, coffee, and cola drinks). The focus in this section is on drugs that can have very damaging effects. However, there are many drugs that have positive effects on behaviour. These include drugs used in therapy (e.g. anti-anxiety drugs, anti-depressant drugs, and drugs used to control the symptoms

The study of drugs with a focus on their psychological effects is known as psychopharmacology. It is in part biology, physiology, biochemistry, medicine, and psychiatry.

of conditions such as schizophrenia). There is a detailed discussion of such drugs in Chapter 26.

Psychologists have been particularly interested in **psychoactive drugs**, which alter psychological or mental processes. There are many different ways to categorise psychoactive drugs, but any such categorisation is likely to exaggerate the similarities among drugs placed in the same category. According to Hamilton and Timmons (1995), three of the main categories are as follows:

1. Depressants: these drugs (e.g. alcohol; barbiturates) produce feelings of relaxation and drowsiness; they tend to have what is known as a sedative effect.
2. Stimulants: these drugs (e.g. amphetamine; caffeine; nicotine) produce a state of alertness, and can increase feelings of confidence.
3. Hallucinogens: these drugs (e.g. LSD) produce mental distortions and hallucinations, and can cause a range of psychotic symptoms.

Drugs affect our behaviour by influencing neurotransmitters, as was described in the previous section. As mentioned earlier, some drugs (known as agonists) increase the effects of a given neurotransmitter. Other drugs (known as antagonists or blockers) reduce the effects of a neurotransmitter.

Addiction

A key issue when discussing drugs and behaviour is that of addiction. It has been argued that addiction can be based on physical dependence or on psychological dependence. **Physical dependence** occurs when the body needs a given drug and there are severe withdrawal symptoms if the drug is no longer available. **Psychological dependence** is a state that occurs in the absence of physical dependence. It involves a state in which taking a given drug is so pleasurable and not taking it causes such withdrawal symptoms that the individual is addicted.

It used to be assumed that most drug addiction involves physical dependence. According to that view (Pinel, 1997, p.340)

physical dependence traps addicts in a vicious circle of drug taking and withdrawal symptoms. The idea was that drug users whose intake has reached a level sufficient to induce physical dependence are driven by their withdrawal symptoms to self-administer the drug each time they attempt to curtail their intake.

This view is still popular among many non-experts, but it does not seem to fit the facts. For example, many addicts are put through a process of **detoxification**, in which the drug to which they are addicted is gradually withdrawn until it has disappeared from their bodies and they suffer no withdrawal symptoms. According to physical-dependence theories, this should stop the addiction. In fact, however, most addicts whose physical dependence has been removed start taking drugs again shortly thereafter.

The general failure of detoxification programmes has led most experts to favour the notion of psychological dependence based on the pleasurable effects of drugs. Some idea of the strength of psychological dependence can be obtained from this statement by a drug addict (Pinel, 1997, p.341): "If I could get more money, I would spend it all on drugs. All I want is to get loaded. I just really like shooting dope. I don't have any use for sex; I'd rather shoot dope. I like to shoot dope better than anything else in the world."

Many addicts continue to take drugs even though the drugs themselves do not seem to create much pleasure. According to Robinson and Berridge (1993), this can be explained by distinguishing between the pleasurable effects of drugs and the *anticipated* pleasure of taking drugs. Initially, drugs are taken because of their pleasurable effects, but in addicts they are taken mostly because of the anticipated pleasure.

KEY TERMS

Psychoactive drugs: drugs that alter psychological processes.

Physical dependence: a state in which the body requires a given drug, and in which removal of the drug causes various withdrawal symptoms; it is also known as physiological dependence.

Psychological dependence: a state in which taking a given drug produces intense pleasure and/or not taking the drug causes serious withdrawal symptoms in the absence of physical dependence.

Detoxification: a process in which drugs are gradually withdrawn from addicts until they have no drugs in their bodies and experience no withdrawal symptoms.

Methadone is sometimes prescribed for the treatment of heroin addiction. However it can itself be addictive, and does not lead to reduced withdrawal symptoms when used in a programme of gradual drug withdrawal. List the possible advantages and disadvantages of prescribing methadone to existing drug addicts. What are the ethical issues involved here?

Depressants

There are several depressant drugs including alcohol and the barbiturates. We will focus on alcohol, which is used by hundreds of millions of people around the world. It is regarded as a depressant drug, because it reduces neural firing at moderate doses and above. How does alcohol do this? It has various effects on the nervous system (Pinel, 1997, p.332):

> *It reduces the flow of calcium into neurons by acting on calcium channels, increases the action of the inhibitory neurotransmitter GABA by acting on the GABA receptor complex, increases the number of binding sites for the excitatory neurotransmitter glutamate, reduces the effects of glutamate at some of its receptor subtypes, and interferes with second messenger systems inside neurons.*

Small amounts of alcohol typically make people feel less anxious, more relaxed, and less inhibited. In large quantities, alcohol has a sedative effect on many people, but it makes others argumentative and aggressive. Consumption of

> As is the case with many drugs, consuming an unusually large or unaccustomed amount of alcohol can lead to death from alcohol poisoning.

very large amounts of alcohol causes loss of co-ordination, socially unacceptable behaviour, and even unconsciousness. People who consume a large amount of alcohol over a short period of time subsequently experience alcohol withdrawal syndrome consisting of three stages. First, they experience headaches, nausea, sweating, and abdominal cramps about five hours after drinking has stopped. Second, they experience convulsions which can last for several hours about one day after drinking has stopped. Third, there is **delirium tremens**, which involves hallucinations, agitation, delusions, and high temperature.

High doses of alcohol can make people aggressive and violent. For example, most murders are committed by people who have been drinking (Bushman & Cooper, 1990). It is not clear exactly why alcohol makes people aggressive, but it probably reduces the control that people normally exhibit over their feelings of anger.

> **KEY TERM**
> **Delirium tremens**: a state produced by excessive alcohol intake that involves hallucinations, agitation, delusions, and high temperature.

Alcohol and driving

The effects of alcohol on driving performance are of special importance to society. Drew, Colquhoun, and Long (1958) found in the laboratory that surprisingly small doses of alcohol disrupted driving performance by slowing reaction times, reducing steering efficiency, and by lowering attention to speedometer readings. The notion that alcohol impairs driving ability has been confirmed repeatedly. Sabey and Codling (1975) considered the effects of the introduction of legislation in Great Britain putting a legal limit on the level of alcohol in the blood. In the year after the legislation was introduced, there was a 36% decrease in the number of people killed on the roads during the main drinking hours of 10pm to 4am. This figure should be compared against a reduction of only 7% in fatalities for the hours 4am to 10pm.

Hockey (1983) summarised the negative effects of alcohol on performance. Alcohol reduces alertness, decreases speed of performance, reduces accuracy of performance, and reduces short-term memory capacity. As a result, alcohol impairs performance on nearly all tasks.

The introduction of limits on the permitted level of alcohol in the blood for British drivers resulted in a significant fall in the number of deaths due to road accidents during the main drinking hours (10pm to 4am).

Discussion points

1. Do you think that the law should be changed to reduce the amount of alcohol that drivers are allowed to drink?
2. Why are many drivers confident of their driving ability after having had a lot to drink, when the evidence indicates the opposite?

An important issue is to distinguish between effects of alcohol that are due to its effects on the nervous system and those that are due to expectations about its effects. This has

When conducting research into the use and effects of alcohol, what safeguards would you bear in mind when selecting participants?

been addressed by giving some people non-alcoholic drinks that they are led to believe are alcoholic. It has generally been found that the expectations within any given culture have a strong impact on behaviour (see Hull & Bond, 1986). For example, male participants who thought they had drunk alcohol reported higher sexual arousal and less guilt when exposed to sexually arousing stimuli, regardless of whether or not they had actually consumed any alcohol (Hull & Bond, 1986).

Alcoholism

Some people become alcoholics as a result of their addiction to alcohol. Cloninger (1987) argued that there are two kinds of alcoholics: (1) steady drinkers, who drink virtually every day and find it very hard to abstain from drinking; and (2) binge drinkers, who drink only occasionally, but cannot stop drinking and they have started. Far more men than women are alcoholics. Why do people become alcoholics? Cloninger et al. (1985) carried out an adoption study to assess the relative importance of heredity and environment. There was a major effect of heredity on steady drinking in men but not in women: adopted men tended to become steady drinkers if their biological father was a steady drinker, but the drinking behaviour of members of their adoptive family had no effect. Cloninger et al. found that binge drinking in males and females depended on both heredity and environment. Binge drinkers tended to have a biological parent who was a binge drinker *and* one or more heavy drinkers in their adoptive family.

Ethical considerations obviously prevent many approaches to the study of alcohol abuse, but the case study approach has proved very valuable.

There are many serious consequences of alcoholism. It can cause cirrhosis of the liver. It can also cause severe damage by preventing the liver from metabolising the vitamin thiamine. Thiamine deficiency leads to the loss of brain neurons, and this eventually produces amnesia or memory loss in the form of **Korsakoff's syndrome**. Patients suffering from this syndrome have great difficulties in acquiring new knowledge about the world and about themselves and their experiences, and so they have poor long-term memory in those areas. However, their ability to learn and to remember motor skills is usually intact. In view of the many negative effects of alcohol, it is not surprising that it is at least partly responsible for 3% of all deaths in the United States.

Opiates

Among the opiates are to be found some of the most dangerous and addictive drugs. The opiates are based on opium, which is a sticky resin produced by the opium poppy. Morphine is one of the ingredients of opium, and heroin and codeine can both be produced from morphine. As McIlveen and Gross (1996) pointed out, heroin was developed because soldiers who were given morphine to relieve pain tended to become

The morphine that was used in the nineteenth century in war hospitals sometimes resulted in addiction.

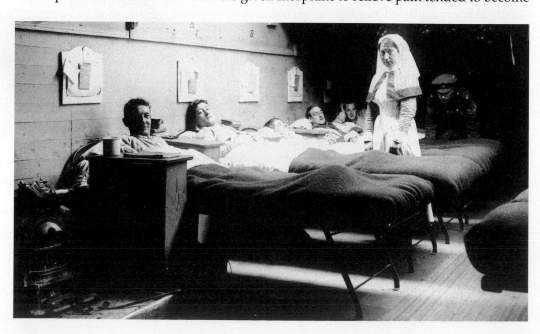

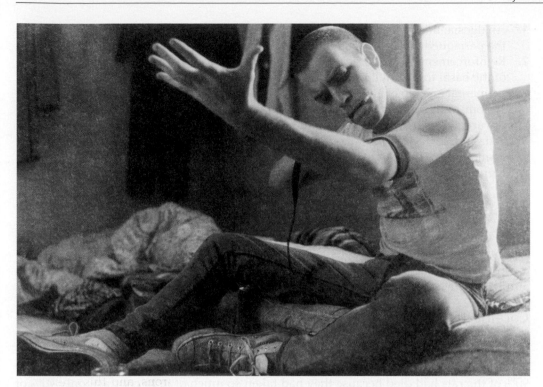

In the film *Trainspotting*, Ewan McGregor portrays a character who struggles to overcome his dependence on heroin.

addicted to it. This led the Bayer drug company to develop heroin as a substitute drug at the end of the nineteenth century. However, it soon emerged that heroin was as addictive as morphine.

What are the effects of the opiates? Heroin, the most commonly used opiate, produces an almost immediate feeling of euphoria and extreme well-being, followed by feelings of relaxation and contentment. Morphine produces some of the same effects, and is also very effective as an analgesic or painkiller. However, there are very serious consequences of repeated use of these drugs, such as a general increase in hostility and aggression, and a reduced ability to get on with other people. Those who take heroin on a regular basis develop tolerance to it, meaning that a given amount of the drug has less and less effect. Not surprisingly, this growing tolerance leads most users of heroin to take increasingly large amounts of it in order to experience feelings of euphoria.

Heroin users rapidly become physically and psychologically addicted to it. As a result, they find it very difficult to stop taking heroin, even though they recognise that it is an extremely dangerous and expensive drug. If heroin users do manage to stop, they experience a wide range of withdrawal symptoms. These include agitated behaviour, increased heart rate, sweating, insomnia, and uncontrollable leg movements. However, the withdrawal symptoms are generally not very dramatic. As Carlson (1994, p.584) pointed out, to stop taking heroin "is not as painful as most people believe; withdrawal symptoms have been described as similar to a bad case of flu." The main reason why heroin users find it so hard to give up the habit is because of their psychological dependence on it as a source of euphoric feelings.

What are the effects of the opiates on the brain? In general terms, what happens is that opiates such as heroin stimulate specialised opiate receptors in different parts of the brain. Why do these opiate receptors exist? The reason is that there are a number of naturally occurring or endogenous opiates. Two examples of opiates that occur naturally in the body are **encephalin** and β**-endorphin**.

Four of the main effects of repeated use of heroin are as follows: analgesia or absence of pain; reinforcement or reward; sedation; and hypothermia or reduction of body temperature. There appear to be separate opiate receptors associated with each of these effects:

The β-endorphins produced by the human body are natural opiates that can trigger the same feeling of euphoria as some opiates. Prolonged and extreme exercise produces this effect in a safer way.

1. Analgesia: this is produced via opiate receptors in a part of the midbrain known as the periaqueductal grey matter.
2. Reinforcement: the reinforcing effects of opiates occur via opiate receptors in a part of the basal forebrain known as the nucleus accumbens and in the ventral tegmental area; the neurotransmitter dopamine is involved in the brain's reward system, and opiates activate dopaminergic neurons and so trigger the brain's reward system (Matthews & German, 1984).
3. Sedation: there are relevant opiate receptors in the mesencephalic reticular formation.
4. Hypothermia: there are opiate receptors for hypothermia in the preoptic area.

Stimulant drugs

There are numerous stimulant drugs which increase activity within the sympathetic nervous system. Cocaine, amphetamine, ecstasy, nicotine, and caffeine are just some examples of stimulant drugs. In our discussion, we will focus on cocaine, and amphetamine.

Cocaine

Cocaine is a powerful drug that has very strong reinforcing properties. Some evidence of its power was reported by Bozarth and Wise (1985). Rats could press a lever in order to administer cocaine to themselves. After 25 days of unlimited access to cocaine, over 90% of the rats had died because they had taken so much of it. In contrast, only 40% of rats who had unlimited access to heroin died over the same period of time.

People who have taken cocaine say that it makes them feel euphoric, very wide-awake, and powerful. It also influences their behaviour, typically making people more talkative and energetic. Sigmund Freud often took cocaine. In 1885 (p.9), he described "the exhilaration and lasting euphoria, which in no way differs from the normal euphoria of the healthy person ... You perceive an increase of self-control and possess more vitality and capacity for work."

> **Change over time**
>
> Attitudes to drugs of all types have changed and will continue to change over time. When Freud first tried cocaine he was enthusiastic about its use as a therapeutic drug, and recommended it to many people, including his friends and family. His close friend Fleischl became severely addicted to cocaine, which eventually contributed to his death (Stevens, 1989). Nowadays cocaine would not be seen as therapeutically useful.
>
> In the 1960s and 1970s, amphetamines were prescribed to suppress appetite and help in weight loss. However, once the dramatic side-effects of amphetamine use became known, this practice waned, and is now regarded as very dangerous.

The positive effects tend to wear off within about 30 minutes or so, producing feelings of depression and extreme tiredness. These negative after-effects of taking cocaine are sometimes known as "crashing". People who take cocaine on a regular basis often experience psychotic symptoms such as hallucinations, paranoid delusions, and mood disturbances.

Repeated use of cocaine leads to addiction. This does not seem to be due to physical dependence. Cocaine users who stop taking cocaine do not generally show any withdrawal symptoms, nor do they develop tolerance for cocaine while they are taking it. However, there is psychological dependence based on the reinforcing or rewarding effects of cocaine.

Amphetamine

The effects of amphetamine use are similar to those of cocaine. Amphetamine makes people feel very alert, aroused, and full of energy. One difference from cocaine is that these effects typically last for several hours rather than 30 minutes or so. When the effects of the amphetamine wear off, there is a similar crashing to that found with cocaine. Persistent use of amphetamines can produce psychotic symptoms and high levels of anger and aggression.

The effects of amphetamine on behaviour were summarised by Hockey (1983). Amphetamine in moderate doses increases the speed of performance, but this is sometimes achieved at the cost of an increase in errors. There is increased attentional selectivity, in the sense that less important environmental stimuli tend to be ignored. Finally, there is a reduction in the capacity of short-term memory.

Amphetamine can also have effects on emotional states. For example, consider the classic work of Schachter and Singer (1962) on emotion. They found that doses of amphetamine increased emotional reactions, provided that the participants did not attribute their state of arousal to the amphetamine. However, it has proved hard to replicate these findings (see Chapter 6).

As was mentioned when discussing the opiates, the neurotransmitter dopamine is involved in the brain's reward system. It follows that **dopamine agonists** (drugs that increase dopamine activity) should stimulate this reward system. Cocaine and amphetamine are both dopamine agonists, which largely accounts for their addictive properties.

Hallucinogens

Hallucinogens are drugs that produce visual hallucinations, illusions, and other distortions of thinking. Some of the hallucinogens are naturally occurring, whereas others are synthetic or manufactured substances. Naturally occurring hallucinogens include psilocybin, which is found in magic mushrooms, and mescaline, which comes from the peyote cactus. Manufactured hallucinogens include lysergic acid diethylamide or LSD, dimethyltryptamine or DMT, and phencyclidine or PCP.

> Drugs that are prescribed for therapeutic use are rigorously tested and titrated (given in measured doses). However, these safeguards do not apply to the illegal use of substances such as amphetamines and hallucinogens. What are some possible consequences?

Hallucinogenic drugs have a wide range of effects on those who take them. Halgin and Whitbourne (1997, p.441) concluded that these drugs

cause anxiety, depression, ideas of reference [misinterpreting trivial remarks as having personal significance], fear of losing one's mind, paranoid thinking, and generally impaired functioning. Also prominent are perceptual changes such as the intensification of perceptions, feelings of depersonalisation, hallucinations, and illusions. Physiological responses may include dilation of the pupils, increased heart rate, sweating, heart palpitations, blurred vision, tremors, and uncoordination.

During the 1960s Timothy Leary, a professor at Harvard University, described drugs such as LSD as "mind-expanding", and advocated their use. He advised people to "tune in, turn on, and drop out", much to the consternation of the establishment.

> **KEY TERMS**
> **Dopamine agonists**: drugs that stimulate activity of the neurotransmitter dopamine.
> **Hallucinogens**: drugs that produce visual hallucinations and distorted thoughts.

One of the effects of repeated use of hallucinogens is a condition known as hallucinogen persisting perception disorder, which is typically found when no hallucinogens have been taken for some weeks. It involves flashbacks, hallucinations, delusions, and mood changes, many of them resembling the effects of hallucinogenic intoxication.

Of the various hallucinogens, most is known about LSD or "acid". It was discovered towards the end of 1943 by a scientist called Albert Hoffmann. He swallowed the drug extract of a fungus which he thought might help people with breathing difficulties. Unfortunately, the drug gave him vivid hallucinations on his way home. According to Hoffmann, "It was so unusual that I really got afraid that I had become insane." In the 1960s, LSD played a central role in the drug culture that started with a Harvard University professor, Timothy Leary, in the United States.

When someone has taken LSD, the resultant "trip" typically lasts for between 4 and 12 hours. One of the dangers of taking LSD is that the distorted thought processes it produces can delude people into thinking strange things, for example that they can fly or jump safely from the top of a tall building. If such delusions are acted on, they can cause death. Repeated use of LSD does not seem to lead to physical dependence, and when people stop taking it there are few if any withdrawal symptoms. It is not altogether clear whether LSD can cause psychological dependence.

> **Other risks**
>
> When many different drugs are bought and sold for illegal use, they are often "cut" or mixed with other substances, such as talcum or even scouring powder, in order to increase the seller's profits. The risks of practices like these are obvious: it is never clear just what substance a person may be taking, and if that person should need medical care it would be equally unclear to staff trying to decide on an effective course of treatment.

Some of the effects of PCP or "angel dust" resemble those of LSD, but it is a more dangerous drug in some ways. PCP can make people aggressive and violent, and it can produce some of the symptoms of schizophrenia. Worst of all, it can produce high blood pressure, convulsions, and even coma.

What are the effects of hallucinogenic drugs on the brain? LSD, and probably the other hallucinogens as well, have an effect on the serotonin system (Carlson, 1994). More specifically, LSD blocks serotonin receptors, and as a result there is a reduction in the neurotransmission of serotonin. It is also known that serotonin is involved in the control of dreaming (Carlson, 1994). If we put these facts together, it seems likely that some of the effects of LSD on the brain produce dreaming even though the individual is awake.

Marijuana or cannabis

Marijuana is the name given to the dried leaves of the *Cannabis sativa* or hemp plant, which is grown mainly in warm climates. The main active ingredient in this plant is delat-9-tetrahydrocannabinol or THC. However, marijuana contains dozens of other chemicals resembling THC, and some of them may also have effects on the brain. Hashish or hash also contains THC. It is more powerful than marijuana or cannabis, because it contains THC taken from the resin of the plant. THC binds to receptors that are located in various regions of the brain, including the hippocampus, cerebellum, the caudate nucleus, and the neocortex (Matsuda et al., 1990).

Marijuana or cannabis has been taken for its effects on the mind for thousands of years according to Chinese records. It is usually smoked in a cigarette-like joint, but it can also be eaten or injected. The effects of the drug last for about two hours, but THC remains in the body for several days thereafter.

What are the effects of marijuana or cannabis on mental processes and behaviour? The evidence indicates that its psychological effects are surprisingly varied, and seem to depend in part on the expectations of the person taking it. The effects of small doses tend to be rather subtle. According to the National Commission on Marijuana and Drug Abuse (1972, p.68), someone who has had a small dose of marijuana

may experience an increased sense of well-being: initial restlessness and hilarity followed by a dreamy, carefree state of relaxation; alteration of sensory perceptions including expansion of space and time; and a more vivid sense of touch, sight, smell, taste, and sound; a feeling of hunger, especially a craving for sweets; and subtle changes in thought formation and expression.

High doses of marijuana or cannabis have more negative effects. There is poor co-ordination; an inability to concentrate; social withdrawal; impaired short-term memory; sensory distortion; watery eyes; and slurred speech. Some of these effects influence an individual's ability to drive a car. In a study of fatal car accidents in Alabama, it was found that 17% of drivers had taken cannabis (Fortenberry et al., 1986). However, in order to interpret this finding properly we would need to know what percentage of all drivers have taken cannabis. Cannabis use causes drivers to be relatively slow at realising that they should stop, but has little or no effect on their reaction time once they have decided to stop (Moskowitz, Hulbert, & McGlothin, 1976).

Marijuana or cannabis is typically not very addictive, and any withdrawal symptoms (e.g. nausea; sleep disturbance) tend to be mild and short-lived. However, many people do use cannabis regularly over long time periods, and it has been argued that there are various negative effects of such long-term use. First, those who smoke cannabis sometimes have impaired respiratory functioning in the form of coughs, asthma, and bronchitis. However, it appears that it is the inclusion of tobacco and nicotine in what is smoked that causes these effects. Up until the early years of the twentieth century, doctors used to prescribe cannabis for asthmatics, because its muscle-spasm relaxing properties actually *improved* respiratory functioning.

Second, it has been claimed that cannabis reduces the level of motivation, and prevents people from working effectively. However, there is little evidence to support this claim. For example, Brill and Christie (1974) found that the academic performance of college cannabis users and non-users was the same. However, prolonged heavy use of cannabis may lead to lethargy.

Third, it has been suggested that long-term use of cannabis in males reduces the level of the male sex hormone testosterone, and thus impairs sexual functioning. However, most of the evidence does not support these suggestions (see Pinel, 1997). Fourth, it has been argued that cannabis use can lead to physical disease, because it causes impaired functioning of the immune system and because it produces increased heart rate. However, once again the evidence is unconvincing.

> **Ethical issues**
> Some people have claimed that smoking cannabis can alleviate painful symptoms in some conditions such as multiple sclerosis. Given the drawbacks of regular cannabis use, would it be ethically acceptable to legalise this use?

PERSONAL REFLECTIONS

- The central nervous system, the peripheral nervous system, and the endocrine system have been discussed separately for purposes of communication. However, it is very important to remember that these three systems typically function in an integrated and co-ordinated way. I am impressed by the complexity of the body's functioning, and am well aware of the fact that it has only been possible to present an oversimplified view in this chapter

- I think there is a danger of assuming too strongly that we are slaves to our own physiological systems, and that psychological factors are unimportant. For example, homeostatic mechanisms normally keep our weight fairly constant, but psychological stress can cause our weight to increase or decrease dramatically. In my opinion, it is important to know the detailed processes of the nervous system and the endocrine system for some purposes, but not for others. For example, does knowledge of the sodium–potassium pump tell us anything about people's social behaviour?

- I think that drug studies can shed more light on the nervous system than is generally realised. Such studies allow us to manipulate experimentally (and precisely) the levels of various neurotransmitters, and then to observe the detailed effects on behaviour.

S U M M A R Y

Nervous system

The nervous system contains all the nerve cells in the body, most of which are neurons specialised to conduct electrical impulses. The nervous system is divided into the central nervous system (brain and spinal cord) and the peripheral nervous system. The brain has three major regions (forebrain; midbrain; and hindbrain). The forebrain is divided into the telencephalon and the diencephalon, the midbrain consists of the mesencephalon, and the hindbrain is divided into the metencephalon and the myencephalon. The telencephalon plays a crucial role in virtually all cognitive activities, and the diencephalon contains the hypothalamus and the thalamus. The hypothalamus is involved in the control of body temperature, hunger, and thirst, and the thalamus is a relay station for sensory signals. The mesencephalon contains the tectum (which forms part of the visual and auditory systems) and the tegmentum (which contains part of the reticular formation and is also involved in movement control). The metencephalon is involved in consciousness and the precise control of movements. The myencephalon contains the medulla; it is involved in the control of respiration and the relaying of signals. The peripheral nervous system consists of the somatic nervous system (concerned with interactions with the external environment) and the autonomic nervous system (concerned with the body's internal environment). The autonomic nervous system is divided into the sympathetic nervous system and the peripheral nervous system. The former is involved when energy and arousal are needed, whereas the latter is involved when energy conservation is required.

Endocrine system

The endocrine system consists of various glands including the pituitary, thyroid, parathyroid, and adrenal glands, and the pancreas and gonads. The endocrine glands secrete hormones. Most of the endocrine system is controlled by the hypothalamus. There are direct connections between the hypothalamus and the anterior pituitary gland. It is the "master gland" of the body, and releases numerous different hormones. The gonads are the sexual glands of the body; they secrete androgens, estrogens, and gestagens. The adrenal glands secrete various corticosteroids. The thyroid gland produces the hormone thyroxin, which increases the body's metabolic rate. The pancreas secretes insulin (which controls the level of glucose in the blood) and glucagon (which stimulates the release of glucose into the blood).

Influences of the three systems

The central nervous system, peripheral nervous system, and endocrine system combine to create a constant internal state in the body known as homeostasis. Homeostasis applies to body temperature, the body's water supply, oxygen concentration, supply of nutrients, and so on. The regulation of body temperature involves the hypothalamus. It also involves the sympathetic nervous system when the temperature is too low, and the parasympathetic nervous system when the temperature is too high. Sleep probably serves various homeostatic functions, including permitting energy conservation and allowing tissue repair to occur.

Neural and synaptic activity

The resting membrane potential of a neuron is about –70mV. When neurons fire, they release chemicals or neurotransmitters which cross the synapses and affect the receptors on adjacent neurons. Neurotransmitters alter the membrane potential of adjacent neurons, which decreases or increases the chances of receptive neurons firing and producing an action potential. At the start of an action potential, sodium ions enter the neuron, followed by potassium ions being driven out. There are two main types of receptors that respond to neurotransmitters: ion-channel linked receptors and G-protein linked receptors. There are five classes of neurotransmitters. They have only short-lived effects on synapses because of re-uptake and enzymatic degradation.

Drugs and behaviour

Three of the main categories of drugs are as follows: depressants; stimulants; and hallucinogens. Opiates such as heroin and morphine produce feelings of euphoria followed by contentment. Prolonged use can lead to hostility, aggression, and an inability to get on with others, and there is psychological dependence. There are separate opiate receptors in the brain associated with the analgesic, reinforcing, sedative, and hypothermic effects of opiates. Stimulant drugs include cocaine and amphetamine. Cocaine makes people feel euphoric, powerful, and very wide-awake, and they become talkative and energetic. Repeated use produces psychological dependence and various psychotic symptoms (e.g. hallucinations). The effects of amphetamine are similar. Cocaine and amphetamine are dopamine agonists, and dopamine affects the brain's reward system. Hallucinogens such as LSD and PCP produce hallucinations, illusions, and other distortions of thinking. Prolonged use of hallucinogens can produce anxiety, paranoid thinking, and aggression, and PCP can produce convulsions and coma. The hallucinogens affect the serotonin system, as a result of which some of their effects resemble dreaming while awake. Cannabis contains THC, which can produce relaxation, good humour, increased sexual interest, and increased awareness of what is going on. It can also produce anxiety, poor concentration, social withdrawal, and impaired short-term memory. Prolonged use can lead to reduced reproductive functioning and extreme lethargy.

FURTHER READING

Most of the topics dealt with in this chapter are discussed in an accessible way in J.P.J. Pinel (1997), *Biopsychology (3rd Edn.)*, Boston: Allyn & Bacon. There is more detailed and complex coverage of these topics in N.R. Carlson (1994), *Physiology of behaviour (5th Edn.)*, Boston: Allyn & Bacon. There is a good account of the endocrine system in S. Green (1994), *Principles of biopsychology*, Hove, UK: Psychology Press.

REVISION QUESTIONS

1	Distinguish between the structure and functioning of the central and autonomic nervous systems.	(24 marks)
2a	Explain what is meant by the term homeostasis.	(6 marks)
2b	Discuss the influence of any *two* of the following on homeostasis: • central nervous system • autonomic nervous system • endocrine system.	(18 marks)
3	Discuss the processes involved in neuronal and synaptic activity.	(24 marks)
4	Describe and assess research into the effects of drugs on behaviour.	(24 marks)

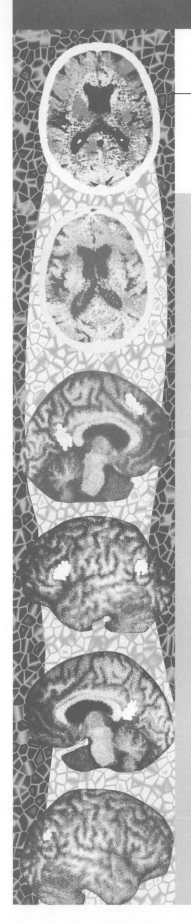

- **Non-invasive techniques**
  Ways of observing the brain in action while we think or speak, etc.

  EEGs and evoked potentials
  Scanning techniques, including CAT, MRI, fMRI, PET, and Squid
  Gabrieli et al.'s fMRI study of the processing of meaning

- **Invasive techniques**
  Changing the way the brain functions by altering it physically.

  Ablations and lesions in animal studies
  Techniques for studying brain damage
  Penfield's work with epileptics

- **Localisation of function**
  What are the different parts of the cerebral cortex, and what do they do?

  The four lobes of the cortex and their functions
  Cerebral control of movement; apraxia

- **Hemisphere asymmetries**
  The different specialised functions of the two halves of the brain.

  Language: Broca's aphasia, Wernicke's aphasia, etc.
  The Wernicke–Geschwind model
  Sperry et al.'s split-brain studies
  Bradshaw and Sherlock's work with normals
  Gainotti's study on mood and emotion

- **Structure and processes of visual perception**
  How the human visual system works and why it is so important.

  Structure of the eye
  Hubel and Wiesel's spatial-frequency theory
  Hierarchical organisation: blindsight
  Zeki's theory of modular processing

- **Colour vision**
  How and why do we see in colour?

  Young–Helmholtz theory
  Opponent-process theory
  Land's study of colour constancy

4

Cortical Functions

The cerebral cortex is the outer layer of the cerebrum in the forebrain. It is only two millimetres thick, but it has great importance for our ability to perceive, think, and use language. There are numerous ways of studying cortical functioning, some of which are non-invasive, meaning that they involve observing the brain in action without disturbing its functioning. Other methods are invasive, in that they involve deliberately interfering with parts of the brain. The most extreme example of an invasive technique is surgically removing part of the brain to observe the effects this has.

We will start by considering various non-invasive techniques for studying cortical functioning. After that, we will move on to some of the major invasive techniques. Psychologists and physiologists now have a wide range of techniques at their disposal. Intensive use of these techniques has led to an increase in our knowledge of brain functioning in recent years.

After that, we discuss what has been learned about the brain by using these techniques. Some parts of the cortex are specialised for certain functions (e.g. language), and we now know much about the locations of these functions.

Finally, we consider the structures and processes involved in visual perception. Vision is vital in our everyday lives, and it is no coincidence that large areas of the cortex are specialised for the processing of visual information.

Non-invasive Techniques

As you read about the various non-invasive and invasive techniques that have been used to study the brain, you may find it hard to decide which techniques are the best. In fact, different techniques are designed for different purposes, and are not usually in direct competition. The techniques vary in their spatial and temporal resolution. Some provide information about the neuronal level of functioning, whereas others tell us about activity over the entire brain. In similar fashion, some techniques provide information about brain activity on a millisecond-by-millisecond basis, whereas others measure brain activity over much longer time periods such as minutes or hours.

There is no single "best level" of spatial or temporal resolution. High spatial and temporal resolutions are advantageous if a very detailed account of brain functioning is required. In contrast, low spatial and temporal resolutions are more useful if a general view of brain activity is needed.

Electroencephalogram (EEG)

The **electroencephalogram** (EEG) is based on electrical recordings taken from the scalp. It was first used by Hans Berger over 65 years ago. Very small changes in electrical activity

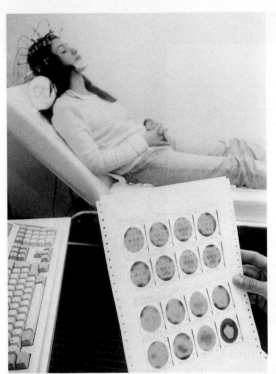

Brain activity recorded using an EEG.

Why has it been so important for scientists and psychologists to determine the locations of various brain functions?

within the brain are picked up by electrodes placed on the scalp. These changes are shown on the screen of a cathode-ray tube by means of an instrument known as an oscilloscope. The pattern of changes is sometimes referred to as "brain waves".

The EEG has proved useful in many ways. For example, it has been found that there are five stages of sleep, varying in terms of the depth of sleep and the presence or absence of dream activity (see Chapter 5). These stages differ in terms of the EEG record, and EEG research was crucial in identifying these stages. It has also proved useful in the detection of epilepsy, damaged brain tissue, and the location of tumours.

The EEG has also been of value in identifying the functions of the two hemispheres of the brain. There is more activity in the left hemisphere than in the right hemisphere when someone is carrying out a language-based task (Kosslyn, 1988). However, the opposite is the case during the performance of a spatial task (Kosslyn, 1988). These findings confirm those from other lines of research, such as studies of brain-damaged patients.

The EEG is a rather blunt instrument in two ways. First, it measures electrical activity in several different areas of the brain at once, and so it is hard to work out which parts of the brain are more and less active. Second, it is an indirect measure of brain activity, because the recording electrodes are on the scalp. The EEG has been compared to trying to hear what people are saying in the next room by putting your ear to the wall.

Suppose we want to know how the brain responds to a given stimulus (e.g. a tone). This can be assessed by extracting what are known as **evoked potentials** from EEG recordings. A stimulus is presented several times, and the EEG recordings from each presentation are then averaged. This is done to distinguish genuine effects of stimulation from background brain activity.

The value of evoked potentials can be illustrated by considering a study by Loveless (1983). The participants were instructed to listen to the stimuli presented to one ear and to ignore those presented to the other ear. Loveless found differences in evoked potentials between attended and unattended stimuli within about 60 milliseconds of stimulus presentation. Thus, attended and unattended stimuli are processed differently in the brain at a very early stage of processing.

How useful are evoked potentials? They provide fairly detailed information about brain activity over time, but do not reveal precisely which regions of the brain are involved.

Brain scanning

In recent years, various brain scanners have been developed to study cortical functioning. The ones we will consider here are computerised axial tomography (CAT scans), magnetic resonance imaging (MRI scans), functional MRI, positron emission tomography (PET scans), and superconducting quantum interference devices (Squid magnetometry).

CAT scans
In order to produce a **CAT scan**, the individual lies on a table with his or her head in the middle of a doughnut-shaped ring. An X-ray beam then goes through the individual's head from front to back, and the level of radioactivity is detected. The level of radioactivity is lower when the X-rays pass through very dense material. To obtain a fairly full picture, the X-ray emitter and detector are moved around the ring to assess the level of radioactivity from different angles.

CAT scans are very useful for detecting tumours, blood clots, and other brain abnormalities. They are also used with accident victims to identify the damaged parts of the brain. CAT scans have clear limitations. They do not permit precise localisation of brain damage; they cannot show the actual functioning of the brain; and they can only be taken in the horizontal plane.

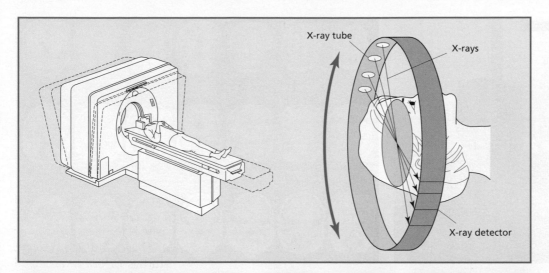

In a CAT scanner, X-rays pass through the brain in a narrow beam. X-ray detectors are arranged in an arc and feed information to a computer that generates the scan image.

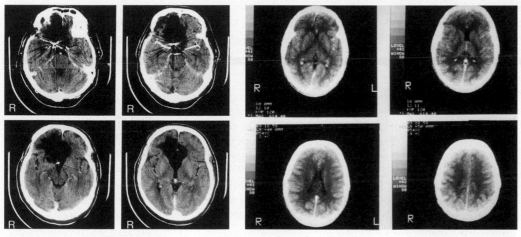

The dark patches on these CAT scans (left) show frontal lobe damage in the brain of a 67-year-old man. Compare these to the undamaged brain of a healthy 16-year-old boy (right).

MRI scans

MRI scans are similar to CAT scans in some ways, but produce clearer and more detailed pictures. What happens in an MRI scan is that radio waves are used to excite atoms in the brain. This produces magnetic changes which are detected by an 11-ton magnet surrounding the patient. These changes are then interpreted by a computer and turned into a very precise three-dimensional picture. MRI scans can be used to detect very small brain tumours.

MRI scans provide more detailed information about the brain than CAT scans. MRI scans can be obtained from numerous different angles, whereas CAT scans can only be obtained in the horizontal plane. However, MRI scans share with CAT scans the limitation of telling us about the structure of the brain rather than about its functions.

Functional MRI

The MRI technology has been applied to the measurement of brain activity to provide **functional MRI**. This approach provides three-dimensional images of the brain with areas of high activity clearly indicated. It is less well known than the PET scan (discussed later), but is more useful. Functional MRI provides more precise spatial information than PET scans, and it also shows changes over much shorter periods of time.

Gabrieli et al.

Gabrieli et al. (1996) used functional MRI to study the parts of the brain involved in the processing of meaning. Their participants were given two tasks to perform: (1) deciding whether words were concrete (referring to objects) or abstract; (2) deciding whether words were in capital letters. They argued that the first task involved the processing of meaning, whereas the second one did not.

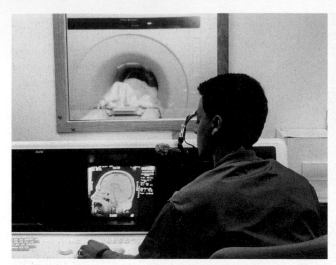

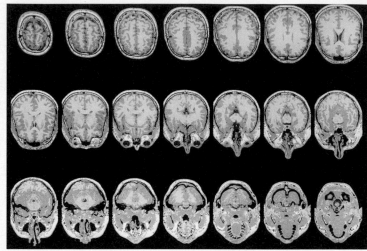

In a MRI scanner, an 11-ton magnet detects magnetic changes in the brain, which are used to generate precise three-dimensional images.

MRI scanning creates "slice" images through the body, useful in detecting brain tumours and cancers. These 21 scans are taken from the top of the head (top left) down to the level of the teeth (lower right).

The key finding was that functional MRI indicated that parts of the left prefrontal cortex were more active when the meaning task was being performed. Gabrieli et al. (1996, p.283) concluded that "the process visualised in left inferior pre-frontal cortex may be thought of as a search for meaning." They also found that the words that had been processed for meaning were recalled much better than the words not processed for meaning. This confirms the prediction from levels of processing theory (see Chapter 13).

In general terms, the findings of Gabrieli et al. confirm the value of functional MRI as a way of studying cognitive processing. More specifically, their findings suggest that activity in the left prefrontal cortex could be used as an independent measure of whether participants are processing meaning.

Discussion points

1. Some of the limitations with functional MRI are discussed next. Do these limitations pose problems for the interpretation of the study by Gabrieli et al.?
2. The two tasks used by Gabrieli et al. may have differed in difficulty level as well as in the processing of meaning. Would it be a good idea to repeat their study using different tasks?

Raichle (1994, p.350) argued that functional MRI has several advantages over other techniques:

> *The technique has no known biological risk except for the occasional subject who suffers claustrophobia in the scanner (the entire body must be inserted into a relatively narrow tube). MRI provides both anatomical and functional information, which permits an accurate anatomical identification of the regions of activation in each subject. The spatial resolution is quite good, approaching the 1–2 millimetre range.*

The main problem with functional MRI is that it assesses blood flow, but blood flow follows neuronal activity in the cortex by almost 1 second. As a result, we do not obtain immediate evidence of brain activity.

PET scans

Of all the new methods, the one that has attracted the most media interest is positron emission tomography or the **PET scan**. The technique is based on positrons, which are the atomic particles emitted by some radioactive substances. A radioactive form of glucose is injected into the body. When part of the cortex becomes active, the radioactive glucose moves rapidly to that place. A scanning device that looks similar to a CAT scanner

KEY TERMS
PET scans: pictures of brain activity based on radioactive glucose levels within the brain; PET stands for positron emission tomography.

measures the positrons emitted from the radioactive glucose. A computer then translates this information into pictures of the activity levels of different parts of the brain. It may sound dangerous to inject a radioactive substance into someone. However, only tiny amounts of radioactivity are involved.

The potential value of PET scans can be seen if we consider the work of Tulving (1989) using a related method. He found that the front part of his brain was most active when personal events were being thought about (episodic memory), whereas the back part of the brain was most active when he thought about his general knowledge of the world (semantic memory). These findings suggest that different parts of the brain are involved in thinking about different kinds of information in long-term memory.

PET scans show us the brain in action, and so they are an advance on CAT and MRI scans. However, they are more limited than is sometimes realised. They tell us which areas of the brain are active, but they do not identify these areas with precision. Furthermore, PET scans indicate the activity levels in different areas of the brain over a period of 60 seconds or more, but not on a moment-by-moment basis.

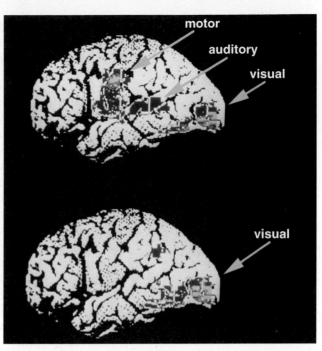

This PET scan shows active areas of the brain involved in reading. The (darker) patches are active areas. Top: The subject is reading aloud. Active regions of the brain are: visual cortex for sight; motor region for speech production; auditory region as the subject hears the sound of their own voice. Bottom: The subject is reading silently, and only the visual cortex is active.

Squid magnetometry

In recent years, a new technique known as **Squid magnetometry** has been developed. Squid stands for superconducting quantum interference device, and it measures very accurately the magnetic flux or field when a group of neurons in the brain is triggered. An important reason for this accuracy is that the skull is completely transparent to magnetic fields, which contrasts with the low electrical conductivity of bone.

There are some problems associated with the use of Squid magnetometry. The magnetic field generated by the brain when thinking is about 100 million times weaker than the Earth's magnetic field, and a million times weaker than the magnetic fields around overhead power cables. As a result, it is very hard to prevent irrelevant sources of magnetism from interfering with the measurement of brain activity. Another problem is that superconductivity requires temperatures close to absolute zero, which means that the Squid has to be immersed in liquid helium at four degrees above the absolute zero of –273°C.

BRAIN SCANNING METHODS: A SUMMARY		
	Advantages	**Limitations**
CAT scan	Can detect damaged parts of the brain in accident victims, as well as tumours and blood clots.	Precise location of damage cannot be determined. Brain function cannot be shown, only structure.
MRI scan	Produces more detailed information and can detect very small tumours.	Brain function cannot be shown, only structure.
Functional MRI	Produces 3D images that provide structural and functional information.	Blood flow follows neuronal activity by about a second. As functional MRI assesses blood flow, it does not give immediate evidence of brain activity.
PET scan	Shows the brain in action and which part is active when different tasks are performed.	Does not provide a moment-by-moment analysis, but shows activity over a 60-second period.
Squid magnetometry	Can produce an accurate image of brain activity because it measures the magnetic field of a group of activated neurons.	Extraneous sources of magnetism may interfere with measurements. The Squid has to be kept at extremely low temperatures.

KEY TERM
Squid magnetometry: a technique for assessing the magnetic flux or field in the brain using a superconducting quantum interference device.

Invasive Techniques

Ablations and lesions

One of the main approaches to finding out the locations of various brain functions is to observe the effects of destroying parts of the brain of an animal. The basic assumption is that whatever abilities are eliminated or greatly impaired after surgery depend on the part of the brain that has been destroyed. We can draw a distinction between ablation and lesion. Ablation involves surgical procedures in which brain tissue is systematically destroyed and often removed. There are various ways in which this can be done. For example, brain tissue can be sucked away through a glass pipette or slender tube attached to a vacuum pump, or it can be removed with a knife, or it can be burned out by inserting electrodes into the brain.

A lesion is a wound or injury. When brain lesions are produced surgically, the amount of tissue destroyed is typically less than with ablation. What generally happens is that a hole is drilled in the skull of an anaesthetised animal. After that, electric current is passed through an electrode, the end of which has previously been inserted into a specified part of the brain. The electric current that is used to create a lesion can be either direct current or based on radio frequency. The former type of current is less useful, because metal ions from the electrode remain in the brain after the electrode has been removed.

How is it known that the tip of the electrode is in the correct place? This is usually achieved by using a stereotaxic apparatus, which fixes the animal's head and provides the experimenter with precise information about the location of the electrode in three-dimensional space. The stereotaxic apparatus is used in conjunction with a stereotaxic atlas containing detailed drawings of the brain and the distances between different parts.

What are some of the problems associated with using studies of animals to draw conclusions about human functioning?

Evaluation

Ablations and lesions can provide very useful information about the functions of different parts of the brain. However, there are various limitations of the surgical approach:

1. It is difficult to interpret the findings because all parts of the brain are interconnected. Suppose, for example, that there are three brain areas A, B, and C adjacent to each other. A given capacity depends on areas A and C, with information being passed between these two areas through area B. Destruction of area B will stop the animal from showing the capacity, even though that area is not directly involved. By analogy, destroying the plug on your television set will stop the set from working, in spite of the fact that the plug is not responsible for producing television pictures.
2. Surgical destruction of a specific area can lead to fairly widespread reduced functioning in adjacent brain areas. This makes it hard to assess the precise importance of the destroyed area.
3. Researchers sometimes fail to destroy the part or parts of the brain they intended to destroy.
4. There are very serious ethical issues associated with the surgical procedures discussed here (see Chapter 29). In many countries, a special licence is required before ablations or lesions can be carried out, and there is regular monitoring to ensure that there is adherence to ethical guidelines.

Brain damage

We have seen that one way of studying the brain is by causing deliberate damage to part or parts of it, but ablation and lesion techniques cannot be used with humans. However, large numbers of people have suffered brain damage because of car accidents, alcohol abuse, strokes, and so on, and evidence from them can be used to understand how the intact brain works. The term **cognitive neuropsychology** is used to describe the area of research concerned with trying to understand the workings of the cognitive system by studying brain-damaged patients and the kinds of impairment associated with brain damage.

We can use techniques already discussed (e.g. CAT, MRI, functional MRI, PET) to find out exactly which parts of the brain are damaged. Before brain scans were available, the damaged brain areas were usually identified in a postmortem examination. Different patients rarely have exactly the same pattern of brain damage. It is often hard to interpret the findings from a series of patients, each of whom differs in terms of brain damage and the pattern of impairment.

When studying people who have suffered brain damage, how would you determine what their functioning was like before the damage occurred? Why is this important?

Single-unit recording

Single-unit recording is a fine-grain technique developed over 40 years ago to permit study of single neurons. A micro-electrode about one 10,000th of a millimetre in diameter is inserted into the brain to obtain a record of extracellular potentials (electrical charges). A stereotaxic apparatus (discussed earlier) is used to ensure that the electrode is in the correct position. Single-unit recording is a very sensitive technique, as electrical charges of as little as one-millionth of a volt can be detected.

The best-known application of this technique was by Hubel and Wiesel (1962). They used the single-unit recording technique with cats to study the neurophysiology of vision when visual stimuli were presented. Their findings are discussed in more detail later in this chapter. In general terms, however, they found that many brain cells respond to very specific aspects of visual stimuli. This discovery influenced many subsequent theories of visual perception.

Electrical stimulation

Electrical stimulation of the brain simply involves applying a weak electric current to the brain through very small electrodes. If this is done carefully, then the brain appears to respond to the current as if it were an actual nerve impulse.

Penfield

Wilder Penfield (1969) carried out numerous operations on epileptic patients. During these operations, he often stimulated the surface of the brain with a weak electric current. The stimulating electrode sometimes caused the patient to re-experience events from his or her past with great vividness. Penfield (1969, p.165) argued that his findings indicated permanent storage of information: "It is clear that the neuronal action that accompanies each succeeding state of consciousness leaves its permanent imprint on the brain. The imprint, or record, is a trail of facilitation of neuronal connections that can be followed again by an electric current many years later."

Close examination of Penfield's data indicates that his conclusions cannot be accepted. Only 7.7% of his patients showed any evidence of recovery of long-lost memories, and the fact that they were epileptic patients means that we cannot be sure that we would obtain the same findings with other groups of people. Penfield emphasised the vividness and the details of the patients' remembered experiences, but in most cases the recollections were rather vague and limited. From a scientific point of view, it is unfortunate that Penfield did not have any independent verification of the events that his patients claimed to remember during electrical stimulation.

Discussion points

1. Why do you think psychologists were excited by Penfield's findings?

2. How could we carry out a study that reduced the problems that Penfield encountered?

Electrical stimulation by means of electrodes has been used in other parts of the brain. Olds and Milner (1954) found that rats would press a lever several hundred times when rewarded by electrical stimulation of the hypothalamus. In later work, it turned out that self-stimulation effects were most dramatic when the area stimulated was in the medial forebrain bundle in the lateral hypothalamus (Olds & Forbes, 1981).

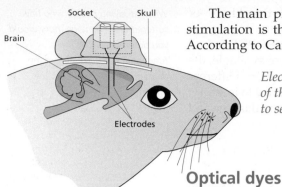

Socket   Skull

Brain

Electrodes

The main problem with interpreting the findings from studies using electrical stimulation is that an electrical stimulus differs in many ways from nerve impulses. According to Carlson (1994, p.196):

> *Electrical brain stimulation is probably as natural as attaching ropes to the arms of the members of an orchestra and then shaking all the ropes simultaneously to see what they can play.*

Optical dyes

There are various ways in which optical dyes have been used to shed light on cortical functioning, of which the most useful is perhaps the technique developed by Blasdel (1992). Part of the skull of monkeys was removed surgically close to the area of the primary visual cortex. After that, a glass window was placed over the primary visual cortex. An optical dye was then injected into the primary visual cortex. This dye was voltage-sensitive, so that it changed colour when an electrical field passed through it. Visual stimuli were then presented to the monkeys, with those cells that responded to the stimuli changing colour. Video recordings were made so that the pattern of colour changes in the primary visual cortex could be analysed in detail.

One of the ways in which Blasdel used this technique was to compare the responses when a stimulus was presented to only one eye. Some cortical cells responded only to left-eye or right-eye stimulation, whereas others responded equally regardless of the eye to which the stimuli were presented.

Electrical stimulation has shown some results, such as rats learning to press a lever to obtain the reward of a pleasurable electrical stimulus to the hypothalamus. An electrical stimulus differs from a nerve impulse, making it difficult to interpret findings.

Control versus involvement

All the methods of studying brain function described here contribute to the debate about the key issue of control versus involvement. When evaluating research we must be aware that it cannot demonstrate for certain whether the part of the brain in question controls a particular behaviour or is merely involved in it.

Localisation of Function

Lashley (1931) studied localisation of function in rats' brains. The rats learned a maze task, after which some part of the cerebral cortex was lesioned. Lashley was trying to discover where in the brain memories were stored. To his surprise, what he found was that the effects of a lesion of a given size were very similar in any part of the brain. This led him to put forward the principle of equipotentiality, according to which all parts of the cerebral cortex are equally involved in the storage of memories. It also led him to propose the principle of mass action, according to which memories are stored throughout the cortex. As we will see, there is much more evidence in humans that different parts of the cerebral cortex are responsible for particular functions.

The human cerebral cortex can be divided up in two main ways. First, it can be divided into four lobes or areas known as the frontal, parietal, temporal, and occipital. The lobes are anatomical regions named for the bones of the skull lying closest to them. The frontal lobe is at the front of the brain, and the occipital lobe is at the back of the brain. The other two lobes are in the middle of the brain, with the parietal lobe at the top and the temporal lobe below it. Second, the entire brain is divided into two hemispheres. This has led to a distinction between the left and right cerebral hemispheres.

Lobes of the cerebral cortex

The four lobes of the cerebral cortex differ somewhat in terms of what they do. Robert Sternberg (1995, p.93) provided a good summary of their functions:

> *higher thought processes, such as abstract reasoning and motor processing, occur in the frontal lobe, somatosensory processing (sensations in the skin and muscles of the body) in the parietal lobe, auditory processing in the temporal lobe, and visual processing in the* ***occipital lobe.***

CASE STUDY: *Computers and the Brain*

Computer technology is developing at a very rapid pace, and it seems now that not only are some computers small enough to fit in your pocket, but the physical movement necessary to interact with the machine may soon be replaced with mental dexterity. Researchers in America have been working on a computer that will be controlled by a person's brain alone. This is not science fiction: the device is being used by a 57-year-old man who is paralysed as a result of a stroke. Tiny implants (glass cones containing miniature electrodes) have been placed in the man's motor cortex, where nerves have been encouraged to grow through them using chemicals extracted from the man's knees. When the nerves grow, they connect to the electrodes, allowing the computer to detect brain signals via a transmitter located just under the man's skull. The man can control the computer cursor just by thinking.

According to Pritchard (1998) this man is now "able to use the system to control a computer cursor to pick phrases on a screen, and communicate with the outside world." At the moment, movement of the cursor is limited to simple up and down, right and left commands, but the benefits to people with severely restricted movement should not be underestimated. This research is just one of the growing number of projects looking at ways in which we can communicate with computers, but what ethical questions might studies like this raise?

Frontal lobe

The frontal lobe contains the primary motor cortex, which is located in the precentral gyrus. It is involved in the planning and control of movements. The connections are between the right hemisphere and the left side of the body, and between the left hemisphere and the right side of the body. The main parts of the secondary motor cortex are just in front of the primary motor cortex. One part of the secondary motor cortex is the supplementary motor area, which is involved in coordinating motor responses. Another part of the secondary motor cortex is the premotor cortex. The motor cortex is considered in more detail later. In addition, the frontal lobe is involved in thinking and reasoning.

Parietal lobe

The parietal lobe contains the primary somatosensory cortex, which is in the postcentral gyrus. This area receives information from various senses about temperature, pain, and pressure, with the connections running from the left side of the body to the right hemisphere, and from the right side of the body to the left hemisphere. Those parts of the body most represented in the primary motor cortex also tend to be well represented in the primary somatosensory cortex. This was discovered by Penfield and Boldrey (1937), who applied electrical stimulation to several parts of the primary somatosensory cortex. Penfield and Boldrey believed that the primary somatosensory cortex was a single area. In fact, it consists of four separate strips, each

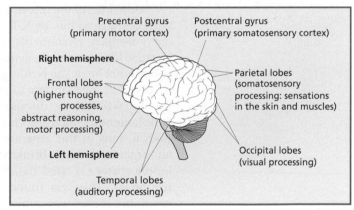

with its own particular sensitivity (e.g. touch; temperature) (Kaas et al., 1981). There is also a much smaller secondary somatosensory cortex, which is adjacent to the primary somatosensory cortex.

Temporal lobe

The temporal lobe is involved in auditory processing. The most important form of this processing is speech perception. Within the temporal lobe, some parts respond most to certain kinds of sound (e.g. those high or low in pitch). The primary auditory cortex is in the lateral fissure of the temporal lobe, and it is surrounded by about six areas of secondary auditory cortex. The primary auditory cortex is organised in vertical functional columns. All of the neurons within a vertical column respond mainly to sounds of similar frequency. Regions towards the front of the primary auditory cortex respond to higher frequencies, whereas those towards the back respond to lower frequencies. The most common effect of damage to the auditory cortex in humans is word deafness. This involves difficulty in perceiving speech and in identifying any sounds that are presented briefly.

Occipital lobe

The occipital lobe is mainly concerned with visual processing. Nerve fibres from the right side of each eye go to the right occipital lobe, whereas those from the left side of each eye

■ Research activity: Complete a table like the one below for each of the cortical areas.

	Location	Functions	Effects of damage
Auditory area			
Somatosensory area			
Visual area			
Motor area			

go to the left occipital lobe. If you are struck on the back of the head close to the occipital area, you will see "stars". The occipital lobe plays a key role in vision, but the temporal and parietal lobes are also involved. Indeed, it has been estimated that as much as 50% of the entire cerebral cortex is devoted to visual processing. There is more coverage of the cortical areas involved in visual processing later in the chapter.

None of the four lobes is devoted exclusively to the processes described so far. Large areas within each lobe are association areas, which link sensory and motor processing. Association areas integrate or organise different kinds of sensory information to produce appropriate behaviour. The frontal association area in the frontal lobes is of great importance. It is centrally involved in complex planning and problem solving.

Motor processes

What would be the likely results of not being aware of the positions of your limbs and body?

As has already been mentioned, most of the areas of the brain involved in motor processes are in the frontal lobes. In general terms, the posterior parietal association cortex receives information from the auditory, visual, and somatosensory systems. As a result, the individual is aware of the locations of objects in the environment and of the positions of his or her limbs and body. Signals then go to the dorsolateral prefrontal association cortex, and then on to the secondary motor cortex, and finally the primary motor cortex.

Some idea of the role of the posterior parietal association cortex comes from patients with damage to this area. They often suffer from **apraxia**, which is an inability to carry out voluntary movements (Benson, 1985). This is not due to any muscular damage, because the same movements are sometimes performed when the patient is not thinking about what he or she is doing. Thus, the posterior parietal association cortex seems to be involved in the planning of movements.

We will briefly discuss two of the areas of the secondary motor cortex. The supplementary motor cortex is involved in co-ordinating motor responses. Monkeys with lesions in this area are still able to reach and grasp, but they cannot do this in an organised way (Brinkman, 1984). The premotor cortex (also in the secondary motor cortex) is used mainly when sensory information is used to determine motor responses. This was found by Colebatch et al. (1991). PET scans revealed that the premotor cortex was active when the participants made hand movements in time to a metronome, but not when they made the same hand movements without a metronome present.

Penfield and Boldrey (1937) studied the primary motor cortex by applying electrical stimulation. They found that most of this area is dedicated to those parts of the body that make the most precise movements (e.g. hands; face). The primary motor cortex occupies a central position in the control of motor movements. However, damage to the primary motor cortex has surprisingly little effect (Pinel, 1997).

Roland (1993) assessed blood flow while individuals performed a variety of motor tasks. His findings reinforce and add to those already discussed. According to Pinel (1997, p.219), Roland's research points to the following conclusions:

> *The posterior parietal cortex provides sensory information to the supplementary motor area and the premotor cortex, the supplementary motor area and the premotor cortex exert most of their influence through the primary motor cortex, the supplementary motor area is responsible for developing and executing programs for controlling the sequencing of patterns of motor output, the premotor cortex modifies existing motor programs on the basis of sensory input, and the primary motor and somatosensory areas can execute a series of simple repeated movements without the contribution of the association or secondary cortex.*

KEY TERM

Apraxia: a condition involving an inability to carry out voluntary movements.

Hemisphere Asymmetries

So far we have discussed the cerebral cortex as if its two hemispheres or halves are very similar in their functioning. However, this is by no means the case. There is much hemispheric specialisation, meaning that the two hemispheres differ in their functions. This produces numerous situations in which there is cerebral dominance, with one hemisphere being mainly responsible for processing information in that situation.

Language

It has been known for more than 100 years that language in the great majority of right-handed people (about 95%) is based mainly in the left hemisphere. In left-handed people, about 70% have language based in the left hemisphere. The remainder of right- and left-handed people either have language mainly in the right hemisphere, or neither hemisphere dominates language.

Speech

Most of the evidence about the brain locations of different language functions has been obtained from patients who have suffered strokes. Strokes involve blood clots that produce an interruption in the blood flow to parts of the brain, and this causes the destruction of brain cells. Stroke patients often suffer from **aphasia**. According to Carlson (1994, p.512) in order to be regarded as suffering from aphasia

> *a patient must have difficulty comprehending, repeating, or producing meaningful speech, and this difficulty must not be caused by simple sensory or motor deficits or by lack of motivation.*

Thus, for example, people who are deaf may find it hard to understand speech, but they are not aphasic.

Broca

In the 1860s, Paul Broca studied patients suffering from what is now known as Broca's aphasia or expressive aphasia. These patients have great difficulty in speaking, and their spoken language tends to be very slow and lacking in fluency. In contrast, their ability to comprehend speech is relatively good, but typically worse than that of someone without brain damage. Patients with Broca's or expressive aphasia have three kinds of problems with speech production (although there are great individual differences in terms of their relative severity):

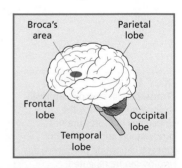

- Anomia: difficulty in finding the right word.
- Agrammatism: difficulty in speaking in a grammatical way.
- Articulation problems: many words are mispronounced.

Broca (1861) argued that expressive aphasia is caused by a lesion in the frontal association cortex, in a region of the brain now known as Broca's area. Broca was partially correct, in that Broca's area is definitely involved in expressive aphasia. However, expressive aphasia is generally only found when brain damage extends beyond Broca's area into adjacent parts of the frontal lobe and subcortical white matter (Damasio, 1989).

Why did Broca underestimate the area of brain involved in expressive aphasia? The area affected by brain damage is often larger than the area in which there is obvious tissue damage. For example, PET scans of aphasic patients with subcortical damage to the basal ganglia have revealed that there can be impaired functioning of apparently "undamaged" parts of the frontal cortex (Metter, 1991). Further evidence that the basal ganglia can be involved in expressive aphasia was obtained by Damasio, Eslinger, and Adams (1984). Patients with damage to the basal ganglia showed most of the symptoms associated with expressive aphasia.

CASE STUDY: *"Tan"*

Paul Broca's first and most famous neurological patient was "Tan": so-called because the only syllables he could utter were "tan-tan". For years Tan was also paralysed on his right side, and became a patient of the surgeon Broca because of an infected bedsore. Broca found that Tan's understanding of speech seemed relatively intact. Broca was curious about why this should be, and when Tan died, Broca performed a post-mortem and found damage in what is now known as Broca's area of the brain. Tan's brain is embalmed and preserved in a museum in Paris, and the damaged area is clearly visible.

KEY TERM
Aphasia: impaired ability to comprehend or to produce language.

Comprehension

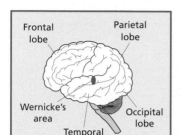

Wernicke's aphasia. A few years after Broca, Carl Wernicke studied stroke patients who were able to speak, but who had very poor ability to understand language. These patients had suffered damage to a part of the left hemisphere in the middle and back areas of the superior temporal gyrus. This later came to be known as Wernicke's area. Patients with Wernicke's or receptive aphasia speak fluently but in an almost meaningless way. Try to guess what was being described by a patient with receptive aphasia who was studied by Geschwind (1979): "Mother is away here working her work to get better, but when she's looking the two boys looking in the other part. She's working another time." In fact, the patient was looking at a picture of a woman with two boys behind her stealing biscuits.

As a result, we cannot test the ability of receptive aphasics to understand speech by asking them to respond verbally. One approach is to ask patients with Wernicke's aphasia to point to specified objects, a task that they find very difficult. Perhaps surprisingly, most patients with Wernicke's aphasia do not seem to realise that they have severe language problems.

Patients with Wernicke's aphasia typically have a number of language problems, with the severity of each problem varying from patient to patient:

* Pure word deafness: spoken words cannot be recognised even though non-speech sounds (e.g. a bird's call) are recognised.
* Word comprehension: difficulties in understanding word meanings.
* Thought expression: difficulties in producing meaningful speech that expresses the speaker's thoughts.

Wernicke's area is part of the auditory association cortex, and so it seems reasonable to assume that this area is involved in pure word deafness or the inability to recognise words. Studies on Wernicke's patients using CAT and MRI scans have provided support for this assumption (Carlson, 1994). However, pure word deafness can also be caused by damage to the primary auditory cortex (which is adjacent to Wernicke's area) or by damage to the axons conveying information from the primary auditory cortex to Wernicke's area.

Transcortical sensory aphasia. Severe problems with word comprehension and with expressing thoughts in speech involve an area behind Wernicke's area close to the meeting point of the temporal, occipital, and parietal lobes. Some of the most convincing evidence for this comes from studies of patients suffering from what is known as **transcortical sensory aphasia**, who have damage to the area just described but not to Wernicke's area. These patients do not understand the meanings of words and cannot produce meaningful speech, but they can repeat words that they hear. As Carlson (1994, p.520) pointed out, "the symptoms of Wernicke's aphasia consist of those of pure word deafness plus those of transcortical sensory aphasia."

Conduction aphasia. We have discussed Broca's area and Wernicke's area separately. However, these two areas are joined by the **arcuate fasciculus**. Damage to this bundle of axons produces what is known as **conduction aphasia**. Patients with conduction aphasia are generally able to understand speech and to speak in a fluent and meaningful way. However, they find it very hard to repeat non-words or unfamiliar words they have heard.

Anomic aphasia. The final type of aphasia that we will discuss is anomic aphasia. Patients with **anomic aphasia** have good speech comprehension and talk both fluently and gram-

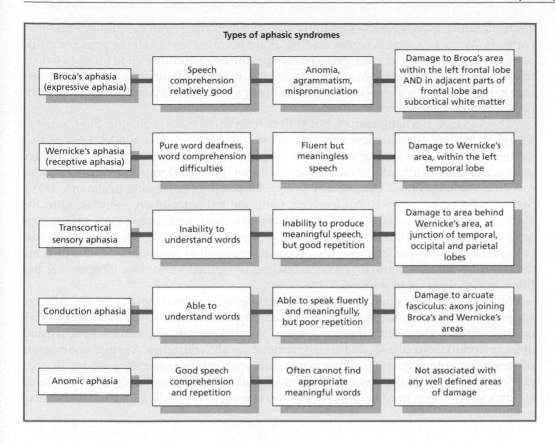

Types of aphasic syndromes

Broca's aphasia (expressive aphasia)	Speech comprehension relatively good	Anomia, agrammatism, mispronunciation	Damage to Broca's area within the left frontal lobe AND in adjacent parts of frontal lobe and subcortical white matter
Wernicke's aphasia (receptive aphasia)	Pure word deafness, word comprehension difficulties	Fluent but meaningless speech	Damage to Wernicke's area, within the left temporal lobe
Transcortical sensory aphasia	Inability to understand words	Inability to produce meaningful speech, but good repetition	Damage to area behind Wernicke's area, at junction of temporal, occipital and parietal lobes
Conduction aphasia	Able to understand words	Able to speak fluently and meaningfully, but poor repetition	Damage to arcuate fasciculus: axons joining Broca's and Wernicke's areas
Anomic aphasia	Good speech comprehension and repetition	Often cannot find appropriate meaningful words	Not associated with any well defined areas of damage

matically. However, they often cannot think of the right words when speaking. For example, here is a patient trying to name a picture of a saw: "Ss ... sahbing ... sah ... I can't say it. I know what it is and I can cut the wood with it and it's in my garage" (Carlson, 1994, p.524).

Which parts of the brain are damaged in anomic aphasia? The evidence suggests that various parts of the brain can be involved. For example, Damasio et al. (1991) studied several patients suffering from anomic aphasia. Patients who had anomia for common nouns had damage to the inferior temporal cortex, whereas those with anomia for proper nouns (names for persons, places, or objects) had damage to the adjacent temporal pole.

Reading and writing

Aphasic patients who find it hard to understand speech generally also have problems in reading, and those whose speech production is deficient have limited writing skills. There are also close similarities in the *specific* problems shown by aphasic patients with respect to these language skills. Thus, for example, Broca's patients whose speech is not grammatical tend to write in an ungrammatical way.

Some patients do not conform to the general pattern described in the previous paragraph. For example, Semenza, Cipolotti, and Denes (1992) studied a female aphasic patient whose comprehension and production of written language were much better than her oral language. Thus, she could understand what she read and could write the names of objects, even though she was unable to make sense of what people said to her and could not say the names of objects. These findings suggest that the parts of the brain used for written language are not exactly the same as those used for oral language, although there is clearly a substantial overlap.

Evaluation

The extensive work on language localisation has led to the Wernicke–Geschwind model (see Pinel, 1997). According to this model, seven areas of the brain are involved in language processing: primary visual cortex; angular gyrus; primary auditory cortex; Wernicke's area; the arcuate fasciculus; Broca's area; and primary motor cortex.

Understanding speech involves auditory signals proceeding from the primary auditory cortex to Wernicke's area, whereas reading aloud involves first of all the primary visual cortex, followed by the angular gyrus (which produces an auditory code for each word), followed by Wernicke's area. In speech production, information proceeds from Wernicke's area to the arcuate fasciculus, and then on to Broca's area, followed by the primary motor cortex, and then the speech muscles.

This model is partially correct, but suffers from three main problems. First, some of the relevant brain areas are less important than is suggested by the model. Lesions that destroy all of Broca's area or most of the arcuate fasciculus typically fail to produce permanent speech difficulties (Rasmussen & Milner, 1975), and much of Wernicke's area can be removed without causing any lasting language impairments (Ojemann, 1979). Second, other areas seem to be involved. Only the left hemisphere is included in the Wernicke–Geschwind model, but PET scans of participants performing various language tasks showed much activity in the right hemisphere (Petersen et al., 1989). Third, the model is too neat and tidy. For example, the processes involved in reading familiar words are usually different from those involved in reading unfamiliar words (see Chapter 14), but this is not allowed for in the model.

Studies of brain-damaged patients have revealed much about the locations of different speech-related functions. However, there is an important limitation of most of the work on brain-damaged patients. Broca's aphasia, Wernicke's aphasia, transcortical sensory aphasia, conduction aphasia, and anomic aphasia are all syndromes. A syndrome consists of various symptoms found together in numerous patients. Syndrome-based approaches *exaggerate* the similarities among different patients allegedly suffering from the same syndrome, and often minimise the similarities among patients claimed to have different syndromes.

What other syndromes can you think of? How might the limitations of the syndrome-based approach to disorders affect diagnosis and treatment?

Split-brain studies

Much of what we know about hemispheric specialisation and cerebral dominance comes from the study of split-brain patients. These patients mostly suffered from severe epilepsy, which can produce collapse and loss of consciousness. The corpus callosum or bridge between the two hemispheres was surgically cut to contain the epileptic seizures within one hemisphere. The corpus callosum is a collection of about 250 million axons connecting sites in one hemisphere with those in the other. There are two other pathways connecting the two hemispheres, but the corpus callosum is far more important in terms of the rapid transmission of information from one hemisphere to another. As a result, split-brain patients provide an exciting way of working out what happens in each hemisphere.

It was not initially realised that cutting the corpus callosum caused any problems for split-brain patients. These patients cannot transfer information from one hemisphere to another, but they can ensure that visual information from the environment reaches both hemispheres by simply moving their eyes around. Thus, careful studies need to be carried out in order to produce convincing evidence of impaired performance. As we will see, such studies have been carried out in the United States by Roger Sperry, Michael Gazzaniga, and their colleagues.

Most of the studies involved presenting visual stimuli in such a way that some information went to the left hemisphere and some information to the right hemisphere. The anatomy of the visual pathways is fairly complex. The fibres from the outer half of each retina go to the same hemisphere, whereas those from the inner half cross over and go the opposite hemisphere. As a result, information presented to the left half of each retina will proceed only to the left hemisphere, and information presented to the right half of each retina will go only to the right hemisphere.

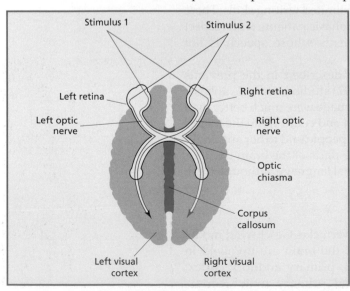

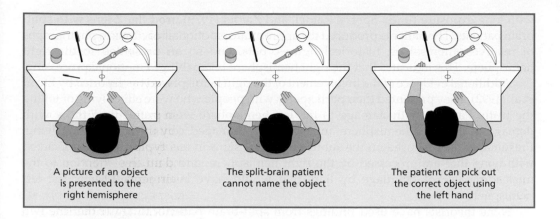

| A picture of an object is presented to the right hemisphere | The split-brain patient cannot name the object | The patient can pick out the correct object using the left hand |

Faces and objects

The following study by Levy, Trevarthen, and Sperry (1972) took advantage of the anatomy of the visual pathways. Split-brain patients were shown faces, in which the left half of one person's face was presented next to the right half of another person's face. These faces were presented very briefly to prevent the eyes moving during presentation. This made sure that information about the right half of the picture went to the left hemisphere, and information about the left half went to the right hemisphere. The patients were asked to say what they had seen. They generally reported seeing the right half of the picture. However, when they were asked to use their fingers to point to what they saw, most of the patients pointed to the left half of the picture. These findings suggest that language is mainly (or exclusively) based in the left hemisphere, whereas the spatial processing involved in pointing to something depends far more on the right hemisphere.

Sperry and his colleagues carried out other similar research. In one study, a picture of an object was presented briefly to the right hemisphere. Split-brain patients could not name the object, presumably because the right hemisphere has very poor language abilities. After that, the patients put their left hands behind a screen to decide which of the objects hidden there corresponded to the picture. Most of the patients were able to do this, because of the good ability of the right hemisphere to process spatial information.

Discussion points

1. Why is this research on split-brain patients regarded as of major importance?

2. Why do we need to be careful when generalising from the performance of split-brain patients to that of other people?

You can test some of Sperry's ideas by doing a simple experiment. You balance a rod on either the right or the left index finger for as long as possible. If right-handed people do this while remaining silent, they can balance the rod longer on the right index finger than on the left. However, if they talk while they try to balance the rod, then the opposite result is obtained: they can now balance the rod longer on the left index finger than on the right. It is as if speaking knocks the rod off the right index finger.

What is happening here? Speech and the right hand are both controlled by the left hemisphere, and so interfere with each other. In contrast, speech and the left hand are controlled by different hemispheres, and so hardly interfere with each other.

If split-brain patients have the chance to make eye movements when presented with visual stimuli, there is a danger that the information will go directly to both hemispheres. As a result, there have been very brief presentations in most studies. This problem was solved by Zaidel. He devised the Z lens that permits visual input to enter only one hemisphere of split-brain patients even

Mary had a little lamb...

with long exposure times. Sperry, Zaidel, and Zaidel (1979) used the Z lens with split-brain patients. The patients produced the appropriate emotional reactions to photographs of relatives, themselves, historical figures, pets, and so on presented to the right hemisphere. This indicates that the right hemisphere is capable of emotional processing.

Additional evidence of the involvement of the right hemisphere was reported by Etcoff et al. (1992). They presented their participants with people who were either lying or telling the truth. Patients with damage to the left hemisphere were better than those with damage to the right hemisphere and non-brain-damaged controls at detecting lying. Presumably they focused on the subtle emotional signs in facial expressions associated with lying that are processed by the right hemisphere, and paid less attention to the misleading use of language by liars that would have been processed by the left hemisphere.

Some theorists have used findings from split-brain patients to argue that the two hemispheres are very different from each other. According to Sperry (1985), the right hemisphere usually processes information in a synthetic fashion (as a whole). In contrast, the left hemisphere processes information in an analytic or logical fashion (bit by bit).

Sperry and others have gone further, and argued that split-brain patients have two minds or streams of consciousness. It is hard to evaluate this claim, but the evidence tends not to support it. If these patients have two minds, then it should be possible to produce a dialogue between these two minds. However, MacKay (1987) argued that this had not happened. According to him, "despite all encouragements we found no sign at all of recognition of the other 'half' as a separate person." One of the patients even asked MacKay, "Are you guys trying to make two people out of me?"

Evaluation

The findings from split-brain patients are dramatic. However, we must not fall into the trap of assuming that the two hemispheres of normal individuals act independently. For those having an intact corpus callosum, information is transferred from one hemisphere to the other in a few milliseconds. As a result, our two hemispheres normally function together in a co-operative fashion. Indeed, even split-brain patients function very well unless special studies are set up to show their limitations.

The split-brain patients studied by Sperry and others had suffered from severe epilepsy over a period of several years, and epilepsy is normally caused by brain damage. This makes it hard to know whether the ways in which they processed information before the operation were the same as in people with intact brains. Most of the patients studied by Sperry were adults at the time of surgical cutting of the corpus callosum. The age at which surgery occurs seems to be important. Lassonde et al. (1991) found that the performance of split-brain patients on various tasks was generally better when the operation took place in childhood rather than later. Presumably the ability of the brain to adapt to cutting of the corpus callosum is greater in younger people.

The notion that the left hemisphere operates in an analytic way whereas the right hemisphere operates in a synthetic way has a grain of truth about it. However, this is clearly a very oversimplified view, in part because a wide range of different processing activities occur *within* each hemisphere. Kimura (1979) put forward a motor theory that may be an advance on the analytic–synthetic theory. According to Kimura, the left hemisphere is specialised for the control of all precise movements, of which speech is merely one example. As predicted, patients with lesions in the left hemisphere who had impaired speech also had reduced ability to make precise facial movements (Kimura & Watson, 1989).

Studies on normals

There are various experimental methods that have been used in normal individuals to study the role of each hemisphere in information processing. For example, there is the divided visual field technique, in which two stimuli are presented at the same time, one to each hemisphere. The stimulus that is detected or reported first provides an indication as to which hemisphere is better able to process information from that kind of stimulus.

What are the subtle facial expressions associated with telling lies?

The auditory equivalent of the divided visual field technique is the dichotic listening task. Two words or other auditory stimuli are presented at the same time one to each ear, and the participants are asked to report what they hear. In interpreting the findings from the dichotic listening task, it has to be borne in mind that information presented to the left ear goes to the right hemisphere first, and information from the right ear proceeds initially to the left hemisphere. However, visual or auditory information that goes initially to one hemisphere will go through the corpus callosum and into the other hemisphere within 100 milliseconds or less.

What has emerged from the relevant research? Green (1994, p.69) has provided a useful summary:

In divided field studies, face recognition, pattern recognition, discriminating brightness and colours, depth perception, and perceiving the orientation of lines all produce a right hemisphere advantage. Words, letters, and digits (numbers) produce a left hemisphere advantage. In dichotic listening studies recognition of environmental sounds, and aspects of music such as duration and emotional tone produce a right hemisphere advantage, whereas spoken digits, words, nonsense syllables, backwards speech, and normal speech all produce a left hemisphere advantage.

Relevant evidence comes from Kimura (1964). She found that the left hemisphere was better at detecting words, but the right hemisphere was better at perceiving melodies.

The findings from studies on normals resemble those obtained from split-brain patients. However, it is hard to interpret the findings. As Cohen (1983, p.237) pointed out:

The observed hemisphere differences may originate at any stage intervening between stimulus input and response output ... Hemispheric asymmetries could be reflecting differences in perception, in analysis, in judgement, or in control of the voice or hand making the response.

Bradshaw and Sherlock

Do hemispheric differences depend on the type of stimulus presented or on the type of processing that the stimulus receives? This issue was addressed by Bradshaw and Sherlock (1982). They presented their participants with faces made up of squares, triangles, and rectangles. On each trial, they had to decide whether a target face had been presented. In one condition, the target was a face in which the features were all close together. In the other condition, the target was a face in which the nose was pointing up.

What did Bradshaw and Sherlock find? The participants were better at detecting the target with the features close together when it was presented to the right hemisphere rather than the left hemisphere. However, the nose target was detected better by the left hemisphere than by the right hemisphere. These findings indicate that hemispheric differences can depend on the type of processing required rather than simply on the type of stimulus. According to Bradshaw and Sherlock, the right hemisphere is good at holistic processing involving the whole stimulus. That is why the closeness of the features was detected more accurately by the right hemisphere. In contrast, the left hemisphere is good at analytic processing, in which a stimulus is processed component by component. That is why the nose target was detected more accurately by the left hemisphere.

Discussion points

1. What important issues were Bradshaw and Sherlock (1982) trying to study?
2. Are there other ways we could test the notion that the right hemisphere engages in holistic processing, whereas the left hemisphere engages in analytic processing?

Hemispheric lateralisation is probably clearest with respect to language. Some of the most convincing evidence that language in normal individuals is mainly a left-hemisphere function is based on the Wada test. What happens is that an anaesthetic is injected into an artery supplying one hemisphere, and the participant is then asked to read aloud. For

CASE STUDY: *Phineas Gage*

The link between emotional state and brain function was famously demonstrated in the case of Phineas Gage, a construction foreman on the American railroad who, on 13 September 1848, was involved in a gruesome accident (Rylander, 1948). An explosive charge went off accidentally, and a metal spike three feet long and one inch thick was driven through Gage's head, entering at his cheek and passing out through the top of his skull. Amazingly, Gage survived his injuries, and his memory, attention, and cognitive processes appeared to be largely unaffected. However, his personality was so badly changed that his employers refused to take him back into work. They wrote that "the balance between his intellectual faculties and animal propensities seems to have been destroyed." Before the accident, Gage had been a well balanced, civilised, and conscientious man, but now he was "fitful, irreverent, indulging at times in the grossest profanity [swearing] ... impatient of restraint or advice when it conflicts with his desires ... A child in his intellectual capability and manifestations, he has the animal passions of a strong man." Poor Gage was so changed that his friends said he was "no longer Gage", and it is reported that he eventually became an exhibit in a circus, probably the only means of earning a living open to him at the time.

over 90% of people, reading aloud is more disrupted when it is the left hemisphere that is anaesthetised rather than the right hemisphere (Green, 1994).

Emotion

There has been much interest in the issue of whether various emotions depend more on the left or right hemisphere. Gainotti (1972) explored this issue by considering patients who had suffered brain damage to only one hemisphere. Patients with damage to the left hemisphere experienced anxiety and aggression, whereas those with damage to the right hemisphere seemed relatively unemotional and indifferent. These findings led him to conclude that emotional experience depends more on the right hemisphere than on the left one. In similar fashion, some studies have found in brain-damaged patients that the right hemisphere was better than the left hemisphere at perceiving mood (Tompkins & Mateer, 1985).

The evidence from other research is rather inconsistent (Green, 1994). However, Davidson et al. (1990) took EEG recordings of their participants as they watched films designed to produce feelings of pleasure or disgust. Feelings of pleasure were associated with greater activity in the left hemisphere, whereas feelings of disgust led to greater activity in the right hemisphere. They concluded that positive emotions have greater left hemisphere involvement, whereas negative emotions have greater right hemisphere involvement.

Summary

Kolb and Whishaw (1990) provided a review of the literature on hemispheric lateralisation. They concluded that there is a left hemisphere dominance for the following functions: words; letters; verbal memory; all language skills; arithmetic; and complex movements. In contrast, there is a right hemisphere dominance for the following functions: faces; emotional expression; non-verbal memory; spatial abilities (e.g. geometry); touch; music; and movement in spatial patterns.

Hemispheric lateralisation (Kolb & Whishaw, 1990)

Left hemisphere dominance	Right hemisphere dominance
Words	Faces
Letters	Emotional expression
Verbal memory	Non-verbal memory
All language skills	Spatial abilities
Arithmetic	Music
Complex movements	Movement in spatial patterns

Structure and Processes of Visual Perception

Why do you think vision could be regarded as the most important of our senses?

Far more of the cortex is devoted to vision than to any other sense modality. Why is that so? There are two main reasons. First, vision is of enormous importance in our lives, and is perhaps even more important than our other senses. Second, the human visual system is engaged in complex processing activities. In the words of Pinel (1997, p.151):

> From the tiny, distorted, upside-down, two-dimensional retinal images projected upon the visual receptors lining the backs of our eyes, the visual system creates an accurate, richly detailed, three-dimensional perception.

Structure of the visual system

KEY TERM
Cornea: a transparent membrane at the front of the eye.

Light waves from objects in the environment pass through the transparent **cornea** at the front of the eye and proceed to the iris, which lies just in behind the cornea and gives the eye its distinctive colour. The amount of light that enters the eye is determined by the pupil, which is an opening in the iris. This is achieved by the pupil becoming smaller when the lighting is very bright, and larger when there is relatively little light. The lens focuses light onto the retina at the back of the eye. Each lens adjusts in shape by a process of **accommodation** to bring images into focus on the retina.

The retina itself is fairly complex. It consists of five different layers of cells: receptors; horizontal cells; bipolar cells; amacrine cells; and retinal ganglion cells. The arrangement of these cells is slightly odd. Light from the lens goes through all of the layers of cells until it reaches the receptor cells at the back, after which the neural message goes back through the layers. Impulses from the retina leave the eye via the optic nerve, which is at the front of the retina. There are two types of receptors in the retina: rods and cones. They are discussed later in the section on colour vision.

Why do we have two eyes? A key reason is because this produces **binocular disparity**, which means that the image of any given object is slightly different on the two retinas. Binocular disparity provides very useful information for the task of constructing a three-dimensional world out of two-dimensional retinal images (see Chapter 11).

Pathways from eye to cortex

The main pathway between the eye and the cortex is the retina-geniculate-striate pathway. This transmits information from the retina to the primary visual cortex or striate cortex via the lateral geniculate nuclei of the thalamus. The entire retina-geniculate-striate system is organised in a similar way to the retinal system. Thus, for example, two stimuli that are adjacent to each other in the retinal image will also be adjacent to each other at higher levels within the system. When the primary visual cortex of blind patients is stimulated by electrodes forming a given shape, they report "seeing" that shape (Dobelle, Mladejovsky, & Girvin, 1974).

Each eye has its own optic nerve, and the two optic nerves meet at the optic chiasma. At this point, the axons from the outer halves of each retina proceed to the hemisphere on the same side, whereas the axons from the inner halves cross over and go to the other hemisphere. Signals then proceed along two optic tracts within the brain. One tract contains signals from the left half of each eye, and the other signals from the right half of each eye.

After the optic chiasma, the optic tract proceeds to the lateral geniculate nucleus, which is part of the thalamus. Nerve impulses finally reach the primary visual cortex within the occipital lobe before speading out to nearby secondary visual cortical areas.

There is one final important feature of the retina-geniculate-striate system. There are two independent channels within this system:

1. The parvocellular (or P) pathway: this pathway is most sensitive to colour and to fine detail; most of its input comes from cones.
2. The magnocellular (or M) pathway: this pathway is most sensitive to information about movement; most of its input comes from rods.

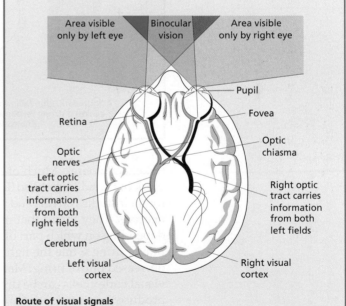

Route of visual signals
Note that all light from the fields left of centre of both eyes (green) falls on the right sides of the two retinas; and information about these fields goes to the right visual cortex. Information about the right fields of vision (grey) goes to the left cortex. Data about the binocular vision go to both cortices.

KEY TERMS
Accommodation: the process of adjusting the shape of the lens to ensure that images are focused on the retina.
Binocular disparity: the difference in the image of any given object on the two retinas.

Edge perception: Primary visual cortex

Most people would not think that the perception of edges is important. However, this view is mistaken. As Pinel (1997, p.163) pointed out, "Edges are the most informative features of any visual display because they define the extent and position of the various objects in it". What are edges? They are the meeting place of two adjacent areas of the visual field.

In order to perceive an edge, there needs to be some kind of contrast between two adjacent areas. Suppose that you look at two adjacent columns, one of which is brighter than the other. What happens in the area around the dividing line or edge between them is that the brighter column looks brighter than it actually is, whereas the darker column looks darker than it is. These illusory stripes are sometimes called Mach bands, and they illustrate what is known as **contrast enhancement**. This phenomenon is caused by **lateral inhibition**, in which the firing of a receptor inhibits the firing of adjacent receptors. Thus, for example, the receptors in the middle of the brighter column fire at a high rate, but they are all subject to lateral inhibition from each other. Receptors in the brighter column that lie close to the edge also fire at a high rate, but they are exposed to relatively little lateral inhibition from the receptors in the darker column. As a result, the part of the brighter column nearest the edge seems brighter than the rest of the column.

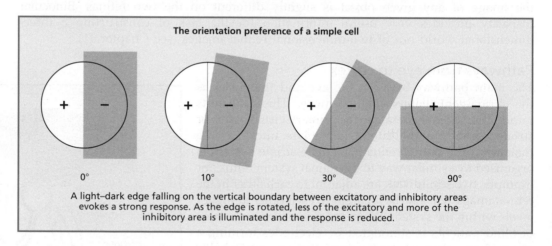

The orientation preference of a simple cell

0°   10°   30°   90°

A light–dark edge falling on the vertical boundary between excitatory and inhibitory areas evokes a strong response. As the edge is rotated, less of the excitatory and more of the inhibitory area is illuminated and the response is reduced.

Hubel and Wiesel. Much of our understanding of basic visual processes stems from the work of David Hubel and Torsten Wiesel (e.g. 1979), who were awarded the Nobel Prize for their studies on cats and monkeys. They used single-unit recording to study individual neurons. They found that many cells responded in two different ways to a spot of light depending on which part of the cell was affected: (1) an "on" response, with an increased rate of firing while the light was on; and (2) an "off" response, with the light causing a decreased rate of firing. Many retinal ganglion cells, lateral geniculate cells, and primary visual cortex cells can be divided into on-centre cells and off-centre cells. On-centre cells produce the on-response to a light in the centre of their receptive field and an off-response to a light in the periphery; the opposite is the case with off-centre cells.

Hubel and Wiesel (1979) discovered the existence of two types of neurons in the receptive fields of the primary visual cortex: simple cells and complex cells. Simple cells have "on" and "off" regions, with each region being rectangular in shape. Simple cells play an important role in detection. They respond most to dark bars in a light field, light bars in a dark field, or to straight edges between areas of light and dark. However, it should be noted that any given simple cell only responds strongly to stimuli of a particular orientation.

There are many more complex cells than simple cells. They resemble simple cells in that they respond maximally to straight-line stimuli that are presented in a particular orientation. However, there are three significant differences:

1. Complex cells have larger receptive fields.

KEY TERMS

Contrast enhancement: facilitated perception of edges by contrast effects produced by lateral inhibition.

Lateral inhibition: a process in which the firing of receptors inhibits the firing of adjacent receptors, thus causing contrast enhancement.

2. The rate of firing of a complex cell to any given stimulus does not depend on its position within the cell's receptive field; in contrast, simple cells are divided into "on" and "off" regions.

3. A majority of complex cells respond to stimulation of either eye, whereas nearly all simple cortical cells respond only to stimulation of one eye (left or right).

Organisation of cells

So far we have talked about the responses of different kinds of cells separately from each other. However, the reality is that there is a definite organisation of these cells. As Pinel (1997, p.168) argued, "Signals flow from on-centre and off-centre cells in lower layer IV to simple cells and from simple cells to complex cells." The primary visual cortex is also organised in that its cells are arranged in functional vertical columns which are at right angles to the cortical layers. The cells within any one column resemble each other in that all of them respond maximally to lines having the same orientation. Functional columns that analyse input from a given part of the retina are gathered together in clusters. Within a cluster, half of the cells respond mainly to stimulation from the left eye, whereas the other half respond mostly to stimulation from the right eye. A block of tissue that analyses visual input from a given part of the visual field contains within it clusters of cells that respond maximally to straight-line stimuli in several different orientations. All in all, there is an impressive level of organisation within the primary visual cortex.

Spatial-frequency theory

Hubel and Wiesel (1979) argued that processing in the visual cortex is based on straight lines and edges. However, it now seems that matters are more complicated. DeValois and DeValois (1988) claimed that processing is actually based on spatial frequency. More specifically, they focused on **sine-wave gratings**. These consist of alternating light and dark stripes of equal width which produce a regular sine wave when the intensity of light across the pattern is plotted. More generally, it is possible to plot the varying intensity of light across any visual stimulus, and this plot can be represented in the form of a sine wave. According to this theory, perception of a scene involves putting together the information from numerous sine-wave gratings.

How do we know that the spatial-frequency theory is an improvement on the approach of Hubel and Wiesel? A key finding is that most cells in the primary visual cortex respond more strongly to sine-wave gratings than to lines and edges. This suggests that the visual cortex is mainly designed to process spatial frequency. However, it should be noted that the two theories are not very different from each other, because "straight-edge stimuli ... can readily be translated into component sine-wave gratings of the same orientation" (Pinel, 1997, p.171).

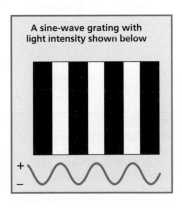

A sine-wave grating with light intensity shown below

Hierarchical organisation in the cortex

In the previous section, we focused on the primary visual cortex, which is located in the posterior region of the occipital lobes. However, other parts of the cortex are also involved in visual processing. In general terms, information from the primary visual cortex proceeds to the secondary visual cortex, and from there to the association cortex. Part of the secondary visual cortex is located in the prestriate cortex in the occipital lobe close to the primary visual cortex. The rest of the secondary visual cortex is in the inferior temporal lobe. The association cortex is distributed in various parts of the cortex, but much of it is in the posterior parietal region.

We have suggested that the primary visual cortex acts as a kind of gateway to later visual processing. As a result, we would expect that patients who have lost their primary visual cortex through injury or disease should be unable to see. In fact, what happens is more complex. Such patients report being blind, but some of them are nevertheless able to perform visual tasks. For example, there was the case of DB, who denied that he could see anything in his left visual field. According to Weiskrantz et al. (1974, p.726), in spite of that

KEY TERM
Sine-wave gratings: patterns of light intensity created by alternating light and dark stripes.

(a) he could reach for visual stimuli [in his left field] with considerable accuracy; (b) could differentiate the orientation of a vertical line from a horizontal or diagonal line; (c) could differentiate the letters "X" and "O".

This phenomenon is known as **blindsight**. It probably occurs because some information passes directly from subcortical structures to the secondary visual cortex without going through the primary visual cortex. This allows patients with blindsight to perform simple visual tasks, but is insufficient to produce conscious awareness.

There are two main streams of information going from the primary visual cortex to other cortical areas: (1) the dorsal stream proceeds to the dorsal prestriate cortex and then on to the posterior parietal cortex; (2) the ventral stream proceeds from the ventral prestriate cortex to the inferotemporal cortex. What are the functions of these two streams? According to Ungerleider and Mishkin (1982), the dorsal stream carries information about object location ("where is it?"), whereas the ventral stream carries information about object identification ("what is it?"). Evidence for this comes from brain-damaged patients (Ungerleider & Haxby, 1994). Patients with damage to structures associated with the dorsal stream can identify objects but cannot reach accurately for them. In contrast, patients with damage to structures of the ventral stream can reach accurately for objects they cannot identify.

Milner and Goodale (1993) argued that the dorsal stream may be of most value in providing an answer to the question, "How do I interact with that object?" rather than to the question, "Where is that object?". Many patients with damage to the dorsal stream who could not pick up objects cleanly could nevertheless describe very precisely their location, size, and shape. In other words, they knew where objects were, but could not use that information effectively.

Modular processing

Zeki (1992, 1993) argued that different parts of the cortex are specialised for different visual functions. In other words, the visual system consists of a number of modules or relatively independent processing units. This is very different to the traditional view, according to which there is a unitary processing system. Zeki (1992) has studied the visual cortex of the macaque monkey. It consists of the primary visual cortex (area V1) and the prestriate cortex (areas V2 to V5). Here are the main functions of these areas according to Zeki:

- V1 and V2: these areas are involved at an early stage of visual perception; they consist of different groups of cells responsive to colour and form, and may be said to "contain pigeonholes into which the different signals are assembled before being relayed to the specialised visual areas" (Zeki, 1992, p.47).
- V3 and V3A: cells in these areas are responsive to form (especially the shapes of objects in motion), but are not responsive to colour.
- V4: the great majority of cells in this area are responsive to colour; many are also responsive to line orientation.
- V5: this area is specialised for visual motion.

Zeki assumed that colour, form, and motion are processed in anatomically separate parts of the visual cortex. The initial evidence came from studies of monkeys. However, evidence from PET scans of brain activity and from the study of brain-damaged patients indicates that the functional specialisation of the visual cortex in humans is similar to that in monkeys.

Zeki (1992) discussed some of his work with PET brain scans. Normal human participants viewing an abstract colour painting showed the most brain activity in the fusiform gyrus, which is an area known as human V4. In contrast, viewing a pattern of moving black-and-white squares led to greatest activity in a

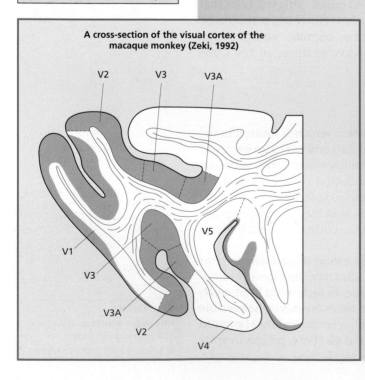

A cross-section of the visual cortex of the macaque monkey (Zeki, 1992)

different area known as human V5. Zeki also found that there was activity in area V5 when his participants viewed a static visual figure known as "Enigma". This is of interest, because this figure creates an illusion of rotating movement. These findings show that motion and colour are processed in different parts of the visual cortex in humans as well as in monkeys. The additional finding that there was much activity in area V1 (and also probably in area V2) with both stimuli suggests that these regions are involved in distributing signals to the relevant specialised areas of the striate cortex.

Discussion points

1. Do you find it surprising that different aspects of visual processing take place in different parts of the cortex?
2. What is left unexplained by Zeki's theory?

If there are anatomically separate brain systems in visual perception, then presumably some brain-damaged patients will have damage to only one of those systems. As a result, they should have very selective impairments in visual perception. There are various conditions involving specific impairments:

- **Achromatopsia**: patients with damage to area V4 have no colour perception; however, their form and motion perception are normal.
- **Akinetopsia**: there is damage to area V5; stationary objects can be seen fairly well, but moving objects are invisible.
- **Chromatopsia**: colour vision is good even though all other aspects of visual perception are much impaired.

There are separate brain systems concerned with motion, form, and colour. This raises the issue of how these different types of information are brought together and integrated. According to Zeki (1992), various processing stages are probably involved:

- Signals proceed from the retina to area V1 via the lateral geniculate nucleus.
- Signals go from area V1 to the various areas of the prestriate cortex specialised for form, motion, and colour processing.
- Signals from the specialised areas of the prestriate cortex are sent back to areas V1 and V2, because these are the areas that have the most precise maps of the visual field.

Cells responding to any given object in the visual field may be distributed throughout area V1. Some form of "binding" is needed to fasten together these distributed sources of information. As yet, little is known of how this is done.

Colour Vision

Why has colour vision developed? After all, if you see an old black-and-white film on television, it is perfectly easy to make sense of the moving images presented to your eyes. There are two main reasons why colour vision is of value to us (Sekuler & Blake, 1994):

- Detection: colour vision helps us to distinguish between an object and its background.
- Discrimination: colour vision makes it easy for us to make fine discriminations among objects (e.g. between ripe and unripe fruit).

In order to understand how we can discriminate about five million different colours, we need to start with the retina. There are two types of visual receptor cells in the retina: cones and rods. There are about six million cones, and they are mostly found in the fovea or central part of the retina. The cones are specialised for colour vision and for sharpness of vision. There are about 125 million rods, and they are concentrated in the outer regions of the retina. Rods are specialised for vision in dim light and for the detection of movement. Many of these differences stem from the fact that a retinal ganglion cell receives input

What might be the evolutionary benefits of colour vision?

> **KEY TERMS**
> **Achromatopsia**: a condition in which there is no colour perception, but intact form and motion perception.
> **Akinetopsia**: a condition in which stationary objects can be seen, but moving objects cannot.
> **Chromatopsia**: a condition in which colour vision is good, but all other aspects of visual perception are impaired.

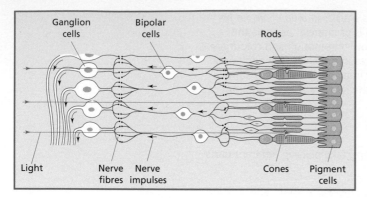

from only a few cones but from hundreds of rods. As a result, only rods produce much activity in retinal ganglion cells in poor lighting conditions, but the disadvantage is that the exact location of the stimulus is less clear.

Young–Helmholtz theory

Cone receptors contain rhodopsin. This is a light-sensitive photopigment which allows the cone receptors to respond to light. According to the component or trichromatic theory put forward by Thomas Young and developed by Hermann von Helmholtz, there are three types of cone receptors differing in the light wavelengths to which they respond most strongly. One type of cone receptor is most sensitive to short-wavelength light, and is most responsive to blue stimuli. A second type of cone receptor is most sensitive to medium-wavelength light, and responds greatly to green stimuli. The third type of cone receptor responds most to long-wavelength light such as that coming from red stimuli. How do we see other colours? According to the theory, many colours activate two or even all cone types. The perception of yellow is based on the second and third cone types, and white light involves the activation of all three cone types.

Dartnall, Bowmaker, and Mollon (1983) obtained strong support for the Young–Helmholtz theory using a precise technique known as microspectrophotometry. The amount of light absorbed by individual cone receptors at different wavelengths was assessed. All three of the types of cone receptor assumed by the Young–Helmholtz theory were found. However, the Young–Helmholtz theory cannot account for all aspects of colour perception. For example, most individuals who are colour blind have problems in perceiving red and green. However, practically no-one has problems with green and blue, and most have a normal ability to perceive red and yellow. These patterns of colour blindness are mysterious from the perspective of the Young–Helmholtz theory. Negative afterimages, which are discussed next, also cannot be explained by the theory.

Opponent-process theory

Ewald Hering (1878) put forward an opponent-process theory. He assumed there are three types of opponent cells in the visual system. One type of cell produces perception of green when it responds in one way and of red when it responds in a different way. A second type

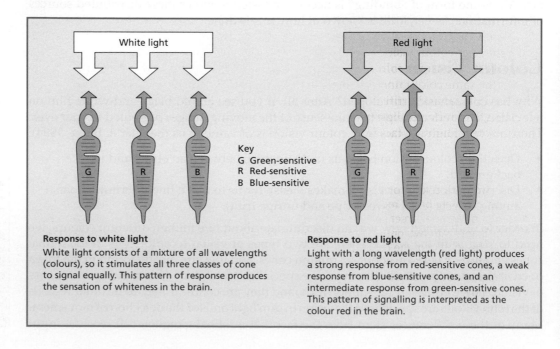

Response to white light
White light consists of a mixture of all wavelengths (colours), so it stimulates all three classes of cone to signal equally. This pattern of response produces the sensation of whiteness in the brain.

Response to red light
Light with a long wavelength (red light) produces a strong response from red-sensitive cones, a weak response from blue-sensitive cones, and an intermediate response from green-sensitive cones. This pattern of signalling is interpreted as the colour red in the brain.

of cell produces perception of blue or yellow in the same way. The third type of cell encodes brightness, and produces white or black.

Some evidence in support of Hering's theory is available from studies of negative afterimages (Pinel, 1997). If you stare at a square of a given colour for several seconds, and then shift your gaze to a white surface, you will see a negative afterimage in the colour predicted from the theory. For example, a green square produces a red afterimage, and a blue square produces a yellow afterimage. In addition, opponent cells have been found in the lateral geniculate nucleus of monkeys (DeValois & DeValois, 1975).

■ Research activity: To see the effects of a negative afterimage, stare at the coloured square for 30 seconds, then look at the white box. What colour do you see?

One of the greatest strengths of the opponent-process theory is that it provides an account of colour blindness. According to the theory, colour blindness typically occurs when there is damage to the cells responsible for the perception of red and green, or to those responsible for the perception of yellow and blue. As a result, colour blindness applies to red and green or to yellow and blue, but not to green and blue together.

Synthesis

The Young–Helmholtz and Hering theories can be combined. The three cone types of the Young–Helmholtz theory send signals to the opponent cells of the Hering theory, and this produces the perception of colour. The short-wavelength cones send excitatory signals to the blue–yellow opponent cells, and long-wavelength cones send inhibitory signals. If the strength of the excitatory signals is greater than that of the inhibitory signals, blue is seen. If the strength of the inhibitory signals is greater, then yellow is seen. The green–red opponent cells receive excitatory signals from the medium-wavelength cones, and inhibitory ones from the long-wavelength cones. Green is seen if the strength of the excitatory signals exceeds that of the inhibitory ones, whereas red is seen if the relative strengths are reversed.

This combined theory is supported by work on colour blindness. As was mentioned earlier, the most common form of colour blindness affects the perception of red and green, which involve the same opponent process. As is predicted by the theory, people with this type of colour blindness typically have a reduced number of medium- or long-wavelength cones (Zeki, 1993).

Which theories of colour vision can best explain colour blindness?

Colour constancy

From what has been said so far, you may have the impression that colour vision can be completely explained in neurophysiological terms. That may be true, but various phenomena of colour vision do *not* depend only on the wavelengths of the light reflected from objects. Consider **colour constancy**, which is the tendency for an object to appear to have the same colour under different viewing conditions. There are marked differences between natural and artificial light. If our perception of colour were based only on the wavelength of reflected light, then the same object would appear redder in artificial light than in natural light. In fact, we generally show colour constancy in such circumstances.

Land

Why do we show colour constancy? The most obvious reason is because of familiarity. We know that post boxes are bright red, and so they look the same colour whether they are illuminated by the sun or by artificial street lighting. However, that is not the whole story. Land (1977) presented his participants with two displays consisting of rectangular shapes of different colours. He then adjusted the lighting of the displays so that two differently coloured rectangles (one from each display) reflected exactly the same wavelengths of light. However, the two rectangles were seen in their actual colours, showing strong evidence of colour constancy in the absence of familiarity. Finally, Land (1977) found that the two rectangles looked exactly the same (and so colour constancy broke down) when everything else in the two displays was blocked out.

KEY TERM
Colour constancy: the tendency for an object to be perceived as having the same colour under varying viewing conditions.

Can you think of examples from your own experience that illustrate the phenomenon of colour constancy?

What was happening in Land's study? According to his retinex theory, we decide the colour of a surface by *comparing* its ability to reflect short, medium, and long wavelengths against that of adjacent surfaces. That is why colour constancy breaks down when such comparisons cannot be made. As would be expected on this theory, there are neurons that respond to differences in the wavelengths of light reflected from adjacent surfaces (Zeki, 1993). These neurons are known as dual-opponent colour cells.

Discussion points

1. Why is colour constancy important?

2. How convincing is the evidence for retinex theory provided by Land (1977)?

PERSONAL REFLECTIONS

- In my opinion, the various brain-scanning techniques such as PET scans and functional MRI have so far proved somewhat disappointing. These techniques have generally only *confirmed* the previous findings of cognitive psychologists (adding information about *where* processes occur), but have not led to brand-new *discoveries*. However, I am gradually coming to accept that this situation may be about to change. The number of brain-scanning studies in cognitive psychology increased about sixfold during the 1990s, and signs are appearing that we are getting closer to major breakthroughs in our understanding of brain functioning. It might be worth a modest bet that the most important progress in psychology in the twenty-first century will be based on technological advances in brain-scanning techniques.

SUMMARY

Non-invasive techniques

Several non-invasive and invasive techniques have been devised to study cortical functioning. These techniques differ greatly in their spatial and temporal resolution. The EEG was of use in identifying the various stages of sleep, but it provides an imprecise and indirect measure of brain activity. Evoked potentials based on EEG recordings indicate the time course of stimulus processing, but not which parts of the brain are most active. There are various types of brain scans, including CAT scans, MRI scans, functional MRI, and PET scans. PET scans and functional MRI show us the brain in action, and so they are an advance on CAT and MRI scans. However, PET scans do not indicate brain activity levels on a moment-by-moment basis. Squid magnetometry is a promising new technique, but it is very complex technically.

Invasive techniques

Ablations and lesions are of use if we assume that whatever abilities are impaired after surgery depend on the part of the brain that has been destroyed. The fact that all parts of the brain are interconnected makes it hard to know precisely *why* destruction of a given area of the brain produces the effects it does. Ablations and lesions cannot be produced in humans, but brain-damaged patients can provide valuable information about localisation of functions in the brain. Single-unit recordings have provided detailed information about the responsiveness of brain cells to different stimuli. Electrical stimulation of the brain can produce the same responses as actual nerve impulses. Optical dyes can be used to identify the responses of cells to stimulation.

Localisation of function

The cerebral cortex can be divided into four lobes or areas: frontal, parietal, temporal, and occipital. It is also divided into two hemispheres. In general terms, higher thought processes and motor processing occur in the frontal lobe, somatosensory processing in the parietal lobe, auditory processing in the temporal lobe, and visual processing in the occipital lobe. The primary auditory cortex is in the lateral fissure of the temporal lobe, and is surrounded by about six areas of secondary auditory cortex. Several areas in the frontal lobes are involved in motor processing. The supplementary motor cortex in the secondary motor cortex is involved in co-ordinating motor responses. The premotor cortex (also in the secondary motor cortex) is involved when sensory information is used to determine motor responses. Most of the primary motor cortex is dedicated to those parts of the body making the most precise movements.

Language functions are mostly based in the left hemisphere. Broca's or expressive aphasia occurs as a result of brain damage to the frontal association cortex and associated areas. Wernicke's or receptive aphasia occurs through damage to the superior temporal gyrus and associated areas. Damage to the arcuate fasciculus, which connects Broca's area with Wernicke's area, produces conduction aphasia. Syndrome-based approaches exaggerate the similarities among patients. Studies on split-brain patients suggest that language processing occurs in the left hemisphere and spatial processing in the right hemisphere. Most of the time, the two hemispheres function co-operatively. Studies on normals indicate that the right hemisphere has an advantage in pattern recognition, face recognition, and colour discrimination, whereas the left hemisphere has an advantage in processing words, letters, and digits. Many hemisphere differences depend on the type of processing rather than the type of stimulus. There is some evidence that positive emotions have greater left hemisphere involvement, whereas negative emotions have greater right hemisphere involvement.

Hemisphere asymmetries

Light falls onto the retina at the back of the eye, from where impulses leave the eye via the optic nerve. The optic nerves of the two eyes join at the optic chiasma. After the optic chiasma, the optic tract proceeds to the lateral geniculate nucleus. There are simple and complex cells within the primary visual cortex. Within the cortex, different areas are specialised for different aspects of visual perception, such as perception of form, motion, and colour. Evidence for this specialisation has come from PET scans and the study of brain-damaged patients.

Structure and processes of visual perception

Colour vision helps the detection of objects and discrimination among objects. Colour vision depends on cones in the retina. There are three types of cone receptors, which differ in terms of the light wavelengths to which they respond most strongly. One type is most responsive to blue, another to green, and the third to red. According to opponent-process theory, there are three opponent processes. One process produces green at one extreme and yellow at the other; another process produces blue and yellow at the extremes; and the third process produces black and white. Signals from the three types of cone receptors activate these processes. The most common form of colour blindness affects the perception of red and green, both of which involve the same opponent process. The existence of colour constancy means that colour perception does not depend only on the wavelengths of the light reflected from objects. Some of the cells in area V4 of the brain show colour constancy.

Colour vision

FURTHER READING

There is very clear and accessible coverage of cortical functions in J.P.J. Pinel (1997), *Biopsychology (3rd Edn.)*, Boston: Allyn & Bacon. Cortical functions are also discussed (but in a more complex way) in N.R. Carlson (1994), *Physiology of behaviour (5th Edn.)*, Boston: Allyn & Bacon. The topics of this chapter are also dealt with in S. Green (1994), *Principles of biopsychology*, Hove, UK: Psychology Press.

REVISION QUESTIONS

1	Discuss methods and techniques that have been used to investigate cortical functioning.	(24 marks)
2	Describe and assess research into localisation of function in the brain (e.g. language; hemisphere asymmetries).	(24 marks)
3	Critically consider the neurophysiological basis of visual perception.	(24 marks)

- **Bodily rhythms**
  The causes of regular patterns such as sleeping–waking or the menstrual cycle.

  Sleep–waking cycle and Schochat et al.'s findings on melatonin
  Jet-leg, PMS, and seasonal affective disorder

- **Sleep**
  Why do we need to sleep? What happens when people are prevented from sleeping?

  Dement and Kleitman's five stages of sleep
  Sleep deprivation studies
  Recovery theories (Oswald, Horne)
  Adaptive theories (Meddis, Webb)

- **Dreaming**
  What are dreams? Do they have any purpose or meaning?

  Freud's wish-fulfilment theory
  Hobson's activation-synthesis theory
  Crick and Mitchison's reverse-learning theory
  Foulkes' cognitive theory
  Hajek and Belcher's study of smokers' dreams
  Winson's survival strategy theory

- **Consciousness**
  Different states of awareness, from thinking and reasoning to absent-mindedness.

  Reber's Consciousness I and II
  Oakley's levels of consciousness
  Baars' work on attention and consciousness
  Psychodynamic approach
  Schizophrenia and identity disorders

- **Hypnosis**
  What happens to people's state of awareness when they are hypnotised?

  Hypnotic susceptibility scales
  Amnesia and analgesia under hypnosis
  Hilgard's neo-dissociation theory
  Wagstaff's non-state theory
  Freud's use of hypnosis
  Hypermnesia and false memory syndrome

5

Awareness

Every day, each one of us experiences a range of different states of awareness. For example, there is clearly an important difference between the waking and sleeping states, and within the sleeping state we need to distinguish between dreaming and non-dreaming. There are also changes in our states of alertness during the course of the day, with many of them depending on various bodily rhythms. There seem to be at least two levels of consciousness, the higher of which involves self-awareness and self-reflection.

There are various ways in which our state of awareness can be altered. Some of these involve drugs, which may be legal (e.g. alcohol) or illegal (e.g. ecstasy). Our state of awareness can also be altered by hypnosis. Much interest has been created in the hypnotic state by the television demonstrations of Paul McKenna and others. Perhaps the key question about hypnosis is the following: does hypnosis produce a special state of awareness? Some psychologists answer "No", whereas others answer "Yes".

Bodily Rhythms

There are numerous bodily rhythms. Most of them can conveniently be divided into biological or physiological rhythms and psychological rhythms. One of the most important bodily rhythms is the sleep–waking cycle, but several other bodily rhythms have a significant impact on human behaviour.

Biological rhythms

Most of the biological rhythms possessed by human beings repeat themselves every 24 hours. The term **circadian rhythms** (from two Latin words meaning "about" and "day") is used to refer to such rhythms.

According to Green (1994), mammals possess about 100 different biological circadian rhythms. For example, temperature in humans varies over the course of the 24-hour day, reaching a peak in the late afternoon and a low point in the early hours of the morning. Other examples of human circadian rhythms are the sleep–waking cycle and the release of hormones from the pituitary gland.

Humans also possess other bodily rhythms, which consist of cyclical variations in various physiological or psychological processes. Apart from circadian rhythms, there are infradian and ultradian rhythms. **Infradian rhythms** involve repeating cycles lasting more than a day. Perhaps the best-known example of an infradian rhythm in humans is the menstrual cycle, which typically lasts about 28 days. The phases of the human menstrual cycle are determined by hormonal changes (see Chapter 3). The key phases are as follows:

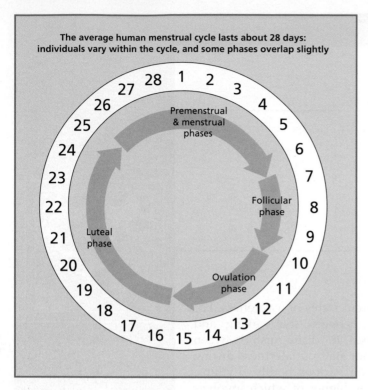

The average human menstrual cycle lasts about 28 days: individuals vary within the cycle, and some phases overlap slightly

- Follicular phase: increased levels of follicle-stimulating hormone cause ovarian follicles to grow around egg cells or ova; then the ovarian follicles start to release estrogens.
- Ovulation phase: the estrogens stimulate the hypothalamus to increase the release of luteinising hormone and follicle-stimulating hormone from the anterior pituitary; the increased level of luteinising hormone causes one of the follicles to rupture and so release its ovum.
- Luteal phase: the ruptured follicle starts to release progesterone; as a result, the lining of the uterus is prepared for the implantation of a fertilised ovum or egg.
- Premenstrual and menstrual phases: the ovum or egg moves into the fallopian tube; if it is not fertilised, progesterone and estradiol levels decrease.

Ultradian rhythms involve cycles lasting less than a day. A good example of an ultradian rhythm is to be found in sleep. As is discussed later in the chapter, there is a characteristic sleep cycle lasting about 90 minutes, and most sleepers work through a number of sleep cycles.

Sleep–waking cycle

The 24-hour sleep–waking cycle is of particular importance, and is associated with other circadian rhythms. For example, bodily temperature is at its highest about halfway through the waking day (early to late afternoon) and at its lowest halfway through the sleeping part of the day (about three in the morning). Why is the sleep–waking cycle 24 hours long? One possibility is that it is strongly influenced by external events such as the light–dark cycle, and the fact that each dawn follows almost exactly 24 hours after the preceding one. Another possibility is that the sleep–waking cycle is **endogenous**, meaning that it is based on internal biological mechanisms or pacemakers.

What links can you see between body temperature and efficient functioning during waking hours?

External factors

How can we decide whether the sleep–waking cycle depends mainly on external or on internal factors? One approach is to study individuals who are removed from the normal light–dark cycle, e.g. by being kept in the dark. Michel Siffree spent two months in a dark cave. At first, there was no very clear pattern in his sleep–waking cycle. Later on, however, he developed a sleep–waking cycle of about 25 hours rather than the standard one of 24 hours (Green, 1994). Wever (1979) discussed studies on participants who spent several weeks or months in a bunker or isolation suite. Most of them settled down to a sleep–waking cycle of about 25 hours.

These findings suggest that the sleep–waking cycle is largely endogenous. However, the fact that there is a discrepancy between the endogenous sleep–waking cycle and the normal sleep-waking cycle indicates that external cues such as changes in light and dark also play a role. The technical term for an external event that partially controls biological rhythms is **zeitgeber** (literally, "time giver").

Internal factors

We know something about the endogenous mechanisms involved in the pacemaker for the sleep–waking cycle. Green (1994, p.136) described it in the following way:

The key pacemaker is the supra-chiasmatic nucleus, part of the hypothalamus. This receives a neural pathway directly from the retina of the eye. It in turn sends axons to the pineal, stimulating the production and release of melatonin [a hormone].

KEY TERMS
Ultradian rhythms: biological rhythms with a cycle of less than one day.
Endogenous: based on internal biological mechanisms.
Zeitgeber: external events that partially determine biological rhythms.

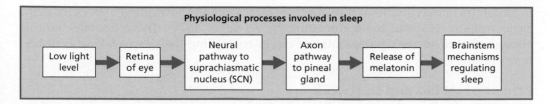

Physiological processes involved in sleep

Low light level → Retina of eye → Neural pathway to suprachiasmatic nucleus (SCN) → Axon pathway to pineal gland → Release of melatonin → Brainstem mechanisms regulating sleep

The neurons of the supra-chiasmatic nucleus (SCN) have a natural circadian firing pattern, and damage to this structure causes circadian rhythms to be eliminated.

More detailed information about the physiological processes involved in sleep is discussed by Cardwell et al. (1996). The fact that there are pathways from the retina to the SCN means that the amount of light striking the eye influences the activity of the SCN. This then leads on indirectly to the release of melatonin from the pineal gland, with more melatonin being released when light levels are low. Melatonin influences the brainstem mechanisms involved in sleep regulation, and so plays a part in controlling the timing of sleep and waking periods.

Schochat et al.

Some of the strongest evidence of the involvement of melatonin in the sleep–waking cycle was reported by Schochat et al. (1997). They made use of the ultra-short sleep–wake paradigm, in which their six male participants spent 29 hours between 7a.m. one day to noon the following day in the sleep laboratory. Throughout that time they spent 7 minutes in every 20 lying down in bed in a completely darkened room trying to sleep. This method allowed Schochat et al. to measure sleep propensity or the tendency to sleep at different times of day. The period of greatest sleep propensity is known as the "sleep gate", and starts in the late evening. Surprisingly, the period of lowest sleep propensity (known as the "wake maintenance zone") occurs in the early evening shortly before the sleep gate.

> **KEY STUDY EVALUATION — Schochat et al.**
>
> Schochat et al.'s results were important in demonstrating that melatonin plays a role in sleep–waking cycles. However, it could be argued that trying to sleep in a laboratory situation is a task that does not have a great deal of ecological validity. The demand characteristics of the experiment and evaluation apprehension may have affected the participants, possibly even at a hormonal level. The sample used by Schochat et al. was also very small, consisting of only six male volunteers, and was not really representative. However, the study, like many others, provides a strong basis for future work.

Schochat et al. measured the levels of melatonin by taking blood samples up to three times an hour during the 29-hour session. The key finding was as follows: "We demonstrated a close and precise temporal relationship between the circadian rhythms of sleep propensity and melatonin; the nocturnal [night] onset of melatonin secretion consistently precedes the nocturnal sleep gate by 100–120 min" (1997, p.367). This close relationship between increased melatonin levels and increased sleep propensity does not prove that they are causally related. However, Schochat et al. discussed other studies that strengthen the argument that melatonin is important in determining sleep propensity. For example, individuals who suffer from insomnia find it much easier to get to sleep when they are given melatonin about two hours before bedtime.

Discussion points

1. What are some of the good features of the study carried out by Schochat et al.?

2. What are the limitations of their approach?

There is recent evidence suggesting that the pigment cryptochrome may be of importance. According to Hawkes (1998, p.9):

> *American scientists have discovered a new light-sensitive pigment [cryptochrome] which is responsible for the body's internal clock. It appears to control the circadian rhythm which regulates functions such as blood pressure, intellectual performance and sleep. The pigment cryptochrome is found in the eye, the skin and the part of the brain responsible for the body clock.*

From what has been said, it might be thought that there is a single endogenous mechanism or internal clock. In fact, matters seem to be more complex than that. Nearly all participants in long-term bunker studies lasting for more than a month show different patterns in the sleep–waking cycle and the temperature cycle (Wever, 1979). These findings indicate strongly that there are separate internal clocks controlling the sleep–waking cycle and temperature.

Effects of jet lag and shiftwork

In our everyday lives, there is usually no conflict between our endogenous sleep–waking cycle and external events or zeitgebers. However, there are situations in which there is a real conflict. Probably the two most important examples of such conflict are jet lag and shiftwork.

Jet lag can be a problem for airline staff who frequently cross time zones in the course of their work.

How would you advise an employer on the most beneficial pattern of shift working?

Jet lag. It is sometimes thought that jet lag occurs because travelling by plane can be time-consuming and tiring. In fact, jet lag occurs only when flying from east to west or from west to east. It depends on a discrepancy between internal and external time. For example, suppose you fly from Scotland to the east coast of the United States. You leave at eleven in the morning British time, and arrive in Boston at five in the afternoon British time. However, the time in Boston is probably midday. As a result of the five-hour difference, you are likely to feel very tired by about eight o'clock in the evening Boston time.

Klein, Wegman, and Hunt (1972) found that adjustment of the sleep–waking cycle was much faster for westbound flights than for eastbound ones, regardless of which direction was homeward. For eastbound flights, re-adjustment of the sleep–waking cycle took about one day per time zone crossed. Thus, for example, it would take about six days to recover completely from a flight to England from Boston.

Why is it easier to adapt to jet lag when flying in a westerly direction? An important reason is that the day of travel is effectively lengthened when travelling west, whereas it is shortened when travelling east. As the endogenous sleep–waking cycle is about 25 hours, it seems reasonable that it is easier to adapt to a day of more than 24 hours than to one of fewer than 24 hours.

Shiftwork. What about shiftwork? As they say, there are only two problems with shift-work: you have to work when you want to be asleep, and you have to sleep when you want to be awake. There are several different types of shift system. Monk and Folkard (1983) identified two major types: (1) rapidly rotating shifts, in which the worker only does one or two shifts at a given time before shifting to a different work time: (2) slowly rotating shifts, in which the worker shifts work time much less often (e.g. every week or month). There are problems with both shift systems. However, rapidly rotating shifts are preferable. They allow workers to maintain fairly constant circadian rhythms, whereas

---

CASE STUDY: *Melatonin and Aircrew*

Melatonin is now available in US chemists and some claim it is the cure for jet lag. Jet lag can lead to fatigue, headache, sleep disturbances, irritability, and gastrointestinal disturbances—all with a potentially negative impact on flight safety. Interestingly, reported side-effects of melatonin use include many similar symptoms. Although some researchers claim melatonin is among the safest known substances, no large clinical evaluations have been performed to evaluate long-term effects.

Scientists believe melatonin is crucial for the functioning of our body clock. Studies suggest that treating jet lag with melatonin can not only resolve sleeping problems but also increase the body clock's ability to adjust to a new time zone. However, those in the medical community advise caution. Melatonin is not a universal remedy for everyone who must travel over many time zones. It is thought by some that it should not be used unless the user intends to spend more than three days in the new time zone. International aircrews will often cover several time zones, typically flying overnight west to east, spending 24 hours on the ground, then returning during the day (east to west). This cycle is likely

to be repeated several times before an extended period of sleep is possible. Melatonin usage to adjust the body clock in these circumstances is viewed by many scientists as inappropriate.

Timing the dose of melatonin is very important. Studies show that resynchronisation of the sleep–waking cycle only occurred if the subjects were allowed to sleep after taking the medication. In those participants unable to sleep after taking melatonin, the circadian rhythm was actually prolonged. More worryingly, melatonin's effect on fine motor and cognitive tasks is unknown and the nature of melatonin's sedative effects are uncertain.

Unfortunately, there are no published clinical studies evaluating flying performance while taking melatonin. The US Armed Forces are actively evaluating melatonin's aeromedical usefulness. Despite ongoing research, no US military service permits the routine use of melatonin by aviators. Significantly, aircrew participating in experimental study groups are not allowed to perform flying duties within 36 hours of using melatonin.

slowly rotating shifts can cause harmful effects through major changes to individuals' circadian rhythms.

Psychological circadian rhythms

So far we have focused mainly on circadian rhythms depending directly on underlying biological or physiological processes. There are other, more psychological rhythms which depend indirectly on basic circadian rhythms. For example, there are fairly consistent patterns of performance on many tasks throughout the day, with a variation of about 10% between the best and the worst level of performance (Eysenck, 1982).

Would you expect to find that industrial accidents are more likely to occur at certain times of day?

The classic work in this area was carried out by Blake (1967). He asked naval ratings to perform several tasks at five different times of day (08.00; 10.30; 13.00; 15.30; and 21.00). For most of the tasks, the best performance was obtained at 21.00, with the second-best level of performance occurring at 10.30. It was found in later studies that peak performance on most tasks is reached at around midday rather than during the evening (Eysenck, 1982).

Why do people perform at their best at midday rather than earlier or later in the day? Relevant evidence was obtained by Akerstedt (1977). Self-reported alertness (assessed by questionnaire) was greatest at about noon, as was the level of adrenaline. Adrenaline is a hormone associated with states of high physiological arousal within the autonomic nervous system (see Chapter 3). However, it should be noted that the notion of physiological arousal is rather vague and imprecise. The evidence suggests that psychological and physiological activation are both high at midday, and this may well account for the peak performance shown at that time. However, these are correlational data, and it is hard to be sure that the high level of midday performance *depends* on activation.

■ Research activity: Design a questionnaire to measure alertness and distribute it to volunteer participants. Ask them to complete it at regular intervals over several days. Analyse the data to see if there are "morning" and "afternoon" people, in terms of levels of alertness. What are the methodological problems you may encounter?

Blake (1967) found that most of his participants showed a clear reduction in performance at 13.00 compared to their performance at 10.30. This reduction in performance occurred shortly after lunch, and is commonly known as the "post-lunch dip". What seems to happen is that the physiological processes involved in digestion make us feel sluggish and reduce our ability to work efficiently.

Infradian rhythms

Infradian rhythms are bodily rhythms for which the cycle time is greater than one day. One of the clearest examples of an infradian rhythm is the menstrual cycle in women. In evolutionary terms, we might expect that women would be most sexually active around the time of ovulation, when they are most fertile. This pattern has been found in newly married African women (Hedricks et al., 1987). However, such a mid-cycle peak in sexuality is rarely reported in studies carried out in Europe or the United States. The likeliest explanation of this difference is that most newly married African women want to become pregnant, whereas most European and American women do not. A relevant issue here is the extent to which women are aware of when they are ovulating.

Pre-menstrual syndrome

Pre-menstrual syndrome or PMS is an important aspect of the menstrual cycle. It refers to the fact that many women experience tension, depression, headaches, and so on in the last few days prior to menstruation. However, about 30–40% of women show little or no evidence of pre-menstrual syndrome. Women are more likely to commit crimes shortly before menstruation than at other times of the month (Dalton, 1964). This is presumably due to pre-menstrual syndrome.

There is reasonable evidence for pre-menstrual syndrome in most cultures (McIlveen & Gross, 1996).

KEY TERM
Pre-menstrual syndrome: symptoms of tension, depression, and so on experienced by many women shortly before menstruation.

Pre-menstrual syndrome
It has been pointed out (e.g. Bunker-Rohrbaugh, 1980) that the definition of a "pre-menstrual syndrome" presents some difficulties. Studies of the syndrome tend to use questionnaires with a negative bias, asking women how "depressed" and "anxious" they feel, as opposed to how "happy". In addition, the attitudes of many Western women to menstruation in general are often negative, as opposed to some non-Western cultures in which it is celebrated. This too may bias research in this area.

This suggests that it is determined by physiological factors (e.g. changing hormone levels) rather than by environmental ones. However, the menstrual cycle itself can be influenced by environmental factors. Reinberg (1967) reported the case of a woman who lived in a dimly lit cave for a period of three months. During that time her menstrual cycle was reduced to just under 26 days.

Circannual rhythms

Circannual rhythms are biological rhythms that last for about one year before repeating. They are more common in some animal species than in humans, and this is especially true of species that hibernate during the winter. Convincing evidence of a circannual rhythm in the gold-mantled ground squirrel was reported by Pengelley and Fisher (1957). They put a squirrel in a highly controlled environment with artificial light on for 12 hours every day, and a constant temperature of 0°C. The squirrel hibernated from October through to the following April, with its body temperature dropping dramatically from 37°C before hibernation to 1°C during hibernation. The circannual rhythm for this squirrel was somewhat less than a year, having about 300 days' duration.

Seasonal affective disorder

Some people suffer from **seasonal affective disorder**, which resembles a circannual rhythm. The great majority of sufferers from seasonal affective disorder experience severe depression during the winter months, but a few seem to experience depression in the summer instead. The evidence suggests that seasonal affective disorder is related to seasonal variations in the production of melatonin, which is a hormone secreted by the pineal gland (Barlow & Durand, 1995). Melatonin is produced primarily at night, and so more is produced during the dark winter months. As would be expected, seasonal affective disorder is more common in northern latitudes where the winter days are very short. Terman (1988) found that nearly 10% of those living in New Hampshire (a northern part of the United States) suffered from seasonal affective disorder, compared to only 2% in the southern state of Florida.

Phototherapy is recommended for the treatment of seasonal affective disorder (Barlow & Durand, 1995). This involves exposing sufferers to about two hours of intense light shortly after they wake up in the morning. It is assumed that this treatment reduces the production of melatonin. However, as Barlow and Durand (1995, p.256) pointed out, the effectiveness of phototherapy "is not yet clear since no controlled studies have been conducted; also the mechanism of action or cause has not been established".

A young seasonal affective disorder sufferer receiving phototherapy from a light box on the right of the picture.

Sleep

Sleep is an important part of all our lives, generally occupying almost one-third of our time. There are various ways of trying to understand sleep. However, the electroencephalograph or EEG is of particular value. In essence, scalp electrodes are used to obtain a continuous measure of brain-wave activity, which is recorded as a trace. Other useful physiological measures include eye-movement data from an electro-oculogram or EOG, and muscle movements from an electromyogram or EMG.

There are two main aspects to EEG activity: frequency and amplitude. Frequency is defined as the number of oscillations of EEG activity per second, whereas amplitude is defined as half the distance between the high and low points of an oscillation. In practice, frequency is used more often than amplitude to describe the essence of EEG activity.

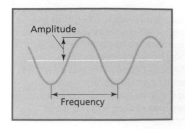

Stages of sleep

The most important finding from physiological studies such as those of Dement and Kleitman (1957) is that there are five different stages of sleep:

- Stage 1: there are alpha waves (waves having a frequency of between 8 and 12 cycles per second) in the EEG, there is slow eye rolling, and reductions in heart rate, muscle tension, and temperature: this stage can be regarded as a state of drowsiness.
- Stage 2: the EEG waves become slower and larger, but with short bursts of high-frequency sleep spindles; there is little activity in the EOG.
- Stage 3: the EOG and EMG records are similar to Stage 2, but the EEG consists mainly of long, slow delta waves with some sleep spindles; this is a deeper stage of sleep than either of the first two stages.
- Stage 4: there is a majority of the long, slow delta waves that are present in smaller amounts in the previous stage, and very little activity in the EOG or the EMG; this is a deeper stage of sleep than any of the first three stages, and it is often known as slow-wave sleep.
- Stage 5: rapid eye movement or REM sleep, in which there are rapid eye movements and a very low level of EMG activity, while the EEG record is like that of Stage 1; REM sleep has been called paradoxical sleep, because it is harder to awaken someone from REM sleep than from any of the other stages, even though the EEG indicates that the brain is very active.

After the sleeper has worked through the first four stages of progressively deeper sleep, he or she reverses the process. Stage 4 sleep is followed by Stage 3, and then by Stage 2. However, Stage 2 is followed by REM sleep (Stage 5). After REM sleep, the sleeper starts another sleep cycle, working his or her way through Stages 2, 3, and 4, followed by Stage 3, then Stage 2, and then REM sleep again. A complete sleep cycle or ultradian cycle lasts about 90 minutes. Most sleepers complete about five ultradian cycles during a normal night's sleep. The proportion of the cycle devoted to REM sleep tends to increase from one cycle to the next.

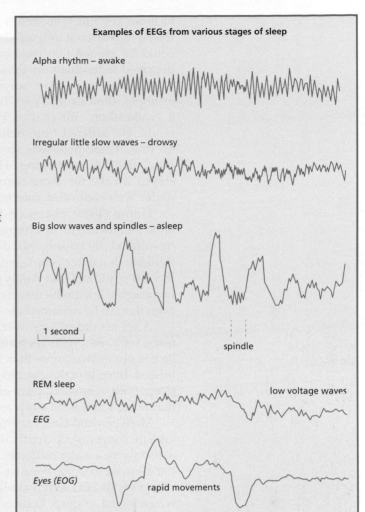

Examples of EEGs from various stages of sleep

Alpha rhythm – awake

Irregular little slow waves – drowsy

Big slow waves and spindles – asleep

1 second

spindle

REM sleep   low voltage waves

EEG

Eyes (EOG)   rapid movements

Discussion points

1. Try to think of some reasons why there are several stages of sleep.
2. The issue of why we need to sleep is considered shortly. Before you read that part of the chapter, guess what some of those reasons might be.

REM sleep

REM sleep is the most interesting stage of sleep. Aserinsky and Kleitman (1955) discovered that it is associated with dreaming. They woke up their participants when they were in REM sleep, and most of them reported that they had just been dreaming. However, dreaming does *not* only occur in REM sleep. About 30% of sleepers in slow-wave sleep report having been dreaming when woken up (Green, 1994). This is a fairly high percentage, even though it is lower than the 70–75% for those awoken from REM sleep.

The dreams reported from REM sleep differ from those from other stages of sleep. Dreams during REM sleep tend to be vivid and detailed, whereas non-REM dreams contain much less detail and are less coherent (McIlveen & Gross, 1996).

Sleep deprivation

We spend about one-third of our lives asleep. This adds up to almost 200,000 hours of sleep in the course of a lifetime. It seems reasonable to assume that sleep must serve one or more key functions, but it has proved hard to discover these functions. One way of trying to work out *why* we sleep is to deprive people of sleep and see what happens. It could be argued that the kinds of problems and impairments experienced by sleep-deprived individuals are those that sleep is designed to prevent.

People often cope surprisingly well when deprived of sleep. Consider, for example, the case of Peter Tripp. He was a New York disc jockey who took part in a "wakeathon" for charity. He managed to stay awake for eight days or about 200 hours. He suffered from delusions and hallucinations (e.g. that his desk drawer was on fire). These delusions were so severe that it was hard to test his precise level of psychological functioning. However, he showed no long-term effects from having stayed awake for more than a week. It should be noted that he was not studied under well-controlled conditions.

Horne (1988) discussed the case of Randy Gardner, a 17-year-old student who remained awake for 264 hours or 11 days in 1964. Towards the end of the 11-day period, he suffered from disorganised speech, blurred vision, and a small degree of paranoia (e.g. thinking that other people regarded him as stupid because of his impaired functioning). In view of the fact that Randy Gardner missed out on about 80–90 hours of sleep, he had remarkably few problems. He was clearly less affected than Tripp by sleep deprivation, even though he remained awake for three extra days.

After his ordeal was over, Randy Gardner slept for 15 hours. He slept longer than usual for a few nights thereafter, before reverting to his normal sleep pattern. However, he did not recover more than 25% (about 20 hours) of the 80 to 90 hours of sleep he had missed. In spite of that, he did recover almost 70% of Stage 4 deep sleep and 50% of REM sleep, with very small recovery percentages for the other stages of sleep. This suggests that Stage 4 and REM sleep are of special importance.

McIlveen and Gross (1996) discussed a study showing the serious consequences of very prolonged sleep deprivation. Rechtschaffen et al. (1983) placed two rats at a time on a disc above a water container. The EEG activity of both rats was monitored. One rat was not allowed to sleep, because the disc started to rotate and caused it to fall in the water whenever its EEG activity indicated that it was starting to sleep. In contrast, the other rat was allowed to sleep, because the disc stopped rotating when its EEG indicated sleep. All of the sleep-deprived rats died within 33 days, whereas the rats that were not sleep-deprived seemed in good health.

How much sleep do you need per night? How do you feel if you have not had enough sleep?

It is hard to be sure whether findings on rats also apply to humans. However, Lugaressi et al. (1986) studied a 52-year-old man who could hardly sleep at all because of damage to parts of his brain involved in sleep regulation. Not surprisingly, he became absolutely exhausted, and was unable to function normally.

REM sleep deprivation

We saw in the case of Randy Gardner that he recovered more of his lost REM sleep than most other stages of sleep. Dement (1960) carried out a systematic study of REM and non-REM sleep. Some of his participants were deprived of REM sleep over a period of several days, whereas others were deprived of non-REM sleep. In general, the effects of REM sleep deprivation were more severe, including increased aggression and poor concentration. Those deprived of REM sleep tried to catch up on the REM sleep they had missed. They started on REM sleep 12 times on average during the first night in the laboratory, but this rose to 26 times on the seventh night. When they were free to sleep undisturbed, most of them spent much longer than usual in REM sleep; this is known as a rebound effect.

Task performance

Ethical issues: Is it possible to study sleep deprivation in humans without encountering ethical difficulties?

The performance of sleep-deprived individuals has been studied systematically in controlled laboratory studies (see Eysenck, 1982, for a review). Sleep deprivation over the first three days or so has few adverse effects on tasks that are complex and interesting. However, sleep-deprived individuals tend to perform poorly on tasks that are monotonous and uninteresting. This is especially the case when these tasks are performed in the early hours of the morning and need to be performed over a longish period of time.

A good example is the vigilance task, in which the participants have to detect signals (e.g. faint lights) which are only presented occasionally.

What do these findings mean? According to Wilkinson (1969, p.39), it is "difficult for us to assess the 'real' effect of lost sleep upon subjects' *capacity* as opposed to their *willingness* to perform." Wilkinson and others found that most of the adverse effects of sleep loss on performance could be eliminated if attempts were made to motivate the participants (e.g. by providing knowledge of results). It thus appears that poor performance by sleep-deprived individuals is usually due to low motivation rather than to reduced capacity.

Effects over time

Impaired performance on boring tasks is the main problem caused by sleep deprivation over the first three nights of sleep loss. During the fourth night of sleep deprivation, there tend to be very short (2–3 second) periods of micro-sleep during which the individual is unresponsive (Huber-Weidman, 1976). In addition, this length of sleep deprivation sometimes produces the so-called "hat phenomenon". In this phenomenon, it feels to the sleep-deprived person as if he or she were wearing a rather small hat that fits very tightly. From the fifth night on, there are delusions as reported by Peter Tripp. From the sixth night on, there are more severe problems such as partial loss of a sense of identity and increased difficulty in dealing with other people and the environment. Some of these symptoms were experienced by Randy Gardner. The term sleep-deprivation psychosis has been used to refer to these symptoms (Huber-Weidman, 1976). However, this is an exaggerated description of the actual symptoms.

Air traffic controllers have to be alert to tiny changes in flashing lights on their screens at all hours of the day or night, but as the lights represent aircraft, motivation to be vigilant remains high.

Why has the focus in this section been almost exclusively on the *psychological* effects of sleep deprivation? The reason is that the physical and physiological effects tend to be rather small. Some of the evidence was reviewed by Eysenck (1982, p.147), who concluded as follows:

> *Sleep deprivation leads to reduced arousal when the environment is relatively unstimulating or monotonous, whereas more inconsistent effects are observed when the situation is demanding or stressful ... Arousal level is determined interactively by sleep deprivation and environmental stimulation.*

Theories of Sleep

Several theories of sleep function have been proposed over the years. However, most of them belong to two broad classes of theory:

1. Recovery or restoration theories.
2. Adaptive or evolutionary theories.

We will consider these two classes of theories. After that, we will discuss the more specific issue of the function of REM or rapid eye movement sleep. In that connection, some of the main theories of REM sleep function will be discussed.

Recovery or restoration theories

An important function of sleep is probably to save energy and to permit the restoration of tissue. This notion is central to various recovery or restoration theories, such as those of Oswald (1980) and Horne (1988). These theories focus on the benefits of sleep for the physiological system. It is also possible that sleep conveys advantages to the psychological system. In other words, sleep may also serve to restore psychological functions.

Important evidence for physiologically based recovery or restoration theories was discussed by Allison and Cicchetti (1976). They surveyed 39 mammalian species to work out the amount of time spent in slow-wave sleep and in REM sleep. Body weight was the best predictor of slow-wave sleep, with smaller mammals having more such sleep. Metabolic rate, which is highly correlated with body weight, was also very predictive of slow-wave sleep. In contrast, vulnerability to danger (e.g. danger of being preyed upon) was the best predictor of the amount of REM sleep, with those most vulnerable having less REM sleep than those least vulnerable.

The key finding from the perspective of recovery theories is the association between metabolic rate and the duration of slow-wave sleep. It is possible to interpret this association in various ways. However, it seems likely that small mammals are in particular need of the energy conservation function of sleep because of their high metabolic rate.

According to Oswald's (1980) recovery theory, slow-wave sleep is useful for recovery processes in the body. As he pointed out, there is a release of growth hormone from the pituitary gland during slow-wave sleep. This stimulates protein synthesis, and so contributes to the repair of tissues within the body. He also argued that important recovery processes occur in the brain during REM sleep. This latter proposal is supported by the finding that newborn infants (who experience enormous brain growth) have a very high percentage of their time asleep devoted to REM sleep (Green, 1994).

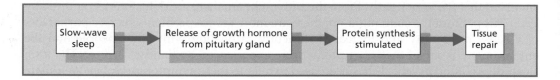

Evidence consistent with Oswald's (1980) recovery theory was reported by Shapiro et al. (1981). They studied runners who had taken part in an ultra marathon covering 57 miles. These runners slept about an hour and a half longer than normal on the two nights after the ultra marathon, and there was an especially large increase in the amount of time devoted to Stage 4 (slow-wave) sleep. It might be imagined that people who take very little exercise would sleep for less time than those who take an average amount of exercise, but there is little or no support for this.

The notion that REM sleep and slow-wave sleep are of great importance is supported by the previously discussed sleep-deprivation study on Randy Gardner. After his long period of sleep deprivation, there was much greater recovery of REM sleep and Stage 4 slow-wave sleep than of the other stages of sleep.

Horne (1988) put forward a recovery theory resembling that of Oswald (1980). The main difference is that he emphasised the fact that members of the human species have periods of relaxed wakefulness during which there are rather low levels of energy expenditure. According to Horne, the repair of bodily tissues occurs during periods of relaxed wakefulness rather than during sleep itself. What evidence supports this position? Horne pointed out that most of Randy Gardner's problems during sleep deprivation were connected with brain processes rather than with other physiological processes in the body. The implication is that sleep is not essential for the repair of bodily tissues.

As was mentioned earlier, one of the possible functions of sleep is to permit restoration of psychological functions. For example, there are various studies in which associations were found between quality of sleep and mood. Insomniacs (who have persistent problems with

Why do you think small species need relatively more slow-wave sleep than larger ones?

How might prey animals benefit from having less REM sleep?

Although studies show that people need extra sleep following extreme exertion, there is no evidence that people who take little or no exercise reduce their sleeping time.

sleeping) tend to be more worried and anxious than people who sleep normally. Such evidence is hard to interpret. However, it is usually assumed that it is more a question of people's worries and concerns disrupting sleep than of disrupted sleep causing worries. Additional evidence was reported by Berry and Webb (1983), in a study in which they assessed self-reported anxiety. When people slept well during a given night, their level of anxiety on the following day was lower than when they had slept poorly.

Naitoh (1975) discussed various studies concerned with the effects of one night's sleep deprivation on mood. The effects were consistently negative. Sleep-deprived individuals described themselves as less friendly, relaxed, good-natured, and cheerful than those who had not been sleep-deprived.

Do you find that some worries and problems recede after a good night's sleep? Is this valid evidence for the function of sleep?

Adaptive or evolutionary theories

According to various theorists (e.g. Meddis, 1979; Webb, 1968), sleep can be regarded as adaptive behaviour favoured by evolution. In particular, the sleep behaviour shown by any species depends on the need to adapt to environmental threats and dangers. Thus, for example, sleep serves the function of keeping animals fairly immobile and safe from predators during periods of time when they cannot engage in feeding and other kinds of behaviour. In the case of those species that depend on vision, it is adaptive for them to sleep during the hours of darkness.

It follows that those species in danger from predators should sleep more of the time than those species that are predators. In fact, however, predators tend to sleep more than those preyed upon (Allison & Cicchetti, 1976). This might seem inconsistent with adaptive theories of sleep. However, species that are in danger from predators might benefit from remaining vigilant most of the time and sleeping relatively little. This seems like an example of having your cake and eating it, in the sense that any pattern of findings can be explained by the adaptive or evolutionary approach!

Interesting evidence that the pattern of sleep is often dictated by the environmental threats faced by animals was reported by Pilleri (1979). Dolphins living in the River Indus are in constant danger from debris floating down the river. As a consequence, these dolphins sleep for only a few seconds at a time to protect themselves from the debris.

Evaluation

How can we decide between recovery and adaptive theories of sleep function? According to most recovery theories, sleep is absolutely essential to well-being. In contrast, sleep is generally rather less crucial according to adaptive theories. There are no reports of human beings who have managed without sleep. However, there are a few reports of individuals who led normal healthy lives in spite of regularly sleeping for very short periods of time each day (e.g. Meddis, Pearson, & Langford, 1973).

Horne (1988) made the important point that sleep probably serves different purposes in different species. Thus, no single theory of the functions of sleep is likely to be adequate. The recovery and adaptive theoretical approaches have been discussed here. The adaptive or evolutionary approach is based on the assumption that sleep is very useful but not essential. This key assumption seems to be inconsistent with two findings: (1) sleep is found in all species; (2) sleep deprivation can have fatal consequences.

On balance, the recovery approach seems to provide a more thorough and well-developed account of sleep. However, it could be argued that these two approaches address somewhat different issues. The recovery approach provides some views on *why* sleep is important, whereas the adaptive approach also focuses on *when* different species sleep.

Bats have very limited vision, relying instead on echolocation to detect prey. They are adapted to a nocturnal pattern, sleeping during the day and hunting at night.

Bearing in mind the two theoretical approaches to sleep, explain why human babies sleep a lot.

When two different approaches address different issues within an area of psychology, is it possible to make a true comparison between them?

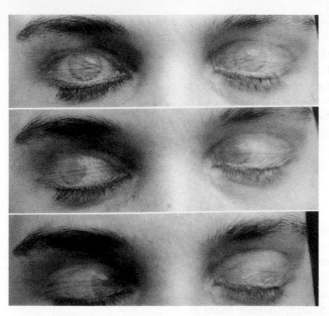

A photo montage illustrating eye movement during REM sleep.

■ Research activity: In small groups, discuss your ideas about the possible functions of dreaming in human beings.

Dreaming

Most dreaming takes place during REM (rapid eye movement) sleep. We can thus use the duration of REM sleep during the night as an approximate measure of how long any given individual spends dreaming. Newborn babies spend about nine hours a day in REM sleep, and adults two hours. The fact that we devote so much time to dreaming (about 700 hours a year) suggests that dreams are likely to fulfil some important function or functions. As we will see, various theorists have tried to identify these functions.

It may not seem as if we spend so much of our time dreaming. The reason is that we forget more than 95% of our dreams. What are these forgotten dreams about? Researchers have obtained some idea by using sleep laboratories, in which sleepers are woken up when the EEG and EOG records indicate that a dream is taking place. The dreams that are normally forgotten tend to be much more ordinary and less strange than the dreams we normally remember (Empson, 1989). This is important, because it shows that the dreams we normally remember are not *representative* or typical of dreams in general. It would thus not be appropriate to produce a general theory of dreaming purely on the basis of the 5% of dreams we normally remember.

Empson (1989) identified various differences between dreaming and waking consciousness. First, dreamers typically feel that they have little or no control over their dreams, whereas we nearly always have a sense of conscious control in our waking lives. However, people occasionally have lucid dreams, in which they know they are dreaming and can sometimes control the dream content. For example, LaBerge, Greenleaf, and Kedzierski (1983) studied a woman who was able to create lucid sex dreams that produced orgasms.

Second, dreams often contain elements that would seem illogical or nonsensical in our waking consciousness. For example, dreams sometimes include impossible events or actions (e.g. someone floating above the ground), and they can also include various hallucinations and delusions.

Third, we tend to be totally absorbed by our dream imagery, reflecting what Empson (1989) described as the "singlemindedness of dreams". However, when we are awake, we can usually stand back from our conscious thoughts and avoid becoming dominated by them.

In what follows, we will be discussing four of the main theories of dreaming. We will start with Freud's classic wish-fulfilment theory, and then move on to activation-synthesis theory, reverse-learning theory, and the cognitive theories of Foulkes and Winson.

Freud's wish-fulfilment theory

Probably the best-known theory of dreaming was put forward by Sigmund Freud (1900). He claimed that all dreams represent *wish fulfilment*, mainly of repressed desires (e.g. sexual). These wish fulfilments are often unacceptable to the dreamer, leading Freud to describe dreams as "the insanity of the night". As a result of the unacceptable desires expressed in dreams, the actual dream and its meaning (the latent content) are generally distorted into a more acceptable form (the manifest content) by the time the dreamer is consciously aware of his or her dream.

Psychoanalysis can be used to uncover the latent content. Indeed, according to Freud, dream analysis provides a *via regia* or royal road to an understanding of the unconscious mind. An important feature of such dream analysis involves working out the meaning of various dream symbols. For example, riding a horse might be a symbol for sex, or a cigar might be a symbol for a penis. However, as Freud himself pointed out, "Sometimes a cigar is only a cigar."

Evaluation

Freud deserves credit for having put forward the first systematic theory of dream function. Probably its greatest strength is that it provides an explanation of the puzzling finding that dreams often seem rather incoherent or even meaningless. In view of the somewhat repressive nature of Austrian society at the end of the nineteenth century, it is likely that some of the dreams of Freud's patients did represent wish fulfilment in a distorted form.

Freud argued that dreams can provide us with vital information about the unconscious thoughts and feelings of the dreamer. Most later theorists have been unwilling to go that far, but have accepted that dreams can tell us something about the thoughts and feelings of the dreamer. For example, it is claimed within activation-synthesis theory (see next section) that dreamers have a "quest for meaning" that leads them to interpret the brain's activity in certain ways.

There are various problems with wish-fulfilment theory. First, it is improbable that there is much repression of unacceptable desires in today's liberal and permissive society. Second, some dreams (nightmares) are very frightening, and it is hard to regard them as wish fulfilling even in a distorted way. Third, the latent content of a dream as identified through psychoanalysis generally seems open to question. In other words, dubious methods are used to identify the latent content of a dream. Although some dreams undoubtedly represent wish fulfilment (and not always in a distorted form!), it is unlikely that all dreams can reasonably be regarded as wish-fulfilling.

Is it possible to test Freud's wish-fulfilment approach to dreams in an empirical way? Is this a strength or a weakness?

Activation-synthesis theory

Hobson and McCarley (1977) were impressed by the fact that the brain is as physiologically active during REM (rapid eye movement) sleep as it is during normal waking life. This led them to put forward the activation-synthesis theory of dreaming. According to this theory, the physiological mechanisms responsible for dreaming produce high levels of activation in several parts of the brain, including those involved in perception, action, and emotional reactions. This activation is essentially random. Those parts of the cortex responsible for producing actions tend to be active in spite of the fact that bodily movements are inhibited during REM sleep. The reason for this is the existence of an output blockade at the top of the spinal column which prevents commands for action being acted upon. In addition, there is inhibited processing of environmental stimuli via an input blockade. However, signals resembling those that normally come from the eyes and the ears are generated within the hindbrain and midbrain structures. Dreamers generally interpret these internally generated signals as if they were produced by external stimuli.

Why might it be advantageous for bodily movements to be restricted during REM sleep?

There is physiological evidence to support the activation-synthesis theory. Research on cats indicated that there is apparently random firing of cells in cats' brains during REM sleep (Hobson, 1988). This then produces activation in the parts of the brain that are used in visual perception and the control of motor movements. However, as motor movements are inhibited during REM sleep, it is hard for the sleeping person to interpret the meaning of activation in those parts of the brain responsible for movement control.

Hobson (1994) developed the activation-synthesis theory. He noted that cortical levels of the neurotransmitters noradrenaline and serotonin are lower during REM sleep than during non-REM sleep or waking life. According to Hobson, these reduced levels of noradrenaline and serotonin prevent the effective use of attentional processes and of the capacity to organise information in a coherent way. This makes it easier for the brain to misinterpret internally generated signals as if they came from external stimuli or from responses. Hobson went on to argue that the problems of attention caused by low levels of noradrenaline and serotonin may explain why we fail to remember the great majority of our dreams.

Hobson (1988) discussed evidence that may help to explain why periods of REM sleep alternate with periods of non-REM sleep. The neurotransmitter acetylcholine causes giant cells in the reticular activating system to fire, and this leads to the onset of REM sleep and to dreaming. When the level of acetylcholine falls, REM sleep ceases until the level builds up again.

How do dreamers react to the high level of random brain activation that occurs during REM sleep? According to Hobson (1988), dreamers try to make sense of it by synthesising or combining the information contained in the bursts of neural activity. As this activity is essentially random, it is often very difficult for dreamers to produce coherent dreams. Indeed, one might wonder how it is possible at all. According to Hobson (1988), "The brain is so inexorably bent upon the quest for meaning that it attributes and even creates meaning when there is little or none in the data it is asked to process." The finding that dreams sometimes lead to creative problem solving can be understood within this theoretical framework.

Evaluation

The greatest strength of the activation-synthesis theory is that it is based on detailed information of the physiological activity of the brain during dreaming. The theory can explain why smells and tastes rarely or never appear in our dreams. The reason is that "the neurons responsible are not stimulated during REM sleep" (McIlveen & Gross, 1996, p.108). The activation-synthesis theory also accounts for the incoherent nature of many dreams. If dreams occur as a result of random activity in the brain, and attentional processes are not functioning effectively, then it is entirely understandable that we often find our dreams hard to understand.

The greatest limitation of the theory is that it does not provide a convincing account of the fact that dreams often possess clear meaning and coherence. It may be true that the brain has a "quest for meaning", but this is hardly a detailed explanation of dream coherence. The theory is also of little value in explaining why it is that so many people have dreams that relate to their present concerns. This is puzzling if dreams are based on *random* brain activity.

Reverse-learning theory

Crick and Mitchison (1983) put forward a challenging approach to dreaming known as reverse-learning or unlearning theory. According to this theory, the main function of dreaming is to get rid of useless information stored in the brain. This information (which they called "parasitic information") uses up valuable space in the cortex, and so dreaming helps to free up space in the cortex for the storage of more useful information. More specifically, according to Crick and Mitchison (1983), there are neuronal networks in the cortex. These networks are strongly interconnected, and this can lead to overloading. The elimination of unimportant information during dreaming allows the neuronal networks to function more efficiently.

What are the physiological processes involved in dreaming and the elimination of unwanted information? According to Blakemore (1988):

> Dreams are, quite literally, a kind of shock therapy, in which the cortex is bombarded by barrages of impulses from the brainstem below, while a different mode of synaptic modification ensures that the unwanted elements of each circuit are unlearned.

It is hard to test reverse-learning theory. However, Crick and Mitchison (1983) claimed that the size of the cortex in different species of mammals provides support for their theory. The only mammals not having the REM (rapid eye movement) sleep associated with dreaming are dolphins and spiny anteaters. As a result, it is likely that these species are unable to get rid of useless information. According to Crick and Mitchison, these species only manage to function effectively because they have an unusually large cortex for mammals of their size.

Evaluation

Reverse-learning theory represents an interesting approach to dream function. If dreaming is simply designed to allow us to erase valueless information, then it makes sense that we rarely remember the content of our dreams. As we have seen, we forget about 95% of our dreams, which is entirely consistent with the reverse-learning theory.

There are some major problems with the theory. First, dreams are often meaningful or significant, whereas it would be predicted by the theory that they should be relatively meaningless. One of the most famous examples of a valuable dream was reported by the chemist Kekule. He had a dream about snakes which revealed to him the ring-like atomic structure of benzine molecules, a problem he was working on at the time. Second, as McIlveen and Gross (1996) pointed out, there is evidence that foetuses engage in something resembling REM sleep. It is hard to believe that they are trying to forget meaningless information before they are even born! However, this work is only relevant if we assume that foetuses are in a dreamlike state when they experience REM sleep.

Cognitive theory: Foulkes

Foulkes (1985) proposed a cognitive theory of dream function that resembles Freud's wish-fulfilment theory. According to Foulkes, dreams express the dreamer's current concerns. These concerns may relate to the wishes emphasised by Freud, but may also relate to fears (e.g. job insecurity; health of a loved one). These concerns are often expressed in a symbolic way rather than directly. For example, students who are concerned they may fail a forthcoming examination may dream about falling over a cliff or tripping over something in the street.

Hajek and Belcher

There is evidence that many dreams are relevant to current concerns. Hajek and Belcher (1991) studied the dreams of smokers who were involved in a programme designed to help them stop smoking. Most of the participants reported dreams about smoking during the course of treatment and for a year afterwards. Most of these dreams were what they called dreams of absent-minded transgressions or DAMITS. In these dreams, engaging in smoking was followed by feelings of panic or guilt.

Hajek and Belcher found that dreaming about smoking seemed to help the ex-smokers. Those who had the most dreams about smoking (and about feeling bad about it) were less likely to start smoking again than those who had few such dreams. However, these are correlational findings, and do not show that the dreams were actually useful.

Discussion points

1. Are most of the dreams that you remember related to your current concerns?

2. If we dream about personally relevant issues, why is it that we remember only a small fraction of our dreams?

Another study showing that current concerns can influence dream content was by Bokert (1970; discussed in McIlveen & Gross, 1996). He reported that people who had been deprived of water tended to have dreams about drinking.

Additional evidence that dreams are often meaningful and of relevance to current concerns was reported by Dement and Wolpert (1958). They compared the dreams of sleepers who were sprayed with cold water with those of sleepers who were not. The former group of sleepers was much more likely to dream about water than was the latter group. Here is an example of one such dream discussed by Dement and Wolpert (1958, p.550):

Have you ever had a dream that has incorporated external stimuli? When and why might this phenomenon be useful?

> *Children came into the room and came over to me asking for water. I had a glass of ice water and I tipped the glass to give it to them. I was sitting, and I spilled the water on myself.*

Evaluation

The notion that dreaming tends to be meaningful and of relevance to some of our current concerns is plausible and in line with much of the evidence. It would seem to follow from Foulkes's theory that it would be useful for us to remember our dreams. It seems puzzling that we remember fewer than 5% of our dreams.

How would Foulkes's theory explain students dreaming about their exams, or patients dreaming about an operation?

There are other problems for Foulkes's cognitive theory. Many dreams seem to lack meaning, and other dreams have no obvious connections to our concerns. The most reasonable conclusion is that Foulkes's cognitive theory helps to explain some dreams, but does not provide a comprehensive account of all types of dream. Finally, his approach is uninformative about the physiological processes involved in dreaming.

Survival strategy theory

Winson (1997) has recently put forward a theory of dreams that resembles Foulkes's cognitive theory. According to Winson:

> *REM sleep is the information-processing period when memories and events of the day are juxtaposed [placed close together] with things that happened in the past to form a strategy for survival. What was this or that like? What better actions can I take in a similar situation in the future? All the indications are that REM sleep plays an important part in our survival.*

There is some support for this theory in the finding that people who are deprived of REM sleep find it hard to remember the key events of the previous day.

■ Research activity: Keep a "dream diary" for two weeks, noting down not only the content of your dreams but also any links you notice to events in your waking life. Which of the four theoretical approaches described here provides the best explanation for your dreams, or does each approach address a different aspect?

Winson argued that the inhibition against movement found during dreaming is important: "If you didn't have this neural block on activity while you sleep, you would attempt to wake up and act out your dreams. Eye movements are not stopped because they don't interfere with sleeping."

Evaluation

It is hard to evaluate survival strategy theory, because relatively few studies have been designed specifically to test it. However, if dreams are designed to provide a survival strategy, it might be expected that most of them would be remembered. The fact that so few dreams are remembered suggests that many dreams do not provide useful guidance for future action.

Consciousness

One of the most important states of awareness is that of **consciousness**. There is increasing agreement that there is more than one level of consciousness. For example, Reber (1993) distinguished between Consciousness I and Consciousness II. Consciousness I allows individual animals "to distinguish between self and not-self" (Reber, 1993, p.135). This is a fundamental form of consciousness, which is probably found in most species.

In contrast, "Consciousness II is characterised by both self-reflection and the capacity to use the knowledge derived from self-reflection to modulate other functions" (Reber, 1993, p.136). Thus, Consciousness II involves self-awareness. It is probably limited only to the human species or to the human and other higher primate species (e.g. chimpanzees).

Oakley (1985) put forward a similar position, and tried to identify those parts of the brain associated with different levels of consciousness. The highest level he proposed was self-awareness, which corresponds to Reber's Consciousness II. According to Oakley, this

KEY TERM
Consciousness: the higher level involves self-awareness and self-reflection, whereas the lower level involves a basic discrimination between self and not-self.

OAKLEY'S (1985) IDENTIFICATION OF BRAIN STRUCTURES WITH LEVELS OF CONSCIOUSNESS

Type of consciousness	Description	Location
Self-awareness	Self-reflection	Neo-cortex of humans and primates
Consciousness	Reasoning and complex learning	Cortex and limbic system
Simple awareness	Classical conditioning (see Chapter 10) and reflexes	Various subcortical structures

is located in the neo-cortex of humans and other primate species. Below that is consciousness (corresponding to Reber's Consciousness I) which is involved in reasoning and complex learning. This is located in the cortex and the limbic system. At the lowest level, Oakley identified simple awareness, which is shown in basic forms of behaviour such as classical conditioning or reflexes. The brain structures involved are found in various subcortical structures in humans and other species.

The distinction between Consciousness II or self-awareness and Consciousness I or consciousness is not always easy to make in practice. In what follows, we will be focusing mainly on Consciousness II or self-awareness. However, it is not always possible to be sure which meaning was intended by any given theorist.

Assessing consciousness

A major difficulty with studying consciousness is that we have no direct knowledge of anyone else's conscious experience. Wittgenstein (1953, paragraph 293) expressed the problems this raises by comparing each person's conscious experience with the contents of a box: "No-one can look into anyone else's box, and everyone says he knows what a beetle is only by looking at his beetle ... It would be quite possible for everyone to have something different in his box ... the box might even be empty."

In spite of these problems, there is fairly general agreement that conscious experience has the following features (Valentine, 1992):

- It is private.
- It can combine information across different sensory modalities.
- It contains information about the results or products of thought processes rather than the processes themselves. For example, if asked to name the capital of France, we think of the answer with no awareness of the processes involved.
- It is constantly changing like a river or stream.

How should we assess an individual's conscious experience? Baars (1997) suggested that researchers should use the following guidelines:

1. The individual's experience should be reported by means of some voluntary response, such as a verbal report.
2. The individual should assert that he or she is reporting his or her conscious experience.
3. There should be independent evidence of some kind that the reported experience is valid and genuine.
4. There should be no social or other pressures on the individual to distort his or her responses.

What kind of independent evidence might Baars have included in the third guideline for researchers?

Consciousness and attention

There are clear links between consciousness and attention. Two clear examples are discussed in Chapter 12. First, there is evidence that prolonged practice at a task leads to the development of automatic processes and a reduction in conscious awareness of how task behaviour is being produced (e.g. Shiffrin & Schneider, 1977). For example, expert typists generally have little or no conscious awareness of where the letters are on the keyboard of a word processor, in spite of having typed each letter thousands of times. The knowledge is "in the fingers", and typists have to mimic the appropriate finger actions to identify the locations of the letters.

What other activities or tasks become automatic after prolonged experience?

The second example of links between attention and consciousness concerns action slips or absent-mindedness (see Chapter 12). An action slip typically occurs when someone fails to attend to (or be consciously aware of) what he or she is doing, and so produces a habitual (but wrong) response. For example, someone normally drives along a given route from work to home, but decides to make a detour and buy some groceries from a supermarket. What often happens in such circumstances is that the person follows the habitual route and misses the turn-off to the supermarket.

Baars (1997) considered the relationship between attention and consciousness by focusing on sentences such as "We look in order to see" or "We listen in order to hear." He argued (1997, p.364) that:

The distinction is between selecting an experience and being conscious of the selected event. In everyday language, the first word of each pair involves attention; the second word involves consciousness.

Thus, the contents of consciousness are often determined by attentional processes. According to Baars, attentional processes resemble selecting a given television channel, and consciousness resembles what then appears on the television screen.

Expert typists have problems using keyboards designed for different languages—they never look at the keys when using the familiar keyboard layout, so a different arrangement of letters upsets their habitual ability.

Functions of consciousness

What are the functions of consciousness? Shallice (1982) argued that it fulfils the following purposes:

- It can be used in decision-making.
- It permits flexibility of behaviour.
- It can be used to control action.
- It can be used to monitor behaviour.

According to Humphrey (1993), consciousness evolved in humans because it made it easier for us to communicate with others and to develop social groups. As Humphrey expressed it:

The first use of human consciousness was—and is—to enable each human being to understand what it feels like to be human and so to make sense of himself and other people from the inside.

Psychodynamic approach

How did Freud know what information was in the unconscious?

Sigmund Freud identified three different levels of consciousness. First, there is the conscious, which is what we are fully aware of at any moment. Second, there is the preconscious, which consists of information that we are not aware of, but could readily become so. Third, there is the unconscious, which consists mainly of traumatic and other anxiety-related information that is very inaccessible to conscious awareness.

Before Freud, it had been generally accepted that psychology was concerned with conscious experience. Since Freud's time, it has been accepted increasingly that consciousness is more limited than we like to think. Two examples will illustrate this point. First, Nisbett and Wilson (1977) presented their participants with an array of essentially identical pairs of stockings, and asked them to decide which pair was best. They were also asked to indicate why they had chosen that particular pair. Most of the participants chose the right-most pair in the array, but practically none of them realised at the conscious level that spatial position had influenced their decision.

Why do you think spatial position influenced the participants' decisions in Nisbett and Wilson's study?

Second, it seems reasonable to assume that visual perception is impossible in the absence of conscious awareness. However, strong evidence that this is not the case has been found in cases of blindsight (see Chapter 4). Brain-damaged patients with blindsight can decide whether a light is present or absent and they can decide where a stimulus is in the visual field. However, they claim that they cannot see anything, and are very surprised that their "guesses" are usually correct (Weiskrantz, 1986).

Schizophrenia

Schizophrenia is a serious condition in which there is a loss of contact with reality, including various delusions and hallucinations (see Chapter 25). For example, some schizophrenics have delusions that their actions are controlled by alien forces. According to Frith and Cahill (1994, p.911), "Such delusions could arise if patients were unable to monitor their own intended actions and thus found themselves performing actions without being aware of any prior intention to do so." In other words, the monitoring function of consciousness may be defective in schizophrenic patients.

Most of the hallucinations experienced by schizophrenics consist of voices saying something of personal relevance to them. McGuigan (1966) suggested that these auditory hallucinations may result from schizophrenics' failure to monitor their own inner speech. The evidence for this was that the patient's larynx was often active during the time the auditory hallucination was being experienced.

Dissociative identity disorder

Some of the complexities of human consciousness can be seen in rare cases of **dissociative identity disorder**, in which an individual has two or more separate personalities. Individuals with this disorder are only consciously aware of one of their personalities or identities at any time. Perhaps the best-known case of dissociative identity disorder is Chris Sizemore, whose life formed the basis of a film called *The Three Faces of Eve*. One of her identities was Eve Black, who was impulsive and promiscuous. A second identity was Eve White. She was very different, being inhibited and conformist in her behaviour. Her third identity was as Jane, who had the most stable character. Eve Black knew of the existence of Eve White, but Eve White did not know about Eve Black. Jane knew about both Eves, and tended to prefer Eve Black.

What causes dissociative identity disorder? Most of those with the disorder suffered sexual abuse in childhood (Ross et al., 1990). Females are more likely than males to experience sexual abuse, and the great majority of individuals with dissociative identity disorder are female. The multiple personalities develop as a result of the attempt to separate off the traumatic experiences of childhood from conscious awareness.

Experimental evidence that individuals with dissociative identity disorder really possess more than one personality was reported by Putnam (1991). The different personalities within individual patients seem to have access to different memories, they perform very differently on personality tests, and they even show physiological differences in stressful situations.

> **KEY TERM**
> **Dissociative identity disorder**: a condition in which an individual has multiple personalities.

The actress Joanne Woodward used different expressions, make-up, and clothes to portray the different "personalities" of Chris Sizemore in the film *The Three Faces of Eve*.

Hypnosis and sleep

According to Gregory (1987) the relationship between hypnosis and ordinary sleep has been widely studied. People often describe being under hypnosis in sleep-like terms, using words like "drowsy" and "lethargy". However, as early as the nineteenth century it was observed that the muscles of hypnotised subjects do not relax as in sleep, so that a person being hypnotised does not drop an object held in the hand. The EEGs of hypnotised subjects do not resemble sleepers in any respect, but are essentially the same as those of people who are awake.

Hypnosis

What is **hypnosis**? The word comes from the Greek word *hypnoun* meaning to put to sleep, but a hypnotised person is not actually asleep. Hilgard (1977) defined it as

the state of consciousness caused in a subject by a systematic procedure for altering consciousness, usually carried out by one person (the hypnotist) to alter the consciousness of another (the subject).

Hypnosis can also be defined as a state of heightened suggestibility which may or may not represent an altered state of consciousness. You may find this definition a little unsatisfactory, because it does not make it clear whether the hypnotic state is very different from the normal waking state. However, this definition is favoured because there has been much controversy on this precise issue.

How can we produce the hypnotic state? It can be achieved in many people by induction procedures based on suggestions for sleep and relaxation. Initially, the participant may be asked by the hypnotist to focus on a given target (e.g. a swinging pendulum; a spot of light). When the participant's attention is directed fully on the target, the hypnotist suggests to the participant that he or she is feeling relaxed and sleepy. The suggestion is also made that the participant's arms and legs are feeling heavy and relaxed. Typically, about 10 or 15 minutes are spent in trying to produce the passive and sleeplike hypnotic state. After that, more time is spent in assessing the depth or strength of the hypnotic state that has been created.

Susceptibility to hypnosis

There are large individual differences in susceptibility to hypnosis. These individual differences can be assessed by scales such as the Stanford Hypnotic Susceptibility Scale or the Harvard Group Scale of Hypnotic Susceptibility. These scales consist of various suggestions (e.g. "Your hand is heavy, and you can't hold it up"; "You will forget what I have just said"). The number of these suggestions that are followed by the individual provides a measure of his or her susceptibility to hypnosis.

While being hypnotised, participants are often asked to focus on a moving object.

We will consider the Stanford Hypnotic Susceptibility Scale as a concrete example of how to assess susceptibility to hypnosis. It consists of 12 items or suggestions. Some of the suggestions are fairly easy and followed by many people (e.g. imagine that a fly is buzzing around your head, and try to brush it away). Other suggestions are more difficult and are only followed by a small percentage of people (e.g. negative visual hallucination, in which the individual can no longer see a small box following the hypnotist's suggestion). About 5% of people come out as highly susceptible to hypnosis on the Stanford Hypnotic Susceptibility Scale, and about one in ten show practically no signs of susceptibility.

What kinds of people are particularly susceptible to hypnosis? According to McIlveen (1995), they tend to be fantasy-prone, meaning that they report having a large number of vivid fantasies. They also tend to score highly on absorption, which McIlveen (1995, p.11) defines as "the tendency to become deeply involved in sensory and imaginative experiences." However, absorption only predicts hypnotic susceptibility among people who are expecting to undergo hypnosis (McIlveen, 1995). Another characteristic of those who have high hypnotic susceptibility is that they are more willing than most to take orders from others.

What about the effects of age and gender on hypnotic susceptibility? There are no gender differences in susceptibility to hypnosis. However, age differences have been

KEY TERM
Hypnosis: a state of heightened suggestibility that may or may not represent an altered state of consciousness.

found. The peak age for susceptibility is about 10, and there is a progressive reduction in susceptibility during adolescence and early adulthood.

The hypnotic state

The hypnotised individual seems to be in a fairly passive and sleep-like state. However, EEG recordings of brain-wave activity indicate that the hypnotic state does not resemble sleep. The physiological measures that have been used to understand the hypnotic state include respiration rate, skin temperature, skin resistance, and blood pressure, as well as the EEG. Disappointingly little has emerged from this line of research. As Wagstaff (1994, p.995) concluded

> *most researchers ... now seem to agree that the quest to find a unique correlate of the hypnotic state has not been very successful. Physiological changes do often occur following hypnotic induction or hypnotic suggestions, but they seem to be explicable in other ways; for example, they may be due simply to normal changes in attention ..., or the achievement of a relaxed state.*

Various phenomena have been reported in the hypnotic state. Some (e.g. active reliving of past lives) are highly improbable, but others deserve careful consideration. We will consider four such phenomena:

1. Hypnotic amnesia.
2. Hypnotic analgesia.
3. Trance logic.
4. Attentional narrowing.

Hypnotic amnesia

Hypnotised individuals are sometimes instructed to forget what they have just learned or done. They generally show a high level of forgetting in those circumstances; this forgetting is known as **hypnotic amnesia**. It is not forgetting in the ordinary sense, because the "forgotten" information is usually remembered when the hypnotised person is given a release signal (e.g. "Now you can remember"). The most striking example of such forgetting is known as **post-hypnotic amnesia**. Hypnotised individuals are told they

> **KEY TERMS**
> **Hypnotic amnesia**: temporary forgetting in hypnosis caused by suggestion.
> **Post-hypnotic amnesia**: forgetting of the events of a hypnotic session by hypnotised individuals as a result of a suggestion given by the hypnotist.

CASE STUDY: *Stage Hypnosis*

In recent years, shows featuring hypnosis have become more common, both on television and on stage. On 12 December 1994 the House of Commons held a debate on the alleged harm suffered by some participants in public performances of stage hypnotism, which led to a full review of the current Hypnotism Act (1952) and subsequent tightening of legislation.

The panel of experts placed advertisements in five journals requesting clinicians to submit any relevant medical evidence. There were 25 reported cases of harm related to performances of stage hypnotism over the previous 25 years. In four of these cases the problems complained of were physical ailments linked to accidents on the stage; two participants fell from the stage while under hypnosis, and two others fractured bones in their hands while acting out hypnotic suggestions. In the remaining cases, identifying whether there was a link between an ailment and previous participation in stage hypnosis was not straightforward. Frequent complaints were of headaches, dizziness and persistent tiredness, resulting in feelings of lethargy. Some participants reported difficulty in sleeping or disturbed sleep, and feelings of depression were mentioned in half the cases.

In seven of the cases serious psychological problems such as severe depression, post-traumatic stress disorder, and chronic paranoid schizophrenia were diagnosed. Some cases received considerable press coverage. However, it was decided that the evidence suggests there is

not a significant problem directly associated with stage hypnotism. Although a number of individuals have suffered following participation in stage hypnosis, most people who choose to attend or participate in demonstrations of stage hypnotism find them enjoyable and suffer no ill-effects.

Apart from obeying the authority of the hypnotist, other social factors are present in stage hypnosis such as audience pressure and pressure from other volunteers. Studies indicate that these factors play a part in the undesirable effects experienced by some individuals. It seems that some participants will find the process of performing frivolous acts on stage in front of a large crowd, and the feeling of loss of control over their own actions, disturbing. In addition, the intermittent bouts of physical exertion and relaxation that form part of many shows may themselves cause some participants to feel tired and experience headaches or dizziness. However, as these side-effects might equally be experienced following a variety of other activities, it is difficult to say that they are a direct result of stage hypnosis.

The law now recommends that all individuals should be aware that some people, particularly those with a history of emotional problems and vulnerable mental health, can find the experience of being hypnotised and then asked to perform actions in front of an audience unpleasant or distressing.

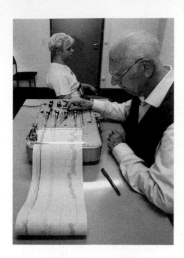

Coe (1989) found that when hypnotised individuals were questioned using a lie detector, they remembered whatever they had been told to forget under hypnosis.

will forget the entire hypnotic session when they come out of the hypnotic state. Post-hypnotic amnesia is shown by most individuals. It is not permanent forgetting, because the events of the hypnotic session can usually be recalled when the individuals are hypnotised again and instructed to try to remember what happened the last time they were hypnotised.

A phenomenon related to post-hypnotic amnesia is known as **post-hypnotic suggestion**. What happens is that the hypnotist gives an instruction to a hypnotised individual to carry out some action when the signal is given (e.g. start sneezing when the hypnotist says hay fever). The hypnotist tells the hypnotised person that he or she will not remember the instruction. The signal is given when the person is back in the normal waking state. He or she carries out the specified action, but does not remember the post-hypnotic suggestion.

The simplest explanation of hypnotic amnesia is that hypnotised individuals either do not try to remember or that they distract themselves from the memory task. Evidence consistent with these explanations was reported by Coe (1989). He found that hypnotic amnesia usually disappeared when the participants were instructed to be honest, attached to a lie detector, and shown a videotape of their own performance. Wagstaff (1977) found that participants who were allowed to indicate that they were role-playing rather than in a hypnotic trance usually showed no evidence of hypnotic amnesia.

Hypnotic analgesia

The phenomenon of **hypnotic analgesia** is shown when a hypnotised individual experiences little or no pain when exposed to a very painful situation. As early as 1842, a British surgeon called Ward reported a striking example of hypnotic analgesia. He claimed to have amputated a man's leg without causing him any pain simply by using hypnosis!

In a typical study on hypnotic analgesia, the painful situation involves the participants putting their hand into ice-cold water or having a pressure stimulus applied to them. Suggestions that pain will not be experienced are usually more effective when given in the hypnotic state than in the normal state (Hilgard & Hilgard, 1983). However, as Wagstaff (1994) pointed out, the same participants were often used in the hypnotic and normal states. In order to conform to what they perceive to be the experimenter's wishes, the participants may deliberately avoid using pain-reducing strategies in the normal state.

Another possible explanation of hypnotic analgesia is that it depends on compliance or faking. Spanos et al. (1990) administered a painful stimulus to their participants. Those who were led to believe subsequently that they were hypnotised at the time reported less pain than those who believed they were not hypnotised, and this difference was found regardless of whether they were actually hypnotised when receiving the painful stimulus.

More evidence that hypnotic analgesia may be a suspect phenomenon was reported by Pattie (1937). First of all he told hypnotised individuals that they would feel nothing in one hand. Next he asked them to interlock the fingers on their two hands. They were then told to twist their arms around so that it would be hard for them to know which hand any given finger was on. Finally, Pattie touched some of their fingers, and asked the participants to indicate how many times their fingers had been touched. They included touches to fingers on both hands, indicating that they still had feeling in the allegedly "anaesthetised" hand.

Trance logic

Another phenomenon associated with the hypnotic state is that of **trance logic**. This refers to the finding that hypnotised individuals do not display logical consistency in their thinking. For example, there is what Orne (1959) called the "double hallucination" response: when hypnotised individuals look at someone, and are told to hallucinate that person standing somewhere else, they typically report seeing the person and the hallucinated image at the same time. Another example of trance logic occurs when hypnotised individuals are asked to imagine that someone is sitting on an empty chair. They usually report seeing the chair through the person. In contrast, non-hypnotised individuals who have been asked to act as if they were hypnotised (simulators) do not show trance logic.

There has been some dispute about the existence and significance of trance logic. There are several studies in which there was no difference between hypnotised participants and simulators on the double hallucination response (DeGroot & Gwynn, 1989). An important issue is what hypnotised individuals mean when they say they can see someone and their hallucinated image at the same time. If hypnotised individuals are given the choice, they usually prefer to claim that they "imagined" the hallucinated image rather than "saw" it (Spanos, 1982). This suggests that the double hallucination effect is less dramatic than is often supposed.

Attentional narrowing

The next phenomenon we will consider is **attentional narrowing**, which involves a reduction in the processing of environmental information. For example, hypnotised individuals instructed to pay attention only to the hypnotist will often report being unaware of what other people are saying. Does this attentional narrowing mean that hypnotised individuals are *actually* processing less environmental information? Interesting evidence was reported by Miller, Hennessy, and Leibowitz (1973). They presented hypnotised participants with the Ponzo illusion (discussed more fully in on page 280). People in the normal waking state report that the top rectangle is longer than the bottom one, in spite of the fact that they are actually the same length. Miller et al. made use of hypnotic suggestion so that the hypnotised individuals reported that they could no longer see the slanting lines at the sides. However, they still reported the normal Ponzo illusion. Thus, they were processing information about the slanting lines even though they were not aware of doing so.

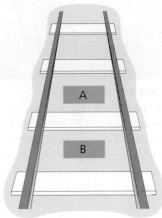

The Ponzo illusion

The Ponzo illusion—as rectangles A and B are the same size on the retinal image, the more distant rectangle (A) must actually be larger than the nearer one (B).

Altered state theories

The crucial question about hypnosis is whether it represents a special, altered state of consciousness. The most prominent advocate of the view that it does is Ernest Hilgard (1986), who put forward a **neo-dissociation theory**. According to this theory (McIlveen, 1996, p.24), what happens in hypnosis is that there is

> *a dissociation (or division) of consciousness into separate channels of mental activity. This division allows us to focus our attention on the hypnotist and, simultaneously, enables us to perceive other events peripherally (or "subconsciously").*

Hilgard (1986) argued that what we say and do in the normal state is under conscious control, but that most of this conscious control disappears in the hypnotic state. Hypnotic phenomena occur because there is a dissociation (separating off) of one part of the body's system from the rest by means of amnesic barriers. For example, hypnotised individuals exposed to painful stimuli typically exhibit the normal physiological responses associated with pain, even though they report experiencing little or no pain. This suggests that the part of the brain registering conscious awareness of pain is separated off from those parts registering basic physiological responses.

How would you measure a hypnotised person's physiological responses to pain?

The hidden observer phenomenon

Hypnotised individuals often report their experiences as involving an absence of conscious control. For example, they describe their obedience to the hypnotist's instructions as involving involuntary actions rather than planned and deliberate ones. According to Hilgard (1986), more direct evidence for his neo-dissociation theory comes from the **hidden observer phenomenon**, which can be observed in hypnotised individuals. This involves taking a hypnotised person and giving him or her the following instructions: "When I place my hand on your shoulder, I shall be able to talk to a hidden part of you that knows things are going on in your body, things that are unknown to the part of you to which I am now talking ... You will remember that there is a part of you that knows many things that are going on that may be hidden from either your normal consciousness or the hypnotised part of you" (Knox et al., 1974, p.842).

KEY TERMS

Attentional narrowing: an apparent reduction in the amount of environmental information being processed during hypnosis.

Neo-dissociation theory: Hilgard's theory, according to which one part of the body is separated off from other parts in the hypnotic state.

Hidden observer phenomenon: an effect in which the experiences of part of the hypnotised person's mind differ from those of the rest of his or her mind.

The cold pressor test—most people can only keep their arm in ice-cold water for 25 seconds, but hypnotised individuals who have been told that they will not feel any pain can keep their arm in the water for about 40 seconds.

A good example of the hidden observer phenomenon was discussed by Hilgard (1986). He used the cold pressor test, in which the participant's arms are kept in ice-cold water for as long as possible. Most people can only tolerate this for about 25 seconds. However, hypnotised individuals who are told that they will not experience any pain keep their arms in the water for about 40 seconds, and report much less pain than non-hypnotised individuals. The hidden observer, who was told to "remain out of consciousness", reported a very intense experience of pain. In other words, the consciousness of these hypnotised individuals seemed to divide into two parts.

Hilgard has used the neo-dissociation theory to explain some of the phenomena of hypnosis. Hypnotic amnesia may occur because the "forgotten" memories are dissociated or separated from conscious control, and so cannot be retrieved voluntarily. There is also evidence of dissociation with hypnotic analgesia, in which suggestions that pain will not be experienced are often effective when given in the hypnotic state. As we have seen, Hilgard used the hidden observer technique with the cold pressor test. He found that the "hidden part" reported higher levels of pain than were reported for other parts of the body. According to Hilgard (1986), only the hidden part is not protected from awareness of pain by an amnesic barrier. Spanos (1989) argued that hypnotised individuals simply report what they think they should report. He found that "hidden observers" can be led to report high or low levels of pain depending on the expectations they have been given.

Discussion points

1. Does the neo-dissociation theory seem to you to provide a good account of hypnosis?

2. How could we tell whether hypnotised individuals are simply saying what they think they should say?

Bearing in mind what you know of the mechanisms of demand characteristics and evaluation apprehension, who do you think might be closer to the truth, Hilgard or Spanos?

On the face of it, the illogical responses given by hypnotised participants in trance logic can easily be explained by the neo-dissociation theory. All that needs to be assumed is that different parts of consciousness are being accessed separately during hypnosis, so that hypnotised individuals do not notice the inconsistencies in what they report. There is some doubt whether the reported hallucinations in trance logic really indicate what hypnotised individuals think they are seeing (Spanos, 1982). However, when they are instructed to be honest, hypnotised individuals typically report that their hallucinations are more vivid than those of non-hypnotised individuals (Bowers, 1983).

Evaluation

Hilgard's (1986) neo-dissociation theory provides an account of many of the phenomena observed in the hypnotic state. The notion that hypnosis involves an altered state is a popular one among the public at large. On the face of it, the existence of the hidden observer phenomenon seems to provide good support for the theory.

On the negative side, it has proved rather hard to obtain strong evidence in favour of the theory. Most demonstrations of the hidden observer phenomenon can be explained on the basis that hypnotised individuals report what they think they are expected to say. Most of the other phenomena found in hypnotised individuals can be explained in simple terms that do not involve talking of dissociation and amnesic barriers. However, as is discussed next, there is some evidence to at least suggest that the hypnotic state is a different state of consciousness from the normal waking state.

Non-state theories

Several theorists (e.g. Wagstaff, 1991) have argued that the hypnotic state is not substantially different from the normal waking state. Their theories can be regarded as non-state theories. There are some differences among non-state theorists. However, as Wagstaff (1994, p.993) pointed out *non-state theorists argue that hypnotic phenomena are readily explicable in terms of more mundane psychological concepts, mainly from the areas of social and cognitive psychology, such as attitudes, expectancies, beliefs, compliance, imagination, attention, concentration, distraction, and relaxation.*

Wagstaff (1991) argued that the behaviour of hypnotised individuals can be explained by assuming there are three stages in their response to the hypnotic situation:

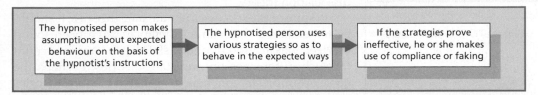

There are two powerful arguments in favour of the non-state approach to hypnosis. First, nearly all of the phenomena associated with hypnosis have also been observed in non-hypnotised individuals. What has generally been used is the "real–simulator" design, in which hypnotised individuals are compared with those simply instructed to pretend to be hypnotised. Another approach is to use a task-motivated control group, in which the participants are told to do their best to experience hypnotic suggestions even though they have not been hypnotised. With either design, those who pretend to be hypnotised can mimic most of the behaviour of hypnotised individuals.

If the hypnotic state is really different from the normal waking state, then we might expect to find that measures of brain activity would differ in the two states. In fact, no differences are generally found (Sarbin & Slayle, 1972). The similarities are especially clear when brain activity under hypnosis is compared against that in states of relaxation or meditation. Council and Kenny (1992) argued that hypnotic procedures and relaxation training produce essentially the same state of consciousness. Their evidence consisted of self-reports of their experiences and thoughts from participants who were in a hypnotised or relaxed state.

Can you see any similarity between a task-motivated control group and a group of people who volunteer to take part in a stage hypnosis show?

There are some exceptions to the general rule that the behaviour of hypnotised individuals is found in non-hypnotised controls. McIlveen (1995) discussed a study in which the participants were either hypnotised or told to behave as if they had been hypnotised. Both groups were told they would touch their forehead with their hand whenever they heard the word "experiment". The highly susceptible hypnotised participants responded appropriately 70% of the time and hypnotised participants in general responded 30% of the time. In contrast, the participants who only pretended to have been hypnotised responded appropriately only 8% of the time.

Gross (1996, p.88) mentioned some other findings suggesting that hypnosis produces an altered state of consciousness. According to him, "touching the skin with a pencil may cause blisters if the participant has been told it is red hot." However, it has proved hard to obtain such findings under controlled laboratory conditions.

Evidence opposed to non-state theories was reported by Kinnunen, Zamanky, and Block (1995). They compared the physiological responses of hypnotised individuals and those pretending to be hypnotised (simulators). Kinnunen et al. (1995) measured skin conductance to assess the level of deception or lying when the participants were asked about their conscious experiences. There was more evidence of deception among the simulators than among the hypnotised participants, presumably because the simulators knew that they were only pretending to have certain experiences. Perhaps of greatest importance, the evidence suggested that hypnotised individuals were not lying about their experiences.

■ Research activity: In small groups, discuss the ways in which people who have never studied hypnosis and have never been hypnotised might answer the following questions:

• What is it like to be hypnotised?
• How do hypnotised people behave?

Without any knowledge of hypnosis, on what do people base their views?

Second, it is generally accepted that hypnotised individuals are highly suggestible. This implies that many phenomena associated with hypnosis can be explained simply as attempts to conform to the wishes of the hypnotist, rather than by bringing in notions of hypnosis as an altered state of consciousness.

Ethical issues: What ethical problems arise in the use of hypnosis by doctors or police officers?

Evaluation

The fact that most of the phenomena associated with hypnotic states can also be found in individuals simply pretending to be hypnotised is strong evidence in favour of non-state theories. It is certainly the case that there are strong similarities between the hypnotic state and the states associated with relaxation or meditation. Non-state theories also have the advantage that they provide simple explanations of hypnotic phenomena that require none of the complex mechanisms identified within neo-dissociation theory.

In spite of the successes of non-state theories, it should be remembered that some differences have been found between waking and hypnotic states. It is hard to account for such differences on non-state theories. Perhaps the most appropriate conclusion is that non-state theories explain most, but not all, of the findings, and that the search for an adequate account of hypnotic phenomena continues.

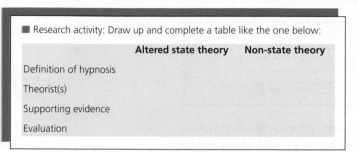

■ Research activity: Draw up and complete a table like the one below:

	Altered state theory	Non-state theory
Definition of hypnosis		
Theorist(s)		
Supporting evidence		
Evaluation		

Applications

Sigmund Freud developed psychoanalysis as a form of therapy at the end of the nineteenth century. He was very concerned to find ways of gaining access to his patients' traumatic and painful memories stored in the unconscious. One method Freud used was dream analysis, which was discussed earlier in the chapter. However, the method he used first was hypnosis. Freud and Breuer (1895) treated a 21-year-old woman called Anna O, who suffered from various neurotic symptoms such as paralysis and nervous coughs. Hypnosis uncovered a repressed memory of Anna hearing the sound of dance music coming from a nearby house as she was nursing her dying father, and her guilty feeling that she would rather be dancing than looking after her father. Her nervous coughing disappeared after that repressed memory reappeared.

In spite of Freud's initial enthusiasm for hypnosis, he gradually started to make more use of dream analysis and of free association in therapy. Why did he desert hypnosis? One reason was because he found that it was very hard to hypnotise many of his patients. Another reason was because the memories produced under hypnosis were often unreliable, in the sense that it was not clear that the events remembered had actually happened.

Memory retrieval

Another area in which hypnosis has been applied is that of criminal justice. The media have reported numerous cases in which hypnosis seems to have been remarkably effective in bringing forgotten memories to light. For example, the Israeli National Police Force and many other police forces have used hypnosis to collect relevant evidence from eyewitnesses about matters such as car number plates and the physical features of wanted criminals. The term **hypermnesia** has been used to refer to the enhanced memory allegedly created by hypnosis.

Does hypermnesia really exist? In general terms, the hypnotic method is nothing like as effective in enhancing memory as has been claimed. The hypnotised individual is less cautious than normal in his or her reported memories. For example, hypnotised individuals will confidently "recall" events from the future! However, the reduced cautiousness of the hypnotised individual means that some genuine memories that could not otherwise be recalled come to light under hypnosis. The obvious problem is to tell which of the memories reported by hypnotised individuals are genuine and which are false.

Relevant evidence was reported by Putnam (1979). He showed people a videotape of an accident involving a car and a bicycle. They were then asked a series of questions, some of which contained misleading information. Some of the participants were asked these questions while hypnotised, whereas others were not hypnotised. The hypnotised participants made more errors in their answers than did

Putnam (1979) used a videotape of scenes like this to test the memory of eyewitnesses. He asked hypnotised and non-hypnotised participants about their memories of the accident and the events leading up to it, and found that the hypnotised individuals made more errors in their answers than those who had not been hypnotised. The hypnotised people were also more suggestible—i.e. giving positive answers to misleading questions.

the non-hypnotised ones, and this was especially the case with the misleading questions. These findings led Putnam (1979, p.444) to conclude that participants are "more suggestible in the hypnotic state and are, therefore, more easily influenced by the leading questions."

Hypnosis has been used to assess the validity of **false memory syndrome**, in which adults mistakenly claim to have had traumatic experiences (e.g. sexual abuse) during childhood. In recent unpublished work, Green and Lynn asked hypnotised individuals whether they had heard any loud noises during a good night's sleep. In fact, practically none of them had actually heard a loud noise. Some of the participants were warned that hypnosis can cause people to misremember what has happened, whereas the others were not. Afterwards, when they were no longer hypnotised, the participants were asked whether they had heard a loud noise. Of those who had not been warned, 44% reported hearing a loud noise; in contrast, only 28% of those warned did so. These findings suggest that false memories can be planted in the mind, and that specific warnings can reduce the likelihood of such "memories" occurring.

How safe do you think it would be to convict someone of a crime on the basis of evidence from a witness under hypnosis?

PERSONAL REFLECTIONS

- Issues concerning consciousness and states of awareness are among the most important in psychology, but they are very difficult to resolve. The central problem is that we generally have to rely on an individual's reports of his or her state of awareness, since we lack any proper independent evidence. However, one of my dreams is that brain-scanning techniques will develop to the point at which they can supply crucial evidence about an individual's current state of awareness.

SUMMARY

Circadian rhythms (e.g. sleep–waking cycle) have a cycle of about 24 hours. Infradian rhythms (e.g. menstrual cycle) have a cycle of more than one day, and ultradian rhythms (e.g. sleep) have a cycle of less than a day. The sleep–waking cycle is largely endogenous, but it also depends on external events or zeitgebers. We experience problems when there is a conflict between our endogenous sleep–waking cycle and zeitgebers; examples are jet lag and shiftwork. Circannual rhythms are involved in species that hibernate, and in seasonal affective disorder. There is a psychological

Bodily rhythms

KEY TERM
False memory syndrome: mistaken memories of patients that they have had traumatic experiences during childhood.

circadian rhythm, with task performance typically peaking in the late morning. There are detectable patterns of mood change through the menstrual cycle (e.g. pre-menstrual tension).

Sleep

Physiological measures such as the EEG, EOG, and EMG have indicated that there are five stages of sleep. Of particular importance are Stage 4 sleep (which is slow-wave and deep) and Stage 5 or REM sleep, during which most dreaming occurs. Sleep deprivation typically produces few physiological effects. However, it can impair performance on monotonous tasks, lead to micro-sleep, and produce some hallucinations and delusions. According to recovery or restoration theories, sleep permits the restoration of tissue and energy saving. In support, mammalian species with high metabolic rate tend to have more sleep than those with low metabolic rate. According to adaptive or evolutionary theories, sleeping behaviour is determined by the need to adapt to environmental threats (e.g. predators). Sleep seems to be essential rather than merely desirable, thus supporting recovery or restoration theories.

Dreaming

Dreaming occurs mainly during REM sleep. Adults dream about two hours per night, but forget more than 95% of their dreams. Dreams that are normally forgotten tend to be less strange than those normally remembered. According to Freud's wish-fulfilment theory, dreams represent the fulfilment of mainly repressed desires. This produces major differences between the dream information consciously remembered (the manifest content) and the information in the dream itself (the latent content). Frightening dreams do not seem to involve wish fulfilment, and the methods used to identify the latent content of a dream are dubious. According to the activation-synthesis theory of Hobson and McCarley, there is a high level of essentially random brain activation during REM sleep. Dreamers try to make sense of their activation by synthesising or combining the information contained in the bursts of neural activity. The activation-synthesis theory has the advantage of being based on detailed information about brain processes, but the disadvantage that it does not explain adequately the existence of coherent dreams. According to Crick and Mitchison's reverse-learning or unlearning theory, the main function of dreaming is to eliminate useless information stored in the brain and so free up space in the cortex. It is hard in this theory to account for meaningful dreams. According to cognitive theories, dreams express current concerns. It is certainly true of many dreams, but other dreams do not seem to reflect the dreamer's concerns or they are simply meaningless.

Consciousness

There is a higher level of consciousness involving self-awareness and self-reflection, and a lower level of consciousness used in complex learning and reasoning. The higher level is located in the neo-cortex, whereas the lower level is in the cortex and limbic system. The contents of consciousness are often determined by prior attentional processes. The higher level of consciousness is used to monitor and control behaviour, and to allow behavioural flexibility. Freud emphasised the limitations of consciousness, and this general view is supported by research on brain-damaged patients (e.g. those with blindsight). Schizophrenics have deficits in consciousness based on a poor ability to monitor their own intended actions. Patients with dissociative identity disorder have multiple personalities, but are only consciously aware of one personality at any given time.

Hypnosis

The passive and sleeplike hypnotic state is produced by the hypnotist making a series of suggestions designed to relax the individual concerned. Individuals who are fantasy-prone, high on absorption, and willing to accept orders tend to be most susceptible to hypnosis. EEG recordings indicate that the hypnotic state does not resemble sleep. Deeply hypnotised individuals show a range of interesting phenomena, including hypnotic amnesia, hypnotic analgesia, and trance logic. According to Hilgard's neo-dissociation theory, hypnotic phenomena occur because there is a dissociation or separating off of one part of the body's system from the rest by means of amnesic barriers. This theory provides an account of many of the phenomena observed in the hypnotic state, but most of these phenomena can be explained in simpler terms. Other theorists argue that the hypnotic state does not differ very much from the normal waking state. According to this non-state approach, hypnotised individuals make assumptions about their expected behaviour on the basis of the hypnotist's instructions, and they try to behave as expected. If need be, they resort to compliance or faking.

FURTHER READING

The topics dealt with in this chapter are analysed in an accessible way in J.P.J. Pinel (1997), *Biopsychology (3rd Edn.)*, Boston: Allyn & Bacon. Some of the key aspects of awareness are discussed by N.R. Carlson (1994), *Physiology of behaviour (5th Edn.)*, Boston: Allyn & Bacon. There is a good review of work on hypnosis by G.F. Wagstaff (1994), Hypnosis, in A.M. Colman (Ed.), *Companion encyclopedia of psychology, Vol. 2*, London: Routledge.

REVISION QUESTIONS

1	Examine and assess research into physiological factors involved with *either* bodily rhythms *or* states of awareness.	(24 marks)
2	Compare and contrast *two* theories of sleep.	(24 marks)
3a	Explain what psychologists mean by the term hypnosis.	(6 marks)
3b	Describe and analyse research studies that have been carried out into hypnosis.	(18 marks)

- **Motivation**
  What is it that starts, steers, and then stops our behaviour?

Theories of hunger
Rogers and Blundell's study of the positive-incentive theory of hunger
Theories of thirst
McDougall's instinct theory of motivation
Murray's need-press theory
Hull's drive-reduction theory
Maslow's hierarchy of needs
Latham and Yuki's study on goal theory

- **Emotion**
  The mechanisms and processes behind our feelings.

The Papez–MacLean limbic model
Brain surgery and emotion
James–Lange theory of emotion
Cannon–Bard theory
Schacter and Singer's cognitive labelling theory
Lazarus's cognitive appraisal theory
Parkinson's four-factor theory

- **Stress**
  The sources and effects of stress in our lives and how to deal with them.

Selye's general adaptation syndrome
Holmes and Rahe's Social Readjustment Rating Scale
Friedman and Rosenman's Type A study
Stress and the immune system
Biofeedback, drug treatment, and social support
Meichenbaum's stress inoculation training
Endler and Parker's multidimensional coping inventory

6

Motivation, Emotion, and Stress

This chapter is concerned with key areas of psychology: motivation; emotion; and stress. The study of motivation concerns the issue of *why* people behave in the ways they do. We can only really understand someone else when we begin to appreciate the motivational forces driving their behaviour. Emotion is also a vital part of psychology. Imagine for a moment how empty your life would be if you never experienced positive feelings of love, joy, and happiness. Even negative emotions such as anxiety and anger have their uses. For example, we usually become anxious when a situation may be dangerous, so the experience of anxiety warns us to be on our guard.

What about stress? If the media are to be believed, the pressures of everyday life are so great that most of us are highly stressed nearly all the time. No-one denies that millions of people suffer stress. However, people may have become too concerned about it. For example, some people who spend a lot of money on the National Lottery have received stress counselling because their failure to win is making them poor. In addition, many of those who have won fortunes on the National Lottery have also received stress counselling because of the pressures produced by having millions of pounds!

Motivation

Motivation is highly relevant to the following:

- Direction of behaviour: the goal or goals being pursued.
- Intensity of behaviour: the amount of effort, concentration, and so on, invested in behaviour.
- Persistence of behaviour: the extent to which a goal is pursued until it is reached.

A definition including these ingredients was put forward by Taylor et al. (1982, p.160):

> *Motivation ... is generally conceived of by psychologists in terms of a process, or a series of processes, which somehow starts, steers, sustains and finally stops a goal-directed sequence of behaviour.*

If someone is very hungry, we would expect their behaviour to be directed towards the goals of finding and eating food, we would expect them to put in much effort, and we would expect them to continue looking for food until they found some.

A key notion in the biopsychological approach to motivation is that of a regulatory mechanism maintaining some internal characteristic at a fairly constant level in spite of external variability. This is known as **homeostasis** (see Chapter 3). For example, humans

KEY TERM
Homeostasis: the process of maintaining a reasonably constant internal environment.

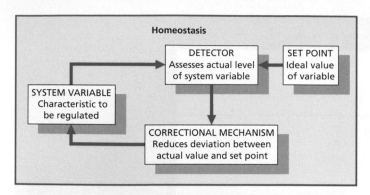

Homeostasis

SYSTEM VARIABLE
Characteristic to
be regulated

DETECTOR
Assesses actual level
of system variable

SET POINT
Ideal value
of variable

CORRECTIONAL MECHANISM
Reduces deviation between
actual value and set point

Standardised eating times are the norm, with work and social schedules being planned around them.

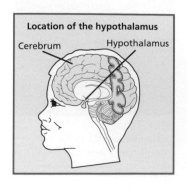

Location of the hypothalamus

Cerebrum   Hypothalamus

possess a regulatory mechanism that maintains our internal bodily temperature at a given level even when there are very large variations in external temperature. Eating and drinking behaviour both depend on regulatory mechanisms to some extent. As was discussed in Chapter 3, regulatory mechanisms involve a system variable (the characteristic to be regulated), a set point (the ideal value for the system variable), a detector that assesses the actual value of the system variable, and a correctional mechanism that reduces any deviation between the actual value and the set point.

Hunger

Most people's body weight changes little over time. Thus, they are able to regulate or control their body weight, even though it may be at a weight above the ideal. What factors determine when we start and stop eating? Social and cultural factors are very important in relatively affluent parts of the world. For example, people often eat because it is the normal time for lunch or dinner, or because other people are eating. However, physiological factors are also important, and it is to such factors that we now turn.

Hypothalamic theory

Early research on animals suggested that the hypothalamus plays a major role in regulating eating behaviour. It was claimed (e.g. Anand & Brobeck, 1951) that the lateral nucleus of the hypothalamus is a feeding centre, which is responsible for initiating food intake. In contrast, the ventromedial nucleus of the hypothalamus is a satiety centre, which causes eating to stop.

A lesion (small cut) in the feeding centre should reduce feeding, whereas a lesion in the satiety centre should lead to increased feeding. Anand and Brobeck found that lesions to the lateral nucleus stopped rats from eating, so they lost weight rapidly. Hetherington and Ranson (1942) observed the effects of lesions to the ventromedial nucleus. The rats started to eat much more than they had done previously, and their weight often doubled as a result.

Hoebel and Teitelbaum (1966) found that lesions to the ventromedial nucleus were followed by two phases: the dynamic and the static. Rats ate many times the normal amount of food during the dynamic phase, which usually lasted between four and twelve weeks. During the subsequent static phase, however, there was no further increase in body weight, with food consumption being regulated to maintain the weight reached at the end of the dynamic phase.

The hypothalamic theory of hunger is no longer accepted. Lesions to the lateral hypothalamus lead to reduced drinking as well as to reduced eating, and they also make animals generally unresponsive to stimuli (Pinel, 1997). Therefore, it cannot simply be regarded as a feeding centre.

The ventromedial hypothalamus is not a satiety centre for various reasons. First, lesions to the ventromedial hypothalamus typically damage other related areas. Damage to some of these areas (e.g. the ventral noradrenergic bundle; the paraventricular nuclei) can also cause obesity. Second, rats with lesions in the ventromedial hypothalamus become obese, but do not seem very hungry in some ways. For example, lesioned rats are more willing than control rats to eat tasty food, but they will not work as hard as controls to gain access to it (Teitelbaum, 1957). Third, a major effect of lesions to the ventromedial hypothalamus is to increase body fat. Han, Feng, and Kuo (1972) found that lesioned rats gained more body fat than control rats given the same amount of food. Lesioned animals eat a lot because the food they eat goes into body fat and contributes relatively little to their immediate energy needs.

Glucostatic theory

The hypothalamic theory did not provide a detailed account of the kinds of information used by the hypothalamus to produce eating behaviour or its cessation. Mayer (1955) put forward the glucostatic theory to fill this gap. According to this theory, there are specialised neurons known as glucostats, which measure the level of blood glucose. Glucostats produce high rates of firing when the availability of glucose is low, and these high rates of firing result in hunger.

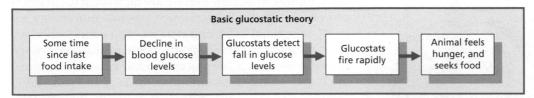

Basic glucostatic theory

Some time since last food intake → Decline in blood glucose levels → Glucostats detect fall in glucose levels → Glucostats fire rapidly → Animal feels hunger, and seeks food

Evidence supporting the glucostatic theory was reviewed by Campfield and Smith (1990). There is generally a decline in blood glucose levels shortly before rats start eating, but this does not prove that falling glucose levels cause eating behaviour. However, Campfield and Smith discussed other studies in which a small injection of glucose into rats' veins delayed eating, provided that this was done when blood glucose levels were going down. The overall evidence is somewhat inconsistent. For example, eating behaviour is often unaffected even by large infusions of glucose (see Pinel, 1997).

Where are the glucostats or glucose-sensitive receptors located? They are found in the brain and in the liver (Carlson, 1994). For example, Russek (1971) injected a dog with glucose either into the jugular vein of the neck or directly into the liver. Glucose injected into the jugular vein did not affect the dog's food intake, whereas glucose injected into the liver prevented eating for several hours.

So far we have ignored the role of insulin. Blood glucose levels fall abruptly shortly before animals start eating because of an immediately preceding 50% increase in insulin secretion. An injection increasing insulin secretion produced a fall in glucose levels and eating behaviour (Campfield & Smith, 1990). The importance of insulin was also shown by Woods et al. (1979). Regular infusions of insulin into the lateral ventricles of baboons produced a 70% reduction in their food intake.

Lipostatic theory

Hunger can be produced by low levels of glucose. Glucose is one of the major nutrients (substances providing nourishment), but there are two others: lipids or fatty acids, and amino acids. According to the lipostatic hypothesis (e.g. Nisbett, 1972), eating behaviour is initiated when the hypothalamus receives information that the levels of lipids or fatty acids are low.

Lipoprivation (depriving cells of lipids) causes hunger, especially when combined with glucoprivation (depriving cells of glucose). Friedman, Tordoff, and Ramirez (1986) gave rats moderate doses of chemicals producing either lipoprivation or glucoprivation. There was a marked increase in food intake when both chemicals were given together, but much smaller effects when only one chemical was used.

Where are the receptors that detect low levels of lipids or fatty acids? Ritter and Taylor (1990) found that hunger produced by a lack of fatty acids was eliminated by cutting the vagus nerve as it enters the abdominal cavity. This suggests that there are lipid-sensitive receptors in or close to the abdominal cavity.

Cessation of eating

Why do we stop eating? There are social pressures to eat meals of a certain size, but there are also internal physiological processes. Deutsch and Gonzalez (1980) found that the stomach plays an important role. They operated on rats to insert an inflatable cuff that

What factors other than social or cultural ones might motivate you to eat?

could be used to prevent food from leaving the stomach. When five millilitres of the stomach contents were removed artificially, the rats consumed almost exactly five millilitres more of the liquid diet in order to compensate for what had been lost.

There is other strong evidence that the stomach plays a role. Receptors in the gastrointestinal tract respond to ingested food by causing the release of peptides. Several of these peptides send satiety signals to the brain and lead to a cessation of eating. Relevant evidence was reported by Gibbs, Young, and Smith (1973). They injected the peptide cholecystokinin into hungry rats, and found that this led to reduced eating. Similar findings have been obtained for several other peptides.

The Prince Regent: a well-known glutton.

Evaluation

It is tempting to assume that we are motivated to eat when our energy level falls significantly below our energy set point or optimal level, and that we stop eating when we have returned to our set point. Some of the theories we have discussed (e.g. the glucostatic and lipostatic theories) are based on those assumptions. In fact, as Pinel (1997) argued, the set-point approach with its homeostatic emphasis is inadequate. When most people in Western societies eat meals, they have no significant physiological or energy deficits (e.g. glucose levels; fat deposits). For most of us, hunger has more to do with social and cultural factors (e.g. expected mealtimes) than it has with basic physiological processes.

Studies on sham feeding provide strong evidence against homeostatic theories. In these studies, animals are operated on so that the food they eat passes along a tube and out of the body rather than going to the stomach. In spite of the fact that the animals (e.g. rats) are not obtaining any energy from their food, they initially eat only the amount of their usual diet that they have been used to eating (Weingarten & Kulikovsky, 1989). Such findings indicate that eating behaviour is only very imperfectly controlled by restoring energy levels.

Positive-incentive theory

Positive-incentive theory (e.g. Rolls & Rolls, 1982) is more in line with the evidence than is the set-point or homeostatic approach. According to positive-incentive theory, hunger levels are determined by the anticipated pleasure of eating. Numerous factors influence the level of anticipated pleasure; they include the anticipated flavour of the food, the length of time since the last meal, the time of day with respect to normal mealtimes, blood glucose levels, and so on. In other words, basic physiological processes and social factors both contribute to our feelings of hunger.

Strong support for positive-incentive theory was reported by Rogers and Blundell (1980). They compared the eating behaviour of rats offered their normal diet and those offered what is known as a cafeteria diet, which consists of a variety of palatable foods. In this study, the rats on a cafeteria diet were offered bread and chocolate in addition to their normal diet.

What were the findings? The rats given the cafeteria diet had an average increase of 84% in their daily calorie intake. After 120 days on their new diet, these rats showed an average increase of 49% in their body weight. These findings (although based only on rats) may help to explain why there has been a dramatic increase in the number of very fat or obese people in the Western world. They suggest that an important part of the explanation is that the ready availability of foods that satisfy our

Cafeteria diet

preferences for fatty, sweet, and salty tastes encourages us to eat more than we should, as would be expected on positive-incentive theory. In contrast, set-point or homeostatic theory cannot readily explain why so many people become obese.

Discussion points

1. Consider which aspects of our eating behaviour are explained by positive-incentive theory. For example, the kinds of tastes associated with desserts are very different from those associated with main courses.
2. Do you feel that positive-incentive theory has relevance for your patterns of eating?

Thirst

Various theories of thirst have been proposed. About one-third of the water in the human body is found outside cells and so is extracellular, with the remaining two-thirds being inside cells and so intracellular. Water (whether inside or outside cells) contains dissolved substances, of which the most important is sodium or salt. Water containing many substances is said to have high osmotic pressure, whereas water with few substances has low osmotic pressure.

The cell membrane is semi-permeable. This means that water can pass through it, but not the dissolved substances in the water. When there is water on both sides of a semi-permeable membrane, then water in the solution having the lower osmotic pressure will pass through to the solution having the higher osmotic pressure. This continues until the osmotic pressure inside and outside the cells is the same; the process involved is known as osmosis. Water deficits can occur either intracellularly or extracellularly. Rolls, Wood, and Rolls (1980) found in various species that intracellular deficits have more effect on drinking behaviour. When they eliminated the intracellular deficit in water-deprived animals by injections, this reduced the amount of drinking by 75%. In contrast, eliminating the extracellular deficit reduced drinking by only about 15%.

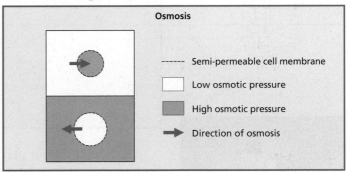

There are two major ways in which water deprivation leads to thirst. First, water deprivation produces a greater concentration of sodium in the extracellular water than in the intracellular water. This leads via osmosis to water leaving the cells. These changes are detected within the lateral preoptic area of the hypothalamus by osmoreceptors. This leads to thirst *directly* by activating the relevant neural circuits. It also leads *indirectly* to thirst. Antidiuretic hormone is released, leading to conservation of the body's water supplies and feelings of thirst.

Second, water deprivation results in a reduction in blood volume. Blood-flow receptors detect this reduction, and they trigger kidney function directly. Baroreceptors or blood pressure receptors in the wall of the heart also detect reduced blood volume, and they affect the functioning of the kidneys by increasing the release of antidiuretic hormone. Antidiuretic hormone reduces the amount of urine produced in the kidneys, and it also leads to the release of the hormone renin. In turn, renin leads to the formation of the peptide hormone angiotensin II in the blood. Angiotensin II produces increased blood pressure and also leads to the release of the hormone aldosterone. Aldosterone leads the kidneys to reabsorb sodium, which has the effect of preventing additional decreases in blood volume.

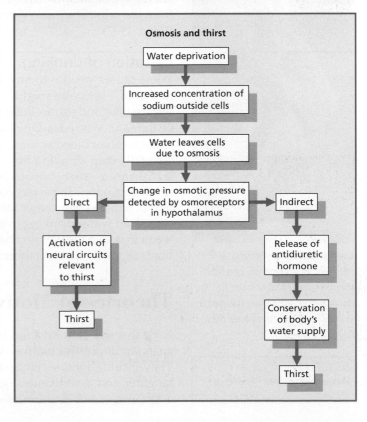

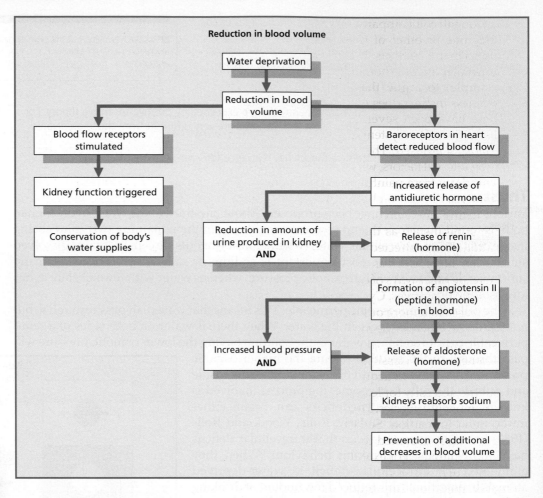

Reduction in blood volume

Water deprivation

Reduction in blood volume

Blood flow receptors stimulated

Baroreceptors in heart detect reduced blood flow

Kidney function triggered

Increased release of antidiuretic hormone

Conservation of body's water supplies

Reduction in amount of urine produced in kidney
AND

Release of renin (hormone)

Formation of angiotensin II (peptide hormone) in blood

Increased blood pressure
AND

Release of aldosterone (hormone)

Kidneys reabsorb sodium

Prevention of additional decreases in blood volume

The hypothalamus plays a key role in thirst and drinking behaviour. Lesions of the lateral hypothalamus have been found to eliminate drinking in response to water loss from the cells. They also eliminate drinking in response to a reduction in blood volume (Pinel, 1997).

Cessation of drinking

What causes people to stop drinking water? Considerations of homeostasis and the notion of a set point might lead to the assumption that people keep drinking until the intracellular and extracellular water levels are restored to normality. However, that cannot be the case. Much drinking in humans occurs in the absence of any significant deficits in water levels or blood volume. In addition, people who do drink in response to fluid deficits generally stop drinking before the water has had time to be absorbed into the body. In fact, there are satiety (satisfaction) receptors in the mouth and in the intestines which cause drinking to stop. These receptors become satiated especially rapidly when the taste of the liquid remains the same; this is known as sensory-specific satiety. Rolls et al. (1980) compared water drinking in rats who were offered either water on its own or flavoured water in which the flavour changed frequently. Rats in the latter group drank almost three times as much water as those in the former group.

Theories of Motivation

Early theories of motivation attached great importance to the notion of **instinct**, which is an innate impulse or motive. According to McDougall (1912), there are numerous instincts. They include food-seeking, sex, curiosity, fear, parental protectiveness, disgust, anger, laughter, self-assertiveness, gregariousness, acquisitiveness, rest, migration, appeal for assistance, comfort, submissiveness, and constructiveness.

Even people experiencing severe thirst will stop drinking, and feel that they have had enough to drink, before their body has had a chance to absorb the water they have consumed.

KEY TERM
Instinct: an innate impulse or motive.

McDougall could apparently account for all behaviour by attributing it to the attempt to satisfy one or other of these instincts. However, it does not make much sense to identify so many instincts. It is improbable that constructiveness or submissiveness are fundamental motives. Another problem is that there is a great danger of circular argument. For example, to argue that someone is being self-assertive because of their self-assertiveness instinct does not really explain their behaviour!

There have been several attempts since McDougall to classify or categorise our various motives. One system is based on the distinction between motives that are *internally* and *externally* aroused. The motives for food, water, sleep, and elimination all depend largely on internal factors, whereas motives such as a desire to avoid extreme temperatures or to withdraw from painful stimulation are triggered off by external stimuli. However, most motives depend on both internal and external factors. For example, although the goal of eating often involves internal physiological conditions, it is also affected by external stimuli such as the sight of appetising food. Another clear example is sexual motivation. This is affected by sex hormones in the bloodstream, but it is also influenced by external factors such as the availability of an attractive and willing partner.

There are other ways of categorising motives. One way is to categorise them into cyclic and non-cyclic motives. Cyclic motives are those where the motivational force increases and decreases in a more or less regular way over time. The needs to sleep and to eat are cylic motives, whereas the motive to avoid painful stimulation is not. Cyclic motives tend to be internally aroused, whereas non-cyclic motives are externally aroused.

Can you think of any other motives that are cyclic or non-cyclic?

Another way of classifying motives is into primary or basic and secondary or acquired. Primary motives appear without the necessity for learning, and are found in nearly every member of a species. They include the needs for food, drink, and elimination. Secondary motives are learned, and it is usually assumed that their existence owes much to primary motives. For example, many people regard the acquisition of money as an important goal in its own right. However, the initial importance of money is simply as a way of being able to satisfy primary motives, such as those for food and drink.

■ Research activity: How would you categorise the possible motives for the following behaviours?

- Studying for exams
- Working for money
- Voluntary work
- Going to a party
- Getting married
- Having children

Need-press theory

Henry Murray (1938) argued in his need-press theory that we have 20 manifest needs. These needs include dominance, achievement, affiliation, play, sex, aggression, and nurturance. Each need has a desire or intended effect, feelings, and actions associated with it. For example, the dominance need involves the desire to control or influence other people, feelings of confidence, and actions designed to influence and persuade others. In order to understand someone's behaviour, we have to take account of **press**, which consists of those features of the environment relevant to need-satisfaction. For example, the need for dominance can only be satisfied when there are other people around who are willing to be influenced.

How can needs be measured? The Thematic Apperception Test was developed by Murray (Morgan & Murray, 1935). It consists of a number of pictures (e.g. a young man turned away from an older woman). The individual taking the test is told to say what is happening in the picture, what led up to the situation, and what will

■ Research activity: Using the example of a picture of a young man turned away from an older woman, devise some possible explanations that illustrate the range of motives people might demonstrate in the Thematic Apperception Test.

happen subsequently. These stories are usually interpreted in a rather flexible and subjective fashion to identify the individual's underlying motives and conflicts. Murray (1938, p.529) developed the Thematic Apperception Test as part of "an attempt to discover the covert (inhibited) and unconscious (partially repressed) tendencies of normal persons."

McClelland, who worked with Murray, developed a measure of need for achievement based on the ways in which pictures were interpreted. Need for achievement was defined

KEY TERM
Press: those environmental characteristics that are relevant to need-satisfaction.

as a need to do things better or to surpass standards of excellence. Those who score highly on need for achievement tend to prefer moderately difficult tasks (which provide a challenge) to ones that are either very easy or very hard (Koestner & McClelland, 1990). They also prefer work activities where they are responsible for the outcome. Evidence for the validity of measures of need for achievement was discussed by Koestner and McClelland (1990). Societies high on need for achievement had higher levels of productivity and economic growth than societies low on need for achievement.

McClelland et al. (1953) carried out an interesting cross-cultural study on need for achievement. They collected the folk tales of eight Native American cultures and rated them for achievement motivation. They also rated the cultures for the amount of training in independence received by the children. The level of need for achievement was much higher in cultures that encouraged independence.

Cross-cultural issues: How do you think need for achievement might relate to collectivistic and individualistic cultures?

Evaluation

The approach to motivation adopted by Murray and by McClelland is concerned with important needs. Need for achievement has been found to predict job success, and to account for some of the differences among cultures. On the negative side, the Thematic Apperception Test and the measures of need for achievement developed by McClelland have fairly low reliability and validity. Thus, they do not measure needs consistently and do not predict behaviour very accurately. Many of the needs identified by Murray have not been studied in detail, and so it is hard to evaluate the overall success of the need-press theory.

Drive theories

Woodworth (1918) introduced the notion of **drives**, by which he meant the motivational forces that cause individuals to be active and to strive for certain goals. One of the first drive theories of motivation was homeostatic drive theory. This theory was based on the notion of homeostasis, which was used by Cannon (1929) to refer to the processes by which we maintain a reasonably constant internal environment. As we have seen, there are regulatory or homeostatic mechanisms involved in hunger and thirst. However, it is not at all clear that homeostatic drive theory can account for other forms of motivation. Before evaluating homeostatic drive theory, however, we will consider a related type of drive theory.

Hull (1943) put forward drive-reduction theory, in which he argued that there is an important distinction between needs and drives. Needs are essentially physiological in nature; they include hunger, water, and so on. In contrast, drives are less physiological and more psychological, and they are based on needs.

Hull's approach was called drive-reduction theory because it was assumed that behaviour is motivated by the attempt to reduce one or more drives. Drive reduction is reinforcing or rewarding, so that animals and humans learn to behave in ways that produce drive reduction. For example, if a young child learns that eating biscuits from a jar in the kitchen reduces hunger drive, then he or she will show an increased tendency to return to the biscuit jar when hungry.

If one of our drives is anxiety, and we are motivated to reduce it, what types of behaviour would this explain?

A central assumption in drive-reduction theory was that an individual's behaviour in a given situation is determined by drive or motivation, and by what he or she has learned (habits). This led to the equation that the tendency to respond = drive × habit. Hull later added further assumptions about the role of incentives and other factors. However, he still maintained that behaviour depends mainly on a combination of motivation (drive) and learning (habit).

Evaluation

Homeostatic drive theory can account for some aspects of hunger and thirst. However, the whole drive theory approach is inadequate. Why is this so? First, there are many exceptions to the notion that all behaviour is directed towards drive reduction. Much human behaviour is based on curiosity, and it is hard to regard curiosity as involving the reduction of either a drive or a need. Rats who receive electrical stimulation of a particular part of the brain (the hypothalamus) in return for pressing a lever will do so thousands of times an hour for several hours (Olds & Milner, 1954). Again, no physiological need is reduced by this behaviour.

Second, the theoretical approach was based largely on studies with other species, especially rats. It is possible (if unlikely) that rats, dogs, and other species are largely motivated to reduce physiological needs and drives. However, it is improbable that this is true of humans. For example, the humanistic psychologist Maslow argued that humans are motivated in part by cognitive needs (such as curiosity), aesthetic or artistic needs, and the need for self-actualisation (see next section). Whether or not one agrees with the humanistic approach, the forces that motivate humans are much more numerous than those included in drive theories.

Third, there is very little recognition in drive theories that cognitive factors play an important role in human motivation. Some theorists (e.g. Locke, 1968) have argued that motivation depends in large measure on the goals we set. For example, someone who is firmly committed to obtaining a B grade in A-level psychology is likely to be more motivated (and will work harder) than someone who is only concerned about passing. This aspect of motivation was ignored by Cannon and by Hull.

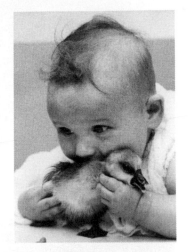

Food-seeking or curiosity?

Abraham Maslow

According to the humanistic psychologist Abraham Maslow (1954, 1970), most theories of motivation are very limited. They deal with basic physiological needs such as hunger and thirst, or with the need to avoid anxiety. However, such theories generally omit many important needs relating to personal growth. Maslow addressed these issues by putting forward a theory based on a *hierarchy of needs* (see Chapter 2). Physiological needs or requirements, including those for food and drink, are at the bottom level of the hierarchy, with safety needs immediately above them. In the middle of the hierarchy are needs for affection and intimacy. Above that level, there is the need for esteem, with the need for self-actualisation (or fulfilling one's potential) at the top of the hierarchy.

Maslow regarded all the needs towards the bottom of the hierarchy as deficiency needs, because they are designed to reduce inadequacies or deficiencies. Needs towards the top of the hierarchy (e.g. self-actualisation) represent growth needs, and are designed to promote personal growth. The key notion of self-actualisation was described as follows by Maslow (1954):

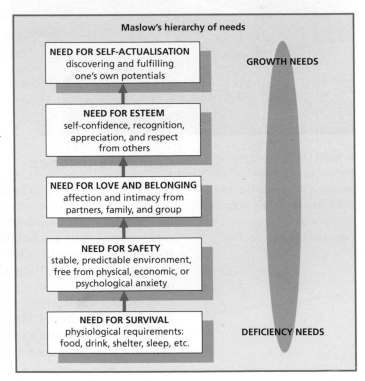

Maslow's hierarchy of needs

NEED FOR SELF-ACTUALISATION
discovering and fulfilling one's own potentials

NEED FOR ESTEEM
self-confidence, recognition, appreciation, and respect from others

NEED FOR LOVE AND BELONGING
affection and intimacy from partners, family, and group

NEED FOR SAFETY
stable, predictable environment, free from physical, economic, or psychological anxiety

NEED FOR SURVIVAL
physiological requirements: food, drink, shelter, sleep, etc.

GROWTH NEEDS

DEFICIENCY NEEDS

A musician must make music, an artist must paint, a poet must write, if he is to be ultimately at peace with himself. What a man can be, he must be. This need we may call self-actualisation.

According to Maslow (1954, 1970), people only focus on their growth needs after their deficiency needs have been met. An implication of this view is that fewer people manage to satisfy their growth needs than to satisfy their deficiency needs. Maslow (1970) estimated that Americans satisfy about 85% of their physiological needs, 70% of their safety needs, 50% of their belongingness and love needs, 40% of their self-esteem needs, and only 10% of their self-actualisation needs.

Aronoff (1967) tested the prediction that higher needs will only emerge when lower needs are satisfied. He compared fishermen and cane cutters in the British West Indies. Fishermen worked on their own. They generally earned more than cane cutters, who worked in groups. Cane cutting was a more secure job, because the rewards fluctuated much less than for fishermen, and because cane cutters were paid

Can you name some people who, in your opinion, have become self-actualised?

Aronoff (1967) found that most West Indian fishermen had their security and esteem needs met, and this enabled them to handle an income and lifestyle that was less predictable than cane cutting.

even when unwell. According to Maslow's theory, it should be mainly those whose security and esteem needs were met who chose the more challenging and responsible job of fisherman. This prediction was confirmed by Aronoff (1967).

Evaluation

The greatest strength of Maslow's approach to motivation is that it is more comprehensive than other approaches. More specifically, the needs for self-actualisation and for esteem seem very important, but were not included in most earlier theories of motivation. However, the notion of self-actualisation is vague, and it has proved hard to develop good ways of measuring it. Maslow may have been overly optimistic in his assumption that everyone has the potential to become a self-actualiser. The fact that the average British person spends 25 hours a week watching television suggests that there are many people whose motivation for personal growth is not enormous! Another limitation is that the influence of the environment in facilitating the development of self-actualisation is not emphasised enough. In fact, individuals who become self-actualised usually owe much to environmental factors such as schooling, training, supportive parents, and so on.

Cognitive theories

How does motivation in humans differ from motivation in other species? Humans are often motivated by long-term goals (e.g. passing examinations), whereas other species typically focus on short-term goals (e.g. finding food). This aspect of human motivation was recognised by Locke (1968, p.159). According to his goal theory, the key factor in motivation is the goal. Locke (1968) defined the goal as "what the individual is consciously trying to do." The goal that someone has set himself or herself can be assessed by direct questioning.

How does goal setting relate to performance? According to Locke (1968, p.162), there is a straightforward relationship between goal difficulty and performance: "the harder the goal the higher the level of performance." This happens because people try harder when difficult goals are set.

Latham and Yukl

Evidence supporting goal theory was reported by Latham and Yukl (1975). They divided workers whose job was cutting and transporting wood into three categories:

1. Workers simply instructed to "do your best" (do-your-best groups).
2. Groups assigned to a specific hard goal in terms of hundreds of cubic feet of wood per week (assigned groups).
3. Groups in which everyone participated in setting a specific hard production goal (participative groups).

Latham and Yukl found that the do-your-best groups set the easiest goals, and so were predicted to have the poorest performance. In contrast, the participative groups set the hardest goals, and so should have performed the best. As predicted, the do-your-best groups averaged 46 cubic feet of wood per hour; the assigned groups averaged 53 cubic feet; and the participative groups averaged 56 cubic feet. These differences may not seem very large. However, the work performance of the participative groups was almost 22%

greater than that of the do-your-best groups, and any company would be delighted to increase the productivity of its workers by 22%!

Discussion points

1. Why do you think that goal theory is perhaps the most widely used theory of motivation in occupational psychology?

2. What do you think are the weaknesses of Locke's approach (see later for some of my thoughts)?

Goal theory has also been applied to the effects of incentive on performance. According to Locke et al. (1968, p.104), "Incentives such as money should affect action only if and to the extent that they affect the individual's goals and intentions." Support for this hypothesis was obtained by Farr (1976) in a study on speed of card sorting. Providing financial incentives led to the setting of much higher goals and to increased sorting speed.

Locke et al. (1981) reviewed the evidence on goal theory. Goal setting had led to improved performance in about 90% of studies, especially under the following conditions:

• Goal commitment: individuals accept the goal that has been set.
• Feedback: information about progress towards goals is provided.
• Rewards: goal attainment is rewarded.
• Ability: individuals have sufficient ability to attain the goal.
• Support: management or others provide encouragement.

Evaluation

Goal setting and goal commitment are often important in determining the level of performance, as predicted by goal theory. Goal theory also sheds some light on individual differences in motivation and performance: highly motivated workers set higher goals and are more committed to them than are poorly motivated workers.

However, Locke's goal theory is rather limited. For example, an individual's goal level is seen as corresponding to his or her conscious intentions, but people's motivational forces are not always open to conscious awareness. Another limitation is that goal theory ignores some potential disadvantages of setting high goals and being committed to those goals. These disadvantages include various negative emotional states such as anxiety, stress, and frustration. Another limitation is that major motivating forces such as hunger and thirst are not considered.

How does Locke et al.'s list of five conditions relate to your own experience of short-term and long-term goals (e.g. studying psychology)?

Emotion

The study of emotion is of great importance within psychology. However, it is not easy to define. According to Drever (1964, p.82), emotion involves

> *bodily changes of a widespread character—in breathing, pulse, gland secretion, etc.—and, on the mental side, a state of excitement or perturbation, marked by a strong feeling.*

We can go beyond Drever's definition to identify the following components of emotion:

• Cognitive or thinking: emotions are usually directed towards people or objects (e.g. we are in an anxious emotional state because the situation is dangerous), and we know the situation is dangerous rather than harmless as a result of thinking.
• Physiological: there are generally a number of bodily changes involved in emotion; many of them (such as increased heart rate, increased blood pressure, increased respiration rate, sweating) occur because of arousal in the sympathetic division of the autonomic nervous system or hormonal activity within the endocrine system (see Chapter 3).

Facial expressions associated with emotion are generally recognised across cultures.

- Experiential: the feeling that is experienced, which can only be assessed in the human species.
- Expressive: facial expression and other aspects of non-verbal behaviour such as bodily posture.
- Behavioural: the pattern of behaviour (e.g. fight or flight) produced by an emotional state.

Brain systems in emotion

Papez circuit

Many parts of the brain are involved in emotion. The first systematic attempt to identify the key brain systems involved in emotion was made by Papez (1937). He studied cases of rabies, a disease that typically produces high levels of aggression. This increased aggression seemed to be associated with damage to the hippocampus. Papez combined this information with findings from studies of brain-damaged individuals to propose the **Papez circuit** as the basis of emotion. As McIlveen and Gross (1996, p.153) pointed out, this circuit "forms a closed loop running from the hippocampus to the hypothalamus and from there to the anterior thalamus. The circuit continues via the cingulate gyrus and the entorhinal cortex back to the hippocampus."

The Papez circuit is oversimplified. For example, there seem to be subtle differences in the functions of different parts of it. Flynn (1976) studied the effects of electrical stimulation of various parts of the hypothalamus in cats. Cats responded with a quiet, biting attack when one area was stimulated, but with an affective (emotional) attack involving claws and hissing when another area was stimulated.

Papez–MacLean limbic model

MacLean (1949) suggested some improvements in the Papez–MacLean limbic model. This model differed from the original Papez circuit in that the role of the cingulate gyrus was reduced, and there was increased emphasis on the role of the amygdala and the hippocampus. Part of the reason for this emphasis on the amygdala came from the work of Kluver and Bucy (1939). Monkeys with the anterior temporal lobe removed became less aggressive, showed little fear, tended to put objects in their mouths, and engaged in more sexual activity. This pattern of behaviour is known as the Kluver–Bucy syndrome, and depends mostly on damage to the amygdala, which lies within the temporal lobe. In humans, the damage can be due to tumours or head injuries.

As a result of work such as that of Kluver and Bucy (1939), "psychosurgeons" in the United States carried out numerous operations on criminals serving jail sentences. Many of these operations were amygdalotomies, in which parts of the amygdala were destroyed.

KEY TERM
Papez circuit: a brain circuit or loop involved in emotion, based on the hypothalamus, hippocampus, and thalamus.

This was done by putting fine wire electrodes into the amygdala through a small hole drilled in the skull, and then passing strong electric currents through the electrodes. These amygdalotomies generally reduced fear and anger in those operated on, but they often had very unfortunate side-effects. For example, Thomas R was a 34-year-old engineer who suffered delusions and became unable to work after surgery. He was found on one occasion walking about with his head covered by bags, rags, and newspapers. He justified this behaviour by saying that he was frightened that other bits of his brain might be destroyed. Thankfully, amygdalotomy is very rarely carried out nowadays.

More is now known about the role of the amygdala in emotion. According to LeDoux (1989), the amygdala is the brain's "emotional computer", and is involved in assessing the emotional significance of stimuli. LeDoux discussed evidence based on studies of monkeys in which the neurons connecting the amygdala with either vision or hearing were lesioned or cut. The monkeys could still see and hear stimuli, but they were no longer able to assess the emotional importance of those stimuli.

LeDoux (1995) has put forward a modified version of the limbic theory of emotion. According to him, information about emotional stimuli is relayed to the thalamus. After that, two rather separate brain circuits are involved. First, there is a rapid emotional response based on information passing from the thalamus to the amygdala, which often leads to autonomic and endocrine changes. These changes are then interpreted by the cortex. Second, there is a slower emotional response based on the direct transmission of information from the thalamus to the cortex.

What happens when there is a conflict between the emotional reactions generated by the two brain circuits? An example might be the experience that many people have in a dentist's waiting room: "I feel very anxious even though there is nothing to be frightened about." In such cases, the first circuit based on the amygdala is indicating a high level of anxiety, whereas the second circuit based on a direct link between the thalamus and the cortex is not.

Evaluation. The limbic system is involved in emotion. However, limbic theories of emotion are limited in various ways. First, most of the evidence is based on a few emotions such as fear and anger or rage. The role of the limbic system in other emotions (e.g. love; grief) is less clear. Second, most studies have been carried out on other species. The brain systems involved in human emotion are probably more complicated than those involved in emotion in other species. Third, and related to the second point, humans have a larger area of cortex and much more developed cognitive systems than other species. This is important in emotion. For example, we can become anxious merely by thinking about some unpleasant future events (e.g. sitting examinations), which is presumably much less true of other species. It is an advantage of LeDoux's (1995) theory that it focuses more than previous theories on the role of the cortex in emotion.

Frontal lobes

The frontal lobes are also involved in emotion. This was perhaps first suspected as a result of a terrible injury sustained by a dynamite worker called Phineas Gage (see page 86). He was ramming a charge of dynamite into a hole with a steel rod when there was an explosion, and the steel rod was driven through his orbitofrontal cortex and the top of his head. He turned from a hard-working and serious man into someone who was rather childish and unconcerned. Thus, the accident seemed to have reduced his experience of emotion.

About a hundred years later, Jacobsen, Wolfe, and Jackson (1935) removed the frontal lobes of a chimpanzee called Becky. Jacobsen et al. (1935, pp.9–10) described how, before the operation, when Becky made an error "she immediately flew into a temper tantrum, rolled on the floor, defaecated and urinated." After the operation, she "showed no evidence of emotional disturbance." A Portuguese neuropsychiatrist, Egas Moniz, was impressed by these findings. He developed frontal lobotomies to destroy parts of the frontal lobes or cut them off from the rest of the brain. Frontal lobotomies were carried out on tens of thousands of people, and were successful in reducing anxiety, obsessions, and compulsions. As a result, Moniz was awarded the Nobel Prize in 1949. However, the

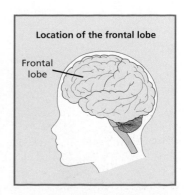

Location of the frontal lobe

Frontal lobe

operation produced very serious side-effects. The patients typically failed to experience normal emotions any more, and most were unemployable after surgery. In view of these side-effects, frontal lobotomies are no longer carried out.

Evaluation. The frontal lobes seem to play a role in deciding on the personal meaning of situations and in producing the appropriate emotional reactions. They are connected to the other brain systems we have discussed, because outputs from the frontal lobes go to the amygdala, the hippocampus, and the hypothalamus. The fact that several areas of the brain are known to be involved in emotion reminds us that emotions depend on the integrated functioning of the brain rather than solely on certain small parts of it. That fact alone should have suggested to Moniz and others that frontal lobotomies were unlikely to prove very effective. In addition, such operations raise major ethical issues, because it is very hard to justify changing someone's personality so dramatically.

Theories of Emotion

James–Lange theory

The first major theory of emotion was put forward independently in the United States by William James and in Denmark by Carl Lange. For obvious reasons, it came to be known as the James–Lange theory. According to the theory, the following states are involved in producing emotion:

*   There is an emotional stimulus (e.g. a car coming rapidly towards you as you are crossing the road).
*   This produces bodily changes (e.g. arousal in the autonomic nervous system).
*   Feedback from the bodily changes leads to the experience of emotion (e.g. fear or anxiety).

These three stages can be seen in the following example taken from James (1890): "I see a bear, I run away, I feel afraid." Stage 1 is seeing the bear, running away is stage 2, and feeling afraid is stage 3.

Evidence supporting the James–Lange theory was reported by Hohmann (1966). He studied 25 paralysed patients who had suffered damage to the spinal cord; this damage greatly restricted their awareness of physiological arousal. For those patients with the least ability to experience arousal, there was a large reduction in their emotional experiences of anger, grief, and sexual excitement. In the words of one patient, "Sometimes I act angry when I see some injustice. I yell and cuss and raise hell ... but it just doesn't have the heat to it that it used to. It's a kind of mental anger."

Later research has generally not confirmed the findings of Hohmann (1966). Bermond et al. (1991) found that most patients with spinal damage reported *increased* intensity of emotions. They even reported that the bodily symptoms of emotion were as great as before they were injured. These findings suggest that feedback from bodily changes is *not* needed for emotion to be experienced.

According to the James–Lange theory, the emotion we experience depends on the specific bodily changes that occur. Thus, each emotion should have its own pattern of bodily changes. There is some support for this view. Smiling is associated with happiness, crying with misery, and running away with fear. Ax (1953) compared the physiological responses to fear and to anger. Fear was created by telling the participants that they might receive an unpleasant electric shock, and anger was created by having a technician make a series of rude and unkind remarks. The physiological responses of fear were similar to those produced by the hormone adrenaline, whereas the responses of anger were like those produced by a combination of adrenaline and noradrenaline.

What are the physiological responses associated with adrenaline?

Evaluation

As predicted by the James–Lange theory, physiological changes can occur before we experience emotion. However, the theory is inadequate in various ways. First, we often experience emotion before the bodily changes have occurred, rather than afterwards as the theory predicts. In other words, emotions can be triggered directly by an emotional stimulus rather than indirectly via bodily changes.

Second, the assumption that there is a distinctive pattern of bodily changes associated with every emotional state is only partially correct. Many different emotional states are associated with a broadly similar state of arousal of the autonomic system, suggesting that the rich variety of emotional experience cannot depend solely on bodily changes.

Would the pattern of arousal of an athlete's autonomic nervous system before a race indicate a single emotional state?

Third, the theory states that an emotional stimulus produces a series of bodily changes. However, very little is said about how this happens. It was only later theorists (e.g. Lazarus, 1966) who considered in detail how the ways in which the situation is interpreted produce physiological changes and emotional experiences.

Cannon–Bard theory

The Cannon–Bard theory was put forward as an alternative to the James–Lange theory. When someone is put in an emotional situation, a part of the brain known as the thalamus is activated (see Chapter 3). This is followed by two separate effects: (1) the appropriate emotional state is experienced; and (2) another part of the brain (the hypothalamus) is activated, producing physiological changes such as arousal in the sympathetic division of the autonomic nervous system.

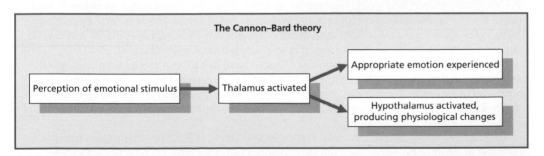

According to the Cannon–Bard theory, our feelings are not determined by the level of physiological arousal. As a result, this theory has no problem with the fact that our experience of emotion can occur before the relevant bodily changes have taken place. However, it does have problems with Hohmann's (1966) findings on patients with damage to the spinal cord. If perception of the bodily changes in emotion has no effect on emotional experience, it is hard to explain why such patients show much reduced emotionality. However, as we have seen, it has proved hard to repeat Hohmann's findings (e.g. Bermond et al., 1991).

Evaluation

The Cannon–Bard theory is very limited in a number of ways. First, the evidence generally suggests that the experienced intensity of emotional states depends in part on the level of physiological arousal (Reisenzein, 1983). Second, the theory tells us nothing about how we decide whether a given situation is emotional. This is an important omission, because there are many ambiguous situations (e.g. hearing a noise outside in the middle of the night) which can be interpreted as being emotional or non-emotional. These limitations were addressed in cognitive labelling theory, to which we now turn.

Cognitive labelling theory

Schachter and Singer (1962) started the modern era in emotion research with their very influential cognitive labelling theory. It was one of the first theories of emotion to focus on cognitive factors. Their main proposal was that there are two factors, both of which are essential for emotions to be experienced:

• High physiological arousal.
• An emotional interpretation of (or label for) that arousal.

According to Schachter and Singer (1962), an emotional state will not be experienced if either of these two crucial factors is missing. A study by Maranon (1924) fits that prediction. The participants were injected with adrenaline, a drug whose effects are like those of a naturally occurring state of arousal. When they were asked how they felt, 71% simply reported their physical symptoms with no emotional experience. Most of the remaining participants reported "as if" emotion, i.e. an emotion lacking its normal intensity. Why did almost none of the participants report true emotions? They interpreted (or labelled) their state of arousal as having been produced by the drug, and so failed to attach an emotional label to it.

Schachter and Singer

Schachter and Singer (1962) carried out an expanded version of Maranon's (1924) study. All the participants were told the study was testing the effects of the vitamin compound "Suproxin" on vision. In fact, they were injected with either adrenaline (to produce arousal) or a salt-based solution having no effect on arousal. Some of those given adrenaline were correctly informed about the effects of the drug. Others were misinformed or uninformed (being told simply that the injection was mild and would have no side-effects). After the injection, the participants were put in a situation designed to produce either euphoria (joy) or anger. This was done by putting them in the same room as someone who acted in a joyful way (making paper planes and playing paper basketball) or in an angry way (reacting to a very personal questionnaire).

Which groups were the most emotional? It should have been those groups who were given adrenaline (and so were very aroused), but who would not interpret the arousal as having been produced by the drug. Thus, it was predicted that the misinformed and uninformed groups given adrenaline should have been most emotional. The findings broadly supported the predictions, but many of the effects were rather small.

One of the reasons why the study by Schachter and Singer (1962) did not produce strong effects may be because those given the salt-based solution may have become physiologically aroused by being put into an emotional situation. If so, they would have had the high arousal and emotional labels, which together produce an emotional state. Schachter and Wheeler (1962) argued that the way to stop people becoming aroused was to give them a depressant drug that reduces arousal. The participants were given a depressant, or adrenaline, or a substance having no effects, and were told in each case that the drug had no side-effects. They then watched a slapstick film called *The Good Humour Man*. As predicted, those given adrenaline (and thus aroused) found the film the funniest, whereas those given the depressant (and thus de-aroused) found it least funny.

Ethical issues: What ethical difficulties would need to be overcome if you wished to replicate Schachter and Singer's study today?

Discussion points

1. How does the approach adopted by Schachter and Singer differ from those of previous theorists?
2. What are the weaknesses with this research and this theoretical approach (see next section for some ideas)?

Evaluation

Schachter and Singer (1962) were right to argue that cognitive processes are important in determining *whether* emotion will be experienced, and in determining *which* emotion will be experienced. Their cognitive labelling theory led several other theorists to develop cognitive approaches to emotion, and so their theory has been very influential.

On the negative side, it has proved very hard to repeat the findings of Schachter and Singer (1962). Marshall and Zimbardo (1979) found that large doses of adrenaline reduced (rather than increased) their participants' happiness in the euphoria or joy condition. Perhaps a high level of arousal is generally regarded as unpleasant. Another problem is that the situation used by Schachter and Singer is very artificial. In our everyday lives, we rarely experience high levels of arousal that are hard to interpret.

As the theory predicts, emotional intensity tends to be greater when the level of physiological arousal is high. However, the effect of arousal on emotional intensity is often much weaker than would be expected theoretically (Reisenzein, 1983).

Lazarus's cognitive appraisal theory

Most theorists nowadays no longer accept cognitive labelling theory as an adequate account of emotion. However, it is fairly generally accepted that Schachter and Singer (1962) were right to emphasise the role of cognitive processes in emotion. One of the most influential cognitive approaches to emotion was put forward by Lazarus (1982, 1991). According to Lazarus (1982, p.1021), "Cognitive appraisal (of meaning or significance) underlies and is an integral feature of all emotional states." This contrasts with the view of Zajonc (1984, p.117): "Affect and cognition are separate and partially independent systems and ... although they ordinarily function conjointly, affect could be generated without a prior cognitive process."

Do you think Zajonc was correct in stating that emotion could be generated without prior cognition?

It has not proved possible so far to obtain clear evidence on the issue of whether cognitive processes always precede emotional reactions to stimuli. However, Zajonc (1980) discussed several studies that he believed provided support for his theoretical position. In these studies, melodies or pictures were presented either very briefly below the level of conscious awareness or while the participants were involved in a task. Even though these stimuli could not be recognised in a later memory test, the participants still tended to choose previously presented stimuli rather than similar new ones when asked to select the ones they preferred.

According to Zajonc (1980), these studies indicate that there can be a positive emotional reaction to previously presented stimuli (as assessed by the preference judgements) even when there is no evidence of cognitive processing (as assessed by recognition memory). This phenomenon is known as the "mere exposure" effect. One problem with these studies is that they do not have much obvious relevance to ordinary emotional states. The participants made superficial preference judgements about fairly meaningless stimuli of little relevance to their personal lives, and so only minimal emotion was involved. Another problem is Zajonc's assumption that the absence of recognition memory means that the stimuli were not processed cognitively. This conclusion only makes sense if we assume that cognitive processing must be conscious, which very few cognitive psychologists would be willing to do.

According to Lazarus (1982, 1991), cognitive appraisal of the situation can be subdivided into three more specific forms of appraisal:

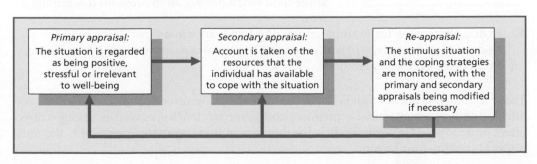

Some of the earliest evidence indicating the importance of cognitive appraisal was reported by Speisman et al. (1964). The participants were shown a film of a Stone Age ritual in which adolescent boys had their penises deeply incised. Cognitive appraisal was manipulated by varying the soundtrack of the film. Denial was produced by indicating that the film did not show a painful operation, and intellectualisation was produced by considering matters from the perspective of an anthropologist viewing strange native customs. There was also a control condition in which there was no soundtrack. The participants in the denial and intellectualisation conditions were less anxious than those in the control condition in terms of physiological measures (e.g. heart rate).

Evaluation

Studies such as the one by Speisman et al. (1964) have shown that emotional reactions to situations can be changed if cognitive appraisals are changed. However, there are various problems with cognitive appraisal theory. First, it can be very hard to assess an individual's cognitive appraisals of a situation, because they may occur below the level of conscious awareness (Lazarus, 1991). Second, the studies carried out by Lazarus and others are rather artificial. The participants typically sit passively in an initially unemotional state while they are exposed to emotionally threatening stimuli. In such situations, it is clear that cognitive appraisals can affect emotional responses. In the real world, however, it is likely that the causality can go in the opposite direction, with emotional states influencing the process of cognitive appraisal. Third, it is unlikely that emotional experience depends only on cognitive appraisal. As is discussed next, it is probable that other factors (e.g. bodily reactions) also play a part in determining emotional experience.

Synthesis: Four-factor theory

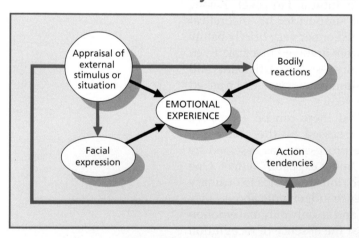

■ Research activity: To test Parkinson's theory concerning facial expressions, practise with a partner trying to express extreme anger while smiling broadly.

The major theories of emotion we have considered are generally thought of as being in competition with each other. However, none of them can be regarded as providing complete accounts of emotion. It is increasingly argued that what is needed is a theory combining elements of previous theories. As an example, we can take the four-factor theory of emotion put forward by Parkinson (1994). According to this theory, emotional experience depends on four separate factors:

1. Appraisal of some external stimulus or situation: this is the most important factor, and is the one emphasised by Lazarus (1982, 1991).
2. Reactions of the body (e.g. arousal): this is the factor emphasised in the James–Lange theory.
3. Facial expression: the importance of this factor was shown in a study by Strack, Martin, and Stepper (1988) in which participants were more amused by cartoons when adopting a facial expression close to a smile than when having an expression resembling a frown.
4. Action tendencies: for example, preparing to advance in a threatening way is associated with anger, whereas preparing to retreat is associated with fear (Frijda, Kuipers, & ter Schure, 1989).

These four factors are not independent of each other. Cognitive appraisal of the situation affects bodily reactions, facial expression, and action tendencies, as well as having a direct effect on emotional experience. It is for this reason that cognitive appraisal is the most important of the four factors.

Stress

We will make a start by considering the meaning of the term "stress". Selye (1950) defined stress as "the nonspecific response of the body to any demand". However, this definition is not very useful, because the nature of the stress response depends on the situation, and the definition does not consider adequately the factors causing stress.

Driving is particularly stressful for a learner driver.

According to the transactional model (Cox, 1978), stress depends on the interaction between an individual and his or her environment. This approach leads to a definition such as that of Steptoe (1997, p.175): "Stress responses are said to arise when demands exceed the personal and social resources that the individual is able to mobilise." Thus, for example, driving is stressful to a learner driver, because he or she has limited ability to meet the demands of handling a car in traffic. Driving is not stressful to experienced drivers, because they are confident that their driving ability will allow them to cope with most driving situations.

What are the effects of stress? Many of the effects are physiological in nature, and that is why stress is considered within biopsychology. However, other changes also occur inside stressed individuals. There are four major kinds of effects associated with the stressed state: emotional; physiological; cognitive; and behavioural. Here are some specific examples of what stress looks like:

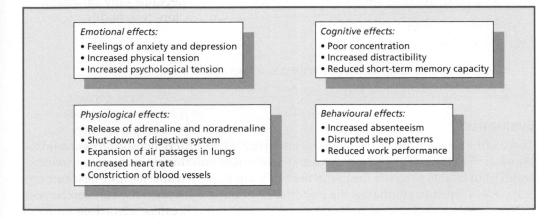

Emotional effects:
- Feelings of anxiety and depression
- Increased physical tension
- Increased psychological tension

Cognitive effects:
- Poor concentration
- Increased distractibility
- Reduced short-term memory capacity

Physiological effects:
- Release of adrenaline and noradrenaline
- Shut-down of digestive system
- Expansion of air passages in lungs
- Increased heart rate
- Constriction of blood vessels

Behavioural effects:
- Increased absenteeism
- Disrupted sleep patterns
- Reduced work performance

General adaptation syndrome

Most of our emotional reactions have evolved because they are adaptive and functional in some way. However, it has often been argued that stress has a range of very negative effects. Why, then, has the stress reaction evolved? According to Hans Selye (1950), stress is useful in the short term, but it can become very damaging if it lasts for long periods of time.

Selye studied hospital patients with various injuries and illnesses. He noticed that they all seemed to show a similar pattern of bodily response. Selye called this pattern the **general adaptation syndrome**. He argued that it consisted of three stages:

1. Alarm reaction stage: there is activation of the anterior pituitary adrenal cortex system. This can be triggered by the hypothalamus secreting a peptide called corticotrophin-releasing factor, which stimulates the anterior pituitary gland. As a result, adrenocorticotrophic hormone (ACTH) is released from the anterior pituitary, and this triggers the release of hormones known as glucocorticoids from the adrenal cortex, with these hormones producing the stress response. Glucocorticoids are so called because they have great effects on glucose metabolism. They help to break down protein and convert it to glucose, they help to make fats available for energy, and they increase the rate of blood flow. As a result, the individual is ready for fight or flight.

2. Resistance stage: the physiological efforts to deal with stress that started in the alarm reaction stage are at full capacity. However, as this stage proceeds, the parasympathetic nervous

KEY TERM
General adaptation syndrome: the bodily response to stress, consisting of three stages: alarm reaction; resistance; and exhaustion.

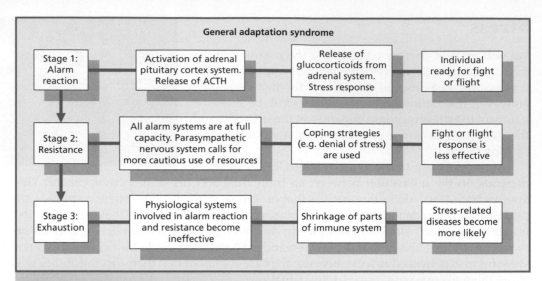

system (which is involved in energy-storing processes) calls for more careful use of the body's resources. There is also much use of coping strategies, e.g. denying that the situation is stressful.

3. Exhaustion stage: eventually the physiological systems used in the alarm reaction and resistance stages become ineffective, and stress-related disease (e.g. high blood pressure; asthma; heart disease) becomes more likely. In extreme cases, there is enlargement of the adrenal cortex, shrinkage of parts of the body's immune system (e.g. the spleen and thymus), and bleeding stomach ulcers.

Discussion points

1. Why do you think the work of Selye has been so influential?
2. What are the weaknesses of his work (see next section for my thoughts)?

Evaluation

There are two main physiological systems involved in producing the stress response (Pinel, 1997). Selye identified one of them (based on the anterior pituitary and the adrenal cortex), but tended to ignore the role of the sympathetic nervous system (see next section). Selye was correct to emphasise the importance of the glucocorticoids. This can be seen clearly in adrenalectomised individuals who cannot produce the normal amounts of glucocorticoids. When they are exposed to a stressor, they have to be given additional quantities of glucocorticoid in order to survive (Tyrell & Baxter, 1981).

Selye assumed that the physiological effects of stress are very similar regardless of the stressor. In fact, the stress response often varies somewhat depending on the type of stressor. For example, Mason (1975) compared the reactions to stressors varying in the degree of how much fear, anger, or uncertainty they created. The various stressors produced different patterns of adrenaline, noradrenaline, and corticosteroid secretion.

What might be an active response to stress?

Another limitation of Selye's approach is that he assumed that people respond in a *passive* way to stressors. In fact, people typically react to stressors in an active way. According to Mason (1975) there is an active process of psychological appraisal when people confront a stressor, and this process helps to determine the physiological response of the body. For example, Symington et al. (1955) compared the physiological responses of two groups of dying patients, consisting of those who remained conscious and those who were in a coma. There were many more signs of physiological stress in the patients who remained conscious, presumably because they engaged in stressful psychological appraisal of their state.

Other physiological effects

Stress has very widespread physiological effects, only some of which were identified by Selye (1950). In addition to the involvement of ACTH and the glucocorticoids, the sympathetic nervous system triggers the release of hormones such as adrenaline, noradrenaline, and the corticosteroids from the adrenal medulla. These hormones increase blood flow to the muscles, they increase heart and respiration rate, they reduce activity in the digestive system, they increase the release of clotting factors into the bloodstream to reduce blood loss in the event of injury, and so on. Adrenaline affects glucose metabolism, by increasing the availability of the nutrients stored in muscles to become available to provide energy. Noradrenaline is a neurotransmitter within the brain as well as a stress hormone. There are increased levels of noradrenaline in various parts of the brain (e.g. hypothalamus; frontal cortex) when rats are exposed to stressful situations (Carlson, 1994).

The effects of stressors on the sympathetic nervous system and the endocrine system can be very useful in the short term. As with the glucocorticoids, adrenaline and noradrenaline equip the person or animal for fight or flight. However, there can be negative long-term consequences. Adrenaline and noradrenaline increase the output of the heart, which causes an increase in blood pressure. If this occurs over long periods of time, it can lead to cardiovascular disease.

Stress and illness

It is generally believed that stress can play a part in causing various illnesses, and much of the available evidence supports this belief. Cohen, Tyrrell, and Smith (1991) carried out a well-controlled study in which the participants were given nasal drops containing cold viruses. Those who had the highest level of stress (they had experienced many negative life events and felt out of control) were almost twice as likely to develop colds as those with the lowest level of stress. There is also evidence that stress can help to cause gastric ulcers. Stress often increases the secretion of hydrochloric acid, and also weakens the defences of the gastrointestinal tract against it. As a result, gastric ulcers can develop (Pinel, 1997).

Apart from cardiovascular disease and gastric ulcers, what other illnesses could be stress-related? How would you try to establish a causal relationship between stress and illness?

Stress and life events

Early work on life events was carried out by Holmes and Rahe (1967). They found that patients tended to have experienced several life events in the months before the onset of illness. This led them to develop the Social Readjustment Rating Scale, on which people indicate which out of 43 life events have happened to them over a period of time (usually six or twelve months). These life events are assigned a value in terms of their likely impact. Here are various life events taken from this scale, with their associated life change units in brackets:

Death of a spouse	(100)
Divorce	(73)
Marital separation	(65)
Prison	(63)
Death of a close family member	(63)
Change in eating habits	(15)
Holiday	(13)
Minor violations of the law	(11)

Why are holidays treated as stressful life events? According to Holmes and Rahe (1967), any change (whether desirable or undesirable) can be stressful. The evidence from numerous studies using the Social Readjustment Rating Scale is that people who have experienced events totalling more than 300 life change units over a period of one year are more at risk for a wide range of physical and mental illnesses. These illnesses include heart attacks, diabetes, TB, asthma, anxiety, and depression (Martin, 1989). However, the correlations between life change units and susceptibility to any particular illness tend to be rather low, indicating a weak association between life events and illness.

There are various problems with evidence obtained from use of the Social Readjustment Rating Scale. First, it is often not clear whether life events have caused some stress-related illness, or whether stress caused the life events. For example, stress may cause a change in eating habits

rather than a change in eating habits causing stress. Second, the impact of most life events varies from person to person. For example, marital separation may be less stressful for someone who has already established an intimate relationship with someone else. Some measures take account of the context in which people experience life events. For example, this is true of the Life Events and Difficulties Schedule (LEDS; see Harris, 1997). Third, the assumption that desirable life events can cause stress-related illnesses is not generally supported (Martin, 1989).

Discussion points

1. What are the main reasons why some life events are much more stressful than others?
2. What criticisms have been made of the approach adopted by Holmes and Rahe (see next section for some ideas)?

Change can be stressful, even the usually pleasant ones associated with going on holiday.

Indirect evidence that stressful life events can play a role in life-threatening diseases was reported by Tache et al. (1979). Cancer was more common among adults who were divorced, widowed, or separated, than among those who were married. The most likely explanation is that those who were not married were more stressed because of a lack of social support. However, it is hard to establish causal relationships from such data. Perhaps those who were divorced or separated were more vulnerable to stress than those who were married, and this stress vulnerability played a role in the collapse of their marriages.

Type A behaviour pattern

Two cardiologists, Meyer Friedman and Ray Rosenman (1959) argued that individuals with the **Type A behaviour pattern** are more stressed than Type B individuals, and so are more likely to suffer from coronary heart disease. The Type A behaviour pattern has been defined by Matthews (1988, p.373) as including

> *extremes of competitive achievement striving, hostility, aggressiveness, and a sense of time urgency, evidenced by vigorous voice and psychomotor mannerisms.*

In contrast, Type B behaviour is more relaxed, and lacks the features found in Type A behaviour.

Bearing in mind the characteristics of a Type A person, what types of careers would most suit such a personality type?

The Type A behaviour pattern was initially assessed by means of the Structured Interview. This assessment procedure makes use of two main kinds of information: (1) the answers given to the questions asked during the interview; and (2) the individual's behaviour, including aspects of his or her way of speaking (e.g. loudness; speed of talking). The individual's tendencies towards impatience and hostility are assessed by the interviewer deliberately interrupting the person being interviewed from time to time. The Type A behaviour pattern has also been assessed by various self-report questionnaires (e.g. the Jenkins Activity Survey).

The notion that Type A individuals are more likely than Type B individuals to suffer from coronary heart disease was tested in the Western Collaborative Group Study (Rosenman et al., 1975). The findings were striking. Of nearly 3200 men who had no symptoms of coronary heart disease at the outset of the study, Type As were nearly twice as likely as Type Bs to have developed coronary heart disease over the following $8^1/_2$ years. This remained so, even when account was taken of various other factors (e.g. blood pressure; smoking; obesity) which are known to be associated with heart disease.

One of the limitations of the Western Collaborative Group Study as reported by Rosenman et al. (1975) was that it was not clear which aspect of the Type A behaviour pattern was most closely associated with heart disease. This issue was addressed by Matthews et al. (1977). They re-analysed the data from the Western Collaborative Group

KEY TERM
Type A behaviour pattern: forms of behaviour involving impatience, time pressure, competitiveness, and hostility.

Study, and found that coronary heart disease was most associated with the hostility component of Type A.

Why is Type A (or its hostility component) associated with heart disease? As Ganster et al. (1991, p.145) pointed out, it has often been assumed that "chronic elevations of the sympathetic nervous system [in Type As] lead to deterioration of the cardiovascular system." Ganster et al. put their participants into stressful situations and recorded various physiological measures, including blood pressure and heart rate. Only the hostility component of Type A was associated with high levels of physiological reactivity. These findings, when combined with those of Matthews et al. (1977), suggest that high levels of hostility produce increased activity within the sympathetic nervous system, and this plays a role in the development of coronary heart disease.

Some researchers have failed to find any relationship between Type A and coronary heart disease. This has led a number of psychologists to doubt the importance of the Type A behaviour pattern as a factor in causing heart disease. However, Miller et al. (1991) reviewed the literature, and found that many of the negative findings were obtained in studies using self-report measures of Type A behaviour. Studies using the Structured Interview with initially healthy populations reported a mean correlation of +0.33 between Type A behaviour and coronary heart disease, indicating a moderate relationship between the two variables.

Cross-cultural issues: Do you think there are likely to be cultural differences in the prevalence of Type A and B individuals (i.e. between individualistic and collectivistic cultures)?

Mechanisms: How does stress cause illness?

There is good evidence that stress can increase the chances of someone becoming ill. There are two major ways in which stress can cause illness:

1. Directly, by reducing the body's ability to fight illness.
2. Indirectly, by leading the stressed individual to adopt an unhealthy lifestyle (e.g. increased smoking and drinking).

Immune system

There is increasing evidence that stress can cause illness by impairing the workings of the **immune system**. This system consists of cells distributed throughout the body that fight disease, and the term **psychoneuroimmunology** is used to refer to the study of the effects of stress and other psychological factors on the immune system. Stress can affect the immune system in a fairly direct way. Alternatively, it can affect the immune system indirectly via an unhealthy life style. Cells in the immune system have receptors for various hormones and neurotransmitters that are involved in the stress response, so it is easy to see how the physiological stress response could influence the functioning of the immune system.

How does the immune system work? The cells within the immune system are known as white blood cells (**leucocytes**). These cells identify and destroy foreign bodies (**antigens**) such as viruses. In addition, the presence of antigens leads to the production of antibodies. **Antibodies** are produced in the blood. They are protein molecules that attach themselves to antigens, and mark them out for later destruction.

There are several kinds of white blood cells or leucocytes within the immune system, including T cells, B cells, and natural killer cells. T cells destroy invaders, and T-helper cells increase immunological activity. These T-helper cells are attacked by HIV, which is the virus causing AIDS. B cells produce antibodies. Natural killer cells are involved in the fight against both viruses and tumours.

Evidence that stress can change the immune system was reported by Schliefer et al. (1983). They compared the functioning of the immune system in the husbands of women who died from breast cancer. The husbands' immune system functioned less well after

> **KEY TERMS**
> **Immune system**: a system of cells within the body that is involved in fighting disease.
> **Psychoneuroimmunology**: the study of the effects of stress and other psychological factors on the immune system.
> **Leucocytes**: white blood cells that find and destroy antigens.
> **Antigens**: foreign bodies such as viruses.
> **Antibodies**: protein molecules that attach themselves to invaders, marking them out for subsequent destruction.

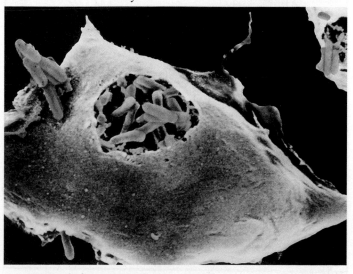

A macrophage cell—one of the scavenger cells in the immune system—engulfing M. Tuberculosis bacteria.

their wives had died than before, showing the impact of bereavement on the immune system.

Stress can affect natural killer cell cytotoxicity, which is of major importance in the defence against various infections and cancer. Reduced levels of natural killer cell cytotoxicity have been found in people who are highly stressed, including students facing important examinations, bereaved individuals, and those who are severely depressed (Ogden, 1996). Goodkin et al. (1992) studied natural killer cell cytotoxicity in HIV-positive homosexual men who had no physical symptoms when tested. The level of natural killer cell cytotoxicity was higher among those men who had plenty of vitamin A in their diet and who drank little alcohol. These findings may reflect an indirect effect of stress on the immune system, with the most stressed men adopting a less healthy lifestyle than the others in terms of diet and alcohol use. In addition, those HIV men who had an active coping style involving focusing on (and expressing) their emotions had higher levels of natural killer cell cytotoxicity than those with other coping styles. This indicates a direct effect of stress on the immune system.

There are other ways in which psychological factors can influence the functioning of the immune system. Arnetz, Wasserman, and Petrini (1987) studied women who were stressed because they were unemployed. Some were provided with a social support programme, whereas the others were not. Immune functioning was better in those women receiving social support.

What types of social support would help to reduce stress?

Evaluation. There is convincing evidence that stress can produce changes in the immune system, and there is also good evidence that stress can increase the probability of individuals developing various physical illnesses. This evidence is not conclusive. As Bachen, Cohen, and Marsland (1997) concluded, "It is not yet clear that either the nature or magnitude of immunological change found in PNI [psychoneuroimmunology] research bears any relevance to increased disease susceptibility." One reason for caution is that the functioning of the immune system in most stressed individuals is within the normal range. Another reason for caution is that the immune system is very complex, and so the quality of an individual's immune system is hard to assess. Finally, it is likely that changes in the immune system will have much more effect on health among those whose immune systems are already weakened (Bachen et al., 1997).

Stress can lead to an unhealthy lifestyle.

KEY TERM
Pathogens: agents that cause physical illness.

Lifestyle

Stress can cause illness in an indirect way via changes to lifestyle. In technical terms, stressed individuals may be more likely to expose themselves to **pathogens**, which are agents causing physical illness. People who are stressed tended to smoke more, to drink more alcohol, to take less exercise, and to sleep less than people who are not stressed (Cohen & Williamson, 1991). For example, adolescents who experience high levels of stress are more likely to start smoking than those whose lives are less stressful (Wills, 1985). Adults are more likely to resume smoking after having given up when they experience a high level of stress in their lives (Carey et al., 1993). So far as alcohol is concerned, there is much support for tension reduction theory. According to this theory, tension in the form of anxiety, fear, or depression leads to an increase in alcohol consumption in order to reduce the level of tension. There is reasonable support for this theory (Ogden, 1996).

Evidence that illness depends on lifestyle as well as on stress was reported by Brown (1991). The effects of stress in the form of negative life events were compared in students who were high in physical fitness and those low in physical fitness. Stress almost trebled the number of visits to the health clinic made by unfit students, but had little effect on visits made by those who were physically fit.

Methods of Reducing Stress

There are dozens of ways in which people try to reduce their stress level. Many of these ways are psychological in nature:

1. Cognitive restructuring to think more positively about life's problems.
2. Social support from friends and family.
3. Time management training to prevent numerous activities having to be performed in a very short period of time.

In spite of the existence of these psychological methods for reducing stress, we will focus mainly on methods that are designed to reduce stress by means of changes within the physiological system. The two main physiologically oriented methods we will consider are biofeedback and anti-anxiety drugs. After that, there is a brief discussion of the major psychological methods.

Biofeedback

Biofeedback is often used to reduce stress. In essence, **biofeedback** is "a technique for transforming some aspect of physiological behaviour into electrical signals which are made accessible to ... awareness (usually vision or audition)" (Gatchel, 1997, p.198). For example, an auditory or visual signal might indicate whether an individual's heart rate is too high or about right. The individual is also trained in techniques that have been found to reduce physiological aspects of stress. For example, there is relaxation training, part of which involves breathing in a regular and calm way.

Biofeedback training involves three stages:

1. Developing an awareness of the particular physiological response (e.g. heart rate).
2. Learning ways of controlling that physiological response in quiet conditions; this can include providing rewards for successful control in addition to feedback.
3. Transferring that control into the conditions of everyday life.

It seems unlikely that we would be able to exert voluntary control over apparently involuntary processes such as blood pressure. Consider, however, the famous escapologist Harry Houdini. He managed to escape when he was securely shackled, with his clothes and body having been searched thoroughly to ensure he was not hiding any keys. How did he do it? He held a key suspended in his throat, and regurgitated it when no-one was looking. The natural reaction to having an object stuck in your throat is to gag. However, Houdini had spent hours practising with a small piece of potato on a string until he was able to control his gag reflex.

Biofeedback can produce short-term reductions in heart rate, blood pressure, skin temperature, and brain-wave rhythms. This happens in spite of the fact that we cannot control *directly* our heart rate and blood pressure, because they are controlled automatically by the autonomic nervous system. However, it is possible to exert control *indirectly*. For example, breathing deeply, using

Learning to relax is one of the major foci of yoga, which is used by many people to counteract stress.

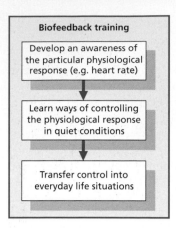

Biofeedback training

Develop an awareness of the particular physiological response (e.g. heart rate)

↓

Learn ways of controlling the physiological response in quiet conditions

↓

Transfer control into everyday life situations

methods of relaxation, or simply moving around can produce changes in various physiological measures.

Biofeedback has produced significant long-term reductions in stress in everyday life, even though people have no direct feedback about their current physiological state. However, caution is needed when considering the evidence. As Gatchel (1997, p.199) pointed out, "There have been claims for the therapeutic efficacy of biofeedback which have been grossly exaggerated and even wrong."

It is hard to *interpret* the beneficial effects of biofeedback. Relaxation training is often given along with the biofeedback, making it hard to tell whether it is the biofeedback or the relaxation training that is more effective. Biofeedback may lead to benefits by producing a sense of control rather than through purely physiological mechanisms.

Drug treatment

One way of reducing people's level of stress is by giving them anti-anxiety drugs. The most used anti-anxiety drugs are the benzodiazepines such as Valium and Librium. There are benzodiazepine receptors in the brain which form part of the GABA receptor complex. The benzodiazepines increase the activity of the neurotransmitter GABA, which inhibits activation throughout the nervous system. The benzodiazepines are very effective at reducing anxiety, and it is for this reason that they are used by hundreds of millions around the world.

In spite of the effectiveness of the benzodiazepines, they have several unwanted side-effects. They often have sedative effects, and can make people feel drowsy. In addition, the benzodiazepines can cause cognitive and memory impairments, they sometimes lead

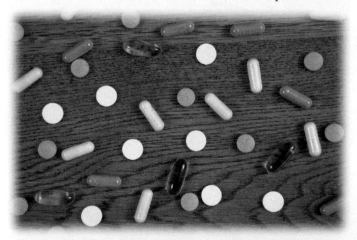

to feelings of depression, and they can interact unpredictably with alcohol (Ashton, 1997). As a result, individuals taking benzodiazepines are more likely to be involved in accidents. Finally, many people become dependent on benzodiazepines, and find it hard to stop taking them. Sudden removal of benzodiazepines can lead to a return of the initial symptoms of intense stress and anxiety.

A more recent anti-anxiety drug, buspirone, offers some advantages over benzodiazepines. It is a serotonin agonist, meaning that it facilitates the effects of the neurotransmitter serotonin. It does not have the sedative effects of benzodiazepines, and there are no marked withdrawal symptoms. However, buspirone produces some side-effects such as headaches and depression (Goa & Ward, 1986).

Anti-anxiety drugs can be very effective at reducing intense feelings of stress. However, they do not address the problems causing the stress, and they can have unfortunate side-effects. The recommendation is that the benzodiazepines should generally be limited to short-term use of no more than four weeks (Ashton, 1997). It is also recommended that they should only be given to individuals with severe anxiety symptoms, and the drugs should be given in the minimal effective doses. Individuals who have become dependent on benzodiazepines should have their dosage reduced gradually. The good news is that about 70% of dependent users of benzodiazepines who are motivated to give them up manage to do this for periods of several years or more (Ashton, 1997).

Social support

It has often been claimed that social support can help to provide protection against stress. Before discussing the evidence, however, we need to consider definitions of social support. Schaefer, Coyne, and Lazarus (1981) argued that the term social support has two rather different meanings:

1. Social network: the number of people who are available to provide support.
2. Perceived support: the strength of social support that can be provided by these individuals.

According to Schaefer et al., the effects of these types of social support on health and well-being are very different. Perceived support (basically the quality of social support) is positively related to health and well-being, whereas social network (basically the quantity of social support) is unrelated to well-being. Social network can even be negatively related to well-being, because it is very time-consuming and demanding to maintain a large social network.

The importance of perceived social support was shown by Brown and Harris (1978). They found that 61% of severely depressed women had experienced a very stressful life event in the previous nine months, compared with only 25% of non-depressed women. However, many women managed to cope with severe life events without becoming depressed. Of those women who experienced a serious life event, 37% of those without an intimate friend became depressed, against only 10% of those who did have a very close friend.

The effects of social support on physical well-being were studied by Nuckolls, Cassel, and Kaplan (1972) in a study on pregnant women. They made use of a general measure of psychosocial assets including measures of social network and perceived support. Women exposed to many stressful life events were much more likely to have medical complications during pregnancy if they had low psychosocial assets.

Stress inoculation training

Several forms of cognitive therapy have been devised for the treatment of clinical anxiety and depression (see Chapter 26). The essence of this approach to therapy is to replace negative and irrational thoughts (e.g. "I am totally incompetent") with positive and rational ones (e.g. "I can achieve many things if I try hard enough"). Cognitive therapy is used with patients who are already suffering from high levels of anxiety and/or depression. Meichenbaum (1977, 1985) argued that we should use cognitive therapy *before* people become very anxious or depressed rather than afterwards. This led him to develop stress inoculation training.

There are three main phases in stress inoculation training:

1. Assessment: the therapist discusses the nature of the problem with the individual, together with the individual's perception of how to eliminate it.
2. Stress reduction techniques: the individual learns various techniques for reducing stress, such as relaxation and self-instruction. The essence of self-instruction is that the individual practises several coping self-statements such as "If I keep calm, I can handle this situation" or "Stop worrying, because it's pointless".
3. Application and follow-through: the individual imagines using the stress reduction techniques learned in the second phase in difficult situations, and/or engages in role play of such situations with the therapist. Finally, the techniques are used in real-life situations.

Meichenbaum (1985) developed some of his earlier ideas on stress inoculation training. In particular, he put more emphasis on some of the cognitive processes involved. For example, he argued that it is important to consider the ways in which individuals think about the situations that they find especially stressful.

Meichenbaum (1977) compared his stress inoculation technique against a form of behaviour therapy known as desensitisation (see page 716). These methods were applied

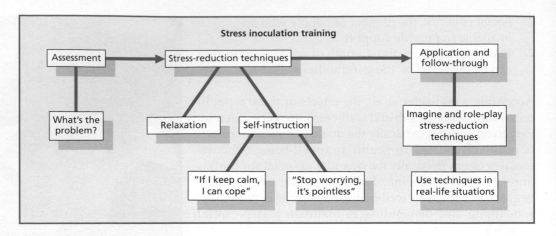

to individuals who suffered from both snake phobia and rat phobia, but treatment was only provided for one phobia. Both forms of treatment were effective in reducing or eliminating the phobia that was treated. However, stress inoculation also greatly reduced the non-treated phobia, whereas desensitisation did not. The implication is that self-instruction easily generalises to new situations, which makes it more useful than very specific forms of treatment.

Evaluation

Why do you think stress inoculation training is less valuable in highly stressful situations? How might this problem be addressed?

Stress inoculation has proved to be fairly effective in reducing the stress that people experience in moderately stressful situations. However, it is of less value when treating individuals who are highly stressed or exposed to very stressful situations. Individuals differ in how easy they find it to use coping self-statements in stressful situations.

Coping strategies

Individuals show consistent individual differences in the coping strategies they used to handle stressful situations. Endler and Parker (1990) devised the Multidimensional Coping Inventory to assess three major coping strategies:

Can you think of a behavioural example for each type of strategy (e.g. leaving a red telephone bill unopened)?

- Task-oriented strategy: this involves obtaining information about the stressful situation and about alternative courses of action and their probable outcome; it also involves deciding priorities and acting so as to deal directly with the stressful situation.
- Emotion-oriented strategy: this can involve efforts to maintain hope and to control one's emotions; it can also involve venting feelings of anger and frustration, or deciding that nothing can be done to change things.
- Avoidance-oriented strategy: this involves denying or minimising the seriousness of the situation; it also involves conscious suppression of stressful thoughts and their replacement by self-protective thoughts.

Individuals who are high in the personality dimension of trait anxiety, and thus experience much stress and anxiety, tend to use the emotion-oriented and avoidance-oriented strategies rather than the task-oriented strategy (Endler & Parker, 1990). The situation is very different in those with the Type A behaviour pattern. They have a strong tendency to use the task-oriented strategy, even when it is not appropriate (Eysenck, 1994a).

Which kind of coping strategy is most effective in reducing stress? There is no simple answer, because the effectiveness of any coping strategy depends on the nature of the stressful situation. In general terms, task-oriented coping tends to be most effective when the individual has the resources to sort out the stressful situation. On the other hand, emotion-oriented coping is preferable when the individual cannot resolve the situation (Eysenck, 1994a).

Avoidance-oriented strategy

PERSONAL REFLECTIONS

- In my opinion, the biopsychological approach tells us more about *how* motivation, emotion, and stress occur than about *why* they occur. It is easy to be impressed by the detailed physiological processes involved, and to lose sight of the ways in which motivation, emotion, and stress all depend on the psychological, social, and cultural context.

- I think that motivation is both one of the most important and the least understood areas in psychology. There is general agreement that an assessment of motivation is very valuable in personnel selection. However, it has proved very hard to devise valid measures that will predict how hard someone will work. What is generally of most value is the individual's work record so far, on the basis that the past often predicts the future. It is disappointing that theories of motivation do not allow us to improve on that simple approach.

SUMMARY

Motivational factors help to determine the direction, intensity, and persistence of behaviour. It used to be argued that the lateral nucleus of the hypothalamus is a feeding centre, whereas its ventromedial nucleus is a satiety centre. This hypothalamic theory is oversimplified. Eating often occurs after a decline in blood glucose levels, or when the levels of lipids or fatty acids are low. Cessation of eating depends in part on a nutrient-monitoring system in the stomach. Positive-incentive theory is more adequate than a homeostatic approach to hunger. Thirst occurs when water leaves the cells, and the detection of this leads to the release of antidiuretic hormone. Water deprivation also produces a reduction in blood volume, and this affects the kidneys directly and by increasing the release of antidiuretic hormone. Satiety receptors in the mouth and intestines cause drinking to stop.

Motivation

According to Murray, we have 20 manifest needs, and their expression depends on environmental factors or "press". Some of these needs have been measured by the Thematic Apperception Test. The most explored of Murray's needs is need for achievement. The Thematic Apperception Test has low reliability and validity. Drive theories are based on the notion of homeostasis. These theories can account for hunger and thirst, but are of little relevance to curiosity, self-actualisation, and so on. Maslow argued for a hierarchy of needs ranging from deficiency needs to growth needs. This approach is comprehensive, but the impact of the environment is not emphasised enough, and some of the concepts (e.g. self-actualisation) are vague. According to Locke's goal theory, high levels of motivation and performance require the setting of hard goals and commitment to those goals. Locke only focused on conscious intentions, and tended to ignore negative effects of goal setting and commitment (e.g. anxiety if performance does not match up to the goal).

Theories of motivation

Emotion consists of cognitive, physiological, experiential, expressive, and behavioural components. The Papez circuit based on the hippocampus, hypothalamus, and thalamus was suggested as the basis of emotion. This was later modified into the Papez–MacLean limbic model, in which there was more emphasis on the role of the amygdala. More recently, LeDoux argued that there are two brain systems involved in emotion: one involves the amygdala and autonomic and endocrine changes, and the other involves direct transmission of information from the thalamus to the cortex. Limbic theories of emotion are most relevant to fear and anger, and tend to de-emphasise the role of the cortex in emotion. The frontal lobes are also involved in emotion.

Emotion

According to the James–Lange theory, experienced emotion depends on feedback from the bodily changes produced by an emotional stimulus, with each emotion having its own

Theories of emotion

pattern of bodily changes. However, we often experience emotion before the relevant bodily changes have occurred, and many different emotional states are associated with a broadly similar state of autonomic arousal. According to the Cannon–Bard theory, emotional stimuli lead to activation of the thalamus and this produces two separate effects: (1) emotional experience; and (2) activation of the hypothalamus and autonomic arousal. The fact that the experienced intensity of emotional states often depends on the level of physiological arousal is inconsistent with the theory. According to cognitive labelling theory, emotion will be experienced only when there is high physiological arousal and that arousal is given an emotional interpretation. Many studies have provided only weak evidence for the theory, and the effects of arousal on emotional intensity are often much weaker than predicted. According to Lazarus, emotional experience depends on cognitive appraisal of significant stimuli.

Stress

Stress produces a range of emotional, physiological, cognitive, and behavioural effects. According to Selye, responses to stress form the general adaptation syndrome, which consists of an alarm reaction stage, a resistance stage, and an exhaustion stage. In fact, stress reactions are more variable than Selye assumed, and depend in part on the nature of the stressor. Stress activates the anterior pituitary adrenal cortex system, and it also activates the sympathetic nervous system. Stressful life events are associated with numerous illnesses, but this may not be a causal link. It has been argued that people with the Type A behaviour pattern are more stressed than those with the Type B behaviour pattern. The main evidence is that individuals high in the hostility component of Type A are susceptible to coronary heart disease. Stress can cause changes in the immune system, and these changes may help to cause disease. Some of these effects occur because stressed individuals tend to have an unhealthy lifestyle in terms of diet, smoking, alcohol consumption, and so on. There are three main coping strategies that individuals use to handle stress: task-oriented coping; emotion-oriented coping; and avoidance-oriented coping.

A positive emotional state can help people deal with day-to-day stress.

Biofeedback has been used to reduce stress. It works in the short term, but it is less clear that biofeedback can produce long-term reductions in stress in everyday life. Anti-anxiety drugs are also used to reduce stress. Benzodiazepines can have sedative effects, and their sudden removal can lead to intense anxiety. A newer drug, buspirone, does not have these disadvantages, but it is can produce headaches and depression. Anti-anxiety drugs reduce stress, but they do not address the problems causing stress. They should be used for short periods of time in low doses. Psychological methods based on social support and control are effective in reducing stress.

Methods of reducing stress

FURTHER READING

There are full accounts of motivation (Chapter 10) and emotion and stress (Chapter 17) in J.P.J. Pinel (1997), *Biopsychology (3rd Edn.)*, Boston: Allyn & Bacon. Detailed information about motivation and emotion is provided in Chapters 11–13 of N.R. Carlson (1994), *Physiology of behaviour (5th Edn.)*, Boston: Allyn & Bacon. There are brief discussions of the topics covered in this chapter in S. Green (1994), *Principles of biopsychology*, Hove, UK: Psychology Press.

REVISION QUESTIONS

1   Consider and analyse research into the relationship between brain systems and motivation.   (24 marks)

2a Critically consider *one* physiological theory of emotion.   (12 marks)

2b Critically consider *one* non-physiological theory of emotion.   (12 marks)

3   Discuss *either* theories *or* research findings relating to the physiological effects of stress.   (24 marks)

4   "Many methods have been proposed in the search to reduce the stressful effects of being alive, and a rough division would be into those directly affecting physiological reactivity and those intervening at the psychological level ... Combinations of the two are probably most successful" (Green, 1994). Critically consider the extent to which psychological evidence supports this statement.   (24 marks)

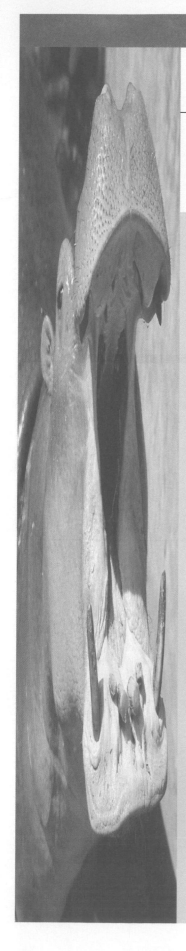

- **Evolution of behaviour**
  Some explanations for the ways in which different animals and birds behave.

  Krebs and Davies' theory
  Malthus, and Darwin's theory of natural selection
  Grier and Burk's theory of change

- **Competition for resources**
  When a resource like food is in short supply, why do some individuals fare better than others?

  Huntingford and Turner's features of territory
  Milinski's work with sticklebacks
  Gill and Wolf's study of sunbirds
  Huntingford and Turner's territoriality theory

- **Predator–prey relationships**
  How hunters and hunted succeed and fail.

  Grier and Burk's list of tactics
  Krebs and Davies' search image theory
  Prey adaptations: crypsis, polymorphism, startling, edibility, and mimicry

- **Symbiotic relationships**
  Different species that live together and benefit each other.

  Isack and Reyer's honeyguide study
  Preston's study of fish
  Thompson's theory of symbiotic relationships

7
Evolution and Behaviour

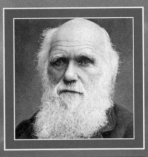
Charles Darwin, 1809–1882.

This chapter is concerned with some of the factors that determine the behaviour of non-human animals. Charles Darwin in 1859 put forward the theory of evolution, which focused on the role of natural selection, heredity, and the evolution of species. We consider applications of this general approach to the evolution of behaviour in various species.

Of crucial importance for the members of every species is the need to have access to adequate resources, especially of food. An important part of the theory of evolution is based on the notion that there will generally be competition for resources. In order to survive and to reproduce, the members of a species need to be able to compete effectively for resources.

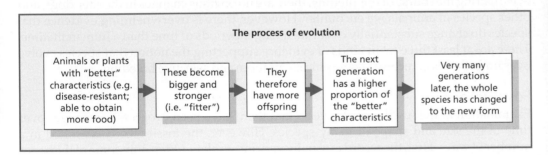

The process of evolution

| Animals or plants with "better" characteristics (e.g. disease-resistant; able to obtain more food) | → | These become bigger and stronger (i.e. "fitter") | → | They therefore have more offspring | → | The next generation has a higher proportion of the "better" characteristics | → | Very many generations later, the whole species has changed to the new form |

The process of evolution has led to various relationships between the members of different species. The most common relationship is that of predator and prey, with the members of one species trying to kill and eat the members of the other species. This produces strong evolutionary pressures on the prey species to protect itself more effectively against predation. When this happens, it produces evolutionary pressures on the predator species to develop new strategies for capturing members of the prey species. Sometimes the members of two species will develop positive relationships, in which they both benefit from the actions of the other species.

Evolution of Behaviour

Probably the most important question in comparative psychology is the following: "Why do the members of any given species behave in a certain way?" There are usually several different answers to that question. For example, some species of birds may sing in the spring because this attracts mates for breeding purposes, which is important for the preservation of the species. However, they may also sing because the increasing length of the day in the spring triggers off changes in hormone levels.

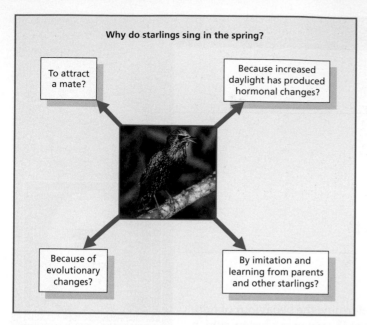

Why do starlings sing in the spring?

- To attract a mate?
- Because increased daylight has produced hormonal changes?
- Because of evolutionary changes?
- By imitation and learning from parents and other starlings?

Tinbergen (1963) developed this line of argument. He argued that there are often *four* kinds of answers to the question of why the members of a species behave as they do. We will follow Krebs and Davies (1993) in considering these four kinds of answers with respect to the issue of why starlings sing in the spring:

1. Survival value: starlings sing to attract mates for breeding.
2. Causation: starlings sing because of the hormonal changes produced by the lengthening day in spring.
3. Development: starlings sing because they have heard their parents and other starlings singing.
4. Evolutionary history: starlings sing complex songs as a result of evolutionary change from previous generations of birds singing simpler songs.

It is tempting to ask which of these four answers is the correct one. In fact, *all* of the answers are correct. There are various levels of explanation for animal behaviour, and all of these levels need to be considered in order to provide a complete account. In this chapter, however, we will focus mainly on the impact of a species' evolutionary history on the current behaviour of its members.

Species: Fixed or changing?

It used to be argued that every species is separate from every other species, and that it remains fixed over time. This argument seems to be supported by the evidence of our own eyes. During the course of our lifetime, there are no obvious changes in the cats, dogs, and other species of animals we encounter. However, there is overwhelming evidence that species do change substantially over much longer periods of time than a human lifetime. There are at least three main kinds of evidence supporting the notion that species evolve over time: the fossil record; geographical variation; and selective breeding.

Fossil record

Examination of the fossil record reveals that there have been progressive changes over time in the size and shape of many species. However, the fossil record is limited in a number of ways. First, the record is usually very incomplete. Often only some of the bones have been preserved, and there may be gaps in the record extending over thousands or tens of thousands of years. Second, the fossil record at best provides evidence only about the

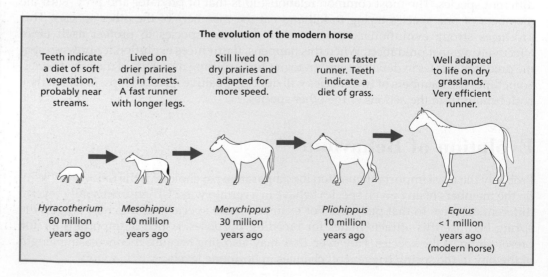

The evolution of the modern horse

Teeth indicate a diet of soft vegetation, probably near streams.	Lived on drier prairies and in forests. A fast runner with longer legs.	Still lived on dry prairies and adapted for more speed.	An even faster runner. Teeth indicate a diet of grass.	Well adapted to life on dry grasslands. Very efficient runner.

| *Hyracotherium* 60 million years ago | *Mesohippus* 40 million years ago | *Merychippus* 30 million years ago | *Pliohippus* 10 million years ago | *Equus* < 1 million years ago (modern horse) |

Ichthyosaurus: a marine reptile from the Jurassic era. Fossil records give us clues to what an animal looked like, but not how it behaved.

hard parts of an animal, and so it is often not easy to work out in detail what the animal looked like. Third, the fossil record cannot tell us about the behaviour of the members of a species. It is sometimes possible to make well-informed guesses about their behaviour, but that is all.

Geographical variation

The notion that each species remains unchanged over time seems improbable in the light of geographical variation. As Ridley (1995, p.21) pointed out:

> At any one place, species do appear as discrete groups of organisms, but if a species is traced across the world its appearance can usually be seen to change from place to place. House sparrows, for example, vary in size, bodily proportions, and colouration across the United States, and the house sparrows of North America visibly differ from those of Europe.

Charles Darwin travelled thousands of miles on the scientific survey ship *HMS Beagle*, and his observations of geographical variation within species played a part in the development of his theory of evolution.

Selective breeding

Selective breeding also supports the view that species can change over time. Darwin (1859) was impressed by the way in which breeding programmes can produce, for example, either race horses that are light and lean or farm horses that are large and strong. Darwin himself bred pigeons, and observed changes in them from one generation to the next. He argued that the changes produced artificially by selective breeding are like those that occur under more natural conditions.

Natural selection and adaptation

We have seen that there is convincing evidence that species can change considerably over long periods of time. What is needed is an explanation of the *processes* involved in producing these changes. Darwin (1859) provided such an explanation in his theory of natural selection. This theory was based on five major assumptions:

1. Variation: individuals within a species differ from each other in their physical characteristics (e.g. height) and in their behaviour.
2. Heritability: at least some of the variation among members of a species is inherited; as a result, offspring tend to resemble their parents more than other members of the species.

Examples of modern selective breeding can be visually obvious (e.g. pedigree dogs) or less so (e.g. strawberries that are resistant to the cold). Modern wheat is the result of over 2000 years of selective breeding from grasses. Can you think of other examples of selective breeding in our current environment?

All dogs have the same distant ancestors, but selective breeding has resulted in major variations.

Numbers of descendants after many generations

Year	Generation	Number of descendants
2000	1st	3
2025	2nd	9
2050	3rd	27
2075	4th	81
2100	5th	243
2125	6th	729
2150	7th	2187
2175	8th	6561
2200	9th	19,683
2225	10th	59,049
2250	11th	177,147
2275	12th	531,441
2300	13th	1,594,323

Based on a new generation every 25 years, where each descendant has three surviving children. This situation is hypothetical as some people do not have three children due to early death, sterility, or choice.

3. Competition: the members of most species produce far more offspring than can survive. Darwin worked out that a pair of elephants could have about 19 million descendants alive 750 years after their birth if there were no problems of survival. In fact, there is competition for mates, food, and places to live.
4. Natural selection: the members of a species which survive the process of competition and go on to breed will tend to have characteristics that are better suited to the environment than those which do not. Thus, there is natural selection or survival of the fittest (in the sense of survival or reproductive success rather than physical fitness).
5. Adaptation: as a result of the process of natural selection, successive generations will tend to be more and more adapted to their environment. They will possess characteristics that allow them to obtain food and to reproduce.

Cheetahs are the fastest land animals and catch their prey using amazing bursts of speed. They can reach 70mph (110kph) but tire after about 400 metres.

Darwin was greatly influenced by the work of Malthus (1798). Malthus emphasised the notion that the human population tends to increase considerably over time, whereas the earth's resources (e.g. land; food) either cannot increase or do so only slowly. Malthus worked out what would happen if a couple had three children, all of their children had three children, and so on. After 12 generations, the original couple would have more than 250,000 descendants. After 25 generations, this would increase to over 5 million, a figure that makes me feel guilty at having three children of my own! Malthus and Darwin were both pessimistic about the chances of any species showing reproductive restraint. As a result, Darwin reasoned, what must happen is that there will be ever-increasing competition for finite resources.

Changes within a species

How do the assumptions of Darwin's theory of natural selection explain changes within a species? The crucial notion is that the environment will often only allow those members of a species having certain characteristics to survive. Suppose, for example, that a speedy predator eats mainly the members of a given species. If only the fast-moving members of the prey species survive, then that species should evolve over the generations in the direction of becoming faster moving on average.

Darwin (1859) assumed that evolutionary change would generally happen relatively slowly over periods of hundreds or thousands of years. However, the fossil record suggests that changes can occur fairly rapidly. As a result, Gould (1981) argued that a species will sometimes have fairly brief periods of rapid development in between long periods of relative stability. He described this notion as **punctuated equilibrium**. Recent research has identified the genes that permit such rapid development.

Grier and Burk (1992) addressed the issue of why it is some aspects of behaviour seem to have changed much more than others during the course of evolution. They identified four main reasons why evolutionary change might be rapid for some categories of behaviour:

1. Changes in those aspects of behaviour may allow a more efficient use of the available resources.

KEY TERM

Punctuated equilibrium: the notion that long periods of relative stability for a species are punctuated by short-lived periods of rapid change.

Deep sea octopus

In a study of deep sea life, Wider, Johnsen, and Balser (1999) described one octopus species that lives at depths of 900 metres and feeds on prey too small to grasp with tentacles. The usual suckers on octopus tentacles are therefore redundant and do not have the muscles in this species that are normal in shallow-water octopuses. Instead, the sucker-like pads have developed light-emitting cells, which produce the bluish light typical of bioluminescence and attract prey.

2. Competition may lead to more specialised forms of behaviour.
3. Forms of behaviour that are of use with respect to other members of the same species (e.g. courtship; communication) may be especially likely to show evolutionary change.
4. Forms of behaviour between the members of two species (e.g. predator–prey interactions; host–parasite interactions) may be subject to rapid change by both species.

In contrast, forms of behaviour tend to be stable over the generations when there would be no advantage in changing them. They are also stable because a superior form of behaviour has simply not appeared in the species in question.

Adaptation is imperfect

It might be thought that the processes of natural selection and adaptation would tend to make the members of a species almost perfectly suited to their environment. This is not what Darwin actually believed. According to Darwin (1872, p.163):

> *Natural selection tends only to make each organic being as perfect as, or slightly more perfect than, the other inhabitants of the same country with which it comes into competition ... Natural selection will not produce absolute perfection.*

Behaviour is sometimes not well adapted to the environment because the environment has changed recently. For example, it is speculated that the behaviour of the dinosaurs became fatally non-adaptive after a large meteor hit the earth 65 million years ago.

It is much harder for species to adapt to their environment when it is changing rapidly. Numerous species have experienced enormous changes in recent years because of the speed at which the human species is destroying their environment. According to Sir Robert May (1998), "Looking towards the immediate future, three different approaches to estimating impending rates of extinction suggest species' life expectancies of 200 to 400 years." In contrast, the average lifespan for a species before the arrival of the human species was about 5 to 10 million years. May (1998) pointed out that what is happening "represents a sixth great wave of extinction fully comparable with the Big Five mass extinctions of the geological past [including the one that wiped out the dinosaurs]. But

One theory about the disappearance of the dinosaurs is that they failed to adapt to changes in world climate brought about when a massive meteor hit the earth.

CASE STUDY: *The Milk Thief*

In 1949 doorstep delivery of bottled milk was becoming increasingly popular. Previously, milk had been decanted into the householder's own jugs and containers, but the new method involved a glass bottle with a foil cap. Housewives began to complain that someone or something was piercing and peeling back the foil cap, and stealing the cream from the top of the milk. As this epidemic of thefts spread, it was discovered that the culprits were several species of tits, the main offenders being blue tits who had discovered a new food source. The behaviour was widespread for ten years or so, during which time householders learned that a solution was to leave a cup on the doorstep for the milkman to put over the top of the milk bottle. Gradually the milk thefts ceased to be a problem.

However, at about the same time, blue tits began another unusual behaviour. Entering houses and factories, they would embark on an orgy of paper-tearing, ripping up strips of any paper they found: wallpaper, toilet rolls, parcel wrappings, newspapers, and so on. There seemed to be no obvious reward for this behaviour, and scientists were baffled. One explanation put forward by the British Trust for Ornithology was that, because the birds could find so much food so easily, their hunger was satisfied before their hunting drive, so they were imitating tearing bark from trees in search of prey. Before anyone could agree on the true explanation for this odd behaviour, it too died out, and milk-stealing and paper-tearing by blue tits is now almost unknown.

it is different, in that it results from the activities of a single other species rather than from external environmental changes."

An important reason why species are imperfectly adapted to their environment was identified by Maynard Smith (1976). He argued that natural selection typically produces *stable* behavioural strategies, even when these strategies are not ideal. When an individual animal interacts with other animals, its most adaptive behaviour depends very much on how the other animals behave.

Maynard Smith considered whether it is more adaptive for animals to be hawks (very aggressive and inclined to fight) or doves (avoiding conflict and fighting). In principle, the most adaptive strategy would be for all animals to be doves. However, in the real world, that is a risky strategy because of the danger of invasion by hawks. The most adaptive strategy in practice is for there to be a mixture of hawks and doves, and this is what is found in many species. Maynard Smith referred to this as an **evolutionarily stable strategy**. This is "a strategy which when adopted by most members of the population cannot be beaten by any other strategy" (Krebs & Davies, 1993, p.149).

Do you think the adaptive strategy of a mixture of hawks and doves also applies to the human species?

Evidence

Uniformitarianism. Most of the evidence for natural selection is rather indirect. The reason for this is because the processes involved occur over such long periods of time that they cannot be observed directly. Those who use the fossil record or other historical evidence endorse the assumption of **uniformitarianism**. This is the notion that biological and physical processes operate in the same uniform way over time. If we accept the notion of uniformitarianism, then our observations in the present allow us to make inferences about the past.

There is a constant danger of observing what a given species is like now and making up an "explanation" that sounds plausible but lacks evidence. For example, we might guess that giraffes have long necks because in the long distant past only those giraffes with long necks were able to reach up high enough to obtain food. Hailman (1992, p.127) was very critical of this approach:

The colouration, anatomy, physiology, and behaviour of animals seem so well suited to the environments in which they live that natural selection "must" have adapted the animals to their environments. Come on, can't we do better than that?

KEY TERMS

Evolutionarily stable strategy: a behavioural strategy that works effectively and is stable over time provided that most members of a species adopt it.

Uniformitarianism: the notion that biological and other processes operate in the same constant way over time.

The peppered moth. What has often been regarded as fairly direct support for some of the assumptions of Darwin's theory was obtained by H.B.D. Kettlewell in the 1950s (see Ridley, 1995). He studied two variants of the peppered moth, one of which was darker than the other. The difference in colour is inherited, with the offspring of the darker type being on average darker than those of the lighter type. Both types of peppered moth are eaten by birds such as robins and redstarts that rely on sight to detect them. Kettlewell observed the moths when they were on relatively light lichen-covered trees and when they were on dark, lichen-less trees in industrially polluted areas. The lighter-coloured

moths survived better on the lighter trees and the darker-coloured moths survived better on the darker trees.

Colour variants of the peppered moth.

According to Darwin's theory, the number of darker moths should increase if there is an increase in the proportion of dark trees. Precisely this happened in England due to the industrial revolution, when pollution killed the lichen and coated the trees with sooty deposits. The proportion of peppered moths that were dark apparently went from very low to over half in a period of about 50 years. However, the evidence that there were few dark peppered moths in the late nineteenth century comes from moth collections. As Hailman (1992, p.126) pointed out, "Those collections were not scientific samples but were made by amateurs ... Perhaps they did not like ugly black moths."

Kittiwakes. Good evidence for the theory of evolution comes from studies on gulls. There are about 35 species of gulls, and most of them show great similarities in their behaviour. Nearly all these species nest on the ground, but kittiwakes nest on narrow ledges which are a long way above ground level. Cullen (1957) found that the chicks of most gull species start to roam about away from the nest within about one day of hatching. In contrast, the

Roaming behaviour in kittiwake chicks would seriously damage the survival of the species.

chicks of kittiwakes remain in their nests. The evolutionary significance of this difference is fairly clear. The chicks of kittiwakes might kill themselves if they moved around on narrow ledges, whereas the chicks of other gull species can often avoid danger by running away from it.

Empid flies. The courtship behaviour of various species of empid flies can easily be explained in evolutionary terms. In some species, male flies give prey wrapped in silk to the female during courtship. This is effective, but has the disadvantage that the male has to exert energy to obtain the prey. In other species, the male gives the female nothing. This has the disadvantage that the male is some-times eaten by the female, probably because the female is not distracted by the presence of the prey wrapped in silk. In evolutionary terms, the optimal behaviour for the male would be to distract the female without the need to catch any prey. Precisely this happens in other species of empid flies, in which the male gives the female an empty silk balloon (Kessel, 1955).

Links between environment and behaviour. One of the best ways of testing evolutionary notions is to study numerous species that differ in their behaviour. The researcher tries to work out which environmental differences have produced the behavioural differences among species. According to Grier and Burk (1992, p.143):

> *This approach is considered as strong or nearly as strong as the genuinely experimental method. In essence, one is merely taking advantage of experiments that have already taken place in nature where there is a sufficiently large sample size to reduce the impact of spurious correlations.*

Male frogs use precopulatory guarding to ensure that mating is successful.

Ridley (1983) made use of this approach. There are numerous species in which the male hangs on to the female for periods of time ranging between days and weeks before fertilisation occurs. This is known as precopulatory guarding, and it is found in arthropods (e.g. spiders and crustaceans), frogs, and toads. Ridley argued that precopulatory guarding might develop through natural selection in species in which the females are receptive for mating for fairly brief but predictable periods of time. On the other hand, precopulatory guarding would not be found in species where the females are continuously receptive for mating or where their receptivity occurs at unpredictable times. His key finding was that these predictions were confirmed in 399 out of 401 species.

Evaluation

Mechanisms of heredity. It is generally accepted that Darwin's (1859) theory of natural selection is essentially correct as far as it goes. However, he did not provide an account of the *mechanisms* involved in heredity. We now know that genes determine what is inherited, and so Darwin's theory can be re-expressed in terms of the involvement of genes. In the words of Krebs and Davies (1993, pp.9–10):

> *The individual can be regarded as a temporary vehicle or survival machine by which genes survive and are replicated ... the most successful genes will be those which promote most effectively an individual's survival and reproductive success ... As a result, we would therefore expect individuals to behave so as to promote gene survival.*

Evidence that genetic factors can have powerful influences on behaviour comes from artificial selection experiments. In such experiments, animals are bred so as to produce separate strains that behave very differently from each other. For example, Berthold et al. (1990) carried out a selection study on blackcaps, 75% of whom were migratory and 25% of whom were resident. They mated migratory birds with other migratory birds, and they mated resident birds with other resident birds. After six generations, they produced two separate strains that were either 100% migratory or 100% resident. It is claimed that selection experiments show in an exaggerated form the workings of evolution.

Can you think of everyday examples of artificial selection?

Altruism. According to Darwin's theory, individual animals should behave in a selfish fashion to compete successfully against other individuals, and so ensure the survival of their genes in the future. However, animals often seem to show altruistic behaviour, which is behaviour that benefits other animals but at some cost to the animal itself or to its reproductive potential. One of the clearest examples of such altruism is found in social insect societies, in which most of the insects do not try to reproduce themselves (see Chapter 9).

   The existence of altruistic behaviour is contrary to evolutionary theory as put forward by Darwin (1859). However, it can be explained in terms of evolution. The key notion is that an individual animal's close relatives share many of its genes. As a result, its motivation to ensure that its genes are transmitted to the next generation can be achieved by helping

Does the kin selection strategy also apply to human beings?

its close relatives to reproduce. This strategy is known as **kin selection**. That seems to explain the apparently altruistic behaviour of social insects.

Adaptation. According to Darwin's theory, the characteristics possessed by individual animals serve the function of making them well adapted to their environment. However, some species possess characteristics that do not seem to serve any useful purpose. For example, the long tail or train of peacocks makes them vulnerable to attack by predators because it reduces their mobility. It now appears that peacocks' long tails or trains are more functional than used to be thought (see Chapter 8). Peahens find the peacock's long train attractive, and so peacocks with long trains have greater reproductive success than those with short trains. Not only do the peacocks spread out their trains as a mating display, they also shake them noisily to draw attention to them.

The peacock's long tail, apparently an evolutionary error, has an important role to play in attracting a mate.

Competition for Resources

When resources such as food are in short supply, individual animals need to compete for those resources. In nature, there are often several factors that together determine how individuals compete for resources. However, we will start by considering two simple possibilities: competition by exploitation and competition by resource defence. After that, we will consider some examples of species that make use of these forms of competition.

Exploitation

Exploitation means using up resources. According to the simplest model of exploitation, individuals go to the place or habitat that offers them the greatest access to resources. The key point is that the best habitat is not always the one that contains the most resources. Krebs and Davies (1993) took the simple example of an environment with a rich habitat and a poor one. Initially, it is best for all individuals to go to the rich habitat. However, the resources of the rich habitat will be increasingly used up as more and more individuals go to it. There will come a point at which newcomers will do better to go to the poor habitat, which has the advantages of less competition and less depletion of resources.

Suppose that we assume that the numbers of animals at each habitat are such that each individual has equal access to resources. This state of affairs is known as the **ideal free distribution**. It is an ideal distribution because it will only happen when the animals have good or ideal information about the availability of resources at the various habitats. It is a free distribution because it is based on the assumption that all of the animals are free to go to whichever habitat they prefer. In nature, animals often defend a habitat in an aggressive way, and so the assumption is not justified.

Exploitation: the best habitat is not always the one that contains the most resources.

Resource defence

Resource defence involves some animals keeping others away from resources by displays of aggression or by

This wolf will react aggressively towards any stranger attempting to share its kill.

fighting. What typically happens is that the first animals to arrive at a rich habitat set up territories, which they then defend against animals that arrive later on. A **territory** can be regarded more generally as any area that is defended by one or more animals. A territory can be set up for feeding purposes, for mating purposes, for raising young, and so on.

Huntingford and Turner (1987) argued that there are four key features defining the existence of a territory:

1. The animal or animals defending a territorial area display aggressive behaviour towards other animals.
2. Animals defending a territory limit their aggressive behaviour to a given area.
3. The territory or defended area is only used by the animal or animals defending it.
4. The aggressive or dominant behaviour displayed by animals defending their own territory changes to submissive behaviour when they enter another territory.

Evidence: Exploitation

In your experience, how do pet animals show what they consider to be their territory?

Some studies on exploitation of resources have obtained evidence of an ideal free distribution. Milinski (1979) put six sticklebacks into a tank. Prey were dropped into the water at each end of the tank, with twice as many prey being available at one end as at the other. An ideal free distribution in these circumstances would involve four sticklebacks being at the end of the tank with the greater resources. That was precisely what Milinski found.

The study by Milinski was a controlled laboratory study. Evidence of an ideal free distribution under natural conditions was reported by Power (1984). She studied the behaviour of armoured catfish in a stream in Panama. These fish eat algae, which are found mostly in sunny pools. The catfish tended to gather in the sunny pools, and the relative numbers in sunny and shady pools were in agreement with the ideal free distribution.

It is very common in nature for the competition for resources to involve both exploitation and resource defence. For example, animals may decide which habitat to go to for resources on the basis of exploitation, but the amount of resources obtained by each animal in any given habitat may depend on resource defence.

Whitham (1980) studied habitat selection in the aphid. In the spring, females settle on leaves that provide juices they need to reproduce successfully. Larger leaves provide more juices than smaller leaves, and so the largest leaves are the ones that are occupied first. Whitham's findings were in agreement with the ideal free distribution. More female aphids settled on the large leaves than on the small ones, so that the average reproductive

Milinski's study: at the start, two-thirds of the prey were available at one end of the tank. Subsequently, two-thirds of the sticklebacks moved to the place with greater prey resources, showing an ideal free distribution.

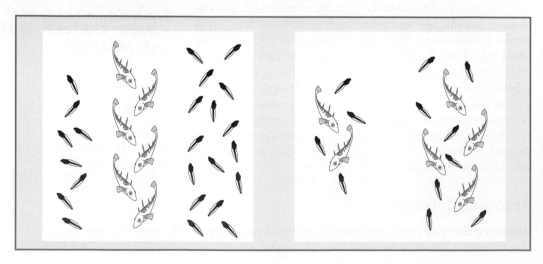

KEY TERM
Territory: an area that is defended by one or more animals.

success in terms of the number of offspring did not depend on whether the habitat was good or poor.

The findings discussed so far have conformed to the ideal free distribution. However, here even though the *average* access to resources and reproductive success did not depend on the nature of the habitat, there was also evidence that some individuals within any given habitat had access to more resources than others. Some parts of the leaf provide more juices than others, and female aphids kicked and pushed each other in order to occupy the best positions on the leaf. These findings indicate that resource defence played a part in the competition for resources.

Evidence: Resource defence

Krebs (1971) reported evidence of resource defence in great tits. Their best breeding habitat is in oak woodland. The oak woodland is filled rapidly with defended territories in the spring, so that late-arriving great tits have to occupy the much poorer habitat provided by hedgerows. When great tits were taken away from the oak woodland, others from the hedgerows moved in rapidly to replace them. This suggests that it was resource defence that forced them to inhabit hedgerows.

The members of some species compete for resources by means of resource defence or defending their territory, but the members of other species do not. What determines whether or not animals make use of resource defence? Brown (1964) argued for the importance of **economic defendability**, which is the notion that a territory will be defended whenever the benefits are greater than the costs. In the section on territorial contests we will see how a group of red deer stags assesses the costs of defending their territory.

Gill and Wolf

It is hard in many species to work out the benefits and costs associated with territorial defence. However, this can be done in some species of birds. Gill and Wolf (1975) looked in detail at the behaviour of the golden-winged sunbird in East Africa. Sunbirds extract nectar from *Leonotis* flowers. They can obtain this nectar either by defending patches of these flowers against competitors, or by foraging for it. Defended territories generally consisted of between 1000 and 2500 flowers, and there was more nectar on the defended flowers than the non-defended ones.

Gill and Wolf worked out the costs of territorial defence, foraging, and sitting on a perch in terms of the number of calories per hour they required. Territorial defence used up far more calories per hour than the other activities. However, territorial defence took less time than foraging, and it provided access to flowers containing more nectar. According to the notion of economic defendability, sunbirds should engage in territorial defence when the gain in terms of additional nectar outweighs the cost in terms of using up calories. In general terms, that is exactly what was found by Gill and Wolf. However, it is important to note that the sunbirds did *not* work out the number of calories per hour involved in different activities before deciding what to do. The information actually used by sunbirds when deciding whether to defend their territory or to forage for food remains unclear.

Discussion points

1. Can psychologists always work out the precise benefits and costs of territorial defence?
2. How could we extend this type of research? For example, we could put small weights on the backs of sunbirds to increase the cost of territorial defence in terms of calories.

Size of territory

We have seen so far that the notion of economic defendability is of value in predicting whether animals will defend territories. However, it would be useful to be able to make

Great tits prefer a woodland habitat, but when all available woodland territory is used up, they will find other areas.

more detailed predictions. For example, what is the size of the territory that animals will choose to defend? It might be thought that animals would defend a large territory, because large territories contain more resources than small ones. However, it takes more energy to defend a large territory, and so the benefits of extra resources may be outweighed by the costs of its defence.

This issue was considered by Carpenter, Paton, and Hixon (1983). They studied rufous hummingbirds who were migrating southwards through California, and who needed to make up the weight lost on their journey. These birds often changed the size of their territory between one day and the next. Carpenter et al. found that the hummingbirds showed more weight gain when they defended a medium-sized territory than when they defended one that was either large or small. These findings suggest that the best defended territory is of medium size.

How might Carpenter et al. have assessed the size of the hummingbirds' territory from day to day?

Sharing

All the examples of resource defence considered so far have involved individuals defending a territory. However, there are many cases in which two or more individuals of the same species combine forces to defend the same territory. Davies and Houston (1981) studied pied wagtails. These birds feed on insects washed up on the banks of rivers. Individual wagtails generally go around their territory a number of times each day, taking about 40 minutes each time. Sometimes two pied wagtails defend the same territory, with the territory owner permitting a "satellite" territory owner to join it. This has the advantage that the territory is defended better against intruders. However, it has the disadvantage that each bird is only able to feed on about half of the insects within the territory. Davies and Houston worked out that the advantages of sharing would outweigh the costs when many insects were being washed up on the river bank, and when there were many intruders. As predicted, sharing was much more common in those circumstances than when there were fewer insects being washed ashore and fewer intruders.

Resource defence: Theory

Most theoretical approaches have focused on the notion of economic defendability, with its emphasis on identifying the benefits and costs associated with resource defence. Huntingford and Turner (1987) identified several benefits and costs that jointly determine whether a territory possesses economic defendability. Some of the main potential benefits of territoriality are as follows:

A male hippopotamus "gapes" to warn off intruders to its territory.

- Decreased risk of predation (being attacked by predators).
- Food resources last longer, because fewer animals have access to them.
- Renewable food resources are used more slowly, and so can be harvested more efficiently.
- Animals may have greater reproductive success because of the resources available within the territory.
- Offspring are raised in a more favourable environment.

Huntingford and Turner identified the following major costs of territoriality:

- It may be necessary to remove the previous owner before taking over a territory.
- Defending a territory may require the expenditure of much energy.
- Defending a territory may take up considerable amounts of time.
- Defending a territory may risk injury or even death.

It is often thought that animals will typically strive to maintain their territory over long periods of time. However, it follows from the notion of economic defendability that territories will often be abandoned when circumstances change so as to reduce the benefits of the territory and/or increase the costs. This was shown clearly in the study by Davies and Houston (1981) on pied wagtails. Territory owners used four different territorial strategies at different times. When the food resources in the territory were very low, they abandoned it completely. When the food resources were fairly low, they spent all their time in the territory. When the food resources were abundant, but there was much intrusion by other birds, they allowed a second or satellite bird to join them in the territory (see earlier). When the food resources were abundant, but there was little risk of intrusion, the pied wagtails did not devote time to defending their territory.

Do you think Huntingford and Turner's lists of benefits and costs would also have applied to early humans?

Territorial contests

The decision as to whether it is worth defending a territory often depends on the likelihood of the territory owner being successful in a territorial contest against an intruder. In most species, the winner of any territorial contest tends to be the larger animal (Huntingford & Turner, 1987). When the two animals are the same size, then the owner or resident is more likely to win. For example, Burk (1984) studied territorial contests in male Caribbean fruit flies. When both flies were the same size, the owner won just over 70% of the contests.

Keep-out behaviours. There are various reasons why territorial contests are rare in many species. One reason is because of the existence of keep-out behaviours that may be visual or auditory. Peek (1972) studied male red-winged blackbirds, who defend their territories by showing off their red and yellow shoulder patches and by loud vocalisations. Blackbirds that had their shoulder patches covered with black polish were less successful at keeping out intruders. In similar fashion, blackbirds that were operated on to prevent them vocalising were also less able to prevent intruders from entering their territory.

> **Red deer displays**
>
> The red deer colony on the Scottish island of Rhum show clear ritual in their mating and territorial contests. The ritual has several stages, each of which acts as an assessment of an opponent's strength. A stag can leave the contest at any time by backing off and turning away, thereby escaping serious injury. First, the two contesting stags perform a parallel walk, side by side up and down a stretch of land. They appear to be assessing each other visually. If the contest continues, the stags stop walking and stand to bellow or roar. They can make a fearsome amount of noise, which appears to be another way of demonstrating strength. The next stage involves mock rushes at the other animal, followed by physical contact using their bodies and antlers. If contests reach this point, serious injury can result, even leading to the death of an animal, so this final stage is only embarked on when both stags assess their strength and fighting ability as likely to bring success. Because success brings territory and a harem of females, it is a powerful reward.

Ritualised aggression may not involve any contact between the protagonists.

Ritualised aggression. Another reason why no-holds-barred territorial contests are fairly rare is because of **ritualised aggression**. This involves an animal producing stereotyped aggressive displays to deter other animals from attacking it. One of the key purposes of ritualised displays is that they permit animals to assess each other's fighting ability without serious risk of injury or death. For example, a cat defending its territory will arch its back, erect its fur, and make menacing noises at other cats. Male frogs and toads wrestle each other to decide who has the best territory, and beetles push each other to assess which is the stronger (Krebs & Davies, 1993).

True aggression. Ritualised aggression may be the norm, but vicious fighting often occurs when resources are scarce or valuable. For example, up to 10% of male musk oxen die every year as a result of fierce fights over females. More dramatically, male fig-wasps inside a fig fruit often kill each other in fights to decide who will mate with female fig-wasps. According to Krebs and Davies (1993, p.157), one fig fruit "was found to contain 15 females, 12 uninjured males and 42 damaged males who were dead or dying from fighting injuries. Damage included legs, antennae and heads completely bitten off, holes in the thorax, and eviscerated [disembowelled] abdomens."

> **KEY TERM**
> **Ritualised aggression**: stereotyped rituals involving aggressive displays designed to deter other animals from fighting.

Predator–Prey Relationships

According to Krebs and Davies (1993), there is a kind of "arms race" over time between predators and their prey. Natural selection during evolution should produce predators who are increasingly well equipped to detect and to capture their prey. However, natural selection should also lead to changes in the prey, so that they are better able to avoid detection or to escape from predators. The term **coevolution** is used to refer to the notion that evolutionary changes in predator and prey species depend in part on changes in the other species. According to Grier and Burk (1992, pp.268–269):

> *The effects of predator–prey coevolution on animal behaviour and morphology [form and structure] are so pervasive that it has even been theorised to be one of the main factors in, for example, the evolution of the vertebrates.*

There can be serious consequences, leading to extinction of their species, if either predators or prey fail to adapt rapidly enough, so it is of great importance for both predators and prey not to fall behind in the evolutionary arms race. Dawkins and Krebs (1979) argued that the pressures are often greater on the prey rather than on the predators. According to them, "A fox may reproduce after losing a race against a rabbit. No rabbit has ever reproduced after losing a race against a fox. Foxes who often fail to catch prey eventually starve to death, but they may get some reproduction in first."

In what follows, we will see some of the methods used by predators, as well as some of the defensive methods that have been developed by prey. There is a surprising variety of methods used by both predators and by prey. Some of these methods depend in a direct way on evolutionary change. For example, many species have developed acute senses of seeing, hearing, or smelling. Other species have developed physically, becoming able to move more quickly or becoming stronger and heavier. Other methods are more subtle, depending on various forms of trickery.

There are various stages in the predator–prey relationship. Endler (1991) identified five stages, as follows: encounter; detection; identification; approach; and consumption. Any given adaptation by predators or by prey is typically of most relevance to one or other of these stages.

Adaptations by predators

Tactics

Grier and Burk (1992) list seven methods used by predators when trying to catch prey. Perhaps the most obvious method is by simply chasing and pursuing the prey. Another method is to force the prey to keep moving until it is exhausted. This method is often used when the prey might prove dangerous if attacked before it is exhausted.

Stalking and ambushing are used by many species of cats. Some other species (e.g. chameleons; mantids) achieve success at stalking and ambushing by blending in with their background so they are hard to see. An unusual form of stalking and ambushing is used by anglerfish. They display a bait that looks very much like a small fish. If a prey moves close to this bait, the anglerfish moves rapidly to catch it (Pietsch & Grobecker, 1978).

Predators sometimes achieve more success at hunting in groups. Such communal hunting is found in lions, wolves, killer whales, communal spiders, and other species. Detailed evidence on the effects of group size on hunting success in lions was reported by Schaller (1972). When lions hunted gazelle, wildebeest, zebra, or other prey on their own, their overall success rate was only 15%. This increased to 29% when two lions hunted together, and to 37% when three lions hunted together. The success rate decreased somewhat when there were more than three lions in the hunting group.

Seven methods used by predators to catch prey (Grier & Burke, 1992)

1. Groping and flashing: this involves using feet or feelers.
2. Stalking and ambushing.
3. Chase and pursuit.
4. Interception of flight path.
5. Exhaustion of prey.
6. Tool use to get prey.
7. Communal hunting.

KEY TERM

Coevolution: evolutionary changes in predator and prey species that depend on changes in the other species.

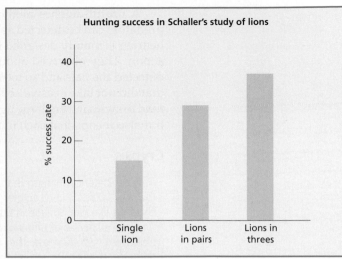

Hunting success in Schaller's study of lions

Angler fish attract their prey by displaying a mock "bait".

Search image

Krebs and Davies (1993) identified additional ways in which predators can become more successful at catching prey. Predators may develop more effective ways of searching for prey by improved visual acuity. Alternatively, they may learn to find prey more easily by forming a **search image**, which involves learning more about the visual features of their prey. Forming a search image may also involve improved attentional processes. Evidence for the development of a search image in chicks was reported by Dawkins (1971). The prey consisted of coloured rice grains which were presented on a background that was either the same or a very different colour to the grains. The chicks initially found it hard to detect the prey when it was the same colour as the background. After a few minutes, however, they started to detect and to eat the prey more quickly, suggesting that the chicks had formed an appropriate search image.

Subduing prey

Krebs and Davies (1993) also pointed out that some predators become more effective by developing better ways of subduing prey they have caught. Prey can be subdued and killed in various ways. Predators can use their teeth or beak to bite or tear their prey, or they can use their claws to open them up. Another possibility is squeezing or suffocating prey by the use of constriction, as with many species of snakes. Finally, predators such as stingrays, venomous snakes, and scorpions use stinging or poison to subdue and kill their prey.

Success rates

Predators are often not very successful at catching prey. Success rates are hard to calculate accurately, in part because it is not always clear to an observer whether an act of predation has been tried. In addition, success rates vary considerably depending on the predator and prey species involved. However, a typical hunting success rate for a predator is about 30% (Grier & Burk, 1992), indicating that about two-thirds of predation attempts end in failure. In the next section, we consider some of the ways in which prey manage to avoid being caught by predators.

Adaptations by prey

Tactics

According to Grier and Burk (1992), there are at least 11 major methods used by prey to defend themselves against predators. The most obvious method is to run, swim, or fly faster than the predator, so that the prey cannot be caught. Another fairly obvious method is for the prey to make unpredictable movements so that it is hard for the predator to follow it. This method is used by moths when trying to escape from bats.

KEY TERM
Search image: detailed learning about the visual features of prey by predators.

A useful defence method is to develop more sensitive perceptual abilities so that predators can be detected as early as possible. Roeder and Treat (1961) argued that moths' hearing is mainly designed to detect bats' calls and alert them to the need to take escape action. They observed about 400 encounters between bats and moths. The moths that detected the bats and so took evasive action were much more likely to survive than those that did not take evasive action. A different tactic is used by small reef-dwelling fish. They tend to swim in very large tightly packed shoals. This mass may serve to distract predators, but also means that each individual fish has a greater chance of escaping predation.

Crypsis

Another defence method that has proved useful in many species is known as **crypsis**, in which the prey's colouring resembles that of the setting in which it is generally found. In other words, crypsis is like camouflage in that it makes it harder for the predator to detect its prey.

Various species of underwing moths have forewings that look very similar to the bark of the trees on which they rest. They generally seem to make the camouflage most effective by orienting themselves so that the patterning on their forewings matches that on the bark as closely as possible. Evidence that crypsis is, indeed, effective in reducing the ability of predators such as blue jays to detect the moths was reported by Pietrewicz and Kamil (1981). They presented slides to blue jays in a testing apparatus. An underwing moth was present in some of the slides but not in others, and the moth was shown against a background that either resembled the moth's forewings or was rather different. The blue jay was rewarded with a mealworm every time it correctly detected a moth. The blue jays detected over 90% of the moths presented against a different background, but only about 10% of the moths presented against a very similar background. These findings show clearly that crypsis or camouflage in prey can be a very effective defence against predators.

It might be thought that crypsis or camouflage in prey will only be an effective defence when it is very hard for predators to detect them. However, this is not so. Erichsen et al. (1980) presented great tits with a mixture of large prey that took a few seconds to detect and small prey that were easy to detect. When the easily detected prey were encountered often, the great tits tended to eat them and to ignore the large cryptic prey. Thus, even fairly poor crypsis or camouflage will be very useful to a species if it makes some other prey more profitable to predators.

Discussion points

1. Can you think of other species that make use of camouflage?

2. How do you think that crypsis or camouflage developed in those species that possess it?

Polymorphism

Underwing moths do not only have crypsis or camouflage as a defence against predators. The forewings of many species of underwing moths show **polymorphism**; that is, they differ somewhat in colour among the members of that species. Suppose that a predator forms a search image (see earlier) of the colour pattern of the first moth it finds, and then looks for further moths having the same colour pattern. If that is the case, then polymorphism would help prey to avoid detection.

This notion was tested by Pietrewicz and Kamil (1981). Blue jays were presented with slides consisting of either members of only one species of underwing moth or a random mixture of members of two species. The blue jays showed a rapid improvement in their ability to detect the moths when they were all of the same species, but there was no improvement when the moths came from two differently coloured species. These findings suggest that predators who encounter polymorphic prey find it hard to form a useful search image of their prey.

Startling a predator

The forewings of underwing moths look like tree bark. In contrast, their hindwings tend to be brightly coloured. In order to escape detection, the moths normally rest with their hindwings covered by their forewings. When they are disturbed by a predator, the moths suddenly expose their hindwings. This may startle the predator, and thus give the moth the chance to escape. The advantage of brightly coloured hindwings may be that they startle the predator more than would hindwings lacking colour.

Schlenoff (1985) tested these ideas. She presented blue jays with models of moths in which the hindwings suddenly became visible. Blue jays who were initially exposed to models with grey hindwings had a startle response to brightly coloured hindwings. However, blue jays who initially saw brightly coloured hindwings were not startled when shown grey hindwings. Thus, brightly coloured hindwings do cause predators to become startled. Schlenoff also found that blue jays were no longer startled when exposed repeatedly to the same brightly coloured hindwings. However, the startle response returned when differently coloured hindwings were presented. These findings make sense of the fact that underwing moths have a great variety of colour patterns in their hindwings.

Edibility

Some species of prey are brightly coloured all over, and do not show any tendency towards crypsis or camouflage. It is a little puzzling that such prey have colouring that makes it very easy for predators to detect them. The puzzle is largely solved when it is realised that such prey are often distasteful. Evidence that it is useful for distasteful prey to be easily detected or conspicuous was reported by Gittleman and Harvey (1980). Chicks were presented with breadcrumbs which had been made distasteful by dipping them in quinine sulphate and mustard powder. Initially, the chicks ate more of the breadcrumb prey when they were easily detected rather than hard to detect or cryptic. However, the conspicuous or easily detected prey were eaten much less than the cryptic prey later on. Presumably chicks find it easier to avoid distasteful prey when it is conspicuous than when it is cryptic.

Mimicry and confusion

The fact that predators learn to avoid distasteful or inedible prey lies behind the development of Batesian mimicry in some species. Batesian mimicry involves the members of an edible species having the same warning colours and patterns as the members of an inedible species. This is found in various beetles and flies. For example, bombardier beetles resemble crickets, and ladybeetles look like roaches. Batesian mimicry generally works best when there are more members of the inedible species than of the mimicking one. If this is not the case, then predators may eat several mimics before encountering a member of the inedible species.

The warning coloration of this edible wasp beetle mimics that of a real wasp to deter predators.

The term "mimicry" suggests that the prey species deliberately adopts a particular pattern or colour. Is this so?

Mertensian mimicry is another way in which prey can defend themselves against predators. It involves the members of a prey species behaving in ways resembling those of a species that is dangerous to the predator. For example, some species of snakes make themselves seem more dangerous by hissing, shaking their tails, or making striking movements (Grier & Burk, 1992). Rowe, Coss, and Owings (1986) found that burrowing owls make hissing sounds that are like those of rattlesnakes.

Another way in which prey can avoid being captured and eaten by predators is by creating confusion effects. Grier and Burk (1992) describe two examples of such effects. Octopuses that are being attacked emit a large amount of black ink, which makes it very hard for predators to see them. Geese that are being attacked by an eagle often use their wings to splash water all around them to confuse the eagle.

Adaptations and counter-adaptations

As was mentioned earlier, we can only understand predator–prey relationships by focusing on coevolution. In other words, the evolutionary adaptations of predators depend on the changing behaviour of their prey, and the adaptations of prey likewise depend on the changing behaviour of their predators. We will reconsider some of the evidence in this context.

Predators have adapted in various ways to make it easy for them to detect their prey. Adaptations include improved visual and auditory sensitivity, and the ability to form search images. It is obviously very much in the interests of prey species *not* to be easily detected. This has led to various counter-adaptations by prey species, such as crypsis and polymorphism.

Predators generally want to get as close as possible to their prey before they are detected. This can be done by blending in with their background. It can also be done by approaching their prey slowly and almost silently and/or by making sure they are downwind of their prey. One of the main counter-adaptations by prey species is to develop more sensitive perceptual abilities (e.g. hearing in moths), so that they can detect predators when they are still at some distance.

When predators have detected their prey, they usually move swiftly to capture it. For example, this is the case with lions and tigers. Many prey species have developed counter-adaptations to reduce their chances of being captured after detection. For example, octopuses and geese create confusion effects. Other counter-adaptations include looking like the members of an inedible species and behaving like the members of a more dangerous species. Some harmless hover-flies have black and yellow striped bodies that resemble wasps.

Many predator species have developed various adaptations so that they can subdue and kill their prey. These adaptations include sharp teeth and/or claws, powerful bodies to squeeze prey, and the ability to sting or poison prey. Many prey species have developed counter-adaptations. Some species of rodents and insects attack predators in an aggressive way. Other prey species develop spines or hard shells which protect them.

Symbiotic Relationships

As Grier and Burk (1992, p.291) pointed out, "Organisms of most species simply go about their business and do not interact with most of the other organisms surrounding them." As we have seen, most relationships between members of different species are of the predator–prey kind. However, there are many examples of less aggressive relationships between species. **Symbiotic relationships** involve the members of two different species behaving in ways that benefit each other (the word "symbiosis" means living together). The two most important kinds of symbiotic relationship are mutualism and commensalism. **Mutualism** involves interactions between the members of different species that are of benefit to both the participants. In contrast, **commensalism** involves interactions that are of benefit to one participant but which do not benefit or harm the other.

Do you think humans have anything approaching a symbiotic relationship with another species? If so, which one(s)?

There is a close similarity between symbiotic relationships on the one hand and reciprocal altruism on the other hand (see Chapter 9). The main difference is that symbiotic relationships involve individuals of different species helping each other, whereas reciprocal altruism involves mutual helping between members of the same species.

Evidence

Most symbiotic relationships provide the benefit of food to one of the participants and a different benefit (e.g. protection from predators; bodily hygiene) to the other participant. Some examples of this type of symbiotic relationship will be considered before moving on to other types. For example, there is a symbiotic relationship between groupers and wrasses. Groupers are large fish and wrasses are small cleaner fish. A grouper allows a wrasse to enter its mouth to remove skin parasites and other small eligible items. When the wrasse has finished, the grouper allows it to swim out of its mouth without trying to harm it. The grouper gains because it loses the parasites from its mouth, and the wrasse gains because it is being provided with a meal.

There are other species in which symbiosis involves the removal of parasites. For example, cowbirds often spend much of their time removing insects that have become lodged in the hair or skin of giraffes or other large African animals. In return, cowbirds gain access to a rich source of food.

An example of a symbiotic relationship: during feeding the remora sucker removes parasites from the white tip reef shark.

Isack and Reyer (1989) discussed one of the relatively few cases in which humans are involved in a symbiotic relationship with the members of another species. The greater honeyguide (a species of bird) leads the Borans of Kenya to honeybee colonies or hives, which are often not easily visible from a distance and can be located deep inside hollow trees. The birds do this by flying and perching in such a way as to indicate the direction and distance of a hive. The Borans remove the honey. They benefit because the average time taken to find a hive is 3.2 hours with the assistance of the birds compared to almost 9 hours without their assistance. The birds eat the bee larvae and wax. They benefit because most of the hives are only accessible to them with human help.

Preston (1978) studied a form of mutualism that did not involve feeding. There is a symbiotic relationship between goby fish and shrimp, in that the shrimp digs a hole in which they both live. The goby fish gains the benefit of somewhere safe to live, and the shrimp gains the benefit that the goby warns of danger. The shrimp maintains contact with the goby fish by means of its antennae, and the goby gives a tactile warning signal with its fins.

Most symbiotic relationships benefit both of the participants, but such relationships can be exploited by the members of other species. For example, blenny are small fish that look like cleaner fish, and resemble them in their behaviour. As a result of this resemblance, blenny are able to approach closely to host fish. They then take a bite out of the host fish rather than providing a cleaning service.

How do symbiotic relationships develop?

It is usually easy to see the advantages of symbiotic relationships to the members of the two species involved. However, it is harder to work out how such relationships between different species became established in the first place. It is often hard to form co-operative relationships between members of the same species, and it would seem that this would be even harder to achieve between two species. Thompson (1982, p.61) argued that most symbiotic relationships develop out of antagonistic encounters:

> *If it is unlikely that individuals can avoid a specific antagonistic interaction, then selection will favour individuals that have traits causing the interaction to have at least less of a negative effect on them. This selection regime sets the stage for the evolution of the interaction towards commensualism or mutualism.*

Why do antagonistic encounters need to be unavoidable for them to lead to the development of a symbiotic relationship? If such encounters are avoidable, then the members of the weaker species are likely to make use of avoidance behaviours so as to reduce the chances of injury or death.

Springett (1968) discussed an example of a symbiotic relationship developing out of antagonistic encounters. Burying beetles and colliphora flies compete with each other to lay their eggs on dead mice. The flies are more successful in this competition, as the beetle larvae do not survive when flies are present. However, the overall situation is to the benefit of all, because the mites carried by beetles eat the eggs of the flies, and this allows the beetles to survive.

Thompson (1982) argued that the development of symbiotic relationships (e.g. mutualism) depends on various factors in addition to unavoidable antagonistic encounters:

1. The environment should be physically stressful, as for example by providing very limited food supplies; this provides motivation for symbiotic relationships to occur.
2. The level of survival of members of the two species should be intermediate; if it is low, then encounters with other species are too risky; if it is high, then there are no clear advantages in seeking encounters with members of another species.
3. Social species (e.g. social insects; birds) that have various ways of communicating with others are more likely to form symbiotic relationships than are non-social species.

Evaluation

Thompson (1982) has suggested various factors that are likely to be involved in the development of symbiotic relationships. His suggestions are consistent with most of the evidence, and help to explain why it is that such relationships are more common among social insects and birds than most other species. However, there is an inevitable problem with testing any theoretical ideas about the ways in which symbiotic relationships develop. It is very rarely possible to observe these relationships in the process of developing, and so it is only possible to speculate on why and how they occur.

PERSONAL REFLECTIONS

*   It is often easy to provide evolutionary explanations for the patterns of behaviour exhibited by the members of a species. However, that does not prove that the explanations are correct. My own view is that there is generally a grain of truth in such explanations, but that a full account of any species' behavioural patterns requires consideration of numerous other factors such as the current environment, social interactions among members of the species, and so on. The fact that evolutionary explanations can rarely be submitted to direct experimental test further indicates the need for caution before accepting them as valid.

SUMMARY

Evolution of behaviour

According to the theory of natural selection, there is variation among the members of a species, and at least some of the variation is inherited. Genes determine what is inherited. There is competition for mates, food, and places to live, leading to natural selection or survival of the fittest. As a result of natural selection, successive generations of a species tend to be increasingly adapted to their environment. However, adaptation is imperfect, in part because of evolutionarily stable strategies. The evolutionary history of most species shows punctuated equilibrium. Evolutionary theory has been supported by research on gulls and other species. Darwin's original theory has some problems in explaining the existence of altruistic behaviour and the fact that some species possess characteristics that do not seem to serve any function.

Individuals within a species can compete for resources either by exploitation or by resource defence. In the absence of aggression by other animals and given adequate knowledge of the location of resources, competition by exploitation can lead to an ideal free distribution in which each individual has equal access to resources. With resource defence, some animals are kept away from resources by displays of aggression or by fighting to defend a territory. Whether or not a species makes use of resource defence depends on economic defendability, which is the notion that a territory will be defended if the benefits exceed the costs. Benefits include reduced risks of predation and parasitism, and longer-lasting food supplies. Costs include the time and effort involved in territory defence, and the risk of injury when defending the territory. Medium-size territories are usually best, because large ones are hard to defend and small ones provide few resources. As predicted by the notion of economic defendability, territories are often abandoned if the environmental circumstances change.

Competition for resources

Predators and their prey are engaged in an evolutionary arms race, with predators becoming better equipped to detect and capture their prey, and prey becoming better able to avoid detection and/or to escape from predators. This is known as coevolution. Predators use various methods such as forming search images, chasing and pursuing, exhausting their prey, stalking and ambushing, communal hunting, and using sharp teeth and/or claws to subdue and kill their prey. Some prey species develop more sensitive perceptual abilities, whereas others develop crypsis, or polymorphism, or are distasteful to predators. Other prey adaptations include looking like the members of an inedible species or behaving like the members of a more dangerous species.

Predator–prey relationships

There are several cases in nature in which the individuals from two species help each other. In most cases, one of the participants receives the benefit of food, whereas the other one receives protection from predators, bodily hygiene, or some other benefit. Most symbiotic relationships seem to develop out of unavoidable antagonist encounters. Their emergence is most likely when the environment is physically stressful, the species have an intermediate level of survival, and they are social species with various communication responses.

Symbiotic relationships

FURTHER READING

There are very good accounts of the topics discussed in this chapter in J.W. Grier and T. Burk (1992), *Biology of animal behaviour (2nd Edn.)*, Dubuque, IO: W.C. Brown. Most of the topics are dealt with in detail by J.R. Krebs and N.B. Davies (1993), *An introduction to behavioural ecology (3rd Edn.)*, Oxford: Blackwell. The evolutionary determinants of behaviour are considered in an accessible way by M. Ridley (1995), *Animal behaviour (2nd Edn.)*, Oxford: Blackwell. A readable account of current perspectives on evolutionary theory is provided by R. Dawkins (1989), *The selfish gene (2nd Edn.)*, Oxford: Oxford University Press.

REVISION QUESTIONS

1a Outline the main assumptions of evolutionary concepts. (8 marks)
1b Assess their effectiveness in explaining the behaviour of non-human animals. (16 marks)
2 Discuss research evidence on the factors involved in resource defence. (24 marks)
3 Critically consider research evidence on the adaptations exhibited by predators and by prey in predator–prey relationships. (24 marks)

- **Sexual reproduction and parental investment**
  The advantages of producing new generations of offspring that are genetically diverse and how survival of offspring is ensured.

  Advantages of anisogamy over isogamy
  Genetic diversity
  Trivers' definition of parental investment
  Primate studies by Clutton-Brock and Harvey
  Sex-role reversal in various species

- **Sexual selection**
  Why do some individuals succeed in mating whereas others do not?

  Clutton-Brock and Albon's red deer study
  Andersson's study of tail length in birds
  Fisher's hypothesis
  Zahavi's handicap hypothesis
  Sociobiological approach to human sexual selection
  Cross-cultural meta-analysis by Buss

- **Mating systems and parental care**
  The reasons why some species bond in pairs for life, whereas others are promiscuous.

  Monogamy, polygyny, polyandry, and promiscuity in various species
  Wilson's four factors affecting parental care

- **Parent–offspring conflict**
  Who wins when the interests of parents and offspring are in conflict?

  Trivers' theory of weaning conflict
  Haplodiploidy; work by Trivers and Hare
  Hrdy's study of infanticide in monkeys
  Grier and Burk's theories of bird infanticide

Reproductive Strategies

Why does sexual reproduction exist? That may seem like an odd question, but it is one that has been considered in detail by biologists. Perhaps the main reason for focusing on this question is because of the various disadvantages associated with sex. In the words of Grier and Burk (1992, p.319):

> Sexual behaviour involves the expenditure of large amounts of time and energy, and its conspicuousness often increases the risk of predation (not to mention the danger from sexually transmitted parasites and pathogens). Worst of all, from an evolutionary standpoint, sexual reproduction is a particularly inefficient method of passing on one's particular alleles [genes].

Female aphids can reproduce by parthenogenesis and all the offspring are genetically identical to the parent.

The reasons for regarding sexual reproduction as inefficient are discussed shortly.

The overwhelming majority of species reproduce by means of sexual reproduction. However, there are a few species that reproduce in other ways. For example, in aphids (an order of insects), females reproduce by means of **parthenogenesis**. This is a type of reproduction in which the unfertilised ovum or egg develops into an individual without a male being involved. It has the additional odd feature that all the offspring of the female produced in this way are genetically identical to her. It should be noted that aphids do not always reproduce in this way.

There are considerable differences in reproductive strategies across species. In some species, the members of one sex compete with each other for mating rights. In others, the members of one sex develop characteristics that are attractive to the opposite sex to increase their chances of mating successfully. As we will see, there are several mating systems and strategies that are used by different species, with the choice being largely determined by the benefits and costs of each system or strategy. Of importance to many of these issues is the extent to which male and female parents invest resources of food, time, and effort in their offspring.

Sexual Reproduction and Parental Investment

We all know about some of the main processes involved in sexual reproduction. However, biologists focus on rather different processes. According to the definition offered by Krebs and Davies (1993, p.175), "Sexual reproduction entails gamete formation by meiosis and the fusion of genetic material from two individuals." Some of the terms in this definition need to be considered. First, a gamete is a reproductive cell (e.g. a spermatozoon or sperm; an ovum or egg) that can undergo fertilisation. Second, meiosis is a type of cell division in which a nucleus divides into four nuclei, each containing half of the chromosome number of the original nucleus. Third, the two individuals involved are a male and a

KEY TERM
Parthenogenesis: reproduction by a female without a male being involved; all the offspring are genetically identical. From the Greek "parthenos" (virgin) and "genesis" (meaning begun or produced).

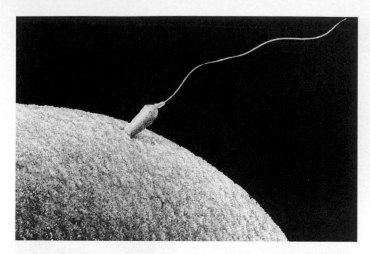

female. In nearly all species, males produce gametes or sperm that are very tiny, numerous, and mobile, whereas females produce gametes or eggs that are large and immobile.

We need to distinguish between anisogamy and isogamy. **Anisogamy** is a type of sexual reproduction in which the gametes of the two sexes are dissimilar. It is very much the dominant type of sexual reproduction and occurs in our own species, as shown in the photograph here. In contrast, **isogamy** is a rare type of sexual reproduction in which the two gametes are of the same size. Paramecium, a tiny freshwater organism, is an example of a species in which reproduction involves isogamy.

Fertilisation of a human egg by a sperm, an example of anisogamy, where the gametes of the two sexes are dissimilar.

Genetic diversity

Why are the offspring of most species produced by means of sexual reproduction rather than by, say, parthenogenesis? The most important reason is that sexual reproduction produces genetic diversity. As can be seen in large human families, two parents typically produce offspring who differ significantly in terms of height, shape, intelligence, and personality. This is due in large measure to the fact that the precise genetic make-up of each child is different, except in the case of monozygotic or identical twins.

The value of genetic diversity can be seen if we compare it against the identical offspring produced by parthogenesis. If the environmental conditions remain constant, then parthogenesis may be an excellent reproduction strategy. However, the environmental conditions often change in unpredictable ways, and genetic diversity maximises the chances of the members of a species being able to cope with such changes. A key part of the environment consists of other species which may act as predators. If predator species are continually evolving more effective ways of catching their prey, then it is vitally important for prey species to show genetic diversity and so develop better defences. The situation is similar for predator species, which need to evolve biologically in order to be well equipped to catch prey species that are improving their defences.

> **Insecticides**
>
> An illustration of the advantages of genetic diversity is the use of insecticides in agriculture. When these chemicals are used to kill insect pests there will always be a few individual insects that do not die. This is because their own genetic make-up includes a resistance to that particular chemical. The species survives and the resistant insects go on to breed a new generation that inherits their resistance.

Why is anisogamy so common?

In order for an individual's genes to be passed on to the next generation, it is necessary for his or her gametes to survive for long enough for them to be involved in sexual reproduction. One strategy for achieving this is to produce a few large gametes that are designed to survive in an unfriendly environment. This strategy is used by females with their eggs. Another strategy is to produce large numbers of very mobile gametes so that one or more of them may fertilise the female's eggs before this is done by another individual. This strategy is used by males with their sperm. Anisogamous species such as our own "hedge their bets" by combining both strategies.

There are various important consequences of anisogamy. In most species, females produce relatively few eggs, whereas males produce very large numbers of sperm. Indeed, it has been worked out that there are enough sperm in a typical male ejaculation to fertilise about 500 million females. Thus, each female gamete is much more important than each male gamete or sperm. Females can usually maximise their reproductive success by providing food and care for their offspring. In contrast, males can often maximise their reproductive success by fertilising several females rather than by caring for their offspring.

How does the evolution of the horse (described on page 160) demonstrate the advantages of genetic diversity in a prey species?

KEY TERMS
Anisogamy: sexual reproduction in which the gametes of the two sexes are dissimilar.
Isogamy: sexual reproduction in which the gametes of the two sexes are of the same size.

Parental investment

Females typically differ from males in having a higher level of **parental investment**. Parental investment was defined by Trivers (1972) as "any investment by the parent in an individual offspring that increases the offspring's chance of surviving (and hence reproductive success) at the cost of the parent's ability to invest in other offspring." Parental investment can take many forms. The nutrients contained in eggs are an important form of parental investment, but such investment also includes retaining eggs in the body, providing embryos with food through a placenta, and building a nest to shelter the eggs and/or the offspring. After the offspring have been born, parental investment can involve feeding them, defending them against predators, and spending time providing them with knowledge relevant to their future survival.

Female and male investment

In mammals, female investment in her offspring is greater than male investment, because of the female's efforts during pregnancy. For example, female elephant seals are pregnant for several months before giving birth to a pup that may weigh as much as 50kg or 8 stone. After the pup is born, the mother loses up to 200kg or 31 stone in weight during the first few weeks of feeding.

What are the implications of the greater parental investment of females than males? As Trivers (1972) pointed out:

> *Where one sex invests considerably more than the other, members of the latter will compete among themselves to mate with members of the former.*

Elephant seal pups can weigh as much as 50kg (8 stone) at birth.

Thus, we would expect in most species that males would compete with each other for the right to mate with females rather than vice versa. The reason is that females have more to lose from having offspring from an unsuitable mate, and so they are more careful in their choice of mate.

Some of the notions that we have discussed can be related to the views of Alexander and Borgia (1979). They started off by defining reproductive effort as the total resources (such as energy and time) that an animal uses in producing offspring and ensuring their survival. They argued that reproductive effort consists of mating effort (the resources allocated to obtaining mates) and parental effort (the resources allocated to feeding and rearing offspring). In those terms, the males of most species put most of their reproductive effort into mating effort, whereas females focus more on parental effort.

In most species, females invest more than males in their offspring, and so males compete with each other to mate with females. One prediction that follows from this analysis is that males should tend to be larger and heavier than females, so that they are equipped to compete with each other. Clutton-Brock and Harvey (1977) reported information about the relative weight of males and females in numerous primate species. In about 90% of these species, the average weight of males was greater than that of females. If males are heavier than females because of the need for them to compete for females, then the weight advantage of males should be greater in polygamous species in which some males mate with several females. The findings of Clutton-Brock and Harvey were in line with that prediction (see also the study of soay sheep described later in the chapter).

Mate selection

Some of the ideas discussed so far can help to explain why the members of the sex with the greater parental investment favour some members of the opposite sex over others. The central notion is that those individuals who can contribute the most resources

Male sticklebacks who are aggressive towards other males also tend to be most aggressive in defence of their nests.

The male tern feeds the female while he is courting her, and the amount of feeding may predict how good a provider he will be for the chicks when they hatch.

towards parental investment should be chosen most often. There is much evidence for this. For example, Thornhill (1980) studied hangingflies, in which the males offer prey to the females. Females generally have sex with males offering prey, but the duration of mating is determined by the size of the prey. As a result, females do not receive any sperm from males who offer small prey, but they receive large amounts of sperm from males who offer large prey.

We can see that it is in the female's interests to mate with males who will provide the greatest parental investment. However, there is a problem here. Most of the parental investment provided by males occurs *after* conception has occurred, by which time it is too late for the female to change her mind! What happens in many species is that the courtship behaviour of males allows females to predict the likely level of parental investment they will provide later on. For example, female sticklebacks prefer to mate with males who are most aggressive in their behaviour towards other males. This makes sense, because males who are most aggressive towards other males also tend to be aggressive in defending their nests against predators (Huntingford, 1976). In similar fashion, the amount of feeding provided by male terns during courtship predicts the amount of feeding of the chicks that they will subsequently provide (Wiggins & Morris, 1986).

Sex-role reversal

It is important to note that Trivers (1972) did not argue that females in every species would have greater parental investment than males. His key notion was that the sex having more parental investment would tend to be more selective and choosy when mating than would the other sex. This will generally be females, because they can make eggs and become pregnant, and female mammals can provide their offspring with their own milk. However, there are several ways in which males can contribute to parental investment. They can build nests, incubate eggs, defend the young against predators (as does the male stickleback) and they can find food for their offspring to eat. If we could find species in which the parental investment of the male is greater than that of the female, the females of such a species should compete with each other for males. There are a number of species in which this happens, as is discussed next.

Mormon crickets living in high-density groups often have to cope with the problem of food scarcity. This makes it hard for females, who need access to good food supplies in order to make eggs. In such circumstances, male Mormon crickets make a major contribution to parental investment by providing a spermatophore or capsule containing sperm for the female. This is a valuable source of food. Gwynne (1981) found that female Mormon crickets often fought each other for access to a male having a spermatophore. The males seemed to be selecting their mates, because they were more likely to accept heavier than lighter females. This makes evolutionary sense, because heavier females are able to produce more offspring.

There is a rather different kind of parental investment by males in spotted sandpipers. The incubation of the eggs and care of the brood are very largely carried out by the males rather than the females. As a result, female spotted sandpipers compete for males by making aggressive displays and by fighting each other. Female sandpipers are about 20% heavier than male sandpipers, presumably because they have to compete with each other for mating purposes.

Cases of sex-role reversal provide especially good support for the notion that parental investment plays an important role in determining whether males or females are more selective in their mating patterns. They indicate clearly that the reason why females in most species are more selective than males in their choice of mating partners is because of their greater parental investment rather than simply because they are female.

> **Sex-role reversal in sticklebacks**
>
> Classic research by Tinbergen (1951) clearly showed that male sticklebacks not only invest heavily in parenting, but also have to work hard to attract mates. The male finds and defends his territory, builds a nest, and then approaches a female and tries to lead her into the nest. If he is successful and she lays her eggs in the tunnel-like nest, the male fertilises them. By then the female has moved on, and the male guards the nest, fans currents of water through it, and for a while protects the young after they have hatched.

Evaluation

The ideas discussed in this section represent a significant change from previous ones about sexual reproduction. It used to be believed that the males and females of most species co-operated with each other during the processes of reproduction and rearing of offspring. This co-operation was explained as being of benefit to both males and females, because their offspring inherit 50% of their genes from each parent. However, as we have seen, it is now appreciated that there are various conflicts between the sexes. According to Krebs and Davies (1993), "The outcome of this sexual conflict is often more akin to exploitation by one sex of the other than to mutual co-operation."

The notion that one of the results of anisogamy is that the females of most species have a greater parental investment than the males has proved of value. However, it is not always easy to obtain a precise measure of parental investment. In addition, the notion of parental investment does not explain the behaviour of all species. As Cardwell et al. (1996) pointed out, there are species of pipefish in which the females produce larger gametes than the males, but they compete with each other for males rather than the other way around.

Clutton-Brock and Vincent (1991) argued that the behaviour of these pipefish can be explained in terms of potential reproductive rate. In the great majority of species, males have a much greater potential reproductive rate than females, and it follows that males compete with other males for right of access to females. In the case of pipefish, the males carry their offspring in a small cavity in their body. This limits the number of offspring that female pipefish can produce, because without this obstacle they could produce many more offspring. In a sense, the potential reproductive rate of female pipefish is greater than that of male pipefish. The general notion favoured by Clutton-Brock and Vincent is that members of the sex with lower potential reproductive rate will compete with each other to mate with members of the opposite sex. This notion explains the behaviour of pipefish, and may be of general value in understanding the behaviour of many other species.

Sexual Selection

In most species, some individuals enjoy more reproductive success than others. This raises the issue of **sexual selection**, which was defined by Darwin (1871) as "the advantage which certain individuals have over others of the same sex and species solely in respect to reproduction." As we have seen, there are marked differences in most species between males and females in mate selection, with males competing for females rather than females competing for males. Females in most species can only raise a few offspring in a season or a lifetime, and so it is important for them to mate with the most suitable males. In contrast, males in most species can mate with numerous females, and so it is less important for them to be selective.

In most species, it is the female rather than the male who is mainly responsible for raising the offspring. This is a further reason why females are more selective than males

> **KEY TERM**
> **Sexual selection**: selection for characteristics that increase mating success.

Using words like "preferring", "selecting", and "choosing" a mate may imply a conscious decision by the species concerned. How could this difficulty of description be overcome?

in their choice of mate. It follows that sexual selection should be less intense when parental investment is about the same for males and females. As Krebs and Davies (1993) pointed out, there is equality of parental investment in many species of monogamous birds (those having only one mate), with males and females both being involved in feeding their offspring. As predicted, the forces of sexual selection are weaker in such species than in others.

It follows from the discussion so far that there are basically two forms of sexual selection. First, there is **intrasexual selection**, in which same-sexed members (typically male) of a species compete to mate with opposite-sexed members of that species. Second, there is **intersexual selection**, in which the members of one sex (generally female) select or choose mates of the opposite sex.

Intrasexual selection

The most obvious way in which two males compete directly to mate with a female is by fighting or other forms of aggressive behaviour, which could help to explain why males are larger than females in most species of mammals and birds. We will start by looking at some examples of intrasexual selection based on aggression. After that, we consider examples of other ways in which such selection is achieved.

Aggressive behaviour

Aggressive behaviour in red deer was studied by Clutton-Brock and Albon (1979). Stags compete for females during the autumn rutting season. First, two males start by roaring. If the male who has a harem of females roars faster than his challenger, that is usually the end of the competition. Second, the two males walk parallel to each other. They do this so that they can assess each other, especially with respect to body size. If one stag is much larger than the other, then the contest will often end at that point. Third, the two males lock antlers, and try to push each other. The larger stag generally wins.

Why does the competitive behaviour of male stags often fail to lead to a fight? The main reason is that there can be real risks associated with fighting. The most obvious risk is that of injury, with about 25% of male deer being permanently injured from fighting. So far as the male with the female harem is concerned, there is the risk that other stags may try to steal some of these females while he is fighting. In view of these risks, it makes sense for stags to avoid fights unless they have a reasonable chance of winning. This explains why stags engage in roaring (they have to be in good condition to roar well), and why they inspect each other closely before deciding to fight.

Discussion points

1. How could this behaviour by male stags have developed in evolutionary terms?

2. Would it be preferable if stags behaved in a different way towards each other?

Stags usually avoid fighting unless they have a chance of winning, so the combatants are generally evenly matched.

An important factor in determining whether the male of most species will fight is an assessment of how aggressive or inclined to attack the other male seems to be. Aggressive males will often adopt a particular posture. For example, the male herring gull's beak points downwards when it is being aggressive, whereas it is held more horizontally when it is anxious (Tinbergen, 1959). As McFarland (1985) pointed out, one might expect that there would be a lot of cheating, with males simply adopting a threatening posture in order to deter other males from fighting them. In fact, however, cheating is not widespread. Perhaps the reason is that an aggressive posture would not have any meaning if cheating were common, and so it would simply be ignored.

> **Soay sheep**
> Research by Brian Preston at University of Stirling (Motluk, 1999) parallels the findings on stag behaviour. The three-year study of 100 wild soay sheep on St Kilda's Isle, Scotland, showed that the larger rams were most successful in mating, seeing off the smaller rams so that they could mate 10 or more times a day. Blood tests on the lambs showed that the majority born from matings that took place early in the five-week reproductive season in November and December were fathered by the bigger rams. However, lambs born from matings in the last two weeks of the season had an equal chance of being fathered by bigger or smaller rams. This shows that at the beginning of the mating season the bigger rams were more successful, and selection was for heaviness. The later fall in success rates could be explained by the larger rams actually running out of sperm: too much success leading to failure!

Sperm competition

There are several species in which intrasexual selection takes the form of sperm competition. This involves males trying to prevent each other's sperm from fertilising the female's eggs. For example, consider one particular species of dragonfly (*Orthetrum cancellatum*). Female dragonflies of this species have a special sac in their body, in which sperm are stored for later use. Every male dragonfly has a barbed whip at the end of his penis. This is used to remove any sperm left by other males before he mates with the female and leaves his sperm in the sac.

What other reasons might there be for the relative absence of cheating by less aggressive males?

Parker (1978) looked at sperm competition in dungflies. A male dungfly will often kick or push another male off a female dungfly while they are mating, and will then mate with her himself. In order to see which of the two males was more likely to produce offspring, Parker sterilised some of the males. The sterile male could still fertilise the female's eggs, but the eggs would not hatch. If the first male to mate was normal, but the second male was sterile, then only about 20% of the eggs hatched. However, if the first male was sterile, but the second was normal, then about 80% of the eggs hatched. These findings indicate that the second of two male dungflies to mate with a female will usually win the sperm competition. This explains why a male dungfly who has mated often sits on top of the female and protects her until she has laid her eggs.

> **Mating by proxy**
> Researcher Matt Gage of Liverpool University was studying an insect pest, the flour beetle, which destroys stored grain (Walker, 1999). He hoped to find clues to methods of control from the reproductive cycle of the beetles, and he stumbled on a strange strategy of "mating by proxy". This appears to stem from the crowded populations of flour beetles, which are highly promiscuous. The males mate with many females in just a few minutes, and so the females have a succession of matings. Each male uses his spiny genitalia to scrape out the previous male's sperm before replacing it with his own. The ousted sperm stick to the outside of the male's genitalia and survive the journey to the next female where they are deposited. According to Gage, one in eight females was fertilised by a male with which they had not mated. So far, it seems that this strategy is unique in the animal world.

Other forms of competition

Intrasexual selection in a few species takes very unusual forms. Abele and Gilchrist (1977) observed the mating habits of *Monoliformes dubius*, which is a worm that lives in rats' intestines. Males of this species apply cement to the female's genital opening after they have mated with her. This is done to prevent other male worms from fertilising her. They also have the charming habit of applying cement to the genital areas of other males, so that they cannot mate.

Intrasexual selection takes the form of a kind of homosexual mating in a species of insect known as *Xylocoris maculipennis*. Mating normally involves a male entering the female's body wall and injecting her with sperm. However, a male insect sometimes injects sperm into another male in a similar way (Carayon, 1974). When the injected male next mates with a female, there is a chance that the sperm of the other male will fertilise her eggs.

Alternative strategies

You may have got the impression that intrasexual selection within any given species always operates in the same way. In fact, that is often not the case. For example, Howard (1978) studied male bullfrogs. When two males fought, it was nearly always the larger bullfrog

The call of a large male bullfrog is intended to attract females. However, smaller males may also be attracted, in the hope of mating with one of the females drawn by the calls.

How can we be sure of the motivation behind the behaviour of the female Caribbean fruit fly?

Can you explain why Andersson's approach is more convincing than one based on correlational evidence?

that won the fight. This suggests that smaller male bullfrogs should adopt a different strategy. What Howard found was that intermediate-sized bullfrogs did not defend their territories. When challenged by another bullfrog, they moved away and made their mating calls elsewhere. As a result, they had reasonable mating success. Finally, the smallest (and youngest) males stayed close to large males. Occasionally they managed to mate with a female who had been attracted by the call of the large male.

Intersexual selection

Intersexual selection occurs when the members of one sex (typically female) choose or select mates of the opposite sex. There are numerous factors that can form the basis of intersexual selection (see Grier & Burk, 1992, for details). For example, it makes sense that a female should select males who are best able to fertilise her eggs. Sivinski (1984) studied female Caribbean fruit flies, who normally prefer to mate with large males. However, they selected small males who had not mated rather than large males who had just mated, because the latter would be less likely to fertilise their eggs.

It also makes sense that females should choose to mate with males who can provide good resources, rather than with males providing poor resources. Evidence for this was reported by Thornhill (1980). Hangingfly males offer insects to females before mating. The length of time that females copulated with males (and the amount of sperm that was transferred) was much greater when large prey rather than small prey was offered.

Physical characteristics

Perhaps the most interesting form of intersexual selection occurs when some characteristic (e.g. a long tail) evolves over the generations because it is attractive to members of the opposite sex. For example, the males of several species (e.g. peacocks; birds of paradise) are elaborately adorned, and their adornment seems to make them more attractive to females for mating purposes. This form of intersexual selection may seem straightforward, but it is not really so. For example, the peacock's very long and large tail reduces its chance of escaping from a predator. In addition, it has to eat more because of the weight of its tail.

It seems reasonable to assume that such adornments have developed because females find them attractive. However, it is always useful to have good evidence for any assumption. Andersson (1982) studied long-tailed widow birds in Kenya. The male of the species is fairly small (about the size of a sparrow), but its tail is about 40 centimetres or 16 inches in length. Andersson cut the tails off some males to reduce their length to about 14 centimetres or 6 inches. He lengthened the tails of other males by sticking the detached pieces of tail on to them with superglue, making their tails about 65 centimetres or 26 inches long.

Andersson then measured mating success by counting the number of nests in each male's territory. The males with the artificially lengthened tails had the greatest mating success, indicating that female widow birds are attracted to long tails in male birds. This evidence is convincing, because Andersson experimentally manipulated the length of the tail rather than simply relying on correlational evidence.

Discussion points

1. Why is the research by Andersson of particular value?

2. Do you think that this research provides a good explanation of long tails in male widow birds?

Bird song

Catchpole, Dittami, and Leisler (1984) studied intersexual selection based on correlational evidence that male European sedge warblers who sang the most elaborate songs tended to mate before those with less elaborate songs. Female warblers who were brought into the laboratory responded more to large than to small repertoires. This suggests that male warblers with large repertoires of songs are more attractive to females.

Theoretical approaches

Fisher's hypothesis. One of the main theoretical approaches to intersexual selection is Fisher's hypothesis. According to Fisher (1930), during the early stages of the evolution of a species, females are attracted to those features of males that have survival value. For example, birds having fairly long tails may be better at flying and so at finding food than those with short tails. If the genes determine tail length, then successive generations of males will have increasingly long tails. In addition, females will tend to develop a gene leading them to prefer longer tails in males, because their sons will be more likely to find a mate and so preserve their mother's genes. During the course of evolution, female choice of mate will tend to be based mainly on producing attractive sons who will have the greatest chance of being attractive to females when they grow up. Male birds will not continue for ever to show increased tail length, because having a very long tail threatens their survival in the face of predators.

According to Fisher's hypothesis, why will successive generations of male birds have longer tails?

The handicap hypothesis. The main alternative to Fisher's hypothesis is Zahavi's (1977) handicap hypothesis. According to this hypothesis, a male adornment such as a long tail is a handicap in terms of survival. Females prefer males with long tails *because* a long tail is a handicap. The argument is that a male bird that is able to survive in spite of having a significant handicap is likely to be superior to other birds. Thus, females who prefer handicapped males may be selecting those who tend to possess good genes for survival.

The basic notion behind the handicap hypothesis can be seen if we consider a concrete example. Suppose that two men are running around a track at the same speed, but one of them is carrying a heavy load. We would probably assume that the man handicapped by the load is stronger and fitter than the other man.

Hamilton and Zuk (1982) put forward a specific version of the handicap hypothesis. They argued that males are only likely to have a long tail or other sexual adornment if they are in good health. Thus, male animals with these adornments are attractive to females because they are likely to be free of diseases.

Moller (1990) tested Hamilton and Zuk's version of the handicap hypothesis. He studied barn swallows in Denmark. First of all, Moller showed that female swallows prefer males with long tails. He did this by finding that males with artificially lengthened tails paired up more quickly with female swallows than did normal males. Then he found that baby swallows reared in nests containing numerous blood-sucking mites were more likely to have reduced growth or to die than were those raised in nests with relatively few mites. Finally, he found that male swallows with long tails had offspring with fewer mites on them than did males with short tails. In other words, as predicted by the handicap hypothesis, male barn swallows with longer tails are healthier than those with shorter tails, because they have greater resistance to parasites such as blood-sucking mites.

Human sexual selection

Sociobiological approach

Human sociobiologists such as Wilson (1975) have argued that many of the factors determining sexual selection in animal species also apply to humans. Human males can maximise their reproductive success by having sex with numerous females. In contrast, females can bear only a limited number of children, and they invest heavily in each one during the nine months of pregnancy and for several years thereafter. It follows that women should be more selective than men in their choice of sexual partners. They should prefer men who have good resources, and who are willing to be committed to them over long periods of time. When a child is born, there is no doubt about the identity of the mother, but that of the father may be uncertain. In evolutionary theory, males should be unwilling to invest resources (e.g. time; money) in a child that does not possess any of their genes. As a result, males should value chastity in females more highly than females do in males.

Do observations like those
described by Westen constitute
proper evidence for the
sociobiological account of human
sexual selection?

As Westen (1996, p.706) pointed out, there are many features of the sociobiological or evolutionary account which seem to fit with our observations of others:

Consider the Casanova who professes commitment and then turns out a few months later not to be ready for it; the man who gladly sleeps with a woman on a first date but then does not want to see her again, certainly not for a long-term relationship; or the women who only date men of high status and earning potential.

Cross-cultural evidence

One way of testing the sociobiological theory of human sexual selection is by carrying out a cross-cultural study of preferred characteristics in mates. If the theory is correct, there should be clear differences in those characteristics preferred by men and by women, and these differences should be consistent across cultures. Some support for these predictions was reported by Buss (1989b), who obtained data from 37 cultures in 33 countries. He found that males in virtually every culture preferred females who were younger than them, and so likely to have good reproductive potential. In contrast, females in all cultures preferred males who were older, and thus more likely to have good resources. As predicted, females rated good financial prospects in a potential mate as more important than did males. It could be argued that males should value physical attractiveness in their mates more highly than females, because of its association with reproductive potential. In 36 out of 37 cultures, males valued physical attractiveness in mates more than did females. Finally, males tended to value chastity in a potential mate more than did females, but the difference between the sexes was not significant in 38% of the cultures sampled.

The findings of Buss (1989b) are of key importance, but they are less clear-cut than they seem for two main reasons. First, they do not actually show that sex differences in mate preference are consistent across cultures. In fact, there were much smaller sex differences in more developed cultures than in less developed ones on most measures, including preferred age differences, importance of financial prospects, and the value of chastity in a mate. Second, the sociobiological approach is more concerned with behaviour than with the preferences assessed by Buss. In fact, the actual average age difference between husband and wife across cultures was 2.99 years, which is similar to the preferred age differences for males (2.66 years) and for females (3.42 years). However, it is by no means clear that there would be this level of agreement between preferences and behaviour for the other measures obtained by Buss.

Discussion points

1. Does this research provide strong support for the sociobiological approach?
2. Why do you think that sex differences in mate preference vary between Western and non-Western cultures?

Evaluation

Buss's (1989b) findings are interesting and important, especially the apparently consistent sex differences in the factors that are most valued in a mate. His findings are consistent with those of Davis (1990), who considered the content of personal advertisements in newspapers. Women advertising for a mate tended to emphasise their physical beauty and to indicate that they were looking for a high-status, wealthy man. In contrast, men emphasised their wealth or other resources, and made it clear that they were looking for a physically attractive younger woman. In other words, women regard men as "success objects", whereas men regard women as "sex objects".

What are the potential weaknesses
of using personal ads in
newspapers as a research source?
Are people always honest in the
wording of their ads?

More evidence supporting the prediction from sociobiological theory that females should be more selective than males in their choice of sexual partners was reported by Clark and Hatfield (1989). Attractive male and female students approached students of the opposite sex, and asked each student if he or she would sleep with them that night. As you have probably guessed, this offer was received much more eagerly by male students than by female ones. None of the female students accepted the invitation, whereas 75% of the male students did.

In the human species, do you think
"a sexual partner" means the same
as "a mate" in other species?

If we consider human sexual behaviour and reproduction more generally, there are several findings that are hard to account for in evolutionary or sociobiological terms. Here are a few examples:

- Extra-marital affairs among females.
- The existence of homosexuality, as it does not lead to reproduction and gene survival.
- The fact that married couples in affluent countries with good resources are having few children on average, which is inconsistent with the notion of individuals maximising their reproductive success.

In general, it is assumed within the evolutionary or sociobiological approach that human sexual selection should change very little from one generation to the next. In fact, there were enormous changes within many Western cultures during the course of the twentieth century, and there was much talk of the "sexual revolution". It is not clear how such changes in sexual habits can be explained in evolutionary terms. Overall, the evolutionary or sociobiological approach seems to be oversimplified and unable to account for the complexities of human sexuality.

Mating Systems and Parental Care

There are substantial differences among species in their mating systems and their provision of parental care. A mating system is "the way in which male and female sexual behaviours interact in a species" (Grier & Burk, 1992, p.359). According to Krebs and Davies (1993), there are four main kinds of mating system, which will be considered in detail later in this section:

1. **Monogamy**: there is a pair bond between a male and a female, which may last for an entire breeding season or even a lifetime; often both parents protect the eggs or young, and co-operate in rearing the offspring.
2. **Polygyny**: a male mates with several females, whereas a female usually mates with only one male; females are more likely than males to provide the parental care.
3. **Polyandry**: a female mates with several males, whereas a male usually mates with only one female; in this mating system, males generally provide the parental care.
4. **Promiscuity**: males and females both mate with several members of the opposite sex; parental care may be provided by members of either sex.

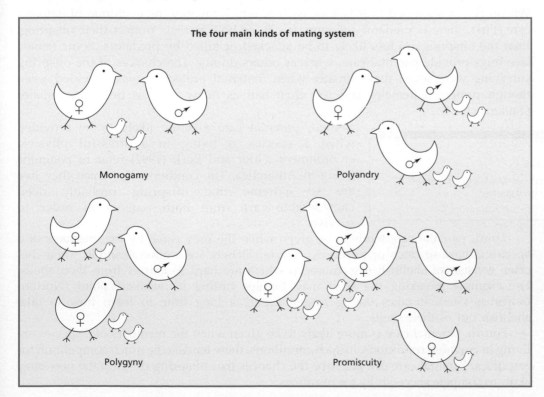

The four main kinds of mating system

Monogamy

Polyandry

Polygyny

Promiscuity

The most common form of mating system is different for different classes of vertebrates. Most species of birds are monogamous, with parental care being shared by the parents. Most species of mammals are polygynous, with the female being mainly or solely responsible for parental care. In contrast, fish tend to engage in promiscuity, and it is mostly the male who is involved in parental care. As we will see, it is often an over-simplification to suppose that all of the members of a given species use the same mating system.

According to Krebs and Davies (1993), the choice of mating system for a given species depends very much on **ecology**, that is, the relationship between animals and their environment. An aspect of the environment that is often important is the availability of food. One of the reasons why most species of birds are monogamous is because food is fairly scarce, and two parents working together can provide much more food for their offspring than can a single parent. However, many species of birds that are fruit or seed eaters adopt a polygynous mating system, because food supplies are so great during the summer months that only one parent is needed to feed the offspring.

Parental care

There are links between the mating system adopted by a species and the provision of parental care. In general terms, species in which both parents provide a lot of parental care are more likely to be monogamous than species in which very little parental care is provided. If only one parent provides most of the parental care, then that parent is less likely than the other parent to mate with numerous other opposite-sexed members of the species.

The amount of parental care provided varies dramatically from one species to another. The greatest amount of parental care is found in birds, mammals (including humans), and the eusocial or highly social insects. In all of these species, the parents devote large amounts of time and effort to providing their offspring with food, nests or other shelters, defence against predators, and so on.

Wilson's four factors

Wilson (1975) identified four factors, each of which favours the evolution of parental care. First, there is predator pressure. If one or both parents protect their offspring, then the offspring are less likely to be attacked or killed by predators. Some female lace bugs provide parental care, whereas others do not. The chances of the offspring surviving were seven times greater when maternal protection was provided, even though protecting females laid less than half as many eggs as deserting females (Tallamy, 1984).

Second, parental care is more likely to be provided when a species is living in a stressful physical environment. Grier and Burk (1992) refer to penguins living in Antarctica. The conditions in which they live are so extreme that offspring probably need considerable care from both parents in order to survive.

Third, parental care tends to be given when the prey eaten by the members of a species is hard to catch or to process. Oystercatchers are a good example. Their diet often consists of shellfish (e.g. mussels) which are hard to extract from their shells. For example, breaking the shell may involve hitting its weakest point (Norton-Griffiths, 1969). It takes young oystercatchers a long time to learn how to take shellfish out of their shells.

Fourth, parental care is more likely to be given when the members of a species are living in crowded conditions. In such conditions, there tends to be much competition for resources. Parental care can improve the chances that offspring develop the necessary skills to compete successfully for resources.

Parental responsibilities have to be taken seriously in the Antarctic.

■ Research activity: Wilson's four factors

In small groups, discuss and list points from Wilson's four factors of parental care that might apply to our own species.

KEY TERM
Ecology: the relationship between organisms and their environment.

Who provides the care?

We have considered some of the factors that determine how much parental care is likely to be provided. It is also of importance to focus on the issue of *who* provides the parental care. What determines whether it is the male, or the female, or both parents? Some of the factors involved can be seen in various species of fish.

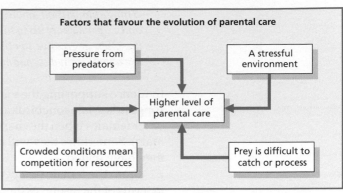

Factors that favour the evolution of parental care

In bony fish and amphibians, an important factor in determining who provides parental care is whether there is internal or external fertilisation. Gross and Shine (1981) reported that female care is much more common than male care when there is internal fertilisation. In contrast, male care is found more frequently than female care when there is external fertilisation. These differences can be explained by assuming that *association* with the embryos prepares a parent to provide care later on (Gross & Shine, 1981). The female is always more closely associated with the embryo when there is internal fertilisation. With external fertilisation, the female fish's eggs are generally laid in the male's territory, and so the male is more closely associated than the female with the embryos. Males can defend their territory and offer parental care at the same time.

Other physiological factors are also important. Consider, for example, lactation. Female mammals are designed to provide milk for their offspring, and this means that they provide most of the parental care when their offspring are young. In addition, female mammals have internal fertilisation, which as we have seen tends to increase female involvement in parental care. In many species of mammals (including the human species), males play some part in providing parental care. This generally happens when the males can carry some of their offspring, or when they can help in feeding the young.

We have seen that there are several general factors that help to determine the mating system and type of parental care provided by any species. We now consider each of the main mating systems in turn.

Monogamy

About 90% of bird species are monogamous. Why is this so? According to Lack (1968, p.225), it happens because "each male and each female will, on average, leave most descendants if they share in raising a brood." This explanation seems to apply to many species of seabirds and birds of prey, in which males and females co-operate during the incubation of the female's eggs. If one of the partners dies or is removed, then the breeding is unsuccessful. However, the presence of both partners is less essential in many species of songbirds. For example, removal of a male song sparrow from the nest caused breeding success to be reduced to only 51% of that found when both parents were present to feed the offspring (Smith, Yom-Tov, & Moses, 1982). Thus, male parental care was valuable but by no means essential.

One of the problems with Lack's views is that many species of birds are actually less monogamous than he assumed. It is only in recent years that it has been possible to establish paternity in a very clear way by making use of a technique known as DNA fingerprinting. Birkhead and Moller (1992) reported on the use of DNA fingerprinting in several bird species. For purple martins and indigo buntings, 35% of the offspring resulted from extra-pair matings, and the figure was 28% for red-winged blackbirds. In contrast, there were no cases of offspring produced by extra-pair matings in the fulmar, willow warbler, or wood warbler.

Krebs and Davies (1993) considered the issue of why most species of birds are monogamous, or at least fairly monogamous. According to them, male birds generally have limited chances to mate with several females. Krebs and Davies (1993, p.226) identified two reasons for this:

strong competition among males may make it difficult for a male to gain a second female; and … females are likely to suffer in polygyny through the loss of male help and [so] females are often aggressive to other females which may decrease the chance that their partners are able to gain a second mate.

Evidence supporting the views of Krebs and Davies has been found in various species of songbirds. Male songbirds are very willing to desert their female partner and to mate with other females when the chance presents itself (e.g. through the removal of a neighbouring male). Sometimes they will provide food for the offspring of various females with whom they have mated.

From the female perspective, a key factor is the extent to which male territories vary in terms of the resources they provide. If some male territories are much better than others, then females may do better to be the second or third mate of a male with a good territory than to be the only mate of a male with a poor territory. On the other hand, monogamy is likely to make more sense if male territories do not vary much in quality.

Polygyny

Polygyny (in which a male mates with several females) is of obvious benefit to the males of most species, because it maximises the chances of their genes surviving. However, it is less clear that it benefits females, because it is likely to reduce the amount of parental care that is provided by the male. Why is it, then, that polygyny occurs in many species? An influential answer to this question was provided by Verner and Willson (1966) in their polygyny threshold model. According to this model, females will tend to choose polygyny when the costs of having to share the male's parental care with other females are outweighed by the benefits of moving to a better territory. More specifically, if a paired male has a much better territory than an unpaired male, then it is in the interests of the female to mate with the paired male.

> Verner and Willson's model suggests that choice of mating system depends on circumstances. Do you think their approach is a valid one? Consider your answer after you have read the descriptions of all four mating systems.

Ezaki (1990) reported findings from a study on great weed warblers which supports the position of Verner and Willson. The percentage of male weed warblers who are polygynous varies from year to year, but averages out at about 50%. Those males who were polygynous tended to have the best nest sites, which were those in dense reeds offering good protection from predators. Ezaki compared the breeding success of monogamous females in poor nest sites against that of second females of polygynous males. If anything, the second females had more breeding success, indicating that they had not suffered because of polygyny.

There are other reasons why polygyny develops. For example, if several females live close together, it may be possible for one male to defend them and to mate with all of them. This form of polygyny is found in red deer and elephant seals (see Grier & Burk, 1992).

Polygyny may also develop when females of a species agree on which males are the most attractive. This is seen in a clear form in what are known as leks. A **lek** consists of several males in a fairly small area, to which females come only for mating purposes. A few of the males usually mate with numerous females, whereas other males are much less successful. Leks were originally observed in species of birds (e.g. grouse), but have since been found in some species of fish, mammals, amphibians, and insects.

Beehler and Foster (1988) provided an explanation of lek formation in their hotshot model. According to this model, dominant males (the hotshots) attract females to their territories. Non-dominant males move close to these hotshots, presumably because they expect that the presence of several females in the lek will allow them to enjoy some

Seals commonly practise polygyny, in which several females are defended and mated by one male.

mating success. In support of their model Beehler and Foster found that males often move closer to those males who attract the largest numbers of mates. However, as Grier and Burk (1992, p.369) pointed out, "It seems likely that lek formation occurs for several reasons."

So far we have assumed that females choose the polygynous mating system. However, there is evidence that females sometimes become involved in that mating system without realising that the male has already mated with another female. Alatalo et al. (1981) found that male pied flycatchers sometimes mate with a second female after having established a nesting territory with another female. The fact that the nesting territory of the second female is usually several hundred metres away from that of the first female suggests that the male is trying to deceive the second female. This interpretation of the findings was supported by Alatalo et al. (1990). They found that female pied flycatchers could not discriminate between males who had already mated and those who had not. It is perhaps worth mentioning that polygyny based on deception is not unknown in the human species!

Polyandry

Polyandry is less common than either monogamy or polygyny, and is found mainly in a few species of birds and fish. The main reason why some species are polyandrous is because it maximises the reproductive success of the female. Consider the case of the spotted sandpiper. Female sandpipers typically compete with each other to defend large territories in which there may be several males incubating different clutches (Lank, Oring, & Maxson, 1985). Female sandpipers mate with several males because they rarely produce more than four eggs in a clutch, and this would limit their reproductive success if they were monogamous. In fact, female sandpipers mate with up to five males, and so have been known to lay up to 20 eggs within a six-week period. As female sandpipers want to mate with several males, they compete with each other for males. In order to help them to compete, female sandpipers are about 25% larger than male sandpipers.

Oring (1986) argued that it is important to distinguish between classical polyandry and co-operative polyandry. In classical polyandry, each male sets up its own breeding site, and the female divides her time among these sites. Thus, spotted sandpipers provide an example of classical polyandry. In co-operative polyandry, various males co-operate with one female on a single breeding effort. The Tasmanian native hen shows this form of polyandry. Brothers typically mate with the same female, and large groups of hens help each other in defending territory, nest building, and taking care of the chicks (see page 208).

Why does polyandry exist? Classical polyandry may occur because males are better than females at providing parental care. Another possibility is that there are more males than females available for breeding, and so it is easier for females to find several mates. Co-operative polyandry may be found when the environmental conditions are extreme, and so it is better for three or more adults to contribute towards the protection and feeding of the offspring.

The Tasmanian hen is an example of co-operative polyandry: various males co-operate with one female in a single breeding effort.

Promiscuity

It has often been assumed that the males of most species benefit from mating with several females, but that females do not usually benefit from multiple matings. In fact, it is now increasingly recognised that there are often significant benefits in females mating with several males. Halliday and Arnold (1987) identified several advantages, including the following: (1) it may produce greater genetic diversity in the offspring; (2) it may persuade a number of males to guard the brood; and (3) it may reduce the negative effects of males engaging in sexual competition.

Some dunnocks or hedge sparrows engage in promiscuity, but others engage in monogamy, polygyny, and polyandry (Davies & Lundberg, 1984). Male dunnocks obtain the largest possible territory, and female dunnocks establish a territory sufficient to provide several feeding sites. Mating generally takes place between dunnocks with overlapping territories. Monogamy tends to be found when a female territory only overlaps with the territory of a single male, whereas polyandry is found when a female territory overlaps those of two males. In similar fashion, polygyny occurs when a male has a large territory that overlaps with those of two females. Finally, promiscuity is found when two or three males share a territory which overlaps with those of two or more female dunnocks.

The form of mating system shown by dunnocks clearly depends on the size of their territories. What determines territory size? Female territories tend to be small when food is plentiful, but they are large when food is not readily available. Davies and Lundberg (1984) supplied extra food, and found that this produced the expected changes in territory size and an increase in polygyny and monogamy.

Evaluation

The notion of mating systems is a valuable one. There are very large differences in sexual behaviour in different species, but most of the observed patterns conform to one of the four mating systems we have discussed. However, an approach based on mating systems exaggerates the extent to which sexual behaviour is similar within any given species. More specifically, this approach ignores the considerable individual differences in sexual behaviour within a species. An alternative approach is based on mating strategies. According to this approach, the sexual behaviour of individual males and females of a given species depends on the precise circumstances in which they find themselves. In essence, those who favour the mating systems approach assume that the sexual behaviour shown by male and female members of a species is predictable solely on the basis of the species to which they belong. In contrast, those who favour the mating strategies approach argue that predicting sexual behaviour requires knowledge of the environment in which males and females have to exist as well as the species to which they belong.

Some of the evidence we have already considered is more consistent with the strategy approach than with the systems approach. For example, work based on DNA fingerprinting has shown that many species of birds are less monogamous than used to be believed (Birkhead & Moller, 1992). More strikingly, dunnocks can exhibit monogamy, polygamy, polygyny, or monogamy (Davies & Lundberg, 1984). In general terms, the pattern of sexual behaviour that is adopted by individuals depends on the costs and benefits involved, such as food availability.

The importance of food availability is suggested in work on passerines (types of birds) (Lack, 1968). Insect-eating passerines are monogamous, whereas about 25% of seed- and fruit-eating passerines are polygynous. The likeliest explanation is that insects are usually less available than seeds and fruit, and so it is important for the survival of the offspring that both parents provide insects for them.

There are other factors in addition to food availability that help to determine the mating system adopted by any individual. These factors include the following: competition among males; the presence of predators; territorial resources; and the extremeness of the environment. Thus, the sexual behaviour exhibited by the members of most species depends on an assessment of the costs and benefits of various mating systems. In other words, sexual strategies are generally flexible and adapted to the environmental conditions rather than conforming closely to the mating system that any given species is "supposed" to follow.

Parent–Offspring Conflict

It seems natural to assume that parents in all species will devote themselves to looking after their offspring. This would appear to make sense in terms of the notion of inclusive fitness, i.e. maximising the probability of the individual's genes being passed on to future

What advantages and disadvantages might there be for humans in the four types of mating systems: monogamy, polygyny, polyandry, and promiscuity?

generations. However, there is often a balance to be drawn. If there is a substantial parental investment in the care of their current offspring, this may greatly reduce the parents' future reproductive success. As a result, it follows from evolutionary theory that there will be situations in which there is great conflict between the needs of parents and the needs of their offspring.

Robert Trivers (1974) provided an important and influential theoretical account of parent–offspring conflict. He pointed out the existence of an important *genetic asymmetry*: parents are equally related genetically to each of their offspring, but the offspring are twice as related to themselves as their siblings. As a result, offspring typically want more than their fair share of parental investment, whereas parents try to invest their resources equally among their current offspring. Parents often go further, and try to retain some resources for future offspring rather than giving them all to their current offspring (see next section).

Siblings competing for food.

Conflict during weaning

The approach favoured by Trivers (1974) can be used to explain the conflicts between parents and offspring in many species that occur during weaning. At that time, the offspring typically demand more food than before. However, there are various reasons why mothers want their offspring to be weaned off their milk. First, in order to maximise their reproductive success, mothers may need to keep some of their resources for future offspring (Trivers, 1974). Second, and related to the first reason, the physiological demands on mothers who are lactating or producing milk tend to be very great. Indeed, they are often even greater than the demands associated with pregnancy. The female body has to provide not only the proteins, fats, minerals, etc. that are in the milk, but also the energy to produce the milk itself.

Evidence of parent–offspring conflict during weaning can be seen in rhesus monkeys (Hinde, 1977). For the first several weeks of their lives, contacts with their mother are generally broken off by the infants. After about 15 weeks, their mother increasingly rejects their advances, and prevents them from making contact with her nipple.

According to the theoretical approach of Trivers (1974), many parent–offspring conflicts occur because of mothers' needs to maximise their reproductive success. It follows that there might be fewer such conflicts with older parents who are at, or close to, the end of their reproductive lives. Evidence for this was reported by Trivers (1985) in a study on California gulls. Older parents provided more feedings per hour to their offspring than did younger parents, and they also spent more time defending their offspring.

Who wins parent–offspring conflicts?

Parents are larger and stronger than their offspring, and so it might be thought that parents would usually win in any parent–offspring conflict. Theoretical reasons for assuming that parents would win parent–offspring conflicts were put forward by Alexander (1974). According to him, offspring who are successful at winning conflicts with their parents would tend to have offspring that inherited the ability to manipulate their parents successfully. This might have an adverse effect on their ability to reproduce successfully, and so would not make evolutionary sense.

Successfully manipulative offspring...

In fact, the evidence indicates that matters are actually more complex. Offspring may try to win a conflict about food by pretending to be very hungry and so persuading their parents to give them more food than their siblings. Another form of deception is practised by herring gulls. When they are about three months of age, they try to obtain food from their parents by stooping and withdrawing their heads to appear smaller than they actually are. Grier and Burk (1992, p.386) argued that the best situation in evolutionary terms would be one in which individuals are "successfully manipulative offspring when young and successfully manipulative parents when old."

Haplodiploidy

Trivers and Hare (1976) reported an interesting case in which parent–offspring conflict was resolved in favour of the offspring. They studied a number of ant species in which, as in the honeybee, sex is determined by a mechanism called haplodiploidy. The essence of **haplodiploidy** is that males are derived from unfertilised eggs, whereas females are derived from fertilised eggs. As Trivers and Hare pointed out, this produces the odd situation that females are three-quarters related to their sisters, but only one-quarter related to their brothers. As a result, it would be to the advantage of the female worker ants if the queen ant produced more queens than male drones. More specifically they would benefit from a ratio of three queens to one male drone. In contrast, the queen is half related to her sons and to her daughters, and so it would be in her interests for the ratio to be one queen to one drone.

Trivers and Hare (1976) found in several ant species that the actual ratio was usually the three to one favoured by the female workers. How can this be, given that the queen can decide whether her eggs are fertilised? The main reason is that workers look after the brood, and they tend to care for future queens at the expense of future drones. However, the queen sometimes wins this parent–offspring conflict. In a species of wasps known as *Polistes metricus*, the reproductive sex ratio is one to one. Queens produce males early on in the season when there are relatively few female workers around to influence the reproductive sex ratio. Later in the season, queens increasingly produce queen daughters as a result of the influence of their worker daughters.

Haplodiploidy and honeybees

In honeybees the queen bee is female. She mates with one of the male bees (drones) and lays three types of eggs. The majority are fertilised eggs, which hatch into worker bees that are female but sterile. As their name suggests, they forage for pollen and nectar, store food in the hive, and care for the queen's eggs, larvae and pupae. The worker bees form the majority in the hive. A few unfertilised eggs are laid by the queen, and these develop by parthenogenesis into the male drones. Occasionally a third type of egg is laid by the queen. This egg is fertilised, and when it hatches is fed a special diet before developing into a new queen bee.

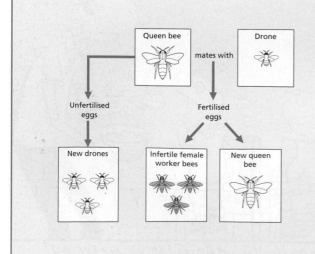

Haploid and diploid numbers

Most cells have an even number of chromosomes in each nucleus, as the chromosomes there are in pairs. This paired number is known as the diploid number, and in human cell nuclei it is 46, or 23 pairs of chromosomes. Half the diploid number, i.e. one chromosome of each pair, is the haploid number, and haploid nuclei are usually found in gametes such as egg cells and sperm.

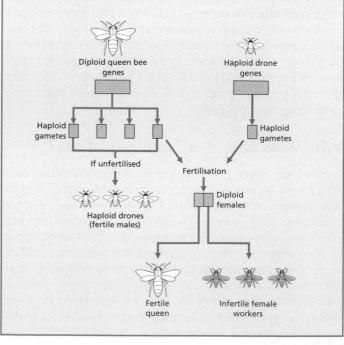

In sum, neither parents nor offspring can be relied on to triumph in conflicts between them. Parents sometimes win, offspring sometimes win, and at other times the solution is a form of compromise.

Discussion points

1. What are the unusual features of haplodiploidy?

2. Why is it of value to study species in which there is haplodiploidy?

Infanticide

Infanticide (the deliberate killing of infants) is a striking example of conflict between adults and young. It is found mainly in species in which one or more males defend a larger number of females. For example, Halliday (1980) described the behaviour of lions in Tanzania. Each pride typically consists of two or three males and about ten females. When the males controlling a pride are defeated by other males, the new leaders of the pride kill all of the cubs within the pride. Why does this infanticide happen? One reason is that this brings the females back into estrus or sexual receptivity more rapidly. This allows the new males to make them pregnant, and so produce their own offspring. Another reason is that the cubs that are in the pride when it is taken over share no genes with the new males. As a result, the new males' attempts to preserve their genes for future generations would not be helped by allowing the cubs to survive.

Hrdy

Hrdy (1977) studied Hanuman langur monkeys. These monkeys generally live in groups of about 25, consisting of one adult male plus several related females and their offspring. Hrdy observed several instances of infanticide, which generally occurred shortly after a change in the resident male. Why did infanticide occur? The reasons are similar to those in lions. A resident male remains in control of a group of monkeys for 27 months on average. This may sound like a long time, but offspring only become independent about 24 months after they have been conceived. The new resident male needs to kill the existing infants when he takes over in order to maximise the chances that his own offspring will be independent before he is replaced by another male.

Infanticide is also common in several species of birds (e.g. hawks; owls) in which the chicks hatch at different times. What typically happens (especially when there are two chicks) is that the firstborn receives more than its share of the food provided by its parents. In many cases, the

> **KEY TERM**
> **Infanticide:** the deliberate killing of an infant.

In a pride of lions, a new leader will often kill the cubs of the previous leader.

younger chick slowly starves to death, after which it may be fed to the firstborn chick by its parents. The older chick sometimes hastens the death of its sibling by attacking it.

We have seen that infanticide can have benefits for males. However, there are no obvious benefits for females in having their offspring killed. Hrdy found that female langur monkeys tried to prevent infanticide in various ways. Sometimes several females would fight the resident male when he was trying to kill one of the offspring. Some females left the troop of monkeys until their offspring became independent. Pregnant females often have sex numerous times with the new resident male, presumably so that he may be fooled into thinking that their offspring are his rather than those of the previously dominant male.

Discussion points

1. What are some of the main reasons why infanticide occurs?

2. Why is infanticide thankfully rare in the human species?

There is another way in which the females of some species prevent infanticide from happening. Spontaneous abortions have been found in wild mares who mate with non-dominant stallions (Berger, 1983), and whose offspring might be killed by the dominant stallion. The logic seems to be that this stops the investment of additional resources that would probably be lost later through infanticide.

Why is infanticide so common in some species in spite of the defensive strategies used by females? According to Grier and Burk (1992, p.340):

> *The balance of circumstances favours the infanticidal male; preventing infanticide requires constant vigilance by several females, but successful infanticide requires only a few seconds of carelessness and a quick bite with the canine teeth.*

Birds

Why do the parents of some bird species allow their younger or youngest offspring to die through deliberate under-feeding? According to Grier and Burk (1992), there are two main strategies that may be involved:

1. Parental insurance strategy: more than one chick is produced in case the firstborn chick fails to survive.

2. Opportunistic strategy: if the food supply is poor, then the firstborn receives most of it; if the food supply is very good, then the other chicks can be given enough food for them to survive as well as the firstborn.

An adult egret perching on the back of a buffalo in an East African swamp.

Some species use the first strategy, whereas other species use the second. The parental insurance strategy is used by species such as black eagles and lesser spotted eagles. In these species, the younger chick nearly always dies shortly after hatching, provided that the firstborn has survived. The opportunistic strategy is used by species such as the tawny owl. The younger chick or chicks in tawny owls generally survive if food is plentiful (see Grier & Burk, 1992).

Mock and Parker (1986) studied some of the complexities of the opportunistic strategy in egrets. Egret parents often allow older egret chicks to kill their younger siblings (this is known as siblicide). If shortage of food is responsible for such killings, then they should happen more often when the size of the brood is large than when it was small. This was found by Mock and Parker. However, chicks in a brood of one (singletons) were much less likely to survive than chicks in larger broods. Parents tended to commit infanticide by abandoning nests containing only one chick, especially early in the breeding season. As a result, only 26% of singletons born early in the season survived, compared to 55% of those born towards the end of the season.

Why did egret parents sometimes commit infanticide when they had a single chick? This happened because they established another nest if there was enough time left in the breeding season. This strategy, unpleasant though it sounds, makes evolutionary sense in terms of the parents' long-term reproductive success.

Evaluation

Evolutionary explanations for infanticide are generally convincing, especially when looked at from the male perspective. It seems to occur mainly in those species in which male adults can best ensure their own reproductive success by infanticide. The fact that there are strong reasons for infanticide raises the issue of why it is not more common than is actually the case. Grier and Burk (1992) provided two explanations. First, there are some species in which the female is larger than the male, and so she is able to prevent males from committing infanticide. Second, two conditions need to be satisfied to make infanticide favoured by evolutionary pressures: (1) a reasonable probability that the dominant male or males in a group will be displaced by other males at some time; (2) a long period of time when the female is feeding her offspring during which she cannot become pregnant. These conditions are found mainly in certain mammal species, and it is in those species that most cases of infanticide are found.

In spite of the success of evolutionary explanations, there are some issues that have not been addressed fully. For example, infanticide is so much against the interests of females that it might have been expected that they would have developed more successful strategies for preventing it. In addition, it is not entirely clear how males know that offspring are not theirs, and are therefore candidates for infanticide. They may rely on the unfamiliar odour of the cubs, or they may have some memory of their own sexual history. In many cases, we simply do not know what information they are using.

PERSONAL REFLECTIONS

- Much is now known about the key general evolutionary principles that influence the mating systems or strategies used by different species. In my opinion, however, more needs to be done to bridge the gap between these principles and the actual sexual behaviour of animals. For example, many species have a dominant mating system with numerous exceptions, and we need to understand more precisely *why* these exceptions occur.
- The reproductive strategy adopted by any given animal depends on evolutionary principles *and* on some kind of cost–benefit analysis of different strategies based on the circumstances in which it finds itself. More research is required on the interaction between principles and circumstances.
- Too often we only have a vague idea of the information that is actually determining the sexual behaviour of a given species. For example, how do the females of a species decide that one male is likely to provide greater parental investment than another?

SUMMARY

The dominant type of sexual reproduction is anisogamy, in which the gametes of the two sexes are dissimilar. This generally takes the form of females producing relatively few eggs, whereas males produce very large numbers of sperm. As a result, females can maximise their reproductive success by providing greater parental investment than males. An important consequence of the greater parental investment of females is that

Sexual reproduction and parental investment

there is competition among males for the right to mate with females rather than vice versa. The need to compete for females may explain why males in most species weigh more than females. In species in which the parental investment of the male is greater than that of the female, the females compete with each other for males. A different view is that members of the sex with lower reproductive rate will compete for members of the opposite sex.

Sexual selection

There are various ways in which males can compete with each other for females, but there are two main possibilities: intrasexual selection and intersexual selection. Intrasexual selection often takes the form of fighting or other aggressive behaviour, but it can involve sperm competition or applying cement to other males' genital areas. Intersexual selection can involve males evolving an adornment or other characteristic that is attractive to females. Males of several bird species have long tails. These tails may have evolved originally because they had survival value. Another possibility is that a long tail is a handicap, and a bird that survives with such a handicap is likely to possess good genes for survival. There is some evidence from cross-cultural research that the evolutionary or sociobiological viewpoint is relevant to human sexual selection. However, this is more the case in less developed cultures, and extra-marital affairs and homosexuality are hard to explain in evolutionary terms.

Mating strategies and parental care

Birds tend to be monogamous, mammals tend to be polygynous, and fish are mostly promiscuous. Both parents usually provide parental care in monogamous species, females generally provide most of the parental care in polygynous species, and parental care may be provided by either sex in promiscuous species. The choice of mating system depends on various factors, such as the relationship between animals and their environment, and physiological factors (e.g. internal versus external fertilisation; mother providing milk). Polygyny is chosen by females when the costs of having to share the male's parental care with other females are outweighed by the benefits of gaining access to valuable resources (e.g. food). The variety of mating patterns within many species suggests that it may be preferable to think in terms of mating strategies rather than mating systems.

Conflict between parents and offspring often occurs at the time of weaning, with the offspring demanding more food than ever and parents trying to keep some resources for future offspring. There are striking conflicts between adults and offspring in prides of lions, with the new male leader often killing all the cubs. Infanticide serves the interests of the male lion, but not those of the females or of the species. Infanticide is most common in species in which dominant males are likely to be replaced, and when females who are feeding their offspring have a long period of time during which they cannot become pregnant.

Parent–offspring conflict

FURTHER READING

There are well-written accounts of the topics discussed in this chapter in Chapters 11 and 12 of J.W. Grier and T. Burk (1992), *Biology of animal behaviour (2nd Edn.)*, St. Louis: Mosby. The various issues related to sexual reproduction are dealt with in detail by J.R. Krebs and N.B. Davies (1993), *An introduction to behavioural ecology (3rd Edn.)*, Oxford: Blackwell. A straightforward account of reproductive strategies and sexual behaviour is provided in Chapter 8 of M. Ridley (1995), *Animal behaviour (2nd Edn.)*, Oxford: Blackwell.

REVISION QUESTIONS

1   Critically consider research on the role of sexual selection in the evolution of animal behaviour.   (24 marks)

2   Discuss evidence on gender differences in parental investment in non-human species.   (24 marks)

3a   Describe *either* mating strategies *or* social organisation in non-human species.   (8 marks)

3b   Critically consider views on the evolution of the system you have described.   (16 marks)

4   Discuss evolutionary explanations for parent–offspring conflict in non-human species.   (24 marks)

- **Altruism**
  Are animals selfish? Why do bees commit suicide when they sting?

  Maynard–Smith's kin selection
  Hamilton's rule
  Sherman's study of ground squirrels
  Altruism in eusocial insects
  Axelrod and Hamilton's Prisoner's dilemma analogy; reciprocity
  Mutualism and manipulation

- **Sociality**
  The advantages and disadvantages of living in groups.

  Avoiding predation and obtaining food
  Ward and Zahavi's theory of "information centres"
  Caraco et al.'s model of optimum group size
  Disadvantages: competition, disease, etc.

- **Imprinting**
  Why newly hatched geese will follow the first thing they see.

  Lorenz's studies on geese
  Later modifications by Sluckin and Suomi

- **Bonding**
  Helpless newborn mammals need close bonds with their parents in order to survive.

  Harlow's "cloth mother" monkey studies

- **Signalling systems and communication**
  How and why animals communicate with members of their own species.

  Chemical, visual, auditory, and tactile signals
  Ritualised behaviour
  Deception
  Von Frisch's studies on honeybee communication
  Herman et al.'s dolphin studies
  Whale song studies

9
Kinship and Social Behaviour

The human species is a very social one. Most of us spend much of our time interacting with family and friends, helping others, and so on. Surely the same cannot be said of other species? It is probably true that social behaviour is more common in humans than in members of other species. However, some aspects of social behaviour are found in many species. For example, it is common for animals to spend their time in groups.

As we will see in this chapter, there are major differences between the human and other species in the *reasons* for belonging to groups. For most animal species, the key reasons are to increase the chances of reproducing and having enough food to eat.

According to evolutionary theory, individuals behave so as to maximise their own reproductive success. This makes it easy to understand why individuals compete for mates or for access to food or other resources. However, the members of many species also exhibit social behaviour of direct benefit to others (but costly to the individual). Such altruistic behaviour is puzzling, because it seems on the face of it to be inconsistent with evolutionary theory. Possible explanations of altruistic behaviour are discussed in this chapter.

Special kinds of social behaviour are shown between mothers and offspring in many species. One of the processes involved is imprinting, in which offspring follow the first moving object they see. Another important process is bonding or attachment, which involves offspring developing a close attachment with one or both parents. Bonding is found in primates and various other species. Imprinting and bonding may have developed because they help to increase the chances of the offspring surviving into adulthood.

An important part of social behaviour in animals involves the use of signalling systems to communicate information. Different species have developed very different kinds of signalling system based on visual, auditory, chemical, and tactile signals. These signalling systems are used to communicate important information about the sources of food, the presence of predators, and so on. Each of these forms of signalling system possesses its own advantages and disadvantages.

Altruism

Many species show evidence of **altruism** or apparent altruism in their behaviour. Altruistic behaviour is of benefit to other animals, but is costly to the animal itself. Krebs and Davies (1993, p.265) defined altruism as "acting to increase another individual's lifetime number of offspring at a cost to one's own survival and reproduction." This definition is rather limited, because the benefits and costs of altruistic behaviour do not have to be as extreme as suggested by Krebs and Davies.

Examples of altruistic behaviour are the suicidal sting of the honeybee and birds' alarm calls which serve to warn others that a predator is nearby, but which also tell the predator

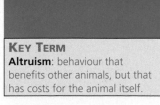

Attached to the honeybee's sting is a sac of venom. When the bee attacks, it leaves its sting in its victim, along with the venom sac. Once the bee has lost its sting, it dies, so defending the hive in this way could be seen as altruism.

What examples can you suggest for possible altruistic behaviour in our own species?

where they are. It is hard to account for the existence of altruism or apparent altruism in terms of Darwin's (1859) theory of natural selection (see Chapter 7). Animals who show altruistic behaviour are less likely than other animals to produce many offspring, but reproductive success is of central importance to the theory of natural selection. It would seem to follow that the processes of natural selection would lead to the gradual disappearance of altruism. Why hasn't this happened?

One possible answer to this question is that natural selection operates at the level of the group or species. For example, birds' warning calls help to ensure the survival of a flock of birds even if they reduce the chances of survival of the bird making the calls. This line of reasoning may sound convincing, but there is a problem with it. Selfish individuals in a group composed mainly of altruists would have greater reproductive success than would the altruists. Thus, selfishness would be favoured by natural selection, and would probably eliminate altruism.

There are various ways of explaining altruism. According to Krebs and Davies (1993), there are four main reasons why animals sometimes exhibit altruistic behaviour. These are as follows:

1. Kin selection: an individual can increase its genetic representation in future generations by providing help to its close relatives.
2. Reciprocity: one individual behaves altruistically towards a second individual, with the expectation that the second individual will return the favour in the future.
3. Mutualism: two individuals may both behave in an altruistic fashion at the same time because they both gain from co-operation.
4. Manipulation: an individual is misled or manipulated by the other individual into behaving in an apparently altruistic way.

We will consider these four reasons in turn.

Kin selection

Darwin (1859) focused on the individual as the unit of natural selection, and it is difficult from that perspective to account for altruistic behaviour. It may make more sense to regard the gene as the unit of selection. Offspring inherit half of their genes from their father and half from their mother. Suppose that it is more important to ensure that those genes survive than to ensure that a given individual survives. As Gross (1996, p.413) pointed out, this provides a simple explanation for altruistic behaviour:

> *If a mother dies in the course of saving her three offspring from a predator, she will have saved 1½ times her own genes (since each offspring inherits one half of its mother's genes). So, in terms of genes, an act of apparent altruism can turn out to be extremely selfish.*

Parental care and altruism

"Bringing up baby" involves heavy costs to many animal parents: in mammals this includes biological investment in egg production, growth and development of the foetus in the womb, milk production after birth, time and effort spent in care and defence, etc. In birds there is a similar amount of investment in nest building, egg production, incubation, feeding, etc. These behaviours could be argued to be of no benefit to the parents directly, and so could come under the heading of altruism. This altruism is even more marked if the parents are assisted by other family members, i.e. others who share the same genes. Mumme (1992) observed a type of Florida jay whose older broods acted as helpers with younger offspring, with the result that the younger brood had a greatly increased survival rate.

Maynard Smith (1964) introduced the term **kin selection**, which is very relevant to the discussion. It refers to "the process by which characteristics are favoured due to their beneficial effects on the survival of close relatives, including offspring and non-descendant kin" (Krebs & Davies, 1993, p.266). The term "kin" covers all of an individual's relatives. As we will see, kin selection may well be the most important reason for the evolution of altruism.

Genetic closeness
A key implication in kin selection is that altruistic behaviour is more likely to be shown towards genetically close relatives than to other individuals. This idea was summed up

by the geneticist J.B.S. Haldane. He argued that he would be willing to sacrifice his own life for the sake of two of his brothers or eight of his cousins.

We can understand more clearly what is involved in kin selection by considering the notions of direct and indirect fitness. **Direct fitness** is fitness in terms of gene survival gained through production of offspring, whereas **indirect fitness** is fitness in terms of gene survival gained through helping the survival of non-descendant kin such as siblings, cousins, nephews, and nieces. According to Hamilton (1964), the main reason why animal altruism exists is because of the addition of indirect fitness to direct fitness. The combination of these two forms of fitness is known as inclusive fitness. According to Grier and Burk (1992, p.457), **inclusive fitness** is

> *(1) an individual's reproductive success, plus (2) the extra reproductive success its relatives had because of its behaviour, devalued in each case by the coefficient of relatedness of the relative to the individual, minus (3) the extra offspring the individual had (if any) because of the help it received from its relatives.*

Hamilton (1964) brought together many of the ideas we have been discussing. According to Hamilton's rule, the necessary conditions for the evolution of altruism can be expressed in the following formula:

$$B/C > 1/r$$

In this formula, B is the benefit to the animal receiving help, C is the cost to the altruistic animal, and r is the coefficient of relatedness. The coefficient of relatedness is based on the fact that each parent has a one-half chance of having the same allele or gene as each of its offspring, and the same is true of siblings. In contrast, grandparents and grandchildren have a one-fourth chance of having the same allele, and first cousins have a one-eighth chance.

It follows from Hamilton's rule that close relatives are more likely to be helped than distant ones. However, distant relatives will receive altruistic help if the benefits are large and/or the costs to the altruistic animal are small. Hamilton's rule may be of use in explaining why parents are much more likely to behave in an altruistic way towards their offspring than is one sibling towards another. We cannot explain this in terms of the coefficient of relatedness, which is the same in both cases. According to Hamilton's rule, it is likely that the difference occurs because offspring benefit more than siblings from altruistic behaviour, or because the costs of altruism are less for parents than for siblings.

Sherman

Evidence supporting the notion of kin selection was reported by Sherman (1977) in a study of Belding's ground squirrels in the United States. When the squirrels are only a few weeks old, the young males go off in different directions, whereas the young females typically stay near the area in which they were born. Females who are closely related rarely fight each other, and co-operate to defend each other's young from attackers. However, unrelated ground squirrels drag approximately 80% of the young squirrels from their burrows, and then kill them. As these squirrels are not close relatives to the young squirrels that are killed, considerations of kin selection do not apply.

Sherman also studied alarm calls in squirrels when a predator (e.g. weasel; coyote) was approaching. These alarm calls represent altruistic behaviour, because squirrels giving an alarm call increased their chances of being attacked by the predator. As predicted from the kin selection notion, females were much more likely to give these alarm calls when there were close relatives nearby than when only unrelated squirrels were in the area. Those who benefited from the alarm calls were usually the offspring of the squirrel making the calls. However, alarm calls were also given when only parents or non-descendant relatives (e.g. sisters) were nearby. These findings are exactly in line with the notion that altruistic behaviour is more likely to occur when it serves the interests of close relatives than when it does not.

Giving an alarm call alerts other ground squirrels to the presence of a predator, but alerts the predator to the caller's presence and position at the same time.

KEY TERMS
Direct fitness: fitness in terms of gene survival gained through production of offspring.
Indirect fitness: fitness in terms of gene survival gained through helping non-descendant kin.
Inclusive fitness: an individual's reproductive success together with the additional reproductive success of its relatives produced by its behaviour (taking account of the genetic similarity between the individual and its relatives).

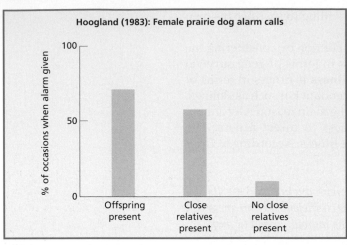

Hoogland (1983): Female prairie dog alarm calls

(bar chart; y-axis: % of occasions when alarm given, scale 0–100; x-axis categories: Offspring present ≈71, Close relatives present ≈58, No close relatives present ≈10)

Alarm calling

Hoogland (1983) looked at alarm calls in black-tailed prairie dogs, which live in groups known as coteries. Within each coterie there is usually one adult male, three or four adult females, and their offspring. In order to persuade the prairie dogs to give alarm calls, Hoogland presented a stuffed badger, which is a predator of prairie dogs. Female dogs gave the alarm call on 71% of occasions when their offspring were in the coterie, on 58% of occasions when there were only non-descendant close relatives (e.g. siblings) in the coterie, and on only 10% of occasions when no close relatives were present. The figures were similar for male dogs: 51%, 49%, and 25%, respectively. The key finding was that alarm calling was almost as frequent when only non-descendant relatives would benefit as it was when descendant ones were in the coterie. This indicates that altruistic behaviour is shown towards both descendant and non-descendant relatives, which is as predicted from the notion of kin selection.

Pairs and trios

Strictly speaking, kin selection refers to behaviour that increases the chances of survival of related members of the species. The limitation of studies on alarm calls is that we cannot work out in any detail their effects on survival of relatives. A more relevant study was carried out by Maynard Smith and Ridpath (1972). Tasmanian native hens form either pairs (one male, one female) or trios (two males, one female) for breeding purposes. In the trios, the two males are usually brothers, with one of them being dominant over the other. The dominant male will generally allow his brother to mate with the female hen. According to kin selection, this co-operative behaviour should occur provided it is beneficial in terms of the number of offspring produced. Maynard Smith and Ridpath found that the average number of surviving offspring among first-year breeders were 3.1 for trios against only 1.1 for pairs, and the figures were 6.5 and 5.5 for experienced breeders. Detailed calculations based on kin selection suggested that the number of offspring was sufficiently higher for trios than for pairs to justify the brothers' co-operative behaviour.

Eusocial insects

The most striking evidence of altruistic behaviour is found among the eusocial or highly social insects, which include all of the ants and termites and several species of wasps and bees. These insects co-operate in nest building, they engage in group foraging to obtain food for the group, there is co-operative care of the young, and the nest is aggressively defended against invaders. Probably the best-known example of such defence is the altruistic suicide of honeybees. When a honeybee stings an invader, its entire sting apparatus is ripped out, causing the bee to die.

Why do eusocial insects behave in such altruistic ways? The single most important reason stems from the fact that most species of eusocial insects have a system of sex determination known as haplodiploidy. **Haplodiploidy** involves males developing from unfertilised eggs, whereas females develop from fertilised eggs (see Chapter 8). Under haplodiploidy, the female offspring of a common father get all of his genes, and they also share half of the genes from their common mother. As a result of this unusual arrangement, a female's relatedness to her sisters is 0.75, but her relatedness to her own offspring is only 0.5. This means that she can maximise the chances of her genes surviving by helping her mother (so that her mother produces more sisters for her) rather than by reproducing herself.

Ants co-operate to bring large amounts of food back to the main group.

How do we know that the altruistic behaviour of eusocial insects depends on haplodiploidy? Key evidence is that elaborate altruistic societies have developed in 11 insect species in which there is haplodiploidy, but in only one species (diploid termites) in which there is not. However, haplodiploidy cannot be the only factor involved in producing complex altruistic societies. Haplodiploidy is also found in solitary parasitic wasps which do *not* form themselves into altruistic societies. What other factors are involved? It is likely that a high level of danger from predators and the need to build complex nests play a part in the development of complex societies (Grier & Burk, 1992).

Kin recognition

We have seen that individuals in many species are more likely to behave in an altruistic way when close relatives or kin will benefit than when only non-relatives will gain. This suggests that they can recognise which members of their species are kin and which are not. How does this kin recognition occur? A key point is that individuals are by no means always accurate on this issue. For example, there are several species of birds in which the parents will ignore their own offspring if they are put outside their nest. However, if a cuckoo or other bird deposits an egg inside their nest, they will look after the bird when it hatches as if it were their own. These observations suggest that individuals tend to regard any other animal living in their home as kin even if there is no close physical resemblance.

"Well, he lives in our home, so I guess he must be one of us."

Holmes and Sherman (1982) tested the notion that animals treat those they have grown up with as kin. The pups of ground squirrels were assigned to four kinds of rearing group: siblings reared by one mother; siblings reared by different mothers; non-siblings reared together by one mother; and non-siblings reared by different mothers. When they had grown up, pairs of squirrels selected in various ways from these groups were put together. Animals that had been reared together rarely behaved aggressively to each other, and it made no difference whether or not they were genetically related. Animals that had been reared apart behaved much more aggressively towards each other than did animals that had been reared together. It did not matter whether the animals in the pair were genetically related, except that two sisters who had been reared apart were less aggressive towards each other than were unrelated females reared apart. Thus, the behaviour of squirrels towards each other is based more on whether they have lived close to each other than on whether or not they are kin.

From your own experience, does a form of kin recognition apply to the behaviour of some household pets?

In sum, it is often hard for individuals to be certain whether another member of their species is or is not kin. However, the simple assumption that anyone living in the same nest or other home is kin is generally correct. If a special study is set up in which the young of a species are brought up with non-relatives (e.g. Holmes & Sherman, 1982), then animals will make mistakes. However, these kinds of situations rarely arise in nature.

Evaluation

There is strong evidence that much altruistic behaviour in animals depends on kin selection. However, it should be noted that there are some complicating factors. First, animals cannot work out the coefficient of relatedness, and so they make use of "rules of thumb" such as that all those in the same nest are closely related. Second, even when altruistic behaviour is influenced by kin selection, it is often also influenced by

Young ground squirrels reared together behave as if they were genetically related, and are less aggressive towards each other as adults than are related squirrels who have been brought up apart.

Anthropomorphism

The term "anthropomorphism" means ascribing human characteristics to animals or inanimate objects. In Western cultures there are many stories where non-human animals (and even inanimate objects such as trains!) are described as thinking, feeling, and talking just as we do. There is nothing wrong with this in everyday life, nor with the way in which we discuss other animals such as our domestic pets being "happy" or "fed up", for instance. However, we do need to beware when trying to be objective, for example when doing research. It is not possible to know whether or not an animal is pleased or annoyed in the sense that human beings can be, or whether they have human-style emotions, or can think as we do. There is little or no evidence that they do. We need to take care to avoid thinking, speaking, and writing about animal behaviour in human terms during our research, as we cannot ascribe human thoughts or emotions to other species.

Reciprocity in baboons

In baboon tribes the most successful males in the group mate most often with the females. However, Packer (1977) observed altruistic co-operation between young males. One of them would distract the dominant male—a risky business, as the dominant male is always larger and stronger. The other young male would seize the opportunity to mate with the partner of the dominant male. It seems the favour would be returned on a later occasion, giving both young males the chance of mating and fathering offspring.

KEY TERM

Reciprocity: altruistic behaviour by one animal towards a second, with the second returning the favour later.

environmental factors. For example, the presence of dangerous predators may increase the chances that the members of a species will behave altruistically towards each other. Third, we need to be careful when trying to apply the findings from animal species to our own. Humans often behave in an altruistic way because they experience empathy or understanding of the feelings of others (see Chapter 22). In contrast, most altruism in animal species is based on survival of the individual's genes, and almost certainly has nothing to do with empathy at all.

Reciprocity

Trivers (1971) argued that an animal will behave altruistically towards other animals when this increases the chances that the other animals will then behave altruistically towards it. He used the term delayed reciprocal altruism to refer to this state of affairs. The most obvious problem with delayed reciprocal altruism (or **reciprocity** as it is also known) is the possibility of cheating. If someone behaves altruistically towards you, but you then refuse to help that person, then you have gained overall but they have lost.

Axelrod and Hamilton (1981) discussed the problem of achieving co-operation or reciprocity in terms of the "prisoner's dilemma" (see boxed text). This was originally devised to understand human behaviour, but can easily be applied to other species. The basic idea is that each individual animal will do better if it behaves selfishly rather than co-operatively. However, it is better for them if they both co-operate than if they both act in a selfish way. As Axelrod and Hamilton pointed out, if two animals meet only once, then their best strategy is to behave in a selfish way. However, if they meet numerous times, then other strategies can become more effective.

Axelrod (1984) asked 62 scientists to suggest winning strategies for the prisoner's dilemma. The most effective strategy was tit for tat. It involved the individual co-operating on the first occasion. On the second occasion, the individual behaved as the other individual had on the first occasion. After that, the individual simply copied the behaviour of the other individual on the previous occasion. This tit-for-tat strategy works because it encourages the other animal to be co-operative, while discouraging it from being selfish.

The Prisoner's Dilemma

This game holds a particular fascination for psychologists, because it tests co-operation between people: the outcome of the game always depends on the choices both people make and the degree of co-operation between them. In its typical format, the players are given the hypothetical situation of being arrested for working together to commit a crime. The two "prisoners" are kept apart, and each is questioned by the "police". The same suggestion is made to each one: if he or she (A) will agree to confess and give evidence against the other prisoner (B), then A will be released and B will be severely punished. Each player has two choices: to keep silent in co-operation with their partner, or to defect and confess all.

Both players gain when they co-operate with each other, as each will receive the same small punishment (there being little or no evidence against either). If both players confess, they both lose, because there is now evidence against them both and the penalties will be more severe. However, if one remains silent and the other confesses, the confessor

gets away without a penalty while the other player receives the severe punishment. The dilemma is, of course, that one person can never be sure of the other person's decision.

Research activity

Try to simulate the prisoner's dilemma in groups of three. Two people take the prisoner roles, and the third acts as "judge", allocating points. Each prisoner must be unable to see or hear what the other prisoner decides, but can be told their scores at the end of each trial. A scoring method could be:

Both keep silent (co-operation):	Each scores 5 points
A keeps silent, but B confesses:	A loses 10 points. B gains 10 points.
B keeps silent, but A confesses:	B loses 10 points. A gains 10 points.
Both confess:	Each scores no points.

Try the experiment in two conditions: one with no hints, and one using Axelrod's tit-for-tat strategy.

The tit-for-tat strategy is very effective, and it is an easy strategy for animals to use. However, it is not very clear how this strategy could become established in a species in the first place. Axelrod and Hamilton (1981) suggested that it might be directly linked to kin selection. Considerations of kin selection indicate that co-operative behaviour or reciprocity would be most likely to evolve between close relatives. It could then be that co-operative or reciprocal behaviour is used to identify relatives from non-relatives.

Evidence

Krebs and Davies (1993) discussed various examples of reciprocity. Fischer (1980) considered spawning in the black hamlet fish, which possesses both male and female characteristics. The fish form pairs, in which one fish releases some eggs, which are then fertilised by the other fish. The two fish then swap roles, and they continue to alternate roles over a two-hour period. The value of this rather complicated method of spawning is that cheating can be detected at an early stage. Fischer found that when one fish in the pair refused to co-operate, the other fish would not release any more eggs, and would simply swim away.

Reciprocity was also found in vampire bats in Costa Rica (Wilkinson, 1984). He formed one large group of bats from two roosts, both of which consisted of unrelated individuals. A bat was removed and denied access to blood. It was then put back into the group. It was far more likely to be given blood by a familiar bat from its roost than by an unfamiliar bat from the other roost. This is as expected, because reciprocity is more likely between animals that know each other. Of particular importance, the starving bat that was given blood by another bat was more likely to give blood to that bat in future than to other bats.

Mutualism

Mutualism is like reciprocity in that it involves two animals behaving in altruistic or co-operative ways towards each other. The difference is that both animals obtain benefits at the same time with mutualism, but the benefits for one of the animals are delayed in the case of reciprocity.

Packer et al. (1991) studied mutualism in prides of lions in Tanzania. In each pride, there are usually a number of related females and between two and six males. The advantage for males of being in a pride is that it increases their chances of reproducing. When there were only two males in a pride, both of them fathered a number of offspring. This suggests the existence of mutualism, or co-operation between them. Mutualism was less obvious when there were more males in a pride. In such prides, at least one of the males did not father any offspring. This can be explained in terms of kin selection. All the males in a large pride were close relatives. As a result, the genes of the males who did not father any offspring survived through the reproductive success of the other males in the pride.

Manipulation

Sometimes what looks like altruism actually occurs because the animal behaving in an altruistic way has been tricked by the animal that benefits from the altruistic behaviour. Perhaps the best-known example of such **manipulation** is the way in which cuckoos can persuade birds of other species to act as hosts by hatching their eggs and caring for their offspring. The female cuckoo places one egg in the host nest, and removes one of the eggs that was already there. After the cuckoo hatches, it rapidly ejects all of the host eggs from the nest.

This manipulation on the part of cuckoos is carefully designed so that the host bird will be less likely to reject the cuckoo's egg. Davies and Brooke (1988) used model cuckoo eggs. They found that the host birds are more likely

Once a cuckoo's egg has been accepted by the host birds, the chick will try to push all the other chicks out of the nest to ensure its own survival.

to reject eggs if they see a stuffed cuckoo on its nest, if the eggs are not like their own eggs, or if they are laid in the nest before the host birds have laid their own eggs. The behaviour of cuckoos placing their eggs in host nests is such as to maximise the chances that the eggs will be accepted by the host birds.

Sociality

Numerous species of animals live in groups at least part of the time, and the term **sociality** is used to refer to this tendency. As you might imagine, there are many different reasons why animals choose to live in groups. However, two reasons are of major importance: (1) avoiding predation (being killed and eaten by a predator); and (2) obtaining adequate amounts of food. If the members of a species are less likely to be attacked and killed by a predator, or more likely to have enough food to eat, by belonging to a group, then they will generally join a group.

We will start by considering the evidence relating to these advantages of group membership. After that, some of the disadvantages of belonging to groups will be discussed. Finally, we consider how information about the benefits and costs of group membership can be combined to explain group size.

Advantage: Avoiding predation

Evidence that groups can be formed in order to reduce the risk of attack by predators was reported by Seghers (1974). He studied guppies swimming in various streams in Trinidad. They showed a much greater tendency to keep close together in groups when there were many predators than when there were only a few.

Scanning
How does living in a group help to protect individual animals from being attacked by predators? Some of the advantages relate to scanning for predators. In a study on ostriches, Bertram (1980) found that each ostrich spent less time scanning or looking around for possible predators when in a flock than when on its own. In spite of that, the proportion of the time during which at least one ostrich was scanning for predators was slightly higher in flocks or groups.

Rapid detection of predators
Group scanning is often more effective than individual scanning in the rapid detection of predators. Kenward (1978) found that solitary pigeons usually only reacted to an

Ostriches in groups have more time to forage for food as each individual spends less time scanning for predators. Sharing the scanning duties means that the entire group is better protected than any ostrich on its own.

approaching goshawk when it was very close to them. In contrast, pigeons in large flocks of more than 50 birds reacted on average when the goshawk was still about 40 yards or 37 metres away. Goshawk attacks on solitary pigeons had an 80% success rate, whereas this fell to 10% when goshawks attempted to take birds from flocks of 20 or more.

In Bertram's (1980) study on ostriches, he found that ostriches living in groups are much less likely than solitary ostriches to be eaten when attacked by lions. The reason is that lions only kill one ostrich in a successful attack. However, larger and more visible groups of ostriches may be more likely to be attacked by predators than are ostriches on their own.

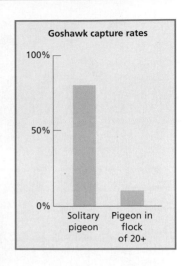

Goshawk capture rates

The dilution effect

The notion that any given animal is more likely to survive a predator's attack when in a group than on its own is called the **dilution effect**. This effect has been found in several species other than ostriches, including monarch butterflies and semi-wild horses. Calvert et al. (1979) considered the effects of attacks by birds on monarch butterflies, which gather on trees in very large numbers. They found that the chances of a butterfly being eaten by a bird were higher in relatively small roosts than in large ones. The dilution effect was strong enough to outweigh the possible disadvantage that large butterfly roosts were more readily detected by birds.

The selfish-herd effect

Another advantage of group living is what is known as the **selfish-herd effect** or you-first effect. This effect occurs when animals in the centre of a group are safer from predators than those on the outside. A good example of the selfish-herd effect is found in bluegill sunfish. A major predator for this species is snails, which eat their eggs. Gross and MacMillan (1981) counted the numbers of snails in sunfish nests that were either in the centre or at the edge or periphery of the colony. There were twice as many snails in peripheral nests as in central nests. However, there were only half as many snails in peripheral nests as in solitary nests, so there were advantages of group living even for sunfish in peripheral nests.

The selfish-herd effect: deer at the centre of the group are more shielded from attack.

Mobbing

The examples we have considered so far have shown that there can be real advantages of living in groups even when the animals in a group behave in a passive way towards predators. However, there are some species in which the animals belonging to a group combine forces to attack predators. For example, consider the case of black-headed gulls, which are attacked by crows. Gulls in the middle of a large colony will often jointly mob a crow, thus reducing the chances that its attack will be successful (Kruuk, 1964).

In sum, there are a number of ways in which animals living in group are protected from predators. These ways include the following: (1) less time spent scanning for predators; (2) more rapid detection of predators; (3) dilution effect; (4) selfish-herd effect; and (5) active defence against predators (e.g. mobbing).

Advantage: Obtaining food

As was mentioned earlier, an animal joining a group may increase its chances of having enough food to eat. Consider, for example, the case of spotted hyenas trying to catch wildebeest calves. Kruuk (1972) found that hyenas on their own were only successful on 15% of attempts, whereas pairs of hyenas succeeded on 74% of attacks. The main reason why pairs of hyenas were so successful was because one hyena distracted the mother wildebeest while the other one caught the calf.

KEY TERMS
Dilution effect: the reduced chances of an individual being killed by a predator in a large group rather than in a small group or on its own.
Selfish-herd effect: the tendency for animals in the centre of a group to be in less danger from predators than those on the periphery.

Pairs of hyenas are more than twice as successful than single hyenas when they hunt together, so co-operation is a good strategy even if they eventually have to share the catch.

Information exchange among ravens?

Marzloff, Heinrich, and Marzloff (1996) studied ravens, which roost in large groups overnight in the pine forests of western Maine in the USA. Ravens are scavengers, and fly off each morning searching for carcasses of animals. Observations showed that if some birds found a large carcass (such as a deer) and fed on it before returning to the roost, the next day the flock would follow them back to the carcass and feed there for several days until the bones were picked clean. Was some information being communicated at the roost site about the food source? How this took place or what these signals might be has not yet been discovered.

It has sometimes been argued that lions hunt in groups because this increases their success in catching prey. However, some of the evidence is inconsistent with that argument. For example, Packer (1986) found that lions in larger groups consume *less* food per day than do lions in small groups of two, or on their own. Why, then, do lions hunt in groups? According to Packer, lions spend much time scavenging rather than hunting, and it is easier for large groups of lions to defend any carcasses they find from other lions or from hyenas.

When it is hard to find good sources of food (e.g. it is widely scattered), animals in a group may obtain useful information from each other about the best places to search for food. This is found in honeybees, which make use of a complex form of communication based on waggle dances (discussed in more detail later in the chapter). These waggle dances are very effective. The average bee hive rears about 150,000 bees each year, with the bees consuming 45 pounds of pollen and 130 pounds of honey. As Seeley (1985) pointed out, "To collect this food … a colony must dispatch its workers on several million foraging trips, with these foragers flying 20 million kilometres overall."

Ward and Zahavi (1973) claimed that the nesting colonies and communal roosts of many bird species resemble "information centres". The basic idea is that birds can discover good food sources by following birds that have been successful in obtaining food. The term "information centre" is rather misleading. It suggests that the birds co-operate unselfishly with each other, whereas they are simply using other birds' information for their own purposes.

The notion of an information centre was tested by DeGroot (1980) on two groups of weaver birds. One group was trained to find water in one out of four compartments, and the other group was trained to find food in one of the other compartments. After that, the two groups of birds were put together and deprived of water or of food. As predicted by Ward and Zahavi (1973), the birds who did not know where water (or food) was to be found followed those who did have the crucial information.

In sum, there are various ways in which living in groups can allow animals to obtain adequate food. It can make it easier to find food, to catch food, or to defend food from other animals.

Other advantages

There are other advantages of group living, of which the most important is probably protection from hostile members of the same species. According to Wrangham and Rubenstein (1986), many species form themselves into polygynous groups (one male with several females) for that reason. These species include lions, horses, and chimpanzees. The male in such groups acts as a kind of "hired gun" to protect the females in his group from the hostile actions of other males of the same species.

In many species, such protection is very valuable. For example, consider what happens when a pride of lions is attacked by other males. If these males succeed in taking over the pride, then the lion cubs are usually killed by them (Halliday, 1980). It is thus very much in the interests of female lions to belong to a fairly large group to minimise the risks of this happening.

Another advantage of social living is known as the Fraser Darling effect. This effect occurs when young animals in groups start reproducing earlier than those on their own, as a result of the social stimulation they receive from other members of the group. This effect was found in colonial seabirds by Fraser Darling (1938). As a result of early reproduction, the animals involved may be able to have additional broods, and so increase their reproductive success.

Disadvantages

From what has been said so far, it might be thought that living in groups produces only advantages for animals. This is not at all the case. As Alexander (1974) pointed out, "There is no automatic or universal benefit from group living. Indeed, the opposite is true: there are automatic and universal detriments." According to Alexander, the two major detriments or disadvantages are as follows: (1) competition for food and reproduction; and (2) increased rates of parasitism and disease.

Competition

We will start by considering the effects of group living on competition for food. Even if the animals within a group on average capture more prey than those on their own, it is still possible that some individuals in the group do *less* well than they would have done on their own. This was shown clearly by Major (1978) in a study of the jack, which is a predatory fish. The average jack in a five-fish group captured about 60% more Hawaiian anchovy than when hunting on its own. However, the fish at the front of the hunting group did much better than any of the others, and the fourth and fifth fish in the group did worse than jack hunting alone.

Perhaps the most obvious cost of feeding in a group is the likelihood that the animals within the group will compete with each other for the food sources. This was shown clearly in a study by Reichert (1985) on the African social spider. When the number of spiders in the feeding group was six, each spider consumed only about 60% as much food per day as spiders on their own. The number of eggs produced by each spider also decreased in larger groups, so group living had an adverse effect on spiders' reproductive success.

Evidence of how animals respond to competition for food sources was obtained by Elgar (1986) in a study on house sparrows. When one house sparrow finds a source of food, it usually gives a "chirrup" call which brings other sparrows to the spot to form a flock. The chirrup call was much more likely to be given when bread was available in the form of numerous crumbs than when the same amount of bread was in a lump. There would be much greater competition within the flock for food if it were hard to divide it up (e.g. a lump of bread) than if it were not. Fierce competition for food was avoided by the first sparrow spotting the lump of bread failing to alert other sparrows to its existence.

One of the obvious costs of competition for food and other resources is an increase in various forms of aggressive behaviour. For example, the average number of aggressive encounters among white-tailed and black-tailed prairie dogs was about 60% higher in large colonies than in small ones (Hoogland, 1979).

Parasitism and disease

What about the problems of parasitism and disease in large groups? Hoogland (1979) studied rodent fleas in white-tailed and black-tailed prairie dogs. The average number of fleas in each burrow was greater when the prairie dogs were organised into larger groups. This is an important issue, because these fleas are carriers of the bubonic plague, which is fatal. Further evidence that large groups are more at risk from parasites is discussed in the next section.

Other disadvantages

There are other possible disadvantages of group living. For example, it is often easier for predators to detect groups of animals than animals on their own. This was shown by Andersson and Wicklund (1978). They studied fieldfares, a species of small birds which sometimes nest in colonies and sometimes individually. There were much greater effects of predation on the colonial nests than on the solitary ones.

"Mum! Mum! Over here! Mum! Over here!"

Another disadvantage of group living is the possibility of parents caring for offspring other than their own. For example, McCracken (1984) found that at least 17% of female Mexican free-tailed bats were caring for the wrong offspring. This is not altogether surprising, because very large numbers of young bats are left close together while the mothers fly off to find food.

Benefits and costs: Influence on group size

We have already considered some of the main benefits and costs associated with living in groups. The next step is to try to use this information to work out the best or optimal size of a group, in which the benefits are maximised while the costs are minimised. Some progress in that direction was made by Brown and Brown (1986), who looked at cliff swallows in Nebraska. These swallows nest in colonies of between 1 and 3000 pairs, and they feed on swarms of insects. The main benefit of being in a colony is the information about food sources provided by other birds. Birds that had just been successful in finding food were followed on their next trip by other birds on 44% of occasions, against only 10% for birds that had just been unsuccessful.

What are the costs to cliff swallows of being in a large colony? Chicks are often attacked by swallow bugs, which reduce the rate of growth of the chicks. The number of bugs per nest is greater in larger colonies than in smaller ones. Brown (1988) fumigated some of the nests with an insecticide to kill the bugs, and found that the chicks in the fumigated nests grew more quickly in larger colonies than in small ones. However, there was no relationship between size of the colony and growth rate in the chicks in the nests that were not fumigated. These various findings suggest that the greater problem with swallow bugs in large colonies than in small ones is a significant factor in holding down the average colony size. When the bugs were removed by the use of insecticide, the overall benefits of large colonies were greater than those of small colonies.

Caraco et al.

Caraco, Martindale, and Pulliam (1980) put forward an influential model of group size based on winter flocks of small birds. Their starting point was that these birds have to divide up their time among various activities in an attempt to avoid starvation and attack from predators. Some of Caraco et al.'s main theoretical assumptions were as follows:

1. Birds divide their time among scanning for predators, fighting for food, and feeding; only one of these activities can be carried out at any one time.

2. The time that each bird spends scanning decreases as the group size increases, because the task of detecting predators is spread around more birds.

3. Birds spend more time fighting and behaving aggressively in larger groups, because of the greater frequency with which other birds are encountered.

4. Birds spend more time feeding in flocks of medium size than in small or large flocks, because birds in small flocks devote much time to scanning and those in large flocks to fighting; thus, the best or optimal size for a flock is usually neither large nor small.

Caraco et al. studied the amount of time that yellow-eyed juncos in winter flocks in Arizona spent in scanning and in fighting. Each bird spent less time scanning and more time fighting in large flocks than in small ones. Caraco et al. also tested some other predictions of the model, all of which were supported by the evidence. First, they found that providing additional cover for the birds in the form of a bush led to reduced scanning and increased fighting and feeding. Second, increasing the chances of the birds being attacked by a predator (a hawk) led to increased scanning. Third, higher temperatures made it easier for dominant birds to find enough to eat, which gave them the time to evict subordinate birds. This led to reduced flock size. Fourth, increased food supply led to decreased flock size and to an increase in the amount of time that dominant birds behaved aggressively.

Discussion points

1. What are the strengths of this model (see next section for some of my thoughts)?

2. What are the weaknesses of the model (see next section)?

Evaluation

Caraco et al. (1980) identified the main activities of flocks of small birds. They also showed how the amount of time devoted to each of these activities could be influenced by flock size, with their various theoretical assumptions being supported by the evidence. Finally, they provided good reasons why the best size of a flock is usually neither small (because too much time is spent scanning) nor large (because too much time is spent fighting).

On the negative side, the model is too simple. As we saw earlier in the chapter, there are advantages of flocking over and above those emphasised in the model. For example, there is the dilution effect and there is the possibility of increased vigilance when the flock is large. In addition, the evidence of Caraco et al. (1980) indicated that the average flock size was 3.9 birds, whereas the size that would have led to the greatest feeding time would have been 6 or 7 birds. Why was there this difference between the actual flock size and the best or optimal size? As Krebs and Davies (1993) pointed out, there are various reasons why the actual size of a flock will not be optimal. For example, a solitary bird may join a flock that is already of optimal size, because it will benefit by having more feeding time even though the existing members of the flock will lose slightly.

Imprinting

During the 1930s and 1940s, a number of scientists including Konrad Lorenz and Niko Tinbergen developed an approach to comparative psychology known as **ethology**. The basic idea behind the ethological approach was that the best way to understand another species is to observe members of that species in their natural surroundings. One of their main discoveries was the existence of **imprinting**. This is the tendency among the young of some species of birds to follow the first moving object they see, and to continue to follow it thereafter. Imprinting is found in **precocial species** of birds, in which the newborn are able to move around. Imprinting helps to ensure that the newborn stay close to their mother rather than wandering off into danger, and so it has clear evolutionary value.

Lorenz (1935) provided evidence for imprinting in a study on newborn geese. For half of the geese, their mother was the first moving object they saw, whereas for the other half it was Lorenz. The newborn geese showed a strong tendency to follow the first living creature they saw regardless of whether it was their mother or Lorenz. According to Lorenz, imprinting possesses two other key features:

1. There is a critical period, in that imprinting is only possible during the first few hours after hatching.

2. It is irreversible, in that a bird will remain imprinted to the same creature for its lifetime.

Subsequent research has indicated that Lorenz's assumptions are not correct. If young birds are kept in

Imprinting

The BBC television series *Supernatural* used imprinting as a means of obtaining spectacular close-up film of geese in flight. A member of the production company made sure he was the first thing a group of goslings saw when they hatched, and from then on the birds followed him everywhere, even into the office! When the geese were young adults, their adopted "parent" took to the skies as a passenger in a microlite aircraft. The geese followed and flew alongside, allowing him to film their flight to produce a truly breathtaking sequence for the television series.

Imprinted geese flying behind microlite for *Supernatural* series.

isolation for the first several days of their lives, they show imprinting thereafter, even though it is well after the end of the alleged critical period. Such findings led Sluckin (1965) to propose replacing the term "critical period" with the less extreme notion of "sensitive period". According to Sluckin, imprinting occurs more easily early in a bird's life than later, but can still be achieved when the bird is older.

There are also doubts about the notion of irreversibility. If a bird imprints to an unnatural object, then it is sometimes possible for the imprinting to shift later on to the mother or other natural object (Staddon & Ettinger, 1989).

Lorenz (1935) assumed that imprinting only occurs in a small number of species of precocial birds. However, there is growing evidence of imprinting-like phenomena in numerous other species. Species as diverse as dogs, humans, fish, and sheep seem to show at least some signs of imprinting (Suomi, 1982).

In sum, imprinting is a widespread phenomenon. However, it does not operate in nearly as rigid a way as Lorenz assumed. There is no fixed critical period, and imprinting is by no means always irreversible.

Bonding

Altricial species are ones in which the young are helpless when they are born, and require a considerable amount of parental care in order to survive. Most species of mammals are altricial, including humans and monkeys. In view of the fact that young mammals are often vulnerable and unable to look after themselves for the first several months or years of their lives, it is important that they are closely attached to one or both of their parents in order to ensure their survival. The term **bonding** or attachment is used to refer to the process by which young members of altricial species develop a close relationship with one or both of their parents.

Studies of monkeys

There is good evidence that bonding typically occurs in the great majority of mammals. Some of the factors involved in bonding in monkeys were identified by Harry Harlow (1958). He created two substitute monkey mothers. One was a "cloth mother" that was warm and soft to the touch, whereas the other "mother" was made of wire mesh. Infant monkeys who were separated from their real mothers shortly after birth greatly preferred the softer cloth mother to the wire mother. On average, they spent 18 hours a day cuddling against the cloth mother, compared with under two hours a day against the other mother. This preference remained even when the infant monkeys could only obtain milk from the wire mother.

In other studies, Harlow showed that the baby monkeys were very strongly attached to the cloth mother. He created four "monster mothers", all of which were covered with cloth. One gave the infants blasts of air; the second shook so violently that the infants were often shaken off; the third contained a catapult that flung the infants away from it; and the fourth had a set of metal spikes which poked through the fabric from time to time. The baby monkeys became disturbed when they first experienced the unpleasant aspects of each monster mother. However, as soon as the monster mothers returned to normal, the baby monkeys almost immediately started cuddling them again.

Do infant monkeys have the same kind of attachment for cloth mothers as for their real mothers? The answer is "yes" according to Harlow (1958): "Love for the real mother and love for the surrogate [substitute] mother appear to be very similar ... the infant monkey's affection for the real mother is strong, but no stronger than that of the experimental monkey for the surrogate cloth mother, and the security that the infant gains from the presence of the real mother is no greater than the security it gains from a cloth surrogate."

What happens when infant monkeys are prevented from bonding with their parents? Harlow and Mears (1979) reported that there were far-reaching effects when baby monkeys were not allowed to see or to interact with other monkeys for the first several months of life. When a number of monkeys isolated in this way were brought together, they behaved very aggressively. Some of them froze in strange postures, made meaningless repetitive movements, or simply stared into space. Another effect of isolation was on the monkeys' sex lives. When a sexually experienced male monkey was placed in the same area as some previously isolated female monkeys, the male was unsuccessful in making any of the females pregnant.

Harlow and Mears also reported some more encouraging findings. Some of the negative effects on baby monkeys of being prevented from bonding with their mother were reduced when a substitute mother was present. There were also beneficial effects when isolated monkeys were put in the company of younger, normally reared monkeys. However, when isolated monkeys were placed with normally reared monkeys of the same age as themselves, they were unable to cope. They froze with fear, and hardly interacted at all with the normal monkeys.

Evidence that a lack of bonding or attachment with the mother at an early age need not have permanent effects was obtained by Melinda Novak (reported in Harlow & Mears, 1979). She studied monkeys who had been isolated for the first 12 months of life. These monkeys were placed with normally reared monkeys who were less than one-third of their age, so that the isolated monkeys would not be frightened of them. Over a period of two years, there was a gradual disappearance of undesirable behaviour by the isolated monkeys, and a slow increase in play and social contact.

In sum, bonding is an important process that normally develops over a period of months in the young. It typically develops much more slowly than imprinting, which can occur in a matter of minutes. Bonding is much more easily achieved during the early months of life than later on. However, some of the negative effects produced by a lack of bonding early in life can be removed later on.

KEY STUDY EVALUATION — Harlow

Monkeys are social animals who usually live in quite large groups. This means that Harlow's studies could be criticised on two grounds: modern ethical considerations would make this experimental approach hard to justify, but the studies could also be methodologically flawed. The baby monkeys were doubly deprived, so that causality is not clear. Their subsequent behaviour could have been caused by either maternal or social deprivation, or both.

Discussion points

1. Why do you think this research by Harlow is so highly regarded?
2. Do you think that what Harlow found in monkeys is also true of humans?

Signalling Systems and Communication

Nearly all species communicate with members of their own species by means of signals. Many species also communicate with the members of other species (e.g. predators or prey species). These signals can take many forms: they may be visual, auditory, chemical, or tactile.

Human communication is usually intentional. In other words, the individual who is communicating tries to have a given effect on the person or people to whom the communication is addressed. It is very hard to tell whether animal communication is intentional, and so definitions of communication in animals do not refer to intentionality. We will consider two definitions of communication here. Burghardt (1970) argued that communication "occurs when one organism emits a stimulus that, when responded to by another organism, confers some advantage ... to the signaller or its group." According to Krebs and Davies (1993, p.349), communication is "the process in which actors use specially designed signals or displays to modify the behaviour of reactors."

The key notion that is common to both definitions is that communication requires that the behaviour of the receiver be altered in some way by it. This approach to communication has the advantage that we can observe the receiver's behaviour, and so tell whether communication has occurred.

Why do animals communicate? As Grier and Burk (1992) pointed out, there are many reasons. However, there seem to be four major functions of animal communication:

In what ways do human beings communicate unintentionally?

KEY TERMS
Altricial species: a species in which the young are helpless when they are born, and need a lot of parental care for months or years.
Bonding: the process by which the young of altricial species establish a close attachment with one or both parents; parents also form strong attachments to their offspring.

Classes and species

Vertebrates are divided into five classes, each of which contains a very large number of individual species.

Vertebrates
(animals with backbones)

| Fish | Amphibians | Reptiles | Birds | Mammals |

| Herring, Cod, etc. | Frog, Newt, etc. | Snake, Lizard, etc. | Hawk, Pigeon, etc. | Rat, Human, etc. |

---

1. Survival: for example, alarm and distress signals are used to warn of predators.
2. Reproduction: for example, signals are used during courtship, pair formation, and pair maintenance.
3. Territory boundaries and social spacing: for example, aggressive threat, defensive threat, and submissive signals are used between members of a species.
4. Food: for example, signals can be given indicating where there is a good food supply.

Human communication fulfils all of these functions, together with many others. An important difference between communication in humans and in animals is that we often communicate about events from the past or what might happen in the future. In contrast, animals typically communicate about the here and now, relating to issues of immediate importance.

It might be thought that the number of different signals would be much higher in some classes of species (e.g. mammals) than in others (e.g. birds). However, the evidence does not really support this view. The average number of different signals is slightly higher in mammals than in birds, and in birds than in fish (Moynihan, 1970). There is much more variability between different species of mammals, birds, or fish than between different classes of species.

We will next consider some of the general features of signalling systems in animals. After that, we will discuss specific features of signalling in various species.

Sensory channels

As has already been mentioned, the main sensory channels used for animal communication are the chemical, visual, auditory, and tactile.

Chemical signals

Most chemical signals are called pheromones, and were probably developed before signals in other sensory channels. Chemical signals have various advantages over other signals. Receivers can detect chemical signals even in darkness or when there are numerous objects between sender and receiver. In addition, chemical signals often last for a long time, and are hard for predators to detect and interpret. On the downside, chemical signals can last too long and so interfere with later chemical signals, and it can take longer to create chemical signals than other kinds of signal.

Pheromones

The function of many pheromones is to attract the opposite sex for mating. Gardeners can now use this mechanism to catch garden pests by buying traps baited with female pheromones from the insect species concerned. The males flock to the traps and are killed before they have the opportunity to reproduce.

Visual signals

Many signals produced by animals are visual in nature. According to Grier and Burk (1992, p.528), there are several advantages associated with the use of visual communication:

(1) it is transmitted instantaneously; (2) it may carry a large amount of information, assuming the receiver's eyes and brain are capable of processing it all; (3) it is highly directional, permitting the source to be located; and (4) some aspects, such as body colouration, are permanent ... needing to be produced only once.

What are the disadvantages of visual signals? First, they are only effective under reasonable lighting conditions. Second, they are not generally detectable by receivers over long distances.

Auditory signals

Auditory signals (which are produced by numerous species) possess various advantages. Unlike visual signals, they can be used in the dark. In addition, they can contain much more meaning than chemical signals, and the process of communication is generally fast and efficient. On the negative side, animals often need to use a lot of energy to produce auditory signals. For example, some species of insects lose 2–3% of their body weight during prolonged calling (Dodson et al., 1983). Other problems are that predators can usually detect auditory signals, and auditory signals become very distorted over long distances.

Tactile signals

Tactile signals, which involve touching, are mostly used in combination with other kinds of signals. Tactile signals are used when offspring want to be fed by their parents, during grooming, or to indicate that an individual wants to be carried. Tactile communication has the advantage that it does not depend on complex structures such as those involved in sending and receiving auditory signals. It has the disadvantage that it can only be used in situations in which direct contact between two animals is possible.

Other channels

A few species of fish make use of electrical signals. For example, various species of electric fish communicate with each other by means of electrical signals. These signals are used during courtship, and are also used when dominance hierarchies are being set up (Hagedorn & Heiligenberg, 1985).

Overview

Different species of animals vary in terms of the main sensory channel used for purposes of communication. According to Wilson (1975), most reptiles, fireflies, and fishes tend to make more use of the visual channel than of the chemical or auditory channels. Frogs, mosquitoes, and cicadas rely mostly on the auditory channel, and moths and protozoans use mainly the chemical channel. Other species are harder to categorise. Many species of birds rely about equally on the visual and auditory channels, and humans make most use of the auditory channel, followed by the visual channel, with relatively little reliance on the chemical channel.

There are often fairly obvious reasons for the channel preferences of a given species. For example, roe deer living in open spaces use mainly visual signals to mark their territories. However, in dense forests their visual signals would not be seen. As a result, they make use of loud calls and scents placed in their territory to warn other animals.

Sometimes, animals send signals in more than one modality at a time. For example, ants use chemical signals in the form of odour trails so that other ants will follow them (Holldobler, 1971). At the same time, they use head movements to indicate whether they are leading to food (side-to-side movements) or to a nest site (backwards-and-forwards movements).

It does not make much sense to ask which sensory channel is the best for communication purposes. Each channel has its own advantages and disadvantages, and effective use of any channel requires that the sender and receiver both possess the appropriate structures (e.g. a larynx; ears; eyes). In general terms, less complex species tend to have more limited sensory abilities than more complex ones, and rely more on chemical and tactile signals.

Cockroach trails

Researchers at the University of Florida in Gainesville, USA, found that some cockroaches follow their own dirt trails. As they wander about, they defaecate, and other cockroaches also follow this trail, perhaps because it is likely to lead to a food source (Guterman, 1998).

Ritualisation

The signals made by many species tend to be stereotyped, exaggerated, and repetitive. These signals have developed through evolution so that they communicate information more effectively to other animals. The process involved in the progressive development of signals is known as **ritualisation**.

Why does ritualisation occur? One key reason is to reduce ambiguity and make sure that the receiver understands the meaning of the signal. For example, the posture adopted

KEY TERM
Ritualisation: the evolutionary process by means of which signals come to be more effective at communicating information to other animals; ritualised signals tend to be stereotyped, exaggerated, and repetitive.

The way in which a male fiddler crab waves its claw may differentiate one species from another during courtship.

What sort of human behaviour could count as signalling?

Vervet monkeys respond to each other's alarm calls by taking refuge in the nearest tree.

by a dog is very different depending on whether it is fearful or trying to appear threatening. A fearful dog crouches near the ground, whereas a threatening dog stands erect. The submissive posture is likely to lead to less conflict and so less chance of sustaining injury. Another example of ambiguity reduction is found in the courtship displays of various species of fiddler crabs, in which the male crabs wave their enlarged claw. In some species, there is a rapid series of short claw waves, whereas in others there are only a few, long-lasting claw waves. The patterns of claw waves presumably differ from one species to another in order to make sure that there is no confusion between species.

Deception

According to the principles of natural selection, animals should only use signals when doing so provides them with an advantage. As a result, signalling animals will often try to manipulate the behaviour of other animals. This may involve deception, and be to the disadvantage of the animal receiving the signal. An example of this is the signalling behaviour of young cuckoos who beg for food from their foster parents. If those on the receiving end of attempts at manipulation by signalling show resistance, then signals may become more exaggerated and stereotyped in order to overcome this resistance.

Zahavi (1987) argued that it is very important for animals receiving signals to be able to detect dishonest signals, and so only honest signals will last. Fitzgibbon and Fanshaw (1988) reported a clear example of an honest signal. When Thompson's gazelles in East Africa are approached by a predator, they often engage in stotting, which consists of odd leaping movements. The rate of stotting provides an honest indication of the gazelle's ability to escape. Gazelles that stot at a high rate are less often caught by predators than are gazelles that stot at a low rate.

There are some signals that are not honest. Mantis shrimps have powerful forelimbs which they spread out in a threat display. This is usually an honest signal. However, mantis shrimps shed their hard outer protective covering every two months, and this makes them soft and vulnerable for a few days. They continue to use their threat display during this vulnerable period, even though it is not an honest signal of their ability to fight (Adams & Caldwell, 1990).

Mantis shrimps and most other species that make use of deceptive signals are probably not being dishonest in a deliberate way. A possible exception in the vervet monkey was reported by Cheney and Seyfarth (1990). These monkeys have an alarm call indicating that a leopard is approaching. This causes other monkeys in the group to climb up the nearest tree. A monkey called Kitui was observed giving this call when a male monkey from another group was approaching, but there was no leopard in sight. This caused the strange male to climb a tree, and so stopped him from interfering with the group. On two of these occasions, Kitui walked along the ground giving the leopard call, which he would not have done if he had really thought there was a leopard in the area.

Many animal signals are fixed or stereotyped. However, the signals of some species are surprisingly variable. The fulmar, a species of seabird, makes several different threat signals when competing for fish. According to Enquist (1985), these various threat signals can be understood in terms of cost and effectiveness. Those signals which are most effective in causing the competitor to retreat, such as rushing from behind, are also mostly costly in terms of energy expenditure. In contrast, the less effective signals (e.g. wing raising) are least costly. Which signal is chosen seems to depend on how important food is to the bird at the time.

Communication in birds

As was mentioned earlier, most species of birds communicate much information through the auditory modality. The precise nature of their songs often depends on the kind of environment in which they live. Hunter and Krebs (1979) made recordings in several countries of the territorial songs of great tits living in dense forest or in open woodland or parkland. Birds in an open environment had songs with higher maximum frequency, notes which repeated more rapidly, and a wider range of frequencies than did birds living in the forest. This effect was so strong that the songs of great tits in English parkland were more like those of great tits in Iran than those of birds in a dense English forest.

Why does the type of environment or habitat have such large effects on birdsong? Wiley and Richards (1978) argued that the songs of birds are designed so that they can be heard by other birds with as little distortion as possible. Distortion can occur in forests because of echoes or reverberations from parts of trees. Such echoes are stronger if there are high-frequency sounds in the song, or if the song contains rapidly repeated notes. In contrast, distortion is most likely to occur in an open environment because gusts of wind cause the song to sound softer or louder from moment to moment.

It follows from the analysis of Wiley and Richards that bird songs in forest conditions should contain low-frequency sounds. They should also consist of pure notes or of trills (quavering sounds) with notes spaced out in time. On the other hand, bird songs in open spaces should consist of high-frequency sounds and should be in the form of rapid trills. The songs of most bird species are in line with these predictions.

Communication in honeybees

Probably the most important kind of information that honeybees need concerns the locations of good sources of food. As a result, they have a well-developed ability to communicate information about where food is to be found. The classic work in this area is by von Frisch (1950). He analysed carefully over 6000 occasions on which a honeybee that had located food returned to its hive and communicated this information to the other bees by moving in specific ways. This was normally done on a vertical surface. When the food was within about 100 metres, the honey bee simply moved around in a circle. When the food was further away, the bee performed a waggle dance in the form of a figure-of-eight. In this figure-of-eight pattern, the central line indicates the direction of the food source. More specifically, it represents the angle between the hive, the position of the sun, and the food.

How is the distance of the food source communicated in the waggle dance? This distance is indicated by the speed with which the bee dances, with slower speeds being found when the food source is a long way away. The bee dances at the rate of about 25 figures-of-eight per minute when the food source is 500 metres away, compared to about eight per minute when food is 10,000 metres away.

How well are the other bees able to make use of the information contained in the waggle dance? Von Frisch's findings suggested that the bees made fairly effective use of it. He found that over 60% of the bees went to the food sources that were closest to the hive rather than to ones that were farther away. The speed with which they reached these food sources suggests that the waggle dance had provided the bees with valuable information. However, it is possible that some of the bees found the nearest food sources through smell or vision rather than because of observing a waggle dance.

It used to be assumed that bees responded in an automatic way to the waggle dance. However, it now looks as if matters may not be so simple. Gould (1992) found that bees were very unwilling to use the information in the dance to fly to nectar that had been placed in a boat in the middle of a lake. This may have been because it seemed improbable that food would be found in the middle of a lake, or because bees do not like to fly over water.

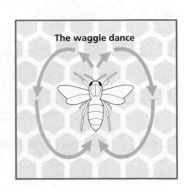

The waggle dance

Discussion points

1. How might bees have developed this complex system of communication?

2. What problems do you think von Frisch might have had in making his observations?

Cetacean research

Cetaceans (dolphins and whales) have developed a large brain, with that of the dolphin having a relatively large area of cortex. It has often been argued that these creatures are highly intelligent. As a result, attempts have been made to understand their communication systems and to teach them aspects of language.

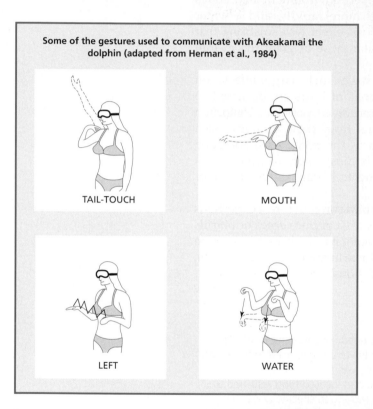

Some of the gestures used to communicate with Akeakamai the dolphin (adapted from Herman et al., 1984)

TAIL-TOUCH

MOUTH

LEFT

WATER

"Well, I simply trained them to give me fish by pressing this over and over again."

Dolphins

Dolphins make various sounds. Some of these sounds consist of sequences of clicks and rattles, whereas others are whistles, squeaks, groans, and chirps. These sounds allow communication between dolphins. For example, Bright (1984) recorded the sounds made by a male dolphin while it was being captured. When these sounds were played to other dolphins in the same group, they swam away rapidly.

Herman, Richards, and Wolz (1984) studied language learning in bottlenosed dolphins. One of them, Akeakamai, was trained in a visual language based on gestures made by a trainer. There was an emphasis on grammar in this language, in the sense that word or symbol order made a difference to the meaning being expressed by the trainer. Akeakamai became very proficient at fetching a given object from among a large number after a training programme in which she was rewarded for responding correctly. She was also able to take one object to another in response to the trainer's gestures. After a lot of training, Akeakamai was presented with new sentences describing combinations of actions that she had not carried out before. She showed her comprehension ability by performing these actions correctly.

Herman et al. (1984) studied another bottlenosed dolphin called Phoenix. He was trained on a language like that used with Akeakamai, except that it was expressed by means of short, computer-generated noises. Phoenix displayed a good ability to respond correctly to instructions in this language, and was good at taking account of word order.

Impressive evidence of communication between dolphins was reported by Bastion (1967). Two dolphins were kept in separate tanks. They could not see each other, but were within hearing range. One dolphin was taught to press a paddle in order to obtain a reward. When the other dolphin was tested, it was immediately able to perform the task correctly. This suggests that the first dolphin had somehow managed to communicate relevant information about the task to the second dolphin.

In sum, dolphins show some ability to understand language and to grasp the basics of grammar. More research is needed to find out whether they can develop their language abilities further than this.

Whales

Humpback whales communicate with each other by means of elaborate "songs" or combinations of sounds. The notes of the songs are long, and the sounds have an echoing quality about them. Each song lasts for up to 30 minutes, and is then repeated. Typically, whale songs have about six themes, but the number ranges between four and ten. A large group of humpback whales will all sing the same songs. In a long-term study, Payne and Payne (1985) found that the songs changed over time.

The exact meaning of these songs is not known. However, whales sing mainly during their breeding season. It has also been found that whales are most likely to "sing" when they are rounding up fish, coming together as a group, or moving off in different directions.

Some light was shed on the meanings of whale calls by Tyack (1983). When he played tape recordings of whale songs to other whales, they tended to disperse. Whales within a group make calls to each other when they are observing a competition between two males for the attention of a female. When Tyack played a tape recording of such calls to whales, they immediately became very excited.

In sum, most (or all) of the calls made by humpback whales seem to be designed to communicate with other members of their group. Thus, their calls probably serve various social functions.

PERSONAL REFLECTIONS

- There is no doubt that significant progress has been made in understanding phenomena such as apparent altruism, sociality, and the development of signalling systems. However, most of the research in this area has involved making observations of animals' behaviour, and there has been a relative lack of controlled experimentation. As a result, the evidence that is available is generally consistent with the theories, but is not especially convincing.

SUMMARY

Altruism is hard to explain, because animals who behave altruistically often have less reproductive success than those who do not. The main explanation for altruism is kin selection. According to this notion, an individual's altruistic behaviour should be directed towards his or her close relatives, because this can help to ensure the survival of that individual's genes. Kin selection depends on being able to identify kin. Animals often seem to assume that any animal living in the same nest or home is kin. Altruism can also be based on reciprocity, which involves a tit-for-tat strategy. Other reasons for altruistic behaviour are mutualism and manipulation.

Altruism

Sociality

Animals generally join groups in order to avoid predation, to obtain adequate amounts of food, or to protect themselves against other members of their own species. Groups protect against predation because scanning for predators is shared among group members. In addition, each animal is more likely to survive an attack because of a dilution effect, or because of the selfish-herd effect. Animals in a group may obtain more food because being in a group makes it easier to find or to catch prey, or to defend prey that has been caught. However, there can be costs of being in a group, such as competition among group members to eat any food that is obtained, and there are increased dangers from parasites and disease. The best size of a group of animals is usually neither small (because too much time is spent scanning for predators) nor large (too much time is spent fighting).

Imprinting

Imprinting is found in precocial species of birds, in which the newborn are able to move around. It helps to ensure that they stay close to their mother, and thus increases their chances of survival. In contrast to the views of Lorenz, there is no fixed critical period during which imprinting can occur, and imprinting is not always irreversible.

Bonding

Bonding or attachment is very common in altricial species, in which the young are helpless when they are born. It helps to ensure their survival. There is evidence that bonding in primates occurs because the mother's touch is soft rather than because she provides her offspring with milk. Bonding normally develops over a period of months, and is most easily achieved during the early months of life. Some of the negative effects produced by a lack of bonding early in life can be removed later on.

Animal signals are used to communicate about the here and now rather than the past or the future. These signals can be visual, auditory, chemical, or tactile. Each type of signal has its own advantages and disadvantages. Many signals are ritualised, that is, they are stereotyped, exaggerated, and repetitive. Ritualisation often develops as a way of reducing ambiguity. Most signals are honest, but some are deceptive. The songs of bird species depend on their natural habitat. They are designed to minimise problems such as echo effects or varying amplitude. Honey bees communicate the direction and distance of a food source by means of a complex dance. It used to be thought that bees responded automatically to the dance, but that now seems unlikely. Dolphins have shown good ability to understand a range of artificial, language-like communications and to grasp some of the basic elements of grammar. Some language skills have also been found in whales.

Signalling systems and communication

FURTHER READING

J.W. Grier and T. Burk (1992), *Biology of animal behaviour (2nd Edn.)*, St. Louis: Mosby. There is extensive coverage of many of the topics in this readable book. Chapter 14 is concerned with altruism, Chapter 13 with sociality, and Chapter 15 with animal communication and signalling systems. J.R.Krebs and N.B. Davies (1993), *An introduction to behavioural ecology (3rd. Edn.)*, Oxford: Blackwell. Most of the topics discussed in this chapter are dealt with in detail in this book.

REVISION QUESTIONS

1   Critically consider the view that altruistic behaviour is genetically determined.   (24 marks)
2   Discuss the benefits and costs to animals of living in groups.   (24 marks)
3a Describe the main forms of attachment that develop between parents and offspring.   (8 marks)
3b Critically consider *two* theories of parent–offspring attachment.   (16 marks)
4   Using evidence, discuss explanations of signalling systems used in communication in
    non-human animals.   (24 marks)

- **Classical conditioning**
  Why does your mouth water at the thought of your favourite food?

  Pavlov's salivating dogs
  Kamin's work on expectation
  Garcia's discovery of one-trial learning

- **Operant conditioning**
  People tend to keep on doing things that are rewarded and stop doing things that are not rewarded.

  Skinner's rat box; schedules of reinforcement
  Shaping and latent learning
  Punishment and avoidance learning
  Seligman's learned helplessness theory
  Abramsom et al.'s attribution theory

- **Foraging**
  Searchers and ambushers: how animals find food.

  Zach's study of optimal foraging theory
  Foraging goals in birds and bees

- **Homing and migration**
  How do some birds, fish, and insects find their way home over very long distances?

  Studies of fish, birds, and Monarch butterflies
  Use of magnetic information, the sun, landmarks, odours, and the stars

- **Animal language**
  Can other species be taught human languages?

  The views of Skinner and Chomsky
  Hayes and Hayes' study of Viki
  Gardner and Gardner's work with Washoe
  Terrace's study of Nim Chimpsky
  Patterson's study of Koko
  Savage-Rumbaugh et al.'s work with Kanzi

- **Evolutionary explanations of human behaviour**
  Can our social behaviour be explained in evolutionary terms?

  Wilson's sociobiology theory
  Trivers' theory of parent–offspring conflict
  Dawkins' selfish gene theory

228

10

Behaviour Analysis

Most of this chapter is concerned with key aspects of animals' learning and behaviour that are essential for survival. If the members of most species are to survive, they need to be able to find food and to find their way home. The ability to learn from experience is of relevance here, because those species that have the greatest learning ability (e.g. humans) tend to be well equipped for survival.

Comparative psychologists have been interested in exploring the learning abilities of other species under laboratory conditions. Many years ago, the behaviourist approach was dominant. This approach was concerned with the detailed study of learning and behaviour. As a result, much research was devoted to studies of classical and operant conditioning in other species. As these are fairly simple and basic forms of learning, it is not surprising that most species can easily be conditioned.

Language learning is much more complex than the learning involved in conditioning. As a result, attempts to teach language to animals have focused very largely on apes. The work in this area is somewhat controversial. However, it is clear that apes can be taught some (but probably not all) of the basic features of language.

It is very important for animals to forage or search for food without using too much energy and while avoiding predators. As we will see in this chapter, most animals are efficient foragers, and their foraging ability improves with experience and learning. However, there are various reasons why their foraging is often not completely efficient. As with language learning, the complexities of foraging behaviour cannot readily be explained in conditioning terms.

Many species of birds and fishes migrate over long distances, and need to find their way home. Species vary in terms of the kinds of information they use when homing, and much ingenuity has been used to work out precisely how the members of any given species travel accurately over long distances. As we will see, there are several kinds of information that animals can use in their homing behaviour, with the precise information that is used varying across species. The homing behaviour of many species is very efficient from an early age, but learning processes probably play some role.

Evolutionary explanations, starting with those provided by Charles Darwin, have proved of great value in understanding much of animal behaviour. Some sociobiologists have argued that evolutionary explanations are equally applicable to human behaviour. This is a controversial issue. The main arguments for and against the sociobiologists' position are analysed later in the chapter.

Classical Conditioning

Imagine that you have to go to the dentist. As you lie down on the reclining chair, you may feel frightened. Why are you frightened before the dentist has caused you any pain?

Learned associations

Imagine something nice, something delicious, your favourite food. Is it strawberries, chocolate, a barbecue, a curry? Think about it and visualise it, and you will find your mouth is watering! There is no such food nearby, you cannot really see, smell, or taste it, but you have learned that you love this food and this learned association has made you salivate. This will not happen if you are presented with a food you have never seen before, as you have not learned an association to it. If your most disliked sort of food were actually presented to you, your mouth would not water either. A different association would have been learned, and possibly a different response too.

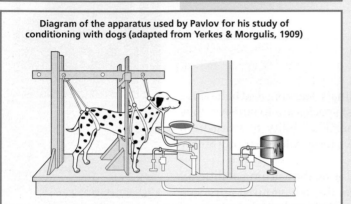

Diagram of the apparatus used by Pavlov for his study of conditioning with dogs (adapted from Yerkes & Morgulis, 1909)

The sights and sounds of the dentist's surgery lead you to expect or predict that you are shortly going to be in pain. In other words, you have formed an *association* between the neutral stimuli of the surgery and the painful stimuli involved in drilling. Such associations are of central importance in classical conditioning.

Basic findings

The best-known example of classical conditioning comes from the work of Ivan Pavlov (1849–1936). Dogs (and other animals) salivate when food is put in their mouths. In technical terms, what we have here is an unlearned or **unconditioned reflex** involving a connection between the unconditioned stimulus of the food in the mouth and the unconditioned response of salivation. Pavlov found he could train a dog to salivate to other stimuli. In some of his studies, he presented a tone (the training or conditioned stimulus) just before food on a number of occasions, so that the tone signalled that food would be arriving soon. Finally, he presented the same tone (the conditioned stimulus as a test) on its own without any food following, and found that the dog salivated to the tone. In technical terms, the dog had learned a **conditioned reflex**, in which the conditioned stimulus (the tone) was associated with the unconditioned stimulus (sight of food), and the conditioned response was salivation.

Pavlov discovered a number of features of classical conditioning. One of these was generalisation. The conditioned response of salivation was greatest when the tone presented on its own was the same as the tone that had previously been presented just before food. A smaller amount of salivation was obtained when a different tone was used. **Generalisation** refers to the fact that the strength of the conditioned response (e.g. salivation) depends on the similarity between the test stimulus and the previous training stimulus.

Pavlov also identified the phenomenon of **discrimination**. Suppose that a given tone is paired several times with the sight of food. The dog will learn to salivate to the tone. Then another tone is presented on its own. It produces a smaller amount of salivation than the first tone through generalisation. Next the first tone is paired with food several more times, but the second tone is never paired with food. Salivation to the first tone increases, whereas that to the second tone decreases. In other words, the dog has learned to discriminate between the two tones.

Another key feature of classical conditioning is **experimental extinction**. When Pavlov presented the tone on its own several times, he found that there was less and less salivation. In other words, the repeated presentation of the conditioned stimulus in the absence of the unconditioned stimulus removes the conditioned response. This finding is known as experimental extinction.

Extinction does not mean that the dog or other animal has lost the relevant conditioned reflex. Animals brought back into the experimental situation after extinction has occurred produce some salivation in response to the tone. This is known as **spontaneous recovery**. It shows that the salivary response to the tone was inhibited rather than lost during extinction.

Discussion points

1. Can you think of reasons *why* Pavlov's dogs behaved in the way they did (see next section)?
2. Why were the behaviourists such as Watson (see Chapter 2) so interested in Pavlov's findings?

Explanations of classical conditioning

Time factors

What is going on in the classical conditioning situation? It is crucial for an association to be formed between the conditioned and unconditioned stimuli. In order for that to happen, it is important for the two stimuli to occur close together in time. Conditioning is usually greatest when the conditioned stimulus is presented a short time (about half a second) before the unconditioned stimulus, and stays on while the unconditioned stimulus is presented. If the unconditioned stimulus is presented shortly before the conditioned stimulus, there is little or no conditioning. This situation is known as **backward conditioning**.

What is important is that the conditioned stimulus (i.e. the tone) allows the dog to *predict* that the unconditioned stimulus (i.e. food) is about to be presented. The tone provides a clear indication that food is about to arrive, and so it produces an effect (i.e. salivation) which is similar to that produced by the food itself. Experimental extinction or the disappearance of salivation occurs when the tone no longer predicts the arrival of food. This explains why backward conditioning is so ineffective. If the conditioned stimulus is only presented after the unconditioned stimulus, then it cannot predict its arrival.

Expectation

Kamin (1969) showed that classical conditioning depends on expectation. The animals in the experimental group received light paired with electric shock, and learned to react with fear and avoidance when the light came on. The animals in the contrast group had no training. Then both groups received a series of trials with a light–tone combination followed by shock. Finally, both groups received only the tone. The contrast group responded with fear to the tone on its own, but the experimental group did not.

What is going on here? The experimental animals learned that light predicted shock, and so they ignored the fact that the tone also predicted shock. The contrast animals learned that the tone predicted shock, because they had not previously learned something different. The term **blocking** is used to refer to what happened with the experimental animals: a conditioned stimulus does not lead to conditioning if another conditioned stimulus is already being used to predict the onset of the unconditioned stimulus.

Rescorla and Wagner (1972) proposed a theory of classical conditioning which accounts for blocking and many other phenomena. According to their theory, conditioning depends on the discrepancy between obtained and expected reinforcement. In the study by Kamin (1969), the shock was fully predicted by the light. Adding the tone did not introduce any discrepancy between obtained and expected reinforcement, and so there was no conditioning to the tone.

Evaluation of classical conditioning

Classical conditioning is an important form of learning. Phobias (strong fears of certain objects or situations) can be produced in humans through classical conditioning. However, most human learning is not based on classical conditioning. In laboratory studies of classical conditioning, a *passive* animal is presented with various conditioned and unconditioned stimuli. In real life, on the other hand, learning typically involves the animal or human interacting *actively* with the environment.

One-trial learning

Classical conditioning is more complex than used to be thought. It used to be assumed that classical conditioning occurs only after many training trials, and that the unconditioned stimulus must follow the conditioned stimulus very closely in time. Garcia, Ervin, and Koelling (1966) discovered a dramatic exception to these assumptions. Indeed, it was such an exception to what generally happens that many psychologists at first refused to accept the findings, and Garcia had great difficulty in publishing them.

Garcia et al. (1966) studied taste aversion. Rats have a strong preference for sweet-tasting foods. Some were given saccharin-flavoured water followed by a drug that caused intestinal illness several hours later. This produced one-trial learning, with the rats only needing to be sick once in order to avoid drinking the water thereafter. Why was

Ethical issues: Do you think Kamin's study would face difficulties in gaining ethical permission today?

> **KEY TERMS**
> **Backward conditioning**: the situation in which the unconditioned stimulus is presented just before the conditioned stimulus in classical conditioning.
> **Blocking**: the failure of a conditioned stimulus to produce a conditioned response because another conditioned stimulus already predicts the presentation of the unconditioned stimulus.

The vapourer moth caterpillar is poisonous, and any animal eating it will be ill or even die. Potential predators must learn to avoid these caterpillars quickly, to minimise loss. If too many are eaten before the predators learn to avoid them, then the brightly coloured signalling strategy is not working.

conditioning so rapid in this case? Animals are biologically prepared to learn to behave in ways that will ensure the survival of the species, and it is clearly important for animals to learn to avoid poisoned food.

Natural associations

The early behaviourists assumed that the strong associations needed for classical conditioning could be formed between almost any conditioned stimulus and any unconditioned stimulus. This notion has been disproved, because some associations are much easier to form than others. In one study, rats learned to associate saccharin-flavoured water with illness produced by X-rays, but they did not learn to associate light and sound with illness. Rats naturally learn to associate taste with illness, but they are not equipped biologically to associate external stimuli like light and sound with illness.

Language

Does telling a person with spider-phobia that there is nothing to fear bring about the end of their phobia?

Classical conditioning is much less important in humans than in other species. A major reason for this is that humans possess language. With other species, extinction usually occurs only slowly and over a fairly long period of time. With humans, simply telling them that the unconditioned stimulus will not be presented again can produce immediate extinction (Davey, 1983). The key point here was expressed by Mackintosh (1994, p.392):

> *People have rather more efficient, language- or rule-based forms of learning at their disposal than the laborious formation of associations between a CS [conditioned stimulus] and a US [unconditioned stimulus]. Even behaviour therapy, one of the apparently more successful attempts to apply principles of conditioning to human affairs, has given way to cognitive behaviour therapy or simply cognitive therapy.*

Biological value

According to Grier and Burk (1992, p.719), "Although usually studied in the laboratory with artificial CSs [conditioned stimuli] such as ringing bells or flashing lights, classical conditioning clearly is a natural phenomenon with real biological value." Taste aversion is one clear example of the biological value of classical conditioning. Grier and Burk also argued that classical conditioning is involved when predators learn to associate certain sounds or smells with potential prey. However, much more research needs to be done before we have a clear picture of the relevance of classical conditioning to the lives of animals living in the wild.

Operant Conditioning

In everyday life, people are often persuaded to behave in certain ways by the offer of some reward or reinforcement. For example, students at school deliver the morning papers because they are paid, and amateur athletes take part in competitions because of the praise they receive for performing well. These are merely two examples of what is known in psychology as operant conditioning or instrumental conditioning. Much of operant conditioning is based on the **law of reinforcement**: the probability of a given response occurring increases if that response is followed by a reward or positive reinforcer such as food or praise.

> **KEY TERM**
> **Law of reinforcement**: the probability of a given response being produced is increased if it is followed by reward or a positive reinforcer.

Basic findings

The best-known example of operant conditioning is provided by the work of B.F. Skinner (1904). He placed a hungry rat in a small box (often called a Skinner box) containing a lever. When the rat pressed the lever, a food pellet appeared. The rat slowly learned that food could be

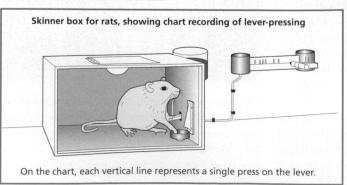

Skinner box for rats, showing chart recording of lever-pressing

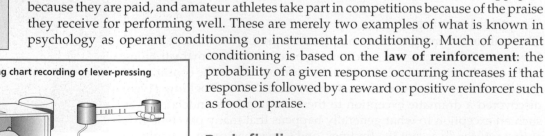

On the chart, each vertical line represents a single press on the lever.

obtained by lever pressing, and so pressed the lever more and more often. This is a clear example of the law of reinforcement. The effects of a reward or positive reinforcer are greater if it follows shortly after the response has been produced than if it is delayed.

The probability of a response has been found to decrease if it is not followed by a positive reinforcer. This phenomenon, discussed earlier, is known as experimental extinction. As with classical conditioning, there is usually some spontaneous recovery after extinction has occurred.

There are two major types of positive reinforcers or rewards: primary and secondary reinforcers. **Primary reinforcers** are stimuli that are needed to live (e.g. food; water; sleep; air). **Secondary reinforcers** are rewarding because we have learned to associate them with primary reinforcers. Secondary reinforcers include money, praise, and attention.

Schedules of reinforcement

It seems reasonable that we tend to keep doing things that are rewarded and to stop doing things that are not rewarded. However, Skinner (1938) found some complexities in operant conditioning. We have looked so far at *continuous reinforcement*, in which the reinforcer or reward is given after every response. However, it is rare in everyday life for our actions to be continuously reinforced. Consider what happens with partial reinforcement, in which only some of the responses are rewarded. Skinner discovered four main schedules of partial reinforcement:

- **Fixed ratio schedule**: every nth (e.g. fifth; tenth) response is rewarded; workers who receive extra money for achieving certain targets are on this schedule.

- **Variable ratio schedule**: every nth response is rewarded on average, but the gap between two rewarded responses may be very small or fairly large; this schedule is found in fishing and gambling.

- **Fixed interval schedule**: the first response produced after a given interval of time (e.g. 60 seconds) is rewarded; workers who are paid regularly every week are on this schedule — they receive reward after a given interval of time, but do not need to produce a specific response.

- **Variable interval schedule**: on average, the first response produced after a given interval of time (e.g. 60 seconds) is rewarded; however, the actual interval is sometimes shorter than this and sometimes longer; as Gross (1996) noted, self-employed workers whose customers make payments at irregular times are rewarded at variable intervals, but they do not need to produce a specific response.

It might be thought that continuous reinforcement (with reward available after every response) would lead to better conditioning than partial reinforcement. In fact, the opposite is the case. Continuous reinforcement leads to the lowest rate of responding, with the variable schedules (especially variable ratio) leading to very fast rates of responding. This helps to explain why gamblers often find it hard to stop their addiction.

What about extinction? Those schedules of reinforcement associated with the best conditioning also show the most resistance to extinction. Thus, rats who have been trained on the variable ratio schedule will keep responding in extinction (in the absence of reward) longer than rats on any other schedule. Rats trained with continuous reinforcement stop responding the soonest. One reason why continuous reinforcement leads to rapid extinction is that there is a very obvious shift from reward being provided on every trial to reward not being provided at all. Animals trained on the variable schedules are used to reward being provided infrequently and irregularly, and so it takes much longer for them to realise that they are no longer going to be rewarded for their responses.

Discussion points

1. Can you think of some examples of situations in everyday life involving the various schedules of reinforcement?
2. What are the limitations of Skinner's operant conditioning approach (see Evaluation section)?

KEY TERMS
Primary reinforcers: rewarding stimuli that are needed to live (e.g. food; water).
Secondary reinforcers: stimuli that are rewarding because they have been associated with primary reinforcers; examples are money and praise.
Fixed ratio schedule: a situation in which every nth response is rewarded.
Variable ratio schedule: on average every nth response is rewarded, but there is some variation around that figure.
Fixed interval schedule: a situation in which the first response produced after a given interval of time is rewarded or reinforced.
Variable interval schedule: on average the first response produced after a given interval of time is rewarded, but with some variation around that time interval.

Although these gamblers have no idea when or if they will receive a payout, they continue to play. This is an example of the most successful reinforcement schedule—variable ratio reinforcement.

Shaping

One of the features of operant conditioning is that the required response has to be made before it can be reinforced. How can we condition an animal to produce a complex response that it would not produce naturally? The answer is by means of **shaping**, in which the animal's behaviour moves slowly towards the desired response through successive approximations. Suppose we wanted to teach pigeons to play table tennis. To start with, they would be rewarded for making any contact with the table-tennis ball. Over time, their actions would need to become more and more like those involved in playing table tennis for them to be rewarded. In this way, Skinner actually persuaded pigeons to play a basic form of table tennis!

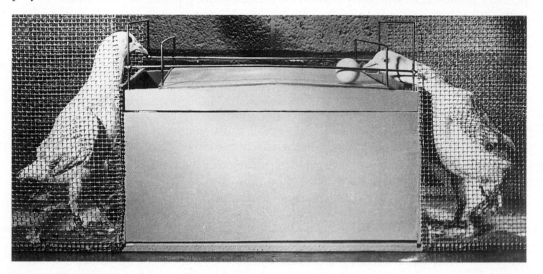

Latent learning

There are clear links between learning and performance. The easiest way of knowing that someone has learned something is by observing appropriate changes in their behaviour. However, it is possible for learning to occur without any obvious effects on performance or behaviour if positive reinforcement is not provided. This is known as **latent learning**.

Several studies of latent learning have focused on rats running in mazes. Rats who explore a maze but receive no food reward for doing so seem from their behaviour to have learned very little. However, when food is provided in the goal box at the end or centre of the maze, the rats run rapidly to it, thus indicating that latent learning has occurred. In one study, Tolman and Honzik (1930) compared maze running in rats who had received no reward over the first 10 days with rats who had been rewarded every day. When the former group started to receive food reward, their performance rapidly improved to the level of the latter group. Thus, latent learning can be as good as learning based on operant conditioning.

The main problem with studies of latent learning was raised by Hilgard and Marquis (1961, p.233):

> *It is never possible to state with complete certainty that a given experiment has accomplished its primary objective, that of temporarily eliminating reinforcement for one group of subjects in the experiment.*

Punishment

So far we have considered the effects of positive reinforcers or rewards on performance. However, operant conditioning can also involve unpleasant or *aversive stimuli*, such as electric shocks or failure feedback. Humans and other species learn to behave in ways that reduce their exposure to aversive stimuli, just as they learn to increase their exposure to positive reinforcers or rewards.

KEY TERMS
Shaping: using reward or reinforcement to produce progressive changes in behaviour in a desired direction.
Latent learning: learning which does not influence performance until positive reinforcement is provided.

Operant conditioning in which a response is followed by an aversive stimulus is known as **punishment training**. If the aversive stimulus occurs shortly after the response, then it has the effect of reducing the likelihood that the response will be produced in future. If there is substantial delay, however, then the effects of the aversive stimulus are much reduced.

Skinner argued that punishment can suppress certain responses for a while, but it does not produce new learning. Estes (1944) reported findings supporting this view. Two groups of rats learned to press a lever for food, and were then given a series of extinction trials. One group was given a strong electric shock for every lever press during the early stages of extinction, but the other group was not. The punishment reduced the rate of responding for a while (suppression). However, in the long run the two groups produced the same number of responses. This suggested that the effects of punishment are short-lived.

It is certainly not the case that punishment always has only temporary effects on behaviour. One of the features of the study by Estes was that the only way in which the rats could obtain positive reinforcement was by pressing the lever. Punishment usually has a more lasting effect when it is possible to obtain positive reinforcement with some response other than the one that has been punished. For example, a child who is punished for putting his or her elbows on the table at mealtime is most likely to stop doing this if he or she is also rewarded for sitting properly.

Avoidance learning

Nearly all drivers stop at red traffic lights because of the possibility of aversive stimuli in the form of an accident or trouble with the police if they do not. This is a situation in which no aversive stimulus is presented if suitable action is taken, and it is an example of **avoidance learning**. Many aversive stimuli strengthen any responses that stop the aversive stimuli being presented; they are known as *negative reinforcers*.

Avoidance learning can be very effective, as was shown by Solomon and Wynne (1953). Dogs were placed in a two-compartment apparatus. A change in the lighting served as a warning that a strong electric shock was about to be presented. The dogs could avoid being shocked by jumping into the other compartment. Most dogs received a few shocks at the start of the experiment. After that, however, they generally avoided the shock for the remaining 50 or more trials.

Mowrer (1947) put forward a two-process learning theory to account for avoidance learning. According to this theory, the first process involves classical conditioning. The pairing of neutral (e.g. walls of the compartment) and aversive stimuli (electric shock) produces conditioned fear. The second process involves operant conditioning. The avoidance response of jumping into the other compartment is rewarded or reinforced by fear reduction.

Two-process theory provides a plausible account of avoidance learning. However, there are some problems with the notion that the avoidance response occurs to reduce fear. Dogs in the Solomon and Wynne study typically responded to the warning signal in about 1.5 seconds, which is probably too little time for the fear response to have developed. After the avoidance response occurred regularly, the dogs did not behave as if they were anxious. Thus, it is hard to argue that their avoidance behaviour was motivated only by fear reduction.

Learned helplessness

Seligman (1975) studied another form of learning based on aversive stimuli. Dogs were exposed to electric shocks they could not avoid. After that, they were put in a box with

CASE STUDY: *Punishment*

Using punishment alone to affect behaviour is regarded by most psychologists today as a technique that is morally and ethically dubious. When this belief is added to research that has shown how punishment on its own has at best only short-lived effects, it is surprising that punishments are still used in so many situations, from family life to warring nations.

Many cultures, such as our own, still use punishment to deal with criminal offenders. Fines or prison sentences are serious punishers in their own right, but research suggests that they would be more effective if linked to some kind of reward for not re-offending. Figures from the Central Statistical Office (1996) show that punishment alone does not have much success. In England and Wales between 1987 and 1990, three in every five males sent to prison became re-offenders, and in 1991 75% of young male offenders had been reconvicted within two years; 12% within three months of their release from prison.

If a small child is misbehaving in a supermarket, parents will sometimes offer sweets as a pacifier. Which kind of reinforcement is this? What is the likely outcome in terms of the child's behaviour?

Can you think of other everyday examples of avoidance learning?

KEY TERMS
Punishment training: a form of operant conditioning in which the probability of a response being made is reduced by following it with an unpleasant or aversive stimulus.
Avoidance learning: a form of operant conditioning in which an appropriate avoidance response prevents presentation of an unpleasant or aversive stimulus.

a barrier in the middle. The dogs were given shocks after a warning signal, but they could escape by jumping over the barrier into the other part of the box. In fact, most of the dogs passively accepted the shocks, and did not learn to avoid or escape them. Seligman used the term **learned helplessness** to refer to passive behaviour in situations in which unpleasant stimuli could be escaped or avoided by appropriate action. Seligman also found that dogs who had *not* previously received unavoidable shocks rapidly learned to avoid the shocks by jumping over the barrier as soon as the warning signal was presented. These dogs were simply showing avoidance learning.

Attribution theory

Seligman (1975) argued that the learned helplessness seen in dogs is very similar to the passive helplessness shown by humans suffering from some kinds of clinical depression. A cognitive account of the processes involved in learned helplessness was offered by Abramson, Seligman, and Teasdale (1978). In their attribution theory, they argued that people might attribute failure to an internal cause (themselves) or to an external cause (other people; the situation). In addition, they might attribute failure to a stable cause that was likely to continue in the future or to an unstable cause that might change soon. Finally, people might attribute failure to a global cause (relevant to many situations) or to a specific cause (relevant only to one situation). Abramson et al. argued that people suffering from learned helplessness tend to attribute failure to internal, stable, and global causes. Thus, they feel personally responsible for failure, they think the factors leading to the current failure will continue in the future, and they think those factors will influence other situations.

Evaluation of operant conditioning

What examples of operant conditioning can you recognise from your own upbringing?

Operant conditioning is often very effective. It is possible to control the behaviour of humans and other species by clever use of reinforcement. For example, the training of circus animals is largely based on the principles of operant conditioning. Operant conditioning has also been used successfully in the treatment of various mental disorders. For example, there is the token economy, in which patients are rewarded for producing desirable behaviour of various kinds. This token economy approach has been used with several kinds of patients including schizophrenics (see page 717).

Operant conditioning has been shown in numerous species (see Grier & Burk, 1992). For example, Boycott (1965) trained octopuses to avoid crabs (part of their normal diet). This was done by presenting the octopus with a white square and a crab, and then giving the octopus an electric shock. The octopuses were not shocked when there was no white square, and they learned to take crabs when there was no danger of receiving a shock. Similar operant conditioning procedures were used to train octopuses to take crabs and avoid fish, or vice versa.

Insight learning

One of the most obvious weaknesses of the conditioning approach is that there are several kinds of learning that do not seem to depend on conditioning principles. Latent learning, which has already been discussed, is an example, but there are others. The Gestaltists studied a phenomenon known as **insight learning**, which involves a sudden restructuring or reorganisation of a problem. Insight learning (also called the "aha experience") was studied by Kohler (1925). For example, an ape was placed in a cage with some sticks, none of which was long enough to reach a banana he wanted. Suddenly, he joined two sticks together, and was then able to reach the banana. Birch (1945) studied apes brought up in captivity, and found little evidence of insightful problem solving in them. He pointed out that Kohler's apes had spent part of their lives in the wild, and so might have slowly learned the abilities that looked like sudden insight.

Observational learning

Bandura (1977) argued for the importance of **observational learning**. This is learning that is based on imitating the behaviour of others, especially if their behaviour is seen to be rewarded. Bandura et al. (1963) showed observational learning in young children who watched a film in which a female adult behaved aggressively or non-aggressively towards a large inflated clown known as a Bobo doll. After they had watched the film, the children played with the doll. Those who had seen the adult behave aggressively towards the doll were much more likely to treat it aggressively themselves. (Bandura's work is discussed more fully on pages 602–603.)

Bandura argued that the entire operant conditioning approach was very limited. According to him (1977, p.12):

An example of observational learning—attacking a Bobo doll.

> *Psychological theories have traditionally assumed that learning can occur only by performing responses and experiencing their effects. In actuality, virtually all learning phenomena resulting from direct experience occur on a vicarious [second-hand] basis by observing other people's behaviour and its consequences for them.*

Equipotentiality

Skinner seems to have believed that virtually any response could be conditioned in any stimulus situation; this is known as **equipotentiality**. In fact, some forms of operant conditioning are much more difficult to produce than others. Breland and Breland (1961) tried to train a pig to insert a wooden token into a piggy bank for reward. What happened was that the pig picked up the token, but then repeatedly dropped it on the floor. In the words of Breland and Breland, the pig would "root it, drop it again, root it along the way, pick it up, toss it in the air, drop it, root it some more, and so on." They argued that their findings showed evidence of instinctive drift, meaning that what animals learn tends to resemble their instinctive behaviour.

What kinds of behaviour would be most easy to condition in rats and mice?

Convincing evidence that instinctive behaviour plays a much larger role in operant conditioning than Skinner believed was provided by Moore (1973). He took films of pigeons pecking at keys for either food or water reward. Students were then asked to decide what the reward was by looking at the films of the pigeons' pecking behaviour. They were correct 87% of the time. Birds pecking for food usually struck the key with an open beak, and made sharp, vigorous pecks. When pecking for water, the pigeons had their bill closed and there was a more sustained contact with the key.

Explanatory deficiencies

According to Skinner, operant conditioning involves forming an association between a given response and a reinforcer. However, as Mackintosh (1994) pointed out, matters are often more complex than that. He gave the example of a rat that is trained to press a lever in a Skinner box in order to obtain sucrose pellets. After that, the rat eats sucrose pellets in a different place. This is followed by an injection of lithium chloride

> ### Ecological validity
> Many of the early conditioning experiments would also be criticised today because of their lack of ecological validity. Normal behaviour is unlikely to be produced in abnormal situations, and most of the experiments described here could not be regarded as providing normal situations for the animals involved.

which conditions an aversion to sucrose pellets. Finally, the rat refrains from pressing the lever in the Skinner box, even though nothing has been done to weaken directly the lever-pressing response.

Mackintosh (1994, p.382) argued that this example illustrates a very important limitation of Skinner's views on operant conditioning:

> *Conditioning is not reducible to the strengthening of new reflexes or stimulus–response connections by the automatic action of a process of reinforcement. It is more profitably viewed as the process by which animals detect and learn about the relationship between events in their environment, be those events stimuli, responses, or reinforcers.*

In similar fashion, Bandura (1977) argued that "Reinforcement serves principally as an informative and motivational operation rather than as a mechanical response strengthener."

> **KEY TERM**
> **Equipotentiality**: the notion that any response can be conditioned in any stimulus situation.

Foraging

Virtually all animals engage in **foraging**, which involves various kinds of behaviour designed to provide enough food for them to eat. We can divide animal foragers into searchers and ambushers. Searchers move around the environment in an active way while foraging, whereas ambushers remain in a given place and try to catch their prey there. Successful foraging involves a range of different activities. It starts with finding a suitable source of food. If the food source is living, then the animal may have to pursue, capture, and kill it. After that, the foraging animal has to handle the prey or prepare it for eating.

Feeding is of vital importance to animals, and so they need to use effective foraging strategies. More specifically, they need to make various decisions during the course of foraging, such as the following:

- What kind or kinds of food are suitable?
- What is the best search strategy for finding prey?
- How should prey be captured and killed?
- How should killed prey be prepared for eating?
- How much food should be eaten?

Some of the issues relating to foraging overlap with those of relevance to predator–prey relationships (see Chapter 7). However, there are some important differences. In particular, foraging is a much broader topic than predator–prey relationships, and it is more concerned with the detailed behaviour shown by animals as they try to obtain food.

Animal foragers: searcher and ambusher.

Optimal foraging theory

Several theories of feeding behaviour have been put forward over the years. However, the dominant approach is known as optimal foraging theory (optimal means best). This theory was originally proposed by MacArthur and Pianka (1966) and by Emlen (1966). In essence, it is claimed within optimal foraging theory that we can understand the foraging behaviour of the members of any species by considering the benefits and costs of different foraging strategies. More specifically, foraging behaviour is designed to maximise the benefits and to minimise the costs. It is to be expected that learning and experience will enable the members of a species to become more successful at maximising the benefits and minimising the costs.

According to the theory, there can be various kinds of *benefits* and *costs*. However, the major benefits usually consist of the number of calories consumed. The major costs are generally in the form of expenditure of energy, but can include the risks of being attacked by predators and the use of time.

It is clear that efficient foraging in the sense of maximising benefits and minimising costs is very desirable (or even essential) if there is a limited supply of food. This follows fairly directly from Darwin's notions of natural selection and survival of the fittest. However, optimal foraging theory goes beyond Darwin in at least two ways. First, it is predicted by optimal foraging theory that animals will forage in an efficient way even when food is plentiful. Second, there is more emphasis within optimal foraging theory on the types of foraging behaviour shown by individual members of a species.

According to optimal foraging theory, all aspects of animals' foraging behaviour should be efficient and optimal. Animals should seek the most suitable type of food, and they should search for it in an efficient way. Finally, they should allocate their time efficiently across different areas in which food might be found. However, no-one expects the foraging behaviour of animals to be entirely efficient and optimal. Animals have limited sensory systems, and they rarely have full knowledge of their environment and of the availability of food within it. In other words, there are various constraints on

KEY TERM

Foraging: the various actions performed by animals in their attempts to find suitable food.

animals' foraging behaviour. As a result, their foraging strategies are likely to be fairly efficient rather than optimally efficient.

Evidence

According to optimal foraging theory, we can understand foraging behaviour by carrying out a cost–benefit analysis. Zach (1979) provided a good example of this approach. He studied the behaviour of northwestern crows that feed on whelks in Canada. A crow will select a large whelk, and then drop it on a rock to get at the food inside. A whelk needs to be dropped more times to break it if it is dropped from a low height, which suggests that it should be dropped from a good height. However, crows have to expend energy in flying upwards to drop a whelk. According to Zach's calculations, the best trade-off between the number of drops and energy expenditure occurs at a drop height of five metres. This corresponded closely to the crows' actual behaviour.

Zach also considered the size of whelks chosen by the crows. Larger whelks have the disadvantage over smaller ones that they are harder to carry and there are fewer of them. However, they have two advantages: (1) their shells are easier to break; (2) they provide more food. Zach worked out that it would be most efficient for the crows to choose the larger whelks, and that is precisely what they did.

Discussion points

1. How do you think this behaviour by crows may have developed in the course of evolution?

2. Could there be other benefits and costs in addition to obtaining food and using up energy, respectively?

Goss-Custard (1977a) obtained evidence that the redshank, a wading bird, operates on the basis of costs and benefits. He focused on redshank that were feeding only on polychaete worms. The redshank consistently ignored small worms, and ate only the larger ones. If there were numerous large worms, then they also tended to ignore worms of intermediate size. Their behaviour showed maximum efficiency of energy expenditure, because large worms provide more energy than small ones in return for the effort expended on foraging.

In a further study, Goss-Custard (1977b) found that the foraging behaviour of the redshank is not always predictable from a simple cost–benefit analysis. When the crustacean *Corophium* was available as well as polychaete worms, most of the birds preferred to feed on *Corophium*. Goss-Custard worked out the birds' energy expenditure and the energy content of their prey. It turned out that the redshank would have obtained at least twice as much energy by feeding on worms rather than on *Corophium*. There was obviously some other attractive feature of *Corophium* (e.g. their taste).

According to optimal foraging theory, the precise foraging activities of animals should be those that are most efficient in the circumstances. This issue was addressed by Grubb (1977). He studied ospreys, whose foraging activities include hovering in a fixed position and looking out for prey while flying or gliding. Hovering is the most costly foraging activity in terms of energy expenditure, but it is generally the most successful in terms of the chances of catching prey. Hovering is the most efficient foraging strategy when the conditions are good, and it is the one usually used by ospreys. When the conditions are bad (e.g. poor visibility), other strategies can become more efficient, and ospreys tend to switch to them.

For many species, foraging behaviour is strongly influenced by the potential danger of being attacked by predators. When sparrows are feeding in an open field, their rate of feeding depends on the number of birds in the flock (Barnard, 1980). The feeding rate was slower when the flock was small, presumably because each bird had to spend more time scanning for predators. When the sparrows were feeding in a cattle shed, where there was

Part of a squirrel's foraging strategy is to gather more food than it can eat while it is plentiful, and to store it for when food is scarce.

much less danger from predators, their feeding rate was much less affected by the number of birds in the flock (Barnard, 1980).

There are still other factors that influence foraging behaviour. When the air temperature is 25°C (77°F) or greater, bumblebees will forage small blossoms, such as wild cherry, as well as small cranberry and rhododendron. At lower temperatures, however, they stop foraging for the smaller flowers. Why is this? The bees need to heat their thorax by shivering at lower temperatures. This leads them to ignore flowers that provide only small amounts of nectar, such as wild cherry.

Goals of foraging behaviour

We have seen that foraging behaviour shows clear evidence of being influenced by benefits and costs. However, there is a complicating factor. In order to assess benefits and costs with precision, we need to know what the animal's goal is in its foraging behaviour. As we will see, there are clear differences in the goals of starlings and of worker honey bees (Krebs & Davies, 1993).

The foraging behaviour of starlings suggests that they are trying to maximise the rate of delivery of food to their offspring, while taking account of their energy costs during foraging. It might be thought that a starling would achieve this goal by loading itself up with as much food as possible in its beak before flying back to the nest. This is not so, because it is less efficient at finding food when its beak is nearly full. More specifically, starlings hunt for food (mostly leatherjackets, the larvae of the crane fly) by pushing their closed beaks into the ground, and then spreading their beaks to expose the leatherjackets that are close to the surface. It becomes harder to do this when their beaks already contain several leatherjackets.

Use of phrases such as "achieving goals" and "trying to maximise rates" suggests a conscious effort on the part of the animal or bird. How far is this true?

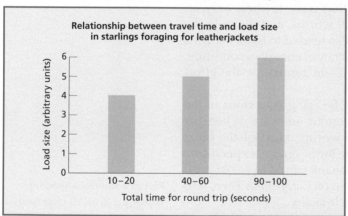

Kacelnik (1984) obtained strong evidence that starlings are trying to maximise the delivery rate of food to their offspring. He argued that two factors were important:

1. Travelling time: the time taken to fly to the feeding site and then return.
2. Loading curve: this reflects the fact that it takes longer and longer to find each additional leatherjacket as the number caught previously increases.

Kacelnik argued that these two factors are related: it is worth the while of starlings who have spent a long time travelling to the feeding site to accept the diminishing returns of the loading curve to return home with several prey. He tested this by dropping mealworms through a plastic pipe at longer and longer intervals to mimic the usual loading curve. These mealworms were presented at distances of between 8 and 600 metres from the nest. As predicted, the average load size was higher at the longer distances than at the shorter distances (about six mealworms versus three or four, respectively).

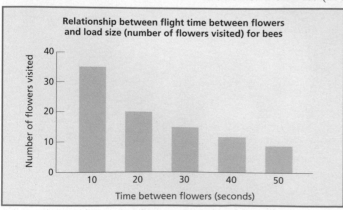

Schmid-Hempel et al. (1985) studied the foraging behaviour of worker honey bees, and found that it could *not* be explained in terms of maximising the rate of delivery of food. The bees collected smaller loads of nectar when they had to fly longer distances, and this seemed to occur because they were trying to maximise the efficiency with which they used their energy. For these bees, the problem with flying long distances with a large nectar load was that it used up a lot of their energy, and thus became inefficient. Schmid-Hempel showed the importance of this factor by attaching tiny weights to the bees' backs. Bees with weights attached collected less nectar than did those without. The importance to bees of conserving energy is also shown by the fact that those who carry heavy loads have shorter lifespans than those who do not.

In sum, as the graphs have shown, we should not assume that the goals of foraging are the same for each and every species. In order to understand foraging behaviour, we must take account of the characteristics of each species, such as the need for bees to try to conserve their energy.

Evaluation

Foraging behaviour is determined by several factors. It often comes close to maximising the benefits in terms of the energy value of the food and/or the taste of the food, and to minimising the costs in terms of energy expenditure, time spent on foraging, and the dangers of being attacked by predators. In other words, optimal foraging theory has been supported by much of the evidence. Some of the failures of optimal foraging theory have also been of value. They have led researchers to look for the kinds of constraints that can prevent animals from foraging in an efficient way.

In spite of the successes of optimal foraging theory, there are various problems with it. First, it is often hard to measure the various benefits and costs of foraging behaviour. As a result, it is sometimes unclear whether the foraging behaviour of a given species is optimal or not.

Second, foraging behaviour needs to be considered within a broader context than is provided by traditional versions of optimal foraging theory. Animals often have to take account of the actual or potential presence of predators, they may have to focus on defending their territory, and their behaviour may be affected by competing foragers. Thus, foraging behaviour is not determined only by calorific benefits and costs, but also by other kinds of demands and dangers. For example, dominant juncos (American birds) forage in a fairly optimal or efficient way, but the foraging behaviour of subordinate juncos is much less efficient because they have to cope with interference from dominant individuals (Caraco et al., 1980).

Third, there are several well-documented cases in which foraging behaviour is very inefficient. For example, animals often fail to forage optimally when they find themselves in an unfamiliar environment. For example, the foraging behaviour of starlings in their familiar environment consists of energetic activities such as digging for mealworms hidden below ground level. Their foraging behaviour remains the same when they are placed in an unfamiliar environment in which some mealworms are plainly visible (Inglis & Ferguson, 1986).

Fourth, optimal foraging theory is concerned with information about the distribution of prey, the energy costs of capturing different kinds of prey, the locations of predators, and so on. Those who favour optimal foraging theory tend to focus on all the information that is *potentially* available to animals rather than on the information that is *actually* available to them. This can lead to misinterpretations. The foraging behaviour of an animal may look inefficient to a theorist armed with all the relevant information, but may actually be efficient in the light of the information known to the animal concerned.

Fifth, rather little is known of *how* animals use the information available to them. It is likely that they use simple rules of thumb such as "Catch the largest worm you can see", and that these rules of thumb produce only an approximation to optimal foraging. At present, we have little knowledge of the rules of thumb used by any species.

Homing and Migration

Several species of birds are able to find their way home even over distances of hundreds or thousands of miles. This is known as **homing**, and it is closely related to migration. **Migration** has been defined as "long-distance travel, usually with a return, to specific locations" (Grier & Burk, 1992, p.243). Migration is found in many species of birds and fishes, and generally involves large numbers of animals travelling together. The distances involved can be very impressive. Some examples are given by Grier and Burk (1992).

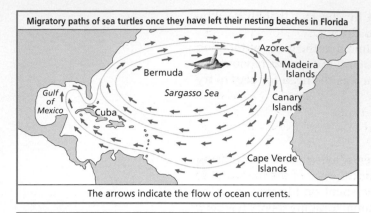

Migratory paths of sea turtles once they have left their nesting beaches in Florida

Azores
Madeira Islands
Bermuda
Gulf of Mexico
Sargasso Sea
Cuba
Canary Islands
Cape Verde Islands

The arrows indicate the flow of ocean currents.

Monarch butterflies

Every winter millions upon millions of Monarch butterflies fly to Mexico from the USA and Canada (Cocker, 1998). Records show that one butterfly was tagged near Brighton, Ontario and was later found 2135 miles away in Mexico (see also case study on page 244).

Golden plovers have been known to fly 2400 miles nonstop from Labrador in Canada to South America, and an arctic tern was discovered in the Antarctic 9000 miles away from the place in Russia at which it was ringed.

There are several costs associated with migration. Migrating long distances can use up a lot of energy, there is the risk of getting lost, and migrating animals may be caught by predators while on their travels. In view of these costs, why then does migration occur at all? There must be significant rewards involved to outweigh the costs of migration. Seasonal variations in temperature, availability of food, and so on, seem to be important. In general terms, migration makes sense if the food (and other) resources available in the place to which animals migrate are better than those available at the place from which they start. For example, many species of birds live in northern parts of the world which become very cold and inhospitable during the winter months. Migrating southwards offers the prospect of having better access to food.

There can be other advantages associated with migration. For example, there may be better breeding territories in the area of migration than in the original area. In addition, competition from another species may be less in the migration area.

Fish

There are several species of fish that migrate over long distances. Two of these species, which have been studied in most detail, are eels and salmon. Atlantic eels live in rivers in western Europe and close to the eastern coast of North America. However, they breed in the Sargasso Sea, which is in the western part of the Atlantic ocean. When the young hatch, they drift for at least a year until they reach a river. As you might imagine, it is very hard to track the movements of eels over thousands of miles. As a result, it is not surprising that it is not known in detail how the eels find their way to the Sargasso Sea.

More is known about the homing behaviour of salmon. Salmon hatch in streams and rivers, but then spend several years in the ocean hundreds or thousands of miles away. After that, they show an amazing ability to return for breeding purposes to the stream or river in which they were hatched. How do salmon manage to return to the home stream or river? Evidence discussed by Hasler (1986) indicates that salmon make use of the fact that each stream has its own distinctive odour. Young salmon learn the odour of their stream, and their memory of this odour directs their homing behaviour. When salmon could not use their sense of smell because their noses were plugged, their ability to home was greatly disrupted (see Hasler, 1986).

In another study, young salmon were exposed to one of two artificial odours before being released into Lake Michigan. Then two streams running into the lake were scented with one of the artifical odours, and attempts were made to monitor which salmon returned to which stream. More than 90% of the recovered fish went to the stream that had the odour to which they had been exposed when young (Grier & Burk, 1992). These findings show convincingly that homing behaviour in salmon is influenced by smell.

Birds

Homing pigeons are the best known of the species of homing birds. However, there are several others. For example, pied flycatchers breed in the northern part of Europe and migrate to Africa for the winter. In one study (Berndt & Sternberg, 1969), it was found that a majority of the birds returned very close to where they had been hatched during the breeding season. In another study, a Manx shearwater was flown by plane from England to the east coast of the United States. It managed to find its way back to its nest in 12 days (Matthews, 1953).

Does the migratory and homing behaviour of birds depend on heredity or on experience? The answer varies from one species to another. As Grier and Burk (1992) pointed out, the direction in which European storks cross the Mediterranean seems to be determined by heredity. Schuz (1971) took advantage of the fact that young storks in western Europe fly in a southwesterly direction, whereas those further east fly in a southeasterly direction. He took stork eggs from the east and moved them to nests in western Europe. The young storks flew in a southeasterly direction, rather than the southwesterly direction of storks whose parents were from western Europe. Differences in heredity presumably underlie these differences in direction of flying.

Evidence that heredity and experience can both be important was reported by Perdeck (1958). Starlings from northern and eastern Europe tend to migrate in a southwesterly direction during the autumn. Perdeck arranged for young and adult starlings to be transported from the Netherlands to Switzerland. When they were released, the young starlings simply flew in a southwesterly direction. As a result, they arrived in parts of Europe much further south than is normal for starlings. In contrast, the adult starlings adjusted their flying direction to take account of the fact that they had been displaced. They flew in a northwesterly direction, and arrived at their normal destination.

What might be the reason for the difference in behaviour between young and adult starlings in Perdeck's study?

What mechanisms are involved in homing?

We have seen that many bird species are very good at homing. The key issue is to understand the mechanisms that allow birds to fly very long distances with such accuracy. Much of this research has focused on homing pigeons, but relevant findings from other species will also be considered.

There are two important general points to be made at the outset. First, it would be wrong to assume that all species of homing birds use the same mechanisms to navigate accurately. Second, some bird species can use various mechanisms in homing, with the one chosen at any given time being determined by the precise circumstances.

Magnetic information. Homing pigeons make use of various kinds of information to guide them. There is strong evidence that information from the earth's magnetic field is used. Lednore and Walcott (1983) attached an electromagnetic coil to the heads of pigeons in order to disrupt their ability to use magnetic information. This prevented the pigeons from returning home on overcast days, but not on sunny ones. The implication is that pigeons can make use of information from magnetism or from the sun's position to guide their homing behaviour.

Lednore and Walcott used experienced pigeons. Inexperienced pigeons are much less able to navigate accurately on the basis of magnetic information alone, and seem to need information from the sun's position as well (Keeton, 1974). These findings indicate that learning and experience play an important role in the development of precise navigation.

More evidence that pigeons use magnetic information to help them navigate was reported by Walcott and Green (1974). They fitted electro-magnetic coil caps to the heads of homing pigeons. Magnetic fields were then produced by connecting the coils to small batteries. When the pigeons were tested on overcast days, they flew in the correct direction with a certain direction of current flow in the electro-magnetic coils. When the direction of the current was reversed, the pigeons flew in the opposite direction.

Other bird species also make use of magnetism. Wiltschko (1972) studied caged European robins that were exposed to changed magnetic fields. Their direction of movement was affected by these changes, indicating that they were making use of magnetic information.

The sun's position. We saw in the study by Lednore and Walcott (1983) that pigeons can use information about the sun's position to find their way home. Further relevant evidence has been obtained by the use of **clock shifting**. In essence, pigeons or other birds are exposed to artificial light. This light is turned on and off in such a way as to create an artificial day that starts and ends a few hours earlier (or later) than the natural day. After a while, the bird's circadian rhythm or sleep–waking cycle (see Chapter 5) shifts in line with the artificial day. It is assumed that birds exposed to such clock shifting will

KEY TERM
Clock shifting: this involves changing an animal's internal daily rhythms relative to external time.

CASE STUDY: *Monarch Butterflies*

Clock shifting has also been used to test Monarch butterflies' homing abilities. Colonies fly from the eastern and western USA and Canada to Mexico. Perez, Taylor, and Jander (1977) clock-shifted migrating Monarchs by six hours and compared them to a laboratory control group. The results showed a statistically significant orientation to the sun in flight direction.

On the other hand, grains of magnetic material have been found in the bodies of adult Monarchs (Cocker, 1998), and the area of Mexico to which they migrate is rich in iron ore. Its magnetic reading is 90–100 times greater than normal. This would seem to suggest that Monarchs are using their own compass-like ability as well as their sun-map to home in on a natural magnetic beacon as their winter site.

misinterpret information about the sun's position, because they perceive the time as being several hours earlier or later than is actually the case.

Keeton (1974) used clock shifting to produce a six-hour shift in the circadian rhythm or sleep–waking cycle of homing pigeons. When the pigeons were released on a sunny day, they set off about 90° away from the homeward direction. In contrast, they showed normal homing behaviour on overcast days. These findings suggest that the pigeons chose to use information from the sun's position when possible, but the shifted circadian rhythm made them misinterpret that information.

Landmarks. It might be thought that pigeons would make use of visual information to guide their homeward flight, perhaps making use of landmarks identified on the outward trip. However, pigeons released repeatedly from the same site very rarely fly the same route twice. This suggests that they do not carefully follow a series of landmarks. More convincing evidence was reported by Walcott and Schmidt-Koenig (1971). They fitted pigeons with translucent lenses before releasing them 80 miles away from home. The lenses prevented the pigeons from identifying landmarks. However, most of them either found the way home or at least set off in the right direction. Most strikingly of all, pigeons that have been clock shifted have been known to fly in completely the wrong direction even when their home loft is visible from the point of release (Keeton, 1974)!

Other bird species seem to make more use of visual information. Gannets who were moved to an unfamiliar location tended to fly around over increasingly large areas in a rather random fashion. When they happened to fly over familiar territory, they rapidly found their way back home (Griffin, 1955).

Odours. Papi (1982) argued that homing pigeons make use of olfaction, i.e. information about odour. He and his colleagues have reported various studies supporting this viewpoint. For example, homing behaviour is impaired in pigeons whose nostrils have been plugged or whose olfactory nerves have been cut. However, it has proved hard to repeat these findings. It may well be the discomfort and pain caused to the pigeons that disrupt their homing behaviour, rather than the specific effects on the olfactory system. There are other problems with Papi's theory, including the difficulty of explaining how information about odour could be used at long distances.

The stars. Some bird species make use of information about the stars for navigational purposes. For example, Bellrose (1958) compared the flight paths of mallards who were released on clear or overcast nights. The mallards all flew in the same direction on clear nights, but were disoriented and flew around aimlessly on overcast nights. Indigo buntings also make much use of information from the stars, but many other species (e.g. swans) do not.

Evaluation

We have seen that information about the earth's magnetism, the position of the sun, visual landmarks, the positions of the stars, and possibly olfactory information can be used for purposes of navigation. Experienced homing pigeons seem to rely on information from the sun's position if it is available. If it is not available, they use information about the earth's magnetic field. These sources of information are very useful in guiding pigeons in the right general direction. When they have flown fairly close to home, then they probably use visual landmarks to reach the loft.

In spite of the progress that has been made, there is much that remains unclear. For example, *what* is the precise information that birds obtain from the position of the sun, the earth's magnetic field, the positions of the stars, and so on? *How* is that information used to allow birds to arrive at their destination? In general terms, birds need to know the direction in which home lies, as well as at least its approximate distance. In addition, they need to know how to travel in the desired direction. In other words, birds require both a map and a compass.

There has been some controversy as to whether the sun is used as a map or as a compass. According to the map–compass hypothesis (Kramer, 1953), birds use the position of the sun only as compass information. Evidence supporting this hypothesis was reported by Keeton (1974). Clock shifting was used to move pigeons' internal clocks back by six hours. They were then transported just over 60 miles to the south, and released at mid day. Assume that the pigeons knew that their home was to the north, and that they used the position of the sun to tell them how to fly north. The clock shifting made the time appear to be six in the morning rather than the actual mid day, and the sun is in the east early in the morning. According to the map–compass hypothesis, the pigeons should have flown 90° to the left of the sun in the mistaken belief that they were going northwards. That is precisely what happened.

> There are many stories, some of which have been made into films, in which household pets have travelled extremely long distances alone to return to former homes. Assuming that such animals do have some "sense of direction", what possible explanations can you give for how this sense might function?

Animal Language

Some of the forms of communication used by other species were considered in detail in Chapter 9. In general terms, other species do not seem to possess anything resembling human language. However, the fact that other species do not possess language does not necessarily mean that they cannot acquire it. Several attempts have been made to teach apes the basic features of human language, and the findings from such attempts are discussed here. It has generally been assumed that apes are the only non-human species that might be able to learn human language.

The issue of whether language can be taught to other species has some theoretical interest. According to Skinner (1957), spoken language is learned in very much the same way as other responses. In other words, utterances that are rewarded or reinforced tend to be strengthened, whereas those that are not rewarded are weakened. As a result, there is nothing special about language, and thus there is no reason why language should not be learned by other species (see Chapter 14).

In contrast, Chomsky (1959, 1965) claimed that language is a unique system. It cannot be acquired by other species, because language learning can only occur in species having various innate linguistic mechanisms. According to Chomsky (1959), only the human species has such innate mechanisms, and they form part of the so-called **language acquisition device**. This language acquisition device is sufficiently general that it is of value to someone trying to learn any out of the hundreds of human languages.

We will now consider the evidence from some of the main studies on apes.

> ■ Research activity: Before reading this section, try to write a working definition of "language". Would you include things like bird calls, or the signalling given by a peacock's tail? What about "body language"? How would Sign Language or Braille fit into your definition?

KEY TERM
Language acquisition device: an innate mechanism found only in the human species which allows us to develop language.

Hayes and Hayes

Keith and Catharine Hayes brought up a chimpanzee named Viki, and spent six years trying to teach her to speak (Hayes, 1951). At the end of that time, Viki could only say four words: "momma"; "poppa"; "up"; and "cup". Her teachers had to push her lips and mouth into the correct positions at first. However, she finally learned to position her lips and mouth with her own hands to produce the sounds.

This study was poorly designed. It is not at all natural for chimpanzees to make much use of their vocal cords. Humans can produce about 100 distinct sounds, but chimpanzees can produce only about a dozen. As we will see, later studies abandoned the attempt to make chimpanzees communicate in the same way as humans.

Gardner and Gardner

Attempts to teach language to chimpanzees started in earnest in 1966. Allen and Beatrice Gardner began to teach American Sign Language to a 1-year-old female chimpanzee called Washoe. After four years of training, Washoe knew 132 signs, and she could arrange them in novel ways. For example, when she saw a swan she signed "water bird". There was also evidence that she had grasped some of the elements of grammar. She signed "tickle me" much more often than "me tickle", and "baby mine" more often than "mine baby". Washoe also showed the ability to apply the signs she had learned in new situations. For example, she initially learned the sign "open" with reference to a door. After that, she used the sign in the presence of cupboards, drawers, and boxes. In view of what Washoe learned to do, the Gardners concluded that she had learned language.

We should be cautious about accepting the conclusions of Gardner and Gardner (1969). Terrace et al. (1979) carried out a detailed analysis of Washoe's behaviour as revealed in a film that was made about her. Most of the grammatical sequences of signs produced by Washoe occurred when she simply imitated the signs that had just been produced by her teacher. The ability to imitate is very different from the ability to grasp grammatical rules. In addition, many of the signs that Washoe learned are the same as gestures that occur naturally in apes. These include "tickle" (signed by tickling), "hug" (signed by hugging), and "scratch" (signed by scratching). On the other hand, the Gardners have pointed out that Terrace's conclusions were based only on a short film, not the full record of Washoe's behaviour throughout their study.

Terrace

One of the most thorough attempts to teach sign language to an ape was made by Herbert Terrace (1979). He and his associates tried to teach American Sign Language to a chimpanzee called Nim Chimpsky (a rather feeble pun on Noam Chomsky). Between 18 and 35 months of age, Nim was observed signing over 19,000 utterances consisting of two or more signs. Analysis of the two-sign combinations consisting of a transitive verb and "me" or "Nim" showed that Nim chose the verb-first order 83% of the time (e.g. "tickle Nim" rather than "Nim tickle").

Most humans sometimes use language to deceive others, and Nim was also able to do this. He noticed that his teachers were very responsive when he signed either "dirty" (meaning he needed to go to the toilet) or "sleep" (meaning that he was tired). He started to use these signs when they were obviously not appropriate, probably because he was bored and wanted more attention.

Nim's achievements looked much less impressive when his performance was compared to that of young children. Children initially produce utterances containing about one-and-a-half words on average. However, this rapidly increases to an average of four or more words per utterance. In contrast, the average length of Nim's utterances remained very steady at about one-and-a-half signs for the whole of the period between 26 and 46 months. In other words, Nim remained at a low level of language achievement, which is greatly exceeded by most young children.

How might you relate Nim's attention-seeking signing to what you have learned about conditioning?

There was another major difference between Nim's language and that of young children. Among children just starting to talk, under 20% of their utterances consist of imitations of their parents' expressions, and about 30% are spontaneous. In contrast, 40% of Nim's signings were merely imitations of what his teacher had just signed, and only 10% were spontaneous. Thus, Nim used language in a much less creative and spontaneous way than even very young children.

There are various possible reasons why Terrace found less evidence of language learning than other researchers (e.g. Gardner & Gardner, 1969) who have made use of American Sign Language. First, Terrace (1979) took more care than previous researchers to distinguish between "true" use of language and mere imitation. Second, a large number of volunteers were used by Terrace in the attempt to teach language to Nim, and some of them may not have been very competent. This could have limited the amount of language acquired by Nim. Third, Terrace had studied with Skinner, and so may have applied the techniques of operant conditioning to Nim. Such techniques are more likely to produce an imitative rather than spontaneous use of language.

Patterson

Patterson (1979) trained a female gorilla called Koko in a modified version of American Sign Language. She had mastered over 400 signs by the age of 10, which is much more than has been achieved by most other apes. She showed some ability to generalise beyond what she had been taught. For example, she was taught the sign for "straw" in the sense of a drinking straw, but then applied it to similar-looking objects such as plastic tubes and cigarettes.

One of Koko's most impressive achievements was her ability to create novel combinations of signs. For example, she signed "white tiger" to indicate a zebra, "false mouth" to mean nose, and "eye-hat" to mean mask. The productivity or creativity involved in these sign combinations is one of the main criteria for genuine language. She also showed some evidence of displacement, or the ability to refer to events that were not currently happening. For example, on one occasion she seemed to be apologising for having bitten someone three days earlier, and on another occasion she used the phrase "dirty toilet" as an insult.

On the negative side, Koko showed little evidence of having mastered syntax or the grammatically correct ordering of words. In addition, most of her communications were rather brief, and were certainly much shorter than is the case with even young children. Thus, Koko only exhibited some of the features of language.

Savage-Rumbaugh et al.

The chimpanzees studied by the Gardners and by Terrace were common chimpanzees (*Pan troglodytes*). It has been claimed that bonobo apes (*Pan paniscus*) are more intelligent than common chimpanzees. As a result, Savage-Rumbaugh et al. (1986) decided to study language in a male bonobo ape called Kanzi. In contrast to previous studies based on American Sign Language, Kanzi was taught using a keyboard containing geometric symbols known as lexigrams. Those working with Kanzi sometimes used the keyboard themselves, and sometimes they spoke to him in English.

Most of the earlier work on language learning in great apes had focused on language production rather than on language comprehension. In contrast, Savage-Rumbaugh et al. were as concerned with Kanzi's comprehension skills as with his ability to produce language. One reason for this is that language comprehension develops more quickly and easily in young children than does language production, and the same might be the case with great apes.

Sometimes Kanzi received spoken instructions through headphones.

Sue Savage-Rumbaugh holds a board displaying lexigrams that Kanzi uses to communicate with her.

In 17 months, Kanzi learned to understand nearly 60 of these symbols, and he was able to produce nearly 50 symbols. After prolonged training, Kanzi mastered the use of 150 different symbols. Savage-Rumbaugh et al. found that Kanzi had developed good comprehension skills. He responded correctly every time to 109 words on a speech comprehension test, and behaved appropriately to 105 action–object utterances (e.g. "Kanzi, go get me a knife").

Kanzi's language learning was greater than that of Washoe, Nim Chimpsky, or Koko. He understood the difference between "Chase Kanzi" and "Kanzi chase". He could even make fairly subtle distinctions, such as that between "Put the pine needles in your ball" and "Can you put the ball on the pine needles?". However, as with Nim Chimpsky, he differed from young children in that the length of his utterances did not increase over time. Indeed, most of his utterances consisted of a single lexigram.

Discussion points

1. How impressed are you by Kanzi's command of language?
2. What are the limitations in the achievements of Kanzi and other apes (see below)?

Evaluation

The issue of whether or not apes can be taught language is important in a number of ways. In principle, it should help to resolve the theoretical controversy between Skinner (1957) and Chomsky (1959) that was discussed earlier. In addition, work on this issue may provide some insights into the nature of language.

On the negative side, it is rather artificial to try to teach chimpanzees human language systems to which they are not adapted. It is perhaps unfortunate that so much of the research has made use of a version of American Sign Language that is particularly artificial. The grammatical structure of American Sign Language is different from that of spoken languages, and the version of it used in research is simplified and distorted from the original. As a result, Benderly (1980) concluded as follows: "This rather impoverished form is really not a language, but a manual code for English."

We can only decide whether or not apes have succeeded in acquiring language if we have some criteria for defining language. Hockett (1960) put forward a large number of such criteria, some of which are as follows:

- Semanticity: the words or other units must have meaning.
- Arbitrariness: there must be an arbitrary connection between the form or sound of the word and its meaning.
- Displacement: language can be produced in the absence of the object or objects being described.
- Prevarication: there is an ability to tell lies and jokes.
- Productivity: there is an essentially infinite number of different expressions that can be communicated.

According to Harley (1995, p.14), "If we look at them [attempts to teach apes a human-like language] in terms of Hockett's design features, at first sight all the important ones appear to be present." However, as Harley went on to point out, there is only weak evidence for some of the

"He says the downturn in world trade is adversely affecting banana supply, and warrants a reduction in interest rates".

criteria. For example, apes do not often show displacement, and very rarely refer to objects that have not been seen for a long time. They also show much less evidence of productivity than do most humans.

How else can we evaluate the language performance of chimpanzees? According to Harley (1995, p.18), "A great deal comes down to a comparison of the performance of apes with that of children, and there is considerable disagreement on how well apes come out of this comparison." There are various ways in which the language performance of apes falls short of that of young children. First, apes do not often use language spontaneously, and they very rarely ask questions. Second, the average length of their utterances is much less than that of most young children. Third, there is very little evidence that apes use language to help them think. Fourth, apes use language to refer to the here-and-now, and rarely refer to objects that are not visible or have not been seen for some time.

Chimpanzees have shown only a modest ability to learn language because they have only a limited need or wish to communicate. As Savage-Rumbaugh et al. (1986) concluded:

> *Symbols have merely served to replace or accompany non-verbal gestures the chimpanzee would otherwise employ ... chimpanzees, even with intensive linguistic training, have remained at the level of communication they are endowed with naturally—the ability to indicate ... that they desire you to perform an action upon them or for them.*

It is hard to come to any definite conclusions. However, the fact that most human children as young as 2 years old have a much greater command of language than any trained ape suggests that no ape has developed language in the full sense. Another reason for doubting the language ability of chimpanzees was offered by Chomsky (quoted in Atkinson et al., 1993):

> *If an animal had a capacity as biologically advantageous as language but somehow hadn't used it until now, it would be an evolutionary miracle, like finding an island of humans who could be taught to fly.*

Evolutionary Explanations of Human Behaviour

We saw in Chapters 7, 8, and 9 that the Darwinian or evolutionary approach has contributed much to our understanding of the behaviour of many different species. Members of the human species share more than 98% of their genetic make-up with some other species, such as apes and chimpanzees. In addition, the major regulatory genes are remarkably similar across nearly all species, including the human species. As a result, it is natural to consider whether Darwin's biological and evolutionary approach can usefully be extended to provide an understanding of human social behaviour.

Edward Wilson (1975) put forward a version of evolutionary theory designed to apply to the human species, and by so doing established what is known as **sociobiology**. The key assumption of sociobiology is that "individuals should act to maximise their inclusive fitness. Inclusive fitness refers to the number of descendants left in future generations, including those of relations as well as direct descendants" (Smith, 1983, p.224). In more general terms, sociobiologists argue that much of human behaviour is determined by genetic factors and by the goal of preserving one's genes in the future. In other words, the goal of gene survival is allegedly involved when humans weigh up the benefits and costs of different forms of social behaviour. Evolutionary psychologists are in general agreement with sociobiologists, but perhaps apply the Darwinian approach in a broader way.

Wilson (1975, p.156) attached enormous significance to the role of genetic factors in determining human behaviour: "Only small parts of the brain represent a *tabula rasa* [clean slate]; this is true even for human beings. The remainder is more like an exposed negative, waiting to be dipped into developer fluid." Later statements of the sociobiological position

Looking back at your working definition of language, do you think it is still adequate? How would you change it, if at all, in the light of all these animal studies?

KEY TERM
Sociobiology: the notion that human behaviour is strongly influenced by the goal of survival of one's genes.

How does Wilson's statement tie in with notions of "biological preparedness" (where a species is prepared through evolution to learn some things but not others)?

have included more of a recognition that environmental factors also matter, but still emphasise the role of heredity.

Sociobiology developed in part out of ethology. **Ethology** is concerned with the study of animals in their natural environments, and ethologists such as Lorenz and Tinbergen argued that much animal behaviour depends on inherited capacities and responses (see Chapter 9). The sociobiologists and the ethologists both believe in the relevance of Darwinian evolutionary theory to humans, but sociobiologists have been more inclined to interpret most human social behaviour in evolutionary terms.

It has been claimed that the sociobiological approach can provide an explanation for numerous social phenomena. These phenomena include altruism, incest taboo, conformity, ethical behaviour, exploitative capitalism, tribal warfare, territoriality, gender differences in behaviour, fear of other races, and so on. For example, Wilson (1975) argued that men are biologically more aggressive and have greater spatial ability than women. As a result, "even with identical education and equal access to all professions, men are likely to continue to play a disproportionate role in political life, business, and science."

Wilson's comments were made in the mid-1970s, when the women's movement was burgeoning. Do you think statements like this would be so acceptable today?

Those who adopt an evolutionary approach often assume that nearly all human behaviour is adaptive and serves some valuable purpose. However, this assumption is probably wrong. As Cardwell et al. (1996, p.533) pointed out, the human appendix serves no useful purpose at all. They argued that "each living organism is made up of a hotch-potch of solutions which had some non-ideal starting point." Part of the reason for this is that major cultural and social changes tend to occur much more rapidly than genetic changes produced by evolutionary pressures over long periods.

Some specific examples of the evolutionary approach applied to human behaviour are considered next. They include sexual selection (discussed in more detail in Chapter 8), parent–offspring conflict, and male aggression.

Sexual selection

According to the sociobiologist Symons (cited in Eysenck, 1990):

> *With respect to sexuality, there is a female human nature and a male human nature ... Men and women differ in their sexual nature because throughout the immensely long hunting and gathering phase of human evolutionary history the sexual desires and dispositions that were adaptive for either sex, were for the other, tickets to reproductive oblivion.*

Wilson (1975) claimed that women and men adopt different sexual strategies because women have to devote a considerable amount of time to their offspring, both during pregnancy and thereafter. In contrast, men can maximise their reproductive potential by having sex with numerous women. Women can be sure that any child they produce is really theirs, whereas men lack this certainty. As a result, men feel a need to control female sexuality so that they can be as sure as possible that any child they protect is carrying their genes.

As is discussed in Chapter 8, a major problem with this approach to human sexual selection is that it de-emphasises the importance of social and cultural influences. There have been enormous changes in human sexual behaviour and in sexual attitudes during the past 50 years, and these changes simply cannot be explained in evolutionary terms.

Parent–offspring conflict

Trivers (1974) put forward a very influential theory about the evolutionary basis of parent–offspring conflict (see Chapter 8). Parents and offspring have various common interests, but there are good reasons why conflicts should develop. According to Trivers, such conflicts can even develop between the mother and her unborn foetus. An important source of parent–offspring conflict that was emphasised by both Trivers (1974) and Wilson (1975) is a crucial genetic asymmetry. Parents are equally related genetically to each of their children, but the children are twice as genetically related to themselves as to their siblings. As a result, according to Wilson (1975, p.343), "there is likely to evolve a conflict between parents and offspring in the attitudes towards siblings: the parent will encourage more altruism than the youngster is prepared to give."

It is possible to apply some of these ideas to the strange finding that the average weight of newborn babies is rather less than it should be to maximise their chances of survival. It can be argued that it helps to preserve the mother's resources, and so increases her chances of having further children.

Before birth

Cardwell et al. (1996) discuss in detail some of the ways in which parent–offspring conflict may reveal itself before the child is born. Profet (1992) focused on the feelings of nausea or morning sickness that pregnant women often experience. These feelings tend to occur after the mother has eaten something that is toxic or poisonous for the foetus. There are various foods that are toxic to foetuses but not to most adults, because they have gradually developed an immunity to them over the years. According to Profet, what we have here is an effective system in which the foetus causes moderate discomfort to its mother, which leads her to stop eating whatever foods have toxic properties for the foetus. It is also possible that the unexpected cravings that mothers have for certain foods may occur when the foetus is receiving an insufficient supply of certain minerals or other nutrients.

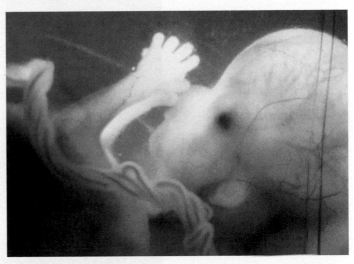

Conflict between parent and offspring may even begin before birth, as the foetus competes with its mother for resources or causes discomfort to her, leading her to change her behaviour.

Haig (1993) argued that some of the medical conditions suffered by pregnant women occur because of the foetus's demands for food. For example, pregnant women sometimes suffer from pre-eclampsia or gestational diabetes due to the actions of the foetus. Pre-eclampsia involves high blood pressure and abnormal weight gain. It seems to result from the foetus sending cells into its mother's arteries to increase its blood-borne resources.

Gestational diabetes in the mother occurs when the foetus secretes lactogen into her bloodstream. This desensitises the mother to insulin and can create temporary diabetes. However, there is benefit to the foetus. It has greater access to glucose from the mother. This provides it with an increased food supply, and allows it to establish a layer of fat as food reserves. This is a clear example of parent–offspring conflict, because the foetus gains directly at the expense of the mother.

Childhood

Parent–offspring conflict is common during the years of childhood. Young children make use of numerous strategies such as crying, temper tantrums, running away, refusing to eat, refusing to defaecate, and so on to gain the attention of their parents. These manipulative strategies seem to be used more often when there are two or more children in the family. As was pointed out earlier, Trivers (1974) argued that children with siblings want to have more than their fair share of their parents' attention, which parents are generally unwilling or unable to provide. According to Trivers:

> *Conflict during socialisation need not be viewed solely as conflict between the culture of the parent and the biology of the child; it can also be viewed as conflict between the biology of the parent and the biology of the child.*

Comparisons with other species

It is possible to obtain some insight into parent–offspring conflicts in humans by considering what happens in other mammalian species. Cardwell et al. (1996) discuss three stages of parent–offspring conflict in baboons. First, the mother baboon will initially provide substantial resources to her offspring, who could not survive without her resources (e.g. food) and protection. Second, when her offspring is old enough to feed itself, the mother becomes less willing to continue to provide it with her milk. At this

Newborn baboons could not survive without their mother's protection and provision of food. However as the baby gets larger and stronger, the mother gradually withdraws her milk, and the baby is encouraged to separate from her.

stage, the mother is likely to provide fewer resources than the infant desires. Third, parent–offspring conflict tends to increase as the infant continues to make demands on its mother, but she becomes more and more hostile in her response.

Some of the elements of parent–offspring conflict in baboons seem to be present in humans. Human parents initially provide all the resources of food, protection, and attention required by the infant. Later in development, adolescents often display hostility towards their parents as they continue to demand resources from their parents, while at the same time seeking increased independence.

Evaluation

The various adverse effects on the mother produced by the foetus's demands for food provide convincing evidence of parent–offspring conflict produced by evolutionary pressures for survival. However, there is a problem in interpreting parent–offspring conflicts stemming from children wanting more resources from their parents than their siblings receive. This could be due to the greater genetic similarity of a child to itself than to its siblings, as Trivers (1974) and Wilson (1975) have suggested. On the other hand, it may depend more on social and cultural factors than on basic evolutionary pressures.

It is commonly assumed that adolescence is a stage during which parent–offspring conflicts are at a peak. However, the extent of these conflicts is often exaggerated (see Chapter 18). For example, Larson et al. (1996) found that there was a reduction in the level of positive emotion experienced in family interactions during the early stages of adolescence, but this recovered to childhood levels later in adolescence.

Male aggression

Several attempts have been made to explain the greater aggressiveness of males than of females in evolutionary terms. For example, Spriggs (1998) argued that male aggression was favoured in the course of evolution for various reasons. First, our ancestors were hunter gatherers living in groups, and aggression was needed to capture wild animals to provide food. Second, the most aggressive males were able to ensure the survival of their genes by using force on females. Third, females may have preferred males who were aggressive for mating purposes. According to Spriggs (1998), the result of these evolutionary pressures was as follows: "Since evolutionary success was built on the foundation of the aggressive male and responsive female, evolution continued to favour those social groups dominated by 'naturally selecting' cultures in which this aggression and response dominated."

Spriggs went on to argue that male aggression was of more value to the hunter-gatherer societies of thousands of years ago than it is to modern societies. The dangers of high levels of male aggression include sexual abusiveness and what he termed the male "criminal" mind. There are supposed to be various indicators of this "criminal" mind. The neurotransmitter serotonin is lower in animals in stressful environments, and our male ancestors were exposed to the stresses of hunting wild animals. As a result, men tend to have lower levels of serotonin. Men have higher levels than women of the sex hormone testosterone, and adolescent boys who are aggressive and anti-social in their behaviour have especially high levels of testosterone (Olweus, 1985). Finally, male criminals tend to have a low resting heart rate (Spriggs, 1998). This made evolutionary sense in the past when successful hunters were those who were able to remain still and quiet before attacking their prey.

Sports involving physical aggression are more common among males than females, which could reflect higher levels of aggression in males. However, many cultures disapprove of the expression of aggression by females, while applauding controlled aggression shown by males in appropriate settings.

Evaluation

The evolutionary explanation of male aggression makes sense of some of the findings. However, there is little or no direct evidence to support it. It is not clear that there are large sex differences in aggression (see page 599). Eagly and Steffen (1986) reviewed the literature, and found there is only a small tendency for men to be more aggressive than women. Bjorkqvist et al. (1992) found that male adolescents showed more physical aggression than females, but female adolescents showed more indirect aggression (e.g. malicious gossip). Tieger (1980) reviewed developmental trends in aggression, and found that there is very little evidence of sex differences in aggression below the age of 5. This suggests that any later sex differences in aggression may depend on socialisation processes rather than on basic biological factors.

Most of the evidence on aggression and levels of testosterone and serotonin is correlational in nature. That makes the findings hard to interpret. It is possible that low serotonin levels or high testosterone levels lead to aggression, but it is also possible that aggression leads to low serotonin and high testosterone levels (Durkin, 1995).

Why are correlational findings hard to interpret?

The notion that continued male dominance in many societies is due to greater strength and aggression is dubious. Human dominance tends to depend on prestige and reputation rather than on brute strength. As Durkin (1995) wittily remarked, "If physical strength alone were critical to social status, we would all have a lot more respect for the elephant."

Sociobiology: Other evidence and evaluation

It is rarely possible to submit the assumptions of sociobiology to experimental test. What sociobiologists such as Wilson (1975) and Dawkins (1976) have typically done instead is to provide speculative sociobiological explanations (or "evolutionary stories") of various aspects of human behaviour. For example, there are many societies in which the mother's brother plays a much more active role in bringing up her child than does her husband. If there is a reasonable chance that the husband is not the father, then the genetic link between the mother's brother and the child will often be greater than that between the "father" and the child. It follows from the sociobiological perspective (with its emphasis on inclusive fitness) that the mother's brother should have more of an investment in the child.

Genes and genetics

Dawkins (1976) argued that several aspects of human social behaviour can be explained by assuming that the main purpose in life is to pass on one's genes. For example, it explains why step-parents tend to be hostile to their step-children and why people are unpleasant to strangers. The obvious counter-argument is that many step-parents behave in a loving way towards their step-children. In addition, it is fairly common for strangers to be treated in a friendly and helpful way.

The greatest strength of the sociobiological approach is that it acknowledges the role played by genetic factors in human social behaviour. Genetic factors help to determine individual differences in intelligence and personality (see Chapters 27 and 28). Beyond that, genetic factors influence many other aspects of human behaviour. It is even possible to predict who will get divorced on the basis of genetic factors (Plomin, 1997)! However, the sociobiologists exaggerate the importance of genetic factors. Heredity typically has a modest *indirect* influence on human social behaviour, whereas situational and cultural factors have a large *direct* influence.

Heredity vs. culture

Sociobiologists argue that there are strong evolutionary pressures that lead to altruism in the human and other species. They claim that the evidence indicates that altruism is a common feature of most species (see Chapter 9). However, it is important to distinguish between biological altruism (which is determined by basic evolutionary pressures) and psychological altruism (which is determined by the need to preserve a culture). Biological altruism may be found in most species, but the human species is probably the only one that shows psychological altruism.

Sociobiologists typically offer *retrospective* accounts of the evolution of human society and behaviour. These accounts tend to be circular. It is claimed that human behaviour conforms to Darwinian theory because it is adaptive and functional. How do we know

that human behaviour is adaptive? If it were not adaptive, we would not be here today to discuss it! This is a weak and unconvincing line of argument at best.

Most psychologists believe that human social behaviour is influenced much more by the development of knowledge and culture than by biological or genetic factors. Indeed, the enormous changes in human social behaviour over the past 100 years or so can only be explained by environmental and cultural factors. Even the founder of psychobiology, Edward Wilson, admitted in 1978 that cultural factors have been more important than biological ones in the evolution of the human species over the past 100,000 years:

> *Human social evolution is more cultural than genetic. Nevertheless, I consider that the underlying emotion of altruism, expressed powerfully in virtually all human societies, is the consequence of genetic endowment.*

Several aspects of contemporary Western society are inconsistent with the sociobiological approach. For example, the average family size has gone down in many countries in spite of increasing prosperity, which is contrary to the notion of maximising the survival of one's genes. Another example is the fact that most adoptions take place outside the family. This large investment of resources cannot be explained in terms of the survival of one's family genes.

Human sociobiology offers only a modest understanding of human social behaviour. As Smith (1983, p.240) concluded:

> *It seems likely that "naive" human sociobiology has most relevance to earlier phases of human evolution, and to less complex societies, and has a much more limited application in its unmodified form to modern industrial societies.*

Few experts believe any more that human social behaviour can simply be explained in the same biological and evolutionary terms as the behaviour of other species. As Durkin (1995, p.29) pointed out:

> *Most contemporary ethologists and sociobiologists with interest in humans acknowledge the distinctiveness of this species in terms of its capacities to reflect consciously on its behaviours and social structures and to take deliberate steps to adjust them.*

PERSONAL REFLECTIONS

- I think that Skinner is probably the most overrated psychologist of all time. It is true that animal and human behaviour can be influenced in predictable ways by operant conditioning. However, language acquisition, complex human thinking, long-term goals and planning, and so on are fundamental to human psychology but depend very little on conditioning principles. Thus, Skinner's approach is very limited.
- Until the 1970s and 1980s, evolutionary theory had much less impact on psychology than it deserved. More recently, however, there is a danger that the pendulum has swung too far the other way, with evolutionary explanations being offered of almost all forms of human behaviour. In my opinion, several factors jointly influence most human behaviour, and it is important not to exaggerate the importance of evolutionary factors.

SUMMARY

Classical conditioning is a type of learning in which a pre-existing unconditioned reflex is used as the basis for forming a new conditioned reflex. It is of key importance that the conditioned stimulus predicts the arrival of the unconditioned stimulus in order for conditioning to occur. Classical conditioning is sometimes involved in the development

Classical conditioning

of phobias. However, classical conditioning is of less importance in humans than in other species, because we have more efficient forms of learning based on language and on rules.

Operant conditioning

Much of operant conditioning is based on the law of reinforcement, according to which the probability of a given response being produced increases when it is followed by reward or reinforcement. There are several schedules of reinforcement based on providing reward only after a certain amount of time has elapsed or a certain number of responses have been produced. Other forms of operant conditioning are punishment training (in which the probability of a response is reduced by following it with an aversive stimulus) and avoidance learning (in which producing an appropriate response prevents the presentation of an aversive stimulus). Operant conditioning is very effective in many situations. However, it is sometimes hard to produce good conditioning, because what animals learn tends to resemble their instinctive behaviour. Skinner argued that operant conditioning involves a simple strengthening or weakening of responses. In fact, animals learn about the relationships among events in their environment.

Dog trainers often make use of operant conditioning techniques. The desired behaviour is rewarded, sometimes with food treats, and the animal is praised. Part of a dog trainer's role involves teaching the dog's owner to give clear and unambiguous commands. You could say the owners are receiving some operant conditioning as well!

Foraging

According to optimal foraging theory, foraging behaviour can be understood in terms of a cost–benefit analysis. The benefits usually consist of the amount and nutritional value of the food obtained, and the costs consist of the expenditure of time and energy, and the risk of being attacked. It is important to understand the goals of foraging behaviour. In many species, the goal is to maximise the rate of delivery of food to their offspring, but honey bees try to maximise the efficiency with which they use their energy. Foraging behaviour is often less efficient than is predicted by optimal foraging theory. Some of the reasons for this are as follows: (1) animals have to deal with predators and competing foragers; (2) animals often only have access to some of the relevant information about food sources; (3) most animals probably base their foraging behaviour on rules of thumb.

Homing and migration

Homing pigeons make use of various kinds of information to guide their homeward flights. They use information about the sun's position, but on overcast days they make use of information about the earth's magnetic field. Homing pigeons do not seem to make much use of landmarks, except when they are close to home. More remains to be discovered about precisely *what* information is used by homing pigeons and about *how* they use it. Migration, generally en masse over large distances, has significant rewards of resources to compensate the costs.

Chimpanzees and bonobo apes have been taught some of the basic elements of language such as vocabulary and simple grammar, and they show some ability to comprehend and to produce language. However, most of their utterances are very short, and they use language in a less spontaneous way than young human children. It is doubtful whether any animals have mastered language in terms of the range of criteria for language proposed by Hockett and others.

Animal language

Sociobiologists argue that much human behaviour is influenced by the goal of ensuring the survival of one's genes, and that biological and genetic factors determine human social behaviour. This approach has been applied to sexual selection, parent–offspring conflict, male aggression, and so on. Biological factors often have an indirect influence on human behaviour, but it is determined much more by cultural factors. The argument that human social behaviour has evolved because it is adaptive tends to be circular. A steady decrease in family size in recent years, and the fact that most adoptions occur outside the family, are hard to explain in evolutionary terms.

Evolutionary explanations of human behaviour

FURTHER READING

Theory and research on conditioning are discussed in N.J. Mackintosh (1994), *Companion encylopedia of psychology, Vol. 1*, London: Routledge. There is excellent coverage of the topics of foraging and homing, as well as a short discussion on the evolutionary determinants of human behaviour in J.W. Grier and T. Burk (1992), *Biology of animal behaviour (2nd Edn.)*, Dubuque, IO: W.C. Brown. A thorough account (but sometimes hard to follow) of most of the topics discussed in this chapter is presented in J.R. Krebs and N.B. Davies (1993), *An introduction to behavioural ecology (3rd Edn.)*, Oxford: Blackwell. There are interesting views on evolutionary determinants of human behaviour in K. Durkin (1995), *Developmental social psychology*, Oxford: Blackwell.

REVISION QUESTIONS

1	Critically consider *two* theories of learned behaviour.	(24 marks)
2	Compare explanations of *either* homing behaviour *or* foraging.	(24 marks)
3	Using evidence, discuss attempts by psychologists to teach language to primates.	(24 marks)
4	Describe and evaluate evolutionary explanations of *two* aspects of human behaviour.	(24 marks)

- **Perceptual development**
  How newborn babies learn to make sense of the world around them.

  Butterworth and Cicchetti's moving room
  The visual preference study by Fantz
  Gibson and Walk's visual cliff
  Studies of size and shape constancy
  Piaget's approach
  Gibson and Spelke's differentiation theory
  Shaffer's three stages

- **Perceptual organisation**
  Theories of the ways in which we distinguish depth, size, colour, and movement in what we see.

  Navon's investigation of Gestalt laws
  Wertheimer's point-light experiment
  Johansson's study of common fate

- **Space or depth perception**
  How we use the two-dimensional images on our retinas to perceive a three-dimensional world.

  Monocular and binocular cues
  Kanizsa's illusory square
  Stereopsis
  Bruno and Cutting's three strategies

- **Visual constancies**
  How do we know that a distant car is a real one and not a small toy?

  The Ames room
  Land's retinex theory; colour constancy

- **Pattern recognition**
  Using information from memory to recognise, for example, the face of a friend in a crowd.

  Feature theories (e.g. Neisser)
  Structural descriptions (e.g. Bruce & Green)
  Marr's computational theory; 3D
  Biederman's recognition-by-components theory

- **Theories of perception**
  Ideas about how human visual perception works.

  Gibson's theory of direct perception
  Constructivist theory (e.g. Helmholtz)
  Gregory's misapplied size-constancy theory; the Ponzo illusion; Muller–Lyer figures
  Neisser's cyclic theory

- **Individual, social, and cultural variations**
  Does what we perceive depend on our experiences?

  Field dependence and trait anxiety
  Social and cross-cultural studies

11

Perceptual Processes

Seeing the world about us and making sense of it seems very easy. For example, we do not have to think much to know that we are on the pavement, and that there are several cars moving in both directions on the road. In fact, making sense of (or perceiving) the environment is a major achievement. Some of the complexities of perception will be discussed in this chapter, together with some of the processes involved in perceptual development.

What do we mean by the term **perception**? According to Roth (1986, p.81):

The term perception refers to the means by which information acquired from the environment via the sense organs is transformed into experiences of objects, events, sounds, tastes, etc.

A distinction is sometimes drawn between perception and sensation, with **sensation** referring to the basic uninterpreted information presented to our sense organs. It has been argued that sensation occurs before perception, but it is more realistic to assume that they generally overlap in time. The general view nowadays is that the processes involved are so complex that there is little value in trying to divide them up neatly into sensation and perception.

Perceptual Development

How much can the newborn baby (or neonate) see and hear? It used to be assumed that the answer was "very little". William James, towards the end of the nineteenth century, described the world of the newborn baby as a "buzzing, blooming confusion, where the infant is seized by eyes, ears, nose and entrails all at once." This suggests that the infant is bombarded by information in all sense modalities, and cannot attach meaning to this information. That view greatly underestimates the capabilities of infants. Many basic perceptual mechanisms are working at a very early age, and infants are not merely helpless observers of their world.

Research methods

It is hard to assess perception in infants, because they cannot tell us what they can see or hear. However, several methods to assess the perceptual abilities of infants have been developed:

- Behavioural method. Various behavioural measures can be taken to discover what infants can perceive. For example, Butterworth and Cicchetti (1978) tested infants

A drawing of the Butterworth and Cicchetti moving room. The walls and ceiling of the room can be moved, although the floor is fixed. The children experience loss of balance, swaying forwards or backwards depending on which way the room appears to move.

Why is it an advantage to use a newborn baby in experiments about perception?

in a room in which the walls and the ceiling moved towards and away from them. The infants lost balance, and this loss of balance was always in the expected direction. If the room moved towards them, they swayed forwards, whereas they swayed backwards if the room moved away from them.

- Preference method. Two or more stimuli are presented together, and the experimenter simply observes which stimulus attracts the most attention. If infants systematically prefer one stimulus to another, this indicates that they can discriminate between them. This method was used by Fantz (1961) in research discussed later.

- Habituation method. A stimulus is presented repeatedly until the infant no longer attends to it; this is known as **habituation**. When the infant shows habituation to one stimulus, he or she is shown a different stimulus. If the infant responds to the new stimulus, he or she must have discriminated between the two stimuli.

- Eye-movement method. The eye movements of infants can provide information about their visual perception. For example, if infants are presented with a moving stimulus, the tracking response or optokinetic nystagmus can be recorded. This indicates whether or not they can distinguish between the moving stimulus and the background against which it is presented. Alternatively, infants can be presented with a visual stimulus, and the pattern of eye movements can be photographed and then examined. Maurer and Salapatek (1976) found that one-month-old infants looked at the edges and contours of a human face, whereas two-month-olds focused in a more systematic way on the internal features such as the eyes, nose, and mouth.

- Physiological method. Various physiological measures can be used. One way of telling whether infants can discriminate between two stimuli is to measure their visual evoked potentials (brain-wave activity) to each stimulus. Alternatively, if infants show different patterns of heart rate and/or breathing rate to two stimuli, this suggests that the infants perceive the two stimuli to be different. As we will see later, heart rate can also indicate whether infants are frightened or merely interested in a visual stimulus.

- Visual reinforcement method. The basic idea is that the infant is given control over the stimulus or stimuli presented to it. For example, Siqueland and DeLucia (1969) gave infants a dummy that was wired up so that their sucking rate could be assessed. A stimulus may be presented only for as long as it continues to produce a high sucking rate, being replaced when it does not. Alternatively, infants can be presented with one stimulus when their sucking rate is high and another stimulus when it is low.

Studies of perceptual development

Visual preference

Fantz (1961) devised the visual preference task, which has proved to be one of the most effective ways of studying infant perception. In essence, two visual stimuli are presented to the infant at the same time, with one being presented to the infant's left and the other to the right. The amount of time spent looking at each stimulus is recorded. If an infant consistently looks at one stimulus more than the other, this selectivity is thought to show the existence of perceptual discrimination.

Fantz showed infants (aged between four days and five months) head-shaped discs.

Infants of all ages looked most at the realistic face and least at the blank face. On the basis of such studies, Fantz (1966, pp.171–173) arrived at the following sweeping conclusions:

The findings have tended to destroy ... the myth—that the world of the neonate is a big booming confusion, that his visual field is a form of blur, that his mind is a blank slate, that his brain is decorticate, and that his behaviour is limited to reflexes or undirected mass movements. The infant sees a patterned and organised world which he explores discriminatingly within the limited means at his command.

Findings from the visual preference task do not really justify these conclusions. At an experimental level, the difference in time spent looking at the real and the scrambled faces was fairly small in the study by Fantz (1961). At an interpretive level, it is hard to know whether infants look at the real face because it is a face or because it is a complex, symmetrical visual stimulus. However, Dannemiller and Stephens (1988) made use of computer-generated faces that were constructed so as to control for these factors. Thus, for example, they produced human faces and patterns that had the same level of complexity and symmetry. Three-month-old infants preferred human faces, thus confirming Fantz's findings under well-controlled conditions.

Discussion points

1. Do you think Fantz interpreted his findings in an exaggerated way?
2. Can we tell exactly *why* an infant looks at a face?

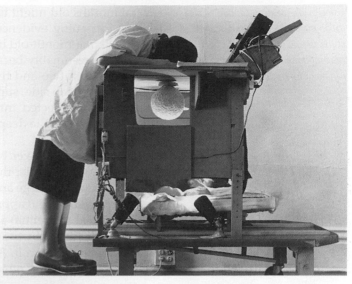

The experimental apparatus used by Fantz to observe how infants respond to visual stimuli.

Do you think the Dannemiller and Stephens study had more ecological validity than the Fantz study? Why might the computer-generated faces still be unlike a real human face?

Depth perception

The visual cliff. Gibson and Walk (1960) also argued that infants possess well-developed perceptual skills. They designed a "visual cliff", which was actually a glass-top table. A check pattern was positioned close to the glass under one half of the table (the "shallow" side) and far below the glass under the other half (the "deep" side). Infants between the ages of 6½ months and 12 months were placed on the shallow side of the table, and encouraged to crawl over the edge of the visual cliff on to the deep side by being offered toys or having their mothers call them. Most failed to respond to these incentives, suggesting that they possessed at least some of the elements of depth perception.

Gibson and Walk tested the performance of other species on their visual cliff. Most species (including chicks under one day old) avoided the deep side of the visual cliff, suggesting that some aspects of depth perception may be inborn. However, four-week-old kittens who had been reared in the dark did not avoid the deep side, nor did rats who could detect the glass with their whiskers.

Research on the visual cliff does not necessarily indicate that depth perception is innate. Infants who are

A drawing of Gibson and Walk's "visual cliff". Babies between 6½ and 12 months of age were reluctant to crawl over the "cliff" edge, even when called by their mothers, suggesting that they perceived the drop created by the check pattern.

Using evidence from (a) babies and (b) animals in Gibson and Walk's study, would you say that depth perception was more likely to be innate or learned?

several months old might have learned about depth perception from experience. There is some intriguing evidence pointing to the importance of learning in the visual cliff situation. Nine-month-old infants had faster heart rates than normal when placed on the deep side, presumably because they were frightened (Campos et al., 1978). However, infants between two and five months actually had *slower* heart rates than usual when placed on the deep side, suggesting that they were not frightened. This slowing of heart rate probably reflected interest, and it certainly indicates that they detected some difference between the deep and shallow sides of the visual cliff situation.

Retinal image size. Bower et al. (1970) obtained more convincing evidence that infants have some aspects of depth perception. They showed two objects to infants under two weeks old. One was large and approached to within 20 centimetres of the infant, whereas the other was small and approached to 8 centimetres. The two objects had the same retinal size (i.e. size at the retina) at their closest point to the infant. In spite of this, the infants were more disturbed by the object that came closer to them, rotating their heads upwards and pulling away from it. Apparently these infants somehow made use of information about depth to identify which object posed the greater threat.

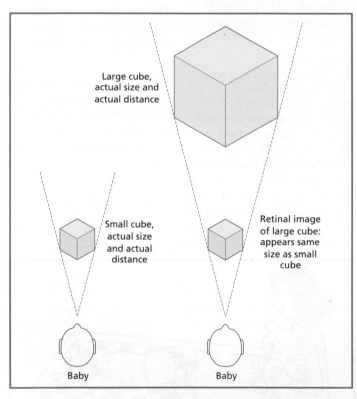

Large cube, actual size and actual distance

Small cube, actual size and actual distance

Retinal image of large cube: appears same size as small cube

Baby

Baby

Two cubes of different sizes may project retinal images of the same size, depending on their distance from the viewer. Bower used this effect to test depth perception and size constancy in infants.

Size and shape constancy

Nearly all adults display *size constancy* and *shape constancy*. Size constancy means that a given object is perceived as having the same size regardless of its distance from us, and shape constancy means that an object is seen to have the same shape regardless of its orientation. Thus, we see things "as they really are", and are not taken in by variations in the information presented to the retina. This is more of an achievement than might be supposed, because the retinal image of an object is very much smaller when the object is a long way away from us. It is of interest to discover whether infants show evidence of size and shape constancy.

Size constancy. Bower (1966) studied size constancy in infants between 75 and 85 days of age. The first stage of the experiment involved teaching the infants to look at a 30-centimetre cube placed about one metre from them. Bower then compared the length of time spent looking at the same cube placed three metres from the infant and a 90-centimetre cube placed three metres away. The former stimulus had the same size as the original cube, but a much smaller retinal image. In contrast, the latter stimulus had a much greater real size, but the same retinal size as the original cube. Some size constancy was shown, because the infants were almost three times more likely to look at the former than at the latter stimulus object. However, they failed to show complete size constancy, because they were more likely to look at the 30-centimetre cube when it was placed one metre away rather than three metres away.

Shape constancy. Evidence for shape constancy in three-month-old infants has been found using the habituation method (Caron, Caron, & Carlson 1979). Some infants were presented repeatedly with a square forming a trapezoidal shape on the retina until they habituated or lost interest in it. After that, they were presented with a real trapezoid, in which they showed an immediate interest. Thus, they had habituated to the real shape rather than to the retinally presented shape.

Innate or learned? Are the perceptual skills of size and shape constancy innately determined? As Bower was studying infants who were two or three months of age, they may have learned at least some of the skills involved. However, the exploratory and reaching activities that might lead to the learning of relevant perceptual skills do not usually start in earnest until infants are at least three months of age. It makes evolutionary sense for infants to display size and shape constancy at a young age, because this helps them to perceive the world accurately rather than inaccurately.

Piaget's approach

According to Piaget, children up to the age of 2 are in the sensori-motor stage of development. Infants acquire their knowledge of the world mainly by acting on it through mouthing, grasping, and manipulating objects. During this stage, thought and action are almost identical to each other. The main implication of this approach is that the development of perception depends to a large extent on the infant's growing mobility and ability to act on the environment. For example, depth perception should be acquired when the infant starts crawling and interacting directly with its surroundings.

Piaget exaggerated the importance of action in the development of perception. Arterberry, Yonas, and Bensen (1989) showed infants between the ages of five and seven months two identical objects placed on a grid that created the illusion of depth. The two objects were actually the same distance away, but seven-month-old infants reached for the object that looked closer, whereas the five-month-olds did not. The key finding was that those infants who had had the most experience of crawling showed no more depth perception than the others.

Meadows (1986) discussed other findings that do not seem to fit well with Piaget's theoretical approach. For example, five-month-olds do not generally reach for objects that are out of reach, even though they have only limited experience of moving around their environment.

Differentiation theory

According to the differentiation theory (e.g. Gibson & Spelke, 1983), the stimuli presented to our senses contain all the information needed for accurate perception. Perceptual development involves learning to identify the crucial features of any stimulus, as can be seen in a study by Gibson (1969). Children aged between 4 and 8 were asked to select from 13 figures the only one that was identical to a standard stimulus figure. The other 12 figures differed slightly from the standard figure in various ways. Some differed in orientation (i.e. the figure was rotated or inverted), and others differed in perspective (i.e. the figure appeared slanted or tilted backwards).

What did Gibson find? The number of errors decreased with age, and the pattern of errors changed. Perspective errors were very common at all ages, but orientation errors showed a sharp decrease between the ages of 4 and 8. These findings may reflect the children's acquisition of the skills involved in reading and writing. Stimulus orientation is not important when a child looks at a toy from different angles, but is crucial in reading and writing for differentiating letters (e.g. the letters b, d, p, and q differ mainly in orientation). In contrast, perspective changes are of little importance whether children are trying to identify objects or letters.

Much evidence indicates that children become progressively better at differentiation. However, perceptual development involves more than that. Fluent readers perceive the meaning of the sentences they read, and that involves much more than simply differentiating letters from each other.

Evaluation

Infants are unexpectedly good at performing a wide range of perceptual tasks. For example, they show good discrimination on the visual preference task, and they exhibit some aspects of depth perception in the visual cliff situation. In addition, they are reasonably good at size and shape constancy.

Slater (1990, p.262) summarised the perceptual skills of infants in the following way:

No modality [none of the senses] operates at adult-like levels at birth, but such levels are achieved surprisingly early in infancy, leading to recent conceptualisations of the

If you look at a coin standing on its edge or lying flat on a table, how do you know it is a coin when the image your eye receives differs depending on the coin's position? If you hold the same coin at arm's length and bring it slowly towards you, the coin appears to become larger as it gets closer. How do you know it hasn't really changed in size?

Which of Piaget's concepts (see Chapter 16) links with shape constancy?

"competent infant"... early perceptual competence is matched by cognitive incompetence, and much of the reorganisation of perceptual representation is dependent upon the development and construction of cognitive structures that give access to a world of objects, people, language, and events.

Shaffer (1993) argued that there are three stages of perceptual development during the first year:

THREE STAGES OF PERCEPTUAL DEVELOPMENT DURING FIRST YEAR OF LIFE		
Period	**Stage**	**Infant can:**
0–2 months	Stimulus seeking	discriminate between visual stimuli
2–6 months	Form constructing	perceive numerous forms and shapes
6–12 months	Form interpretation	make sense of what they perceive

What is the role of maturation in the development of perceptual processes?

Most research provides only limited information about the perceptual abilities of infants. The habituation and physiological methods tell us which stimuli can be discriminated by infants, and the preference and visual reinforcement methods also tell us which stimuli are preferred by infants. However, these methods generally do *not* tell us in detail how the stimuli are perceived and interpreted. The eye-movement and behaviour methods sometimes provide more information about the significance of stimuli for infants, but leave many questions unanswered. For example, infants of eight months will not crawl over the deep side of the visual cliff, and their heart rate goes up when they are placed on the deep side. These findings indicate clearly that infants find *something* disturbing about the visual cliff, but do not show that they perceive depth like adults.

Perceptual Organisation

Knowledge about perceptual organisation has helped in the design of aesthetically pleasing working environments and visual display panels that are easy and effective to use.

Visual perception is nearly always highly organised. Our visual world consists of objects arranged meaningfully in three-dimensional space. This happens so naturally and effortlessly that it is hard to believe that organised perception is a substantial achievement. The fact that computers can be programmed to play high-level chess, but still cannot mimic the visual skills of even fairly primitive animals, supports this idea.

The information that arrives at the sense receptors is confusing and disorganised. In the case of vision, there is usually a mosaic of colours, and the retinal sizes and shapes of objects in the environment may correspond very poorly to their actual sizes and shapes.

Computers may be programmed to surpass human abilities in specific tasks, but they cannot possess the full range of human skills.

Perceptual organisation requires good depth perception, an ability to recognise objects, an ability to detect movement, and an ability to perceive the sizes and colours of objects accurately. These abilities are discussed in what follows.

Gestaltist approach

The first systematic study of perceptual organisation was carried out by the Gestaltists ("*Gestalt*" is German for "organised whole"). They were a group of German psychologists (including Koffka, Köhler, and Wertheimer) who emigrated to the United States between the two World Wars. They were especially interested in the issue of *perceptual segregation*, i.e. our ability to work out which parts of the visual information presented to us belong together and thus form separate objects. A key aspect of perceptual segregation is the division of the visual field into the figure (central focus of attention) and the ground (everything else).

Principles of perceptual organisation

The Gestaltists proposed several laws of perceptual organisation. However, their most basic principle was the *law of Prägnanz*, which was expressed as follows by Koffka (1935, p.110):

> *Psychological organisation will always be as "good" as the prevailing conditions allow. In this definition the term "good" is undefined*

In fact, Koffka was unduly vague in his definition. The Gestaltists actually regarded a good form as being the simplest or most uniform of the various possible organisational structures.

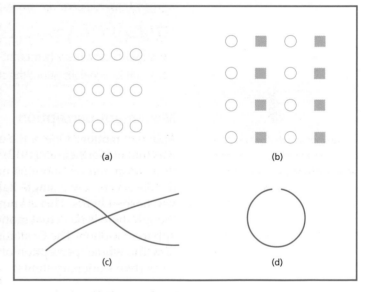

The Gestaltist approach can be seen most clearly if we consider some concrete examples. Pattern (a) is most naturally seen as three horizontal arrays of dots. This illustrates the Gestalt law of proximity, according to which visual elements that are close to each other will tend to be grouped together. In pattern (b), vertical columns rather than horizontal rows are seen. This fits the law of similarity, according to which similar visual elements are grouped together. In pattern (c), we see two crossing lines rather than a V-shaped line and an inverted V-shaped line. This fits the law of good continuation, which states that those visual elements producing the fewest interruptions to smoothly curving lines are grouped together. Finally, pattern (d) fits the law of closure, according to which the missing parts of a figure are "filled in" to complete it. All these laws can be regarded as more specific statements of the fundamental law of Prägnanz.

Evidence for the importance of grouping was reported by Pomerantz and Garner (1973). The participants were presented with stimuli consisting of two brackets arranged in various ways. The task was to sort the stimuli into two piles as fast as possible depending on whether the left-hand bracket was "(" or ")". In spite of the fact that the participants were instructed to ignore the right-hand bracket, they found it impossible to do this when the two brackets were groupable (e.g. because both brackets were similar in orientation or were close to each other). The evidence for this consisted of slower sorting times for groupable stimuli than for non-groupable ones.

Where do organisational processes come from? The Gestaltists argued that most perceptual organisation reflects the largely innately determined functioning of the perceptual system. However, this is unlikely to be the whole story. Our everyday experiences teach us that those visual elements which are similar and close to each other typically belong to the same visual object, but visual elements that are dissimilar and far apart do not.

```
S                S
S                S
S                S
S                S
S                S
SSSSSSSSSSSSS
S                S
S                S
S                S
S                S
S                S
```

The whole and the parts

One of the key assumptions made by the Gestaltists was that "the whole is more than the sum of its parts". Exactly what they meant by this is a little obscure. However, a testable implication is that the overall Gestalt or whole may be perceived before its parts. This sounds like putting the cart before the horse, because it has usually been assumed that the individual parts or features of a visual stimulus are processed before the overall object is identified. Navon (1977) presented his participants with rather strange stimuli. One was a large letter H formed out of numerous little Ss. In addition, there was a large letter H formed from little Hs, and a large letter S formed from little Ss.

The task on each trial was to identify either the single large letter or the small letters as rapidly as possible. The time taken to identify the large letter was not affected by whether the small letters were the same as the large letter. In contrast, the time taken to identify the small letters was much longer when the large letter differed from them than when it was the same. This happened because information about the whole (i.e. the identity of the large letter) was available before information about the parts (i.e. the identity of the small letters).

Navon's research suggested that early perceptual processing identifies the most important objects. Subsequent perceptual processing then provides more fine-grained analysis of their detailed structure. However, perceptual processing does not always proceed in this fashion. Kinchla and Wolfe (1979) used stimuli constructed in the same way as those of Navon, but they varied the overall size of the stimuli. Their participants heard the name of a letter and were then presented with a visual stimulus. They had to respond "yes" if either the large letter or the small letters matched the letter they had heard. When the overall stimulus was fairly small, the participants were faster to detect a match with the large letter than with the small letters. This finding resembles those of Navon (1977) in indicating that the large letter is processed first. However, precisely the opposite finding was obtained when the overall stimulus was five times larger. Thus, the parts are processed faster than the whole with large stimuli.

Discussion points

1. What determines whether the whole comes before the parts or vice versa?
2. What is ingenious about the stimuli used by Navon?

Movement perception

Apparent motion. One of the earliest studies on perception carried out by the Gestaltists was that of Wertheimer (1912). There were two lights in a dark room. When one light was flashed on and off about 50 milliseconds before the other light was flashed on and off, the observers saw a single light appear to move through the dark space separating the two flashed lights. This is known as **apparent motion**, because motion is perceived even though there is no actual motion. Anyone who has ever watched a film has experienced apparent motion. The Gestaltists were interested in apparent motion, because it showed how the whole (perception of motion or movement) could be more than the sum of its parts (two stationary lights).

The law of common fate. The Gestaltists also put forward the law of common fate, according to which visual elements that seem to move together are grouped together. Johansson (1973) attached lights to each of the joints of an actor wearing dark clothes. This actor was then filmed as he moved around in a dark room. Observers saw only a meaningless display of lights when the actor was at rest, but they perceived a moving human figure when he walked around. This was in spite of the fact that they could not see anything except the lights.

Cutting and Kozlowski (1977) found that observers were good at identifying themselves and others from point-light displays. Kozlowski and Cutting (1978) reported that observers were right about 65% of the time when guessing someone's sex from point-light displays. The observers took account of the fact that men swing their shoulders more than their hips when walking, whereas women show the opposite tendency.

The importance of movement detection. The importance of being able to detect movement was shown clearly in the case of a female patient, LM, who had suffered brain damage.

In the cinema, what we perceive to be a moving picture is a series of stationary pictures, each one slightly different, presented in rapid succession.

KEY TERM

Apparent motion: the illusion of movement created when similar stationary stimuli are presented in rapid succession.

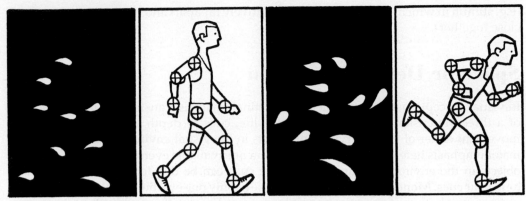

Johansson attached lights to an actor's joints. While the actor stood still in a darkened room, observers could not make sense of the arrangement of the lights. However, as soon as he started to move around, they were able to perceive the lights as defining a human figure.

She was good at locating stationary objects by sight, and had good colour discrimination, but her movement perception was extremely poor. As a result (Zihl et al., 1983, p.315):

> She could not cross the street because of her inability to judge the speed of a car, but she could identify the car itself without difficulty. "When I'm looking at the car first, it seems far away. But then, when I want to cross the road, suddenly the car is very near."

Corollary discharge theory. How can we tell whether changes in the retinal image produced by an object are due to movement of the object or to movement of our eyes? According to corollary discharge theory (e.g. Richards, 1975), the visual system compares the movement registered on the retina with signals about eye movements. When your brain sends a message to your eye muscles, it also sends a copy (known as a corollary or resulting discharge) to the part of the visual system concerned with movement perception. Then whether movement of the retinal image is due to movement in the environment or simply to movement of the eyes can be determined.

Simple evidence supporting corollary discharge theory comes if you press the side of your eyeball gently. There is movement in the retinal image unaccompanied by commands to the eye muscles. As a result, this movement is interpreted by the visual system as being produced by movement in the environment.

However, corollary discharge theory does not provide a complete account of movement perception. As Tresilian (1994, p.336) pointed out, the theory predicts that

> if the eyes are stationary in the head as the head rotates, the resulting image motion will be interpreted as motion of the environment, yet everyone knows that this does not happen.

Thus, we do not rely only on information about eye movements to perceive a stable environment. Movement of the entire retinal image is usually attributed to movement of the head or eye, whereas movement of part of the retinal image is interpreted as movement of an external object.

Evaluation

The Gestalt laws of organisation seem reasonable. However, they have attracted much criticism. The laws are only descriptive statements which fail to explain *why* similar visual elements or those close together are grouped. Another limitation is that most of the Gestalt laws relate mainly to the perceived organisation of two-dimensional patterns. Other factors come into play with three-dimensional scenes. For example, it may only be possible to separate out the figure of a chameleon from its background when it moves. Finally, it is hard to apply the Gestalt laws of organisation to certain complex visual stimuli

This dried-out lake bed is an example of a real-life texture gradient. As the earth slants away from the viewer, the pattern seems to get smaller and less distinct.

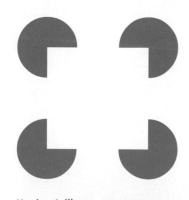

Kanizsa's illusory square—although no square is present, people see the diagram as if it were four black circles with a white square lying on them.

(e.g. stimuli in which similar elements are relatively far apart and dissimilar elements are close together).

Space or Depth Perception

In visual perception, the two-dimensional retinal image is transformed into perception of a three-dimensional world. In everyday life, cues to depth are often provided by movement either of the observer or of objects in the visual environment. However, the major emphasis here will be on depth cues that are available even if the observer and the objects in the environment are static. These cues can be divided into monocular and binocular cues. **Monocular cues** require the use of only one eye, but can also be used when someone has both eyes open. Such cues clearly exist, because the world still retains a sense of depth with one eye closed. **Binocular cues** are those that involve both eyes being used together.

Monocular cues

There are various monocular cues to depth. They are sometimes known as **pictorial cues**, because they are used by artists trying to create the impression of three-dimensional scenes. One such cue is *linear perspective*. Parallel lines pointing directly away from us seem closer together as they recede into the distance (e.g. railway tracks). This convergence of lines can create a powerful impression of depth in a two-dimensional drawing.

Another aspect of perspective is known as *aerial perspective*. Light is scattered as it travels through the atmosphere, especially if the atmosphere is dusty. As a result, more distant objects lose contrast and seem somewhat hazy.

Another cue related to perspective is *texture*. Most objects possess texture, and textured objects slanting away from us have what Gibson (1979) called a texture gradient. This is an increased gradient (rate of change) of texture density as you look from the front to the back of a slanting object. For example, if you look at a large patterned carpet, the details towards its far end are less clear than those nearer to you.

A further cue is *interposition*, in which a nearer object hides part of a more distant object. Evidence of the power of interposition is provided by Kanizsa's (1976) illusory square. There is a strong subjective impression of a white square in front of four black circles. We make sense of the four sectored black discs by perceiving an illusory interposed white square.

Yet another cue to depth is provided by *shading*, or the pattern of light and dark on and around an object. Flat, two-dimensional surfaces do not cause shadows, and so shading provides good evidence for the presence of a three-dimensional object.

Another cue to depth is *familiar size*. If we know an object's actual size, then we can use its retinal image size to provide an estimate of its distance. When participants looked at playing cards through a peephole, large ones looked further away than they actually were, whereas undersized playing cards looked closer than was really the case (Ittelson, 1951).

The final monocular cue is *motion parallax*. This is based on the movement of an object's image over the retina. Consider, for example, two objects moving left to right across the line of vision at the same speed, but one object is much further away from the observer than the other. In that case, the image cast by the nearer object would move much faster across the retina.

Binocular cues

There are three other depth cues which are available only to those with binocular vision. These cues (*convergence*, *accommodation*, and *stereopsis*) lose any effectiveness they may have when objects are more than a short distance away:

1. Convergence refers to the fact that the eyes turn inwards to focus on an object to a greater extent when the object is very close.
2. Accommodation refers to the variation in optical power produced by a thickening of the lens of the eye when focusing on a close object.
3. Stereopsis is stereoscopic vision depending on the disparity in the images projected on the retinas of the two eyes.

There has been controversy about the value of convergence as a cue to distance. The findings have tended to be negative when real objects are used. Accommodation is also of very little use. Its potential value as a depth cue is limited to the region of space immediately in front of you. However, distance judgements based on accommodation are inaccurate, even when the object is at close range (Kunnapas, 1968).

The importance of stereopsis was shown by Wheatstone (1838), who was the inventor of the stereoscope. What happens in a stereoscope is that separate pictures or drawings are presented to the observer so that each eye receives the information it would receive if the objects depicted were actually presented. Stereoscopic vision produces a strong depth effect.

Hold a pen at arm's length; its image will be quite clear. However, as you bring the pen closer to your face, the image will blur because your eyes will no longer be able to converge and focus accurately beyond a certain point.

Combining information from cues

So far, we have considered depth cues one at a time. In the real world, however, we generally have access to several depth cues, and so we need to know how information from various cues is combined and integrated. Bruno and Cutting (1988) identified three strategies that might be used by observers who had information available from two or more depth cues:

1. Additivity: all the information from different cues is simply added together.
2. Selection: information from one cue is used, with information from the other cue or cues being ignored.
3. Multiplication: information from different cues interacts in a multiplicative way.

Bruno and Cutting studied depth perception in a series of studies in which visual displays were observed through one eye only. Their participants had access to four sources of information about depth (e.g. interposition) when making decisions about the distance

Close one eye and line up a finger with a point in front of you. Then open the eye that was closed and close the other one. The finger appears to jump from one position to another. This is a result of the two retinas receiving slightly different images.

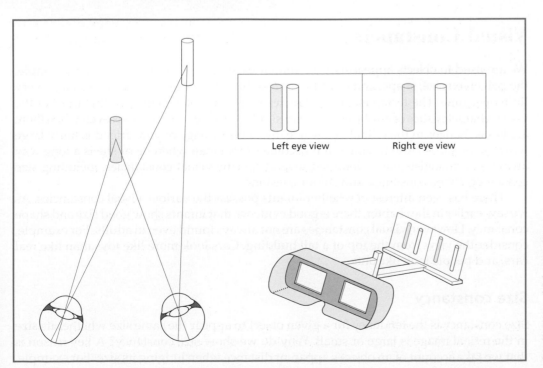

Left eye view   Right eye view

As the eyes are set a short distance apart, each eye receives a slightly different image from the same scene. The difference in the retinal images, at identical places on each eye, is called binocular disparity. The brain makes use of these slight differences as one way of registering spatial depth. This is the principle of the stereoscope, where photographs taken from slightly different angles, corresponding to the position of each eye, appear to the viewer to fuse as a single three-dimensional image.

The two stages of the playing-card experiment, as discussed by Woodworth and Schlosberg. When the viewer looks at the first set-up, the card at the back looks farther away (which it is). However, when the front card has been clipped, and the position of the cards rearranged, the back card looks as if it overlaps the front card. The cue of familiar size, telling the viewer that the smaller card must be farther away than the bigger card, is overridden by the cue of interposition, suggesting that the card that appears to obscure part of the other one must be nearer to the viewer, despite its size.

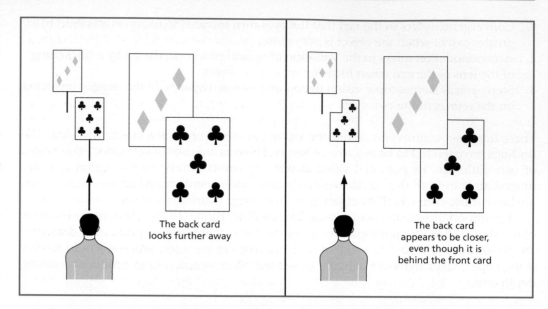

The back card looks further away

The back card appears to be closer, even though it is behind the front card

of various objects. The participants used the additivity strategy, because they made equal use of all the four sources of information.

It is usually sensible to combine information from depth cues in an additive fashion. Any depth cue provides inaccurate information sometimes, and so relying totally on one cue would often lead to error. In contrast, taking account of all of the available information is usually the best way to make sure that depth perception is accurate. However, there are rare cases in which the selection strategy is used. Woodworth and Schlosberg (1954) discussed a study in which two normal playing cards of the same size were attached to stands, with one card being closer to the observer. The observers viewed the two cards monocularly, and the farther card looked more distant. In the next, crucial phase of the study, the corner of the nearer card was clipped, and the two cards were arranged so that the edges of the more distant card seemed to fit exactly the cutout edges of the nearer card. With monocular vision, the more distant card seemed to be in front of, and partially obscuring, the nearer card. In this case, the cue of interposition overwhelmed the cue of familiar size.

Visual Constancies

We are used to objects appearing very similar each time we look at them. For example, the perceived size, shape, and colour of a close friend of yours are likely to change very little over time. The term **visual constancies** is used to refer to the fact that most of the visual characteristics of an object look very similar on different occasions even when there are large changes in the retinal image (e.g. the retinal image of your friend is fairly large when he or she is close to you, but it becomes very small when he or she is a long way away). Psychologists have identified several specific visual constancies, including size constancy, shape constancy, and colour constancy.

There has been interest in whether infants possess the various visual constancies. As we saw earlier in the chapter, there is good evidence that infants show good size and shape constancy. However, visual constancies are not always found even in adults. For example, consider the view from the top of a tall building. Cars look more like toys than like real cars, and people look like ants.

Size constancy

Size constancy is the tendency for a given object to appear the same size whether its size in the retinal image is large or small. Why do we show size constancy? A key reason is that we take account of an object's apparent distance when judging its size. For example,

KEY TERM
Visual constancies: an object's size, shape, colour, and so on, are perceived as remaining fairly constant or unchanging in spite of large variations in the retinal image.

an object may be judged to be large even though its retinal image is very small if it is a long way away. The fact that size constancy is often not shown when we look at objects on the ground from the top of a tall building or from a plane may occur because it is hard for us to judge distance accurately.

One of the factors influencing size constancy is familiar size. For example, we know that most adults are between about 1.60 and 1.85 metres tall. We can use this information about familiar size to make accurate assessments of size regardless of whether the retinal image is very large or very small. Evidence of the importance of familiar size was obtained by Schiffman (1967). Observers viewed familiar objects at various distances in the presence or absence of depth cues. Their size estimates were accurate even when depth cues were not available, because they made use of their knowledge of familiar size.

According to the size–distance invariance hypothesis, people work out an object's size by combining information about its retinal size with information about its perceived distance. This theory was supported by Holway and Boring (1941). Participants sat at the intersection of two hallways. The test circle was presented in one hallway, and the comparison circle was presented in the other one. The test circle could be of various sizes and at various distances, and the participants' task was to adjust the comparison circle so that it was the same size as the test circle. Their performance was very good when depth cues were available. However, it became poor when depth cues were removed by placing curtains in the hallway and requiring the participants to look through a peephole.

If size judgements depend on perceived distance, then size constancy should not be found when the perceived distance of an object is very different from its actual distance. The Ames room provides a good example. It has a peculiar shape: the floor slopes, and the rear wall is not at right angles to the adjoining walls. In spite of this, the Ames room creates the same retinal image as a normal rectangular room when viewed through a peephole. The fact that one end of the rear wall is much further from the viewer is disguised by making it much higher. The cues suggesting that the rear wall is at right angles to the viewer are so strong that someone walking backwards and forwards in front of it appears to grow and shrink as he or she moves about!

Have you ever been disappointed when taking a photograph of a distant object (for example, a rock star on stage at a large stadium venue)? Perhaps you expected the person to be much closer than he or she turned out to be in the picture. Why does this happen?

What does the fact that the viewer "sees" the impossible in the Ames room (i.e. a person who grows and shrinks) tell you about the importance of perceived distance and familiar size?

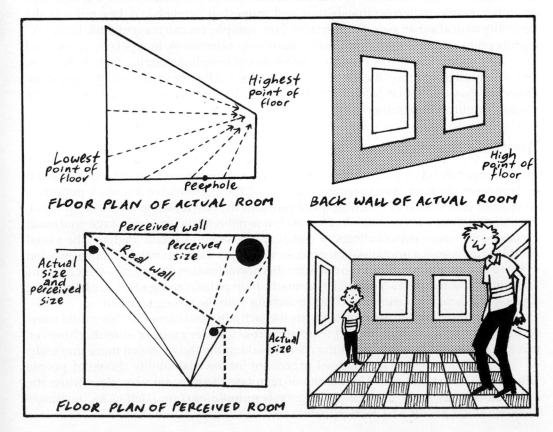

Left: Drawing of the real dimensions and angles used in the Ames room; **Right:** The Ames room as seen through the peephole.

Colour constancy

Colour constancy is the tendency for an object to appear to have the same colour regardless of the light reflecting from it. For example, the light reflected from objects when they are illuminated by artificial lighting is usually yellower than when they are illuminated by the sun. However, this generally has very little effect on the objects' perceived colour (Sekuler & Blake, 1994).

If we see snow on the ground at night, how do we know it is really white when it appears to be much darker?

Why do we show colour constancy? One reason is that we have learned over the years that most objects tend to have a particular colour. For example, English people know that pillar boxes are red, and so they look red even at night under poor lighting conditions.

Land (1977) argued in his retinex theory that we perceive a surface's colour accurately by comparing the light reflected from it against that from adjacent surfaces (see Chapter 4). He obtained evidence for this theory by using two visual displays. The lighting was arranged so that two rectangles having different colours reflected the same wavelengths of light. In spite of this, the two rectangles were seen as different, and their true colours were perceived. It follows from Land's theory that colour constancy would not be found if information about the light reflected from adjacent surfaces were not available. When everything in Land's visual display apart from the two differently coloured rectangles was blocked out, they seemed to have the same colour.

Colour constancy works best when we are viewing objects in natural light from the sun. It tends to break down when we look at objects in artificial light having a restricted wavelength distribution. As Sekuler and Blake (1994) pointed out, some supermarkets exploit this fact by illuminating their meat products so they look redder than is actually the case.

Pattern Recognition

Pattern recognition is concerned with the identification of two-dimensional and three-dimensional visual stimuli. It is very important, because it allows us to make sense of the environment. Some research on two-dimensional stimuli has focused on the recognition of alphanumeric patterns (alphabetical and numerical symbols). A key point is the flexibility of the human perceptual system. For example, we can recognise the letter "A" rapidly and accurately in spite of great variations in orientation, in typeface, in size, and in writing style. How is this possible? Advocates of template theories, feature theories, and structural description theories have put forward different answers to this question. However, they agree that pattern recognition involves matching information from the visual stimulus with information stored in memory.

Template theories

What features might distinguish the template for a cow from the template for a horse? Or would both of these fit only an "animal" template?

The key idea behind template theories is that there is a miniature copy or template stored in long-term memory corresponding to each of the patterns we know. A pattern is recognised on the basis of which template provides the best match to the stimulus input. This kind of theory is very simple. However, it is not realistic, in view of the enormous variations in visual stimuli allegedly matching the same template. Perhaps the visual stimulus undergoes a normalisation process, which produces an internal representation in a standard position, size, and so on. After this normalisation process, the search begins for a matching template. Normalisation might help pattern recognition for letters and digits, but it would sometimes produce matching with the wrong template.

Perhaps there is more than one template for each letter and numeral. This would allow accurate matching of stimulus and template across a wider range of stimuli. However, this success would be achieved at the cost of making the theory much more unwieldy.

Template theories are ill equipped to account for the adaptability shown by people when recognising patterns. Limitations of template theories are very clear when the stimulus belongs to an ill-defined category (e.g. buildings). In such cases, no single template could possibly be enough.

If the first example is your "template" for the category "buildings", it is easy to see how adaptable humans have to be when recognising other examples of the same group.

Feature theories

According to feature theorists, a pattern consists of a set of features or attributes. For example, a face could be said to possess features such as a nose, two eyes, a mouth, a chin, and so on. The process of pattern recognition is assumed to begin with the individual features from the visual stimulus. This set of features is then combined, and compared against information stored in long-term memory.

In the case of a letter such as "A", feature theorists might argue that its crucial features are two straight lines and a connecting cross-bar. This kind of approach has the merit that visual stimuli varying greatly in size, orientation, and minor details may still be identifiable as instances of the same pattern.

Feature analysis

Feature theories have been tested in studies of visual search, in which a target letter has to be found as rapidly as possible in a block of letters. Neisser (1964) compared the time taken to detect the letter "Z" when the distractor letters consisted of straight lines (e.g. W, V) or contained rounded features (e.g. O, G). Performance was faster in the latter condition, presumably because the distractors shared fewer features with the target letter Z.

Neisser's classic research suggested that feature analysis plays a major role in letter perception. However, Harvey, Roberts, and Gervais (1983) argued that other factors are also involved. They studied spatial frequency, which is low when alternating light and dark bars are close together, but high when they are further apart. Letters (e.g. "K" and "N") having several features in common were not confused, whereas letters with similar spatial frequencies but few common features were confused.

EXAMPLE OF ARRANGEMENT OF LETTERS	
List 1	List 2
IMVXEW	ODUGQR
WVMEIX	GRODUQ
VXWIEM	DUROQG
MIEWVX	RGOUDQ
IWVXEM	UGQDRO
IXEZVW	GUQZOR
VWEMXI	ODGRUQ
MIVEWX	DRUQGO
WXEIMV	UQGORD

Neisser used stimuli like these to measure the time it took for people to detect the letter Z. He found that they took less time to find it in the block of rounded letters than in the block of "straight line" letters.

Context and expectations

Feature theories ignore the effects of context and of expectations. Weisstein and Harris (1974) asked their participants to detect a line that was embedded either in a briefly flashed three-dimensional form or in a less coherent form. According to feature theorists, the target line should always activate the same feature detectors, and so the coherence of the form in which it is embedded should not affect detection. In fact, target detection was best when the target line was part of a three-dimensional form. Weisstein and Harris called this the "object-superiority effect", and this effect is inconsistent with many feature theories.

Pattern recognition does not depend solely on listing the features of a stimulus. For example, the letter "A" consists of two oblique uprights and a dash. However, these three features can be presented in such a way that they are not perceived as an A, like this: \ / – . Thus, we need to consider the *relationships* among features.

Limitations

The limitations of feature theories are clearer with three-dimensional stimuli. Observers can usually recognise three-dimensional objects even when one or more of the main features are hidden from view. This is hard to explain if features are crucial for recognition.

If you were planning to replicate Neisser's experiment, would the design be repeated or independent (see Chapter 31)? Which statistical test would you use to compare the mean times for each condition (see Chapter 32)?

Structural descriptions

Theories based on structural descriptions are more adequate than template and feature theories. Structural descriptions consist of propositions, which are the smallest units to which we can assign a meaning. According to Bruce and Green (1990, p.186), "such propositions describe the nature of the components of a configuration and make explicit the structural arrangement of these parts." For example, a structural description of a capital letter T might include the following: there are two parts; one part is a horizontal line; one part is a vertical line; the vertical line supports the horizontal line; the vertical line bisects the horizontal line.

Structural descriptions are more complete than those provided by a feature analysis. Structural descriptions focus on key aspects of stimuli and ignore the others. For example, the structural description of the letter T does not include propositions referring to the lengths of the vertical and horizontal lines. The reason is that the letter T can be recognised in spite of wide variations in the lengths of its two lines.

Limitations

Imagine being in a busy shopping mall trying to identify a friend in the crowd. Which theory of pattern recognition would you find most relevant: template, feature, or structural description?

In sum, the approach based on structural descriptions is superior to that based on templates or features. However, it is not clear how the structural description formed from a visual stimulus is matched with the relevant stored structural descriptions. Furthermore, structural descriptions suffer from the limitation that they do not take contextual information into account.

Marr's computational theory

Marr (1982) proposed a computational theory of visual perception and pattern recognition. According to this theory, visual processing produces a series of representations or descriptions. These representations provide increasingly detailed information about the visual environment. The three main kinds of representation are as follows:

- Primal sketch: this provides a two-dimensional description of the main light-intensity changes in the visual input, including information about edges, contours, and indistinct forms, or blobs.
- $2\frac{1}{2}$-D sketch: this provides a description of the depth and orientation of visible surfaces, making use of information provided by shading, texture, motion, binocular disparity, and so on.
- 3-D model representation: this provides a three-dimensional description of the shapes of objects and their relative positions; it differs from the $2\frac{1}{2}$-D sketch in that the description does not depend on the observer's viewpoint.

3-D model representation

The faces–goblets ambiguous figure. When you concentrate on the faces alone, the concavities make it easy to identify the forehead, nose, lips, and chin. But when you see the goblet, the concavities suggest the base, stem, and bowl.

For the purposes of understanding pattern or object recognition, it is most important to consider Marr's **3-D model representation**. He assumed that object recognition involves matching information from a 3-D model representation against object information stored in long-term memory. Thus, for example, an object is recognised as a dog if the information in the 3-D model representation matches stored information about the characteristics of dogs more closely than those of any other object.

Marr and Nishihara (1978) argued that the basic units for describing objects should be cylinders having a major axis. These units are organised in a hierarchical way, with high-level units providing information about object shape, and low-level units providing more detailed information.

How does the perceiver identify the major axes of an object? According to Marr and Nishihara, concavities (areas where the contour points into the object) are identified first. Some evidence that concavities are important was reported by Hoffman and Richards (1984). They studied the faces–goblet ambiguous figure. When one of the faces is seen, the concavities make it easy to identify the forehead, nose, lips, and chin. In contrast, when the goblet is seen, the concavities define its base, stem, and bowl.

KEY TERM
3-D model representation: in Marr's theory, a three-dimensional description of the shapes of objects, which is independent of the observer's viewpoint.

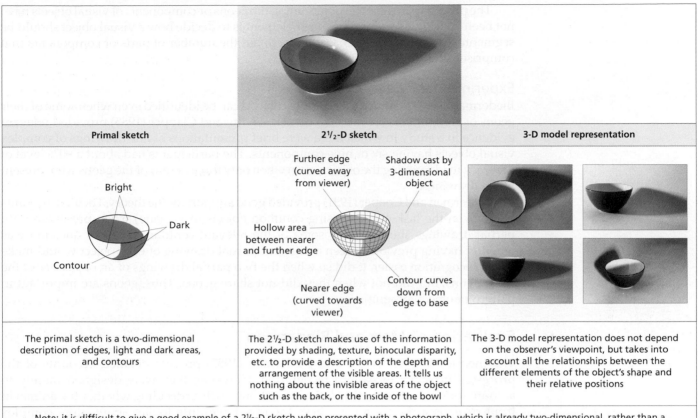

Primal sketch	2½-D sketch	3-D model representation
The primal sketch is a two-dimensional description of edges, light and dark areas, and contours	The 2½-D sketch makes use of the information provided by shading, texture, binocular disparity, etc. to provide a description of the depth and arrangement of the visible areas. It tells us nothing about the invisible areas of the object such as the back, or the inside of the bowl	The 3-D model representation does not depend on the observer's viewpoint, but takes into account all the relationships between the different elements of the object's shape and their relative positions

Note: it is difficult to give a good example of a 2½-D sketch when presented with a photograph, which is already two-dimensional, rather than a real object. Our own knowledge about the geometry and function of bowls tends to interfere with our attempts to describe only what we are actually seeing, rather than what we know is also present!

Recognition-by-components theory

Biederman (1987) put forward a more detailed theory of pattern recognition. He assumed that objects consist of basic shapes or components known as "geons" (geometric ions). Examples of geons are blocks, cylinders, spheres, arcs, and wedges. According to Biederman, there are about 36 different geons, which may sound like rather few. However, we can identify enormous numbers of spoken English words, even though there are only about 44 phonemes in the English language. The reason is that these phonemes can be arranged in almost endless different orders, and the same is true of geons.

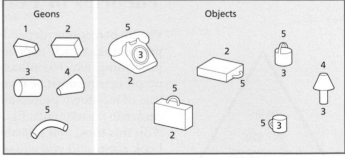

Some examples of Biederman's volumetric primitives called "geons". Note how different objects can be created by combining the same geons in different orientations.

The richness of the object descriptions provided by geons stems partly from the different possible spatial relationships among them. For example, a cup can be described as an arc connected to the side of a cylinder. A bucket can be described by the same two geons, but with the arc connected to the top of the cylinder.

Stored representations

So far we have focused only on the stage involving the determination of the components or geons of a visual object and their relationships. When this information is available, it is matched with stored object representations or structural models containing information about the nature of the relevant geons, their orientations, sizes, and so on. The identification of any given visual object is determined by whichever stored object representation provides the best fit with the component- or geon-based information obtained from the visual object.

The processes involved in determining the geons or components of visual objects have not been considered so far. One major element is to decide how a visual object should be segmented or divided up in order to work out the number of parts or components that comprise it.

Experimental evidence

Biederman (1987) assumed that complex objects can be identified even when some of their geons or components are missing. Biederman, Ju, and Clapper (1985) provided relevant evidence in a study in which there were brief presentations of line drawings of complex visual objects having six or nine components. The participants had about a 90% level of accuracy in identifying the objects, even when only three or four of the geons were present in the drawings.

Biederman and Cooper (1991) provided good support for the theory. Their participants were given the task of recognising common objects (e.g. piano) when presented with partial drawings showing only some of the relevant contours. The key question was whether having previously seen a different partial drawing of each object would make object recognition easier. It did so when the two partial drawings of an object *shared* the same geons, but did not when they did not share geons. Thus, geons are important in pattern or object recognition.

Evaluation of Marr and Biederman

The theories of Marr (1982) and Biederman (1987) provide detailed accounts of the processes involved in pattern recognition. However, they were designed mainly to account for unsubtle perceptual discriminations, such as deciding whether the animal in front of us is a dog or a cat. These theories have little to say about more complex discriminations, such as identifying which one out of a varied collection of cups is the one we normally use. Furthermore, these theories tend to ignore the role played by *context* in pattern recognition. It is easier to recognise an object when it fits the context than when it does not, but the theories of Marr and Biederman do not fully explain why this should be the case.

Theories of Perception

Visual perception depends on two types of processing. First, there is **bottom-up processing**, which depends directly on external stimuli. Second, there is **top-down processing**, which is influenced by an individual's knowledge and expectations. Bottom-up processing must be involved in visual perception, but it is less clear that the same is true of top-down processing. A simple illustration of the role of top-down processing is shown in the triangular figure here. Look now before you read on. Unless you are familiar with this trick, you probably read the message in the triangle as "Paris in the spring". Look again, and you will see that the word "the" is repeated. Your expectation that it is a well-known phrase (i.e. top-down processing) overrides the information available in the stimulus (i.e. bottom-up processing).

Perception often involves a mixture of bottom-up and top-down processing. An especially clear demonstration of this comes from a study by Bruner, Postman, and Rodrigues (1951), in which the participants expected to see ordinary playing cards presented very briefly. When black hearts were presented, some of them claimed to have seen purple or brown hearts. Here we have an almost literal blending of the black colour based on bottom-up processing with the red colour based on top-down processing, due to the expectation that hearts will be red.

Some theorists have emphasised the importance of either bottom-up or top-down processing to visual perception. For example, Gibson (1950, 1966, 1979) focused on bottom-up processes. According to his theory of direct perception, the information provided by the visual environment permits the individual to move around and to interact directly with that environment without internal processes being involved. In

PARIS
IN   THE
THE   SPRING

KEY TERMS
Bottom-up processing: processing that is determined by external stimuli rather than by an individual's knowledge and expectations.
Top-down processing: processing that is affected by an individual's knowledge and expectations rather than directly by the stimulus.

contrast, Neisser (1967) and Gregory (1972, 1980) focused on top-down processes. According to their constructivist theory, perception is an active and constructive process which is much influenced by hypotheses and expectations. These theories are considered in some detail next.

Gibson's theory of direct perception

Optic flow

Gibson's interest in visual perception started during the Second World War. He was given the task of preparing training films showing the problems pilots experience when landing. Gibson (1950) found that there are **optic flow patterns**: the point towards which the pilot is moving (called the "pole") seems motionless, with the rest of the visual environment apparently moving away from that point. The further any part of the landing strip is from the pole, the greater is its apparent speed of movement. According to Gibson, the sensory information available to pilots in optic flow patterns provides them with unambiguous information about their direction, speed, and altitude.

Gibson was so impressed by the wealth of sensory information available to pilots in optic flow patterns that he devoted himself to an analysis of the information available in other situations. He argued that texture gradients provide useful information about depth: objects slanting away from you have an increased gradient (rate of change) of texture density as you look from the near edge to the far edge.

Pilots now train on computer simulators, learning how to interpret information from the optic flow about speed, height, and direction, and gaining an understanding of how the plane will react in certain situations.

Optic array

Gibson (1966, 1979) put forward a general theory of visual perception. His starting point was the notion that the pattern of light reaching the eye can be thought of as an **optic array** containing all the visual information available at the retina. This optic array provides unambiguous information about the layout of objects in space. This information comes in many forms, including optic flow patterns and texture gradients. Perception involves "picking up" the rich information provided by the optic array in a direct fashion with little or no information processing involved.

Perception and action

Of particular importance in Gibson's theory was the assumption that there is a close relationship between perception and action. An observer can obtain valuable information about the environment by moving about. For example, optic flow patterns only exist when the individual is in movement. Previous researchers in visual perception had minimised the importance of movement, in part because of the artificial laboratory studies they carried out. For example, they often prevented movement of the eyes relative to visual displays by using chin rests or other restraints.

Invariants

Gibson argued that important aspects of the optic array remain the same when observers move around their environment; these are known as **invariants**. The pole (the point towards which someone is moving) is an example of an invariant. Another example is the horizon ratio relation: the ratio of an object's height to the distance between its base and the horizon is invariant regardless of its distance from the viewer. According to Gibson, this invariant helps to maintain size constancy.

Resonance

How do people "pick up" or detect the invariant information provided by the optic array? According to Gibson, there is a process of **resonance**, which he explained by analogy to the workings of a radio. In most houses throughout the Western world, there is almost non-stop electromagnetic radiation from various radio transmitters. When a radio set is

KEY TERMS
Optic flow patterns: perceptual effect in which the visual environment appears to move away from the point towards which a person is moving.
Optic array: in Gibson's theory, the pattern of light reaching the eye.
Invariants: in Gibson's theory, those aspects of the visual environment that remain the same as an observer moves.
Resonance: in Gibson's theory, the process used to detect invariant information in the environment.

switched on, there may be only a hissing sound. If tuned properly, however, speech or music will be clearly heard. In Gibson's terms, the radio is now *resonating* with the information contained in the electromagnetic radiation.

The analogy suggests we can pick up information from the environment in a fairly automatic and effortless way if we are attuned to that information. The radio operates as a single unit, in the sense that damage to any part of its circuitry would stop it working. In a similar way, Gibson argued that the nervous system works as a single unit when perceiving.

Affordance

A key part of visual perception involves attaching meaning to the visual information provided to the eyes. It is usually assumed that we perceive a meaningful environment due to the involvement of relevant knowledge stored in long-term memory. Gibson (1979) disagreed with this assumption. He argued that all the potential uses of an object (which he called their **affordances**) are directly perceivable. For example, a ladder "affords" ascent or descent, and a chair "affords" sitting. The notion of affordances was even applied to postboxes by Gibson (1979, p.139):

> *The postbox ... affords letter-mailing to a letter-writing human in a community with a postal system. This fact is perceived when the postbox is identified as such.*

Most objects give rise to more than one affordance, with the particular affordance influencing behaviour being determined by the perceiver's current state. Thus, a hungry person will perceive the affordance of edibility when presented with an orange, and so will eat it. A person who is angry may detect the affordance of a projectile, and so throw the orange at someone.

The notion of affordances is very important to Gibson's theory. It forms part of his attempt to show that all the information needed to make sense of the visual environment is directly present in the visual input. In addition, it conforms to the notion that there is a close relationship between perception and action.

Evaluation

Perception and action. The main strength of Gibson's theory is its emphasis on the notion that the visual environment provides much more information than had previously been thought. He was right in assuming that the moment-by-moment changes in the optic array occurring when we are in movement provide very useful information about the layout of the visual environment. Most previous theorists had de-emphasised the importance of movement, and had carried out studies in which the visual environment and the participant were both motionless.

Accuracy of perception. Gibson argued that the wealth of information provided in the optic array means that perception is nearly always accurate. What about laboratory studies showing that visual perception can be very inaccurate? According to Gibson, such studies (e.g. of visual illusions) typically involve either very brief stimulus presentations or impoverished stimuli, and so have little relevance to everyday perception. He was right to argue that it can be unwise to assume that the findings from artificial laboratory situations apply to ordinary perception.

Oversimplification. On the negative side, the processes involved in identifying invariants in the environment, in discovering affordances, and in producing resonance, are much more complex than Gibson indicated. According to Marr (1982, p.30), the major shortcomings of Gibson's analysis result

> *from a failure to realise two things. First, the detection of physical invariants ... is exactly and precisely an information-processing problem ... And second, he vastly under-rated the sheer difficulty of such detection.*

Would you class Gibson's theory as a reductionist one (see Chapter 2)? Why is this?

KEY TERM
Affordances: in Gibson's theory, the possible uses of objects, which are claimed to be given directly in the sensory information provided by the stimulus.

"Seeing as". Gibson's theoretical approach applies much better to some aspects of visual perception than to others. This key issue can be approached in terms of the distinction between "seeing" and "seeing as". Fodor and Pylyshyn (1981) clarified this distinction by considering someone called Smith, who is lost at sea. He sees the stars in the night sky, including the Pole Star. However, what may be crucial to his survival is whether he sees the Pole Star as the Pole Star or as just another star. In other words, "seeing as" involves attaching *meaning* to what is being seen. Gibson's notion of affordances was an unsuccessful attempt to explain the meaningfulness of perception. Gibson provided a valuable account of *seeing*, but had little of interest to say about *seeing as*.

Gibson's theory does not account for visual illusions, for example "seeing" water on the road on a very hot day.

The role of memory. A final weakness of Gibson's approach was his notion that no internal representations (e.g. memories) are needed to explain perception. Bruce, Green, and Georgeson (1996) referred to the work of Menzel (1978) to show the problems flowing from Gibson's position. Chimpanzees were carried around a field, and were shown the locations of 20 pieces of food. When each chimpanzee was then released, it moved around the field picking up the food efficiently. As there could be no relevant information in the light reaching the chimpanzees (because they were now moving independently rather than being carried), they must have made use of stored information in long-term memory to guide their search. This is contrary to the assumptions made by Gibson.

> **Internal representation and perception**
>
> According to Gibson, a meaningless mark on a piece of paper (e.g. ~) should be enough visual information to permit identification. We could certainly identify it as a squiggle, but if we were to see a note on someone's doorstep that read "A pint of ~ please", we could interpret it correctly using our internal representations from previous experiences of notes on doorsteps. Gibson's theory does not address this issue.

Constructivist theory

Helmholtz (1821–1894) argued that the inadequate information provided by the senses is augmented by *unconscious inferences*, which add meaning to sensory information. He assumed that these inferences were unconscious, because we are usually unaware that we are making inferences while perceiving. Helmholtz's constructivist approach to perception has been developed by theorists such as Gregory (1972, 1980) and Neisser (1967).

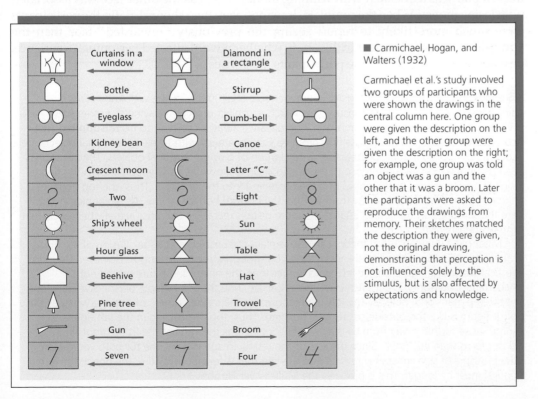

■ Carmichael, Hogan, and Walters (1932)

Carmichael et al.'s study involved two groups of participants who were shown the drawings in the central column here. One group were given the description on the left, and the other group were given the description on the right; for example, one group was told an object was a gun and the other that it was a broom. Later the participants were asked to reproduce the drawings from memory. Their sketches matched the description they were given, not the original drawing, demonstrating that perception is not influenced solely by the stimulus, but is also affected by expectations and knowledge.

When you see an object such as a table, information from your senses will tell you its size, shape, and colour, but you will need to add meaning to this sensory information to know what the object is used for.

Our senses can be deceived by suggestion, such as when hypnosis and relaxation techniques are used as methods of pain relief (Chapter 5).

The following assumptions are made by most constructivist theorists:

- Perception is an active and constructive process; according to Gordon (1989, p.124), it is "something more than the direct registration of sensations ... other events intervene between stimulation and experience."
- Perception is not directly given by the stimulus input, but rather involves internal hypotheses, expectations, and knowledge, as well as motivational and emotional factors; sensory information is used as the basis for making informed guesses or inferences about the presented stimulus and its meaning.
- Because perception is influenced by hypotheses and expectations that will sometimes be incorrect, perception is prone to error.

Other studies: Emotional and motivational factors

Solley and Haigh (1958) examined the role of emotional factors in perception. In two sessions, one before and one after Christmas, they asked children aged between 4 and 8 to draw Santa Claus. As Christmas approached the Santa drawings became larger and more elaborate, but after Christmas the drawings were much smaller (see page 792). The emotions involved in anticipating Christmas affected how the children depicted Santa and his presents.

Motivational factors were examined by Sandford (1936). Some participants were deprived of food on the day of Sandford's study and then given a word-completion task. Most hungry participants produced BREAD as the word to complete B——D, whereas non-deprived participants tended to produce the word BORED!

The flavour of this theoretical approach was captured by Gregory (1972). He claimed that perceptions are constructions "from the fragmentary scraps of data signalled by the senses and drawn from the brain memory banks, themselves constructions from the snippets of the past." Thus, the inadequate information supplied to the sense organs is used as the basis for making inferences or forming hypotheses about the visual environment.

Ittelson (1952) provided an illustration of how expectations can influence perception, based on the Ames distorted room discussed earlier in the chapter. The room has a very strange shape, but our perception of it is strongly influenced by our expectation that rooms are rectangular. As a result, someone standing in the rear right corner appears to be much taller than someone standing in the rear left corner.

Constructivist theorists argue that an observer's hypotheses and expectations can be influenced by motivational and emotional factors. Supporting evidence was reported by Schafer and Murphy (1943). They used drawings in which an irregular line had been drawn vertically through a circle so that each half of the circle could be seen as the profile of a different face. At the start of the study, each face was presented on its own. One face in each pair was associated with winning money, whereas the other face was associated with losing money. When the complete drawings were then shown briefly, the participants were much more likely to report seeing the previously "rewarded" face than the "punished" one. It is not clear in this study whether reward affected perceptual experience, or whether it only affected the participants' responses.

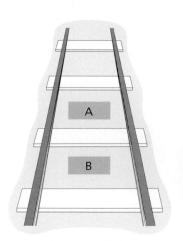

The Ponzo illusion

Gregory (1970) used the constructivist approach to explain many of the well-known visual illusions. He started with size constancy, in which an object is seen as having the same size whether it is looked at from a short or a long distance away. According to his **misapplied size-constancy theory**, the processes that produce size constancy with three-dimensional objects are sometimes applied inappropriately to the perception of two-dimensional objects. The basic ideas can be understood with reference to the Ponzo illusion shown here. The long lines in the figure look like railway lines or the edges of a road receding into the distance. Thus, the top horizontal line can be seen as further away from us than the bottom horizontal line. As rectangles A and B are the same size in the retinal image, the more distant rectangle (A) must actually be larger than the nearer one (B).

Misapplied size-constancy theory can also explain the best-known visual illusion of all, the Muller–Lyer illusion. The vertical lines in the two figures are the same length. However, the vertical line in the figure on the left looks longer than the one in the figure on the right. According to Gregory, the Muller–Lyer figures can be thought of as simple perspective drawings of three-dimensional objects. The left figure looks like the inside corners of a room, whereas the right figure is like the outside corner of a building. Thus, the vertical line in the left figure is in some sense further away from us than its "fins", whereas the vertical line in the right figure is closer to us than its "fins". Since the size of the retinal image is the same for both vertical lines, the principle of size constancy tells us that the line that is further away (i.e. the one in the left figure) must be longer. This is precisely the Muller–Lyer illusion.

Gregory argued that figures such as the Ponzo and the Muller–Lyer are treated in many ways as three-dimensional objects. Why, then, do they seem flat and two-dimensional? According to Gregory, cues to depth are used automatically whether or not the figures are seen to be lying on a flat surface. Support for this viewpoint comes from the finding that the two-dimensional Muller-Lyer figures do indeed appear three-dimensional when they are presented as luminous models in a dark room. According to Gregory, it is only when these (and other) figures are presented on a flat surface that we do not perceive them as three-dimensional.

It might be thought that the depth cues of two-dimensional drawings would be less effective than those of photographs. Supporting evidence was reported by Leibowitz et al. (1969). They studied the Ponzo illusion, and found that the extent of the illusion was significantly greater with a photograph than with a drawing.

Discussion points

1. Is it likely that any single theory of the visual illusions will explain all of them?

2. What grounds are there for doubting Gregory's misapplied size-constancy theory (see Evaluation)?

The Muller–Lyer illusion

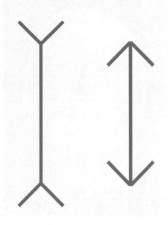

Evaluation

Gregory's misapplied size-constancy theory is ingenious, and has been regarded as the most adequate theory of the visual illusions. However, Gregory's claim that luminous Muller–Lyer figures are seen three-dimensionally by everyone is incorrect. It is puzzling that the Muller–Lyer illusion can still be seen when the fins on the two figures are replaced by other attachments, such as circles or squares (see Eysenck & Keane, 1995). Such evidence was interpreted by Matlin and Foley (1997) as supporting the incorrect comparison theory, according to which our perception of visual illusions is influenced by parts of the figure that are not being judged. Thus, for example, the vertical lines in the Muller–Lyer illusion may seem longer or shorter than their actual length simply because they form part of a large or small object.

Evidence supporting incorrect comparison theory was reported by Coren and Girgus (1972). The magnitude of the Muller–Lyer illusion was greatly reduced when the fins were in a different colour to the vertical lines. Presumably this made it easier to ignore the fins when deciding on the relative lengths of the two vertical lines.

The strongest evidence that Gregory's theory is incomplete was reported by DeLucia and Hochberg (1991). They used a three-dimensional display consisting of three 2-foot high fins on the floor. Even though it was obvious that all the fins were at the same distance from the viewer, the typical Muller–Lyer effect was obtained. You can check this out for yourself by placing three open books in a line so that the ones on the left and the right are open to the right and the one in the middle is open to the left. The spine of the book in the middle should be the same distance from the spines of the other two books.

Variants on the Muller–Lyer illusion

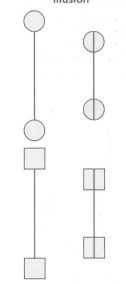

Outline any illusions you have encountered in everyday life. Have these experiences helped your understanding of the nature of perception?

General evaluation

Top-down processes based on expectations, hypotheses, and so on can have a considerable influence on visual perception. Many theorists, such as Gibson, have emphasised the importance of bottom-up processes, and constructivist theorists have performed the valuable service of demonstrating that top-down processes should not be ignored. However, there are some serious problems with the constructivist approach, and the three main ones are discussed here.

Accuracy

Constructivist theorists predict that perception will often be in error, whereas it is typically accurate. If we always use hypotheses and expectations to interpret sensory data, how is it that these hypotheses and expectations are correct nearly all the time? The obvious answer is that the environment provides much more information than the "fragmentary scraps of data" assumed by constructivist theorists.

The spine of the middle book is closer to the spine of which other book? Now check your answer with a ruler.

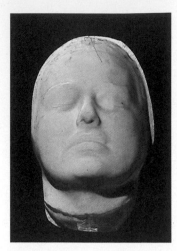

This photograph shows the inside of a hollow mask of a face, but it is very difficult to perceive it as seen "from the back". The viewer tends to perceive it as if they were seeing it from the front.

Artificial stimuli

Many of the studies carried out by constructivist theorists make use of artificial or unnatural stimuli. As Gordon (1989, p.144) pointed out, such studies involve

> *the perception of patterns under conditions of brief exposure, drawings which could represent the corners of buildings, glowing objects in darkened corridors ... none of these existed in the African grasslands where human perceptual systems reached their present state of evolutionary development.*

Consider, for example, studies involving the very rapid presentation of visual stimuli. Brief presentation reduces the impact of bottom-up processes, thus allowing more scope for top-down processes to operate.

Hypotheses

Constructivist theorists assume that the hypotheses formed by perceivers are the "best guesses" in the light of the available information. However, it is often very hard to persuade observers to change their hypotheses. For example, there is Gregory's (1973) "hollow face" illusion. In this illusion, observers looking at a hollow mask of a face from a distance of about one metre report seeing a normal face. Even when observers know that it is a hollow face, they still report that it looks normal.

Synthesis: Neisser's cyclic theory

Neisser (1976) provided a synthesis of the direct and constructivist approaches to perception in his cyclic theory. He assumed that there is a perceptual cycle involving schemata, perceptual exploration, and the stimulus environment. Schemata contain collections of knowledge derived from past experience serving the function of *directing* perceptual exploration towards relevant environmental stimuli. Such exploration often leads the perceiver to *sample* some of the available stimulus information. If the information obtained from the environment fails to match information in the relevant schema, then the information in the schema is modified appropriately.

The perceptual cycle described by Neisser includes elements of bottom-up and top-down processing. Bottom-up processing is represented by the sampling of available environmental information which can modify the current schema. Top-down processing is represented by the notion that schemata influence the course of the information processing involved in perception.

Schemata

The key notion in Neisser's theory is that of schemata or organised knowledge. According to the theory, schemata should reduce the need to analyse all aspects of a visual scene. Evidence for this was reported by Biederman, Glass, and Stacy (1973).

Test the Biederman et al. experimental findings for yourself. Show the scene on the right to someone who has not already seen these pictures, very briefly (Biederman used one-tenth of a second), and see what objects they can recall. Try the random arrangement on the left on someone else, for the same time period. Again, see how many objects they can remember. Why do you have to show the two pictures to different people? How might this affect your findings?

Participants were able to recall almost half the objects in photographs of familiar scenes (e.g. a city street) after viewing them for only one-tenth of a second, because the relevant schema could be used easily. In contrast, when the objects were arranged randomly in the photograph, participants found it much harder to identify and to remember them.

Friedman (1979) reported good evidence that visual perception is influenced by schemata. Participants were presented with detailed line drawings of scenes (e.g. a kitchen; an office). The duration of the first look was almost twice as long for unexpected as for expected objects, indicating the role of schemata in processing expected objects. It is easier to perceive objects that fit our schemata than objects that do not.

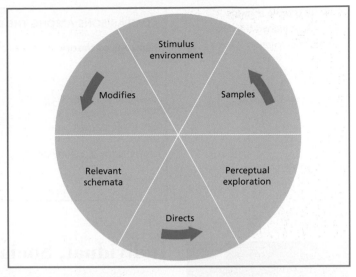

The **perceptual cycle** as proposed by Neisser (1976).

Evaluation

Neisser's (1976) cyclic theory combines some of the best features of the direct and constructivist approaches to perception. Perception often involves top-down processes as well as bottom-up processes, and both types of processes are incorporated into Neisser's perceptual cycle. Another strength of Neisser's theory is its emphasis on schemata. Schema-relevant objects are generally perceived and remembered much better than schema-irrelevant objects.

Neisser's cyclic theory is very sketchy, and fails to specify in any detail the processes involved in perception. More specifically, we are not told in detail how relevant schemata direct perceptual exploration, how perceptual exploration determines what is to be sampled in the stimulus environment, or how processing of the stimulus environment then modifies the relevant schemata. Theories such as those of Marr (1982) and Biederman (1987) indicate that we need much more complex and detailed theories to understand human perception properly.

Draw up a table showing comparisons among the different theories of perception.

COMPARISONS AMONG THE DIFFERENT THEORIES OF PERCEPTION

Features of theory	Direct theories	Constructivist theories	Synthesis
Major concepts			
Top-down or bottom-up?			
Generally learned or innate?			
Stored knowledge needed?			
Weaknesses			

Individual, Social, and Cultural Variations

If visual perception depends on experience and on expectations as claimed by constructivist theorists, then we would expect to find individual, social, and cultural variations in perception. All these factors can influence perception, especially the meaning or significance that is obtained from external stimuli. For example, people from all social and cultural backgrounds probably perceive the actual movements of football players playing a match in the same way. However, only those who are familiar with the game perceive the significance of a player running into an offside position.

Individual variations

Numerous factors cause individual variations in perception, but we will consider only two: field dependence and trait anxiety.

Field dependence

Field dependence is a perceptual style in which perception is distorted by background or contextual factors. Witkin (1967) argued that there is an important distinction between field dependence and field independence, in which perception is free from distortion by environmental factors. One way of assessing field dependence is by using the tilted room test, in which the room and the chair in which the participant is sitting are moved in different directions. The participant's task is to adjust the chair back into the upright position. Field-dependent people take more account of the tilted room than do field-independent. Thus, their perception is more influenced by *external* factors, whereas that of field-independent people is more influenced by *internal* factors (e.g. sense of balance).

There are two problems with this approach. First, different measures of field dependence do not usually correlate highly with each other (Eysenck, 1977). Second, there is overlap between field dependence and intelligence, with field-independent people tending to be more intelligent than field-dependent people (Vernon, 1972). As a result, it is often not clear whether individual variations in perception are due to field dependence or to intelligence.

Trait anxiety

Some people perceive the world in a positive or optimistic way, whereas others perceive it in a negative or pessimistic way. For example, for some a glass is half full, whereas for others it is half empty. There is much evidence that individuals high in **trait anxiety** (a personality dimension relating to the experience of anxiety) see things more negatively than those low in trait anxiety (Eysenck, 1997). Derakshan and Eysenck (1997) videotaped participants while they gave a public talk. After that, the participants and independent judges viewed the videotapes, and provided ratings of behavioural anxiety. Those high in trait anxiety perceived their behaviour as more anxious than it seemed to the judges, but the opinion of those low in trait anxiety did not differ from that of the judges.

KEY TERMS
Field dependence: a perceptual style in which perception is distorted by background or contextual factors.
Trait anxiety: a personality dimension concerned with individual differences in susceptibility to anxiety.

Social variations

Social variations in perception were studied by Bruner and Goodman (1947). Rich and poor children estimated the sizes of coins. The poor children overestimated the size of every coin. This may reflect the greater value of money to poor children. However, a simpler explanation is that rich children are more familiar with coins, and this made them more accurate in their size estimates. Ashley, Harper, and Runyon (1951) modified the study in an ingenious way. They hypnotised adult participants into believing they were rich or poor. The size estimates of the coins were larger when the participants were in the "poor" state. These findings suggest that poor participants do not overestimate coin sizes purely because of a lack of familiarity, and indicate the importance of social factors in perception.

Witkin et al. (1962) found that social factors influenced the perceptual styles of field dependence and field independence. Males tended to be field independent, and thus their visual perception was relatively unaffected by distracting stimuli. In contrast, females tended to be field dependent. Witkin et al. also reported that children brought up by domineering parents tended to be field dependent, whereas those brought up by more liberal parents were field independent. As mentioned earlier, however, it is hard to measure field dependence properly (Eysenck, 1977).

Do the findings of studies like those of Bruner and Goodman support the perceptual theories of Gibson or Gregory?

Cultural variations

Witkin and Berry (1975) extended research on field dependence to include cross-cultural variations in perception. They distinguished between two types of culture or society:

1. Hunter/gatherer societies, in which small groups move about in search of food.
2. Farming/pastoral societies, in which members of the group remain in the same place, tending flocks and/or raising crops.

The children in hunter/gatherer societies tend to be field independent, whereas those in farming/pastoral societies tend to be field dependent. It could be argued that the clear, undistorted perception of the world associated with field independence is more important in hunter/gatherer societies.

Use of visual illusions

Much of the evidence on cross-cultural variations in perception is based on various visual illusions. Segall, Campbell, and Herskovits (1963) argued that the Muller–Lyer illusion would only be perceived by those with experience of a "carpentered environment" containing numerous rectangles, straight lines, and regular corners. People in Western societies live in a carpentered environment, but Zulus living in tribal communities do not. Rural Zulus did not show the Muller–Lyer illusion. However, this finding might simply mean that rural Zulus cannot interpret two-dimensional drawings. This is unlikely in view of another of Segall et al.'s findings. They studied the horizontal–vertical illusion, which involves overestimating vertical extents relative to horizontal ones in a two-dimensional drawing. Rural Zulus showed the horizontal–vertical illusion to a greater extent than Europeans, presumably because of their greater familiarity with large open spaces.

Other researchers have produced different findings. Gregor and McPherson (1965) compared two groups of Australian Aborigines. One group lived in a carpentered environment, but the other group lived in the open air and had very basic housing. The two groups did not differ on either the Muller–Lyer or the horizontal–vertical illusion. Cross-cultural differences in visual illusions may depend more on training and education than on whether or not a given group lives in a carpentered environment.

The eye of the beholder? Are the animals in this picture large animals against a distant background, or small animals close up?

Do cultural variations in perception support the view that we process information in a top-down or a bottom-up way?

Additional evidence of cross-cultural differences in perception was reported by Turnbull (1961). His subject was a pygmy who lived in dense forests, and so had limited experience of looking at distant objects. This pygmy was taken to an open plain, and shown a herd of buffalo a long way away. He stated that the buffalo were insects, and refused to believe that they really were large animals. Presumably he had never learned to use some of the depth cues described earlier in the chapter in the way that people in other cultures do. However, this study is limited because only one person was studied, and it is not clear if he had seen buffalo before.

More evidence of cross-cultural differences was reported by Annis and Frost (1973) in a study on Canadian Cree Indians. Some of them lived in tepees out in the countryside, and some of them lived in cities. Annis and Frost argued that those who lived in cities would be exposed mainly to vertical and horizontal lines in their everyday lives, whereas those living in tepees would come across lines in all orientations. Both groups were asked to decide whether two lines were parallel. Cree Indians living in tepees were good at this task no matter what angle the lines were presented. In contrast, those living in cities did much better when the lines were horizontal or vertical than when they were at an angle. These findings suggest the importance of relevant experience to visual perception.

Allport and Pettigrew (1957) made use of an illusion based on a nearly rectangular or trapezoidal "window" fitted with horizontal and vertical bars. When this "window" revolves in a circle, it looks like a rectangular window moving backwards and forwards. People living in cultures without rectangular windows tended not to experience the illusion. Zulus living in rural areas were less likely than Europeans or Zulus living in urban areas to see a rectangle moving backwards and forwards.

Use of drawings

Most adults in Western societies are able to interpret two-dimensional drawings and pictures as showing three-dimensional scenes. However, black children and adults in South Africa with little previous experience of such drawings find it very hard to perceive depth in them (Hudson, 1960). There are problems with such cross-cultural research. Deregowski, Muldrow, and Muldrow (1972) found that members of the Me'en tribe in Ethiopia did not respond to drawings of animals on paper, which was an unfamiliar material for them. This might suggest that they had poor ability to make sense of two-dimensional representations. However, when the tribespeople were shown animals drawn on cloth (a familiar material to them), they were generally able to recognise the animals correctly.

Evaluation

There is evidence for individual, social, and cultural variations in perceptual organisation. Individuals differ in perceptual style, there are social differences in parenting and experiences, and cultures differ in their main activities and in the perceptual experiences of their members.

There are three major limitations with the research in this area. First, it is often hard to interpret the findings. For example, cross-cultural differences in perception could be due to several factors, because the experiences of people living in different cultures differ in numerous ways. In future, groups not showing a visual illusion (e.g. the Muller–Lyer) could be studied to find out what kinds of learning experiences they need to show the illusion. The fact that even pigeons show the Muller–Lyer illusion (Malott et al., 1967)

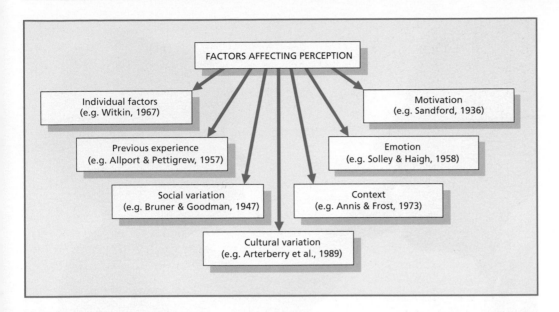

suggests we should be careful about assuming that cultural factors are of major importance in determining how the illusion is seen.

Second, most studies are limited because they rely on self-report measures. For example, individuals high in trait anxiety may exaggerate how anxious their own behaviour is because of low self-esteem rather than because that is what they actually perceive. Some apparent cross-cultural differences in perception may occur because of cultural differences in the ability to report perceptual experiences in an accurate way. Other cross-cultural differences may depend on differences across languages rather than because of actual differences in perception.

Third, much cross-cultural research has focused on two-dimensional visual illusions, and such limited research may tell us little about cultural differences in everyday perception. It is probable that there are large cultural differences in the significance attached to various visual stimuli. For example, members of many African cultures can make much more sense of complex patterns of footprints than members of Western societies.

Cross-cultural issues: What is ethnocentrism? Why does ethnocentrism lead to limitations in the interpretations of findings of cross-cultural studies?

Cultural variations in perception present us with evidence that perception is learned. Use Turnbull's study of the pygmy to describe why this should be.

PERSONAL REFLECTIONS

- In my opinion, the British psychologist David Marr has contributed more than anyone else in the last 50 years to our understanding of visual perception. His main insight was that visual perception (which seems easy and effortless to us) actually involves a considerable number of complex processes. He then proceeded to identify many of these processes, and was the first person to show how the visual system constructs three-dimensional representations of objects. His achievements were outstanding, even though he died in 1980 at the tragically young age of 35.

SUMMARY

There are several methods available for studying perceptual development, including the habituation and preference methods. Infants show an early preference for the human face over other stimuli. Studies on the visual cliff indicate that infants who are several months old possess at least some of the elements of depth perception. Infants also show some ability to display size and shape constancy. Perceptual development depends in part on the infant's active involvement with the environment, and in part on a process of differentiation.

Perceptual development

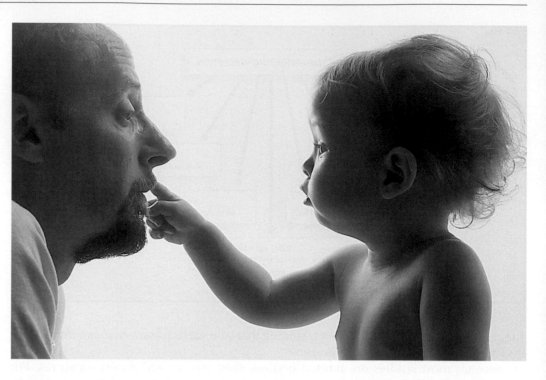

Perceptual organisation

The Gestaltists emphasised perceptual segregation and the law of Prägnanz. Further laws (e.g. those relating to proximity, similarity, good continuation, and closure) all illustrate the law of Prägnanz. These laws are descriptions rather than explanations. The Gestaltists also assumed that the whole is more than the sum of its parts, and some evidence supports this assumption.

Space or depth perception

Space perception depends on various monocular cues such as pictorial cues, linear perspective, aerial perspective, texture, interposition, shading, familiar size, and motion parallax. It also depends on binocular cues, of which stereopsis is easily the most important. Information from cues is normally combined in an additive way, but occasionally information from one cue is ignored.

Visual constancies

Most of the visual characteristics of objects look very similar under changes in viewing conditions. For example, most people exhibit size constancy, shape constancy, and colour constancy. These constancies develop early in life, and enable us to perceive a fairly unchanging world in spite of large variations in the retinal image.

Pattern recognition

Template theories of pattern recognition have not proved successful. Feature theories emphasise the processing of individual features or attributes, but tend to ignore context and expectation effects. Theorists such as Marr and Biederman have put forward theories of pattern recognition based on structural descriptions. Marr identified three kinds of representation (primal sketch; $2^1/_2$-D sketch; and 3-D model representation), and Biederman argued that objects consist of basic shapes or components known as geons. These theories explain unsubtle discriminations and tend to ignore the role of context in pattern recognition.

Theories of perception

Gibson in his theory of direct perception emphasised that the information provided by the environment is generally sufficient to allow individuals to move freely around. He argued that some aspects of optic array remain the same or invariant when observers move around. He also argued that the potential uses of an object (called affordances) are directly perceivable. Gibson minimised the complexity of the processes underlying visual perception. Constructivists such as Gregory and Neisser argue that perception involves hypotheses, expectations, and knowledge. They claim that motivational and emotional factors can influence perception. The top-down processes discussed by constructivists do influence perception. However, the fact that visual perception is rarely in error suggests that these processes are used less often than is assumed by constructivists.

There is evidence of individual, social, and cultural variations in perception. Some individual variations depend on perceptual style and personality. The Muller-Lyer illusion tends not to be found in societies lacking a carpentered environment. The differing visual experiences across cultures influence visual perception in a number of ways. Of particular importance, people in Western societies find it easier than those elsewhere in the world to interpret two-dimensional drawings and pictures as showing three-dimensional scenes because of extensive relevant experience. Problems include difficulties in interpreting cultural differences, and too much reliance on two-dimensional figures and self-report measures of perception.

Individual, social, and cultural variations

FURTHER READING

M.W. Eysenck (1993), *Principles of cognitive psychology*, Hove, UK: Psychology Press; Chapter 2 of this book provides basic coverage of visual perception for introductory level students. V. Bruce, P.R. Green, and M.A. Georgeson (1996), *Visual perception: Physiology, psychology, and ecology (3rd Edn.)*, Hove, UK: Psychology Press; most of the topics discussed in this chapter are discussed in detail in this book, and it contains a very good account of Gibson's approach to perception. R. Sekuler and R. Blake (1994), *Perception (3rd Edn.)*, New York: McGraw-Hill; this book has good accounts of many topics in visual perception.

REVISION QUESTIONS

1	Distinguish between constructivist and direct theories of perception.	(24 marks)
2	Describe and assess methods that have been used to study perceptual development.	(24 marks)
3a	Describe *two* theories of perceptual organisation.	(12 marks)
3b	Analyse research evidence on which these theories are based.	(12 marks)
4	Consider and analyse cultural variations in perceptual organisation.	(24 marks)

- **Focused auditory attention**
  How we select, process, and remember one sound against a background of many.

  Cherry's "cocktail party" effect; shadowing
  Broadbent's filter theory
  Treisman's attenuation theory
  Deutsch and Deutsch's modification
  Johnston and Heinz's compromise position

- **Focused visual attention**
  Selecting and processing one visual image from among many.

  LaBerge's zoom-lens model
  Treisman's feature integration theory

- **Divided attention**
  How easy is it to perform two different tasks at the same time?

  Central capacity interference theory
  Bourke et al.'s four-task study
  Predictive testing

- **Automatic processing**
  Some tasks are practised so often that they become automatic, e.g. typing, or driving a car.

  The Stroop effect
  Shiffrin and Schneider's mapping studies
  Logan's instance theory

- **Action slips**
  When attention processes fail, people may do things they did not intend to do in an "absent-minded" way.

  Reason's diary study
  Hay and Jacoby's paired associates study
  Sellen and Norman's schema theory

12

Attention and Performance

How does divided attention affect work performance?

The term "attention" has been used in various ways. Sometimes it is used to mean concentration. However, it is most often used to refer to the ability to select part of the information available in the environment for further processing. This latter meaning was emphasised by William James (1890, pp.403–404):

> Everyone knows what attention is. It is the taking possession of the mind, in clear and vivid form, of one out of what seem several simultaneously possible objects or trains of thought. Focalisation, concentration, of consciousness are of its essence. It implies a withdrawal from some things in order to deal effectively with others.

There are links among attention, arousal, and alertness. Consider, for example, someone who is drowsily sitting in a comfortable chair. He or she is in a state of low arousal or alertness, and in this state will probably attend little to the environment. Attention is generally "voluntary" in the sense that we decide what to attend to. However, it can be "involuntary" when we are presented with a novel, surprising, or intense stimulus such as a car backfiring.

Eysenck and Keane (1995) argued that there is an important distinction between focused attention and divided attention. **Focused attention** is studied by presenting people with two or more stimulus inputs at the same time, and instructing them to respond to only one. Work on focused attention can tell us how well people can select certain inputs rather than others. It also allows us to study the nature of the selection process and the fate of unattended stimuli. Focused attention is involved when students taking examinations have to try to avoid being distracted by other students, noises outside the room, and so on.

Divided attention is studied by presenting two stimulus inputs at the same time, with the instructions indicating that all stimulus inputs should be attended to and responded to. Studies of divided attention (also known as dual-task studies) provide useful information about an individual's processing limitations. They may also tell us something about attentional mechanisms and their capacity. An everyday example of divided attention is when students do their homework while listening to music. Is it really possible to do both things at once?

We can also learn much about the workings of attention by studying **action slips**, which are actions that are not carried out as intended. Various factors can produce action slips, but the most important one is a failure to attend sufficiently to what we are doing.

My most serious action slip occurred when I was trying to copy 25,000 words from one storage place in my computer to another which had nothing in it. These two storage places were represented by very similar icons on the computer screen, and I managed to copy nothing into the storage place containing 25,000 words. As a result I was left with nothing in either storage place!

KEY TERMS
Focused attention: a situation in which participants try to attend to only one stimulus input and to ignore all others.
Divided attention: a situation in which participants try to perform two different tasks at the same time. Investigated using dual-task studies.
Action slips: actions that occur, but were not intended.

Many psychologists (and non-psychologists) assume that all the phenomena of attention depend on a single attentional system. This is most unlikely to be the case, as was pointed out by Allport (1993, pp.203–204): "There is no uniform function, or mental operation (in general, no one causal mechanism) to which all so-called attentional phenomena can be attributed ... It seems no more plausible that there should be one unique mechanism, or computational resource, as the causal basis of all attentional phenomena than that there should be a unitary causal basis of thought, or perception, or of any other traditional category of folk psychology."

What do you think Allport might have meant by "folk psychology"?

Some evidence for Allport's (1993) position comes from studies of brain-damaged patients having problems with attention. Many of them experience difficulties with respect to some attentional abilities, but not to others. Posner and Petersen (1990), for example, used such findings to argue that there are at least three separate visual attentional processes:

- The ability to disengage attention from a given visual stimulus.
- The ability to shift attention from one target stimulus to another.
- The ability to engage attention on a new visual stimulus.

KEY STUDY EVALUATION — Focused auditory attention

The research by Colin Cherry is a very good example of how a psychologist, noticing a real-life situation, is able to devise a hypothesis and carry out research in order to explain a phenomenon, in this case the "cocktail party" effect. Cherry tested his ideas in a laboratory using a shadowing technique and found that participants were really only able to give information about the physical qualities of the non-attended message (whether the message was read by a male or a female, or if a tone was used instead of speech). Cherry's research could be criticised for having moved the real-life phenomenon into an artificial laboratory setting. However, this work opened avenues for other researchers, beginning with Broadbent, to elaborate theories about focused auditory attention.

How do we distinguish and follow one conversation out of many in situations like this?

Focused Auditory Attention

Colin Cherry, when he was working in an electronics research laboratory at the Massachusetts Institute of Technology, became interested in the "cocktail party" problem. The problem is to explain how it is that we can follow just one conversation when several people are all talking at once. Cherry (1953) found that our ability to do this involves making use of physical differences between the various auditory messages to select the one of interest. These physical differences include differences in the sex of the speaker, in voice intensity, and in the location of the speaker. When Cherry presented two messages in the same voice to both ears at once (thereby removing these physical differences), the participants found it very hard to separate out the two messages purely on the basis of meaning.

Cherry also carried out studies using a **shadowing task**, in which one auditory message had to be shadowed (repeated back out loud) while a second auditory message was presented to the other ear. Very little information seemed to be obtained from the second or non-attended message. Listeners rarely noticed when that message was spoken in a foreign language or in reversed speech. In contrast, physical changes such as the insertion of a pure tone were usually detected, and listeners noticed the sex of the speaker and the intensity of sound. The conclusion that unattended auditory information receives almost no processing was supported by other evidence. For example, there is very little memory for words in the unattended message, even when they are presented 35 times each (Moray, 1959).

Discussion points

1. Are you surprised by any of Cherry's findings?
2. Why do you think that Broadbent (discussed next) found Cherry's findings of great interest?

Broadbent (1958) discussed findings from what is known as the **dichotic listening task**. What usually happens is that three digits are presented one after the other to one ear, while at the same time three different digits are presented to the other ear. After the digits have been presented, the participants try to recall them in whatever order they prefer. They show a clear preference for recalling the digits ear by ear rather than pair by pair. Thus, for example, if 496 were presented to one ear and 852 to the other ear, recall would be 496852 rather than 489562. It should be mentioned that there is no need to use digits with the dichotic listening task: all kinds of verbal stimuli can be used.

Broadbent's filter theory

Broadbent (1958) put forward the first detailed theory of attention. It was also one of the first information-processing theories. What characterises an information-processing theory? In essence, the information-processing approach is based on the following major assumptions:

- Information made available by the environment is processed by a series of processing systems (e.g. attention; perception; short-term memory).
- These processing systems transform the information in various systematic ways (e.g. we see 2 x 4 and we think 8).
- The aim of research is to specify the processes and structures (e.g. long-term memory) underlying cognitive performance.
- Information processing in people resembles that in computers.

Broadbent's (1958) filter theory used findings from the shadowing task and the dichotic listening task to propose a filter theory of attention. The key assumptions in this theory were as follows:

- Two stimuli or messages presented at the same time gain access in parallel (at the same time) to a **sensory buffer**, which contains information for a short period of time before it is attended to or disappears from the processing system.
- One of the inputs is then allowed through a filter on the basis of its physical characteristics, with the other input remaining in the buffer for later processing.
- This filter is needed to prevent overloading of the limited-capacity mechanism beyond the filter; this mechanism processes the input thoroughly.

If we can model attention processes on a computer, does this mean that humans process information in the same way as computers?

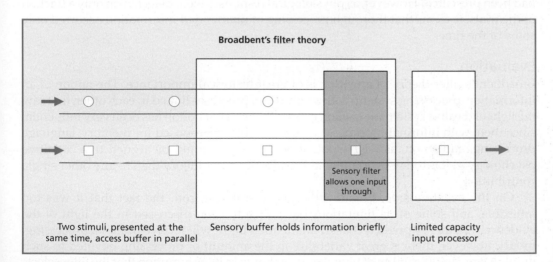

Broadbent's filter theory

Two stimuli, presented at the same time, access buffer in parallel | Sensory buffer holds information briefly | Limited capacity input processor

Sensory filter allows one input through

This theory handles Cherry's basic findings, with unattended messages being rejected by the filter and thus receiving very little processing. It also accounts for performance on Broadbent's original dichotic listening task, because it is assumed that the filter selects one input on the basis of the most obvious physical characteristics distinguishing the two inputs (i.e. the ear of arrival). However, it does not explain other findings. For example, it is assumed within filter theory that the unattended message is *always* rejected at an early stage of processing, but this assumption is wrong. The original shadowing studies involved participants with no previous experience of shadowing messages. As a result, they had to devote nearly all of their processing resources to the shadowing task. Underwood (1974) asked participants to detect digits presented in either the shadowed

Everyday applications

What application might work like Donald Broadbent's have in everyday life? Broadbent became interested in the mechanisms and problems of attention because of his experiences in the RAF during the Second World War, while trying to devise ways to enable radar and air-traffic controllers to work to maximum efficiency. Air-traffic controllers faced the difficult task of selecting and concentrating on one message from a pilot, against a background of many conflicting messages. The vital importance of effective attentional mechanisms in situations like this is only too obvious, even more so today as air traffic becomes ever heavier.

or the non-shadowed message. Participants who had not done the task before detected only 8% of the digits in the non-shadowed message. In contrast, an experienced researcher in the area was able to detect 67% of the non-shadowed digits.

The two messages were very similar (i.e. both auditorily presented verbal messages) in early studies on the shadowing task. Allport, Antonis, and Reynolds (1972) found that the degree of similarity between the two messages had a major impact on memory for the non-shadowed message. When shadowing of auditorily presented passages was combined with auditory presentation of words, memory for the words was very poor. However, when shadowing was combined with picture presentation, memory for the pictures was very good (90% correct). If two inputs differ clearly from each other, then they can both be processed more thoroughly than was allowed for on Broadbent's filter theory.

Broadbent (1958) assumed that there was no processing of the meaning of unattended messages, because the participants had no conscious awareness of their meaning. However, this leaves open the possibility that meaning might be processed without awareness. Von Wright, Anderson, and Stenman (1975) gave their participants two auditorily presented lists of words. They told the participants to shadow one list and to ignore the other one. When a word that had previously been associated with electric shock was presented on the non-attended list, there was sometimes a noticeable physiological response. There was the same effect when a word very similar in sound or meaning to the shocked word was presented. These findings suggest that information in the unattended message was processed in terms of both sound and meaning. The most striking finding was that these physiological reactions occurred even though the participants were not consciously aware that the previously shocked word or its associates had been presented. However, as physiological responses were detected on only a fraction of the trials, it seems that thorough processing of unattended information occurred only some of the time.

Evaluation

Broadbent's filter theory of attention is of great historical importance. The notion of an information-processing system, with a number of processes linked to each other, first saw the light of day in a systematic fashion in filter theory. That notion has been very influential since then, with information-processing systems being proposed for memory, language processing, and so on, as well as attention. Indeed, it could be argued that cognitive psychology as it is today owes more to Broadbent's filter theory than to any other single contribution.

On the negative side, Broadbent's theory suffered from the fact that it was too inflexible, and some of its limitations have already been discussed in the light of the evidence. The theory predicts that an unattended input will receive minimal processing. In fact, however, there is great variability in the amount of processing devoted to such input. A similar inflexibility of filter theory is shown in its assumption that the filter selects information on the basis of physical features of the input. This assumption is supported by the tendency of participants in the dichotic listening task to recall digits ear by ear. However, a small change in the basic task produces very different results. Gray and Wedderburn (1960) made use of a version of the dichotic listening task in which "who 6 there" might be presented to one ear at the same time as "4 goes 1" was presented to the other ear. The preferred order of report was not the usual ear by ear; instead, it was determined by meaning (e.g. " who goes there" followed by "4 6 1"). Thus, selection can occur either *before* or *after*

■ Research activity: Dichotic listening

You will need two personal stereos: one playing a tape (perhaps an audio book) featuring a man's voice and the other featuring a woman's voice. It should be possible to use the headsets to set up your own dichotic listening apparatus, in which one ear hears the male voice and the other the female voice at the same time. Try to "shadow" one of the voices, repeating what is said out loud. How much can you recall of the other voice? The procedure could be repeated with two male voices, or two female voices, or even using a foreign-language tape. How would you present your findings?

the processing of information from both inputs. The fact that selection can be based on the meaning of presented information is inconsistent with filter theory.

Alternative theories

Treisman's theory

Treisman (1964) proposed an attenuation theory of attention, in which the processing of unattended information is attenuated or reduced. In Broadbent's filter theory, it was proposed that there is a bottleneck early in processing. In Treisman's theory, the location of the bottleneck is more flexible. It is as if people possess a "leaky" filter which makes selective attention less efficient than was assumed by Broadbent (1958).

Let us consider Treisman's theory in a little more detail. Stimulus processing proceeds in a systematic fashion, starting with analyses based on physical cues, and then moving on to analyses based on meaning. If there is not enough processing capacity to allow full stimulus analysis, then some of the later analyses are left out of the processing of unattended stimuli. This theory neatly predicts Cherry's (1953) finding that it is usually the physical characteristics of unattended inputs (e.g. sex of the speaker) that are noticed rather than their meaning.

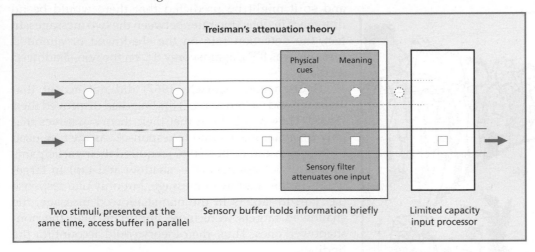

The extensive processing of unattended sources of information that was embarrassing for filter theory can be accounted for by Treisman's attenuation theory. However, the same findings were also explained by Deutsch and Deutsch (1963). They claimed that all stimuli are analysed fully, with the most important or relevant stimulus determining the response. This theory is like filter theory and attenuation theory in assuming the existence of a bottleneck in processing. However, it places the bottleneck closer to the response end of the processing system.

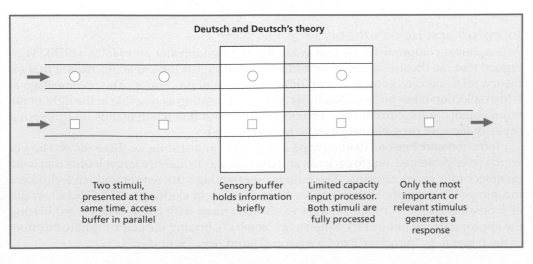

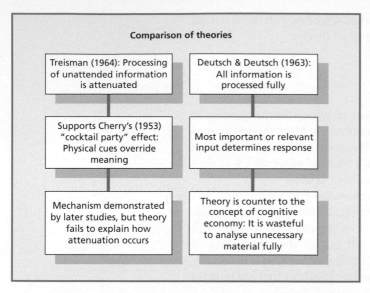

Comparison of theories

Treisman (1964): Processing of unattended information is attenuated

Deutsch & Deutsch (1963): All information is processed fully

Supports Cherry's (1953) "cocktail party" effect: Physical cues override meaning

Most important or relevant input determines response

Mechanism demonstrated by later studies, but theory fails to explain how attenuation occurs

Theory is counter to the concept of cognitive economy: It is wasteful to analyse unnecessary material fully

Only important input leads to responses...

It has proved very hard to decide conclusively between the theoretical positions of Treisman and of Deutsch and Deutsch. Treisman's theory seems more plausible in some ways. The assumption made by Deutsch and Deutsch that all stimuli are analysed completely, but that most of the analysed information is lost almost at once, seems rather wasteful. In fact, studies by Treisman and Geffen (1967) and by Treisman and Riley (1969) provided support for attenuation theory rather than the theory of Deutsch and Deutsch (1963).

In the study by Treisman and Geffen (1967), the participants shadowed one of two auditory messages, having been told to tap whenever they detected a target word in either message. According to attenuation theory, there should be reduced analysis of the non-shadowed message, and so fewer targets should be detected in that message than in the shadowed one. According to Deutsch and Deutsch, there is complete processing of all stimuli, and so it might be predicted that there would be no difference in detection rates between the two messages. In fact, the detection rate on the shadowed or attended message was 87%, against only 8% on the non-shadowed message.

Deutsch and Deutsch (1967) did not accept that Treisman and Geffen's (1967) findings had disproved their theory. They pointed out that their theory assumes that only *important* inputs lead to responses. As the task used by Treisman and Geffen (1967) required their participants to make two responses (i.e. shadow and tap) to target words in the shadowed message, but only one response (i.e. tap) to targets in the non-shadowed message, the shadowed targets were more important than the non-shadowed ones. Thus, their theory could account for the findings.

Treisman and Riley (1969) retaliated by carrying out a study in which exactly the same response was made to targets in either message. Their participants were told to stop shadowing and to tap whenever they detected a target in either message. Many more target words were detected in the shadowed message than on the non-shadowed one, a finding that is hard to explain using the theory of Deutsch and Deutsch.

Johnston and Heinz's theory

A reasonable compromise position was adopted by Johnston and Heinz (1978). They argued that the theories we have considered so far are too inflexible. According to their theory, selection can occur at several different stages of processing. The precise stage at which selection takes place is usually as early in processing as possible in the light of the requirements of the current task. The reason for this is that the demands on processing capacity increase progressively as selection is delayed.

Johnston and Wilson (1980) carried out a study to test some of these ideas. Pairs of words were presented, one to each ear, and the task was to identify target words that were members of a given category. The targets were ambiguous words with two different meanings. For example, if the category were "articles of clothing", then "socks" would be a possible target word. Each target word was paired with a non-target word biasing the appropriate meaning of the target (e.g. "smelly"), biasing the inappropriate meaning of the target (e.g. "punches"), or by a neutral word (e.g. "Saturday").

When the participants did not know which ear the targets would arrive at (divided attention), target detection was improved by appropriate non-targets and impaired by inappropriate non-targets. Thus, when attention had to be divided between the two ears, the non-targets were processed for meaning. In contrast, when the participants knew that all the targets would be presented to the left ear (focused attention), target detection was unaffected by the appropriateness or otherwise of the non-target word presented at the same time. This suggests that non-targets were not processed for meaning in the focused attention condition. These various findings indicate that the amount of processing received by non-target stimuli is no more than is necessary to perform the main task.

Focused Visual Attention

One of the most common ways of thinking about focused visual attention is by comparing it to a spotlight. In both cases, everything within a relatively small area can be seen clearly, whereas anything lying outside the spotlight's beam is harder or impossible to see. Various refinements on this basic idea have been suggested. According to Broadbent (1982, p.69), we should

> *think of selectivity as like a searchlight, with the option of altering the focus. When something seems to be happening ... the beam sharpens and moves to the point of maximum importance.*

In similar fashion, Eriksen (1990) developed a **zoom-lens model**. He argued that attention is generally widely distributed, but it can zoom in on certain parts of the visual field if it is necessary to obtain maximum information from them.

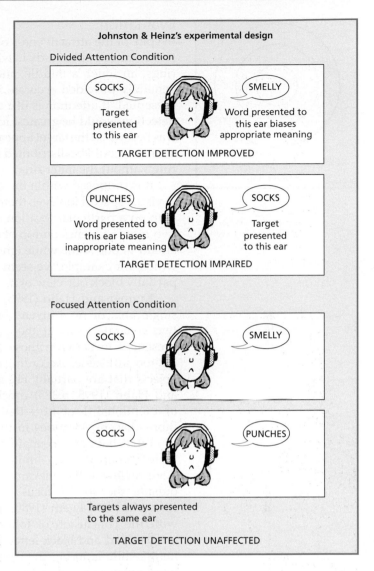

Johnston & Heinz's experimental design

The zoom-lens model

The notion of an adjustable attentional beam was investigated by LaBerge (1983). The participants were presented with five-letter words, and they had to perform one of two tasks. One task required them to focus on the entire word, because they had to decide the category to which the word belonged. The other task only required the participants to focus on the middle letter, because they were asked to categorise that letter.

In order to decide *where* the participants were attending, LaBerge sometimes presented a probe stimulus requiring a rapid response in the spatial position of one of the five letters of the word, immediately after the word had been presented. He assumed that the probe would be responded to more quickly when it fell within the central attentional beam than when it did not. When the participants had been asked to categorise the middle letter, the reaction time to the probe was significantly faster when it was presented in the spatial position of the middle letter than when it was presented anywhere else. This suggests that the attentional beam was very narrow in that condition. In contrast, the speed of response to the probe was influenced very little by its spatial position when the task involved categorising the word. This suggests that the attentional beam was very broad in that condition. Overall, the findings indicate that the attentional spotlight is of flexible width depending on the precise requirements of the task.

Since LaBerge's study was carried out in a laboratory setting with little resemblance to real-life situations, does it have ecological validity?

Discussion points

1. Does LaBerge provide convincing evidence that attention is like a zoom lens?
2. What are the limitations of LaBerge's approach (see Evaluation)?

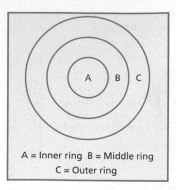

A = Inner ring   B = Middle ring
C = Outer ring

Evaluation

In spite of the attractiveness of the zoom-lens model, it has some limitations. Juola et al. (1991) carried out a study in which a target letter was presented in one of three concentric rings: an inner, a middle, and an outer ring. The participants were given a cue that generally provided accurate information as to the ring in which the target would be presented. If attention is like an adjustable spotlight, then speed and accuracy of target detection would be greatest for targets presented in the inner ring. In fact, performance was best when the target appeared in the ring that had been cued. This suggests that visual attention could be distributed in an O-shaped pattern to include only the outer or middle ring without the inner ring.

It is proposed within the zoom-lens model that the focus of attention is a given *area* in visual space. However, there is evidence indicating that we often focus on *objects* rather than on a particular location. For example, Neisser and Becklen (1975) placed films of two moving scenes on top of each other. They found that the participants could easily attend to one scene while ignoring the other one. This corresponds to everyday life, in which, for example, we seem able to attend to a building while ignoring the trees that partially block our view of it.

Kramer and Hahn (1995) argued that attention does not have to be focused on a single area or on a given object. They found that their participants could attend to two separate areas at the same time, while ignoring distracting stimuli that were presented in between those two areas. They argued that the zoom-lens model was far too inflexible. According to them, attention can be focused on a single area, on objects that are partially obscured by other stimuli, or on two separate areas. Kramer and Hahn (1995, p.385) concluded that their findings "suggest a remarkable degree of attentional flexibility—that is, the ability to divide attention among noncontiguous [non-adjacent] locations in the visual field."

What happens to unattended visual stimuli? According to the zoom-lens model, there should be very limited processing of such stimuli. Johnston and Dark (1986, p.56) reviewed the relevant evidence, and came to the following conclusion: "Stimuli outside the spatial focus of attention undergo little or no semantic processing." Francolini and Egeth (1980) were among those reporting findings that are consistent with the conclusion of Johnston and Dark. They gave their participants a circular array of red and black letters or numerals, and told them to count the number of red items while ignoring the black items. Performance speed was reduced when the red items consisted of numerals conflicting with the answer, but there was no interference effect from the black items. These findings suggested that there was little or no processing of the to-be-ignored black items.

Francolini and Egeth made the apparently reasonable assumption that a lack of interference from the to-be-ignored stimuli showed that they were not processed. This assumption is incorrect. Driver and Tipper (1989) carried out a similar study to that of Francolini and Egeth (1980). However, they used more sensitive measures, and found that the meaning of to-be-ignored stimuli was processed.

In sum, the meaning of unattended visual stimuli is processed at least some of the time. There may be less extensive processing of unattended than of attended stimuli, but unattended stimuli do typically receive some processing.

Visual search

Progress in understanding some of the underlying processes involved in focused visual attention has come

Is attention focused on the object or the location?

from studies of **visual search**. In visual search tasks, the participants are presented with a visual display containing several different stimuli, and have to decide as rapidly as possible whether a target stimulus (e.g. number 4) is present. An example from everyday life might be looking at a school photograph and trying to find yourself. Even if there are dozens of people in the photograph, it usually takes very little time to find your image.

Classic research on visual search was reported by Neisser (1964). He presented his participants with lists of letters, and asked them to detect the letter "Z". Performance was faster when the distractor letters contained rounded features (e.g. S, B, P, O, etc.) than when they consisted of straight lines (e.g. E, H, T, L, etc.), presumably because the distractors shared fewer features with the target letter Z in the former condition (see Chapter 11). There was a great increase in speed with practice, suggesting that target detection was becoming automatic.

Feature integration theory

Treisman (1988) put forward a *feature integration theory* to account for the findings from visual search studies. The theory involves a distinction between objects and features of objects (e.g. colour, size, outlines). Some of the key aspects of this theory are as follows:

Picking out one unfamiliar face from all these children might take some time, but how quickly would you locate your own face if you were in the picture?

- The visual features of objects in the environment are processed rapidly in parallel (i.e. all at the same time) without attention being required; this is the first stage of processing.
- The features are then combined to form objects (e.g. a red chair; a purple flower) by means of a slow, serial (i.e. one after another) process; this is the second stage of processing.
- Focused attention on the location of an object provides the "glue" which permits objects to be formed from combined features.
- Features can also be combined on the basis of stored knowledge (e.g. "strawberries are red").
- In the absence of focused attention or relevant stored knowledge, features will be combined in a random fashion; this can produce odd combinations of features known as *illusory conjunctions*.

Treisman and Gelade (1980) reported findings that are relevant to the predictions of feature integration theory. If the target stimulus in a visual search task is defined in terms of a single feature (e.g. something blue), then only the first stage of processing should be needed. As the first stage of processing occurs in parallel, the speed of detection should hardly be affected by the number of items in the display. The findings should be very different, however, if the target is an object defined by a *combination* of features (e.g. a green letter T); these are conjunctive targets. In this case, the second stage of processing and focused attention would be involved. As focused attention operates in a serial fashion, detection speed should be much slower when there are several items in the visual display than when there are few. The findings in positive trials (i.e. when the target was present) were precisely as predicted. The findings in negative trials (i.e. when the target was absent) are of less relevance.

According to feature integration theory, there should be illusory conjunctions or incorrect combinations of features when attention is not focused on the critical part of a

How and when could you relate feature integration theory to your everyday experience of life?

> **KEY TERM**
> **Visual search**: a task in which a visual target or targets must be located as quickly as possible from among distractors.

visual display. However, illusory conjunctions should not occur when stimuli receive focal attention. Precisely this pattern of results was reported by Treisman and Schmidt (1982).

In spite of the successes of feature integration theory, it does not provide a full account. Treisman and Sato (1990) proposed a modification of the basic theory. They argued that the degree of similarity between the target and the distractors is a factor influencing visual search time. They claimed (with supporting evidence) that visual search for a target defined by more than one feature is usually limited to those distractors having at least one of the features of the target. For example, if you were looking for a green circle in a display containing green triangles, black circles, and black triangles, then you would ignore black triangles. This contrasts with the views of Treisman and Gelade (1980), who argued that none of the stimuli would be ignored in such circumstances.

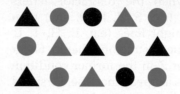

Divided Attention

As was indicated earlier in the chapter, divided attention or dual-task studies involve the participants trying to perform two tasks at the same time as well as possible. It is of importance in such studies to find out how successfully the two tasks can be performed together. Everyday experience indicates that some tasks can be combined successfully, such as when an experienced motorist drives a car and holds a conversation at the same time. In other cases, however, dual-task performance is often poor. For example, when someone tries to rub their stomach with one hand while patting their head with the other, there can be a complete disruption of performance. These anecdotal examples indicate the need to consider in detail the factors determining how well two tasks can be performed together.

Task similarity

When we think of pairs of activities that can be performed well together, we tend to think of examples in which the two activities are dissimilar (e.g. driving and talking; reading and listening to music). There is much evidence indicating the importance of task similarity. A relevant study by Allport et al. (1972) was discussed earlier in the chapter. They found that participants repeating back prose passages while learning auditorily presented words had poor long-term memory for the words, but they were able to repeat back prose passages and remember pictures presented at the same time.

There are various ways in which two tasks can be similar or dissimilar. Wickens (1984) reviewed the evidence on dual-task performance. He came to the conclusion that two tasks interfere with each other if they make use of the same stimulus modality (e.g. visual or auditory), if they make use of the same stages of processing (e.g. input, internal processing, and output), or if they rely on related memory codes (e.g. verbal or visual).

Response similarity is also important. McLeod (1977) asked his participants to do a tracking task with manual responding at the same time as carrying out a tone-identification task. Some participants had to respond vocally to the tones, whereas others responded with the hand not involved in the tracking task. Performance on the tracking task was worse when there was high response similarity (manual responses on both tasks) than when there was low response similarity (manual responses on one task and vocal ones on the other).

■ Research activity: Doing two things at once

The physical task of rubbing your stomach with one hand while patting the top of your head with the other has been used for amusement by children for generations. However, being able to do this well has been suggested as a good indicator of suitability for training as a helicopter pilot, where it is essential to be able to carry out different tasks with each hand! List everyday examples where people are required to do two tasks at the same time. Now consider whether you can actually write an essay while listening to music. Would there be any difference if you listened to a talk radio station? If you feel there would be a difference, can you explain this?

Practice

Common sense indicates that the old saying "Practice makes perfect" is very relevant to dual-task performance. For example, learner drivers find it almost impossible to drive and to hold a conversation at the same time, but expert drivers find it easy. Support for this common-sense position was obtained by Spelke, Hirst, and Neisser (1976) in a study on two students called Diane and John. These students had two hours' training a week for four months on various tasks. Their first task was to read short stories for comprehension at the same time as they wrote down words to dictation. At first, they found it very hard to do these two tasks together. After six weeks of training, however, they were able to read as rapidly and with as much comprehension when taking dictation as when only reading. In addition, the quality of their handwriting had also improved.

Spelke et al. found that Diane and John could recall only 35 out of the thousands of words they had written down at dictation. Even when 20 successive dictated words formed a sentence or came from the same semantic category (e.g. four-footed animals), the two students were unaware of it. Spelke et al. gave them further training. As a result, they learned to write down the names of the categories to which the dictated words belonged while maintaining normal reading speed and comprehension.

When two complex tasks are performed well together, it is usually found that the skills involved have been highly practised. For example, expert pianists can play from seen music while repeating back or shadowing heard speech (Allport et al., 1972), and an expert typist can type and shadow at the same time (Shaffer, 1975). Such levels of performance are impressive. However, it should be noted that some signs of interference are present in the data from these experts (Broadbent, 1982).

The effects of practice: pianist and entertainer Liberace combined chatting to an audience with playing the piano for many years in his stage and television shows.

Task difficulty

It is harder to perform two tasks together when they are difficult or complex than when they are simple. For example, Sullivan (1976) gave her participants the task of shadowing an auditory message and detecting target words on another auditory message at the same time. When the shadowing task was made harder by using a more complex message, fewer targets were detected on the other message.

There are two problems with research on the effects of task difficulty on dual-task performance. One problem is that there are several ways in which one task can be harder than another one. As a result, it is not easy to assess task difficulty with any precision. The other problem is that a task that is hard for one person may be very easy for another. An expert word processor finds typing very easy and undemanding, whereas someone who is just learning to type finds it very hard.

Think back over your own life. Which tasks that you once found extremely hard have now become easy and "overlearned"?

Theoretical accounts

We have seen that the extent to which two tasks can be performed successfully together depends on various factors. As a rule of thumb, two dissimilar, highly practised, and simple tasks can typically be performed well together, whereas two similar, novel, and complex tasks cannot. In addition, having to perform two tasks together rather than separately often produces entirely new problems of co-ordination. For example, moving your forefinger in front of you in a circular fashion is very easy. It is also very easy to move both forefingers around in a circular fashion if they both move in the same direction (i.e. both clockwise or anti-clockwise).

However, it is harder to move one forefinger clockwise around an imaginary circle while the other forefinger moves anti-clockwise, because the two tasks interfere with each other and resist coordination (see Duncan, 1979).

Central capacity interference theory

The simplest theoretical explanation of dual-task performance is the *central capacity interference theory*, which has been favoured by Norman and Bobrow (1975) and by other theorists. There are two crucial assumptions made by this theory:

* There is some central capacity (attention or effort), which has limited resources.
* The ability to perform two tasks together depends on the demands placed on those resources by the two tasks.

It follows that dual-task performance will be poor if the two tasks require more resources than are available. However, the two tasks will be performed successfully if their combined demands for resources are less than the total resources of the central capacity.

Four-task study

Bourke, Duncan, and Nimmo-Smith (1996) provided some of the most convincing evidence for the notion that there is a general capacity that plays a part in determining how well two tasks can be performed together. First of all, they selected four tasks that were designed to be as different as possible from each other:

1. Random generation: the participants were told to try to generate letters at random so they did not form words.
2. Prototype learning: the participants had to work out the features of two patterns or prototypes from seeing various exemplars.
3. Manual task: the participants were told to screw a nut down to the bottom of a bolt and back up to the top, and then down to the bottom of a second bolt and back up, and so on.
4. Tone task: the participants had to detect the occurrence of a given "target" tone.

The participants were given two of these tasks to perform at a time, and were told that one task was of more importance than the other. The basic argument was as follows: if there is a central or general capacity, then the task making most demands on this capacity will interfere most with all three of the other tasks. In contrast, the task making fewest demands on this capacity will interfere least with all three of the other tasks.

What did Bourke et al. find? First, they found that these very different tasks did interfere with each other. Second, they discovered that the random generation task interfered the most overall with the performance of the other tasks, and the tone task interfered the least. Third, and of greatest importance, the random generation task consistently interfered most with the prototype, manual, and tone tasks, and it did so whether it was the primary or the secondary task. The tone task consistently interfered least with each of the other three tasks. In other words, the findings were very much in line with the predictions of a general capacity theory.

The main limitation of the study by Bourke et al. is that they did not shed light on the nature of the central capacity. As they admitted (1996, p.544), "The general factor may be a limited pool of processing resource that needs to be invested for a task to be performed. It may be a limited central executive that coordinates or monitors other processes and is limited in how much it can deal with at one time ... The method developed here deals only with the existence of a general factor in dual-task decrements, not its nature."

KEY STUDY EVALUATION — Bourke et al.

As we have seen, the four tasks used by Bourke et al. are very different from each other. If performance depended only on very specific processes, then there would presumably have been little or no interference between tasks. The fact that there was considerable interference is strong evidence for a general central processing capacity. It may have occurred to you that participants with special expertise might have found it easier to combine some of the tasks, for example, a mechanic might be very good at handling nuts and bolts. However, the participants were recent university students, and lacked special expertise for any of the tasks.

Discussion points

1. Is it surprising that these very different tasks interfered with each other?
2. Why do you think that the random generation task interfered the most with other tasks, whereas the tone task interfered the least?

Task difficulty and practice. How does the central capacity interference theory account for the main findings from studies of dual-task performance? The fact that task difficulty is an important factor poses no problem for the theory, because task difficulty is defined simply as the demands placed by the task on the resources of the central capacity. The finding that two demanding tasks (e.g. reading for comprehension and writing at dictation) can sometimes be performed successfully together (e.g. Spelke et al., 1976) seems contrary to the spirit of the central capacity theory. However, complex tasks can usually only be performed well together after a substantial amount of practice, and the demands on central resources may be reduced through practice. As is discussed in the next section, prolonged practice can lead to some processes becoming automatic and thus not requiring central resources.

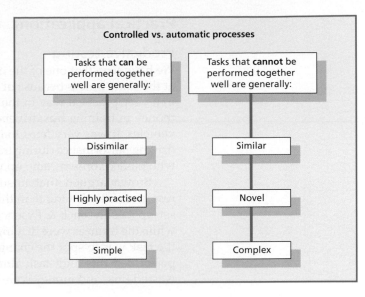

Task similarity. The central capacity interference theory can account for the effects of task difficulty and practice. However, it cannot handle some of the effects of task similarity. This can be seen if we consider a study by Segal and Fusella (1970). Their participants had to detect a weak visual or auditory signal while maintaining a visual or an auditory image. As there were two signal-detection tasks and two imagery tasks, there were four possible combinations of tasks.

Performance on the auditory signal task was better when it was combined with the visual imagery task than when it was combined with the auditory imagery task. According to central capacity theorists, this means that the visual imagery task is easier and less demanding of resources than the auditory imagery task. However, inspection of the findings for the visual signal task points to the opposite conclusion. Here performance was better when the visual signal task was combined with the auditory imagery task, suggesting that the auditory imagery task requires fewer resources than the visual imagery task.

Theory of specific mechanisms
Allport (1989) argued that there are various specific processing mechanisms, each of which has limited capacity. This allows us to make sense of the fact that the degree of similarity between two tasks helps to determine how well they can be performed together. Similar tasks typically compete for the same specific processing mechanisms, and this competition disrupts performance. In contrast, dissimilar tasks tend to use different mechanisms, and so are much less likely to interfere with each other.

Allport's general approach can be illustrated by considering someone who is trying to drive a car and to hold a conversation at the same time. Car driving involves a number of specific skills involving visual perception and motor responses, whereas holding a conversation involves language skills and retrieving information stored in long-term memory about the topic of conversation. It is because such different skills are involved that people are able to drive and to talk at the same time.

Combined theory
Eysenck (1984) argued that a theory combining aspects of central capacity interference theory and the theory of specific mechanisms may be more adequate than either theory on its own. According to this view, the effects of task difficulty on dual-task performance are due largely to attention or the central processor, whereas the effects of similarity are due to specific processing resources. The effects of practice occur because tasks that initially require much use of attention or the central processor no longer do so after much practice.

Practical applications

Predictive testing

We have seen that one of the main reasons why people find it hard to perform two tasks at the same time is because of limited resources. This notion was applied by Ivor Brown in a very practical way in the 1960s. A bus company in England was spending a lot of money in training bus drivers, many of whom failed the driving test for public service vehicles. It was very hard to identify those who were going to fail on the basis of their driving performance during training, because it did not differ noticeably from that of those who passed. Brown came up with an ingenious solution.

Brown argued that unsuccessful trainees were having to put more attentional resources into driving than the successful ones. He tested this idea by using a dual-task set-up (see Eysenck & Eysenck, 1981). A set of eight digits was read every few seconds while the trainees were driving. Each set differed in one digit from the preceding set, and the task was to spot the changed digit. Those trainees who later passed the driving test performed this digit task almost twice as well as those who failed. As a result, much wasted time and money were saved.

Effects of anxiety

Ethical issues: What ethical considerations are involved in studies like the one by Weltman et al. (1971)?

When people are working in a potentially dangerous environment, they become more anxious. What are the effects of anxiety on our ability to carry out two tasks at the same time? You might imagine that anxiety would impair performance on both tasks, but what actually happens is more complex. Weltman, Smith, and Egstrom (1971) made their participants anxious by fooling them into believing that the diving chamber they were in had descended to a depth of 60 feet (18 metres). They were given the main task of detecting small gaps in rings and the subsidiary task of detecting a light when it came on. Anxiety had no effect on performance of the main task, but impaired performance on the subsidiary task. This can best be explained by assuming that the adverse effects of anxiety can be compensated for to some extent by putting most of the available attentional resources into the main task at the expense of the subsidiary one. This may explain why pilots in an emergency situation sometimes ignore vital information that is not normally needed in order to fly safely.

Learning attention management

Gopher (1993) argued that attention management in dual-task situations is a skill that can be learned. He tested this argument using a computer game called *Space Fortress*. This involves controlling the movements of a space ship, firing missiles to destroy a fortress, and avoiding being destroyed. Some Israeli air force cadets were given attentional training on the game, focusing on one task component at a time (e.g. firing missiles). These cadets were twice as likely as other cadets to become qualified pilots within 18 months. This happened in spite of the fact that real flying is much more demanding than *Space Fortress*. What the cadets trained on the game had learned was how to control their attention effectively.

Training in attention management (also known as Nintendo Zelda).

Automatic Processing

As was pointed out earlier, practice often has a dramatic effect on performance. It has often been assumed that this occurs because some processing activities become automatic as a result of prolonged practice. Some of the main criteria for **automatic processes** are as follows:

- They are fast.
- They make no demands on attention.
- They are not available to consciousness.
- They are unavoidable, in the sense that they always occur when an appropriate stimulus is presented.

KEY TERM
Automatic processes: processes that typically occur rapidly, do not require attention, and for which there is no conscious awareness.

It has proved hard to find many processes satisfying all of these criteria. For example, the requirement that automatic processes make no demands on attention means that they should have no effect at all on the performance of any attention-demanding task being carried out at the same time. In fact, this is rarely the case (see Hampson, 1989, for a review).

The Stroop effect

Problems with the unavoidability criterion were identified by Kahneman and Henik (1979). They studied the Stroop effect, in which the naming of colours in which words are printed is slowed down by using colour words (e.g. the word BLACK printed in green). This Stroop effect has often been regarded as involving unavoidable and automatic processing of the colour words. Thus, when you see the word BLACK printed in green, it is hard to inhibit the tendency to say "black" even though you have been instructed to name the ink colours. However, Kahneman and Henik found that the Stroop effect was much larger when the distracting information (i.e. the colour name) was in the same location as the to-be-named colour rather than in an adjacent location. Thus, the processes producing the Stroop effect are not always totally unavoidable.

BLACK	**GREEN**	**BLACK**
GREEN	**GREEN**	**BLACK**
BLACK	**GREEN**	**GREEN**
GREEN	**BLACK**	**BLACK**

> ■ Research activity: The Stroop effect
>
> To carry out the Stroop task you will need two sheets of paper, four coloured pens (red, green, yellow, blue) and a stopwatch.
>
> On one sheet of paper, write the colour names red, green, yellow, blue in random order, a total of five times each. However, each colour name must be written in a different colour, e.g. the word "red" written in green ink.
>
> On the other sheet of paper, construct a second list that looks the same as the first one, but where the words are not colour names but other words that occur with the same frequency, e.g. boat, clock, etc.
>
> The experiment will be a repeated measures design, so you need to counterbalance the list presentation (Participant 1 receives List 1 then List 2: Participant 2 receives List 2 then List 1, and so on). The instructions you devise should ask your participants to say the names of the ink colour in each list as rapidly as possible without making any errors. Any errors that are made should be corrected.
>
> Record the times taken and decide how to present your results. Do they concur with those of Kahneman and Henik?

Skill acquisition

Some of the clearest evidence for automatic processes comes from studies of skill acquisition. Consider, for example, the development of touch-typing skills. As Fitts and Posner (1967) pointed out, there seem to be three stages involved. First, there is the cognitive stage, during which typists rely on rules of which they are consciously aware (e.g. move the index finger of the left hand to the right to type the letter g). Second, there is the associative stage, in which typing errors are gradually detected and eliminated. Third, there is the autonomous stage, in which typing becomes fast, accurate, and automatic.

The evidence shows very clearly that typing speed increases greatly with practice, so that a fairly skilled typist can make one keystroke every 60 milliseconds (Fitts & Posner, 1967). However, what is crucial is that the *nature* as well as the *speed* of the processes involved changes with training. This is most obvious in the autonomous stage, because most typists in that stage type with very little conscious involvement and can no longer verbalise the rules they used to rely on. This is certainly true in my case. I have typed about three million words in my life, but find it very hard to tell anyone where any given letter is on the keyboard!

Additional evidence that skilled typing largely relies on automatic processes was reported by Shaffer (1975). He found that skilled typists could shadow or repeat back what was said to them with very little effect on their typing performance. He also found that skilled typists could engage in a conversation while typing without it causing much impairment of typing speed or accuracy.

Skilled touch typists can hold a conversation and attend to other stimuli with very little effect on their typing speed or accuracy.

Controlled vs. automatic processes

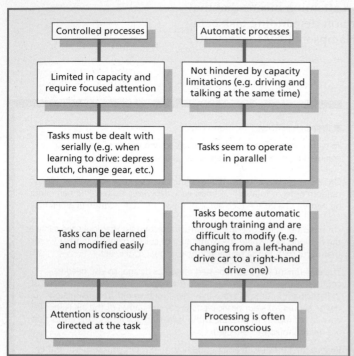

Controlled processes	Automatic processes
Limited in capacity and require focused attention	Not hindered by capacity limitations (e.g. driving and talking at the same time)
Tasks must be dealt with serially (e.g. when learning to drive: depress clutch, change gear, etc.)	Tasks seem to operate in parallel
Tasks can be learned and modified easily	Tasks become automatic through training and are difficult to modify (e.g. changing from a left-hand drive car to a right-hand drive one)
Attention is consciously directed at the task	Processing is often unconscious

Shiffrin and Schneider (1977) and Schneider and Shiffrin (1977) put forward a theory based on the distinction between controlled and automatic processes. According to their theory, controlled processes are of limited capacity, require attention, and can be used flexibly in changing circumstances. Automatic processes suffer no capacity limitations, do not require attention, and are very hard to modify once they have been learned.

Schneider and Shiffrin (1977) tested these ideas in a series of studies. Their basic situation was one in which the participants memorised one, two, three, or four items (consonants or numbers); this was called the memory set. They were then shown a visual display containing one, two, three, or four items (consonants or numbers). Finally, they had to decide rapidly whether there was any item that was present in both the memory set and the visual display.

Of crucial importance was the distinction between *consistent mapping* and *varied mapping*. With consistent mapping, only consonants were used as members of the memory set, and only numbers were used as distractors in the visual display (or vice versa). Consider someone who was given only numbers as members of each memory set. If a number was seen in the visual display, it had to be a member of the current memory set. According to Schneider and Shiffrin (1977), the participants' years of practice at distinguishing between letters and numbers allowed them to perform the consistent-mapping task in an automatic fashion. With varied mapping, the memory set consisted of a mixture of consonants and numbers, and so did the visual display. In this condition, it is not possible to use automatic processes.

In order to clarify this key difference between consistent mapping and varied mapping, we will consider a few examples of each:

Consistent mapping

Memory set	Visual display	Response
H B K D	4 3 B 7	Yes
H B K D	9 2 5 3	No
5 2 7 3	J 5 D C	Yes
5 2 7 3	B J G H	No

Varied mapping

Memory set	Visual display	Response
H 4 B 3	5 C G B	Yes
H 4 B 3	2 J 7 C	No
5 8 F 2	G 5 B J	Yes
5 8 F 2	6 D 1 C	No

There was a large difference in performance between the consistent and varied mapping conditions. The number of items in the memory set and the visual display had very little effect on decision time with consistent mapping, but had a large effect with varied mapping. According to Schneider and Shiffrin (1977), performance in the consistent-mapping condition reflects the use of automatic processes operating in parallel. On the other hand, performance in the varied mapping condition reflects the use of attentionally demanding controlled processes operating in a serial fashion. The more items that have to be considered, the slower the decision time.

The notion that automatic processes develop as the result of prolonged practice was studied by Shiffrin and Schneider (1977). They used consistent mapping, with the memory set items always being drawn from the consonants B to L, and the distractors in the visual display always being drawn from the consonants Q to Z, or vice versa. There were 2100 trials, and the dramatic improvement in performance over these trials presumably reflected the development of automatic processes.

After automatic processes had developed, there were a further 2400 trials with the reverse consistent mapping. Thus, for example, if the memory set items had been drawn from the first half of the alphabet during the initial 2100 trials, they were taken from the second half of the alphabet during the subsequent 2400 trials. Reversing the consistent mapping greatly impaired performance. The impairment was so great that it took almost 1000 trials for performance to recover to its level at the very start of the experiment. These findings indicate that it is hard to abandon automatic processes that have outlived their usefulness.

What are the relative advantages and disadvantages of automatic and controlled processes? The greatest advantages of automatic over attentional processes are that they operate much more rapidly, and that many automatic processes can take place at the same time. However, automatic processes are at a disadvantage when there is a change in the environment or in the prevailing conditions, because they lack the adaptability and flexibility of controlled processes. The fact that we possess both automatic and controlled processes allows us to respond rapidly and appropriately to most situations.

> **KEY STUDY EVALUATION — Schneider and Shiffrin**
>
> Schneider and Shiffrin's work on controlled and automatic processing is another good example of a theory being tested and supported by the use of experiments. Interestingly, some advertising has made use of similar combinations of letters and numbers to good effect, for example the film "SE7EN" (Seven), which demonstrates how difficult it can be to override the automatic process of reading. The research by Schneider and Shiffrin supplies confirmation of what may seem obvious, that some processes become automatic with time, but it does not specify how or what is actually occurring.

Discussion points

1. How useful is this research by Shiffrin and Schneider (see next for some pointers)?
2. Think of some examples of automatic and controlled processes in your everyday life.

Evaluation

The work of Shiffrin and Schneider (1977) and of Schneider and Shiffrin (1977) is important at the theoretical and experimental levels. Theoretically, they drew a clear distinction between automatic and controlled processes, and this distinction has proved very influential. Experimentally, they provided reasonably convincing evidence that the speed of performance can be much affected by whether it is based on automatic or controlled processes.

On the negative side, there is a puzzling discrepancy between theory and data with respect to the identification of automaticity. The theoretical assumption that automatic processes operate in parallel and place no demands on capacity means there should be a slope of zero (i.e. a horizontal line) in the graph relating decision speed to the number of items in the memory set and/or in the visual display when automatic processes are operating. In fact, decision speed was slower when the memory set and the visual display both contained several items.

The greatest weakness of Shiffrin and Schneider's theoretical approach is that it describes rather than explains. The claim that some processes become automatic with practice does not tell us much about what is actually happening. Practice may simply lead to a speeding up of the processes involved in performing a task, or it may lead to a change in the nature of the processes themselves. Cheng (1985) argued that participants in the consistent mapping conditions did not search through the memory set and visual display looking for a match. If, for example, they knew that any consonant in the visual display had to be an item from the memory set, then they simply scanned the visual display looking for a consonant without any regard to which consonants were actually in the memory set. Cheng was probably right, but we cannot tell for sure on the basis of the data provided by Shiffrin and Schneider.

Look back at the examples of consistent and varied mapping given earlier. Do you think Cheng's argument is correct?

Instance theory

We have seen that Shiffrin and Schneider (1977) did not really explain *how* automatic processes develop through practice. Logan (1988) put forward an instance theory that was designed to fill this gap. This theory was based on five main assumptions:

1. Separate memory traces are stored away each time a stimulus is presented and processed.
2. Practice with the same stimulus leads to the storage of increased information about the stimulus, and about what to do with it.
3. This increase in the knowledge base with practice permits rapid retrieval of relevant information when the appropriate stimulus is presented.

4. "Automaticity is memory retrieval: performance is automatic when it is based on a single-step direct-access retrieval of past solutions from memory" (Logan, 1988, p.493).
5. In the absence of practice, responding to a stimulus requires thought and the application of rules; after prolonged practice, the appropriate response is stored in memory and can be accessed very rapidly.

This theoretical approach provides a useful account of many aspects of automatic processing. Automatic processes are fast because they require only the retrieval of "past solutions" from long-term memory. Such processes have little or no effect on the processing capacity available to perform other tasks, because the retrieval of heavily over-learned information is fairly effortless. Finally, there is no conscious awareness of automatic processes because few processes intervene between the presentation of a stimulus and the retrieval of the appropriate response.

Action Slips

Action slips involve the performance of actions that were not intended. At the most general level, action slips usually result from failures of attention. This is recognised at a common-sense level in the notion of "absent-mindedness". Before discussing theoretical accounts of action slips, however, we will describe some of the main categories. See whether your own action slips seem to fit these categories.

Diary studies

One way of studying action slips is to collect hundreds of examples by means of a diary study. Reason (1979) asked 35 people to keep diaries of their action slips over a two-week period. Over 400 action slips were reported, most of which belonged to five major categories.

In the study, 40% of the slips involved *storage failures*, in which intentions and actions were either forgotten or recalled incorrectly. Here is one of Reason's examples of a storage failure (1979, p.74): "I started to pour a second kettle of boiling water into a teapot of freshly made tea. I had no recollection of having just made it."

A further 20% of the errors were *test failures*, in which the progress of a planned sequence was not monitored adequately at crucial junctures or choice points. Here is an example (Reason, 1979, p.73): "I meant to get my car out, but as I passed through the back porch on my way to the garage I stopped to put on my Wellington boots and gardening jacket as if to work in the garden."

Subroutine failures accounted for another 18% of the errors; these involved insertions, omissions, or re-orderings of the various stages in an action sequence. Reason (1979, p.73) gave this example: "I sat down to do some work and before starting to write I put my hand up to my face to take my glasses off, but my fingers snapped together rather abruptly because I hadn't been wearing them in the first place."

The remaining two categories occurred only rarely in the diary study. *Discrimination failures* (11%) consisted of failures to discriminate between objects (e.g. mistaking icons on a computer screen).

Programme assembly failures (5%) involved inappropriate combinations of actions. For example, "I unwrapped a sweet, put the paper in my mouth, and threw the sweet into the waste bucket" (Reason, 1979, p.72).

Evaluation

A diary study such as the one by Reason (1979) provides valuable information about the kinds of action slips that occur in everyday life. However, there are various reasons for not attaching much significance to the reported percentage for each category of action slip. First, the figures are based on those action slips that were detected, and we simply do not know how many cases of each kind of slip were never detected. Second, in order to interpret the percentages, we need to know the number of occasions on which each kind of slip might have occurred but did not. Thus, the small number of discrimination failures may reflect either good discrimination or a relative lack of situations requiring fine discrimination.

Another problem is that two action slips may be categorised together because they seem superficially similar, even though the underlying mechanisms are actually different. Grudin (1983) carried out videotape analyses of substitution errors in typing, in which the key next to the intended key was struck. Some substitution errors involved the correct finger moving in the wrong direction, but others involved an incorrect key being pressed by the finger that normally strikes it. According to Grudin, the former kind of error is due to faulty execution of an action, whereas the latter is due to faulty assignment of the finger. Thus, we would need more information than is usually available in diary studies in order to identify such subtle differences in underlying processes.

> ■ Research activity: Diary study
>
> Conduct your own diary study: over an agreed time period (one or two weeks) keep a diary listing every example of your own action slips and any that you observe happening to other people. Can you fit your action slips into the same categories as Reason suggested? Did you encounter any problems with this type of methodology? The Evaluation section may help you here.

Laboratory studies

In view of the problems with diary studies, it might be argued that laboratory studies offer a way of obtaining more precise data. However, potential disadvantages with the laboratory approach were identified by Sellen and Norman (1992). They pointed out (p.334) that many naturally occurring action slips occur

> when a person is internally preoccupied or distracted, when both the intended actions and the wrong actions are automatic, and when one is doing familiar tasks in familiar surroundings. Laboratory situations offer completely the opposite conditions. Typically, subjects are given an unfamiliar, highly contrived task to accomplish in a strange environment. Most subjects arrive motivated to perform well and ... are not given to internal preoccupation ... In short, the typical laboratory environment is possibly the least likely place where we are likely to see truly spontaneous, absent-minded errors.

However, in spite of these problems with laboratory studies, some interesting findings have been obtained (see next section).

Hay and Jacoby

Hay and Jacoby (1996) argued that action slips are most likely to occur when two conditions are satisfied:

1. The correct response is *not* the strongest or most habitual one.
2. Attention is not fully applied to the task of selecting the correct response.

For example, suppose you are looking for your house key. If it is not in its usual place, you are likely to waste time by looking there first of all. If you are late for an important appointment as well, you may find it hard to focus your attention on thinking about other places in which the key might have been put. As a result, you may spend a lot of time looking in several wrong places.

Hay and Jacoby tested this theoretical approach in a study in which the participants had to complete paired associates (e.g. knee: b _ n _). Sometimes the correct response on a basis of a previous learning task was also the strongest response (e.g. bend), and sometimes the correct response was *not* the strongest response (e.g. bone). The participants had either one second or three seconds to respond. Hay and Jacoby argued that action slips would be most likely when the

Hay and Jacoby's research looked at action slips in a laboratory setting. There has been little experimental research in this area. Action slips can be seen to be important in real-life settings. For example, consider a technician on a battleship who has to decide whether an approaching target is hostile or not. Hay and Jacoby found that action slips were most likely to occur when the correct response was not the strongest and had to be made rapidly. This would suggest that for the battleship technician the necessity for speed and previous practice in responding to mainly hostile targets may make an action slip (attacking a non-hostile target) more likely.

correct response was not the strongest one, and when the response had to be made rapidly. As predicted, the error rate in that condition was 45% against a mean of only 30% in the other conditions.

Why is the research by Hay and Jacoby (1996) of major importance? As they themselves pointed out (p.1332), "Very little has been done to examine action ... slips by directly manipulating the likelihood of their occurrence in experimental situations. In the research presented here, we not only manipulated action slips, but also teased apart the roles played by automatic and intentional responding in their production."

Discussion points

1. Does the approach of Hay and Jacoby seem to explain any action slips you have had lately?

2. Are there limitations of the laboratory-based approach used by Hay and Jacoby?

Theories of action slips

Several theories of action slips have been proposed, including those of Reason (1992) and Sellen and Norman (1992). In spite of differences between these theories, Reason (1992) and Sellen and Norman (1992) agree that there are two modes of control:

- An automatic mode: motor performance is controlled by schemas or organised plans; the schema that determines performance is the strongest one available.
- A conscious control mode: this involves some central processor or attentional system; this mode of control can override the automatic control mode.

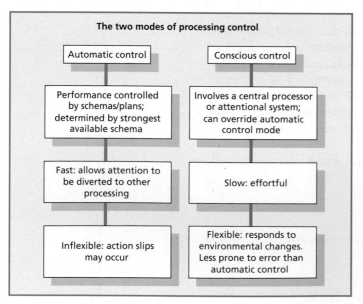

The two modes of processing control

Automatic control

Performance controlled by schemas/plans; determined by strongest available schema

Fast: allows attention to be diverted to other processing

Inflexible: action slips may occur

Conscious control

Involves a central processor or attentional system; can override automatic control mode

Slow: effortful

Flexible: responds to environmental changes. Less prone to error than automatic control

The advantages of automatic control are that it is fast and that it permits attentional resources to be devoted to other processing activities. Its disadvantages are that it is inflexible, and that action slips occur when there is too much reliance on this mode of control. Conscious control has the advantages that it is less prone to error than automatic control, and that it responds flexibly to environmental changes. However, it operates fairly slowly, and is an effortful process.

According to this theoretical analysis, action slips occur when someone is in the automatic mode of control and the strongest available schema or motor programme is the wrong one. The involvement of the automatic mode of control can be seen in many of Reason's (1979) action slips. One common type of action slip involves repeating an action because the first action has been forgotten (e.g. brushing one's teeth twice in quick succession; trying to start a car engine that has already been started). As we saw earlier in the chapter, unattended information is held very briefly and then forgotten. When brushing one's teeth or starting a car occurs in the automatic mode of control, it would be predicted that later memory for what has been done should be very poor. As a result, the action would often be repeated.

Schema theory

Sellen and Norman (1992) proposed a schema theory, according to which actions are determined by hierarchically arranged **schemas** or organised plans. Note that the term schemas is being used in a different way from that typically found in theories of memory (see Chapter 13). The highest-level schema represents the overall intention or goal (e.g. buying a present), and the lower-level schemas correspond to the actions involved in achieving that goal (e.g. taking money out of the bank; taking the train to the shopping centre). Any given schema determines action when its level of activation is high enough, and when the appropriate triggering conditions exist (e.g. getting into the train when it stops at the station). The activation level of the schemas is determined by current intentions and by the immediate situation.

Why do action slips occur according to schema theory? There are a number of possible reasons. First, there may be errors in the formation of an intention. Second, there may be faulty activation of a schema, leading to activation of the wrong schema, or to loss of activation in the right schema. Third, the situation may lead to faulty triggering of active schemas, leading to action being determined by the wrong schema.

Many of the action slips recorded by Reason (1979) can be related to schema theory. For example, discrimination failures can lead to errors in the formation of an intention, and storage failures for intentions can produce faulty triggering of active schemas.

Although these acrobats have practised these actions thousands of times, the consequences of any action slips are too serious for the actions to become purely automatic.

Evaluation. It could be argued that action slips are special events produced by their own mechanisms. However, it is probably better to argue (as is done within schema theory) that action slips are "the normal by-products of the design of the human action system" (Sellen & Norman, 1992, p.318). In other words, there is a single action system which normally functions well, but occasionally produces errors in the form of action slips.

Recent theories of action slips emphasise the notion of automatic processing. However, automatic processes are hard to define. More needs to be discovered about the factors leading to automatic processes being used at the wrong time. Recent theories predict correctly that action slips should occur most often with highly practised activities, because automatic processes are most likely to be used with such activities. However, action slips are much more common with actions of minor importance than those regarded as very important. For example, many circus performers carry out well-practised actions, but the element of danger ensures that they do not make use of the automatic mode of control. Recent theories do not seem able to explain such facts.

Performance efficiency

It could be argued that humans would make fewer action slips, and would perform more efficiently, if they made less use of the automatic mode of control. This is a rather suspect argument. Reason's (1979) diarists reported an average of only one action slip per day, which does not suggest that they were behaving inefficiently. The great advantage of the automatic mode of control is that it leaves the attentional system free to think about the past, to make plans for the future, and so on. Finally, action slips usually have a very small disruptive effect on everyday life.

PERSONAL REFLECTIONS

- It used to be thought by most psychologists that nearly all information processing required the use of the limited resources of attention and conscious awareness. That view sounds sensible and in line with our everyday experience, but it is wrong. There is much processing of unattended visual and auditory stimuli, and dual-task studies reveal that our limited attentional resources can be bypassed by developing automatic processes. We typically exaggerate the importance of the attentional system, because we are unaware of all the other processes going on below the level of conscious awareness.

SUMMARY

Concept of attention

There is an important distinction between focused attention, in which only one stimulus input is responded to, and divided attention, in which all stimulus inputs should be attended to and responded to. Attention is often thought of as consisting of a single, unitary system; in fact, it actually involves a number of different processes.

Focused auditory attention

People are good at following one auditory message and ignoring a second one presented at the same time, provided that there are physical differences between them (e.g. sex of the speaker; location of the speaker). Very little information on the unattended message is usually remembered, but sensitive measures indicate that some processing of the meaning of the unattended message may occur. People generally process as much of the "unattended" message as they need to in order to identify the input to which they want to attend.

Focused visual attention

Focused visual attention can be compared to a spotlight with a variable beam. This view is an oversimplification, because attention can be used more flexibly than a spotlight. Visual stimuli outside the attentional beam receive limited processing, but this can include information about their meaning. According to feature integration theory, the visual features of objects are processed in parallel, and then combined by focused attention to form objects.

Divided attention

Studies on divided attention indicate that we can sometimes perform two tasks at once with no apparent problem, but other pairs of tasks are almost impossible to perform at the same time. Some of the important factors determining dual-task performance include task similarity, task difficulty, and amount of practice. Many of the findings can be

Considering the research on divided attention, what is your view on whether car drivers should use mobile phones while driving along?

accounted for by the central capacity interference theory. There also seem to be specific processing mechanisms.

Why does practice usually lead to a great improvement in dual-task performance? It can lead to the development of automatic processes, which in theory are rapid, do not rely on attention, are unavailable to consciousness, and are unavoidable. In practice, few processes satisfy all these criteria. Automatic processes often depend on stored knowledge that permits rapid retrieval of past solutions.

Automatic processing

Diary studies indicate that many action slips depend on storage failures or test failures. Laboratory research suggests that action slips are most likely when the correct response is not the strongest one, and when attention is not fully applied to the ongoing situation. Some theorists distinguish between an automatic control mode and a conscious control mode. According to schema theory, actions are determined by hierarchically arranged schemas or organised plans.

Action slips

FURTHER READING

The topic of attention is discussed thoroughly in Chapter 3 of M.W. Eysenck (1993), *Principles of cognitive psychology*, Hove, UK: Psychology Press. There is more detailed coverage of the topics discussed here in Chapter 5 of M.W. Eysenck and M.T. Keane (1995), *Cognitive psychology: A student's handbook (3rd Edn.)*, Hove, UK: Psychology Press. The whole subject of attention research is dealt with in a clear way in E.A. Styles (1997), *The psychology of attention*, Hove, UK: Psychology Press.

REVISION QUESTIONS

1   Discuss *two* theories of focused attention. (24 marks)
2a Explain what psychologists mean by divided attention. (6 marks)
2b Discuss *two* studies that have been made of divided attention. (12 marks)
2c Assess what insights these *two* studies have given us into the nature of divided attention. (6 marks)
3   Describe and evaluate research evidence into automatic processing. (24 marks)
4a Define the term action slip. (6 marks)
4b Describe and criticise *two* theories of performance deficits (e.g. action slips; dual-task limitations). (18 marks)

- **Memory stores**
  A theory of the structure of human memory in which there are a number of different stores.

  Atkinson and Shiffrin's multi-store model
  Brown and Kulik's flashbulb memories

- **Working memory**
  A theory of memory in which the short-term memory store is replaced by a more complex system.

  Baddeley and Hitch's working memory model
  Hitch and Baddeley's dual task study

- **Memory processes**
  Does how we process information affect how well we remember it?

  Craik and Lockhart's levels-of-processing theory
  Craik and Tulving's work on elaboration
  Eysenck's studies of distinctiveness
  Morris et al.'s transfer-appropriate processing theory

- **Long-term memory**
  The different kinds of long-term memory systems.

  Tulving's episodic and semantic memory
  Graf and Schacter's explicit and implicit memory
  Cohen and Squire's declarative and procedural knowledge

- **Organisation of information in long-term memory**
  How is the mass of knowledge in long-term memory arranged?

  Collins and Quillian's semantic memory networks
  Collins and Loftus' spreading activation theory
  Bartlett's schema theory

- **Why do we forget?**
  The processes of forgetting

  Trace decay theory (Jenkins and Dallenbach)
  Interference theory (Underwood and Postman)
  Cue-dependent forgetting (Tulving and Pearlstone)
  Repression (Freud)
  Reber's work on implicit memory
  The Brown–Peterson paradigm

- **Practical applications**
  Theories of memory applied to real-life situations, e.g. eyewitness testimony, revising for exams.

  Loftus and Palmer's eyewitness studies
  Ley's medical information studies
  Mnemonic techniques

13

Human Memory

Human memory involves the encoding, storage, organisation, and retrieval of information about our lives and experiences.

How important is memory? Imagine if we were without it. We would not recognise anyone or anything as familiar. We would not be able to talk, read, or write, because we would remember nothing about language. We would have the same lack of knowledge as newborn babies.

We use memory for numerous purposes. It allows us to keep track of conversations, to remember telephone numbers while we dial them, to write essays in examinations, to make sense of what we read, and to recognise people's faces. The richness of memory suggests that we have a number of memory systems. This chapter explores in detail some of the proposed sub-divisions of human memory.

There are close links between learning and memory. The existence of memory depends on previous learning, and learning can most clearly be demonstrated by good performance on a memory test. Learning and memory involve a series of three stages:

1. Encoding, which involves the processes that occur during the presentation of the learning material.
2. Storage, in which as a result of encoding, some information is stored within the memory system.
3. Retrieval, which involves recovering or extracting stored information from the memory system.

Those interested in learning focus on encoding and storage, whereas those interested in memory concentrate on retrieval. However, all these processes depend on each other.

There is an important distinction between *structure* and *processes*. Structure refers to the way in which the memory system is organised, whereas processes are the activities taking place within the memory system. Structure and processes are both important. However, theorists differ in the emphasis they put on these two aspects of the memory system.

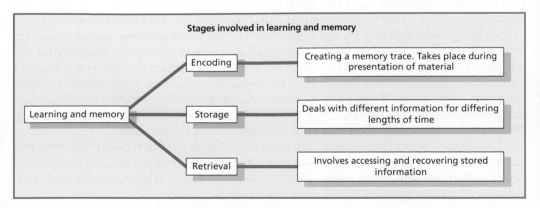

Stages involved in learning and memory

Learning and memory
- Encoding — Creating a memory trace. Takes place during presentation of material
- Storage — Deals with different information for differing lengths of time
- Retrieval — Involves accessing and recovering stored information

315

This chapter is also concerned with practical applications of memory research. We will be focusing later on eyewitness testimony, recall of medical information, and mnemonic strategies to aid long-term memory.

Memory Stores

Atkinson and Shiffrin (1968) argued that the basic structure of the memory system consisted of a number of memory stores:

- Sensory stores: stores associated with a single modality (e.g. vision; hearing) which hold information very briefly.
- Short-term store: a store of very limited capacity which holds information for only a few seconds.
- Long-term store: a store of essentially unlimited capacity which can hold information over extremely long periods of time.

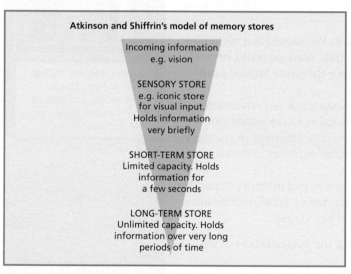

According to the theory, information from the environment is initially received by the sensory stores. Some of this information is attended to, and processed further, by the short-term store. In turn, some of the information processed in the short-term store is transferred to the long-term store. Long-term storage of information often depends on rehearsal, with a direct relationship between the amount of rehearsal in the short-term store and the strength of the stored memory trace.

The multi-store approach was based on a number of structural and processing assumptions. The memory stores themselves form the basic structure, and processes such as attention and rehearsal control the flow of information between the memory stores. However, the main emphasis was on structure.

Sensory stores

Our senses are constantly bombarded with information, most of which does not receive any attention. If you are sitting in a chair as you read this, then information about touch from that part of your body in contact with the chair is available. However, you have probably been unaware of that information until now. Information in every sense modality persists for some time after the end of stimulation. This makes it easier to extract its most important aspects for further analysis.

The sensory store in the visual modality is known as the **iconic store**. When Sperling (1960) presented a visual array consisting of three rows of four letters each for 50 milliseconds, he found the participants could name only four or five letters. However, they claimed to have seen many more letters. Sperling wondered whether this meant that visual information in the iconic store had faded before most of it could be reported.

Sperling tested this idea by using a tone to cue the participants to report the letters from only *one* row. The total information available was estimated by multiplying the number of letters recalled by three (there were three rows). When the tone was presented immediately before or after the onset of the visual display, nine letters were available. However, performance dropped to six letters when the tone was heard 0.3 seconds after the presentation of the display, and it fell to 4.5 letters with an interval of one second. Thus, information in the iconic store decays within about 0.5 seconds.

The sensory store in the auditory modality is known as the **echoic store**. Suppose you are reading a book when someone asks you a question. You might ask, "What did you say?", and at the same time realise that you actually know what has been said. This "playback" facility depends on the workings of echoic memory.

A related effect was explored by Treisman (1964). Her participants shadowed (repeated back aloud) the message presented to one ear while ignoring a second message presented to the other ear. When the second or non-shadowed message was in advance of the shadowed message, the two messages were only recognised as being the same when they were within two seconds of each other. This suggests that unattended auditory information in the echoic store only lasts for about two seconds. However, other estimates are rather longer.

Short-term and long-term stores

Trying to remember a telephone number for a few seconds is an everyday example of the use of the short-term store. It illustrates two of its key features:

1. Very limited capacity.
2. Fragility of storage, as distraction causes us to forget the number.

It is hard to estimate the capacity of short-term memory. There are two main ways in which its capacity has been assessed: span measures, and the recency effect in free recall. An example of a span measure is digit span, in which the participants have to repeat back immediately a list of random digits in the correct order. The span of immediate memory is generally "seven, plus or minus two", whether the units are numbers, letters, or words. According to Miller (1956), about seven **chunks** (integrated pieces or units of information) can be held in short-term memory. For example, "IBM" is one chunk for those familiar with the company name International Business Machines, but three chunks for everyone else.

The capacity of short-term memory depends more on the number of chunks than on the number of words. Simon (1974) found that the memory span was 7 words for unrelated words, whereas it was 22 words for 8-word phrases. These figures correspond to seven and three chunks, respectively. Thus, Miller (1956) was wrong to assume that the capacity of short-term memory in chunks always remains the same.

The recency effect is measured in studies of free recall, in which the participants recall the words from a list in any order immediately after it has been presented. The **recency effect** is defined by the fact that the last few items in a list are usually much better remembered than items from the middle of the list. Glanzer and Cunitz (1966) found that counting backwards for only 10 seconds between the end of list presentation and the start of recall virtually eliminated the recency effect, but otherwise had no effect on recall. The two or three words affected by the recency effect were in the short-term store at the end of list presentation, and so were in a fragile state. In contrast, the other items were in the long-term store, and so were unaffected by the task of counting backwards.

The participants recalled the first few items much better than those from the middle of the list. This is known as the **primacy effect**. Why is there a primacy effect? The words at the start of the list are rehearsed more than those from the middle. This was shown by Rundus and Atkinson (1970), who asked their participants to rehearse out loud any of the words they wanted to during list presentation.

The recency effect suggests that the capacity of the short-term store is about two or three items. However, span measures indicate a capacity of about seven items. Why do these two techniques produce different results? One reason relates to different patterns of rehearsal. Participants carrying out a span task rehearse as many items as possible, whereas those asked to learn a list for free recall rehearse only a few items at a time. The recency effect and span measures both indicate that the capacity of short-term memory is strictly limited. In contrast, no effective limits on the capacity of long-term memory have been discovered.

> ■ Research activity: Read quickly through the following list of digits once. Cover the list and try to write the digits down.
>
> 7 3 5 1 5 6 9 8 2 7 4
>
> How many did you remember in the correct order? This is one way of measuring your memory span. Now try the following digits:
>
> 1 9 3 9 1 0 6 6 1 8 0 5 1 2 1 5
>
> More digits, but if you recognised the "chunks" you should have remembered them all:
>
> 1939 Start of Second World War
> 1066 Battle of Hastings
> 1805 Battle of Trafalgar
> 1215 Signing of the Magna Carta
>
> Did you find any primary or recency effects when you tried to recall the list of digits? Try the test again with this in mind.

KEY TERMS
Chunks: integrated units of information.
Recency effect: good free recall of the last few items in a list based on information in the short-term store.
Primacy effect: the high level of recall of the first items in a list in free recall; it depends mainly on extra rehearsal.

The strongest evidence for a distinction between short-term and long-term memory has come from the study of brain-damaged patients. Amnesic patients (discussed later in the chapter) have poor long-term memory for many kinds of information. However, they have almost normal short-term memory as assessed by digit span and by the recency effect in free recall (e.g. Baddeley & Warrington, 1970). A few brain-damaged patients have good long-term memory but impaired short-term memory. Shallice and Warrington (1970) studied KF, who suffered brain damage as a result of a motorcycle accident. KF had no problem with long-term memory, but his digit span was only two items. These findings suggest that different parts of the brain are involved in short-term and long-term memory.

The evidence from brain-damaged patients does not completely support the Atkinson and Shiffrin (1968) model. They assumed there was only one short-term store, but studies by Warrington and Shallice (1972) and by Shallice and Warrington (1974) indicated that matters are more complex. Warrington and Shallice (1972) studied KF further. His short-term forgetting of auditory letters and digits was much greater than his forgetting of visual stimuli. Shallice and Warrington (1974) found that KF's short-term memory deficit was limited to verbal materials (e.g. letters; words), and did not extend to meaningful sounds (e.g. cats mewing). Thus, only some aspects of short-term memory were impaired in KF. According to Shallice and Warrington (1974), KF's problems centred on what they called the "auditory-verbal short-term store".

A major distinction between the short-term and long-term stores concerns the ways in which forgetting occurs. As is discussed later in the chapter, forgetting in short-term memory depends on diversion of attention and interference. In contrast, forgetting from long-term memory depends mainly on cue-dependent forgetting (discussed later).

Evaluation

The multi-store model provided a systematic account of the structures and processes involved in human memory. The notion that there are three different kinds of memory store was based firmly on evidence that there are important differences among the stores:

The idea that there is a single long-term memory store has been questioned. Imagine how difficult it could be to retrieve a specific item from the confusion shown here, let alone to retrieve your knowledge of it from all the varied memories you have stored in your life.

1. Temporal duration.
2. Storage capacity.
3. Forgetting mechanism.
4. Effects of brain damage.

The multi-store model is very oversimplified. It was assumed there is a single short-term store and a single long-term store. These assumptions have been disproved, as we will see later in the chapter. Consider, for example, the assumption that there is a single long-term memory store. There is an enormous wealth of information stored in long-term memory, including knowledge that Emma Thompson is a film star, that 2 + 2 = 4, that we had fish and chips for lunch yesterday, and perhaps information about how to ride a bicycle. It seems improbable that all this knowledge is stored within a single long-term memory store.

According to the model, the main way in which information is stored in long-term memory is through rehearsal in the short-term store. However, most people devote very little time to active rehearsal, even though they are constantly storing away new information in long-term memory. **Flashbulb memories**, consisting of long-lasting and vivid memories of highly significant events, seem to contradict the notion that thorough processing in the short-term store is needed for good long-term memory. For example, millions of people have flashbulb memories of the death of Diana, Princess of Wales, remembering clearly where and how they learned of her death. Such memories may be especially vivid if they are thought about frequently (see Eysenck & Keane, 1995).

KEY TERM

Flashbulb memories: accurate and long-lasting memories formed by significant public or personal events.

CASE STUDY: *Flashbulb Memories*

There has been much research into what have been called "flashbulb memories" (Brown & Kulik, 1977). This research was first prompted by the assassinations of President John Kennedy and Martin Luther King in America. People in the USA and all over the world, when asked about these terrible events, found that they not only recalled the event clearly, but could remember in great and often trivial detail where they were, who they were with, and what they were doing when they heard the news. Brown and Kulik argued that when a nationally or internationally important event occurs, this leads to the event being imprinted on the memory like a flash photograph. Others have argued that these trivial details are recalled because of the number of times the story is retold.

Following the death of Diana, Princess of Wales, it seems likely that eventually this event will be studied in terms of the memories people have for hearing the initial news and for events that occurred during the following week. These studies will clearly have to consider the possible ethical implications of causing people distress once again, and may

therefore have to be delayed for quite some time. Methodological requirements may mean that it will be necessary to wait at least until media inquests and debates subside.

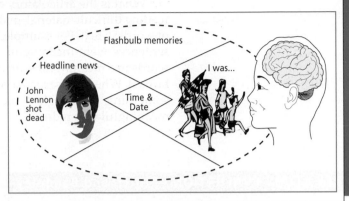

In general terms, the multi-store model is too rigid and inflexible. There is a tendency to minimise the active involvement of the individual in learning and remembering information.

Working Memory

One of the reasons why the multi-store model fell into disfavour was because its account of short-term memory was oversimplified. Baddeley and Hitch (1974) argued that the concept of the short-term store should be replaced with that of working memory. According to them, the working memory system consists of three components:

- Central executive: a modality-free component of limited capacity; it is like attention.
- Articulatory or phonological loop: this holds information briefly in a phonological (i.e. speech-based) form; in the revised version of the model, the loop is divided into a phonological store which is directly concerned with speech perception and an articulatory process linked to speech production.
- Visuo-spatial scratch (or sketch) pad: this is specialised for spatial and/or visual coding.

The most important component is the **central executive**. It has limited capacity, and is used when dealing with most cognitive tasks. The **articulatory loop** and the **visuo-spatial sketch pad** are slave systems used by the central executive for specific purposes. Most is known about the articulatory loop, which was studied by Baddeley, Thomson, and Buchanan

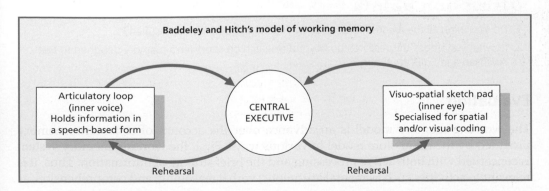

Baddeley and Hitch's model of working memory

(1975). They asked their participants to recall immediately sets of five words in the correct order. Their ability to do this was better with short words than with long ones. Further investigation of this *word-length effect* showed that the participants could recall as many words as they could read out loud in two seconds. This suggested that the capacity of the articulatory loop is determined by time duration in the same way as a tape loop.

What is the articulatory or phonological loop used for in everyday life? It is used in reading difficult material, making it easier for readers to retain information about the order of words in text. For example, Baddeley and Lewis (1981) asked their participants whether sentences were meaningful. Some of the sentences were not meaningful because two words in a meaningful sentence had been switched round (e.g. "The tree flew up into the birds"). When the participants were prevented from using the articulatory loop by saying something meaningless repeatedly, their ability to decide whether sentences were meaningful was reduced.

Hitch and Baddeley

KEY STUDY EVALUATION — Hitch and Baddeley

Working memory was proposed by Baddeley and Hitch as an alternative to the multi-store structural model of short-term memory. Baddeley and Hitch carried out research using the dual-task technique. The assumption that lies behind this technique is that each of the processors has only a limited capacity to process information. If two tasks using the same processor are carried out concurrently, performance on one or both of the tasks will be impaired. This research is an example of how theorising about a concept such as working memory can lead to the development of a hypothesis and controlled research.

Intuitively this research may make sense to us, by suggesting that there are different ways of dealing with different forms of information. The concept of working memory is an active rather than a passive process, and can be used to explain real-life situations, such as reading and doing mental arithmetic. It can also explain short-term memory problems experienced by brain-damaged patients. However, there are always difficulties in using research from patients with brain damage to support a theory (as, for example, in Shallice & Warrington's study of KF). It is difficult, if not impossible, to assess precisely what the short-term memory function of a person would have been prior to the event or accident that leads to them being assessed by psychologists.

■ Research activity: Try the dual-task technique yourself. Read a page in a book you have not read before. You should find that you have understood what was being written about, and could explain what you have read to another person. Now turn to a different page and try to read it while saying "the, the, the" aloud repeatedly. You may find that you have some difficulty in understanding the text, and your reading rate may have been reduced. Can you explain what you have read to someone else this time? If you can, how would you explain this?

The working memory model can be used to predict whether or not two tasks can be performed successfully at the same time. Every component of the working memory system has limited capacity, and is relatively independent of the other components. Two predictions follow:

1. If two tasks make use of the same component, they cannot be performed successfully together.
2. If two tasks make use of different components, it should be possible to perform them as well together as separately.

Hitch and Baddeley (1976) tested these predictions. Their participants carried out a verbal reasoning task, which involved deciding whether each in a set of sentences provided a true or a false description of the letter pair that followed it (e.g. B is followed by A: BA). It was assumed that this task would make extensive use of the central executive.

At the same time, the participants either had to say "the" repeatedly, say the sequence "one two three four five six" over and over again, repeat a different random string of digits out loud every trial, or there was no additional task. They were given this additional task before each trial on the reasoning task was presented. It was assumed that saying "the" or "one two three four five six" repeatedly would involve only the articulatory loop, because little thought or attention is involved. In contrast, saying six random digits involves the central executive as well as the articulatory loop. Thus, saying six random digits should interfere with performance on the verbal reasoning task, but saying six digits in sequence or saying "the" should not. As predicted, reasoning performance was slowed down by the additional task only when it involved using the central executive (i.e. six random digits).

Discussion points

1. Do you think all the assumptions made by Hitch and Baddeley are justified?
2. In what ways does this research go beyond research on short-term memory designed to test Atkinson and Shiffrin's theory?

Evaluation

The working memory model is an advance over the account of short-term memory provided by the multi-store model in various ways. First, the working memory system is concerned with both active processing and the brief storage of information. Thus, it is relevant to activities such as mental arithmetic, verbal reasoning, and comprehension, as well as to traditional short-term memory tasks. Second, the working memory model accounts for many findings (e.g. those of Hitch & Baddeley, 1976) which are hard to explain within the multi-store approach. Third, the working memory model views verbal rehearsal as an *optional* process that occurs within the articulatory or phonological loop. This is more realistic than the central importance of verbal rehearsal in the multi-store model.

On the negative side, little is known about the central executive. It has limited capacity, but this capacity has not been measured accurately. It is argued that the central executive is "modality-free" and used in many different processing operations, but the precise details of its functioning are not known. In real life, many accidents are caused when the demands on a pilot or driver are so great that the capacity of the central executive is exceeded. Some practical research in this area is discussed in Chapter 12.

Memory Processes

Suppose you were interested in looking at the effects of learning processes on long-term memory. One method that has often been used is to present several groups of participants with the same list of nouns, and to ask each group to perform a different activity or orienting task. The tasks used range from counting the number of letters in each word to thinking of an appropriate adjective for each word.

> **Ethical issues: Deception**
> Of course, it is unethical to deceive participants about the purpose of an experiment. However, this can be overcome to some extent by asking the participants *after* the study whether they had been distressed at the deception. If so, the study could be stopped. In reality, however, it is unlikely that the minor deception involved in incidental learning would be distressing to anyone.

If the participants were informed that their memory was going to be tested, they might realise that a task such as simply counting the number of letters in each word would not allow them to remember much. There would thus be a natural temptation to process the words more thoroughly. In order to control the participants' processing activities, the experimenter does not tell them about the memory test (this is **incidental learning**). Finally, the participants are unexpectedly asked for recall. As the various groups learn the same words, any differences in recall must reflect the influence of the processing tasks.

Hyde and Jenkins (1973) used the approach just described. Words were either associatively related or unrelated in meaning, and different groups performed each of the following five orienting tasks:

* Rating the words for pleasantness.
* Estimating the frequency with which each word is used in the English language.
* Detecting the occurrence of the letters "e" and "g" in the list words.
* Deciding whether the list words fitted sentence frames.
* Deciding the part of speech (noun, verb, etc.) appropriate to each word.

Half the participants in each condition were told to learn the words (intentional learning), whereas the other half were not (incidental learning). Then there was a test of free recall.

Rating pleasantness and rating frequency of usage presumably involve semantic processing (processing of meaning), whereas the other three orienting tasks do not. Recall was 51% higher after the semantic tasks than the non-semantic tasks with the associatively unrelated words. With the list of associatively related words, there was an 83% superiority for the semantic tasks. Surprisingly, incidental learners recalled the same number of words as intentional learners. Thus, what matters is the nature of the processing activity at the time of learning.

Levels-of-processing theory

Craik and Lockhart (1972) put forward levels-of-processing theory. They assumed that the attentional and perceptual processes operating at the time of learning determine what is stored in long-term memory. They also assumed that there are various levels of processing,

> **KEY TERM**
> **Incidental learning**: learning that occurs in the absence of instructions that there will subsequently be a memory test.

■ Research activity: Try to construct a list of words that have approximately the same frequency of usage. Now think of questions to ask that will involve deep processing (e.g. Is this the opposite of … ?) or shallow processing (e.g. Does this word include the letter G?). It will be easier if your questions have yes/no answers. Divide the list in half, give each half to a naive participant, such as a member of your family, and ask the questions. Take the list away and give the participant a blank piece of paper for a free recall test. Your findings should be in line with those of Craik and Lockhart: deep processing should lead to better recall.

ranging from shallow or physical analysis of a stimulus (e.g. detecting specific letters in words) to deep or semantic analysis. The crucial notion of depth of processing was clarified by Craik (1973, p.48): " 'Depth' is defined in terms of the meaningfulness extracted from the stimulus rather than in terms of the number of analyses performed upon it."

The key theoretical assumptions made by Craik and Lockhart (1972) were as follows:

- The depth of processing of a stimulus has a substantial effect on its memorability.
- Deeper levels of analysis produce more elaborate, longer lasting, and stronger memory traces than do shallow levels of analysis.

The findings of Hyde and Jenkins (1973), as well as many other findings, are in line with these assumptions. However, it became apparent that the approach was over-simplified, and so various modifications were proposed.

Elaboration

Craik and Tulving (1975) found that elaboration of processing (the amount of processing of a particular kind) is important. In one study, the participants were presented on each trial with a word and a sentence containing a blank, and asked to decide whether the word fitted into the incomplete sentence. Elaboration was manipulated by varying the complexity of the sentence frame between the simple (e.g. "She cooked the _____ ") and the complex (e.g. "The great bird swooped down and carried off the struggling _____ "). Cued recall was twice as high for words accompanying complex sentences, suggesting that elaboration benefits long-term memory.

Later studies indicated that memory depends on the kind of elaboration as well as on the amount of elaboration. Bransford et al. (1979) presented either minimally elaborated similes (e.g. "A mosquito is like a doctor because they both draw blood") or multiply elaborated similes (e.g. "A mosquito is like a raccoon because they both have heads, legs, jaws"). Recall was much better for the minimally elaborated similes. Thus, the nature and degree of precision of semantic elaborations are relevant when predicting recall.

Distinctiveness

Eysenck (1979) argued that long-term memory is affected by distinctiveness of processing. Memory traces that are distinctive or unique in some way will be more readily retrieved than memory traces closely resembling others. Eysenck and Eysenck (1980) tested this theory by using nouns having irregular grapheme–phoneme correspondence (i.e. words not pronounced in line with pronunciation rules, such as "comb" with its silent "b"). The participants performed the shallow or non-semantic orienting task of pronouncing such nouns as if they had regular grapheme–phoneme correspondence (e.g. pronouncing the "b" in "comb"), which produced distinctive and unique memory traces. This was the non-semantic, distinctive condition. In the non-semantic, non-distinctive condition, nouns were simply pronounced in their normal fashion. In the semantic, distinctive and the semantic, non-distinctive conditions, nouns were processed in terms of their meaning.

On an unexpected test of recognition memory, words in the non-semantic, distinctive condition were much better remembered than those in the non-semantic, non-distinctive condition. Indeed, they were remembered almost as well as the words in the two semantic conditions. These findings show the importance of distinctiveness.

Distinctiveness depends in part on the context in which a given stimulus is processed. For example, the name "Smith" if presented in the list "Jones, Robinson, Williams, Baker, Smith, Robertson" would not be distinctive, but it would stand out in the following list: "Zzitz, Zysblat, Vangeersadaele, Vythelingum, Smith, Uwejeyah" (for which I am indebted to the London Telephone Directory). It would be fairly easy to manipulate distinctiveness in this way and to observe its effects on long-term memory if you wanted to carry out an experiment in this area.

Evaluation

Processes occurring at the time of learning have a major impact on long-term memory. That sounds obvious, but few studies before 1972 considered learning processes and their effects on memory. It is also of value that elaboration and distinctiveness of processing have been identified as factors influencing learning and memory.

On the negative side, it is hard to decide whether a particular orienting task involves shallow or deep processing. This problem occurs because of the lack of any independent measure of processing depth. Hyde and Jenkins (1973) assumed that estimating the frequency of usage of words involves deep or semantic processing, but they had no real evidence for this assumption. A related point is that participants may not stop at the expected level of processing. For example, if you were asked to count the numbers of "e"s and "g"s in your own name, it is likely that you would think about yourself in a meaningful way as well as doing the task.

Some evidence does not support levels-of-processing theory. Morris, Bransford, and Franks (1977) argued that stored information is remembered only to the extent that it is of *relevance* to the memory test. Participants had to process words in terms of their meaning or in terms of their sound. Some of them were tested by a rhyming recognition test. On this test, participants had to select words that rhymed with list words, with the list words themselves not being presented. For example, if the word "whip" was on the rhyming test and the word "ship" had been in the list, participants should have selected it because it rhymed with a list word.

Morris et al. (1977) found that recognition memory was much better for words that had been processed in terms of their sound than for those that had been processed for meaning. This disproves the prediction of levels-of-processing theory that deep processing is always better than shallow processing. The reason is that processing the meaning of the list words was of little help when the memory test required the identification of words rhyming with list words. The information acquired from the shallow rhyme task was far more relevant, and so memory performance was higher in this condition.

Morris et al. argued that their findings supported a transfer-appropriate processing theory. According to this theory, different kinds of processing lead learners to acquire different kinds of information about a stimulus. Whether the stored information leads to later retention depends on the *relevance* of that information to the memory test.

The levels-of-processing approach *describes* rather than *explains*. Craik and Lockhart (1972) argued that deep processing leads to better long-term memory than shallow processing. However, they failed to provide a detailed account of *why* deep processing is so effective.

Why would lists of people's names be unsuitable material for use in research into memory processes?

Long-term Memory

The multi-store model of memory proposed by Atkinson and Shiffrin (1968) was discussed earlier in the chapter. According to that theory, there is only a single long-term memory store. However, it is improbable that all the knowledge we possess is stored in exactly the same form in a single long-term memory store. If there is more than one long-term store, we need to work out the number and nature of long-term stores that we possess. Some of the main suggestions are discussed next.

Episodic and semantic memory

Tulving (1972) argued for a distinction between two types of long-term memory: episodic memory and semantic memory. **Episodic memory** has an autobiographical flavour, referring to the storage of specific events or episodes occurring in a particular place at a particular time. Memories of what you did yesterday or what you had for lunch last Sunday are examples of episodic memory. In contrast, **semantic memory** contains information about our stock of knowledge of the world. Tulving (1972, p.386) defined semantic memory as

KEY TERMS

Episodic memory: long-term memory for autobiographical or personal events, usually including information about the time and place of an episode or event.

Semantic memory: organised knowledge about the world and about language stored in long-term memory.

a mental thesaurus, organised knowledge a person possesses about words and other verbal symbols, their meanings and referents, about relations among them, and about rules, formulas, and algorithms for the manipulation of these symbols, concepts, and relations.

Tulving (1989) obtained some support for the distinction between episodic and semantic memory. A small dose of radioactive gold was injected into the bloodstream of volunteers, including Tulving himself. They thought about personal events or about information in semantic memory (e.g. the history of astronomy). Blood flow in different areas of the brain was recorded. Episodic memory was associated with a high level of activation of the frontal cortex, whereas semantic memory was associated with a high level of activation in the posterior or back regions of the cortex. The fact that different parts of the brain were most active during retrieval of episodic and semantic memories fits the view that there are at least partially separate episodic and semantic memory systems.

Evaluation

How useful is the distinction between episodic and semantic memory? There is a clear difference in *content* between the information in episodic and semantic memory. However, it is less clear that there is a difference in the *processes* involved. Episodic and semantic memory depend heavily on each other. For example, remembering what you had for lunch last Sunday basically involves episodic memory. However, semantic memory is also involved, in that your knowledge of the world is needed to identify the different kinds of food you ate.

Explicit and implicit memory

The memory tests discussed in this chapter (e.g. free recall; cued recall; recognition) all involve the use of direct instructions to the participants to retrieve specific information. Such memory tests are tests of **explicit memory**, which "is revealed when performance on a task requires conscious recollection of previous experiences" (Graf & Schachter, 1985, p.501). Graf and Schachter contrasted explicit memory with **implicit memory**, which "is revealed when performance on a task is facilitated in the absence of conscious recollection."

How would you test participants' recognition memory for a word list?

Tulving, Schachter, and Stark (1982) carried out a study on implicit memory. Their participants learned a list of rare words (e.g. "toboggan"). One hour or one week later, they filled in the blanks in word fragments to make words (e.g. _ O _ O _GA _). The solutions to half the fragments were words from the list, but the participants were not told this. As conscious recollection of the list was not required on the word-fragment test, it can be regarded as a test of implicit memory. The participants completed more of the fragments when the solutions matched list words than when they did not, thus providing evidence for implicit memory.

Tulving et al. (1982) found differences between implicit memory and explicit memory in the form of recognition memory. Recognition memory was much worse after one week than after one hour, whereas fragment-completion performance did not change significantly over time.

Ethical issues: Claparède's observations give us an insight into the nature of memory and amnesia, but was his behaviour ethical?

The usefulness of the distinction between explicit and implicit memory can be explored by studying brain-damaged patients suffering from **amnesia.** These patients have severe problems with long-term memory. What is important here is that these problems are mainly with explicit memory rather than implicit memory. This can be seen in a story told by Claparède (1911). He hid a pin in his hand before shaking hands with an amnesic patient. After that, she was reluctant to shake hands with him, but was embarrassed that she could not think of any reason for her reluctance. Her behaviour indicated implicit memory, but this occurred in the absence of explicit memory of the incident.

KEY TERMS
Explicit memory: memory based on conscious recollection.
Implicit memory: memory not based on conscious recollection.
Amnesia: partial loss of long-term memory, usually caused by brain damage.

More evidence that amnesic patients show less forgetting in implicit memory was reported by Graf, Squire, and Mandler (1984). Memory for list words was tested in four ways. Three tests were standard explicit memory tests (free recall; cued recall; recognition), but the fourth (word completion) involved implicit memory. On the word-completion task, the participants were given three-letter word fragments (e.g. STR___), and wrote down the first word they thought of starting with those letters. Implicit memory was assessed by the extent to which the word completions corresponded to words from the previous list. The amnesic patients did much worse than normal controls on all the explicit memory tests. However, they performed as well as the controls on the implicit memory test.

What is the difference between free recall tests and cued recall tests?

Evaluation

The distinction between explicit and implicit memory is important in both normals and amnesic patients. However, it is often not easy to find out whether participants are or are not making use of conscious recollection, which is the crucial defining feature of explicit memory. Another limitation of work in this area is that it tells us little about the *structures* involved in explicit and implicit memory. This issue is addressed in the next section.

Declarative and procedural knowledge systems

Cohen and Squire (1980) argued that long-term memory is divided into two memory systems: declarative knowledge and procedural knowledge. This distinction is related to that made by Ryle (1949) between "knowing that" and "knowing how". **Declarative knowledge** corresponds to knowing that. Thus, for example, we know that we had roast pork for Sunday lunch, and we know that Paris is the capital of France. **Procedural knowledge** corresponds to knowing how, and refers to the ability to perform skilled actions (e.g. how to ride a bicycle; how to play the piano) without the involvement of conscious recollection. Explicit memory depends largely or wholly on the declarative knowledge system, whereas implicit memory depends on the procedural knowledge system.

According to Cohen and Squire (1980), amnesic patients have severe impairment of the declarative memory system, but have an intact procedural memory system. Declarative memory consists of episodic and semantic memory, and amnesic patients find it hard to acquire new episodic and semantic memories. Most of the learning that amnesics find easiest involves motor or other skills which can be regarded as largely procedural. The tasks on which amnesics have been shown to acquire skills

■ Research activity: State whether the following involve procedural or declarative knowledge.

- Your name
- Driving a car
- The capital city of Japan
- The value of m² when m = 6
- Balancing on one leg

Think of some other examples of procedural and declarative knowledge.

are very varied. They include the following: dressmaking; billiards; finger mazes; tracking a moving target on a pursuit rotor (involving a rotating turntable); jigsaw completions; and reading mirror-reversed script (Eysenck & Keane, 1995).

Studies of the reading of mirror-reversed text show the procedural learning abilities of amnesic patients. In these studies, it is possible to distinguish between general improvement in speed of reading produced by practice and more specific improvements produced by re-reading the same groups of words or sentences. Cohen and Squire (1980) reported that amnesics demonstrated general and specific improvement in reading mirror-reversed script.

Squire, Knowlton, and Musen (1993) argued that the main brain structures underlying declarative or explicit memory are located in the hippocampus and related structures in the medial temporal lobes and the diencephalon. This view was supported by Squire et al. (1992). They used PET scans, and found that blood flow in the right hippocampus was much higher when the participants were performing a declarative memory task (cued recall) than a procedural memory task (word-stem completion).

It has proved harder to identify the brain structures involved in procedural or implicit memory, because implicit memory consists of a large collection of skills and processes. Squire (1987) argued that there are five major types of procedural or implicit learning:

KEY TERMS
Declarative knowledge: knowledge relating to "knowing that", including episodic memory and semantic memory.
Procedural knowledge: knowledge relating to "knowing how", including motor skills.

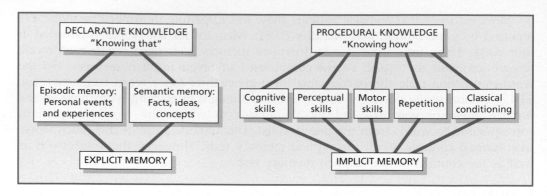

- Cognitive skill learning.
- Perceptual learning.
- Motor skill learning.
- Repetition learning.
- Classical conditioning.

Evaluation

The evidence indicates that the single long-term store proposed by Atkinson and Shiffrin (1968) needs to be replaced by two separate long-term memory systems. One of these systems is concerned with declarative knowledge, and the other with procedural knowledge. Retrieval from the declarative knowledge system typically involves explicit memory, and amnesic patients show poor performance. Retrieval from the procedural knowledge system typically involves implicit memory, and amnesic patients perform normally or very nearly so.

Organisation of Information in Long-term Memory

Memory is usually highly organised. Furthermore, the more organised information is in memory, the better we remember it. The existence of organisation in memory can be easily shown. A categorised word list is prepared containing a number of words belonging to several categories (e.g. four-footed animals; sports; flowers; articles of furniture). The list is then presented in a random order (e.g. tennis, cat, desk, golf, carnation, and so on), followed by a test of free recall in which the words can be written down in any order. The words are not written down in a random order. Instead, they are recalled category by category. This is known as **categorical clustering**, and it shows the way in which presented information is structured and organised in line with the knowledge stored in long-term memory.

Categorical clustering is a useful tool for sorting and storing a mass of information. Imagine how difficult it would be to find anything in a supermarket if goods were organised by colour or size.

KEY TERM
Categorical clustering: the tendency to free recall categorised word lists category by category.

Why does categorical clustering occur? One possibility is that the list words are organised during learning. Alternatively, our knowledge of categories is used to organise the list words at the time of retrieval. Evidence that organisational processes occur during learning was obtained by Weist (1972). A categorised word list was presented in a random order, followed by a test of free recall. Weist asked his participants to rehearse out loud during learning, and he recorded their overt rehearsal. The patterns of overt rehearsal indicated that organisation into categories occurred during learning. Weist also found that the more organised the rehearsal, the better the participant's level of recall.

Mandler (1967) discovered that organisational processes are at work even with lists of random words. Participants sorted words into between two and seven categories. When they had sorted the words consistently, they were asked to provide recall. Recall was poorest for those who had used two categories, and increased by about four words per extra category used. Thus, those who used seven categories recalled about 20 more words than those who used only two. According to Mandler, those participants who used several categories in sorting were imposing more organisation on the list than were those who used only a few; this is termed **subject-imposed categorisation**. Mandler (1967, p.328) concluded that, "memory and organisation are not only correlated, but organisation is a necessary condition for memory."

In our discussion of organisation, we will make use of Tulving's (1972) distinction between episodic memory and semantic memory. Episodic memory is basically autobiographical memory, whereas semantic memory is general knowledge about the world and about language. We will assume that information in semantic memory is highly organised, and that categorical clustering reflects this underlying organisation.

Collins and Quillian: Semantic memory networks

In spite of the fact that semantic memory contains hundreds of thousands or millions of items of information, we can generally answer questions about that information very rapidly. For example, we can decide in about one second that a sparrow is a bird, and it takes the same length of time to think of a fruit starting with the letter "p". Semantic memory normally operates very efficiently because it is highly organised or structured.

The first systematic theory of semantic memory was put forward by Collins and Quillian (1969). They assumed that semantic memory is organised into a series of hierarchical networks. The major concepts in each network (e.g. animal, bird, canary) are represented as nodes, and properties or features (e.g. has wings; is yellow) are associated with each concept. Why is the property "can fly" stored with the bird concept rather than with the canary concept? According to Collins and Quillian, it would waste space in semantic memory to have information about being able to fly stored with every bird name. If those properties shared by nearly all birds (e.g. can fly; has wings) are stored only at the bird node or concept, this produces cognitive economy. The underlying principle is that property information is stored as far up the hierarchy as possible to minimise the amount of information stored in semantic memory.

Collins and Quillian (1969) tested their theory by using a speeded verification task, in which the participants had to decide as rapidly as possible whether sentences were true or false. It should be possible to decide very rapidly that the sentence, "A canary is yellow" is true, because the concept (i.e. "canary") and the property (i.e. "is yellow") are stored together at the same level of the hierarchy. In contrast, the sentence "A canary can fly", should take longer, because the concept and the property are separated by one level in the hierarchy. The sentence "A canary has skin" should take even longer, because there are two levels separating the concept and the property. As predicted, the time taken to respond to true sentences lengthened as the separation between the subject of the sentence and the predicate became greater.

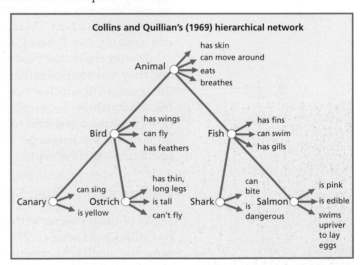

Collins and Quillian's (1969) hierarchical network

■ Research activity: Study Collins and Quillian's hierarchical network. Which of the following sentences should be verified most quickly, and which should take the longest?

• A salmon is an animal.
• Sharks can bite.
• Salmon is edible.

Evaluation

The theory proposed by Collins and Quillian (1969) provides a potential explanation of the hierarchical organisation observed in numerous memory experiments. Bower et al. (1969) asked their participants to learn 112 words belonging to four hierarchies, each of which consisted of four levels. The minerals hierarchy had the word "minerals" at the top level, "metals" and "stones" at the next level, "rare", "common", "alloys", "precious", and "masonry" at the third level, and several specific minerals at the fourth level (e.g.

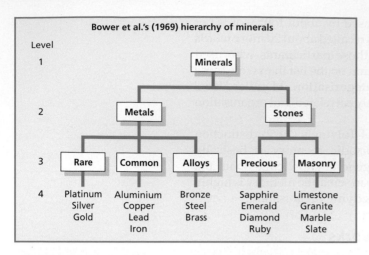

Bower et al.'s (1969) hierarchy of minerals

■ Research activity: Which are the atypical or unrepresentative category members?

Thrush, Eagle, Chicken, Penguin, Sparrow, Ostrich

What else might affect decision times in a categorisation task involving these words? Would different people have different ideas about typicality (e.g. an English person and an Inuit person)?

platinum; copper; steel). When the words were presented in their hierarchies, the participants recalled 73 words on average, compared to only 21 when the words were arranged randomly.

The theory correctly assumes we often use inferences to find the correct answer in semantic memory. For example, the information that Leonardo da Vinci had knees is not stored directly in our semantic memory. However, we know that Leonardo da Vinci was a human being, and that human beings have knees. Thus, we can confidently infer that Leonardo da Vinci had knees. This is the kind of inferential process proposed by Collins and Quillian (1969).

The theory also suffers from various problems. A sentence such as "A canary is yellow" differs from "A canary has skin" not only in the hierarchical distance between the concept and its property, but also in terms of familiarity. Conrad (1972) equated the various groups of sentences for familiarity, and found that the hierarchical distance between subject and predicate had very little effect on the time to verify each sentence.

There is another problem with the theory, relating to the prediction that the time required to decide that a member of a category does belong to that category should be the same regardless of how typical or representative of that category that member is. Thus, for example, it should take no longer to decide that "A chicken is a bird" is true than to make the same decision for "A robin is a bird". In fact, verification times are faster for the more typical members of a category (see Eysenck & Keane, 1995).

In sum, the hierarchical networks proposed by Collins and Quillian are too inflexible, and they make logical rather than psychological sense. According to Collins and Quillian, the speed with which we can access information in semantic memory is determined by the relationships of concepts to each other based on their dictionary meanings. In practice, however, speed of access to information in semantic memory depends to a great extent on how we use language, and on the experience or familiarity we have with different combinations of concepts.

Collins and Loftus: Spreading activation

Many of the problems with Collins and Quillian's (1969) network theory were resolved by Collins and Loftus (1975) in their spreading activation theory. According to this theory, semantic memory is organised on the basis of semantic relatedness or semantic distance. Semantic relatedness can be measured by asking people to decide how closely related pairs of words are. Alternatively, people can be asked to list as many members as they can of a given category; those members produced most often are the ones most closely related to the category.

According to the theory, the appropriate node in semantic memory is activated whenever someone sees, hears, or thinks about a concept. This activation then spreads most strongly to concepts that are closely related semantically. For example, activation would pass strongly from "robin" to "bird" in the sentence "A robin is a bird", because "robin" and "bird" are closely related semantically. This would permit the individual to decide rapidly that the sentence is true.

Evidence in support of spreading activation theory has come from studies on lexical decision, in which the participants have to decide whether a letter string is an English word. Meyer and Schvaneveldt (1971) presented two letter strings together, and the participants' task was to respond "yes" only if both letter strings formed words. Decisions were made much more quickly on yes trials when the two words were semantically related (e.g. doctor nurse) than when they were unrelated (e.g. doctor tree).

Evaluation

Spreading activation theory has proved more successful than the approach of Collins and Quillian (1969). In many situations, performance is determined by semantic relatedness rather than by the location of concepts within hierarchies. As is predicted by spreading activation theory, the activation of any given concept leads to the automatic activation of semantically related concepts. However, as Baddeley (1990, p.333) pointed out, the theory accounts for the data, "at the expense of assuming a very complex network and a set of elaborate processing rules."

Spreading activation theory does not provide a full account. In our everyday lives, we use the information in semantic memory in many different ways, and spreading activation is only one out of several processes. Spreading activation is basically an automatic process that does not rely on conscious awareness or control. Thus, spreading activation theory sheds little light on the processes involved in thinking about the concepts in semantic memory.

Spreading activation theory deals with individual concepts in semantic memory. However, much of the information in semantic memory is in the form of schemas, which are organised packets of information (see next section). An example of a schema would be our knowledge of schools (e.g. who works in them; how they are organised; what they are for; and so on). Spreading activation theory does not cover complex kinds of information such as schemas.

Bartlett: Schema theory

Bartlett (1932, p.213) argued that memory is determined not only by the information actually presented, but also by the relevant past knowledge the person possesses:

> *Remembering is ... an imaginative reconstruction, or construction, built out of the relation of our attitude towards a whole active mass of organised past reactions or experience.*

He argued that prior knowledge is stored in the form of **schemas**, and that schemas are involved in trying to reconstruct what we have read or heard. Thus, schemas provide one of the main ways in which information in memory is organised.

How does learning occur in a schema-based system? According to Rumelhart and Norman (1981), schema learning occurs in three ways:

1. Accretion: A new example of an existing schema is recorded, and added to the relevant schematic information in long-term memory.
2. Tuning: Concepts in a schema are elaborated and refined through experiences indicating that the existing schema is not adequate.
3. Restructuring: A new schema is created, often with reference to a similar, pre-existing schema.

Unfortunately, there is very little evidence on the processes of accretion, tuning, and restructuring.

Testing Bartlett's theory

How can we show the impact of prior knowledge or schematic knowledge on memory? Bartlett (1932) asked people to learn material producing a *conflict* between what was presented and the reconstructive processes based on knowledge of the world. If, for example, people read a story taken from a different culture, then prior knowledge might produce distortions in the remembered version of the story, making it more conventional and acceptable from the standpoint of their own cultural background.

In one study, Bartlett asked English participants to read a North American Indian folk tale called "The War of the Ghosts", after which they tried to recall the story. Part of the story was as follows:

One night two young men from Edulac went down the river to hunt seals, and while they were there it became foggy and calm. Then they heard war-cries, and they thought: "Maybe this is a war-party." They escaped to the shore, and hid behind a log. Now canoes came up, and they

KEY TERM
Schemas: organised sets of information or knowledge stored in long-term memory.

KEY STUDY EVALUATION — Bartlett

Sir Frederic Bartlett believed in taking a constructionist approach to memory, that is, he saw people as taking an active approach to memorising and recalling memories. The memory itself is therefore a construction, integrating past experiences with new input. Bartlett's research was carried out early in the twentieth century and yet, as he was interested in how people's memories worked in real-life situations, he was very up-to-date. It can be argued that his experiments are much more ecologically valid than those involving recall of syllables or lists of words. However, this research, like much qualitative work, has difficulties in classifying data, such as the types of recall errors made. More recently there has been a resurgence of everyday memory studies within the Bartlett tradition, but in ways that make it easier to analyse the data that emerge.

■ Research activity: In small groups, write your own schemas for the following:

• Catching a train
• Buying a newspaper
• Starting school

How easy was it to agree on a uniform pattern of events? Were any of the themes easier to agree on than the others? Why might this be?

heard the noise of paddles, and saw one canoe coming up to them. There were five men in the canoe, and they said: "What do you think? We wish to take you along. We are going up the river to make war on the people."

What did Bartlett find? The participants' recall distorted the content and style of the original story, and these distortions increased over successive recalls. Most of the recall errors were in the direction of making the story read more like an ordinary English story. Bartlett used the term **rationalisation** to refer to this type of error. Other distortions of memory included flattening (failing to recall unfamiliar details) and sharpening (elaboration of certain details).

Bartlett (1932, p.78) did not give very specific instructions to his participants: "I thought it best ... to try to influence the subjects' procedure as little as possible." Thus, some of the distortions observed by Bartlett may have been due to conscious guessing rather than to actual memory errors. There is some force in this argument, because instructions stressing the need for accurate recall eliminated almost half of the errors usually found (Gauld & Stephenson, 1967).

Support for Bartlett (1932) has come from several studies. Sulin and Dooling (1974) asked their participants to read a story, having told them it was about either Adolf Hitler or Gerald Martin (a fictitious character). Afterwards, they were given a test of recognition memory, and asked to decide whether each sentence in the test had been presented in the story. The key sentences were those that had *not* been presented, but which referred to well-known facts about Adolf Hitler. Those participants who had been told the story was about Hitler were much more likely to claim mistakenly that these key sentences had been in the original story. Thus, their prior knowledge about Hitler produced distortions in their recall.

Bartlett used the term "schema" vaguely, and never obtained good evidence about the kinds of information contained in any given schema. Bower, Black, and Turner (1979) addressed this issue. They argued, for example, that most people have a restaurant schema. In other words, they have clear expectations about the sequence of events likely to take place during a restaurant meal. They asked several people to list the most important events associated with having a restaurant meal, and found that most included the following events in their list: sitting down; looking at the menu; ordering; eating; paying the bill; and leaving the restaurant. Bower et al. (1969) carried out the same exercise for other schemas, and found that the contents of any given schema tended to be fairly uniform from one person to the next.

Discussion points

1. Why do you think that Bartlett's research has been so influential?
2. Do you think that the kinds of errors and distortions observed by Bartlett would be found with other kinds of material (see next section)?

Evaluation

Prior knowledge can produce systematic distortions in our memory for stories. The notion that this prior knowledge is usually stored in the form of schemas or organised packets of information is widely accepted. One of the main criticisms of Bartlett's schema theory is that he used stories from an unfamiliar culture to find good evidence of systematic distortions in memory. However, Bransford (1979) argued that people *constantly* use schematic knowledge when they engage in inference drawing, in which missing information in a message is guessed at on the basis of relevant information. After people have drawn an inference, they will often think later on that the inference formed part of the information presented to them, and this will lead to distortions of memory.

Bransford discussed one of his studies on inference drawing. The participants were presented with simple stories (e.g. "When the man entered the kitchen, he slipped on a wet spot and dropped the delicate glass pitcher on the floor. The pitcher was very expensive and everyone watched the event with horror"). On a later test of recognition

KEY TERM

Rationalisation: the tendency for story recall to be distorted to conform to cultural conventions.

memory, the participants often claimed that they had heard the sentence, "When the man entered the kitchen, he slipped on a wet spot and broke the delicate glass pitcher when it fell on the floor." Their schematic knowledge of pitchers encouraged them to draw the inference that the pitcher broke, and this led to errors in long-term memory.

Bartlett (1932) argued that schemas affect the retrieval process rather than the comprehension process. In fact, schemas influence *both* processes (Eysenck & Keane, 1995). Schema theory goes too far in the direction of claiming that memory is usually inaccurate. We often remember accurately the personal remarks that others make about us, and actors and actresses need to remember their lines perfectly. Such phenomena are not easily explained by schema theory, with its emphasis on the ways in which schemas change what has been presented in systematic ways.

Why Do We Forget?

Our memory for what happened in the past tends to become worse as time goes by. Hermann Ebbinghaus (1885) produced the first clear experimental evidence for increased forgetting over time. In his studies, Ebbinghaus was both the experimenter and the only participant. He learned a list of meaningless items known as nonsense syllables (e.g. MAZ; TUD) until he could recall all of them. He later re-learned the list until he could again recall all of them. Ebbinghaus measured his level of remembering at different retention intervals by the reduction or saving in the number of trials required for complete recall between the original and second learning (the savings method).

Ebbinghaus's memory was very good at short retention intervals, but became steadily worse at longer retention intervals. There was a large increase in forgetting over the first hour after learning, after which forgetting increased more slowly. It is easy to describe the time course of forgetting, but harder to identify the reasons for forgetting. In what follows, we will discuss some of the main factors in forgetting. The later section on practical applications of memory deals with some areas of everyday life in which forgetting can have serious consequences.

Is forgetting always a bad thing? Do we need to remember everything?

Trace decay theory

Forgetting might be due to gradual decay of the memory traces produced by basic processes within the brain: "The persisting images suffer changes which more and more affect their nature" (Ebbinghaus, 1885). It has proved hard to study these physiological changes directly. As a result, tests of trace decay theory have been somewhat indirect. They have addressed the theoretical assumption that forgetting depends on the length of the retention interval rather than on the events occurring during the retention interval.

Jenkins and Dallenbach (1924) asked two students to recall nonsense syllables at intervals between one and eight hours. The students were either awake or asleep during the retention interval. There was much less forgetting when the students were asleep during the retention interval than when they were awake. This is inconsistent with trace decay theory. It suggests that most forgetting is due to interference from other events, with such interference being much greater when people are awake than when they are asleep.

In fact, the findings obtained by Jenkins and Dallenbach (1924) cannot be accepted at face value. In the asleep condition, the students learned the material in the *evening*, whereas their learning usually occurred in the *morning* in the awake condition. Thus, the high level of forgetting in the awake condition could have occurred either because the students were awake throughout the retention interval, or because learning is worse in the morning. Hockey et al. (1972) unconfounded these factors. The rate of forgetting was rapid during daytime sleeping, suggesting that forgetting depends mostly on the time at which learning occurs.

In sum, there is very little support for trace decay theory. If all memory traces are subject to decay, it is surprising how well we can remember many events that happened several years ago and which are rarely thought about or rehearsed. For

What were the independent, dependent, and confounding variables in Jenkins and Dallenbach's study?

After reorganising the contents of kitchen cupboards, you may find yourself looking for something in its old location, even weeks after everything has been moved. This is an example of interference—memory for the old location is interfering with memory for the new one.

example, most people remembered in detail for some years what they were doing when they heard the news of Mrs Thatcher's resignation in 1990 (Conway et al., 1994). Accurate and long-lasting memories for very significant events are known as flashbulb memories (discussed earlier in the chapter). However, trace decay may play some causal role in forgetting.

Interference theory

If you had asked psychologists during the 1930s, 1940s, or 1950s what caused forgetting, you would probably have received the answer "Interference". It was assumed that memory can be disrupted or interfered with by what we have previously learned or by what we will learn in the future. When previous learning interferes with later learning and retention, this is known as **proactive interference**. When later learning disrupts memory for earlier learning, this is known as **retroactive interference**.

Interference theory has been tested by means of paired-associate learning. The early research involved nonsense syllables, but more recently words have generally been used. The participants are initially presented with several pairs of words (e.g. cat–tree; candle–table). The first word in each pair (e.g. cat; candle) is known as the stimulus term, and the second word (e.g. tree; table) is the response term. Learning continues until the participants can recall each response term when presented with the stimulus term.

The participants then learn a second list of paired associates. Evidence for proactive interference can be obtained by later testing for recall of the second list of paired associates, and comparing memory performance against that of control participants who did not learn the first list. Retroactive interference is assessed by testing for recall of the first list of paired associates, with performance in this condition being compared with that of participants who were not required to learn the second list. Proactive and retroactive interference is revealed by the extent to which the performance of the experimental group is lower than that of the control group.

There is strong evidence for both kinds of interference when the same stimulus terms are used in both lists of paired associates, but with the response terms differing (Underwood & Postman, 1960). However, little proactive or retroactive interference is found when different stimulus terms are used in the two lists (Underwood & Postman, 1960).

It is unlikely that interference theory has much applicability to everyday life. Substantial interference is found only when two different responses are attached to the same stimulus. This happens occasionally in everyday life. It is illustrated by the case of the nineteenth-century German psychologist Hugo Munsterberg, who moved his pocket-watch from one pocket to another. When provided with the appropriate stimulus (e.g. "What time is it?"), Munsterberg would often fumble about in confusion, and put his hand into the wrong pocket.

According to interference theory, learning a second response to a given stimulus causes the first response to be unlearned. This seems to occur under laboratory conditions, but not with associations learned outside the laboratory. The participants in a study by Slamecka (1966) produced free associates to various stimulus words. In other words, they said whatever associations came to mind. Then the stimulus words were paired with new responses, which should have caused unlearning of the free associates. However, when Slamecka asked his participants to recall their free associates, there was no sign of the predicted retroactive interference.

There is another reason why interference theory no longer enjoys much popularity. A central interest of cognitive psychologists is in the *processes* involved in learning and memory, but interference theory has very little to say about them.

What explanation could you suggest for Slamecka's finding that interference theory does not always apply in real life?

Cue-dependent forgetting

According to Tulving (1974), there are only two major reasons for forgetting. First, there is trace-dependent forgetting, in which the information is no longer stored in memory.

KEY TERMS
Proactive interference: current learning and memory being disrupted by previous learning.
Retroactive interference: subsequent learning disrupting memory for previous learning.

Trace decay theory emphasised this form of forgetting. Second, there is **cue-dependent forgetting**, in which the information is in memory, but cannot be accessed. Such information is said to be available (i.e. it is still stored) but not accessible (i.e. it cannot be retrieved).

Evidence of the importance of cue-dependent forgetting was provided by Tulving and Pearlstone (1966). Long lists of words belonging to several different categories (e.g. articles of furniture; four-footed animals) were presented. The participants were then asked to write down what they could remember (non-cued recall). After that, they were given all the category names as cues, and were again asked to write down the list words. The participants recalled up to three or four times as many words with cued recall as they could recall with non-cued recall. The relatively poor performance with non-cued recall occurred because the helpful cues presented in cued recall were absent; in other words, there was a substantial amount of cue-dependent forgetting.

Tulving and Psotka (1971) compared the cue-dependent approach with interference theory. There were between one and six word lists, with four words in six different categories in each list. After each list had been presented, the participants free-recalled as many words as possible. That was the original learning. After all the lists had been presented, the participants tried to recall the words from *all* the lists that had been presented. That was total free recall. Finally, all the category names were presented, and the participants tried again to recall all the words from all the lists. That was total free cued recall.

There was apparently strong evidence for retroactive interference in total free recall, because word recall from any given list decreased as the number of other lists intervening between learning and recall increased. This finding would be interpreted within interference theory by assuming that there had been unlearning of the earlier lists. However, this interpretation does not fit with the findings from total cued recall. There was essentially no retroactive interference or forgetting when the category names were available to the participants. Thus, the forgetting observed in total free recall was basically cue-dependent forgetting.

The studies of cue-dependent forgetting that we have considered so far have involved *external* cues (e.g. presenting category names). However, cue-dependent forgetting has also been shown with *internal* cues (e.g. mood state). Information about current mood state is often stored in the memory trace, and there is more forgetting if the mood state at the time of retrieval is different. The notion that there should be less forgetting when the mood state at learning and at retrieval is the same is generally known as **mood-state-dependent memory**. This was shown amusingly in the film *City Lights*, in which Charlie Chaplin saves a drunken millionaire from attempted suicide, and is befriended in return. When the millionaire sees Charlie again he is sober, and fails to recognise him. However, when the millionaire becomes drunk again, he catches sight of Charlie, treats him like a long-lost friend, and takes him home with him. The next morning, when the millionaire is sober again, he forgets that Charlie is his invited guest, and gets his butler to throw him out.

People tend to remember material better when there is a *match* between their mood at learning and at retrieval. The effects are stronger when the participants are in a positive mood than a negative mood (Ucros, 1989). They are also greater when people try to remember events having personal relevance.

Some psychologists have argued that all forgetting is cue-dependent forgetting, claiming that there is permanent storage of information. Loftus and Loftus (1980) found that 84% of psychologists and 69% of non-psychologists believed in permanent storage. There is little evidence to support this strong position. It is probably popular because we cannot disprove the notion of permanent storage. It is possible that information is still stored somewhere in long-term memory, even if it cannot be retrieved. At present, the most appropriate conclusion is probably that most (but not all) forgetting is cue-dependent.

The findings on cue-dependent forgetting and on mood-state-dependent memory indicate that forgetting occurs when the information available at the time of retrieval does

Can you apply Tulving and Pearlstone's research to your study of psychology? Try to think of "cues" that you can use to organise recall around.

Bearing in mind that the effects of mood on recall are stronger when the individual has a positive mood when learning and retrieving, can you think of applications for this research? For example, efforts made by advertisers to link products to positive-mood-inducing devices.

The film *City Lights* illustrates the concept of mood-state-dependent memory.

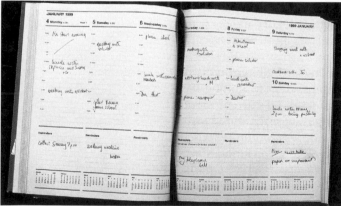

not match or "fit" the information contained in the memory trace. Tulving (1979, p.408) used this notion to put forward his **encoding specificity principle**:

The probability of successful retrieval of the target item is an ... increasing function of informational overlap between the information contained in the retrieval cue and the information stored in memory.

Thus, the greater the similarity between the information contained in the retrieval cue and in the memory trace, the higher the probability that the individual will remember the information he or she is seeking.

The encoding specificity principle is hard to test, because we do not usually know how much "informational overlap" there is between retrieval cue and memory trace. According to the encoding specificity principle, retrieval (or its opposite, forgetting) occurs fairly rapidly and with little thinking involved. However, retrieval often involves problem-solving activities. For example, if asked what you were doing last Friday, you might reply: "Let's see, on Friday I usually play badminton, but last week was half-term, and so I went to see *Titanic* with a friend."

Repression

One of the best known approaches to forgetting is the repression theory advanced by Sigmund Freud. According to Freud (1915, p.86), the essence of **repression** "lies simply in the function of rejecting and keeping something out of consciousness." Freud argued that much forgetting is motivated by the desire to keep anxiety-provoking memories out of conscious awareness. However, he used the term "repression" in a number of different ways. Freud sometimes defined repression as the inhibition of the capacity for emotional experience. According to this definition, repression can occur even when there is conscious awareness of unpleasant memories.

KEY TERMS
Encoding specificity principle: the notion that memory is best when there is a large overlap between the information available at the time of retrieval and the information in the memory trace.
Repression: Freud's notion that very anxiety-provoking material is kept out of conscious awareness.

It is hard to test Freud's theory. It is impossible ethically to make use of the anxiety-producing and traumatic events involved in repression. Experimental attempts to demonstrate the phenomenon of repression typically involve creating anxiety to produce forgetting or repression. After that, the anxiety is removed to show that the repressed information is still in long-term memory (the "return of the repressed"). In practice, failure feedback (telling the participants their memory-task performance is poor) has usually been used to produce anxiety. Anxiety has then been removed by reassuring the participants the failure feedback was false. Failure feedback often leads to impaired memory, but it is not clear that repression is involved. As Holmes (1990) has pointed out, the participants may think about their failure and the reasons for it rather than devoting all their efforts to the memory test.

More convincing evidence for repression has come from repressors, who have low scores on trait anxiety (a personality factor relating to susceptibility to anxiety) and high scores on defensiveness (see Chapter 27). According to Weinberger, Schwartz, and Davidson (1979), those who score low on trait anxiety and on defensiveness are the truly low-anxious, those high on trait anxiety and low on defensiveness are the high-anxious, and those high on both trait anxiety and defensiveness are the defensive high-anxious.

All four groups were studied by Myers and Brewin (1994). They measured the length of time taken to recall negative childhood memories. Repressors were much slower than any of the other groups. This did not happen because repressors had enjoyed the happiest childhoods: they reported having experienced the most indifference and hostility from their fathers.

There is also non-experimental evidence of repression. Large numbers of adults seem to have repressed memories for sexual abuse which they suffered in childhood. For example, Herman and Schatzow (1987) found that 28% of a group of female incest victims reported severe memory deficits from childhood, and such repressed memories were most frequent among women who had suffered violent abuse. There is often no concrete evidence to confirm the accuracy of repressed memories. Brewin et al. (1993, p.94) discussed the issues involved, and came to the following conclusion: "Provided that individuals are questioned about the occurrence of specific events or facts that they were sufficiently old and well placed to know about, the central features of their accounts are likely to be reasonably accurate." However, it must be borne in mind that the whole issue of recovered memories of abuse is very sensitive. It raises major ethical and legal issues concerning the therapist's responsibilities, the effects of accusations on other members of the family, and so on.

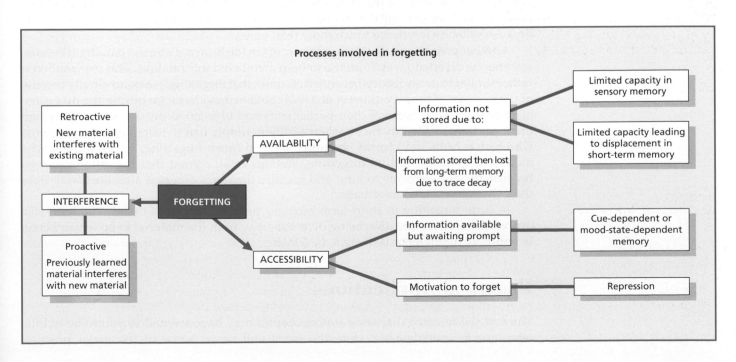

Processes involved in forgetting

Implicit memory

So far we have been discussing the factors that influence explicit memory, which depends on conscious recollection. What about implicit memory, which does not depend on conscious recollection? Reber (1993) argued that implicit learning and memory are generally more robust than explicit learning and memory, and so less affected by forgetting. Meudell and Mayes (1981) asked participants to search cartoons for specified objects. Seventeen months later, the participants were generally poor at recognising the cartoons (explicit memory). However, they found the objects more quickly than on the previous occasion (implicit memory). Thus, the factors producing forgetting in explicit memory did not do so for implicit memory.

Reber (1993) argued that implicit learning and memory are more resistant than explicit learning and memory to the effects of brain damage. As we have seen, the evidence from amnesic patients (e.g. Claparède, 1911; Graf et al., 1984) supports this position. Why does brain damage cause more forgetting in explicit memory than in implicit memory? According to Reber (1993), the brain systems involved in implicit learning and memory developed earlier in evolution than did those involved in explicit learning and memory, and they have become increasingly robust over the generations. In contrast, the brain systems involved in explicit learning and memory rely heavily on conscious awareness, which is rather vulnerable and fragile. Regardless of whether Reber is right or wrong, the factors producing forgetting in explicit memory have less effect on implicit memory.

Short-term memory

Most theories of forgetting focus on long-term memory. However, there has been some interest in identifying the factors producing forgetting in short-term memory. The key findings come from the Brown–Peterson paradigm. In this paradigm, three consonants (e.g. F B M) are presented, followed immediately by a three-digit number. The participant's task is to count backwards by threes from the number until the signal is given to recall the consonants. Consonant recall is generally almost 100% if there is no retention interval, but it falls to only 10–20% with a retention interval of 18 seconds.

What causes forgetting in the Brown–Peterson paradigm? One possibility is that retroactive interference is involved, with the digits being sufficiently *similar* to the consonants to produce interference. Evidence supporting that point of view was reported by Reitman (1971). The participants carried out either a syllable detection task or a tone detection task during the retention interval. Those who performed the syllable detection task had much lower recall than those who performed the tone detection task, presumably because syllables interfered much more than tones.

Another possibility is that forgetting occurs in the Brown–Peterson paradigm because attention is diverted away from the to-be-remembered information. This explanation is rather similar to decay theory, because it assumes that forgetting can occur simply because of the passage of time. Watkins et al. (1973) obtained evidence favouring the diversion-of-attention theory. Some of their participants had to listen to musical notes, then hum them, and finally identify them, whereas others simply had to listen to the notes. Those who had to hum and identify the notes showed much forgetting, whereas those who merely listened showed no forgetting. Watkins et al. argued that forgetting occurred because the requirements to hum and identify the notes diverted attention away from the to-be-remembered information.

In sum, forgetting in short-term memory probably depends mainly on decay-like processes based on attention being diverted away from the material to be remembered. In addition, interference is likely to be a factor.

Practical Applications

Much of the research discussed in this chapter may have seemed to you to be of little relevance to everyday life. Here the focus will be on some of the major practical applications of our knowledge of human memory. There are several advantages to studying everyday memory. First, such research is more likely than laboratory research to have direct applicability to everyday life. Second, it is important to consider the functions served by memory in our lives. Third, research into everyday memory provides a test-bed for theories of memory developed from laboratory research.

There are some disadvantages in everyday memory research. First, there is often poor control of the conditions in which learning occurs. Second, we often cannot assess the accuracy of everyday memories. Third, everyday memory research has failed to produce many new theoretical insights into human memory (Eysenck & Keane, 1995). In fact, the first two limitations do not apply to most of the research we will be discussing, which was conducted under well-controlled conditions.

Eyewitness testimony

Many innocent people have been put in prison purely on the basis of eyewitness testimony. Mistakes by eyewitnesses may occur because of what happens at the time of the crime or incident, or because of what happens thereafter. Perhaps the most obvious reason for mistaken testimony is because the eyewitness was not paying enough attention to the incident. Eyewitness testimony also tends to be more limited when the crime is violent. Loftus and Burns (1982) showed participants two filmed versions of a crime (including or excluding a violent incident). Inclusion of the violent incident caused impaired memory for details presented up to two minutes earlier. The memory-impairing effects of violence would probably be greater in real life, because the presence of violent criminals might endanger the eyewitness's life.

Post-event information

Some studies have focused on the fragility of eyewitness memories and the ways in which such memories can be distorted *after* the incident. Loftus and Palmer (1974) showed their participants a series of projected slides of a multiple-car accident. The participants then answered specific questions. Some were asked "About how fast were the cars going when they smashed into each other?", whereas for others the verb "hit" was substituted for "smashed into". The estimated speed was affected by the verb used, averaging 41 mph when the verb "smashed" was used versus 34 mph when "hit" was used. Thus, the information implicit in the question affected memory, even though the questions apparently differed only slightly.

One week later, all the participants were asked the following question: "Did you see any broken glass?" There was actually no broken glass, but 32% of the participants who had been asked previously about speed using the verb "smashed" said they had seen broken glass. In contrast, only 14% of the participants asked using the verb "hit" said they had seen broken glass. Thus, the change of only one word in a question heard a week earlier had a major effect on the participants' memory!

KEY STUDY EVALUATION — Loftus and Palmer

This research was carried out by showing participants film of a multiple-car accident. Methodologically, this study was well controlled, although, as is common, students were used as participants and it could be argued that students are not necessarily representative of the general population. However, the experiment lacks ecological validity, in that the participants were not real-life witnesses, and it could be said that the emotional effects of being a real-life witness could affect recall. The study has real-life applications, particularly in respect of the credence given to eyewitness testimony in court, and the use of taped interviews in police stations.

Loftus and Zanni (1975) showed that even small differences in the way in which a question is asked can have a marked effect. They showed their participants a short film of a car accident. Some of them were asked "Did you see a broken headlight?", whereas others were asked "Did you see the broken headlight?" There was no broken headlight in the film, but the latter question implies there was. Only 7% of those asked about *a* broken headlight said they had seen it, against 17% of those asked about *the* broken headlight.

Discussion points

1. How confident can we be that such laboratory-based findings resemble what would be found in the real world?
2. What are some of the practical implications of this research?

Explanation

How does misleading post-event information distort what eyewitnesses report? Bartlett's schema theory provides an answer. Bartlett (1932) argued that retrieval involves a process of reconstruction, in which all the available information about an event is used to reconstruct the details of that event on the basis of "what must have been true". New information that is relevant to a previously experienced event can affect recollection by providing a different basis for reconstruction.

Another possibility is that eyewitnesses simply respond as they think the experimenter wants them to respond. If the experimenter asks, "Did you see the broken headlight?", this suggests there was a broken headlight which the experimenter would expect observant eyewitnesses to have noticed. When the participants in a study simply behave in expected ways, this is known as responding to the **demand characteristics** of the situation. Lindsay (1990) tried to eliminate demand characteristics by telling some of his participants that the post-event information was wrong. Memory for the incident was still distorted by the post-event information, suggesting that this information had genuinely changed memory.

A major limitation of most studies on the effects of post-event information is that they have focused on memory for peripheral details (e.g. presence or absence of broken glass). As Fruzzetti et al. (1992) pointed out, it is harder to distort eyewitnesses' memory by misleading post-event information for key details (e.g. the murder weapon) than for minor details.

Other factors

The most important findings on eyewitness testimony are those that are obtained consistently, and differ from what might be expected from common sense. Kassin, Ellsworth, and Smith (1989) asked experts in eyewitness testimony to identify the findings that they believed to be well established and also asked them to state whether or not they believed the findings were common sense. For most of the well-established findings, only a very small number of experts (percentages in brackets) thought that they conformed to a common-sense view.

- An eyewitness's confidence is not a good predictor of his or her identification accuracy (3%).
- Eyewitnesses tend to overestimate the duration of events (5%).
- Eyewitness testimony about an event often reflects not only what the eyewitness actually saw, but also information they obtained later on (7.5%).
- There is a conventional (i.e. Ebbinghaus-type) forgetting curve for eyewitness memories (24%).
- An eyewitness's testimony about an event can be affected by how the questions put to that witness are worded (27%).
- The use of a one-person line-up increases the risk of misidentification (29%).

Implications for police procedures

It follows from the research we have discussed that the questions asked during a police interview may distort an eyewitness's memory, and thus reduce its reliability. What happened until fairly recently in the United Kingdom was that an eyewitness's account of what had happened was repeatedly interrupted. The interruptions made it hard for the eyewitness to concentrate fully on the process of retrieval, and thus reduced recall. As a result of psychological research, the Home Office issued guidelines recommending that police interviews should proceed from free recall to general open-ended questions, concluding with more specific questions.

Are there any other changes that have been (or should be) introduced to improve eyewitness testimony? Geiselman et al. (1985) argued that interview techniques should take account of some basic characteristics of human memory:

- Memory traces are complex, and contain various features and/or kinds of information.

KEY TERM
Demand characteristics: cues used by participants to try to work out what an experiment is about.

- The effectiveness of a retrieval cue depends on the extent to which the information it contains overlaps with information stored in the memory trace; this is the encoding specificity principle (see earlier).
- Various retrieval cues may permit access to any given memory trace; for example, if the name of an acquaintance cannot be retrieved, it may be recalled if other information is used as a retrieval cue (e.g. forming an image of him or her; thinking of the names of the person's friends).

Geiselman et al. used these considerations to develop the basic cognitive interview. The eyewitness tries to recreate mentally the context that existed at the time of the crime, including environmental and internal (e.g. mood state) information. The eyewitness then simply reports everything he or she can think of relating to the incident, even if the information is fragmented. In addition, the eyewitness reports the details of the incident in various orders, and from various perspectives (e.g. that of another eyewitness).

Geiselman et al. compared the effectiveness of the basic cognitive interview with that of the standard police interview. The average number of correct statements produced by eyewitnesses was 41.1 using the basic cognitive interview, compared to only 29.4 using the standard police interview. Fisher et al. (1987) devised an enhanced cognitive interview, and showed it was more effective than the basic cognitive interview. The enhanced cognitive interview includes the main aspects of the basic cognitive interview. However, it also makes use of the following recommendations (Roy, 1991, p.399):

Investigations should minimise distractions, induce the eyewitness to speak slowly, allow a pause between the response and next question, tailor language to suit the individual eyewitness, follow up with interpretive comment, try to reduce eyewitness anxiety, avoid judgemental and personal comments, and always review the eyewitness's description of events or people under investigation.

Remembering medical information

It is important that patients should remember the information provided by their doctors, and should act on it appropriately. However, patients often forget much of the medical information they have been told, and this can have adverse effects on their health.

Ley (1978, 1997) discussed systematic investigations of memory for medical information. His first task was to discover which items of information were well remembered and which were poorly recalled. Most of his findings were predictable from earlier laboratory studies. The initial information given by the doctor was well remembered (this is the primacy effect, see earlier). Items of information rated as most important by the patients were recalled better than those rated least important, presumably because they were processed more thoroughly. Another predictable finding was that patients forgot a greater percentage of statements as the number presented by the doctor increased. This follows from our limited ability to process information. As might be expected, memory performance for medical information tended to be higher with recognition memory than when recall was used.

Information that was organised explicitly into categories (e.g. medicines to take) was remembered better than the same information presented in an unorganised way. As we saw earlier in the chapter, organised information is easier to remember, because it corresponds to the structure and organisation of long-term memory. Patients with more medical knowledge remembered more of what the doctor said than did the less knowledgeable, presumably because they found it easier to engage in

From what you have learned so far about recall, what practical advice would you give to doctors to improve recall of information by patients?

Ley's investigations of patients' memory for medical information found that much of the information given by doctors was forgotten. As a result, he came up with a list of recommendations for improving recall through better presentation of information.

elaborative processing. As would be expected by psychologists (but not perhaps by medical doctors), simply repeating information had relatively little effect on the amount recalled. The reason is that repetition of a statement is unlikely to change the depth or elaboration of processing.

Having established that memory for medical information in everyday settings obeys the same principles as memory for other kinds of information, Ley (1978) put forward various recommendations for doctors. First, he argued that the most important information, i.e. advice and instructions, should be given first. Second, the importance of the advice and instructions should be emphasised. Third, doctors should use short words and sentences. Ley (1978) found that patients often found it hard to understand the information contained in medical booklets. He compared two booklets on weight loss, one of which used long words and sentences and the other of which used short words and sentences. Obese women reading the former booklet lost 8 pounds on average, compared to 15 pounds for those reading the latter booklet. These effects reflect greater compliance with, as well as greater understanding of, the latter booklet. Ley (1997) found across 13 studies that simplifying the way in which medical information was presented increased recall by 55% on average.

Fourth, the information should be organised into explicit categories (e.g. "These are the tests that will be done"). Fifth, repeat the information, even though the effects are likely to be small. Sixth, doctors should be as specific as possible. For example, they should tell an overweight patient "You must lose 20 pounds" rather than "You must lose weight". This last point was based on a study by Bradshaw et al. (1975). Specific statements were more than twice as likely as general statements to be remembered.

Ley (1988) prepared a booklet for medical practitioners based on these recommendations. Before the general practitioners received the booklet, their patients recalled about 55% of what they said. Afterwards, that figure increased to 70%.

Ley (1997) added a further recommendation based on research in Australia. Some smokers bought packets of cigarettes, all of which had the same health warning on them. Other smokers were exposed to four different health warnings in rotation. Of those in the former group, 92% recalled the health warning. In contrast, over 50% of those in the latter group recalled no more than one warning. The recommendation is not to overload people with information.

Ley's recommendations

1. Give advice and instructions first
2. Emphasise importance of advice and instructions
3. Use short words and sentences
4. Organise information into explicit categories
5. Repeat information
6. Be specific
7. Do not overload people with information

Mnemonic techniques

Of all the practical applications of memory research, techniques for improving memory are potentially of greatest use. **Mnemonic techniques** (i.e. techniques designed to aid memory) have been developed, and have a lengthy history going back to the ancient Greeks.

Method of loci

The Greeks invented the **method of loci** (the method of locations), which enables people to remember a large number of items in the correct order. The first step is to memorise a set of locations, such as places along a familiar walk. Mental imagery is then used to associate each of the items in turn with a specific location. When the individual wants to recall the items, he or she carries out a "mental walk", simply recalling what is stored at each location along the walk. You might remember the items on a shopping list by imagining each item at a different place along the walk (e.g. a loaf of bread at the entrance to the park).

"One is a bun"

The method of loci is basically a peg system, with the items being associated with convenient "pegs" (e.g. locations on a walk). A more recent peg system is based on the one-is-a-bun rhyme (e.g. one is a bun; two is a shoe; three is a tree). Mental imagery is used to associate the first item to be remembered with a bun, the second item with a shoe, and so on. The advantage of this method over the method of loci is that you can rapidly produce any specific item (e.g. the fifth). This method doubles recall compared to conventional learning strategies (Morris & Reid, 1970).

Why is the one-is-a-bun mnemonic so successful? According to Ericsson (1988), there are three requirements for very high levels of memory performance:

- Meaningful encoding: the information should be processed meaningfully, relating it to pre-existing knowledge; this is reminiscent of the levels-of-processing theory.
- Retrieval structure: cues should be stored with the information to aid later retrieval; this is reminiscent of the encoding specificity principle.
- Speed-up: there is extensive practice so that the processes involved in encoding and retrieval occur rapidly.

How to use the "one-is-a-bun" mnemonic

Peg Rhyme	Standard Visual	Item to be remembered	Mnemonic Version
One-is-a-bun		Screwdriver	
Two-is-a-shoe		Ticket	
Three-is-a-tree		Newspaper	

The one-is-a-bun mnemonic provides meaningful encoding, because what needs to be learned is related to a meaningful rhyme that the learner already knows. It also provides a retrieval structure, because the items in the rhyme (e.g. bun; shoe) provide effective and specific retrieval cues. It also involves interactive imagery. It is unfortunate that we do not know the relative contributions of meaningful encoding, retrieval structure, and interactive imagery to the success of the one-is-a-bun mnemonic.

The keyword method is another mnemonic technique. It has been applied extensively to the task of acquiring foreign vocabulary. First, an association is formed between each spoken foreign word and an English word or phrase sounding like it (the keyword). Second, a mental image is created in which the keyword acts as a link between the foreign word and its English equivalent. For example, the Russian word "*zvonok*" is pronounced "zvah-oak", and it means "bell". This can be learned by using "oak" as the keyword, and forming an image of an oak tree covered with bells.

One is a bun
Two is a shoe
Three is a tree
Four is a door
Five is a hive
Six is sticks
Seven is heaven
Eight is a gate
Nine is a vine
Ten is a hen

Keyword method

The keyword technique is more effective when the keywords are provided than when learners provide their own. In a study by Atkinson and Raugh (1975), the participants were presented with 120 Russian words and their English equivalents. The keyword technique produced much better memory for the Russian words at a short retention interval and six weeks after learning.

SQ3R

What about strategies for learning complex, integrated material? Morris (1979) discussed SQ3R, which stands for Survey, Question, Read, Recite, Review (see Chapter 1). The initial Survey stage involves skimming through the material, trying to construct a framework that will help comprehension. In the Question stage, the learner asks himself or herself questions based on the various headings in the material. The material is read thoroughly at the Read stage, keeping the questions from the previous stage in mind. The material is re-read at the Recite stage, with the learner describing the essence of each section to himself or herself after it has been read. Finally, the learner reviews what has been acquired from the stimulus material.

The SQ3R method has proved very effective (see Morris, 1979). It is based on several theories of memory. The Survey stage is designed to activate relevant knowledge schemas and to provide an organisational structure to aid learning and memory. The Question and Read stages are designed to produce deep or semantic processing and elaborative processing. Finally, the Recite and Review stages test the reader's ability to retrieve the

Which of the mnemonic techniques could you use to enhance your ability to recall complex information such as used in your study of psychology?

information under examination-like conditions. That makes sense, because what we can remember depends very much on the conditions of retrieval (encoding specificity principle).

Evaluation

Do you use any personal mnemonic techniques other than those described? How might they link to the various theories of memory you have learned about?

Most mnemonic techniques are limited. They allow us to remember long lists of unrelated items. However, with the exception of the SQ3R method, they do not help much with the complex learning required to remember the contents of a book. However, mnemonic techniques are very useful under certain circumstances (e.g. harassed teachers trying to remember the names of their students).

The other main limitation with most mnemonic techniques is that it is often not known in detail exactly *why* they are effective. However, Ericsson (1988) has identified three important factors (listed earlier) that are often associated with very high levels of memory performance.

PERSONAL REFLECTIONS

- In my opinion, there has been much progress in our understanding of human memory in recent years. We now have much more realistic views about how short-term and long-term memory work, and the oversimplified theories of yesteryear have been abandoned.
- Perhaps the greatest progress has come in our understanding of everyday memory and the practical applications of memory associated with it. Thirty years ago, laboratory studies of memory seemed to have nothing to say about memory in everyday life, and I am delighted the gulf is closing rapidly.

SUMMARY

Memory stores

Theories of learning and memory focus on the successive stages of encoding, storage, and retrieval; they also focus on the structure of human memory and the processes operating on that structure. According to the multi-store theory, there are separate sensory, short-term, and long-term stores; this theory is oversimplified, especially the notion that there are unitary short-term and long-term stores.

Working memory

Baddeley argued that the short-term store should be replaced by a working memory system consisting of a central executive, an articulatory or phonological loop, and a visuo-spatial scratch (sketch) pad; this system is used for both active processing and brief storage of information.

Memory processes

According to levels-of-processing theory, depth of processing, elaboration of processing, and distinctiveness of processing are major determinants of long-term memory. The main problem is that the focus was too much on learning processes and not enough on retrieval processes.

Long-term memory

Tulving argued that long-term memory should be divided into episodic and semantic memory. Episodic and semantic memory differ in terms of content, but it is less clear that they differ in terms of the processes involved. There is an important distinction between explicit and implicit memory, as is shown by the finding that amnesic patients have poor explicit memory but intact implicit memory. Explicit memory depends on a declarative knowledge system, whereas implicit memory depends on a procedural knowledge system. Evidence from amnesic patients supports this distinction.

Semantic memory is highly organised on the basis of semantic relatedness or semantic distance. This organisation is reflected in phenomena such as categorical clustering and subject-imposed organisation. Knowledge in long-term memory is organised into schemas. The kinds of errors made in recall reflect the influence of underlying schemas. For example, people often mistakenly believe that the inferences they made during comprehension were actually presented. The notion of a schema is rather vague, and schema theory seems to predict more memory errors than are found.

Organisation of information in long-term memory

Forgetting may depend in part on trace decay, but there is a lack of convincing evidence. Long-term memory is generally so good that it is unlikely that trace decay is a major factor in forgetting. Forgetting depends in part on proactive and retroactive interference. However, although it is easy to obtain strong interference effects in the laboratory, it is unlikely that interference is of much importance in everyday life. Cue-dependent forgetting is probably the most important cause of forgetting, in which the information available at the time of retrieval does not match that stored in the memory trace; the cues can be external or internal (e.g. mood state). Forgetting from short-term memory depends on diversion of attention and interference.

Why do we forget?

Eyewitness testimony can easily be distorted by post-event information. The basic cognitive interview and the enhanced cognitive interview are designed to avoid that problem, and are based on the notion that memory traces contain a number of different kinds of information. Various mnemonic techniques (e.g. method of loci; one-is-a-bun; keyword technique; SQ3R) have been shown to be effective in improving memory. Most of these techniques are limited to memory for lists of words, and so lack general usefulness.

Practical applications

FURTHER READING

Nearly all the topics discussed in this chapter are dealt with in Chapter 4 of M.W. Eysenck (1993), *Principles of cognitive psychology*, Hove, UK: Psychology Press. A much fuller account of human memory is contained in M.W. Eysenck and M.T. Keane (1995), *Cognitive psychology: A student's handbook (3rd Edn.)* Hove, UK: Psychology Press. Several key topics in memory are discussed in an accessible way in J.A. Groeger (1997), *Memory and remembering: Everyday memory in context*, Harlow, UK: Addison Wesley Longman.

REVISION QUESTIONS

1	Compare and contrast *two* models of memory.	(24 marks)
2	"The notion that memory should be divided into short-term memory systems is valuable but rather oversimplified … If we look to the future … it is likely that additional short-term and long-term stores will be discovered" (Eysenck, 1994). Describe and evaluate psychological research that has shown us how information is organised in memory.	(24 marks)
3a	Outline *two* psychological theories of forgetting.	(12 marks)
3b	Assess the practical applications of these *two* theories.	(12 marks)
4a	Outline *two* practical applications of memory research.	(6 marks)
4b	Discuss the research evidence on which these applications are based.	(18 marks)

- **Language acquisition**
  How young children learn to communicate through language.

  Chomsky's theories
  The critical period hypothesis
  Skinner's reinforcement approach

- **Language comprehension**
  Understanding speech and the written word.

  Bransford and Johnson's schema studies
  McKoon and Ratcliff's minimalist hypothesis
  Graesser et al.'s search-after-meaning theory
  Van Dijk and Kintsch's theory of comprehension

- **Language production**
  Speaking and writing.

  Grice's co-operative principle
  Garrett's five-level model
  Hayes and Flower's theories of writing

- **Reasoning**
  How human beings think about problems and try to solve them.

  Braine et al.'s abstract-rule theory
  Wason's selection task
  Categorical reasoning
  Johnson-Laird's mental models theory
  Wason's inductive reasoning task

- **Decision making and judgement**
  Theories about how we decide between different options.

  Utility theory
  Tversky and Kahneman's study of loss aversion
  Tversky's elimination-by-aspects theory
  Simon's satisficing theory
  Tversky and Kahneman's studies of judgement and probability

- **Language and thought**
  Does the way we think depend on our use of language?

  Watson's approach
  The Whorfian hypothesis
  Hunt and Agnoli's modified Whorfian hypothesis
  Piaget, Vygotsky, and Fodor
  Bernstein's two language codes

14

Language and Thought

Without language, we would be unable to carry on with our everyday lives. Most of our social interactions with other people rely very heavily on language, and a good command of language is vital for all students. We are much more knowledgeable than people of previous generations, and the main reason is because knowledge is passed on from one generation to the next in the form of language. One of the main advantages we have over other species is our language ability.

According to Sternberg (1995), language can be defined as "an organised means of combining words in order to communicate." Parrots may say certain words, but they are not really using language. What they say is not organised, and does not involve combining words to pass on a message to others.

Three major areas of language research are dealt with in what follows. First, there is language acquisition, which is concerned with understanding how it is that young children so rapidly develop a good command of language. Second, there is language comprehension. When we read or listen to someone talking, we generally find it reasonably easy to make sense of the written or spoken sentences involved. Psychologists have studied in some detail the processes involved in comprehension. Third, there is language production. Most people are good at communicating their thoughts by speaking and by writing. As with comprehension, psychologists have been interested in studying the processes involved in language production.

Finally, we consider the complex issue of the relationship between language and thought. Several theorists have argued that language influences thought in various ways, and some of these theories are considered in the light of the evidence.

Organisations like the United Nations rely on language to improve co-operation between nations.

Why do you think language is so important as a means of communication for human beings?

Language Acquisition

Perhaps the most remarkable achievement of young children is the breathtaking speed with which they acquire language. By the age of 2, most children use language to communicate hundreds of messages. By the age of 5, children who may not even have started to go to school have mastered most of the grammatical rules of their native language. However, very few parents are consciously aware of the rules of grammar. Thus, young children simply "pick up" the complex rules of grammar without the benefit of much formal teaching.

Stages of language development

Language development can be divided into *receptive language* (language comprehension) and *productive language* (language expression or speaking). One-year-old children (and adults as well) have better receptive language than productive language. We

Cross-cultural issues: Do different cultures think differently as a consequence of different forms of language, or are these different language forms a result of variations in the ways people live? How would you go about examining this "chicken and egg" situation?

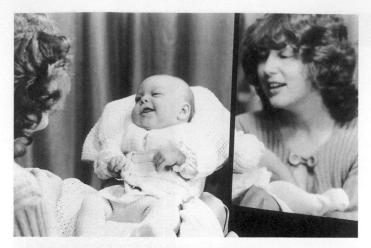

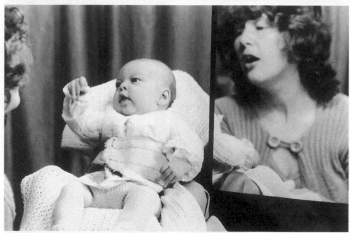

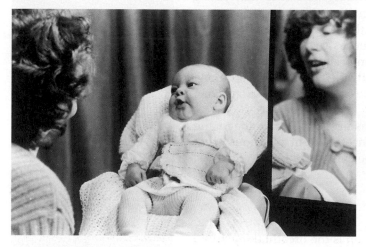

A six-week-old girl smiles at her mother's face, then responds to gentle baby-talk with cooing vocalisation and a conspicuous hand movement. In the third picture the mother is imitating the preceding vocalisation of her baby. From Olson (1980).

How do you think parents learn to decipher the meaning of early vocalisations?

underestimate the language skills of children if we assume that their speech reflects all the knowledge of language they have learned.

Children need to learn at least four kinds of knowledge about language (Shaffer, 1993):

- Phonology: the sound system of a language.
- Semantics: the meaning conveyed by words and sentences.
- Syntax: the set of grammatical rules indicating how words may and may not be combined to make sentences.
- Pragmatics: the principles determining how language should be modified to fit the context (e.g. we speak in a simpler way to a child than an adult).

Children usually learn about language in the order listed. They first of all learn to make sounds, followed by developing an understanding of what those sounds mean. After that, they learn grammatical rules and how to change what they say to fit the situation.

Early vocalisations

Newborn babies cry when they are distressed. When they are about three weeks of age, they produce "fake cries", which seem to occur in the absence of any distress. It is not known for sure why these fake cries are produced, but the reason may be because infants enjoy listening to their own voices. Infants between the ages of about three and five weeks start to coo. This involves producing vowel-like sounds (e.g. "ooooh") over and over again. Between four and six months of age, infants start to babble. Babbling consists of combinations of vowels and consonants that do not seem to have any meaning for the infants.

The babbling of infants up to about six months of age is rather similar in all parts of the world and in deaf infants as well as hearing ones. However, by about eight months of age, infants start to show some differences in their babbling which reflect the language they have heard. Indeed, adults can sometimes guess accurately from their babbling whether infants have been exposed to French, Chinese, Arabic, or English (De Boysson-Bardies, Sagart, & Durand, 1984).

One-word stage

Categories. Up until the age of about 18 months, young children are limited to single-word utterances. Nelson (1973) studied the first 50 words used by infants, and put those words into categories. The largest category was classes of objects (e.g. cat; car). The next largest category was specific objects (e.g. Mummy; Daddy). The other four categories used by young children were (in descending order of frequency): action words such as "go" and "come"; modifiers (e.g. "mine"; "small"); social words (e.g. "please"; "no"); and function words (e.g. "for"; "where").

Almost two-thirds of the words used by young children refer to objects or to people. Why is this so? Children refer to things of interest to them, which are mainly the people and objects that surround them.

Mistakes with meanings. Young children often make mistakes with word meanings. Some words are initially used to cover more objects than they should. This is known as **over-extension**. It can be embarrassing, as when a child refers to every man as "Daddy". The opposite mistake, in which the meaning given to a word covers too few objects, is known as **under-extension**. For example, a child may think that the word "cereal" refers only to the brand of cereal the family eats for breakfast.

More meaning in one word. McNeill (1970) referred to the one-word stage as the **holophrastic period**. In this period, young children try to convey much more meaning than their utterances would suggest. For example, an infant who says "ball" while pointing to a ball may mean that he or she would like to play with the ball. McNeill claimed that infants produce one-word utterances because they have a limited attention span and a small vocabulary.

It is hard to test McNeill's notion of a holophrastic period. In its favour is the fact that young children often suggest by their actions or by their tone of voice that they are trying to communicate more than just one word. On the other hand, young children have very limited cognitive development. This must restrict their ability to have complex ideas.

Children should have mastered around 27–45 phonemes (speech sounds) by the age of about 18 months. What might impair this rate of development?

Telegraphic period

The second stage of language development is the **telegraphic period**. It begins at, or shortly after, 18 months of age. Its name arises because the speech of children in this stage is rather like a telegram. Telegrams used to cost so much per word, and so senders of telegrams made them short. Content words such as nouns and verbs were included, but function words such as "a", "the", "and", pronouns, and prepositions were left out. The same is true of the speech of young children. However, they leave out even more than was left out of a telegram. For example, they generally omit plurals and tenses.

Even though young children are largely limited to two-word utterances, they can still communicate a wide range of meanings. One reason for this is that a given two-word utterance can mean different things in different situations. For example, "Daddy chair" may mean "I want to sit in Daddy's chair", "Daddy is sitting in his chair", or "Daddy, sit in your chair!".

Pivot words and open words. Braine (1963) found that early speech consists of two main classes of words: *pivot words* and *open words*. Pivot words always occur in the same place within an utterance, they are few in number, and they are used very often. In contrast, open words appear in different places in different utterances, they are numerous, and each open word is used rarely. Most telegraphic utterances consist of a pivot word plus an open word, and this seems to be a rule that children use. Braine recorded these examples of a

EARLY LANGUAGE ACQUISITION				
Age	**0–6 months**	**6 months–1 year**	**1–2½ years**	**2–5 years**
Babbling	✓			
Some phonemes learned	✓	✓		
First spoken word		✓		
Beginning of grammatical rules			✓	
Basic rules of grammar acquired				✓

pivot word followed by an open word from one child: all clean; all done; all dressed; all messy.

Basic order rule. Another way in which telegraphic speech is based on rules was identified by Roger Brown (1973). He argued that young children possess a basic order rule: a sentence consists of agent + action + object + location (e.g. "Daddy eats lunch at home"). Their two-word utterances follow the basic order rule. For example, an utterance containing an agent will be in the order agent–action (e.g. "Daddy walk") rather than the reverse ("walk Daddy"). Similarly, action and object will be spoken in the order action–object (e.g. "drink Coke"). Children all over the world construct two-word utterances obeying the basic order rule.

Brown's basic order rule illustrates the child's early use of syntax (sentence construction). Its universal quality suggests that language development at this stage may have strong innate features.

Subsequent developments

Children's language develops considerably between 2½ years and 5 years of age. The most obvious change is in the mean length of utterance, which is usually measured in terms of the number of morphemes (meaningful units) produced. Another important change is based on the learning of what are known as grammatical morphemes. These include prepositions, prefixes, and suffixes (e.g. "in", "on", plural -s; "a"; "the"). All children learn the various grammatical morphemes in the same order (de Villiers & de Villiers, 1973). They start with simple ones (e.g. including "in" and "on" in sentences) followed by more complex ones (e.g. reducing "they are" to "they're"). The grammatical morphemes are basically rules that can be applied to several situations.

Over-regularisation. Are children simply imitating the speech of adults rather than actually learning rules? Evidence that they are not comes from children's grammatical errors. A child will say, "The dog runned away", which is a sentence that parents and other adults are unlikely to produce. Presumably the child makes that mistake because he or she is applying the rule that the past tense of a verb is usually formed by adding -ed to the present tense. Using a rule in situations in which it does not apply is known as **over-regularisation**.

This is a wug

Now there is another one. There are two of them. There are two _____.

It could be argued that over-regularisation occurs because children imitate what other children say. However, this cannot explain the findings of Berko (1958). Children were shown two pictures of an imaginary creature. They were told, "This is a wug. This is another wug. Now there are two ...". Berko found that even young children produced the regular plural form "wugs", in spite of the fact that they had never heard the word before.

Increasing sophistication. Between the ages of 2½ and 5, children start to use more complex sentences containing a number of ideas. When my daughter Fleur was 2 years old, we were crossing the Channel when I pointed out to her what I thought was a boat. Her (entirely accurate) reply was "Daddy, that's not a boat, it's a yacht."

Pragmatics. Finally, children at this stage develop a good grasp of pragmatics, in which what they say fits the situation. Shatz and Gelman (1973) analysed the speech of 4-year-old children when talking about a new toy to a 2-year-old or to an adult. The 4-year-olds used complex sentences when talking to the adult. However, they used short sentences when talking to the young child, and focused on holding its attention (e.g. "Look at this!").

Nativist theories of child language

How do young children learn the complexities of language so rapidly and easily? Nativist theorists argue that infants are born with knowledge of the structure of human languages. For example, Chomsky (1965) argued that humans possess a **language acquisition device**, which consists of innate knowledge of grammatical structure.

KEY TERMS

Over-regularisation: applying grammatical rules to situations in which they do not apply.

Language acquisition device: innate knowledge of grammatical structure, which is used to assist language learning.

Surface structure and deep structure

In developing this notion, Chomsky distinguished between the surface structure and the deep structure of a sentence. The surface structure is based on the actual phrases used in a sentence, whereas the deep structure reflects its meaning. For example, the sentence, "Visiting relatives can be boring", has only one surface structure. However, it can mean either that it is sometimes tedious to visit relatives, or that relatives who come on a visit can be boring. The two meanings of this and other sentences are distinguished in the deep structure.

The distinction between surface and deep structure is also important in sentences such as "The man wrote the book", and "The book was written by the man". The meaning of these two sentences is very similar, but this similarity is clear only in the deep structure.

Chomsky (1965) introduced the notion of a **transformational grammar**. This allows us to transform the meaning, or deep structure, of a sentence into the actual words in the sentence (the surface structure). According to Chomsky, this transformational grammar is innate, and forms a key part of the language acquisition device.

Universal grammar

Chomsky (1986) later replaced the notion of a language acquisition device with the idea of a universal grammar. According to Chomsky, there are "linguistic universals", which are features found in nearly every language. There are substantive universals and formal universals. Substantive universals concern categories that are common to all languages; noun and verb categories are examples of substantive universals. Formal universals are concerned with the general form of syntactic or grammatical rules.

Word order is a good example of a linguistic universal. Consider the preferred word order for expressing the subject, verb, and object within sentences. There are six possible orderings, two of which (object–verb–subject; object–subject–verb) are very rarely found among the world's languages (Greenberg, 1963). The most popular word order is subject-object-verb (44% of languages), followed by the subject-verb-object word order found in English (35% of languages). Greenberg found that the subject precedes the object in 98% of languages.

Where do linguistic universals come from? Chomsky (1986) argued they are innate, but there are other possibilities. Consider the linguistic universals of nouns and verbs, with nouns referring to objects and verbs to actions. Perhaps objects and actions are distinguished in all languages simply because the distinction is such an obvious feature of the environment.

The language acquisition device is an innate precursor to language acquisition—rather like a chess board without the pieces. The chess pieces represent words (symbols). The squares on the board are the basis for grammatical constructs. Meaning is only communicated by using both the words and the grammar.

List alternative sentences that convey the same meaning (e.g. "The house in which I live" or "The house I live in"), in which the surface structure differs, but the deep structure is the same.

EVALUATION — Chomsky

Chomsky's concern with linguistic structures tends to emphasise correct linguistic acquisition rather than everyday speech, which often includes non-grammatical sentences.

The syntax of a sentence may transform the meaning of a collection of words, but it is the meaning itself that most concerns psychologists.

Language is socially constructed as well as a psychologically constructed medium of communication. So it carries with it important signals that extend beyond one-to-one communication. For example, advertisers use the word "natural" to describe a cosmetic, but this is loaded with social meaning rather than just an accurate description of the contents of a bottle. Here the structure of the utterance is of less importance than the meaning that is conveyed by the word "natural".

Critical period hypothesis

Did you find it easier to learn your native language as a young child than other languages that you learned later? It probably seems that it was much easier to learn your own language. According to Lenneberg (1967) and other nativists, this common experience supports the "critical period hypothesis". According to this hypothesis, language learning depends on biological maturation, with language learning being easier before puberty.

According to Lenneberg (1967), the two hemispheres of the brain have the same potential at birth. However, their functions become more specialised and rigid over the years, with language functions typically being located mainly in the left hemisphere. It follows that damage to the left hemisphere at an early age can be overcome by language functions moving to the right hemisphere. This would be harder if the brain damage occurred during adolescence, by which time language is well established in the left hemisphere.

KEY TERM
Transformational grammar: in Chomsky's theory, what allows the meaning of a sentence to be turned into the words actually used in the sentence.

Two types of aphasia resulting from brain injury

Broca's aphasia: the person has greater difficulties in producing speech and in writing than in comprehending language.

Wernicke's aphasia: the person has greater difficulties in understanding the content of speech and written text rather than in speaking.

Cross-cultural issues: What factors might influence the speed at which young children learn a second language when they move to another country?

Aphasia

Lenneberg (1967) claimed support for the critical period hypothesis from studies on **aphasia**, which involves some loss of language due to brain injury (see Chapter 4). Some children who become aphasic before puberty recover most or all of their lost language functions. Recovery is especially likely if the brain damage occurs before the age of 5. In contrast, brain damage after puberty is often followed by only slow and partial recovery of language. However, other aphasic children fail to support the critical period hypothesis, with the recovery of language functioning being comparable at all ages from early childhood to early adulthood (Harley, 1995).

Second language learning

The critical period hypothesis has been used to explain why second language learning seems to be harder for older children and adults than for younger children. In fact, adults actually have an initial advantage over children when it comes to learning a second language, but children eventually outperform adults. Snow and Hoefnagel-Hohle (1978) studied American families in their first year in Holland and found that 3- and 4-year-old children made less progress at learning Dutch than did older children and adults. Newport (1994) looked at second language learning over a longer period of time in Asian immigrants to the United States. The younger the children were when they entered the country, the better was their ability to learn complex rules of grammar and other aspects of English.

Deprived children

In principle, the best way to test the critical period hypothesis is to consider children who have little chance to learn language during their early years. There have been various reports on wild or feral children who were abandoned at birth. For example, there was the "Wild Boy of Aveyron", who was found in an isolated place in the south of France. A French educationalist, Dr Itard, tried to teach the child language, but he only managed to learn two words. Language development in another deprived child is described in the case study "Genie", below.

The evidence suggests there is a critical period for the learning of syntax, and the same is true of phonological learning, for example, how to pronounce the words of a language. However, there is less evidence of a critical period for the learning of vocabulary, and many language skills can be acquired after the critical period. As Harley (1995) concluded, it is reasonable to argue for a weakened version of the critical period hypothesis, according to which some aspects of language are harder to acquire outside the critical period.

Environmental theories

Skinner (1957) claimed that language is acquired by means of **operant conditioning**, in which learning is controlled by reward or reinforcement (see Chapter 10). According to this approach, only those utterances of the child that are rewarded or reinforced become stronger. Language develops through a process of **shaping**, in which responses need to become progressively closer to the correct response to be rewarded.

KEY TERMS
Aphasia: loss of language to a greater or lesser extent following brain injury.
Operant conditioning: a form of learning that is controlled by reward or reinforcement.
Shaping: a form of operant conditioning in which responses need to become closer and closer to what is desired in order to be rewarded.

CASE STUDY: *Genie*

Genie spent most of her time up to the age of 13 in an isolated room (Curtiss, 1977). She had practically no contact with other people, and was punished if she made any sounds. After Genie was rescued in 1970, she learned some aspects of language, especially vocabulary. However, she showed very poor learning of grammatical rules. There are problems in interpreting the evidence from Genie. She was exposed to great social as well as linguistic deprivation, and her father's "justification" for keeping her in isolation was that he thought she was very retarded. Thus, there are various possible reasons for Genie's limited ability to learn language.

Ethical issues: Deprivation studies are useful examples from which we can draw some inferences, but they rarely provide data that can be regarded as scientific. What are some of the ethical issues that arise from looking at the effects of deprivation? Should the psychologist be concerned with compensation for deprivation experienced, e.g. linguistic support for individuals like Genie?

Do the ethical problems concerning work like this outweigh any practical advancement of our understanding as psychologists?

Imitation is often involved, with the child trying to repeat what his or her parent has just said. This is known as an **echoic response**. Children imitate particular words spoken by their parents and by others, and they also imitate grammatical structures that they hear. Skinner also focused on tacts and mands. A **tact** is involved when the child is rewarded for producing a sound that resembles the correct pronunciation of a word. A **mand** is involved when the child learns a word whose meaning has significance for him or her.

Children do sometimes learn words by imitation or because they are rewarded for saying certain words or sentences. However, detailed analysis of the language behaviour of young children provides evidence against Skinner's theory. Brown, Cazden, and Bellugi (1969) observed the interactions between middle-class American parents and their young children. Parents rewarded or reinforced the speech of their children on the basis of its accuracy or truth rather than the grammar used. According to Skinner's theory this should produce adults whose speech is very truthful but ungrammatical. In fact, of course, the speech of most adults is grammatical but not always very truthful.

Most children develop an excellent command of language very rapidly. Many experts (e.g. Chomsky, 1959) doubt whether such rapid language acquisition would be possible on the basis of imitation and reinforcement. It can take some time to learn a single word via reinforcement, and yet children learn thousands of words and a good understanding of grammar.

It seems to follow from Skinner's approach that children should tend to imitate or copy what they have heard other people say. In fact, the telegraphic speech of children under the age of 2 does not usually closely resemble the utterances of other people. As children's language develops, it tends to become more and more creative. Children will often produce sentences that they have never heard before.

Finally, and most importantly, Skinner focused mainly on the learning of specific responses (e.g. pressing a lever; saying a word) by reinforcement. However, much of the knowledge of language possessed by children is not in the form of specific responses at all. They know a lot about grammatical rules, but it does not make much sense to argue that a grammatical rule is a response that can be rewarded. We saw evidence of the learning of rules in the phenomenon of over-regularisation.

Motherese

The most important environmental factor in language acquisition is the nature of the social interaction between the mother, or primary carer, and her child. Most mothers adopt a style of speaking to their children known as **motherese**. This involves using very short, simple sentences, which gradually become longer and more complex as the child's own use of language develops (Shatz & Gelman, 1973). In order to help their children, mothers typically use sentences that are slightly longer and more complicated than the sentences produced by her child (Bohannon & Warren-Leubecker, 1989).

Mothers, fathers, and other adults also help children's language development by means of expansions. These consist of fuller and more grammatical versions of what the child has just said. For example, a child might say "Cat out", with its mother responding "The cat wants to go out".

Evidence that the way in which the mother talks to her child has an impact on its language development was reported by Harris et al. (1986). They found that 78% of what mothers said to their 16-month-old children related to the objects to which the children were attending. However, the situation was different in a group of children whose language development at the age of 2 years was poor. Among these children, only 49% of what mothers said to their children at the age of 16 months related to the object of the child's attention.

The language development of children is greatly helped by conversations with adults involving motherese, expansions, and so on. However, it is not certain that this kind of

> ■ Research activity: In groups of 4–5 people, choose one person and a topic about which they feel confident enough to talk for a while. Observe how their speech changes in response to rewards (smiles, nodding, eye contact, body language, oral responses).
>
> 1. Do they respond to the rewards?
> 2. How do they respond in terms of their use of language (less formal, more precise)?
>
> A high degree of change may indicate a response to learning, or may be a consequence of their high level of sociability. Which do you think is more likely?

Ethical issues: How can we study the effects of poor parent–child communication without causing harm?

KEY TERMS
Echoic response: learning of words by children through imitation.
Tact: a form of language learning in which saying a word almost correctly leads to a reward.
Mand: this refers to a word that is learned because its meaning is of significance in the child's life.
Motherese: the short, simple sentences used by mothers when talking to their young children.

What factors might determine whether mothers converse with their child about the object of the child's attention?

What does Harris' research tell us about the role of language in young children's social development?

help is needed for normal language development. As Shaffer (1993) pointed out, there are several cultures (e.g. the Kaluli of New Guinea) in which adults talk to children as if they were adults. In spite of this, children in these cultures seem to develop language at about the normal rate.

Language Comprehension

Most psychologists assume the comprehension processes involved in reading resemble those involved in speech comprehension. Supporting evidence was reported by Daneman and Carpenter (1980). Individuals with good reading skills tended to have good speech comprehension skills, suggesting that both kinds of skill involve the same processes. In spite of the similarities between reading and speech comprehension, there are important differences:

- Only when reading is it possible to look back to increase understanding of what has been presented; indeed, about 10% of all eye movements during reading are backwards (Rayner & Sereno, 1994).
- It is harder to identify the individual words in speech than in text. Speech typically consists of a continuously changing pattern of sound with few periods of silence. This produces the segmentation problem, which involves deciding how the continuous stream of sound should be divided up into words.
- Speakers may provide useful cues to syntactic or grammatical structure (known as **prosodic cues**) based on variations in pitch, intonation, stress, and timing. (Just how important prosodic cues are is emphasised in the case study "The President's Speech," below.)
- Reading is often easier than listening to speech, because writers express themselves more clearly than speakers.

Parsing

Parsing involves working out the grammatical structure of a sentence. A key issue is whether meaning influences the initial parsing of a sentence. This issue has been studied

KEY TERMS
Prosodic cues: the cues to grammatical structure provided by a speaker; these cues are based on variations in pitch, stress, and timing.
Parsing: the process of working out the grammatical structure of a sentence.

CASE STUDY: *The President's Speech*

In Oliver Sacks' well-known text *The man who mistook his wife for a hat* (1986, p.76), he describes the reaction of some of his hospital patients to a speech made by Ronald Reagan, the former President of the United States:

What was going on? A roar of laughter from the aphasia ward, just as the President's speech was coming on, and they had all been so eager to hear the President speaking …

There he was, the old Charmer, the Actor, with his practised rhetoric, his histrionisms, his emotional appeal—and all the patients were convulsed with laughter. Well, not all: some looked bewildered, some looked outraged, one or two looked apprehensive, but most looked amused. The President was, as always, moving—but he was moving them, apparently, mainly to laughter. What could they be thinking? Were they all failing to understand him? Or did they, perhaps, understand him all too well?

The aphasia patients were intelligent people who suffered from a severe form of memory disorder that meant they were not able to understand words as such, even though they did understand what was being said to them. They managed to derive meaning from "extra-verbal cues" such as tone of voice, intonation, emphasis, and inflection, in addition to visual cues such as gestures, facial expression, and posture. If the patients were presented with mechanical speech that was devoid of any such non-verbal cues,

the patients would not be able to understand what was being said to them.

The fact that these aphasic patients were able to understand people talking to them despite the actual words holding no meaning for them suggests that natural speech consists of more than just words, and understanding utterances involves more than simple word recognition. It has been said (Sacks, 1986) that you cannot lie to a person with aphasia because they cannot grasp your words and therefore cannot be deceived by them, but they understand what you are saying based on the non-verbal cues that accompany the words.

So, why did the aphasic patients laugh at the President's speech? Despite Ronald Reagan's career as an actor he was not able to deliver as convincing a speech in non-verbal terms as he did in verbal terms. The aphasic patients were acutely sensitive to the non-verbal cues given out by the President but unaware of the meaning of his actual words and as such they responded to the falseness of the expressions, gestures, intonation, and cadence of his speech. The glaring improprieties with which the speech was delivered made them react spontaneously as they were not deceived by the words of the President. Most were amused, some were outraged, and some confused or worried by what they understood from the President's non-verbal manner—hence the roar of laughter in the ward when the President delivered his speech.

by using ambiguous or "garden-path sentences". Here is an example: "Since Jay always jogs a mile seems like a short distance". It is easy to assume mistakenly that Jay always jogs a mile.

According to the garden-path model (e.g. Rayner, Carlson, & Frazier, 1983), the meaning of a sentence is *not* involved in its initial parsing. Rayner et al. presented sentences such as "The performer sent the flowers was very pleased with herself" and "The florist sent the flowers was very pleased with herself". If meaning plays a part in parsing, then the former sentence should be easier to read. In fact, the participants took the same length of time to read each sentence.

Taraban and McClelland (1988) favoured a different approach. According to their content-guided theory, meaning is typically involved in the initial parsing of a sentence. They presented sentences such as "The reporter exposed corruption in the government", and "The reporter exposed corruption in the article". The last word was processed faster in the former sentence, presumably because it was more in line with the reader's expectations.

It seems that meaning has little or no effect on initial sentence parsing when one particular grammatical structure is strongly implied, as in the study by Rayner et al. (1983). However, meaning can have a powerful influence on the initial parsing when no single grammatical structure is strongly implied, as in the study by Taraban and McClelland (1988).

Schemas

In order to comprehend language, we use **schemas** or organised packets of information stored in long-term memory. This can be shown at an anecdotal level. When I first visited the United States, I was baffled by the commentaries on baseball games. I could understand every word and sentence at some level, but full comprehension was impossible because of my imperfect knowledge of the rules of baseball.

Hilary Mordey Can't Quite Believe It

Getting to work nowadays takes her just 10 minutes, a far cry from the 19 years she spent commuting from Thames Ditton in Surrey to John Lewis' branch in Oxford Street.

From the *Bristol Evening Post*

Ambiguous sentences may be the result of too little attention to grammar.

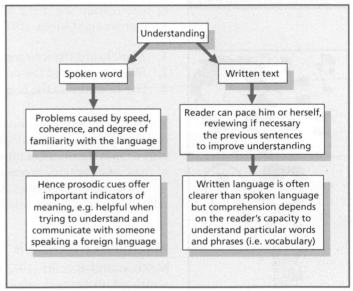

Bransford and Johnson

Experimental evidence of the importance of schemas to comprehension was reported by Bransford and Johnson (1972, p.722). They presented their participants with a passage written so that the underlying schema was hard to identify:

The procedure is actually quite simple. First you arrange items into different groups. Of course one pile may be sufficient depending on how much there is to do. If you have to go somewhere else due to lack of facilities, that is the next step; otherwise, you are pretty well set. It is important not to overdo things. That is, it is better to do too few things at once rather than too many. In the short run this may not seem important but complications can easily arise. A mistake can be expensive as well. At first, the whole procedure will seem complicated. Soon, however, it will become just another facet of life. It is difficult to foresee any end to the necessity for this task in the immediate future, but then, one never can tell. After the procedure is completed one arranges the materials into different groups again. They can then be put into their appropriate places. Eventually, they will be used once more and the whole cycle will then have to be repeated. However, that is part of life.

Participants given this passage on its own found it hard to understand. The reason was presumably because they could

KEY TERM
Schemas: organised packets of knowledge stored in memory.

KEY STUDY EVALUATION — Bransford and Johnson

It could be argued that this study distorts its material in order to mislead participants into making incorrect deductions. For example, not only are many things left out of the passage, but pronouns and phrases have been included to obscure the meaning or suggest other meanings. Some phrases used could not be described as neutral in terms of meaning. Use of "After the procedure", for example, implies a formal task using a recognised skill, not a personal and familiar task like doing the washing.

However, Bransford and Johnson succeed in demonstrating the importance of schemas in deciphering language and the centrality of cultural influences. It would be interesting to translate the passage into another language and run the same study in another culture. Would participants experience the same amount and types of difficulties in making sense of the text?

not relate the information in the passage to their relevant knowledge stored in long-term memory in the form of schemas. On the other hand, those who were provided with the underlying schema in the form of the title, "Washing clothes", found it fairly easy to comprehend.

Discussion points

1. Did you manage to make sense of the passage before knowing the title?

2. How did Bransford and Johnson produce a passage that can be understood phrase by phrase, but overall seems to make little sense?

Inference drawing

An important example of the crucial role played by schematic knowledge is the process of inference, which involves using schemas to fill in the gaps in text or speech. Some idea of how readily we make inferences can be seen from the following story taken from Rumelhart and Ortony (1977):

1. Mary heard the ice-cream van coming.
2. She remembered the pocket money.
3. She rushed into the house.

You probably made various assumptions or inferences: Mary wanted to buy some ice-cream; ice-cream costs money; Mary had some pocket money in the house; and Mary had only a limited amount of time to find some money before the ice-cream van arrived. None of these assumptions is actually stated.

How many inferences do we normally draw? Some theorists argue that we draw relatively few, whereas others think that this is an underestimate.

Minimalist hypothesis

McKoon and Ratcliff (1992) put forward their "minimalist hypothesis", according to which relatively few inferences are made automatically. In addition, some inferences are made in pursuit of the reader's goals; these are known as strategic inferences. Evidence in line with the minimalist hypothesis was reported by Dosher and Corbett (1982). They wanted to know whether participants presented with a sentence such as "Mary stirred her coffee" would draw the inference that she used a spoon. The inference was not drawn under normal reading conditions. However, when the participants were told to guess the instrument being used (e.g. spoon), the appropriate inferences were drawn.

These findings indicate that whether an inference is drawn can depend on the reader's intentions or goals. The findings also suggest that even fairly obvious inferences are not always drawn. You have to infer the instrument used in stirring coffee to have a full understanding of the sentence "Mary stirred her coffee". However, the evidence shows that such inferences are not usually drawn.

Cross-cultural issues: Inferences based on simple statements such as "She joined in the group's mourning following his death" would vary enormously between different cultures. You may be able to think of instances when you have made incorrect inferences from something you read or heard while within a culture other than your own.

Evaluation

The minimalist hypothesis clarifies which inferences are, and are not, automatically drawn when reading a text. Another strength of the minimalist hypothesis is that it emphasises the distinction between automatic and strategic inferences. The notion that many inferences will be drawn only if they are consistent with the reader's goals in reading is important.

On the negative side, it is not always possible to predict from the hypothesis which inferences will be drawn. For example, McKoon and Ratcliff (1992) argued that automatic inferences will be made if the necessary information is "readily available", but it is hard to measure availability.

Search-after-meaning theory

Graesser, Singer, and Trabasso (1994) argued that the minimalist hypothesis underestimated the number of inferences that are drawn. They proposed a search-after-meaning theory based on the following assumptions:

- Reader goal assumption: the reader constructs a meaning for the text that addresses his or her goals.
- Coherence assumption: the reader tries to construct a meaning for the text that is coherent.
- Explanation assumption: the reader tries to explain the actions, events, and states referred to in the text.

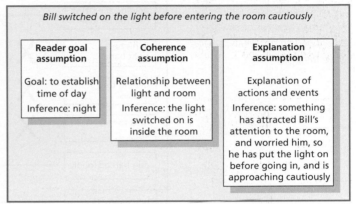

Readers will not search after meaning if their goals do not require the construction of a meaning representation of the text (e.g. if they are proofreading); if the text seems to lack coherence; or if they do not possess the necessary knowledge to make sense of it. Graesser et al. discussed the available evidence. More inferences are normally drawn than would be predicted on the minimalist hypothesis. At present, the search-after-meaning theory probably provides the most adequate account of the inferences drawn in reading.

Text comprehension

Most of the research discussed so far has focused on comprehension of single sentences or short passages. In fact, of course, much of our reading is of longer texts such as stories and books. Our comprehension of, and memory for, such texts is very selective, in that we focus on the central theme rather than on unimportant details. Gomulicki (1956) asked one group of participants to write a summary of a story that was visible in front of them. He asked a second group to read the story, and then to recall it from memory. A third group were shown the summaries and the recalls, and were generally unable to tell which were which. Thus, what is extracted from a story and then remembered closely resembles a summary in its emphasis on the main theme of that story.

Propositions and short-term memory

Van Dijk and Kintsch (1983) put forward a theory to explain *why* the key ideas in stories are most likely to be remembered. According to them, the propositions (the smallest units of meaning to which we can assign a truth value; generally phrases or clauses) within a story are entered into a short-term working buffer of limited capacity. When the buffer contains a number of propositions, the reader or listener tries to relate them to each other in a coherent way. Those propositions that are highly relevant to the main theme tend to be stored for a fairly long time in the buffer. The reason is that such propositions are well connnected to other propositions in the buffer, and so keeping them in the buffer makes it easier to understand the story. As a result of spending a long time being processed in the buffer, thematic propositions are remembered well.

Van Dijk and Kintsch argued that the comprehension processes used in text processing produce two main structures. First, there is the microstructure, which is the level at which the propositions from the text are formed into a connected structure. Second, there is the macrostructure, which consists of an edited version of the microstructure combined with schematic information.

Evaluation

There is reasonable evidence for the distinction between microstructure and macrostructure, and it is likely that proposition-like representations are involved in text

An illustration of how our comprehension is assisted by discarding non-essential information and making additional inferences.

The story reads: A little boy, wearing a brown jumper and green shorts, was walking in a park, holding the string of a red balloon in his hot right hand. Behind the bushes next to the path, a dog barked loudly. The boy jumped, then began to cry as he saw the red dot getting smaller and smaller above the trees.

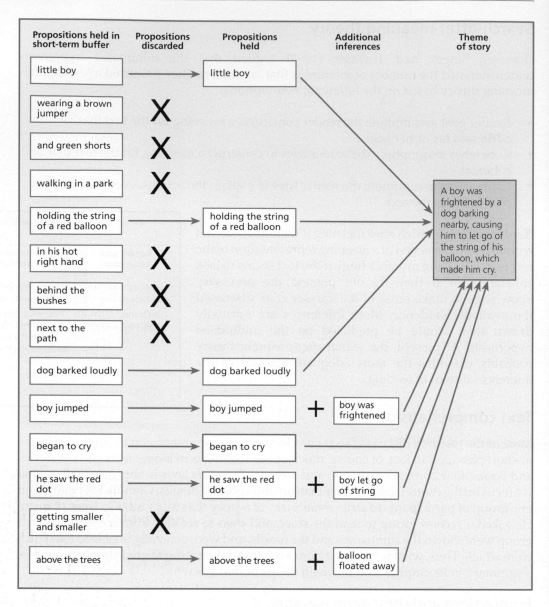

comprehension. What is especially important is the notion that propositions relating to the main theme are well remembered because they spend more time in the working buffer. On the negative side, the theory does not spell out the details of how propositions are formed. Furthermore, it is not clear how schematic knowledge interacts with textual information to produce the macrostructure.

Language Production

Much more is known about language comprehension than about language production. This is partly because it is easier for an experimenter to exercise control over the material to be comprehended than it is to constrain someone's language production. In addition, language production cannot be considered purely from the perspective of a theory of language. Language production is clearly a motivated activity. People speak and write to make friends, to influence people, to convey information to others, and so on.

The two forms of language production considered here are speaking and writing. Speaking has been studied in more detail than has writing. The fact that most people spend far more of their time talking than writing may be relevant, as it is of more practical value to understand the processes involved in speaking than in writing.

Speaking

Speech as communication

For most people (unless there is something seriously wrong with them), speech nearly always occurs as conversation in a social context. In other words, we speak because we want to communicate with other people. Grice (1967) argued that the key to successful communication is the **Co-operative principle**, according to which speakers and listeners must try to be co-operative.

In addition to the Co-operative principle, Grice (1967) proposed four maxims that the speaker should heed:

- Maxim of quantity: the speaker should be as informative as necessary, but not more so.
- Maxim of quality: the speaker should be truthful.
- Maxim of relation: the speaker should talk about things that are relevant to the situation.
- Maxim of manner: the speaker should make his or her contribution easy to understand.

Quantity. Some evidence that speakers heed the maxim of quantity was discussed by Olson (1970). He pointed out that what needs to be said depends on the context. Thus, it is not possible to account for what someone says simply by focusing on what the speaker wants to describe (often called the referent). We also need to know the objects from which the referent is to be distinguished. If most of the players on a football team are boys, with only one girl, we can say "The girl is good at football", and listeners will know which player we mean. If it is an all-girl team, however, we must be more specific, e.g. "The red-haired girl is good at football."

Common ground. In applying the maxim of quantity, the speaker has to take account of the "common ground" (Clark & Carlson, 1981). The common ground between two people consists of their mutual beliefs and knowledge, and is usually greater between friends. If a speaker and his or her listener have several friends in common, then it may be reasonable for the speaker to say "John bought Kevin's old car". However, if the listener does not know who Kevin is, and only knows John as Dr Wilding, then the speaker will say something like "Dr Wilding bought the blue car parked outside your office".

Conversational turns. Brennan (1990) studied some of the factors determining who talks when. One common way in which a conversation moves from one speaker to another is by means of an *adjacency pair*. In an adjacency pair, what the first speaker says provides a strong invitation to the listener to take up the conversation. A question followed by an answer is a very common example of an adjacency pair. If the first speaker completes what he or she intended to say without producing the first part of an adjacency pair, then the next turn goes to the listener who speaks first. If none of the listeners speaks, then the first speaker is free to continue with another turn (known as a *turn-constructional unit*).

Processes in speech production

It is hard to identify the processes involved in speech production. One reason is that they occur rapidly, as we normally produce two or three words per second on average. How can we study the processes involved? One approach is to ask participants to speak on a particular topic, and to make a tape recording. Another approach is to make collections of everyday speech errors. As Dell (1986, p.284) pointed out, "The inner workings of a highly complex system are often revealed by the way in which the system breaks down."

■ Research activity: Choose a simple subject and produce examples of speakers who conform to or violate each of Grice's maxims. For example: Quantity—speaker might make instructions too succinct to be understood, or talk about things in too much detail in a boring way.

The importance of common ground is clear if you overhear a conversation between two friends on a bus or train. Because you lack the common ground that they share, it can be very hard to understand what they are saying to each other.

■ Research activity: Devise two brief scripts of conversations between two friends that demonstrate adjacency pairs and turn-constructional units.

What effect might listener error (mis-hearing) have on this type of research?

Collections of speech errors have been reported by various psychologists (e.g. Garrett, 1975). The errors in these collections were personally heard by the researcher himself. This procedure poses some problems. There may be systematic biases, because some kinds of error are easier to detect. Thus, we should be sceptical about percentage figures for the different kinds of speech errors. In addition, most people make relatively few errors when speaking, and these few errors may not be a good basis for working out what is involved in normal speech production.

Information about speech errors can be used to form theories of speech production. The classic theory was put forward by Garrett (1976, 1984), with modifications of that theory still being current. Accordingly, we will focus on Garrett's theoretical approach.

Garrett

Garrett (1976, 1984) argued that speech production is much more complex than it might seem. According to his model, there are five different levels of representation involved in speaking a sentence. These levels typically occur in the following sequence:

- Message-level representation: this is an abstract representation of the ideas the speaker wants to communicate.
- Functional-level representation: this is an outline of the proposed utterance having grammatical structure; the slots for nouns, adjectives, and so on, are allocated, but no words fill the slots.
- Positional-level representation: this differs from the previous representation, because it contains the words of the proposed sentence.
- Phonetic-level representation: this contains information about the ways in which words in the intended sentence are pronounced.
- Articulatory-level representation: this contains a set of instructions for articulating the words in the sentence in the correct order.

According to this theory, the speaker engages in elaborate forward planning before speaking. This can be tested by considering the kinds of errors that people make while talking. If, for example, sounds or words from the end of a sentence intrude into the early part of a sentence, then this provides evidence of forward planning. A classic error of this type is the spoonerism, which was named in honour of the Reverend William Archibald Spooner. The essence of a **spoonerism** is that the initial letter or letters of two words are transposed. Among the Reverend Spooner's famous utterances are the following: "The Lord is a shoving leopard to his flock" and "You have hissed all my mystery lectures". Cynics have claimed that Spooner spent many hours thinking up such errors, but some people do produce them spontaneously.

Other errors also show the existence of forward planning. An **anticipation error** occurs when a word is spoken earlier in the sentence than it should be (e.g. "The school is at school"). A similar type of error is the **exchange error**, in which two items within a sentence are swapped (e.g. "This is the happiest life of my day").

The sentence "I want a biscuit" broken down into Garrett's five levels of representation.

KEY TERMS
Spoonerism: speech error in which the initial letter(s) of two words are transposed.
Anticipation error: speech error in which a word is spoken earlier than it should be in a sentence.
Exchange error: speech error in which two words in a sentence are switched around.

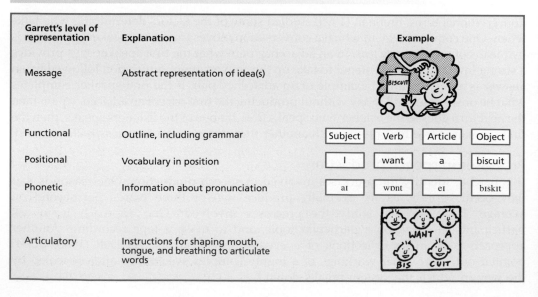

Garrett's level of representation	Explanation	Example
Message	Abstract representation of idea(s)	
Functional	Outline, including grammar	Subject / Verb / Article / Object
Positional	Vocabulary in position	I / want / a / biscuit
Phonetic	Information about pronunciation	aɪ / wɒnt / eɪ / bɪskɪt
Articulatory	Instructions for shaping mouth, tongue, and breathing to articulate words	

Pre-planning of speech is also indicated by speakers' pauses. Most people pause for about 40 or 50% of their total speaking time. These pauses occur mainly between one clause and the next, and reflect the time taken to decide what to say next and how to say it. Although pausing is very common in speech production, it may be wondered whether it is as essential to normal speech as Garrett's (1984) theory implies. This issue was studied by asking people telling stories to reduce the number of their long pauses. As a result, the repetition of words and even of whole phrases doubled. Thus, unfilled pauses are of great value in the planning of spontaneous speech.

According to the theory put forward by Garrett (1976, 1984), speakers decide on the grammatical structure of a proposed utterance in the functional-level representation. They then select the right words to fit into that structure in the subsequent position-level representation. Given this sequence, it would be possible for the grammatical structure of a spoken sentence to be correct, even though some of the words within it were incorrectly positioned. This is found with **morpheme-exchange errors**. In such errors, the roots or basic forms of two words are switched, leaving the grammatical structure unchanged (e.g. "He has already trunked two packs" instead of "He has already packed two trunks").

Discussion points

1. What problems are there with using people's speech errors to work out how speech production normally occurs?
2. Is it good or bad that we make some errors when speaking?

KEY STUDY EVALUATION — Garrett

Garrett's model indicates that speech production involves a series of unconscious (and possibly automatic) processes designed to turn thought into language. These processes include forward planning about what is to be said over the next few seconds, and it is during this forward planning that errors can occur. In general terms, the study of speech production provides an interesting way of looking at some of the links between thought and language.

One of the problems with Garrett's model is that most of its predictions relate to the kinds of errors that we expect to find in speech production. It is less easy to apply the model to fluent and error-free speech production. However, it seems reasonable to assume that most of the forward planning in speech production occurs while the speaker is pausing. As might be expected, pauses are generally followed by the fluent production of a sentence or major part of a sentence.

An issue that is raised by Garrett's model is whether everyone actually plans what they are going to say in great detail. We all know people who seem to speak without thinking! More seriously, there is evidence that young children and some brain-damaged patients with language difficulties make less use of forward planning than most adults. How do we know? The reason is that very few of their speech errors are those associated with forward planning (e.g. anticipation errors; exchange errors).

Why is human speech production prone to error? According to Dell (1986), it is the price we pay for having such a flexible speech-production system. Its flexibility allows us to produce novel sentences. Most speech errors involve novelty, but novelty of an unwanted kind. If we had a very rigid speech-production system, it might prevent errors from occurring, but we would produce very stereotyped utterances.

Writing

Writing makes use of many processes that are also used in other cognitive activities. It involves memory retrieval plus goal setting, planning, problem solving, and evaluation. Thus, writing should not be regarded as quite separate from other language and non-language activities.

Levels of analysis

The processes involved in writing can be considered at a number of different levels. At the most specific level, we can focus on individual words. At the most general level, we can focus on the overall structure of a piece of writing, and on the writer's major goal or goals. At an intermediate level, we can focus on the processes between goal setting and writing sentences.

Protocol analysis

How can we study the processes involved in writing, most of which are not directly observable? One method is **protocol analysis**, in which writers verbalise their thoughts during writing, and a tape recording is made of these verbalisations. In addition, all of the notes made by the writer are assessed. Hayes and Flower (1980) used protocol analysis successfully with a writer who was unusually aware of the processes he used when writing. He started by generating information, after which he organised the information. Finally, he translated the information into written sentences.

Drawbacks of protocol analysis. Protocol analysis can only provide information about those processes of which the writer is consciously aware. Writers do not know how they search

---

KEY TERMS

Morpheme-exchange errors: speech errors in which the roots of two words are switched, but the grammatical structure is correct.
Protocol analysis: a method for studying writing based on the writer's verbalisations of his or her thoughts during writing, plus any notes made by the writer.

long-term memory for ideas, or how they set about organising the information retrieved from memory. Asking writers to verbalise their thoughts may disrupt some of the processes normally used in writing.

Theory of writing

Hayes and Flower (1986) argued that there are three key processes involved in writing:

■ Research activity: Compare the composition of a poem with writing a speech to be delivered in public, considering their differences in terms of planning, construction, and re-writing.

- Planning process: this involves producing ideas and organising them into a writing plan to satisfy the writer's goals.
- Sentence-generation process: this involves turning the writing plan into the actual writing of sentences.
- Revision process: this involves evaluating what has been written; this can occur at a specific level (e.g. individual words or phrases), or at a more general level (e.g. the structural coherence of the writing).

Why do you think Hayes and Flower found that good writers can use knowledge in a more flexible way than less competent writers?

Planning. Writing plans depend on the writer's knowledge about the topic in question. However, they are also influenced by other factors. Experts are often very poor at organising their ideas into an understandable form. This happens in part because their expertise distances them from the problems experienced by the non-expert.

According to Hayes and Flower (1986), strategic knowledge plays a major role in the formation of a writing plan. Strategic knowledge concerns ways of organising the goals and sub-goals of writing to form a coherent writing plan. Hayes and Flower found that good writers use strategic knowledge in a flexible way. The structure of the writing plan often changes during the writing period as new ideas occur to the writer, or dissatisfaction grows with the original plan. Hayes and Flower suggested that people who suffer from writer's block tend to stick rigidly to their original writing plan. If the plan proves inadequate, then the writing process grinds to a halt.

Adults with much knowledge of a topic and those with only a little were compared by Hayes and Flower. Experts produced more goals and sub-goals, and so formed a more complex overall writing plan. However, the greatest difference between experts and non-experts was in plan integration: experts' goals were much better integrated.

Sentence generation. There is often a large gap between the writing plan and the actual writing. Kaufer, Hayes, and Flower (1986) compared the outlines that writers produced with the essays they then wrote. The essay was always at least eight times longer than the outline. The use of protocol analysis allowed Kaufer et al. to study sentence generation. Here is a verbal protocol of a writer engaged in writing (the dashes indicate a definite pause; the numbers identify the different fragments):

> *The best thing about it is (1) _____ what? (2) Something about using my mind (3) _____ it allows me the opportunity to (4) _____ uh _____ I want to write something about my ideas (5) _____ to put ideas into action (6) _____ or _____ to develop my ideas into (7) _____ what? (8) _____ into a meaningful form? (9) Oh, bleh! _____ say it allows me (10) _____ to use (11) _____ Na _____ allows me _____ scratch that. The best thing about it is that it allows me to use (12) _____ my mind and ideas in a productive way (13).*

> Final written sentence: *The best thing about it is that it allows me to use my mind and ideas in a productive way.*

In this protocol, fragments 12 and 13 formed the written sentence. The earlier fragments 1, 4, 6, 7, 9, and 11 were attempts to produce parts of the sentence.

Kaufer et al. compared experts and average writers. Both groups accepted about 75% of the sentence parts they verbalised, and those that were changed were typically those that had just been produced. However, the two groups differed in the length of the average sentence part that was proposed. The length was 11.2 words for the expert writers, compared with 7.3 words for the average writers. Thus, good writers make use of larger units or "building blocks".

Revision. Expert writers differ from non-expert writers in the amount of time they spend revising. Surprisingly, expert writers tend to spend longer than non-expert writers in revision. Matters become clearer, however, if we look at how the two groups regard the revision process. Expert writers focus on the coherence and structure of the arguments expressed, whereas non-expert writers focus on individual words and phrases. It is much harder to modify the overall structure of a text than to change individual words.

Faigley and Witte (1983) considered the revisions made by writers. Of the revisions made by experienced adult writers, 34% involved a change of meaning, compared to only 12% of the revisions made by inexperienced college writers. Presumably, experienced writers are more concerned with the broad issues of coherence and meaning.

Further differences between expert and non-expert writers were found by Hayes et al. (1985). Expert writers detected about 60% more problems in a text than did non-experts. Of the problems that were detected, the expert writers correctly identified the problem in 74% of cases, compared to only 42% for the non-expert writers. Surprisingly, both groups often re-wrote sections of the text without working out what was wrong with the original version.

Evaluation. Hayes and Flower (1986) have contributed to our understanding of the processes involved in writing. Of particular interest is their comparison of more and less skilled writers. This has helped to identify the specific processes and strategies used in skilled writing, and has produced practical advice for those lacking adequate writing skills. The research of others (e.g. Kellogg, 1988) has confirmed that the planning process is of great importance in determining writing quality.

There are some doubts as to whether the three processes of planning, sentence generation, and revision can be neatly separated from each other. For example, planning and sentence generation are often very bound up with each other. Hayes and Flower largely ignored the fact that writing has an important social dimension, and is designed to communicate with others (Kellogg, 1990). Another criticism is that the protocol analysis used by Hayes and Flower does not provide information about processes occurring below the level of conscious awareness.

Writing expertise

Skilled writers differ from less skilled ones during the planning, sentence generation, and revising stages of writing. However, individual differences in writing ability probably depend mostly on planning processes. Bereiter and Scardamalia (1987) argued that two major strategies are used in the planning stage: the knowledge-telling strategy and the knowledge-transforming strategy. The *knowledge-telling strategy* involves the writer simply writing down everything that he or she knows about a topic. There is no real planning or attempt to organise the information for the reader's benefit. In the words of a 12-year-old child who used the knowledge-telling strategy (Bereiter & Scardamalia, 1987, p.9):

> *I have a whole bunch of ideas and write them down until my supply of ideas is exhausted. Then I might try to think of more ideas up to the point when you can't get any more ideas.*

The *knowledge-transforming strategy* is more complex. It involves asking questions about the writing goals (e.g. "Can the main ideas be expressed more simply?"). It also involves considering issues about the specific information to be included (e.g. "The case of Smith vs. Jones strengthens the argument").

Writers using a knowledge-transforming strategy should produce more organised texts than those produced by using a knowledge-telling strategy. Well-organised texts contain high-level main points that describe important themes. Those writers who produce a high-level main point should be more likely to use the knowledge-transforming strategy. In support, Bereiter, Burtis, and Scardamalia (1988) found that writers who produced a high-level main point used on average 4.75 different knowledge-transforming processes during planning. In contrast, those who produced a low-level main point used only 0.23 knowledge-transforming processes.

Writing and schooling: The quality of a piece of writing seems to depend on the amount of practice by the writer. So writing difficulties may be overcome if the person can devote enough time to practising. This has important implications for all levels of the educational process, and might influence educationalists to encourage young children who are experiencing difficulties in writing to spend more time on this, rather than less.

■ Research activity: Choose a paragraph from one of your own essays that is "knowledge-telling" and try to convert it to "knowledge-transforming" text. This will involve thinking more analytically about your knowledge and transforming it so that it engages more deeply with the essay question. (See the example overleaf.)

> **TASK: WRITE AN OUTLINE FOR A TRAVEL ARTICLE ON SAN FRANCISCO**
>
> | Knowledge-telling strategy | Knowledge-transforming strategy |
> |---|---|
> | • It's in California
• Golden Gate Bridge
• Earthquakes
• Chinatown
• Foggy
• Gay community
• Victorian houses
• Ferries
• Hippie culture | • Theme of article: diversity of city caused by
  • Geography—earthquakes, bay
  • History—trade
  • Climate—compare rainfall with rest of California
  • Population—long-established racial mix; tolerance of alternative lifestyles |

Reasoning

One of the great advantages that humans have over other species is that we are much better at reasoning. Two major forms of reasoning have been identified: **deductive reasoning** and **inductive reasoning**. Deductive reasoning consists of drawing conclusions which follow logically provided that certain statements are assumed to be true. **Syllogisms** involve deductive reasoning. They are logical tasks consisting of two statements or *premises* (e.g. "London is in England"; "England is in the United Kingdom") and a *conclusion* (e.g. "London is in the United Kingdom"). The task is to decide whether the conclusion follows logically from the premises.

Inductive reasoning involves drawing a general conclusion from specific information. This conclusion may be true, but is not certain to be correct. For example, a turkey might draw the conclusion "Each day I am fed", because this has been true every day of his life. However, if tomorrow is Christmas Eve, then he may be in for a rude shock!

In what follows, we will discuss some aspects of deductive and inductive reasoning. Much of the interest in this area is in trying to work out the processes that people use when confronted by various kinds of reasoning problem.

Deductive reasoning

Conditional reasoning

There are many ways of studying deductive reasoning. One of the most popular is to use conditional reasoning problems. Here is an example: "If it is raining, then Fred gets wet" and "It is raining" are the two premises. These two premises taken together permit the valid inference or conclusion "Fred gets wet". This example is based on one of the most important rules of inference, known as *modus ponens*: given the premise, "If A, then B", and also given A, it is valid to infer B. Another major rule of inference is *modus tollens*: from the premise "If A, then B", and the premise "B is false", the conclusion "A is false" follows validly. (See diagram opposite).

The validity of a given conclusion depends only on logical principles: it does not matter whether the conclusion is actually true in the world. For example, if we accept the premises "If she is a woman, then she is Aristotle" and "She is a woman", then the conclusion "She is Aristotle" is valid. The fact that Aristotle was a man is irrelevant to the logical validity of the conclusion.

Two other inferences are worth considering at this stage. The first is called *affirmation of the consequent*, and the second is called *denial of the antecedent*. Here is an example of affirmation of the consequent:

Premises:
If it is raining, then Fred gets wet
Fred gets wet

Conclusion:
Therefore, it is raining

KEY TERMS

Deductive reasoning: a form of reasoning in which definite conclusions follow provided that certain statements are assumed to be true.

Inductive reasoning: a form of reasoning in which a general conclusion is drawn from specific information; this conclusion cannot be shown to be necessarily true.

Syllogisms: problems consisting of two statements or premises followed by a conclusion that may or may not follow logically from the statements.

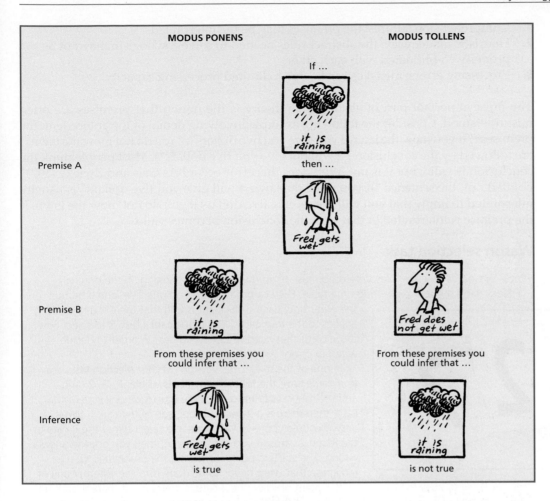

MODUS PONENS   MODUS TOLLENS

If ...

Premise A   then ...

Premise B

From these premises you   From these premises you
could infer that ...   could infer that ...

Inference

is true   is not true

Here is an example of denial of the antecedent:

Premises:
If it is raining, then Fred gets wet
It is not raining

Conclusion:
Therefore, Fred does not get wet

Do you think the conclusions are valid? In a study by Evans, Clibbens, and Rood (1995), using abstract versions of the above, 21% of their participants accepted the affirmation of the consequent inference, and over 60% accepted the denial of the antecedent inference. In fact, however, they are both invalid. In the first syllogism, it does not have to be raining in order for Fred to get wet. He might have jumped into a swimming pool or someone might have turned a hose on him. The same line of reasoning shows why denial of the antecedent is also not valid.

Conditional reasoning is prone to error when it comes to affirmation of the consequent or denial of the antecedent. The typical finding in studies on modus ponens and modus tollens is that very few errors are made with modus ponens, but the error rate often exceeds 30% with modus tollens (Evans et al., 1995). Part of the reason for this difference is that we lack practice in thinking about what is not the case.

Theoretical accounts

How can we account for the errors made in conditional reasoning? Braine, Reiser, and Rumain (1984) put forward an abstract-rule theory. According to their theory, people make use of abstract rules when engaged in conditional and other forms of reasoning. There are three major reasons why errors occur:

1. Comprehension failures: the premises may be misinterpreted.
2. Heuristic inadequacy: the abstract rules needed to solve a syllogism may not be properly co-ordinated with each other.
3. Processing errors: mistakes can be due to limited processing capacity.

The most important part of abstract-rule theory is the notion that premises are often misunderstood. Consider the following example involving denial of the antecedent: the premises ("If you mow the lawn, I will give you five dollars"; "You do not mow the lawn") are followed by the conclusion ("I will not give you five dollars"). Most people think the conclusion is valid, but it is not. Why does this error occur? As Geis and Zwicky (1971) pointed out, the sentence "If you mow the lawn, I will give you five dollars" is usually interpreted to imply that you will not receive five dollars if you do not mow the lawn. If the premise is interpreted in that way, the conclusion becomes valid.

Wason selection task

Peter Wason devised the Wason selection task to study deductive reasoning. In the original version, there are four cards lying on a table. Each card has a letter on one side, and a number on the other side. Each participant is told that there is a rule which applies to the four cards. The participant's task is to select only those cards that need to be turned over in order to decide whether or not the rule is correct.

In one of the most used versions of this selection task, the four cards have the following symbols visible: R, G, 2, and 7, and the rule is as follows: "If there is an R on one side of the card, then there is a 2 on the other side of the card". What answer would you give? Most people select either the R card or the R and 2 cards. If you did the same, then you got the answer wrong. The starting point for solving the problem is to recognise that what needs to be done is to see whether any of

Rule: If there is an R on one side of the card, then there is a 2 on the other.

Which cards do you need to turn over (pick as few as possible) in order to decide if the rule is correct?

the cards *fail* to obey the rule. From this point of view, the 2 card is irrelevant. If there is an R on the other side of it, then all that this tells us is that the rule *might* be true. If there is any other letter, then we have found out nothing about the validity of the rule.

The correct answer is to select the cards with R and 7 on them. This answer is produced by only about 5–10% of university students. The reason why the 7 card is necessary is that it would definitely disprove the rule if it had an R on the other side.

There are some similarities between Wason's selection task and typical conditional reasoning. The selection of the 7 card follows from the modus tollens rule of inference: from the premises "If there is an R on one side of the card, then there is a 2 on the other side" and "The 7 card does not have a 2 on it", it follows logically that the 7 card should not have an R on the other side. If it does, then the premise specifying the rule must be incorrect.

Wason and Shapiro (1971) argued that the abstract nature of the Wason task makes it hard to solve. They used four cards (Manchester, Leeds, car, and train), and the rule was, "Every time I go to Manchester I travel by car". The task was to select only those cards that needed to be turned over to prove or disprove the rule. The correct answer that the Manchester and train cards need to be turned over was given by 62% of the participants, against only 12% when the task was presented in its abstract form.

Wason and Shapiro's findings suggest that the use of concrete and meaningful material makes it easier to reason accurately. However, problems for this view emerged from a study by Griggs and Cox (1982). They used the same tasks as Wason and Shapiro (1971) with American students in Florida. They failed to find a greater success rate for the meaningful task, presumably because most American students have no direct experience of Manchester or Leeds.

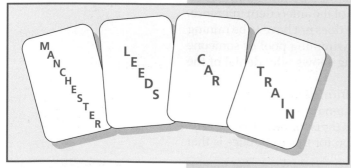

A more concrete version of the Wason selection task.

These findings led Griggs and Cox to propose a memory cueing hypothesis, according to which people perform better on a reasoning task when it relates to their own experience. They obtained support for this hypothesis in their second study in which 73% of the same students produced the correct answer when the rule corresponded to the Florida law on drinking, and so was relevant to their experience. The rule stated that "If a person is drinking beer, then the person must be over 19 years of age".

Griggs and Cox found that memory cueing is not the only important factor. They asked their participants to imagine that they were store managers responsible for checking sales receipts. They had to test the rule "If a purchase exceeds $30, then the receipt must be approved by the department manager". The participants had no direct experience of checking sales receipts, but about 70% of them solved the problem correctly.

Cheng and Holyoak (1985) explained the findings of Griggs and Cox (1983) in terms of pragmatic reasoning schemata, which are abstract rules relating to permission and obligation. We are often exposed to situations involving permission (e.g. to have permission to enter university, it is necessary to achieve certain examination results) and obligation (e.g. if there is an accident, then someone in authority must be informed). As a result, we have learned pragmatic reasoning schemata or rules that allow us to solve versions of the Wason task involving permission or obligation.

There are various factors determining the level of performance on the Wason task. Reasoning on this task is more likely to succeed if the participants have had relevant specific experiences or if the task allows the use of pragmatic reasoning schemata.

Discussion points

1. Why do you think most people find the original version of the Wason selection task so difficult?

2. How can the Wason selection task be made easier?

Evaluation

The Wason selection task has been studied in dozens of studies, with the findings generally suggesting that people's reasoning is irrational and illogical. However, Evans, Over, and Manktelow (1994) argued that we should distinguish between two kinds of rationality. Rationality$_1$ involves reasoning leading to the achievement of one's goals, whereas rationality$_2$ involves reasoning in conformity to a system such as logic. Wason's selection task assesses only rationality$_2$. It is thus entirely possible that most people possess rationality$_1$. According to Evans et al. (1994, p.184):

Cross-cultural issues: What Evans refers to as rationality$_1$ may be more prone to cultural variation than rationality$_2$. This could be examined in a cross-cultural sample using a task like the shopping and letter-posting example given below. What might the findings reveal about the significance of experience in determining individual responses?

> *The notion of rationality which really matters to people is rationality$_1$. People in general do have this to a fair degree, as they do tend to be reasonably good at achieving most of their goals.*

Categorical reasoning

Categorical reasoning makes use of syllogisms (that is, two statements followed by a conclusion that may be valid or invalid), and is concerned with membership in categories.

How might your actions differ if you reason using rationality$_1$ rather than rationality$_2$ in this situation?

Goals	• to leave college and catch the train from the station • to post a letter in the letterbox on the way • to collect some heavy shopping at the supermarket on the way	
Information	• the supermarket is closer to the college than the station • the letterbox is closer to the station than the college • the walk from the supermarket to the station is slightly longer if you go via the letterbox	
Plan of action	**Rationality$_1$** • first post the letter • double back to the supermarket • then to the station	**Rationality$_2$** • go to the nearest destination first (the supermarket) • then to the letterbox • then to the station
Reasoning	If I get rid of the letter first, I won't have to carry the shopping as far, even though I walk further overall.	This is the shortest overall route, and involves no backtracking.

STATION

LETTERBOX

SUPERMARKET

COLLEGE

Rationality$_1$ ⟶
Rationality$_2$ ⟶

Here is an example of a categorical reasoning task:

Premises:
All animals are mortal
All men are animals

Conclusion:
Therefore, all men are mortal

This conclusion is valid because it follows logically from the two premises.

Errors. People often make errors on categorical reasoning tasks. One reason for this is **belief bias**, which is the tendency to accept believable conclusions and to reject unbelievable conclusions whether or not the conclusions are actually valid. Newstead et al. (1992) found evidence for belief bias. They also found that their participants were more accurate at deciding whether a conclusion was valid when it was unbelievable. Why did this happen? Newstead et al. argued that people form one or more **mental models**, which are representations of the state of affairs described in the premises (see the next section for more details). Participants usually formed only one mental model if it led to a believable conclusion, and this often led to errors. In contrast, processing was more thorough when the first mental model led to an unbelievable conclusion, with the participants going on to form additional mental models. This more thorough processing reduced the number of errors.

Strategies. Ford (1995) argued that different people use different strategies to solve categorical syllogisms. She asked people to think out loud while solving each syllogism, and then to use pencil and paper to explain in detail how they had reached their conclusion. Verbal reasoning was used by 35% of the participants, who seemed to focus on the inference rules of logic such as modus ponens and modus tollens. In contrast, 40% of the participants favoured spatial reasoning. They produced drawings in which the relationships among the terms in the problem were shown in spatial terms. For example, the premise "All cats are animals" might be shown as a large circle labelled "animals" with a small circle labelled "cats" contained within it. The remaining participants used a variety of strategies, but showed no clear preference for verbal or spatial reasoning.

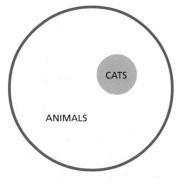

A diagrammatic solution to thinking about the premise "All cats are animals."

Mental models

Probably the most influential theoretical approach to deductive reasoning based on mental models was put forward by Johnson-Laird (1983). In order to show how mental models are formed, we will consider some examples taken from Eysenck and Keane (1995):

Premises:
The lamp is on the right of the pad.
The book is on the left of the pad.
The clock is in front of the book.
The vase is in front of the lamp.

Conclusion:
The clock is to the left of the vase.

According to Johnson-Laird, people use the information contained in the premises to form a mental model like this:

book	pad	lamp
clock		vase

It is easy to see from this model that the conclusion that the clock is to the left of the vase is valid. In many cases, however, there will be more than one mental model that is consistent with the premises:

Premises:
The lamp is on the right of the pad.
The book is on the left of the lamp.
The clock is in front of the book.
The vase is in front of the pad.

Conclusion:
The clock is to the left of the vase.

Mental model 1:   Mental model 2:

book   pad   lamp   pad   book   lamp
clock   vase   vase   clock

Someone who formed only mental model 1 would mistakenly conclude that the clock must be to the left of the vase. However, it would be clear to someone who formed both mental models that the clock is not necessarily to the left of the vase.

Some of the key features of Johnson-Laird's theory of mental models can be summarised as follows:

* Comprehension of the premises of a problem leads to the formation of one or more mental models representing the state of affairs indicated by the premises.
* The model or models that are formed are used to produce a novel conclusion not directly specified in the premises.
* There is a check to decide whether there are any additional models of the premises that invalidate the novel conclusion.
* The above three processes all depend on the processing resources of working memory (see Chapter 13). In particular, errors are likely to occur when several mental models have to be formed and held in working memory.

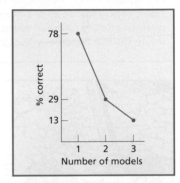

Evidence that the limited capacity of working memory can lead to errors in reasoning was reported by Johnson-Laird. Participants indicated what conclusions followed validly from sets of premises, and Johnson-Laird varied the demands on working memory by manipulating the number of mental models consistent with the premises. Seventy-eight per cent drew the valid conclusion when the premises only allowed the formation of one mental model. This figure dropped to 29% when two mental models were possible, and to 13% with three mental models.

When there is only one possible valid conclusion from a set of premises, most participants can select the right one. When there are two or more possible conclusions, it becomes more difficult to select them all.

Inductive reasoning

Wason (1960) devised an interesting inductive reasoning task. He told his participants that the three numbers 2 4 6 conformed to a simple relational rule. They had to generate sets of three numbers, and to provide reasons for each choice. After each choice, the experimenter indicated whether the set of numbers conformed to the rule that the experimenter had in mind. The task was to discover the nature of the rule. Since the rule was apparently very simple, namely, "three numbers in ascending order of magnitude", it might be guessed that most people would have solved it rapidly. In fact, only 21% of the participants were correct with their first attempt.

Performance on this problem was poor because most people thought of a hypothesis that was too specific (e.g. the second number is twice the first, and the third number is three times the first). They then generated sets of numbers consistent with that hypothesis (e.g. 6 12 18; 50 100 150). Participants following this strategy assumed it must be correct, because their original hypothesis was constantly confirmed. According to Wason, what people should have done was to look for sets of numbers that would *disconfirm* their hypothesis. Failure to try hypothesis disconfirmation

Imagine that you have to make a journey as quickly as possible. There are two alternative routes. Your first decision is based on mileage (one route is 20 miles, the other 25 miles). Later you discover that there are more junctions and traffic lights on the shorter of the two routes. You then have to revise your assessment of the journey. Finally, you discover that the traffic is heavier on the longer of the two routes.

What conclusions do you come to at each stage of this decision process? To what extent do your findings correspond with those of Johnson-Laird?

prevented the participants from replacing their initial hypotheses, which were too narrow and specific, with the correct general rule.

Tweney et al. (1980) showed how performance on the 2-4-6 problem could be improved. The participants were told that the experimenter had two rules in mind, one of which generated "DAX" triples and the other of which generated "MED" triples. They were also told that 2-4-6 was a DAX triple. The DAX rule was as in the Wason (1960) study, and the MED rule was the rule that generated all other sets of three numbers. The participants then generated sets of three numbers, and with each set following *either* the DAX rule *or* the MED rule. More than 50% of the participants produced the correct rule on their first attempt. Why was the approach taken by Tweney et al. so successful? They argued that the participants worked out the DAX rule by *confirming* the MED rule rather than by *disconfirming* the DAX rule.

Following the MED rule involves calculation rather than pattern. Numbers usually involve calculation when they are given in ascending forms rather than as a problem. Bearing this in mind, try to generate three sets of numbers that do not fit the DAX rules.

Application of Popper's argument

The hypothesis "All swans are white" can be disproved by the existence of just one black swan. If a scientist who wanted to test this hypothesis did not look for black swans, he or she might falsely conclude that all swans are indeed white. Thus scientific research into the colour of swans should begin by trying to refute the null hypothesis "Not all swans are white".

I wish I'd decided to check that it wouldn't explode if it wasn't heated, rather than the other way round!

Evaluation

Wason (1960) claimed that his findings on the 2-4-6 problem showed evidence of confirmation bias, which is of relevance to the ways in which scientific research is carried out. He argued that scientists generally try to confirm an existing hypothesis rather than to disconfirm it. The disadvantages of this approach to science were pointed out by Popper (e.g. 1969; see Chapter 28). According to Popper, hypotheses cannot be confirmed, they can only be disconfirmed or falsified.

Evans (1989) disagreed with Wason. He argued that the participants may have been trying to produce positive tests of their hypotheses rather than simply trying to confirm them. He gave the example of a scientist who wants to test the hypothesis that all metals expand when heated. The sensible way of proceeding would be to heat one metal after another to see whether each one expands. Thus, positive testing is often valuable in scientific research. Evans concluded that people may have a bias towards positive testing rather than towards confirmation, and thus that Wason may have misinterpreted his own findings.

Decision Making and Judgement

In everyday life, we have to make numerous decisions and judgements. How do we do it? In order to answer this question, we will consider some examples.

Utility theory

Suppose that a rare disease found mainly in Asia is expected to kill 600 people in the United States. There are two possible programmes of action to fight the disease. It is estimated that Programme A will save 200 lives, whereas Programme B offers a $\frac{1}{3}$ probability that all 600 people will be saved, and a $\frac{2}{3}$ probability that no-one will be saved.

Which of the two programmes is preferable? If we think rationally, then we should take account of the **expected utility** or expected value of each option. This can be worked out by using the following equation:

Expected utility = (probability of a given outcome) x (utility of that outcome)

In this example, the expected utility of Programme A is 1 x 200 = 200 people saved, and the expected utility of Programme B is 0.33 x 600 = 200. Thus, the two programmes are equally useful. In fact, Tversky and Kahneman (1987) found that 72% of their participants chose Programme A. This suggests that their decisions were not made on purely rational grounds. This was further supported when they gave other participants exactly the same problem expressed slightly differently: if Programme A is used, then 400 people will die: if Programme B is used, then there is a ⅓ probability that nobody will die, and a ⅔ probability that 600 people will die. Even though this is the same problem, only 22% of the participants chose Programme A.

Framing the problem

In the problem we have what is known as a **framing effect**, meaning that the decision is influenced by the phrasing or frame in which the problem is presented. Why did the participants show a framing effect? In the first version of the problem, Programme A is framed in a positive way, with an emphasis on the number of lives that will be saved. In the second version, in contrast, the emphasis is on the people who will die.

Loss aversion

The study by Tversky and Kahneman shows that we do not always behave in line with expected utility. There are many other situations in which people do not make use of expected utility. For example, most people show evidence of **loss aversion**, which is the tendency to be much more sensitive to losses than to gains. Kahneman and Tversky (1984) asked participants whether they would accept a bet that involved them winning $20 if a coin came up heads, but paying $10 if it came up tails. The bet should be accepted according to utility theory, but most of the participants rejected it. Thus, they showed loss aversion.

Alternatives to utility theory

Elimination by aspects. Tversky (1972) put forward an elimination-by-aspects theory, according to which the decision maker eliminates options by considering one relevant attribute after another. Someone buying a house may first of all consider the attribute of geographical location, eliminating from further consideration all those houses not lying within a given area. He or she may then consider the attribute of price, eliminating all those properties costing above a given figure. This process continues attribute by attribute until there is only one option left. This strategy has the advantage that it does not involve difficult or complex thinking. However, it suffers from the disadvantage that the option that is selected depends on the order in which the attributes are considered.

You'll have to drop her to catch me, so are you feeling lucky, punk?

■ Research activity: Consider the plans you may have for a future career. In deciding on that career, apply Tversky's elimination-by-aspects theory, then compare it to the application of satisficing theory. Which approach do you feel is more convincing? Are there any non-rational factors that might override a decision such as this?

Satisficing. Simon (1978) argued for a different approach known as satisficing theory. This theory is of most use when the various options become available at different points in time. An example is trying to decide who to marry. According to the theory, decision makers set a minimum acceptable level. The first option (i.e. boyfriend or girlfriend) to reach that level is selected. If the initial level of acceptability is set too high or too low, it can be adjusted upwards or downwards to make it more realistic.

Payne (1976) studied the ways in which people choose a flat or apartment from information presented on cards. Most of them started off by using techniques such as elimination by aspects and satisficing to reduce the number of possibilities being considered. After that, they focused on the remaining options in a more thorough way.

Reasonableness. Other theorists have argued that people make decisions that are reasonable or justified. Tversky and Shafir (1992) gave their participants the task of deciding whether to buy an attractive package holiday in Hawaii. All the participants were told to imagine that they had just taken a difficult examination. Some were told to imagine that they had passed the examination, some that they had failed the examination, and the rest that they did not know whether they had passed or failed.

Of those participants who had passed the examination, 54% decided to buy the holiday. They had the justification that they deserved to celebrate their success. Of those who had failed, 57% bought the holiday, presumably as a consolation for their disappointment. Of those who did not know what had happened, only 32% decided to buy the holiday. It was hard for the participants in this condition to think of a good justification for taking the holiday when they were in a state of uncertainty.

Summary

We do not generally make decisions in the rational or logical way proposed by utility theory. We are influenced by non-rational factors such as the phrasing or framing of a problem, loss aversion, the desire to be able to justify our decisions, and so on. The precise strategies that we use vary from problem to problem. However, our decision making often makes use of elimination by aspects and/or satisficing. These strategies are not ideal, but usually work fairly well in practice.

Judgement under uncertainty

Kahneman and Tversky (1973) argued that people often make poor decisions or judgements because they ignore relevant information. Suppose you read in an encyclopaedia that a physical complaint from which you are suffering is one of the symptoms of a rare and unpleasant disease. Suppose further that one person in 5000 has the disease, that the probability of having the physical symptom if you are suffering from the disease is 0.7, and that the probability of having the symptom without also having the disease is 0.01. What is the probability that you have the disease? Most people would argue that there was a high probability that they were suffering from the disease. In actual fact, however, the correct probability is only about 0.014.

Representativeness

How might the representativeness heuristic apply to:

1. *The popularity of the National Lottery.*
2. *Travel by plane in preference to car/boat/train.*

Why are the probability judgements so inaccurate in this situation? According to Kahneman and Tversky, people decide between various possibilities by considering which one seems to be most representative of, or consistent with, the evidence. In other words, they use a rule of thumb known as the "representativeness heuristic", according to which representative or typical instances of a category are judged to be more probable than unrepresentative ones. What is left out of account is the base-rate information. In the example, this refers to the relative numbers of people suffering from, and not suffering from, the disease. As the number of non-sufferers from the disease is vastly greater than the number of sufferers (4999 out of 5000 people versus 1 out of 5000), this greatly reduces the probability that a person with the physical symptom will actually be suffering from the disease.

Kahneman and Tversky (1972) tested use of the representativeness heuristic, using the following problem:

All the families having exactly six children in a particular city were surveyed. In 72 of the families, the exact order of births of boys (B) and girls (G) was G B G B B G. What is your estimate of the number of families surveyed in which the exact order of births was B G B B B B?

The best estimate is 72, because the probability of having a boy or a girl is the same at 0.5. Thus, any sequence of six children is as likely as any other sequence. However, most of the answers were much lower than 72. According to Kahneman and Tversky, the participants used the

CASE STUDY: *Picking Lottery Numbers*

In general, people have a very poor understanding of randomness and probability, as evidenced by the types of numbers commonly selected in the UK National Lottery. Even people who claim to understand that any given number is as likely to come up as any other will be heard to despair: "Oh, I'll never win with that—four numbers in a row!", or "All my numbers are bunched up under 20—I'd better spread them out a bit to get a better pattern." In fact, statistics suggest that you're actually better off picking numbers with a skewed or bunched appearance: you're no more likely to win, but in the unlikely event that you do, you'll be less likely to have to share your prize with anyone else!

representativeness heuristic: the birth order G B G B B G seems more likely than the birth order B G B B B B because it is more representative of the numbers of males and females in the population, and because it appears to be more random.

Tversky and Kahneman (1983) produced even more striking evidence of the kinds of error that can result from using the representativeness heuristic. They found what they called the "conjunction fallacy". The participants were told that an imaginary person called Linda is a former student activist, single, very intelligent, and a philosophy graduate. They were then asked to estimate the probability of her being a bank teller, a feminist, or a feminist bank teller. Most said it was more likely that Linda was a feminist bank teller than a bank teller. This cannot be correct, because the category of bank tellers includes all feminist bank tellers.

Relevance

Do people always rely on the representativeness heuristic and ignore base-rate information? According to Tversky and Kahneman (1980), base-rate information is often used when its causal relevance is made clear. They told their participants that there were two taxi companies in a town, the Blue Company and the Green Company. There was an accident involving a taxi, and the participants' task was to decide the probability that the taxi had been blue. Some participants were told that 50% of the taxis in the town were blue and the other 50% were green, but that 85% of the taxi-related accidents involved green taxis. They were also told that a witness claimed that a blue taxi was involved, but there was a 20% chance that he was mistaken. When the causal relevance of the base-rate information (i.e. the percentage of accidents caused by blue taxis) was made obvious, the participants used that information. Most of them were fairly close to the correct figure of a 59% chance that a blue taxi was involved. When the causal relevance of the base-rate information was not made clear, most participants claimed mistakenly that there was an 80% probability that the taxi was blue.

Availability heuristic

Tversky and Kahneman (1973) studied another heuristic or rule of thumb known as the "availability heuristic". According to this heuristic, probability judgements are sometimes made on the basis of how available relevant examples are in long-term memory. They asked their participants whether each of five letters of the alphabet (K, L, N, R, and V) occurs more often in the first or the third position in English words. All five letters appear in the third position in more words, but the participants mostly argued that each letter appears more often in the first position. This finding depends on the availability heuristic: it is much easier to generate words starting with a given letter than those having the same letter in the third position.

How might you go about testing the strength of the availability heuristic in determining how people make judgements?

Media coverage

Lichtenstein et al. (1978) found that the availability heuristic is used in everyday life. They argued that our judgements about the probabilities of different kinds of lethal events are influenced by the amount of media coverage given to them. Causes of death that receive considerable media coverage (e.g. murder) are judged to be more common than causes of death that receive little publicity (e.g. suicide), even when the less reported lethal events are actually more common. The reason is that we can more readily think of examples of the lethal events that are discussed at length in the media.

Evaluation

The greatest strength of the approach adopted by Kahneman and Tversky is that it captures some of the processes involved in making judgements. We often use rules of thumb or heuristics in our thinking, with important information (e.g. base-rate information) being ignored. In other words, our judgemental thinking is often less precise and rational than we imagine.

How problems are expressed. One weakness in the approach of Kahneman and Tversky is that we are sometimes more capable of making accurate judgements than is predicted by their approach. For example, Fiedler (1988) repeated the conjunction fallacy finding of Tversky and Kahneman (1983; see earlier). About 75% of the participants argued that it was more likely that Linda was a feminist bank teller than that she was a bank teller. However, when other participants were asked to estimate how many out of a hundred people like Linda would be feminist bank tellers and how many would be bank tellers, about 75% argued correctly that more would be bank tellers! If small changes in the wording of a problem can produce major changes in judgemental accuracy, then we must be cautious in interpreting the available findings.

Laboratory studies. A second weakness of the approach is that it is based too much on artificial laboratory studies. According to Koehler (1996), we are more likely to make use of base-rate information if we have obtained this information through direct experience rather than simply being provided with it in the laboratory. Christensen-Szalanski and Bushyhead (1981) looked at the use of base-rate information by doctors who had found from experience that pneumonia has a low base-rate. These doctors made considerable use of this base-rate information when deciding on a diagnosis.

Lack of a theory. A final weakness of the approach is that there is no proper theory of what is involved. For example, it seems that use of the availability heuristic involves information retrieved from long-term memory. However, little is known of the processes involved in such retrieval or of the ways in which the retrieved information influences probability judgements.

Language and Thought

So far we have generally treated language and thought as if they were separate. However, there are close links between them. As we will see, there has been some controversy as to the relationship between language and thought. Some have argued that language determines thought, whereas others have argued that thought determines language. Still others have argued that the relationship is more complex than either of those possibilities.

Watson's approach

One of the earliest attempts to provide a theoretical account of the relationship between language and thought was made by the behaviourists. John Watson, the founder of behaviourism, argued that thinking was nothing more than inner speech. It may be true that most people sometimes engage in inner speech when thinking about difficult problems, but that is a far cry from Watson's dogmatic position.

The ludicrous nature of Watson's theory was revealed in a witty comment made by the philosopher Herbert Feigl. According to him, Watson "made up his windpipe that he had no mind". Evidence destroying Watson's theory was provided by Smith et al. (1947). Dr Smith showed great bravery by allowing himself to be given a curare derivative (curare was the poison used by American Indians on their arrowheads). This paralysed his entire musculature, so that an artificial respirator had to be used to keep him alive. Because the curare totally prevented any sub-vocal speech, it should also have prevented him from thinking. In fact, he reported that he had been able to think about what was going on around him while paralysed.

John Watson, the American psychologist and founder of behaviourism.

Whorfian hypothesis

An influential theory on the relationship between thought and language was put forward by Benjamin Lee Whorf (1956). He was a fire prevention officer for an insurance company, but spent his spare time working in linguistics. Whorf was much influenced by the obvious differences among the world's languages. For example, Arabic has numerous words describing camels and their disgusting habits, and the Inuit Eskimos have various words to describe snow. In the Thai language, verbs do not have tenses as they do in English. As a result, Thai people often find it hard to use verbs correctly in English to refer to the past or to the future.

Does language influence thinking?

Whorf was impressed by these differences among languages. According to his "linguistic relativity hypothesis", language determines (or has a major influence on) thinking. In the words of Whorf (1956, pp.212–213), the linguistic system is

> not merely a reproducing instrument for viewing ideas but rather is itself the shaper of ideas, the program and guide for the individual's mental activity, for his analysis of impressions, for his synthesis of his original stock in trade. Formulation of ideas is not an independent process ... but is part of a particular grammar and differs, from slightly to greatly, as between different grammars. We dissect nature along lines laid down by our native language.

Three hypotheses

It is hard to test this hypothesis. Some clarification of the theoretical issues involved was offered by Miller and McNeill (1969). They argued that there are *three* different hypotheses concerning the effects of language on psychological processes. The strong hypothesis (the one put forward by Whorf) claims that language determines thinking. The weak hypothesis states that language affects perception. Finally, the weakest hypothesis makes the more modest claim that language influences memory, with information that is easily described in a given language being remembered best. Of these three hypotheses, the weakest hypothesis has been tested most often.

As Gross (1996) pointed out, one of the few attempts to test the strong hypothesis was reported by Carroll and Casagrande (1958). They studied Navaho children who spoke only Navaho; Navaho children who spoke Navaho and English; and American children who spoke only English and whose families were of European descent. The importance of form or shape is emphasised more in the Navaho language. For example, Navaho verbs to do with picking up or touching objects differ depending on the shape of the object being handled. According to the strong hypothesis, children who know the Navaho language should show form recognition before those who do not. In fact, the children who spoke only Navaho showed form recognition at the earliest age. However, those who spoke Navaho and English were slower to acquire form recognition than those who spoke only English. Thus, the findings provided mixed support for the strong hypothesis.

Colour words

Apparent support for Whorf's position was obtained by Lenneberg and Roberts (1956). Zuni speakers, who are North American Indian people who come from West New Mexico, made more mistakes in recognising yellows and oranges than did English speakers. As the Zuni language differs from English in having only a single word to describe yellows and oranges, it could be argued that the limited Zuni language caused the memory problems.

Later research produced findings less favourable to Whorf's hypothesis. Heider (1972) used as her starting point the fact that English (and other languages) have the same basic 11 colour words, and for each hue there is a best or focal colour. The importance of these focal colours is shown by the finding that English speakers usually find it easier to remember focal colours than non-focal ones. If language affects memory, then different results should be obtained with the Dani. They live in New Guinea, and their language has only two basic colour words: "mili" for dark, cold colours, and "mola" for bright, warm colours. In spite of this, the Dani people showed better recognition memory for focal than for non-focal colours.

Heider's findings are suspect, because the focal colours she used were more perceptually distinct than the non-focal colours. Lucy and Schweder (1979) eliminated this problem, and found that focal colours were *not* remembered any better than non-focal ones. However, an effect of language on perception was reported by Kay and

■ Research activity: The colour red has the greatest number of variations. Make a list of words that describe a type of red, e.g. crimson, etc. Compare your list with other people's. How would you account for any marked differences between you and your fellow students or family and friends?

Kempton (1984). Their participants were presented with colour chips that were intermediate in colour between blue and green. English speakers exaggerated the differences between colour chips that differed only slightly, whereas speakers of the Mexican–Indian language Tarahomara did not. Why was there this difference? English speakers seem to have categorised some chips as blue and others as green and this literally coloured their judgement. Speakers of Tarahomara did not use exaggeration, because there are no words for blue and green in their language.

Perception and memory

Additional evidence that language can influence perception and/or memory was obtained by Carmichael, Hogan, and Walters (1932). They showed their participants a series of drawings, and told them that each one resembled some well-known object. For example, the same drawing could be labelled as a crescent moon or the letter "C" (see page 279). The participants' subsequent reproductions from memory were influenced by the verbal labels provided for each object.

Evaluation

Whorf's original linguistic relativity hypothesis cannot be accepted. There are various reasons for this. First, he tended to exaggerate the differences among the world's languages. For example, Inuit Eskimos may indeed have various words for snow, but there are several in English as well. Second, there is little evidence that differences between languages have much influence on thought. What is more likely is that the different environmental conditions experienced by different cultures influence what they think about, and this affects the ways in which their language develops. Third, as Greene (1975) pointed out, it is easy to attach too much significance to the expressions in a given language. For example, users of English talk about the foot of a mountain, but they are well aware that it is very different from a person's foot.

Modified Whorfian hypothesis

Hunt and Agnoli (1991) put forward a modified version of the Whorfian hypothesis. According to Hunt and Agnoli (1991, p.379):

Different languages lend themselves to the transmission of different types of messages. People consider the costs of computation when they reason about a topic. The language that they use will partly determine those costs. In this sense, language does influence cognition.

Thus, any given language makes it easy to think in certain ways, but hard to think in other ways.

Some of the findings we have already discussed are consistent with this modified Whorfian hypothesis. For example, consider Carmichael et al.'s (1932) finding that verbal labels influenced memory. This probably happened because the participants found it easier to rely on those labels when remembering. If it had been essential to remember the drawings accurately, then they might have used more demanding processing strategies.

An example of how language can influence thinking was provided by Hoffman, Lau, and Johnson (1986). Bilingual English-Chinese speakers read descriptions of individuals. These descriptions were deliberately prepared to conform to either Chinese or English stereotypes of personality. For example, there is a stereotype of the artistic type in English, consisting of a mixture of artistic skills, moody and intense temperament, and bohemian lifestyle, but this stereotype does not exist in Chinese. After they had read the descriptions, the participants were asked to provide free impressions of the individuals described.

Bilinguals thinking in Chinese made use of Chinese stereotypes in their free impressions, whereas bilinguals thinking in English used English stereotypes. Thus, the inferences we draw can be much influenced by the language in which we are thinking.

Additional evidence that language can influence habits of thought was reported by Ervin-Tripp (1964) in a study on Japanese-American bilinguals. When they were given sentence-completion or word-association tests, their performance resembled that of Japanese-only speakers when they responded in Japanese. However, their answers were like those of English-only speakers when they responded in English.

Evaluation

Hunt and Agnoli (1991) have provided a plausible cognitive account of the Whorfian hypothesis, and there is a fair amount of evidence consistent with it. However, what is lacking is a systematic programme of research to show clearly that language influences thought in the ways specified by Hunt and Agnoli.

Piaget

According to Piaget, children can only think effectively when they have developed certain cognitive operations and structures (see Chapter 16). For example, suppose that a young child is shown two glasses of the same size and shape containing the same amount of liquid. All the liquid from one of the glasses is then poured into a different glass that is taller and thinner. The child is then asked if the two glasses contain the same amount to drink (this is known as a conservation task). Children below the age of 7 will often mistakenly argue that there is more liquid in the new, tall glass ("because it's higher") or in the original glass ("because it's wider"). Solving the problem requires the cognitive operation of **reversibility**, which involves the ability to undo (or reverse) mentally some operation that has been carried out. Older children realise that the liquid in the new glass could be poured back into the original glass, and thus that the two glasses contain the same amount of liquid.

In children's education we tend to base our assessment of the child's understanding of concepts like reversibility on the language that they use, either verbal or written. Can you think of any arguments for and against this that might demonstrate uncertainty about the relationship between language and thought?

Piaget argued that cognitive operations and structures develop in the course of maturation. Where does language fit in? According to Piaget, thinking influences language development much more than language development influences thinking. Some evidence for this was reported by Sinclair-de-Zwart (1969). She used the two-glass conservation task with children, who were also given various language tests relevant to the conservation task (e.g. "This is tall but it's thin; this is short but it's wide"). On the language tests children who solved the conservation problem did much better than those who did not, suggesting that there are important links between language and thought.

Sinclair-de-Zwart's key finding was on those children who failed the conservation problem. Only about 10% of these children who were taught the conservation-relevant language showed evidence of conservation thereafter. Thus, language does not benefit thinking very much, and a full understanding of language can only be achieved *after* the relevant cognitive operations and structures are in place.

Vygotsky

According to the Russian Lev Vygotsky, thought and language in the very young child are separate and independent activities. Infants can think before they acquire language, and their early attempts at language often involve repeating what an adult has said without any understanding. Things change when the child reaches the age of 2, when "thought becomes verbal and speech rational" (Vygotsky, 1962).

There are further developments between the ages of 2 and 7. During that time, language develops two rather different uses: (1) it has the *internal* function of being used to monitor and to direct internal thoughts; and (2) it has the *external* function of being used to communicate to others what has been thought about internally. Children up until the age of 7 cannot distinguish clearly between these two functions of language. As a result, they produce what is known as **egocentric speech**. According to Vygotsky, egocentric speech serves "mental orientation, conscious understanding; it helps in

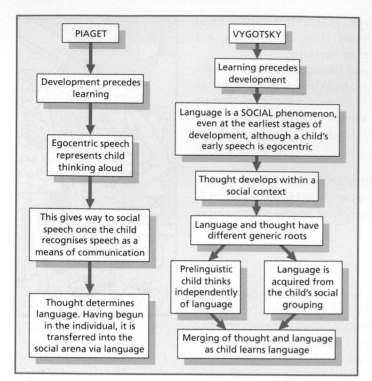

overcoming difficulties, it is speech for oneself, intimately and usefully connected with the child's thinking. In the end it becomes inner speech."

Vygotsky 's basic position is that language and thought are initially independent, but become interdependent during childhood. As Harley (1995) pointed out, it is hard to evaluate the significance of Vygotsky's theory because it is expressed rather vaguely and has not been submitted to detailed testing. There is more detailed information on Vygotsky's theory in Chapter 16.

Fodor

Fodor (1983) argued there is a module or cognitive system dedicated to language processing. He also argued that this language-processing system exhibits information encapsulation, meaning that it functions independently of other modules.

An important implication is that the process of language comprehension is not influenced by non-linguistic information (e.g. thoughts). As a result, it would be expected that language comprehension should proceed in an entirely bottom-up or stimulus-driven way. In fact, however, top-down processes can affect the processes involved in speech comprehension. For example, Warren and Warren (1970) presented their participants with a recording in which part of a word had been deleted. The participants heard one of the following sentences (the asterisk indicates the deleted portion):

It was found that the *eel was on the axle.
It was found that the *eel was on the shoe.
It was found that the *eel was on the table.
It was found that the *eel was on the orange.

All the participants heard the same speech sound (i.e. "*eel"), but their top-down processes based on the sentence context led them to perceive it differently. Those listening to the first sentence heard "wheel", those listening to the second sentence heard "heel", whereas those exposed to the third and fourth sentences heard "meal" and "peel", respectively.

Fodor's theoretical position seems too extreme. However, the fact that brain damage often affects only language processes rather than cognition generally suggests that there are processing systems dedicated to language (see Chapter 4). Furthermore, as Harris (1990, p.203) pointed out:

> *Language processing has to be largely independent of other cognitive activities. For, if it were not, we would hear only what we expected to hear and read only what we expected to read.*

Social factors: Bernstein

Bernstein (1973) argued that children's use of language is determined in part by the social environment in which they grow up. He distinguished between two language codes or patterns of speech: the restricted code and the elaborated code. The *restricted code* is relatively concrete and descriptive. It is also rather context-dependent, in the sense that it is hard to understand unless one knows the context in which it is being used. In contrast, the *elaborated code* is more complex and abstract, and can easily be understood in the absence of contextual information.

Bernstein (1973, p.203) gave the following examples of the two codes based on descriptions of four pictures like those on the next page:

- Restricted code: "They're playing football and he kicks it, and it goes through there. It breaks the window and they're looking at it and he comes out and shouts at them because they've broken it. So they run away and then she looks out and she tells them off."

- Elaborated code: "Two boys are playing football and one boy kicks the ball and it goes through the window. The ball breaks the window and the boys are looking at it, and a man comes out and shouts at them because they've broken the window. So they run away and then that lady looks out of her window, and she tells the boys off."

Bernstein argued that middle-class children generally use the elaborated code, whereas working-class children use the restricted code. However, many middle-class children can use both codes, whereas many working-class children are limited to the restricted code. The lack of an elaborated code may limit the thinking of working-class children. Teachers in school typically use the elaborated code, and this may disadvantage working-class children.

Evidence that working-class children may have restricted language development was reported by Bernstein (1961). Middle-class and working-class boys who obtained high scores for non-verbal intelligence (e.g. spatial and mathematical ability) were compared on verbal intelligence based on the use of language. The middle-class boys performed equally well on both kinds of intelligence, whereas the working-class boys obtained lower scores for verbal intelligence. Bernstein argued that the discrepancy between verbal and non-verbal intelligence showed by the working-class boys was due to their reliance on the restricted language code.

Hess and Shipman (1965) studied American mothers and their four-year-old children. Middle-class mothers used language interactively to discuss issues with their children via questions and answers. In contrast, working-class mothers used language to give orders to their children, and there was less exchange of ideas.

> **KEY STUDY EVALUATION — Bernstein**
>
> Bernstein's research has been applied to the study of Black English. Both pieces of research focus on the importance of social context. Bernstein is making an objective assessment of the style of language spoken by children in school, and the apparent disadvantage that working-class children suffer as a consequence of their style of speech. This is not an accurate assessment of their abilities and cannot be used as an indicator of their academic potential. However, teachers who use the elaborated, formal, or public codes of speech sometimes assume that this is the case. As a consequence of the informal or restricted speech codes of many working-class children, they find it hard to relate to the language of the classroom. Cultural factors also apply in the case of some, but not all, ethnic minority children.

Cross-cultural issues: Caution must be taken to avoid generalising results such as Hess and Shipman's to class and race.

Discussion points

1. How adequate is it to divide language into a restricted code and an elaborated code?
2. What seem to be the main differences between the restricted and elaborated codes?

Evaluation

There is evidence for the distinction between the elaborated and restricted codes. However, Bernstein's views are over-simplified. There are probably several codes, with the elaborated and restricted codes representing the extremes. At the very least, it is likely that many people use a mixture of the two codes in their everyday speech. Bernstein seems to assume that the elaborated code is superior to the restricted code. In fact, as Harley (1995, p.348) pointed out, "[It] is far from obvious that the working class dialect is impoverished compared to the middle class dialect: it is just different."

PERSONAL REFLECTIONS

- In my opinion, it is very odd that language (which is of enormous importance) was hardly studied during the first 50 years or so of experimental psychology. This may have happened because the behaviourists wanted to focus on the similarities between humans and other species. Alternatively, it may have happened because the behaviourist emphasis on observable stimuli and responses was unsuitable for studying internal language processes.

• There have been major practical implications of our growing understanding of language. For example, there has been much progress in improving the language abilities of children with physical and sensory handicaps, as well as those with dyslexia (see Chapter 23).

S U M M A R Y

Language acquisition

Young children pass through a one-word stage and a telegraphic period, followed by the learning of grammatical morphemes and pragmatics. Chomsky argued that humans possess a language acquisition device consisting of innate knowledge of grammatical structure. Subsequently, he favoured the notion of a universal grammar. According to the critical period hypothesis, language learning depends on biological maturation. The evidence supports a weakened version of this hypothesis, according to which some aspects of language (e.g. phonological learning) are harder to acquire outside the critical period.

Language comprehension

Language comprehension often involves bridging and elaborative inferences. Most of the inferences that are drawn are those that are needed in order for readers to achieve their reading goals.

Language production

Speakers should take account of the maxims of quantity, quality, relation, and manner. Speech production involves much forward planning. According to Garrett, there are five levels of representation involved in speaking: message-level representation; functional-level representation; positional-level representation; phonetic-level representation; and articulatory-level representation. These levels usually occur in the order indicated. Evidence for Garrett's approach comes from the study of speech errors (e.g. spoonerisms; exchange errors). The processes involved in writing have been studied by means of protocol analysis, in which writers verbalise their thoughts during writing. According to Hayes and Flower (1986), writing involves planning, sentence-generation, and revision

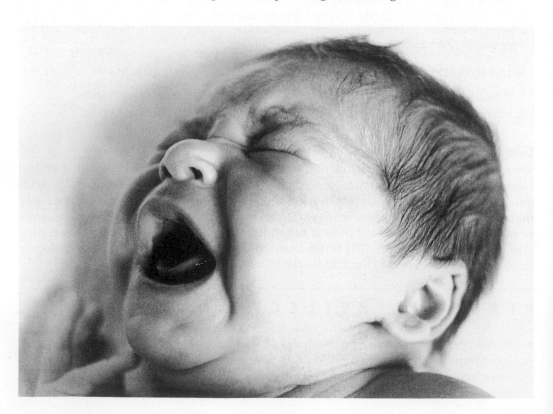

Babies cry as soon as they are born, to signal distress, but three weeks later they start to produce "fake cries" when they are clearly not in distress. It may be that infants enjoy listening to their own voices.

processes. Expert writers use a knowledge-transforming strategy during the planning process, whereas novice writers tend to use a knowledge-telling strategy. Expert writers tend to generate larger sentence parts than non-expert writers, and they tend to spend longer in revision.

Reasoning

Many errors tend to be made in conditional reasoning. According to abstract-rule theory, these errors can be due to comprehension failures, heuristic inadequacy, or processing errors. Performance on the Wason selection task is error-prone, but tends to improve if the participants have had relevant specific experiences or if the task allows use of pragmatic reasoning schemata. Categorical reasoning is liable to belief bias, and can involve either spatial or verbal reasoning. Mental models are often formed when people try to solve reasoning problems. Inductive reasoning can involve confirmation bias or positive testing, with people being reluctant to try to disconfirm their hypotheses.

Decision making and judgement

Rational decision making would involve taking account only of the expected utility or expected value of each option. In fact, this is rarely the case, as is shown by framing effects and loss aversion. Elimination-by-aspects theory and satisficing theory provide more plausible accounts of decision making. People generally attach importance to being able to justify any decision. Judgements under uncertainty are influenced by various rules of thumb such as the representativeness heuristic and the availability heuristic.

Language and thought

According to Whorf's linguistic relativity hypothesis, language determines (or has a major influence on) thinking. This overstates the case, but any given language does tend to make it easy to think in certain ways but hard to think in other ways. Bernstein argued that there is an important distinction between a restricted and an elaborate code of language, with working-class children tending to use the former and middle-class children the latter.

FURTHER READING

M.W. Eysenck (1993), *Principles of cognitive psychology*, Hove, UK: Psychology Press; Chapters 5 and 6 in this book contain discussions of most of the topics covered in this chapter. K.J. Gilhooly (1995), *Thinking: Directed, undirected and creative (3rd Edn.)*, London: Academic Press; there are thorough discussions of the major types of thinking in this book. T.A. Harley (1995), *The psychology of language: From data to theory*, Hove, UK: Psychology Press; most aspects of language are dealt with very thoroughly in this book, and it is written in a clear fashion, but is rather complicated in parts.

REVISION QUESTIONS

1	Compare and contrast *two* theories of language acquisition.	(24 marks)
2	Critically consider what psychological research has shown us about the nature of language comprehension.	(24 marks)
3a	Describe *two* models of human thought.	(12 marks)
3b	Assess the extent to which research has supported these models.	(12 marks)
4	"Human beings ... are very much at the mercy of the particular language which has become the medium of expression for their society. We see and hear and otherwise experience very largely as we do because the language habits of our community predispose certain choices of interpretation" (Sapir, 1941).	
	"Language can in some circumstances facilitate thought but ... it does not determine it in the sense of precluding other ways of thinking ... The evidence suggests that changing language will not, on its own, have a great effect on people's attitudes and thoughts" (Newstead, 1995).	
	In the light of psychological evidence, critically consider which of these two opposing views is more accurate.	(24 marks)
5	Describe and analyse social and cultural variations in language in relation to thought.	(24 marks)

- **Sociability**
  How and why infants begin to be friendly towards adults and other infants.

  Parten's six types of play behaviour
  Mueller and Lucas's three-stage theory
  Parenting style and genetic factors

- **Attachment**
  How close emotional relationships begin to develop.

  Freud's theory
  Harlow's study of monkeys
  Dollard and Miller's learning theory
  Ethological and ecological approaches
  Ainsworth and Bell's strange situation studies

- **Effects of deprivation**
  How does a lack of emotional care affect children's development?

  Bowlby's maternal deprivation hypothesis
  Tizard's studies of institutionalised children

- **Enrichment**
  Providing extra care and stimulation can give children an advantage as they grow up.

  Project Head Start
  The Milwaukee project
  Carolina Abecedarian project
  Cultural and subcultural effects
  Pretence

- **Cross-cultural differences in child-rearing**
  People from different cultures vary in the ways they bring up their children.

  Cross-cultural strange situation findings
  Attachment style
  Development of intelligence across cultures

15

Early Socialisation

Much of infants' early learning is in the area of social development. Two aspects of this learning are of special importance: sociability and attachment. **Sociability** is the tendency to interact in a friendly and positive way with other people, whereas an **attachment** is a fairly strong and long-lasting emotional tie to another person. Most children as they grow up are sociable with many other children and adults, but they typically only form attachments to a small number of people (e.g. their parents). In the following two sections, we consider the processes involved in the development of sociability and of attachment.

Children's development can be greatly affected by the kind of environment to which they are exposed. There has been much concern that deprivation (and especially maternal deprivation) may have severe long-term effects on children socially and intellectually. Of course, the environment can also be very favourable, and psychologists have looked at the effects of enrichment on children's development. As we will see, children are often affected in various ways by deprivation and by enrichment.

Children's social and emotional development depends in part on their parents' child-rearing practices. Styles of child-rearing vary considerably across cultures, and this makes it important to carry out cross-cultural studies. As might be expected, child-rearing practices tend to reflect the dominant values of the culture, and so this is one way in which parents pass on those values to the next generation.

Sociability

Infants show signs of sociability (e.g. smiling; attention-seeking) at a very early age. As early as six weeks old, they tend to protest if an adult leaves them on their own (Schaffer & Emerson, 1964). After that, infants become more and more sociable, displaying a wider range of sociable behaviour with an increasingly large number of other people.

Sociability with care-givers

The fact that sociability develops early in life is easily explained from an evolutionary perspective. Infants and young children are almost helpless, and thus are heavily reliant on other human beings if they are to survive and develop normally. This helps to explain why it is that two-day-old infants can recognise their mothers (Bushnell, Sai, & Mullin, 1989), and why infants start to smile at an early age (Durkin, 1995). The sociability shown by infants may be of crucial importance in leading to close attachments with their mother or other major care-giver.

Even six-month-old children show social interaction.

How many people do you feel attached to?

How many people do you feel social with?

KEY TERMS
Sociability: the tendency to interact in a friendly and positive way with other people.
Attachment: a fairly strong and long-lasting emotional tie to another person.

381

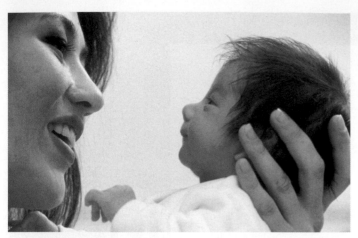

Infants start to smile at an early age, which may be a crucial factor in developing close attachments to their care-giver.

Infants start to play with each other at about six months old and gradually improve their communication as they develop physical, cognitive, and language skills.

Sociability with other infants

In this section, we will focus on the development of sociability towards other infants. Infants show an interest in other infants at a very young age. When they are only two months old, they will often look at other infants, and one or two months later they start to touch other infants. When infants are about six months old, they smile at other infants and make noises. As they become more mobile, they start to crawl towards other infants, or they follow them around the room. By the time they reach their first birthday, infants use gestures with other infants, they imitate each other, and they laugh in the presence of other infants (Vandell & Mueller, 1980).

The importance of other infants in the development of sociability has been shown in studies in which infants are observed in the same room as their mother and another infant. Becker (1977) found that nine-month-old infants paid more attention to the other infant than to their mother or their toys. When they met the other infant again, they showed even more interest, and played in more complex ways.

Observations such as these indicate that infants are sociable in terms of being interested in other infants. Do they show proper social behaviour in the sense of having proper interactions with other infants? The answer to this question seems to be "yes", at least by the time infants are six months old. Infants of that age tend to adjust the frequency with which they touch other infants so that it matches the frequency with which they themselves are touched. In addition, the moods of six-month-old infants become more similar as they play together (Nash, 1988).

Infants between the ages of 6 and 12 months become better able to communicate with each other, because they are developing physical, cognitive, and language skills. As a result, when two infants nearing their first birthday are together, they often show good co-ordination of behavioural activities such as gesturing, vocalising, and looking (Durkin, 1995).

There are significant increases in co-operative play during the second year. Children start to play games that involve turn-taking, and they begin to talk to each other in ways that resemble conversations (Durkin, 1995).

Parten

The study of sociability in children between the ages of 2 and 5 owes much to the work of Parten (1932). She identified six categories of play behaviour on the basis of observations of children:

1. Unoccupied behaviour: the child is not playing, and is not attending to the activities of other children.
2. Solitary play: the child plays on his or her own and shows little or no interest in other children.
3. Onlooking behaviour: the child displays genuine interest in the play activities of other children, but his or her play activities are not integrated.
4. Parallel play: the child plays with other children, but his or her play activities are not integrated with those of other children.
5. Associative play: the child plays with other children, and his or her behaviour is partially integrated with that of other children.
6. Co-operative play: the child plays as a member of a group of children behaving co-operatively and in an organised way.

Parten (1932) found that parallel play was more common than any other category of behaviour at all ages between 2 and 5. However, there were some significant changes during the preschool years. The more sociable forms of behaviour (associative play; co-operative play) increased in frequency, whereas the non-sociable forms such as solitary play and onlooking behaviour became less common. According to Bakeman and Brownlee (1980), children who engage in parallel play generally want to engage in group play, but are unsure how to achieve that goal. They obtained support for this view by finding that parallel play is often followed by group play, but is rarely followed by solitary play.

Discussion points

1. Do you think that Parten identified the main categories of play behaviour?

2. How easy is it to distinguish between play aggression and real aggression?

Shea (1981) videotaped 3- and 4-year-olds in the playground during their first 10 weeks at nursery school, and found that sociability increased over that time. The children's behaviour was assessed on five dimensions: aggression; rough-and-tumble play; frequency of peer interaction; distance from the teacher; and distance from the nearest child. There were clear indications that the children became more sociable over time. There was a decrease in the distance from the nearest child and in aggression, and an increase in rough-and-tumble play, frequency of peer interaction, and in distance from the teacher. The increases in sociability were greater in those attending the nursery school for five days a week than in those attending for only two days, indicating that it was the experience of nursery school rather than maturation that was producing most of the changes.

Stage approach

Mueller and Lucas (1975) focused on the early stages of the development of sociability. They suggested that infants go through three stages:

- Object-centred stage: infants pay at least as much attention to a toy as they do to each other.
- Simple interactive stage: infants are now more interested in other infants, and will often try hard to influence the behaviour of another infant.
- Co-ordinated interactions stage (18 months upwards): infants gaze and smile at each other, and they start to co-operate to achieve common goals (e.g. playing games that require two people).

Brownell and Carriger (1990) argued that infants need to have some sense of themselves as individuals to reach the stage of co-ordinated interactions. They assessed the sense of self in two ways: (1) by seeing whether infants' behaviour suggested that they could recognise themselves in a mirror; and (2) by observing whether they could discriminate photographs of themselves from photographs of other infants. Their key finding was that infants began to have co-ordinated interactions at about the same time as they showed evidence of a sense of self.

Why are some young children much more sociable than others? As Shaffer (1993) pointed out, there are several factors that seem to be involved. Some of the main ones are discussed next.

Ainsworth's theory

Attachment and sociability refer to rather different aspects of social behaviour (attachment is described in more detail later). However, as Ainsworth (1979) argued, it is possible that children who show secure attachment to their mother will tend to be more sociable than children who lack a secure attachment. Evidence fitting this theory was reported by Waters, Wippman, and Sroufe (1979). They assessed infants' attachment behaviour at the age of 15 months, and then observed their social behaviour at nursery school at the age of 3½ years. The securely attached children were clearly more sociable than those who were insecurely attached. For example, they were more popular with other children, they were more sensitive to the feelings of other children, and they were much more likely to start play activities.

■ Research activity: Observing children at a nursery or preschool playgroup. Remember that ethically you must obtain permission from the head teacher or manager.

Construct a table showing male and female children, and note the number of examples of Parten's six categories of play.

This task might be made easier with the use of video recordings, or more than one observer, but remember to check for inter-rater reliability.

Children attending nursery school are more likely to develop proper social behaviour in relation to other infants. One example of this is that nursery school children are more likely to engage in non-aggressive rough-and-tumble play.

How would you devise a study to test whether infants can recognise themselves in a mirror? Would you expect self-recognition to occur at the same time developmentally across different cultures (suggesting a genetic link) or at different times (implicating environmental factors)?

More evidence that attachment is related to sociability was reported by Main and Weston (1981). They exposed infants to a friendly stranger dressed in a clown's outfit. Infants who were securely attached to both parents showed the most sociability in this situation, followed by those who were securely attached to one parent. The infants who were not securely attached to either parent responded in the least sociable way.

Parenting style

It seems reasonable that the ways in which parents treat their young children should affect their children's level of sociability. According to Shaffer (1993, p.471)

> *parents who are warm and supportive and who require their children to follow certain rules of etiquette (for example, "Be nice"; "Play quietly"; "Don't hit") are likely to raise well-adjusted sons and daughters who relate well to both adults and peers ... By contrast, permissive parents who set few standards and exert little control over their children often raise youngsters who are aggressive and unpopular with their peers ... boys who have overprotective mothers are quite sociable when interacting with adults but are often anxious and inhibited around their peers.*

Much of the sociable behaviour shown by young children consists of playing with other children. As a result, it seems likely that the parents' style of playing with their children affects how sociable they are with other children. Vandell and Wilson (1987) studied nine-month-old infants. Infants whose mothers allowed them to help to decide what play activities should occur were more responsive when playing with other infants. MacDonald and Parke (1984) obtained similar findings with children between the ages of 3 and 5. They found that children who had unfriendly interactions with other children tended to have parents who controlled playmaking with them by giving commands and ignoring their wishes.

Genetic factors

Sociability has been identified in adults as an important trait forming a major part of the personality dimension of extraversion (Eysenck & Eysenck, 1985). About 30–40% of individual differences in most important personality traits are due to genetic factors (see Chapter 27). As a result, it is reasonable to assume that individual differences in sociability among young children depend at least to some extent on heredity.

Evidence relevant to this hypothesis has been reported by Matheny (1983) and by Daniels and Plomin (1985). Matheny assessed social smiling and fear of strangers in

monozygotic or identical twins and in dizygotic or fraternal twins. The twins were tested at 18 and 24 months of age. At both ages, the identical twins were much more similar than the fraternal twins. These findings suggest strongly that heredity partially determines sociability in infants.

Daniels and Plomin (1985) carried out a study on shyness in young adopted children. The biological mothers of shy children tended to be lower in sociability than were the biological mothers of non-shy children. Daniels and Plomin also found that the adoptive children of shy mothers were low in sociability; indeed, the association was somewhat stronger than between the children and their biological mothers. The findings for biological mothers point to the involvement of genetic factors, whereas those for adoptive mothers indicate the importance of environmental factors.

Attachment

According to Shaffer (1993), an attachment is "a close emotional relationship between two persons, characterised by mutual affection and a desire to maintain proximity [closeness]." In the normal course of events, the main attachment of the infant is to its mother. However, strong attachments can be formed to other people with whom the infant has regular contact (Schaffer & Emerson, 1964). This is generally the father, but is sometimes other relatives. The first attachment that infants form in early childhood is very important because it is the starting point for their lifelong social and emotional involvements with other people. It gives them an idea of what they might expect from adults as they grow up.

Evidence that infants often form attachments to their father as well as their mother was obtained by Weston and Main (1981). They used the Strange Situation procedure (described later) with 44 infants. Of these infants, 12 were securely attached to both parents, 11 were securely attached only to their mother, 10 were securely attached only to their father, and 11 were insecurely attached to both parents.

Schaffer and Emerson (1964) argued that infants go through three stages in the early development of attachments to others:

1. The *asocial* stage, which lasts for about the first six weeks of life. During this stage, emotional behaviour such as smiling or crying does not seem to be directed specifically at any given individual.
2. The stage of *indiscriminate attachment*, which lasts between about the ages of about six weeks and seven months. During this stage, the infant seeks attention from numerous different people, and is generally content when he or she receives attention.
3. The stage of *specific attachments*, which starts at about seven months of age and continues to eleven months. The infant in this stage typically forms a strong attachment to one individual, but good attachments to others often follow shortly thereafter.

STAGES OF ATTACHMENT		
Asocial stage	**Indiscriminate attachment**	**Specific attachments**
0–6 weeks	6 weeks–7 months	7 months–11 months
Smiling and crying, not directed at any special individuals	Attention sought from different individuals	Strong attachment to one individual

The development of these strong attachments depends jointly on the warm and loving responsiveness of the mother and on the positive responses (e.g. smiling) of the infant. In order for an attachment to develop between an infant and its mother, it is first of all necessary for it to be able to recognise its mother and to discriminate her from other adults. Evidence that two-week-old infants can recognise their mother's face and voice was reported by Carpenter (1975). He set up a situation in which infants looked at a face while hearing a voice. Sometimes the face and the voice belonged to the same person, and sometimes they did not. The infants looked at the face for the longest time when it was the mother's face, and when it was accompanied by her voice. More convincing evidence that the infants recognised their mother's face and voice was obtained when they were presented with their mother's face but an unfamiliar voice, or vice versa. Most of the infants found this distressing, and rapidly looked away from the face.

There are some problems of interpretation with Carpenter's study, because those rating the behaviour of the infants knew which condition was being used at any time. However, improved versions of Carpenter's design have been used in several later studies. According to Durkin (1995, p.54), "the evidence points consistently to the conclusion that infants can discriminate between their mother and other female strangers at a very early age."

Ethical issues: Might Carpenter have predicted that infants would become distressed by seeing their mother's face and hearing another voice? If so, is this study really ethical?

How could this problem with the interpretation of Carpenter's study have been overcome?

Although the wire mother on the left is where the baby monkey receives his food, he runs to the cloth mother for comfort, when he is frightened by the teddy bear drummer (Harlow, 1959).

Do you think there are problems with generalising about behaviour from one species to another that might diminish the importance of this study?

There is striking evidence that babies as young as two days old can recognise their mother's face. Bushnell et al. (1989) presented two-day-old babies with the faces of their mother and a female stranger until they had spent a total of 20 seconds fixating on one of the faces. Almost two-thirds of them showed a preference for their mother over the stranger, indicating that they had some ability to recognise their own mother.

We will now consider some of the major theories of attachment. They are discussed approximately in the order in which they were put forward, starting with the earliest theories and moving on to more recent ones.

Psychodynamic approach

Sigmund Freud (1924) put forward a very simple account of the infant's attachment to its mother: "The reason why the infant in arms wants to perceive the presence of its mother is only because it already knows by experience that she satisfies all its needs without delay." In other words, babies are initially attached to their mothers because they are a source of food as well as a source of comfort and warmth.

Freud's views on early attachment stemmed from his theory of psychosexual development (see Chapter 2). According to that theory, the first stage of psychosexual development is the oral stage. This lasts for about 18 months, and during it the infant obtains much of its satisfaction through oral experiences such as sucking the mother's breast. As a result, Freud (1924, p.188) argued that the mother's status was "unique, without parallel, established unalterably for a whole lifetime as the first and strongest love-object and as the prototype of all later love-relations".

Evaluation

Attachment behaviour in babies does *not* depend only on the provision of food. Harry Harlow (1959) carried out a series of studies on very young monkeys. These monkeys had to choose between two surrogate (or substitute) mothers, one of which was made of wire and the other of which was covered in cloth. Milk was provided by the wire mother for some of the monkeys, whereas it was provided by the cloth mother for the others. The findings were clear-cut. The monkeys spent most of their time on the cloth mother even when she did not supply milk (see Chapter 9).

It could be argued that Harlow's work on monkeys is not relevant to the study of human attachment. However, Schaffer and Emerson (1964) found with about 40% of human infants that the adult who fed, bathed, and changed the infant was not the person to whom the infant was most attached. Thus, there is not the simple link between food and attachment behaviour that was assumed by Freud. Infants were most likely to become attached to adults who were responsive to them, and who provided them with much stimulation in the form of touching and playing.

Ethical issues: Harlow's study

Harlow carried out a series of experiments with rhesus monkeys who were reared in isolation. These are monkeys who come from a highly social background. After the experiments were completed, the monkeys exhibited severely disturbed behaviour. At the time, the distress caused to the monkeys was seen as acceptable in the light of the possible benefits of understanding how attachment develops. However it is unlikely that such a study would be allowed to proceed today because of stricter ethical guidelines for research using non-human participants.

Learning theory and social learning theory

According to the learning theory put forward by Dollard and Miller (1950), all humans possess various primary drives such as hunger and thirst. In addition, there are secondary or learned drives, which arise out of primary drives. For example, an infant's attachment to its mother may involve a secondary drive that evolves as a result of the mother providing it with primary rewards in the form of food. These primary and secondary drives determine what is rewarding or reinforcing. Mothers may be rewarded when they make their offspring smile or stop crying. One of the limitations of this theoretical approach is that infants often become attached to adults who are not involved in feeding or basic care-giving (Schaffer & Emerson, 1964).

A more sophisticated version of this type of theory is the social learning theory put forward by Hay and Vespo (1988). According to them, attachment occurs because parents "deliberately teach their children to love them and to understand human relationships" (p.82). How do parents achieve these goals? Some of the main ways are as follows:

- Modelling: children learn to imitate the affectionate behaviour shown by their parents.
- Direct instruction: parents teach their children in a direct and explicit way to attend to them and to show affection.
- Social facilitation: parents watch their children carefully and provide assistance as and when necessary.

Evaluation

The greatest strength of the social learning approach is that it has led to a detailed consideration of the interactional processes that occur between parents and children. In addition, at least some of the attachment learning shown by infants does depend on processes such as modelling, direct instruction, and social facilitation. On the negative side, as Durkin (1995) pointed out, the strong emotional intensity of many parent–child attachments is not really explained by social learning theorists.

Ethological approach: Bonding

The ethologists studied animals in their natural environment. One ethologist (Konrad Lorenz) found that the young of some species of birds tended to follow the first moving object they saw, and they continued to follow it thereafter. This is known as **imprinting**. It only occurs during a short critical period in the bird's life. When imprinting has occurred, it tends to be irreversible, in the sense that the bird will continue to follow the object on which it is imprinted (see also Chapter 9).

According to Bowlby (1969), something like imprinting occurs in infants. He discussed the notion of monotropy, according to which human infants have an innate tendency to form strong bonds with one particular individual. This will usually (but not always) be the infant's mother. He also argued that there is a critical period during which the infant's attachment to the mother or other care-giver must take place. This critical period ends at some point between 1 and 3 years of age. After that, it is no longer possible to establish a powerful attachment to the mother or other person.

Evidence

Klaus and Kennell (1976) were in general agreement with Bowlby (1958) that early bonding between infant and mother is of great importance. More specifically, they argued that there is a sensitive period immediately after birth in which bonding can occur through skin-to-skin contact. Klaus and Kennell compared the progress of two groups of infants. One group only had routine contact with their mothers during regular feeding sessions throughout the first three days of life, whereas the other group had extended contact for several hours a day with their mothers over the first three days.

When the mothers returned to the hospital one month later, there was evidence that more bonding had occurred in the extended contact group than in the routine contact group. During feeding, the extended-contact mothers cuddled and comforted their babies more, and they also maintained more eye contact with them. Even one year later, the extended-contact mothers still behaved in a more soothing and involved way with their infants.

Later research generally failed to repeat the findings reported by Klaus and Kennell (1976). Durkin (1995) pointed out that most of the mothers in the original study were

Ethical issues: Do you think there are any ethical questions concerning this type of study?

> **KEY TERM**
> **Imprinting**: a strong tendency for the young of some species (e.g. geese) to follow and to bond with the first moving object they encounter.

unmarried teenagers from disadvantaged backgrounds. The extended-contact mothers may have become more involved with their babies than the routine-contact mothers because of the special attention they received, rather than because of the hours of skin-to-skin contact they had with their babies. The general view nowadays is that the relationship between mother and baby develops and changes over time rather than being fixed shortly after birth.

Cross-cultural evidence supports these conclusions. Lozoff (1983) reported that mothers were no more affectionate towards their babies in cultures that encouraged early bodily contact between mother and baby. Furthermore, mothers in cultures in which early nursing is typical did not show greater bonding with their babies than did mothers in other cultures.

Klaus and Kennell suggested that prolonged skin-to-skin contact between baby and mother gave rise to greater bonding. However, recent research, including cross-cultural studies, indicates that other forms of attention also promote bonding.

Ecological theory

Bronfenbrenner (1979) put forward an ecological theory that was designed to provide a framework within which to understand human development. Bronfenbrenner argued that too much research on children had taken place in laboratories, making developmental psychology "the science of the strange behaviour of children in strange situations with strange adults." He proposed the notion that development occurs within a set of environmental structures arranged "like a set of Russian dolls" (p.3). There are four basic structures or systems:

- Microsystem: this consists of parent–child interactions, family, friends, and other groupings with which the child comes into direct contact.
- Mesosystem: this consists of the inter-relationships among the settings with which the child is familiar (e.g. family and school).
- Exosystem: this consists of factors (e.g. parents' workplaces; mass media) that have an impact on the child, but not through direct experience.
- Macrosystem: this consists of the general beliefs and ideology of the culture.

This ecological approach is attractive for two reasons. First, it helps to integrate the closely related areas of developmental and social psychology. Second, it identifies more of the numerous factors influencing children's development than most developmental theories. The most obvious limitation of the ecological approach is that it does not lead to many precise and testable predictions.

■ Research activity: Prepare a chart comparing the theories involved in explanations of socialisation and attachment in infants.

	Psychodynamic approach	Learning and social learning theories	Ethological approach	Ecological approach
Main researcher(s)				
Evidence for this approach				
Evidence against this approach (if any)				
Ethical and/or methodological issues in main research				

Ainsworth and Bell

In order to develop a full understanding of infants' attachment behaviour, we need to have good ways of measuring it. Ainsworth and Bell (1970) developed the Strange Situation procedure. The infant (normally about 12 months old) is observed during a sequence of eight short episodes. For some of the time, the infant is with its mother. At other times, it is with its mother and a stranger; or just with a stranger; or on its own. The child's reactions to the stranger, to separation from the mother, and to being re-united with its mother are all recorded.

The infant's reactions to these episodes allow its attachment to its mother to be placed in one of three categories:

1. **Secure attachment**: the infant is distressed by the mother's absence. However, it rapidly returns to a state of contentment after the mother's return, immediately seeking contact with her. There is a clear difference in the infant's reaction to the mother and to the stranger. About 70% of American infants show secure attachment.

2. **Resistant attachment**: the infant is insecure in the presence of the mother, and becomes very distressed when the mother leaves. It resists contact with the mother upon her return, and is wary of the stranger. About 10% of American infants are resistant.

3. **Avoidant attachment**: the infant does not seek contact with the mother, and shows little distress when separated from her. The infant avoids contact with the mother upon her return. The infant treats the stranger in a similar way to the mother, often avoiding him or her. About 20% of American infants are avoidant.

Resistant attachment is shown when a baby resists contact with his or her mother after being left. The baby cries and tries to twist away from the mother.

Why do some infants have a secure attachment with their mother, whereas others do not? According to Ainsworth's (1982) care-giving hypothesis, the sensitivity of the mother (or other care-giver) is of crucial importance. Ainsworth, Bell, and Stayton (1971) found that most of the mothers of securely attached infants were very sensitive to their needs, and responded to their infants in an emotionally expressive way. In contrast, the mothers of resistant infants were interested in them, but often misunderstood their infants' behaviour. Of particular importance, these mothers tended to vary in the way they treated their infants. As a result, the infant could not rely on the mother's emotional support.

Finally, there are the mothers of avoidant infants. Ainsworth et al. (1971) reported that many of these mothers were uninterested in their infants, often rejecting them and tending to be self-centred and rigid in their behaviour. However, some mothers of avoidant infants behaved rather differently. These mothers act in a suffocating way, always interacting with their infants even when the infants did not want any interaction. What these two types of mothers have in common is that they are not very sensitive to the needs of their infants.

Discussion points

1. What are the strengths of the experimental approach used by Ainsworth?
2. What factors determine infants' attachment style (see next section)?

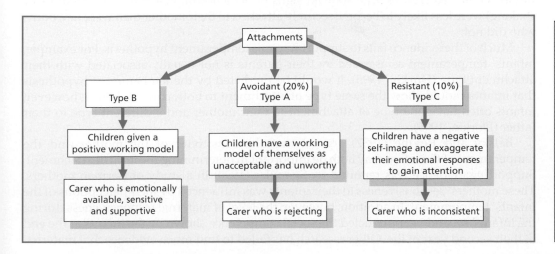

Attachments

Type B	Avoidant (20%) Type A	Resistant (10%) Type C
Children given a positive working model	Children have a working model of themselves as unacceptable and unworthy	Children have a negative self-image and exaggerate their emotional responses to gain attention
Carer who is emotionally available, sensitive and supportive	Carer who is rejecting	Carer who is inconsistent

Care-giving hypothesis

Research following on from that of Ainsworth et al. (1971) has tended to support the care-giving hypothesis. Durkin (1995, p.97) drew the following conclusion from the relevant studies:

> These studies have supported the broad claim that characteristics of the care-giving environment, particularly maternal sensitivity and the harmony of the customary interaction style, are associated with attachment type in the direction that Ainsworth claims.

Does infant attachment predict social behaviour later in childhood? The evidence is mixed. Bates, Maslin, and Frankel (1985) found that attachment style at 12 months did not predict the presence of behaviour problems at 3 years of age. However, Elicker et al. (1992) found links between attachment style in infancy and social interactions several years later at school. Most of the evidence supports the hypothesis that early attachment behaviour predicts later social and emotional development. According to Ainsworth, this happens because a strong early attachment provides a secure base for social development. However, it is also likely that most children who have a secure attachment with their mother during infancy continue to do so in subsequent years, and this may be why infants who are securely attached show better social development during childhood.

Evaluation

Much research has confirmed the usefulness of the Strange Situation test, and of the three types of attachment identified by Ainsworth and Bell (1970).

However, Main and Solomon (1986) argued that a small number of infants display a fourth type of attachment, which they called disorganised and disoriented. These infants seemed to lack any coherent strategy for coping with the Strange Situation, and their behaviour was often a confusing mixture of approach and avoidance.

The Strange Situation procedure is generally carried out in the laboratory, and so it can be argued that it represents a rather artificial approach to the study of attachment behaviour. Bronfenbrenner (1979) pointed out that infants' attachment behaviours are typically much stronger in the laboratory than they are at home, indicating that the laboratory setting does influence attachment. However, as we have seen, much of importance has been learned from studies using the Strange Situation procedure.

The temperament hypothesis. The care-giving hypothesis has been criticised because it overemphasises the role played by the care-giver in the development of attachment and ignores the part played by the infant. Jerome Kagan (1984) focused on the role played by the infant's temperament or personality in determining its attachment to the mother. Evidence that the infant's temperament may be important was reported by Belsky and Rovine (1987). Newborns who showed signs of behavioural instability (e.g. tremors or shaking) were less likely to become securely attached to their mother than were newborns who did not.

Much of the evidence fails to support Kagan's temperament hypothesis. For example, infants' temperament as assessed by their parents is not usually associated with their attachment type (Durkin, 1995). It would be predicted by the temperament hypothesis that infants should show the same type of attachment to both parents. In fact, however, infants often have one type of attachment to their mother and a different type to their father (Durkin, 1995).

Belsky and Rovine (1987) argued that the sensitivity of the mother and the temperament of the infant may both be important in determining the form of attachment. Supporting evidence was reported by Spangler (1990) in a study of German mothers. These mothers' responsiveness to their infants was influenced by their perceptions of the infants' temperament. In addition, however, the level of maternal responsiveness during the infants' second year predicted the social competence shown by the infants at the end of their second year of life. Other research has failed to find much evidence that maternal sensitivity is of importance. Seifer et al. (1996) carried out a longitudinal study in which infants were studied with their mothers at 6, 9, and 12 months of age. The key finding was as follows: "Maternal sensitivity was ... unrelated to Strange Situation classification" (p.12).

Cross-cultural issues: Different cultures may place different values on the characteristics displayed by the children. The children may be displaying the behaviour normally rewarded by the mother.

Effects of Deprivation

We have already considered some of the factors that determine the nature of the attachment that a young child forms with its mother or other care-giver. In the real world, of course, there are circumstances such as divorce or death of a parent that can disrupt the child's attachments or even prevent them from being formed at all. In this section of the chapter, we will discuss the effects on the young child of being separated from one or more of the most important adults in its life. However, it should be borne in mind that deprivation can have severe effects on much older children as well. For example, it has been found that girls whose mothers had died before they reached the age of 12 were much more likely than other girls to become severely depressed in adult life (Brown & Harris, 1978).

Maternal deprivation hypothesis

John Bowlby (1907–1990) was a child psychoanalyst who focused on the relationship between mother and child. According to Bowlby (1951), "an infant and young child should experience a warm, intimate and continuous relationship with his mother (or permanent mother-figure) in which both find satisfaction and enjoyment." No-one would disagree with that. However, Bowlby went on to put forward the more controversial maternal deprivation hypothesis. According to this hypothesis, breaking the maternal bond with the child during the early years of its life is likely to have serious effects on its intellectual, social, and emotional development. Bowlby also claimed that many of these negative effects of maternal deprivation are permanent and irreversible.

Short-term effects

Most studies have focused on the long-term effects of deprivation. However, we will first consider some of the short-term effects. Even fairly brief separation from the mother has severe emotional effects on the child. Robertson and Bowlby (1952) studied young children who were separated from their mother for some time, often because she had gone into hospital. They found that there were three stages in the child's response to separation:

1. Protest, which is often very intense; the child cries much of the time, and sometimes seems panic stricken.
2. Despair, involving a total loss of hope; the child is often apathetic and shows little interest in its surroundings.
3. Detachment, during which the child seems to behave in a less distressed way. If the mother re-appears during this stage, she is not responded to with any great interest.

Separation from the mother can have severe emotional effects on a child. The first stage of the child's response to the separation is known as protest: an intense period during which the child cries for much of the time.

It used to be thought that children in the third stage of detachment had adjusted fairly well to separation from their mother. However, it seems that the calm behaviour shown by the child often hides underlying distress. The indifference shown by the child when its mother reappears is generally apparent rather than real, as is shown by the fact that the child will re-establish an attachment to the mother over time.

   Is it inevitable that short-term separation will produce these negative effects? Evidence reported by Robertson and Robertson (1971) suggests that it is not. They looked after, in their own home, a number of young children who had been separated from their mothers, and took various steps to minimise any distress the children might experience. First, they ensured that the children visited their home some time before the actual separation, so that they could become familiar with their

How might Robertson and Robertson's findings be used to help children who have to spend time in hospital or short-term foster care?

Recent news reports have highlighted deprivation in Romanian orphanages, with many children demonstrating anaclitic depression, having received basic sustenance but little human warmth or contact.

new surroundings. Second, they did their best to provide the children with the kind of daily routine with which they were familiar. Third, they discussed the children's mothers with them. This approach proved successful, with the children showing much less distress than do most separated children.

Evidence

Orphans. Bowlby's maternal deprivation hypothesis was based in part on the work of Spitz (1945) and Goldfarb (1947). Spitz visited several very poor orphanages and other institutions in South America. Most of the children in these orphanages received very little warmth or attention from the staff, as a result of which they became apathetic. Many of the children suffered from **anaclitic depression**, a state involving resigned helplessness and loss of appetite.

Goldfarb (1947) compared two groups of infants from a poor and inadequately staffed orphanage. One group had spent only the first few months of their lives there before being fostered. The other group consisted of infants who had spent three years at the orphanage before fostering. Both groups were tested at various times up to the age of 12. Those children who had spent three years at the orphanage did less well than the other on intelligence tests. They were less socially mature, and they were more likely to be aggressive.

The findings of Spitz (1945) and Goldfarb (1947) provide less support for the maternal deprivation hypothesis than Bowlby assumed. The institutions they studied were deficient in several ways, with the children suffering from a general lack of stimulation and attention as well as maternal deprivation. As a result, we cannot interpret the findings: they may be due to absence of the mother, or they may be due to presence of poor institutional conditions, or to some combination of both factors.

EVALUATION — Bowlby

Bowlby based his maternal deprivation hypothesis on his study of 44 juvenile thieves. These were adolescents who were attending a child guidance clinic. Bowlby compared this group with 44 other adolescents who were emotionally disturbed but who had not been convicted of a criminal offence. Bowlby found that 17 of the 44 juvenile thieves had been separated from their mother for a period of at least a week before they reached the age of 5. His work has been criticised on the grounds that the study was methodologically flawed, lacking true control groups and with problematic sampling. Bowlby himself later accepted that he might have overstated his case. It now seems more probable that it is the formation of an attachment itself to anyone, not just the mother, that is important.

Long-term effects. Bowlby (1946) presented evidence that maternal deprivation can have severe long-term effects. He compared juvenile delinquents who had committed crimes with other emotionally disturbed adolescents who had not committed any crimes. Thirty-two per cent of the juvenile delinquents, but none of the emotionally disturbed adolescents, showed **affectionless psychopathy**, which is a disorder involving a lack of guilt and remorse. Bowlby found that 64% of the juvenile delinquents with affectionless psychopathy had experienced deprivation in early childhood. In contrast, only 10% of the juvenile delinquents *without* affectionless psychopathy had been maternally deprived. These findings suggested that maternal deprivation can lead to affectionless psychopathy. However, these findings were not repeated in later studies.

Deprivation and privation

Rutter (1981) argued that Bowlby's (1946) findings on affectionless psychopathy should be reinterpreted. He pointed out that there is an important difference between deprivation and privation. **Deprivation** occurs when a child has formed an important attachment, but is then separated from the major attachment figure. In contrast, **privation** occurs when a child has never formed a close relationship with anyone. Many of Bowlby's juvenile delinquents had experienced several changes of home and of principal care-giver during their early childhood. This indicated to Rutter (1981) that their later problems were due to privation rather than deprivation as Bowlby had claimed. Rutter (1981) argued that the effects of privation are much more severe and long-lasting than those of deprivation. He concluded that privation often leads to *an initial phase of clinging, dependent behaviour, followed by attention-seeking, uninhibited, indiscriminate friendliness and finally a personality characterised by lack of guilt, an inability to keep rules and an inability to form lasting friendships.*

Monotropy hypothesis

According to Bowlby's **monotropy hypothesis**, infants form only one strong attachment, and this is typically to the mother. This is often not the case. Schaffer and Emerson (1964), in a study mentioned before, visited the homes of babies several times during their first year of life. They measured the infant's attachment to various adults on the basis of its level of protest when separated from each adult. By the age of 10 months, 59% of infants had formed more than one attachment, and the figure rose to 87% by the age of 18 months. At the older age, only about half of the infants were mainly attached to their mother, with 30% being mainly attached to their father. Thus, relatively few children only have a strong attachment to their mother as was assumed by Bowlby.

Reasons for deprivation

Bowlby (1951) argued that deprivation in and of itself causes long-term difficulties. In contrast, Rutter (1981) suggested that the effects of deprivation depend on the precise reasons for the separation. In some of his own research, Rutter studied boys aged between 9 and 12 years of age who had been deprived of their mothers for a period of time when they were younger. In general, the well-adjusted boys had been separated because of factors such as housing problems or physical illness. In contrast, the maladjusted boys had mostly been separated because of problems with social relationships within the family (e.g. psychiatric illness). Thus, it is mostly family discord rather than separation as such that causes difficulties for children.

Tizard

Bowlby (1951) argued that the negative effects of maternal deprivation could not be reversed or undone. However, much of the available evidence does not support his argument, and indicates that even privation does not always have permanent effects. Some of the most thorough evidence on this issue was reported by Tizard (1977), Tizard and Hodges (1978), and Tizard (1986). They studied children who spent up to the first seven years of their lives in an institution. Each child had been looked after on average by 24 different care-givers by the age of 2. The lack of opportunity to form a strong, continuous relationship with any one adult meant that they suffered from maternal deprivation. In spite of this, the children had a mean IQ of 105 at the age of 4½. Thus, the institutions probably did not hold back the children's cognitive development.

The progress of these children was also studied at the ages of 8 and 16. Some of them had returned to their own families, whereas others had been adopted. Most of the adopted children had formed close relationships with their adoptive parents. This was less true of the children who returned to their own families, because their parents were often not sure they wanted to have their children back. Both groups of children experienced difficulties at school. According to Tizard and Hodges (1978, p.114), they had "an almost insatiable desire for adult attention, and a difficulty in forming good relationships with their peer group."

Hodges and Tizard (1989) found that the family relationships of the adopted children at the age of 16 were as good as those of families in which none of the children had been removed from the family home. However, the 16-year-olds who had returned to their families showed little affection for their parents, and their parents were not very affectionate towards them. Both groups were similar in their relationships with other adolescents of the same age. They were less likely than other children to have a special friend or to regard other adolescents as sources of emotional support.

Discussion points

1. What has the research of Tizard added to our knowledge of the effects of deprivation?
2. How might we account for the different patterns of behaviour shown by adopted children and children who returned to their families?

KEY TERM
Monotropy hypothesis: the notion that infants have an innate tendency to form strong bonds with their mother; put forward by Bowlby.

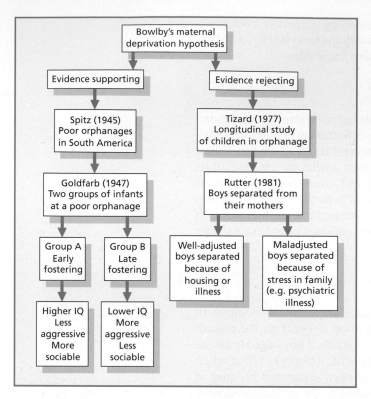

Bowlby's maternal
deprivation hypothesis

Evidence supporting

Spitz (1945)
Poor orphanages
in South America

Goldfarb (1947)
Two groups of infants
at a poor orphanage

Group A
Early
fostering

Group B
Late
fostering

Higher IQ
Less
aggressive
More
sociable

Lower IQ
More
aggressive
Less
sociable

Evidence rejecting

Tizard (1977)
Longitudinal study
of children in orphanage

Rutter (1981)
Boys separated from
their mothers

Well-adjusted
boys separated
because of
housing or
illness

Maladjusted
boys separated
because of
stress in family
(e.g. psychiatric
illness)

Extreme privation

A few researchers have looked at the effects of very extreme privation and isolation on children. It is surprising how resilient these children seem to be. Koluchova (1976) studied identical twins who had spent most of the first seven years of their lives locked in a cellar. They had been treated very badly, and were often beaten. They were barely able to talk, and relied mainly on gestures other than speech. The twins were fostered at about the age of 9. By the time they were 14, their behaviour was essentially normal. By the age of 20, they were of above average intelligence, and had excellent relationships with the members of their foster family.

Curtiss (1989) discussed the case of Genie (see also page 350), who spent most of her childhood in a cupboard at her home in Los Angeles. She had had very little contact with other members of her family, and was discouraged from making any sounds. She was found in 1970 when she was 13½ years old. She had not been fed adequately, could not stand erect, and had no social skills. At that time, she did not understand language and could not speak. Genie was given a considerable amount of education and assistance in the years after she was found. Her ability to perform tasks that did not depend on language improved rapidly, and reached normal levels on several perceptual tasks (Curtiss, 1989).

Unfortunately, Genie's language skills failed to reach normal adult levels. She developed a fairly large vocabulary, but she generally spoke in short, ungrammatical sentences, and did not understand sentences that were complex grammatically. Her social skills remained limited, in part because "her use of intonation was poor, and only people who knew her well could understand much of what she was trying to say" (Curtiss, 1989, p.216).

Freud and Dann (1951) provided interesting evidence that young children who form strong attachments with other young children can avoid severe damage resulting from the loss of both parents and living in terrible circumstances (see page

Orphaned children held in concentration camps who underwent terrible experiences in their early lives showed rapid social and language development once they had been removed from the camps. These children were photographed awaiting their release from Auschwitz in January 1945.

861). They studied six war orphans whose parents had been murdered in a concentration camp when they were only a few months old. The infants lived together in a deportation camp for about two years until the age of 3, and had very distressing experiences such as watching people being hanged. In this camp, they were put in the Ward for Motherless Children, and had very limited contact with anyone other than each other. After the camp was liberated at the end of the Second World War, they were flown to England. When they were freed from the camp, the children had not yet developed speech properly, they were underweight, and they expressed hostility towards adults. However, they were greatly attached to each other. According to Freud and Dann (1951, p.131):

> The children's positive feelings were centred exclusively in their own group ... They had no other wish than to be together and became upset when they were separated from each other, even for short moments.

As time went by, the six children became attached to their adult care-takers. In addition, they developed rapidly at a social level and in their use of language. It is hard to say whether their early experiences had any lasting adverse effects. One of them (Leah) received psychiatric assistance, and another (Jack) sometimes felt very alone and isolated (Moscovitz, 1983). However, it would not be exceptional to find similar problems in six adults selected at random.

In sum, the evidence indicates that most of the adverse effects of maternal deprivation or privation can be reversed, and that children are more resilient than Bowlby believed. However, the case of Genie suggests that the ability to develop normal adult language skills may be partially lost if language development is held back throughout the years of childhood.

CASE STUDY: *The Riley Family*

Jean Riley (54) and her husband Peter (58) adopted two children from Romania who are now aged 17 and 9. Cezarina, when they first saw her, was cross-eyed, filthy, and about four years behind in her physical development. First Cezarina's physical problems had to be sorted out, but from then on she made good progress. However, Cezarina is "laid back" about things that seem important to Jean and Peter. Jean understands this attitude, though, because clearly examinations seem less important when a child has had to struggle to survive.

According to Jean, Cezarina is bright, but needs to have information reinforced over and over again. She has also struggled to understand jokes and sarcasm, although this may be due to difficulties with learning the language. Jean sees Cezarina as naive and emotionally immature. Cezarina says herself that initially she was frustrated because she couldn't communicate. She does see herself as being different from other girls, although she likes the same things, such as fashion and pop music. Jean runs The Parent Network for the Institutionalised Child, a group for people who have adopted such children. Cezarina has partly recovered from her poor early experiences. (Account based on an article in *Woman*, 21 September 1998.)

An important study has been carried out by Rutter et al. (1998) on 111 Romanian children adopted in the UK before the age of 2. The children arrived with severe developmental impairment, but in two years their progress has been described as dramatic.

These findings provide further support for the notion that most children are able to recover even from very difficult and distressing childhoods.

Enrichment

We have seen that attempts to eliminate the adverse effects of severe deprivation have often been surprisingly effective. The success of those attempts suggests that providing an enriched environment for children who are only moderately deprived might also be successful. Probably the best known of such attempts was Project Head Start, which was introduced in the United States during the 1960s. However, there have been various other enrichment programmes such as the Milwaukee project and the Carolina Abecedarian project, and they will also be considered.

Project Head Start

Project Head Start was an enrichment programme for young disadvantaged children. It focused on the provision of extensive preschool education, but was sometimes extended to provide care and education for the children's parents. Medical and nutritional advice was also included.

Head Start programmes typically produced increases in IQ scores of about 10 points in a short period of time (Lazar & Darlington, 1982), and there were also beneficial effects on educational achievement. However, these gains in IQ tended to disappear when the children moved on to school.

Head Start programmes differed considerably in terms of the competence of the teachers involved and the level of resourcing available. Schweinhart and Weikart (1985) concluded that the benefits of good Head Start programmes included *improved intellectual performance during early childhood, better scholastic placement and improved scholastic achievement during the elementary school years; and, during adolescence, a lower rate of delinquency and higher rates of both graduation from high school and employment at age 19.*

Once they start school, children who have attended preschool classes have a range of advantages over children who have not. The Head Start enrichment programme also produced benefits, but these were no greater than those provided by preschool attendance.

The findings of Lee et al. (1990) suggested that Project Head Start or preschool gave children who attended them an advantage over other children. Does this research have implications for social policy in society today?

Lee et al. (1990) carried out a 20-year follow-up on children who had taken part in a Head Start programme, or had attended preschool, or had done neither. The benefits of the Head Start programme had reduced over the years, but those who had been involved in it still showed some advantages compared to those who had not and who had not attended preschool either. However, there was very little difference between those who had taken part in Head Start and those who had attended preschool.

Why was Project Head Start of only modest benefit in the long term? A major limitation of Head Start was that many children spent only a few hours a week actively participating in the programme. As a result, it is perhaps unsurprising that a year or two of full-time schooling caused many of the benefits of Head Start to disappear.

Milwaukee project

The most obvious way of improving on Head Start programmes is to devise an enrichment programme that involves much more intensive involvement by the children exposed to it. Precisely this was done in the Milwaukee project (Heber et al., 1972), which involved the infants of 40 black mothers of low social class with IQs below 75. The mothers and infants were divided into two groups (experimental and control), with only the experimental group receiving the intervention. So far as the infants were concerned, this involved an intensive, five-days-a-week daycare programme which started when the infants were only three months old. The programme focused on reading, mathematics, language, and problem solving, but also involved the provision of social support. So far as the mothers were concerned, the intervention consisted of workshops to improve their home-keeping and parenting skills, plus training in the skills needed to obtain a job.

What were the findings of the Milwaukee project? The children in the experimental and control groups had the same average IQ during the first 18 months of the project. However, there was an enormous gap of 30 points in mean IQ at the age of 5½ (124 vs. 94), and this gap only reduced to about 20 points during the years that the two groups spent at school. These findings are dramatic, in that they suggest that enrichment programmes can produce very large long-term effects. However, it is not clear whether we should accept the findings at face value. As Berryman et al. (1991, p.133) pointed out

some doubt surrounds the Milwaukee project since its results have seldom been published in refereed journals. Charles Locurto refers to the project as the "mystery in Milwaukee" for this reason: he also calls it the "miracle in Milwaukee".

Carolina Abecedarian project

One of the reasons for doubting the findings of the Milwaukee project is because the findings from the rather similar Carolina Abecedarian project were much less impressive. In the Carolina Abecedarian project, Ramsey, Bryant, and Suarez (1985) studied disadvantaged children whose mothers had IQs between 70 and 85. Some of these children received a five-day-a-week educational programme which started when they were only a few weeks old and continued until they were 5. There was also a control group of similarly disadvantaged children who did not receive the educational programme.

The mean IQ of children in the programme was much higher than that of the control children at the age of 3 (102 vs. 84, respectively). There was still a fairly large gap in IQ between the two groups at the age of 5 (102 vs. 93, respectively), and a difference was still found at the age of 12. However, comparison with the findings from the Milwaukee project indicates that the beneficial effects of the intervention on IQ at the age of 5 were only about one-third as great in this study.

Other groups were also studied in the Carolina Abecedarian project, for example, disadvantaged children who received the intervention programme between the ages of 5 and 8 (Campbell & Ramey, 1994). The benefits of the programme were much smaller among these children, presumably because they had already started school.

Discussion points

1. How impressive are the findings of the Carolina Abecedarian project?

2. What light does this project shed on the nature–nurture controversy with respect to intelligence?

Adoption studies

Some of the most convincing evidence that an enriched environment can improve intelligence and educational achievement has come from adoption studies. Schiff et al. (1982) studied children who had been abandoned at birth, whose biological parents were unskilled workers. These children were placed with successful professional families at about four months of age, and their mean IQ several years after adoption was 109. In contrast, the mean IQ of their biological half-siblings who were brought up by their biological parents was only 95. In other words, the enriched environment experienced by the adopted children raised their mean IQ by 14 points. In addition, the rate of school failures was only about one-quarter as great among the adopted children as among their half-siblings.

Another adoption study producing similar findings was reported by Capron and Duyne (1989; see pages 434 and 742). They considered adopted children whose biological parents were of low socio-economic status. Half of these children were adopted by families of high socio-economic status, and the other half were adopted by families having low socio-economic status. Several years after adoption, the former group of children had a mean IQ that was 11 points higher than that of the latter group (107 vs. 92, respectively).

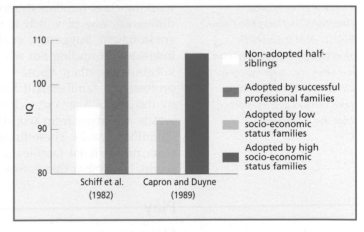

"Hot house" children

Project Head Start, the Milwaukee project, and the Carolina Abecedarian project were all designed to provide enrichment programmes for disadvantaged children. It is also possible to provide enrichment programmes for children of average or above average ability. Walmsley and Margolis (1987) argued that such programmes can be very effective. According to them, young children who receive intensive instruction in basic skills from their parents can develop abilities years earlier than most children. They used the term **"hot house" children** to refer to such children.

Walmsley and Margolis implied that all children could develop exceptional abilities if they were provided with an enriched learning environment. There is no evidence that that is the case. However, it is certainly true that the great majority of children with exceptional academic achievements have received intensive instruction and encouragement from their parents. Thus, an enriched environment is a necessary but not a sufficient requirement for exceptional achievement in children.

The relevant evidence on "hot house" children was discussed by Howe (1988). He came to the following conclusion:

KEY TERM

"Hot house" children: children of average or above average ability who have exceptional levels of achievement because of intensive instruction at an early age.

The babies of parents who make conscientious efforts to promote the early acquisition of basic skills will show accelerated development. Moreover, providing that the parental support and encouragement is not abruptly terminated after early childhood, the effects of accelerated development will be cumulative and long-lasting.

Cultural and subcultural effects

Enrichment has generally been considered in terms of specific programmes directed at given groups. However, there is also evidence that enrichment can be effective in a much more general way. For example, Flynn (1987) compared IQs from one generation to the next in 14 countries. His key finding was that there were substantial increases in mean IQ in virtually all of the countries he considered. Presumably these changes occurred because of improved social and educational opportunities. The encouraging implication is that enrichment can produce large benefits to intelligence within entire societies. However, it is possible that at least some of the gains reported by Flynn were due to greater familiarity with intelligence tests rather than to a genuine increase in intelligence.

Parents can provide their children with an excellent start in acquiring skills if they support and encourage attempts to learn through play.

Vocabulary and social class

Children from middle-class families tend to have higher IQs than children from working-class families (Sternberg, 1985). There are several possible reasons for this difference, one of which is that middle-class families provide an enriched learning environment. Suggestive evidence was reported by Hart and Risley (1995), who were interested in finding out why 3-year-olds from professional families had much larger vocabularies than those from other families. They found that children from professional families had heard more than 30 million words directed towards them by the age of 3, whereas children from families on welfare had heard only 10 million words. Children from working-class families were intermediate, having heard about 20 million words. These findings do not prove that the larger vocabularies of children from professional families were due to their enriched language environment, but it seems likely that this is one of the relevant factors.

How could an enriched language environment be applied in playschools and reception classes? (Bear in mind the research generated by Project Head Start and other enrichment programmes, and the possible link between those benefits and an enriched language environment.)

Play

Many theorists have argued that play helps children to develop intellectually and socially, and so can be regarded as a form of enrichment. Piaget and Inhelder (1969) distinguished between practice play and symbolic play. Practice play, which is found in infants, involves repeating actions over and over again in order to perfect them. In contrast, symbolic play is found somewhat later in development. Symbolic play involves pretending that an object or person is other than it really is. For example, a child may pretend that a seashell is a cup, or that he or she is a pirate or train driver. According to Piaget and Inhelder, symbolic play allows children to develop their powers of imagination.

Piaget and Inhelder argued that an important function of symbolic play is to allow children to play various roles (e.g. teacher; parent), and this helps them to learn more about the social world in which they live. For example, children often engage in symbolic play to resolve conflicts they have experienced. Piaget and Inhelder gave the following example (1969, p.60):

If there is a [disciplinary] scene at lunch ... one can be sure that an hour or two afterward it will be re-created with dolls and brought to a happier solution. Either the child disciplines her doll ... or in play she accepts what had not been accepted at lunch

such as finishing a bowl of soup she does not like, especially if it is the doll who finishes it symbolically.

Suggestive evidence of the enriching effects of play was reported by Dansky (1980). He initially divided preschool children into two groups on the basis of how often they engaged in pretend play. Then he observed these children as they played with objects that are not normally used in play; these objects included matchboxes and paper clips. The key finding was that the children who often engaged in pretend play used these unusual play objects in more original and creative ways.

How might original and creative play help to prepare children for adult life?

More evidence that pretend play can have beneficial effects was obtained by Connolly and Doyle (1984). Preschool children who engaged most often in pretend play tended to be more popular with other children and more advanced socially than those who rarely became involved in pretend play.

There is a limitation with the studies of Dansky (1980) and Connolly and Doyle (1984). They obtained essentially correlational evidence that high levels of pretend play were associated with various desirable outcomes (e.g. popularity). However, that does not prove that the desirable outcomes occurred as a result of pretend play.

Evaluation

The findings from enrichment programmes for disadvantaged children are fairly consistent. There are generally fairly rapid increases in IQ and in educational achievement, but these beneficial changes tend to disappear during the early years of full-time schooling. Adoption studies have confirmed that enrichment can increase IQ for children born into disadvantaged families. There is also evidence that average and above average children can show more rapid development of abilities if their parents provide them with intensive instruction.

Limitations

In spite of the consistency in the findings, the research on enrichment is limited in several ways. First, we do not know in detail *why* and *how* enrichment has its effects on children's development. It is likely that enrichment programmes work mainly because children are given detailed teaching in reading, mathematics, and so on. However, enrichment programmes may also help to motivate children so that they work harder when they go to school. In similar fashion, children adopted by successful professional families probably benefit in several ways. There may be social and emotional benefits, as well as educational and motivational ones.

Emphasis on IQ

Second, there has been too much focus on changes in IQ as a measure of the effectiveness of enrichment programmes. IQ as assessed by most intelligence tests provides a somewhat narrow measure of intellectual ability. The use of IQ as a measure is often defended because high IQ is a good predictor of academic success at school. However, there is evidence (Miller & Bizzell, 1983) that high IQ scores produced through intervention programmes are less predictive of school success than are high IQ scores occurring "naturally". It is not known why this is the case, but the clear implication is that a high IQ produced via enrichment does not mean the same as the same IQ occurring in the absence of enrichment.

Cross-cultural factors

Third, most of the enrichment programmes have been carried out in the United States, and so it is not clear whether the findings obtained are applicable in other cultures. A key reason why the disadvantaged children in these studies showed clear short-term benefits from enrichment programmes was probably because they would not otherwise have received any form of preschool or nursery education. Enrichment programmes might well have less effect in societies in which nearly all young children attend nursery school.

Child-rearing practices vary from culture to culture. Although in the UK it would be unacceptable to expect children as young as these rubbish collectors to earn their own livings, in Bangladesh this may be the only way to ensure the child and the family can afford enough to eat.

Cross-cultural Differences in Child Rearing

So far in this chapter the focus has been largely on the processes of early socialisation among young children in the United States and the United Kingdom. As we will see shortly, it would be wrong to assume that social development in infants in other parts of the world occurs in the same way. There are substantial differences in child-rearing practices from one culture to another, and these differences inevitably have effects on children's social behaviour. Studies using the Strange Situations test have been carried out in several different cultures, and these cross-cultural findings will be discussed in some detail.

Unproven causality

However, two cautions are needed before we proceed. First, when we discover interesting cross-cultural differences in child-rearing practices and in children's behaviour and development, it is tempting to conclude that the former have caused the latter. However, cross-cultural studies have not made use of the experimental method. Such studies are essentially correlational, and so it has *not* been shown that there are causal relationships between child-rearing practices and children's development.

Different, therefore better?

Second, it is dangerous to assume that some cultures have better child-rearing practices than others. Full account needs to be taken of the appropriateness of a culture's child-rearing practices within that particular culture. For example, parents may spend very little time looking after their children if the society to which they belong is very poor and under threat. An example of this is found among deprived families in the north east of Brazil (Scheper-Hughes, 1992). Children in this area who fail to develop at the normal rate typically receive very little care if they become ill. This sounds very harsh. However, it becomes much more understandable when one realises that these families are living in such difficult conditions that about 50% of the children die before the age of 5. In those circumstances, it may be sensible to give proper care only to those children who have the best chance of survival.

The dangers of trying to impose cultural values were shown by Raven (1980) in a Home Visiting project in Edinburgh. In this project, working-class mothers were encouraged to adopt what was regarded as the middle-class approach of communicating very frequently with their children. The main effect was that the mothers became less confident of their own mothering skills. As Meadows (1986, p.183) commented, "Some part of what is 'good parenting' depends on what society outside the family allows to, and demands of, the child and family" (p.183). In other words, child-rearing practices develop because they "work" within that culture.

In what follows, we will initially focus on cultural effects on social development. After that, we will consider cultural effects on intellectual development.

Child-rearing practices

Some studies have found important similarities across cultures in terms of child-rearing practices, whereas others have not. Among those studies reporting similarities was one by Keller, Scholmerich, and Eibl-Eibesfeldt (1988). They observed mothers and their infants in four cultures: German; Greek; Yanomani Indian; and Trobriand Island. The patterns of eye contact and conversations between mothers and infants were very similar in all four cultures.

In contrast, Rabain-Jamin (1989) found that French mothers and West African mothers living in Paris treated their 10- to 15-month-old infants rather differently. Native French mothers spoke more to their children. They were also more likely to integrate verbal and non-verbal information, for example, by naming and talking about an object while pointing to it. The essence of the difference in child-rearing practices was expressed in the following words by a West African mother: "We give toys to play with. You give them toys to teach, for the future. We feel that children learn better when they are older" (1989, p.303).

Cross-cultural issues: How does this West African approach differ from "hot-housing", described earlier?

When would we expect to find cultural differences in child-rearing practices? Such differences typically reflect differences in terms of the cultural expectations of older children and adults. For example, consider the differences between French and West African mothers reported by Rabain-Jamin. As Durkin (1995) pointed out, the expectation within French culture is that children will devote several years to formal education, with high-level language skills forming an important part of that education. In contrast, the expectation within West African culture is that children will become equipped at a fairly young age to handle the practical demands of everyday living. The differences in child-rearing practices seem well designed to achieve these cultural goals.

The Western approach to child rearing generally involves the care-givers adapting their speech and their behaviour to suit the child's stage of development. The approach is different in Samoa, in that adults do not simplify their language when addressing infants. They sing or speak in a rhythmical way to children, and they show little interest in trying to clarify the precise meaning of what children are saying. Why do Samoan adults adopt this approach? Samoan society is one in which status means a lot, and young children have low status. As a result, it is not thought appropriate for high-status adults to modify their speech and behaviour for the benefit of those of much lower status.

Cross-cultural issues: Compare the Samoan approach to that of the West African mother, and to Western enrichment programmes.

Cultural values

Child-rearing practices in different cultures are of importance in passing on cultural values from one generation to the next. For example, it has often been argued that human societies differ in terms of their emphasis on individualism versus collectivism (e.g. Hofstede, 1980; see Chapter 28). Individualistic cultures (such as the American) focus on personal achievement, whereas collectivistic cultures (such as the Japanese and Chinese) focus on group effort and co-operation. Bornstein et al. (1990) found that Japanese mothers encouraged their babies to attend to them, after which the mothers directed their child's attention to some aspect of the environment. In contrast, American mothers provided support and encouragement to their babies, regardless of whether they attended to the environment or to their mother. These findings indicate cultural differences in social development. They suggest that Japanese mothers focus mainly on the interpersonal development of their infants, whereas American mothers focus on developing initiative in their infants.

Why do you think parents are likely to encourage either personal achievement or group effort in cultures as diverse as America and Japan?

Similar findings were reported by Harwood and Miller (1991). They found that Anglo-American mothers reacted favourably to signs of independence on the part of their infants, which fits with the individualistic British and American cultures. In contrast, Puerto Rican culture is more collectivistic, and mothers in that culture reacted favourably to obedient and social behaviour by their infants.

Some of the strongest evidence that child-rearing practices can influence social development by fostering collectivism was reported by Bronfenbrenner (1970). He interviewed 12-year-olds in the former Soviet Union, Great Britain, the United States, and what was then West Germany. Some of the children were told that their interview answers would be entirely confidential, whereas others were told that only their peers would know what they had said, and still others were informed that the results would be shown at a parent–teacher meeting.

One of Bronfenbrenner's key findings was that the answers of the Soviet children revealed much less anti-social behaviour in every condition than did those of any of the other three groups of children. The German, British, and American children were more willing to admit to anti-social behaviour when they thought only their peers would know what they had said, whereas the Soviet children refused to admit to anti-social behaviour even in that condition. In those days, the Soviet educational system was designed to make children develop a sense of collective belonging, and this provides the most obvious explanation of the very low level of anti-social behaviour admitted to among Soviet children.

Parental style

Baumrind (1980) argued that there are two basic dimensions of parenting style:

- Permissive–demanding: this dimension is concerned with the degree of parental control over children.
- Accepting–rejecting: this dimension is concerned with the degree of parental affection.

Baumrind's approach is relevant here, because the two parenting dimensions she proposed have been observed in nearly all human societies (Rohner & Rohner, 1981).

Collectivistic and individualistic societies tend to differ in terms of parenting style along the permissive–demanding dimension (Triandis, 1993). As we saw in the previous section, parents in collectivistic societies tend to be relatively demanding, because they want their children to become co-operative and obedient members of society. In contrast, parents in individualistic societies tend to be permissive, in order to encourage their children to become independent. Children in collectivistic and individualistic cultures respond to these child-rearing practices. For example, children in South Korea (a moderately collectivistic culture) regard parents who are accepting and demanding as much more loving than parents who are accepting and permissive (Rohner & Pettengill, 1985).

What about the accepting–rejecting dimension? Cross-cultural studies indicate that children in virtually all societies do better in terms of social development if their parents are accepting rather than rejecting. Parental rejection is associated with aggression, delinquency, difficulty in maintaining intimate relationships, and moodiness (Rohner, 1986). Rohner (1975) carried out a large cross-cultural study in which cultures were assessed for parental acceptance versus rejection. Across cultures, there was a correlation of +0.72 between parental acceptance and self-esteem in children, indicating an almost universal tendency for high self-esteem in children to be associated with parental acceptance. Cultures with accepting or loving parents also had children who were low in hostility (a correlation of -0.48) and low in dependence (a correlation of -0.30).

Cross-cultural differences

Infant attachment styles in various cultures have been studied using the Strange Situation test devised by Ainsworth and Bell (1970). Findings for infants in the United States, Israel, Japan, and Germany were reported by Sagi et al. (1991). Their findings for the American infants were similar to those reported by Ainsworth and Bell (1970): 71% of them showed secure attachment, 12% showed anxious and resistant attachment, and 17% were anxious and avoidant.

The Israeli infants behaved rather differently from the American ones. Secure attachment was shown by 62% of them, 33% were anxious and resistant, and only 5% were anxious and avoidant. These infants lived in a kibbutz or collective farm, and were looked after much of the time by adults who were not part of their family. However, they had a close relationship with their mothers, and so tended not to be anxious and avoidant.

Japanese infants are treated very differently from Israeli infants. Japanese mothers practically never leave their infants alone with a stranger. In spite of the differences in child-rearing practices in Japan and Israel, the Japanese infants showed similar attachment styles to the Israeli ones. Two-thirds of them (68%) had a secure attachment, 32% were anxious and resistant, and none was anxious and avoidant. The complete absence of anxious and avoidant attachment may have occurred because the infants were faced with the totally new situation of being on their own with a stranger.

Israeli and Japanese children showed anxious and resistant attachment for rather different reasons. Israeli children are accustomed to being separated from their mother, but they rarely encounter complete strangers. Thus, their resistant behaviour was due to the presence of the stranger. In contrast, Japanese children are practically never separated from their mother, and this was the main cause of their resistant attachment behaviour.

The notion that Japanese infants behave as they do because they have not had the experience of being separated from their mother receives support from a study by Durrett et al. (1984). They focused on families in which the mothers were pursuing careers, and so had to leave their children in the care of others. The children of these mothers showed a similar pattern of attachment styles to that found in the United States.

Finally, the German infants showed a different pattern of attachment to the other three groups of infants. Only 40% of them were securely attached, which was less than the number of infants (49%) who were anxious and avoidant. The remaining 11% were anxious and resistant. Grossmann et al. (1985) obtained very similar findings. They suggested that German culture requires keeping some interpersonal distance between parents and children. As Grossmann et al. (1985, p.253) expressed it, "the ideal is an independent, nonclinging infant who does not make demands on the parents but rather unquestioningly obeys their commands."

Further evidence on why it is that German children are less likely to be securely attached than infants from other cultures was reported by Sagi and Lewkowicz (1987). German parents regarded some aspects of securely attached behaviour in a negative way as indicating that the infants were spoiled.

The very different child-rearing practices in the United States, Israel, Japan, and Germany seem to have a significant impact on infants' attachment styles. However, it is noteworthy that about two-thirds of infants in the United States, Israel, and Japan show secure attachment to their mothers. This suggests that the goal of producing securely attached children can be reached in various ways.

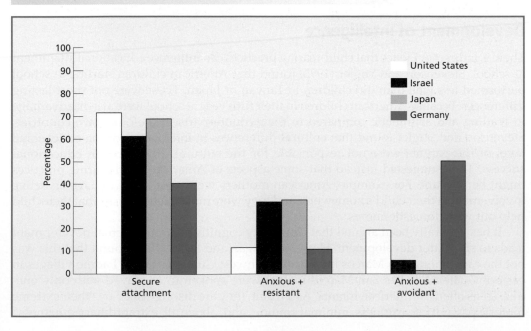

Attachment studies

Van IJzendoorn and Kroonenberg (1988) carried out a meta-analysis of the various studies on the Strange Situation. One of their key findings was that the variation in findings *within* cultures was $1^1/_2$ times greater than the variation *between* cultures. The notion that there is a *single* British or American culture is undoubtedly an oversimplification: in fact, there are several sub-cultures within most large countries. Van IJzendoorn and Kroonenberg also found that the overall percentages of children showing each of the three attachment styles across all of the studies were fairly close to Ainsworth's original figures.

In spite of the above findings, some generalisations about cultural differences are possible. According to Durkin (1995, p.106):

> While Type Bs [securely attached] are the most common type, Type As [avoidant] are relatively more common in Western European countries, while Type Cs [resistant] are relatively more frequent in Israel and Japan.

Evaluation

There are basically two main ways of interpreting cross-cultural differences in infant attachment style. First, the findings may tell us something important about cultural differences in the relationship between infants and their mothers and about child-rearing practices. Second, as Cole and Cole (1993, pp.235–236) pointed out, it is possible that

> cultural differences in the meaning attached to the strange situation make it difficult to infer the true nature of the emotional bonds between the mothers and their children, leading to false conclusions when patterns discovered in one culture are used to reason about another.

We cannot be sure which interpretation is more valid. However, the fact that there are plausible associations between mothers' behaviour and their infants' attachment styles suggests that the findings can largely be accepted at face value.

Development of intelligence

There is indirect evidence that child-rearing practices can influence educational attainment at school. Stevenson and Stigler (1992) found that American children starting at school performed less well than did children in Taiwan or Japan. These were not short-lasting differences, because American children in their fifth year at school were at a disadvantage in reading and arithmetic compared to their counterparts in the other two countries. Stevenson and Stigler found that cultural differences in intelligence or the educational level of the parents were not responsible for the cultural differences in educational success. They suggested instead that some aspects of American child-rearing practices might be relevant. For example, American mothers were least likely to have an active involvement in their child's homework, and they were most likely to insist that their child help out with domestic chores.

It has generally been argued that slow early cognitive and intellectual development leads to slow later development. However, Kagan and Klein (1973) found that this was not the case among San Marcos infants in northwest Guatemala or in Ladino villages in eastern Guatemala. The San Marcos infants were spoken to or played with only one-quarter as often as American infants. As a result, they are distinguished by "their extreme motoric passivity, fearfulness, minimal smiling, and, above all, extraordinary quietness"

Cross-cultural issues: Is Stevenson and Stigler's evidence consistent with the type of culture involved (i.e. individualistic or collectivist)?

(Kagan & Klein, 1973, pp.949–950). After about the age of 15 months, these infants begin to play with other children, and their cognitive development proceeds rapidly. According to Kagan and Klein (p.947), they observed "active, gay, intellectually competent 11-year-olds."

The Ladino infants were treated in a similar way. They only showed meaningful speech at the age of 2½, which is about one year later than American children. Most other aspects of cognitive development were also greatly delayed. However, their cognitive development was essentially normal by the age of 11. Kagan and Klein (1973, pp.960–961) concluded as follows:

> *Infant retardation seems to be partially reversible and cognitive development during the early years more resilient than had been supposed ... There are few dumb [foolish] children in the world if one classifies them from the perspective of the community of adaptation, but millions of dumb children if one classifies them from the perspective of another society.*

PERSONAL REFLECTIONS

- Brown (1965) argued that socialisation is "the meeting ground of social science, of general psychology, and of the psychology of personality. It may reasonably be designated the central topic of social psychology." I would not disagree with that. The evidence on socialisation (especially evidence from cross-cultural studies) suggests to me that children are fairly adaptable. They show good socialisation and cognitive development across a wide range of child-rearing practices. If true, that means that parents do not have to worry about every last detail of their interactions with their young children.

Below: "Socialisation is the meeting ground of social science."

SUMMARY

Sociability

The development of sociability involves an object-centred stage, a simple interactive stage, and a co-ordinated interactions stage. Securely attached infants are more sociable than those who are insecurely attached. Children tend to be more sociable if their parents do not control their playmaking. Twin studies indicate that genetic factors play a part in determining individual differences in children's sociability.

Attachment

The main attachment of an infant is usually to its mother, but there are often strong attachments to other people with whom the infant has regular contact. There are three stages in the early development of attachment to others: the asocial stage; the stage of indiscriminant attachment; and the stage of specific attachments. According to the psychodynamic approach, babies are initially attached to their mother because she is a source of food. In fact, there is not the simple link between food and attachment behaviour that was assumed by Freud. According to Bowlby, infants have an innate tendency to form strong bonds with one particular individual, and there is a critical period (ending by the age of 3) during which this bonding must occur. In fact, the relationship between mother and baby develops over time rather than being fixed shortly after birth. Evidence from the Strange Situations test indicates that there are three main types of attachment of infants to their mother: secure attachment; anxious and resistant attachment; and anxious and avoidant attachment. According to Ainsworth's care-giving hypothesis, the sensitivity of the mother (or other care-giver) is of crucial importance in determining the type of attachment. This hypothesis ignores the part played by the infant, and may exaggerate the importance of the mother's sensitivity or responsiveness.

Effects of deprivation

According to Bowlby's maternal deprivation hypothesis, breaking the child's bond with its mother in early life has severe long-term effects on its social, emotional, and intellectual development. There are also short-term effects in the form of protest, despair, and detachment. However, the effects of privation are generally more severe than those of deprivation, and only a few children show a strong attachment to their mother. Deprivation is much more likely to lead to long-term difficulties when it occurs because of problems with social relationships within the family than when it is due to physical illness or housing problems. Bowlby argued that the adverse effects of maternal deprivation are generally irreversible. Most studies on children who have experienced extreme privation and isolation have failed to support the notion of irreversibility.

Enrichment

Several enrichment programmes for young disadvantaged children have been used in the United States. These programmes include Project Head Start, the Milwaukee project, and the Carolina Abecedarian project. There was generally a rapid increase in IQ and an improvement in educational performance, but these benefits were reduced or disappeared during the early school years. Significant gains in IQ have also been reported in adoption studies in which children from disadvantaged families were adopted by successful professional families. There is some evidence that average and above average preschool children can benefit from intensive instruction provided by their parents. The key limitation of most of the research is that it is not clear *how* enrichment had its effects on children's development.

Cross-cultural differences in child rearing

Cultural differences in child-rearing practices typically reflect differences in terms of adults' cultural expectations and values. Parents in collectivistic societies tend to be demanding, and to want their children to be obedient and co-operative. In contrast, parents in individualistic societies tend to be permissive, and to want their children to become independent. Cultures vary in terms of parental acceptance or rejection, but rejection is almost universally associated with undesirable outcomes in the children (e.g. low self-esteem; delinquency; aggression). Child-rearing practices can also affect educational attainment at school. However, cognitive development is resilient, with slow early development within a culture often being followed by a normal rate of cognitive development. Most infants in most cultures have a secure attachment style. However, an avoidant attachment style is more common in Western Europe than elsewhere, whereas a resistant style is relatively more common in Israel and Japan. The key limitation with most cross-cultural studies is that it is not possible to show causal relationships.

FURTHER READING

Chapter 3 in K. Durkin (1995), *Developmental social psychology: From infancy to old age,* Oxford: Blackwell, contains a good account of theory and research on attachment behaviour and maternal deprivation. Enrichment is considered in some detail in J.C. Berryman, D. Hargreaves, M. Herbert, and A. Taylor (1991), *Developmental psychology and you*, Leicester: BPS Books. The early development of sociability and attachment is discussed fully in Chapter 11 of D.R. Shaffer (1993), *Developmental psychology: Childhood and adolescence (3rd Edn.)*, Pacific Grove, CA: Brooks/Cole.

REVISION QUESTIONS

1a	Explain what psychologists mean by *either* attachment *or* sociability.	(6 marks)
1b	Outline *one* theory of attachment or sociability development.	(6 marks)
1c	Evaluate the extent to which psychological research has supported this theory.	(12 marks)
2	"It is sometimes argued that although early acceleration may be possible, it will not have a positive effect in the long run. The phrase 'early ripe, early rot' expresses the kinds of concerns that underlie this point of view" (Howe, 1995). Critically consider whether psychological research into enrichment has shown support for this concern or whether it is unfounded.	(24 marks)
3a	Describe cultural differences that have been found to occur in child-rearing.	(12 marks)
3b	Assess the effects these differences have been shown to have.	(12 marks)

- **Piaget's theory**
  Swiss psychologist Jean Piaget believed that children develop skills stage by stage.

  Piaget's stage theory of development
  Conservation tasks
  Three mountains task
  Hughes' hidden policeman task
  McGarrigle and Donaldson's teddy bear conservation study

- **Vygotsky's theory**
  Russian Lev Vygotsky emphasised the social context in which children develop.

  Vygotsky's theory of zones of proximal development
  Wood et al.'s scaffolding theory
  Berk's work on inner speech

- **Information-processing approach**
  Some theorists believe development involves increasing mental power, or M-power.

  Case's three kinds of cognitive schemes
  Pascual-Leone's M-power

- **Practical applications to education**
  How do theories of cognitive development affect our schooling?

  Piaget's theory and self-discovery
  Vygotsky's theory and peer tutoring
  Task analysis and error analysis

- **Development of intelligence-test performance**
  What do IQ tests measure and what do the results really mean?

  Binet and Simon's IQ tests
  Twin studies
  Capron and Duyne's adoption study
  Environmenal factors; the HOME inventory
  The Rochester study

16

Cognitive Development

Children change and develop in almost every way in the years between infancy and adolescence. However, some of the most dramatic changes take place in terms of cognitive development. The first systematic theory of cognitive development was proposed by Jean Piaget (1896–1980). However, there are several other major theoretical approaches to cognitive development, including those of Vygotsky and the information-processing theorists.

One reason why it is important to study cognitive development is because of its relevance to education. If we can understand the processes involved in learning and cognitive development, then it should be possible to improve the educational system for the benefit of students of all ages.

Cognitive development depends in part on children's level of intelligence, and on the way in which measured intelligence develops during childhood. There has been some controversy as to the relative importance of genetic and environmental influences in determining intelligence-test performance, and the relevant evidence is discussed later. This controversy is of some importance, because it may influence the ways in which individual children should be taught.

Piaget's Theory

Jean Piaget put forward the most thorough account ever offered of cognitive development. Indeed, such is the richness of his contribution that only a sketchy account can be provided here.

Piaget was interested in how children learn and adapt to the world. In order for adaptation or adjustment to occur, there must be constant interactions between the child and the outside world. According to Piaget, two processes are of key importance:

- **Accommodation**: the individual's cognitive organisation is altered by the need to deal with the environment; in other words, the individual adjusts to the outside world.
- **Assimilation**: the individual deals with new environmental situations on the basis of his or her existing cognitive organisation; in other words, the interpretation of the outside world is adjusted to fit the individual.

The clearest example of the dominance of assimilation over accommodation is play, in which reality is interpreted according to the individual's whim (e.g. a stick becomes a gun). In contrast, dominance of accommodation over assimilation is seen in imitation, in which the actions of someone else are simply copied.

An example of the dominance of assimilation over accommodation —pretending that cardboard boxes are vehicles.

Jean Piaget, 1896–1980.

There are two other key Piagetian concepts: schema and equilibration. **Schema** refers to organised knowledge used to guide action. The first schema infants develop is the body schema, when they realise there is an important distinction between "me" and "not me". This body schema helps the infant in its attempts to explore and make sense of the world.

Equilibration is based on the notion that the individual needs to keep a stable internal state (equilibrium) in a changing environment. When a child tries unsuccessfully to understand its experiences in terms of existing schemas, there is an unpleasant state of *disequilibrium* or lack of balance. The child then uses assimilation and accommodation to restore a state of equilibrium or balance. Thus, disequilibrium motivates the child to learn new skills and knowledge to return to the desired state of equilibrium.

We can distinguish between two kinds of theorists in the area of child development. One group argues that cognitive development only involves changes in the amount of knowledge available to the child, and the efficiency with which that knowledge is used in thinking. According to such theorists, there are no fundamental differences in cognition during development. The second group of theorists (e.g. Piaget) claim that the ways of thinking found in adolescence are very different from those of early childhood.

Piaget argued that all children pass through various stages. His stage theory is discussed in detail later. However, some of its main assumptions are as follows: First, there must be sufficient changes in cognitive development to permit the identification of separate cognitive stages. Second, while the ages at which different children attain any given stage can vary, the sequence of stages should remain the same for all. Third, the cognitive operations and structures defining a stage should form an integrated whole.

Stage theories can potentially explain the complexities of developmental change. However, they can overestimate the differences between stages and underestimate the variations within a given stage. Piaget accepted that children in a given stage do not always adopt the mode of thought typical of that stage, and he coined the term **horizontal decalage** to refer to this.

Stage theory

Piaget argued that there are four major stages of cognitive development. The first is the *sensori-motor stage*, which lasts from birth to about 2 years of age. The second is the *pre-operational stage*, spanning the years between 2 and 7. The third is the *concrete operations stage*, which usually occurs between the ages of 7 and 11 or 12. The fourth stage is the *formal operations stage*, which follows on from the stage of concrete operations.

According to Piaget, very young children deal with the environment by manipulating objects. Thus, sensori-motor development is basically *intelligence through action*. After that, thinking becomes dominated by *perception* during the stage of pre-operational thought. From 7 years onwards, thinking is more and more influenced by logico-mathematical considerations. During the stage of concrete operations, logical reasoning can only be applied to objects that are real or can be seen. During the stage of formal operations, the older child or adult can think logically about potential events or abstract ideas.

Sensori-motor stage (0–2 years)

This stage of cognitive development lasts from birth to about 2 years of age, with the infant learning a great deal by moving around. Initially, the baby's schemas consist largely of inborn reflexes such as sucking. However, these reflexes change somewhat with experience. For example, babies learn at a very early age to alter the shape of their lips so that they can suck more efficiently.

The key achievement of this stage is **object permanence**. This involves being aware that objects continue to exist when they are no longer in view. In the early part

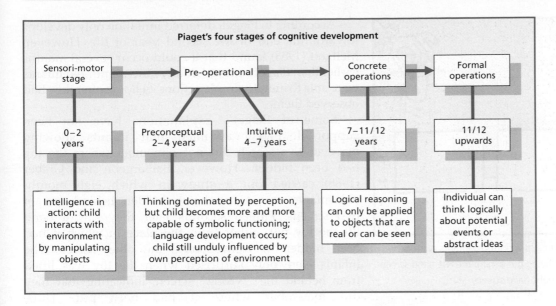

Piaget's four stages of cognitive development

In the left-hand picture, the baby is reaching for a toy he can see. In the right-hand one, he searches in the same place for it, although in fact it is hidden under the paper on his right.

of the sensori-motor stage, the infant has no awareness at all of object permanence: it is literally a case of "out of sight, out of mind". Object permanence develops as the child actively explores his or her environment. Towards the end of its first year, the infant starts to display what is known as **perseverative search**. This involves the infant searching for a concealed object in the place in which it was found some time earlier, rather than in the place in which it was last seen. According to Piaget, this happens because the infant does not regard the object as existing independently of the infant's own behaviour. Perseverative search shows some features of object permanence. However, full object permanence is only achieved towards the end of the sensori-motor stage.

The development of imitation is a major achievement of the sensori-motor stage. Imitation allows the infant to add considerably to the range of actions of which it is capable. It develops slowly, becoming more precise over time. Towards the end of the sensori-motor stage, the infant shows evidence of **deferred imitation**, which is the ability to imitate behaviour that was seen before.

What reflexes are babies born with, and how might they develop into a conscious activity?

How could the development of a baby's first words be explained in terms of imitation?

Evaluation of the sensori-motor stage. Piaget identified many of the main kinds of learning shown by infants during the first two years. However, he underestimated the abilities of infants in a number of ways. For example, Bower (1982) hid a toy behind a screen. When the screen was lifted a few seconds later, the toy was no longer there. Infants who were three or four months old showed surprise. This suggests that some aspects of object permanence are present much earlier than was claimed by Piaget. This was also found by Bower and Wishart (1972). They made an object disappear from sight by removing all light from it. However, infra-red television cameras revealed that very young children reached out for the object in the correct direction, suggesting that they had at least some aspects of object permanence.

KEY TERMS
Perseverative search: mistakenly searching for an object in the place in which it was previously found, rather than the place in which it is currently hidden.
Deferred imitation: in Piaget's theory, the ability to imitate behaviour that was observed at an earlier time.

Baillargeon and Graber found that eight-month-old infants were surprised when a cup they had seen being put behind the left-hand screen was then retrieved from behind the right-hand screen.

According to Piaget, deferred imitation only develops towards the end of the second year of life. However, Meltzoff (1988) found that it could occur several months earlier than Piaget believed. Many nine-month-old infants were able to imitate simple actions 24 hours after they had observed them.

Some of Piaget's explanations have not been supported. Piaget assumed that infants showing perseverative search did not remember where the toy had been hidden. However, Baillargeon and Graber (1988) carried out a study in which eight-month-old infants saw a toy being hidden behind one of two screens. Fifteen seconds later they saw a hand lift the toy out, either from the place in which it had been hidden or from behind the other screen. The infants were only surprised when the toy was lifted from behind the "wrong" screen, indicating that they did remember where it had been put. Thus, perseverative search does *not* occur simply because of faulty memory.

There is another problem with Piaget's explanation of perseverative search. He argued that perseverative search occurs because young children believe that an object's existence depends on their own actions. It follows from this explanation that children who only passively observed the object in its first location should *not* show perseverative search. In fact, infants show as much perseverative search under those conditions as when they have been allowed to find the object in its first location.

Pre-operational stage (2–7 years)

The child who completes the sensori-motor stage of cognitive development is still not capable of "true" thought. This child operates largely at the level of direct action, whereas the pre-operational child becomes more and more capable of symbolic functioning. The development of language is associated with the cognitive advances of pre-operational children. However, Piaget regarded language development as largely a consequence of more fundamental cognitive changes, rather than as itself a cause of cognitive advance.

Children show considerable cognitive development during the five years covered by the pre-operational stage. Accordingly, Piaget divided the pre-operational stage into two sub-stages: the preconceptual (2–4 years) and the intuitive (4–7 years). Two of the cognitive differences between children at the *preconceptual* and *intuitive* stages involve *seriation* and *syncretic thought*.

Seriation tasks require children to arrange objects in order on the basis of a single feature (e.g. height). Piaget and Szeminska (1952) found that preconceptual children found this very hard to do, and even intuitive children often used a trial-and-error approach.

Syncretic thought can be revealed on tasks where children are asked to select various objects that are all alike. Intuitive children tend to perform this task accurately, for example selecting several yellow objects or square objects. Preconceptual children show syncretic thought. The second object they select is the same as the first on one dimension (e.g. size), but then the third object is the same as the second on another dimension (e.g. colour). Thus, syncretic thought occurs because young children focus on two objects at a time, and find it hard to consider the characteristics of several objects at the same time.

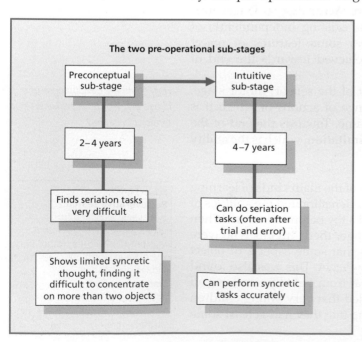

The two pre-operational sub-stages

Preconceptual sub-stage	Intuitive sub-stage
2–4 years	4–7 years
Finds seriation tasks very difficult	Can do seriation tasks (often after trial and error)
Shows limited syncretic thought, finding it difficult to concentrate on more than two objects	Can perform syncretic tasks accurately

Conservation tasks

Pre-operational children are unduly influenced by their own perception of the environment. They tend to pay attention to only one aspect of the total situation (this is called **centration** by Piaget). The way in which centration produces errors is shown in studies of conservation. **Conservation** refers to the understanding that certain aspects of a visual display do not vary in spite of changes in perceptual aspects. In his classic studies on conservation of quantity, Piaget presented children with two glasses of the same size and shape containing the same quantity of liquid. Once the child has agreed that there is the same quantity of liquid in both glasses, the liquid from one of the glasses is poured into a different glass that is taller and thinner.

The child is then asked if the two glasses (the original one and the new one) contain the same amount to drink, or if one contains more. Pre-operational children fail to show conservation. They argue either that there is more liquid in the new container ("because it's higher") or that there is more liquid in the original glass ("because it's wider"). In either case, the child centres or focuses on only one dimension (height or width).

The pre-operational child fails on conservation tasks partly because of centration. However, the child also lacks crucial internalised cognitive operations, according to Piaget. Two cognitive operations are of special relevance to conservation tasks: reversibility and decentration. **Reversibility** involves the ability to undo, or reverse mentally, some operation that has been carried out. Reversibility allows the realisation that the effect of pouring liquid from one container into another could be negated by simply pouring the liquid back into its original container. **Decentration** involves the ability to take account of two or more aspects of a situation at the same time. In the case of conservation of quantity, it involves considering height and width together.

Discussion points

1. Think of some reasons why Piaget's research on conservation has attracted so much interest.

2. What are the limitations of Piaget's research (see Evaluation section)?

KEY STUDY EVALUATION — Conservation

Piaget used the conservation of liquid task to show that pre-operational children lack the internalised cognitive operations of reversibility and decentralisation. However, it might be interesting to try the same experiment with children from a non-Western environment, such as the bush people of the African Kalahari desert, who are not likely to be familiar with glass beakers filled with water. Would they show conservation or not? Would a lack of conservation necessarily mean that these children could not decentre?

Piaget argued that the thinking of pre-operational children is characterised by egocentrism. **Egocentrism** is the tendency to assume that one's way of thinking about things is the only possible way. Piaget studied egocentric thinking in pre-operational children by using the three mountains task. Children looked at a model of mountains, and then decided which picture showed the view that would be seen by someone looking at the display from a different angle. Children younger than 8 nearly always selected the photograph of the scene as they themselves saw it. According to Piaget, this error occurred because of their inability to escape from an egocentric perspective.

Egocentrism also involves a lack of differentiation between the self and the world, which makes the child unable to distinguish clearly between psychological and physical events. This produces:

* Realism: the tendency to regard psychological events as having a physical existence.
* Animism: the tendency to endow physical objects and events with psychological qualities.
* Artificialism: the tendency to consider that physical objects and events were created by people.

Piaget (1967, p.95) provided the following example of realism in a conversation with a child called Engl:

> *"Where is the dream whilst you are dreaming?" "Beside me." "Are your eyes shut when you dream? Where is the dream?" "Over there."*

Piaget's three mountains task required children to reverse a complicated image in their heads. Do you think a failure to do this shows egocentricity?

A drawing of the model used in Piaget's three mountains task. Children were shown the model from one angle, then shown photographs of the model from other viewpoints, and asked to choose which view someone standing at one of the other labelled points would see. Pre-operational children usually selected the view from the point at which they themselves had seen the model.

Give a definition of operant discrimination learning and how it might be demonstrated in Wheldall and Poborca's study.

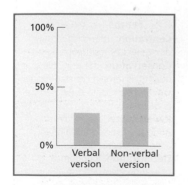

Percentages of children aged 6–7 years who showed conservation on the two versions of Piaget's conservation task (Wheldall & Poborca, 1980).

Children show animism when they claim that the wind feels it when it blows against a mountain. Young children often attribute consciousness to all things. An example of artificialism concerns my daughter Fleur at the age of three. We were on Wimbledon Common, and I told her that the sun would come out when I had counted to ten. When it did so, she was very confident that Daddy could control the sun, and often begged me to make the sun appear on gloomy days!

Evaluation of the pre-operational stage. Piaget identified several limitations in the thinking of pre-operational children. He also provided a theoretical account, arguing that children at this stage lack important cognitive operations (e.g. reversibility). However, Piaget greatly underestimated the cognitive abilities of pre-operational children. For example, Wheldall and Poborca (1980) claimed that children often fail on conservation tasks because they do not understand the question. Accordingly, they devised a non-verbal version of the liquid conservation task. This version was based on operant discrimination learning: the child was rewarded for making the correct choice, and language was not involved. Only 28% of their 6- and 7-year-old participants showed conservation with the standard verbal version, but 50% did so when tested on the non-verbal version. These findings suggest that misunderstanding of language is one factor involved in non-conservation. However, the fact that one-half of the participants were non-conservers with the non-verbal version indicates that other factors must also be involved.

Bruner, Olver, and Greenfield (1966) argued that pre-operational children may fail to show conservation because they are influenced too much by the altered appearance of the visual display. First, they used the standard version of the liquid conservation task. Then they placed two beakers of different shapes behind a screen with only the tops of the beakers visible. Next water was poured from one beaker into the other behind the screen. When asked whether there was the same amount of water in the second beaker as there had been in the first, children of all ages between 4 and 7 showed much more evidence of conservation than they had in the standard version of the task. Finally, the children were given the standard conservation task for the second time. The percentage of 5-year-olds showing conservation more than trebled from 20% on the first test under standard conditions to about 70% on the second test.

Bruner et al. questioned the children about the reasons for their judgements on the conservation task. Children who nearly always showed conservation claimed that the water was the same, suggesting that a sense of identity is necessary (if not sufficient) for conservation. In addition, focusing on the issue of identity by asking the question "Is it still the same water?" led to a marked increase in the number of children showing conservation.

Field (1981) also obtained evidence that the sense of identity is important. Identity involves realising that an object remains the same after it has been transformed. Field gave some four-year-old children training in the operations of reversibility and decentration, whereas others were given identity training. Only 35% of the children trained in reversibility and decentration showed conservation a few months later, compared to 70% of those who received identity training. These findings suggest that Piaget was mistaken in his emphasis on reversibility and decentration.

Hughes (1975) argued that poor performance on the three mountains task occurred because the task did not relate to children's experience. He tested this argument by using a piece of apparatus in which two walls intersected at right angles to form what looked like a plus sign. A boy doll and a policeman doll were put into the apparatus, and the child was asked whether the policeman doll could see the boy doll. After that, the child was told to hide the boy so that the policeman could not see him. Nearly all the children could do this, and any errors were corrected. Finally, a second policeman was used, and the children were told to hide the boy doll so that neither of the policemen could see him. According to Piaget, the children should have hidden the boy so that they themselves could not see him, and so should have failed the task. In fact, Hughes found that 90% of children between the ages of 3^1/$_2$ and 5 performed the task successfully. Hughes concluded that the main reason why performance was much higher on his task than on the three mountains task used by Piaget was because his task was much more meaningful and interesting for young children.

Concrete operations stage (7–11 years)

Piaget argued that the shift from pre-operational to concrete operational thinking involves an increasing independence of thought from perception. Underlying this shift is the development of various cognitive operations of a logical or mathematical nature, including the actions implied by mathematical symbols (e.g. $+, -, \div, \times, >, <, =$). The most important cognitive operation is reversibility, which involves the ability to cancel out the effects of a perceptual change by imagining the opposite change. During the concrete operations stage, children can use the various cognitive operations only with respect to specific concrete situations. In the subsequent stage of formal operations, thinking is freed from the immediate situation.

A drawing of the two policemen version of Hughes' (1975) experimental set-up, in which the child is asked to hide a boy doll where neither of the policemen can see him. According to Piaget's egocentrism theory, children should hide the boy doll in sections A or B, where they themselves can't see him, but in fact Hughes found that 90% of children put the doll in section C—the only one the policemen cannot see.

Piaget argued that cognitive operations are usually combined or organised into a system or structure. For example, the operation "greater than" cannot really be considered independently of the operation "less than". Someone will fail to grasp the full meaning of "A is greater than B" unless he or she realises that this statement means that "B is less than A". Piaget coined the term *grouping* to refer to such sets of logically related operations.

What kinds of tasks can children perform in the concrete operations stage that they could not perform previously? One example is based on the notion of *transitivity*, which allows three elements to be placed in the correct order. For example, if Mark is taller than Peter, and Peter is taller than Robert, then it follows from the notion of transitivity that Mark is taller than Robert. Concrete operational children can solve problems such as this one, but they cannot apply the notion of transitivity to abstract problems.

Piaget argued that children should find it easier to achieve conservation on some tasks than on others. Conservation of number (e.g. realising that two rows of objects contain the same number of objects even when the objects are closer together in one row than in the other) involves fairly simple operations. All the child has to do is to pair each object in one row with an object in the other row. In contrast, consider conservation of volume. This can be tested by placing two identical balls of clay into two identical transparent containers filled to the same level with water. One ball of clay is then moulded into a new shape, and conservation is shown if the child realises that this will not change the amount of water it displaces. Conservation of volume is said to be harder to achieve than conservation of number because it involves taking account of the operations involved in the conservation of liquids and of mass. As predicted, conservation of volume is generally attained some years after conservation of number (e.g. Tomlinson-Keasey et al., 1979).

One of the tasks used to test conservation of number. Children are asked if there are the same number of beads in the two rows before and after they are rearranged.

According to Piaget, most children acquire the various forms of conservation in the same order. First comes conservation of number and liquid at the age of about 6 or 7. Then comes conservation of substance or quantity and of length at about 7 or 8, followed

This apparatus tests conservation of volume. Children are asked if the liquids will be at the same level again when the new shape of clay is put back into the glass. Conservation of volume is not usually attained until about the age of 11 or 12.

What can you do now that you were not able to do before you were 11?

Examples of propositional operations are tasks like algebra and trigonometry.

by conservation of weight between the ages of 8 and 10. Finally, there is conservation of volume at about the age of 11 or 12.

Evaluation of the concrete operations stage. Children between the ages of 7 and 11 typically learn a range of cognitive operations related to mathematics and to logic. However, Piaget's approach is limited. Children during the concrete operations stage acquire an enormous amount of new knowledge, which contributes to their cognitive development. Much of this knowledge owes little to either mathematics or to logic. Piaget underestimated the importance of specific experiences in determining performance on conservation tasks. For example, children often show conservation of volume for substances with which they are familiar some time before they show conservation of volume for less familiar ones (Durkin, 1995). This is inconsistent with Piaget's stage-based account of cognitive development.

Formal operations stage (11 upwards)

Formal operational thought involves the ability to think in terms of many possible states of the world. This permits an escape from the limitations of immediate reality. Thus, adolescents and adults in the formal operations stage can think in an abstract way, as well as the concrete way found in the previous stage of cognitive development.

Inhelder and Piaget (1958, p.279) put forward the following suggestions for deciding whether someone is using formal operations:

> *Analyse the proofs employed by the subject. If they do not go beyond observation of empirical correspondences [observable similarities], they can be fully explained in terms of concrete operations, and nothing would warrant our assuming that more complex thought mechanisms are operating. If, on the other hand, the subject interprets a given correspondence as the result of any of several possible combinations, and this leads him to verify his hypotheses by observing their consequences, then we know that propositional operations are involved.*

In other words, most or all of the possible combinations of factors are considered in formal operational thinking, whereas only a small number of combinations is considered in concrete operational thinking.

What kinds of problems have been used to study formal operational thought? One task used by Piaget involved presenting the participants with a set of weights and a string that could be lengthened or shortened. The goal was to work out what determines the frequency of the swings of a pendulum formed by suspending a weight on a string from a pole. The factors that are likely to be considered include the length of the string, the weight of the suspended object, the force of the participant's push, and the position from which the pendulum is pushed. In fact, only the length of the string is relevant.

When pre-operational children are presented with this problem, they typically argue mistakenly that the strength of the push they give to the pendulum is the main factor. Concrete-operational children often argue that the frequency of swinging of the pendulum is affected by the length of the string, but they cannot isolate that factor from all the others. In contrast, many formal-operational

Children were asked to work out what would affect the frequency of the swings of the pendulum (how many times it would go back and forth in a given period). They were asked to consider changing the weights on the pendulum, the length of the string, how hard they pushed it, and which direction it was pushed in.

children manage to solve the problem. According to Piaget, the ability to solve the pendulum problem requires an understanding of a complicated combinatorial system.

Evaluation of the formal operations stage. It is probable that Piaget greatly exaggerated the role played by logico-mathematical structures in adolescent and adult thought. Adults in their everyday lives typically deal with problems that have no single perfect solution, and that cannot be solved simply by the rigorous use of logic. Thus, a detailed understanding of mathematics and of logic is of limited value in most adult thinking.

General evaluation of Piaget's theory

Piaget's theory was an ambitious attempt to explain how children move from being irrational and illogical to being rational and logical. The notion that children learn certain basic operations (e.g. reversibility), and that these operations then allow them to solve a wide range of problems, is a valuable one. No-one before Piaget had provided a detailed account of the ways in which children's thinking changes.

We have seen that much of the evidence that Piaget obtained about children's cognitive development is flawed. He used the clinical method, which involves the experimenter discussing the task with the child in an unstandardised and rather unscientific way. A major problem with the clinical method is that it makes considerable demands on the language ability of the child. As a result, Piaget often underestimated the cognitive abilities of children.

What problems does the clinical method pose for anyone attempting to carry out a longitudinal study of a child's development?

Some of the major assumptions on which Piaget's theory is based are inadequate:

1. Cognitive development occurs in stages.
2. Performance depends almost entirely on competence.
3. Cognitive development depends on maturational processes.

Piaget assumed that all children go through the same sequence of four major cognitive stages. One of the great dangers with stage theories is that the differences between stages will be *overestimated*, whereas those within stages will be *underestimated*. For example, Piaget assumed that children who show conservation of quantity for one material possess the operation of reversibility. As a result, they should show conservation with other materials. In fact, children generally show conservation of quantity for familiar materials some time before they show it for unfamiliar materials. Thus, successful performance depends on *specific* learning experiences as well as on the *general* cognitive operations emphasised by Piaget. In essence, cognitive development proceeds in a much more unsystematic way than Piaget assumed.

Piaget argued that children who fail to solve a problem lack the necessary cognitive structures or competencies. There is an important distinction between performance (which is what the individual actually does) and competence (which is the underlying

RESEARCH THAT HAS CHALLENGED PIAGET'S FINDINGS

Author	Developmental Stage	Operation or Function	Findings	How does this challenge Piaget?
Bower	Sensori-motor	Object permanence	Ability present at 3–4 months	Infants demonstrate object permanence much earlier than predicted
Hughes	Pre-operational	Egocentrism	Decentred thought present at 3–5 years	Children perform better if the task is meaningful to them
Durkin	Concrete operational	Conservation of volume	Children can conserve substances with which they are familiar	Inconsistent with Piaget's stage theory which does not account for cultural differences

knowledge). As Shaffer (1993, p.268) pointed out, Piaget had a tendency "to equate *performance* with *competence* (and to ignore other factors that influence children's responses)." Donaldson (1978) drew a distinction between embedded and disembedded language. Embedded language is very much bound up in ongoing events, whereas disembedded language is not. Donaldson argued that children find it much harder to show the abilities they possess when problems are presented in disembedded language. In other words, the gap between competence and performance is greater when disembedded language is used. In similar fashion, students often find mathematics and statistics difficult, because they tend to be disembedded from the immediate experience of students.

McGarrigle and Donaldson

McGarrigle and Donaldson found that when an experimenter rearranged one of a pair of rows of counters, relatively few six-year-old children thought that the two rows still contained the same number of counters. However, when a teddy bear appeared to mess up the counters accidentally, most children said that the numbers in the rows were still the same.

McGarrigle and Donaldson (1974) showed that there can be a large discrepancy between competence and performance. They presented six-year-old children with two rows of counters. All the children agreed that there were equal numbers of counters in each row. In one condition, the experimenter deliberately messed up one of the rows. Only 16% of the children showed number conservation (i.e. argued that there were the same number of counters in each row). This finding suggests that very few of the children had the underlying competence necessary to show number conservation. However, the findings were very different in a second condition, in which a "naughty teddy bear" messed up one of the rows in what looked like an accidental way. In this condition, 62% of the children showed conservation.

Why did McGarrigle and Donaldson find such a large difference between the two conditions? The high level of performance in the "naughty teddy" conditions occurred because most of the children had a general understanding of number conservation. In the other condition, the fact that the experimenter deliberately altered the situation may have led the children to assume that the experimenter *intended* to change the number of counters in one of the rows. Whether or not that is correct, the fact remains that performance in that condition failed to reflect the underlying level of competence.

Discussion points

1. Why do you think that McGarrigle and Donaldson found such a large difference between their two conditions?
2. What problems for Piaget's theory arose from his failure to distinguish carefully between performance and competence?

The notion that children may fail to show number conservation because they think the experimenter intended to change the number was further supported by Light et al. (1979). They tested five- and six-year-olds in pairs, with both members of each pair being given glass beakers of the same size and containing the same number of pasta shells. They were told the shells would be used to play a competitive game, and so it was essential they had the same number. Then the experimenter pretended to notice that one of the beakers had a badly chipped rim and so might be dangerous to handle. The shells were then transferred to another beaker of a different shape, and the children were asked whether the number of shells in each beaker was the same. Conservation was shown by 70% of the children in this incidental transformation condition, against only 5% in a standard intentional transformation condition. Presumably the change seemed less important when it was seen as merely incidental.

Why might the fact that the children were told it was essential to have the same number of pasta shells be a confounding factor in Light et al.'s study?

Piaget (1970) assumed that maturation of the brain and of the nervous system plays an important role in allowing children to move through the successive stages of cognitive development. He also assumed that new cognitive structures can develop when there is a *conflict* between what the child expects to happen and what actually happens. These assumptions are too vague to be of much value in understanding the forces producing cognitive development. Piaget provided a detailed *description* of the major changes in cognitive development, but he did not offer an adequate explanation. He told us *what* cognitive development involves, but not *why* or *how* this development occurs. However, Piaget's approach has given rise to much research, and he remains the most significant theorist on cognitive development.

Vygotsky's Theory

Lev Vygotsky (1896–1934) was a Russian psychologist who emphasised the notion that cognitive development depends very largely on social factors. According to Vygotsky (1981, p.163):

> *Any function in the child's cultural development appears twice, or on two planes. First, it appears on the social plane, and then on the psychological plane.*

As Durkin (1995) pointed out, the child can be thought of as an apprentice who learns directly from social interaction and communication with older children and adults who have the knowledge and skills that the child lacks. This approach is very different from Piaget's, where the emphasis is on the individual acquiring knowledge through a process of self-discovery.

Lev Semeonovich Vygotsky, 1896–1934.

Vygotsky's four stages

Vygotsky argued that there are four stages in the formation of concepts. He identified these four stages on the basis of a study in which children were presented with wooden blocks provided with labels consisting of nonsense symbols. Each nonsense syllable was used in a consistent way to refer to blocks having certain characteristics, such as circular and thin. The children were given the concept-formation task of deciding on the meaning of each nonsense syllable. Vygotsky's four stages were as follows:

1. Vague syncretic stage: the children failed to use systematic strategies and showed little or no understanding of the concepts.
2. Complex stage: non-random strategies were used, but these strategies were not successful in finding the main features of each concept.
3. Potential concept stage: systematic strategies were used, but they were limited to focusing on one feature at a time (e.g. shape).
4. Mature concept stage: systematic strategies relating to more than one feature at a time were used, and led to successful concept formation.

Zone of proximal development

One of the key notions in Vygotsky's approach to cognitive development is the **zone of proximal development**. This was defined by Vygotsky (1978, p.86) as

> *the distance between the actual developmental level as determined by independent problem solving and the level of potential development as determined through problem solving under adult guidance or in collaboration with more capable peers.*

In other words, children who seem to lack certain skills when tested on their own may perform more effectively in the social context provided by someone with the necessary knowledge. Skills shown in the social situation but not the isolated one fall within the zone of proximal development.

Left to his own devices, could this boy make his sister a birthday cake? His mother uses scaffolding to create a situation in which he can begin to move into a zone of proximal development.

Scaffolding

Wood, Bruner, and Ross (1976) developed Vygotsky's notion of a zone of proximal development. They introduced the concept of **scaffolding**, which refers to the context provided by knowledgeable people such as adults to help children to develop their cognitive skills. An important aspect of scaffolding is that there is a gradual withdrawal of support as the child's knowledge and confidence increase.

Moss (1992) reviewed a number of studies concerned with the scaffolding provided by mothers during the preschool period. There were three main aspects to the mothers' scaffolding strategies. First, the mother instructed her child in new skills that the child could not use on its own. Second, the mother encouraged her child to maintain useful problem-solving tactics that it had shown spontaneously. Third, the mother tried to persuade the child to discard immature and inappropriate forms of behaviour.

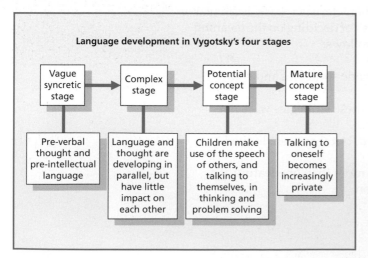

Language development in Vygotsky's four stages

Vague syncretic stage	Complex stage	Potential concept stage	Mature concept stage
Pre-verbal thought and pre-intellectual language	Language and thought are developing in parallel, but have little impact on each other	Children make use of the speech of others, and talking to themselves, in thinking and problem solving	Talking to oneself becomes increasingly private

KEY TERMS

Scaffolding: the context provided by an adult or other knowledgeable person which helps the child to develop its cognitive skills.

Intersubjectivity: a process by which two individuals with different views about a task adjust those views so they become more similar.

Language development

Vygotsky attached great importance to the development of language. He argued that language and thought are essentially unrelated during the first stage of development. As a result, young children have "pre-intellectual speech" and "pre-verbal thought". During the second stage, language and thought develop in parallel, and continue to have very little impact on each other. During the third stage, children begin to make use of the speech of others and talking to themselves (private speech) to assist in their thinking and problem solving. An important notion here is that of **intersubjectivity**. This refers to the process by which two individuals whose initial views about a task are different move towards an agreed understanding of what is involved.

Finally, private speech is used routinely in problem solving, and language plays a part in the development of thinking. In other words, language becomes more and more central to cognitive development over the years. Private speech is initially spoken out loud, but then becomes more and more internal. Language generally plays a crucial role when children learn from social interactions with others. Some of the processes involved were described by Berk (1994, p.62):

When a child discusses a challenging task with a mentor [someone providing guidance], that individual offers spoken directions and strategies. The child incorporates the language of those dialogues into his or her private speech and then uses it to guide independent efforts.

Evidence for Vygotsky's approach

Scaffolding

There is considerable experimental evidence that approaches to teaching based on the zone of proximal development and on scaffolding can be very effective. For example Conner, Knight, and Cross (1997) studied the effects of scaffolding on two-year-olds, who were asked to perform various problem-solving and literary tasks. Most previous studies had focused only on mothers' scaffolding, but Conner et al. also considered fathers' scaffolding. Mothers and fathers were equally good at scaffolding, and the quality of scaffolding predicted the children's performance on the various tasks during the teaching session.

If scaffolding is to be of real value in education, then clearly its beneficial effects need to last well beyond the original teaching session. Accordingly, Conner et al. conducted a follow-up session. They found that the children who had originally received better scaffolding continued to perform better than those who had received poor scaffolding.

Social context

Wertsch et al. (1980) obtained evidence supporting Vygotsky's view that learning initially emerges in a social context. Mothers and their children between the ages of 2 and 4 were given the task of building a truck so that it looked like a model they could refer to. When the mothers of the younger children looked at the model, this was followed by their children looking at the model on about 90% of occasions. However, the older children's looking behaviour was much less influenced by what their mothers were doing. Thus, social factors in the form of the mother's looking behaviour had much more impact on younger than on older children, as would be expected according to Vygotsky's theory.

Inner speech

Vygotsky's notion that inner speech can be of value in thinking has received support. In one study (Hardyck & Petrinovich, 1970), participants read an easy or difficult text. Half of them were told not to use inner speech, whereas the remainder were free to do so. Comprehension of the difficult text was significantly higher when the participants were allowed to use inner speech, but the use of inner speech did not affect comprehension of the easy text. This is consistent with other evidence indicating that inner speech is of most value when tasks are difficult (Eysenck & Keane, 1995). Behrend et al. (1992) used whispering and observable lip movements as measures of inner speech. Children who used the most inner speech tended to perform difficult tasks better than children who made little use of inner speech.

Children who make use of inner speech tend to perform better on difficult or novel tasks than children who do not use much inner speech.

Berk

Convincing evidence of the important role played by inner speech was reported by Berk (1994). She found that six-year-olds spent an average of 60% of the time talking to themselves while solving problems in mathematics. Those whose speech contained numerous comments about what needed to be done on the current problem did better at mathematics over the following year. This confirmed Vygotsky's view that self-guiding speech can make it easier for children to direct their actions. Presumably this self-guiding speech made it easier for the children to focus their attention on the task in hand.

Vygotsky argued that private speech diminishes and becomes more internal as children's level of performance improves. Berk (1994) discussed a study in which four- and five-year-old children made building bricks models in each of three sessions. As predicted by Vygotsky, the children's speech become increasingly internalised from session to session as their model-making performance improved. Thus, as Vygotsky assumed, private speech is of most value to children when they are confronted by novel tasks that they do not fully understand.

KEY STUDY EVALUATION — Berk

The usefulness of Vygotsky's theory of diminishing speech depends on what is meant by "speech". For example, some children with learning difficulties are unable to speak but can perform quite well on many types of tasks. Children who are born profoundly deaf and whose families are hearing often find speech difficult or impossible to acquire, but their intelligence is sometimes unimpaired. It is interesting to speculate whether deaf children of deaf parents who grow up using sign language can use signs as their own private "speech" in the way intended by Vygotsky.

Evaluation of Vygotsky's approach

There are several significant strengths of Vygotsky's theoretical approach. As he argued, children's cognitive development does depend importantly on the social context and on guidance provided by adults and other children. Piaget underestimated the importance of the social environment, and Vygotsky deserves credit for acknowledging the key role it plays in cognitive development. It follows from Vygotsky's approach that there should be major differences in cognitive development from culture to culture, whereas Piaget argued that children everywhere go through the same sequence of cognitive stages in the same order. There is limited evidence for the universal stages emphasised by Piaget (see Eysenck, 1984), but there are also important cultural differences in cognitive development.

There are several limitations with Vygotsky's theoretical approach. First, he has been criticised for exaggerating the importance of the social environment. Children's rate of cognitive development is determined by their level of motivation and interest in learning, as well as by the social support they receive.

Second, the account he offered is rather sketchy. He did not make it clear precisely what kinds of social interaction were most beneficial for learning (e.g. general encouragement versus specific instructions). According to Durkin (1995, p.380), the followers of Vygotsky "offer only superficial accounts of how language is actually used in the course of social interactions."

Third, social interactions between, for example, parent and child do not always have beneficial effects. Indeed, social interactions can make matters worse rather than better. As Durkin (1995, p.375) pointed out, "People confronted with an opposing point of view ... dig their heels in, get hot under the collar, refuse to budge, exploit their knowledge as a source of power and control, and so on."

Fourth, Vygotsky assumed that social interactions enhanced cognitive development because of the instruction that was provided. However, there are other reasons why children benefit from social interactions. Light et al. (1994) found on a computer-based task that children learned better in pairs than on their own, even when the other child was merely present and did not say anything. This is known as *social facilitation*, and occurs because the presence of others can have a motivational effect.

Fifth, it would seem from Vygotsky's account that nearly all learning should be fairly easy provided that children receive the appropriate help from adults and other children. In fact, young children often take months or years to master complex skills even when they are well supported in their schools and homes. This suggests that there are genuine constraints on children's learning that were ignored by Vygotsky.

Vygotsky developed his theory during the last ten years of his life, before he died of tuberculosis at the tragically early age of 38. At least some of the weaknesses of his approach might have been resolved had he lived longer.

Does social facilitation only apply to young children? Are there times when it might also apply to older individuals?

Information-processing Approach

Most cognitive psychologists have made use of the information-processing approach in their attempts to understand cognition in adults (Eysenck & Keane, 1995; see Chapter 2). According to this approach, there is an information-processing system consisting of a small number of *processes* (e.g. attention) and of *structures* (e.g. long-term memory). This system is used in flexible ways to handle all kinds of cognitive tasks ranging from simple mathematics to reading a novel, and from studying French to playing chess. More specifically, it is assumed by information-processing theorists that external stimuli are attended to, then perceived, and then various thought processes (e.g. problem solving) are applied to them. Finally, a decision is made as to what to do with the stimuli, and some kind of response is produced.

What are the implications of the information-processing approach for understanding cognitive development? As Meadows (1994, p.702) pointed out, there are various possible ways in which cognitive development might occur within this approach. It might involve:

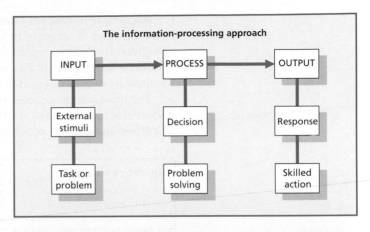

> *Development of basic processes, of the information base they are applied to, of the structure of the sequence in which basic processes are used, of the executive control of the whole system, or of combinations of these.*

Thus, for example, children may develop attentional or perceptual skills as they grow up, the capacity of short-term memory may increase, their problem-solving skills may improve, and so on.

One of the most obvious differences between children and adults is in the size of the knowledge base: on most tasks, adults possess much more relevant knowledge than children. Does this make a difference? Evidence that it can was reported by Chi (1978), who carried out a study on 10-year-old children who were skilled chess players and on adults who knew little about chess. The adults had much better digit recall than the children, but the children's ability to recall chess positions was more than 50% better than that of the adults. The finding that the children recalled chess positions better than the adults indicates the

importance of relevant knowledge. Adults generally have superior cognitive processes and ability to perform tasks, and the only obvious advantage possessed by the children was their greater knowledge of chess.

One of the key features of cognitive development from the information-processing perspective is a great increase in **automatic processes**, that is, processes that occur rapidly and with minimal use of processing capacity. Good examples can be found in reading and arithmetic. For most older children and adults, the processes involved in identifying words or simple multiplication (e.g. 5 × 6) are essentially automatic and effortless. For children who are just starting school, these cognitive activities can be very demanding. The basic processes underlying reading and arithmetic become automatic as a result of prolonged practice.

Can you recall trying to master a skill, such as multiplication or telling the time, which seemed impossible to grasp but is now automatic?

Approach of Case and Pascual-Leone

Pascual-Leone (1984) and Case (1974) were both strongly influenced by Piaget's theoretical approach. They agreed with Piaget that children actively structure their understanding, and that children move from pre-concrete to concrete thinking, and then on to abstract thinking. However, their views differed from those of Piaget in some important ways.

Neo-Piagetian theory

First, they argued that it was desirable to consider cognitive development within an information-processing approach. Second, they claimed that it was preferable to focus on specific components of cognitive processing rather than the more general schemas emphasised by Piaget. Third, they argued that much of cognitive development depends on an increase in mental capacity or mental power. These areas of agreement and disagreement with Piaget led them to develop a neo-Piagetian theory of cognitive development.

> **KEY TERM**
> **Automatic processes**: processes that occur rapidly and with minimal use of processing capacity.

According to Pascual-Leone (1984), a key aspect of mental capacity is "M". This refers to the number of schemes or units of cognition that a child can attend to or work with at any given time. M increases as children grow up, and this is one of the main reasons for cognitive development. Pascual-Leone assumed that increased M or processing capacity resulted from neurological development.

The information-processing approach of Pascual-Leone and Case revolves around the notion of scheme or basic unit of cognition, which resembles Piaget's schema. Case (1974) identified three kinds of scheme:

Figurative schemes	Operative schemes	Executive schemes
Internal representations of items of information with which a subject is familiar or of perceptual configurations he or she can recognise	Internal representations of function (rules), which can be applied to one set of figurative schemes in order to generate a new set	Internal representations of procedures which can be applied in the face of particular problem situations, in an attempt to reach particular objectives
For example: recognising one's own school from a photograph	For example: deciding that two photographs depict the same school	For example: looking at a work colleague and deciding whether to use an operative scheme related to work goals or an operative scheme related to social goals

According to this theory, a child's ability to solve a problem depends on four basic factors. First, there is the range of schemes that the child has available. Second, there is the child's M-power or mental capacity, which increases with age. Third, there is the extent to which the child uses all of its available M-power. Fourth, there is the relative importance that the child gives to perceptual cues on the one hand and to all other cues on the other.

How do children acquire new schemes? Case (1974) suggested that they can be formed by modifying existing schemes. Alternatively, new schemes can be acquired by the combination or consolidation of several existing schemes.

Experimental evidence

This theory can be applied to many of Piaget's findings. For example, Piaget found that children below the age of 7 generally did not realise that the amount of water remains the same when it is poured from one container into another that is taller and thinner. According to Piaget, this is because these children do not understand the logic of conservation. According to Pascual-Leone (1984), this is often because the children do not have enough mental capacity to hold all the relevant schemes in mind. Suppose that the conservation task were made easier by filling the containers with beads and allowing children to count the number of beads. Piaget would still expect the children to fail, because they have not learned the underlying logic, whereas Case and Pascual-Leone would predict more success, because the demands on mental capacity have been reduced. When this study was carried out, the findings supported the neo-Piagetians rather than Piaget (Bower, 1979).

The value of this approach can also be seen in a study discussed by Case (1992). Children and adolescents aged between 10 and 18 were asked to draw a picture of a mother who was looking out of the window of her home and could see her son playing peekaboo with her in the park on the other side of the road. The younger participants found it very hard to do this. They could draw the mother in the house and the boy in the park, but they did not seem to have enough mental capacity to integrate the two parts

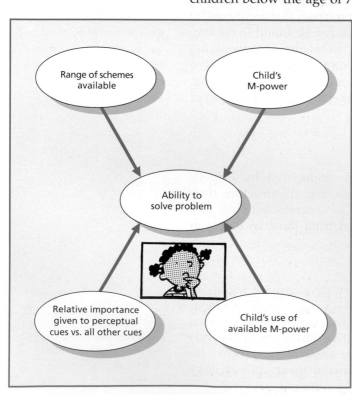

of the drawing. In contrast, the older participants did produce an integrated drawing, because they had greater M-power.

Evaluation

There are some clear advantages to this theory compared with Piaget's approach. First, the information-processing approach has been applied with great success to the study of adult cognition, and it is reasonable to extend that approach to children's cognition. Second, Piaget argued that children fail to solve problems because they lack the necessary logical or other structures, rather than because of processing limitations. It is argued correctly within the theory of Case and Pascual-Leone that many problem-solving failures in children depend on processing limitations or insufficient M-power. Third, the concepts (e.g. different types of schemes) used by theorists such as Case and Pascual-Leone tend to be easier to measure than the schemas included in Piaget's theory.

On the negative side, there are problems in testing the theory. First, it is often hard to work out how many schemes are required to solve a task, or to decide how many schemes are actually being used by a given child.

Second, it is not at all easy to calculate someone's mental capacity. There is a danger of assuming that success results from sufficient mental capacity and failure results from insufficient mental capacity, without actually measuring mental capacity at all. When that happens, the findings are simply re-described rather than explained.

Third, it is very hard to distinguish between changes in strategies and changes in M-space or mental capacity. As Meadows (1986, p.41) pointed out, "Attempts to measure the size of M-space have to hold strategy and strategy demands constant if they are to distinguish between changes in the size of M-space and changes in the way a stably-sized space is used." In fact, Case (1985) admitted that children's cognitive development may depend more on changing strategies than on basic mental capacity.

If schemas are hypothetical structures, why might this be a limitation of theories that include them?

COMPARISON OF THE THREE MAIN APPROACHES		
Information-processing	**Vygotsky**	**Piaget**
Children's intellectual development is explained in terms of automatic processes	Children are participating in an interactive process whereby knowledge becomes individualised through socially and culturally determined knowledge	Children's intellectual development can be seen in terms of the individual's adaptation to the environment

Practical Applications to Education

The theories of cognitive development put forward by Piaget, by Vygotsky, and by information-processing theorists have been very influential in the field of education. In this section of the chapter, we will focus on some of the ways in which their ideas have had an impact on education in schools. However, it is worth noting that many of the educational methods discussed are also used very successfully by parents and others outside the school context.

Piaget's approach

Piaget himself did not focus very much on the usefulness of his theory for educational practice. However, many people working in education have done precisely that. The Plowden Report in 1967 suggested that some of Piaget's ideas should be used in schools. Years later, the Nuffield Science approach to education was based on the Piagetian notions that children should be actively involved in learning, and that concrete practical work should precede the more abstract aspects of science. Next we consider three of the main ways in which Piagetian theory has been applied in education (see Gross, 1996).

1. What can children learn?

According to Piaget, what children can learn is determined by their current stage of cognitive development. In other words, it is very much limited to what they are "ready"

to learn. More specifically, children can only deal successfully with tasks that make use of the various cognitive structures and operations they have already mastered.

This prediction has received little support. Several attempts have been made to teach concrete operations to preschool children. The ability to perform concrete operational tasks is normally learned at about the age of 7. Thus, it should not be possible on Piagetian theory for much younger children to perform them successfully. However, provision of suitable training to four-year-olds usually leads to reasonably good performance on such tasks (Brainerd, 1983). In other words, Piaget seems to have underestimated the ability of children to cope with new kinds of intellectual challenge.

2. How should children be taught?

According to Piaget, children learn best when they engage in a process of active **self-discovery**. Children apply the processes of assimilation and accommodation to their active involvement with the world around them. Teachers can encourage this by creating a state of disequilibrium, in which the child's existing schemas or cognitive structures are shown to be inadequate. Disequilibrium can be created by asking children difficult questions, and by encouraging them to ask questions.

Some of these ideas can be applied to playgroup practices and to children playing with toys. According to Piaget, children will obtain the most benefit from playgroups and from toys when they are actively involved in a process of self-discovery. In what Piaget called mastery play, the child uses new motor schemas in several different situations. This helps to strengthen the child's learning.

Piaget's preferred educational approach can be contrasted with the more traditional approach, in which the teacher provides relatively passive children with knowledge. Piaget argued that this approach (sometimes called **tutorial training**) is much less effective than self-discovery. In his own words, "Every time we teach a child something, we prevent him from discovering it on his own."

Brainerd (1983) reviewed the relevant studies. He concluded that, "although self-discovery training can produce learning, it is generally less effective than tutorial learning." Meadows (1994) arrived at a similar, but broader conclusion: "Piagetian theory emphasises the individual child as the virtually independent constructor of his own development, an emphasis that under-values the contribution of other people to cognitive development and excludes teaching and cultural influences."

Socio-cognitive conflict. The notion of disequilibrium was developed by neo-Piagetians such as Doise and Mugny (1984). They argued that cognitive development involves the resolution of **socio-cognitive conflict**, which is produced by exposure to the differing views of others. In other words, they emphasised social factors in learning more than did Piaget.

Evidence indicating the importance of socio-cognitive conflict was reported by Ames and Murray (1982), in a study on children of 6 and 7 who had failed on conservation tasks. Some of the children were given corrective feedback, and others were exposed to children who already knew about conservation. Still others were paired with children who had also failed to conserve, but who had provided a different wrong answer from the one they had produced. Children in the last condition showed the greatest improvement in ability to conserve. Presumably this happened because socio-cognitive conflict and the need to consider the task in detail were greatest in this condition.

The neo-Piagetians also emphasised the importance of **social marking**, which involves conflict between an individual's cognitive understanding and some social rule. Doise et al. (1981) studied conservation of liquid in children between the ages of 4 and 6 who did not initially show conservation. Social marking was induced in some pairs of children by reminding them of the social rule that both children deserved the same reward. Other pairs of children were not reminded of this rule. The children in the social marking

Cross-cultural issues: Most children in Western societies spend many years in school. What implication might this have for trying to apply such a universal theory to all children?

KEY TERMS

Self-discovery: an active approach to learning in which the child is encouraged to use his or her initiative in learning.

Tutorial training: a traditional approach in which the teacher imparts knowledge to fairly passive students.

Socio-cognitive conflict: intellectual conflict produced by exposure to the differing views of others.

Social marking: conflict between an individual's cognitive understanding and a social rule.

condition saw a conflict between the social rule and the apparently different amounts of liquid in the two containers, and this helped them to show conservation.

3. What should children be taught?

Piaget claimed that cognitive development depends very much on children learning a range of schemas or cognitive structures (e.g. operations). Many of these schemas are based on mathematical or logical principles. It follows that it should be useful for children to study mathematics and logic, as well as science subjects that provide illustrations of these principles at work. Of crucial importance is the notion that the learning material must not be too complex and far removed from the child's existing schemas. According to Piaget, children can only learn effectively when they possess the relevant underlying schemas.

The major weakness of Piaget's position is that the cognitive structures he emphasised are of rather limited value for many kinds of learning. It is not clear that concrete and formal operations are of much relevance to the learning of foreign languages or of history. Thus, his approach applies only to a small number of subjects taught at school.

Which school subjects are difficult to link with Piaget's theory? Which subjects fit well with the theory?

Evaluation

In sum, Piaget's ideas have influenced educational practice in several countries. However, the available evidence indicates that this influence has been of limited value. In some cases (e.g. tutorial training), the more traditional approach seems to be superior to Piaget's alternative approach.

Vygotsky's approach

Vygotsky's key contribution to educational practice was the notion that children typically learn best in a social context in which someone who is more knowledgeable carefully guides and encourages their learning efforts. Thus, children can be regarded as apprentices who are taught the necessary skills by those who already possess them, by means of scaffolding. Effective teachers or tutors will generally reduce their control over the learning process when children are performing successfully, but will increase their control when children start making errors.

Vygotsky's ideas are relevant at home as well as in the school environment. Some parents do not make use of scaffolding, and do not discuss issues with their children in a way appropriate to their level of understanding. As a result, the children tend to have poor concentration, and find it hard to develop activities (Meadows, 1994).

To be an effective tutor, this father needs to avoid interfering while his son is managing alone, but be prepared to help when the boy gets stuck.

Peer tutoring

According to Vygotsky, it is important for those involved in educating children to focus on the children's zone of proximal development. It could be argued that the ideal tutors are children who are slightly older and more advanced than the children being taught. Such tutors have useful knowledge to communicate to the children being taught. They should also remember the limitations in their own knowledge and understanding when they were one or two years younger. The approach we have just described is known as **peer tutoring**, and it has become increasingly popular in schools.

Peer tutoring is generally effective. Barnier (1989) looked at the performance of six- and seven-year-olds on various spatial and perspective-taking tasks. Those who were exposed to brief sessions of peer tutoring with seven- and eight-year-old tutors performed better than those who were not. The benefits of peer tutoring have been found in various cultures. Ellis and Gauvain (1992) compared seven-year-old Navaho children and Euro-American children who performed a maze game. They were tutored by either one or two nine-year-old tutors working together. The children from both cultures benefited more

Peer tutoring: a girl teaches her younger sister to count.

Think back to your own experiences at school: which method helped you learn most successfully?

Does thinking about the ideas underlying a task link more closely with the Piagetian or the information-processing approach?

from the paired tutors than from the individual ones, and the benefit was the same in both cultures. There were some cultural differences in the teaching style of the tutors: the Euro-American tutors gave many more verbal instructions, and were generally less patient.

Collaboration and conflict

Forman and Cazden (1985) found that collaboration as recommended by Vygotsky and conflict as recommended by the neo-Piagetians both have a role to play. They studied nine-year-olds who had to carry out an experiment on chemical reactions. Collaboration among the children was very useful early on when the apparatus had to be set up. Later on, however, when they had to make decisions about how to carry out the experiment (e.g. which combinations of elements would produce which effects), conflict seemed to be more useful than collaboration. An important implication of this study is that any given teaching method is likely to work better in some situations than in others.

Learning through play

Vygotsky also argued that children can learn much through play. According to Vygotsky (1976, p.552):

> *In play, the child functions above his average age, above his usual everyday behaviour, in play he is head high above himself.*

Why is this? A key reason is because children at play generally make use of some aspects of their own culture. For example, they may pretend to be a firefighter or a doctor, or they may play with toys that are specific to their culture. This relationship to their own culture enhances learning.

Evaluation

There is convincing evidence that the scaffolding provided by peers or by teachers can be very effective in promoting effective learning at school. However, the Vygotskyan approach has various limitations. First, as Durkin (1995, p.375) pointed out, the whole approach is based on the dubious assumption that, "helpful tutors team up with eager tutees to yield maximum learning outcomes." In fact, as Salomon and Globerson (1989) pointed out, there are several reasons why this assumption is often incorrect. For example, if there is too much status difference between the tutor and the learner, the learner may become uninvolved in the learning process. Another possibility is what Salomon and Globerson called "ganging up on the task", in which the tutor and learner agree that the task is not worth doing properly.

Second, Durkin (1995) argued that the Vygotskyan approach may be better suited to some kinds of tasks than to others. Many of the successful uses of scaffolding have been on construction tasks of various kinds. In contrast, Howe, Tolmie, and Rodgers (1992) studied peer tutoring on a task concerned with understanding motion down an incline. Peer tutoring was of very little benefit, whereas thinking about the underlying ideas proved useful.

Third, the main focus of the Vygotskyan approach to education is on the contribution made by the tutor or expert to the understanding of the child or apprentice. In fact, it is probable that the success or otherwise of scaffolding depends crucially on the responsiveness of the tutor to the thoughts and actions of the child. In other words, those who favour Vygotsky's approach sometimes emphasise *external* factors in learning (e.g. the instructions given by the tutor) while minimising *internal factors* (e.g. the child's knowledge and activities).

Information-processing approach

Task analysis and error analysis

There are several implications of the information-processing approach for education. The most important one is that teachers should engage in a careful task analysis of the information they want to communicate to the children in their class. This is valuable in ensuring that the material is presented in the most effective way. It is also of value in identifying the reasons why some children perform a task inaccurately. If teachers have a clear idea of the information and processes needed to perform the task, they can analyse children's errors to see which rules or processes are being used wrongly. We will consider concrete examples of these implications.

Reading and mathematics. Information-processing researchers have shown that there are two different ways in which people can read individual words:

1. Use is made of rules to translate the written letters and syllables of the word into sound patterns.
2. The word and its pronunciation are found in long-term memory; this approach works best with fairly familiar words.

These two ways correspond to two methods of teaching reading: the phonic method, in which the word is broken down into parts (e.g. c-a-t), and the look-and-say or whole-word method. Many teachers used to favour one method or the other, but it is increasingly recognised that the process of learning to read can be speeded up by using a combination of the two methods.

How was spelling taught in your school? What rules of spelling do you remember?

Brown and Burton (1978) used errors to identify children's problems in mathematics (see Cardwell et al., 1996). They used the term "bug" to refer to the systematic errors in the arithmetic rules used by children. For example, a child might claim that $736 - 464 = 372$ and that $871 - 663 = 218$ because he or she is using the mistaken rule that subtractions in the hundreds, tens, and units columns are never affected by what has happened in the column to the right. Brown and Burton devised computerised games that provided teachers with training in identifying bugs. As a result, teachers detected bugs more quickly than before, and they appreciated that some errors in mathematics are due to faulty rules rather than simply to lack of attention.

Other implications

Other implications are as follows (see Cardwell et al., 1996):

1. Parts of the information-processing system, especially those concerned with attention and short-term memory, have very limited capacity. As a result, it is important that teachers present tasks in such a way that these limited capacities are not overloaded. The development of automatic processes is very useful in this connection.
2. Children benefit from gaining **metacognitive knowledge** about cognitive processes; such knowledge involves understanding the value of various cognitive processes (e.g. knowing that processing of meaning will enhance long-term memory).
3. Tasks that involve **implicit learning** need to be taught in a different way from other tasks. Implicit learning was defined by Seger (1994, p.163) as "learning complex information without complete verbalisable knowledge of what is learned." There is often little value in giving people explicit instructions on implicit learning tasks (see discussion that follows).

Implication 1. With respect to the first implication, Beck and Carpenter (1986) argued that children often find it hard to understand what they read because their processing capacity is focused on identifying individual words and parts of words. Accordingly, they gave children huge amounts of practice in identifying and making use of sub-word units such as syllables. This led to substantial increases in the speed and accuracy of word recognition, and also produced enhanced comprehension of reading material.

The two approaches to reading (phonic and whole-word) are used separately or together in the wide variety of materials available for teaching and developing reading skills.

KEY TERMS
Metacognitive knowledge: knowledge about the usefulness of various cognitive processes relevant to learning.
Implicit learning: complex learning that occurs without the learner being able to verbalise clearly what he or she has learned.

Implication 2. Children and even adults often lack important metacognitive knowledge. For example, they realise that words that have been processed for meaning are more likely to be remembered than words that have not (see Chapter 14), but they greatly underestimate the increased probability of recall (Eysenck & Keane, 1995).

In order to understand a text fully, readers need to focus on the structure of the text, including identifying its main theme. However, children typically lack this metacognitive knowledge, and focus on individual words and sentences rather than the overall structure. Palincsar and Brown (1984) gave children specific training in thinking about the structure of the texts they were reading. This led to a significant increase in their comprehension ability.

Implication 3. Berry and Broadbent (1984) used a complex implicit learning task in which a sugar-production factory had to be "managed" to maintain a specific level of sugar output. This task involved implicit learning, because most of those who learned to perform the task effectively were unable to explain the principles underlying their performance. Of key importance, Berry and Broadbent found that giving their participants very explicit instructions about how to control sugar production did not improve performance. Children improve their performance on implicit learning tasks by performing them repeatedly with feedback, rather than by being told what to do.

Evaluation

The information-processing approach has proved of use in education. Its greatest value is that it provides techniques for identifying the processes and strategies required to complete tasks successfully. However, the approach is limited in several ways. First, there are many tasks where it is hard to identify the underlying processes. Second, it is often hard to assess accurately the capacity limitations of any given child, and so the point at which overload will occur is not easy to predict. Third, the information-processing approach often indicates *what* processes are involved in performing a task without specifying *how* children can learn to acquire those processes.

SUMMARY OF THE DIFFERENT APPROACHES TO EDUCATION		
Piaget	**Vygotsky**	**Information-processing**
Child-centred ("discovery learning")	Teacher–child interaction ("social learning")	Development of skills, strategies, and rules

Development of Intelligence-test Performance

What is intelligence?

This section of the chapter is concerned with the factors involved in the development of children's intelligence-test performance. An obvious starting point is to consider the meaning of intelligence (see also Chapter 27). According to Sternberg (1985, p.45), intelligence is

> *mental activity directed towards purposive adaptation to, and selection and shaping of, real-world environments relevant to one's life.*

There tends to be a gap between such definitions of intelligence and tests of intelligence. Sternberg offered a broad definition of intelligence, which includes the ability to cope successfully with life. In contrast, most intelligence tests measure basic cognitive abilities such as thinking, problem solving, and reasoning. These cognitive abilities are of value when coping with life, but successful individuals tend also to possess various "streetwise" skills not assessed by most intelligence tests.

Tests of intelligence

The first proper test of intelligence was devised by Binet and Simon in 1905. Binet was asked to devise an intelligence test that would allow mentally retarded children to be identified at as young an age as possible. The reason for this was so that such children could be given special educational facilities to remedy their mental retardation. Binet and Simon made use of various tests such as anagrams and providing a precis of a story, which were intended to assess high-level cognitive skills. According to Binet and Simon (1916, p.42–43):

Street skills such as the commercial, bargaining, and economic abilities these children possess are not measured by conventional intelligence tests.

> *To judge well, to comprehend well, to reason well, these are the essential activities of intelligence. A person may be a moron or an imbecile if he is lacking in judgement; but with good judgement he can never be either.*

The most common measure of intelligence is the intelligence quotient or IQ, obtained from an intelligence test (see Chapter 27). This is a measure of general intelligence that does not take account of the fact that some people are much more intelligent in some ways than others. For example, consider the case of a boy called Christopher. His tested IQ was 75 or less, which is substantially below the population average of 100. In spite of that, he could speak 17 languages, and many of them fluently (Smith & Tsimpli, 1991).

Class and cultural differences

Another limitation of intelligence tests is that there are various reasons why they may underestimate children's intelligence. First, children may not be well motivated to do their best. Zigler et al. (1973) studied the intelligence-test performance of preschool children from poor and middle-class backgrounds. Those from poor backgrounds showed gains of almost 10 points of IQ after a play session or when tested a second time, indicating that their IQ assessed in the normal way was an underestimate. In contrast, middle-class children showed a much smaller increase of about 3 IQ points when given a play session or tested a second time.

How and why might some children be motivated to perform well in IQ tests?

Second, most intelligence tests are devised by white, middle-class psychologists from Western societies. As a result, the tests they produce may underestimate the intelligence of those from other cultures or social backgrounds. Some support for this point of view was reported by Williams (1972), who devised the Black Intelligence Test of Cultural Homogeneity (BITCH). This test was aimed at black American children, and white American children did less well on this test than most standard ones.

Third, intelligence tests do not take account of the fact that cultures vary in the skills that are valued. For example, Serpell (1979) compared the performance of English and Zambian children on two tasks. The English children did better at a drawing task, whereas the Zambian children did better on a wire-shaping task.

Why do you think drawing might be less valued than a practical skill like wire-shaping in some cultures?

Heredity and environment

Why are some children more intelligent than others? At the most general level, there are only two factors that could be responsible: heredity and environment. Heredity consists of each person's genetic endowment, and environment consists of the situations and experiences encountered by people in the course of their lives. It is generally assumed that individual differences in intelligence depend on both heredity and environment. As we will see, many psychologists have tried to determine the relative importance of heredity and environment in determining intelligence. However, the Canadian psychologist Donald Hebb argued that this is an essentially meaningless issue. He claimed that it is like asking whether a field's area is determined more by its length or by its width. Of course, its area depends equally on both length and width. In similar fashion, Hebb argued, intelligence depends equally on both heredity and environment.

Hebb's argument is perhaps not as convincing as it sounds. Even though it is clear that the area of a field depends equally on its length and width, we can still reasonably ask whether the areas of different fields vary more because of differences in their lengths or in terms of their widths. In the same way, we can ask whether individual differences in intelligence depend more on differences in genetic endowment or on environmental differences.

Those who believe in the importance of heredity draw a distinction between the **genotype** and the **phenotype**. The genotype is the genetic potential with which an individual is endowed, whereas the phenotype consists of an individual's observable characteristics. So far as intelligence is concerned, we cannot access the genotype. All that can be done is to assess the phenotype by means of administering an intelligence test.

Twin studies

The best method of assessing the relative importance of heredity and environment in determining individual differences in intelligence is to conduct a twin study. There are two kinds of twins: **monozygotic twins** and **dizygotic twins**. Monozygotic twins derive from the same fertilised ovum, and have essentially identical genotypes. It is for this reason that they are often called identical twins. Dizygotic twins derive from two different fertilised ova. As a result, their genotypes are no more similar than those of ordinary siblings. Dizygotic twins are sometimes called fraternal twins.

What would we expect to find in a twin study? If heredity is very important, then monozygotic twins should be considerably more similar in intelligence than dizygotic twins. On the other hand, if environmental factors are all-important, then monozygotic twins should be no more alike than dizygotic twins.

What does the evidence suggest? A review based on 111 studies was published by Bouchard and McGue (1981; see pages 741–742). They left out the findings from Burt's (1955) study, because there is clear evidence that he made up some or all of his data. The mean correlation coefficient for monozygotic twins was +0.86, indicating that monozygotic twins are generally very similar to each other in intelligence. The mean correlation coefficient for dizygotic twins was +0.60, indicating only a moderate degree of similarity in intelligence.

The fact that monozygotic twins were much more similar in intelligence than dizygotic twins suggests that heredity is of major significance in determining intelligence. However, that is on the assumption that the degree of environmental similarity experienced by monozygotic twins is the same as that experienced by dizygotic twins. However, monozygotic twins are treated in a more similar fashion than dizygotic twins in the following ways: parental treatment; playing together; spending time together; dressing in a similar style; and being taught by the same teachers (Loehlin & Nichols, 1976). When these data were considered in detail by Kamin (1981), it emerged that there was an effect of similarity of treatment on similarity of intelligence in the form of IQ.

Twins who live apart

In a few twin studies, use has been made of monozygotic twins brought up apart in different families. Such twin pairs would seem to be of particular value in deciding on the relative importance of genetic factors and of environment in determining intelligence. Those arguing that genetic factors are of most importance would expect such twins to resemble each other closely in intelligence. In contrast, those favouring an environmentalist position would argue that placing twins in different environments should ensure that they are not similar in intelligence. According to Bouchard and McGue's (1981) review, the mean correlation coefficient for monozygotic twins brought up apart is +0.72.

The findings from monozygotic twins brought up apart seem on the face of it to provide convincing evidence for the importance of genetic factors. However, there are problems with the evidence. Many monozygotic twins brought up apart were, in fact, brought up in different branches of the same family. Other monozygotic twins were actually brought up together for several years before being separated. Thus, many pairs

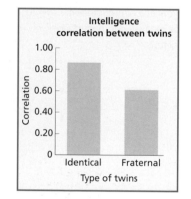

Intelligence correlation between twins

of monozygotic twins actually experience rather similar environments. As a result, at least some of the similarity in IQ of monozygotic twins brought up apart is due to environmental rather than genetic factors. However, the monozygotic twins in the Minnesota Study of Twins Reared Apart were separated in infancy and reared in different environments. In spite of this, their IQs correlated at about +0.75 (Bouchard et al., 1990).

The Collister twins: identical twin brothers, married to identical twin sisters.

Evaluation

The evidence from twin studies suggests that individual differences in intelligence are about 50% due to genetic factors and 50% due to environmental factors. However, there are at least three reasons for being cautious about accepting this conclusion. First, there are problems with many of the studies, and it is often unclear whether environmental similarity has been properly controlled.

Second, intelligence is assessed by means of IQ obtained from standard intelligence tests. It is debatable whether IQ is an adequate measure of intelligence.

Third, the role of heredity in determining individual differences in intelligence tends to increase with age. According to Plomin (1990), about 30% of individual differences in intelligence among children are due to heredity, and this figure increases to 50% in adolescence, and to more than 50% in adult life. This puzzling change may occur because environmental differences are smaller among adults than among children.

Can you give examples of large differences in environment between communities living in the same society?

Fourth, the figure of 50% of individual differences in intelligence being due to heredity applies only to the small number of cultures that have been studied so far. The more similar the environmental factors experienced by those living in a given culture, the greater will be the effect of genetic factors in determining individual differences in intelligence. Indeed, if everyone in a society were exposed to precisely the same environmental conditions, then all individual differences in intelligence would be due to genetic factors! On the other hand, in societies in which there are enormous environmental differences between various sections of the community, the role of genetic factors in producing individual differences in intelligence would be rather small.

Adoption studies

Another method of assessing the role of genetic and environmental factors in intelligence is by means of adoption studies. The measured intelligence of adopted children might depend more on genetic factors (e.g. the intelligence of its biological parents) or it might depend more on environmental factors (e.g. the intelligence of its adoptive parents).

Horn (1983) discussed the findings from the Texas Adoption Project, which involved almost 500 adopted children. The correlation between the adopted children and their biological mothers for intelligence was +0.28, indicating that there was only a moderate degree of similarity in intelligence. The correlation between the adopted children and their adoptive mothers was even lower at +0.15. Both of these correlations are so low that it is hard to make any definite statements about the role played by heredity and environment.

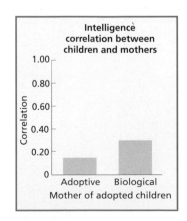

The correlations between adopted children and their adoptive mothers, and between adopted children and their biological mothers are so low that they do not allow us to make any definite statements about the role played by heredity and environment in intelligence.

Change over time

Loehlin, Horn, and Willerman (1989) found that there were some differences in the findings when the adopted children were tested again 10 years later. Shared family environment between the adopted children and their adoptive mothers was reduced in importance, whereas genetic factors had a greater influence on the adopted children's intelligence than had been the case 10 years earlier.

The notion that shared family environment has less influence on intelligence as children become older received additional support in a review by Plomin (1988). He reported that the correlation between genetically unrelated children growing up together in adoptive families was about +0.30 for intelligence when they were still children. However, the correlation dropped to zero in adolescence and adulthood. The major reason for this change is presumably because environmental factors outside the home become increasingly important from adolescence onwards. The zero correlation indicates that the influence of any environmental factors within the home does not seem to be long-lasting.

Capron and Duyne

Capron and Duyne (1989) reported a very impressive adoption study. They made use of four very different groups of adopted children. These groups involved all four possible combinations of biological parents of high or low socio-economic status and adoptive parents of high or low socio-economic status. The predictions are fairly straightforward. The measured intelligence of the adopted children should depend mainly on the socio-economic status of the biological parents if genetic factors are of more importance, but should depend mostly on the socio-economic status of the adoptive parents if environmental factors are more important. In fact, the effects of the socio-economic status of the biological and of the adoptive parents were much the same. These findings suggest that genetic and environmental factors were of about equal importance in determining the intelligence of the adopted children.

This study is important for various reasons. First, it is hard to interpret the findings from most adoption studies because of **selective placement**, which involves adoption agencies placing adopted children into families resembling those of their biological parents in terms of educational and social backgrounds. When there is selective placement, it is hard to disentangle the effects of heredity and environment. The design of the study by Capron and Duyne largely eliminated the issue of selective placement. Second, the use of groups in which there was a large difference between the socio-economic status of the biological parents and that of the adoptive parents is unusual, but has the advantage of making it easier to assess the relative impacts of heredity and environment.

Discussion points

1. Why is the study by Capron and Duyne of importance?
2. Are adoption studies more or less useful than twin studies in trying to decide on the relative importance of heredity and environment in determining individual differences in intelligence?

Evaluation

The findings of Capron and Duyne (1989) are consistent with those from twin studies in suggesting that about 50% of the variance in intelligence scores is due to genetic factors. However, less clear findings have emerged from other adoption studies (e.g. Horn, 1983), in part because of the problems of interpretation posed by selective placement. In many studies, some of the correlation between adopted children and their biological parents is due to selective placement rather than to genetic factors.

Environmental factors

We have seen from the findings of twin and adoption studies that environmental factors are of major importance in producing individual differences in measured intelligence. Somewhat more direct evidence for the role of the environment comes from studies in

GENERAL CRITICISMS OF IQ TESTS, ADOPTION STUDIES, AND TWIN STUDIES		
IQ tests	**Adoption studies**	**Twin studies**
Debatable whether IQ is an adequate measurement of intelligence	Selective placement makes it hard to determine the effects of heredity and environment	Environmental similarity often ocurs
Cultural differences not always considered	Heredity is less well controlled than in twin studies	Twins raised separately actually raised by different branches of the same family
		Twins had spent some years together before being separated

which entire communities have gone through large-scale environmental changes. Wheeler (1932, 1942) studied the members of an isolated community in Tennessee in the United States. This community gradually became more integrated into society as schools and roads were built, and communications with the outside world developed. The children in this community originally had a mean IQ of 82. Ten years later, the children's mean IQ was 93.

The limitation of Wheeler's study is that we do not know which of the many environmental changes within the Tennessee community studied were of most importance in affecting intelligence. As might be expected, there is good evidence that the amount of schooling is important.

Ceci (1991) reviewed studies showing that children who start school after the age of 6 have lower IQs than other children. In addition, children's IQs are lower if they miss long periods of schooling through illness or some other reason, and there is a small decline in IQs over the summer holiday.

The HOME inventory

What is needed is to compare several different aspects of the environment in terms of the effects they have on children's level of intelligence. One suitable measure is the Home Observation for Measurement of the Environment (or HOME) inventory. This inventory provides measures in the following six environmental categories:

A stimulating environment has been said to encourage a child's development. What might this environment include?

- Emotional and verbal responsivity of parent.
- Avoidance of restriction and punishment.
- Organisation of physical and temporal environment.
- Provision of appropriate play materials.
- Parental involvement with child.
- Opportunities for variety in daily stimulation.

Gottfried (1984) has addressed the issue of which of these aspects of the home environment have the greatest impact on children's IQs. The evidence from a number of studies indicated that provision of appropriate play materials, parental involvement with the child, and opportunities for variety in daily stimulation predicted children's subsequent IQs better than did any of the other three aspects.

There is a potential problem with this approach. The findings discussed by Gottfried are correlational in nature, and so they cannot be used to show that a stimulating home environment actually increases children's IQs. It is possible that more intelligent parents are more likely than less intelligent ones to provide a stimulating home environment for their children, and that it is the parental intelligence rather than the home environment they provide which is of importance.

Yeates et al. (1983) addressed the causality issue in a longitudinal study of young children. The mother's IQ predicted children's IQs at the age of 2 better than did scores on the HOME inventory. However, the HOME inventory predicted the IQs of the same children at the age of 4 better than did the mother's IQ. These findings suggest that a stimulating home environment is beneficial for children's intellectual development, and that this beneficial effect becomes stronger as children develop.

The Rochester study

Sameroff et al. (1993) reported the findings of the Rochester Longitudinal Study, in which hundreds of children were followed from birth to adolescence. They identified 10 environmental factors which jointly accounted for 49% of individual differences in IQ. These factors were as follows:

- Mother has a history of mental illness.
- Mother did not go to high school.
- Mother has severe anxiety.
- Mother has rigid attitudes and values about her child's development.
- Few positive interactions between mother and child during infancy.
- Head of household has a semi-skilled job.
- Four or more children in the family.
- Father does not live with the family.
- Child belongs to a minority group.
- Family suffered 20 or more stressful events during the child's first four years of life.

Evaluation

The studies discussed in this section indicate that major environmental changes can produce significant changes in IQ. Thus, they strengthen the notion that intelligence depends to a major extent on environmental factors. However, it has not proved possible to determine precisely which aspects of the environment are most effective in influencing intellectual development. For example, consider the findings of Sameroff et al. (1993). They found that environmental factors such as mother not going to high school and head of household having a semi-skilled job were associated with low IQ in the children. This does not prove a causal relationship. It is possible that genetic factors play a part in producing these environmental factors *and* in producing low IQ in the children.

PERSONAL REFLECTIONS

- In my opinion, one of the greatest contributions that psychology could make to society is in the development of more effective ways of teaching children. Piaget, Vygotsky, and information-processing theorists have all made significant contributions. However, the available research is so limited and piecemeal that the potential usefulness of these approaches in the classroom has not been established. It would be better for decisions about teaching methods to be based on sound psychological evidence rather than on the whims of politicians.

SUMMARY

Piaget's theory

According to Piaget, a state of equilibrium or balance is achieved through processes of accommodation and assimilation. He put forward four stages of cognitive development: sensori-motor, during which development is intelligence through action; pre-operational, during which thinking is dominated by perception; concrete operations, during which logical thinking is applied to objects that are real or can be seen; and formal operations, during which logical thinking can be applied to potential events or abstract ideas. Piaget underestimated the cognitive abilities of children, he underestimated the piecemeal and unsystematic nature of cognitive development, and he described rather than explained cognitive development.

Vygotsky's theory

Vygotsky emphasised the notion that cognitive development depends very largely on social factors. What children can achieve with the assistance of others is generally more than they can achieve on their own; the difference between the two is the zone of proximal development. Scaffolding plays an important role in cognitive development. Social learning is not always effective, and Vygotsky underestimated the contribution of the individual child to his or her own cognitive development.

Information-processing approach

According to the information-processing approach, cognitive development is associated with an increase in knowledge, increased automatic processing, and an increase in mental capacity or M-power. Case argued that there are three kinds of schema or basic units of cognition: figurative; operative; and executive. Within his theory, over time children increase their range of schemes, their M-power, and their ability to use their M-power. It is hard to assess which schemes are being used and to measure M-power.

According to Piaget, what children can learn is determined by their current stage of cognitive development. He claimed that children learn best when engaged in a process of active self-discovery. He also argued that the study of subjects such as mathematics, logic, and science is valuable for the development of cognitive schemas. In general, active self-discovery is less effective than the more traditional approach of tutorial training. The neo-Piagetians attach much importance to conflict, and especially socio-cognitive conflict, as a way to promote effective learning at school. According to Vygotsky, scaffolding provided by teachers or by peer tutors is an effective form of learning. The evidence suggests that conflict works well with some learning tasks, whereas scaffolding is more effective with others. According to the information-processing approach, teaching should be based on a sound understanding of the knowledge and processes required to perform different tasks. Teaching should also focus on preventing overload of short-term memory, on analysing the errors made by children, on developing children's metacognitive knowledge, and on avoidance of explicit instructions on implicit learning tasks.

Practical applications to education

Most intelligence tests measure basic cognitive abilities, but not "streetwise" skills. Twin studies have been used to assess the relative importance of heredity and environment in determining individual differences in intelligence. Identical twins tend to be more similar than fraternal twins in intelligence, with most findings suggesting that about 50% of individual differences in intelligence are due to heredity. However, this figure only applies to the specific cultures in which the studies were carried out, and it relies on the assumption that intelligence tests are a good measure of intelligence. Adoption studies generally confirm the findings of twin studies, but they have the disadvantage that neither genetic nor environmental factors can be assessed accurately. Environmental factors such as provision of appropriate play materials, parental involvement with the child, and variety in daily stimulation are all associated with increased IQ, but it is hard to prove that there is a causal link.

Development of intelligence-test performance

FURTHER READING

There is good coverage of most aspects of cognitive development in K. Durkin (1995), *Developmental social psychology: From infancy to old age*, Oxford: Blackwell. The information-processing approach is discussed fully by D.R. Shaffer (1993), *Developmental psychology: Childhood and adolescence (3rd Edn.)*, Pacific Grove, CA: Brooks/Cole. Factors associated with the development of intelligence test performance are discussed by M.W. Eysenck (1994a), *Individual differences: Normal and abnormal*, Hove, UK: Psychology Press.

REVISION QUESTIONS

1a	Outline *two* theories of cognitive development.	(12 marks)
1b	Analyse the research evidence on which *one* of these theories is based.	(12 marks)
2	Discuss applications of cognitive research to education (e.g. classroom practices).	(24 marks)
3	Discuss the contribution of genetic and environment factors to how well individuals perform on intelligence tests.	(24 marks)

17

Social Behaviour in Development

As children grow up, they have a developing sense of who they are and of their place in society. In this chapter, we will consider how this happens with respect to moral development, the development of gender, and the development of the self. What these three forms of development have in common is that they depend on the child's increasing involvement with society:

* Moral development occurs when the child begins to take account of the needs and wishes of other people.
* The development of gender occurs as the child comes to realise that society has various expectations of him or her as a consequence of being a boy or a girl.
* The development of self occurs when the child becomes aware of himself or herself as an individual, and begins to understand the views that other people have of him or her.

There has been much disagreement about the ways in which the child's increasing socialisation lead to these three forms of development. In this chapter we will be focusing on three of the major approaches: the psychodynamic, cognitive-developmental, and social learning theories.

Moral Development

We will deal here with the various stages of moral development. What is meant by the term "morality"? According to Shaffer (1993), **morality** implies "a set of principles or ideals that help the individual to distinguish right from wrong and to act on this distinction."

Why is morality important? Society cannot function effectively unless there is some agreement on what is right and wrong. Of course, there are moral and ethical issues (e.g. animal experiments) on which individual members of a given society have very different views. However, if there were controversy on all major moral issues, society would become chaotic.

Shaffer argued that human morality has three components. First, there is the *emotional component*. This is concerned with the feelings (e.g. guilt) associated with moral thoughts and behaviour. Second, there is the *cognitive component*. This is concerned with how we think about moral issues, and make decisions about what is right and wrong. Third, there is the *behavioural component*, which is concerned with how we behave. It includes the extent to which we lie, steal, cheat, or behave honourably.

Why should we distinguish among these components? First, there is often a significant difference between two components. We may know at the cognitive level that it is wrong to cheat, but we may still cheat at the behavioural level. Some people lead blameless lives

SHAFFER'S COMPONENTS OF HUMAN MORALITY		
Emotional	**Cognitive**	**Behavioural**
Feelings associated with moral behaviour	How we think about moral issues, and decide between right and wrong	How we behave
Theorist: Freud	Theorists: Piaget Kohlberg	Theorists: Bandura Mischel
Approach: Psychodynamic	Approach: Cognitive-developmental	Approach: Social learning

(behavioural component), but still feel guilty (emotional component). Second, the distinction among different moral components is useful in comparing theories of moral development. Freud emphasised the emotional component, Piaget and Kohlberg focused on the cognitive component, and social learning theorists concentrated on the behavioural component.

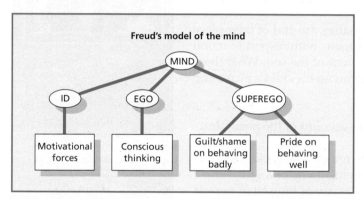

Freud's model of the mind

Psychodynamic theory

Sigmund Freud (1856–1939) argued that the human mind consists of three parts: the id, ego, and superego (see Chapter 2). The id deals with motivational forces (e.g. the sexual instinct); the ego is concerned with conscious thinking; and the superego is concerned with moral issues. The superego is divided into the conscience and the ego-ideal. Our conscience makes us feel guilty or ashamed when we have behaved badly, whereas our ego-ideal makes us feel proud of ourselves when we have behaved well in the face of temptation.

Freud suggested that the superego develops at the age of 5 or 6. Boys develop sexual desires for their mother, leading to an intense rivalry with their father. This state of affairs is known as the **Oedipus complex**. It makes boys feel very fearful, because they are much weaker than their father. This situation is resolved through the process of **identification**, in which boys imitate or copy the beliefs and behaviour of their father. As part of the identification process, boys adopt their father's moral standards, and this leads to the formation of the superego. According to Freud, the superego is "the heir of the Oedipus complex".

According to Freud, a similar process occurs in girls at about the same age. They develop an **Electra complex** based on their desires for their father. This complex is resolved by girls through identification with their mother and through adopting her moral standards. Freud claimed that girls do not identify with their father as strongly as boys identify with their mother. As a result, girls develop weaker superegos than boys. This is an example of gender bias, an issue that is discussed in more detail later in this chapter. However, Freud admitted that, "the majority of men are far behind the masculine ideal [in terms of superego strength]."

Freud developed his ideas about the Oedipus complex at a time when lone-parent families were very rare. What bearing do you think this may have had on his theorising?

Evidence

The main evidence available to Freud consisted of the accounts of his patients as they tried to remember their childhood. Such evidence is weak because of its reliance on patients' fallible memories. Another problem, identified by Meadows (1986, p.162) was that

> *there could be no refuting evidence since a demonstration that a person did not experience an Oedipus complex, feel penis-envy, etc., might be taken as evidence for the perfect repression [motivated forgetting] of the person's Oedipus complex, penis-envy, etc.*

Freud argued that fear of the same-sexed parent was of crucial importance in the development of the superego. Thus, parents who are aggressive and administer a lot of

KEY TERMS
Oedipus complex: in Freudian theory, the notion that young boys desire their mother sexually and so experience rivalry with their father.
Identification: in Freudian theory, children's imitation of the beliefs and behaviour of the same-sexed parent.
Electra complex: in Freudian theory, the notion that young girls desire their father.

punishment might be expected to have children with strong superegos. In fact, the opposite seems to be the case. Parents who make the most use of spanking and other forms of punishment tend to have children who behave badly and who experience little guilt or shame (Hoffman, 1988). However, the evidence is only damaging to Freud if we assume that fear of the same-sexed parent depends entirely on the *actual* levels of punishment used by parents. According to Freud, children who *believe* mistakenly that they are punished a lot would be expected to develop a strong superego, but this was not taken into account by Hoffman (1988).

Freud's hypothesis that girls have weaker superegos than boys has been disproved. Hoffman (1975) discussed a number of studies in which the behaviour of children on their own was assessed in order to see whether they did the things they had been told not to do. There was no difference between boys and girls in most of the studies. When there was a sex difference, it was the girls (rather than the boys) who were better at resisting temptation. However, it could be argued that ability to resist temptation is not a good measure of superego strength.

Cross-cultural studies have confirmed the findings of Hoffman (1975). Snarey (1985) reviewed 17 studies from 15 different countries around the world. Sex differences in moral development were found in only three of those studies.

Freud's theory suggests that punishment should develop a strong superego in the child. However, children who receive a lot of physical punishment tend to behave badly and experience little guilt or shame.

Evaluation

Freud put forward the first detailed theory of moral development. His basic assumptions that parents have a major influence on the moral development of their children, and that many moral values are acquired in the early years of life, are correct. However, most of his specific hypotheses are wrong.

There are several inadequacies with Freud's theory. First, he exaggerated the role of the same-sexed parent in the development of children's morality. The evidence indicates that the other-sexed parent and other children also generally play an important role (Shaffer, 1993).

Freud attached too much weight to emotional factors in morality and not enough to the cognitive processes that help to determine moral behaviour. Theorists such as Piaget and Kohlberg argued that such cognitive processes are the key to moral development. It could also be argued that Freud neglected the behavioural component of morality, which was studied in depth by the social learning theorists.

Freud claimed that children make more dramatic progress in moral development at about the age of 5 or 6 than they do in later childhood or adolescence. In fact, there are large changes in moral reasoning between the ages of 10 and 16 (e.g. Colby et al., 1983, see the later section describing Kohlberg's theory).

Freud's methods

The main source of evidence used by Freud was adults' memories of their childhood. However, not only is this evidence prone to distortion by the person who is remembering, it also cannot be proved or disproved. Freud did not see child patients, but dealt with parents, sometimes only through letters, which has led to speculation about his interpretations of particular behaviours. Freud claimed that the Oedipus and Electra complexes were unconscious phases that a child passed through on his or her way to identifying with the same-sex parent. However, if these phases are unconscious we have no way of proving that they did in fact happen, except indirectly through interpretations of children's behaviour.

A more general criticism of the psychodynamic approach stems from the way in which the theories are formulated. Freud's theory tends to "work backwards", for example, the result leads to the formation of a hypothesis. Freud did not so much predict behaviour as analyse it once it had happened. Finally, the period in which Freud was working must be considered. His patients mostly came from middle-class families, which at the time were ruled by strict disciplinarian regimes. At this point in history, the family would have had the most influence on the developing child. However, today outside pressures such as peer groups, school, and even television may prove as influential as the family in a child's development.

Cognitive-developmental theory: Piaget

According to Jean Piaget (1896–1980), children's thinking goes through a series of stages (see Chapter 16). The early stages focus on what the child can see and hear, whereas the later stages involve the ability to think in an abstract way about possible events that may never happen. Piaget argued that children's moral reasoning also proceeds through a number of different stages.

Piaget began to develop his ideas about moral reasoning by playing marbles with children of different ages. He was interested in seeing how well they understood the rules of the game, how important they thought it was to obey those rules, and so on. His observations led him to propose the following stages of moral development:

PIAGET'S STAGES OF MORAL DEVELOPMENT		
Premoral	**Moral realism (Heteronomous morality)**	**Moral relativism (Autonomous morality)**
0–5 years old	5–10 years old	10 years upwards
Little understanding of rules and other aspects.	Rigid thinking: rules must be obeyed. Actions are judged by their consequences.	Development of flexibility in moral issues. Understanding that people differ in moral standards. Rules can be broken and wrong behaviour is not always punished.
	Belief in: • Expiatory punishment • Immanent justice	Belief in: • Reciprocal punishment

1. Premoral period (0–5 years): children in this stage have very little understanding of rules or other aspects of morality.
2. Stage of moral realism or heteronomous morality (heteronomous means "subject to externally imposed rules") (5–10 years): children at this stage are rather rigid in their thinking—they believe that rules must be obeyed no matter what the circumstances (e.g. it's wrong to tell a lie even if it will spare someone's feelings). Children at this stage think that rules are made by important other people (e.g. parents), and that how bad an action is stems from its consequences, rather than from the actor's intentions. There are two other key features of the moral reasoning of children at this stage. First, they believe in **expiatory punishment**: the naughtier the behaviour, the greater should be the punishment. However, there is no idea that the punishment should fit the crime. For example, a child who drops a freshly baked cake on the floor should be spanked rather than having to help to bake another cake. Second, children between the ages of 5 and 10 strongly favour the notion of fairness. This leads them to believe in *immanent justice*, which is the idea that naughty behaviour will always be punished in some way.
3. Stage of moral relativism or autonomous morality (10 years upwards): children at this stage think in a more flexible way about moral issues. They understand that moral rules evolve from human relationships, and that people differ in their standards of morality. They also understand that most rules of morality can be broken sometimes. If a violent man with a gun demands to be told where your mother is, it is perfectly acceptable to tell a lie and say that you do not know. There are other major differences from the previous stage. First, the child now thinks that the wrongness of an action depends far more on the individual's intentions than on the consequences of his or her behaviour. Second, children in this stage believe in **reciprocal punishment** rather than expiatory punishment. Thus, the punishment should fit the crime. Third, children in this stage have learned that people often behave wrongly but manage to avoid punishment. Thus, they no longer believe in immanent justice.

Why does moral reasoning change during childhood? According to Piaget, there are two main factors involved. First, young children are egocentric in their thinking, seeing the world only from their own point of view. At about the age of 7, they become less egocentric. Their growing awareness of the fact that other people have a different point of view allows them to develop more mature moral reasoning. Second, older children develop flexible ideas of morality because they are exposed to the different views of other children of the same age. This leads them to question their own values. In contrast, most younger children have rather rigid ideas of morality. What counts as good or bad behaviour is determined very much by the reactions of their parents.

Evidence

Children in most Western societies go through Piaget's stages of moral development in the order specified by Piaget (Shaffer, 1993). There is also evidence to support many of the details of the theory. For example, Piaget argued that children in the stage of moral realism judge actions by their consequences rather than by the actor's intentions. Piaget (1932) obtained evidence for this. Children in this stage were told about a boy called John who opened a door, and by so doing broke 15 cups on the other side of the door. They were also told about Henry, who broke one cup while trying to reach some jam. Even though John had no idea there were any cups there, he was still regarded as being naughtier than Henry because he broke more cups.

Other evidence indicates that Piaget underestimated the ability of children in the stage of moral realism to take account of the actor's intentions. Costanzo et al. (1973) used stories in which the characters had good or bad intentions, and in which the outcomes were positive or negative. As Piaget had found, young children almost always ignored the actor's intentions when the consequences were negative. However, they were as likely as older children to take account of the actor's intentions when the consequences were positive.

Piaget argued that children at the stage of moral realism follow the rules of parents and other authority figures in an uncritical way. However, this only applies to certain parental rules, such as those about honesty and stealing. They are much less willing to allow their parents to make and enforce rules about who they may have as their friends or what they should do in their free time (Shaffer, 1993).

Can you think of any situations in which adults might also disregard someone's intentions if the consequences of their actions were negative?

Evaluation

Piaget was right that there are close links between cognitive development in general and moral development in particular. Another strength of his theoretical approach is that most children in Western societies show the shift from moral realism to moral relativism predicted by Piaget. He also developed research in the area of moral development by devising short stories to illustrate moral points.

On the negative side, young children have more complex ideas about morality than was assumed by Piaget, and some of their moral thinking is more advanced than he claimed. Piaget's assumption that 10- and 11-year-old children have reached an adult level of moral reasoning is incorrect. This was shown in a study by Colby et al. (1983) (described later), who found large changes in moral thinking between the ages of 10 and 16.

Finally, Piaget focused on children's views concerning moral issues, and so he dealt with their knowledge of how they ought to behave. However, their thinking may be rather different from their actual behaviour when faced with a moral dilemma. More generally, Piaget tended to neglect the behavioural component of morality (which was studied by social learning theorists). He also paid little attention to the emotional component of morality (which was emphasised by Freud).

Cognitive-developmental theory: Kohlberg

Lawrence Kohlberg (1927–1987) agreed with Piaget that we need to focus on children's cognitive structures to understand how they think about moral issues. However, Kohlberg's theory differs in several ways from that of Piaget. For example, Kohlberg believed that moral reasoning often continues to develop through adolescence and early adulthood.

Evidence

The main experimental approach used by Kohlberg involved presenting his participants with a series of moral dilemmas. Each dilemma required them to decide whether it is preferable to uphold some law or other moral principle, or to reject the moral principle in favour of some basic human need. To make clear what Kohlberg (e.g. 1963) did, we will consider one of the moral dilemmas he used:

Group pressure can sometimes lead children to behave in unacceptable ways, for example stealing sweets.

In Europe, a woman was dying from cancer. One drug might save her, a form of radium that a druggist in the same town had recently discovered. The druggist was charging 2000 dollars, ten times what the drug cost him to make. The sick woman's husband, Heinz, went to everyone he knew to borrow the money, but he could only get together about half of what the drug cost. He told the druggist that his wife was dying and asked him to sell it cheaper or let him pay later. But the druggist said "No". The husband got desperate and broke into the man's store to steal the drug for his wife.

The moral principle in this dilemma is that stealing is wrong. However, it was the good motive of wanting to help his sick wife that led Heinz to steal the drug. It is precisely because there are powerful arguments for and against stealing the drug that there is a moral dilemma.

Kohlberg used evidence from such moral dilemmas to develop his theory. He followed Piaget in assuming that all children follow the same sequence of stages in their moral development. However, Kohlberg's three levels of moral development (with two stages at each level) do not correspond closely to Piaget's:

Level 1: Pre-conventional morality. At this level, what is regarded as right and wrong is determined by the rewards or punishments that are likely to follow, rather than by thinking about moral issues. Stage 1 of this level is based on a *punishment-and-obedience orientation*. Stealing is wrong because it involves disobeying authority, and leads to punishment. Stage 2 of this level is based on the notion that the right way to behave is the way that is rewarded. There is more attention to the needs of other people than in Stage 1, but mainly on the basis that if you help other people, then they will help you.

Level 2: Conventional morality. The greatest difference between Level 1 and Level 2 is that the views and needs of other people are much more important at Level 2 than at Level 1. At this level, people are very concerned to have the approval of others for their actions, and to avoid being blamed by them for behaving wrongly. At Stage 3, the emphasis is on having good intentions, and on behaving in ways that conform to most people's views of good behaviour. At Stage 4, children believe that it is important to do one's duty, and to obey the laws or rules of those in authority.

Level 3: Post-conventional or principled morality. Those at the highest level of post-conventional or principled morality recognise that the laws or rules of authority figures should sometimes be broken. Abstract notions about justice and the need to treat other people with respect can override the need to obey laws and rules. At Stage 5, there is a growing recognition that what is morally right may differ from what is legally right. Finally, at Stage 6, the individual has developed his or her own principles of conscience. The individual takes into account the likely views of everyone who will be affected by a moral decision. Kohlberg (1981) described this as a kind of "moral musical chairs". In practice, it is very rare for anyone to operate most of the time at Stage 6.

Think of an example to illustrate each of Kohlberg's six stages.

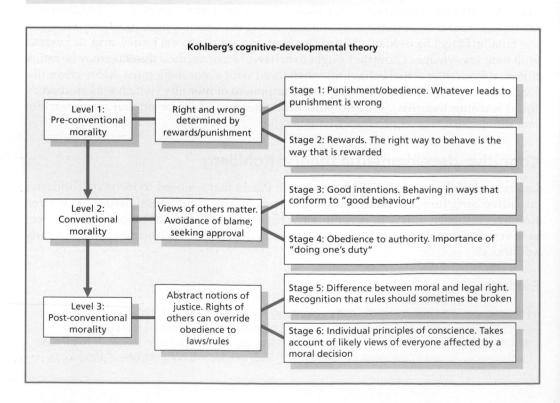

Kohlberg's cognitive-developmental theory

Level 1: Pre-conventional morality	Right and wrong determined by rewards/punishment	Stage 1: Punishment/obedience. Whatever leads to punishment is wrong
		Stage 2: Rewards. The right way to behave is the way that is rewarded
Level 2: Conventional morality	Views of others matter. Avoidance of blame; seeking approval	Stage 3: Good intentions. Behaving in ways that conform to "good behaviour"
		Stage 4: Obedience to authority. Importance of "doing one's duty"
Level 3: Post-conventional morality	Abstract notions of justice. Rights of others can override obedience to laws/rules	Stage 5: Difference between moral and legal right. Recognition that rules should sometimes be broken
		Stage 6: Individual principles of conscience. Takes account of likely views of everyone affected by a moral decision

Kohlberg assumed that all children follow the same sequence of moral stages. The best way of testing this assumption is to carry out a longitudinal (long-term) study to see how children's moral reasoning changes over time. Colby et al. (1983) conducted a 20-year study of 58 American males. There was a substantial drop in Stage 1 and Stage 2 moral reasoning between the ages of 10 and 16, with a compensatory increase in Stage 3 and Stage 4 moral reasoning occurring during the same time period. Most impressively for Kohlberg's theory, all of the participants progressed through the moral stages in exactly the predicted sequence.

Snarey (1985) reviewed 44 studies from 26 cultures. People in nearly all cultures go through the stages of moral development identified by Kohlberg in the same order. There was little evidence for any stage-skipping or for people returning to an earlier stage of moral development.

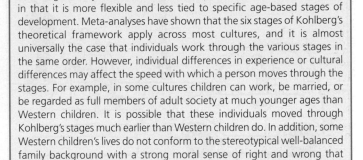

KEY STUDY EVALUATION — Kohlberg

Kohlberg's theory addresses some of the problems of Piaget's approach, in that it is more flexible and less tied to specific age-based stages of development. Meta-analyses have shown that the six stages of Kohlberg's theoretical framework apply across most cultures, and it is almost universally the case that individuals work through the various stages in the same order. However, individual differences in experience or cultural differences may affect the speed with which a person moves through the stages. For example, in some cultures children can work, be married, or be regarded as full members of adult society at much younger ages than Western children. It is possible that these individuals moved through Kohlberg's stages much earlier than Western children do. In addition, some Western children's lives do not conform to the stereotypical well-balanced family background with a strong moral sense of right and wrong that seems to lie behind some of Kohlberg's stages. This may also have a profound effect on a child's moral development.

Kohlberg's claim that the moral thinking of any given individual will be consistently at the same stage has not been supported. Rubin and Trotter (1977) gave their participants several moral dilemmas, and found that many of them responded very differently from one dilemma to the next.

Kohlberg assumed that certain kinds of general cognitive development must occur before an individual can advance a stage in his or her moral reasoning. For example, those whose moral reasoning is at Stage 5 make use of abstract principles (e.g. of justice), which presumably requires them to be good at abstract thinking. Tomlinson-Keasey and Keasey (1974) found that those girls of 11 and 12 who showed Stage 5 moral reasoning were good at abstract thinking on general tests of cognitive development. However, some of the girls could think abstractly, but failed to show Stage 5 moral reasoning. Thus, the ability to think abstractly is a necessary (but not sufficient) requirement for someone to attain Stage 5 or post-conventional morality.

Discussion points

1. How adequate do you find Kohlberg's use of moral dilemmas to study moral development (see Evaluation section)?

2. What do you think of Kohlberg's stage-based approach to moral development?

Evaluation

Nearly all children in all cultures work through the various stages of moral reasoning in the order specified by Kohlberg. Thus, the theory seems to be on the right lines. It has the advantage over Piaget's theory that it provides a more detailed and accurate account of moral development.

On the negative side, most people do not seem to develop beyond Stage 4 (Shaver & Strong, 1976). In addition, it has proved difficult to make a clear distinction between Stage 5 and Stage 6 moral reasoning (Colby et al., 1983).

Kohlberg focused on the verbal responses when his participants were given artificial moral dilemmas, rather than on actual moral behaviour. People's responses to those dilemmas may not predict how they would behave in real-life situations. The evidence is somewhat inconsistent. Santrock (1975) found that children's level of moral reasoning did not predict whether they would cheat when given the chance. However, there is more evidence among adults that the stage of moral reasoning can predict behaviour.

Kohlberg (1975) compared cheating behaviour among students at different levels of moral reasoning. About 70% of the students at the pre-conventional level were found to cheat, compared to only 15% of those at the post-conventional level. Students at the conventional level were intermediate (55%).

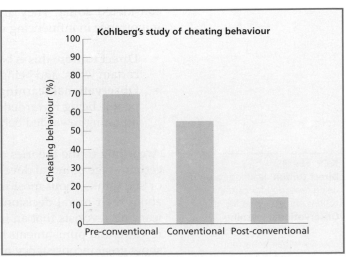

People may show great inconsistency of behaviour in different situations.

Finally, Kohlberg did not consider the emotional component of morality in any detail. For example, the development of emotions such as shame and guilt is important within moral development.

Cognitive-developmental theory: Gilligan

Carol Gilligan (1977, 1982) proposed a theory in response to what she regarded as the sexist bias of Kohlberg. Kohlberg initially based his theory on interviews with male participants, which suggests that bias may have been introduced. In addition, Kohlberg reported that most women were at Stage 3 of moral development, whereas men were at Stage 4.

Gilligan (1982) argued that boys develop the *morality of justice*, in which they focus on the use of laws and moral principles. In contrast, girls develop the *morality of care*, in which their main focus is on human well-being and on compassion for others. According to Gilligan, Kohlberg showed sexist bias by regarding the morality of justice as superior to the morality of care.

Evaluation

There is little evidence to support Gilligan's position. Kohlberg did sometimes find that women were at a lower stage of moral reasoning than men. However, Walker (1984) found in a review of 54 American studies that there were sex differences in moral development in only 8 of them.

Convincing evidence that men and women are actually very similar in their moral reasoning has been found in studies in which people discuss moral dilemmas they have experienced. In contrast to what would be predicted on Gilligan's (1982) theory, men as well as women focus on interpersonal responsibility and the well-being of others at least as much as they consider laws and justice (Walker, de Vries, & Trevethan, 1987). There may be some small sex differences in moral reasoning, but they are outweighed by the similarities.

Social learning theory

Social learning theorists such as Albert Bandura (1977) and Walter Mischel (1970) proposed a social learning theory approach which differs from any of the theories considered so far. They argued that learning experiences of two types are of special importance in influencing moral behaviour:

* **Direct tuition**: this is based on being rewarded or reinforced for behaving in certain ways, and being punished for behaving in other ways.
* **Observational learning**: moral behaviour can be learned by observing other people being rewarded or punished for behaving in certain ways, and then imitating rewarded behaviour.

According to the theories of Freud, Piaget, and Kohlberg, any given individual is at a certain stage of moral development at a particular time, and this determines the way he or she thinks about most moral issues. As a result, there is a high level of consistency about their moral decisions in different situations. In contrast, it is assumed by social learning theorists that an individual's behaviour in any situation is determined by the rewards and punishments he or she has received in similar situations. Thus, people may show great inconsistency of behaviour in different situations.

According to Bandura (1977, 1986), children's moral behaviour changes through development as a result of their experiences. It also changes because there is a shift from *external* to *internal* control. Young children are greatly influenced by the rewards and punishments they receive or see others receive. Older children move in the direction of **self-regulation**, in which they reward themselves for meeting internal standards of behaviour and experience a sense of failure if they do not meet those standards.

Evidence

Evidence that moral reasoning can be influenced by observational learning was reported by Bandura and McDonald (1963). Children between the ages of 5 and 11 were exposed to a model who made opposite moral judgements to them, and who was praised by the experimenter for his or her views. After that, the children were tested on their own. Most of them adopted the model's moral standards, and these effects lasted for at least one month.

According to social learning theory, there should be inconsistency of moral behaviour across situations. Hartshorne and May (1928) looked at stealing, cheating, and lying in 12,000 children between the ages of 8 and 16. They claimed that there was great inconsistency of behaviour. For example, children who lied in one situation were not particularly likely to cheat in another situation. However, a re-analysis of Hartshorne and May's data indicated that the children showed *some* behavioural consistency (Burton, 1976). For example, children who lied in one situation tended to lie in other, related situations, and the same was true for cheating and stealing. In addition, Hartshorne and May (1928) studied children, and there is evidence (Blasi, 1980) that consistency of moral behaviour increases between childhood and adulthood.

Parke (1977) carried out a study on the effects of punishment on moral behaviour. Children received punishment (a soft or unpleasantly loud buzzer) every time they touched an attractive toy. After that, the experimenter left the room. Children were more likely to resist the temptation to play with the attractive toys when the noise was loud than when it was soft. Parke also found that providing children with good reasons why they should resist temptation was effective, perhaps because it made it easier for them to use self-regulatory processes of self-reinforcement for avoiding temptation.

Parke (1977) found that if children heard an unpleasant loud noise when they tried to touch a toy, eventually the temptation to play with it was reduced.

Evaluation

Social learning theory differs from cognitive-developmental theories in its emphasis on the social factors influencing moral development, and in its focus on moral behaviour rather than moral reasoning. Social learning theorists have shown that moral behaviour is influenced by reward, punishment, and observational learning. As predicted, moral behaviour (especially that of children) has sometimes been found to show inconsistency from one situation to another.

Social learning theory has various limitations. First, it is hard within the theory to understand how general moral principles (e.g. justice; fairness) are learned. Social learning theory does not make it clear how moral development occurs, or why it is that most people go through the same stages of moral development.

Second, most research on moral behaviour carried out by social learning theorists consists of short-term laboratory studies. As a result according to Miller (1993, p.228):

We know much more about the variables that can affect the learning of social behaviours [e.g. moral behaviour] than about what variables actually operate in the lives of children or what behaviours actually occur at various ages.

What are the limitations of studying moral behaviour in the laboratory environment?

KEY TERM
Self-regulation: a process of self-reward if an internal standard of performance is achieved, but with feelings of failure if it is not achieved.

Would you consider that any human behaviour is consistent from one situation to another?

Third, the social learning approach focuses very much on the behavioural component of morality at the expense of the cognitive component studied in depth by Piaget and by Kohlberg. It also neglects the emotional component that was emphasised by Freud. As a result, social learning theorists provide us with a rather narrow view of moral development.

Parental role in moral development

The child's early stages of moral development depend very much on its parents. Hoffman (1970) identified three major styles used by parents in the moral development of their children:

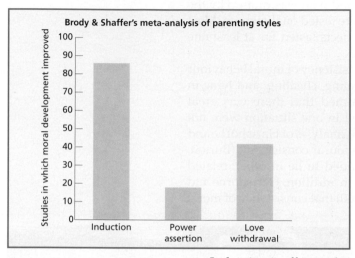

Brody & Shaffer's meta-analysis of parenting styles

1. Induction: explaining why a given action is wrong, with special emphasis on its effects on other people.
2. Power assertion: using spankings, removal of privileges, and harsh words to exert power over a child.
3. Love withdrawal: withholding attention or love when a child behaves badly.

Brody and Shaffer (1982) reviewed studies in which parental style influenced moral development. Induction improved moral development in 86% of those studies. In contrast, power assertion improved moral development in only 18%, and love withdrawal in 42%. As power assertion had a negative effect on moral development in 82% of the studies, it is a very ineffective parenting style. Power assertion produces children who are aggressive and who do not care about others (Zahn-Waxler et al., 1979).

Induction is effective because it provides the child with useful information that helps the development of moral reasoning. Another reason is that induction encourages children to think about other people. Considering the needs and emotions of others is of vital importance if moral development is to occur.

The findings tell us there is an association between parental use of induction and good moral development. The main reason for this association is probably that inductive parenting benefits children's moral development, but that may not be the whole story. Children who are well behaved are more likely to be treated in a reasonable, inductive

THEORIES OF MORAL DEVELOPMENT		
Theory	**Methods**	**Criticisms**
Psychodynamic	Personal accounts from adults about their childhood experiences.	Relies on accuracy of person's memory. Many of Freud's hypotheses have been proved wrong.
Piaget's cognitive-developmental theory	Telling short stories to illustrate moral points revealed a shift from moral realism to moral relativism.	Piaget may have underestimated the young child's ability to take account of people's intentions. Piaget ignored the behavioural and emotional components of morality.
Kohlberg's cognitive-developmental theory	Through the use of artificial dilemmas, Kohlberg described six stages of moral development that seem to be stable across most cultures.	Most people do not seem to develop beyond stage 4. The distinction between stages 5 and 6 is not clear. Kohlberg also placed little emphasis on the behavioural and emotional components of morality.
Social learning theory	Observational studies and laboratory-based work examined children's moral behaviour rather than moral reasoning.	Theory does not show how general moral principles, e.g. fairness, are learned. Laboratory studies often do not reflect real life. The approach ignores the cognitive and emotional components of moral development.

way by their parents. In contrast, children who are badly behaved and aggressive may cause their parents to use power assertion. Thus, parenting style affects children's behaviour, but children's behaviour may also affect parenting style.

Gender Development

When a baby is born, a key question everyone asks is, "Is it a boy or a girl?" As the baby develops, the ways in which it is treated by its parents and other people are influenced by its sex. In the fullness of time, the growing child's thoughts about itself and its place in the world are likely to depend in part on whether it is male or female. This section is concerned with some of these issues.

> ■ Research activity: Gender stereotypes
>
> Make a list of stereotypes that are often used to describe males and females. Now categorise these in terms of gender or biology. Are there any that could be supported by evidence, and what evidence could be considered valid?

Here are some of the key terms we will be using:

- **Sexual identity**: this is determined by the biological factors that have made us male or female; it can usually be assessed from the genitals.
- **Gender identity**: this is a child's or adult's awareness of being male or female; it is socially rather than biologically determined, and emerges during the early years of childhood.
- **Sex-typed behaviour**: the forms of behaviour deemed fitting for members of each sex within a given culture.

Observed sex differences

Some ideas about sex-typed behaviour are in decline. Few people accept any more that men should go out to work and have little to do with looking after the home and the children, whereas women should stay at home and concern themselves only with home and children. However, many stereotypes still exist. It is important to consider the actual behaviour of boys and girls. Do the sexes really differ in their behaviour?

Eleanor Maccoby and Carol Jacklin (1974) reviewed the relevant research. They concluded that there were only four differences between boys and girls for which there was convincing evidence:

- Girls have greater verbal ability than boys; this difference has been found at most ages during childhood.
- Boys have greater visual and spatial abilities than girls.
- Boys have greater arithmetical ability than girls, but this difference only appears during adolescence.
- Boys are more aggressive than girls physically and verbally.

> **KEY TERMS**
> **Sexual identity**: maleness or femaleness based on biological factors.
> **Gender identity**: organised beliefs about the sexes.
> **Sex-typed behaviour**: the kinds of behaviour regarded as suitable for males and females within a culture.

As Shaffer (1993) pointed out, later research has indicated that there are some other sex differences in behaviour. Girls show more emotional sensitivity than boys. For example, girls from the age of about 5 are more interested than boys in babies, and respond more attentively to them. Girls have less developmental vulnerability than boys, with more boys showing mental retardation, language disorders, and hyperactivity.

Most observed sex differences in behaviour are fairly modest. However, there is increasing evidence in Britain that girls are outperforming boys in nearly all subjects. In 1997, the percentages of 14-year-old girls and boys reaching the expected standards in different subjects were as follows (boys' percentages in brackets): modern foreign languages: 67% (51%); history: 62% (50%); geography: 63% (54%); design and technology: 64% (49%); and information technology: 52% (47%).

In general, there are fewer and smaller differences between the sexes than is generally assumed. Why is there this gap between appearance and reality? We tend to

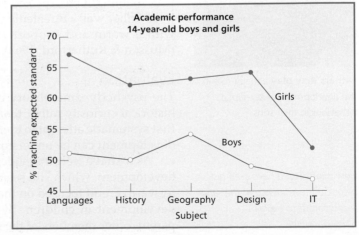

misinterpret the evidence of our senses to fit our stereotypes. Condry and Condry (1976) asked college students to watch a videotape of an infant. The ways in which the infant's behaviour was interpreted depended on whether it was referred to as David or Dana. The infant was said to be "angry" in its reaction to a jack-in-the-box if it had been called David, but "anxious" if it had been called Dana.

Psychodynamic theory: Freud

Part of Freud's psychodynamic theory was designed to account for gender development. Most theories of gender development are based on the assumption that environmental and cultural influences are of crucial importance. In contrast, Freud de-emphasised such influences, arguing that "anatomy is destiny".

As we saw earlier in the chapter, Freud argued that boys develop an Oedipus complex, in which they have sexual desires for their mother combined with intense fear of their father. Part of this fear arises because boys think that their fathers may castrate them. The Oedipus complex is resolved by a process of identification with the father. According to Freud, identification plays a major role in the development of sex-typed behaviour.

Freud (1933) argued that girls are "mortified by the comparison with boys' far superior equipment", for which they blame their mother. Girls develop an Electra complex, in which they have sexual desires for their father and regard their mother as a rival. Girls develop sex-typed behaviour because they are rewarded by their father, who is the central focus of their affection.

Chodorow (1978) developed an alternative psychodynamic theory, according to which most young children develop a close relationship with their mother. This relationship then sets the pattern for future relationships. Girls can develop a sense of gender identity based on their close relationship with another female (their mother). By so doing, they associate femininity with feelings of closeness. In contrast, boys have to move away from their close relationship with their mother in order to develop gender identity, and this can make them regard masculinity and closeness as not being associated.

Fathers may play a major role in the development of sex-typed behaviour in their sons.

How might Freud have used his focus on the influence of the same-sexed parent to explain homosexuality?

Evidence

There is some evidence that the father plays a major role in the development of sex-typed behaviour in boys. Boys whose fathers are missing during the time at which the Oedipus complex develops (around the age of 5) showed less sex-typed behaviour than boys whose fathers were present throughout (Stevenson & Black, 1988). There is also evidence (discussed later) that there are major changes in gender development at around the age of 5.

Freud's psychodynamic theory of the development of gender identity is incorrect in nearly all other respects. His account tells us more about his powers of imagination than about what actually happens. There is no real evidence that boys fear castration or that girls regret not having a penis. Freud argued that the identification process depends on fear, so it might be expected that a boy's identification with his father would be greatest if his father was a threatening figure. In fact, however, boys tend to identify much more with a warm and supportive father than with an overbearing and threatening one (Mussen & Rutherford, 1963).

Evaluation

The psychodynamic theory of gender development should be regarded largely as a historical curiosity rather than as a useful theoretical contribution. However, it was the first systematic attempt to identify a series of developmental stages within which gender development can be understood.

As we have seen, the evidence has generally failed to support Freud's views on gender development, which still seem very speculative one hundred years after they were put forward. Freud focused on the influence of the same-sexed parent in influencing gender development in children. By so doing, he ignored the impact of the opposite-sexed parent, other members of the family, and other children.

Freud's general approach was limited in various ways, as can be seen if we relate it to other theoretical approaches. The emphasis in Kohlberg's cognitive-developmental theory and in gender-schema theory (discussed next) is more on the cognitive factors involved in gender development. The emphasis in social learning theory (also discussed later) is more on the behavioural aspects of gender development.

Cognitive-developmental theory: Kohlberg

Lawrence Kohlberg (1966) put forward a cognitive-developmental theory of the development of sex-typed behaviour. The essence of his approach can be seen by contrasting it with social learning theory, which is discussed later on. According to Kohlberg (1966, p.85), "the child's sex-role concepts are the result of the child's active structuring of his own experience; they are not passive products of social training."

There are other important differences between social learning theory and Kohlberg's theory. According to social learning theory, children develop a gender identity as a result of attending to same-sex models. According to Kohlberg, the causality goes in the other direction: children attend to same-sex models because they have already developed a consistent gender identity. It follows from this theory that children find it rewarding to behave in line with their consistent gender identity. In the words of Kohlberg (1966, p.89), "I am a boy; therefore I want to do boy things; therefore the opportunity to do boy things ... is rewarding." In contrast, social learning theorists argue that rewarding behaviour is behaviour that *others* regard as appropriate.

Do behaviours that are considered "boy things" and "girl things" remain constant over time? Are there illustrative examples from your childhood as compared to your parents' childhoods?

The notion of gender identity is of great importance within Kohlberg's cognitive-developmental theory. Children go through three stages in the development of gender identity:

1. Basic gender identity (age 2 to $3\frac{1}{2}$ years): boys know they are boys, and girls know they are girls. However, they believe it would be possible to change sex.
2. Gender stability ($3\frac{1}{2}$ to $4\frac{1}{2}$ years): there is an awareness that sex is stable over time (e.g. boys will become men), but less awareness that sex remains stable across different situations, such as wearing clothes normally worn by members of the opposite sex. When a doll was dressed in transparent clothes so there was a discrepancy between its clothing and its genitals, children in this stage decided on its sex on the basis of clothing (McConaghy, 1979).
3. Gender consistency ($4\frac{1}{2}$ to 7 years upwards): children at this stage realise that sex remains the same over time and over situations. This is like Piaget's notion of conservation (see Chapter 16).

KOHLBERG'S STAGES IN THE DEVELOPMENT OF GENDER IDENTITY		
Basic gender identity	**Gender stability**	**Gender consistency**
2–3 ½ years	3½–4 ½ years	4½–7 upwards
Aware of sex, but believes it can change.	Aware that sex is stable over time, but not over situations.	Realises sex remains the same, regardless of time or situation.

Evidence

There is evidence that children do, indeed, progress through the three stages proposed by Kohlberg. In a cross-cultural study, Munroe, Shimmin, and Munroe (1984) found that children in several cultures had the same sequences of stages on the way to full gender identity.

One of the predictions of Kohlberg's theory is that children who have reached the stage of gender consistency will pay more attention to the behaviour of same-sex models than children at earlier stages of gender development. Slaby and Frey (1975) tested this prediction. Children between the ages of 2 and 5 were assessed for gender consistency, and assigned to a high or a low gender consistency group. They were then shown a film of a male and a female performing a variety of activities. Those who were high in gender consistency showed a greater tendency to attend to the same-sexed model than did those low in gender consistency.

More evidence of the importance of gender consistency was reported by Ruble, Balaban, and Cooper (1981). Preschoolers high and low in gender consistency watched television commercials in which toys were represented as being suitable for boys or for girls. These advertisements had more effect on the attitudes and behaviour of boys and girls high in gender consistency.

Evaluation

Gender identity does seem to develop through the three stages proposed by Kohlberg. As predicted by the theory, the achievement of full gender identity increases sex-typed behaviour. In more general terms, the notion that gender development involves children actively interacting with the world around them is valuable, as is the notion that how they interact with the world depends on the extent to which they have developed a consistent gender identity.

There are various problems with Kohlberg's theory. First, sex-typed behaviour is shown by most boys and girls by the time of their second birthday. This is several years before they have reached gender consistency, and so it cannot be argued that *all* sex-typed behaviour depends on gender consistency.

Second, Kohlberg (1966, p.98) argued that, "the process of forming a constant sexual identity is ... a part of the general process of conceptual growth." This approach tends to ignore the external factors (e.g. reward and punishment from parents) that determine much early sex-typed behaviour. More generally, Kohlberg's focus was too much on the individual child, and not enough on the social context that largely determines gender development.

Third, Kohlberg probably exaggerated the importance of cognitive factors in producing sex-typed behaviour. Huston (1985) pointed out that Kohlberg's theory leads to the prediction that there should be a close relationship between cognitions about gender and sex-typed attitudes and behaviour. In fact, the relationship is not very strong, and is weaker in girls than in boys. It is not clear how these findings can be explained by Kohlberg.

Cognitive-developmental theory: Gender-schema theory

Martin and Halverson (1987) put forward a rather different cognitive-developmental theory known as gender-schema theory. They argued that children as young as 2 or 3 who have acquired basic gender identity start to form **gender schemas**, which consist of organised sets of beliefs about the sexes. The first schema that is formed is an in-group/out-group schema, consisting of organised information about which toys and activities are suitable for boys and which are suitable for girls. Another early schema is an own-sex schema containing information about how to behave in sex-typed ways (e.g. how to dress dolls for a girl). Some of the processes involved in the initial development of gender schemas may include those emphasised by social learning theorists.

A key aspect of gender-schema theory is the notion that children do not simply respond passively to the world. What happens instead is that the gender schemas possessed by children help to determine what they attend to, how they interpret the world, and what they remember of their experiences. In other words, as Shaffer (1993, p.513) argued, "Gender schemas 'structure' experience by providing an organisation for processing social information."

Evidence

According to the theory, gender schemas are used by children to organise and make sense of their experiences. If they are exposed to information that does not fit one of their schemas (e.g. a boy combing the hair of his doll), then the information should be distorted to make it fit the schema. Martin and Halverson (1983) tested this prediction. They showed five- and six-year-old children pictures of schema-consistent activities (e.g. a girl playing with a doll) and schema-inconsistent activities (e.g. a girl playing with a toy gun).

Schema-inconsistent activities were often misremembered one week later as schema-consistent (e.g. it had been a boy playing with a toy gun).

Another study that supports gender-schema theory was reported by Bradbard et al. (1986). Boys and girls between the ages of 4 and 9 were presented with gender-neutral objects such as burglar alarms and pizza cutters. They were told that some of the objects were "boy" objects, whereas others were described as "girl" objects. There were two key findings. First, children spent much more time playing with objects that they had been told were appropriate to their sex. Second, even a week later the children remembered whether any given object was a "boy" or a "girl" object.

A study by Masters et al. (1979) also supports gender-schema theory. Young children of 4 and 5 were influenced in their choice of toy more by the gender label attached to the toy (e.g. "It's a girl's toy") than by the sex of the model seen playing with the toy. As Durkin (1995) pointed out, children's behaviour seems to be influenced more by the schema, "This is a boy's toy" or "This is a girl's toy" than by a desire to imitate a same-sexed model.

Schema-consistent activities

Schema-inconsistent activities

Evaluation

One of the main strengths of gender-schema theory is that it helps to explain why children's sex-role beliefs and attitudes often change rather little after middle childhood. The gender schemas that have been established tend to be maintained because schema-consistent information is attended to and remembered. Another strength of the theory is its focus on the child as being actively involved in making sense of the world in the light of its present knowledge.

The limitations of gender-schema theory resemble those of Kohlberg's theory. The theory emphasises too much the role of the individual child in gender development, and de-emphasises the importance of social factors. In addition, it is likely that the importance of schemas and other cognitive factors in determining behaviour are exaggerated within the theory. Another problem is that the theory does not really explain *why* gender schemas develop and take the form they do.

Finally, it is assumed within the theory that it should be possible to change children's behaviour by changing their schemas or stereotypes. In fact, as Durkin (1995, p.185) pointed out, "greater success has been reported in attempts to change concepts than attempts to change behaviour or behavioural intentions." In a similar way, many married couples have *schemas* relating to equality of the sexes and equal division of household chores, but this rarely has much effect on their *behaviour*.

Think about your own family. Are there specific domestic chores that are done by particular members of the family? Can they be categorised by gender?

Social learning theory

According to social learning theory (e.g. Bandura, 1977, 1986), the development of gender occurs as a result of the child's experiences. In general terms, children learn to behave in ways that are rewarded by others and to avoid behaving in ways that are punished by others. This is known as direct tuition, and was discussed earlier in the chapter. As society has expectations about the ways in which boys and girls should behave, the operation of socially delivered rewards and punishments will tend to produce sex-typed behaviour.

Bandura also argued that children can learn sex-typed behaviour by observing the actions of various models of the same sex, including other children, parents, and teachers. This is known as observational learning, and was also discussed earlier in the chapter. It has often been argued that much observational learning of sex-typed behaviour in children depends on the media, and especially television.

Parents may try to discourage what they see as sex-inappropriate behaviour in a variety of ways. Climbing trees while wearing a skirt is more difficult than in trousers or shorts.

Evidence

Sex-typed behaviour is learned in part through direct tuition. Fagot and Leinbach (1989) carried out a long-term study on children. Parents encouraged sex-typed behaviour and discouraged sex-inappropriate behaviour in their children even before the age of 2. For example, girls were rewarded for playing with dolls, and discouraged from climbing trees. Those parents who made the most use of direct tuition tended to have children who behaved in the most sex-typed way. However, these findings are not altogether typical. Lytton and Romney (1991) reviewed numerous studies on the parental treatment of boys and girls. There was a modest tendency for parents to encourage sex-typed activities, but boys and girls received equal parental warmth, encouragement of achievement, discipline, and amount of interaction.

Direct tuition is also used by other children. Fagot (1985) studied the behaviour of children aged between 21 and 25 months. Boys made fun of other boys who played with dolls or with a girl, and girls did not like it when one of them started playing with a boy. There are similar pressures from their peers among older children in the years before adolescence. Those who fail to behave in a sex-typed way are the least popular (Sroufe et al., 1993).

Observational learning was studied by Perry and Bussey (1979). Children aged 8 or 9 watched male and female adult models choose between sex-neutral activities (e.g. selecting an apple or a pear). Afterwards, they tended to make the same choices as the same-sex models. These findings suggest that observational learning plays an important role in gender development. However, Barkley et al. (1977) reviewed the literature, and found that children showed a bias in favour of the same-sex model in only 18 out of 81 studies.

Children between the ages of 4 and 11 watch about three hours of television a day, which adds up to 1000 hours a year. It would be surprising if this exposure had no impact on children's views of themselves and on sex-typed behaviour via observational learning. Most of the research indicates there is a modest link between television watching and sex-typed behaviour. Frueh and McGhee (1975) studied the television-viewing habits of children aged between 4 and 12. Those children who watched the most television tended to show more sex-typed behaviour in terms of preferring sex-typed toys. However, this is only correlational evidence, and so we do not know that watching television led to sex-typed behaviour.

Television programmes that showed men and women taking part in non-traditional sex-typed activities have been found to produce some attitude changes among viewers, but effects on behaviour were small.

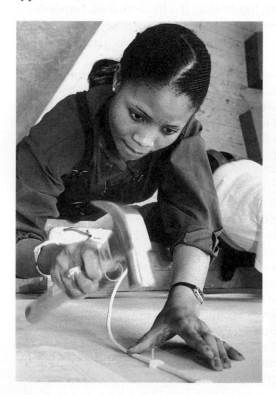

Williams (1986) examined sex-role stereotypes in three towns in Canada nicknamed: "Notel" (no television channels); "Unitel" (one channel); and "Multitel" (four channels). Sex-role stereotyping was much greater in the towns with television than in the one without. During the course of the study, Notel gained access to one television channel. This led to increased sex-role stereotyping among children.

Some of the strongest evidence that television can influence gender development was reported by Johnston and Ettema (1982). In the *Freestyle* project, there was a series of television programmes in which non-traditional opportunities and activities were modelled. These programmes produced significant attitude changes away from sex-role stereotypes, and these changes were still present nine months later. However, the effects on behaviour were rather small.

Do you think the Canadian study by Williams (1986) would be able to demonstrate a causal relationship between television and sex-role stereotyping? What other factors in the children's lives might have played a part?

Evaluation

One of the strengths of the social learning approach is that it takes full account of the social context in which the development of gender occurs. As social learning theorists have claimed, some sex-typed behaviour occurs because it has been rewarded, and sex-inappropriate behaviour is avoided because it has been discouraged or punished. There is also evidence that observational learning is important, but perhaps more with older than with young children.

There are several limitations of social learning theory. First, as Durkin (1995, p.179) pointed out:

> ■ Research activity: Content analysis
>
> In small groups, choose one or two children's television programmes that are currently being shown. Analyse the contents of the programmes for sex-role stereotyping and sex-typed behaviour using observational techniques. Your results can then be pooled for general analysis.
>
> If possible, carry out the same study on children's television programmes from the past, many of which are now available on videotape. What differences, if any, do you find between the two?

Research into the effects of the principal mechanisms emphasised by the theory (parental reinforcement, modelling) has not led consistently to the conclusion that they have a major influence.

Second, social learning theorists seem to regard young children as *passive* individuals who are taught how to behave by being rewarded and punished. In reality, children make an active contribution to their own development. The criticism that the active involvement of children in their gender development is ignored by social learning theorists is most relevant to the initial version of social learning theory. It does not apply so well to Bandura's (1986) social cognitive theory, in which the emphasis is on the self and the role it plays in influencing behaviour.

Third, social learning theorists mistakenly assume that learning processes are very similar at any age. For example, consider young children and adolescents watching a film in which a man and a woman are eating a meal together. The observational learning of the young children might focus on the eating behaviour of the same-sexed person, whereas the adolescents might focus on his or her social behaviour. Approaches such as Kohlberg's cognitive-developmental theory and gender-schema theory are better equipped to explain developmental changes in learning and cognition.

Fourth, social learning theory focuses on the learning of *specific* ways of behaving. This ignores the fact that there is also a considerable amount of *general* learning. For example, children seem to acquire gender schemas (organised beliefs about the sexes; Martin & Halverson, 1987), and it is hard to explain how this happens in terms of social learning theory.

Biological theories

There are various obvious biological differences between boys and girls. These biological differences produce hormonal differences between the sexes at a very early stage of development. For example, the male sex hormone testosterone is present in greater amounts in male than female foetuses from about the age of six weeks, whereas the opposite is the case for the female sex hormone estrogen (see Durkin, 1995). It has been argued that basic biological and hormonal factors are important in gender development, and in the development of greater aggressiveness in boys than in girls. However, as Willerman (1979) pointed out:

One should not expect too much of the genetic differences between males and females. The two sexes have forty-five/forty-six of their chromosomes in common, and the one that differs (the Y) contains the smallest proportion of genetic material.

Ethical issues: What might be some of the ethical problems encountered by researchers conducting studies into the links between sexual identity and biology?

The ideal way of testing biological theories of gender development would be to study individuals in which there is a clear distinction between sexual identity (based on biological factors) and the way in which they are treated socially. Thus, for example, if an individual was born a boy but was treated as a girl, would biological or social factors be more important in their gender development? The ideal study has not been carried out, but approximations to it are discussed next.

Evidence

Suggestive evidence in support of the biological approach to gender development has been obtained in animal studies. For example, Young, Goy, and Phoenix (1964) gave doses of testosterone to pregnant monkeys. This male sex hormone produced greater aggressiveness and higher frequency of rough-and-tumble play in the mothers' female offspring.

Money and Ehrhardt

Money and Ehrhardt (1972) discussed cases of females who were exposed to male sex hormones prior to birth. Even though their parents treated them as girls, they tended to be tomboys. They played and fought with boys, and avoided more traditional female activities. In addition, they preferred to play with blocks and cars rather than with dolls. However, many of these girls were given the hormone cortisone to prevent them from becoming too masculine anatomically. One of the effects of cortisone is to increase activity level, and this may have made their behaviour more like that expected of boys.

Evidence that social factors can override biology was also reported by Money and Ehrhardt. They studied male identical twins, one of whom had his penis very severely damaged during circumcision. He had an operation at the age of 21 months to make him anatomically a girl. His parents treated him like a girl, and this affected his behaviour. He asked for toys such as dolls and a doll's house, whereas his brother asked for a garage. He was neater and more delicate in his behaviour than his identical twin.

There was a follow-up study by Diamond (1982) on the identical twin who grew up as a girl. The findings of this study suggested that biological factors are important. The girl had few friends, did not feel securely female or male, and believed that life was better for boys than for girls.

Discussion points

1. Can studies of such unusual cases tell us about ordinary gender development?
2. Do these cases persuade you that biological factors play a part in gender development?

There are rare cases in which the development of biological gender is complex. For example, about 500 people in Britain have what is known as testicular feminising syndrome. They are male in the sense that they have male chromosomes and testicles. However, their bodies do not respond to the male sex hormone testosterone. As a result, they develop a female body shape and their breasts develop. Mrs DW has testicular feminising syndrome. In spite of her male chromosomes, she looks like a woman, she is married with two adopted children, and she has succeeded in her role as a woman (Goldwyn, 1979).

Imperato-McGinley et al. (1974) studied a family in the Dominican Republic. Four of the sons in the family appeared biologically to be female when they were born, and they were reared as girls. However, at the age of about 12, they developed male genitals and started to look like ordinary adolescent males. In spite of the fact that all four of them had been reared as girls, and had thought of themselves as females, they seemed to adjust well to the male role. According to Gross's account (1996, p.584), "They have all taken on male roles, do men's jobs, have married women and are accepted as men." These findings suggest that biological factors can be more important than social ones.

Evaluation

Most of the evidence we have considered suggests that biological factors play some role in gender development. Of particular interest are those studies in which there is a fairly direct conflict between biological and social factors, as was the case with the four children in the family from the Dominican Republic. It seemed as if biological factors outweighed social factors. However, it needs to be remembered that the relevant evidence has been obtained from very unusual cases, and it is hard to know whether the findings obtained can be generalised to the ordinary population.

It is important to note that biological theories cannot provide more than a partial explanation. Such theories do not explain the impact of social factors on gender development, and they do not account for the substantial changes in gender roles that have occurred in Western societies in recent decades. As Durkin (1995, p.173) pointed out:

> Biological theories stress the demands of parenting and the possible implications of possible differences in abilities, but have little to say about the other distinguishing characteristic that has evolved in this [human] species: its ability to articulate, share, reflect upon, and change its social practices.

Cultural differences

In Western societies, boys are encouraged to develop an *instrumental role*, in which they are assertive, competitive, and independent in their behaviour. In contrast, girls are encouraged to develop an *expressive role*, in which they are co-operative, supportive, and sensitive in their dealings with other people. These are stereotypes, of course, and we have already seen that there are rather small differences in actual behaviour.

There have been great changes in most Western societies in recent years. In the mid-twentieth century, many fewer women than men went to university. Nowadays the number of female university students exceeds that of male students in several countries. There is a similar pattern in employment. In spite of these changes, many of the old stereotypes have changed very little. Bergen and Williams (1991) found in the United States that stereotypical views of the sexes in 1988 were remarkably similar to those expressed in 1972.

In most Western societies, there are now more female than male university students.

Evidence

Socialisation pressures in 110 non-industrialised countries were explored by Barry, Bacon, and Child (1957). They considered five characteristics:

- Nurturance (being supportive).
- Responsibility.
- Obedience.
- Achievement.
- Self-reliance.

There was more pressure on girls than on boys to be nurturant in 75% of the non-industrialised societies, with none showing the opposite pattern. Responsibility was regarded as more important in girls than in boys in 55% of the societies, with 10% showing the opposite. Obedience was stressed for girls more than for boys in 32% of societies, with 3% showing the

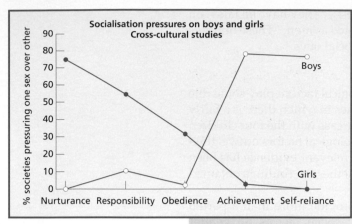

opposite. There was more pressure on boys than on girls to acquire the other two characteristics. Achievement was emphasised more for boys in 79% of societies (3% showed the opposite), and self-reliance was regarded as more important in boys in 77% of societies, with no societies regarding it as more important in girls.

These findings indicate that the sex-role stereotypes of females being expressive and males being instrumental are very widespread. Related findings were obtained by Williams and Best (1990). Similar gender stereotypes to those found in the United States were present in 24 other countries in Asia, Europe, Oceania, Africa, and the Americas.

Discussion points

1. Are you surprised at the cross-cultural similarities in expectations of males and females?
2. Why do you think there are such consistent gender-specific expectations?

Do you think there are countries that appear to have the most and the least gender-related behaviour? On what evidence do you base your decisions?

It would be a mistake to ignore cultural differences altogether. Margaret Mead (1935) studied three tribes in New Guinea. In the Mundugumor tribe, both men and women adopted the aggressive, instrumental style of behaviour that is supposed to be more characteristic of males. In the Arapesh tribe, both sexes adopted the caring, expressive style commonly associated with females. Most dramatically, the females in the Tchambuli tribe behaved in an assertive and independent fashion, whereas the males were nurturant and dependent.

Evaluation

Most cross-cultural studies have indicated that the cultural expectations and stereotypes for boys and girls are surprisingly similar in otherwise very different cultures. However, it is worth noting that there may be large differences between *expectations* and actual *behaviour*. What is needed is more cross-cultural research in which the behaviour of boys and girls of different ages is observed in a systematic way. It is possible, for example, that people living in individualistic societies feel less pressure than those living in collectivistic societies to behave in the gender-appropriate ways expected within their culture.

Development of the Self

As children grow up, they become increasingly aware of themselves and of the ways in which other people think of them. In other words, they develop a sense of self. In order to set the scene for this section of the chapter, it is useful to distinguish between two terms referring to the self:

■ Research activity: List 20 answers to the question "Who am I?". Now make a list of 20 words that you think other people would use to describe you. Are the lists the same? If not, why do you think there are differences?

- **Self-concept**: this is all of the thoughts and feelings about the self; it combines self-esteem and **self-image** (the knowledge an individual has about himself or herself).
- **Self-esteem**: this is the evaluative aspect of the self-concept; it concerns how worthwhile and confident an individual feels about himself or herself.

The self-concept is broader in meaning than self-esteem, but the terms overlap considerably with each other. Whichever aspect of the self-concept we consider, there is generally an emotional reaction (positive and negative). This emotional commitment to the self underlies self-esteem, self-image, and self-concept.

The self-concept is influenced by numerous factors. However, our relationships with other people are of crucial importance. Charles Cooley (1902) used the term "looking-glass self" to convey the idea that the self-concept reflects the evaluations of other people. In other words, we tend to see ourselves as others see us. Those of greatest importance in our lives (e.g. partners; parents; close friends) have most effect on our self-concept.

The idea that the self-concept emerges as a result of our interactions with other people was developed by George Herbert Mead. According to Mead (1934):

KEY TERMS
Self-concept: the total set of thoughts and feelings about the self; it consists of self-esteem and self-image.
Self-image: the part of the self-concept conerned with the knowledge that an individual has about himself or herself.
Self-esteem: the part of the self-concept concerned with the feelings that an individual has about himself or herself.

The self is something which ... is not initially there at birth but arises in the process of social development. That is, it develops as a result of his relations to that process as a whole and to other individuals within the process.

William James (1890) drew a distinction between two aspects of the self-concept: the "I" or self as the subject of experience, and the "me" or self as the object of experience. In essence, young children begin to develop a sense of being separate from other people. This is the "I" or existential self as Lewis (1990) called it. After that, the "me" or categorical self (Lewis, 1990) develops. This involves an awareness of the self as an object that can be perceived by others. So far as we know, no other species develops a categorical self. The categorical self is very similar to the self-concept, which is "based on experiences of oneself *as if seen from an outside perspective*" (Baars, 1997).

Early childhood

It is hard to study the development of the self-concept in early childhood. Young children do not have sufficient command of language to express any thoughts they might have about themselves. However, one interesting way of considering some of the early stages in the development of a sense of self is to hold infants up to a mirror. The crucial point is the one at which they recognise their own reflection. Chimpanzees learn to recognise themselves in a mirror, but macaques, baboons, and gibbons do not (Gallup, 1979).

Chimpanzees can learn to recognise themselves in a mirror and use the mirror to investigate parts of themselves they cannot easily see.

According to Lewis and Brooks-Gunn (1979), there are at least four stages in the infant's reactions to mirror images:

1. Up to three months of age, there is little or no reaction to their own image or that of anyone else.
2. At about four months of age, infants will reach out and touch the mirror image of another person or a toy, because they do not understand that they are only looking at a reflection.
3. At 10 months of age, infants will reach behind them if they see in the mirror that a toy is being placed behind their back; however, they have little or no sense of self, in that they will not attempt to remove a red dot from their nose.
4. From the age of 18 months, young children do remove a red dot from their nose when they see it in the mirror; a few months after that, they respond "Me" when asked to identify their reflection in the mirror: this is the first convincing evidence that a self-concept is starting to emerge.

Lewis et al. (1989) argued that many emotions (which they called "self-referential emotions") involve thinking about oneself in relation to others. For example, we feel embarrassed when we feel we have behaved in a way that someone else finds inappropriate. They tested for the presence of self-referential emotions in young children by observing their reactions when dancing in front of an adult. They also tested for the presence of aspects of a self-concept by using the mirror test to see whether the young children would rub a red dot off their nose. It was mostly the children who recognised themselves in the mirror who became embarrassed when asked to dance. The implication is that self-recognition in the mirror and the presence of self-referential emotions both reflect the development of the self-concept.

Why do you think failure to remove a red dot from the nose when looking in a mirror indicates the lack of a sense of self?

Middle childhood

With older children, it is possible to ask them to describe themselves in some detail. This was done by Damon and Hart (1988) in a large-scale study on children between the ages of 4 and 15. There were various common themes at all ages, with physical features, activities, social characteristics, and psychological characteristics all being included in most self-descriptions. However, there was a progressive increase in the complexity of the self-concept throughout the age range studied. Damon and Hart identified three different levels of the self-concept:

1. Categorical identification (4–7 years): at this level, children describe themselves in terms of various categories (e.g. "I am 7 years old", "I'm happy").

2. Comparative assessments (8–11 years): at this level, self-descriptions are often based on comparisons with other children (e.g. "I'm smaller than most children"; "I'm cleverer than other children").

3. Interpersonal implications (12–15 years): at this level, the impact of children's characteristics on their relationships with other people tends to be included in their self-descriptions (e.g. "I'm very sociable, so I have a lot of friends"; "I understand people, so they come to me with their problems").

What emerges very clearly from Damon and Hart's study is that children increasingly think of themselves in relationship to other people as they grow up. In other words, the self-concept becomes more and more defined in social terms. An important way in which our self-concept is influenced by other people is by means of **social comparison**, in which we judge our performance with reference to the performance of others. Ruble et al. (1980) studied the use of social comparison in children aged between 5 and 9. The children threw balls into a concealed basketball hoop, and were told how their performance compared to that of other children. Children of 9 judged how good they were at this game by taking account of other children's performance. Younger children did not make use of social comparison.

It seems likely that Ruble et al. would have told some children in their study that their performance was poor. Are there any ethical difficulties here? How would you have addressed them?

Discussion points

1. Why does the self-concept become more complex during the course of development?
2. Are there any problems with a stage-based account of the development of the self-concept?

DAMON AND HART'S LEVELS OF THE SELF-CONCEPT		
Categorical identification	**Comparative assessments**	**Interpersonal implications**
4–7 years	8–11 years	12–15 years
Self-description in terms of categories.	Self-description based on comparisons.	Self-description includes the impact of their characteristics on relationships with others.
e.g. I am 7 years old.	e.g. I'm taller than others in my class.	e.g. I'm very sociable, so I have lots of friends.

Psychodynamic theory

Freud did not have a proper theory of the development of the self-concept. The closest he came to it was with his notion of identification, which was discussed earlier in the chapter. The basic idea is that boys and girls at the age of 5 or 6 identify with the same-sexed parent, meaning that they imitate the attitudes and behaviour of that parent. Within the Freudian approach, the process of identification plays a key role in the child's emerging sense of self.

Freud's views on identification have not stood the test of time. First, Freud assumed that different aspects of personal identity develop together during the process of identification: regarding oneself as male or female; behaving in ways that are appropriate to one's sex; and sexual orientation. The reality is more complex (Durkin, 1995).

Second, research does not support these views. Maccoby (1992, p.18) reviewed the findings, and concluded that

the yield of the work with respect to the theory of identification was disappointing ... no consistent relationships were found among characteristics that ought to have been linked by their common origins in the process of identification.

KEY TERM
Social comparison: deciding how well we are doing by comparing ourselves against other people.

For example, it seems to follow from Freud's account that school-age children should closely resemble their same-sexed parent, but this is generally not the case (Maccoby & Jacklin, 1974).

Third, Freud tended to ignore the social factors that are crucial in the development of the self. Indeed, it was in large measure Freud's neglect of social factors that led another psychodynamic theorist, Erik Erikson, to develop an alternative theory. This theory is discussed next.

Erikson's psychosocial theory

Erikson's (1959) starting point was the notion that conflicts between the natural processes of maturation and the expectations of society create various crises that the child must try to resolve. Erikson's theory of psychosocial development resembled Freud's theory of psychosexual development in some ways, but its emphasis was much more on the role of social factors and on the development of the ego. There are eight stages of psychosocial development. Everyone goes through these stages in the same order, but people vary enormously in terms of how successfully they cope with each stage. Each stage has possible positive and negative outcomes associated with it; children who have negative outcomes have to deal with their unresolved crises later in life.

The first four of Erikson's stages are as follows (the remainder are discussed on pages 476–477).

- Stage 1 (age 0–1 years): the infant develops either trust or mistrust in itself and others; the mother or mother figure is the central person in the child's life.
- Stage 2 (age 2–3 years): the child either becomes more independent or has a sense of shame and doubt. Erikson (1959, p.102) described "the sinister forces which are leashed and unleashed, especially in the guerilla warfare of unequal wills; for the child is often unequal to his own violent drives, and parent and child unequal to each other." The parents are the central figures.
- Stage 3 (4–5 years): the child shows initiative or experiences guilt. According to Erikson (1959, p.74), "Being firmly convinced that he *is* a person, the child must now find out *what kind* of a person he is going to be … he wants to be like his parents, who to him appear very powerful and beautiful, although quite unreasonably dangerous." The family is of central importance.
- Stage 4 (6–12 years): the child shows industry and works hard or develops a sense of inferiority. According to Erikson (1959, p.82), the child's approach during this stage is, "I am what I learn." This learning takes place at school and in friends' houses as well as at home, because the child's social world is expanding.

Children generally show a mixture of the positive and negative outcomes identified here. For example, most infants in Stage 1 develop some trust as well as some mistrust. Children for whom the outcomes of each stage are mainly positive develop a stronger and more positive sense of self than children for whom most of the outcomes are negative.

Evidence. Erikson relied heavily on clinical evidence to provide support for his theory, in his role as a practising therapist. Although such evidence can indicate that a theory is on the right lines, it is generally too anecdotal and imprecise to confirm the details of a theory. However, there is some experimental evidence providing indirect support for aspects of Erikson's theory. For example, Erikson argued that trust was a positive outcome of

What are the major drawbacks of using mainly clinical evidence to formulate a theory, as Erikson did?

PSYCHOSOCIAL DEVELOPMENT—ERIKSON'S STAGES 1–4				
Stage	Age	Positive characteristics	Negative characteristics	Social focus
1	0–1	Trust in self and others	Mistrust in self and others	Mother
2	2–3	Becoming independent	Sense of shame and doubt	Parents
3	4–5	Shows initiative	Experiences guilt	Family
4	6–12	Shows industry	Sense of inferiority	School, friends, home

Stage 1, whereas mistrust was a negative outcome. The work of Ainsworth on attachment behaviour is relevant (see pages 383 and 389). Ainsworth and Bell (1970) identified three forms of attachment of an infant to its mother. Secure attachment, which is most useful for the infant's psychological development, involves a high level of trust. In contrast, the less desirable resistant attachment and avoidant attachment both involve mistrust and anxiety.

Erikson's general notion that the development of the self during Stage 4 (ages 6 to 12) is increasingly influenced by friends and by schoolmates has received support in the work of Damon and Hart (1988) discussed earlier. For example, children between the ages of 8 and 11 are much more likely than those between 4 and 7 to describe themselves in comparison to other children.

Evaluation. Erikson's psychosocial theory possesses various significant strengths. First, its focus on social processes and the development of the ego greatly enlarged the scope of psychodynamic theory. Second, the notion that children face a series of conflicts or crises, with the consequences for their sense of self depending on how well these conflicts are resolved, is a valuable one. Third, Erikson would seem to be correct in arguing that most of the conflicts experienced by infants lie within the family, whereas later conflicts (e.g. in Stage 4) spread out to include school and peers.

There are several limitations of the theory. As Miller (1993, p.172) pointed out:

Erikson's theory does not explain in any detail how a child moves from stage to stage or even how he resolves the crisis within a stage. It states what influences the movement (for example, physical maturation, parents, cultural beliefs, to what extent earlier crises were resolved), but not specifically how the movement comes about.

Second, there is little convincing evidence for Erikson's theory. As Dworetzky (1996, p.369) pointed out

hard scientific proof for Erikson's theory is not easy to come by because of the difficulty of examining each of Erikson's stages under controlled laboratory conditions or by other scientific methods.

Why is it so difficult to examine a theory like Erikson's in a scientific way?

Third, one reason why it is hard to test Erikson's theory is because most of the evidence is correlational. For example, suppose we find that children who show signs of independence at Stage 2 develop a stronger sense of self in later childhood than those who do not. This does not prove that independence at Stage 2 *caused* a strong sense of self.

Fourth, there is a danger with any stage theory that it presents far too tidy an account of what happens. For example, a conflict between trust and mistrust is said to be central only to the first stage of development, but it could well be argued that this conflict keeps recurring through most people's lives.

Social learning theory

Most social learning theories have been concerned with the factors determining behaviour in specific situations. As a result, general notions like the self were ignored. However, Bandura (1977, 1986) expanded the scope of such theories by introducing the notion of **self-efficacy**, which refers to an individual's perception or assessment of his or her ability to cope satisfactorily with given situations. According to Bandura (1977, p.391), self-efficacy judgements are concerned "not with the skills one has but with judgements of what one can do with the skills one possesses."

Self-efficacy is regarded as being predictive of several aspects of behaviour. According to Bandura (1977, p.194):

Given appropriate skills and adequate incentives ... efficacy expectations are a major determinant of people's choice of activities, how much effort they will expend, and how long they will sustain effort in dealing with stressful situations.

KEY TERM
Self-efficacy: an individual's assessment of his or her ability to cope with given situations.

A child who has previously been successful in a situation is more likely to expect to succeed again, whereas one who has previously done poorly may be reluctant to put in much effort or show much interest.

Bandura (1986, p.41) argued that this approach to the self is more useful than one based on a very general self-concept. The reason is that the self-concept "does not do justice to the complexity of self-efficacy perceptions, which vary across different activities, different levels of the same activity, and different situational circumstances."

An individual's sense of self-efficacy in any given situation depends on four factors:

1. That individual's previous experiences of success and/or failure in that situation.
2. Relevant vicarious experiences, based on observing someone else cope successfully or unsuccessfully with the situation; this is observational learning.
3. Verbal (or social) persuasion: your feelings of self-efficacy may increase if someone argues persuasively that you have the skills needed to succeed in that situation.
4. Emotional arousal: high levels of arousal are often associated with anxiety and failure, and can serve to reduce feelings of self-efficacy.

Bandura's theoretical approach has several implications for the development of the self-concept:

What other effects might high levels of emotional arousal have, for example in a competitive sports situation?

1. Children develop numerous specific self-efficacy perceptions as a result of their successes and failures in different situations. In a sense, children develop an increasing number of "selves" as they experience more and more people and situations.
2. The fact that children's feelings of self-efficacy vary from situation to situation means that there is no general self-concept.
3. In order to predict whether children will feel generally good or bad about themselves and their abilities, it is necessary to have detailed information about their successes, failures, observational learning experiences, exposure to verbal persuasion, and so on.
4. As children develop, they make increased use of what Bandura (1986) termed self-regulation. Children who are self-regulated set themselves standards of performance. If they achieve these standards, there is a process of self-reinforcement through which they reward themselves. If they fail to match up to their own internal performance standards, then feelings of failure and guilt are created.

Evidence

There is much evidence from studies of children to show the importance of observational learning. Children who saw someone else (the model) behave aggressively and being rewarded for this showed observational learning, in that they then behaved aggressively themselves (Rosekrans & Hartup, 1967). Those children who saw the aggressive model punished did not behave aggressively because of the potential threat of punishment.

In a general sense, Bandura's approach leads to the prediction that children should develop more "selves" as they develop friendships with more people. Relevant evidence was reported by Harter and Monsour (1992). They asked children of 12, 14, and 16 to describe themselves with their parents, with their friends, and at school. Among the 12-year-olds, about one-third of the attributes they used to describe themselves in their relationship with the parents were also used to describe themselves with friends and at school. In contrast, 16-year-olds tended to describe themselves very differently in the three situations, suggesting that they had developed a number of selves. These findings are consistent with the claim of William James (1890, p.294) that people have many selves: "he [an individual] has as many different selves as there are distinct groups of persons about whose opinion he cares."

Do you think William James's description of a person with multiple "selves" is a useful one? Would you say it applied to you?

The importance of self-efficacy was shown by Bandura and Cervone (1983). Their participants performed a task, and then indicated how satisfied or dissatisfied they would be with the same level of performance during a subsequent session. Those high in self-efficacy exerted much more effort than those low in self-efficacy in the second session, and this was especially the case among participants who were dissatisfied with their initial level of performance.

One of the clearest predictions from Bandura's theory is that children and adults who have a strong perception of self-efficacy in one situation will not necessarily be high in self-efficacy in other situations. It has been found in several studies that individuals vary considerably in self-efficacy from situation to situation (Bandura, 1986).

Evaluation

The most important difference between Bandura's social learning theory and other theories is the notion that people possess more and more different "selves" as they experience an increasing number of situations and activities. This does not seem consistent with the fairly simple views of the self held by most children and adults. This discrepancy may well be due to the limitations of conscious awareness, as was claimed by Baars (1997). He referred to "the extraordinary oversimplification that seems to characterise our self-concept." There is no strong evidence, but Bandura (1986) may well be right that our sense of a single, integrated self is an illusion.

The greatest limitation of the social learning theory approach is that it is not specifically a *developmental* theory. In other words, Bandura does not spell out in detail how children's thinking about the self changes in the course of development. The *amount* of information about the self undoubtedly increases during childhood, as Bandura suggests. However, theorists other than Bandura (e.g. Erikson) argue convincingly that the *kinds* of information children possess about the self also change during development, and this is an important omission from social learning theory.

Cognitive-developmental theory: Harter

Harter (1982, 1987) put forward a theoretical approach to the development of self-esteem. He argued that children in early childhood have a rather incoherent sense of self. However, they generally have a very positive view of themselves. During the years of middle childhood, children's level of self-esteem tends to decrease somewhat. This is due, at least in part, to the fact that their self-esteem is increasingly influenced by the opinions of others (e.g. friends and teachers at school), whose views may be more realistic than those of the individual child.

Harter also emphasised the importance of children's assessments of self-competence. As part of the developmental process, children become concerned about their level of competence in an increasing number of areas. This reflects their growing involvement with society as they start going to school, developing friendships, and so on. Harter argued that children's level of self-esteem depends in large measure on their perceived self-competence. Children who regard themselves as competent in most ways tend to have higher self-esteem than those who regard themselves as incompetent.

Evidence

The development of self-esteem was studied by Harter and Pike (1984) and by Harter (1982). In the study by Harter and Pike, children between the ages of 4 and 7 were presented with pairs of pictures. They were told to indicate the member of each pair that corresponded more closely to themselves. The pictures related to the four areas of cognitive competence, physical competence, peer acceptance, and maternal acceptance. The children's responses indicated that they assessed their self-esteem in terms of two categories: (1) competence (cognitive and physical); and (2) acceptance (peer and maternal).

Harter assessed self-esteem in children between the ages of 8 and 12 by giving them the Harter Self-esteem Scale. These children made use of more aspects of self-esteem than did the younger children studied by Harter and Pike. They were able to distinguish among cognitive, social, and physical competence, in addition to general self-worth (e.g. "I am a good person").

Harter (1987) extended this line of work. Children rated themselves in five areas: scholastic competence; athletic competence; social acceptance; physical appearance; and behavioural conduct. They also gave a rating of global self-esteem. Incompetence in any area was associated with low self-esteem, and this was especially the case when the incompetence was in an area that the children regarded as important. Thus, for example, poor athletic competence had little effect on self-esteem among children who were not very interested in sport.

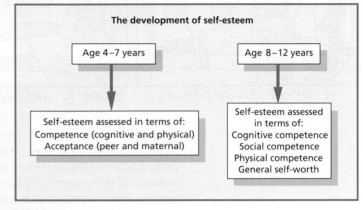

Discussion points

1. What are the problems with relying on self-reports to assess self-esteem?
2. Does it seem reasonable to assume that self-esteem and competence are closely linked?

Evaluation

Harter has shown clearly that there are close links between children's ratings of competence in various areas and their level of self-esteem. He also demonstrated that the number of areas in which children try to be competent increases as they enter more fully into society. These are both important contributions.

One limitation of Harter's approach is that it is based very largely on children's self-reports. In order for these self-reports to be valid, the children concerned must have had detailed conscious awareness of themselves, and must have answered honestly. It may be doubted whether either requirement was satisfied.

Another limitation of Harter's findings is that they are mostly correlational in nature. Harter assumed that feelings of incompetence produce low self-esteem. However, he did not exclude the possibility that low self-esteem made children underestimate their level of competence.

Factors influencing self-esteem

What determines the child's level of self-esteem? Coopersmith (1967) studied boys aged between 10 and 12, and found that how they were treated by their parents was important. The parents of boys with high self-esteem tended to have the following characteristics:

- They had general acceptance of their children.
- They set clearly defined limits on their children's behaviour.
- They allowed their children to control their own lives and to behave with reasonable freedom within those limits.

The findings of Coopersmith suggest that children with high self-esteem have parents who provide them with the opportunity to control themselves and their environment.

General acceptance

Clearly defined limits

Reasonable freedom

Children's level of self-esteem also depends in part on genetic factors. Pedersen et al. (1988) carried out a very large twin study using monozygotic or identical twins and dizygotic or fraternal twins brought up together and apart. They concluded that 31% of individual differences in neuroticism (a personality dimension concerned with anxiety, tension, and depression) were due to genetic factors. The relevance of this is that self-esteem is higher in those low in neuroticism than in those high in neuroticism (Eysenck & Eysenck, 1985).

In sum, there are various factors that jointly determine any child's level of self-esteem. The parenting style of the parents may well be of most importance, but genetic factors also seem to play a role.

PERSONAL REFLECTIONS

- What I find missing from most work on moral development, gender development, and development of the self is a proper consideration of individual differences. Stage-based theories tell us about the similarities in development shown by children, but they can blind us to the differences. For example, moral development differs considerably between children who become juvenile offenders and those who spend much of their time in charity work. Thus, we need to understand the factors producing individual differences as well as those producing similarities across children.

SUMMARY

Moral development

There are emotional, cognitive, and behavioural components associated with morality. Freud emphasised the notion that moral development depends on children's identification with the same-sexed parent at about the age of 5 or 6. This is a very limited theory. According to Piaget, children's moral reasoning goes through three major stages. Moral development occurs as children become less egocentric and more influenced by their peers. Children have more complex and mature ideas about morality than Piaget assumed. Piaget focused on moral reasoning rather than moral behaviour. Kohlberg expanded Piaget's theory in his six-stage theory. This theory has been supported cross-culturally, but it assumes more within-individual consistency than exists, and it tells us more about moral reasoning than moral behaviour. According to social learning theory, moral behaviour depends on direct tuition and observational learning. Reward and punishment can influence moral behaviour as predicted, and there is evidence for the inconsistency of moral behaviour across situations predicted by the theory. However, it is not really a developmental theory, and it does not account for the learning of general moral principles.

Most societies have expectations about the attitudes and behaviour of males and females. However, there are fewer and smaller differences between the sexes than is generally assumed. According to psychodynamic theory, anatomy is destiny, meaning that gender development is largely determined by biological factors. Freud argued that identification with the same-sexed parent plays a major role in the development of sex-typed behaviour. The evidence does not support this. According to social learning theory, gender development occurs through direct learning and observational learning. As predicted, sex-typed behaviour sometimes occurs because it is rewarded, whereas sex-inappropriate behaviour is avoided because it is discouraged. Social learning theorists focus on learning specific forms of behaviour rather than on general types of learning, and they tend to regard children as passive rather than active. According to Kohlberg's theory, children develop gender identity in three stages: basic gender identity; gender stability; and gender consistency. There is evidence for these three stages, and the achievement of gender consistency leads to the predicted increase in sex-typed behaviour. However, Kohlberg focused too much on the internal processes involved in the development of gender identity and not enough on external factors (e.g. rewards). According to gender-schema theory, young children who have acquired basic gender identity start to form gender schemas. Information that is inconsistent with gender schemas tends to be misremembered. There is limited support for biological theories of gender development. Stereotypes of females being nurturant and males being instrumental are very widespread across cultures.

Gender development

There is an "I" (the self as the subject of experience) and a "me" (the self as the object of experience). Children's reactions to their mirror images suggest that their sense of self starts to develop towards the end of their second year. The self-concept becomes increasingly complex in the course of development, and contains more interpersonal implications. According to Erikson's psychosocial theory, children's sense of self depends on the ways in which they resolve the conflicts arising at each stage of development. It is hard to evaluate this theory, in part because the available evidence is mostly correlational. Social learning theorists such as Bandura deny the existence of a general self-concept, arguing instead that self-efficacy perceptions depend on specific previous successes and failures, and on observational learning. Harter argued that children's self-esteem depends on their perceived competence in five domains. Children whose parents accept them, who set clearly defined limits on their behaviour, and who permit them to develop a sense of control, tend to be high in self-esteem.

Development of the self

FURTHER READING

The various forms of development discussed in this chapter are discussed in an informed way in K. Durkin (1995), *Developmental social psychology: From infancy to old age*, Oxford: Blackwell. Other useful textbook references are D.R. Shaffer (1993), *Developmental psychology: Childhood and adolescence (3rd Edn.)*, Pacific Grove, CA: Brooks/Cole, and J.P. Dworetzsky (1996), *Introduction to child development (6th Edn.)*, New York: West Publishing Company.

REVISION QUESTIONS

1   Compare and contrast the psychodynamic and cognitive-developmental theories of moral development. (24 marks)

2a Outline *two* theories of gender development. (12 marks)
2b Analyse the evidence on which *one* of these theories is based. (12 marks)

3   In 1902, Cooley formulated a looking glass theory of self. "He argued that 'the self that is most important is a reflection, largely from the minds of others'. It is as if we project ourselves into the minds of people watching us to see how people perceive us" (Jackson & Humphreys, 1995). Discuss whether or not psychological evidence supports this view of the development of the self. (24 marks)

- **Adolescence**
  Does being a teenager automatically mean having a hard time?

  Erikson's theory of identity crisis
  Marcia's four identity statuses
  Meilman's support for Marcia's theory
  Cross-cultural differences

- **Personality change in adulthood**
  How we continue to develop and change throughout our adult lives.

  Erikson's later stages
  Levinson's life cycle theory
  Roberts and Newton's interview study

- **Adjustment to old age**
  Does growing old necessarily mean doing less?

  Cumming and Henry's disengagement theory
  Activity theory (e.g. Havighurst)
  Reichard et al.'s interview study

- **Life events in adulthood**
  The major events in most people's lives and how they can affect us.

  Holmes and Rahe's Social Readjustment Rating Scale
  Effects of parenting, divorce, bereavement, and unemployment

18

Adolescence, Adulthood, and Old Age

It is natural to assume that the most dramatic developmental changes occur during the years of infancy and early childhood. That may be true, but it is also true that important developmental changes are found throughout life. It is generally accepted that adolescence is a time of major change, but what about middle age and old age? Middle-aged people often have to deal with severe life events such as redundancy or divorce. As people move into their 50s and 60s, they are often faced with the problems of retirement, frequently combined with a reduced standard of living. As people move into old age, they may have to cope with the death of their husband or wife, and they may experience serious health problems.

Psychologists increasingly recognise that development continues from birth to death. Textbooks in developmental psychology used to consider human development only up to adolescence. In recent years, however, there has been a rapid increase in textbooks on what is known as developmental life-span psychology covering people's entire lives. Most of the life span is considered in this chapter, all of the way from adolescence to old age.

Ageing is not necessarily synonymous with withdrawal from society.

Adolescence

It is often assumed that adolescence is a very "difficult" period of life, with adolescents being highly stressed and moody. It is further assumed that adolescents are stressed because they have to cope with enormous changes in their lives. Some of these changes are in sexual behaviour following puberty. There are also large social changes, with adolescents spending much more time with others of the same age and much less time with their parents than they did when they were younger. Adolescence is also a time at which decisions need to be made about the future. Adolescents need to decide which examinations to take, whether or not to apply to university, what to study at university, and so on.

Adolescence is certainly a period of change, and adolescents do have various pressures on them. However, as we will see, it is *not* true that adolescents are especially stressed, and they are at no greater risk of being in crisis than adults of all ages.

When does adolescence begin and end? It is convenient to assume that it covers the teenage years from 13 to 19. However, some girls enter puberty at the age of 10 or 11,

and so become adolescent before they become teenagers. There are also numerous 20- and 21-year-olds who continue to exhibit many of the signs of adolescence. Adolescence cannot only be defined in terms of age, because some people enter and leave adolescence years earlier than others. In spite of these considerations, we will assume that the stage of development known as adolescence largely centres on the teenage years.

Erikson's theory

Erikson (1902–1994) was a psychoanalytically oriented theorist, whose ideas about adolescence stemmed from his observations of emotionally disturbed adolescents during therapy. His views have been influential, and have helped to create the general impression that most adolescents are stressed and uncertain about themselves and about the future.

Erikson (1950, 1968, 1969) argued that adolescents typically experience identity diffusion, which involves a strong sense of uncertainty. They need to achieve a sense of identity, which can be defined as "a feeling of being at home in one's body, a sense of 'knowing where one is going', and an inner assuredness of anticipated recognition from those who count" (Erikson, 1950, p.165). Adolescents find it hard to do this, because they are undergoing rapid biological and social changes, and they need to take major decisions in almost all areas of life (e.g. future career). In other words, adolescents typically face an **identity crisis**, because they do not know who they are, or where they are going. Erikson (1950, p.139) argued that the typical adolescent thinks about himself or herself in the following way: "I ain't what I ought to be, I ain't what I'm gonna be, but I ain't what I was."

Erikson (1969, p.22) spelled out in more detail what is involved in this identity crisis:

> Adolescence is not an affliction but a normative crisis, i.e. a normal phase of increased conflict ... What under prejudiced scrutiny may appear to be the onset of a neurosis is often but an aggravated crisis which might prove to be self-liquidating and, in fact, contributive to the process of identity formation.

What do psychologists mean by identity? What is an identity crisis?

Thus, Erikson seemed to think that it was almost essential for adolescents to go through an identity crisis in order to resolve the identity issue and move on to the formation of a stable adult identity.

According to Erikson (1968), the identity diffusion or uncertainty experienced by most adolescents has four major components:

1. Intimacy: adolescents fear commitment to others because it may involve a loss of identity.
2. Diffusion of time: this "consists of a decided disbelief in the possibility that time may bring change and yet also of a violent fear that it might" (Erikson, 1968, p.169).
3. Diffusion of industry: this involves either an inability to concentrate or enormous efforts directed towards a single activity.
4. Negative identity: this involves "a scornful and snobbish hostility towards the role offered as proper and desirable in one's family or immediate community" (Erikson, 1968, p.173).

Erikson (1969) assumed that there are some important differences between males and females in identity development: females develop a sense of identity later than males, allegedly because they realise that their identity and social status will depend very much on the type of man they choose to marry. It is unlikely that a theorist would make such assumptions in the greatly changed society in which we now live.

One final point needs to be made about Erikson's theoretical approach. Adolescence typically lasts for several years, and an identity crisis could possibly develop at any

A scornful and snobbish hostility towards the role offered in one's family.

point within the teenage years. According to Erikson (1968), however, an identity crisis is more likely to occur in late adolescence than at any earlier time.

Evidence

Some of the evidence is consistent with the notion that adolescents experience high levels of stress. Smith and Crawford (1986) found that more than 60% of students in secondary school reported at least one instance of suicidal thinking, and 10% had attempted suicide. In fact, suicide is the third-leading cause of death among Americans aged between 15 and 24. However, there are fewer suicides among young adults than among middle-aged adults.

One of the implications of Erikson's theory is that adolescents should have low self-esteem because of the uncertainties they face. However, the evidence does not support this. If there are changes in self-image during adolescence, those changes are more likely to be positive than negative (Marsh, 1989). Of course, some adolescents do show reduced self-esteem, but this is only common among those who experience several life changes (e.g. change of school; divorcing parents) in a fairly short period of time (Simmons et al., 1987).

There is also little evidence that adolescents are highly emotional. Larson and Lampman-Petraitis (1989) assessed the emotional states of American children between the ages of 9 and 15 on an hour-by-hour basis. The onset of adolescence was not associated with increased emotionality.

The evidence generally indicates that problems are more likely to occur early rather than late in adolescence. For example, Larson et al. (1996) found that boys experienced less positive emotion in their family interactions at the ages of 12 and 13, and girls did the same at the ages of 14 and 15. After that, however, the level of positive emotion increased in late adolescence back to the level of childhood.

Some studies have addressed the issue of sex differences in identity formation. Douvan and Adelson (1966) obtained support for Erikson's position. Adolescent girls had greater problems than adolescent boys with identity development, and this seemed to be because they focused on the changes in their lives that would result from marriage. In contrast, Waterman (1985) reviewed several studies, and concluded that there was only "weak and inconsistent evidence" that boys and girls follow different routes to identity achievement.

Evaluation

Erikson was correct in his argument that adolescents and young adults typically experience major changes in identity, and that these changes can cause uncertainty and doubt. However, Erikson overstated the case when he focused on the notion of an identity crisis that adolescents go through. Offer et al. (1981, pp.83–84) reviewed the literature, and came to the following measured conclusion:

Cross-cultural issues: Schooling and literacy vary across cultures. There are also cognitive differences, e.g. reasoning and problem-solving skills are culturally biased.

Why should a number of critical life changes reduce an adolescent's self-esteem?

■ Research activity: Erikson's theory

Consider Erikson's theory in the context of other variables in an adolescent's life:

1. In-groups: What major stresses, influences, and decisions are part of an adolescent's life?
2. Do you think that most adolescents accomplish identity formation adequately? If not, why not?
3. Erikson's theory is a stage theory. Can one scheme fit all individuals?

CASE STUDY: Anne Frank

Anne Frank was a Jewish teenager in the Netherlands during the Second World War. She and members of her family spent two years hiding from the occupying Nazis in a secret annexe at the back of a warehouse in Amsterdam, during which time Anne kept a diary of day-to-day events and her thoughts and feelings. Anne was 13 years old when the family went into hiding, and she experienced the difficulties faced by all adolescents as well as the almost unbearable situation of being confined with seven other people, facing hunger, boredom, and the constant fear of discovery. After a year and a half in the secret annexe, Anne wrote:

Everyone thinks I'm showing off when I talk, ridiculous when I'm silent, insolent when I answer, cunning when I have a good idea, lazy when I'm tired, selfish when I eat one bite more than I should, stupid, cowardly, calculating, etc., etc. All day long I hear

nothing but what an exasperating child I am, and although I laugh it off and pretend not to mind, I wish I could ask God to give me another personality, one that doesn't antagonize everyone.

After the war, only one member of Anne Frank's family had survived; her father Otto, who edited and published his daughter's diaries. Because of the social climate of the time (1947) Otto Frank edited out many references Anne had made to her sexual feelings and some passages in which she wrote with anger and sometimes hatred about her mother and other family members. A new edition of the diaries, published in 1997, gives a fuller picture of Anne Frank as a normal adolescent, struggling to come to terms with all the changes in her extraordinary and tragically short life.

The most dramatic ... findings are those that permit us to characterise the model American teenager as feeling confident, happy, and self-satisfied—a portrait of the American adolescent that contrasts sharply with that drawn by many theorists of adolescent development, who contend that adolescence is pervaded with turmoil, dramatic mood swings, and rebellion.

Most of Erikson's theorising was about male adolescents, and he had relatively little to say about female adolescents. This led Archer (1992, p.29) to argue as follows:

A major feminist criticism of Erikson's work is that it portrays a primarily Eurocentric male model of normality.

Erikson initially argued that identity in males and females differed for biological and anatomical reasons, for example, he referred to the "inner space" or womb as the basis for female identity. However, he changed his mind somewhat thereafter. Erikson (1968, p.273) argued that

nothing in our interpretation ... is meant to claim that either sex is doomed to one ... mode or another; rather ... these modes "come more naturally".

Erikson did not carry out any experimental studies to test his theoretical ideas. The ideal approach would have been to conduct a longitudinal or long-term study in which people were observed over a period of years starting before adolescence and continuing until after adolescence. In fact, as was mentioned earlier, Erikson relied mainly on his observations of adolescents undergoing therapy. He obtained evidence of an identity crisis in this biased sample, but this does not mean that all adolescents are the same.

Erikson seemed to believe that nearly all adolescents experience a similar identity crisis. In fact, however, there are enormous individual and cultural differences in the adolescent experience (Durkin, 1995). For example, Weinreich (1979) reported findings on different groups of adolescent girls in the United Kingdom. Immigrant girls (especially those from Pakistani families) had higher levels of identity diffusion than did girls from the dominant culture. It is fairly common to find that adolescents from ethnic minorities take longer to achieve identity status, perhaps because their lives are more complex and confusing than those of the majority group (Durkin, 1995).

Finally, Erikson's views merely *describe* what he regarded as typical of adolescent thinking and behaviour. He did not provide a detailed *explanation* of the processes responsible for creating an identity crisis, nor did he indicate in detail the processes responsible for resolving it.

EVALUATION — Erikson

While searching for an identity, adolescents are already having to cope with physiological changes, changing roles, relationships, the prospect of future work and/or education, and other pressures. All this as they try to discover who they really are, and how they are seen by others.

Erikson uses all these areas of uncertainty, and more, to suggest an identity crisis that adolescents are bound to go through. He has been criticised for his concept of a single identity, and for his research sampling, which has been seen as too small in number and too male-biased.

Erikson's ideas about identity have been termed oversimplified, and more elaborate accounts have been given by Marcia and others. Marcia recognised that multiple identities are possible. Others have criticised the fact that Erikson only offers the option that adolescents must go through a crisis.

Erikson was one of the first to develop a stage account of human development, but his stage theories fail to take individual differences fully into account. One stage or plan cannot apply to all people, and much evidence suggests that no two people with basically the same environment will behave in the same way.

Marcia's theory

James Marcia (1966, 1980) was much influenced by Erikson's (1963) notion that adolescents are likely to experience an identity crisis. However, he argued that better methods of assessing adolescents' state of identity diffusion or identity formation were needed. He also argued that Erikson's ideas were oversimplified, and that there are actually various different ways in which adolescents can fail to achieve a stable sense of identity.

Marcia's first assumption was that each adolescent has an identity status. In order to decide on each individual's identity status, Marcia made use of a semi-structured interview technique exploring the three areas of occupational choice, religion, and political ideology. Four identity statuses were proposed, based on the individual's position on each of two dimensions: (1) Have various alternatives been considered seriously in each of the

How does a semi-structured interview differ from use of a questionnaire?

three areas?; and (2) Have firm commitments been made in those areas? Marcia (1967, p.119) defined the key terms here as follows:

Crisis refers to times during adolescence when the individual seems to be actively involved in choosing among alternative occupations and beliefs. Commitment refers to the degree of personal investment the individual expresses in an occupation or belief.

The four identity statuses are as follows:

1. **Identity diffusion**: identity issues have not been considered in detail and no firm commitments have been made for the future.
2. **Foreclosure**: identity issues have not been considered seriously, but future commitments have been made in spite of this.
3. **Moratorium**: there has been an active exploration and consideration of alternatives, but no definite future commitments have been made; this corresponds to Erikson's identity crisis.
4. **Identity achievement**: various alternatives have been carefully considered, and firm future commitments have been made.

Marcia (1966) assumed that adolescents would tend to move from one of the low-identity statuses (diffusion and foreclosure) to one of the high-identity statuses (moratorium and achievement). Adolescents would change their identity status because of the growing external and internal pressures on them to enter the adult world.

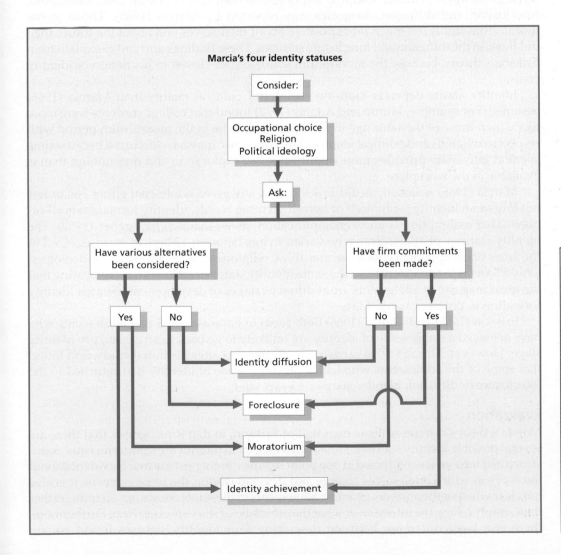

Meilman

Some support for Marcia's general approach was reported by Meilman (1979). He assessed the identity statuses of young males ranging in age between 12 and 24 using Marcia's semi-structured interview technique. All of the 12- and nearly all of the 15-year-olds had one of the low-identity statuses. Among the 15-year-olds, 64% had identity diffusion and 32% had foreclosure. Among the 18-year-olds, 48% had identity diffusion and 24% had foreclosure, with 20% having identity achievement. The percentage of identity achievers increased to 40% among the 21-year-olds, and to 56% among the 24-year-olds.

There are two surprising features of Meilman's findings. First, large numbers of people in their early 20s had still failed to achieve a stable identity, indicating that problems over identity are often by no means confined to the years of adolescence. Second, it appears that only a small minority of individuals at any age is in the moratorium period, suggesting that an identity crisis is fairly infrequent during or after adolescence.

Discussion points

1. Does it make sense to put adolescents and young adults into one of only four categories (see later)?

2. What confidence can we have in the opinions expressed by the participants in semi-structured interviews?

Evidence

One of the key differences between Marcia's theory and that of Erikson is that Marcia argued that there are different ways in which an adolescent can fail to have achieved a sense of identity. Evidence that it is important to distinguish among the moratorium, foreclosure, and diffusion categories was reported by Marcia (1980). Those in the moratorium status felt much more positive about themselves and about the future than did those in the diffusion and foreclosure statuses. These findings are hard to explain from Erikson's theory, because the moratorium status comes closest to his notion of identity crisis.

Identity status depends more on social and cultural factors than Marcia (1966) assumed. For example, Munro and Adams (1977) found that college students were more likely than those of the same age in full-time work to be in the moratorium period with respect to religious and political identity. This difference may have occurred because time spent at university provides more opportunity for exploration and questioning than is available in the workplace.

Marcia (1966) assumed, as did Erikson, that any given adolescent either has or has not forged an identity for himself or herself. In other words, identity formation is all-or-none. That assumption is an oversimplification, as was shown by Archer (1982). The identity statuses of adolescents who varied in age between 12 and 18 were assessed in the areas of occupational choice, gender roles, religious values, and political ideologies. Only 5% of these adolescents had the same identity status in all four areas, indicating that the great majority of adolescents are at different stages of development towards identity formation in different areas of life.

Erikson (1968) and Marcia (1966) both seem to have assumed that adolescents who have achieved a stable sense of identity are unlikely to go back to an earlier, pre-identity stage. However, Marcia (1976) carried out a follow-up after his initial study, and found that some of the adolescents who had achieved a sense of identity had returned to the foreclosure or diffusion identity status six years later.

Evaluation

Marcia's theory is more realistic than that of Erikson, in that it recognises that there are several possible identity statuses. However, it is open to most of the same criticisms. Semi-structured interviews conducted at one point in time cannot provide much evidence about the ways in which adolescents change and develop during the teenage years. It is also not clear whether the answers given by adolescents in these interviews are accurate, rather than simply telling the interviewer what they think he or she expects to hear. Furthermore, there is a large difference between describing four identity statuses found among

Marcia used semi-structured interviews to assess adolescents' identity status. What might be a better method to choose?

adolescents and explaining in detail how these statuses arise and are replaced by other statuses.

Marcia's whole approach is rather limited. This was shown by Archer (1992, p.33), who asked the following awkward question:

> *Why do we expend all this energy conducting these interviews, listen to these people share life stories, and then walk away with only these four little letters—"A" for identity achievement, "M" for moratorium, "F" for foreclosure, and "D" for identity diffusion?*

From your own experience, do you think Erikson was right, or do you prefer Marcia's more elaborate ideas?

Some studies have focused on the factors within the family that may lead adolescents to have different identity statuses. Adolescents in either the identity achievement or moratorium statuses tend to have affectionate parents and the freedom to be individuals in their own right (Waterman, 1982). Adolescents in the identity foreclosure status tend to have close relationships with domineering parents, and those in the identity diffusion status tend to have distant relationships with aloof or uninvolved parents (Waterman, 1982).

Cross-cultural differences

Adolescents in the United States and other Western societies generally take several years to achieve a clear sense of adult identity. However, that does not necessarily mean that similar processes are at work in other cultures. Markus and Kitayama (1991) drew a distinction between societies in which there is an independent construal of the self and those in which there is an interdependent construal of the self. Societies (such as the United States or western Europe) with an independent construal of the self tend to be described as individualistic, egocentric, and self-contained. Societies (such as those in the Far East) with an interdependent construal of the self are described as collectivistic, connected, or relational. In the latter societies, many of the key decisions of early adulthood are not taken directly by the individual concerned. For example, there may be an arranged marriage, and the individual may be expected to do the same job as his or her father or mother. In such societies, the whole nature of adolescence is different from that in individualistic societies.

In adolescence there are "developmental universals" such as puberty. Are developmental changes universal in adulthood?

Evidence that adolescence in the Western sense is not universal was discussed by Condon (1987) in his analysis of the Inuit of the Canadian arctic at the start of the twentieth century. In that society, young women were regarded as adult at puberty. By the time of puberty, they were usually married, and soon thereafter started to have children. Young men were treated as adult when they could build an igloo, hunt large animals on their own, and support themselves and their families. The difficult living conditions in the arctic meant that there was no time for teenagers to spend several years thinking about what they were going to do with their lives.

Difficult living conditions may force adolescents to move straight from childhood to adulthood in order to survive.

Personality Change in Adulthood

Even casual observation indicates that adults vary enormously in terms of the paths their lives take from the end of adolescence to old age. Some of these differences occur because of differences in personality, motivation, and interests, and some occur because of unexpected and unwanted life events (e.g. divorce; unemployment; illness). However, most adults form close relationships with others, most have one or more children, and most have jobs for much of their adult lives, suggesting that there may be some common life themes running through most people's adulthood. Theorists such as Erikson and Levinson have focused on these common themes, and used them as the basis for identifying the major stages of development in the adult years.

Erikson's theory

As we saw in Chapter 17, Erikson identified four stages to cover childhood. Erikson (1950, 1968) divided life during adolescence and adulthood into four further stages, each of which has its own developmental crisis. As with the earlier stages, each of the stages of adolescence and adulthood has a positive outcome and a negative outcome. Those who achieve only a negative outcome at one stage find it harder to cope during subsequent stages. The adolescence and adult stages are as follows (the ages for each stage are very approximate):

1. Stage 5. Adolescence (13–19 years): this is the stage during which individuals strive to avoid role confusion and develop a sense of identity. The social focus is on peer groups.
2. Stage 6. Early adulthood (20–30 years): this is the stage during which most adults commit themselves to a love relationship and to intimacy; other adults develop a sense of isolation. The social focus in this stage is on friendships.
3. Stage 7. Middle adulthood (30–60 years): this is the stage during which most adults commit themselves to productive and socially valuable work (including bringing up their own children and being concerned with others within society), or they become stagnant and self-centred. Erikson described these two extremes as generativity and stagnation. Generativity refers to "the interest in establishing and guiding the next generation" (Erikson, 1959, p.97). The social focus is on the household.
4. Stage 8. Old age (60 years onwards): adults in this stage try to make sense of their lives. If they are successful in doing so, they gain wisdom; if they cannot do this, then they experience despair. The social focus is on humankind.

PSYCHOSOCIAL DEVELOPMENT—ERIKSON'S STAGES 5–8					
Stage	Name	Age	Positive characteristics	Negative characteristics	Social focus
5	Adolescence	13–19	Identity	Role confusion	Peer group
6	Early adulthood	20–30	Intimacy	Isolation	Friends
7	Middle adulthood	30–60	Generativity	Stagnation	Household
8	Old age	60+	Wisdom	Despair	Humankind

In general terms, Erikson seems to have assumed that these three stages of adulthood applied universally to both sexes and to all cultures. However, Erikson (1968) did accept that there were often some differences between men and women in the sequence of stages. For example, men typically achieve a sense of identity before they achieve intimacy with a sexual partner during the stage of early adulthood. In contrast, Erikson argued that most women do not fully achieve a sense of identity until they have found a potential husband. According to him, the reason is that women's identity depends in part on the nature of the man she wishes to marry.

Evidence and evaluation

Erikson was one of the first psychologists to attempt the difficult task of providing a stage account of the whole of human development, and so he helped to open up the psychology of adulthood as an area of study. It is now generally accepted that people do develop and show significant psychological changes throughout their lives rather than simply during childhood.

Erikson's account of adult developmental changes is very sketchy. For example, it is doubtful that it makes much sense to argue that a single stage of development (middle adulthood) covers 30 years of an adult's life.

There is some evidence to support Erikson's assumption that men are more likely than women to achieve identity before intimacy. In a study on undergraduate students (reported in Bee, 1994), very few men showed intimacy without identity. In contrast, 52% of women who had not achieved identity nevertheless showed intimacy.

Different generations of people are brought up with slightly different values and aspirations, so how would this distort a general stage theory such as Erikson's?

Erikson hypothesised that it is harder for parents to provide their children with a sense of purpose to carry them through adult life when the society in which they are living is going through a period of rapid change. Erikson studied the child-rearing practices of Sioux and Yurok Indians, who were experiencing great social change. He found supporting evidence for his hypothesis in these societies (cited in Cardwell et al., 1996).

The most serious problem with stage-based accounts of development is that they imply that most people change and develop in the same ways. There is plentiful evidence that this is not correct. Neugarten (1975) discussed clear evidence that key developmental changes tend to occur at an earlier age for working-class men than for middle-class men. Working-class men tend to get married, have children, and have a full-time job during their early 20s, whereas middle-class men often delay settling down and getting married until their 30s.

The other major problem with Erikson's approach is that it was based on rather limited data. Erikson made use of detailed biographical case studies, such as his biographies of Martin Luther and Mahatma Gandhi, and on his clinical experiences. His approach has the disadvantage that information is obtained from only a small and unrepresentative sample of adults. It also has the disadvantage that Erikson had to rely on whatever information happened to be available (e.g. letters and other documents). It was hard for him to compare different individuals, because he did not have information from the same questionnaires or other measuring instruments as a basis for comparison.

Levinson's theory

Daniel Levinson (1978, 1986) argued that there is a **life cycle**, which consists of a sequence of periods spanning adult life. According to Levinson (1986, p.4), the notion of a life cycle "suggests that there is an underlying order in the human life course; although each individual life is unique, everyone goes through the same basic sequence." Many leading authorities such as Freud and Piaget assumed that development is essentially complete at the end of adolescence. In contrast, Levinson proposed that development continues during adulthood and old age.

Levinson (1986, p.6) also argued that there is a **life structure**, which he defined as "the underlying pattern or design of a person's life at a given time." In trying to understand an adult's life structure, it is of crucial importance to focus on his or her relationships with other people who matter to them, and on the ways in which these relationships change over time. What are the main components in the life structure? Levinson (1986, p.6) found that

> *only one or two components—rarely as many as three—occupy a central place in the structure. Most often, marriage-family and occupation are the central components of a person's life, although wide variations occur in their relative weight and in the importance of other components.*

According to Levinson's theory, the life cycle consists of a sequence of eras. Each era has its own psychological and social characteristics, and each era "makes its distinctive contribution to the whole." The move from one era to the next does not occur rapidly. Instead, there are cross-era transitions, which last for about five years and which span the time period from the end of one era to the start of the next. Finally, there are also important changes within each era.

The detailed structure of the life cycle is given next. The ages that are given for each part of the life cycle are the most common ones, but in practice there is a range of about two years above and below each figure. Here is the proposed structure:

1. Era of pre-adulthood (0–22 years): this is the era of most rapid development, as it spans infancy, childhood, and adolescence; the years between 17 and 22 form the early adult transition, in which there is the start of early adulthood as the individual begins to behave as an adult in an adult world.

■ Research activity: Using two separate decades such as the 1950s and 1980s, examine how Erikson's theory might or might not be relevant to people's experiences.

Do you think Neugarten's theories would apply in non-Western cultures, or across time, e.g. to men in the 1920s?

What is an unrepresentative sample? How and why should researchers safeguard against this?

Neugarten found that working-class men are more likely than middle-class men to marry early and have children.

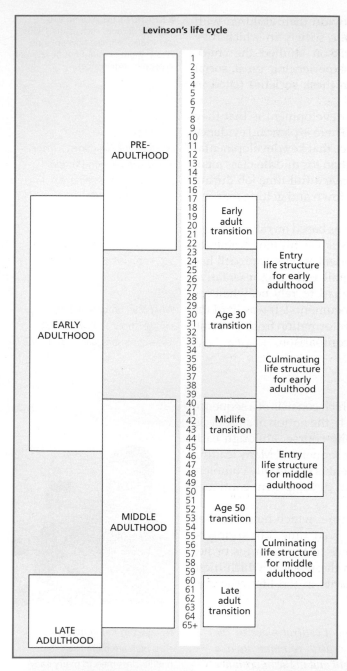

Levinson's life cycle

PRE-ADULTHOOD

EARLY ADULTHOOD

MIDDLE ADULTHOOD

LATE ADULTHOOD

1–16

17 Early adult transition
22 Entry life structure for early adulthood
28 Age 30 transition
33 Culminating life structure for early adulthood
40 Midlife transition
45 Entry life structure for middle adulthood
50 Age 50 transition
55 Culminating life structure for middle adulthood
60 Late adult transition
65+

2. Era of early adulthood (17–45 years): according to Levinson (1986, p.5), this is "the era of greatest energy and abundance and of greatest contradiction and stress." This era starts with the early adult transition (17–22 years), during which the individual forms a Dream, which comprises his or her major life goals. According to Levinson (1978, p.92), "If the Dream remains unconnected to his life it may simply die, and with it his sense of aliveness and purpose." The early adult transition is followed by the entry life structure for early adulthood (22–28 years), which is the time during which an initial attempt is made to construct an adult lifestyle. This is followed by the age 30 transition (28–33 years), which is a time for reconsidering and modifying the entry life structure. After that come the culminating life structure for early adulthood (33–40 years), which is the time for trying to realise key aspirations, and the midlife transition (40–45 years), which brings the era of early adulthood to a close and initiates the era of middle adulthood. In this period of transition, people often feel that their lives will never match their dreams. In other words, they have a midlife crisis.

3. Era of middle adulthood (40–65 years): this era starts with the midlife transition, followed by the entry life structure for middle adulthood (45–50 years), during which the individual develops a life style for middle age. This is followed by the age 50 transition (50–55 years), during which the life structure from the previous period is reconsidered and modified. The culminating life structure for middle adulthood (55–60 years) is the established life structure towards the end of this era. It is followed by the late adult transition (60–65 years), which spans the end of the era of middle adulthood and the start of the era of late adulthood.

4. Era of late adulthood (60–? years): this era begins with the late adult transition, and then moves on to periods concerned with the inevitable adjustments required because of retirement, declining health, and so on.

Early adulthood

Middle adulthood

Late adulthood

Two extreme positions are possible with respect to the life cycle. One extreme is to argue that adult development proceeds from one life structure to the next, with a rapid transition between successive structures. The other extreme is to argue that adult development involves almost constant change, with very little stability in the form of life structures being present. Levinson (1986) adopted a compromise position, according to which most adults spend about an equal amount of time in fairly stable life structures and in states of transition or change.

How can we decide the extent to which an individual's life structure has been satisfactory? There are two factors that need to be considered. First, there is the level of success or failure that the individual has had in his or her dealings with the external world. Second, there is the impact of the life structure on the inner self; for example, has the individual had to ignore or neglect some of his or her major desires?

Evidence

Levinson (1978) originally obtained evidence for his theory from interviews with 40 men in their 30s and 40s. There were ten novelists, ten biologists, ten factory workers, and ten business executives. All of the men were interviewed several times for a total of 10–20 hours over a three-month period in order to explore in detail the ways in which their life structures had developed during adulthood. He interviewed them again two years later, and also interviewed most of their wives. Some years later, Levinson carried out a similar study on 45 women. According to Levinson (1986), both studies indicated a surprisingly great tendency for everyone to proceed through the same periods and eras at about the same ages.

From your own experience, how would you evaluate Levinson's theory?

Roberts and Newton

Roberts and Newton (1987) considered findings based on detailed interviews with 39 women. Nearly all of them experienced a transition between the ages of 17 and 22, they had a Dream during that stage, and they went through a transition at about the age of 30. However, there were some important differences between these women and the men studied by Levinson (1978). Men's Dreams tended to revolve around careers, whereas those of women were more complex. Women's Dreams typically included both personal goals (e.g. career) and interpersonal goals (e.g. obligations to others; providing support for a "special man").

How did women resolve this conflict between personal and interpersonal goals? According to Roberts and Newton, many women who have focused mainly on their careers up to the age of 30 start to switch their attention to marriage and family, whereas those who spent their 20s pursuing marriage and family goals begin to think seriously about a career. Thus, the structure of the life cycle is broadly similar in men and women, but there are some important differences in terms of the Dream and major goals.

Discussion points

1. What reasons are there for assuming that young men and young women might have different goals and aspirations?
2. Do you think that there might also be important differences in the structure of the life cycle in individuals from different social classes or from different cultures?

Evaluation

The interview method used by Levinson (1986) poses various problems. First, people may not remember clearly what happened to them 20 years earlier. Second, what people say about the past may be deliberately distorted. Third, when the interviewer has a particular theory in mind, this can influence the kinds of questions that are asked and the kinds of answers provided by those being interviewed. Fourth, the fact that Levinson (1978) did not interview anyone who was more than 47 years old in his study on men limits what he can usefully say about men in their 50s and 60s.

Critics of Levinson's theory have often argued that there is no real evidence for a midlife crisis during the early 40s. For example, Vaillant (1977) collected longitudinal data over a period of several years on Harvard graduates. He found that some men did divorce, change jobs, or they suffered depression at midlife. However, the frequency of these major changes was about the same throughout adulthood, and there was no real evidence that the early 40s were an unusually difficult or stressful time.

Finally, there is a desperate need for cross-cultural studies in this area, because the structure of the life cycle is likely to be very different in other cultures. For example, there are societies in which life expectancy is only about 40 years. In such societies, it would make little sense to think of the period between 17 and 45 as forming early adulthood! There are other societies in which women are more or less prohibited from working, and this must influence the Dreams of women in such societies.

Adjustment to Old Age

Do you think that intellectual decline is an inevitable feature of old age?

One of the greatest changes during the course of the twentieth century was the dramatic increase in the number of older people in most Western societies. In the United States, for example, the average life span increased by 26 years during the twentieth century, and the proportion of people over 65 increased from 1 in 30 to about 1 in 6. As a result of this enormous increase in the number of old people, there has been a growth of interest in trying to understand the ways in which they adjust to the ageing process.

Adjustment to old age is hard for many reasons. Older people have typically retired from paid employment, their friends and close relatives may die, their physical health is declining, and they have reduced opportunities to be involved in society. In addition, they have to cope with negative stereotypes of old age. Goldman and Goldman (1981) asked more than 800 children in various Western countries their views on old age. Goldman and Goldman (1981, p.408) concluded that the mere figures

Do you think that society's stereotypes of older people lead to a self-fulfilling prophecy effect?

> *do not convey the revulsion and often disgust expressed about old age by many children of all ages. Descriptions of wrinkled skin, sickness, feebleness and increasing fragility were often accompanied by grimaces and emotional negativisms.*

Older people recognise the negative view of them held by society. Graham and Baker (1989) asked students and people in their 60s to indicate the status level of people of different ages. Both groups agreed that status level is low in young children, rises among those in their teens, 20s, and 30s, and declines in older people. The status level of 80-year-olds was as low as that of 5-year-olds.

What do old people regard as of most importance to allow them to enjoy a good quality of life? Ferris and Branston (1994) found that relationships, social networks, and good health were the three most important factors. The importance of social support was also found by Russell and Catrona (1991). Elderly people with little social support were more likely to develop depressive symptoms over a one-year period. Many old people have very little money, and so financial security is another important factor. Krause et al. (1991) found in America and in Japan that elderly people with financial problems experienced depression and a sense of worthlessness.

Disengagement theory

Cumming and Henry (1961) put forward the disengagement theory. According to the theory, there are various reasons why older people become less and less actively involved in society. Some of the reasons are due to factors beyond the control of the individual, such as compulsory retirement, deaths of relatives and friends, and children moving away from home. In addition, many older people choose to reduce the scope of their social lives, spending more and more of their time on their own. According to Cumming and Henry, progressive disengagement is the best way of adjusting to old age.

These theoretical ideas were developed by Cumming (1975). He argued that there is a gradual shrinkage of the

---

■ Research activity: Form groups to address the following questions and report your findings:

1. Is growing old a one-way ticket to decline?
2. If you were designing a study of older people, what design features would you include and why?
3. Do psychologists feel the same now as they have in the past about such issues as intelligence and memory capacities in the older person?
4. Has the way society deals with the older person changed in recent years?

life space in older people. This happens as they come to occupy fewer roles and have social interactions with fewer people. In addition, society has fewer expectations of older people with respect to those roles that they do continue to occupy. Finally, older people actively disengage from most of society, and this is the appropriate way of coping with external and internal pressures. The external pressures include a reduced need by others for the skills and abilities the older person possesses, and the internal pressures include deteriorating physical health and a decreasing level of concern about other people.

Evidence

Cumming and Henry (1961) provided some support for their disengagement theory. They carried out a five-year study on people between the ages of 50 and 90 living in Kansas City in the United States. They found substantial evidence that older people do progressively disengage from society. Somewhat different conclusions emerged from a follow-up study on over half of the original sample by Havighurst et al. (1968). They found that older people showed increasing disengagement as they aged. However, those who remained most socially active and involved tended to be the most contented, which is inconsistent with disengagement theory.

Illness, loneliness, and an unwillingness or inability to cope with day-to-day problems may lead older people to move to sheltered housing or a retirement home.

Two findings of Havighurst et al. were more supportive of disengagement theory. First, they found that some of those studied were *disengagers*, meaning that they had chosen to disengage themselves from social activities, but were nevertheless happy. Second, in spite of their declining levels of social engagement, older adults were less likely than younger ones to experience loneliness.

Evidence that older people cope with stressful situations in a more passive and disengaged way than younger people was reported by Folkman et al. (1987). Elderly people reported using passive and emotion-focused coping strategies in stressful situations, whereas younger people tended to prefer active, problem-focused coping strategies.

Do you think that progressive disengagement occurs naturally, due to the factors mentioned in the text, or do people choose to disengage?

Some categories of elderly people show signs of disengagement. For example, individuals who have always been rather reclusive tend to disengage in their later years (Maddox, 1970). Lieberman and Coplan (1970) found evidence for disengagement during the last two years of life. However, in many cases this disengagement was forced on the individual by ill-health and was not a voluntary choice.

Studies in the United Kingdom and Australia have found that the majority of elderly people do not show the social disengagement predicted by Cumming and Henry (1961). For example, many of them remain very active socially through the church or through community organisations (see Durkin, 1995).

Cultural differences

There are important cultural differences in the extent to which older people disengage from society. In many non-Western cultures, elderly people tend to be actively involved in society, and they are given respect and authority because of their age (Tout, 1989). For example, elderly women in India generally maintain an active role in the lives of their community (Merriman, 1984). However, this is not the case with all non-Western cultures. Nomadic peoples who are frequently moving on from one place to the next often show little respect towards the elderly, because they reduce the mobility of the entire group (Tout, 1989).

Recent studies suggest that the majority of elderly people do not show social disengagement, but instead remain socially active.

As the years go by, so Western influences are spreading throughout much of the world. This has led to a marked reduction in the extended family with the grandparents at its head in numerous cultures in Africa and Asia. The growing tendency towards social exclusion of elderly people in some of these cultures was observed by Turnbull (1989) among the Ik people of Uganda. They have experienced a number of stressful social and economic circumstances, which are responsible in part for growing hostility towards the elderly. When outsiders offered help (e.g. medication) to elderly members of the Ik people, considerable resentment was shown towards them for providing assistance to the "dead".

Evaluation

Older people generally show some signs of disengagement from society, although the extent of this disengagement is often less than was suggested by Cumming (1975). In addition, there are more signs of disengagement among older people shortly before death. However, it seems likely that disengagement occurs more because of external factors (e.g. retirement) than because older people *want* to disengage themselves from society.

One of the greatest limitations of disengagement theory is that it is based on the implicit assumption that all older adults are basically similar. This assumption is incorrect, because there are important personality and cultural factors that determine whether or not older people will disengage. It is known that adult personality changes only modestly during the adult years (Conley, 1984), and so those who are sociable and extroverted during the years of early adulthood and middle age are likely to remain sociable and socially engaged into old age. In contrast, there are many middle-aged people who are unsociable, and so are likely to become disengaged years before they reach old age (Bee, 1994). In other words, individual differences in personality allow us to predict fairly well whether any given person will or will not disengage in later life.

Disengagement theory also fails to take cultural factors into account. We have seen that there are significant cultural differences in the ways in which older people are regarded. Of particular importance here is the distinction between individualism and collectivism (Triandis, 1994). In Western societies, with their individualistic emphasis on personal achievement, older people with their declining powers are likely to be at least partially rejected by society. In the collectivistic societies of Asia and Africa, on the other hand, the greater emphasis on co-operation and supportive groups leads to older people remaining more integrated and engaged with society (Triandis, 1994).

Cardwell et al. (1996) make the interesting point that there may be cohort or generational effects. Those who are elderly now grew up in a society that was much less affluent, in which medical treatment was less developed, and in which life expectancy was less. In contrast, those who are currently young or middle-aged are likely on average to be more secure financially and healthier when they become elderly. It is thus possible that any tendency towards disengagement among the current elderly may be greatly reduced in following generations.

Images of old people change with the times. In the 1880s far fewer people survived into their 70s. How would theories such as disengagement theory have applied to people who had no welfare system to help them in their old age? In the 1940s life expectancy had improved for many reasons, and in the 1990s staying young in outlook and being active were the goals for many aged 70 and over.

CASE STUDY: *Wisdom in Old Age—Laurens van der Post*

Laurens van der Post was born in South Africa in 1906 and died in 1996 at the age of 90. He spent his childhood in Africa, where he developed a closeness with and a fascination for the culture and beliefs of the native people of the Kalahari desert. Later he sailed on a whaling ship and then undertook a long voyage to Japan, which in the 1930s was closed to many Westerners. During the Second World War he fought in the South-East Asian jungle and was taken prisoner by the Japanese. After the war he travelled the world and wrote many books, both fiction and non-fiction, about the cultures and countries he came to know. He was a friend and admirer of the psychiatrist and psychologist Carl Jung.

All this varied experience led van der Post to become a writer and thinker who was deeply concerned with human spirituality, and in his later years he was regarded as a mentor by many people, including the Prince of Wales. In his old age he was valued for his wisdom and insight in a way that is rare in Western society, although it is interesting to note that much of his early life was spent in close contact with non-Western cultures. In a collection of conversations with a friend published in 1986 (Pottiez, 1986, p.146) van der Post is described as " ... like a white Bushman and the earth is your hunting ground." Van der Post himself responds:

I do not know ... but I think one's whole life is a search ... the whole of life consists of making your way back to where you came from and becoming reunited with it in greater awareness than when you left it; by then adding to it your own awareness, you become part of the cosmic awareness.

Activity theory

Havighurst (1964) and other theorists have put forward a different approach to ageing, known as activity theory. According to this theory, older people become somewhat disengaged from society, not because they choose to, but because that is the way that they are treated by society. For example, many workers are forced to retire against their wishes because they have reached the age of 60 or 65, or for some other reason. It is assumed within activity theory that the best strategy for older people to adopt is to remain as active as they can. This involves hanging on to as many of the activities they were involved in during middle age for as long as possible.

Do you think that self-perception could affect the way some people cope with ageing?

Of particular importance is the need to keep involved in numerous different roles within society, trying to replace any roles that have disappeared with new ones. In other words, they need to maintain their "role count". This can be done by starting new hobbies, joining clubs (e.g. a theatre club), or babysitting their grandchildren.

How would you evaluate activity theory? Perhaps you can think of individuals who fit this profile, but does it apply to everyone?

Evidence

Evidence that activity theory describes older people better than does disengagement theory was reported by Atchley (1977), who argued that "most people continue to do in retirement the same kinds of things they did when they were working." Atchley reported on the percentages of men and women continuing to fulfil various social roles in their 70s and beyond. Among men aged between 70 and 74 (the figures for men aged 75 and over are in brackets), 76% (71%) had contact with close relatives, 72% (71%) had the role of friend, 48% (36%) that of neighbour, and 24% (21%) that of worker. Among women aged between 70 and 74 (the figures for older women are in brackets), 56% (50%) had contact with close relatives, 60% (83%) had the role of friend, 52% (50%) that of neighbour, and 16% (17%) that of

Social roles and the elderly (Atchley, 1977)

worker. Thus, most elderly people in the United States have a variety of active social roles.

Heckhausen (1997) presented evidence that older people remain active and motivated in their lives. He studied three groups of people (20- to 35-year-olds; 40- to 55-year-olds; and those 60 plus) in terms of primary control, which consists of active attempts to change the external world in line with the individual's desires. His key finding was as follows: "primary control striving remains stable across the life span, even though the opportunities for primary control decrease in old age" (p.183). However, there were some age differences in terms of the areas in which the participants tried to exercise primary control. Older people focused more than younger ones on the areas of health, leisure, and community, but they focused less on family, financial, and work goals.

Langer and Rodin (1976) studied elderly people living in nursing homes. Those who were encouraged to be active and to look after themselves as much as possible had greater

In what ways can living in an institution affect a person psychologically?

psychological well-being and lived longer than those who were less active. In similar fashion, Yaguchi et al. (1987) found that old people in Japan who remained physically active had higher levels of morale and more life satisfaction than those who were not physically active.

Evaluation

Perhaps the greatest strength of activity theory is that it is based on the recognition that there are important continuities between middle age and old age. In other words, most of the needs and motivational forces that lead middle-aged people to be actively involved in society still apply when they move into old age. Further support for activity theory comes from the frequent finding that the most contented older adults tend to be those who are the most active (e.g. Havighurst et al., 1968; Langer & Rodin, 1976).

The main weakness of activity theory is that it is greatly oversimplified. It takes little or no account of individual differences in personality. Some older adults (such as the disengagers in the Havighurst et al. study) deliberately reduce their activity level and disengage from society, because they find that this approach suits them. Activity theory also pays little attention to several factors other than activity level which contribute towards the adjustment made to old age. These factors include physical health, financial security, close relationships, and a strong social network.

Most elderly people are less active than middle-aged people, and so it might be expected that they would be less content as a result. In fact, however, the level of contentment in elderly people is similar to that in the middle-aged (see Durkin, 1995).

Surprising numbers of active elderly people take up as a retirement hobby something related to their working life, for example ex-railway men volunteering to drive steam trains.

Synthesis

A central weakness with both disengagement theory and activity theory is that they are based on the oversimplified assumptions that all older people are essentially alike and are exposed to similar circumstances. Stuart-Hamilton (1994, p.127) put forward a more realistic hypothesis

> *disengagement and activity theory describe the optimal strategy for some but not all elderly individuals, and which is the better depends upon a variety of factors, such as: financial circumstances (e.g. can one afford an active lifestyle?); health (e.g. does one still have the vigour for some hobbies?); and personality types (e.g. a lifelong introvert may hate an active lifestyle).*

Reichard et al.

The notion that there are different ways of coping successfully with old age was supported by Reichard et al. (1962). They interviewed 87 Americans aged between 55 and 84, and identified five personality types. Two of these (hostility, in which others are blamed for one's misfortune; and self-hatred, in which the hostility is turned on oneself) were associated with poor adjustment to old age. In contrast, the other three personality types were associated with fairly successful adjustment to old age:

- Constructiveness: this involves coming to terms with the losses of old age, and continuing to interact positively with others.
- Dependent or "rocking chair": this involves regarding old age as a time of leisure, and being reliant on others to provide assistance.
- Defensiveness: this involves remaining very active, as if pretending that old age has not arrived.

The findings of Reichard et al. are relevant to the disengagement and activity theories. The dependent personality style clearly possesses elements of disengagement, whereas the defensive personality style is primarily based on activity. Thus, we have evidence here that both theories apply reasonably well to certain individuals.

Discussion points

1. Is it possible that personality is more important than age in determining an individual's outlook on life?
2. Does it make sense to assign all old people to one or other out of five categories?

The disengagement and activity theories both assume that adjustment to old age depends more on *what* you do than on *who* you are. However, there is strong evidence that who you are in terms of personality has a substantial effect on psychological well-being. Costa and McCrae (1980) argued that happy people are those who experience many pleasant emotions and few negative ones. They also argued that those high on extraversion or sociability experience more pleasant emotions than introverts, and that those high on neuroticism (a personality dimension involving being anxious and depressed) experience many

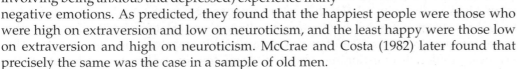

As if pretending that old age has not arrived...

negative emotions. As predicted, they found that the happiest people were those who were high on extraversion and low on neuroticism, and the least happy were those low on extraversion and high on neuroticism. McCrae and Costa (1982) later found that precisely the same was the case in a sample of old men.

Do you think life events tend to occur in clusters?

Life Events in Adulthood

Social Readjustment Scale

Most adults experience several stressful life events over the years. Close relatives may die, they may get divorced, they may become unemployed, and so on. What are the effects of such life events on those who experience them? Holmes and Rahe (1967) addressed this issue. They developed the Social Readjustment Rating Scale, on which people indicate which out of 43 life events have happened to them over a period of time (generally six months or twelve months). These life events are assigned a value (out of 100) in terms of their likely impact (for a full description and examples see pages 147–148). You may or may not be surprised to learn that holidays and Christmas are regarded as sources of stress. However, Holmes and Rahe argued that any change (whether desirable or undesirable) can be stressful. Thus, for example, they included marital reconciliation (45 life-change units), gain of a new family member (39), and outstanding personal achievement (28) among the 43 life events.

Christmas, supposed to be a happy time for joyful family get-togethers, can be a source of considerable stress.

There have been numerous studies using the Social Readjustment Scale. Those individuals experiencing events totalling more than 300 life-change units over a period of one year or so are more at risk for a wide range of physical and mental illnesses. These illnesses include heart attacks, diabetes, TB, asthma, anxiety, and depression. The correlations between life-change units and susceptibility to any particular illness tend to be rather low, rarely exceeding about +0.30.

Evaluation

The approach adopted by Holmes and Rahe (1967) has been very influential, and numerous questionnaire measures of life events have been developed. Their basic assumption that severe life events will increase the probability of being affected by a stress-related illness is a reasonable one that is supported by most of the evidence.

■ Research activity: In groups or singly, evaluate Holmes and Rahe's study bearing in mind the following:
• Methodological problems
• Other studies in the same area
• Ethical issues
• Personality variables and individual differences
• Context and social networks
• Perceived control
• Self-report and retrospective studies
• The role of memory
• Balance: interaction between desirable and undesirable events

On the negative side, there are four key problems with use and interpretation of the Social Readjustment Scale.

Direction of causality. First, it is often not clear whether life events have caused some stress-related illness, or whether stress caused the life events. For example, stress may play an important part in producing life events such as marital separation, change in sleeping habits, or change in eating habits. Schroeder and Costa (1984, pp.859–860) found that

when health-related, neuroticism-related, and subjective items were included in the life event measure, the customary low-to-moderate correlation with reported illness was obtained. However, ... when these contaminated items were excluded, the remaining items were not correlated with illness, which suggests that illness is essentially independent of the occurrence of life event changes.

Individual variation. The impact of most life events varies from one person to another. For example, marital separation may be less stressful to someone who has already established an intimate relationship with someone else, and who long ago ceased to have any affection for his or her spouse. Brown and Harris (1982) addressed this issue by developing a semi-structured interview approach to life events. This involves detailed questioning about life events in order to understand the background *context*. The likely impact of any given life event on the average person in that context is then assessed. This approach is superior to self-report approaches, but is much more time-consuming.

Memory problems. Memory failures can reduce the usefulness of the Scale. People often cannot remember minor life events from several months ago. Jenkins, Hurst, and Rose (1979) asked their participants to report the life events that had occurred during the same six-month period, on two occasions nine months apart. Their total scores were about 40% lower on the second occasion than the first. One way of reducing this problem is to use a structured interview approach in which the interviewer asks several questions about the occurrence and dating of events. Brown and Harris (1982) found that there was much less forgetting when this approach was used.

Desirable vs. undesirable events. Holmes and Rahe (1967) assumed that desirable life events could cause stress-related illnesses. However, most of the evidence does not support that assumption (Paykel, 1974). According to Martin (1989, p.198):

Do you think that stress is always a negative factor in people's lives?

Desirable events have generally been found to be nonsignificantly related to a variety of dependent measures, and the general consensus at present is that life event measures should include only undesirable events.

Parenting

Is the inclusion of gaining a new member of the family as a stressful event inconsistent with Martin's view (given earlier).

Gaining a new member of the family is one of the more stressful life events in the Social Readjustment Scale (Holmes & Rahe, 1967). This may seem surprising. However, becoming a parent involves numerous changes in lifestyle, a marked reduction in free time, and a considerable increase in responsibility. It also produces a change of role, with parents defining themselves and being defined by others as occupying the roles of father and mother. As Bee (1994) pointed out, parents with young children have much less time for each other. As a result, they have fewer conversations with each other, less sex, and spend less time doing routine chores together.

Could parenting style be a factor in the reduction in time couples spend together when a baby is born?

These factors help to explain why studies carried out in Western societies consistently indicate that the arrival of the first child reduces marital satisfaction (e.g. Reibstein & Richards, 1992). This adverse effect is found in all religious groups, races, and at all educational levels (Eysenck, 1990). It is stronger in women than in men, in part because women often expect that the father will provide more assistance with the baby than turns out to be the case (Ruble et al., 1988). Indeed, the only clear exception is provided by white people who feel that the ideal number of children in a family is at least four! There is also evidence of the "empty nest" syndrome, in which marital satisfaction increases somewhat after the last child has left home (Eysenck, 1990).

Why do so many adults decide to have children? Turner and Helms (1983) put forward several reasons. First, children provide a sense of achievement. Second, they allow parents to give and to receive love. Third, having children is a cultural expectation in many societies. Fourth, children can give their parents a sense of importance.

The arrival of a new baby is stressful for both parents.

Cross-cultural issues: What effect do you think extended families in non-Western cultures might have on the findings of studies like those of Reibstein and Richards, or Ruble et al.?

Relevant factors

The extent to which parents adjust successfully or unsuccessfully to the arrival of a baby depends on several factors. For example, working-class parents show less dissatisfaction with parenthood than do middle-class parents (Russell, 1974). A possible reason for this is that becoming a parent is more likely to have a serious disruptive effect on the career plans of middle-class women.

As might be expected, the extent to which mothers are satisfied with the role of mother influences their reactions to their children. Lerner and Galambos (1985) carried out a study in the United States, and found that children are more likely to be rejected if their mother is dissatisfied with her role. In addition, the children are more likely to become difficult to handle.

Couples differ in how well they adjust to the demands of parenting. Couples who are psychologically close before the birth of their first child are most likely to adjust well to its arrival. For example, couples whose interactions were most positive during the months of pregnancy, and who showed respect to each other when conflicts arose, dealt most successfully with their roles as parents (Heinicke & Guthrie, 1992). Fathers feel more positive about their role and mothers behave more warmly towards their children in couples who confide in each other (Cox et al., 1989).

The age and financial circumstances of parents are also important in determining how well they adjust to having a baby. Couples who are young and who have adequate amounts of money tend to be happier parents than couples who are older and poorer (Bee & Mitchell, 1984).

Evaluation

It is very hard to draw general conclusions from research on parenting. There are two main reasons. First, the impact of a baby on its parents depends on numerous factors. These factors include social class, the attitude of the mother to her new role, the psychological closeness of the parents, the extent to which the parents confide in each other, the age of the parents, and the financial means of the parents. Other factors that are likely to be important are whether the baby was planned and whether or not the parents have other young children.

Second, the three people in the basic family (father, mother, child) typically interact in complex ways with each other. As a result, it is usually hard to work out exactly *why* any given couple finds parenting a stressful experience. For example, a married couple may argue that parenting is stressful because their child cries a lot and behaves badly. However, it is possible that the child's mother has not behaved with enough warmth and sensitivity to produce secure attachment of the child to its mother (see Chapter 15). In other words, it is often hard to establish cause and effect.

How would you design a study to look at how couples adjust to being parents? What ethical issues might be involved?

When divorce was rare and carried a social stigma, cards such as these were unheard of. However, 40% of marriages in Britain now end in divorce.

What effect do you think the social climate in 1969 might have had on the responses people gave in Bradburn's study? Do people always tell the truth in situations like this?

Divorce

Divorce is becoming increasingly common in Western societies. Almost 40% of marriages in Britain end in divorce, and the figure is even higher in the United States. Divorce is especially likely during the first five years of marriage, and other "danger periods" are after 15 and 25 years of marriage (Gross, 1996).

Divorce is the second most stressful life event after death of one's spouse according to the Social Readjustment Scale (Homes & Rahe, 1967). Divorced people tend to have worse mental and physical health than married people (Buunk, 1996). Indeed, their general health is even worse than that of people who are widowed or who have never married.

Information on happiness levels as a function of marital status was obtained by Bradburn (1969) in an American study. Bradburn found that 35% of married men and 38% of married women said they were "very happy", which was much higher than the figures for never-married men and women (18% in both cases). In turn, the never-married were more likely than the separated, divorced, or widowed to indicate that they were "very happy". At the other end of the scale, fewer than 10% of married people said they were "not too happy", compared to over 30% of divorced people, and 40% of separated people. These findings may be due to divorce causing unhappiness, but it is also possible that unhappy people are more likely to get divorced.

The stressfulness of divorce depends on a variety of factors. Buunk (1996, p.371) concluded that:

> *Individuals who had a less close relationship with their former partner, who took the initiative to break up or divorce, who are embedded in social networks, and who at present have a satisfying, intimate relationship, are relatively better off. In addition, certain personality characteristics, including high self-esteem, independence, tolerance for change, and egalitarian [favouring equality] sex-role attitudes, facilitate coping with the situation of being divorced.*

The impact of divorce often differs for men and women. Women are likely to suffer more in some ways, because they often lose more financially and have to accept greater parental responsibilities (Rutter & Rutter, 1992). On the other hand, men are less likely than women to initiate divorce proceedings, and they tend to have weaker support networks (Gross, 1996).

Stages

It has been argued that those getting divorced tend to go through a series of stages during the divorce process. For example, Bohannon (1970) proposed the following six stages:

1. Emotional divorce: the marriage disintegrates psychologically amid conflict and recrimination.
2. Legal divorce: the marriage ends officially and legally.
3. Economic divorce: the assets of the divorced couple are divided up.
4. Co-parental divorce: issues relating to custody of any children of the marriage and access rights to them are decided.
5. Community divorce: the necessary changes are made to relationships with family and friends.
6. Psychic divorce: the two divorced people adjust separately to the new state of affairs.

As with most stage theories, it may be doubted whether everyone who gets divorced works their way neatly through these six stages in the specified order.

Can you use the concept of loss to link divorce with bereavement and other critical life events?

Evaluation

The effects of divorce vary greatly depending on the personalities of those involved, on the nature of the previous relationship between them, and on the existence (or otherwise) of another intimate relationship and a strong social network. The available evidence is limited. Divorced people are less happy and more stressed than non-divorced people, and this could occur because divorce makes people stressed, or because stressed and unhappy people seek divorce. We don't know exactly what is going on, but there is evidence that certain kinds of people tend to divorce. For example, identical twins whose co-twin has divorced are rather more likely to become divorced than identical twins whose co-twin has not divorced (Plomin, 1997). The genetic factors that play a part in determining who becomes divorced may also tend to produce negative emotional states.

Bereavement

According to the Social Readjustment Scale (Holmes & Rahe, 1967), bereavement in the form of death of one's spouse is the most stressful life event that people experience. There are several reasons for this. For most married people, death of their spouse causes considerable emotional trauma, because they have lost the central relationship in their lives. In addition, it typically also requires great changes in the life structure of the bereaved person. Finally, bereavement also has a major impact on the bereaved person's social identity. They lose their role as partner in a marriage, and adopt the lesser role of widow or widower. This can pose particular problems in those societies in which social life is organised mainly around married couples.

Stroebe et al. (1982) argued that the loss of one's spouse affects the survivor's social functioning in four main ways:

1. Loss of social and emotional support: this is the key loss.
2. Loss of social validation of personal judgements: an individual's spouse can help to make them confident about the correctness of their views.
3. Loss of material and task supports: in most marriages, there is some role differentiation, with the husband and wife focusing on different tasks and activities; after bereavement, the survivor has to take on the tasks done hitherto by the spouse.
4. Loss of social protection: the spouse can no longer defend the survivor from unfair treatment by other people.

Stages

Parkes (1986) argued that bereaved people go through a series of stages following the death of their spouse. First, there is a period of shock and numbness. Second, there is a period of an intense longing for the dead spouse. Third, there is a prolonged period of depression and general hopelessness. Fourth, the bereaved person does what is possible to construct a new life for himself or herself.

Ramsay and de Groot (1977) argued that the processes involved in coming to terms with bereavement do not occur in the predictable ways assumed by stage theorists. According to them, there are nine components of grief which may occur in various different orders: (1) shock or numbness; (2) disorganisation or an inability to plan sensibly; (3) denial (e.g. expecting the dead spouse to arrive home); (4) depression; (5) guilt at having neglected the dead spouse or having treated him or her badly; (6) anxiety about the future; (7) aggression (e.g. towards the doctors or members of one's family); (8) resolution or acceptance of what has happened; (9) reintegration or reorganisation of one's life.

It has often been suggested that the final stage of grief involves recovery from bereavement. However, Stroebe et al. (1993) argued that total recovery is often not possible: "if there has been a strong attachment to a lost loved one, emotional involvement is likely to continue, even for a lifetime."

Evidence

Nearly everyone who is bereaved experiences a range of grief reactions. Indeed, there are still signs of grief and other negative emotions $2^1/_2$ years after bereavement (Thompson et al., 1991). However, bereavement is somewhat less stressful if the person who died had been ill for some time beforehand (Eisdorfer & Wilkie, 1977). Bereavement is also less

Do you think that we deal with death in the same way as people did 100 years ago? What differences are there and what psychological consequences could there be?

stressful on average when the bereaved person is old rather than young (Stroebe & Stroebe, 1987). An important part of the reason for this is probably that the loss is more likely to be unexpected when the person who died was young.

Stroebe et al. (1982) reported evidence that those who have been bereaved are at increased risk of death from cirrhosis of the liver, accidents, strokes, coronary heart disease, and violence. Widowers are more at risk than widows so far as deaths from cirrhosis of the liver and violence are concerned. Gallagher-Thompson et al. (1993) carried out a longitudinal study, in which they confirmed that bereaved men and women are at increased risk of premature death. They also found that the bereaved who died were less integrated socially than those who did not: their spouse had been the main person in which they confided; they had small social networks; and they were generally less involved in social activities.

Cross-cultural issues: Do you think that Gallagher-Thompson et al.'s findings would apply equally to non-Western cultures? What cross-cultural differences might you expect to find?

It is much more common for the wife to be bereaved than for the husband. About 85% of married people who are bereaved are widows, against only 15% who are widowers. It is often argued that men find it harder to adjust to loss of their spouse than do women (Cavenaugh, 1994). One reason is that, for many men, their wife is their only close friend, whereas women tend to have a wider circle of friends. Another reason is that many men lack the housekeeping and cooking skills needed to look after themselves properly. Men tend to be older than women when they are widowed, and this makes it harder for them to cope. In view of this evidence, it is only to be expected that bereaved men are more likely than bereaved women to suffer from ill health and rapid death (Bury & Holme, 1991).

The effects of widowhood on women depend to a large extent on the nature of the relationship they had with their husband. Women who have defined themselves in terms of their husband experience a loss of identity, and generally find it very hard to adjust to widowhood (Lopata, 1979). In contrast, those whose lives have had a broader focus cope better and do not suffer much loss of identity. There is also evidence that widows who have strong relationships with other people (especially their own children) manage to adjust more successfully than those who do not (Field & Minkler, 1988).

Another difference between the sexes is that women who are bereaved are less likely than men to remarry. Lopata (1979) reported that widows are often reluctant to surrender their independence, and they are also concerned about the possibility of being widowed for a second time. In contrast, men often favour remarriage because they find it harder than women to achieve psychological closeness with people outside the home.

It is possible that sex differences in reactions to bereavement are in decline. As Stuart-Hamilton (1994, p.121) suggested, "the current societal re-evaluation of gender roles may eradicate whatever differences there are."

Unemployment

Not surprisingly, the psychological effects of unemployment tend to be negative. For example, Hepworth (1980) compared employed and unemployed British men on a measure of general distress containing items about feelings of anxiety, depression, worthlessness, hopelessness, and so on. The distress scores of the unemployed men were nearly six times higher than those of the employed ones. According to Warr (1987), unemployment typically causes a rapid fall in psychological well-being, followed by further deterioration. After that, there is a plateau of poor psychological well-being, which is reached three to six months after job loss.

Unemployment also has negative physical effects. Moser et al. (1984) carried out a 10-year longitudinal study on males who were aged between 15 and 64 at the start of the study. Men who were unemployed initially were significantly more likely than employed men to die during the course of the study, and this was especially so for death by suicide or lung cancer. As Warr (1987) pointed out, the increased risk of lung cancer may have arisen because unemployed men tend to smoke more than those in employment.

In spite of the fact that unemployment generally has negative effects, the size of these effects depends on the circumstances in which unemployed people find themselves. For

Unemployment can cause a rapid fall in psychological well-being.

example, unemployment is likely to be especially damaging to a relatively poor middle-aged person who is supporting a large family and who has little chance of finding another job. In contrast, unemployment will have less impact on someone who is wealthy and who was due to retire shortly in any case. Warr (1987) pointed out that about 10% of unemployed men actually report an improvement in their health since losing their jobs. This mostly happens because their jobs damaged their physical health, but some unemployed men reported improved psychological health as well.

What psychological effects can long-term unemployment have?

Why does unemployment typically impair psychological and/or physical health? Warr (1987) argued that there are nine environmental factors that influence psychological well-being, with unemployment tending to change all of these factors for the worse. The nine factors are as follows:

What reasons might there be for the improvement in mental health reported by 10% of men who lost their jobs?

1. Availability of money: unemployed people typically have less money at their disposal.
2. Opportunity for control: unemployed people are less able to behave as they choose.
3. Opportunity for skill use: this generally decreases as a result of unemployment.
4. Goals and task demands: unemployment reduces the demands on people, and can make their behaviour less purposeful and goal-directed.
5. Variety: unemployed people tend to have less variety and change in their everyday lives than those in employment.
6. Physical security: unemployed people may worry about the loss of adequate housing or may be unable to pay for fuel for heating and lighting.
7. Opportunity for interpersonal contact: unemployed people typically have social contact with fewer people than do employed people.
8. Environmental clarity: unemployed people tend to be more uncertain about the future than those in employment.
9. Valued social position: unemployed people lose the socially approved role they filled when they were employed, and this can cause reduced self-esteem.

One of the key predictions from Warr's approach is that unemployed people who manage to construct lives involving variety, opportunities for control and for skill use, goals and task demands, opportunity for social contact, and a valued social position should be best able to cope with a period of unemployment. This prediction was supported by Fryer and Payne (1984). Unemployed men and women who found satisfying roles in community, religious, or political organisations tended to have good psychological well-being.

Cross-cultural issues: In Western societies people often feel they are defined by the job they do. What effect do you think this has on how people cope with unemployment? How might this vary across cultures?

PERSONAL REFLECTIONS

*   Developmental psychology used to be concerned only with the period between birth and adolescence, presumably because the most obvious and dramatic developmental changes occur during that time. However, it actually makes much more sense to accept that change and development occur throughout the whole of human life. Most life-span developmental psychology focuses on the *similarities* among people as they move through adulthood and into old age. What is missing is an emphasis on the *differences* in development that are found among adults. In other words, what I would like to see in the future is a systematic attempt to understand why adults differ considerably in the types of development they show during the adult years.

SUMMARY

Adolescence roughly covers the teenage years, but is better defined in psychological terms rather than by age. Erikson argued that adolescents experience an identity crisis, because of identity diffusion or uncertainty revolving around intimacy, diffusion of time, diffusion

Adolescence

of industry, and negative identity. He also argued that females have greater problems than males with identity development. The evidence provides little support for the notion of a universal identity in adolescence or for sex differences in identity development. Erikson relied too much on limited observations of a biased sample of emotionally disturbed adolescents. Marcia argued that there are four identity statuses based on thorough thinking in key areas of life and firm commitments in those areas. There is support for the existence of these identity statuses, but they are less all-or-none than Marcia suggested. Erikson and Marcia both described rather than explained what happens in adolescence, and they ignored individual and cultural differences in the adolescent experience.

Personality change in adulthood

According to Erikson's theory, there are three major stages after adolescence: early adulthood; middle adulthood; and old age. The first stage revolves around intimacy vs. isolation, the second stage around generativity vs. stagnation, and the third stage around wisdom vs. despair. This theory is very sketchy, and it mistakenly implies that most people change and develop in the same ways. It is based on limited data from biographical case studies. According to Levinson, the life cycle consists of a series of eras, with lengthy cross-era transitions. The main eras are those of pre-adulthood, early adulthood, middle adulthood, and late adulthood. The evidence for this theory comes mainly from interview data, which are retrospective and may be biased. Levinson's assumption that virtually everyone experiences a midlife crisis has received little support.

Adjustment to old age

According to social disengagement theory, older people become less actively involved in society in part because they choose to become disengaged, and because it is the best strategy. However, older people who remain the most active tend to be the most contented. There is less disengagement in many non-Western cultures. Social disengagement theory de-emphasises individual differences in personality and preferred lifestyle. According to activity theory, older people should remain as active as possible. This theory recognises that there are important similarities between middle age and old age. Activity theory takes little or no account of individual differences in personality.

Life events in adulthood

Serious life events show some tendency to be followed by physical and mental illness. It is often hard to assess the direction of causality, and there are individual differences in the meaning of any given life event. Parenting tends to reduce marital satisfaction, because it reduces the parents' free time and increases their responsibilities. Divorced people tend to have worse mental and physical health than married ones. The divorce process involves various stages, starting with emotional divorce and legal divorce, and ending with community divorce and psychic divorce. Bereavement in the form of death of one's spouse is the most stressful life event, and can lead to premature death as well as grief. It causes a period of shock and numbness, followed by intense longing for the dead spouse, followed by a long period of depression, followed by the construction of a new life. Men often find it harder to cope with bereavement than do women. Unemployment has negative mental and physical effects. These effects occur because unemployment reduces the availability of money, control, opportunities for skill use, variety, and so on.

FURTHER READING

Chapters 15 to 19 of K. Durkin (1995), *Developmental social psychology: From infancy to old age*, Oxford: Blackwell, deal with theories of adolescence, adulthood, and old age in some detail. The changes that occur in old age are discussed fully by I. Stuart-Hamilton (1994), *The psychology of ageing: An introduction (2nd Edn.)*, London: Jessica Kingsley. The strengths and weaknesses of methods for studying life events are discussed fully by R.A. Martin (1989), Techniques for data acquisition and analysis in field investigations of stress, in R.W.J. Neufeld (Ed.) (1979), *Advances in the investigation of psychological stress*, New York: Wiley.

REVISION QUESTIONS

1   Critically consider what psychological research has told us about social development in adolescence.   (24 marks)

2   Describe and evaluate *two* theories of personality change in adulthood.   (24 marks)

3   Discuss ways in which it has been shown that people adjust to old age.   (24 marks)

4   Consider and analyse psychological research that has been carried out into the effects of life events in adulthood (e.g. parenting, divorce, bereavement, unemployment).   (24 marks)

- **Theories of social cognition**
  Do people define themselves by the
  groups they feel they belong to?

  Tajfel's social identity theory
  *Moscovici's definition of social
  representations*
  Cultural identity theories

- **Attribution theory**
  How we arrive at our opinions about
  other people's behaviour.

  *Jones and Davis's correspondent inference
  theory*
  Kelley's attribution theory
  *Gilbert et al.'s study of the fundamental
  attibution error*
  The actor–observer effect
  Self-serving bias

- **Prejudice and discrimination**
  What is the difference between these
  two terms? What are stereotypes?

  Allport's theory
  LaPiere's American study
  Macrae et al.'s stereotyping study
  Bodenhausen's cognitive approach

- **Theories of prejudice**
  Are some people born prejudiced?

  *Dollard et al.'s frustration–aggression
  hypothesis*
  Adorno et al.'s E- and F- scales
  Sherif's group conflict studies
  Runciman's theory of relative deprivation
  Aboud's social developmental theory

- **Reduction of prejudice and
  discrimination**
  Different approaches to changing
  people's prejudiced behaviour.

  Aronson and Osherow's jigsaw classroom
  The Wexler Middle School study
  *Brewer and Miller's decategorisation
  theory*
  *Experiencing prejudice: Weiner and
  Wright*
  Monteith's self-regulation approach

19

Social Cognition

What are the factors that cause us to behave in certain ways in social situations? Numerous factors are at work, including our personalities, our previous experiences in similar situations, the expectations of others, and our relationships with them. Social psychologists increasingly argue that one important way of understanding social behaviour is by studying the ways in which individuals think about themselves, about the groups to which they belong, and about other groups in society. Thus, they are interested in social cognition, which has been defined as "the way that we think about and interpret social information and social experience" (Hayes, 1993, p.159).

This chapter is concerned with some of the major aspects of social cognition. Two of the most influential theories, especially within Europe, are social identity theory and the theory of social representations. These theories are discussed, together with the related issue of cultural identity. After that, some of the main errors and biases in social cognition are described and examined. These errors and biases are important, because they introduce systematic distortions into our perceptions of our own behaviour and the behaviour of others. Finally, prejudice and discrimination are discussed with respect to the factors producing and maintaining them, followed by an analysis of ways in which prejudice and discrimination can be reduced.

Theories of Social Cognition

Much of social psychology is concerned with issues such as the factors responsible for individual and group identities, and the ways in which our knowledge of the world is acquired. The theories discussed in this section deal with such issues. What these theories have in common is their emphasis on the social and cultural context. At the risk of over-simplification, social psychologists used to argue that attitudes develop on an individual basis as people acquire more and more information about the world. The contemporary view is that attitudes and beliefs about the self and about the world depend in a profound way on social communication.

This section is concerned with social identity theory, social representations, and cultural identity. A key notion in social identity theory is that *who* we think we are is defined in a major way in social terms by the groups to which we belong. According to the theory of social representations, much of our knowledge of the world depends on our social interactions with others. According to views on cultural identity, an individual's feelings and beliefs about himself or herself depend importantly on his or her sense of cultural identity as a member of some larger cultural group. Thus, the thoughts that we have about ourselves, about our place in society, and about the world about us are all greatly influenced by social factors.

How many different groups do you belong to? Are some more important than others? Suggest some reasons for this.

Members of the Elvis Presley Fan Club in Blackpool.

Which of the groups that you belong to meets your need for self-enhancement?

Social identity theory

Social identity theory was put forward by Henri Tajfel (1978, 1981). According to this theory, we have a need to understand and to evaluate ourselves. This is achieved by self-categorisation, in which we think of ourselves as belonging to a number of categories. Of particular importance, everyone has a number of **social identities**, based on the different groups with which they identify. These social identities can include racial group, nationality, work group, gender, social group, and so on. Thus, for example, an individual may identify herself as a female, as a student, as a member of a netball team, and as a Londoner, all at the same time.

The other main ingredient in social identity theory is the need for self-enhancement. People try to increase their self-esteem by regarding the groups with which they identify as being superior to all other groups. In a nutshell, the key assumption of social identity theory is that how good we feel about ourselves depends on how positively we view the groups with which we identify.

Evidence

It is assumed within social identity theory that we have a strong need to form social identities. The most striking finding to emerge from Tajfel's studies is that a social identity can be formed with amazing ease. In one of his studies, 14- and 15-year-old boys estimated the number of dots seen in brief exposures. They were then assigned at random to one of two minimal groups: the over-estimators or the under-estimators. After that, they awarded points (which could be exchanged for money) to other individuals who were identified as belonging to the same group or to the other group. Nearly all the boys awarded more points to members of their own group than to members of the other group.

Ingroup favouritism. A similar amount of ingroup favouritism was found even when the participants were told they had been put into groups on a random basis (e.g. by the toss of a coin). Ingroup favouritism has also been found when judgements of likeableness/unlikeableness had to be made. The participant's own group was consistently judged as being more likeable than the other group.

There is evidence of ingroup favouritism in the real world. Brown (1978) reported a study of factory workers, who were highly motivated to maintain the wage differentials between their department and others in the same factory. This remained the case, even when this would lead to a reduction in their own earnings.

Why do people discriminate between an ingroup and an outgroup even with minimal groups? Doise (1976) argued that part of what is involved is **categorical differentiation**. The basic idea is that we exaggerate the differences between our group and other groups. We do this because it allows us to simplify and to organise our social worlds.

Self-esteem. Why do people favour their group over other groups? According to social identity theory, they do this because it increases their sense of social identity and boosts their

self-esteem. These notions were tested by Lemyre and Smith (1985). All their participants were put into groups at random. Some were then allowed to give rewards to members of either an ingroup or an outgroup. The other participants had to give rewards either to one of two ingroups or to one of two outgroups. Those participants who were able to discriminate in favour of an ingroup over an outgroup had higher self-esteem than those unable to discriminate in that way.

Further evidence of a link between social identity and self-esteem was reported by Hirt et al. (1992). They studied college students who were very keen fans of their basketball team. When the team was defeated, their self-esteem and feelings of competence were reduced. Those whose sense of social identity is less bound up with a team sometimes use psychological distancing to cope with its defeats. Cialdini et al. (1976) phoned students several days after their college team had lost a game of American football. The students mostly used the pronoun "they" to describe the team's defeat. In contrast, they used the pronoun "we" when their team had won, and they further showed a sense of social identity by wearing college scarves and other college clothing. However, not all the findings are as supportive of the theory. Brown (1996, p.548) reviewed the evidence, and concluded as follows: "the social-identity hypothesis that self-esteem is an important variable controlling or being controlled by intergroup discrimination cannot be unambiguously sustained."

Evaluation

Group membership and social identity have powerful effects on attitudes towards the self, the ingroup, and outgroups. As predicted by social identity theory, people often develop a sense of social identity because it increases their self-esteem.

The findings from minimal-group studies have been interpreted as indicating the importance of social identity. Rabbie, Schot, and Visser (1989) argued that self-interest can also determine behaviour in the minimal-group situation. Some participants were told that they would only receive only what outgroup members gave them. These participants showed outgroup favouritism, because self-interest outweighed the sense of social identity.

Another limitation of social identity theory is that it is not applicable to some cultures. Wetherall (1982) compared the attitudes and behaviour of white and Polynesian children in New Zealand. As predicted by social identity theory, the white children tended to discriminate in favour of their group and against the Polynesian children. However, the Polynesian children were co-operative towards the white children, and showed very little ingroup favouritism. In some studies (e.g. Mullen et al., 1992), members of poorly regarded minority groups actually showed favouritism towards more highly regarded outgroups. This is the opposite of what is predicted by social identity theory, and indicates that cultures vary in their beliefs and values.

Finally, it is assumed within the theory that most people have several different social identities. More research needs to be done to find out why some identities come to the surface more readily than others, and to explore the factors that determine which social identity is dominant at any given time.

Social representations

Much of our knowledge of the world is not obtained through first-hand experience, but rather is obtained indirectly from social interactions. For example, we may have very definite views about individual members of the royal family even though we have not met them, because we have discussed them with friends. The term **social representations** is often used to refer to such socially derived knowledge. Moscovici (1981, p.181) offered a fuller definition of social representations as

> *a set of concepts, statements and explanations originating in daily life in the course of inter-individual communications. They are the equivalent, in our society, of the myths and belief systems in traditional societies; they might even be said to be the contemporary version of common sense.*

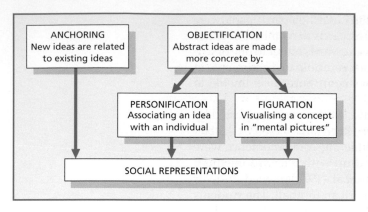

The media often use objectification, e.g. "butter mountain", "millennium bug". List some examples.

How do we form new social representations? According to Moscovici, two key processes are involved: anchoring and objectification. **Anchoring** refers to the way in which new ideas are related closely to existing knowledge and categories. **Objectification** is the process of making abstract ideas more concrete; it has the advantages of making ideas more understandable and easy to remember. According to Moscovici and Hewstone (1983), objectification can involve either personification or figuration. As they pointed out, most people's social representations about psychoanalysis centre on the figure of Sigmund Freud. This is an example of personification. Figuration or visualisation of an abstract idea is involved when we picture the law of gravity in terms of an apple falling on Newton's head.

Why do we rely so heavily on social representations? According to Moscovici (1988, p.215):

> We derive only a small fraction of our knowledge and information from the simple interaction between ourselves and the facts we encounter in the world. Most knowledge is supplied to us by communication which affects our way of thinking and creates new concepts.

In other words, the world is so complex that we often need to make use of the views and knowledge of others to make sense of it. In addition, it is easier for members of a group to communicate with each other if they share numerous social representations.

Evidence

Representations of intelligence. Carugati (1990) found support for some of Moscovici's (1981) ideas in a study on social representations of intelligence among Italian teachers and parents. They regarded intelligence as a gift, which is an example of anchoring a complex concept to what is known. They also used objectification by assuming that individual differences in intelligence can be used to predict future success.

Representations of health. Herzlich (1973) studied the social representations of health and illness in 80 French people by conducting conversational interviews with them. Most of them regarded health as a pool or reservoir within individuals which can be used up. Illness, on the other hand, lies outside individuals and is influenced by lifestyle. Living in a city can produce illness, whereas living in the countryside preserves the pool of health. Advertisers take account of these social representations. Advertisements for health foods typically show charming rural scenes, even though the products being advertised are mostly manufactured in large factories in towns.

Ethical issues: Were there any potential methodological or ethical problems in Jodelet's study?

Representations of mental illness. Jodelet (1991) looked at social representations of mental illness in a French village called Ainay-le-Chateau. This village was chosen because mental patients lived as lodgers in the homes of many of the villagers. Jodelet obtained most of her information from living in the village, but she also carried out in-depth interviews and conducted a large questionnaire survey. Most of the villagers regarded the mental patients as dirty, and notions of dirtiness and contamination loomed large in their social representations of mental illness. Why was this the case? According to Jodelet (1991, pp.143–144)

> dirtiness seems to siphon off the major part of the negativity of insanity and is a less disturbing manifestation of the illness than others. Dirtiness which is due to illness is unthreatening. That alone makes it worth putting up with.

Errors of attribution. In the next section of the chapter, we will consider various attribution biases and errors. For example, there is the actor–observer effect, in which people attribute the behaviour of others to their personality, but attribute their own behaviour to the situation. This effect is usually regarded as applying to individuals. However, Guimond, Begin, and Palmer (1989) argued that errors and biases can develop out of social representations. The normal effect was reversed when poor, unemployed people and social science students were asked to provide reasons for poverty. Unemployed people blamed themselves for being poor, whereas the social science students attributed poverty to society and the situation in which poor people find themselves.

What caused this reversal of the normal actor–observer effect? Presumably the poor had learned the social representations of poverty that are common in society, and the social science students had learned the social representations frequently expressed by social scientists. Thus, knowledge of social representations can eliminate the actor–observer effect.

Evaluation

Our beliefs and knowledge about the world depend to a large extent on our communications with other people. Moscovici (1985, p.95) was probably right to argue that, "Social representations are the outcome of an unceasing babble and a permanent dialogue between individuals." As a result, groups of people and even entire cultures will often share very similar social representations. The notion of social representations is valuable, because it encourages us to search for the social origins of much of our knowledge.

On the negative side, theoretical accounts of social representations are rather vague. In addition, the processes underlying the formation of social representations have not been studied in detail. One of the criteria for a scientific theory is that it should generate hypotheses that are falsifiable (see Chapter 28). This has not happened sufficiently with theories of social representation. One of the few clear predictions is that social representations should be shared across a social group. In fact, this is often not the case. In the study by Carugati (1990), parents who were also teachers held the social representation that intelligence is a gift more strongly than parents who were not teachers. The latter group of parents put more emphasis on the view that intelligence is a quality that can be developed by teachers. However, Galli and Nigro (1987) studied Italian children's social representations of radioactivity shortly after the Chernobyl explosion. The children's representations were very similar, presumably because the explosion had led to considerable discussion about radioactivity and the danger of nuclear power.

Could you hold a conversation with a friend about "global warming" or "BSE"? Where did your knowledge come from? Do you both have beliefs in common?

Cultural identity

Many social psychologists assume that people have one fixed identity, and that this identity is often based on the culture or ethnic group to which they belong. A different approach is favoured by social constructionists. They argue that individuals have a number of identities, and that these identities are flexible. According to social constructionists, human knowledge (including knowledge of our cultural identity or identities) stems from social interactions. Gergen and Gergen (1991, p.78) argued that meanings are constructed as people

collectively generate descriptions and explanations in language ... what we take to be knowledge is not placed within individual minds, nor is it contained within abstract descriptions and explanations ... from the constructionist standpoint, knowledge is part of the co-ordinated activities of individuals.

The social constructionist approach to cultural identity was expressed in the following way by Hall (1990, p.225):

Cultural identity ... is a matter of "becoming" as well as of "being". It belongs to the future as much as to the past. It is not something which already exists ... Cultural identities undergo constant transformation ... they are subject to the continuous "play" of history, culture and power.

What are the limitations of analysing qualitative data?

The most common method for investigating the social constructionist approach is to require the participants to provide a narrative in spoken or written form. This narrative is concerned with the range of attitudes and beliefs that the individual has with respect to cultural identity. Some form of qualitative analysis is then usually applied to the narrative data.

Evidence

Some of the strongest evidence that cultural identities often change over time comes from studies of ethnic groups living within a larger society. Hall (1990) focused on Afro-Caribbean and Asian migrants to Britain. They had to construct or actively create their own cultural identities, which was often difficult. For example, the British historically exerted much power in Jamaica. This had a major influence on the narratives and stories by which Jamaican people (and Jamaican migrants to Britain) came to a sense of cultural identity. As a result, Jamaican migrants often engaged in an internal struggle or fight against the identities that had been imposed upon them.

The Notting Hill Carnival, which has sometimes become a focus for racial violence in the past, is now seen as an example of "achieved ethnic identity", in which West Indian culture is celebrated.

Three stages. Phinney (1993) put forward a theory to explain the ways in which members of a minority group come to establish a cultural or ethnic identity. This theory was based on a review of the relevant research. According to him, there are three stages in cultural or ethnic identity formation:

1. Unexamined ethnic identity: at this stage, minority individuals have often spent little time thinking about cultural identity issues. As a result, they may simply accept the negative stereotypes of their minority group that are commonly accepted by the majority group. This can produce the experience of "self-hate".
2. Ethnic identity search: this stage often starts with an incident that persuades minority individuals to try to reject the negative identity they have accepted so far and replace it with a more positive identity. During this stage, minority individuals may develop an oppositional identity, in which they reject the members of the majority group and their values.
3. Achieved ethnic identity: at this stage, minority individuals obtain confidence in their own cultural or ethnic identity by combining aspects of the dominant culture with pride in their own ethnic group.

When members of a minority group have reached the third stage, they develop a high level of self-esteem and a positive cultural or ethnic identity. This allows them to feel integrated into the larger society and to participate fully in its activities.

Four strategies. Berry (1997) adopted a more pessimistic position. He discussed problems of cultural identity encountered by individuals from ethnic groups (see page 807). Their sense of cultural identity is typically influenced both by the ethnic group to which they belong and by the larger group or culture in which they are living. Individuals differ in how they react. Some individuals retain their own cultural identity and also adopt aspects of the cultural identity of the larger group, thus having at least two cultural identities. This is the integration strategy, which tends to be associated with the greatest psychological well-being (Berry, 1997). This strategy corresponds closely to the third stage of achieved ethnic identity proposed by Phinney (1993). It can be hard to use this strategy effectively if members of the dominant culture have little tolerance for ethnic groups. Other individuals lose their own cultural identity and find

Strategy	Ethnic group culture		Larger group culture	Degree of stress
Integration	RETAINED	+	ADOPTED	Least
Assimilation	ABANDONED	+	ADOPTED	
Separation	RETAINED	+	REJECTED	
Marginalisation	ABANDONED	+	REJECTED	Most

it hard to adjust to the cultural identity of the society in which they live. This marginalisation strategy leads to a loss of cultural identity, and produces a high level of stress.

There are two other strategies that involve focusing on only one cultural identity. Individuals who follow the separation strategy retain the cultural identity of their own ethnic group, but make no attempt to incorporate aspects of the dominant cultural identity. In contrast, those who follow the assimilation strategy adopt the dominant cultural identity and abandon the identity of their ethnic group. These two strategies generally produce less stress than the marginalisation strategy, but more than the integration strategy.

Evaluation

The social constructionist approach to cultural identity has various strengths. First, it recognises the complexity of the views that individuals and groups possess about their own cultural identity. Second, the notion that cultural identity can only be understood in a social context is almost certainly correct. Third, it is reasonable to assume that narratives and stories are important in the construction of cultural identities.

The greatest limitation of the social constructionist approach is that it does not lead to many testable predictions. The other main limitation concerns the methods used by social constructionists to obtain their data. The views that individuals express to interviewers about their sense of cultural identity may be distorted in various ways. For example, they may try to impress, or engage the sympathy of, the interviewer. In addition, they may not be consciously aware of all aspects of their sense of cultural identity.

How would you feel if someone asked you about your sense of cultural identity? How important is this identity to you, and have you ever thought about it before? What are the ethical issues involved in such questions?

Attribution Theory

In our everyday lives, we spend much of our time in the company of other people. It is often important to work out *why* they are behaving in certain ways. For example, suppose that someone you have only just met is very friendly. They may really like you, or they may want something from you, or perhaps they are merely being polite. In order to know the best way of interacting with this person, it is very useful to have a good understanding of the reasons for their apparent friendliness.

According to Heider (1958), people are naive scientists who relate observable behaviour to unobservable causes. We produce **attributions**, which are beliefs about the causes of behaviour. Heider argued that there is a key distinction between internal attributions (based on something within the individual whose behaviour is being observed) and external attributions (based on something outside the individual).

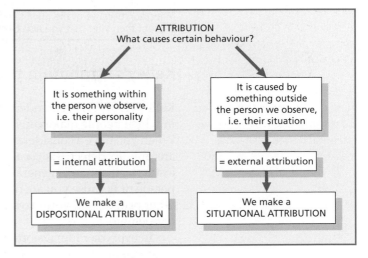

Internal attributions are often called **dispositional attributions**, whereas external attributions are called **situational attributions**. A dispositional attribution is made when we decide that someone's behaviour is due to their personality or other characteristics. In contrast, a situational attribution is made when someone's behaviour is attributed to the current situation.

The distinction between dispositional and situational attributions can be seen if we consider the case of an office worker who is working very slowly and inefficiently. A dispositional attribution would be that he or she is lazy or incompetent. A situational attribution would be that he or she has been asked to do work that is not appropriate to his or her skills.

Since Heider's contribution, various theorists have put forward attribution theories based on his ideas. Two of the most important of such theories are discussed next. First, we consider the correspondent inference theory put forward by Jones and Davis (1965). Second, we deal with Kelley's (1967, 1973) attribution theory.

KEY TERMS
Attributions: beliefs about the causes of behaviour.
Dispositional attributions: deciding that other people's actions are caused by their internal characteristics or dispositions.
Situational attributions: deciding that people's actions are caused by the situation in which they find themselves rather than by their personality.

Correspondent inference theory

According to correspondent inference theory (Jones & Davis, 1965), we use information about people's behaviour and its effects to work out their intentions and their personal dispositions. First, there is the issue of whether the effects of someone's behaviour were intended or not. We decide that effects were intentional if we think that the person knew the consequences of his or her own behaviour, and that he or she had the ability to perform the action required to produce those consequences.

Second, we decide whether the person's behaviour and the underlying intention correspond to some personal disposition within the individual. We are more likely to decide that there is a correspondence when the effects of the behaviour are socially undesirable. For example, if someone is very rude in a social situation, we tend to conclude that he or she is an unpleasant person. On the other hand, if someone is conventionally polite, then we do not feel we have learned much about that person.

In deciding whether someone's behaviour corresponds to an underlying disposition, we also make use of the *non-common effects principle*. If the other person's actions have rare or non-common effects not shared by other actions, then we infer an underlying disposition.

NON-COMMON EFFECTS PRINCIPLE: WHICH CAR WILL YOU BUY?

Car A	Car B	Car C
Lead-free petrol	4-star petrol	Diesel
Power steering	Power steering	Power steering
Air bag	Air bag	Air bag
Expensive to service	Cheap to service	Cheap to service

If you buy Car A, we can infer that lead-free petrol is important to you. You will not have made your decision because of the power steering or air bags, as they are common to the other two cars. We might then infer that you also care about the environment.

Kelley's attribution theory

Think of a time when someone you did not know acted rudely towards you. What did you think about them?

Kelley (1967, 1973) extended attribution theory in various ways. He argued that the ways in which people make causal attributions depend on the information available to them. When you have a considerable amount of relevant information from several sources, you are able to detect the *covariation* of observed behaviour and its possible causes. For example, if a man is generally unpleasant to you, it may be because he is an unpleasant person or because you are not very likeable. If you have information about how he treats other people, and you know how other people treat you, then you can work out what is happening.

In everyday life, we often only have information from a single observation to guide us in making a causal attribution. For example, you see a car knock down and kill a dog. In such cases, you must make use of information about the configuration or arrangement of factors. For example, if there was ice on the road or it was a foggy day, this will increase the chances that you will make a situational attribution of the driver's behaviour.

Covariation

According to Kelley (1967), people making causal attributions use the **covariation principle**. This principle states that "an effect is attributed to a condition that is present when the effect is present, and absent when the effect is absent" (Hewstone & Antaki, 1988, p.115). There are three types of information that we use when deciding why someone has behaved in a given way:

- Consensus: the extent to which others in the same situation behave (or have behaved) in the same way.
- Consistency: the extent to which the person usually behaves in the way he or she is currently behaving.

KEY TERM
Covariation principle: "An effect is attributed to a condition that is present when the effect is present, and absent when the effect is absent" (Hewstone & Antaki, 1988, p.115).

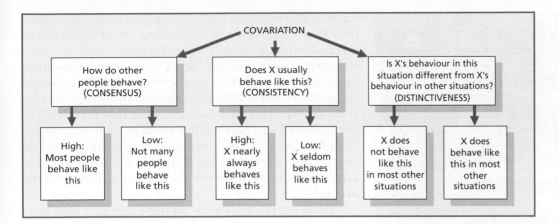

- Distinctiveness: the extent to which the person's behaviour in the present situation differs from his or her behaviour in the presence of other people.

Information about consensus, consistency, and distinctiveness is used to make a dispositional or situational attribution. If someone's behaviour has high consensus, high consistency, and high distinctiveness, then we will probably make a situational attribution. Here is an example: everyone is rude to Bella; Mary has always been rude to Bella in the past; Mary has not been rude to anyone else. Here Mary's behaviour is attributed to the unpleasantness of Bella rather than to her own unpleasantness.

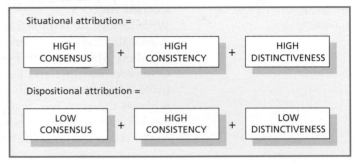

In contrast, we will make a dispositional attribution if someone's behaviour has low consensus, high consistency, and low distinctiveness. Here is an example: only Mary is rude to Susan; Mary has always been rude to Susan in the past; Mary is rude to everyone else.

Fundamental attribution error

One of the best known errors or biases is the **fundamental attribution error**, which is "the tendency to over-emphasise dispositions and to under-emphasise situational factors as causes of behaviour" (Hewstone & Antaki, 1988). In other words, we are biased in the direction of regarding other people's actions as being due to their personality rather than to the situation. For example, interviewers may interpret the nervousness of someone being interviewed for a job as being due to their personality rather than to the stressfulness of the situation.

Evidence
Evidence of the fundamental attribution error was obtained by Jones and Harris (1967). They presented their American participants with short essays either for or against the Castro government in Cuba. The participants were informed either that the essay writers had chosen which side to support (choice condition), or that they had been told to write a pro- or anti-Castro essay as part of an examination on a political science course (no-choice condition). The participants' task was to estimate the essay writer's real attitudes towards Castro.

The participants paid some attention to the situation (whether or not the essay writer had a choice), but less than they should have done. Strictly speaking, nothing can be concluded about the writer's true attitudes in the no-choice condition. However, the participants were greatly influenced by the views expressed by the writer in the no-choice condition.

Suppression of true attitudes
There are doubts as to whether the fundamental attribution error is really fundamental. It is hard to believe that people *always* underestimate the importance of situational factors.

Are we more likely to assume that this man is sleeping rough because of situational factors (he's been taken ill, forgotten his house keys) or dispositional factors (he can't keep a job, he's drunk and rowdy in accommodation, for example)?

Suppose that someone had a strong reason for suppressing their true attitudes. Fein, Hilton, and Miller (1990) tested this in a study in which the participants read an essay written by a student called "Rob Taylor" on a controversial topic. Some of the participants were told that Rob had been assigned to write either in favour of or against a particular point of view. Other participants were told that Rob had been allowed to choose what point of view to express; however, the professor who would be evaluating Rob had very strong views on the topic. Finally, they were told that Rob's essay put forward the same views as those held by his professor.

Those participants who thought that Rob had been assigned a point of view made the fundamental attribution error. Thus, they decided that Rob's true attitudes were those expressed in the essay. In contrast, those participants who thought that Rob had a good reason for hiding his true attitudes (i.e. pleasing his professor) concluded that the views he put forward in his essay did not reflect his true attitudes. Thus, we do not make the fundamental attribution error when it is clear that people have a hidden motive for what they are saying or doing.

Causal factors

What factors are responsible for the fundamental attribution error? The most important is probably **salience**: someone's behaviour is often more salient or prominent than the situation. McArthur and Post (1977) reported evidence for the importance of salience. Observers watched and listened to a conversation between two people. One of those involved in the conversation was made salient by being illuminated by a bright light, whereas the other was made non-salient by being in a dim light. The behaviour of the person who was made salient was rated as being caused more by disposition and less by the situation than was the behaviour of the non-salient person.

Gilbert, Pelham, and Krull

Gilbert, Pelham, and Krull (1988) tried to identify some of the processes involved in the fundamental attribution error. According to their theory, people initially make an automatic dispositional attribution when they observe someone's behaviour. That is sometimes followed by effortful cognitive processing, which may lead them to change their mind and attribute the behaviour to the situation. They tested this theory in a study in which the participants saw a videotape of a woman who was obviously anxious. She was pulling at her hair, shifting in her seat, biting her fingernails, and tapping her fingers. The participants could not hear what the woman was saying, but the topics she was supposed to be discussing were included as subtitles in the videotape. In one condition, the topics were anxiety-provoking (e.g. sexual fantasies; hidden secrets; public humiliation). In the other condition, the topics were fairly neutral (e.g. world travel; fashion trends; ideal holidays). In fact, the participants in both conditions saw exactly the same videotape except for the subtitles.

Half of the participants who watched the videotape were told to memorise the list of topics, whereas the other half simply watched the videotape. After the videotape had been presented, the participants were asked to indicate the extent to which the woman's anxiety was attributable to her disposition. It would seem more reasonable to give a stronger dispositional attribution when the woman was anxious when talking about neutral topics than when she was talking about anxiety-provoking topics, and that is exactly what was found among participants who simply watched the videotape. In contrast, the participants who were given the memory task gave the *same* dispositional attribution regardless of what the woman was talking about. Why did they give a dispositional attribution when the woman was talking about anxiety-provoking topics? According to Gilbert et al. this occurred because these participants were too busy learning the list to engage in the effortful processing needed to produce a situational attribution.

Discussion points

1. Do the findings of Gilbert et al. provide strong support for their theory?

2. Why do you think that people have the fundamental attribution error (see below)?

KEY TERM
Salience: that aspect of a situation or behaviour that is especially prominent or conspicuous.

Why do people possess the fundamental attribution error? According to Gilbert (1995, p.108), there are two main reasons. First, we like to think that life is fair, and using dispositional attributions can help us to preserve that belief:

> *A dispositionist worldview is … a general sense that people do what they do because of the kinds of people they are, and that … whatever happens to them is pretty much their own doing … by and large, we get what we work for, get what we ask for, and get what we deserve.*

Second, we like to think that what happens in our lives is predictable. If the behaviour of other people is determined mainly by their personalities, this makes their future behaviour much more predictable than if their behaviour varied considerably from situation to situation.

Evaluation

On the positive side, people often exaggerate the importance of disposition and minimise that of the situation as causes of behaviour. Sometimes these effects are extreme. For example, most people hugely underestimate the percentage of people who would be prepared to give very strong electric shocks in the Milgram situation, because they assume that only those with a psychopathic disposition would do such a thing (see Chapter 21).

On the negative side, the fundamental attribution error may be less important in everyday life than in the laboratory. In everyday life, we realise that many people (e.g. politicians; secondhand car salespeople) have hidden motives that may influence their behaviour in certain situations.

Cultural differences. The fundamental attribution error may be less common in Asian cultures than in Western ones. As Moscovici and Hewstone (1983) pointed out, most Western cultures emphasise individualism and the notion that individuals should take responsibility for their own actions. Such cultural norms are very much in line with the fundamental attribution error. In contrast, the emphasis in most Asian cultures is on the group rather than on the individual. Supporting evidence was reported by Miller (1984). Adult Americans and Indian Hindus were asked to explain common events, such as the behaviour of a colleague who stole someone else's idea. The Americans showed a strong tendency to favour dispositional explanations over situational ones (40% vs. 18%, respectively), whereas the Indian Hindus preferred situational explanations 40% of the time and dispositional ones only 18% of the time.

Actor–observer effect

Suppose a mother is discussing with her son why he has done poorly in an examination. The son may argue that the questions were unusually hard, that the marking was unfair, and so on. In contrast, his mother may focus on the child's laziness and general lack of motivation. In more general terms, the son sees his own behaviour as being determined by various external or situational factors, whereas his mother focuses on internal or dispositional factors within her son.

Evidence
Jones and Nisbett (1972) argued that the processes involved in this example operate in numerous circumstances. According to them (1972, p.80)

> *there is a pervasive tendency for actors to attribute their actions to situational requirements, whereas observers tend to attribute the same actions to stable personal dispositions.*

This phenomenon is often referred to as the **actor–observer effect** in attribution.

What assumptions do we make about the motives of politicians (such as Gordon Brown, above) when they meet the public?

In what other situations might the other person have hidden motives?

Cross-cultural issues: Attributions that are made by people from a collectivist culture tend to be contextualised. Attributions made by people in individualistic cultures tend to be more focused on personal choice.

Why do you think Indian Hindus favour situational explanations?

KEY TERM
Actor–observer effect: the tendency for actors to attribute their actions to situational factors, whereas observers attribute them to internal or dispositional factors.

Nisbett et al. (1973) carried out various studies on the actor–observer effect. In one study, male college students wrote an essay about why they liked their girlfriend, and another essay about why their best friend liked his girlfriend. When writing about themselves, the students made twice as many situational attributions as dispositional attributions about their girlfriend. In contrast, when writing about their best friend, they used an equal number of situational and dispositional attributions. An example of a situational attribution is liking one's girlfriend because she is cheerful, and an example of a dispositional attribution is liking one's girlfriend because one likes cheerful women.

In another study, Nisbett et al. asked their participants to rate themselves, their best friend, their father, an admired acquaintance, and Walter Cronkite (a well known American television presenter) on a series of trait adjectives (e.g. tense–calm). They could either pick one of the adjectives or argue that it depended on the situation. The participants were much more inclined to say that it depended on the situation when describing themselves than when describing any of the other people. According to Nisbett et al., people are much more aware of the importance of situational factors in determining their own behaviour than in determining that of others.

Causal factors

Why do actor–observer differences in attribution occur? Such differences may depend on the fact that we possess much more information about ourselves than about other people. This may lead us to be aware of the subtle ways in which our behaviour is influenced by the situation, but unaware that the same is true of others. This explanation

has not received much support. For example, participants in the study by Nisbett et al. knew much more about their father and their best friend than about an admired acquaintance or Walter Cronkite, but this did not affect their attributions.

Another possible reason for the actor–observer effect stems from the fact that we can see other people but cannot see ourselves. However, we can see the situation, and this may lead us to exaggerate its importance in determining our behaviour. This notion was tested by Storms (1973). Two participants took part in a "get acquainted" conversation, and two additional participants observed them. Two videos were made of the conversations, one from the actor's point of view, and the other from the observer's point of view. Some of the participants made attributions of the actor's behaviour after watching one of the two videos. The usual actor–observer effect was obtained when actors and observers viewed the video made from their own perspective. However, the opposite pattern of results was obtained when actors and observers viewed the video taken from the opposite perspective. When people observed their own behaviour, they tended to attribute it to dispositional rather than to situational factors.

Were there any possible confounding variables in Storms' study?

Self-serving bias

The actor–observer effect discussed in the previous section does not always apply. Situational attributions are more common for actors than for observers, but differences between actors and observers in dispositional attributions are less commonly found (e.g. Storms, 1973). Another limitation of the notion that actors generally attribute their own behaviour to situational factors is that it does not account for attributions for success. We tend to attribute our success to internal or dispositional factors (e.g. we worked very hard; we have a lot of ability), whereas we attribute our failures to external or situational factors (e.g. the task was very difficult; we didn't have enough time to prepare ourselves). These tendencies to take the credit for success but accept no blame for failure are often described as the **self-serving bias**.

KEY TERM
Self-serving bias: the tendency to take the credit for one's successes, but not to accept blame for one's failures.

Causal factors

Intentions. There are various reasons why we might have a self-serving bias. According to the cognitive account (Miller & Ross, 1975), we usually intend to succeed and do not intend to fail. As a result, we put much effort into the attempt to succeed. If our internal intentions and efforts are confirmed by success, then it is understandable that we attribute our behaviour to internal factors. If our intentions and efforts are thwarted and we fail, then we may tend to argue that obstacles in the situation have prevented our behaviour from matching our intentions.

Motivation. Miller (1976) found that motivational factors play an important role. The participants were given a test of social perceptiveness, and then told on a random basis that they had succeeded or failed. Half of them were told that it was a good test of social skills, whereas the others were told that it was a poor test. Those who believed the test was valid showed much more evidence of a self-serving bias than the others. These findings suggest that the motivation to protect or enhance self-esteem may underlie the self-serving bias.

Depression and low self-esteem. Further support for the role of self-esteem in the self-serving bias comes from the study of depressed individuals. They often fail to show the self-serving bias. Indeed, they tend to exhibit the opposite pattern of attributing failure to internal factors and success to external factors (e.g. Abramson et al., 1978). Depressed individuals have very low self-esteem, and typically feel there is nothing they can do to boost it. In other words, they do not have enough motivation to show the self-serving bias.

Think of something you have recently been successful in achieving. How did you explain your success? Is there also something you have failed to achieve? How did you explain your failure?

Evaluation

There is strong evidence for the self-serving bias. It has the advantage of encouraging us to persevere even when things are going against us. For example, unemployed workers are more likely to find work if they exhibit the self-serving bias, and avoid attributing their failure to obtain a job to their incompetence or lack of skill.

On the negative side, it remains unclear whether the self-serving bias is better explained in motivational terms (enhancing self-esteem) or in cognitive terms (confirmation or non-confirmation of internal intentions and efforts). The self-serving bias is stronger in individualist cultures than in collectivist ones. Kashima and Triandis (1986) asked American and Japanese students to remember detailed information about landscapes shown on slides. Both groups tended to explain their successes in terms of situational factors (e.g. luck) and their failures in terms of task difficulty. However, the Americans were more inclined to explain their successes in terms of high ability than their failures in terms of low ability, whereas the Japanese showed the opposite pattern. Thus, the self-serving bias was more apparent in the American participants.

Prejudice and Discrimination

Many people regard prejudice and discrimination as meaning the same thing. In fact, there is an important distinction between them. **Prejudice** is an attitude, whereas **discrimination** refers to behaviour or action. If someone dislikes a given minority, but does not allow this dislike to affect their behaviour, then that person shows prejudice but not discrimination. According to Baron and Byrne (1991, p.183), prejudice "is an attitude (usually negative) toward the members of some group, based solely on their membership in that group." In contrast, discrimination involves negative actions (e.g. aggression) directed at the members of some group.

> **KEY TERMS**
> **Prejudice**: an attitude, which is usually negative, towards the members of some group on basis of their membership of that group.
> **Discrimination**: negative actions or behaviour directed against members of another group.

Discrimination against specific groups is sometimes aided by distinguishing visual characteristics (skin colour, or style of dress, for example). Sometimes, however, minority group members are not clearly distinguishable from the majority, and are forced to identify themselves. This was the case in Nazi Germany where Jews had to wear a Star of David on their clothing, making them a focus for racial hatred.

Allport's theory

Discrimination against other groups can take various forms. Allport (1954) argued that there are five different stages of discrimination. In certain situations (e.g. Nazi Germany), the level of discrimination increases rapidly from the early stages to the later ones. Here are Allport's five stages:

1. Anti-locution: verbal attacks are directed against some other group.
2. Avoidance: the other group is systematically avoided; this can involve steps to make it easier to identify members of that group (e.g. the Star of David worn by Jews in Nazi Germany).
3. Discrimination: the other group is deliberately treated less well than other groups in terms of civil rights, job opportunities, membership of clubs, and so on.
4. Physical attack: members of the other group are attacked, and their property is destroyed.
5. Extermination: there are deliberate attempts to kill all members of the other group (e.g. the gas chambers built by the Nazis to murder the Jews).

Discrimination and consistency

You may feel that people's attitudes and behaviour are usually consistent. If that were the case, then prejudice and discrimination would occur together. In fact, inconsistency is very common. LaPiere (1934) took a Chinese couple to 250 hotels and restaurants in the United States. They were only refused service on one occasion, which suggests that there was a very low level of discrimination against Chinese people. However, LaPiere then wrote to all of the hotels and restaurants, asking them whether they would accept Chinese people. Only half replied, with 90% of those replying saying they would not. These findings indicate that there was a high level of anti-Chinese prejudice at that time. Presumably the social pressures to accept Chinese people were much greater in a face-to-face situation than when writing a letter.

Prejudice and social desirability

Ethical issues: The participants in the studies reviewed by Jones and Segall were deceived, because the machine could not really tell if they were lying or not. Was this ethical?

Social pressures are also at work when prejudice is measured. Prejudice is mostly assessed by self-report questionnaires. Responses to questionnaires are influenced by social desirability bias, which is the tendency to give socially approved answers. Evidence of such bias was discussed by Jones and Sigall (1971). Whites in the United States expressed positive and non-prejudiced attitudes towards black people on a questionnaire. They were then connected to a *bogus pipeline*. This is a machine with flashing lights, which the experimenter claims allows him or her to monitor the participant's physiological responses and so discover the participant's true opinions. The participants were asked about their attitudes towards black people while connected to this bogus pipeline. They expressed much more negative attitudes towards black people than they had on the questionnaire. It is likely that the answers given in the bogus pipeline condition were closer to their true attitudes.

Stereotypes

> **KEY TERM**
> **Stereotyping**: the tendency to categorise people on the basis of some readily available feature such as skin colour or sex.

It is important when discussing prejudice and discrimination to consider also stereotyping. Taguiri (1969) defined **stereotyping** as the tendency *to place a person in categories according to some easily and quickly identifiable characteristic such as age, sex, ethnic membership, nationality or occupation, and then to attribute to him qualities believed to be typical of members of that category.*

We are more likely to have stereotypes about **outgroups** (groups to which we do not belong) than about **ingroups** (groups to which we belong).

Macrae, Milne, and Bodenhausen

Why do we have stereotypes? The main reason seems to be that stereotypes provide a simple and economical way of perceiving the world. Relevant evidence was reported by Macrae, Milne, and Bodenhausen (1994). They asked their participants to perform two tasks at the same time. One task involved forming impressions of a number of imaginary people when given their names and personality traits. The other task involved listening to information presented on a tape followed by a test of comprehension. Half of the participants were given the chance to use stereotypes by being told the job held by each of the imaginary people in the impression–formation task. The idea was that being told that someone was, for example, a used car salesman or doctor would activate stereotypical information about the kind of person who has that kind of job. The remaining participants were not given this stereotype-relevant information.

The key finding was that the participants who were able to use stereotypes performed better on both tasks. This suggests strongly that the use of stereotypes saves precious cognitive resources, because they provide a convenient (if inaccurate) summary of a person or object.

The stereotypical image of Italian matriarchs being wonderful cooks has given rise to several advertising campaigns for Italian food products.

Discussion points

1. Do the findings of Macrae et al. really show that stereotypes reduce cognitive processing?

2. Are there other reasons why people have stereotypes?

Are stereotypes necessarily always negative or inaccurate?

Part of what is involved is the perception that members of a given outgroup tend to be very similar, whereas those of an ingroup do not. This so-called *outgroup homogeneity effect* was shown by Quattrone and Jones (1980). Students from Princeton University and from Rutgers University saw a videotape of a student allegedly from their own university or from the other university deciding whether to wait alone or with other participants while the experimenter fixed a piece of apparatus. They were then asked to estimate the percentage of other students from the same university as the videotaped student who would make the same choice. The participants tended to guess that nearly all of the students from the other university would make the same decision as the videotaped student. However, this was not the case when the student was from the same university as themselves.

What characteristics do you think each of these people might possess?

Katz and Braly (1933) carried out the first systematic study of stereotyping. They asked students to indicate which characteristics were typical of a series of groups (e.g. Germans; Black Africans; English). There was fairly good agreement that the Germans were efficient and nationalistic, whereas the Black Africans were seen as happy-go-lucky and superstitious.

The greatest problem with this approach is that the task itself *forced* the participants to produce stereotypes, whether or not they actually thought in a stereotyped way. McCauley and Stitt (1978) used a better method in a study on stereotypes of Germans. They asked their participants a series of questions such as, "What percentage of people in the world generally are efficient?" and "What percentage of Germans are efficient?" The average answer to the former question was 50%, whereas it was 63% to the latter one. Thus, it is nonsense to suppose that most people think all Germans are efficient. In fact, the general feeling is that they are somewhat more efficient than other nationalities. This is a much less extreme form of stereotyping.

Stereotypes and prejudice: Cognitive approach

People who regard most or all of the members of some outgroup as having the same stereotyped characteristics tend to be prejudiced against that group. How do stereotypes lead to prejudice? Bodenhausen (1988) put forward a cognitive approach. According to this approach, information consistent with our stereotypes is attended to and stored away in memory, whereas information inconsistent with our stereotypes is ignored and/or forgotten.

Bodenhausen (1988) tested his cognitive approach in two studies based on the notion that many Americans are prejudiced against people of Spanish origin. In his first study, American participants were asked to imagine that they were jurors at a trial. The defendant was described to some of them as Carlos Ramirez, a Spanish-sounding name. To others, he was described as Robert Johnson. The participants then read the evidence, and decided how likely it was that the defendant was guilty. Those who knew him as Carlos Ramirez rated him as more guilty than did those who knew him as Robert Johnson. This suggests that stereotypes lead to biased processing of information.

In his second study, Bodenhausen tried to find out more about the processes involved. He argued that stereotypes might lead the participants to *attend* only to information fitting their stereotype, or it might lead them to *distort* the information to make it support their stereotype. In order to prevent selective attention to stereotype-fitting information, Bodenhausen asked the participants to rate each item of evidence immediately in terms of whether it favoured or did not favour the defendant. Carlos Ramirez was no longer rated as more guilty than Robert Johnson. Thus, stereotypes make us attend to information fitting the stereotype, and cause us to disregard other items of information.

Evaluation

It is often argued that stereotypes are undesirable for two main reasons: (1) they can lead to prejudice; and (2) they represent very oversimplified views of the world, and so are inaccurate and misleading. It is true that negative stereotypes of other groups can be dangerous, and are increasingly regarded as unacceptable. Two obvious examples are sex- and race-based stereotypes. Sexism and racism have caused great damage over the years in terms of both prejudice and discrimination. Laws based on the notion of equal opportunities have been passed in several countries. These laws have had the effect of preventing much of the discrimination that used to exist. However, although active discrimination may have been reduced, there is often much underlying prejudice.

Oversimplification

In spite of the arguments against stereotypes that have just been put forward, it is not the case that all stereotypes lead to prejudice. Stereotypes are often oversimplified, but they help us to make sense of a very complex world. Even the least prejudiced person probably makes use of several stereotypes every day. For example, Brown (1988) pointed out that

We all use stereotypes, usually without even thinking about them, e.g. "Essex girl", "trainspotter", "punk". Make a list of other examples in common use.

most people have stereotypes about night people and day people (those who go to bed early and get up early). We think of night people as being un-conventional and rebellious, whereas day people are thought of as self-controlled and responsible.

A "kernel of truth"

Stereotypes are often inaccurate. However, that is not always the case. For example, Triandis and Vassiliou (1967, p.324) studied people from Greece and from the United States, and came to the following conclusion, "There is a 'kernel of truth' in most stereotypes *when they are elicited from people who have firsthand knowledge of the group being stereotyped.*" McCauley and Stitt (1978) asked various groups of Americans to estimate the percentage of adult Americans in general and the percentage of adult Black Americans who had not completed high school, were born illegitimate, had been the victims of violent crime, and so on. There were differences in the estimates for most of the questions, thus showing the existence of stereotypes. However, McCauley and Stitt compared the estimates against the relevant government statistics. In their answers to about half of the questions, the participants *underestimated* the actual differences between the two groups. These findings provide additional support for the notion that stereotypes often possess a kernel of truth.

Theories of Prejudice

There are several causes of prejudice. However, it can be argued that there are two main categories to which most of these causes belong. First, prejudice may depend on the personality or other characteristics of an individual who is prejudiced. Second, environmental or cultural factors may produce prejudice. For example, a dramatic increase in the level of unemployment within any given country may lead to greater prejudice and discrimination against minority groups within that country. In reality, of course, we may well need to consider the individual and the social and cultural context in which he or she lives in order to understand prejudice fully.

In what follows, we will initially consider some important approaches to prejudice that have focused on the individual. After that, the emphasis shifts to a consideration of the main social and cultural factors responsible for producing prejudice.

In the early 1960s, during a period of high immigration from the West Indies to the UK, the MP Enoch Powell warned of the dangers of social unrest following the distortion of the labour market. His "rivers of blood" speech was taken by many as a call for repatriation of immigrants, and was quoted by both those for and those against immigration.

Psychodynamic approach

Sigmund Freud put forward his psychoanalytic theories at the end of the nineteenth century and the early part of the twentieth century (see Chapter 2). His views were so influential that they led to a number of psychodynamic theories based loosely on his theories. Two psychodynamic theories of prejudice have been put forward: the frustration–aggression hypothesis, and the theory of the authoritarian personality.

Frustration–aggression hypothesis

Dollard et al. (1939) argued that aggression against individuals and groups is caused by frustration. Frustration leads to the build-up of an unpleasant state of arousal, which is released in the form of aggression. It is often not possible to show aggression or hostility towards the source of the frustration, because it is too powerful. This leads to what Freud called *displacement*: the aggression is directed towards a substitute target or scapegoat (e.g. our boss annoys us, so we go home and kick the cat). The frustration–aggression hypothesis in its original form focused on individual levels of frustration, which can vary

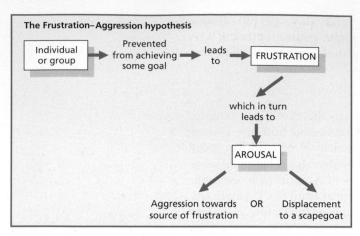

The Frustration–Aggression hypothesis

Individual or group → Prevented from achieving some goal → leads to → FRUSTRATION

which in turn leads to

AROUSAL

Aggression towards source of frustration   OR   Displacement to a scapegoat

Can you think of any similar examples since the Second World War when, as a result of problems such as high unemployment, one group used another as a scapegoat for their frustrations?

considerably from one person to another. However, it was later applied to large groups within society as well as to individuals.

There are many historical examples of scapegoating apparently caused by frustration. Massive inflation and very high levels of unemployment in Germany during the 1920s were followed by the rapid growth of anti-Semitism or anti-Jewish prejudice. Hovland and Sears (1940) argued that drops in cotton prices in the United States reflected increased poverty and led to frustration. They also argued that the number of lynchings (killing a person for an alleged offence, without any legal trial) could be taken as a measure of scapegoating. As predicted by the frustration–aggression hypothesis, those years in which the cotton prices were lowest tended to be the ones with the most lynchings in certain areas of America.

Evaluation. On the positive side, the frustration–aggression hypothesis provides a plausible account of one of the factors causing prejudice. On the negative side, frustration can lead to constructive attempts to remove its source or to a resigned attitude as well as to aggression. In addition, the frustration–aggression hypothesis does not explain why aggression is directed against one particular group (e.g. Blacks) rather than another (e.g. Jews).

Authoritarian personality

Adorno et al. (1950) focused on individual differences in prejudice. According to them, people with an authoritarian personality are most likely to be prejudiced. The **authoritarian personality** includes the following characteristics:

- Rigid beliefs in conventional values.
- General hostility towards other groups.
- Intolerance of ambiguity.
- Submissive attitudes towards authority figures.

Early experiences. Adorno et al. argued that childhood experiences play a key role in the development of the authoritarian personality. Harsh treatment causes the child to have much hostility towards his or her parents. This hostility remains unconscious, because the child is unwilling to admit to it. This causes motivated forgetting, or what Freud called *repression*. The child seems to idealise his or her parents, and in later life acts in a submissive way towards authority figures. However, there is still much hostility lying below the surface. This hostility is displaced on to non-threatening minority groups, and appears in the form of prejudice. Thus, the key theoretical assumption is as follows: the hostility that harshly treated children find hard to express towards their parents is later redirected towards innocent groups.

E-Scale and F-Scale. Adorno et al. devised a number of questionnaires relating to their theory. One of these questionnaires was the Ethnocentrism Scale (E-Scale), ethnocentrism being the belief that one's ethnic group is superior to all others. The scale measures prejudice towards a number of minority groups, including Blacks and Jews. However, the most important questionnaire was the **F (Fascism) Scale**, which was designed to measure the attitudes of the authoritarian personality. A clearer idea of what the F-Scale measures can be seen by looking at a few items: "Obedience and respect for authority are the most important virtues children should learn"; "Most of our social problems would be solved if we could somehow get rid of the immoral, crooked, and feeble-minded people"; "What the youth needs most is strict discipline, rugged determination, and the will to work for family and country".

Adorno et al. obtained various kinds of evidence for the validity of the F-Scale. They gave large groups of people a number of tests and clinical interviews as well as the

F-Scale. Those who scored high on the F-Scale tended to be more prejudiced than low scorers. For example, the F-Scale correlated +0.75 with the Ethnocentrism Scale. As predicted by the theory, high scorers on the F-Scale had been treated more harshly than non-authoritarian individuals during childhood.

More evidence was obtained by Milgram (1974). He found that most people are prepared to give very strong electric shocks to another person when ordered to do so by an authority figure (see Chapter 21). Those with an authoritarian personality are supposed to be submissive to authority, and so they should be especially likely to give powerful electric shocks. As predicted, high scorers on the F-Scale gave stronger shocks than low scorers.

THE NINE PERSONALITY TRAITS OF THE AUTHORITARIAN PERSONALITY, FROM ADORNO ET AL.'S F-SCALE	
Traits	**Description**
Conventionalism	Very conventional, great dislike of change
Authoritarian–Submissive	Deferential to authority
Authoritarian–Aggressive	Very hostile to people who challenge authority
Anti-inception	Very intolerant of behaviour that is "wrong" in any way
Superstition & stereotype	Believes in fate
Power & "toughness"	Has a dominating and bullying manner
Destructiveness & cynicism	Very hostile towards anyone with whom they disagree
Projectivity	Projects own unconscious impulses onto other people
Sex	Has an exaggerated interest in sexual behaviour that is not regarded as "normal"

Cultural differences. The work by Adorno et al. (1950) was carried out in America shortly after the end of the Second World War. It seems likely that some features of the authoritarian personality would vary from one culture to another, and from one time period to another. Some relevant evidence has been reported by Peterson et al. (1993). Americans with an authoritarian personality were strong supporters of family values, and believed very much in the American way of life. Thus, for example, they opposed abortion, argued that homelessness is caused by laziness, and wanted drug dealers to be treated very harshly.

A very different picture emerged from a study of the authoritarian personality in Russia by McFarland et al. (1992). Authoritarian Russians tended to favour continuing communist control of the Soviet Union, a point of view that is almost the opposite of endorsing the American way of life! The findings suggest that those with an authoritarian personality are very conservative. They dislike change, and want those in authority to punish anyone who poses a threat to the existing order. Thus, the beliefs of authoritarian individuals are coloured by the dominant values in their culture.

Evaluation. On the positive side, some individuals are more prejudiced than others, and the F-Scale is a reasonable measure of these individual differences. As is predicted by the theory, childhood experiences help to determine whether someone will develop an authoritarian personality.

On the negative side, there are several problems. First, widespread uniformity of prejudice in certain cultural groups (e.g. anti-Jewish prejudice in Nazi Germany) cannot be explained in terms of the authoritarian personality. Such uniformity depends on social and cultural factors. Second, Adorno et al. (1950) assumed that the authoritarian personality is associated with extreme right-wing views. In fact, those with extreme left-wing views are also rigid and intolerant in outlook (Rokeach, 1960). Third, all of the items on the F-Scale are worded so that agreement with them indicates an authoritarian attitude. As a result, those with an acquiescence response set (a tendency to agree to items regardless of their meaning) seem to be authoritarian. Fourth, Adorno et al. (1950) reported that in-depth interviews with high F-Scale scorers supported their theory. However, the interviewers knew in advance the F-Scale scores of those being interviewed, and this may have distorted the findings.

At the same time as research in America found that authoritarian personalities tended to favour strongly the American way of life, authoritarians in Russia were equally committed to the Communist ideals. This photograph of the Russian leader Khrushchev shows him in a typically authoritarian mood.

Group conflict

According to Sherif (1966), prejudice often results from inter-group conflict. When two groups compete for the same goal, the members of each group tend to become prejudiced against the members of the other group. According to realistic conflict theory, such conflicts of interest cause prejudice.

This theoretical approach developed from the well-known Robber's Cave experiment (Sherif et al., 1961). A total of 22 boys spent two weeks at a summer camp in the United States. They

Sherif et al.'s study has been regarded as very important because it showed ordinary boys acting in different ways towards each other depending on the situation. Competition resulted in dislike and hostility, a common goal led to friendship and good feelings. It might be interesting to speculate about whether the results would have been different if all the participants had been girls. It has been argued that while they are growing up girls are rewarded for co-operation, whereas boys are rewarded for competitiveness. It could also be argued that the participants were not a representative group, in that they were not randomly selected especially for the study.

People who feel strongly about a particular cause are sometimes likely to experience violent clashes with people who do not share the same values.

were put into two groups (called the Eagles and the Rattlers). These groups were told that whichever group did better in various sporting events and other competitions would receive a trophy, knives, and medals. As a result of this competition, a fight broke out between the members of the two groups, and the Rattlers' flag was burned. Prejudice was shown by the fact that each group regarded its own members as friendly and courageous, whereas the members of the other group were thought to be smart-alecks and liars. Prejudice was much reduced when the experimenters replaced the competitive situation with a co-operative one in which the success of each group required the co-operation of the other one.

Similar findings in a different culture were reported by Andreeva in a Russian study. Ingroup favouritism and prejudice increased while boys at Pioneer youth camps were engaged in competitive sports. Andreeva (1984) found that prejudice decreased when the boys co-operated in working on agricultural collectives. In similar fashion, Sherif et al. (1961) found that setting up co-operative tasks reduced prejudice among the boys at the summer camp.

The notion that competition always leads to prejudice and inter-group conflict was rejected by Tyerman and Spencer (1983). They argued that competition only has dramatic effects when those involved have not previously formed friendships, as was the case with the boys in the Sherif et al. and Andreeva studies. Tyerman and Spencer observed scouts who already knew each other well as they competed in groups against each other in their annual camp. Competition did not produce the negative effects observed by Sherif et al. (1961).

Discussion points

1. Why has the study by Sherif et al. been so influential?
2. How important is group conflict as a cause of prejudice?

Relative deprivation

Runciman (1966) argued that we can become prejudiced when there is a gap between what we have done and what we expected to be able to do. He used the term **relative deprivation** to refer to such gaps. When deciding if we are relatively deprived, we often consider our situation or that of groups to which we belong against that of other people or groups. Runciman drew a distinction between two forms of relative deprivation:

1. Egotistic deprivation: this stems from comparisons with other individuals regarded as similar to oneself.
2. Fraternalistic deprivation: this is produced by comparisons between groups rather than individuals. The notion that one's own group is being unfairly treated by comparison with some other group often reflects group norms or expectations of what is fair and just.

Martin Luther King, American civil rights leader, was himself well-educated and of a higher socio-economic status than many of the people on whose behalf he campaigned.

KEY TERM
Relative deprivation: a gap between what we have done and what we expected to be able to do.

We can see the value of the distinction between egotistic and fraternalistic deprivation by considering the leaders of minority groups protesting about the discrimination shown against the group. Such leaders are usually successful individuals who are not egotistically deprived. However, they have a strong sense of fraternalistic or group deprivation. For example, trade union leaders in the United Kingdom who act on behalf of their poorly paid members are usually well paid and successful individuals. In similar fashion, the most militant Blacks in the United States during the 1960s and 1970s tended to be well-educated and of fairly high socio-economic status (Abeles, 1976).

Support for relative deprivation theory was reported by Vanneman and Pettigrew (1972). Those town dwellers in the United States who had the most extreme racist attitudes reported being the most fraternally deprived.

Evaluation

Runciman's (1966) relative deprivation theory (especially the notion of fraternalistic deprivation) helps us to understand prejudice. It is based on group norms, and explains the fact that prejudice is often found in most members of a given group. In addition, the notion of egotistic deprivation explains why the level of prejudice and hostility is greater in some individuals than in others. However, for the theory to be convincing, we would need to know in more detail the processes involved in producing fraternalistic deprivation.

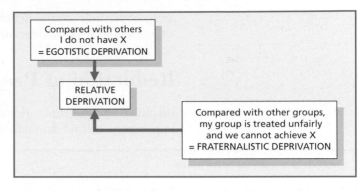

Compared with others
I do not have X
= EGOTISTIC DEPRIVATION

RELATIVE DEPRIVATION

Compared with other groups, my group is treated unfairly and we cannot achieve X
= FRATERNALISTIC DEPRIVATION

Social developmental theory

Aboud (1988) put forward a social developmental theory of prejudice, in which she argued that prejudice is generally greater in younger than in older children. Infants prefer familiar people and tend to distrust strangers. As they grow up, children regard those who are similar to themselves in colour, language, and so on as being more familiar and predictable than those who are dissimilar, and thus as more likeable. When children develop a good command of language, they start to use positive stereotypes for the groups to which they belong and negative stereotypes for other groups. After further cognitive development, older children begin to realise that inner qualities are more important than external features (e.g. skin colour). They also realise that applying a simple stereotype to a large group of people ignores important individual differences within the group.

Evidence

Aboud reviewed the relevant evidence. In some studies, children were presented with various dolls, and asked which was the good doll, or the bad doll, or the doll with which they would like to play. The typical finding was that children between the ages of 4 and 7 showed more ethnic prejudice in their choices than did older children. In later research, it was found that younger children expressed more negative attitudes towards foreigners than did older children (Barrett & Short, 1992). Thus, the findings seem to support Aboud's social developmental theory. However, it is hard to know whether the lower

Ethical issues: What are the ethical issues that need to be taken into account when conducting research with children?

Infants distrust strangers and cling to familiar people.

levels of prejudice found in older children are genuine or whether they simply reflect more awareness of what answers are socially acceptable.

Reduction of Prejudice and Discrimination

Prejudice and discrimination are common in most cultures. It is a matter of considerable importance to find suitable ways for reducing (and ideally eliminating) all forms of prejudice and discrimination. Psychologists have identified various approaches that can be taken, some of which are discussed here. For example, prejudice and discrimination can be reduced if individuals from different groups co-operate to achieve common goals. Alternatively, social contact between groups can also have beneficial effects, especially when attempts are made to blur the boundaries between groups. Finally, there are indications that an effective way of reducing prejudice is to put people on the receiving end of prejudice, so that they can experience for themselves how unpleasant it is.

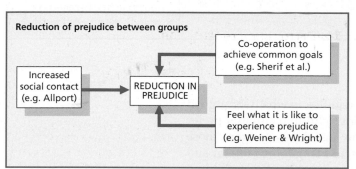

Common goals

It has often been argued that prejudice and discrimination between two groups in conflict can be reduced if they agree to pursue some common goal. This was shown by Sherif et al. (1961) in a study discussed earlier in the chapter. To reduce the conflict between the Rattlers and the Eagles, it was decided that the camp's drinking water should be turned off. In order to restore the supply, the two groups had to combine forces. Several other situations were set up, in which co-operation on a common goal was essential. These situations included rescuing a truck that had got stuck, and pitching tents. As a result of pursuing these common goals, the two groups showed much friendlier attitudes towards each other. In fact, the boys chose as their friends more members of the other group than of their own.

The jigsaw classroom

Aronson and Osherow (1980) tried to reduce prejudice in schools by means of co-operation on common goals. The schools in Austin, Texas had recently been desegregated. This led to concerns about the racial conflict that might result from having black and white children in the same classes. One class of black and white children was divided into small groups for a learning task (e.g. the life of Abraham Lincoln). Within each group, every child was made responsible for learning a different part of the information (e.g. Lincoln's early life; his attitudes towards slavery). Each member of the group then taught what he or she had learned to the other group members. After that, the children received a mark based on their overall knowledge of the topic. This approach was called the **jigsaw classroom**. The reason for this was that all the children had a major contribution to make, just as all of the pieces in a jigsaw puzzle are needed to complete it.

Could raising the competence of the low achievers have been made a common goal in the jigsaw classroom?

The findings with the jigsaw classroom were promising. The children showed higher self-esteem, better school performance, more liking for their classmates, and some reduction in prejudice. However, most of the effects were rather small. There are two likely reasons for this. First, the jigsaw classroom was only used for 45 minutes a day, three days a week, for a six-week period. Second, the groups did not always work in a co-operative way. If the common goals are not achieved, or if the groups co-operating with each other feel they are losing their own identities, then prejudice and discrimination may increase rather than decrease (Brown & Wade, 1987). Additional problems were identified by Rosenfield, Stephan, and Lucker (1981). They used the jigsaw classroom technique, and found that minority group members who were low in competence tended to be blamed for slowing down the learning of the more competent students. Their evidence suggested that this can confirm existing prejudiced attitudes rather than reducing them.

KEY TERM
Jigsaw classroom: an approach to reducing prejudice in which the teacher makes sure that all of the children can contribute to the achievement of classroom goals.

Social contact

According to Allport's (1954) *contact hypothesis*, prejudice can be reduced by increased contact between prejudiced individuals and the groups against which they are prejudiced. There are various reasons why this should be the case. First, stereotypes are based on the assumption that everyone in a given group is very similar, and frequent contact with members of that group disproves that stereotype. Second, interacting with members of another group often makes it clear they are more similar to the prejudiced individual in their attitudes and behaviour than he or she had thought.

Some research findings support the contact hypothesis. For example, Deutsch and Collins (1951) compared the attitudes of black and white American housewives living close to each other with those of housewives living in segregated housing. Prejudice decreased over time for the housewives living close to each other. After a while, their level of prejudice became much less than that of the housewives in segregated housing.

Social contact on its own is not usually enough. As we saw in the summer camp study of Sherif et al. (1961), social contact between the two groups of boys led to conflict rather than to harmony. Even organising a big feast or a large firework display failed to reduce inter-group hostility. Thus, other factors need to be added to social contact if prejudice is to be reduced. Allport (1954) was well aware that contact on its own is not sufficient to produce large reductions in prejudice. He argued that the groups concerned should be involved in a co-operative activity, and that there should be formal institutional support for integration. In addition, Allport felt that contact would be most effective in reducing prejudice when it involved groups having equal status.

> **CASE STUDY:** *New Era Schools Trust*
>
> The New Era Schools Trust (or NEST) runs three boarding schools in South Africa, in Durban, Johannesburg, and Cape Town. The unique aim of all the NEST schools is not only to produce well-educated and personable young people, but also to eliminate any trace of racial prejudice in their students. To achieve this, all races are mixed together from the very first day at school, living and studying alongside each other in a way that is rare even in post-apartheid South Africa. The teachers are similarly multiracial, and there is an equal mix of boys and girls.
>
> Not only are the different races regarded as equal in NEST schools, their cultures are also given equal value. Schools in South Africa have generally taken the view that African culture is irrelevant, and have taught exclusively from a white perspective. At NEST schools the pupils study Xhosa poets as well as Keats, and the lives of Zulu warriors as well as Napoleon. This sense of total equality permeates everything—there are no prefects or top-down discipline, no uniforms or corporal punishment, and everyone takes a hand in doing the chores.
>
> NEST has found that more black parents than white parents wish their children to attend a NEST school. White children tend to have better access to well-equipped schools where they are not required to help clean the dormitories, whereas many black parents are keen for their children to leave the deprivation of the townships to receive their education. This imbalance is lessening, however, as white parents realise what good academic success the NEST schools are achieving. In 1992 their pass rate was 100%, when private white schools and white church schools averaged 90%.
>
> (Based on an article by Prue Leith, *The Times*, May 1993.)

■ Research activity: Try to find examples of social contact between different groups by looking through a selection of newspapers.

Wexler Middle School

One of the most ambitious attempts to test the contact hypothesis in a thorough way was carried out at Wexler Middle School in Waterford in the United States (see Brown, 1986). It involved **desegregation**, that is, members of different groups attended the same school. A large amount of money was spent on the school to provide it with excellent facilities. It was decided that the numbers of black and white students would be about the same, so that it was not regarded as a white school or a black school. Much was done to make all of the students feel equal, with very little streaming on the basis of ability. Co-operation was increased by having the students work together to buy special equipment they could all use.

The results over the first three years were encouraging. There was much less discrimination, with the behaviour of the black and white students towards each other being friendly. However, while there were many black–white friendships, these friendships rarely extended to visiting each other's houses. In addition, some stereotyped beliefs were still found. Black and white students agreed that black students were tougher and more assertive than white students, whereas white students were cleverer and worked harder than black students.

Discussion points

1. Why were the findings from Wexler Middle School more promising than those from other studies (see Evaluation)?
2. Are there ways in which desegregation could be made more effective?

Evaluation

In spite of the success of the study carried out at Wexler Middle School in Waterford, other studies involving desegregation in schools have not worked well. Stephan (1987) reviewed studies on desegregation, and concluded that it often produces increases in white

> **KEY TERM**
> **Desegregation**: the free mixing of members of different racial or other groups (e.g. in schools).

prejudice rather than the desired reduction. In addition, contact between whites and blacks rarely had positive effects on the black students. One of the problems is that white and black students in desegregated schools often keep very much within their own group in the playground and at lunchtime. According to Stephan (1987), desegregation is most likely to lead to reduced prejudice when the students are of equal status, there are co-operative, one-on-one interactions, members of the two groups have similar beliefs and values, and contact occurs in various situations and with several members of the other group. However, these requirements are not usually met in most desegregated schools.

The contact hypothesis has been criticised because it seems to focus too much on changing the prejudiced views of the dominant group and not enough on the attitudes of the minority group. In many cases, contact between the dominant and minority groups involves inter-group anxiety (Stephan & Stephan, 1989). The members of the dominant group are anxious to avoid saying or doing anything that could be regarded as prejudiced, whereas the members of the minority group are anxious that they may be victimised or negatively evaluated. If contact is to lead to reduced prejudice, it is important to consider ways of reducing inter-group anxiety.

In November 1989, in Enniskillen, Northern Ireland, an integrated primary school was opened for children of all religions. What do you think motivated the people of Enniskillen to take this unusual step?

Decategorisation

Brewer and Miller (1984) were in general agreement with the contact hypothesis. However, in their decategorisation theory, they argued that social contact will mainly reduce prejudice when the boundaries between the conflicting groups become blurred or less rigid. When this happens, members of each group are less likely to think of members of the other group in terms of categories or group membership. Instead, they respond to members of the other group as individuals.

Research by Aronson and Osherow (1980) discussed earlier may show the value of decategorisation. They reduced racial barriers in children by having them work together in groups in the "jigsaw classroom". In general terms, teaching methods that focus on co-operative learning and the removal of group barriers are effective in reducing conflicts and prejudice between groups (Slavin, 1983).

Evaluation

Hewstone and Brown (1986) pointed out that decategorisation often works only in a limited way. Decategorisation and co-operation may be very effective in the situation in which they are used. However, the reduction in prejudice often does not extend to other members of the group or to other situations. The techniques used to produce decategorisation involve treating members of the other group as individuals. As a result, there is likely to be a reduction in prejudice towards those individuals rather than towards the group as a whole.

In order for reduced prejudice to generalise from a given individual to his or her group, it may be important to ensure that the individual's group affiliation is clear. Some interesting relevant evidence was reported by Wilder (1984). Students had a pleasant meeting with a student belonging to a rival college. This led to reduced prejudice towards the rival college when the student was regarded as a typical member of that college. However, there was no reduction when he was regarded as atypical. Thus, it is important that individuals are *representative* of the group to which they belong for a general reduction in prejudice to occur.

Have you ever encountered someone from a "rival" group and been pleasantly surprised by what you found?

Experiencing prejudice

People can be prejudiced because they do not know what it feels like to be on the receiving end of prejudice. It follows that prejudice could be reduced by arranging for people to experience prejudice for themselves. Weiner and Wright (1973) tested this notion. White American children aged 9 or 10 were put at random into an orange or a green group, and wore coloured armbands to identify their group membership. On the first day, the orange children were told that they were cleverer and cleaner than the green children, and they were given privileges that were denied to the orange children. The situation was reversed on the second day. On each day, the group that was discriminated against felt inferior, showed reduced self-confidence, and did less well in their schoolwork.

In order to see whether the experience of these children had made them less prejudiced, they were asked whether they wanted to go on a picnic with some black children. Nearly all (96%) of the children agreed. In contrast, only 62% of children who had not been exposed to prejudice agreed to go on the picnic. Thus, experiencing prejudice at first hand can reduce prejudice towards other people.

Self-regulation

Monteith (1993) argued for an approach to prejudice reduction based on self-regulation. According to this approach, even individuals who are not generally prejudiced are likely to have negative stereotypes of various kinds stored away in long-term memory. For example, they may have a stereotype based on the notion that French people are arrogant. When they meet a French person, this stereotype will be activated automatically. This may lead them to behave rudely. If they realise that their behaviour is discrepant from their non-prejudiced outlook, then they are likely to experience feelings of guilt and self-criticism. They may also try to identify the situational cues that led them to behave in a prejudiced way.

An implication of this analysis of prejudiced behaviour is that individuals low in prejudice can eliminate it by regular self-regulation of their thoughts and feelings. This requires being more reflective, and thinking about any stereotypes that are activated automatically *before* they can lead to prejudiced behaviour. Monteith (1993) reported evidence that prejudice can be reduced through the development of self-regulatory mechanisms. However, it should be noted that this approach is only likely to reduce prejudice in those who are initially low in prejudice *and* motivated to avoid prejudiced thinking and behaviour. Indeed, Devine (1995, p.509) admitted that the model "does not directly address the experiences of high prejudiced people."

Evaluation

Much of the research on methods of reducing prejudice has been disappointing. As we have seen, the most common approach based on the contact hypothesis only seems to succeed when the circumstances in which majority and minority groups meet are carefully controlled. More worryingly, even if contact is found to produce beneficial effects, these effects rarely generalise beyond the contact situation. One reason for these disappointing findings is that producing contact between groups is an *indirect* way of trying to change prejudiced attitudes. In contrast, self-regulation has the advantage of trying to change negative attitudes in a *direct* way.

Other major problems with most attempts to reduce prejudice were identified by Devine (1995, p.500):

> *Even though several theoretical explanations have been advanced concerning the processes involved in the acquisition of prejudice, there has been a paucity [lack] of research that uses these theories in order to identify the processes involved in the reduction of prejudice. As a consequence ..., prejudice-reduction techniques seemed to have a "hit-or miss" quality about them; the processes responsible for the technique's successes and failures often were—and remain—unknown.*

Experiencing prejudice as a way of reducing it (Weiner & Wright, 1975)

Why do you think some of the control group did not display prejudice?

What recommendations would you make to the head teacher of a secondary school to help reduce prejudice? How would you then attempt to measure the effectiveness of any changes?

PERSONAL REFLECTIONS

- I am very interested in attributional biases such as the fundamental attribution error. A key question that has not been addressed properly is the following: how do we preserve these biases over the years in the face of evidence indicating that our thinking is wrong? I suspect an important part of the answer is that much of our thinking is intuitive and less rational than we imagine. For example, there has been a study in which the participants were given a complex reasoning problem to solve. Then different groups of them were given different wrong answers that they were assured were correct. Most of the participants were perfectly happy to accept the wrong answer they had been given (see Eysenck, 1998)! Thus, we often fail to consider all the relevant evidence when interpreting situations, and this allows attributional biases to thrive.

SUMMARY

Theories of social cognition

According to social identity theory, individuals have various social identities based on the different groups with which they identify. They try to increase their self-esteem by regarding the groups with which they identify as superior to all other groups. There is ingroup favouritism even with minimal groups; this may reflect social identity or self-interest. Social identity theory is most applicable to Western cultures. According to Moscovici, much of our knowledge of the world takes the form of social representations based on social communication. Social representations can eliminate some attributional biases (e.g. the fundamental attribution error). Theoretical accounts of social representations are hard to test. According to the social constructionists, many people do not have a single fixed cultural identity. Instead, cultural identities evolve over time because of the effects of history, power, and culture. These effects can be seen most clearly in migrant groups.

Attribution theory

According to correspondent inference theory, we tend to decide that there is a correspondence between someone's behaviour and their personal disposition when the effects of his or her behaviour are socially undesirable, or when his or her actions have rare effects. According to Kelley's attribution theory, we decide whether to make a dispositional or situational attribution of someone else's behaviour on the basis of information about consensus, consistency, and distinctiveness. According to the fundamental attribution error, we tend to attribute the behaviour of others to their disposition or personality rather than to situational factors. This error is less likely to be

Having children work in groups helps reduce racial barriers.

found if we suspect that others have hidden motives for their behaviour in a given situation, and it is less common in collectivist cultures than in individualist cultures. According to the notion of actor–observer differences, we tend to attribute our own behaviour to situational factors. This probably happens because we can see the situation but we cannot see ourselves. The self-serving bias may depend on motivational factors (enhancing self-esteem) or it may depend on cognitive factors (confirmation or non-confirmation of intentions)

Prejudice and discrimination

It is hard to measure prejudice and discrimination accurately, in part because of social pressures and social desirability bias. We often have stereotyped views of outgroups. Stereotypes can lead to prejudice, because stereotypes make us attend closely to information fitting the stereotype. Prejudice can stem from frustration, and is more common in individuals with an authoritarian personality. However, widespread uniformity of prejudice in certain cultural groups cannot be explained in terms of the authoritarian personality.

Reduction of prejudice and discrimination

Prejudice and discrimination can be reduced if two groups in conflict successfully pursue common goals. Social contact between groups of equal status can also reduce prejudice. Decategorisation can help by blurring the boundaries between conflicting groups. However, decategorisation often causes a reduction in prejudice towards some individuals in the other group rather than towards the group as a whole. Individuals who are low in prejudice and motivated to eliminate it can do so by self-regulation of their thoughts, especially automatically activated negative stereotypes. Experiencing prejudice at first hand can reduce prejudice.

FURTHER READING

There are good chapters dealing with the issues discussed in this chapter in M. Hewstone, W. Stroebe, and G.M. Stephenson (Eds.) (1996), *Introduction to social psychology (2nd Edn.)*, Oxford: Blackwell. A readable book that deals with social cognition is N. Hayes (1993), *Principles of social psychology*, Hove, UK: Psychology Press. Prejudice and discrimination are discussed in detail by J. Vivian and R. Brown (1994), in A.M. Colman (Ed.), *Companion encyclopedia of psychology, Vol. 2*, London: Routledge.

REVISION QUESTIONS

1	Discuss social representations and social identity theory as explanations of the influence of social factors on perception.	(24 marks)
2a	What do social psychologists mean by the term attribution?	(6 marks)
2b	Discuss errors and biases that have been found to operate in the attributional process.	(18 marks)
3	Critically consider what psychological research has shown us about the origins of social *and/or* cultural stereotypes.	(24 marks)
4a	Consider what psychological research has told us about the origins of prejudice.	(12 marks)
4b	Assess attempts that psychologists have made to reduce prejudice and discrimination.	(12 marks)

- **Liking and loving**
  How to measure liking and loving, and tell them apart.

  Rubin's scales of love and liking
  Sternberg's triangular theory

- **Theories of interpersonal relationships**
  The different psychological approaches to studying relationships.

  Biological theories
  Reinforcement and need satisfaction theory
  Social exchange theory (e.g. Thibaut and Kelley)
  Equity theory (e.g. Hatfield, Argyle)
  Clark and Mills' theory
  Levinger's five-stage model
  Kerckhoff and Davis's filter theory

- **Formation of relationships**
  Why are we attracted to one person and not another?

  Cunningham's features of attractiveness
  Walster et al.'s matching hypothesis
  Proximity and similarity

- **Maintenance of relationships**
  What factors lead to some relationships outlasting others?

  Self-disclosure and commitment
  Maintenance strategies and rules
  Murray and Holmes's storytelling study

- **Dissolution of relationships**
  Why relationships end.

  Models by Lee and Duck
  Duck's risk factors
  Levinger's social exchange theory
  Karney and Bradbury's vulnerability-stress-adaptation model
  Studies of jealousy

- **Components of interpersonal relationships**
  Other kinds of relationships (e.g. mother–child, teacher–student); how we study them and their effects.

  Argyle and Furnham's study of goals and conflicts
  Wish et al.'s study of power
  Post-modern approach (e.g. Wood and Duck)

- **Other aspects**
  Homosexuality, age, mental and physical health.

  Homosexuality
  Anderson et al.'s cross-cultural study
  Bradburn's happiness study

20

Social Relationships

This chapter is concerned with social relationships. It deals with the factors determining whether we are initially attracted to another person, the factors that serve to maintain a friendship or other relationship, and the factors that can lead to its break-up. Several theories have been put forward in an attempt to understand some of the underlying processes in interpersonal relationships, and they are considered in detail. As we will see, there are considerable differences in some aspects of interpersonal relationships (especially marriage) from one culture to another.

How can psychologists study interpersonal relationships? Some issues relating to the early stages of relationships can be studied in the laboratory. For example, suppose we want to know whether physical attractiveness is important in determining initial attraction. We could show our participants photographs of various people, with some biographical information attached to each photograph. We could then see whether willingness to go on a date with each person depended more on their physical attractiveness or on the biographical information.

It is much harder to study the later stages of interpersonal relationships in the laboratory. For example, it is not really possible to study the process of falling in love under laboratory conditions! The fact that proper experiments can rarely be carried out on interpersonal relationships means that other approaches have to be used. Self-report questionnaires are typically used to assess the processes involved in relationships, the level of satisfaction with relationships, and so on. Such questionnaires are open to bias, especially to social desirability bias. This is a tendency to give the socially desirable answers to questions, even when the answers are incorrect. For example, most married couples in the United Kingdom claim to be happily or very happily married. However, the fact that about 40% of marriages end in divorce suggests that many married couples are less happily married than they admit.

Other approaches are also possible. Towards the end of the chapter, we consider the post-modern approach, and examine its recommendations for the study of relationships.

In sum, the topic of interpersonal relationships is one of the most interesting ones in psychology. However, it is a difficult area in which to carry out experiments and to collect valid data. The rest of the chapter shows how psychologists have risen (or failed to rise) to the challenge.

Liking and Loving

Rubin's scales

Our feelings for those with whom we develop social relationships typically include liking and/or loving. A key issue is to try to distinguish between these two feelings. The best-known attempt was made by Rubin (1970), who put forward the Rubin Love Scale and the Rubin Liking Scale. The items on the love scale measure three main factors: (1) desire to help the other person; (2) dependent needs of the other person; and (3) feelings of exclusiveness and absorption. In contrast, the items on the liking scale measure respect for the other person's abilities and similarity of the other person in terms of his or her attitudes and other characteristics.

Rubin's love and liking scales are highly correlated with each other. Sternberg and Grajek (1984) found that liking and loving scores for a lover correlated +0.72, and these scores correlated +0.66 for best friend, +0.73 for one's mother, and +0.81 for one's father. These high correlations mean that Rubin's scales do not discriminate very well between liking and loving.

Sternberg's triangular theory

Sternberg (1986) developed a *triangular theory of love*. According to this theory, love consists of three components: intimacy; passion; and decision/commitment. Sternberg defined them as follows:

> The intimacy component refers to feelings of closeness, connectedness, and bondedness in loving relationships ... The passion component refers to the drives that lead to romance, physical attraction, sexual consummation, and related phenomena in loving relationships. The decision/commitment component refers to, in the short term, the decision that one loves someone else, and in the long term, the commitment to maintain that love.

The relative importance of these three components differs between short-term and long-term relationships. The passion component is usually the most important in short-term relationships, with the decision/commitment component being the least important. In long-term relationships, on the other hand, the intimacy component is the most important, and the passion component is the least important.

Sternberg argued that there are several kinds of love, consisting of different combinations of the three components. Some of the main kinds of love are as follows:

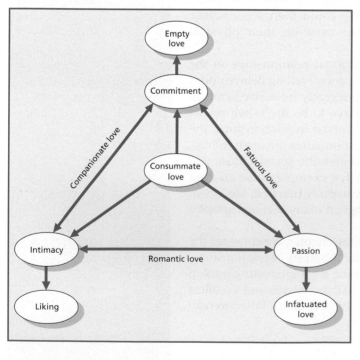

- Liking or friendship: this involves intimacy but not passion or commitment.
- Romantic love: this involves intimacy and passion, but not commitment.
- Companionate love: this involves intimacy and commitment, but not passion.
- Empty love: this involves commitment, but not passion or intimacy.
- Fatuous love: this involves commitment and passion, but not intimacy.
- Infatuated love: this involves passion but not intimacy or commitment.
- Consummate love: this is the strongest form of love, since it involves all three components (commitment, passion, and intimacy).

Levels of love

Who do we tend to love and like the most? Sternberg and Grajek (1984) found that men generally love and like their lover more than their mother, father, sibling closest in age, or their best friend. Women also loved and liked their lover and best friend more than their mother, father, or sibling closest in age. However, women differed from men in that they loved their lover and their best friend of the same sex equally, but liked their best friend more than their lover.

Sternberg and Grajek also found that the amount of love that someone has for one member of their family predicts the amount of love they will have for the other members. For example, people who love their father very much also tend to have high levels of love for their mother and sibling closest in age. However, the amount of love that someone has for their lover or best friend is not predictable from the amount of love they feel for members of their own family.

Can the type of love in a relationship change over time? If so, how and why?

Theories of Interpersonal Relationships

Theories of interpersonal relationships are discussed in this section. It is hard to test these theories. One reason is because many of the processes involved cannot readily be studied in the laboratory. Another reason is the enormous diversity of interpersonal relationships between people. For example, it is important to distinguish among romantic relationships, same-sex friendships, opposite-sex friendships, interpersonal relationships in the workplace, and so on. It is obvious from experience that the processes involved differ considerably from one type of interpersonal relationship to another. It is hard to handle such diversity within a single theory. Many theorists have not been as careful as they might have been in indicating the type or types of interpersonal relationship to which their theory is most applicable.

One of the key features of nearly all interpersonal relationships is that they change over time. In order to understand these changes, we need to focus on the *processes* involved. However, these processes typically occur over long periods of time, and are very hard to observe experimentally.

Biological theories

One way of considering social relationships is in biological or evolutionary terms (see Chapter 8). The central idea is that everyone is motivated to ensure the survival of their genes by means of sexual reproduction. One of the implications of the biological approach is that males and females should both seek sexual partners who are most likely to produce healthy children. This could explain why physically healthy partners are generally preferred to unhealthy ones. Men may tend to prefer women who are younger than themselves because younger women are more likely to be fertile (Buss, 1989b).

What other characteristics would be considered preferable in a partner according to the biological approach?

The biological approach has been extended to account for the close relationships that are often found within families. One of the ways in which an individual can help to ensure the survival of his or her genes is by protecting their relatives so that they will be able to reproduce. For example, children share 50% of their genes with each of their parents. As a result, there are strong biological reasons why parents should devote considerable efforts to looking after their children. The same considerations apply to our relationships with other relatives, with the level of involvement being determined by the genetic similarity. The term **kin selection** is used to describe the notion that survival of an individual's genes is ensured by

helping the survival of close relatives (see Chapter 9).

Some evidence is consistent with the biological approach. Fellner and Marshall (1981) found that 86% of people were willing to be a kidney donor for their children, 67% would do the same for their parents, and 50% would be a kidney donor for their siblings.

Evaluation

Biological theories of relationships help to account for the special nature of the relationships within families, and especially for the enormous amounts of time and

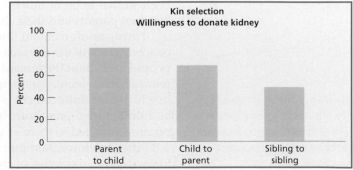

Kin selection
Willingness to donate kidney

Parents invest a lot of time and resources in their children, which may be explained by biological theories of relationships—the parents' chances of passing on their genes are improved if they can help their children to survive and succeed.

resources that most parents devote to their children. However, such theories do not explain most relationships. For example, the notion that romantic relationships have reproduction as their primary goal does not apply to many homosexual relationships, or to heterosexual relationships in which there is no intention to have children.

The greatest limitation of biological theories is that they focus on sexual relationships and ignore non-sexual relationships and friendships. It is hard for such theories to explain why women love their best friend as much as their lover, and like their best friend more (Sternberg & Grajek, 1984). In general terms, biological theories are inadequate to account for interpersonal relationships based on psychological rather than biological needs.

Reinforcement and need satisfaction theory

Reinforcement and need satisfaction theory is based on the notion that a key reason why we form friendships and relationships is because of the rewards or reinforcements that we receive from others. These rewards often consist of approval, smiling, and so on. Foa and Foa (1975) argued that the rewards provided by other people can also include sex, status, love, help, money, and agreement with our opinions. These things may be rewarding because they meet our various social needs. For example, obtaining the approval of others satisfies our need for self-esteem, being comforted satisfies our dependency needs, controlling others meets our needs for dominance, and making love satisfies our sex needs (Argyle, 1988).

List the needs that are being met in the following types of relationship: best friend; parent with child; lover.

Byrne (1971) argued that classical conditioning also plays an important role in determining the effects of reinforcement on interpersonal attraction. He found that positive feelings, or affect, are created when someone expresses similar attitudes to ours, whereas negative affect is produced when someone expresses dissimilar attitudes. Of greatest relevance to his theory, Byrne also found that someone whose picture was present was liked more when the participants listened to someone expressing similar attitudes to their own than when they were listening to dissimilar attitudes. According to Byrne, this resembles the way in which a tone can produce salivation if it is generally followed by the sight of food (see Chapter 10).

Evaluation

We are more attracted to those who provide us with reinforcement than those who do not. For example, individuals who are high on rewardingness (i.e. friendly, co-operative, smiling, warm) are consistently liked more than individuals who are low on rewardingness (Argyle, 1988). However, reinforcement theory does not provide an adequate account of interpersonal attraction for various reasons. First, the theory seems much more relevant to the very earliest stages of attraction than to attraction within an ongoing friendship or relationship. Second, as Argyle pointed out, reinforcement has not been shown to be of much importance in determining the strength of the relationship between parents and their children.

Third, reinforcement theory assumes that people are totally selfish, and only concerned about the rewards they receive. In fact, people are often concerned about other people, and about the rewards that they provide for other people. Fourth, whether or not reinforcement increases interpersonal attraction depends to a large extent on the *context* in which the reinforcement is provided. For example, the need for sexual satisfaction can be fulfilled by a prostitute, but this does not mean that men who resort to prostitutes become attracted to them as people.

Fifth, reinforcement and need satisfaction theories seem of more relevance to the individualistic societies of the Western world than to the collectivistic societies of the

Based on reinforcement theory, how would you advise someone to behave to make a good impression on, or be liked by, someone they have never met before?

non-Western world (see Chapter 28). More speculatively, these theories may tend to be more applicable to men than to women. In many cultures, there is more emphasis on females than on males learning to be attentive to the needs of others (Lott, 1994).

Exchange and equity

Social exchange theory

Social exchange theory (e.g. Thibaut & Kelley, 1959) is similar to reinforcement theory, but provides a more plausible account of interpersonal attraction. It is assumed that everyone tries to maximise the rewards (e.g. affection; attention) they obtain from a relationship, and to minimise the costs (e.g. devoting time and effort to the other person; coping with the other person's emotional problems). It is also assumed that people expect the other person to reward them as much as they reward the other person.

Thibaut and Kelley argued that long-term friendships and relationships go through four stages:

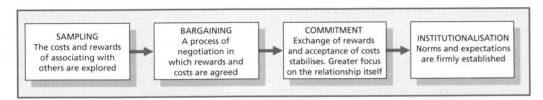

SAMPLING: The costs and rewards of associating with others are explored → BARGAINING: A process of negotiation in which rewards and costs are agreed → COMMITMENT: Exchange of rewards and acceptance of costs stabilises. Greater focus on the relationship itself → INSTITUTIONALISATION: Norms and expectations are firmly established

Additional assumptions are sometimes included in social exchange theory. For example, how satisfied individuals are with the rewards and costs of a relationship will depend on what they have come to expect from previous relationships. In other words, they have a **comparison level** (Thibaut & Kelley, 1959), representing the outcomes they believe they deserve on the basis of past experiences. In addition, their level of satisfaction will depend on the rewards (e.g. affection; sex) and costs (e.g. arguments; loss of control) that would be involved if they formed a relationship with someone else; this is known as the comparison level for alternatives.

Equity theory

Some theorists (e.g. Hatfield, Utne, & Traupmann, 1979) have extended exchange theory to include more of an emphasis on fairness or equity. According to equity theory, people expect to receive rewards from a relationship which are proportional to the rewards they provide for the other person. However, it is assumed within the theory that imbalance can be tolerated if the two people involved in a relationship accept the situation. Walster et al. (1978) expressed the main assumptions of equity theory as follows:

1. Individuals try to maximise the rewards they receive and minimise the costs.
2. There is negotiation to produce fairness; for example, one partner may do the shopping every week to compensate for being away playing sport twice a week.
3. If the relationship is unfair or inequitable, it produces distress, especially in the disadvantaged person.
4. The disadvantaged person will try hard to make the relationship more equitable, particularly when it is very inequitable.

Hatfield et al. (1979) asked newlyweds to indicate the extent to which they felt that they were receiving more or less than they should in view of what they were contributing to the marriage. They were also asked to indicate their level of contentment, happiness, anger, and guilt. The under-benefited had the lowest level of overall satisfaction with their marriage, and tended to experience anger. The over-benefited came next (they tended to feel guilty), and those who perceived their marriage as equitable had the highest level of satisfaction. Men who were over-benefited were almost as satisfied as those in an equitable marriage, but over-benefited women were much less satisfied than women with equal benefit (Argyle, 1988).

What rewards and costs are associated with the following relationships: best friend; parent with child; lover?

What is the difference between equity and equality?

Sharing domestic chores may be a result of negotiation in an equitable relationship, in which each partner feels the other takes their share of responsibilities.

What could be the cause of gender differences such as the one between over-benefited males and over-benefited females?

The finding that those who perceive their marriages as equitable are happiest, and those who perceive themselves as under-benefited are least happy, was replicated by Buunk and VanYperen (1991). However, these findings applied only to those individuals who were high in exchange orientation (i.e. expecting rewards given by one person in a relationship to be followed immediately by rewards given by the other person). Those low in exchange orientation had fairly high marriage satisfaction regardless of whether they were over-benefited, under-benefited, or receiving equal benefit.

Evaluation

Equity theory seems more plausible than exchange theory. It takes more account of the rewards and costs of the other person as well as of the individual himself or herself. The most obvious criticism of both approaches is that they assume that people are very selfish and self-centred in their friendships and relationships. This assumption may possess some validity in an individualistic society such as that of the United States, but is less likely to apply to collectivistic societies. Evidence of cultural differences was reported by Gergen, Morse, and Gergen (1980). European students were found to prefer equality in their relationships, with an equal distribution of rewards. In contrast, American students tended to favour equity, based on a constant ratio of rewards to inputs.

One of the more obvious predictions from equity theory is that the future quality of equitable relationships should be greater than that of inequitable ones. However, there are various studies in which there was no relationship between equity and future quality (see Buunk, 1996).

Much of the research in this area has not proved very informative. Some of the reasons for this were identified by Argyle (1988, p.224):

> [Exchange] theory has led mainly to very artificial experiments ... Research on real-life relationships has been hampered by the difficulty of scaling rewards.

Notions of exchange and equity are more important between casual acquaintances than they are between people who are close friends or emotionally involved with each other. Happily married couples do not focus on issues of exchange or equity. Murstein, MacDonald, and Cerreto (1977) found that marital adjustment was significantly poorer in those married couples who were concerned about exchange and equity than in those couples who were not. Further evidence on this point is discussed in the next section.

Communal relationships

Several theorists have doubted whether intimate relationships can be understood properly in terms of traditional theories. For example, Clark and Mills (1979) argued that there are two major kinds of relationships:

- **Communal relationships**: the main focus is on giving the other person what he or she needs; these relationships typically involve close friends or family members.
- **Exchange relationships**: the main focus is on the notion that what one puts into the relationship should balance what one receives; these relationships usually involve acquaintances or strangers.

According to Clark and Mills, most romantic relationships are not based on the principle of exchange. Those involved in such relationships are much more concerned about being able to meet the needs of the other person than in exchange or reciprocity.

Clark (1984) presented evidence consistent with this proposed distinction between communal and exchange relationships. Male students located sequences of numbers in a matrix with someone called Paula. Each student was told that he and Paula would receive a joint payment based on their performance, and they must decide how much each of them received. Some participants were told that Paula was single and was taking part in the experiment to make friends. The others were told that Paula was married, and that her husband was going to pick her up. Clark predicted that the former participants would tend to think in terms of a possible communal relationship with Paula, whereas the latter participants would expect an exchange relationship.

The participants found that Paula had already circled some sequences of numbers with a felt-tip pen. What was of interest was whether the participants used a pen of a different colour. It was argued that students looking for an exchange relationship would do so, because it would allow them to be paid on the basis of their contribution. In contrast, those seeking a communal relationship should use a pen of the same colour, because they were mainly concerned about their combined efforts. The findings were as predicted. About 90% of those students who thought Paula was married used a felt-tip pen of a different colour, compared to only 10% of those who thought she was single. Clark also found that pairs of friends were less likely than pairs of strangers to use different-coloured pens.

Fiske (1993) extended the line of theorising proposed by Clark and Mills (1979). According to him, there are four types of relationship:

- Exchange: based on reciprocity.
- Communal: based on catering for the other person's needs.
- Equality matching: based on ensuring that everyone receives the same; for example, giving all of the children in a family an ice cream of the same size.
- Authority: based on the notion that one person's orders are obeyed by others.

Discussion points

1. Does the study by Clark and Mills really show that there is a distinction between exchange and communal relationships?
2. Have social psychologists focused too much on exchange relationships and not enough on communal relationships?

Levinger's five-stage model

One of the most important features of relationships and close friendships is that they show dynamic changes over time. Levinger (1980) emphasised these changes in his five-stage or ABCDE model. According to this model, the five successive stages of a relationship are as follows:

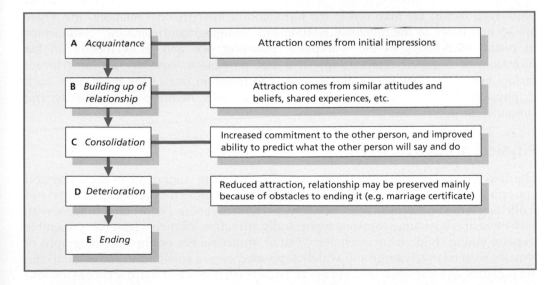

A Acquaintance	Attraction comes from initial impressions
B Building up of relationship	Attraction comes from similar attitudes and beliefs, shared experiences, etc.
C Consolidation	Increased commitment to the other person, and improved ability to predict what the other person will say and do
D Deterioration	Reduced attraction, relationship may be preserved mainly because of obstacles to ending it (e.g. marriage certificate)
E Ending	

Evaluation

The greatest strength of Levinger's model is that it emphasises the notion that relationships and close friendships change in predictable ways over time. However, Levinger regards the sequence of stages of a relationship as occurring in a fixed order, and so focuses on the similarities among relationships. In fact, there are large differences among couples in the progress of their relationships (Brehm, 1992). As a result, it may be preferable to think in terms of flexible phases rather than fixed stages (Brehm, 1992). Levinger's model provides some answers to *what* and *when* questions, telling us what happens during the course of a relationship and when

Do all relationships go through all of Levinger's five stages?

different stages occur. However, it has little to say about *why* questions: Why do relationships go through this set of fixed stages? Why do relationships initially improve over time and then deteriorate?

Filter theory

Do you think factors such as social class, ethnicity, education level, and age are important in the formation and maintenance of relationships?

Kerckhoff and Davis (1962) argued that relationships go through a series of filters, each of which is essential for the relationship to begin or to continue. The first filter revolves around the fact that we only meet a very small fraction of the people living in our area. Most of those we do meet will tend to be of similar social class and education to ourselves, and they may also be of the same racial or ethnic group.

The second filter is based on psychological factors. Kerckhoff and Davis found that the chances of a short-term (under 18-month) relationship becoming more permanent depended most on shared values and beliefs. The third filter is complementarity of emotional needs. The ability to satisfy the other person's emotional needs was the best predictor of survival of long-term relationships that were studied over a seven-month period.

Evaluation

There is considerable evidence that the factors that are important in the early stages of a relationship differ from those that matter later on (see Brehm, 1992), and this is emphasised within filter theory. Another advantage is that it helps us to make theoretical sense of the wide range of factors that influence the formation and maintenance of interpersonal relationships (see later). The main limitation of filter theory is that its focus is on romantic relationships, and thus it tells us little about the factors influencing the development of friendships.

Formation of Interpersonal Relationships

Numerous factors are involved in the formation of interpersonal relationships. There are several types of interpersonal relationships, ranging from romantic relationships to casual friendships in the workplace. However, we will focus mostly on the formation of romantic relationships. It is not possible to consider all the relevant factors here. What has been done instead is to focus on five of the main ones, such as physical attractiveness, proximity, attitude similarity, demographic similarity, and similarity in personality.

Physical attractiveness

Can you think of any famous people who are considered attractive, but who do not meet Cunningham's attractiveness criteria?

The first thing that we generally notice when meeting a stranger is their physical appearance. This includes how they are dressed, and whether they are clean or dirty, and it often includes an assessment of their physical attractiveness. People tend to agree with each other about whether someone is physically attractive. Women whose faces resemble those of young children are often perceived as attractive. For example, photographs of females with relatively large and widely separated eyes, a small nose, and a small chin are regarded as more attractive. However, wide cheekbones and narrow cheeks are also seen as attractive (Cunningham, 1986), and these features are not usually found in young children.

Cunningham also studied physical attractiveness in males. Men having features such as a square jaw, small eyes, and thin lips were regarded as attractive by women. These features can be regarded as indicating maturity, as they are rarely found in children.

Evidence that physically attractive people are thought of as being generally attractive was reported by Brigham (1971). Males and females both argued that physically attractive individuals are poised, sociable, interesting, independent, exciting, and sexually warm.

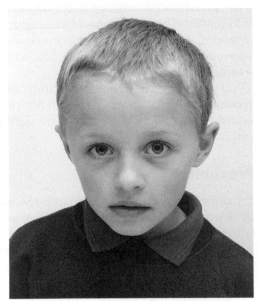

Joan Collins (top left) fits Cunningham's "attractive female" characteristics—note how her features are similar to the little girl's (top right). Pierce Brosnan (bottom left), however, looks very different from the little boy (bottom right).

Walster et al.

Walster et al. (1966) organised a dance at which students were randomly allocated partners of the opposite sex. Half way through the dance, the students filled in a questionnaire giving their views about their partner. These views were compared with judges' ratings of the physical attractiveness of the students. The more physically attractive students were liked more by their partners than were the less attractive students. When Walster et al. asked the students six months later whether they had dated their partners since the dance, they found that partners were more likely to have dated if they were similar in physical attractiveness than if they were dissimilar.

Walster et al. explained their findings as follows. We are initially attracted to those who are beautiful or handsome, but we are realistic about our chances of being found attractive by someone who is much more physically attractive. As a result, we are attracted to those who are about as physically attractive as we are. This is known as the **matching hypothesis**, which was tested by Walster and Walster (1969). They organised another

KEY STUDY EVALUATION — Walster et al.

Walster et al.'s matching hypothesis suggests that people are attracted to those of about the same level of physical attractiveness as themselves. This may indeed be the case in many situations, but it does not take account of many social factors that can also influence who we find attractive. Relationships often occur between people who have different levels of attractiveness but have got to know each other through working together or living nearby. Here mechanisms other than pure physical attractiveness are operating. In other situations, people who are generally considered very attractive may find that others think they are unapproachable. Some people may believe that a less attractive partner will be less likely to stray than a very attractive partner, and so have more confidence in the relationship.

dance. This time, however, the students had met each other beforehand. This may have led them to think more about the qualities they were looking for in a partner. As predicted by the matching hypothesis, students expressed the most liking for those who were at the same level of physical attractiveness.

Discussion points

1. Does the matching hypothesis seem correct in your experience?

2. Why does physical attractiveness play such an important part in dating behaviour and in relationships?

■ Research activity: Use photographs of couples from newspapers and magazines to replicate Murstein's study on the matching hypothesis. This will be a correlational study (i.e. non-experimental). Variations on Murstein's study might include looking at dating couples, couples who have been married for 10 years or more, or homosexual couples. You must bear in mind all the related ethical considerations.

Murstein (1972) obtained further support for the matching hypothesis. The physical attractiveness of engaged couples and those going out together was judged from photographs. There was a definite tendency for the two people in each couple to be similar in terms of physical attractiveness.

Physical attractiveness is of importance in influencing initial attraction for other people. However, some people are much more affected by physical attractiveness than others. Towhey (1979) asked males and females how much they thought they would like a person whose photograph they had seen, and about whom they had read biographical information. The judgements of those scoring high on the Macho Scale (dealing with sexist attitudes, stereotypes, and behaviour) were much influenced by physical attractiveness, whereas those scoring low on the Macho Scale almost ignored physical attractiveness as a factor.

Is physical attractiveness mainly of importance only in the early stages of a relationship? The answer seems to be "no". For example, Murstein and Christy (1976) reported that married couples were significantly more similar than dating couples in physical attractiveness.

Proximity

Proximity or nearness is an important factor in determining our choice of friends. Strong evidence for this was obtained by Festinger, Schacter, and Back (1950). They studied married graduate students who were assigned randomly to flats in 17 different two-storey buildings. About two-thirds of their closest friends lived in the same building. Close friends who lived in the same building were twice as likely to be living on the same floor as the other floor.

The importance of proximity extends to romantic relationships that lead to marriage. Bossard (1932) looked at 5000 marriage licences in Philadelphia. He found there was a clear tendency for those getting married to live close to each other. However, this may be less true today, because people are generally more mobile and travel much more than was the case in the 1930s.

Friendships and relationships are more common between individuals living close to each other, but so are antagonistic relationships. Ebbesen, Kjos, and Konecni (1976) found that most of the enemies of residents in apartment blocks in California lived close by.

Does this concept of proximity apply to your friends?

Friendships arise and are maintained between people who live close to each other, and who enjoy similar leisure pursuits.

Attitude similarity

One of the factors determining interpersonal attraction is attitude similarity. Newcomb (1961) obtained information about the beliefs and attitudes of students. He then used this information to assign student rooms. Some students were given a room with someone of similar attitudes, whereas others were paired with someone having very different attitudes. Friendships were much more likely to develop between students who shared the same beliefs and attitudes than between those who did not (58% and 25%, respectively).

Byrne et al. (1968) found that attitude similarity had much more of an effect on interpersonal attraction when the attitudes were of importance to the individual. They arranged matters so that the other person seemed to have similar attitudes to the participants on either 75% or 25% of the topics. This was done by deliberately providing fake information about the other person. It was only when similarity related to the topics of most importance to the participants that it affected attraction.

Werner and Parmalee (1979) argued that it was not attitude similarity as such that was important. They found that similarity in preference for leisure activities (which is related to attitude similarity) was more important for friendship than was attitude similarity. According to Werner and Parmalee (1979, p.62), "those who play together, stay together."

Do you think that preferring similar leisure activities is important in intimate relationships?

Demographic similarity

Several studies have considered the effects of demographic variables (e.g. age; sex; social class). It has nearly always been found that those who have similar demographic characteristics are more likely to become friends. For example, Kandel (1978) asked students in secondary school to identify their best friend among the other students. These best friends tended to be of the same age, religion, sex, social class, and ethnic background as the students who nominated them.

Similarity in personality

Reasonable similarity in physical attractiveness, attitudes, and demographic variables is found in friends, engaged couples, and married couples. What about similarity in personality? One possibility is that people who have similar personalities are most likely to become involved with each other ("Birds of a feather flock together"). Another possibility is that dissimilar people are most likely to become friends or to marry ("Opposites attract"). Winch (1958) argued for the latter possibility. He claimed that married couples will be happy if they each have complementary needs. For example, if a domineering person marries someone who is submissive, this may allow both of them to fulfil their needs.

Winch found that married couples who were different in personality were happier than those who were similar. However, most of the evidence indicates that similarity of personality is important, and that people tend to be intimately involved with those who are like themselves. Burgess and Wallin (1953) obtained detailed information from 1000 engaged couples, including information about 42 personality characteristics. There was no evidence for the notion that opposites attract. There was significant within-couple similarity for 14 personality characteristics (e.g. feelings easily hurt; leader of social events), but the degree of similarity was not great.

Evaluation of the five factors

There is much evidence that the formation of interpersonal relationships depends very much on several kinds of similarity. Why is similarity so important? Rubin (1973) suggested various answers. First, if we like those who are similar to us, there is a reasonable chance that they will like us. Second, communication is easier with people who are similar. Third, similar others may confirm the rightness of our attitudes and beliefs. Fourth, it makes sense that if we like ourselves, then we should also like others who resemble us. Fifth, people who are similar to us are likely to enjoy the same activities.

Much research in this area is rather artificial. For example, the importance of physical attractiveness has sometimes been assessed by showing participants photographs of people they have never met, and asking them to indicate how much they would like to go out with them. Of course, physical attractiveness is going to have an enormous influence on the results when no other relevant information is available. Interpersonal relationships are formed over time as two people begin to know each other better, but the processes involved have rarely been studied in the laboratory.

A further limitation of most research is that individual differences have been ignored. Some people attach more importance than others to similarity of physical attractiveness, attitudes, and so on, but very little is known about this.

Considering the factors involved in the formation of relationships, what type of person are you likely to form a successful relationship with? Would it be someone like yourself or not?

Maintenance of Relationships

Various factors contribute to the maintenance and development of friendships and relationships. These factors include self-disclosure, commitment, various maintenance strategies, and the following of relationship rules. In contrast, a decline in the level of self-disclosure is typically associated with a reduction in the strength of a relationship.

Self-disclosure

As was discussed earlier in the chapter, Sternberg (1986) identified intimacy as a key component of both liking and loving. **Self-disclosure**, which involves revealing personal and sensitive information about oneself to another person, is of fundamental importance in developing and maintaining intimacy. According to Altman and Taylor's (1973) *social penetration theory*, the development of a relationship involves increased self-disclosure on both sides. People who have just met tend to follow the *norm of self-disclosure reciprocity*, according to which they match the level of self-disclosure of the other person. According to Altman and Taylor, the move towards revealing more about oneself should not be done too rapidly, because the other person may be threatened.

Why is self-disclosure risky in a new relationship?

Depenetration. As a relationship develops, there is less adherence to the norm of self-disclosure reciprocity. In an intimate relationship, the other person is most likely to respond to hearing sensitive personal information by offering support and understanding rather than by engaging in self-disclosure (Archer, 1979). Problems in maintaining a relationship tend to be associated with what Altman and Taylor (1973) called depenetration. **Depenetration** involves abandoning the habit of intimate self-disclosure to the other person across a wide range of topics. It takes two main forms. One form is simply refusing to reveal intimate information to the other person. The other form is talking intimately about only a few topics; these topics are chosen in order to hurt the other person, and usually involve strong negative feelings (Tolstedt & Stokes, 1984).

On average, women disclose more personal and sensitive information about themselves to same-sex friends than men do (Dindia & Allen, 1992).

Gender differences. It is often argued that women tend to have higher levels of self-disclosure in their various relationships than do men. The relevant evidence from 205 studies was reviewed by Dindia and Allen (1992). On average, women self-disclose more than men with their romantic partners of the opposite sex and with their same-sex friends. However, there was no difference between men and women in their self-disclosure levels to male friends. Most of the sex differences in self-disclosure were not large, but the differences did not seem to have become smaller over the past 30 years or so.

Commitment

Commitment, in the sense of a determination to continue the relationship, increases over time. What are the factors leading to the growth of commitment? Rusbult (1980) put forward an investment model, in which he identified three key factors:

1. Satisfaction: the rewards provided by the relationship.
2. Perceived quality of alternatives: individuals will be more committed to a relationship if there are no other attractive options.
3. Investment size: the more time, effort, money, and so on invested in the relationship, the greater will be the commitment.

> **KEY TERMS**
> **Self-disclosure**: revealing personal information about oneself to someone else.
> **Depenetration**: deliberately reducing the amount of self-disclosure to someone else.

Lund (1985) found that the level of commitment depended more on investment size than on satisfaction or rewards. Michaels, Acock, and Edwards (1986) found that commitment to a relationship was stronger when the outcomes received were greater than those anticipated in alternative relationships than when they were smaller. They also found that the extent to which the relationship was equitable did not predict commitment.

There are two limitations with Rusbult's approach. First, the three factors he identifies are not truly independent of each other. For example, individuals who are very satisfied with a relationship are more likely to have a large investment in it. Second, most of the research has focused on short-term rather than long-term relationships (Buunk, 1996).

According to Rusbult's three factors, when is a relationship most likely to fail?

Maintenance strategies

Dindia and Baxter (1987) carried out a thorough study of the strategies used by married couples to maintain their marriages. They found evidence for 49 such strategies, which could be divided into maintenance and repair strategies. Maintenance strategies mostly involved joint activities such as going for walks together or talking about the events of the day, and occurred because they were pleasurable. In contrast, repair strategies involved discussing issues or making difficult decisions, and occurred because there were problems within the relationship.

Dindia and Baxter found differences between those who had been married for only a short period of time, and those who had been married much longer. Newlyweds tended to make more use of maintenance strategies than the long-term married, but the reasons for this are not clear. The positive view is that maintenance strategies are less necessary when two people know each other very well. The negative view is that those who have been married for a long time simply take each other for granted and put less effort into everyday joint activities.

Rusbult, Zembrodt, and Iwaniszek (1986) identified four strategies that people use to deal with conflicts in relationships. Each strategy is active or passive, and constructive or destructive. *Voice* is the active, constructive strategy, in which people discuss their problems and seek answers to the relationship difficulties. *Loyalty* is the passive, constructive strategy, in which people wait and hope that the situation will improve. *Neglect* is a passive and destructive strategy, in which individuals ignore their partners or spend less time with them. Finally, there is *exit*. This is an active and destructive strategy involving individuals deciding to abandon the relationship.

Going for walks together is an example of the kind of maintenance strategy used by couples to maintain their relationship.

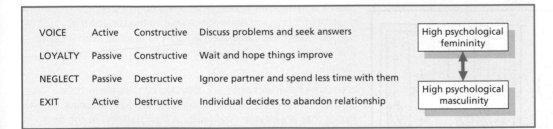

VOICE	Active	Constructive	Discuss problems and seek answers	High psychological femininity
LOYALTY	Passive	Constructive	Wait and hope things improve	↕
NEGLECT	Passive	Destructive	Ignore partner and spend less time with them	High psychological masculinity
EXIT	Active	Destructive	Individual decides to abandon relationship	

What determines the choice of strategy? Rusbult et al. studied lesbian, gay, and heterosexual couples. Individuals with high psychological femininity (warmth, intimacy; concern with interpersonal relations) were much more likely to react constructively to relationship problems than were those with high masculinity (aggressiveness, independence, assertiveness).

Relationship rules

In order to maintain a relationship successfully (whether a romantic relationship, friendship, or whatever), it is necessary for both of the people involved to keep to certain informal relationship rules ("behaviour which it is believed ought or ought not to be performed in each relationship", Argyle, 1988, p.233). Argyle and Henderson (1984) argued that there are four criteria by means of which friendship rules can be identified:

- There should be general agreement that the behaviour indicated in the rule is relevant to friendship.
- The rule should not be applied in the same way to current and former friends.
- Failure to stick to the rule should tend to lead to the abandonment of the friendship.
- The rule should identify some of the ways in which people's behaviour towards close friends and acquaintances differs.

Argyle and Henderson applied these four criteria to study friendship rules in England, Italy, Hong Kong, and Japan. They found that there were six rules that seemed to be of major importance to friendships in all four countries. These were:

1. Trust and confide in the other person.
2. Show emotional support.
3. Share news of success.
4. Strive to make the friend happy when with him or her.
5. Volunteer help in time of need.
6. Stand up for a friend in his or her absence.

Cognitive factors

Murray and Holmes (1993) argued that an important way in which individuals maintain relationships is by means of storytelling, in which the partner's faults are regarded as favourably as possible. This storytelling occurs even in unpromising circumstances. Murray and Holmes studied individuals who claimed that their relationships involved little conflict, and that conflict is harmful to intimacy. Some of them were then informed that there is strong evidence that conflict is beneficial to the development of intimacy. Finally, the participants were asked to write narratives describing the development of intimacy in their relationship.

What happened? The participants who had been told that conflict is advantageous were much more likely to write narratives in which they argued that conflicts and disagreements were valuable. For example, one participant wrote, "I feel he is facilitating our growth by increasingly being able to tell me when he disagrees with my opinions in all areas", and another wrote, "We've had only three disagreements ... we were able to get to the root of the problem, talk it out, and we managed to emerge from it closer than before." Murray and Holmes (1993, p.719) concluded as follows:

We suspect that individuals' continued confidence in their partners ... depends on their continued struggle to weave stories that depict potential faults in their partners in the best possible light.

KEY STUDY EVALUATION — Murray and Holmes

The research by Murray and Holmes is important, because most previous researchers had ignored the role of storytelling in maintaining relationships. However, we need to know more of the factors determining when those involved in relationships will make use of storytelling. There is also the issue of whether the participants really believed what they were writing, rather than simply expressing views that they thought the experimenter wanted them to express.

Discussion points

1. What do you think of the storytelling approach to understanding the maintenance of relationships?
2. Are people aware that they are constructing stories about their partner?

Fincham and Bradbury (1993) argued that the kinds of attributions that married people make about their spouse have an effect on how successfully the marriage is maintained. Husbands and wives who attributed partner's negative behaviour to *internal* characteristics (e.g.

personality) were more dissatisfied with the marriage one year later than were those who attributed it to external factors (e.g. hard work; worries about the family).

Dissolution of Relationships

There are many reasons why relationships come to an end. The reasons that are important in any one case depend on the particular circumstances in which the people concerned find themselves, and on their particular characteristics. It is possible to distinguish between *external* factors (e.g. one partner moves to another part of the country; the appearance of a rival; job loss) and *internal* factors (e.g. the personalities of the two people). Some relationship breakdowns are accompanied by bitter recrimination and even violence, whereas others are handled in a more "civilised" way.

In spite of these differences, it has been argued that similar processes tend to be involved in the dissolution of relationships. We will first consider the break-up of premarital relationships, and then move on to the break-up of marriages.

Premarital relationships

According to Lee (1984), the break-up of premarital relationships should be regarded as a process taking place over a period of time rather than as a single event. More specifically, he argued that there are five stages involved in the process:

- Dissatisfaction: one or both of the partners realise that there are real problems within the relationship.
- Exposure: the problems identified in the dissatisfaction stage are brought out into the open.
- Negotiation: there is much discussion about the issues raised during the exposure stage.
- Resolution attempts: both partners try to find ways of solving the problems discussed in the negotiation stage.
- Termination: if the resolution attempts are unsuccessful, then the relationship comes to an end.

Lee identified these five stages on the basis of a study of over 100 premarital romantic break-ups. The exposure and negotiation stages tended to be the most intense and exhausting stages in the break-up. One of the key findings was that it tended to be those relationships that had been the strongest in which it took the longest time to work through the five stages of dissolution. This makes sense: the more valuable a relationship has been, the harder (and longer) it is worth fighting for its continuation.

Duck (1982) put forward a somewhat similar stage model of the break-up of relationships. He identified four phases or stages of break-up:

- Intrapsychic phase: this involves thinking about the negative aspects of one's partner and of the relationship, but not discussing these thoughts with him or her; this corresponds roughly to Lee's dissatisfaction stage.
- Dyadic phase: this phase involves confronting the partner with the negative thoughts from the intrapsychic stage, and trying to sort out the various problems; this corresponds to Lee's stages of exposure, negotiation, and resolution attempts.
- Social phase: this phase involves deciding what to do now that the relationship is effectively over; it includes thinking of face-saving accounts of what has happened; this corresponds roughly to Lee's termination stage.
- Grave-dressing phase: this phase focuses on communicating a socially acceptable account of the end of the relationship; it is an important phase in terms of preparing the people involved for future relationships.

There are some important differences between Lee's stage theory and Duck's phase theory. Lee's theory focuses mainly on the various processes involved when there is still

How long do you think it would take to pass through all the stages of dissolution described by Duck?

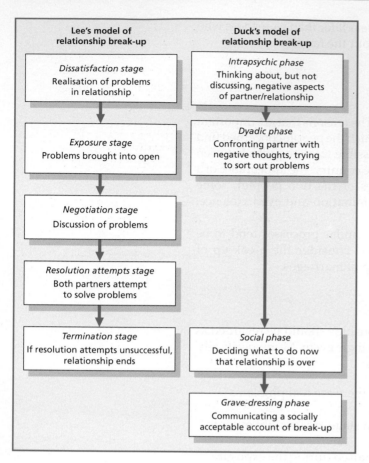

some hope that the relationship can be saved, whereas Duck's theory focuses more on the processes involved after it is clear that the relationship is at an end. It is probable that a six- or seven-stage theory incorporating all of the processes identified in the two theories would provide a more adequate account of relationship break-up than either theory on its own.

Marriage

Studies designed to identify the factors involved in the maintenance and dissolution of marriages can be either cross-sectional or longitudinal. Cross-sectional studies consider what is happening at one point in time, whereas longitudinal studies involve obtaining data during two or more time periods. Longitudinal studies are generally more informative, because they provide information about *changes* over time. Karney and Bradbury (1995, p.18) reviewed the evidence from 115 longitudinal studies, and came to the following conclusions:

In general, positively valued variables—such as education, positive behaviour, and employment—predict positive marital outcomes [in terms of satisfaction and continuation of the marriage], whereas negatively valued variables—such as neuroticism, negative behaviour, and an unhappy childhood—predict negative marital outcomes.

Karney and Bradbury found that most of the variables investigated in the 115 studies had similar effects on husbands and on wives. An important exception was employment. When the husband is employed, this is associated with greater marital satisfaction. However, the opposite is the case when the wife is employed.

Risk factors

What are the disadvantages involved in carrying out longitudinal research?

Duck (1992) also considered the findings from longitudinal studies. He identified several factors that seem to make marriages more fragile and liable to dissolution. First, marriages between people whose parents were themselves divorced are more likely to end in divorce. Second, marriages in which the partners are very young (e.g. teenagers) are less likely to last than marriages in which the partners are older. There are likely to be several reasons why age is a factor. Younger people tend to be less mature, they have not yet developed their adult personality, and they are less likely to have either a steady income or full-time employment.

Third, marriages in which the partners come from very different backgrounds in terms of culture, race, or religion are less stable than those in which the partners come from very similar backgrounds. One reason for this is that the partners may have very different expectations about marriage because of their differing backgrounds. Fourth, marriages between partners from the lower socio-economic groups and/or with lower educational levels are more likely to end in divorce. The partners in such marriages are often very young, which increases the probability of divorce. Fifth, marriages in which the partners have had numerous sexual partners beforehand tend to be less stable. Presumably one reason for this is that those who have had numerous romantic relationships tend to find it harder to produce the long-term commitment needed to make marriage work.

Other factors

The five factors identified by Duck (1992) tell only part of the story. There are successful and stable marriages in which the partners possess all of the vulnerability factors, and there are partners having none of these factors who nevertheless have short-lived marriages. Some of these factors may be more complex than they appear to be. For example, consider the fact that couples with lower educational levels are more likely to divorce. What is important is not really the educational level itself, but rather the reduced prospects of owning their own home and having reasonable full-time jobs which follow from the low level of education.

It is important to note that the data from most longitudinal studies are limited. For example, 75% of the samples used in the longitudinal studies reviewed by Karney and Bradbury (1995, p.17) consisted mainly of middle-class white couples. Karney and Bradbury (1995) identified other limitations:

> *Nearly half of the studies lack the power to detect small effects, even though the effects in question are likely to be* small in many cases. Data have been drawn almost exclusively from self-report surveys and interviews, whereas alternative means of gathering data have yet to be exploited.

Factors likely to make marriage unstable (Duck, 1992)

1. Parents of one or both partners are divorced.

2. Both partners very young.

3. Partners come from very different backgrounds.

4. Partners come from lower socio-economic backgrounds and/or have lower levels of education.

5. One or both partners had numerous sexual partners prior to the marriage.

Theories

Various theories have been put forward to explain the maintenance or dissolution of marriages.

Social exchange theory. Levinger (1976) argued that the chances of a marriage surviving depended on three factors:

1. The attractions of the relationship, such as emotional security and sexual satisfaction.
2. The barriers to leaving the marriage, such as social and financial pressures.
3. The presence of attractive alternatives, such as a more desirable partner.

Divorce is most likely when the marriage has few attractions, there are only weak barriers to leaving the relationship, and there are very attractive alternatives.

One of the advantages of Levinger's social exchange theory is that it helps to explain why marital satisfaction does not strongly predict subsequent divorce (see Karney and Bradbury, 1995). For example, married couples who are dissatisfied may not divorce because there are strong barriers to leaving the marriage and no attractive alternatives. The greatest disadvantage of Levinger's social exchange theory is that it does not explain the processes that cause initially successful marriages to become unsuccessful.

Vulnerability-stress-adaptation model. Karney and Bradbury (1995) put forward a vulnerability-stress-adaptation model of marriage. According to this model, there are three major factors that determine marital quality and stability or duration:

1. Enduring vulnerabilities: these include high neuroticism (a personality dimension concerned with anxiety and depression) and an unhappy childhood.
2. Stressful events: these include short- and long-lasting life events such as illness, unemployment, and poverty.
3. Adaptive processes: these include constructive and destructive coping strategies to resolve difficulties.

A key assumption of the model is that the three factors all affect each other. The use of adaptive processes is influenced by enduring vulnerabilities and by stressful events. For example, married individuals who are high on neuroticism or whose parents divorced tend to have relatively poor adaptive processes, and the stress created by unemployment is associated with more negative and less constructive interactions with spouses (Aubry, Tefft, & Kingsbury, 1990). In addition, enduring vulnerabilities can play a role in creating stressful events. For example, individuals who are very depressed often create stressful

Depressed individuals are likely to create stressful situations in their lives, affecting their relationship with their partner.

conditions in their lives (Hammen, 1991). Adaptive processes can also create stressful conditions. For example, clinically depressed individuals whose spouses were very critical were more likely to suffer relapses than were individuals with less critical spouses (Hooley et al., 1986).

According to the vulnerability-stress-adaptation model (Karney & Bradbury, 1995, p.24), one of the main ways in which a marriage can disintegrate is through the following vicious cycle

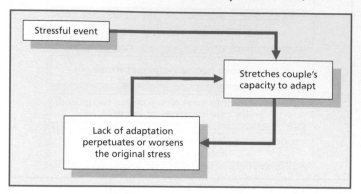

(a) stressful events challenge a couple's capacity to adapt, (b) which contributes to the perpetuation or worsening of those events, (c) which in turn further challenge and perhaps overwhelm their capacity to adapt.

This vicious cycle is most likely to occur in couples having enduring vulnerabilities.

According to Karney and Bradbury (1995), some couples who have enduring vulnerabilities can become stuck in this vicious cycle.

As we saw earlier, numerous factors are associated with the maintenance or dissolution of marriages. One of the strengths of the vulnerability-stress-adaptation model is the way in which most of these factors can be related directly to the three broad variables of enduring vulnerabilities, stress, and adaptive processes. Another strength of the model is that it shows how these three variables can interact in different ways to reduce marital quality.

The greatest limitation of the vulnerability-stress-adaptation model is its emphasis on marital quality or satisfaction as the major determinant of marital stability. As Levinger (1976) argued, factors *external* to the marriage also affect marital stability. These factors include the barriers to leaving the relationship and the presence of attractive alternatives.

Jealousy may be caused by a real rival, but can be just as painful when the jealous partner imagines that he or she has competition.

Jealousy

One of the factors causing the dissolution of a relationship is jealousy. It is triggered by a real or imagined rival, and is a surprisingly common emotion. Eysenck (1990) discussed a study in which 63% of male students and 51% of female students admitted that they were currently jealous.

What factors produce jealousy? Buss et al. (1992) asked students whether they would experience greater distress in response to sexual or to emotional infidelity. Among male students, 60% reported greater distress over a partner's sexual infidelity. In contrast, 83% of the female students said they would be more distressed by emotional infidelity.

The destructive power of jealousy was emphasised by Buss et al. According to them:

The more insecure you are, the more you will be jealous. Jealousy says Abraham Maslow, "practically always breeds further rejection and deeper insecurity" … It is never, then, a function of love but of our insecurities and dependencies. It is the fear of a loss of love and it destroys that very love.

Buss et al. may have overstated their case, but there is some truth in their assertions. Jealousy is typically related to strong feelings of dependence and insecurity about the relationship (Salovey, 1991). It also has the negative effect of reducing the jealous person's level of self-esteem (Mathes, Adams, & Davies, 1985).

Sex differences

Women are more likely than men to end heterosexual relationships, and initiate about two-thirds of divorce proceedings in many Western countries. In general, the partner who initiates the break-up is the one who is less distressed. However, this tendency is much stronger in men than in women (Franzoi, 1996). Why is this so? According to Franzoi, control and power are more associated with the traditional male role than with the traditional female role. As a result, men find it very hard to cope when their partner renders them powerless and out of control by ending the relationship.

Components of Interpersonal Relationships

So far we have focused mainly on personal relationships and on friendships. However, there are numerous other kinds of interpersonal relationships (e.g. mother–child; boss–employee; teacher–student). In this section, we will consider some of the similarities and differences among these different types of relationship.

Goals and conflicts

We can obtain some idea about the motivations underlying different kinds of relationship by studying the goals and satisfactions involved, as well as the conflicts and tensions. Argyle and Furnham (1983) asked their participants to rate nine different relationships in terms of their degree of satisfaction with them on 15 satisfaction scales. Analysis of the data produced three independent factors of material and instrumental help, social and emotional support, and common interests. The relationships highest and lowest on each of these factors were as follows:

Factor	Highest scoring relationships	Lowest scoring relationships
Material and instrumental help	spouse parent same-sex friend	neighbour work associate
Social and emotional support	spouse same-sex friend parent	neighbour work superior work associate
Common interests	spouse same-sex friend opposite-sex friend	neighbour work associate adolescent offspring

These findings are not surprising. They indicate that we obtain the most satisfaction from those relationships (spouse, parent, same-sex friend, opposite-sex friend) that are most important to us. Unimportant relationships (e.g. with neighbours or work associates) are not generally associated with high levels of satisfaction.

Argyle and Furnham also found that the spouse was the greatest source of conflict as well as of satisfaction. It seems reasonable to assume that marital satisfaction will be highest when the rewards greatly exceed the costs. In line with this, Howard and Dawes (1976) found that a simple formula based on the frequency of a major reward (sexual intercourse) minus the frequency of a major cost (angry rows) was a good predictor of marital satisfaction.

Discussion points

1. Different types of relationship obviously differ enormously in many ways. Is it really possible to compare them with each other?

2. What do you think are the main dimensions in terms of which your relationships with other people differ?

Argyle, Furnham, and Graham (1981) asked their participants to indicate the kinds of goals that were important within different relationships. The three goals that emerged most consistently were as follows: (1) social acceptance; (2) the individual's physical well-being; and (3) specific task goals that were appropriate in the given situation. These goals were often not independent of each other, in the sense that the achievement of one goal often made it easier or harder to achieve one of the other goals.

Rules

Most interpersonal relationships are governed by a number of unspoken rules. The rules that people apply to interpersonal relationships vary depending on the nature of the relationship. However, Argyle, Henderson, and Furnham (1985) found that some rules were fairly general when they asked their participants to rate the importance of various rules in each of 22 relationships. The six most generally important rules, in descending order of importance, were as follows:

1. Respect the other person's privacy.
2. Do not discuss with someone else things said in confidence.
3. Look the other person in the eye during conversation.
4. Do not criticise the other person publicly.
5. Do not indulge in sexual activity with the other person.
6. Seek to repay all debts, favours, or compliments.

Would you agree with the order of importance of Argyle et al.'s six rules? Do you think there are any others that are important?

How do we know these rules are actually important? Argyle et al. (1985) studied broken friendships. As predicted, Argyle (1988, pp.233–234) found that:

The lapse of friendship was attributed in many cases to the breaking of certain rules, especially rules of rewardingness and rules about relations with third parties, e.g. not being jealous, and keeping confidences.

Argyle et al. (1986) found that there were some interesting cultural differences in the importance attached to certain rules. For example, participants in Hong Kong and Japan were more likely than those in Britain or in Italy to support rules such as obeying superiors, preserving group harmony, and avoiding loss of face.

What functions are served by rules within interpersonal relationships? According to Argyle and Henderson (1984), some rules help to minimise conflict within relationships, because they indicate what is and is not acceptable. These are known as regulatory rules. There are also reward rules, which are used to ensure that the rewards provided by each person are appropriate. However, as Cardwell et al. (1996, p.37) pointed out, things may well not be so simple:

In a study of intimacy by Wood et al. (1994a) respondents described conflict as energising relationships, heightening individuality, inspiring trust and enriching intimacy.

Of course, conflict cannot always be relied on to improve a relationship!

Power and roles

Wish, Deutsch, and Kaplan (1976) carried out a study to identify the main dimensions along which interpersonal relationships differ. They found four: equal versus unequal; co-operative and friendly versus competitive and hostile; socio-emotional and informal versus task-oriented and formal; and superficial versus intense. Of most interest here is the dimension relating to equality, because unequal relationships are those in which one person has more power ("the capacity to influence another's behaviour", Argyle, 1988, p.235). Relationships that were regarded as equal included close friends, husband and wife, business partners, and team-mates. Relationships that were thought to be very unequal were guard and prisoner, parent and child, and teacher and student.

Can you think of real-life examples where women and men do not have equal power in close relationships? Why is there still inequity?

The relative power of husband and wife within marital relationships is a matter of controversy. According to Argyle (1988), women have more equal power within marriages than used to be the case, in part because they have greater financial independence. However, that is a view that might not meet with universal agreement!

As Hayes (1993, p.2) pointed out:

When we are engaging in social life, we take on "roles" which tell us how we should behave towards other people —essentially, we play our parts and other people play theirs.

In other words, a **role** is "a social part that one plays in society" (Hayes, 1993). The concept of role is very relevant to a discussion of power, because many roles contain the expectation of exerting power or being powerless. For example, an individual filling the role of prison guard is free to exert power, whereas someone filling the role of prisoner is not. This was shown very clearly in the Stanford Prison Experiment (see pages 568–569).

What roles do you fulfil? What sort of power do you possess because of these roles?

Until recent years, it was rare for the female partner in a marriage to hold a publicly more powerful position than her spouse.

Post-modern Approach

Those who favour the post-modern approach (e.g. Wood & Duck, 1995) doubt the value of most research on interpersonal relationships. According to the post-modern approach, relationships need to be considered in terms of the context or environment in which they occur. There are various ways in which the available evidence can be interpreted, and it is hard or impossible to establish that one interpretation is preferable to any other.

Social purpose

Lalljee (1981) put forward related ideas. According to him, we need to consider the underlying social purposes of the explanations that people provide for their behaviour. For example, when two people divorce, they typically explain the disintegration of their marriage in different terms. Each of them tends to suggest that it was the unreasonable behaviour of the other person that led to divorce. In view of people's need to justify their own behaviour to other people, it becomes very difficult to establish the truth. The post-modernists go further, and claim that there is no single "truth" that can be discovered. In the study discussed earlier, Murray and Holmes (1993) showed that storytelling about one's relationship can easily be altered to accommodate awkward facts. This suggests that the truth is a flexible notion.

Discourse analysis

Many post-modernists argue that progress can be made in understanding interpersonal relationships by making use of discourse analysis. **Discourse analysis** involves qualitative analysis of people's written or spoken communications; these are often taped under fairly natural conditions. An interesting example of discourse analysis is contained in the work of Gavey (1992). She studied the coerced sexual behaviour of six women in detail (see Cardwell et al., 1996). Here is part of what one of the women had to say:

He kept saying, just, just let me do this or just let me do that and that will be all. And this could go on for an hour ... So after maybe an hour of me saying "no", and him saying "oh, come on, come on", I'd finally think, "Oh my God ... for a few hours rest, peace and quiet, I may as well".

> **KEY TERMS**
> **Role**: a social part that individuals play when interacting with other people.
> **Discourse analysis**: qualitative analysis of spoken and written communications produced in fairly natural conditions; usually based on tape recordings.

If a person is discussing a personal issue with their partner, a close friend, or a stranger, what sort of differences in approach would you expect to find?

Gavey's evidence suggests that moves towards greater equality of the two sexes still have a long way to go.

This example shows that discourse analysis can provide striking evidence about the nature of relationships. However, Gavey (1992) and others who have used discourse analysis have often obtained evidence from only a small number of participants. This raises the issue of whether the findings obtained can be generalised to larger populations. There are also issues concerning the validity of the procedure. For example, we might expect somone to describe their sexual experiences rather differently to their partner, to a close friend, to an acquaintance, and to a stranger.

Individual, Social, and Cultural Variations

Most of the research on interpersonal relationships has been carried out in Western cultures, especially those of the United States and the United Kingdom. It has also been limited because the focus has been on heterosexual relationships at the expense of homosexual ones, and because voluntary relationships have been studied rather than obligatory ones. According to post-modern theorists, these limitations are very important. They argue that behaviour and communication need to be understood within the context in which they occur, and this context clearly differs considerably from one culture to another, and across different types of relationship.

The crucial point here was made by Moghaddam et al. (1993; cited in Cardwell et al., 1996, p.103):

> *The cultural differences in interpersonal relationships remind us that scientists, like everyone else, are socialised within a given culture ... The cultural values and environmental conditions in North America have led Northern American social psychologists to be primarily concerned with first-time acquaintances, friendships, and intimate relationships.*

What sort of methodological and ethical problems are associated with research into sexual behaviour?

We can readily accept that there are large differences in interpersonal relationships *between* cultures. However, there have also been substantial changes in such relationships *within* many cultures over the centuries. An American doctor, Celia Mosher, asked her middle-class female patients questions about their sexual lives during the latter part of the nineteenth century. Those who were born in the middle of the century described sex as necessary for reproduction, but did not regard it as pleasurable. Those who were born later in the century described sex in much more positive terms, and saw sex as closely linked to passionate love (Westen, 1996).

It is important not to regard some types of relationships as better or worse than others. The relationships that individuals form depend on their personal needs and attitudes, the cultural context in which they live, and so on. As far as we can judge, all the various types of relationships are often very satisfying to the individuals concerned, and that is what matters.

Homosexual relationships

Why has research mainly focused on heterosexual relationships?

Most of the research on romantic relationships has concentrated exclusively on heterosexual couples. However, there are millions of people in the world who are involved in homosexual relationships, and such relationships are increasingly being studied. There are many misconceptions about homosexual relationships, and it is sometimes assumed that such relationships are very different from heterosexual ones. This is not, in fact, the case (see page 806). As Bee (1994; cited by Gross, 1996) pointed out:

> *Gay partnerships are more like heterosexual relationships than they are different. The urge to form a single, central, committed attachment in early adult life is present in all of us, gay or straight.*

The assumption that homosexual and heterosexual relationships are basically similar was described by Kitzinger and Coyle (1995) as liberal humanism (see pages 805–806).

It has often been assumed that homosexual relationships tend to be short-lived and unsatisfactory. In fact, it seems that about 50% of gay men and perhaps 65% of lesbians are in a steady relationship at any one time (Peplau, 1991). Kurdek and Schmitt (1986) measured love for partner and liking for partner in married, heterosexual cohabiting, gay, and lesbian couples. The mean level of love was high in all four types of couple, and did not differ significantly among them. The mean level of liking for partner was also fairly high in all types of couple, but it was somewhat lower for heterosexual cohabiting couples than for any of the other couples.

The liberal humanistic view that homosexual relationships closely resemble heterosexual ones is an oversimplification. Homosexual couples are more likely than heterosexual ones to have additional sexual partners outside the relationship. Among couples together for more than 10 years, 22% of wives, 30% of husbands, 43% of lesbians, and 94% of gay men reported having had sex with at least one person other than their partner (Blumstein & Schwartz, 1983).

In 1996, 175 gay and lesbian couples took part in a formal domestic partners ceremony in San Francisco, similar to the conventional marriage ceremony.

A major difference between homosexual and heterosexual relationships is that more importance is attached to equality of status and power in homosexual relationships. A lack of power equality was found to be a factor in the ending of lesbian and gay relationships but not of heterosexual marriages (Blumstein & Schwartz, 1983).

Another difference is that homosexuals have to contend with the hostility of society. As Kitzinger and Coyle (1995, p.67) pointed out:

Lesbian and gay couples are struggling to build and to maintain relationships in the context of a society which often denies their existence, condemns their sexuality, penalises their partnership and derides their love for each other.

What sort of practical problems might prevent homosexual couples from cohabiting?

As a result, cohabitation is much less common in homosexual relationships than heterosexual ones.

Finally, heterosexual married couples typically stay together for longer than any type of unmarried couple, including gay or lesbian couples. One reason for this is undoubtedly that there is more social, cultural, and religious support for married couples than for unmarried ones.

Cross-cultural issues: What cross-cultural differences might you expect to find in homosexual relationships?

Cultural variations

Physical attributes

It is perhaps natural for us to assume that what is true in our culture about interpersonal relationships is likely to be true in other cultures as well. In fact, this is by no means the case. Consider, for example, the factors influencing whether someone is seen as physically attractive or unattractive. What is regarded as physically attractive is determined to some extent by the current standards of the dominant social group. In the case of the North American culture, light skin is regarded as more attractive than dark skin by a majority of the population. Even African American college students express a preference for lighter skin tones (Bond & Cash, 1992).

Anderson et al.

Standards of physical attractiveness are determined by other factors as well. Anderson et al. (1992) reported an interesting study on female body size preferences in 54 cultures. They divided these cultures into those with a very reliable food supply, those with a moderately reliable food supply, those with a moderately unreliable food supply, and those with a very unreliable food supply. Preferences for different female body sizes were divided into heavy body, moderate body, and slender body. The findings were as follows:

| | Food Supply | | | |
Preference	Very unreliable	Moderately unreliable	Moderately reliable	Very reliable
Heavy body	71%	50%	39%	40%
Moderate body	29%	33%	39%	20%
Slender body	0%	17%	22%	40%

KEY STUDY EVALUATION — Anderson et al.

The research by Anderson et al. is important because it shows that there are considerable cultural differences in preferred female body size. However, we need to remember that this study is correlational in nature, and that we cannot establish causes from correlations. Thus, we cannot be sure that cultural differences in preferred female body size actually depend on the reliability of the food supply rather than on other ways in which cultures differ from each other.

In view of the obsessive focus on slimness in women in Western culture, it comes as a surprise to discover that heavy women are preferred to slender women in the great majority of the cultures studied by Anderson et al., especially those in which the food supply is moderately or very unreliable. How can we explain these cultural differences? Presumably it occurs because heavy women in cultures with unreliable food supplies are better equipped than slender women to survive food shortages, and to provide nourishment for their children. This factor is not relevant in cultures having a very reliable food supply, and in these cultures heavy and slender women were regarded as equally attractive.

Discussion points

1. Why are there such great cultural differences in preferred body shape for women?
2. Are eating disorders likely to be more common in poor countries as they become more affluent?

Relative age

In spite of various cultural differences in standards of physical attractiveness, there are also some important similarities. Buss (1989b) studied 37 cultures around the world, and found that men in all of these cultures preferred women who were younger than themselves, and women preferred men who were older than themselves in all cultures except Spain. Buss also found that the personal qualities of kindness and intelligence were regarded as important in virtually all of the cultures he studied.

There are various possible reasons why men prefer younger women, and women prefer older men. One approach has been put forward by **sociobiologists**, who try to explain human social behaviour in terms of genetic and biological factors. According to sociobiologists (e.g. Buss, 1989b), what men and women find attractive in the opposite sex are those features that maximise the probability of producing offspring and so allow their genes to carry over into the next generation. Younger women are preferred to older ones because older women are less likely to be able to have children. In similar fashion, women prefer older men because they are more likely to be able to provide adequately for the needs of their offspring.

The sociobiological approach is inadequate. First, as Gross (1996) pointed out, sociobiologists do not provide an explanation of why men and women in nearly all cultures regard kindness and intelligence as being more important than age. Second, the factors determining the choice of marriage partner differ considerably from one culture to another. The sociobiologists consistently underestimate the importance of cultural factors in their explanations of social behaviour.

Howard, Blumstein, and Schwartz (1987) tried to explain the preference of men for younger women and of women for older men in social and cultural terms. According to them, women have historically had much lower social status than men. Women who wish to enhance their social status have usually had to do this by marrying

KEY TERM

Sociobiologists: scientists who argue that the roots of social behaviour are to be found in biological and genetic factors.

Marriages with greater partner age difference often have the added disadvantage of being more in the public eye, and can lead to divorce.

an older man of high status. As women were unable to offer high social status because of the structure of society, they needed to offer youth and physical attractiveness instead. Of course, there have been important changes in society in recent years. Far more women than ever before have full-time jobs, and are financially independent from men. It follows from the socio-cultural theory of Howard et al. (1987) that the preference of women for older, high-status men may change as a result. Time will tell.

Romantic love

It has for some time been the case in most Western societies that choice of marriage partner is based largely on romantic love. This was certainly not the case in earlier times. In those days, issues about property and the relative social standing of the families concerned tended to be more important than the emotional feelings of the bride and bridegroom. The increased emphasis on romantic love as the key ingredient in a successful marriage helps to explain the dramatic increase in the divorce rate. The percentage of marriages in the 1990s which ended in divorce in the United Kingdom is about eight times greater than was the case in the 1940s. In addition, there were much greater legal and social barriers to divorce in the 1940s.

In most non-Western cultures, it remains the case that marriages tend to be arranged rather than based on romantic love. Some of the cultural differences in attitudes towards romantic love were studied by Shaver, Wu, and Schwartz (1991). Most Chinese people associate romantic love with sorrow, pain, and unfulfilled affection. In the eyes of Chinese people, the Western view that marriage should be based on romantic love is regarded as unrealistically optimistic.

Cross-cultural issues: What physical features are important in men? Do you think these differ across cultures?

Individualist and collectivist cultures. Goodwin (1995) argued that a key difference between most Western societies and most Eastern societies is that the former tend to be individualistic, whereas the latter tend to be collectivistic. In other words, it is expected in Western societies (especially the United States) that individuals will make their own decisions and take responsibility for their own lives. In Eastern societies, in contrast, it is expected that individuals will regard themselves mainly as part of family and social groups, and that their decisions will be influenced strongly by their obligations to other people. This difference in attitude was summed up by Hsu (1981): "An American asks 'How does my heart feel?' A Chinese asks 'What will other people say?'." As a result, those in individualistic Western societies tend to stress the personality of a potential spouse, whereas those in collectivistic Eastern societies favour arranged marriages based on social status.

Which of Hsu's questions would you consider first when meeting a potential partner? Are they equally important, or not?

Evidence on love and marriage from India, Pakistan, Thailand, Mexico, Brazil, Hong Kong, the Philippines, Australia, Japan, England, and the United States was reported by

In many non-Western cultures, arranged marriages are the norm. Evidence suggests that the average level of marital satisfaction is the same in both arranged marriages and those in which the partners have a free choice.

Levine et al. (1995). Their key finding was that there was correlation of +0.56 between a society's individualism and the perceived necessity of love for the establishment of a marriage. In other words, there was a fairly strong tendency for members of individualistic societies to regard love as more important for marriage than did members of collectivistic societies.

Evidence from 42 hunter-gatherer societies around the world was reported by Harris (1995; cited in Westen, 1996). There was evidence of romantic love in 26 of these societies. However, only six gave individuals complete freedom of choice of marriage partner, with all the others having arranged marriages or at least giving parents the right of veto.

The distinction between individualistic and collectivistic societies should not be taken too far. Even in societies in which arranged marriages are the norm, there is often some restricted element of choice of marriage partner. In individualistic societies, parents often strive to influence the marriage choice of their children.

Are arranged marriages happier or less happy than love marriages? Most of the available evidence indicates that the average level of marital satisfaction is about the same. Yelsma and Athappily (1988) compared Indian arranged marriages with Indian and North American love marriages. In most respects, those in arranged marriages were at least as happy as those in love marriages.

Friendships. There is one other important difference between individualistic and collectivistic societies which applies to friendships. As Goodwin (1995) pointed out, people in collectivistic societies tend to have fewer but closer friendships than do people in individualistic societies. For example, Salamon (1977) studied friendship in Japan and in West Germany. Japanese friendships were much more likely to be ones in which there were no barriers between the friends, so that very personal information could be discussed freely. This is known as the *"shin yin"* relationship.

Effects of Interpersonal Relationships

Interpersonal relationships can obviously have many different kinds of effects on the individuals involved in them. However, most is probably known about the effects of interpersonal relationships (especially marriage) on happiness, on mental health, and on physical health. As a result, these factors will be the focus of this section of the chapter.

Happiness

The high divorce rate and extensive media coverage of marital problems have probably led many people to assume that marriage is a recipe for unhappiness and misery. In fact, most of the evidence suggests exactly the opposite. Before considering the evidence, we need to define the term "happiness". According to Eysenck (1990):

> *If you are asked how happy you are, you might answer on the basis of your thoughts about the general trend of your life (e.g. "Everything's going quite smoothly"; "My life is a complete mess"), or you might answer in terms of your current feelings (e.g. "I feel really pleased right now"; "I feel so depressed and low").*

In the literature, the focus has been on general trends, and so happiness as used in this section means essentially life satisfaction.

Bradburn

Bradburn (1969), in a study carried out in the United States, found that 35% of married men and 38% of married women said that they were "very happy". These figures were much higher than those for never-married men and women (18% for each sex). Of those who had ever been married, but were currently separated, divorced, or widowed, an even smaller percentage was "very happy". For example, only 7% of separated or widowed men said that they were "very happy".

The conclusion that marriage is good for you was strengthened by Bradburn's findings of the percentages of people who admitted that they were "not too happy". Fewer than 10% of married people said that they were "not too happy". This compares to a massive 40% of separated people, as well as over 30% of divorced people. Those who have never been married are less happy than married people. However, they are happier than those who have been married but are no longer in that state, with about 17% of them being "not too happy".

These findings need to be interpreted with care. Divorced people may be less happy than married people mainly because of the fact that they are divorced. However, it is also possible that those who are naturally unhappy and depressed are more likely to become divorced than those who are naturally happy and easy-going.

<table>
<tr><td colspan="2">KEY STUDY EVALUATION — Bradburn</td></tr>
</table>

Bradburn's study found that more married people claimed to be very happy compared to single people, 40% of whom said they were "not too happy". However, the study was carried out in 1969 in the United States, at a time when marriage was the norm, and couples who lived together outside marriage were still regarded as slightly outrageous. The demand characteristics of being asked by a stranger about one's happiness at home may have affected married people's responses, as well as those of single people, who in 1969 were expected to aspire to being married.

Discussion points

1. Why are married people generally happier than those who are not?

2. What are the limitations of self-report measures of happiness?

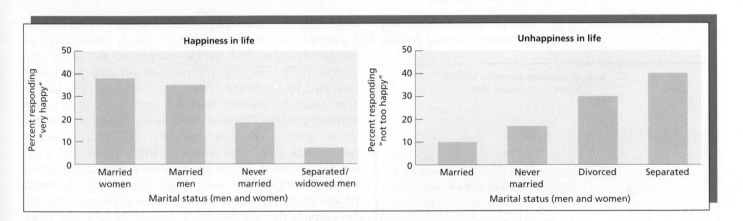

Information about some of the reasons why married people tend to be relatively happy was reported by Argyle and Furnham (1983) in a study already discussed (see pages 541–542). They found three main factors which determine people's level of satisfaction with different kinds of relationships: material and instrumental help; social and emotional support; and common interests. Spouses were rated higher than those in any other kind of non-sexual relationship on all three factors, but especially on material and instrumental help.

There are two additional points that need to be made. First, many of the studies indicating that marriage is associated with high levels of happiness were carried out many years ago. It is possible that marriage has fewer beneficial effects now than it used to have. Second, there has been a dramatic increase in the number of people cohabiting rather than marrying, and a major reason for this is because cohabitors perceive significant disadvantages in the state of marriage. According to Cunningham and Antrill (1995; cited in Cardwell et al., 1996):

Uneasiness about a lifetime commitment to the present partner or to the institution of marriage continually arises in surveys of cohabitors. Women's uneasiness about the institution of marriage now often stems from their awareness that it is still one of the major sites of gender inequality.

Changes during marriage

Marital satisfaction tends to change over the years. It has been reported several times (e.g. Glenn & McLanahan, 1982) that there is a U-shaped relationship between marital

What do you think are the disadvantages and advantages of marriage? Could these explain why more people are cohabiting now?

What do you think a couple's marital satisfaction level might be after 40 years if they had elected to stay childless?

A 50th wedding anniversary celebration.

satisfaction and the length of the marriage. Marital satisfaction declines sharply with the birth of the first child, and only rises again when the last-born child leaves home. One limitation of most of these studies is that married people were usually asked to recall their level of marital satisfaction at different points in the marriage, some of which might have occurred 20 years or more earlier. Obviously, what is recalled over such long periods of time might be inaccurate.

Vaillant and Vaillant (1993) reported a longitudinal study in which married people indicated their level of marital satisfaction at several points over a 40-year period. They found that the husbands' level of marital satisfaction remained at about the same level over the course of the marriage, and that the wives' level of satisfaction showed a modest decline. The difference between their findings and those of most other researchers could be due to the fact that they did not ask their participants to recall feelings from the distant past. However, there was another important difference between their study and those of other researchers. Their male participants were all graduates from Harvard University, and so on average they were very well off. Their affluence may have prevented them from suffering some of the stresses of child rearing.

Mental health

Interpersonal relationships (especially intimate ones) can be very valuable in promoting mental health. For example, married people have much lower rates of mental disorder than single people of the same age (Gove, 1979). Detailed information on this point was provided by Cochrane (1988). He found that the rate of admission to mental hospital was only 0.26% for married people. This was much lower than the rates for those who were not married: 0.77% for single individuals; 0.98% for widowed individuals; and 1.4% for the divorced. There are problems with interpreting these findings. The very high figure for divorced people may well occur in part because people who are developing the symptoms of mental disease are more likely to get divorced in the first place.

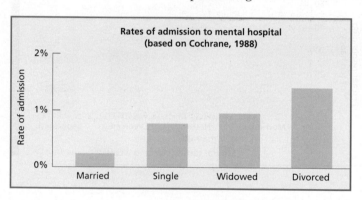

Rates of admission to mental hospital (based on Cochrane, 1988)

Social support

Why do interpersonal relationships have beneficial effects on mental health? An important reason is because of the social support that is provided by friends, lovers, and spouses. Much of the relevant evidence was considered in a meta-analysis of 70 studies by Schwarzer and Leppin (1992). They found that there was an overall correlation of –0.22 between social support and depression, indicating that individuals with the most support are least likely to be depressed. However, some of this effect may occur because depressed people are less likely to receive social support.

What factors could be the cause of higher rates of mental disorder in divorced people?

According to the buffering hypothesis, social support is most effective in improving mental health in stressful conditions. There is some support for this hypothesis. For example, Cohen and Hoberman (1983) found in high stress conditions that individuals high in social support reported only two-thirds as many physical symptoms (e.g. headaches; insomnia) as those low in social support. In contrast, social support had no effect on physical symptoms in low stress conditions.

Thoits (1982) discussed some of the evidence indicating the effectiveness of social support. However, he also pointed out that social support has a number of different dimensions:

* Amount of support.
* Type of support (e.g. emotional versus instrumental).
* Source of support (e.g. spouse; friends; relatives).
* Structure of support networks (e.g. size; accessibility; stability).

Stressful life events

Some of the most convincing evidence for the importance of social support for mental health was reported by Brown and Harris (1978). They studied a sample of over 400 women in south London. Their findings among women who had experienced stressful life events during the preceding year are of particular interest. Only 10% of these women who had a supportive husband became severely depressed, against 41% of women who did not have a supportive husband.

Social support does not always have beneficial effects on mental health. Hobfoll and London (1986) carried out a study during the war between Israel and Lebanon in 1982. Women who had more intimacy with their friends and more emotional support experienced more emotional stress than did those with lower intimacy and support. Why was this? According to Hobfoll and London, women with high levels of support spent a lot of their time discussing exaggerated rumours about the war and its consequences, and this created a kind of "pressure cooker" effect, causing stress.

Physical health

Social support

Some of the most dramatic evidence that social support can have major effects on physical health was reported by Berkman and Syme (1979). Interviews were conducted with 7000 adults in California, focusing on the strength of their supportive social networks. At one extreme were those individuals who lived alone and who had very limited social support from family and friends. At the other extreme were individuals who had strong social networks, including close family ties and several good friends.

Nine years after the initial assessment of the social satisfaction of these Californians, enquiries were made to discover which of them had died during those years. Of the men who were in their fifties at the start of the study, only 10% of those who had the best social support had died during the nine-year period. In contrast, 31% of the men in their fifties with poor social support had died during the same time period. The figures for the female participants were nearly as dramatic. Of those women in their sixties with poor social support, 29% had died, compared to only 10% of those who had strongly supportive social networks.

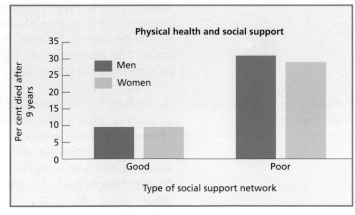

Health practices

How did Berkman and Syme (1979) explain their findings? One possibility is that those participants with poor social support were less likely to take regular exercise, and to eat and drink in moderation. There was some evidence that the poor health practices of those with poor social support did contribute to the shortening of their lives. However, those with strong social networks were more likely than those with weak networks to survive the nine-year period, even when the two groups were matched in terms of health practices, obesity, smoking, drinking, and initial health.

Marriage

Evidence that marriage can serve to preserve physical health was obtained by Lynch (1977). Married people were much less likely than single, divorced, or widowed individuals of the same age to die from several kinds of physical conditions. The illnesses of which this was true included diabetes, stroke, various cancers, cirrhosis of the liver, pneumonia, and tuberculosis. The beneficial effects of marriage on physical health were rather stronger in men than in women.

PERSONAL REFLECTIONS

- Studying social and interpersonal relationships is a nightmare for experimental psychologists. The reason is that it is almost impossible for the researcher to *control* any of the important factors that influence the formation, maintenance, and dissolution of relationships. As a result, all that can normally be done is to *observe* relationships, and to obtain various kinds of correlational evidence. In view of these limitations with most of the research, it is surprising that we know as much as we do about the processes underlying interpersonal relationships.

SUMMARY

Liking and loving

According to Sternberg's triangular theory, love consists of three components: intimacy; passion; and decision/commitment. Liking or friendship involves intimacy but not passion or decision/commitment. The amount of love someone has for one member of their family predicts the amount of love they have for the other members.

Theories of interpersonal relationships

According to reinforcement or need satisfaction theory, we are attracted to people who provide us with reward or reinforcement, but we dislike those who punish us. Some of the main rewards are providing help or money, respect or status, sex, and love. This theory is of most relevance to the initial stages of attraction. It assumes that people are very selfish, and it ignores the context in which reinforcement is provided. According to social exchange theory, people try to maximise the rewards and minimise the costs of interpersonal relationships. According to the similar equity theory, people expect to receive rewards from a relationship that are proportional to the rewards they provide for the other person. Equity theory is more plausible than exchange theory, because it takes more account of the other person's rewards and costs. The exchange and equity theories apply better to exchange relationships than to communal relationships.

Formation of interpersonal relationships

According to the matching hypothesis, we are attracted to those who are about as physically attractive as we are. Support for this hypothesis has been obtained in studies of initial attraction and in married couples. Attitude similarity plays a part in determining interpersonal attraction, as does similarity in preference for leisure activities. Those who are similar in demographic variables (e.g. age, sex, social class) are more likely to become friends. People having similar personalities are most likely to become involved with each other.

Maintenance of relationships

Self-disclosure is of great importance in the initiation and maintenance of relationships, and depenetration is usually involved when a relationship is experiencing problems. Women tend to self-disclose more than men. There seem to be six key friendship rules: trust the other person; show emotional support; share news of success; strive to make the friend happy; offer help in time of need; stand up for a friend in his or her absence.

Dissolution of relationships

Lee (1984) identified five stages in the break-up of premarital relationships: dissatisfaction; exposure; negotiation; resolution attempts; and termination. The exposure and negotiation stages are the most intense and exhausting ones. This theory ignores some of the processes associated with the final break-up (e.g. grave-dressing phase). Divorce is most likely when the partners' parents have divorced, when the partners are very young, when they come from different backgrounds, when they are from the lower socio-economic groups, or when the partners have had numerous previous sexual partners. Jealousy, which is usually related to feelings of dependence and insecurity about the relationship, typically threatens relationships.

People's most significant relationships tend to be associated with the greatest satisfaction in material and instrumental help, social and emotional support, and common interests. Some of the rules governing behaviour within a relationship vary depending on the type of relationship, but other rules are of general applicability (e.g. respect the other person's privacy). Breaking rules often leads to the ending of a friendship. Rules help to minimise conflict and to ensure that the rewards provided by each person are appropriate. One of the main dimensions along which relationships differ is equality–inequality. Unequal relationships are those in which one person has more power, in part because of the role he or she occupies.

Components of interpersonal relationships

The levels of loving and liking are similar in homosexual and heterosexual relationships. However, gay and lesbian couples are more likely than heterosexual ones to base their relationships on the notion of equality. Heterosexual married couples stay together for longer than any type of unmarried couple. Heavy women are overwhelmingly preferred to slender women in cultures having a very unreliable food supply. Men in nearly all cultures prefer women younger than themselves, whereas women prefer men who are older. In most Western cultures, choice of marriage partner is based largely on romantic love. In non-Western cultures, marriages tend to be arranged. People in collectivistic societies have fewer but closer friendships than those in individualistic societies.

Individual, social, and cultural variations

Married people tend to be happier than those who have never married or who are divorced. Happiness with interpersonal relationships depends on material and instrumental help; social and emotional support; and common interests. There is a U-shaped relationship between marital satisfaction and length of marriage. The value of social support for mental health depends on its amount, type, source, and the structure of support networks. People with poor levels of social support tend to die earlier than others, in part because of poor health practices. The beneficial effects of marriage on physical health are greater in men than women.

Effects of interpersonal relationships

FURTHER READING

Chapter 12 in M. Hewstone, W. Stroebe, and G.M. Stephenson (1996), *Introduction to social psychology*, Oxford: Blackwell, gives a good overview of affiliation, attraction, and close relationships. There is an excellent account of social relationships by M. Argyle in M. Hewstone, W. Stroebe, J.-P. Codol, and G.M. Stephenson (1988), *Introduction to social psychology (2nd Edn.)*, Oxford: Blackwell. Interpersonal relationships are discussed in an accessible way by N. Hayes (1993), *Principles of social psychology*, Hove, UK: Psychology Press. Social relationships are also discussed in Chapters 8 and 9 of S.L. Franzoi (1996), *Social psychology*, Madison, WI: Brown & Benchmark.

REVISION QUESTIONS

1 Compare and contrast *two* theories of interpersonal relationships. (24 marks)

2 Discuss insights gained from psychological research into how relationships are formed. (24 marks)

3 Describe and analyse psychological research into the components of interpersonal relationships (for example, the characteristics of relationships such as goals and conflicts, rules and power, and roles). (24 marks)

4 Moghaddam et al. (1993) argue that whereas Western relationships are generally voluntary, individualistic, and often short-term, non-Western ones tend to be involuntary, collectivist, and permanent. Discuss what we have learned about cultural variations in the nature of relationships. (24 marks)

5 Discuss psychological research into the effects that interpersonal relationships have on people (for example on happiness and mental health). (24 marks)

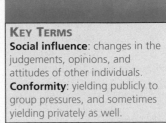

21

Social Influence

What we say, and the way we behave, are influenced by other people. Other people possess useful knowledge about the world, and it is often sensible to take account of what they say. In addition, we want to be liked by other people, and to fit into society. As a result, we sometimes hide what we really think, and try to behave in ways that will meet with the approval of others. These issues relate to **social influence**, which "involves the exercise of social power by a person or group to change the attitudes or behaviour of others in a particular direction. Social power refers to the force available to the influencer to motivate this change" (Franzoi, 1996, p.258).

Social influence takes many forms, some of which are discussed in this chapter. For example, individuals show conformity when they behave in ways that are expected by other members of a group. They also show obedience to authority, when they unthinkingly follow the orders of authority figures. Then there is social power, in which many organisations (e.g. prisons) have power structures that allow some people to dominate others. Finally, social influence is at work in determining the behaviour of individuals in crowds and mobs.

As you read this chapter, think about the individuals and groups that you come into contact with during an average week. Do some of these individuals and groups have more influence over than others over your behaviour? If so, why do you think this might be the case?

Group membership: Even non-conformists may conform to some norms.

Conformity

Conformity can be defined as yielding to group pressures, something that nearly all of us do at least some of the time. Suppose, for example, that you and some of your friends go to see a film. You didn't think the film was much good, but all of your friends thought it was brilliant. You might be tempted to conform by pretending to agree with their verdict on the film rather than being the odd one out. As we will see, conformity to group pressures occurs much more often than most people imagine.

Is conformity undesirable?

As you read about the work on conformity, you may think that conformity to group pressures is undesirable. There are certainly cases in which that is true. For example, consider the case of Rodney King. He was a black man who was assaulted by four Los Angeles police officers. The assault was videotaped by a local resident, and shown in court to the jurors. In spite of the fact that this videotape seemed to show that Rodney King was a victim of police brutality, the police officers were acquitted. Afterwards, one of the jurors, Virginia Loya, admitted that she had changed her vote from guilty to not guilty

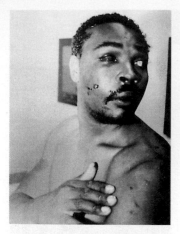

Group decisions can lead people to deny the evidence in front of their eyes. The picture shows Rodney King, victim of a videotaped beating by Los Angeles police officers in 1992. The four police officers involved were indicted a few weeks later.

because of pressures to conform to the views of the other jury members. She did this while remaining unconvinced of their views: "The tape was the big evidence to me. They [fellow jurors] couldn't see. To me, they were people who were blind and couldn't get their glasses clean."

In spite of examples like the Rodney King case, it is not clear that conformity is always undesirable. As Collins (1970, p.21) pointed out:

It would be a mistake to oversimplify the question and ask whether conformity is good or bad. A person who refused to accept anyone's word of advice on any topic whatsoever ... would probably make just as big a botch of his [sic] life ... as a person who always conformed and never formed a judgement on the basis of his own individual sources of information.

Muzafer Sherif

The first major study of conformity was carried out by Muzafer Sherif (1935). He made use of what is known as the **autokinetic effect**. If we look at a stationary spot of light in a darkened room, then very small movements of the eyes make the light seem to move. In Sherif's key condition, the participants were first of all tested one at a time, and then in small groups of three. They were asked to say how much the light seemed to move, and in what direction. Each participant rapidly developed his or her own personal norm. This norm was stable, but it varied considerably between individuals. When three individuals with very different personal norms were then put together into a group, they tended to make judgements that were very close to each other. The fact that a group norm rapidly replaced the personal norms of the members of the group indicates the existence of social influence.

Sherif (1935) also used a condition in which individuals started the experiment in groups of three, and then were tested on their own. Once again, a group norm tended to develop within the group. When the members of the group were then tested on their own, their judgements concerning the movement of the light continued to reflect the influence of the group.

Evaluation of Sherif's study

There are three major limitations with Sherif's (1935) research. First, he used a very artificial situation, and it is not clear how relevant his findings are for most everyday situations. Second, there was no "correct" answer in his situation. It is not very surprising that individuals rely on the judgements of others when they have no clear way of deciding what judgements to make. Third, conformity effects can be assessed more directly by arranging for all but one of the participants in an experiment to give the same judgement, and then seeing what effect this has on the remaining participant. This was done by Jacobs and Campbell (1961) using the autokinetic effect, and they found strong evidence of conformity.

Solomon Asch

KEY TERM
Autokinetic effect: the illusion that a stationary light in a dark room is moving about.

Which line do you think is the closest in height to line X? A, B, or C? Why do you think over 30% of participants answered A?

Solomon Asch (1951, 1956) improved on the work of Sherif (1935). He set up a situation in which usually about seven people all sat looking at a display. They were given the task of saying out loud which one of the three lines A, B, or C was the same length as a given stimulus line, with the experimenter working his way around the group members in turn. All but one of the participants were confederates of the experimenter, and had been told to give the same wrong answer on some trials. The one genuine participant was the last (or the last but one) to offer his or her opinion on each trial. The performance of participants exposed to such group pressure was compared to performance in a control condition in which there were no confederates.

Asch's (1951, 1956) findings were dramatic. On the crucial trials on which the confederates all gave the same wrong answer, the genuine participants also gave the wrong answer on approximately 37% of these trials. This should be compared against an error rate of only 0.7% in the control condition. Thus, the correct answers were obvious, and it might have been expected that nearly all the participants would have given them. However, only about 25% of the participants who were exposed to the wrong judgements of the confederates did not make a single error in the course of the experiment, compared to 95% in the control condition.

Asch (1956) manipulated a number of aspects of the situation in order to understand more fully the factors underlying conformity behaviour. For example, he found that the conformity effect increased as the number of confederates went up from one to three, but there was no increase between three and sixteen confederates. However, other researchers have often found that there is a small increase in conformity as the number of confederates goes up above three (see van Avermaet, 1996, for a review).

Another important factor was whether the genuine participant had a supporter in the form of a confederate who gave the correct answer on all trials, and who gave his or her answers before the genuine participant. Asch (1956) found that the presence of such a supporter produced a dramatic drop in conformity to only 5% of the trials.

Asch's work raises various ethical issues. His participants did not provide fully informed consent, because they were misled about key aspects of the experimental procedures. In addition, they were put in a difficult and embarrassing position. Evidence for this was obtained by Bogdonoff, Klein, Shaw, and Back (1961), who found that the participants in an Asch-type study had greatly increased levels of autonomic arousal. This finding also suggests that the participants were in a conflict situation, in which they found it hard to decide whether to report what they saw or to conform to the opinions of others.

KEY STUDY EVALUATION — Asch

Asch is renowned for his work on conformity. In a situation where the correct answer was obvious, people would agree with an incorrect answer on 37% of trials. Only 25% of Asch's participants gave the correct answer on all the trials despite the incorrect answers of their fellow participants. More people conformed to the views of the confederate participants than gave a correct answer, but the study took place in America in the 1950s before "doing your own thing" came to be regarded as socially acceptable. Also, Asch's participants were put in a difficult and embarrassing position, which may have led to greater levels of conformity due to the particular culture prevailing at the time. When participants had a supporter present, who gave the correct answer before the participant responded, conformity to the incorrect response dropped dramatically to 5% of trials. This suggests that social pressure and feeling of being in a conflict situation may have been a major factor in the unexpectedly high level of conformity in the original study.

Ethical issues: Asch's participants weren't told about the true nature of the study. Was this ethical?

Discussion points

1. Do Asch's findings apply outside the artificial situation he used in his conformity studies?

2. Asch carried out his research in the United States. Why might the findings be different in other cultures (see next)?

Cross-cultural studies

One of the possible limitations of Asch's work on conformity is that it was carried out in the United States in the late 1940s and early 1950s. It has often been assumed that Americans are more conformist than other people. It is also possible that people were more willing to conform in the days before it became fashionable to "do your own thing". Thus, it could be argued that the levels of conformity found by Asch reflected the particular culture prevailing in the United States at that time.

England and the United States. Perrin and Spencer (1980) tried to repeat Asch's study in England in the late 1970s. They found very little evidence of conformity, leading them to conclude that the Asch effect was "a child of its time". However, the low level of conformity may have occurred because they used engineering students who had been given training in the importance of accurate measurement. Smith and Bond (1993) carried out a meta-analysis of studies using Asch's task in the United States. They came to the

When Asch's study was replicated, cross-cultural differences emerged.

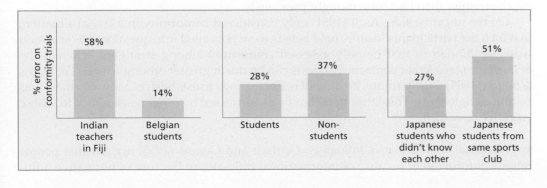

following conclusion (1993, p.124): "Levels of conformity in general had steadily declined since Asch's studies in the early 1950s."

Perrin and Spencer (1981) carried out two more studies on cultural factors in conformity. In one study, the participants were young men on probation, and the confederates of the experimenter who were primed to give the wrong answers were probation officers. The level of conformity was about the same as in the Asch studies. In the other study, the participants and the confederates were both young unemployed men with Afro-Caribbean backgrounds. Once again, conformity levels were comparable to those reported by Asch (1951).

Other participant groups.   There have been over 20 other cross-cultural studies of conformity using Asch's experimental design. The findings from these studies were summarised by Smith and Bond (1993). Asch (1951) found that students gave the wrong answer on 37% of the conformity trials. The average figure was about 30% for the other studies carried out in several parts of the world. The highest figure was 58% wrong answers for Indian teachers in Fiji, and the lowest figure (apart from Perrin & Spencer, 1980) was 14% among Belgian students.

Students and non-students, friends and strangers.   Two interesting points emerge from a more detailed consideration of these conformity studies. First, participants who were students made errors on 26% of conformity trials, whereas non-students made errors on 37% of trials. Why was there this difference? Students may learn to be more independent in their thinking than non-students, or their higher level of intelligence may make them more confident in their opinions.

Second, Williams and Sogon (1984) found that Japanese students made errors on 27% of trials when they did not know any of the other group members, but this increased to 51% when the group members all belonged to the same sports club. These findings suggest that conformity can be much greater if we like and respect other group members than if we do not know them. Asch's (1951) studies on conformity were rather limited because the students were mostly strangers to each other.

Individualism and collectivism.   In general terms, it is possible to distinguish between individualist and collectivist cultures. Individualist societies such as the United Kingdom and the United States emphasise the desirability of individuals being responsible for their own well-being and having a sense of personal identity. In contrast, collectivist cultures (e.g. China) emphasise the priority of group needs over individual ones and having a sense of group identity. Bond and Smith (1993, p.124) carried out a meta-analysis on133 Asch-type studies drawn from 17 countries. Their findings "revealed significant relationships confirming the general hypothesis that conformity would be higher in collectivistic cultures than in individualistic cultures."

Evaluation and theoretical issues

Asch's (1951) research on conformity has had an enormous influence. He found that there are large conformity effects even in an unambiguous situation in which the correct answer is obvious. Indeed, he found that participants on their own only made 0.7% errors on the line-judgement task. He showed convincingly that group pressures to conform are much stronger than had been thought previously.

On the negative side, Asch (1951) only considered conformity in a trivial situation, in which the participants' deeply held beliefs were not called into question. His situation was also limited in that he only assessed conformity among strangers, whereas the evidence suggests that conformity effects can be much greater among friends (Williams & Sogon, 1984). Furthermore, he did not really manage to establish exactly *why* there was so much conformity. This latter issue has been addressed by other researchers, to whose work we now turn.

Informational and normative influence.   Deutsch and Gerard (1955) argued that people might conform either because of informational influence or because of normative influ-

Why do you think students were less likely to conform (26%) than non-students (37%)?

ence. **Informational influence** occurs when an individual conforms because of the superior knowledge or judgement of others. This was presumably involved in Sherif's (1935) work. **Normative influence** occurs when an individual conforms because he or she wants to be liked or respected by the other members of the group. This played an important part in Asch's (1951) studies. A crucial difference between these two types of influence is that informational influence leads people to change their private opinions, whereas normative influence does not.

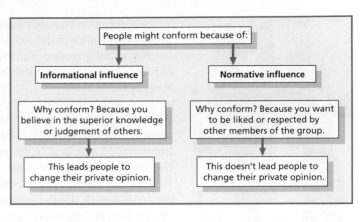

Evidence of informational influence was obtained by Di Vesta (1959). He found that there was more conformity on later trials if the majority gave correct answers on most of the early trials. It was as if the majority demonstrated its competence by being correct, and this persuaded the genuine participant to accept its judgements. Informational influence also seems to have played a part in Asch's (1956) finding that conformity dropped considerably when the genuine participant had a single supporter who always gave the correct answer. Allen and Levine (1971) used a condition in which the informational value of the supporter's judgements was low because he had very poor vision. In this condition, there was a much smaller reduction in conformity than when the supporter had normal vision.

Evidence of the importance of normative influence was reported by Deutsch and Gerard (1955). They increased the interdependence of group members by promising them all a reward in the form of tickets to a Broadway play if they made very few errors. This manipulation produced twice as much conformity as was found when no reward was offered for good group performance.

Moscovici's social influence theory

Kelman (1958) argued that there are three main reasons why someone behaves in a conforming way: compliance; identification; and internalisation.

Compliance involves conforming with the majority in spite of not really agreeing with them. As the conformity is only superficial, compliance stops when there are no group pressures to conform.

Identification occurs when someone conforms to the demands of a given role in society. The conformity generally extends over several aspects of behaviour. For example, stewards and stewardesses on planes try to be cheerful, polite, and helpful to the passengers at all times regardless of how they may actually be feeling. They behave in this way because they are conforming to what is expected of them.

Internalisation occurs when someone conforms because they are really in agreement with the views of those who are seeking to influence them. For example, the parents of a small girl may believe it is very important for her to spend a lot of time with other children. If friends of theirs start sending their daughters to the Brownies, they will probably conform to the suggestion that they might also send their daughter. Conformity based on internalisation is like pushing on an open door, in the sense that the individual is being persuaded to do something he or she really wants to do. As a result, conformity behaviour based on internalisation continues even when there is no external pressure to conform.

Compliance or conversion?

Moscovici (1976, 1980) argued along different lines. He claimed that Asch and others had put too much emphasis on the notion that the majority in a group has a large influence on the minority. In his opinion, it is also possible for a minority to influence the majority. He drew a distinction between compliance and conversion. As we have seen, compliance is involved when a majority influences a minority, and usually involves public agreement with the majority but not private agreement. **Conversion** is how a minority can influence a majority. It involves convincing the majority that the minority's views are correct, and often produces more private agreement than public agreement with the minority.

It is hard to believe that women being allowed to vote was once a minority opinion. The direct action of the suffragette movement in the early part of the twentieth century eventually secured the right for women to vote.

An important real-life example of a minority influencing a majority was the suffragette movement in the early years of the twentieth century. The suffragettes argued strongly for the initially unpopular view that women should be allowed to vote. The hard work of the suffragettes, combined with the justice of their case, finally led the majority to accept their point of view.

Consistency. Moscovici (1976) argued that conversion is most likely to occur when the members of the minority put forward a clear position, and maintain it in a consistent way. Moscovici, Lage, and Naffrenchoux (1969) had previously obtained evidence indicating the importance of consistency. Groups of six participants were presented with blue slides varying in intensity, and each individual had to name aloud a simple colour. Two confederates of the experimenter said "green" either on every trial or on two-thirds of the trials. The percentage of "green" responses given by the majority was 8% when the minority responded in a consistent way, but was only 1% when the minority responded inconsistently.

Why is it important for the members of the minority to be consistent in their opinions? A plausible answer is to be found in Kelley's (1967) attribution theory (see Chapter 19). According to that theory, we try to decide whether other people's behaviour is due to internal causes (e.g. their genuine beliefs) or to external causes (e.g. social pressures). If someone's behaviour differs from that of other people in the same situation, and they consistently behave in that way, then we are likely to infer that it is due to internal causes. Thus, if members of the minority are consistent in their opinions, they are likely to convince the other group members that these opinions are sincere, and so they will be taken seriously.

Nemeth, Swedlund, and Kanki (1974) found that consistency is necessary in order for a minority to influence the majority, but that it is not always sufficient. They essentially replicated the study by Moscovici et al. (1969), but the participants were allowed to respond with all of the colours they saw in the slides rather than only a single colour. There were three conditions of interest:

1. The two confederates of the experimenter said "green" on half of the trials and "green-blue" on the other half in a random way.
2. As (1), except that the confederates said "green" to the brighter slides and "green-blue" to the dimmer slides, or vice versa.
3. The two confederates said "green" on every trial.

Nemeth et al. (1974) found that nearly 21% of the responses of the majority were influenced in condition 2, but that the minority had no influence at all in conditions 1 and 3. The minority had no effect in condition 1 because it did not respond in a consistent way. The minority in condition 3 did respond in a consistent way, but its refusal to use more complex descriptions of the stimuli (e.g. "blue-green") made its behaviour seem rigid and unrealistic.

Evaluation

The evidence indicates that Moscovici (1976, 1980) was correct when he argued that minorities can influence majorities, as well as majorities influencing minorities. There is also some support for his notion that different processes are involved in these two types of influence. More specifically, majorities often influence minorities by producing public agreement or compliance, whereas minorities tend to influence majorities by producing private agreement. However, experts disagree on the extent to which different processes are involved (Van Avermaet, 1988).

Three kinds of conformity effects. Wood et al. (1994b) reviewed numerous studies relevant to Moscovici's theory. They argued that there are three kinds of conformity effects: public influence, in which the individual's

Unquestioning obedience to authority may have catastrophic consequences. The pictures show members of the Nazi Party (left) marching through Nuremberg during the Nazi Party congress in 1935, and (right) survivors of the Auschwitz concentration camp at the end of the war in 1945, following a decade of persecution, imprisonment, and genocide.

behaviour in front of the group changes; direct private influence, in which there is a change in the individual's private opinions about the issue discussed by the group; and indirect private influence, in which the individual's private opinions about related issues change. According to their review, majorities have more impact than minorities on public and direct private conformity. However, minorities tend to have more impact than majorities on indirect private conformity, especially when their opinions are consistent over time.

Obedience to Authority

In nearly all societies, certain people are given power and authority over others. In our society, for example, parents, teachers, and managers are invested with varying degrees of authority. Most of the time, this does not cause any problems. If the doctor tells us to take some tablets three times a day, we accept that he or she is the expert.

Research on obedience to authority differs in at least three ways from research on conformity. First, the participants are ordered to behave in certain ways rather being fairly free to decide what to do. Second, the participant is of lower status than the person issuing the orders, whereas, in studies of conformity, the participant is usually of equal status to the group members trying to influence him or her. Third, participants' behaviour in obedience studies is determined by social power, whereas, in conformity studies, it is influenced mostly by the need for acceptance.

An issue that has been of interest to psychologists for many years is to work out how far most people are willing to go in their obedience to authority. What happens if you are asked by a person in authority to do something that you think is wrong? The lesson of history seems to be that many people are willing to do terrible things when ordered to do so. For example, Adolf Eichmann was found guilty of having played a major role in ordering the deaths of millions of Jews during the Second World War. He denied any moral responsibility, and said he had simply been doing his job. The best-known research on this issue was carried out by Stanley Milgram (1974), and is discussed at length next.

Differences between obedience and conformity

OBEDIENCE	CONFORMITY
Occurs within a hierarchy. Actor feels the person above has the right to prescribe behaviour. Links one status to another. Emphasis is on power.	Regulates the behaviour among those of equal status. Emphasis is on acceptance.
Behaviour adopted differs from behaviour of authority figure.	Behaviour adopted is similar to that of peers.
Prescription for action is explicit.	Requirement of going along with the group is often implicit.
Participants embrace obedience as an explanation for their behaviour.	Participants deny conformity as an explanation for their behaviour.

Stanley Milgram

Stanley Milgram (1974) reported the findings from a long series of studies carried out by him at Yale University. Pairs of participants were given the roles of teacher and learner for a simple learning test. In fact, the "learner" was always a confederate of Milgram. The "teacher" was told to give electric shocks to the "learner" every time the wrong answer was given, and to increase the shock intensity each time. In fact, the apparatus was arranged so that the learner never actually received any shocks, but the teacher did not realise that. At 180 volts, the learner yelled "I can't stand the pain", and by 270 volts the response had become an agonised scream. The maximum intensity of shock was 450 volts. If the teacher was unwilling to give the shocks, the experimenter urged him or her to continue.

Do you think you would have been willing to give the maximum (and potentially deadly) 450-volt shock in this study? Milgram (1974) found that everyone he asked denied that they personally would do any such thing. He also found that psychiatrists predicted that only one person in a thousand would go on to the 450-volt stage. In fact, about 65% of Milgram's participants gave the maximum shock using his standard procedure. This is 650 times as many people as the expert psychiatrists had predicted!

One of the most striking cases of total obedience was that of Pasqual Gino, a 43-year-old water inspector. Towards the end of the experiment, he found himself thinking, "Good God, he's dead. Well, here we go, we'll finish him. And I just continued all the way through to 450 volts."

Milgram (1974) carried out several variations on his basic experiment. He found that there were two main ways in which obedience to authority could be reduced:

1. Increasing the obviousness of the learner's plight.
2. Reducing the authority or influence of the experimenter.

KEY STUDY EVALUATION — Milgram

Milgram's work on obedience to authority is very well known and has always been regarded as rather controversial. Despite predictions by psychiatrists that only one person in a thousand would be prepared to give a fellow human being a 450-volt electric shock, Milgram found that 65% of his participants would do so in a mock teaching and learning situation. Participants did not realise that shocks were not really being given at all. Most of those who used the maximum shock levels did so very reluctantly, showing signs of stress and internal conflict. This may have been due in part to the fact that the study took place in the 1970s, after attitudes to rebellion and individualism had been changed by the social and political movements of the previous decade. Parallels have been drawn between Milgram's findings and the behaviour of people such as Nazi concentration camp guards, who protested that they were only following orders. However, other studies have shown that levels of obedience can be reduced in real-life situations where groups of people challenge authority. Permission to run a study such as Milgram's original one would not be granted today on ethical grounds but his work showed that conformity and obedience depend on many factors.

Why do you think the setting in which the experiments took place made such a difference?

The impact of the first factor was studied by comparing obedience in four situations differing in the obviousness of the learner's plight (the percentage of participants who were totally obedient is shown in brackets):

- Remote feedback: the victim could not be heard or seen (66%).
- Voice feedback: the victim could be heard but not seen (62%).
- Proximity: the victim was only one metre away from the participant (40%).
- Touch-proximity: this was like the proximity condition, except that the participant had to force the learner's hand onto the shockplate (30%).

Milgram (1974) reduced the authority of the experimenter by staging his experiment in a run-down office building rather than at Yale University. The percentage of obedient participants went down from 65% at Yale University to 48% in the run-down office building. The influence of the experimenter was reduced by having him give his orders by telephone rather than having him sitting close to the participant. This reduced obedience from 65% to 20.5%. This effect of distance may help to explain why it is less stressful to kill people by dropping bombs from a plane than by shooting them at close range. Finally, the authority of the experimenter was reduced by having him being apparently an ordinary member of the public rather than a white-coated scientist. This reduced the level of total obedience to 20%.

In a further study, Milgram (1974) made use of three teachers, two of whom were confederates working for the experimenter. In one condition, the two confederates were rebellious and refused to give severe shocks to the learner. In this situation, only 10% of the participants were fully obedient. The fact that two other people were willing to disobey the experimenter reduced the influence of the experimenter over the participants.

Discussion points

1. Do most people simply obey authority in a rather mindless way?
2. What are the main factors determining whether or not there is obedience to authority?

Evaluation and theoretical analysis

Cross-cultural aspects. Milgram's (1974) studies were carried out in the United States, and it is important to know whether similar findings would be obtained in other cultures. The relevant cross-cultural evidence was discussed by Smith and Bond (1993). Unfortunately, key aspects of the procedure varied from one culture to another, and so it is very difficult to interpret the cross-cultural differences in obedience. However, the percentages of participants who were willing to give the most severe shock were very high in several countries. The percentage figure was 80% or higher in studies carried out in Italy, Spain, Germany, Austria, and Holland. These findings suggest that there is substantial obedience to authority in numerous cultures.

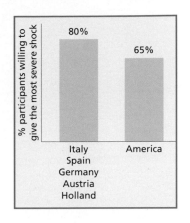

The reasons for obedience. Why are so many people obedient in the Milgram situation? According to Milgram (1974), there are three main reasons:

1. Our experience has taught us that authorities are generally trustworthy and legitimate.
2. The orders given by the experimenter moved gradually from the reasonable to the unreasonable, and so it was hard for the participants to notice when they began to be asked to behave in an unreasonable way.
3. The participants were put into an "agentic" state, in which they became the instruments of an authority figure, and ceased to act according to their consciences. The attitude of those in the agentic state is as follows: "I am not responsible, because I was ordered to do it!"

The importance of Milgram's work. Milgram's research on obedience to authority is of great importance, because of the light it sheds on human behaviour and because of the surprising findings he obtained. However, it seems to portray a very pessimistic view of human nature. According to Milgram (1974):

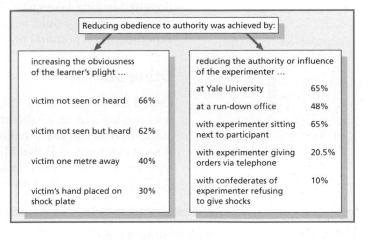

> *The capacity for man to abandon his humanity, indeed the inevitability that he does so, as he merges his unique personality into the larger institutional structures ... is the fatal flaw nature has designed into us, and which in the long run gives our species only a modest chance for survival.*

Milgram (1974) seems to have been unduly pessimistic in his conclusions. Most of the obedient participants indicated in their behaviour that they were experiencing a strong conflict between the demands of the experimenter and the dictates of their consciences. They appeared very tense and nervous, they perspired, they bit their lips, and they clenched and unclenched their fists. Such behaviour does not suggest that they were in an agentic state.

Milgram and others have suggested that there are links between his findings and the horrors of Nazi Germany. However, it is important not to exaggerate the similarities. In the first place, the values underlying Milgram's studies were the positive ones of understanding more about human learning and memory, whereas the values in Nazi Germany were morally vile. Second, most of the participants in Milgram's studies needed to be watched closely in order to ensure their obedience, whereas this was not necessary in Nazi Germany. Third, as we have seen, most of Milgram's participants were in a state of great conflict and agitation. In contrast, those who carried out the atrocities in Nazi Germany typically seemed unconcerned about moral issues.

Attribution. Why was the actual behaviour of the participants in Milgram's studies so different from what most people would have expected? Part of the answer is probably to be found in the **fundamental attribution error**, which is the tendency to

KEY TERM
Fundamental attribution error: the tendency when trying to identify the causes of a person's behaviour to overestimate the role of his or her personal characteristics and to underestimate the role of the situation.

underestimate the role of situational factors in determining behaviour, and to overestimate the role of personality and other personal characteristics. When asked to decide how many people would show total obedience in Milgram's situation, we tend to think along the following lines: "Only a psychopath would give massive electric shocks to another person. There aren't many psychopaths about, and so only a tiny percentage of people would be totally obedient." This line of reasoning focuses exclusively on the individual participant's characteristics. In line with the fundamental attribution error, it ignores the relevant situational factors (e.g. the scientific expertise and status of the experimenter; the insistence of the experimenter that the participant continue to give electric shocks).

Ethics. Finally, it should be noted that Milgram's work poses some important ethical issues. The participants were not told that the study would cause conflict and distress, and so they did not give their informed consent. In addition, they were told that they must remain in the experiment, and so they were not free to leave if that was what they wanted to do. Of central importance to current ethical guidelines is the emphasis that the rights and status of the participant are equal to those of the researcher (see Chapter 29). It has been argued that Milgram totally failed to do this, because his research was specifically designed to see how far the researcher could exploit his superior position to compel participants to behave in ways in which they did not want to behave.

Milgram (1974) made three main points in response to these criticisms. First, all the participants were fully debriefed and given full information about the study. Second, 84% of the participants said they were glad to have been in the experiment, and only 1% regretted having taken part. Third, he argued (and most people agree with him) that the ethical concerns would have much less if nearly everyone had simply disobeyed the experimenter's immoral orders.

Other studies

One of the limitations of Milgram's (1974) research on obedience to authority is that it was carried out in a laboratory situation. It would be useful to study obedience to authority in a real-life situation in order to see whether similar findings can be obtained. A second limitation is that Milgram (1974) found that an authority figure could produce high levels of obedience in individuals, but he did not see whether groups would be similarly obedient. We will consider studies that have addressed these limitations.

CASE STUDY: The My Lai Massacre

The My Lai massacre has become known as one of the most controversial incidents in the Vietnam War. On 14 December 1969 almost 400 Vietnamese villagers were killed in under 4 hours. The following transcript is from a CBS News interview with a soldier who took part in the massacre.

Q. How many people did you round up?
A. Well, there was about forty, fifty people that we gathered in the center of the village. And we placed them in there, and it was like a little island, right there in the center of the village, I'd say ... And ...
Q. What kind of people—men, women, children?
A. Men, women, children.
Q. Babies?
A. Babies. And we huddled them up. We made them squat down and Lieutenant Calley came over and said, "You know what to do with them, don't you?" And I said yes. So I took it for granted that he just wanted us to watch them. And he left, and came back about ten or fifteen minutes later and said, "How come you ain't killed them yet?" And I told him that I didn't think you wanted us to to to kill them, that you just wanted us to guard them. He said, "No. I want them dead." So—

Q. He told this to all of you, or to you particularly?
A. Well, I was facing him. So, but the other three, four guys heard it and so he stepped back about ten, fifteen feet, and he started shooting them. And he told me to start shooting. So I started shooting, I poured about four clips into the group.
Q. You fired four clips from your ...
A. M-16.
Q. And that's about how many clips—I mean, how many—
A. I carried seventeen rounds to each clip.
Q. So you fired something like sixty-seven shots?
A. Right.
Q. And you killed how many? At that time?
A. Well, I fired them automatic, so you can't—You just spray the area on them and so you can't know how many you killed 'cause they were going fast. So I might have killed ten or fifteen of them.
Q. Men, women and children?
A. Men, women and children.
Q. And babies?
A. And babies.

A real-life situation

Hofling et al. (1966) carried out a real-life study in which 22 nurses were phoned up by someone who claimed to be "Dr Smith". They asked the nurses to check that a drug called Astroten was available. When the nurses did this, they saw on the bottle that the maximum dosage of this drug was supposed to be 10mg. When they reported back to Dr Smith, he told them to give 20mg of the drug to a patient.

There were two good reasons why the nurses should have refused to do as they were instructed. First, the dose was double the maximum safe dose. Second, the nurses did not know Dr Smith, and they were only supposed to take instructions from doctors they knew. However, the nurses' training had led them to obey instructions from doctors. There is a clear power structure in medical settings, with doctors in a more powerful position than nurses. As you probably guessed, the nurses were more influenced by the power structure than by the two hospital regulations they were meant to obey. All but one of the nurses did as Dr Smith instructed. When the nurses were asked what other nurses would have done in the circumstances, they all predicted that other nurses would not have obeyed the instructions. This provides evidence that the pressures to show obedience to authority are greater than most people imagine.

Group obedience

Gamson, Fireman, and Rytina (1982) carried out a study in which groups of nine people arrived at a motel to take part in a discussion. They were told that the proceedings would be videotaped by a large oil company that was being sued by a former manager of a petrol station. They were also told that he had been sacked for living with a woman to whom he was not married, but they then discovered that the real reason was that he had spoken out on television against higher petrol prices. When the co-ordinator of the discussion instructed the participants to argue on camera that they were offended by the manager's lifestyle, they refused to do it. In some of the groups, the participants threatened to confiscate the videotapes of the discussion, and to expose the oil company to the media.

Summary

In sum, obedience to authority can be obtained fairly easily in real-life situations. Thus, Milgram's findings are not specific to the laboratory. The findings of Gamson et al. (1982) are encouraging. They suggest that groups of people are often more willing than individuals to challenge the unreasonable demands of authority figures.

Independent Behaviour

We have seen that social pressures to conform or to obey authority can exert powerful effects on people's behaviour. However, some people manage to resist the pressures to conform or to obey and thus exhibit **independent behaviour**. This is easier to do in some circumstances, especially when one or more other people are seen to behave independently. For example, as we have seen, conformity in the Asch situation dropped from 37% to 5% when there was one confederate who gave the correct answer on all trials.

Other people's behaviour

Milgram (1974) carried out a study in which three participants were assigned the teaching role at the same time. One was a genuine participant, whereas the other two were confederates of the experimenter. When the two confederates quit halfway through the study, 90% of the genuine participants followed suit and disobeyed the experimenter. Thus, it is easier to show independent behaviour and resist the pressures to obey authority when you can see other people resisting those pressures.

Individual differences

There are large individual differences between participants in their responses to situations such as those devised by Asch and by Milgram. As we will see, various attempts have

Milgram's (1974) "obedience" experiment. Top left: the "shock box"; top right: the experimenter demonstrating the shock box to the "teacher"; bottom left: wiring the "learner" up to the apparatus; bottom right: one of the "teachers" refusing to continue with the experiment.

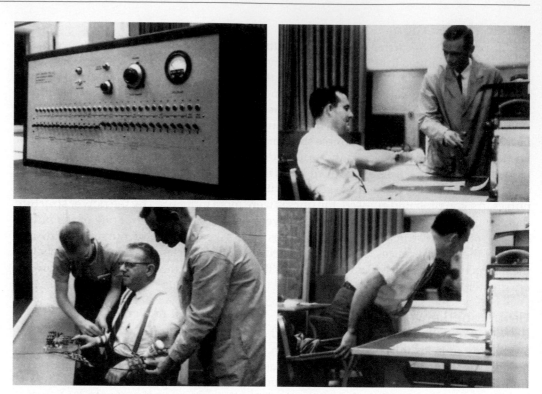

been made to identify the personality and other characteristics of those whose behaviour is independent.

The Milgram situation

About two-thirds of participants in the standard Milgram situation show total obedience to authority, and nearly all the rest obey most of the requests given by the authority figure to administer electric shocks. These findings indicate the the great power of the pressure to obey in the Milgram situation. What about individual differences in obedience to authority? According to van Avermaet (1996, p.525):

> *In the Milgram situation, personality characteristics did not make a lot of difference: his analyses revealed only minor differences between men and women, between people holding different professions or between those scoring differently on personality inventories.*

One of the few exceptions to the generally non-significant findings was reported by Milgram (1974). Those participants who showed signs of independent behaviour tended to have low scores on the F (Fascism) Scale, which is a measure of authoritarian attitudes (see Chapter 19).

The Asch situation

There has been more success in identifying personality characteristics associated with independent behaviour in the Asch situation. Crowne and Marlowe (1964) reported a number of studies in which conformity was assessed in high and low scorers on the Marlowe–Crowne Social Desirability Scale. There has been some controversy about exactly what this scale measures, but it seems in part to assess the need for social approval. As might be expected, those low in need for social approval were more likely to show independent behaviour by refusing to conform in the Asch situation. In other conformity studies (e.g. Stang, 1972) it has been found that individuals high in self-esteem are more likely to behave independently than those low in self-esteem. Wiesenthal et al. (1976) found that those who regarded themselves as highly competent at judgement tasks showed more independent behaviour than those who were less sure of their competence.

Crutchfield (1955) discussed several studies in which individual differences in conformity and independent behaviour were considered. Those who showed independent behaviour tended to be more intelligent than those who conformed. They also had more leadership ability, good insight into their own personalities, and tended to have assertive personalities.

Evaluation

There are two main reasons why some individuals might show more independent behaviour than most other people. First, they may have a high opinion of themselves and of the correctness of their own judgements. This would explain why those high in self-esteem, who believe themselves to be highly competent, who are intelligent, and who have leadership ability, show little conformity behaviour. Second, they may be relatively unconcerned about the approval of others, and so have little motive for submitting to the judgements of other people. This would explain why those low in need for social approval and high in assertiveness may behave in an independent way.

Two final points need to be made. First, the personality and other characteristics of those who show independent behaviour often differ surprisingly little from those who conform. Second, research into independent behaviour is important, because it serves to remind us that conformity behaviour and obedience to authority depend on two factors: (1) the individual; and (2) the social situation.

Social Power

Franzoi (1996, p.258) defined **social power** as "the force available to the influencer to motivate attitude or behaviour change." There are many people who possess social power, including teachers, parents, managers, company directors, and politicians. According to Zimbardo (1973), the topic of power has been almost ignored by psychologists:

> *Power is the most important variable in social psychology and the most neglected ... The great discovery of American behaviourism, namely that responses that are reinforced will increase in frequency, is but a technological footnote to the primary issue of who controls the reinforcers.*

How many types of social power are there?

One influential answer was put forward by Collins and Raven (1969), who identified six forms of social power:

1. Reward power: the power to provide others with various rewards or to withhold them.
2. Coercive power: the power to decide whether others should or should not be punished.
3. Reference power: an individual's power to influence others because of their desire to identify with him or her.
4. Expert power: the power that stems from one person having more relevant knowledge than other people.
5. Legitimate power: the power that comes from having an acknowledged leadership or other role within a social or work organisation.
6. Informational power: power based on having one or more crucial pieces of information.

It is generally accepted that all six forms of social power do exist. For example, the ability of the experimenter to persuade participants in the Milgram situation to obey him or her depends in part on his or her expert power and legitimate power. Matters are less clear in the Asch situation, but the reward power and coercive power of the majority are involved in producing conformity behaviour. Evidence for informational power was reported by Raven and Haley (1980). Nurses and doctors typically used informational power to encourage their colleagues to adhere to hospital policy on the control of infection.

KEY TERM
Social power: the force available to an influencer to change the behaviour and/or attitudes of others.

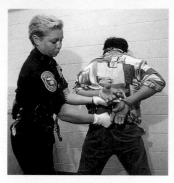

Role or personality? Does our behaviour change with our professional role?

Limitations

There are two major limitations with the approach of Collins and Raven (1969). First, several of these forms of social power tend to be found together. For example, someone who is in a position of legitimate power (e.g. managing director of a company) normally has reward and coercive power as well. Second, Collins and Raven (1969) seem to ignore the social power of individuals who lack all six forms of social power but have a powerful or dominating personality which allows them to influence other people. Schriesham, Hinkin, and Podsakoss (1991) recognised the importance of this factor when they argued that one of the two main forms of social power is personal power. Personal power is based on the ability to make others enthusiastic and the ability to convice others on a course of action.

Two perspectives

In this section and the next, we will consider social power from two main perspectives. First, there is the social power exercised by prison warders, and their treatment of the prisoners in their care. Prison warders possess various forms of social power, including legitimate, reward, and coercive power. A key issue is to decide whether aggressive behaviour by warders is due to their personalities or is due to the prison environment.

Second, there is the social power of leaders. Leaders vary considerably in the forms of social power at their disposal. However, leaders can possess any or all of the six forms of social power identified by Collins and Raven (1969). It is the leader or leaders within any group who has the most social power, even though other members of the group may be able to influence others in a limited way. Key issues are as follows:

1. Do leaders differ from followers in their personalities or other characteristics?
2. What kinds of leaders are most effective?

Stanford prison experiment

In the 1960s, there were numerous reports of problems in American prisons. Many of these reports referred to brutal attacks by prison warders on the prisoners in their care. Why did this brutality occur? One possibility is that those who choose to put themselves into a position of power by becoming prison warders tend to have aggressive or sadistic personalities. Another possibility is that the behaviour of prison warders is due mainly to the social environment of prisons, including the rigid power structure that is found in them.

Philip Zimbardo (1973) studied this issue in what is often referred to as the Stanford prison experiment. Emotionally stable members of society agreed to act as "warders" and "prisoners" in a mock prison. Zimbardo was interested in seeing whether the hostility found in many real prisons would also be found in his mock prison. If hostility were found in spite of not using sadistic warders, this would suggest that the power structure of prisons creates hostility.

In the Stanford prison experiment, attempts were made to make the participants' experience as realistic as possible. Upon arrival at the "Stanford County Prison", the prisoners were stripped naked, skin-searched, deloused, and issued with a uniform, bedding, and basic supplies. The prisoners were only allowed to eat at specified times. They needed the permission of a warder to do almost anything, including writing letters and going to the toilet. In all, there were 16 rules which the warders were asked to enforce.

What went on in the mock prison was so unpleasant and dangerous that the entire experiment had to be stopped after six days instead of the intended fourteen. Violence and rebellion broke out within two days of the start. The prisoners ripped off their clothing, and shouted and cursed at the warders. In return, the guards put down this rebellion violently using fire extinguishers. They also played the prisoners off against one another, and harassed them almost constantly. One of the prisoners showed such severe symptoms of emotional disturbance (disorganised thinking, uncontrollable

KEY STUDY EVALUATION — Zimbardo

Philip Zimbardo's Stanford prison experiment was set up to study the issue of social power. Did brutal treatment of prisoners by warders in American jails depend on the personalities of the warders themselves, or on the nature of the situation in the prison? Zimbardo's participants were stable and well-balanced people who were randomly given the roles of warders and prisoners in a mock prison situation. The study was intended to last 14 days, but had to be stopped after only 6 days because severe violence and disorder broke out. The "warders" began to enjoy their extreme power, and the "prisoners" began to act in a subdued and submissive manner. In his study, Zimbardo showed that situational factors can drastically affect people's behaviour. However, it has been argued that the prison situation is one for which most people have stereotyped ideas that arise from various types of media portrayals. Many people felt that it was ethically wrong to observe the behaviour that took place without intervening, although participants who suffered extreme stress were able to leave the experiment early.

crying, and screaming) that he had to be released after only one day. On the fourth day, two more prisoners showed symptoms of severe disturbance and were released.

There were some interesting changes in the behaviour of the warders and prisoners over time. The prisoners became more and more subdued and submissive, often slouching and keeping their eyes fixed on the ground. At the same time, the use of force, harassment, and aggression by the warders increased steadily from day to day. The warders began to enjoy the power to control other people, and the passive reaction of the prisoners encouraged them to exert more and more power.

What can we learn from the Stanford prison experiment? According to Zimbardo, the experiment showed the great importance of the power structure within prisons. Real prison warders may be somewhat more sadistic than other people. However, the prison environment seems to be the main factor leading to brutal behaviour by warders.

Discussion points

1. Are you surprised by the findings from the Stanford prison experiment?

2. Do you think this study is acceptable ethically?

Evaluation

On the positive side, Zimbardo (1973) managed to show in the Stanford prison experiment that those in a position of power can behave in aggressive and hostile ways even when they have been carefully selected to be emotionally stable. His findings indicate that situational factors (e.g. the power structure of an organisation) can have a decisive effect on people's behaviour.

On the negative side, many critics have argued that it was not acceptable ethically to expose people to such degradation and hostility. Was it reasonable for Zimbardo to stand by while the guards forced prisoners to clean toilets with their bare hands, hosed them with fire extinguishers, and made them do push-ups with a guard standing on their back? Savin (1973) argued that the mock prison was a "hell" (see page 787). In reply, Zimbardo pointed out that he had tried to reduce any negative effects on the participants by holding day-long debriefing sessions, in which the moral conflicts posed by the study were discussed. He also pointed out that most of the participants reported that they had learned valuable things about themselves. It is true that the study was of value. However, it is not clear that this begins to justify the level of degradation and physical assault that happened.

Banuazizi and Mohavedi (1974) raised another problem. According to them, the participants had strong stereotypes of how prison warders and prisoners behave in real prisons, and they simply engaged in role-playing based on these stereotypes. It is true that most people have stereotypes about prison warders and prisoners. However, it is unlikely that the participants were merely "acting out" stereotypically defined roles. If Banuazizi and Mohavedi (1973) were correct, why didn't the participants behave in a stereotypical way from the outset? In addition, the physical abuse and harassment shown by the prison warders seem to have gone a long way beyond what would have been expected from mere play-acting. While acting is most likely in the presence of an audience, Zimbardo (1973) actually found that harassment of prisoners was greater when individual warders were alone with solitary prisoners or out of range of the recording equipment.

Ethical issues: Despite agreeing to take part in the study, several of the "prisoners" in the Stanford experiment were seriously affected during the study. Three of them showed symptoms of emotional disturbance. The experiment was cut short after only six days.

Leadership

It is not easy to provide a good definition of **leadership**. As Stogdill (1974, p.259) pointed out, "There are almost as many definitions of leadership as there are persons who have attempted to define the concept." It has been defined in terms of individual personality characteristics, types of behaviour, group processes, interaction patterns, and so on. However, it is probably most useful to think of leadership in terms of the ability to influence the behaviour and beliefs of group members.

KEY TERM
Leadership: the ability to influence the behaviour and the beliefs of others.

Do leaders share any common characteristics?

Bales (1950) introduced a very influential method for studying status differences within a group. He devised what is known as **interaction process analysis**, in which observers code the behaviour of group members on the basis of a number of categories. Interaction process analysis contains four general behavioural categories, with three sub-categories falling within each categories (sub-categories are shown in brackets):

- Positive socio-emotional behaviour (shows solidarity; shows tension release; agrees).
- Task behaviour (gives suggestion; gives opinion; gives orientation).
- Information exchange (asks for orientation; asks for opinion; asks for suggestion).
- Negative socio-emotional behaviour (disagrees; shows tension; shows antagonism).

Task and social-emotional leaders

Bales and Slater (1955) applied interaction process analysis to the behaviour of small groups. They found that the members of any group varied considerably in terms of the kinds of behaviour they tended to initiate and to receive. More specifically, they found that there were usually two kinds of leader within a group: a task leader and a social-emotional leader. The **task leader** initiated a considerable amount of task behaviour, disagreed with others, and showed antagonism, and received agreement, requests for orientation, opinions, and suggestions, and all types of negative socio-emotional behaviour. In contrast, the **social-emotional leader** initated all types of positive socio-emotional behaviour, asked for orientation, opinions, and suggestions, showed tension, and received solidarity, tension release, orientation, suggestions, and opinions.

Bales and Slater (1955) found that it was rare for the same person to be the task leader and the social-emotional leader. Why is this so? One reason is that any individual is unlikely to possess the different qualities to fulfil both functions adequately. Another reason is that the task leader tends to arouse hostility in other members of the group, and it is difficult for that person to provide effective social-emotional leadership when exposed to so much negative socio-emotional behaviour.

Questionnaire studies

As we have seen, the distinction drawn by Bales between a task leader and a social-emotional leader was based on observations of the behaviour of groups. Essentially the same distinction has been found in questionnaire studies involving the assessment of leaders by members of groups. Likert (1967) identified two broad categories of leader behaviour based on questionnaire assessment: employee-centred and production-centred. There are clear links between employee-centred behaviour and being a social-emotional leader, and between production-centred behaviour and being a task leader.

Evaluation

Most of the studies on task leaders and social-emotional leaders have been carried out in the United States and the United Kingdom. It is clearly of interest to know whether this distinction between two types of leader is relevant in other parts of the world. Nystedt (1996) discussed the evidence. He concluded that most groups have both types of leader in countries such as Finland, Japan, Hong Kong, and Sweden. While this indicates that there is some cross-cultural validity to the distinction between two forms of leadership, it would be valuable to have information from a much wider range of cultures.

There is convincing evidence that leaders contribute more than followers when it comes to developing ways of dealing with the task demands facing the group. There is less evidence that employee-centred or social-emotional skills are of great importance in most groups. Questionnaire findings indicate that group members appreciate it if their leader shows consideration towards them. However, several observational studies (e.g. Lord, 1977) have found little or no evidence of social-emotional leadership.

BEHAVIOUR		TIME										
		1	2	3	4	5	6	7	8	9	10	
Positive social-emotional	Shows solidarity											
	Shows tension release											
	Agrees											
Task	Gives suggestion											
	Gives opinion											
	Gives orientation											
Information exchange	Asks for orientation											
	Asks for opinion											
	Asks for suggestion											
Negative social-emotional	Disagrees											
	Shows tension											
	Shows antagonism											

■ Research activity: Using the categories devised by Bales, observe a member of a discussion group for ten minutes. Classify their behaviour at one-minute intervals, and record your findings on a chart like this one.

How easy was this task? What was the most difficult? Did the person seem to be a social or task leader?

Styles of leadership

Lewin, Lippitt, and White (1939) studied the effects of three styles of leadership on 10-year-old boys in a model-making club. It is important to note that the adult leaders were instructed to adopt a certain style of leadership rather than behaving naturally. Autocratic leaders told the boys what to do, and with whom they were to work. They did not discuss issues with the boys or express an interest in their views. Democratic leaders allowed the boys to choose other boys with whom to work, and encouraged them to make their own decisions. The democratic leaders joined in many of the activities. Finally, laissez-faire leaders had little involvement in the running of the group. They left the boys free to do what they wanted, and did not encourage or criticise them.

Democratic leadership was the most generally successful. The work was carried out well, there was good co-operation among the boys, the boys liked each other, and they carried on working when the leader left the room. Laissez-faire leadership was the least successful. The boys achieved little whether the leader was or was not in the room, they became discouraged when there were problems, and they behaved aggressively to each other. Autocratic leadership led to good work performance, but the boys were aggressive and tended to stop working when the leader left the room.

Cross-cultural issues: Nystedt (1996) concluded that most groups include both task and social emotional leaders in countries such as Finland, Japan, Hong Kong, and Sweden.

Evaluation

There are various limitations of the study by Lewin et al. (1939). First, the democratic style of leadership was regarded as the most acceptable style in the American society in which the study was carried out. It might be much less successful in other cultures. Second, it was found that adults *acting* in an autocratic or laissez-faire way were less successful than those who *acted* democratically. It is possible that autocratic or laissez-faire leadership would be more effective if the leader were *naturally* autocratic or laissez-faire. Third, the democratic style of leadership may be very successful in the unthreatening context of a boys' club. However, a group faced by a sudden emergency requiring rapid decision making might be best served by autocratic leadership.

Trait theory

What determines who fills a leadership role in a group? According to the great man (or person) theory of leadership, also known as the **trait approach to leadership**, leaders possess certain personality or other characteristics which distinguish them from other people. This may seem unlikely if you think of the very different kinds of people who have achieved political leadership. For example, it is not clear that Margaret Thatcher has much in common with Nelson Mandela.

KEY TERM
Trait approach to leadership: the view that leaders differ from followers in a number of characteristics relating to intelligence and personality.

Personality characteristics

Mann (1959) considered studies that had looked at the personality characteristics of leaders. More than 70% of the relevant studies showed a positive relationship between perceived leadership status and intelligence, adjustment, extraversion, dominance, masculinity, and conservatism. However, the relationships were fairly weak. Mann (1959, p.266) concluded that, "in no case is the median correlation between an aspect of personality ... and performance higher than 0.25, and most of the median correlations are closer to 0.15. These correlations suggest that leaders only differ slightly from followers in personality."

Stogdill (1974) came to a similar conclusion in his review of the evidence on the characteristics of leaders. He reported that leaders tend to be slightly more intelligent, self-confident, sociable, dominant, and achievement-orientated than their followers. However, it is important to emphasise that these were all small effects. In other words, it is not possible to predict with any accuracy who will become the leader of a group on the basis of the members' personality traits.

Gender differences

We have consider a number of ways in which leaders may differ from followers. However, perhaps the obvious difference between leaders and followers in most large organisations is that leaders are far more likely to be male than female. Are there consistent gender differences in leadership style that help to explain this fact? In general terms, the answer is "No". Eagly and Johnson (1990) reviewed more than 150 studies of leadership in organisational settings. They found that the similarities in style between male and female leaders were much more obvious than the differences. For example, male and female leaders were equally task-oriented in their approaches. There were small gender differences, in that female leaders were more likely to include followers or subordinates in decision making, and they were less likely than male leaders to be autocratic and domineering. In other words, female leaders tended to display more social-emotional leadership than did male ones.

Evaluation

It is often assumed that the reviews by Mann (1959) and by Stogdill (1974) have shown that the trait approach to leadership is of little value. However, that assumption may be wrong. One of the reasons why correlations between personality measures and leadership are low is because there is poor reliability of measurement. Neither Mann (1959) nor Stogdill (1974) took account of this in their reviews. Lord, De Vader, and Alliger (1986) re-examined data from the studies discussed by Mann (1959), correcting for unreliability of measurement and other factors. The correlation between intelligence and leadership perception increased from +0.25 to +0.50, and that between masculinity–femininity and leadership perception went up from +0.15 to +0.34. Lord et al. (1986, p.407) concluded that "personality traits are associated with leadership perception to a higher degree and more consistently than the popular literature indicates."

The reviews by Mann (1959) and by Stogdill (1974) only addressed the issue of the personality characteristics of those who are perceived to have leadership status. Thus, they tell us nothing about the personality characteristics of those who are effective leaders in terms of improving group performance. Heslin (1964) reviewed studies on personality characteristics associated with effective leadership. He concluded that group performance tends to be better in groups in which the leader has high intelligence and a high level of adjustment.

Additional evidence that some people are better suited than others to the role of leader was reported by Kenny and Zaccaro (1983). There were six group sessions, and no-one worked with the same group members in more than one session. At the end of each session, the members indicated who they preferred as leader. The key finding was that there was a strong tendency for individuals who were preferred as leader in one session to be preferred in the other sessions as well. The implication is that leaders possess qualities not possessed by followers.

Contingency model

In view of the relative failure of the trait approach to leadership, various theorists argued that it is important to study both the leader's behaviour and the situation or situations in which that leadership is exercised. According to this approach, the effectiveness of any particular leadership style is contingent on, or depends on, the conditions in which the group finds itself. As a result, theories within this approach are often described as **contingency models**. Probably the most influential of such contingency models is the one proposed by Fiedler (1967), and that is the one that will be considered in detail.

Fiedler's model

There are four basic components in Fiedler's (1967, 1978) contingency model. One refers to the personality of the leader, whereas the other three refer to characteristics of the situation in which the leader must lead. The leader's personality is assessed on the basis of the leader's liking for the least preferred co-worker. The least preferred co-worker (LPC) scale requires leaders to rate on 18 scales the most difficult person with whom they have had to work (e.g. pleasant–unpleasant; friendly–unfriendly). High scorers (high LPC) on this scale are those who evaluate their least preferred co-worker relatively favourably; they are said to adopt a relationship-orientated or considerate leadership style. In contrast, low scorers (low LPC) are said to be more task-orientated.

The three situational factors included in Fiedler's contingency model jointly determine the leader's level of situational control. These three factors are as follows:

1. Leader-member relations: the relations between the leader and the other members of the group can vary from very good to very poor; this is generally the most important situational factor.
2. Task structure: the amount of structure in the task performed by a group can vary from high structure and goal clarity to low structure and goal clarity.
3. Leader position power: the power and authority of the leadership position are high if the leader can hire and fire, raise pay or status, and has support from the organisation, and are low if these factors are missing.

Is the task-orientated or relationship-oriented style of leadership more effective? Fiedler and Potter (1983) summarised the findings from over 100 studies in which leadership effectiveness was measured by group performance. Task-orientated leaders tend to be more successful than relationship-orientated leaders when the level of situational control

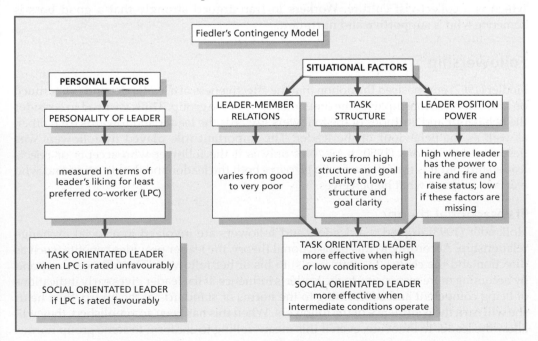

KEY TERM

Contingency models: theories of leadership based on the assumption that the effectiveness of a leadership style depends on the conditions in which the leadership is exercised.

is either high or low. However, relationship-orientated leaders are more successful than task-orientated leaders when the level of situational control is moderate.

Leaders' health. It could be argued that leaders will experience more stress and ill-health when they are placed in work situations in which their style of leadership is not effective. This notion was tested by Chemers et al. (1985). They found that relationship-orientated leaders had more symptoms of ill-health and days of absence when there was a high level of situational control, whereas task-orientated leaders had worse health when there was only a moderate level of situational control. In other words, leaders put into situations in which they find it hard to be effective may suffer ill-health as a consequence.

Evaluation

There is general agreement that the effectiveness of a leader depends on his or her personal characteristics and on various aspects of the situation, and thus that there is no such thing as a good leader for all situations. There is also fairly general agreement that it is important whether the leader is task- or relationship-orientated. However, there are some problems with Fiedler's contingency model. First, the precise meaning of different scores on the LPC scale is not known. Second, the existence of correlations between LPC scores and group performance can be interpreted in more than one way. It may mean that styles of leadership affect group performance, or that the level of group performance has an effect on leadership style.

Third, leadership style is supposed to be a characteristic of the leader, whereas leader-member relations are meant to be a situational factor. This is an over-simplification. The personality and leadership style of the leader are almost bound to have an effect on leader-member relations. Thus, leader-member relations should not be regarded as solely a situational factor.

Cross-cultural issues: Different types of leaders are suited to different cultures. In collectivist cultures where the emphasis is on group rather than individual needs, a good boss was perceived as someone who was supportive and nurturant (Ayman & Chemers, 1983).

Cross-cultural issues. There is another issue relating to Fiedler's contingency model which has not received the attention it deserves. Triandis (1993) pointed out that nearly all of the research on his model has been carried out in individualist cultures, in which individuals pursue their own goals and have a strong sense of personal identity. This could help to explain why task-orientated leaders have been found to be more effective than relationship-orientated leaders across a wide range of situations. In collectivist cultures (such as those of the Far East), the focus is on group rather than individual needs. In such cultures, it may well be that relationship-orientated leaders are preferred to task-orientated leaders. Ayman and Chemers (1983) obtained some relevant evidence in Iran, which is a collectivist culture. Workers in Iran argued strongly that a good boss is someone who is supportive and nurturant.

Followership

Fiedler (1967) emphasised the notion that the effectiveness of a leader depends very much on his or her relationship with the other members of the group. Thus, we need to consider the behaviour and attitudes of the followers towards the leader and towards each other, as well as the behaviour of the leader. The important role played by followers was described by Sanford (1950, p.4): "Not only is it the follower who accepts or rejects leadership, but it is the follower who *perceives* both the leader and the situation and who reacts in terms of what he perceives."

Transactional theory

Hollander (1993) argued that leaders and followers are involved in a social exchange relationship. According to this transactional theory, the leader provides benefits (such as direction and the chance to attain goals) to his or her followers. The followers respond by becoming more responsive to the leader's influence. If the leader gives early indications of being competent and conforming to the norms or standards of the group, then he or she will earn the confidence of the followers. When this has been accomplished, they will allow the leader to innovate, even if this means failing to conform to some group norms.

Cognitive theory

A key notion in transactional theory is that the power and influence of the leader depend to a large extent on his or her ability to gain the support and confidence of his or her followers. Rather similar ideas are contained within the cognitive theory of leadership (see Levine & Moreland, 1995). According to cognitive theory, leadership effectiveness depends on the thoughts or beliefs that leaders and followers have about each other. Leaders make attributions about the behaviour of their followers, and these attributions influence the ways in which they treat their followers. The followers themselves come to have shared beliefs about the behaviour and personality of their leader, and these beliefs then influence how they perceive their leader and the information about him or her that they remember (Levine & Moreland, 1995).

Interaction process analysis

It would be a mistake to regard all followers as being similar in their impact on the functioning of a group. Consider, for example, studies of groups which have made use of the interaction process analysis devised by Bales (1950). As was mentioned earlier, this usually allows us to identify a task leader (who initiates task behaviour) and a social-emotional leader (who initiates positive social-emotional behaviour). However, this kind of analysis also indicates that the followers vary considerably in the extent to which they influence others by initiating task behaviour or positive social-emotional behaviour. In other words, we can use interaction process analysis to rank order all of the members of the group in terms of the amount of leadership-type behaviour they display.

Reactions of followers

The behaviour of followers has a major impact on how favourably leaders are evaluated. In a study by Brown and Geis (1984), the participants watched videotapes of students carrying out a problem-solving task. Some of the participants saw the followers reacting positively to the student leader (e.g. nodding; smiling). The others saw the followers reacting negatively (e.g. expressing doubt; frowning; exchanging dubious glances). The leaders were evaluated more highly in terms of leadership, quality of contributions, and so on when their followers seemed to approve of what they were doing.

Collective Behaviour

It is well known that individuals will often behave differently when they are in a crowd than when they are on their own or with a small group of friends. For

---

CASE STUDY: *The Heaven's Gate Mass Suicide*

The daily papers from 27 March 1997 were full of news that 39 people had committed suicide in a hilltop mansion in Rancho Santa Fe, California. As the story broke, it became apparent that the victims were members of a cult that called itself "Heaven's Gate". The Heaven's Gate cult emerged in the 1970s and was led by Marshall Applewhite and Bonnie Nettles. They were self-described "space age shepherds" who intended to lead a flock of humans to a higher level of existence.

Through the teachings of their charismatic leaders, who claimed to be extraterrestrial representatives of the "Kingdom Level Above Human", the cult members believed their bodies were mere vessels. By renouncing sex, drugs, alcohol, their birth names and all relationships with family and friends, disciples prepared to ascend to space, shedding their "containers", or bodies, and entering God's Kingdom. The cult members were led to believe that the appearance of Comet Hale Bopp was a sign to move on to a more pure existence in outer space.

Investigations revealed that the mass suicide appeared to be a carefully orchestrated event. It took place over three days and involved three groups, proceeding in a calm, ritualistic fashion. Some members apparently assisted others and then went on to take their own dose of a fatal mixture. Lying on cots or mattresses with their arms at their sides,

the victims each carried identification. Each of the members of the organisation gave a brief videotaped statement prior to their death. The essence of the statements was that they believed they were going to a better place.

Three things seem to be essential to the concept of a cult. Members think in terms of "us" and "them", with a total alienation from anyone perceived as "them". Intense, though often subtle, indoctrination techniques are used to recruit and hold members. The third ingredient is the presence of a charismatic cult leader who makes people want to follow his or her beliefs. Cultism usually involves some sort of belief that everything outside the cult is evil and threatening; inside the cult is the safe and special path to salvation through the cult leader and his or her teachings.

The cult leader must be extremely attractive to those who convert. He or she must satisfy the fundamental need to have someone to trust, depend on, and believe in totally. Charismatic leaders like Applewhite and Nettles gave purpose and meaning to the lives of their followers. Unquestioning devotion caused 38 Heaven's Gate cult members to voluntarily commit suicide. Marshall Applewhite was the 39th person to die in the mass suicide.

example, lynch mobs in the south of the United States murdered about 2000 people (mostly blacks) during the first half of the twentieth century. Those involved in these atrocities would almost certainly not have behaved like that if they had not been part of a highly emotional crowd.

Le Bon (1895) was a French journalist who put forward perhaps the first theory of crowd behaviour. According to him, a man who forms part of a crowd

descends several rungs in the ladder of civilisation, he is a barbarian—that is, a creature acting by instinct ... [He can be] induced to commit acts contrary to his most obvious interest and best known habits. An individual in a crowd is a grain of sand amid other grains of sand, which the wind stirs up at will.

Le Bon (1895) referred to the "law of mental unity" that drives a crowd to behave like a mob. He also used the term **social contagion** to describe the way in which irrational and violent feelings and behaviour can spread through the members of a crowd.

Crowds do sometimes behave in senseless ways. However, that is by no means always the case. Consider cases of fires in halls and other public buildings, in which several people died as everyone rushed to escape. At first glance, this may seem like senseless and irrational behaviour. However, it would only make sense for each person to walk slowly to one of the exits if they could trust everyone else to do the same. As that trust is usually lacking, the most rational behaviour is probably to behave like everyone else, and try to be among those first out of the burning building.

Le Bon (1895) exaggerated the mindless of crowds. Part of the reason for the tendency to think that crowds are likely to behave badly is because crowds that are quiet and well behaved receive practically no attention from the media. Thompson (cited in Postmes & Spears, 1998, p.229) discussed the evidence on food riots that had taken place in England during the eighteenth century. According to him, "It is the restraint, rather than the disorder, which is remarkable; and there can be no doubt that the [collective] actions were supported by an overwhelming popular consensus."

Do crowds always lead to negative behaviour?

Evidence on crowd behaviour

Civil disturbance

Reicher (1984) carried out a study on a civil disturbance in the St Pauls area of Bristol, England, which involved the police and the mainly black community. There was a considerable amount of violence, with many people being seriously injured and several police cars destroyed. However, the behaviour of the crowd was much more controlled than might have been imagined. The crowd displayed violence towards the police, but did not attack or destroy local shops and houses. In addition, the actions of the crowd were confined to a small area lying at the heart of the community. If the members of the crowd had simply been intent on behaving violently, then presumably they would have allowed the violence to spread out into the surrounding areas. Finally, those taking part denied that they had lost their identities during the process. Indeed, the opposite was closer to the truth, as they experienced an increased sense of pride in their community.

Reicher (1984) put forward a theory, according to which individuals in a crowd typically attend less than usual to themselves, focusing instead on the situation and the other members of the crowd to provide them with cues as to how to behave. This makes them responsive to group norms. These group norms will sometimes favour taking aggressive action, but very often will favour responsible behaviour.

Football crowds

Further evidence that crowds typically share a social purpose and do not simply behave in a totally unthinking way was reported by Marsh, Rosser, and Harré (1978). They studied the behaviour of football fans in great detail, and found evidence of long-lasting social structures and patterns of behaviour. Those fans who showed the best ability to follow the rules and norms were the most highly regarded and influential members of their group.

In spite of the stereotype of football fans as forming highly aggressive groups, unrestrained fighting between rival fans actually happened very rarely. For example, football fans supporting the home team regarded it as their right to chase fans of the away team away from the ground after the match, but the rival sets of fans usually kept their distance from each other. What generally happens is that football fans use violent language and make threatening gestures, but these activities rarely turn into actual fighting. Where does the physical violence come from at football matches? According to Marsh et al. (1978), most of it consists of isolated incidents involving individuals rather than arising from the violent intentions of a football crowd. However, some account needs to be taken of the personality characteristics of football fans. Russell and Goldstein (1995) compared the male supporters of Utrecht football team with non-fans. They found that the supporters scored significantly higher on a measure of psychopathic or anti-social tendencies.

Demonstrations

Waddington, Jones, and Critcher (1987) considered several cases in which demonstrations did or did not become violent. They argued that the police had a vital role to play in preventing crowd violence. The police should use as little force as possible, and should be seen to be accountable to the local community for their actions. In addition, there needs to be close co-operation between the police and the organisers of demonstrations, with both groups having been thoroughly trained in the skills of communicating with crowds. If it is feasible, the best method of preventing crowd violence is often to allow the crowd to police itself.

Waddington et al. (1987) discussed evidence supporting their view that crowd violence typically depends on the context in which the crowd finds itself, rather than on characteristics of individuals in the crowd. They compared two public rallies held during the miners' strike in Britain in 1984, one of which led to violence and the other of which did not. In contrast to the peaceful rally, the violent one was controlled by the police rather than by the organisers of the rally. The violent rally had not been planned carefully with the police, and insufficient thought had been given to erecting barriers to prevent large numbers of people being forced into a small area.

Mob rule or collective action?

One of the key recommendations made by Waddington et al. was that a full understanding of the behaviour of crowds requires analysis at six different levels:

1. Structural: long-term major underlying issues such as poverty or unemployment.
2. Political/ideological: opposition of members of the crowd to the political and/or ideological views of the current government or other political organisation.
3. Cultural: the beliefs and attitudes that are common in a given culture.
4. Contextual: this level of analysis includes the train of events preceding the demonstration or rally.
5. Spatial: the layout of the area in which the crowd is gathered, which may tend to produce overcrowding or lead to confrontation.
6. Interactional: the specific interactions that occur between individuals, such as rough handling of demonstrators by the police.

The central point made by Waddington et al. was that there are numerous factors that jointly determine whether a crowd will be peaceful or violent. This is a much more sophisticated view than Le Bon's (1895) emphasis on mob psychology.

Crowding and personal space

Overcrowding

It is often argued that people will tend to behave in an aggressive way when there is severe overcrowding. Evidence supporting this view was reported by Loo (1979), who studied the behaviour of young children in a day nursery. The overall level of aggressive behaviour went up as the number of children in the nursery increased. In similar fashion, there are more acts of aggression and riots in prison with a high density of prisoners than in those with a low density (McCain et al., 1980).

Other species

Studies in other species confirm the link between crowding and aggression. Cahoun (1962) carried out a study in which there was a steady increase in the number of rats living in a large enclosure. Even though the rats were well cared for, they grew more and more aggressive as the enclosure became crowded. The level of aggression finally became so high that some of the young rats were killed, and others were simply eaten.

Personal space

Where would you sit...

In order to understand why crowding can cause aggression, it is important to consider the notion of **personal space**. Sommer (1967) defined personal space as "an area with invisible boundaries surrounding a person's body into which intruders may not come". Other psychologists have compared personal space to a buffer zone which affords protection against perceived threats.

Felipe and Sommer (1966) recorded reactions to invasion of personal space in the grounds of a large mental institution. The experimenter walked around the grounds, and sat about 15 centimetres away from any man sitting alone and not involved in any activity. If the man moved his chair, or moved further along the bench, the experimenter moved so as to keep the space between them the same as before. The man typically reacted by facing away from the experimenter, placing his elbows by his sides, mumbling, or laughing nervously. Half of the men took flight within nine minutes of the experimenter sitting beside them, and only 8% did not move at all.

...to work quietly?

Felipe and Sommer (1966) obtained similar findings in an almost empty university library. A female experimenter sat down very close to female college students; 70% of the students left the library within 30 minutes, and only 13% simply stayed put.

The unease caused by invasion of our personal space helps to explain why overcrowding leads to aggression. However, it is perhaps surprising that people are very unlikely to complain about invasion of their personal space. Felipe and Sommer (1966) found that only two of the mental patients and one out of eighty students asked the person invading their space to move away. As Hall (1966b) expressed it, "We treat space somewhat as we treat sex. It is there but we don't talk about it."

...to chat to a friend?

Zones of personal space. Hall (1966) argued that personal space can be divided into four zones. First, there is the *intimate zone*, which extends up to about 18 inches (45 centimetres). Only lovers, close relatives, and very close friends are normally allowed into this zone (social kissing excepted). Second, there is the *personal zone*, which ranges between about 18 inches and 4 feet (1.2 metres). Friends and members of one's family are allowed into this zone. Third, there is the *social zone*, which lies between about 4 feet and 12 feet (3.6 metres). Conversations with acquaintances and work colleagues usually take place in this zone. Fourth, there is the *public zone*, which extends between about 12 and 25 feet (7.6 metres). This is the zone that is often used when someone is giving a talk to an audience.

Cross-cultural issues. It should be noted that the distances in Hall's (1966) four zones apply more to the United States and to northern Europe than to some other parts of the world. Arab cultures, and to some extent Latin American and Mediterranean cultures, tend to favour smaller distances in ordinary conversations. This can produce problems when a northern European or an American talks to an Arab. The former may retreat while the

anonymous or identifiable, and they were given fake information indicating that the group norm was aggressive (loud noise) or non-aggressive (soft noise). According to deindividuation theory, individuals who were anonymous should have behaved more aggressively than those who were identifiable. That was exactly what Mann et al. (1982) found. The theory was also supported by the fact that anonymous participants reported feeling more uninhibited, free, and unselfconscious than identifiable ones.

There was some support for the emergent-norm theory, in that the participants tended to be more aggressive when they were told there was an aggressive group norm rather than a non-aggressive norm. However, the prediction that the level of aggression should be greatest among identifiable participants exposed to the aggressive group norm was not supported. Mann et al. (1982, p.271) concluded as follows: "Our findings suggest that deindividuation theory offers a more compelling explanation than emergent norm theory for the conduct of participants in aggressive crowd actions."

What norms appeared as the public waited to pay their respects to Diana, Princess of Wales?

Postmes and Spears (1998) discussed evidence supporting a modified version of emergent-norm theory. According to their theory, when individuals in a group become deindividuated, they are more likely to behave in accordance with the group norms than with general social norms. Thus, deindividuation may or may not lead to anti-social behaviour by group members depending on the prevailing group norms. Postmes and Spears (1997, p.250) carried out a meta-analysis, and arrived at the following conclusions:

Across 60 studies, there was a small effect of deindividuation manipulations on anti-normative behaviour, defined as transgression [breaking] of general social norms. Moreover, these effects were highly variable. Thus, results on the whole do not warrant deindividuation theory's status as describing a robust group process.

Some of the findings were directly contrary to the theories put forward by Zimbardo (1969) and Diener (1980): "Manipulations of private self-awareness and anonymity ... had no overall effect on anti-normative behaviour" (p.251).

In contrast to the lack of evidence for other theories, the findings from the meta-analysis provided strong support for the theory proposed by Postmes and Spears (1997). This theory has three main assumptions (p.254):

- Deindividuation leads not to a loss of self but only to a decreased focus on personal identity.
- Deindividuation increases responsiveness to situational group norms and context norms.
- Deindividuation is neutral with respect to general social norms.

The findings of Reicher (1984), which were discussed earlier, fit this theory neatly.

Discussion points

1. Do the findings discussed by Postmes and Spears show that the notion of deindividuation on its own does not really explain crowd behaviour?

2. How convincing is the theory put forward by Postmes and Spears?

PERSONAL REFLECTIONS

- In my opinion, the study of social influence is at the heart of social psychology. We all know that our behaviour is often influenced by other people, but social psychologists have shown convincingly that our behaviour is typically influenced by others much more than we realise. As a result, there is only limited value in studying individual behaviour without considering its social context.

- It is very hard to study social influence in crowds and mobs. For obvious reasons, it is not possible to study the behaviour of individuals in crowds in properly controlled conditions. Thus, we still have only a sketchy idea of the processes that lead crowds and mobs to behave in aggressive and anti-social ways. However, it is becoming increasingly clear that crowds generally behave well, and that the media exaggerate the unruliness of crowds.

SUMMARY

Conformity

Many people tend to yield to group pressures, even in unambiguous situations in which the correct answer is fairly obvious but other members of the group give the wrong answer. Conformity can occur because an individual regards others as more knowledgeable or because he or she wants to be liked by others. A minority can influence the majority if it puts forward a clear position and holds firmly to it.

Obedience to authority

Most people are prepared to obey an authority figure, even when he or she makes unreasonable demands. About 60% of people obeyed when told by an experimenter to give very strong electric shocks to the learner in the Milgram situation. There was less obedience when the authority or influence of the experimenter was reduced, or when the obviousness of the learner's plight was emphasised. In spite of their obedience in the Milgram situation, most people clearly experience strong conflicts between the demands of the experimenter and the dictates of their consciences. Most people are surprised at the high level of obedience shown in the Milgram situation. This is largely due to the tendencies to underestimate the role of situational factors in determining behaviour, and to overestimate the role of personality.

Independent behaviour

Independent behaviour in the Milgram situation is only modestly associated with personality characteristics (e.g. low authoritarian attitudes). Independent behaviour in the Asch situation is found in those who have a high opinion of themselves and of the correctness of their own judgements, or who are relatively unconcerned about the

Collective behaviour: What do you do when your personal space is invaded?

approval of others. Research on independent behaviour reminds us that we need to consider the person as well as the situation in order to understand conformity behaviour.

Social power

Prison warders may act in a brutal way towards prisoners because they have aggressive or sadistic personalities, or because of the social environment and rigid power structure found in prisons. In the Stanford prison experiment, Zimbardo found that even emotionally stable mock warders behaved aggressively towards mock prisoners, indicating the impact of situational factors. Many groups have two leaders: a task leader and a social-emotional leader. Leaders tend to be more intelligent, self-confident, sociable, dominant, and achievement-orientated than followers, but the differences are usually rather small. There are important situational factors relevant to leadership, such as leader-member relations, task structure, and leader position power. Followers and leaders are involve in a social-exchange relationship, in which they depend on each other.

Leadership

Many groups have a task leader and a social-emotional leader. It is possible to distinguish among democratic, laissez-faire, and autocratic leadership. Democratic leadership seems to be the most generally successful, and laissez-faire leadership the least successful. There are small but consistent differences in personality between leaders and others. Effective leaders tend to have high intelligence and good adjustment. It has been found that task-orientated leaders are more successful than relationship-orientated leaders when the level of situational control is either high or low, but the opposite is the case when the level of situational control is moderate. Followers vary in terms of the amount of leadership-type behaviour they display, and their behaviour has a major impact on how favourably leaders are evaluated.

Collective behaviour

It has often been argued that crowds behave in senseless ways, but this happens only rarely. People are more likely to behave aggressively when there is severe over-crowding, probably because their personal space is invaded. Personal space can be divided into four zones: the intimate zone; the personal zone; the social zone; and the public zone. People in crowds sometimes lose their sense of personal identity and become anonymous. This can lead to poor monitoring of one's own behaviour, reduced concern about social approval, reduced constraints against behaving impulsively, and a reduced capacity to think rationally. Another possibility is that crowd behaviour is influenced by the emergence of new norms.

FURTHER READING

Most of the topics discussed in this chapter are dealt with in various chapters in M. Hewstone, W. Stroebe, and G.M. Stephenson (Eds.) (1996), *Introduction to social psychology*, Oxford: Blackwell. Two other books providing good coverage of social influence are as follows: N. Hayes (1994), *Principles of social psychology*, Hove, UK: Psychology Press, and S.L. Franzoi (1996), *Social psychology*, Chicago: Brown & Benchmark.

REVISION QUESTIONS

1   "There are rare occasions in science where one particular ... study carried out in a certain field is so definitive or influential that it effectively closes down further research in that field. The view is that the research could not be done better, or that there is little left to be discovered" (Humphreys, 1994). Critically consider the extent to which this view may be true of any piece of research carried out in the field of *either* conformity *or* obedience.   (24 marks)

2   Discuss *two* theories of leadership.   (24 marks)

3   "Collective behaviour, especially crowds and mobs, has been the subject of much empirical and theoretical research. [However, none of the theories] appears to offer a completely adequate account of crowd and mob behaviour" (McIlveen, 1998). Discuss.   (24 marks)

- **Altruism and empathy**
  Understanding someone else's point of view and helping them no matter what the cost.

  Eisenberg et al.'s five-level theory
  Batson et al.'s empathy-altruism study
  Cialdini et al.'s negative-state relief model
  Cross-cultural studies
  Positive and negative influences

- **Bystander intervention**
  What determines whether or not we will help someone in need?

  Darley and Latané's studies
  Latané and Darley's decision model
  Piliavin et al.'s arousal/cost–reward model

- **Aggression**
  Why do human beings sometimes hurt each other on purpose?

  Cultural and individual differences
  Dollard et al.'s frustration–aggression hypothesis
  Baron's negative affect escape model
  Zillmann's excitation-transfer theory
  Bandura's social learning approach
  Gergen's social constructionist approach

- **Reducing and controlling aggressive behaviour**
  Can we do anything to stop this behaviour.

  Punishment
  Modelling and social skills training

- **Media influences on behaviour**
  Do violent films and TV programmes make people behave aggressively?

  Leyens et al.'s study using films
  Longitudinal studies involving TV
  Cognitive priming theory
  Cross-cultural differences

22

Pro- and Anti-social Behaviour

You must have met some people who were very helpful and co-operative, and others who were aggressive and unpleasant. Psychologists use the terms pro-social behaviour and anti-social behaviour to describe these very different ways of treating other people. **Pro-social behaviour** is behaviour that is of benefit to someone else. It includes actions that are co-operative, affectionate, and helpful to others. In contrast, **anti-social behaviour** is behaviour that harms or injures someone else. An individual's personality plays some part in determining whether his or her behaviour is mainly pro-social or anti-social. However, as we will see, aspects of the situation are more important in influencing how we behave towards other people.

The clearest examples of pro-social behaviour involve what is generally called altruism. **Altruism** is voluntary helping behaviour that is costly to the person who is altruistic. It is based on a desire to help someone else rather than on any possible rewards. It has often been assumed that altruism depends on empathy. **Empathy** is the ability to share the emotions of another person, and to understand that person's point of view.

The pro-social behaviour that has probably been studied in most detail is bystander intervention. **Bystander intervention** deals with the factors determining whether the bystanders or witnesses of an incident (e.g. a mugging) help a victim whom they do not know. As we will see, the decision of bystanders about whether or not to lend assistance depends on several factors.

There are a number of different forms of anti-social behaviour. However, psychologists have focused on aggressive behaviour. Violent crime has increased considerably in many Western countries in recent years, and so it is important to understand the factors producing aggression and violence. Of even more practical concern is the need to develop effective ways of controlling and reducing aggressive behaviour.

There were major technological advances during the twentieth century. In terms of changes in pro-social and anti-social behaviour, the most important techno-logical advance was probably television. Hundreds of millions of people spend 20 or 30 hours a week observing the behaviour of others on their television screens. There has been some controversy about the precise impact of television on people's behaviour. However, it is highly probable that massive exposure to television programmes (and especially violent ones) affects the beliefs of viewers in various ways, and may also affect their behaviour. There has been much debate on this topic, particularly with regard to children and violence in the wake of some horrific crimes, and to early language development. The effects of television can also be positive, and can lead to pro-social behaviour. In the same way that seeing people behaving violently on television can produce violent behaviour in viewers, so seeing people behaving in a caring way can increase caring behaviour.

Can you think of any instances of pure altruism? Are the motives behind these instances selfish or unselfish?

Children as young as 18 months may show concern when they see other children in distress.

Altruism and Empathy

The main focus of this section is on altruism, which is behaviour motivated mainly by the desire to help someone else. Altruism often follows from empathy, which involves understanding someone else's point of view. Before considering some of the factors responsible for altruism, we will discuss the related concept of empathy.

Development of empathy

Eisenberg, Lennon, and Roth (1983) put forward a theory of the development of pro-social moral reasoning and behaviour. In this theory, the growth of empathy is seen as a major factor in making children's behaviour more pro-social. According to Eisenberg et al., there are five levels or stages in the development of pro-social reasoning:

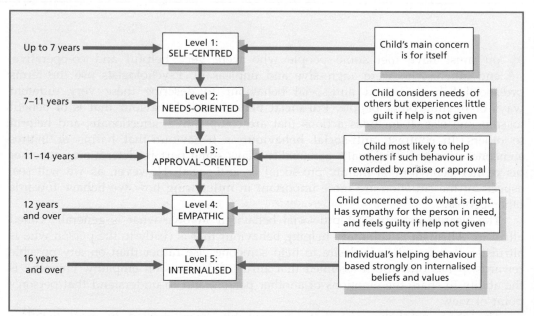

This theory has been tested by asking children of different ages to decide what they would do if faced by various dilemmas. One of the dilemmas was as follows:

One day a girl named Mary was going to a friend's birthday party. On her way she saw a girl who had fallen down and hurt her leg. The girl asked Mary to go to her house and get her parents so that they could come and take her to a doctor. But if Mary did ... she would be late for the party and miss the ice cream, cake, and all the games. What should Mary do?

Eisenberg-Berg and Hand (1979) found that young children tended to be self-centred. Most of them decided that Mary should go to the party and leave the injured girl on her own. In contrast, older children generally decided that it was more important to help the injured girl than to go to the party. Of course, the opinions expressed by children when given such dilemmas may not correspond to their behaviour in everyday life. However, Eisenberg-Berg and Hand obtained some evidence that the level of pro-social reasoning revealed by the dilemmas does predict actual behaviour. Sharing behaviour was more common among children at Level 2 of pro-social reasoning than among those at Level 1.

Eisenberg et al. (1991) found that empathy (which develops during Level 4) plays an important role in producing pro-social thinking. Adolescents given the dilemma about

Mary and the injured girl were more likely to decide that Mary should help if they thought about her feelings of pain and anxiety.

According to the theory of Eisenberg et al. (1983), empathy only develops from about the age of 12. Evidence that empathy may influence pro-social behaviour several years earlier was reported by Zahn-Waxler, Radke-Yarrow, and King (1979). Many children aged between 18 and 30 months showed obvious concern when they saw other children in distress. The infants experienced some aspects of empathy because their mothers had a particular way of dealing with them when they harmed another child. Their mothers emphasised the distress that their behaviour had caused to the other child. The mothers said things such as, "Don't hit Mary—you've made her cry" or "Put that bat down—you've hurt John."

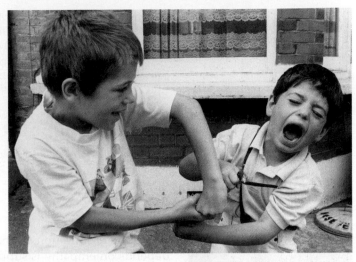

If the mother of an aggressive child emphasises how much the other child is being hurt, the aggressive child is more likely to feel empathy and stop the undesirable behaviour.

Empathy–altruism hypothesis

There are links between empathy and pro-social behaviour during children's development, and Batson (e.g. 1987) argued that the same is true of adults. According to his **empathy–altruism hypothesis**, altruistic or unselfish behaviour is motivated mainly by empathy. He claimed that there are two main emotional reactions that occur when we observe someone in distress (adjectives describing each reaction are in brackets):

- Empathic concern: a sympathetic focus on the other person's distress, plus the motivation to reduce it (compassionate; soft-hearted; tender).
- Personal distress: concern with one's own discomfort, plus the motivation to reduce it (worried; disturbed; alarmed).

Batson et al.

Batson et al. (1981) devised a situation to test the empathy–altruism hypothesis. Female students observed a student called Elaine receiving a number of mild electric shocks. The students were then asked whether they would take the remaining shocks instead of Elaine. Some of the students were told that they were free to leave the experiment if they wanted. The other students were told that they would have to stay and watch Elaine being shocked if they refused to take the shocks themselves. All the students received a placebo drug which actually had no effects. However, the students were given misleading information about the drug, so that they would interpret their reactions to Elaine as either empathic concern or personal distress. (It must be open to doubt whether all the participants believed this somewhat unlikely story!)

Most of the students in the two groups who felt empathic concern offered to take the remaining shocks regardless of whether they could easily escape from the situation. In contrast, most of those who felt personal distress offered to take the shocks when escape was difficult, but far fewer did so when escape was easy. Thus, those feeling personal distress were motivated to help by fear of social disapproval if they did not help, rather than by any real desire to help Elaine.

Batson et al. argued that the students feeling empathic concern helped Elaine for unselfish reasons. However, there are other possibilities. For example, they might have wanted to avoid self-criticism or social disapproval. In order to test this possibility, Batson et al. (1988) carried out a modified version of the 1981 study. Some of the female participants were told that they would only be allowed to help Elaine by taking some of her electric shocks if they did well in a difficult

KEY STUDY EVALUATION — Batson et al.

Batson et al.'s study was intended to test the empathy–altruism hypothesis. However, mechanisms other than empathy may have played a part, including fear of social disapproval, or even the demand characteristics of the experimental situation. The students might easily have guessed that the experimenter was interested in their level of care for another person and behaved in what they thought was the expected or socially acceptable way.

It might also be interesting to speculate on the reasons why psychologists so often use the inflicting of electric shocks in their experiments, even if the shocks are only simulated. Mild shocks are often used in animal experiments, but their use in human experiments often seems contrived and artificial. How often do people find themselves in such a situation in real life?

KEY TERM
Empathy–altruism hypothesis: Batson's notion that altruism is largely motivated by empathy.

mathematical task. Someone who was motivated to help Elaine only to avoid social disapproval and self-criticism might well offer to help, but then deliberately perform poorly on the mathematical task. This could be regarded as taking the easy way out. Many of those feeling personal distress did just that, and performed at a low level on the mathematical task. However, most of the students feeling empathic concern volunteered to help Elaine and did very well on the mathematical task. Their refusal to take the easy way out suggests that their desire to help was genuine.

Discussion points

1. Does this study seem to provide a good test of the empathy–altruism hypothesis?
2. Do you think that someone needs to experience empathy in order to behave altruistically?

Evaluation

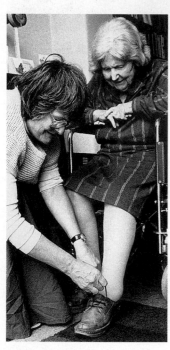

In real life as opposed to experimental situations, altruistic behaviour may involve many years of commitment rather than a brief impulse.

Why might the behaviour of carers not be altruistic?

The basic assumption of the empathy–altruism hypothesis that altruistic behaviour depends on empathy is supported by most of the evidence obtained by Batson and his colleagues. It is also supported by the developmental evidence discussed in the previous section. That evidence suggests that children's thinking and behaviour become more altruistic as their ability to empathise with others increases.

Smith, Keating, and Stotland (1989) argued that the empathy–altruism hypothesis was inadequate. They put forward an empathic joy hypothesis, according to which empathic concern leads people to help a needy person, because this allows them to share in that person's joy at receiving successful help. It is predicted by this hypothesis that those high in empathic concern should be very motivated to learn about their successful acts of helping rather than their unsuccessful ones. However, Batson et al. (1991) found that this was not the case. Indeed, it was those *low* in empathic concern who were most interested in hearing about their successful altruistic behaviour. This, and other, evidence indicates that the empathy–altruism hypothesis is more adequate than the empathic joy hypothesis.

On the negative side, it is hard to be sure that people are offering help for altruistic reasons rather than simply to avoid the disapproval of others, to avoid the feelings of guilt associated with failing to help, or to experience pleasure when the other person has received help. However, Batson and Oleson (1991, p.80) argued that the emerging pattern of findings means that "we must radically revise our views about human nature and the human capacity for caring." That may be overstating matters. As Batson et al. (1983) pointed out, genuine concern for others is often "a fragile flower, easily crushed by egotistic [self-centred] concerns." They provided some evidence for this assertion. Of participants feeling empathic concern, 86% were willing to take Elaine's place when she received mild shocks. However, this figure was reduced dramatically to only 14% when Elaine received painful shocks.

The experimental evidence relating to the empathy–altruism hypothesis is rather limited in some ways. The focus has been on short-term altruistic behaviour that has only a modest effect on the participants' lives. This can be contrasted with real life, in which altruistic behaviour can involve providing almost non-stop care for an ageing relative for several or many years. It is not clear whether the same processes are involved in the two cases.

Negative-state relief model

Cialdini et al. (1987) put forward the **negative-state relief model** to explain why empathy leads to helping behaviour. According to this model, a person who experiences empathy for a victim usually feels sad as a result. They help the victim because they want to reduce their own sadness. Thus, empathic concern should not lead to helping behaviour if steps are taken to remove the sadness that is usually found with empathy. The model also includes the notion that helping is most probable when the rewards for helping are high and the costs are low. Thus, people in an unpleasant mood are more likely to help than those in a neutral mood when helping is easy and very rewarding (e.g. it reduces their unpleasant mood).

The negative-state relief model was tested by Cialdini et al. (1987) using the same situation as Batson et al. (1981). The participants were given a placebo drug having no actual effects. However, the experimenters claimed that the drug would "fix" the participants' mood and prevent it being altered. They predicted that the participants would be less inclined to help the student who was receiving shocks if this would not allow them to reduce their sad feelings. This prediction was supported. Participants feeling empathic concern were less likely to help if they had been given the drug.

Evidence that sadness does not always lead to helping behaviour was reported by Thompson, Cowan, and Rosenhan (1980). When they asked students to imagine the feelings that would be experienced by a friend who was dying, this led to an increase in helping behaviour. However, when they asked the students to imagine their own reactions to this situation, there was no increase in helping behaviour. This suggests that people can be so focused on their own emotional state that they fail to help others in need.

Television programmes aimed at raising money for charity, such as the UK's Comic Relief and Children in Need, rely on high levels of empathic concern among those who are watching.

Evaluation

One of the reasons why empathic concern leads to altruistic behaviour is because altruistic behaviour reduces the helper's negative emotional state (e.g. sadness). However, the negative-state relief model is rather limited. First, it suggests that empathy only leads to altruistic behaviour for the selfish reason that it makes us feel better. Thus, it does not allow for the possibility that we might be motivated by unselfish motives. Second, the evidence indicates that bad moods are far more likely to increase helping behaviour in adults than in children (Franzoi, 1996). Thus, the model does not predict the helping behaviour of children. Third, the model is limited, because it applies only to mild negative feelings. According to the model, intense negative feelings should not lead to helping behaviour.

Cross-cultural and individual differences

Most of the research we have discussed was carried out in the United States. It is dangerous to assume that what is true in one culture is true in other cultures, and this danger is perhaps especially great with respect to altruism. The dominant approach to life in the United States is based on self-interest rather than on any great altruistic concern for others. Darley (1991) described this approach as follows:

Why might the behaviour of people in collectivistic cultures be less altruistic than it first appears?

> *In the United States and perhaps in all advanced capitalistic societies, it is generally accepted that the true and basic motive for human action is self-interest. It is the primary motivation.*

Evidence that this selfish approach is not dominant in all cultures was reported by Whiting and Whiting (1975). They considered the behaviour of young children between the ages of 3 and 10 in six cultures (United States; India; Okinawa, an island in South West Japan; Philippines; Mexico; and Kenya). At one extreme, Whiting and Whiting found that 100% of young children in Kenya were high in altruism. At the other extreme, only 8% of young children in the United States were altruistic. The other cultures were in between the two extremes.

Eisenberg and Mussen (1989) reviewed several studies on cross-cultural differences in altruism. They concluded that there are large differences from one culture to another. In their own words:

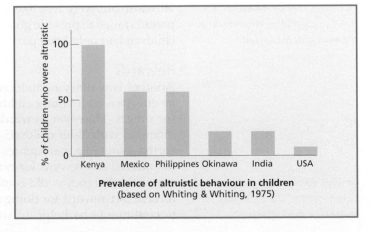

Prevalence of altruistic behaviour in children
(based on Whiting & Whiting, 1975)

Most children reared in Mexican villages, Hopi children on reservations in the Southwest [of America], and youngsters on Israeli kibbutzim are more considerate, kind, and co-operative than their "typical" middle-class American counterparts.

Individualism and collectivism

What do these findings mean? Two main factors are involved. First, industrialised societies such as those in most parts of the United States and Okinawa place much emphasis on competition and personal success. This emphasis is likely to reduce co-operation and altruism. Second, the family structure in non-industrialised cultures such as those of Kenya, Mexico, and the Hopi is quite different from that in industrialised cultures. Children in non-industrialised societies are often given major family responsibilities (e.g. caring for young children), and these responsibilities help to develop altruistic behaviour. Third, it is possible that members of non-industrialised and collectivistic societies expect to receive more co-operation and help from others, in which case their behaviour may be less altruistic than it looks (Fijneman, Willemsen, & Poortinga, 1996; see Personal Reflections at the end of this chapter).

Individual variation

Apart from cultural differences, there are also important individual differences in altruistic behaviour *within* any given culture. Davis (1983) developed an Interpersonal Reactivity Index. This was designed to measure tendencies towards empathic concern (e.g. warmth; compassion) and towards personal distress (e.g. anxiety; uneasiness). He identified the characteristics of those who watched the annual Jerry Lewis muscular dystrophy telethon in the United States, and then gave their time, effort, and money to helping. As would be expected on Batson's empathy–altruism hypothesis, those who scored high on empathic concern were most likely to watch the programme and to help.

Encouraging altruism

Observational learning

How can people be made more altruistic? According to social learning theory, observational learning from models could be an effective technique. Midlarsky and Bryan (1972) tested this notion in a study involving children observing a model giving valuable tokens to a charity. Ten days later, these children were more likely than other children to donate sweets to the same charity.

The importance of observational learning or modelling in everyday life was shown by Rosenhan (1970). He studied white Americans who had worked wholeheartedly in an altruistic way for the civil rights movement during the 1960s. Most of their parents had set them a good example by behaving in a consistently altruistic way, thus providing altruistic models for their children. Rosenhan also studied white Americans who had been less involved in the civil rights movement. Most of their parents had argued in favour of altruism, but were less likely to have behaved in an altruistic way. Thus, most of these parents failed to provide good models of altruistic behaviour. This may explain why their children had only been partly involved in the civil rights movement.

What other factors, apart from modelling, may be the cause of these children's low involvement in the civil rights movement?

Rewards

Another way of trying to increase altruism is by offering rewards for helping. This may be effective with young children who have not yet developed much empathic concern for others. However, rewards or reinforcement can have the opposite effect to that intended with older children. Fabes et al. (1989) promised toys to some children if they sorted coloured paper squares for children who were sick in hospital. Other children were not offered any reward for carrying out the same task. After a while, all of the children were told that they could continue to sort the coloured squares, but that they would not receive any reward for doing so. The children who had been rewarded were less likely to continue to be helpful than those who had not been rewarded. The findings were

At what age, according to Eisenberg et al. (1983), would rewards be most effective?

strongest among those children whose mothers believed in using rewards to make their children behave well.

Why are rewards so ineffective in producing altruistic behaviour? The main reason is that those who are rewarded for behaving helpfully are motivated by the thought of the reward rather than by the desire to help other people. As a result, removal of the rewards often causes the helpful behaviour to stop.

Social norms

The ways in which individuals behave are influenced greatly by **social norms**, which are the expected forms of behaviour within any given society. In order to encourage people to behave more altruistically, it may be necessary to alter some of the social norms within Western cultures. Piliavin et al. (1981, p.254) argued that helping behaviour could be increased by means of re-training:

> In our society, we are trained from an early age to see the problems of others as "none of our business" ... This tendency saves all of us a great deal of emotional distress, but it contributes ... to the increasing alienation and self-absorption of which we all are currently being accused. We may need more training as busybodies; respect for privacy prevents empathic arousal, and directs one's attention to the costs of intervention, specifically the cost of being thought intrusive.

Media influences

There has been considerable public interest in the possibly damaging effects of television violence on children's behaviour (discussed later in the chapter). However, although it has attracted much less interest, there is also evidence that pro-social or helping behaviour shown on television can have beneficial effects on children's behaviour.

Evidence that observational learning from a film can produce beneficial changes in behaviour was reported by O'Connor (1980). Children who avoided playing with other children were shown a film of children playing happily together. Every child who saw the film played more with other children afterwards, and this effect seemed to last for a long time.

Increased pro-social or helping behaviour as a result of watching television programmes has been found in children of various ages. Friedrich and Stein (1973) studied American preschool children, who watched episodes of a pro-social television programme called *Mister Rogers' Neighbourhood*. These children remembered much of the pro-social information contained in the programmes, and they behaved in a more helpful and co-operative way than did children who watched other television programmes with neutral or aggressive content. They became even more helpful if they role-played pro-social events from the programmes.

Sprafkin, Liebert, and Poulos (1975) studied six-year-olds. Some of these children watched an episode of *Lassie*, in which a boy was seen to risk his life in order to rescue a puppy from a mine shaft. Other groups of children saw a different episode of *Lassie*, in which no helping was involved, or they saw an episode of a situation comedy called the *The Brady Bunch*. After watching the programme, all of the children had the chance to help some distressed puppies. However, to do so they had to stop playing a game in which they might have won a big prize. The children who had watched the rescue from the mine shaft spent an average of over 90 seconds helping the puppies, compared to under 50 seconds by the children watching the other programmes.

Baran (1979) studied older children between the ages of 8 and 10. These children watched an episode of *The Waltons*, in which there was much emphasis on helping behaviour. These children were then found to behave in a more helpful or pro-social way than other children who had not seen the programme.

Hearold (1986) reviewed more than 100 studies on the effects of pro-social television programmes on children's behaviour. She concluded that such programmes do generally

Passers-by may hesitate to offer help in case it is considered intrusive or patronising.

Can you think of any social norms that are helping behaviours?

Which past or present television programmes do you consider to be pro-social?

KEY TERM
Social norms: the standards or rules of behaviour for individuals expected by a given society or culture.

make children behave in more helpful ways. Indeed, the beneficial effects of pro-social programmes on pro-social behaviour were on average almost twice as great as the adverse effects of television violence on aggressive behaviour. However, helping behaviour was usually assessed shortly after watching a pro-social television programme. It is not altogether clear whether pro-social television programmes can have long-term effects on children's pro-social behaviour.

Why is children's helping behaviour increased by watching pro-social programmes? One possibility is that observational learning or modelling is involved, with the children simply imitating the pro-social behaviour they have observed. We saw earlier that observational learning can lead to aggressive behaviour (e.g. Bandura, 1965), and the same processes could lead to pro-social behaviour. In a study by Sagotsky, Wood-Schneider, and Konop (1981), children of 6 and 8 saw co-operative behaviour being modelled. Children of both ages showed an immediate increase in co-operative behaviour. However, only the eight-year-olds continued to show increased co-operation seven weeks later.

Bystander Intervention

One of the haunting images of our time is that of someone being attacked violently in the middle of a city, with no-one being willing to help them. This apparent apathy or reluctance to help was shown very clearly in the case of Kitty Genovese. She was stabbed to death in New York as she returned home from work at three o'clock one morning in March 1964. Thirty-eight witnesses watched the murder from their apartments, but none of them intervened. Indeed, only one person called the police. Even that action was only taken after he had asked advice from a friend in another part of the city.

Have you ever been in a situation where someone was in trouble and you did nothing? How did you feel? Can you explain why you did not help?

The police asked the witnesses why they had done nothing to help Kitty Genovese. According to a report in the *New York Times*:

> *The police said most persons had told them they had been afraid to call, but had given meaningless answers when asked what they had feared. "We can understand the reticence of people to become involved in an area of violence," Lieutenant Jacobs said, "but when they are in their homes, near phones, why should they be afraid to call the police?"*

CASE STUDY: *The Kitty Genovese Murder*

At approximately 3.20 in the morning on 13 March 1964, 28-year-old Kitty Genovese was returning to her home in a middle-class area of Queens, New York, from her job as a bar manager. She parked her car and started to walk to her second-floor apartment some 30 metres away. She got as far as a streetlight, when a man who was later identified as Winston Mosely grabbed her. She screamed. Lights went on in the nearby apartment building. Kitty yelled, "Oh my God, he stabbed me! Please help me!" A window opened in the apartment building and a man's voice shouted, "Let that girl alone!" Mosely looked up, shrugged, and walked off down the street. As Kitty Genovese struggled to get to her feet, the lights went off in the apartments. The attacker came back some minutes later and renewed the assault by stabbing her again. She again cried out, "I'm dying! I'm dying!" Once again the lights came on and windows opened in many of the nearby apartments. The assailant again left, got into his car and drove away. Kitty staggered to her feet as a city bus drove by. It was now 3.35 am. Mosely returned and found his victim in a doorway at the foot of the stairs. He then raped her and stabbed her for a third time—this time fatally. It was 3.50 when the police received the first call. They responded quickly and were at the scene within two minutes, but Kitty Genovese was already dead.

The only person to call the police, a neighbour of Ms Genovese, revealed that he had phoned only after much thought and after making a call to a friend to ask advice. He said, "I didn't want to get involved." Later it emerged that there were 38 other witnesses to the events over the half-hour period. Many of Kitty's neighbours heard her screams and watched from the windows, but no-one came to her aid. The story shocked America and made front-page news across the country. The question people asked was why no-one had offered any help, or even called the police earlier when it might have helped. Urban and moral decay, apathy, and indifference were some of the many explanations offered. Two social psychologists, Bibb Latané and John Darley, were unsatisfied with these explanations and began a series of research studies to identify the situational factors that influence whether or not people come to the aid of others. They concluded that an individual is less likely to provide assistance the greater the number of other bystanders present.

Diffusion of responsibility

John Darley and Bibb Latané (1968) were interested in the Kitty Genovese case, and in the whole issue of bystander intervention. They tried to work out why Kitty Genovese was not helped by any of the numerous witnesses who saw her being attacked. According to them, a victim may be in a more fortunate position when there is just one bystander rather than several. In such a situation, responsibility for helping the victim falls firmly on to one person rather than being spread among many. In other words, the witness or bystander has a sense of personal responsibility. If there are many observers of a crime or other incident, there is a **diffusion of responsibility**, in which each person bears only a small portion of the blame for not helping. As a result, there is less feeling of personal responsibility.

A related way of considering what is involved here is to think in terms of social norms or culturally determined expectations of behaviour. One of the key norms in many societies is the **norm of social responsibility**: we should help those who need help. Darley and Latané argued that the norm of social responsibility is strongly activated when only one person observes the fate of a victim. However, it is much less likely to influence behaviour when there are several bystanders.

Darley and Latané

> Darley and Latané tested their ideas in various studies. The participants were placed in separate rooms, and told to put on headphones. They were asked to discuss their personal problems, speaking into a microphone, and hearing the contributions of others to the discussion over their headphones. They were led to think that there were one, two, three, or six people involved in the discussion. In fact, however, all of the apparent contributions by other participants were tape recordings.
>
> Each participant heard that one of the other people in the discussion was prone to seizures, especially when studying hard or taking examinations. Later on, they heard him say, "I-er-I—uh-I've got one of these-er-seizure-er-er-things coming on and-and-and I could really-er-use some help so if somebody would-er-er-help-er-er-help-er-uh-uh-uh [choking sounds] … I'm gonna die-er-er-I'm … gonna die-er-help-er-er-seizure-er … [choking sounds, silence]."

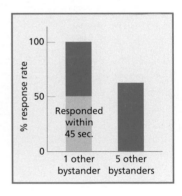

> Of those who thought they were the only person to know that someone was having an epileptic fit, 100% left the room and reported the emergency. However, only 62% of participants responded if they thought that there were five other bystanders who knew about it. Furthermore, those participants who thought they were the only bystander responded much more quickly than did those who thought there were five bystanders: 50% of them responded within 45 seconds of the onset of the fit, whereas none of those who believed there were five other bystanders did so.
>
> Two other interesting findings emerged from the research of Darley and Latané. First, the participants who believed that there were five other bystanders denied that this had had any effect on their behaviour. This suggests that people are not fully aware of the factors determining whether or not they behave in a pro-social or helpful way. Second, those participants who failed to report the emergency were not apathetic or uncaring. Most of them had trembling hands and sweating palms. Indeed, they seemed more emotionally aroused than the participants who did report the emergency.

Discussion points

1. Why do you think the findings of Darley and Latané have had so much influence on subsequent research?
2. Should we be concerned about the artificiality of the situation used by Darley and Latané?

Other factors

In the years since the publication of Darley and Latané's (1968) ground-breaking research, several researchers have identified factors other than diffusion of responsibility which determine whether or not a victim will be helped. We will consider some of these factors, and then proceed to discuss some theories of bystander intervention.

Interpreting the situation

Ambiguous situations. In real life, many emergencies have an ambiguous quality about them. For example, someone who collapses in the street may have had a heart attack, or they may simply have had too much to drink. Not surprisingly, the chances of a bystander lending assistance to a victim are much greater if the situation is interpreted as a genuine emergency. Brickman et al. (1982) carried out a study in which the participants heard a bookcase falling on another participant, followed by a scream. When someone else interpreted the situation as an emergency, the participant offered help more quickly than when the other person said there was nothing to worry about.

Perceived relationships. In many incidents, the perceived relationship between those directly involved can have a major influence on the bystanders' behaviour. Lance Shotland and Margaret Straw (1976) arranged for a man and a woman to stage a fight close to onlookers. In one condition, the woman screamed, "I don't know you." In a second condition, she screamed, "I don't know why I ever married you." When the onlookers thought the fight involved strangers, 65% of them intervened, against only 19% when they thought it involved a married couple. This suggests that bystanders are reluctant to become involved in the personal lives of strangers.

It is likely that one of the reasons why none of the bystanders went to the assistance of Kitty Genovese was because they assumed that there was a close relationship between her and her male attacker. Indeed, a housewife who was among the bystanders said, "We thought it was a lover's quarrel."

Victim characteristics

Most bystanders are influenced by the victim's characteristics. This was shown by Piliavin, Rodin, and Piliavin (1969). They staged incidents in the New York subway, with a male victim staggering forwards and collapsing on the floor. He either carried a black cane and seemed sober, or he smelled of alcohol and carried a bottle of alcohol. Bystanders were much less likely to help when the victim was "drunk" than when he was "ill". Drunks are regarded as responsible for their own plight, and it could be unpleasant to help a smelly drunk who might vomit or become abusive.

Bystander characteristics: Individual differences

What characteristics of bystanders determine the likelihood that they will help a victim?

Skills and expertise. Huston et al. (1981) argued that bystanders who have relevant skills or expertise will be most likely to offer help to a victim. For example, suppose that a passenger on a plane collapses suddenly, and one of the stewardesses asks for help. It is reasonable to assume that a doctor will be more likely to offer his or her assistance than

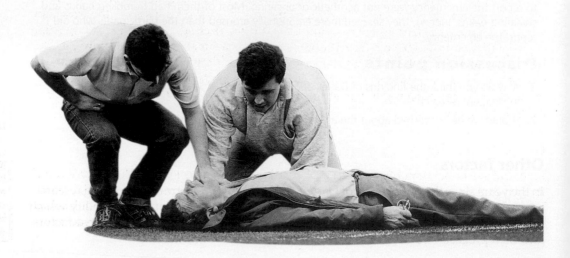

Bystanders who have some relevant skill to offer are more likely to get involved than those who don't know what to do.

someone lacking any medical skills. Huston et al. studied the characteristics of bystanders who helped out in dangerous emergencies. There was a strong tendency for helpers to have training in relevant skills such as life-saving, first aid, or self-defence.

Gender differences. Eagly and Crowley (1986) reviewed the literature on gender differences in helping behaviour. They found that men are more likely than women to help when the situation involves some danger, or when there is an audience. Men are more likely to help women than other men, especially when the women are attractive. In contrast, women are equally likely to help men and women.

Personal values. Schwartz (1977) argued that people possess a range of personal norms, or standards of behaviour based on the values they hold. Some of these norms relate to helping, and to accepting responsibility for the welfare of others. According to Schwartz, individuals who tend to behave in accord with their personal norms experience self-satisfaction, whereas those who do not experience shame and reduced self-esteem. As predicted, Schwartz found that those who were most helpful tended to be those with personal norms relating to helping and to accepting responsibility for others.

Personality factors. It might be expected that bystanders with certain personality characteristics (e.g. sociable; warm-hearted; conscientious) would be more likely to help a victim than those with other personality characteristics (e.g. unsociable; reserved; expedient). There is evidence indicating that those who offer help tend to be other-oriented rather than self-oriented (Dovidio, Piliavin, & Clarke, 1991). However, the effects of personality are typically rather small, especially when there is obviously an emergency.

Perceived similarity

Bystanders are usually most likely to help a victim if he or she is perceived as similar to themselves. However, there are some exceptions. Gaertner and Dovidio (1977) used a situation in which white participants heard a victim in the next room apparently being struck by a stack of falling chairs. When it was not clear whether or not there was an emergency (there were no screams from the victim), the white participants helped a white victim faster than a black one. The findings were different when the victim screamed, and so there was clearly an emergency. In that case, a black victim was helped as rapidly as a white victim.

There is also evidence that people who have heard of research such as Gaertner and Dovidio's study are more likely to intervene and help.

What do these findings mean? They suggest that perceived similarity between the bystander and the victim often influences helping behaviour. However, the effects of perceived similarity can be wiped out by the demands of the situation if it is clear that there really is an emergency.

Other activities

Bystanders do not only take account of the emergency itself. They also take into account the activity they were involved in when they came upon the emergency. Batson et al. (1978) sent their participants from one building to another to perform a task. On the way, they went past a male student who was slumped on the stairs coughing and groaning. Some of the participants had been told that it was important for them to help the experimenter by performing the task, and that they were to hurry. Only 10% of these participants stopped to help the student. However, if the participants were told that helping the experimenter was not very important, and that there was no hurry, then 80% of them helped the student.

Ethical issues: Do you consider there are any ethical problems with studies like that of Batson et al.? Did the participants give their informed consent to take part?

Decision model

How can we make theoretical sense of the various findings on bystander intervention? Latané and Darley (1970) put forward a **decision model**. According to this model, bystanders who lend assistance to a victim do so after working their way through a five-step sequence of decisions, producing a "yes" answer at each step. The complete decision-making sequence is as follows:

> **KEY TERM**
> **Decision model**: Latané and Darley's view that bystanders make a series of decisions before finally helping or not helping a victim.

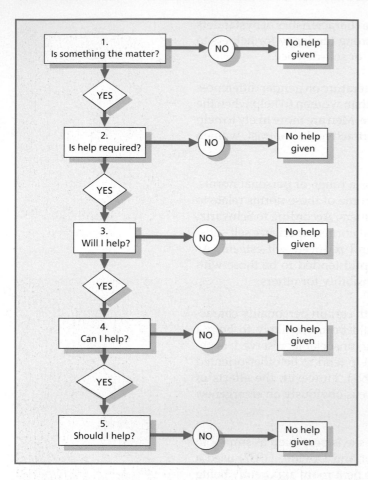

- Step 1: Is something the matter?
- Step 2: Is the event or incident interpreted as one in which assistance is needed?
- Step 3: Should the bystander accept personal responsibility?
- Step 4: What kind of help should be provided by the bystander?
- Step 5: Should the help worked out at step 4 be carried out?

Evaluation

The decision model has two strengths. First, it assumes that there are several different reasons why bystanders do not lend assistance. The experimental evidence that we have discussed provides substantial support for that assumption. Second, the decision model gives a plausible explanation of why it is that bystanders so often fail to help a victim. If bystanders produce a "no" answer at any point in the decision sequence, then help will not be forthcoming.

On the negative side, the model does not provide a detailed account of the processes involved in decision making. For example, it seems reasonable to assume that bystanders who interpret the situation as an emergency and who also accept personal responsibility would nearly always lend assistance to the unfortunate victim. We need to know more about the processes involved when "yes" decisions at steps 1, 2, and 3 are followed by a "no" decision at step 4 or 5.

At each stage in Latané and Darley's decision model, why might a person answer "no"?

Another limitation of the model is that it de-emphasises the influence of emotional factors on the bystanders' behaviour. Bystanders who are anxious or terrified are unlikely to work carefully through the five decision-making stages contained in the decision model.

Arousal/cost–reward model

Piliavin et al. (1981) put forward an **arousal/cost–reward model**. According to this model, there are five steps that bystanders go through before deciding whether or not to assist a victim:

1. Becoming aware of someone's need for help; this depends on attention.
2. Experience of arousal.
3. Interpreting cues and labelling their state of arousal.
4. Working out the rewards and costs associated with different actions.
5. Making a decision and acting on it.

■ Research activity: Complete a table such as this one and rate each situation in order of likelihood of helping.

Devise your own table or use this one to assess the public's views on helping. Compare their responses with Piliavin et al.'s reasons for helping or not helping. Do your results show any sex or age-group differences?

Situation Rating	Costs	Rewards
A pregnant woman drops her shopping bag		
A blind person requests help to cross the road		
There is a car crash on the motorway		
A hitch-hiker is thumbing a lift on a lonely road		

The fourth step is perhaps the most important, and deserves more detailed consideration. Some of the major rewards and costs involved in helping and not helping are as follows:

- Costs of helping: physical harm; delay in carrying out other activities.
- Costs of not helping: ignoring personal responsibility; guilt; criticism from others; ignoring perceived similarity.
- Rewards of helping: praise from victim; satisfaction from having been useful if relevant skills are possessed.
- Rewards of not helping: able to continue with other activities as normal.

Evaluation

The arousal/cost–reward model provides a more complete account than the decision model of the processes involved in deciding whether to provide help. As we saw in our review of the literature, bystanders often seem to take account of the potential rewards and costs associated with helping and not helping. It is also probably true that bystanders are generally more likely to think about the possibility of helping when they experience a state of arousal than when they do not.

On the negative side, it is implied by the arousal/cost–reward model that bystanders spend some time considering all of the elements in the situation and the other demands on their time before deciding what to do. In fact, people faced by a sudden emergency often respond impulsively and with very little thought. Even if bystanders do consider the relevant rewards and costs, it is perhaps unlikely that they consider *all* of them. Another problem with the model is that it is not always the case that a bystander needs to experience arousal before helping in an emergency. Someone with much experience of similar emergencies (such as a doctor responding to someone having a heart attack) may respond efficiently without becoming aroused.

Would you stop to find out what the problem is?

The main goal of the aggression in this picture is to obtain a "reward" by stealing the bag, rather than to hurt someone. This is an example of instrumental aggression.

Aggression

Aggression involves hurting others on purpose. It has been defined as "any form of behaviour directed towards the goal of harming or injuring another living being who is motivated to avoid such treatment" (Baron & Richardson, 1993). The hurting has to be deliberate. For example, someone who slips on the ice and crashes into someone by accident would not be regarded as behaving aggressively.

Psychologists have identified different types of aggression, for example, person-oriented and instrumental aggression. **Person-oriented aggression** is designed to hurt

> **KEY TERMS**
> **Aggression**: behaviour that is designed or intended to harm or to injure another living being.
> **Person-oriented aggression**: aggression that has as its main goal harming another person.

Type of Aggression	Example
Person-oriented	
Instrumental	
Proactive	
Reactive	

■ Research activity: Complete a table such as this one with examples of aggressive behaviours.

someone else, and so causing harm is the main goal. In contrast, **instrumental aggression** has as its main goal obtaining some desired reward (e.g. an attractive toy), with aggressive behaviour being used to obtain the reward.

There is also a distinction between proactive and reactive aggression. **Proactive aggression** is aggressive behaviour that is initiated by the individual to achieve some desired outcome (e.g. gaining possession of an object). **Reactive aggression** is an individual's reaction to someone else's aggression.

It is important to note that aggressive behaviour need not involve fighting or other forms of physical attack. Of course, very young children often resort to physical attacks. However, by the age of 4 or 5, children usually have a good command of language, and they make much use of teasing and other forms of verbal aggression. In the research discussed later, aggression was assessed in several ways, such as aggressive play behaviour, willingness to give electric shocks to someone else, and punching and hitting a doll. The key measurement problem is that aggression involves the *intent* to harm someone or something, and it is often hard to know whether participants intended to cause harm.

Cross-cultural and individual differences

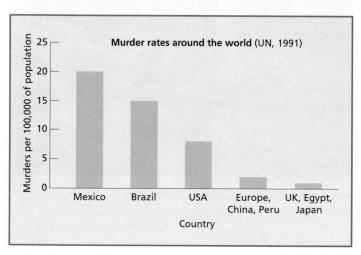

Murder rates around the world (UN, 1991)

The history of the human race indicates that aggression and violence are frequent occurrences. There have been about 15,000 wars in the last 5600 years, which works out at almost 2.7 wars per year. However, there is evidence of cross-cultural differences in the level of aggression. For example, the United Nations in 1991 revealed information about murder rates in different countries. The countries with the worst records were Mexico, with a murder rate of about 20 per 100,000 people, and Brazil (15 per 100,000 people). At the other extreme, the murder rate was only about 1 per 100,000 people in the UK, Egypt, and Japan. Most European countries had low murder rates of about 2 per 100,000, which was about the same as China and Peru. However, the murder rate was 8 per 100,000 in the United States.

Evidence from anthropology

Some of the best-known work on cross-cultural differences in aggression is that of the anthropologist Margaret Mead (1935). She compared three New Guinea tribes living fairly close to each other. In one tribe (the Mundugumor), both men and women were very aggressive and quarrelsome in their behaviour. At times, the Mundugumor had been cannibals who killed outsiders in order to eat them. In a second tribe (the Arapesh), both men and women were non-aggressive and co-operative in their treatment of each other and their children. When they were invaded, the Arapesh would hide in inaccessible parts of their territory rather than fight the invader. In the third tribe (the Tchambuli), the men carved and painted, and indulged themselves with elaborate hairdos, whereas the women were relatively aggressive.

Cross-cultural issues: Does cross-cultural evidence suggest that aggression is due more to nature or to nurture?

Mead (1935) found important cultural differences. However, it is probable that she exaggerated their extent. For example, even in the Tchambuli tribe it was the men who did most of the fighting in time of war.

Gorer (1968) discussed several cultures in which there are low levels of aggression. The Arapesh was one of the cultures, and others were the Lepchas of Sikkim and the Pygmies of central Africa. Within these societies, there is an emphasis on eating, drinking, and sex, but not on achievement or power. Gorer (1968, p.34) summarised the nature of these peaceful cultures as follows: "The model for the growing child is of concrete performance and frank enjoyment, not of ... symbolic achievements or of ordeals to be surmounted."

KEY TERMS
Instrumental aggression: harming another person in order to achieve some desired goal.
Proactive aggression: aggressive behaviour that is initiated by the individual in order to achieve some goal.
Reactive aggression: aggressive behaviour that is produced in response to someone else's aggressive behaviour.

Gender differences

Eagly and Steffen (1986) reviewed numerous studies on gender differences in aggression. There was only a small general tendency for men to be more aggressive than women. Sex differences were greater with respect to physical aggression than verbal and other psychological forms of aggression. Why are men more aggressive than women? According to the evidence discussed by Eagly and Steffen, women feel more guilty and anxious about behaving aggressively. Women are also more concerned about possible danger to themselves if they act in an aggressive way.

Does the evidence reviewed by Eagly and Steffen suggest that gender differences in aggression are due more to nature or to nurture?

The male sex hormone testosterone may play a part in producing higher levels of aggression in men than in women. For example, it has generally been found that men convicted of violent crimes have higher levels of testosterone than non-violent offenders. However, such correlational evidence does not prove that the high levels of testosterone played a part in causing the violent behaviour. More convincing evidence was reported by Hawke (1950). He found that castration led to reduced aggressiveness in male criminals who had been castrated because of their sexually based aggression. He also found that giving these men large doses of testosterone led to a return of aggressive behaviour.

We have seen that men are generally more aggressive than women. However, there seems to be an important exception so far as indirect aggression is concerned. Bjorkqvist, Lagerspetz, and Kaukiainen (1992) studied physical aggression, verbal aggression, and indirect aggression (e.g. gossiping; writing unkind notes; spreading false stories) in adolescent boys and girls. The boys displayed much more physical aggression than the girls, but the girls showed significantly more indirect aggression than the boys. The two sexes did not differ in verbal aggression.

Genetic factors

There is evidence that individual differences in aggressiveness depend in part on genetic factors. McGue, Brown, and Lykken (1992) obtained scores on the aggression scale of the Multi-Dimensional Personality Questionnaire from 54 pairs of identical twins and 79 pairs of fraternal twins. The scores correlated +0.43 for identical twins and +0.30 for fraternal twins. The fact that the correlation was higher for identical twins suggested that genetic factors were of some importance.

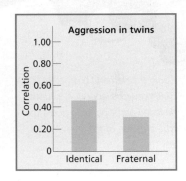

Frustration–aggression hypothesis

Think of occasions when you have behaved aggressively. Many of them probably involved frustrating situations. Dollard et al. (1939) argued in their **frustration–aggression hypothesis** that there are close links between frustration and aggression. In the words of Miller (1941, pp.337–338):

> *the occurrence of aggression always presupposes frustration ... Frustration produces instigations to a number of different types of responses, one of which is an instigation to some form of aggression.*

What types of situation do you find frustrating?

Evidence

Evidence supporting the frustration–aggression hypothesis was reported by Doob and Sears (1939). Participants imagined how they would feel in each of 16 frustrating situations. In one situation, the participants imagined they were waiting for a bus, but the bus driver went past without stopping. Most of the participants reported that they would feel angry in each of the frustrating situations. Of course, anger does not always turn into aggression.

Justified and unjustified frustration. Most of the evidence indicates that the frustration–aggression hypothesis is over-simplified. For example, Pastore (1952) argued that it is important to distinguish between justified and unjustified frustration. According to him, it is mainly unjustified frustration that produces anger and aggression. Doob and Sears (1939) found strong support for the frustration–aggression hypothesis because their

KEY TERM
Frustration–aggression hypothesis: the view that frustration usually leads to aggression, and that aggression is caused by frustration.

situations involved unjustified frustration. Accordingly, Pastore (1952) produced different versions of these situations used by Doob and Sears (1939) involving justified frustration. For example, the situation with the non-stopping bus was rewritten to indicate that the bus was out of service. As predicted, Pastore (1952) found that justified frustration led to much lower levels of anger than did unjustified frustration.

Situational factors. Evidence that aggressive behaviour does not always stem from frustration was reported by Zimbardo (1973). In his Stanford prison experiment (see Chapter 21), the mock prisoners did less and less to frustrate the wishes of the mock warders. However, the mock warders behaved in an increasingly aggressive way against them. In times of war, soldiers often behave aggressively towards the enemy because they are ordered to do so rather than because they are frustrated.

What would happen to soldiers if they did not behave aggressively?

Environmental cues. Berkowitz and LePage (1967) argued that aggressive behaviour does not depend only on frustration. The presence in the environment of aggressive cues also plays a part in making people behave aggressively, and this notion was tested by Berkowitz and LePage. Male university students received electric shocks from another student, who was a confederate working for the experimenter. They were then given the chance to give electric shocks to the confederate. In one condition, a revolver and a shotgun were close to the shock machine. In another condition, nothing was placed nearby. The presence of the guns increased the average number of shocks that were given from 4.67 to 6.07. This is known as the **weapons effect**. According to Berkowitz (1968, p.22):

> *Guns not only permit violence, they can stimulate it as well. The finger pulls the trigger, but the trigger may also be pulling the finger.*

Could the demand characteristics of Berkowitz's laboratory situation have led participants to guess the true purpose of the study?

We need to consider a potential problem with the interpretation of the weapons effect. The presence of the guns may lead the participants to assume that the experimenter wants them to behave in an aggressive way. If so, then only those participants who were suspicious of the experimenter's intentions would show the weapons effect. In fact, the evidence indicates that suspicious participants do *not* show the weapons effect. This suggests that Berkowitz's interpretation of the weapons effect is probably correct.

Cognitive-neoassociation. Berkowitz (1989) revised the frustration–aggression hypothesis in his cognitive-neoassociationistic approach. He argued that an aversive or unpleasant event causes negative affect or emotion (e.g. anxiety; anger). This negative affect activates tendencies towards aggression and towards flight. The behaviour we actually display depends on our interpretation of the situation. Suppose someone knocks into you as you are walking along the pavement. This may cause negative feelings and a tendency towards behaving in an aggressive way. However, if you realise that it was a blind person who knocked into you, your aggressive tendencies are likely to be replaced by feelings of guilt.

According to Berkowitz's (1989) theory, a frustrating situation is one example (but not the only one) of an aversive event. In similar fashion, behaving in an aggressive way is only one of several ways of responding to frustration. This theory is vaguer than the original frustration–aggression hypothesis. However, it is more reasonable than the frustration–aggression hypothesis, and more in line with the available evidence.

Evaluation

The frustration–aggression hypothesis is an advance on the ethological approach, because it considers one of the external conditions (i.e. frustrating situations) causing aggression. The frustration–aggression hypothesis has been turned into a more adequate theory by Berkowitz in his cognitive-neoassociationistic approach. He emphasised the importance of aggressive cues, and the variety of possible responses to frustration.

On the negative side, the frustration–aggression hypothesis is oversimplified. Aggression is much more likely to occur in response to unjustified than justified frustration. Aggression is not always caused by frustration, as can be seen in wartime.

Negative affect escape model

According to Baron's (1977) negative affect escape model, unpleasant stimuli (e.g. noise; heat) usually increase aggressive behaviour, because it provides a way of reducing the negative affect. However, if the unpleasant stimuli become very intense, then there is often less aggressive behaviour as people try to escape or simply become passive.

The findings of Baron and Bell (1976) support the negative affect escape model. They studied the effects of heat on aggression by seeing how willing participants were to give electric shocks to another person. Temperatures within the range 92–95°F (33–35°C) generally increased the level of aggression. However, extreme heat led to a reduced level of aggression towards another person who had provided a negative evaluation of the participant. In those conditions, the participants were very stressed. If they gave shocks to the other person, they would have had to deal with that person's angry reactions, and they felt unable to deal with the added stress.

Other evidence does not support the notion that aggressive behaviour declines when the heat becomes extreme. Anderson (1989) considered the effects of temperature on various forms of aggressive behaviour, such as assault, rape, and murder. There was a steady increase in all of these aggressive acts as the temperature rose, with no indication of any reduction in extreme heat.

Compare the negative affect escape model with the negative-state relief model described earlier.

Do you think using electric shocks in a laboratory is an effective way to model what happens in real life?

Evaluation

It is not known why laboratory tests of the model tend to support it, whereas data from real-life situations do not. One possibility is that it may be easier to escape from unpleasant stimuli in the laboratory than in real life. Another possibility is that provoking stimuli in real life can be much more intense than in the laboratory. As a result, the high levels of negative affect generated by heat or noise are more likely to trigger aggressive behaviour in real life.

Excitation-transfer theory

Zillmann (e.g. 1979) developed an excitation-transfer theory, according to which arousal caused by one stimulus can be transferred and added to the arousal produced by a second stimulus. What is important in determining the emotional reaction to the second stimulus is the way in which the transferred arousal is interpreted. For example, suppose that someone insults you on a very hot day. You might normally ignore the insult. However, because the hot weather has made you more aroused, you may become very aggressive. According to the theory, however, this should *only* happen if you attribute your aroused state to being insulted rather than to the temperature. The notion that the interpretation given to one's arousal level is important resembles the theoretical approach of Schachter and Singer (1962) in their two-factor theory of emotion (see Chapter 6).

The best way to see what is involved in excitation-transfer theory is to consider an experimental example of excitation transfer. In a study by Zillmann, Johnson, and Day (1974), male participants were provoked by a confederate of the experimenter. Half of the participants rested for 6 minutes and then pedalled on a cycling machine for 90 seconds, whereas the other half pedalled first and then rested. Immediately afterwards, all of the participants had the chance to choose the level of shock to be given to the person who had provoked them.

What do you think happened? Zillmann et al. predicted that participants who had just finished cycling would attribute their arousal to the cycling, and so would not behave aggressively towards their provoker. In contrast, those who had just rested for 6 minutes would attribute their arousal to the provocation, and

Why do you think there is increased aggression in situations like the one in the photograph?

KEY STUDY EVALUATION — Zillmann

Like many social psychology experiments, Zillmann's study raises some ethical issues. If participants do not know the true nature of the study, can they give informed consent to take part? Would it be possible to run the experiment if the participants knew of its true intention beforehand? Would those who behaved more aggressively and were prepared to give strong "shocks" have problems later dealing with this probably unwelcome self-knowledge?

so would behave aggressively by delivering a strong electric shock. The results were in line with these predictions.

Discussion points

1. Do you think that excitation transfer happens often in everyday life?
2. Consider ways in which people's attributions of the cause of their arousal could be manipulated.

Evaluation

Unexplained arousal can lead to increased anger and aggression in the way predicted by excitation-transfer theory. However, the theory is rather limited. In real life, we generally know *why* we are aroused, and the theory does not apply to such situations.

Social learning theory

One of the most influential approaches to aggression is the social learning theory approach put forward by Albert Bandura (e.g. 1973). According to this approach, most behaviour (including aggressive behaviour) is learned. In the words of Bandura (1973):

> *The specific forms that aggressive behaviour takes, the frequency with which it is displayed, and the specific targets selected for attack are largely determined by social learning factors.*

Bandura

In Bandura's study the model appeared on a film. What models, apart from those in the media, are children often exposed to?

According to Bandura's theory, observational learning or modelling is of great importance in producing aggressive behaviour. **Observational learning** is a form of learning in which the behaviour of others is imitated or copied. Bandura, Ross, and Ross (1963) carried out a classic study on observational learning or modelling. Young children were shown one of two films. One film showed a female adult model behaving in an aggressive way towards a "Bobo doll". The other film showed the adult model behaving non-aggressively. Those children who had seen the model behave aggressively were much more likely to attack the Bobo doll than were those who had watched the non-aggressive model.

Bandura (1965) carried out another study on aggressive behaviour towards the Bobo doll. One group of children simply saw a film of an adult model kicking and punching the Bobo doll. A second group saw the same aggressive behaviour performed by the adult model, but this time the model was rewarded by another adult for his aggressive behaviour by being given sweets and a drink. A third group saw the same aggressive behaviour, but the model was punished by another adult, who warned him not to be aggressive in future.

Those children who had seen the model rewarded, and those who had seen the model neither rewarded nor punished, behaved much more aggressively towards the Bobo doll than did those who had seen the model punished. It could be argued that the children who had seen the model being punished remembered less about the model's behaviour than did the other groups of children. However, this was shown not to be the case by Bandura. All the children were rewarded for imitating as much of the model's aggressive behaviour as they could remember. All three groups showed the same good ability to reproduce the model's aggressive behaviour. Thus, the children in all three groups showed comparable levels of observational learning, but those who had seen the model punished were least likely to apply this learning to their own behaviour.

KEY STUDY EVALUATION — Bandura

In his classic Bobo doll study, Bandura controlled the behaviour of his adult models. They used novel actions such as hitting the doll with a hammer, or throwing it in the air and saying "Pow! Boom!". These actions were chosen because the children would be unlikely to behave like this spontaneously, so that if the actions were produced, the researchers could be fairly confident that the children were imitating the adult model.

Discussion points

1. What are some of the limitations of this famous research by Bandura (see Evaluation)?
2. How important do you think observational learning is with respect to producing aggressive behaviour?

KEY TERM

Observational learning: a form of learning emphasised by Bandura based on observing and imitating the actions of a model.

Evaluation

Bandura's social learning approach is an important one. Much aggressive behaviour is learned, and observational learning or modelling is often involved. It has been found that children who watch violent programmes on television are more likely to behave in an aggressive way. These studies (discussed later in the chapter) are consistent with social learning theory.

In spite of the successes of social learning theory, there are reasons for arguing that Bandura exaggerated the extent to which children imitate the behaviour of models. Children are very likely to imitate aggressive behaviour towards a doll, but they are much less likely to imitate aggressive behaviour towards another child. Bandura consistently failed to distinguish between real aggression and playfighting, and it is likely that much of the aggressive behaviour observed by Bandura was only playfighting (Durkin, 1995). The Bobo doll is of interest to young children, because it has a weighted base and so bounces back up when it is knocked down. Its novelty value is important in determining its effectiveness. Cumberbatch (1990) reported that children who were unfamiliar with the doll were five times more likely to imitate aggressive behaviour against it than were children who had played with it before. Finally, there are the **demand characteristics**, which are the cues used by participants to work out what a study is about. As Durkin (1995, p.406) pointed out:

> *Where else in life does a 5-year-old find a powerful adult actually showing you how to knock hell out of a dummy and then giving you the opportunity to try it out yourself?*

Bandura's approach is limited in scope. Aggressive behaviour does not depend only on observational learning. People's internal emotional state, their interpretation of the current situation, and their personality are other important factors that need to be taken into account.

Social constructionism

Most of the theories of aggression we have considered so far are based on the assumption that it is fairly easy to decide whether someone is behaving in an aggressive way. However, social constructionists such as Gergen (1997) argue that matters are more complex than that. According to them, we impose subjective interpretations or constructions on the world around us. An example of people interpreting events in different ways can be seen at almost any football game. Tackles that seem like cynical

To one team this looks like a foul; to the other, a justifiable defensive manoeuvre.

Can you think of any recent news items that could be interpreted in different ways according to which side a person supported?

Are there examples of situations in which the norm of reciprocity does not apply?

fouls deserving a sending-off to the supporters of one team are regarded as perfectly fair by the supporters of the other team.

The social constructionist approach as applied to aggression is based on a number of assumptions:

1. Aggressive behaviour is a form of social behaviour, and it is not simply an expression of anger; according to Gergen (1997, p.124), "emotional expressions [of anger] are extended forms of interchange, somewhat like cultural dances."
2. Our interpretation or construction of someone else's behaviour as aggressive or non-aggressive depends on our beliefs and knowledge.
3. Our decision whether to behave aggressively or non-aggressively depends on how we interpret the other person's behaviour towards us.

The first assumption is supported by numerous cases in which an individual behaves aggressively towards someone else some time after being angered by that person. For example, in the days (thankfully past!) when teachers used to cane their students, the caning would often take place days after the student had behaved badly.

The second assumption is supported by the work of Blumenthal et al. (1972). They studied the attitudes of American men towards police and student behaviour during student demonstrations. Students with negative attitudes towards the police judged the behaviour of the police to be violent, whereas the sit-ins and other actions of the students were regarded as non-violent. In contrast, men with positive attitudes to the police did not regard their assaults on students or their use of firearms as violent. However, they condemned student sit-ins as violent acts deserving arrest.

The study by Blumenthal et al. indicates that aggression is not simply a descriptive concept. It is also an evaluative concept, in that our judgement that someone is behaving aggressively depends on the constructions we place on their behaviour. How do we decide whether someone is behaving aggressively? According to Ferguson and Rule (1983), there are three main criteria:

- Actual harm.
- Intention to harm.
- Norm violation, when the behaviour is perceived as illegitimate and against society's norms.

The norm of reciprocity is of particular importance in deciding whether an act is aggressive. According to the **norm of reciprocity**, if someone has done something to you, then you are justified in behaving in the same way to that person. Evidence that the norm of reciprocity applies to aggressive behaviour was reported by Brown and Tedeschi (1976). Someone who initiated a hostile act against another person was seen as aggressive and unfair. In contrast, someone who attacked another person after having been provoked was regarded as behaving fairly and non-aggressively.

The third assumption of the constructionist approach, that we decide whether to behave aggressively towards someone on the basis of our interpretation of their behaviour, was supported in a study by Ohbuchi and Kambara (1985). They studied how people reacted when harm was done to them. People were more likely to retaliate when they believed that the other person intended to hurt them than when they thought that the other person did not realise the pain he or she had caused.

Support for the third assumption in real-life situations was reported by Marsh et al. (1978). They studied violent attacks by students in schools, and found that these attacks were neither random nor spontaneous. The attacks generally occurred in classes with less effective teachers, because the students interpreted this as a sign that the school authorities had written them off. This interpretation (although mistaken) produced anger and aggression.

Evaluation

One of the most valuable aspects of the constructionist approach is the notion that our interpretation or construction of situations and people's behaviour determines our

KEY TERM

Norm of reciprocity: the cultural expectation that it is justified to treat others in the way they treat you.

responses. Such interpretations or constructions depend on our attitudes and beliefs. Thus, we need to distinguish between what actually happens in social situations, and the way in which what happens is perceived and interpreted.

On the negative side, social constructionists seem to exaggerate the differences between different individuals' constructions of what has happened. There are many cases in which nearly everyone would agree that someone is behaving aggressively, for example, if a defenceless old woman is suddenly attacked by a mugger and her handbag is stolen. Some social constructionists such as Gergen go so far as to argue that there is no objective reality at all. According to Gergen (1997, p.119):

Research findings don't have any meaning until they are interpreted, and these interpretations are not demanded by the findings themselves. They result from a process of negotiating meaning within the community.

Most psychologists assume there is an objective reality, which limits or constrains our social constructions. If this assumption is incorrect, then there is no way of deciding whether social constructions are valid or invalid. In that case, the scientific approach to human behaviour is probably doomed to failure (see Chapter 28). Many social constructionists seem to accept that conclusion. According to Burr (1997, p.10):

The criterion of good research [for social constructionists] becomes not whether it describes the truth about people but whether it is enabling [power providing] for them. This abandonment of objectivity as the keystone of psychological science is celebrated by social constructionists.

Episodes of road rage may result when one driver makes the assumption that another has been deliberately aggressive. In fact, the apparently aggressive driver could be lost, in the wrong lane, driving an unfamiliar car, or in the middle of a row with a passenger, and the offensive behaviour could be completely unintentional.

Reducing and Controlling Aggressive Behaviour

There is evidence from crime figures that mugging, rape, and other violent crimes are much more common now than they were a few years ago. This means that it is very important to find effective ways of reducing and controlling aggressive behaviour. Several solutions have been proposed, some of which are considered next.

Catharsis

According to Freud's psychodynamic theory, aggressive energy builds up inside people until it is released in behaviour. It follows that it is better for people to find harmless ways of acting aggressively (e.g. playing sport) rather than allow their aggressive energy to increase to the level at which they become violent. This view is known as the catharsis ("letting off steam") hypothesis.

Most of the evidence does not support the catharsis hypothesis. Indeed, many findings are exactly the opposite of what would be predicted by that hypothesis. Walters and Brown (1963) allowed some children to hit, kick, and punch an inflatable doll to reduce their aggression, whereas other children were not allowed to do so. After that, those who had attacked the doll were much more likely than the other children to behave in an aggressive way towards their classmates.

Another instance when catharsis failed to occur was reported by Mallick and McCandless (1966). Two groups of nine-year-old boys were asked to build a house of bricks to win a prize. One group was prevented from doing this by a disruptive boy, whereas the other group was not. Then some of the boys shot at targets of people and animals, which might be expected to produce catharsis. Finally, all the boys had the chance to give electric shocks to the disruptive boy (no shocks were actually given). Shooting at targets had no effect on aggressive behaviour in terms of shocks given.

Apart from playing sport, what other safe releases for aggression are there?

Do you think that watching a violent film or a boxing match would be cathartic (releasing feelings of aggression)?

Ethical issues: Would Mallick and McCandless's study be considered ethical today?

Incompatible responses

Baron (1977) argued that anger and aggressive behaviour can be reduced by persuading the individual to produce incompatible feelings or responses. He showed the value of this notion in a study in which a confederate of the experimenter tried to cause anger in male motorists by stopping at traffic lights for 15 seconds after they had turned green. Under normal circumstances, 90% of the motorists honked their horns. However, when a female confederate of the experimenter crossed the road wearing a clown mask, only 50% of motorists honked, and the figure fell to 47% when the female confederate crossed the road wearing very revealing clothes.

It is sometimes possible to reduce aggression by inducing incompatible responses. However, this approach is most likely to be successful when someone is experiencing only a small amount of anger, as when held up at traffic lights. It would not be effective if someone were extremely angry, perhaps because their partner had been unfaithful to them.

Punishment

There has been much controversy about the effectiveness of punishment as a way of changing people's behaviour. In one of the most thorough studies, Patterson (1982) seemed to find that punishment was not very effective at all in reducing aggression in children. He studied what happened in the homes of very aggressive boys aged between 3 and 13, as well as what happened in the homes of non-aggressive boys. Punishment and aggression by the parents were more common in the homes of the aggressive boys. The parents of aggressive boys punished their children more often than the parents of non-aggressive boys punished their children, even when the children were well behaved.

There are two main reasons why Patterson obtained the findings he did. First, boys whose parents punish them a lot model their parents' aggressive behaviour in the way assumed by social learning theorists. Second, parents who have a badly behaved and aggressive boy are more likely to punish him than are the parents of a non-aggressive boy.

Discussion points

1. Why is punishment often ineffective in reducing aggressive behaviour?
2. In what circumstances may punishment lead to a reduction in aggression (see next)?

What sort of punishment do you think might be effective in this situation?

Baron (1973) found that the threat of punishment was more effective in reducing aggression when someone was mildly rather than strongly provoked. He allowed male students to give electric shocks to another man who had provoked them either mildly or strongly. Before they did so, they were told that there was a low, moderate, or high probability that this other person would later have the chance to get his own back by giving shocks to them. Those who had been mildly provoked gave much weaker shocks when they thought there was a high probability of retaliation than when the probability was low. In contrast, those who had been strongly provoked gave fairly powerful shocks regardless of the chances of being shocked themselves.

In general, the evidence indicates that punishment is sometimes very effective and sometimes totally ineffective. Baron (1977) has identified some of the requirements for punishment to reduce aggressive behaviour:

1. There should be a very short interval between the aggressive action and the punishment.
2. Punishment should be relatively strong.

3. Punishment should be applied consistently and predictably.
4. The person giving the punishment should not be seen as an aggressive model.
5. The person receiving punishment should understand clearly why he or she is being punished.

Basing your answers on Baron's five requirements, how might you advise a parent on punishing their child for aggressive behaviour?

Modelling

We saw earlier in the chapter that aggressive behaviour can be increased by exposing individuals to others behaving in an aggressive way. According to Bandura (1973), this is an example of the general tendency to imitate or model the actions of others. If so, then exposure to non-aggressive models should reduce aggressive behaviour. This was found by Baron and Kepner (1970). Participants watched someone in the role of a teacher behave in an aggressive or a non-aggressive way towards a learner. When it was their turn to play the role of teacher, the participants imitated the aggressive or non-aggressive behaviour of the model they had observed. However, Bandura did not distinguish clearly between genuine aggression and pretend fighting, and it seems that much of the children's so-called aggressive behaviour was actually only pretend fighting (Durkin, 1995).

It is certainly the case that people often imitate or model the behaviour of others, especially those who seem similar to the observer. However, behaviour that is successful is more likely to be imitated than behaviour that is unsuccessful. For example, if a model is not rewarded for behaving non-aggressively, then observers will not imitate his or her behaviour. One of the limitations with the modelling approach is that it teaches observers specific ways of behaving in specific situations. As a result, they may not behave in the appropriate non-aggressive way in new situations.

Social skills training

People often behave aggressively because they do not have the social skills that would allow them to handle social situations in non-aggressive ways. For example, offering an apology can often reduce the hostility of others and prevent a fight from starting. Guerra and Slaby (1990) gave male and female juvenile delinquents 12 sessions of social skills training. This training covered various activities, such as role-playing non-aggressive behaviour, modelling the pro-social behaviour of others, and working out non-aggressive ways of resolving conflict. The training was successful, in that the delinquents became significantly less aggressive in their behaviour, and they believed less strongly in the value of aggression.

Zahavi and Asher (1978) argued that aggressive children tend to focus on the wrongs that another person has done to them, whereas non-aggressive children focus more on the feelings and thoughts of the other person. In other words, non-aggressive children have more empathy or understanding of others. They

When aggression is not met with aggression, a fight may be avoided.

Approach	Methods of reducing aggressive behaviour
Catharsis	
Incompatible responses	
Punishment	
Modelling	
Social skills training	

■ Research activity: Prepare a table for each of the following situations:
(a) prison;
(b) classroom;
(c) football crowd.

developed a form of social skills training with poorly behaved preschool boys based on the attempt to increase their level of empathy. The boys were told that aggression often hurts other people, that it causes resentment, and that it makes other people unhappy. This social skills training produced a large reduction in aggressive behaviour and a substantial increase in desirable behaviour.

Media Influences on Behaviour

It has been calculated that the average 16-year-old in Western society has seen about 13,000 violent murders on television, and it seems reasonable to assume that this must have some effects on their behaviour. There is, indeed, a positive relationship between the amount of television violence children have seen and the aggressiveness of their behaviour. However, it is hard to interpret such correlational evidence. It may be that watching violent programmes causes aggressive behaviour. On the other hand, it may be that naturally aggressive children choose to watch more violent programmes than non-aggressive children.

Physical and verbal aggression

One of the more thorough studies was reported by Leyens et al. (1975). The participants were juvenile delinquents at a school in Belgium. They lived in four dormitories, two of which had high levels of aggressive behaviour and two of which had low levels. During a special Movie Week, boys in two of the dormitories (one high in aggression and the other low) watched only violent films, whereas boys in the other two dormitories watched only non-violent films.

Ethical issues: Can you see any ethical problems involved in the Leyens et al. study?

There was an increased level of physical aggression among the boys who saw the violent films, but not among those who saw the non-violent films. The findings were more complex for verbal aggression. This increased among boys in the aggressive dormitory who saw violent films, but it actually decreased among boys from the non-aggressive dormitory who saw violent films. A final finding was that the effects of the violent films on aggression were much stronger shortly after watching them

---

CASE STUDY: *Movie Violence*

Since its release in 1994, the film *Natural Born Killers* has been surrounded by controversy and has sparked a long-standing debate about the effect of viewing intense violence on the human mind. The film follows the story of Mickey and Mallory Knox, a young couple who go on a killing spree across America, claiming 52 lives at random. Their flippant attitude towards the crimes they commit is portrayed as exciting and thrilling by the media and as a result their murderous behaviour catches the imagination of a generation of young impressionable people who idolise them. The notion of admiring cold-blooded killers may seem to be far-fetched, but alarming similarities have emerged between the reaction to the fictional Mickey and Mallory and other real-life killers. *Natural Born Killers* has been linked to at least a dozen murders, including two cases in France where the defence has blamed the film as providing inspiration for the crime.

In October 1998 the French courts sentenced Florence Rey to 20 years in prison for her part in a shoot-out that left five people dead. She was committing the crime with her boyfriend, Audry Maupin, who was killed in the shoot-out. Publicity material from the film was found in the flat that Rey shared with her boyfriend at the time of the shootings. The press latched on to this and called the pair "France's Natural Born Killers", and as in the film the vulgarity of the multiple murder was lost and replaced by a glamorous image of rebellion that was both enticing and thrilling. Before long, young Parisians were wearing a picture of the convicted woman on their

T-shirts. This was the first time a real-life murderer had been idolised in public.

Stronger links between the film and a murder were discovered in the case of Véronique Herbert and her boyfriend Sébastian Paindavoine who lured their victim into a trap and then stabbed him to death. There was no motive for the attack and Herbert placed the blame on *Natural Born Killers*. She said, "The film coincided with my state of mind. Maybe I muddled up dream and reality. I wanted to eliminate someone, as if by magic … The idea of killing invaded me." In the light of such a testimony, can anyone deny the link between the sort of violence depicted in *Natural Born Killers* and Herbert and Paindavoine's gruesome act?

The pro-censorship lobby says the film and subsequent murders provide conclusive evidence that screen violence is rapidly translated into street violence. The image of killing, especially in a fictional world where the characters do not have to live with the consequences of their actions, can become a reality. Such allegations against a film cannot be dismissed and the controversy surrounding the subject matter has been fuelled by the similarities between Mickey and Mallory and the real-life murderers. However, there is an argument against censorship which states that *Natural Born Killers* was intended as a satire on the bloodlust of the media and American society and that it is society that should be held responsible for any acts of violence rather than the film itself.

than they were later on. A limitation of this study is that the experimenters did not distinguish clearly between real and pretend aggression.

Longitudinal research

Eron (1982) and Huesmann, Lagerspit, and Eron (1984) reported on a major longitudinal study. First of all, the amount of television watched and levels of aggressiveness were assessed in some young children. Then aggressiveness and the amount of television watched were reassessed in the same participants several years later. One of the key findings was that the amount of television violence watched at a young age predicted the level of later aggressiveness (measured by the number of criminal convictions by the age of 30). This suggests that watching television violence may be one of the causes of aggressive behaviour. In addition, there was evidence that children who were aggressive when young tended to watch more violent television programmes several years later. This suggests that more aggressive individuals choose to watch more violent television programmes.

Absence of television

So far we have considered only studies in which television violence led to increased aggression. However, several studies have found no effect of television on aggression. Of particular interest is evidence obtained in the United States during the early 1950s. The Federal Communications Commission refused to issue any new television licences between the end of 1949 and the middle of 1952. As a result, television arrived in some parts of the United States two or three years before others. According to FBI crime statistics, the level of violent crime was not greater in those areas that had television than in those that did not. Furthermore, the introduction of television into an area did not lead to an increase in violent crime. However, the introduction of television was followed by an increase in the number of thefts (Hennigan et al., 1982). This may have occurred because the advertisements on television made many people more determined to acquire material possessions.

A similar study has recently been carried out on St Helena in the south Atlantic, which is best known for the fact that Napoleon spent the last few years of his life there. Its inhabitants received television for the first time in 1995, but there is no evidence of any adverse effects on the children. According to Charlton (1998):

> *The argument that watching violent television turns youngsters to violence is not borne out, and this study on St. Helena is the clearest proof yet. The children have watched the same amounts of violence, and in many cases the same programmes, as British children. But they have not gone out and copied what they have seen on TV.*

Some of the evidence consisted of secret videoing of the children playing at school. Charlton reported that "Bad behaviour is virtually unheard of in the playground, and our footage shows that what is viewed is not repeated." What are the factors preventing television violence from influencing the children of St Helena? According to Charlton (1998): "The main ones are that children are in stable home, school and community situations. This is why the children on St Helena appear to be immune to what they are watching."

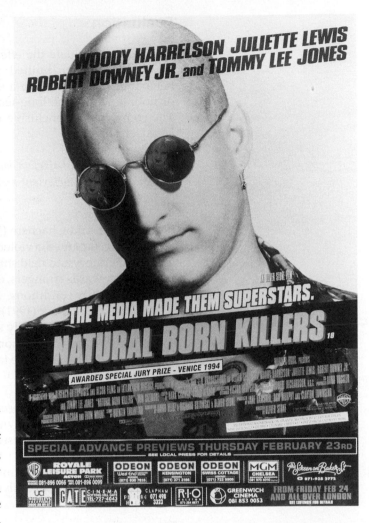

The question of whether or not violence depicted in films and on TV leads to violent behaviour is often discussed and was hotly debated in relation to the Oliver Stone film *Natural Born Killers*. The film itself looks at media focus on violence and how it can be glamorised.

What characters in television programmes do children imitate today? Does such imitation always have negative effects?

Evaluation

It is hard to evaluate the effects of television violence on aggressive behaviour. Many of the studies are limited in scope, focusing only on the short-term effects on behaviour of exposure to a single violent programme. Such studies can tell us little or nothing about the long-term effects of prolonged exposure to violent programmes. The somewhat inconclusive nature of the evidence was summarised by Gunter and McAleer (1990) as

> *the measurement of television's effects ... is highly complex ... we are still a long way from knowing fully the extent and character of television's influence on children's aggressive behaviour.*

Wood, Wong, and Chachere (1991) reviewed 28 laboratory and field studies concerned with the effects of media violence on aggression in children and adolescents. It was found in both laboratory and field studies that exposure to media violence led to more aggressive behaviour towards strangers, classmates, and friends. In general, the effects were stronger under laboratory conditions.

Comstock and Paik (1991) reviewed more than 1000 findings on the effects of media violence. There are generally strong short-term effects, especially with respect to minor acts of aggression. In addition, there seem to be rather weaker long-term effects. They concluded that there are five factors that tend to increase the effects of media violence on aggression:

Bearing in mind Comstock and Paik's five factors, what advice would you give to film makers who do not wish to provoke aggression in their audiences?

1. Violent behaviour is presented as being an efficient way to get what one wants.
2. The person who is behaving violently is portrayed as similar to the viewer.
3. Violent behaviour is presented in a realistic way rather than, for example, in cartoon form.
4. The suffering of the victims of violence is not shown.
5. The viewer is emotionally excited while watching the violent behaviour.

Theoretical accounts

What are some of the possible reasons why aggression might be increased by watching violent television programmes?

Observational learning

According to Bandura's social learning theory, one of the factors is observational learning or modelling. We learn ways of behaving aggressively from observing people on television behaving violently, and this behaviour may be imitated subsequently.

Children are exposed to violent images at an early age and often incorporate them into their play. How well do they distinguish between a play scenario and how they behave in real life?

Reduced responsiveness

As Franzoi (1996) pointed out, another possibility is that we gradually become less responsive to, and emotionally concerned by, acts of violence, because we have seen so many on television. In a study by Thomas et al. (1977), two groups of children watched a videotape of young children behaving aggressively. Their physiological reactions to this videotape were recorded. Those children who had seen a television programme containing much violence just before watching the videotape became less aroused physiologically than did those who had just watched a programme containing no violence. Such reduced responsiveness may be associated with an increased acceptance of violent behaviour.

Cognitive priming

Another reason why media violence may play a part in producing aggressive behaviour is because of *cognitive priming*. The basic idea is that the aggressive cues presented in violent television programmes lead to aggressive thoughts and feelings. When college students were asked to write down their thoughts while watching violent films (e.g. *The French Connection*), they reported numerous aggressive thoughts, increased anger, and a high level of physiological arousal.

Some of the most convincing evidence for the importance of cognitive priming was reported by Josephson (1987). Some Canadian boys were shown a television programme involving violence in the form of a gun battle, in which the snipers communicated with each other by means of walkie-talkies. The other boys watched a non-violent programme about a motorcross team. After they had watched the television programme, all of the boys played floor hockey. Before the game started, the referee gave the boys instructions either by walkie-talkie or in a tape recording. The boys who watched the violent progamme and received instructions by walkie-talkie were more aggressive during the hockey game than were the boys who had watched the same programme but received instructions by tape recording. Thus, the walkie-talkie acted as a cognitive prime or cue to aggression.

Cross-cultural differences

Nearly all research on the effects of media violence has been carried out in the United States or the United Kingdom. As a result, we do not really know whether the findings would be the same in other cultures. One of the few cross-cultural studies was carried out by Huesmann and Eron (1986). They tested children and parents over a period of three years in Finland, Israel, Poland, and Australia. In the first three countries, the amount of television violence that young children had seen predicted their subsequent level of aggression, even when their initial level of aggressiveness was controlled for statistically. However, these findings were not obtained with Australian children. The overall findings suggest that media violence increases aggressive behaviour in most countries.

Even quite small children can show concern when they see others are unhappy.

What sort of physiological reaction does aggression, or seeing aggression, produce?

P E R S O N A L   R E F L E C T I O N S

- In my opinion, many of the studies on altruism and empathy are very artificial, and so their findings may not apply to the real world. For example, would you believe that a drug could fix your mood and prevent it being altered?
- There is good evidence that people in collectivistic societies show much more consideration for others than is the case in individualistic societies. It has generally been assumed that this means that those living in collectivistic societies are more altruistic than those living in individualistic societies. However, Fijneman et al. (1996) found that those living in collectivistic societies expect more help from others than do those living in individualistic societies. As a result, collectivistic and individualistic societies are similar, in that individuals expect to give only a little more help than they expect to receive. It is an interesting question whether this means that people living in collectivistic societies are *not* really altruistic.

S U M M A R Y

The growth of empathy seems to be a major factor in the development of pro-social behaviour in children. According to the empathy–altruism hypothesis, altruistic or unselfish behaviour in adults is motivated mainly by empathy. However, it is hard to know whether people help others for altruistic reasons rather than to avoid feelings of guilt or the disapproval of others. According to the negative-state relief model, people help a victim because they want to reduce the sadness produced by empathic concern. In

Altruism and empathy

general, children in industrialised societies are less altruistic in their behaviour than those in non-industrialised societies. Altruistic behaviour can be encouraged by observational learning or by offering rewards for helping.

Bystander intervention

Bystanders are often less likely to help a victim if there are many other bystanders, because there is a diffusion of responsibility. The chances that bystanders will help also depend on how they interpret the situation, the characteristics of the victim, their expertise and personality, the perceived similarity between the bystanders and the victim, and the importance of the activity that the bystanders were involved in just before the emergency. In general, whether or not bystanders assist a victim depends on the rewards and costs of helping versus not helping.

Aggression

According to the frustration–aggression hypothesis, frustration always produces aggression, and aggression always depends on frustration. This hypothesis is over-simplified, and has been modified by Berkowitz. He argued that an aversive or unpleasant event causes negative feelings which activate tendencies towards aggression and flight. How we then behave depends on our interpretation of the situation. According to the negative affect escape model, unpleasant stimuli usually increase aggressive behaviour, because it provides a way of reducing the negative affect. However, if the negative stimuli become very intense, there is often less aggressive behaviour as people try to escape or simply become passive. According to excitation-transfer theory, unexplained arousal can increase feelings of anger and aggressive behaviour. According to Bandura's social learning approach, aggressive behaviour is learned via observational learning or modelling. This approach de-emphasises the importance of people's internal state, their personality, and their interpretation of the situation. According to social constructionists, our judgement of whether someone is behaving aggressively depends in part on our evaluation of that person (e.g. his or her intentions).

Several ways of reducing and controlling aggressive behaviour have been proposed. Catharsis or letting off steam does not seem to be effective. Persuading the aggressive individual to produce incompatible responses can be useful if the levels of anger and aggression are low. Punishment can be very effective if there is a short interval between the aggressive act and punishment, if the punishment is fairly strong, and if punishment is applied consistently, and if the person being punished understands why he or she is being punished. Other useful approaches include modelling non-aggressive behaviour, and social skills training, in which aggressive individuals learn how to handle social situations in non-aggressive ways.

Reducing and controlling aggressive behaviour

There have been several studies in which it was found that television violence led to increased aggression, but several others in which no effects were observed. In general terms, there are clearer short-term effects of television violence than long-term effects. Aggression may be increased by watching violent programmes for various reasons: observational learning; storage of violence-related information in long-term memory; and reduced responsiveness to violence. Pro-social television programmes generally lead to at least a short-term increase in helping behaviour. This may be due at least in part to observational learning or modelling.

Media influences on behaviour

FURTHER READING

Chapters 13 and 14 in M. Hewstone, W. Stroebe, and G.M. Stephenson (1996), *Introduction to social psychology (2nd Edn.)*, Oxford: Blackwell, provide up-to-date coverage of most of the topics discussed in this chapter. Chapters 11 and 12 in S.L. Franzoi (1996), *Social psychology*, Chicago: Brown & Benchmark, deal with aggression and pro-social behaviour in detail and in an accessible way. Another useful reference is N. Hayes (1993), *Principles of social psychology*, Hove, UK: Psychology Press.

REVISION QUESTIONS

1   Describe and evaluate *two* explanations of altruistic behaviour.   (24 marks)

2   Critically consider the extent to which social psychological theories offer an adequate explanation of aggression.   (24 marks)

3   Discuss what the implications of psychological research are for the reduction *and/or* control of aggression.   (24 marks)

4   "Visitors from Mars might well be forgiven for believing that we have only just discovered media violence ... [but] there has been a long history of moral panics about the harmful effects of popular culture, such as comics and popular theatre in the nineteenth century, followed by the cinema, television, video and computer games. These panics are largely fuelled by the popular press and the claim that things are getting worse ... In this field it is all too easy to scaremonger" (Cumberbatch, 1997). Critically consider whether or not research evidence supports the case for media exerting an influence on anti-social behaviour.   (24 marks)

5   Critically consider what insights psychological research has given us into individual, social, or cultural diversity in pro-social behaviour.   (24 marks)

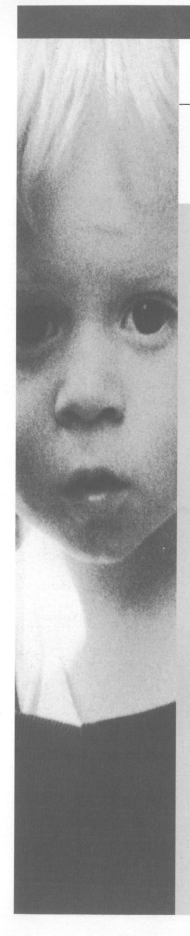

- **Learning difficulties**
  Causes and effects of many forms of learning difficulties.

  DSM-IV definitions
  Genetic and environmental factors
  Academic and social effects

- **Physical and sensory impairments**
  The challenges of blindness, deafness, and cerebral palsy.

  Preisler's longitudinal study of blind children
  Studies of deaf children (e.g. Marschark)
  Peto and Rood's treatment approach to cerebral palsy

- **Attention-deficit hyperactivity disorder**
  When does having lots of energy become a medical problem?

  Definition and possible causes of ADHD
  Problems of diagnosis
  Effects

- **Autism**
  Some children and adults cannot relate to or communicate successfully with other people.

  Kanner's definition of autism
  Butterworth and Jarrett's gaze pattern study
  Diagnosis and causes
  Leslie's theory of mind approach

- **Developmental dyslexia**
  Normally intelligent people sometimes have problems with reading and writing.

  Miles's definition of developmental dyslexia
  The phonological deficit hypothesis
  Causes
  Shaywitz's computer-based therapy

23
Atypical Development

Children differ considerably in their rate of development, with some developing much more quickly than others at the social and cognitive levels. However, it still makes sense to think in terms of stages of development that most children go through at about the same ages (see Chapters 16 and 17). Such stage theories are of less relevance to those children who, for a variety of reasons, are likely to find it harder than their peers to develop at the normal rate. Some of the main categories of such children are as follows:

- Children with learning difficulties, whose general level of intelligence is substantially below average; they are classified by the DSM-IV as having mental retardation (see next section).
- Children with physical and sensory impairments, including those who are blind or deaf or suffering from cerebral palsy.
- Children with emotional and behavioural problems, including attention-deficit hyperactivity disorder, autism, and developmental dyslexia.

Ethical issues: These categories are specific to intellectual, physical, or emotional impairment. What are some of the ethical problems associated with categorising a child in this way?

Some of these groups of children apparently have *specific* impairments or problems, and so it might be thought that their development would be normal in most other respects. As we will see, that tends not to be the case. In fact, most of these groups of children experience severe social, emotional, and cognitive problems. Thus, their development is slow and atypical *in general*.

There are many well-known and successful adults who have coped with one or other of the conditions discussed in this chapter. For example, the Labour MP David Blunkett has had to overcome the problems of blindness, and Jackie Stewart, Michael Heseltine, and Susannah York are among those whose dyslexia has not prevented them from rising to the top of their professions. Barlow and Durand (1995) discussed a 12-year-old American boy called Timothy whose parents moved from China who suffered from autism. In spite of having autistic disorder, he was a gifted violin and piano player.

Those who have any form of disability have to cope with a considerable amount of prejudice from other people. Knight (1998) reported findings showing that nearly one-third of people think that those who are disabled have below-average intelligence. According to Knight, "What we have is an underbelly of, at best, studied indifference and, at worst, active dislocation by wider society from the community of disabled people."

Learning Difficulties

Children who have general learning difficulties are often classified as being "mentally retarded". **Mental retardation** has been defined in various ways, but we will focus on the criteria included in DSM-IV. DSM is short for Diagnostic and Statistical Manual of Mental Disorders, and the fourth version of it was published in 1994. It is produced by the American Psychiatric Association, and is designed to provide an adequate system for classifying mental disorder. It should be noted that the term learning difficulties is in many ways preferable to mental retardation. However, mental retardation will be used here when referring to DSM-IV, because that is the term used there.

Mental retardation is included on Axis II in DSM-IV, meaning that it tends to be long-lasting and hard to treat. The main criterion is an IQ of 70 or less, with four degrees of mental retardation being identified on the basis of the level of intellectual impairment:

Why do you think the term "learning difficulties" is preferable to "mental retardation"?

- Mild mental retardation: IQ level 50–55 up to about 70.
- Moderate mental retardation: IQ level 35–40 up to 50–55.
- Severe mental retardation: IQ level 20–25 up to 35–40.
- Profound mental retardation: IQ level below 20 or 25.

■ Research activity: Labelling

The treatment of people with physical and mental disabilities remains a social issue because of what Knight (1998) refers to as "studied indifference" or "active dislocation". Make a list of disabilities and ailments, in no particular order, e.g. arthritis, Down's syndrome, deafness, schizophrenia. In pairs, choose the name of one of these conditions and list all the characteristics you associate with it. Without revealing the name of the condition to the group, each pair should read out their list of characteristics.

1   How quickly do other members of the group identify the condition?
2   How similar are the words used for different conditions?
3   Does the exercise show that we have an indiscriminate tendency to underrate the intellectual and physical capabilities of disabled individuals, regardless of their disability?
4   What is "labelling" and what are its social consequences?

The level of intellectual functioning in infants is assessed by clinical judgement. For children beyond infancy, it is usually assessed by means of an individually administered intelligence test.

There are two other criteria for mental retardation incorporated in DSM-IV. First, there should be deficits or impairments in present adaptive functioning (ability to match the standards expected of children of that age in that culture) in at least two of the following areas: communication; self-care; home living; social/interpersonal skills; use of community resources; self-direction; functional academic skills; work; leisure; health; and safety. Second, the onset of impaired intellectual functioning should be before the age of 18 years. This criterion excludes people who suffer extensive brain damage in adult life.

Is language always a good medium through which to test intelligence? What other methods are there?

Why does a diagnosis of learning difficulties require poor adaptive functioning as well as an IQ of 70 or less? The main reason is that IQ on its own provides an imprecise measure of whether a child can function effectively in society. For example, a child whose native language is not English may obtain an IQ of under 70 on an intelligence test administered in English, even though he or she functions socially as well as most other children of the same age.

In most Western societies, about 1–2% of children are classified as mentally retarded (or as having learning difficulties). The great majority of these (about 80%) are mildly retarded. About 12% are moderately retarded, 7% are severely retarded, and only 1% are profoundly retarded. About two-thirds of children with learning difficulties are male, and there is a greater incidence of learning difficulties among families of low socio-economic status.

KEY TERM

Mental retardation: a condition in which a child's IQ is below 70 and there is evidence of deficits in adaptive functioning ability. The term "learning difficulties" is preferable.

The notion that an IQ of 70 is at the boundary between the presence and absence of mental retardation or learning difficulties is arbitrary. Why was the figure of 70 chosen? A key measure of the distribution of IQs is the standard deviation. IQs have a normal distribution, and the standard deviation of most intelligence tests is 15 (see Chapter 27). As a result, about 68% of people have IQs within one standard deviation above or below the mean. About 95% have IQs within two standard deviations of the mean, that is, with IQs between 70 and 130. Thus, an IQ of 70 is a convenient boundary, because it is precisely two standard deviations below the average, and covers about 2% of the population. However, it should be borne in mind that intelligence tests are carefully designed so that they produce a normal distribution, and we cannot be sure that intelligence is "really" normally distributed.

Causes of learning difficulties

There are various causes of learning difficulties. About 70% of children with learning difficulties have had no known injury or disease that could account for their condition. Relatively little is known for certain about the causes of learning difficulties in these cases. However, two main explanations have been proposed. The first explanation is that there has been brain damage, but that this brain damage is too slight to be detected by the methods available. It is possible that a trauma at or around the time of birth damages the brain enough to cause permanent damage.

What is the evidence for this explanation? There are indications that synaptic connections in the brains of children with learning difficulties are less complex than those of normal children (Huttenlocher, 1974).

However, such minor physical defects can usually only be detected in examinations conducted after death. With such evidence, it is hard to know whether the physical defect caused the learning difficulties, or whether the learning difficulties caused the physical defect.

The other explanation is based on the fact that intelligence in the form of IQ is normally distributed. As a result, it would be expected that about 2% of children would have IQs below 70 even in the absence of any form of brain damage. According to this approach, low intelligence in the absence of obvious brain damage is due to cultural/familial retardation. For example, Zigler and Cascione (1984) argued that learning difficulties result from a combination of biological and social influences. In other words, the intelligence of most children with learning difficulties depends on heredity and environment in the same way as in the rest of the population (see Chapter 27).

What evidence supports this theory? The fact that learning difficulties tend to run in families is consistent with the theory, and the incidence of learning difficulties is much higher in families of low socio-economic status (Barlow & Durand, 1995). Part of this relationship between learning difficulties and socio-economic status may reflect genetic factors. However, most of it is probably due to the limited stimulation and educational facilities available to many children from poor families.

> **CASE STUDY: *The Black Report***
>
> The Black report (Townsend & Davidson, 1982) studied the link between environmental factors and health. It reported that several studies had concluded that although genetic factors might predispose some infants to congenital defects, environmental factors acted as a trigger. The Black report also found that the nutritional status of mothers, both during their own infancy and before they conceived, correlated positively with rates of perinatal (period immediately before or after birth) death and low birth-weight of babies. Thus a cycle of deprivation may be the underlying cause of genetic defects rather than the genes themselves. The combination of genetic and environmental factors in the incidence of disability makes it difficult to isolate one particular cause.
>
> However, some causal links have been found. For example, spina bifida can be caused by nutritional deficiencies; Down's syndrome is a chromosomal abnormality; and deafness can be the result of a mother being exposed to rubella (German measles) during pregnancy.

Genetic factors

As already stated, 70% of cases of learning difficulties have no known cause. The remaining 30% of children with learning difficulties have suffered some form of illness or brain damage, or they have an inherited condition.

Down's syndrome. About 5% of children with learning difficulties suffer from Down's syndrome, which results from a chromosomal abnormality produced at conception. As the age of the mother increases, so do her chances of having a child with this disorder. Children with Down's syndrome have 47 chromosomes rather than the usual 46 in their cells. This causes them to have moderate or severe learning difficulties and physical weaknesses (especially heart lesions). They also have a small head, and characteristic facial features, including a flat nose, and a small mouth. Many children with Down's syndrome die at an early age. However, the life expectancy for people with Down's syndrome has increased over the past 60 years, from 9 years to over 30 years, with about 25% surviving to the age of 50.

Fragile X syndrome. Fragile X syndrome is an inherited condition that is more common in boys than in girls. It is transmitted through the so-called "fragile X gene" on the X chromosome, and is associated with moderate or severe learning difficulties with speech and other forms of communication. Boys with Fragile X syndrome are more likely than boys with other developmental disabilities to have disturbances in language and motor movements, as well as poor self-control, lack of eye contact, and shyness.

Lesch-Nyhan syndrome. Lesch-Nyhan syndrome is an X-linked genetic disorder which only affects males. The symptoms of this syndrome include tightening of the muscles and self-injurious behaviour (e.g. lip biting) as well as learning difficulties.

Tuberous sclerosis. Tuberous sclerosis is a genetic disorder which occurs once in every 30,000 births. About 60% of children with this disorder have learning difficulties. They also tend to suffer from seizures, and they have small bumps in their skin.

PKU. Disrupted metabolic processes cause learning difficulties in some cases. For example, phenylketonuria or PKU is a disease in which the infant is unable to metabolise the amino acid phenylalanine. As a result, the concentration of phenylalanine increases, and there is permanent brain damage. In addition, there are usually seizures and behaviour problems. PKU is preventable if it is detected early enough. Infants are given a special diet that avoids the chemical phenylalanine. PKU occurs about once in every 14,000 births.

Ethical issues: As genetic screening for disabilities is now routine for couples over the age of 35, the "right to life" debate has become very complex. Issues surrounding abortion and genetic engineering have grown increasingly difficult as medicine becomes more sophisticated.

Tay-Sachs disease. Another metabolic disease is Tay-Sachs disease. It is found most often in the descendants of Eastern European Jews, and causes severe learning difficulties. Sufferers from Tay-Sachs disease show neural degeneration, and death generally occurs before the age of 4.

Other disorders. There are several hundred other genetic disorders, many of which are associated with learning difficulties. However, the numbers of children having most of these other disorders are very small.

Environmental factors

Learning difficulties can also be caused by a variety of environmental factors.

Maternal health. The foetus is vulnerable, especially during the early stages of pregnancy, and it can be harmed by certain drugs and other substances, by maternal malnutrition, or by the mother's infections. For example, learning difficulties can occur if the mother suffers from rubella (German measles) during the first three months of pregnancy. Other infections during pregnancy that can cause problems are herpes simplex and syphilis. Infectious diseases after birth (e.g. encephalitis) can also lead to learning difficulties.

It has been found (Cannon, Barr, & Mednick 1991) that mothers who were exposed to a severe influenza epidemic between the fourth and sixth months of pregnancy were much more likely than others to have children who developed schizophrenia. This finding is of relevance here because schizophrenics tend to have below average intellectual functioning (Barlow & Durand, 1995).

Foetal alcohol syndrome. Learning difficulties can also result from foetal alcohol syndrome. This syndrome occurs when the mother regularly consumes large quantities of alcohol during pregnancy. It is found in between 1 and 3 out of every 1000 births. Children with foetal alcohol syndrome typically have a small head, a short nose and jaw, a long upper lip, and a narrow forehead. Children with this syndrome generally have poor co-ordination, impulsiveness, impairments in speech and hearing, and other cognitive problems (Streissguth, 1994), and these problems often persist into adulthood.

Anoxia. Another environmental factor that can cause learning difficulties is anoxia or lack of oxygen at the time of birth. If there is a prolonged lack of oxygen, learning difficulties often occur because anoxia causes brain damage.

Effects of learning difficulties

As we have seen, there are numerous causes of learning difficulties. As a result, it is only to be expected that the kinds of problems experienced by children with learning difficulties differ considerably. Of course, however, children with severe or profound learning difficulties tend to have more problems than those with mild or moderate learning difficulties, and their problems are more severe. It should also be noted that many children with learning difficulties have impairments in seeing or hearing, and others have poor mobility or difficulties in making precise motor movements.

Academic skills

In view of the fact that the existence of learning difficulties is largely defined in terms of low IQ, it follows that children with learning difficulties typically have problems with school learning of skills such as reading, writing, and mathematics. This is true even of children with mild learning difficulties. However, children with mild learning difficulties can learn skills such as being able to check that they have been given the correct change when shopping, or reading simple books and recipes. Indeed, children with mild learning difficulties can generally develop the academic skills of the average 12-year-old by their late teens. Individuals with severe learning difficulties typically learn to talk, but are unable to learn the academic skills that are taught at school. Children with profound learning difficulties require total care, because they cannot acquire even basic skills.

Cross-cultural issues: Are the skills generally described in the West as "academic" regarded as equally important by all cultures?

Developmental and difference theories. Zigler and Cascione (1984) distinguished between two views of the learning difficulties of children with cultural/familial retardation: the developmental view and the difference view. According to the developmental view favoured by Zigler and Cascione, the cognitive development of children with cultural/familial retardation proceeds in the normal way, but at a slower rate. In other words, their cognitive development is like a slow-motion picture of the same development in normal children. According to the difference view, there are significant differences between children with mild learning difficulties and normal children in the processes involved in cognitive development as well as in the speed of that development.

Mental age. How can we decide between these two points of view? One way is by taking account of **mental age**. A child whose general level of intelligence is the same as that of the average child of 8 has a mental age of 8 regardless of his or her actual age. It follows from the developmental view that children with mild learning difficulties should show the same cognitive abilities as normal children with the same mental age. In fact, this is often not the case. According to Barlow and Durand (1995, p.610):

> at least for some tasks, people with mild mental retardation may do significantly worse than people who are matched with them based on mental age ... people with mild mental

KEY TERM

Mental age: a measure of an individual's general level of intelligence based on comparisons with others; for example, someone with a mental age of 10 has the same level of intelligence as the average 10-year-old.

retardation may in fact differ from people without mental retardation in a way that is not explained just by a developmental delay.

In other words, the difference view is correct, and children with mild learning difficulties may have specific cognitive impairments as well as a generally low level of intelligence.

■ Research activity: Social skills

In groups, list specific skills associated with the following components of social interaction:

- Acknowledgement of others (e.g. make eye contact).
- Regard for well-being of self/others (e.g. walking along the street without colliding).
- Presentation of self to others (e.g. personal hygiene).
- Selecting appropriate responses to others (e.g. smiling).

Discuss the needs of children with learning difficulties when they are learning social skills, with reference to the lists you have made.

Ethical issues: Does the finding of Barlow and Durand justify the segregation of children with disabilities? Do you think children in mainstream schools can learn from sharing their classes with children with learning disabilities?

Music, drama, art, and other forms of creative therapy have been used extensively in the area of special education. Why might these approaches be appropriate for people with learning difficulties?

KEY TERM
Mainstreaming: the policy of teaching children with learning difficulties in ordinary classes whenever possible.

Social skills

Most children with learning difficulties have problems with social skills. Even children who have only mild learning difficulties often find it hard to make and keep friends. Children with more serious learning difficulties typically have a lack of awareness of social conventions. For example, they may be overly friendly, wanting to be hugged by someone they have just met. One reason why children and adults with learning difficulties experience social problems is that psychiatric disorders are about three or four times more common in them than in the normal population (Scott, 1994). Psychiatric disorders are especially common among those with the most serious learning difficulties.

In the United States, attempts have been made to integrate children having learning difficulties with society at large by requiring that they be educated in the least restrictive environment possible. This has led to **mainstreaming**, in which they are taught in classes with normal children, but with access to special teaching as well. There is some evidence that this has improved their academic skills. However, it does not seem to have benefited their social skills. Children with learning difficulties are often teased and ridiculed by their peers, and fail to gain acceptance (Barlow & Durand, 1995).

Communication skills

One of the main reasons why children with learning difficulties have social and interpersonal problems is because of their poor communication skills. Most children with learning difficulties learn to talk, but their ability to express their needs and feelings is very limited. Children who are too disabled to acquire speech are sometimes taught what are known as augmentative communication skills. For example, they might learn sign language or how to indicate what they want by pointing to photographs or drawings of objects and actions.

Self-care skills

Many children with learning difficulties have problems with basic self-care skills such as dressing, eating, keeping clean, and using a telephone. This is especially the case with children having severe or profound learning difficulties, who often have physical disabilities as well as very low intelligence. They can be taught basic self-care skills, but this can require extensive supervision over long periods of time.

Vocational skills

When children with learning difficulties become adults, they often have difficulty in finding a job. One obvious reason for this is that they lack the educational qualifications (e.g. GCSEs; A levels) possessed by many of their peers. However, many individuals with mild learning difficulties do manage to find employment in areas such as the following: clerical work; farming; gardening; packaging; carpentry; and food services. Those with moderate learning difficulties sometimes carry out simple jobs under close supervision in sheltered workshops.

The Green Pepper Cafe in London is a sheltered environment in which adults with learning difficulties can be productive.

Physical and Sensory Impairments

Children suffering from physical and sensory impairments are obviously at a disadvantage in that it is harder for them to achieve normal levels of social, emotional, and cognitive development. We will mainly be considering the effects of blindness, deafness, and cerebral palsy in this section. It is important to note at the outset that many children are unfortunate enough to suffer from more than one kind of impairment. For example, about 75% of children whose primary impairment is cerebral palsy also have learning difficulties, about 30% suffer from deafness, and about 20% suffer from blindness. In the case of children whose primary impairment is blindness, 15% also have learning difficulties. Of those children whose major impairment is deafness, approximately 10% have learning difficulties.

> ■ Research activity: Working in pairs, discuss the difficulties that the following areas might raise for a child who is deaf and for a child who is paraplegic and so unable to walk.
> • Emotional development.
> • Social skills.
> • Cognitive development.

Blindness

There are about 20,000 children in the United Kingdom who are either blind or partially sighted. As might be imagined, children who retain some sight, however limited, develop more rapidly than those who are blind. In addition, children who go blind before the age of 2 typically experience greater developmental problems than children who become blind later in childhood (Pring, 1997).

Everyone knows that it is much more difficult for blind children than for sighted ones to cope with the problems of development. It has often been assumed that their main problems lie in the area of cognitive development and skills such as learning to read. However, that assumption is wrong. As Preisler (1997, p.69) pointed out, "If you ask parents or teachers what they think the most severe or urgent problem is for a blind child, the answer is unanimous: social interaction and friendship with peers." Accordingly, we will start by considering the social problems of blind children.

How would you have to adapt your behaviour if you found that your new baby was blind?

Social problems

Preisler (1997) carried out a long-term or longitudinal study on eight blind children from infancy to the age of 6, and then returned for a follow-up when the children were 10. Detailed evidence was obtained by taking videos in the children's homes and schools, and by interviewing their parents and teachers. Blind children at the age of 5 months behaved as sociably and attentively with their parents as sighted children. After that, however, they began to fall behind. For example, sighted children engage in pretend play with their parents and others when they are between 15 and 18 months of age. In contrast, blind children do not do this until they are almost 2 years old. The most obvious reason why blind children develop socially more slowly than sighted children is because sighted children can read the emotions and intentions of their parents by observing their facial expressions, bodily postures, and actions.

The social problems experienced by blind children tended to increase from the age of 2 onwards when they went to preschool with sighted children. There were very few moments of spontaneous interaction with the sighted children, and they spent most of their time either alone or with adults. Several of the blind children found it so hard to cope with preschool that their social and emotional behaviour became less mature than it had been previously.

The social problems of several of the blind children were greater when they were studied again at the age of 10. All eight of them described themselves as lonely. Even more worryingly, three out of the eight showed clear signs of the kinds of withdrawn behaviour found in autistic children (autism is discussed later in the chapter).

KEY STUDY EVALUATION — Preisler

Preisler's evidence provides valuable in-depth information about the social interactions experienced by blind children, and important detailed information about the development of individuals. Observations taken in naturalistic settings, such as at home, can provide the researcher with vital data about behaviour consistency between one setting and another.

Although Preisler's findings provide interesting insight into the social difficulties experienced by blind children, they lack comparative data, e.g. a group of sighted children from similar backgrounds, and of course the conclusions that can be drawn from such a small sample are limited. Preisler's study does not include social interactions between blind children and their sighted siblings, which could provide insight into how sighted peers adapt to compensate for blindness in others.

While there is evidence that visual cues are of vital importance to the developing child, there are other media through which the infant may learn to adapt to the world. Touch and sound are used extensively to provide stimulation for profoundly disabled children, using music and massage. Blind children may benefit socially from tactile communication; human touch and vocalising help them to feel secure and accepted.

A major finding of Preisler's study was that adults in particular need to focus on the whole child rather than on his or her disability. Failure to do this may lead to passivity and isolation, and could adversely affect the individual's ability to adapt to their environment.

Preisler (1997, p.83) was very concerned that the ways in which teachers and others treat blind children may not be in their best interests:

If too much effort is concentrated on performance and skill, there is a risk that the child will be looked upon as an object, not a subject; that the child will be looked upon as something to form and create, not somebody with his or her own intentions, feelings and motives. The functional disability will be in focus, not the child.

Discussion points

1. What are the strengths of the study by Preisler?

2. What could be done to improve the lives of blind children?

A **blind child** takes over a year to learn the Braille alphabet, and lacks the enormous visual input available to sighted children from picture books, television, and everyday printed material.

■ Research activity: Using no visual material, try to construct a lesson plan for partially sighted students on a topic of your choice.

Reading problems

So far we have considered some of the social problems of blind children. However, they also experience severe problems in other areas, such as learning to read. Sighted children have the advantage of being exposed to thousands of words in picture books, on television, and elsewhere even before they begin to be taught how to read. This gives them a much greater knowledge base in the initial stages of reading.

Most blind children are taught Braille, which involves raised dots that can be interpreted by touch. It typically takes blind children more than a year to learn the Braille alphabet, which is much longer than it takes sighted children to learn the alphabet (Harris & Barlow-Brown, 1997). One reason is that the sense of touch is much less well developed than is that of sight. Another reason is that blind children often learn Braille only at school, whereas sighted children generally spend time at home reading books with their parents.

Other cognitive problems

Apart from problems with learning to read, blind children often cope better than might be expected with other kinds of learning. According to Pring (1997, p.383):

Psychological issues within the area of visual impairment have tended to look for cognitive inabilities caused by the loss of vision ... these do exist but have surprisingly little impact, especially where residual sight can provide a spatial framework.

Blind children's rate of language learning depends very much on the mother. This was shown in a study by Rowland (1983), who studied three blind infants. They said less than sighted infants after their mother's vocalisations. According to Rowland (1983, p.127), the reason was that, "Listening may be so critical to the interpretation of the ... environment that it would be maladaptive for the blind infant to clutter the auditory environment with her own vocalisations." One of the three infants had much faster language development than the other two. The key difference was that the mother of the first infant responded much more often to the vocalisations of her child than did the other two mothers. In other words, it is very important for the mother or primary carer to be sensitive to the needs of her blind child.

Blind children generally master language fairly effectively, even if their rate of progress is slower than for sighted children. According to Landau (1997, p.15), "Blind children do not appear to have difficulty learning the syntax of their native language, nor speaking in sentences that have meaning." However, it has been claimed that there are significant differences between blind and sighted children in their language learning. Dunlea (1989) argued that blind children have a more restricted vocabulary than sighted children, because their experience of the world is more limited. For example, blind children have fewer animal words in their vocabulary than sighted children, but they have more words for household objects. Dunlea also claimed that blind children use verbs in fewer different contexts than do sighted children, again because of their more limited experiences.

Dunlea exaggerated the differences in language learning between blind and sighted children. She also exaggerated the importance of personal experience in acquiring vocabulary. As Landau (1997) pointed out, blind children can learn verbs such as "look" and "see" in spite of the absence of any directly relevant experience.

Mulford (1987) found another difference in vocabulary between blind and sighted children. There are some sounds in English that involve clearly visible mouth movements; they include b, f, and m. There are other sounds such as h, j, k, and x, which do not. Partially sighted and blind children had relatively fewer words in their vocabularies containing sounds based on visible mouth movements, presumably because they cannot use visual information to distinguish among such sounds.

The relationship between language acquisition and the use of visual imagery is an important one. What are the main ways in which blind children's acquisition of language can be assisted?

Coping with blindness

The work of Preisler (1997) and others suggests that what is most needed is for the parents, teachers, and peers of blind children to become more sensitive to their needs. For example, sighted people often fail to pay enough attention to the hand movements of blind children, even though those movements provide valuable information about their interests and preferences. Progress in training sighted people how to interact with blind children has been rather slow. According to Collis and Lewis (1997, p.132):

> *Although at first sight it might seem fairly straightforward to devise intervention programmes to train parents and teachers in appropriate modes of responding, this has proven to be far from straightforward and not particularly successful.*

In essence, it is very hard for sighted people to identify with the needs and problems of blind children.

On a more constructive note, it should be possible to increase the involvement of blind children in play activities. Most forms of children's play depend heavily on vision, but there are games (for example, word games) that do not. Preisler (1997) reported that one teacher started playing a game with a blind child that was so interesting that the sighted children in the class joined in.

Apart from their social problems, blind children also have to cope with the task of learning to read. Harris and Barlow-Brown (1997) have made preliminary attempts to make it easier for blind children to learn Braille. They found that sighted and blind children both learned Braille letters more quickly by touch when the letters were large than when they were of standard size. Presumably this happened because touch is not very sensitive, and so the increase in size made it easier to identify the letters. Of particular interest is the fact that the blind children had no difficulty in transferring their knowledge from the large letters to standard-sized Braille. It thus appears that training on large letters may speed up blind children's rate of learning to read.

Deafness

Very few children have total hearing loss. There is typically some residual hearing, and so the term "hearing-impaired" is often used in preference to "deaf". There have been improvements in detecting the presence of a significant hearing impairment, but many hearing-impaired children are two or three years old before their hearing loss is diagnosed. The great majority (92%) of deaf children are born into families in which both parents have normal hearing. A further 7% have one deaf parent, and the remaining 1% of deaf children have two deaf parents. It is important to distinguish between deaf children with hearing parents and those with at least one deaf parent. The reason is that there is strong evidence (reviewed by Marschark, 1993) that social, cognitive, and language development proceeds more quickly in deaf children with deaf parents than in those with hearing parents.

Why do deaf parents tend to be more successful? There are various reasons. First, deaf parents tend to be more sensitive to the needs of their deaf children. Second, they are better able to communicate without the use of spoken language. Third, deaf parents tend to have greater expectations for, and more involvement in, the education of their

CASE STUDY: *A Deaf Child's Experience*

Deaf children's experience of the world is radically different from that of hearing people's, and their descriptions of this can be revealing as well as poignant. In a collection of descriptions given by deaf people in America, Padden and Humphries (1988, cited and quoted in Brien, 1992, p.9) show how a deaf child's world view develops as he or she uses the information available to "make sense" of things around them. Padden and Humphries (1988, p.21) neatly capture the reasoning processes of a deaf boy called Jim:

Imagine Jim sitting in a room near a door. Suddenly his mother appears, walking purposefully to the door. She opens the door, and there is a visitor waiting on the doorstep. But if the child opens the

door at another time, odds are that there will be no visitor there. How does the child who does not hear the doorbell understand what the stimulus is for the odd behaviour of opening a door and finding someone standing there? We can only guess. We know only that Jim assumed other people had powers not yet discernible to him.

Padden and Humphries are quick to point out that anecdotes such as this do not indicate merely a "naive" world view, but "the unfolding of the human symbolic capacity". Jim will probably never hear the doorbell for himself, but he will quickly learn what such a stimulus represents when it is explained to him in terms he can understand.

How would you have to adapt your behaviour if you found that your new baby was deaf?

deaf children than do hearing parents of deaf children. Gregory and Barlow (1989) provided relevant evidence. Deaf or hearing-impaired mothers responded to their hearing-impaired child's behaviour on 50% of occasions, compared to only 23% for hearing mothers.

In view of the fact that about 90% of deaf children have hearing parents, we will devote most of our coverage to them rather than to deaf children with one or two deaf parents. However, what has been discussed so far makes it clear that the development of deaf children depends on parent-related factors as well as on child-related factors.

Hearing members of a deaf child's family need to learn sign language to communicate among themselves, otherwise the deaf child may be excluded from the bulk of the family's social interaction.

Social problems

Most deaf children experience severe social problems. In the early years of life, many of these problems stem from the fact that it is hard for hearing mothers to adjust to the needs of their deaf children. Part of the problem is communication. For example, it was found in an American study that only about 35% of deaf students used sign language with their families (Jordan & Karchmer, 1986). Another part of the problem is that many mothers find it emotionally disturbing to cope with a deaf child. Henggeler, Watson, and Cooper (1984) studied the hearing mothers of deaf and hearing preschool and early school-age children. The mothers of deaf children tended to be more intrusive, tense, and directive in their communications with their children than were the mothers of hearing children.

As a result of their early experiences, deaf children tend to have problems when adjusting socially to other children at school. In the words of Marschark (1993, p.71):

The average deaf child of hearing parents enters school with a relatively impoverished social repertoire and breadth of social experience relative to hearing peers ... Some frequent, well-established behaviour patterns, such as impulsivity, aggression, and egocentrism [self-centred behaviour] ... influence early school experience with teachers and with other children.

Language problems

Deaf children experience great problems in the acquisition of language. As Mogford (1993, p.131) pointed out, "Although the visual channel allows some compensation, the disruption to the process is evident in virtually every aspect of linguistic development." We will consider the main forms of language in turn, starting with speech comprehension and speech production.

Speech comprehension. Children and adults with normal hearing unconsciously make some use of lip-reading in order to understand what others are saying to them. However, they rely mostly on what they hear rather than what they can see. In contrast, children who have substantial hearing loss have to rely heavily on lip-reading. This is hard to do, because many sounds do not have clear lip movements associated with them, and also because many people do not articulate distinctly. As a result, most deaf children are much slower than hearing children in understanding spoken language.

Speech production. Deaf children also have severe problems with speaking, as is to be expected in view of their problems with understanding the spoken language of others. Conrad (1979) asked teachers to rate the speech of 331 deaf children who were leaving special schools. Almost half (48%) of the deaf children were rated as having speech that was either very hard to understand or unintelligible.

Reading and writing. Most deaf children experience great difficulties in learning to read and write. This can be seen if we consider the percentages of deaf and hearing children in the United States who are functionally illiterate when they leave school. Functional illiteracy is defined as being below the level of reading and writing reached by the average 12-year-old. It is found in over 30% of deaf students leaving school, but in under 1% of hearing students. What is it about learning to read that deaf children find especially difficult? They typically find it hard to convert printed words into sounds, but their greatest difficulties concern vocabulary knowledge and grammatical abilities (Marschark, 1993).

Deaf children also experience significant problems with writing stories and essays. Marschark (1993, p.226) concluded from the evidence that deaf children's written productions appear "concrete, repetitive, and structurally simplistic relative to both the written productions of hearing peers and to their own signed productions."

How important do you think being fluent in a spoken language is for the process of learning to read?

Sign language. So far we have focused on the problems that deaf and hearing-impaired children have with language as it is used by hearing children and adults. In fact, about 80% of deaf children in the United States and the United Kingdom also learn to understand and to communicate by means of sign language. There are various sign languages in every country of the world. In the UK the most important is probably British Sign Language (BSL), with Sign Supported English (SSE) a close second. SSE is useful to deaf people when conversing with hearing English speakers, because as the name suggests it closely follows the word order and grammar of English, whereas BSL has its own separate grammatical structure. Contrary to what is sometimes believed, sign languages are genuine languages of similar complexity to other languages.

Sign languages have clear advantages and disadvantages for deaf children. The greatest advantage is that these languages depend on vision rather than on hearing, and so they are easier for deaf children to learn. The greatest disadvantage is that very few

CASE STUDY: *Life Without Language*

Dr Oliver Sacks is a neurologist and writer who has taken a deep interest in the lives and history of deaf people. In his book *Seeing voices* (Sacks, 1991, pp.45–49) he retells the story of a deaf boy named Jean Massieu who was born in France in the eighteenth century. Massieu was completely without language until the age of 14, when he became a pupil of the Abbé Sicard, a famous teacher of the deaf. Massieu became eloquent in sign language and written French and eventually wrote his autobiography, from which Sacks quotes:

Until the age of thirteen and nine months I remained at home without ever receiving any education ... children my own age would not play with me, they looked down on me, I was like a dog ... I passed the time alone playing with a top or a mallet and ball or walking on stilts.

Sacks describes how Massieu envied other children going to school, and how "he tried to copy the letters of the alphabet with a quill, knowing that they must have some strange power, but unable to give any meaning to them." When Massieu's education eventually began, Sicard showed him drawings of objects and asked the boy to copy them. Then Sicard wrote the name of the object next to the drawing. Massieu was mystified: "He had no idea how lines that did not appear to picture anything could function as an image for objects and represent them with such accuracy and speed." Then, very suddenly, Massieu grasped the significance of written words, and from then on he developed what Sacks describes as "a violent hunger" for names of objects. Once Massieu had names for things, he had some power at last and could begin to manipulate the world that had ignored him for so long.

hearing children or adults know any sign languages, and so its usefulness is largely confined to communicating with other deaf people.

The fact that deaf children struggle to master spoken and written language has general implications for their general development. A good command of the language in common use is of vital importance in coping successfully in most societies, perhaps especially those of the Western world. As Marschark (1993, p.226) concluded

> *deficiencies in writing ability, together with the limitations imposed by lack of reading ability, are centrally involved in dealing with children's generally poor academic performance. At the same time, reading and writing form an essential link to the worlds of social and cognitive interaction, and the consequences of illiteracy have increasing impact on all realms of functioning as deaf children grow up.*

Coping with deafness

Marschark (1993) argued that there are three main factors that need to be taken into account in order to help the development of deaf children. First, there is early language experience. It is of great importance for parents to interact linguistically with their deaf child as much of the time as possible. This is easier for deaf parents to do, but is a crucial goal for hearing parents as well. Second, there is diversity of experience. Deaf children who are exposed to a variety of stimulating environments are the ones most likely to become self-motivating in their learning.

Third, there is social interaction. Deaf children often appear remote and superficial in their social relationships. However, this is much less true of deaf children whose parents put the most effort into developing the social skills of their deaf child. Many of these parents are deaf themselves, but some hearing parents are very effective at interacting socially with their deaf children.

What would be the advantages and disadvantages for a deaf child attending a hearing school?

There are various ways in which the needs of deaf children can be catered for. There have been attempts to integrate deaf children into ordinary hearing schools. However, Marschark pointed out that there are some advantages in sending them to residential deaf schools during the week. Of particular importance, residential schools can make it easier to build up the communication skills needed by deaf children if they are to become fully socialised. Schools for the deaf can also provide a sub-culture in which deaf children feel comfortable, and can provide deaf adults with whom the deaf child can identify. According to Marschark (1993, p.61), the alternative is likely to be worse:

> *Given the relative lack of communication between most hearing parents and their deaf children and the overprotective maternal behaviour patterns frequently exhibited toward deaf ... children, it would be difficult for even a supportive and accepting family to provide a deaf child the full range of interactions available to hearing children during the school years.*

Deaf awareness

The simplest way to help deaf children communicate more effectively is to become deaf aware, and deaf awareness training is now available to hearing people in all walks of life. It is particularly useful to those whose work brings them into contact with the public, such as shop assistants, doctors, solicitors, or bank clerks. The training involves alerting people to the many ways in which they can aid communication, for example by speaking clearly and slowly, but not shouting or mouthing silently, using short simple sentences, making eye contact, and not turning away while speaking. Many points may seem obvious, such as not covering your mouth with your hand while speaking, or not chewing gum, but hearing people often do things like this without thinking. Communication with anyone, disabled or not, is a two-way process and can be facilitated by both participants.

Another approach to helping deaf or hearing-impaired children is what is known as Total Communication. This involves making use of all the potentially available sources of language communication, including sign language, speech, and amplification of sound through the use of hearing aids. Greenberg, Calderon, and Kusche (1984) reported on the use of an intervention programme with preschool deaf children based on Total Communication methods. The intervention programme led to increased mother–child communication during play, and the mothers became more rewarding and better able to gain their children's attention. Of particular interest, the deaf children who had gone through Total Communication were three times more likely than other deaf children to communicate spontaneously in social situations, and they asked four times as many questions.

Cerebral palsy

Cerebral palsy is a condition involving motor impairment caused by non-progressive brain damage. This brain damage is either present at birth or acquired in early childhood. There are various causes of such brain damage, including anoxia or lack of oxygen to the brain, jaundice during the first few weeks of life, bleeding within the brain, and injury. About 0.2% of children have cerebral palsy.

Children with cerebral palsy vary widely in terms of the types of motor deficit they exhibit, and in the severity of their deficits. At one extreme, some children have essentially normal speech and only minor restriction in the movements of one limb. At the other extreme, the most severely disabled children with cerebral palsy have great impairments in every limb and are totally unable to speak. Speech problems are found in about 70% of children with cerebral palsy. As was mentioned earlier in the chapter, about three-quarters of children with cerebral palsy have learning difficulties, one-quarter are blind, and one-quarter are deaf.

Special terms are used to describe some of the main forms of cerebral palsy. For example, the term ataxic cerebral palsy is applied to children who have difficulties with voluntary movements and balance. Athetoid cerebral palsy describes children whose movements are unusual and uncontrollable. Children with spastic cerebral palsy display rigidity in at least one limb and generally have problems with voluntary movements.

Cerebral palsy is the most common cause of two conditions involving impaired speech. One of these conditions is **dysarthria**, which is motor speech impairment caused by lesions within the nervous system. The speech sounds of dysarthric children are typically produced very slowly and in a distorted form. As a result, it is often very hard to understand what they are saying. The other condition is **anarthria**, which is even more severe. Anarthric children cannot speak at all. However, their failure to speak does not necessarily mean that they lack language abilities. Baddeley and Wilson (1985) studied six anarthric individuals, and found that they were all able to make use of silent rehearsal processes.

There are obvious difficulties in assessing the cognitive skills of children with severe forms of cerebral palsy. How might psychologists use computers, music, or art to help in these assessments?

Problems of everyday life

Children with cerebral palsy (especially those with the more severe motor impairments) have various serious problems in their everyday lives. Communication is of vital importance for social and academic development, but many children with cerebral palsy find it extremely difficult to communicate with other people. Severely impaired children are often only able to communicate in various basic ways. For example, they may respond "yes" or "no" to a question by making a motor response such as blinking, or they may indicate what they are interested in by gazing at the appropriate drawing in a display. Children with cerebral palsy have other kinds of problems stemming from their limited mobility. About 50% of children with cerebral palsy are unable to use their legs effectively, and cannot walk by the age of 5. This means that transport needs to be provided both between home and school and also within the school itself. Many children with cerebral palsy have to miss substantial amounts of schooling because they need to be hospitalised for surgery designed to make them more mobile. Some children with cerebral palsy have motor impairments that make it difficult for them to cough. As a result, they may need to be admitted to hospital whenever they suffer from a respiratory complaint.

Many of these children also have other problems. The fact that 75% of children with cerebral palsy have learning difficulties means that most of them have to deal with the problems of everyday living described in the earlier section on learning difficulties.

> With reference to the following areas, what might be the effects of not being able to communicate with other people?
>
> - Social interaction.
> - Emotional life.
> - Establishing and maintaining relationships.

> **KEY TERMS**
> **Cerebral palsy**: this condition is caused by brain damage before or during birth; among the symptoms are reduced muscular functioning and limb weakness.
> **Dysarthria**: partial inability to speak due to brain damage.
> **Anarthria**: inability to speak at all as a result of brain damage.

> **Social participation**
>
> The barriers to social participation by children with cerebral palsy in terms of their physical constraints are compounded by society's response to people who are disabled. Consider the following elements of social prejudice as it affects children with cerebral palsy and their carers:
>
> - Low expectations of physical and intellectual capabilities.
> - Social stigma regarding cerebral palsy.
> - Social isolation.

Practised movements may improve co-ordination skills in children with cerebral palsy.

Coping with cerebral palsy

What can be done to make it easier for children with cerebral palsy to cope with their various problems? The advent of microcomputers has opened up various communication possibilities for them. For example, children with cerebral palsy can often make some movement to control a cursor or movable point on a computer screen so as to select desired items. In addition, they can be trained to write using a modified computer. Even with such assistance, however, it is extremely hard for them to produce essays and other pieces of written work.

Andras Peto and Margaret Rood have put forward separate treatment programmes designed to improve the mobility of children with cerebral palsy. Peto makes use of the method of conductive education, in which a number of children with cerebral palsy spend considerable periods of time practising motor movements. As Cardwell et al. (1996) pointed out, a central goal of conductive education is to produce better motor co-ordination in these children by allowing them to gain better control over their own movements.

Margaret Rood has adopted a rather different approach. According to her, it is valuable for the various muscle groups of children with cerebral palsy to be stimulated in different ways. For example, the children might stretch their muscles at different speeds, or someone else might stroke or rub the muscles. The overall goal is to speed up the rate of motor development.

How effective are the approaches advocated by Peto and by Rood? They certainly seem to be of use, but there is an absence of systematic studies comparing these approaches against others (Cardwell et al., 1996).

Attention-Deficit Hyperactivity Disorder

Most children are rather active, and they tend to have a much shorter attention span than adults. However, there are some children whose high level of activity and/or low level of attention in all situations are such that they are classified as suffering from **attention-deficit hyperactivity disorder** (ADHD). The phrase "in all situations" is important, because there are many normal children who are highly active in a few situations. Klein and Gittelman-Klein (1975) reported that about 75% of those children who seemed to be overactive at school were not so at home or in the clinic.

It is recognised increasingly that children with ADHD differ among themselves in their symptoms. This was incorporated into DSM-IV, which distinguishes three types of ADHD:

- Predominantly inattentive type.
- Predominantly hyperactive type.
- Combined type.

Abnormal or antisocial?

The term "symptoms" suggests that a pathological approach has been applied to what appear to be antisocial forms of behaviour. Read through the text's description of ADHD. To what extent does this imply an emotional–behavioural problem that is suggestive of a mental illness? Could it be argued that what is assumed to be "abnormal" in the case of ADHD is simply socially unacceptable behaviour? In addition, why do you think ADHD is more common in boys than in girls? (For a full description of, and debate about, the concept of abnormality, see Chapter 24.)

The main criterion for a diagnosis of ADHD in DSM-IV is the possession of six or more symptoms of inattention *or* six or more symptoms of hyperactivity/impulsivity, *or* both in the case of the combined type. These symptoms must have lasted for at least six months, they must be maladaptive, and they must be inconsistent with the child's developmental level.

The symptoms of inattention are as follows: often fails to pay close attention or to avoid careless mistakes; often fails to sustain attention; often fails to listen when spoken to directly; often fails to finish schoolwork or duties; often has difficulty in organising tasks and activities; is often reluctant to become involved in tasks (e.g. homework) that need sustained mental effort; often loses things necessary for some activity; is often forgetful in daily activities.

The symptoms of hyperactivity/impulsivity are as follows: often fidgets or squirms; often leaves seat when remaining seated is expected; often runs about or climbs excessively in inappropriate situations; often has difficulty playing or engaging in leisure activities quietly; is often "on the go"; often talks excessively; often blurts out answers before the questions have been finished; often finds it hard to await his or her turn; and often interrupts or intrudes on others.

There are four other criteria for ADHD included in DSM-IV. First, some of the aforementioned symptoms must be present before the age of 7. Second, some impairment due to the symptoms should be found in at least two different settings. Third, there should be clear evidence of clinically significant impairment in social, academic, or occupational functioning. Fourth, the symptoms must not be found exclusively during the course of another disorder, and they must not be better accounted for by another disorder.

Inattention: often fails to listen when spoken to directly.

Hyperactivity: climbs excessively in inappropriate situations.

Who suffers from attention-deficit hyperactivity disorder? There is no doubt that the disorder is much more common in boys than in girls. Anderson et al. (1987) reported that there were over five times as many boys as girls suffering from the disorder. Overall, about 3–5% of children in the United States are diagnosed with the disorder.

Causes of attention-deficit hyperactivity disorder

As with most disorders, it is likely that there are various factors that play a part in the development of ADHD. They can be divided into biological, psychological, and dietary factors. We will consider each of these factors in turn.

Biological factors

There is fairly good evidence that biological factors are involved in the development of attention-deficit hyperactivity disorder. Kendall and Hammen (1995) referred to an unpublished study by Deutsch. He found that 25% of the biological parents of children with ADHD had a history of the disorder, compared to only 4% of adoptive parents. These findings suggest that genetic factors are important. The same conclusion follows from the findings of Goodman and Stevenson (1989). They studied twin pairs in which at least one member of the pair suffered from ADHD. The other twin had the same diagnosis in 51% of identical twins, but in only 33% of fraternal twins. The greater genetic similarity of identical than fraternal twins may account for these findings. However, identical twins may be treated in a more similar way than fraternal twins by their parents, and this may partly explain the findings.

It is useful to know that biological factors are involved in attention-deficit hyperactivity disorder. However, it would be even more useful to have more specific information. There is growing evidence that ADHD is associated with reduced activity in the frontal lobes of the brain, which play a role in the planning and organisation of behaviour. Children with the disorder have decreased blood flow and EEG activity in the frontal lobes (Lou et al., 1989). Adults in whom ADHD started in childhood were found via PET scans to have less brain activity than normal adults while

Are there social and cultural features that correlate with the occurrence of ADHD, or is it randomly distributed throughout the population?

How would we determine whether maladaptive behaviour is a response to environmental factors or has a genetic basis?

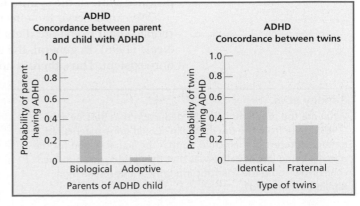

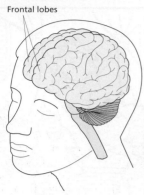

Frontal lobes

What methodological weaknesses are involved in analysing child–parent interactions by the use of observation?

carrying out an auditory-attention task (Zametkin et al., 1990). This reduced brain activity was most apparent in the frontal lobes.

It makes sense that the frontal lobes would be relatively inactive in children and adults with ADHD. As has already been mentioned, the frontal lobes are involved in the planning and organisation of behaviour. Insufficient use of the frontal lobes would lead to the disorganised and impulsive behaviour found in those with ADHD.

Psychological factors

It is possible that the ways in which parents treat their children influence the likelihood that the children will develop attention-deficit hyperactivity disorder. Biological and psychological factors may both be important. Children who are naturally overactive and lacking in attention evoke negative and disapproving behaviour from their parents. In turn, this parental behaviour makes the children's behaviour worse, and this can eventually lead to ADHD.

It has generally been found that the parents of hyperactive children do tend to issue more commands and to interact more negatively with their children than do the parents of normal children (see Davison & Neale, 1996). However, we cannot tell from such evidence whether the negative parental behaviour is causing the children's hyperactive behaviour, whether the children's hyperactive behaviour is causing the negative parental behaviour, or whether the causality goes in both directions.

Barkley et al. (1985) gave hyperactive boys the stimulant drug Ritalin, which reduces most of the symptoms of ADHD. Their key finding was that mothers were less controlling and negative in their behaviour towards their hyperactive sons when the boys had been given Ritalin. This suggests that negative behaviour by the parents of hyperactive children occurs at least in part as a result of their children's disruptive behaviour, and does not cause that disruptive behaviour in the first place.

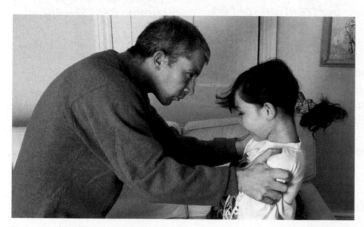

Parents of hyperactive children tend to give more commands than do parents of non-ADHD children, but it is difficult to determine whether this is a causal factor in ADHD, or a result of the parents' difficulty in coping with the hyperactive child.

Ethical issues: What problems might be associated with the prescription of drugs such as Ritalin to children?

It should be mentioned that Ritalin and other similar drugs are somewhat controversial and can produce side-effects such as disturbed sleep and reduced appetite. As Barlow and Durand (1995, p.664) pointed out, "A portion of children with ADHD do not respond to stimulant medications, and most children who do respond do not show gains in the important areas of academic and social skills."

Dietary factors

It has been suggested that various dietary factors may contribute to the development of attention-deficit hyperactivity disorder. For example, Feingold (1975) claimed that food additives have a negative effect on the central nervous system of hyperactive children, and this makes their condition worse. Another suggestion is that refined sugar can produce some of the symptoms of the disorder.

We can observe the effects on hyperactive children of removing food additives or refined sugar from their diets. Some of the relevant evidence is discussed by Davison and Neale (1996). In general, the effects of these kinds of dietary changes are very small or non-existent. Thus, there is no clear evidence that diet plays a significant role in ADHD.

Barkley et al.

What are the problems with the deduction that Barkley et al. (1985) made from the use of Ritalin? Could some parents lack a genuine interest in their child, so that the actual reason for the parents being less negative was that they preferred a subdued child? How could the scientific integrity of this research on Ritalin be improved?

Summary

We have considered some of the main biological, psychological, and dietary factors that may affect the development of attention-deficit hyperactivity disorder. The evidence seems to be strongest for biological factors. Kendall and Hammen (1995, p.511) reviewed the evidence, and came to a similar conclusion:

The growing consensus is that persons with ADHD have a biological predisposition that involves brain function, and that the disorder can be exacerbated by environmental forces (such as complications during pregnancy; family stress).

Effects of ADHD

The primary or main symptoms of ADHD are, of course, failures of attention, an excessive level of activity, and impulsivity. However, many children with ADHD experience a range of other problems that arise directly or indirectly from those primary symptoms. One of the most common of such problems is poor academic performance, a problem that often becomes greater over the school years. According to Barkley et al. (1990a), about 20–25% of children with ADHD have severe difficulties with reading, spelling, or mathematics. Perhaps as a result of these difficulties, adolescents with ADHD are far more likely than other adolescents to leave school before completing their studies (Barkley et al., 1990b).

Children with ADHD tend to have social problems of various kinds. For example, they are often unpopular and rejected by their peers (Carlson, Lahey, & Neeper, 1984). Barkley et al. (1990b) found that ADHD children who had both attentional and behavioural problems were more likely to have social problems than those who had only attentional or behavioural problems. They were at greater risk of developing conduct problems and oppositional behaviour, of having difficulties with other children, and of being put into special classes for behaviour-disordered children.

What is it about children with ADHD that other children find offputting? Erhardt and Hinshaw (1994) found that factors such as intelligence, athletic ability, academic achievement, and physical attractiveness were of little relevance. What mattered was that children with ADHD were perceived as being aggressive and non-compliant.

> ### KEY STUDY EVALUATION — ADHD
>
> A major difficulty with ADHD as a whole lies in the indeterminate nature of its symptoms, which undermines the notion of a unitary syndrome. Identification of primary symptoms should be scientifically based, and this would require accurate and reliable recording of *all* behaviour in *all* situations in order for the diagnosis to be valid. There are both practical and ethical problems associated with this type of research, which would need to be overcome.
>
> Behaviour that is openly exhibited is often an unreliable indicator of the individual's mental activity. It is also open to interpretation and may well be a response to a problem that is operating at a subconscious level.
>
> One way to test the strength of the genetic argument might be to record patterns of behaviour across several situations. The more consistent a person's behaviour, the more a biological causal factor can be suspected.

Discussion points

1. Why do some children with ADHD have such a wide range of social problems?

2. What could we do to make it easier for children with ADHD to adapt?

It is often believed that children with ADHD will grow out of it as they move into adolescence. In fact, children with ADHD typically have problems that last for several years and may persist into adulthood. Barkley et al. (1990a) found that over 70% of children who were diagnosed with ADHD continued to suffer from the disorder when they became adolescents. Some of the most common symptoms shown by these adolescents were the following (the percentages having each symptom are shown in brackets): difficulty following instructions (84%); easily distracted (82%); doesn't seem to listen (80%); difficulty sustaining attention (80%). According to Barkley et al. (1990a), 60% of children diagnosed with ADHD still have some symptoms (e.g. poor concentration) when they become adults.

If the symptoms of ADHD were displayed by a 14-year-old boy and a 30-year-old woman, what cultural and age-based prejudices might affect our interpretation of the two cases? What implications does this have for the classification of ADHD as a recognisable syndrome?

Autism

Autism is generally regarded as the most severe of all the child psychiatric disorders. According to Leo Kanner (1943), the child psychiatrist who first identified it, autism is characterised by "an inability to relate ... in the ordinary way to people and situations ... an extreme autistic aloneness that, whenever possible, disregards, ignores, shuts out anything that comes to the child from outside." In spite of the early work by Kanner, it was only in 1980 with the publication of DSM-III that autism was introduced as an official category.

There are three criteria for autistic disorder in DSM-IV. Six or more symptoms need to be present, with at least two from the first category and one from each of the other categories:

> **KEY TERM**
> **Autism**: a severe disorder involving very poor communication skills and very deficient language development.

Defining autism as a mental disability involves an important distinction between mental impairment that is fixed and that which is treatable, as in the case of mental illness. Why are we more likely to be sympathetic to those who fit into the first category?

1. Qualitative impairment in social interaction: the symptoms include great impairment in the use of multiple non-verbal behaviours (e.g. eye contact); poorly developed peer relationships; a failure to share enjoyment or interests with others; and lack of response to social or emotional behaviour by others.

2. Qualitative impairments in communication: the symptoms include delay in the development of spoken language; reluctance to use speech to initiate or maintain a conversation; stereotyped or repetitive use of language or unusual use of language; and lack of varied spontaneous pretend play or appropriate social imitative play.

3. Restricted repetitive and stereotyped patterns of interests, and behaviour: the symptoms include extreme preoccupation with one or more stereotyped and restricted patterns of interest; compulsive adherence to specific routines or rituals; repetitive motor mannerisms; and persistent preoccupations with parts of objects.

The film *Rainman* has been praised for its attention to detail and for Dustin Hoffman's accurate portrayal of an autistic adult.

Decoupling occurs when children play by separating reality from pretence, e.g. pretending their bedroom is a space capsule. Autistic children are unable to do this.

Three times as many boys as girls suffer from autism, and the majority of autistic children have learning difficulties over and above those produced directly by autism. The onset of autism is typically before the age of 30 months, and is often clearly present even in the first few weeks of life. It is a rare condition affecting only about one child in 2000.

Unlike the overwhelming majority of infants, autistic children do not have an early attachment with their mothers. They rarely smile and generally do not look at their mothers while they are being fed. They even reject attempts by their parents to show affection, refusing to be held or cuddled. When autistic children reach the age of 2 or 3, many of them begin to develop some attachment to their parents. However, the level of attachment is much lower than that shown by other children of the same age.

Autistic children's lack of social involvement extends to their interactions with other children. They rarely play with other children, and generally behave in a very unresponsive way in the presence of other children. Autistic children spend much less time than other children in symbolic play (e.g. pretending that a wooden block is a train engine). As might be imagined from their generally unsociable behaviour, they avoid eye contact. Gaze patterns in autistic children were studied by Mirenda, Donnelflan, and Yoder (1983). They found that autistic children tended not to gaze in order to gain someone's attention, and they rarely gazed so as to direct someone else's attention to an object. In both respects, their gaze patterns were very different from those of normal children.

We have seen in some detail what autistic children do *not* do. What *do* they do? They spend much of their time sitting quietly without becoming involved in any specific social or other activity. They typically give the impression of being totally self-absorbed. Another unusual feature of their behaviour is that they often develop unusually strong attachments to objects (e.g. a blanket; a toy). The most favoured object is carried around wherever they go.

GAZE PATTERNS

The ability to "read" the gaze of others is one that children usually acquire very early, but autistic children are often deficient in this ability. Butterworth and Jarrett (1991) studied children and infants aged between six and eighteen months. They recorded the infants' ability to track their mother's gaze and fixate at the same point. Normal infants' abilities were as follows:

6 months old: Followed mother's gaze but only if she turned her head accordingly.

12 months old: Followed mother's gaze and could locate the precise point of focus, even when the mother moved her eyes without turning her head.

18 months old: Able to follow mother's gaze beyond their immediate field of vision.

These intuitive skills, acquired through quite primitive communication, seem to indicate an understanding of mind. The normal infant has the ability to understand that the other person (in this case the mother) has her own thoughts. The autistic child is unable to achieve this.

Several researchers (e.g. Baron-Cohen, 1994) have argued that the most severe language abnormality shown by autistic children is their insensitivity to the social context. For example, they are often rude without meaning to be, and they do not conform to the turn-taking that is involved in normal conversations. According to Baron-Cohen, autistic children cannot work out the thoughts and intentions of other people, and this prevents them from communicating effectively. One of the features of their speech is what is known as **echolalia**. This involves the child echoing in a rather precise way what he or she has heard someone else say. Another feature of the speech of an autistic child is pronoun reversal, in which the child uses the word "he" or "she" to refer to himself or herself.

> **When autism is diagnosed**
>
> In the case of young (2- to 4-year-old) severely autistic children, speech may be entirely absent. This is sometimes mistaken for deafness until tests prove otherwise. The elimination of the possibility of hearing impairment as a cause of lack of speech, followed by a diagnosis of autism, can cause parents extreme levels of stress. What coping strategies might a parent draw on to deal with such a stressful time? What could be the function of the following in such circumstances?
>
> - Denial.
> - Resistance.
> - Anger.
> - Displacement.
> - Acceptance.

Causes of autism

It is likely that several factors play a part in the development of autism. We will consider some of the evidence relating to three factors. We start with genetic factors, then consider parental style and the theory of mind, and finally look at some possible neurological factors.

Genetic factors

Evidence on the involvement of genetic factors in autism was reported in a twin study by Folstein and Rutter (1978). They studied 11 pairs of monozygotic or identical twins in which one member of each pair was autistic. In four pairs (36%), the other twin was also autistic; this is known as the **concordance rate**. They also studied 10 pairs of dizygotic or fraternal twins in which one member was autistic, and obtained a concordance rate of 0%. The evidence for genetic factors was even greater when cognitive impairments such as delayed speech were considered. The concordance rate was 82% in the monozygotic twins, compared with only 10% in the dizygotic twins (see diagram).

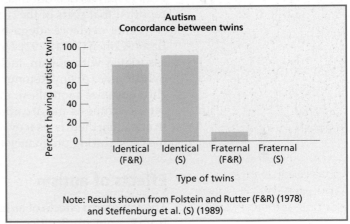

Note: Results shown from Folstein and Rutter (F&R) (1978) and Steffenburg et al. (S) (1989)

Additional evidence for the importance of genetic factors was reported by Steffenburg et al. (1989). They reported a 91% concordance rate in identical twins, compared to 0% in fraternal twins. These findings suggest that genetic factors play a major role in autism.

Parental style

Some early researchers (e.g. Kanner, 1943) argued that a major factor in the development of autism was the behaviour of the parents. More specifically, parents acting in a cold and insensitive way were thought to be more likely than other parents to have an autistic child. However, detailed research has indicated that the parents of autistic children typically behave in very similar ways to other parents (e.g. Cantwell, Baker, & Rutter, 1978). Even if there were evidence that the parents of autistic children did behave in a cold way, this could be due to the unresponsiveness of the child causing the parents' behaviour.

Theory of mind

Leslie (1987) argued that the central problem of autistic children is that they lack an understanding that other people have different ideas and knowledge from their own; this is known as "mind-blindness". They also fail to understand how behaviour is influenced by beliefs and thoughts. According to Leslie, this means that they do not have a theory of mind. As a result, autistic children cannot make sense of the social world, and cannot communicate effectively with other people. According to this theoretical approach, cognitive problems are of primary importance, with social problems occurring as a consequence. This is the opposite of what has normally been assumed, namely, that the social problems are primary and lead on to cognitive problems.

Evidence supporting the theory of mind was reported by Baron-Cohen, Leslie, and Frith (1985). Autistic and normal four-year-old children were presented with the following story:

Sally puts her marble in the basket. Then she goes out. Anne takes Sally's marble, and puts it into her box. Then Sally comes back from her walk. Where will she look for her marble?

How might Piaget have interpreted results such as those of Baron-Cohen et al. (1985)?

Most of the normal children correctly point to the basket, whereas the autistic children point to the box. This happens because they fail to take account of the fact that they possess knowledge that Sally does not. In other words, autistic people find it hard to understand that other children may have a different perspective from their own.

Discussion points

1. Does this approach seem to make sense of autism?
2. Why might mind-blindness lead to social problems?

Brain damage

Evidence that autism may be linked to brain abnormalities or damage has been obtained from studies using brain scans. Rosenbloom et al. (1984), using CAT scans, found that many autistic individuals have unusually large ventricular spaces in the brain. Courchesne et al. (1988) carried out magnetic resonance scans of the brains of autistic children. They reported that parts of the cerebellum were underdeveloped in 82% of cases.

Other evidence suggesting that brain damage may be important was discussed by Baron-Cohen (1994, p.92). He pointed out that there is a wide range of medical conditions associated with autism, including the following: "genetic disorders (such as Fragile X Syndrome, phenylketonuria, tuberous sclerosis, neurofibromatosis, and other chromosomal anomalies); metabolic disorders (such as histidinaemia, abnormalities of purine synthesis and of carbohydrate metabolism); and congenital anomaly syndromes." In addition, there is clear evidence of an association between autism and rubella (German measles) during pregnancy (Baron-Cohen, 1994).

Effects of autism

The long-term effects of autism are generally very serious. About 75% of autistics suffer from learning difficulties, and this greatly reduces their chances of obtaining work. About

CASE STUDY: *Autistic Talents*

Not all aspects of autism are so negative as might be imagined. Some autistic children have startling artistic abilities and can produce drawings in full detail and perspective much earlier than other children.

An autistic girl named Nadia was studied by Selfe (1983). When she was only 5 years old, Nadia could draw realistic pictures of horses, cockerels, and cavalrymen from memory, although she did not speak and had various severe motor problems.

Other talents shown by autistic children and adults include feats of mental arithmetic, for example being able to calculate the day of the week for any given date in the previous 500 years. There have also been gifted autistic musicians who learn to play musical instruments by ear, with no formal training.

These talents may all be linked in some way to the autistic child's narrow focus on the world, through which they can become preoccupied with certain objects or processes in great detail.

Kanner (1943) called gifts like these "islets of ability", which suggests that other aspects of autistic children's intelligence are hidden beneath the surface of a sea of difficulties.

Drawings by 5-year-old Nadia, who is autistic (left) and an average 6½-year-old child (right).

35% of autistics experience depression, and this can start during childhood. These problems, coupled with their greatly retarded social development and poor communication skills, mean that it is very hard for autistic adults to cope with adult life. Lotter (1978) reviewed several studies, and concluded that only between 5% and 17% of autistic children managed to adjust well as adults.

Kanner (1973) reported in detail on the effects of autism in nine adults. Five of them spent most of their lives in institutions, one suffered from epileptic seizures and died at an early age, and one was mute. The other two were in work, but lived at home with their parents and had a very restricted social life.

Various attempts have been made to reduce the adverse effects of autism. One such attempt was the "Natural Language Treatment Programme" which was devised by Koegel, Dell, and Koegel (1987). It was designed to increase the language skills of autistic children by making use of the stimuli and the rewards available in the children's natural environment. Koegel et al. reported that this programme was partially successful. Lovaas (1987) has made use of an operant programme, in which autistic children are rewarded for being less aggressive, for playing with other children, and for talking. A key feature of this programme is that it operates for 40 hours or so a week. Lovaas reported that autistic children in this programme had a mean IQ of 83 at the age of 6, compared to only 55 for control autistic children.

Developmental Dyslexia

The term **developmental dyslexia** is defined as "those difficulties with written and spoken language which are believed to be the results of anomalies of development" (Miles, 1990, p.116). It is important to distinguish this form of dyslexia from acquired dyslexia. Patients with **acquired dyslexia** have lost some of their existing language skills as a result of brain damage (e.g. stroke; injury).

The term "developmental dyslexia" should not be applied to everyone who experiences problems with reading during the course of development. This key point was made very clearly by Ellis (1993, pp.93–94):

> *Central to the concept of developmental dyslexia is the idea of unexpected reading problems; that is, the idea that some children may experience difficulties with the acquisition of reading and writing that cannot be attributed to poor hearing or vision, low intelligence or inadequate educational opportunities.*

How many children suffer from developmental dyslexia? There is no clear answer to this question, because there are differences of opinion about how far a child's reading age should be behind its actual age before the child is called dyslexic. There are also differences of opinion about the definition of low intelligence and what defines inadequate educational opportunities. It is generally believed that reading developmental dyslexia is more common in boys than in girls. However, Shaywitz (1996, p.83) argued as follows: "Boys' reading disabilities are ... identified more often than girls', but studies indicate that such identification is biased. The actual prevalence of the disorder is nearly identical in the two sexes." No convincing evidence for this conclusion was provided.

It has often been argued that words can be read either on the basis of stored information about the whole word (its visual appearance, meaning, and pronunciation) or in a piecemeal way by using rules to translate letters into sounds (see Eysenck & Keane, 1995). For example, you can say the word "cat" correctly either because you recognise it as a familiar word or by working through it letter by letter: c-a-t. This distinction is relevant

According to the Dyslexia Institute, this condition affects 1 in 25 pupils, but dyslexia was omitted from the wording of the 1981 Education Act. Why do you think it has taken so long for educationalists to recognise dyslexia as a specific learning difficulty?

Irregular languages like English cause additional problems for dyslexics. Examples of irregularities of pronunciation in English include:

have→cave
cough→through
bomb→ tomb

There are also words that change pronunciation depending on their context:

He used to live here.
Connect up the live wire.

to developmental dyslexia, and to an important distinction between developmental phonological dyslexia and developmental surface dyslexia. **Developmental phonological dyslexia** is a condition in which reading is based on whole-word information rather than on translating letters into sounds. In contrast, **developmental surface dyslexia** is a condition in which reading is based on translating letters into words rather than on whole-word information.

HM was a female developmental phonological dyslexic who was tested at the age of 17 (Temple & Marshall, 1983). She found it very hard to read three-letter non-words. For example, she read HIB as "hip" and BIX as "back". It is probable that HM made these errors because she had great difficulty in translating letters into sounds.

Allan was a 22-year-old developmental surface dyslexic who was tested by Hanley, Hastie, and Kay (1991). In contrast to HM, he found it easy to read non-words, because he was able to use rules to translate letters into sounds. However, he had problems with irregular words, which do not conform to the letter–sound translation rules. For example, he read BIND as "binned" and SCENE as "sken". These errors occurred because he used letter–sound translation rules on words to which they do not apply.

There are some problems with the notion that all developmental dyslexics are either phonological dyslexics or surface dyslexics. In fact, relatively few dyslexics fall neatly into either category. The great majority of dyslexics have features of both forms of dyslexia (Ellis, 1993). It is thus important to regard terms such as developmental phonological dyslexia and developmental surface dyslexia as convenient labels rather than accurate descriptions of the precise symptoms of any given child.

A theoretical approach to dyslexia

Developmental dyslexics vary in terms of the precise nature of their language problems. However, a theoretical approach that sheds light on most cases of developmental dyslexia is the phonological deficit hypothesis. This can best be understood in the context of work by Bryant and Bradley (1985) and by Shaywitz (1996). Bryant and Bradley argued that a key aspect of learning to read is the ability to translate letters into their corresponding phonemes or sounds. They trained some children to sort words according to their initial and final sounds, whereas others sorted words by meaning. Those children given the sound-based training learned to read more quickly than those given the meaning-based training.

Shaywitz (1996) tested 378 dyslexic and non-dyslexic children on a range of tests. The tests that best distinguished between the two groups were those that assessed phonological processing, that is, the ability to turn letters into sounds. For example, dyslexic children did especially poorly on the Auditory Analysis Test. This requires them to identify the phonemes within a word and then to delete a phoneme from it (e.g. "block" pronounced as "lock").

According to the phonological deficit hypothesis (Shaywitz, 1996, p.80), "when a child is dyslexic, a deficit within the language system ... impairs his or her ability to segment the written word into its underlying phonological components" (p.80). This hypothesis is supported by findings such as those we have just discussed. It seems reasonable to assume on the phonological deficit hypothesis that dyslexics might find it easier to read in languages having a high level of regularity or predictability between sets of letters and speech sounds. There is evidence that the problems of dyslexics are less severe with regular languages such as Spanish and Italian than with irregular languages such as English or Danish (Miles, 1990).

Causes of developmental dyslexia

In order for children to be diagnosed as suffering from developmental dyslexia, they need to have average or above average intelligence, reasonable vision and hearing, and adequate schooling. As a result, it seems unlikely (although not impossible) that developmental dyslexia is caused by environmental problems. The alternative explanation is that developmental dyslexia is caused by biological factors.

Developmental dyslexia tends to run in families, which provides some support for the view that genetic factors are involved. Evidence that the abilities to separate out the sounds in spoken words and to read non-words depend in part on biological factors was reported by Olson et al. (1990). Identical twins were much more likely than fraternal twins to share problems for these specific reading abilities. In other words, the concordance rate was much higher for the identical twins. Cardon et al. (1994) carried out a complex form of genetic analysis, which led them to conclude that a gene on chromosome 6 is responsible for dyslexia. However, even if genetic factors are involved, it does not follow that *all* cases of dyslexia are inherited.

Some insights into the possible causes of developmental dyslexia are also emerging from studies using brain scans. Shaywitz and her colleagues (Shaywitz, 1996) have been using functional magnetic resonance imaging (see Chapter 4). They studied more than 200 dyslexic and non-dyslexic children and adults, and found that phonological processing occurs within the inferior frontal gyrus of the brain. The inferior frontal gyri are in the frontal lobe in areas mainly associated with language. There are significant neural differences between dyslexics and non-dyslexics in this part of the brain. In contrast, functional magnetic resonance imaging did not reveal differences between the two groups in those parts of the brain involved in the identification of letters or gaining access to meaning.

The work of Shaywitz has also helped to explain why females are more likely than males to overcome many of the problems of dyslexia. They found that the left and the right inferior frontal gyrus is involved in phonological processing in females, whereas it was generally only the left inferior frontal gyrus that was activated in males.

How would below average intelligence, inadequate schooling, and defects of vision or hearing affect whether a diagnosis of dyslexia was given?

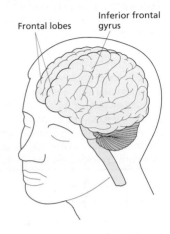

Given the frequency of dyslexia, should schools devote more resources to helping such children? How can schools help to alleviate the stigma associated with dyslexia?

Treatment for dyslexia

It is important to find suitable treatments for dyslexia to improve the reading skills of dyslexic children. It is also important because an inability to read properly often causes dyslexic children to have low self-esteem. This is perhaps especially so if the dyslexia is not diagnosed. For example, consider the case of Jackie Stewart, who was the world champion in Formula One racing on three occasions and then went on to become a very successful businessman. He was laughed at in school because he could not read, and he was very relieved in adult life to discover that this was due to dyslexia rather than to a lack of intelligence.

Many teachers of dyslexic children have favoured the use of a multi-sensory approach to reading. The essence of this approach is that "the pupil needs to listen carefully, to look carefully, and to pay attention both to the mouth movements used in speaking the word and to the hand movements used in writing it" (Miles, 1990, p.120). This approach has proved to be of value.

Computer-based therapy

Shaywitz (1996) discussed a new approach to help language-impaired children, most of whom are dyslexic. As we have seen, dyslexic children find it very hard to identify the phonemes or sounds within spoken or written words. Indeed, it is likely that this is the key problem that prevents dyslexics from learning to read at the normal rate, especially since dyslexic children typically have roughly average intelligence. Paula Tallal and Michael Merzenich developed an approach to the treatment of dyslexia based on this fact. They also took account of the finding that phonemes have to be presented much longer to dyslexic children than to non-dyslexic ones in order to be identified.

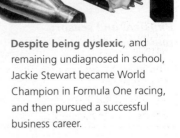

Despite being dyslexic, and remaining undiagnosed in school, Jackie Stewart became World Champion in Formula One racing, and then pursued a successful business career.

KEY STUDY EVALUATION — Dyslexia

Given the precise needs of dyslexic children, a comprehensive programme of diagnosis and support is required. In addition to the presentation of phonemes, as in the Shaywitz study, children require an all-round package that meets their individual needs. Early identification of dyslexia is vital to language improvement and screening at age 7 has been recommended. Other verbal difficulties commonly associated with dyslexia, such as sentence structuring weaknesses and difficulties in distinguishing words that rhyme, could be picked up even earlier, at preschool level.

Apart from earlier identification, a full programme of individual needs should be drawn up and followed. This type of tailor-made approach should attend to all areas of the individual's language deficit, and not just to his or her phonological understanding. Thus, it is recommended that visual and oral skills are involved as well as reading and writing. Fluent oral communication helps to improve self-confidence. Computer skills, including the use of spell-checking, help the individual regain confidence in their abilities. Lastly, public preconceptions about dyslexia sometimes overshadow the considerable variation in difficulty experienced, so it is important to avoid labelling students, who should be treated as individuals.

Tallal and Merzenich devised a computer-based therapy in which similar phonemes such as "pa" and "da" are stretched out in time so that dyslexic children can distinguish between them. They found that 11 children trained in this way showed two years of language development in only one month (Shaywitz, 1996). This computer-based therapy is very promising, but its precise value will only become clear when it has been used on larger groups of children, and when it has been compared systematically against other forms of therapy.

Discussion points

1. How promising does this form of computer-based therapy seem to be?
2. Is it appropriate to focus so much on the problems that dyslexic children have with phoneme identification?

PERSONAL REFLECTIONS

- Hopefully, the work discussed in this chapter will lead to a better understanding of the problems and needs of disabled children, adolescents, and adults. Unfortunately, there is considerable evidence that those who are disabled in any way are not well treated by society. For example, it was found in a British survey in 1998 that 60% of those under the age of 35 had no regular contact with disabled people. What is the answer? According to John Knight, head of policy for Britain's leading disability care charity, Leonard Cheshire Homes, "Sympathy reinforces the impression that they [disabled people] are objects of pity; it makes them feel inadequate; and it injures their sense of pride. What they want is for society to relate to them as ... an individual, not part of a 'disabled lump'."

SUMMARY

Learning difficulties

According to DSM-IV, the criteria for a diagnosis of mental retardation (or learning difficulties) are the following: IQ below 70; deficits or impairments in various areas of adaptive functioning; and an onset of impaired intellectual functioning before the age of 18. There are four degrees of retardation (mild, moderate, severe, and profound), with most children with learning difficulties falling into the mild category. About 70% of children with learning difficulties have cultural/familial retardation, which is believed to be caused by a mixture of biological and social factors. There are numerous other causes of learning difficulties, including tuberous sclerosis, Lesch-Nyhan syndrome, chromosomal aberrations (e.g. Down's syndrome; fragile X syndrome), and metabolic diseases (e.g. PKU; Tay-Sachs disease). Children and adults with learning difficulties (especially those who are severely or profoundly retarded) experience a range of problems. These problems include the following: slowness in acquiring academic skills; deficient social skills; very limited communication skills; difficulties in learning basic self-care skills; and inability to find a job because of a lack of qualifications.

Physical and sensory impairments

The central problems for blind children concern social relationships and friendships with other children. Most blind children of 10 describe themselves as lonely. Blind children acquire language in a fairly normal way, but they have problems in learning to read. It takes blind children over a year to learn the Braille alphabet, mainly because the sense of touch is not well developed. Intervention programmes to train parents and teachers how to interact with blind children have proved only modestly successful. Large-letter versions of Braille speed up letter learning.

Development proceeds more rapidly in deaf children with deaf parents than in those with hearing parents. Deaf children have social problems because of difficulties in communication and narrow social experience. Deaf children have problems in all aspects of spoken and written language, in spite of their use of lip-reading and sign language. Slow language development has adverse effects on their academic and social development. Residential schools and intervention programmes based on Total Communication have proved useful.

Cerebral palsy involves motor impairments caused by non-progressive brain damage. The motor deficits vary widely in their nature and severity, but there are generally problems in speaking. Most cerebrally palsied children have great difficulties with communication, and this disrupts their academic and social development. Microcomputers can be used to assist communication, and Peto and Rood have designed separate programmes to increase the rate of motor development.

Attention-deficit hyperactivity disorder

There are three types of attention-deficit hyperactivity disorder (ADHD): predominantly inattentive type; predominantly hyperactive type; and combined type. Twin studies suggest that genetic factors are involved, and other evidence indicates that the frontal lobes are involved. The parents of ADHD children tend to behave negatively towards them mainly because of the child's disruptive behaviour. Diet does not seem to play a role in ADHD. Children with ADHD perform poorly at school, and they tend to be unpopular because they are aggressive and non-compliant.

Autism

The main criteria for autistic disorder are qualitative impairment in social interaction, qualitative impairment in communication, and restricted repetitive and stereotyped patterns of behaviour, interests, and behaviour. Three times as many boys as girls have autistic disorder. Twin studies indicate that genetic factors are important. Brain scans have shown that parts of the cerebellum are underdeveloped in most autistic children. Attempts have also been made to explain autism by the theory of mind and in terms of cold and insensitive parenting.

Developmental dyslexia

Developmental dyslexics have problems with reading and writing, but their other learning abilities are normal. Developmental dyslexics can be divided into phonological and surface dyslexics. According to the phonological deficit hypothesis, dyslexics' main problem is turning written words into phonemes or sounds. Genetic factors, possibly centring on a gene on chromosome 6, seem to be involved. Computer-based therapy, in which phonemes are stretched out in time, has proved successful.

MP David Blunkett, the first blind person to become a government minister.

FURTHER READING

The most useful general book on atypical development in children is V. Lewis (1987), *Development and handicap*, Oxford: Blackwell. Most of the topics in this chapter are discussed in a readable way in D. Barlow and V.M. Durand (1995), *Abnormal psychology*, New York: Brooks/Cole. Blindness is discussed very fully in V. Lewis and G.M. Collis (1997), *Blindness and psychological development in young children*, Leicester: BPS Books. Key issues associated with deafness are dealt with in M. Marschark (1993), *Psychological development of deaf children*, Oxford: Oxford University Press.

REVISION QUESTIONS

1   Describe and assess psychological research into problems associated with learning difficulties.   (24 marks)
2   Critically consider what we have learned from psychological research into the problems of coping with *either* physical *or* sensory impairments.   (24 marks)
3   Discuss *two* theories relating to the causes of emotional and/or behavioural problems in childhood.   (24 marks)

- **What is abnormality?**
  In order to treat mental disorders, we must first decide how to define abnormality.

  The statistical approach
  Concept of social deviance
  Rosenhan and Seligman's seven features of abnormality
  Cultural context
  DSM and ICD definitions

- **Should we classify?**
  Can mental disorders be labelled in the same way as physical disorders?

  Rosenhan's fake patients study
  Scheff's labelling theory
  Anti-psychiatry views of Szasz and Laing

- **Classification systems**
  The difficulties of compiling any kind of system for diagnosing mental disorders.

  Axes and features of the DSM
  ICD categories

- **Models of abnormality**
  Different ways of deciding why and how mental disorders occur.

  Medical and behavioural models
  Ellis and Beck's cognitive model
  Humanistic model of Rogers and Maslow

- **Cultural and subcultural differences**
  Are the same mental disorders found in every culture?

  Culture-based syndromes, e.g. koro, amok
  Cross-cultural studies of schizophrenia
  Weisz et al.'s suppression–facilitation model
  Cultural, gender, and social class bias

640

24

Models of Abnormality

This palm tree differs from the norm.

Therapists who want to provide treatment for patients with mental disorders must distinguish between normal and abnormal behaviour. Most of them also feel the need to be able to classify or diagnose the symptoms of their patients. In other words, they want to identify the specific mental disorder from which each of their patients is suffering. As we will see, there are many difficulties in the way of devising a satisfactory system for classifying mental disorders. Indeed, it has been argued that the attempt is not worthwhile, because for example, classifying patients does not do justice to each person's unique pattern of symptoms.

Many of the major classificatory systems are based very much on Western conceptions of abnormality and mental disorder. In recent years, however, there has been a growing recognition that it is very important to take account of cultural and subcultural differences. As Westen (1996, p.578) pointed out, "Diagnosis of psychiatric illness always requires knowledge of the patient's culture or subculture." More needs to be done in that direction, because there is evidence of various biases in diagnosis, including cultural bias, gender bias, and social class bias. Some of the reasons for the existence of such biases are discussed towards the end of this chapter (see also Chapter 28).

What Is Abnormality?

The statistical approach

There are several ways in which one might define "abnormality". One way is based on the statistical approach, according to which the abnormal is that which is statistically rare in the population. Consider, for example, trait anxiety (the tendency to experience high levels of anxiety) as assessed by Spielberger's State–Trait Anxiety Inventory. The mean score for trait anxiety is about 40, and only about 1 person in 50 obtains a score higher than 55. Thus, those who score 55 or more can be regarded as abnormal, in the sense that their scores deviate from those of the great majority of the population.

This statistical approach addresses part of what is meant by "abnormality" in the clinical context. However, it is not adequate. There are many people whose scores on trait anxiety are unusually high, but who nevertheless lead contented and fulfilled lives. It would make little sense to argue that they are clinically abnormal. Very low scores on trait anxiety (scores of 25 or less) are also statistically abnormal. However, a low susceptibility to anxiety hardly indicates clinical abnormality.

The statistical approach takes no account of whether deviations from the average are desirable or undesirable. "Abnormality" refers to statistically rare behaviour. However, that behaviour must also be regarded as undesirable and damaging to the individual.

Change over time

Ideas concerning social deviance are subject to change from one generation to the next. For example, giving birth to a child outside marriage in the early part of the twentieth century often resulted in the mother being rejected by her family and society in general. Some women in this situation were even confined in psychiatric institutions for many years because their behaviour was regarded as shocking and unacceptable. Why do you think attitudes like these have changed so dramatically during the last 100 years?

Spitting at policemen would normally be considered unacceptable but may be viewed as less socially deviant during an anti-road protest.

What aspects of your own upbringing would you expect to see changed (and unchanged) in the generation that will follow you?

Abnormal behaviour...?

Social deviance

An important part of what is missing from the statistical approach to abnormality is any consideration of the impact of an individual's behaviour on others. This has led some psychologists to emphasise the notion of social deviance: people who behave in a socially deviant and apparently incomprehensible way that makes others feel uncomfortable should be regarded as abnormal.

Most people who are labelled as clinically abnormal do behave in a socially deviant way. However, clinical abnormality should not be equated with social deviance. There are several different reasons why someone is socially deviant. Some people are socially deviant because they have chosen a non-conformist lifestyle. Others are socially deviant because their behaviour is motivated by high principles (e.g. those in Nazi Germany who spoke out against the atrocities that were being committed, or Russian dissidents who were sent to psychiatric institutions for many years).

There are other problems with attaching too much significance to social deviance. What is regarded by society as deviant or abnormal behaviour varies very much from one culture to another. For example, homosexuality is regarded as a perversion and a criminal offence in some societies, whereas in others (e.g. ancient Greece) it has been tolerated or even encouraged. There have been considerable changes in attitudes towards homosexuality in recent decades in the United Kingdom. Homosexuality between consenting adults was a criminal offence until the 1960s, but has not been so since then. In 1995, the age of consent for homosexual activity was lowered to 18, and there is pressure to lower it further to 16.

Another example of cultural differences was provided by Gleitman (1986). The Kwakiutl Indians engage in a special ceremony in which they burn valuable blankets in order to cast shame on their rivals. If someone in our society deliberately set fire to his or her most valuable possessions, they would be regarded as very odd or mentally ill.

The fact that social deviance should be rejected as the sole criterion of abnormality does not mean that it is entirely irrelevant. After all, people derive much of their pleasure in life from their interactions with other people. As a result, most people find it important for a contented existence to avoid behaving in socially deviant ways that bemuse or upset others.

Abnormality as a concept

Concepts differ very much in their precision. "Abnormality" is an imprecise concept, which is as hard to define as "games". Thus, abnormal behaviour can take different forms, and can involve different features. Moreover, there is no single feature that can always be relied on to distinguish between normal and abnormal behaviour. What is needed is to identify the main features that are more likely to be found in abnormal than in normal individuals. Seven such features were proposed by Rosenhan and Seligman (1989). The more of these features possessed by an individual, the greater the likelihood that he or she will be categorised as abnormal.

Seven features of abnormality

According to Rosenhan and Seligman (1989), there are seven main features of abnormality: suffering; maladaptiveness; vividness and unconventionality; unpredictability and loss of control; irrationality and incomprehensibility; observer discomfort; and violation of moral and ideal standards.

- Suffering. Most abnormal individuals report that they are suffering, and so the presence of suffering is a key feature of abnormality. However, it is not adequate on its own because nearly all normal individuals grieve and suffer when a loved one dies. In addition, some abnormal individuals (e.g. psychopaths or those with anti-social personality disorder) treat other people very badly but do not seem to suffer themselves.

- Maladaptiveness. Maladaptive behaviour is behaviour that prevents an individual from achieving major life goals such as enjoying good relationships with other people or working effectively. Most abnormal behaviour is maladaptive in this sense. However, maladaptive behaviour can occur because of an absence of relevant knowledge or skills as well as because of abnormality.

- Vividness and unconventionality of behaviour. Vivid and unconventional behaviour is behaviour that is relatively unusual. The ways in which abnormal individuals behave in various situations differ substantially from the ways in which we would expect most people to behave in those situations. However, the same is true of non-conformists.

- Unpredictability and loss of control. Most people behave in a fairly predictable and controlled way. In contrast, the behaviour of abnormal individuals is often very variable and uncontrolled, and is inappropriate. However, most people can sometimes behave in unpredictable and uncontrolled ways.

How do attitudes to flamboyant behaviour vary in different circumstances?

- Irrationality and incomprehensibility. A common feature of abnormal behaviour is that it is not clear why anyone would choose to behave in that way. In other words, the behaviour is irrational and incomprehensible. However, behaviour can seem incomprehensible simply because we do not know the reasons for it. For example, a migraine may cause someone to behave in ways that are incomprehensible to other people.

- Observer discomfort. Our social behaviour is governed by a number of unspoken rules of behaviour. These include maintaining reasonable eye contact with other people and not standing too close to other people. Those who see these rules being broken often experience some discomfort. Observer discomfort may reflect cultural differences in behaviour and style rather than abnormality. For example, Arabs like to stand very close to other people, and this can be disturbing to Europeans.

- Violation of moral and ideal standards. Behaviour may be judged to be abnormal when it violates moral standards, even when many or most people fail to maintain those standards. For example, religious leaders have sometimes claimed that masturbation is wicked and abnormal, in spite of the fact that it is widespread.

Rosenhan and Seligman (1989, p.17) also addressed the issue of what is meant by the term "normality", defining it as "simply the absence of abnormality". In other words, the fewer of the seven features of abnormality displayed by individuals in their everyday lives, the more they can be regarded as normal. We should think in terms of degrees of normality and abnormality.

Evaluation

One of the greatest problems with most of the seven features of abnormality proposed by Rosenhan and Seligman is that they involve making subjective judgements. Behaviour that causes severe discomfort to one observer may have no effect on another observer,

...Not when rescuing a cat!

■ Research activity: The seven features of abnormality

Imagine a continuum from extremely abnormal behaviour at one end to normality at the other. At what point does our behaviour become unacceptable? Bearing in mind Rosenhan and Seligman's definitions, consider these experiences. Try to judge the point on the continuum at which such behaviour might start to be regarded as "abnormal".

Suffering: Grief at the loss of a loved one.
Maladaptiveness: Disregard for one's own safety, e.g. taking part in extreme sports.
Vividness and unconventionality: Tattooing or body piercing.
Unpredictability and loss of control: Losing one's temper.
Irrationality and incomprehensibility: Remaining friendly towards someone who is hostile.
Observer discomfort: Laughing at inappropriate times, e.g. when someone is describing a sad event.
Violation of moral and ideal standards: Removing one's clothes to sunbathe on the beach.

Your answers should reflect the following:

• Are we able to say when a behaviour ceases to be normal or safe?

• Are the criteria we use influenced by our cultural and personal backgrounds?

Moral codes

The subjective judgements we make when deciding whether or not a particular form of behaviour is normal are derived from the moral codes or standards that we have observed in the behaviour of significant others. According to Piaget, this forms an essential part of human development. We never become entirely autonomous in our moral thinking. Even as adults our thinking about morality often refers to a collective understanding of the right way to behave in a given situation. Someone who demonstrates a deviation from this may be perceived as either "mad" or "bad".

and behaviour that violates one person's moral standards may be consistent with another person's moral standards.

Another problem with some of the proposed features of abnormality (e.g. irrationality and incomprehensibility; unpredictability and loss of control; vividness and unconventionality) is that they also apply to people who are non-conformists or who simply have their own idiosyncratic style. This issue was addressed in the introduction to the third revised version of the *Diagnostic and Statistical Manual of Mental Disorders* (DSM-III-R), published in 1987 (p.xxii):

Neither deviant behaviour, e.g. political, religious, or sexual, nor conflicts that are primarily between the individual and society are mental disorders unless the deviance or condition is a symptom of a dysfunction (i.e. impairment of function) in the person.

Cultural context

Notions of abnormality vary from one culture to another, and within the same culture at different times. The way in which homosexuality is regarded has altered over successive editions of **DSM**. In DSM-II, which was published in 1968, homosexuality was classified as a sexual deviation. In DSM-III, published in 1980, homosexuality was no longer categorised as a mental disorder. However, there was a new category of "ego-dystonic homosexuality". This was to be used only for homosexuals who wished to become heterosexual. In DSM-III-R, the category of ego-dystonic homosexuality had disappeared. However, there was a category of "sexual disorder not otherwise specified", with "persistent and marked distress about one's sexual orientation" being included. This remains the case in DSM-IV.

The importance of the cultural context can be seen if we return to the seven features of abnormality proposed by Rosenhan and Seligman. Many of the features (e.g. vividness and unconventional behaviour; irrationality and incomprehensibility; observer discomfort) refer to behaviour that is not in accord with the social norms or expectations of the culture. As the social norms or expectations vary across cultures, it follows that abnormality has a somewhat different meaning from one culture to another.

Homosexuality ceased to be categorised as a mental disorder in the 1980 edition of DSM.

DSM and ICD definitions of mental disorder

DSM-IV represents a major attempt to provide an adequate system of classification for mental disorder. According to DSM-IV (1994), mental disorder can be defined as follows:

A clinically significant behaviour or psychological syndrome or pattern that occurs in a person and that is associated with present distress (a painful symptom) or disability (impairment of one or more important areas of functioning) or with a significantly

KEY TERM

DSM: the *Diagnostic and Statistical Manual of Mental Disorders* published by the American Psychiatric Association.

increased risk of suffering death, pain, disability, or an important loss of freedom. In addition, this syndrome or pattern must not be merely an expectable response to a particular event, for example, the death of a loved one.

There is an interesting difference between this definition and the approach adopted by Rosenhan and Seligman. The DSM-IV definition emphasises the individual's distress and suffering, whereas Rosenhan and Seligman attach more significance to the effects of an individual's behaviour on other people. The advantage of the DSM-IV definition is that it excludes individuals who merely behave in a non-conformist way.

Another major classificatory system is the *International Classification of Diseases and Health Related Problems (ICD)*, which is published by the World Health Organisation. According to ICD-10, which was published in 1992, mental disorder implies "the existence of a clinically recognisable set of symptoms or behaviour associated in most cases with distress and with interference with personal functions." This definition resembles that of DSM-IV, in that it focuses mainly on the individual's personal distress rather than on society's reactions to certain atypical forms of behaviour.

Ethical issues: The two major indices used to classify and diagnose mental disorders aim to be objective, but in society there are fears and prejudices against people thus classified. In what ways might individual people and their families be protected from the stigma involved?

Should We Classify?

Nearly all psychiatrists and clinical psychologists accept that abnormality or mental disorder exists. They also accept that those individuals who exhibit abnormal symptoms should receive a psychiatric diagnosis or label which specifies the nature of the abnormality. This psychiatric diagnosis is assumed to be of value when it comes to determining the appropriate form of treatment.

Those who advocate the use of classification typically point to its successful use in the treatment of physical illness. Doctors rarely prescribe any treatment to a sick patient until they have satisfied themselves that they have diagnosed correctly the nature of his or her illness. The substantial increase in longevity in most Western societies over the past 100 years is partly due to the success of this approach.

Are there important parallels between physical illness and mental illness or disorder? It is more difficult to diagnose mental disorders than physical illnesses. Many of the symptoms reported by those suffering from mental disorders are subjective (e.g. "I feel very depressed"; "Life does not seem worthwhile"). This is a real problem, because people may differ considerably in what they mean by being "very depressed". In contrast, doctors trying to diagnose a physical illness often have information about the *signs* of disease (the findings from medical or laboratory tests such as X-rays) as well as about the patient's *symptoms* (their account of the ways in which they feel ill). The findings from medical tests often provide much more precise information than is available to psychiatrists and clinical psychologists. For example, an X-ray can prove that a patient has a broken bone in his or her foot, and a blood test can reveal that someone is suffering from malaria.

There is another important difference between physical illness and mental disorder. The **aetiology** (cause of a disease) of most physical diseases is known, whereas that of mental disorders is usually only partially known. For example, malaria is caused by infected mosquitoes, and a diagnosis of malaria can be confirmed by establishing that the patient has recently visited a part of the world in which there are many infected mosquitoes.

KEY TERMS
ICD: the *International Classification of Diseases and Health Related Problems* published by the World Health Organisation.
Aetiology: the cause of a disease or disorder.

Results of medical tests provide more precise information than is available to psychiatrists and clinical psychologists.

In contrast, psychiatrists or clinical psychologists diagnosing a mental disorder cannot usually check the accuracy of their diagnoses by establishing the cause.

The differences between medical diagnosis and psychiatric diagnosis are often less extreme than has been suggested so far. For example, the only symptom reported by a patient with backache may be a certain amount of pain, and there may be no relevant medical tests that could be carried out. This symptom is as subjective as the symptoms reported by mental patients. Falek and Moser (1975) found that doctors often disagreed among themselves on the diagnoses of physical illness such as angina, tonsillitis, and emphysema. Indeed, disagreement was as great as that for the diagnosis of schizophrenia among psychiatrists. However, the level of agreement among the doctors would undoubtedly have been greater if they had had the results of medical tests available to them before making their diagnosis.

Rosenhan

David Rosenhan (1973) argued that psychiatric classification can be very inaccurate. In his controversial study, eight normal people (five men and three women) tried to gain admission to 12 different psychiatric hospitals. They all complained of hearing indistinct voices which seemed to be saying "empty", "hollow", and "thud". Even though this was the only symptom they claimed to have, seven of them were diagnosed as suffering from **schizophrenia,** which is a very severe condition involving substantial distortions of thought, emotion, and behaviour.

After these eight normal people were admitted to psychiatric wards, all of them said that they felt fine, and that they no longer had any symptoms. However, it took an average of 19 days before they were discharged. For seven of them, the psychiatric classification at the time of discharge was "schizophrenia in remission". This classification carried with it the implication that they might become schizophrenic again in the future.

Rosenhan was not content with having apparently found that the sane can be classified as insane. He next decided to see whether the insane could be classified as sane. He told the staff at a psychiatric hospital that one or more pseudo-patients (normal people pretending to have schizophrenic symptoms) would try to gain admittance to the hospital. No pseudo-patients actually appeared, but 41 genuine patients were judged with great confidence to be pseudo-patients by at least one member of staff. Nineteen of these genuine patients were suspected of being frauds by one psychiatrist plus another member of staff. Rosenhan (1973) concluded, "It is clear that we cannot distinguish the sane from the insane in psychiatric hospitals."

If we accept Rosenhan's conclusions, then attempts at classification appear doomed. However, there are various limitations in his study. The most powerful argument against Rosenhan's findings was provided by Kety (1974), who offered the following analogy:

KEY STUDY EVALUATION — Rosenhan

Rosenhan's research in the early 1970s exposed the imprecision of psychiatric diagnosis. Psychiatrists are often unable to verify patients' symptoms, and can only rely on observable behaviour. A number of observations can be made about Rosenhan's research. First, his findings demonstrate the lack of scientific evidence on which medical diagnoses can be made—a crucial issue when an individual's personal liberty may be at stake. Second, the use of somatic treatments such as drugs and ECT (electro-convulsive therapy) was the subject of much discussion in the 1960s and 1970s. Although Rosenhan's fake patients were not subjected to these treatments, the study underlined the need for caution when making decisions about appropriate types of therapy.

The main concerns about Rosenhan's research are ethical ones. In both studies, professionals were deliberately misled about the true status of patients. The deception of professionals whose job it is to treat people with mental disorders is no more ethically justified than deception of patients or participants in a study. However, it is probable that a more open investigation, with the full knowledge and co-operation of the psychiatrists, would have failed to reveal anything of interest.

A further issue concerns the welfare of the genuine patients. During Rosenhan's second study, it would have been possible for a patient who was exhibiting normal behaviour, but in fact was suffering from a spasmodic mental disorder, to be mistakenly discharged from psychiatric care.

If I were to drink a quart of blood and, concealing what I had done, come to the emergency room of any hospital vomiting blood, the behaviour of the staff would be quite predictable. If they labelled and treated me as having a bleeding peptic ulcer, I doubt that I could argue convincingly that medical science does not know how to diagnose that condition.

Psychiatrists can hardly be blamed for not expecting completely normal people to try to gain admittance to a psychiatric hospital. Errors of diagnosis were made under the very unusual conditions of Rosenhan's (1973) study. However, that does not mean that psychiatrists generally cannot distinguish between the normal and the abnormal.

Rosenhan's findings are actually less dramatic than they seem to be. The diagnosis "schizophrenia in remission" is used very rarely. It suggests that many of the psychiatrists were

KEY TERM

Schizophrenia: a severe condition in which there is a loss of contact with reality, including distortions of thought, emotion, and behaviour.

unconvinced that the patients had really suffered from schizophrenia. This is confirmed by the fact that these normal patients were released within a few days of admission. In those days, many schizophrenic patients spent years in hospital before being allowed to leave.

Discussion points

1. What do you think of Rosenhan's research?

2. Did Rosenhan show that psychiatrists cannot tell the difference between the sane and the insane?

Other problems with classification

A powerful argument against classifying mental disorders was provided by Scheff (1966) in his **labelling theory**. He argued that someone who acquires the stigma (mark of social disgrace) of a psychiatric diagnosis or label will be treated as a mentally ill person. As a result, his or her behaviour may change in directions that make the label more appropriate than it was in the first place. Thus, rather than the symptoms leading to the psychiatric label or diagnosis, it may sometimes be the case that the label plays a part in creating the symptoms.

Rosenhan (1973) found that the way in which someone is treated is influenced by the label they have been given. On numerous occasions, Rosenhan's normal patients with a diagnosis of schizophrenia approached a staff member in their psychiatric ward with a polite request for information. These requests were ignored 88% of the time by nurses and attendants, and 71% of the time by psychiatrists. This unresponsiveness by the psychiatric staff suggests that those who are labelled as schizophrenic are regarded as having very low status. Such treatment could clearly increase the severity of the symptoms experienced by real schizophrenics.

> **Labels and symptoms**
>
> Imagine that you are in a situation where you have been wrongly diagnosed as suffering from a mental disorder such as schizophrenia. How would you react to such a situation? Would you be incredulous? Furious? Tearful? Shocked and withdrawn? How could all those emotions be interpreted by those people whose job it is to assess your mental condition?

The notion that the psychiatric label or classification attached to a patient has little real meaning was taken to its extremes by Thomas Szasz (1962, 1974). His basic argument was that mental illness is a myth. In his own words (Szasz, 1962), "Strictly speaking … disease or illness can affect only the body. Hence, there can be no such thing as mental illness." Why, then, do psychiatrists and clinical psychologists pretend that there is such a thing as mental illness? According to Szasz (1974), society uses stigmatising labels to exclude those whose behaviour fails to conform to society's norms. Such labels include the following: criminal; prostitute; gypsy; foreigner. "Mental illness" is simply a stigmatising label used to exclude non-conformists from society.

Critics of Szasz (e.g. Dammann, 1997) have argued that he used the terms "disease" and "illness" in a very narrow sense, and that it is not reasonable to draw a sharp distinction between physical illness and mental conditions. For example, an outstanding sportswoman who breaks her leg has a physical injury, but is also likely to experience psychological problems as a result.

The Scottish psychiatrist, R.D. Laing agreed with Szasz (1962) that patients are given psychiatric diagnoses because their behaviour is different from that of most other members of society. He argued that it is society rather than the patient that is to blame. According to Laing (1967), "By the time the new human being is 15 or so, we are left with a being like ourselves, a half-crazed creature more or less adjusted to a mad world. This is normality in our present age."

In what way might the effects of labelling be applied to other groups, e.g. football fans? What similarities exist between these other groups and people who have been labelled "mentally ill"?

Cross-cultural issues: Are the norms that society uses to judge people's behaviour stable across different cultures? How might this be relevant to people who settle as immigrants in a different culture from their own?

> **KEY TERM**
> **Labelling theory**: the notion that attaching a psychiatric label to a patient may worsen his or her condition, because he or she is then treated as someone who is mentally ill.

Advantages of classification

If psychiatrists and clinical psychologists avoided any attempt at classification, then they would have to regard each patient as being entirely unique. It would be very hard to develop an understanding of the causes of mental disorder (and of the appropriate form of treatment) if every patient were regarded as being unique. Grouping patients according to their diagnoses provides a good basis for an exploration of the factors responsible for any given form of disorder, and for the development of effective forms of treatment.

Classificatory systems (e.g. DSM) increasingly make some allowance for uniqueness, while also focusing on the ways in which different patients are similar. According to Gelder et al. (1989; cited in Gross, 1996), "The use of classification can certainly be combined with consideration of a patient's unique qualities, indeed it is important to combine the two."

Classification Systems

The starting point for any attempt to classify mental disorders is to identify the patient's symptoms. However, the same (or very similar) symptoms are found in what are otherwise quite different mental disorders. For example, anxiety is a major symptom in generalised anxiety disorder, obsessive-compulsive disorder, and the phobias. As a result, the emphasis in most classificatory systems is not on individual symptoms but on syndromes (sets of symptoms that are generally found together).

The symptom–syndrome approach to abnormality owes much to the work of Emil Kraepelin (1856–1926). In medicine, it is usual to diagnose physical diseases on the basis of physical symptoms, and Kraepelin felt that the same approach was suitable for mental illness. He emphasised the use of physical or behavioural symptoms (e.g. insomnia; disorganised speech) rather than less precise symptoms such as poor social adjustment or misplaced drives.

Different patients rarely present the same symptoms. Thus, patients given the same psychiatric diagnosis (e.g. schizophrenia) differ somewhat from each other in their sets of symptoms. They typically possess only some of the symptoms defining the diagnostic category. There is a grey area in which the fit between a patient's symptoms and those forming the syndrome of a diagnostic category is relatively poor. In such cases, it is hard to know whether or not the diagnostic category is appropriate.

Diagnostic and Statistical Manual: DSM

The current version of the *Diagnostic and Statistical Manual of Mental Disorders* (DSM-IV), published in 1994, is the most widely used classificatory system. The first version of DSM was published in 1952, and was replaced by DSM-II in 1968. The greatest problem with DSM-II was its great unreliability, in the sense that two psychiatrists would often produce very different diagnoses of the same patient. Spitzer and Fleiss (1974) reviewed studies on the reliability of DSM-II. They concluded that reliability reached acceptable levels only with the broad categories of mental retardation, alcoholism, and organic brain syndrome.

DSM-II was so unreliable because many of its symptom definitions were vague. Attempts were made with DSM-III (1980) and DSM-III-R (1987) to offer more precise definitions. For example, DSM-II was vague about the length of time involved in a "major depressive episode". In contrast, DSM-III-R specified that five symptoms (including either depressed mood or loss of interest or pleasure) should be present over a two-week period in order to qualify.

DSM-III and DSM-III-R were also an improvement over earlier versions of DSM in another important way. The two versions of DSM-III focus very much on diagnosing patients on the basis of their observable symptoms. This contrasts with DSM-I and DSM-II, in which there was a strong emphasis on the supposed causes of mental disorders. Thus, there was a shift from a theoretically based approach to one that is more descriptive. That was desirable, because the theories used in the construction of DSM-I and DSM-II were flawed in various ways.

There was another important change between DSM-II and DSM-III. In DSM-II, the diagnosis consisted of a single category or label (e.g. schizophrenia). In contrast, DSM-III,

■ Research activity: Reliability of DSM

Examine the reasons why previous versions of the DSM (DSM-II, III, and III-R) proved to be unreliable. Compare the most recent version to these earlier ones for reliability, writing your answers in the following format:

	Strengths	Weaknesses
DSM-II	Broad categories of mental disorders, e.g. "mental retardation"	Vague definitions of symptoms

Try to use various other reference sources to help make your answer as full as possible.

DSM-III-R, and DSM-IV are all based on a *multi-axial system*, in which the patient is evaluated on five different axes or scales.

Axes and features of DSM

The first three axes or scales of DSM-IV are always used, whereas the last two are optional. Here are the axes:

Axis 1: Clinical disorders: this axis permits the patient's disorder to be diagnosed.

Axis 2: Personality disorders and mental retardation: this axis is used to identify long-term patterns of impaired functioning stemming from personality disorders or mental retardation.

Axis 3: General medical conditions: this axis concerns any physical illness that might influence the patient's emotional state or ability to function effectively.

Axis 4: Psychosocial and environmental problems: this axis is concerned with any significant stressful events that occurred within 12 months of the onset of the mental disorder.

Axis 5: Global assessment of functioning: this axis provides an overall measure of the patient's functioning at work and at leisure on a 100-point scale.

DSM-IV contains over 200 mental disorders arranged into various categories. Here (with brief descriptions) are some of the main categories used in DSM-IV:

> ### KEY STUDY EVALUATION — DSM-IV axes
>
> The five axes of DSM-IV are designed to incorporate a wide variation in causes, symptoms, and behavioural effects of mental disorders. Axis 1, clinical disorders, includes all recognised disorders apart from "personality disorders" and "mental retardation", which are considered to be qualitatively different in origin and prognosis. These two forms of mental disorder are reserved for Axis 2. Axis 3 provides additional evidence of the known connections between physical conditions and psychological disorders, e.g. post-natal depression or long-term alcoholism.
>
> Use of Axes 4 and 5 is not compulsory. They refer more to the social functioning of the individual. Axis 4 acknowledges situational factors that may have occurred recently prior to the onset of a particular problem. A person suffering from PTSD (post-traumatic stress disorder) would necessarily have had a distressing experience in recent months, although even 12 months may not be a long enough time for the disorder to manifest itself. Determining the contribution of life events such as bereavement or divorce presents difficulties, because there may be an interdependent relationship between a person's response to life events and their pre-existing psychological condition. Some personality disorders will occur irrespective of situational factors.
>
> Axis 5 also addresses the social functioning of the individual, but unlike Axis 4 it assesses the person's ability to adapt to the demands of everyday life. Serious maladaption such as violent behaviour or failure to carry out basic personal hygiene would necessitate some sort of intervention.

- Mood disorders: these include depressive disorders and bipolar disorders, in which there are periods of mania or great excitement as well as periods of depression.

- Anxiety disorders: there are 12 anxiety disorders (e.g. panic disorder; generalised anxiety disorder; post-traumatic stress disorder), each of which involves excessive anxiety for certain situations or stimuli.

- Disorders of infancy, childhood, or adolescence: these cover a wide range of disorders (e.g. emotional; physical; behavioural; intellectual); specific examples are mental retardation, depression, and separation anxiety.

- Cognitive impairment disorders: these involve reduced cognitive ability caused by brain damage through disease, injury, or medical condition; examples are dementia (e.g. Alzheimer's disease) and delirium, in which there is a clouding of consciousness.

- Somatoform disorders: these involve preoccupations with the body or with physical illness stemming from psychological causes; examples are somatisation disorder (numerous medical complaints in the absence of actual illness) and conversion disorder (a psychological problem produces a medical complaint which lacks a medical basis).

- Personality disorders: these are long-term, maladaptive patterns of dealing with life (e.g. antisocial personality disorder, in which the rights and needs of others are ignored).

- Impulse control disorder: these are disorders involving difficulties in controlling impulses, which are not featured elsewhere in DSM-IV; an example is kleptomania, which is the psychological compulsion to steal things.

- Schizophrenia and other psychotic disorders: these disorders involve a partial or total loss of contact with reality; schizophrenia with its distortions of thought, emotion, and behaviour, is the most common disorder in this category.

- Sexual disorders: these include orgasm disorders and sexual sadism, in which sexual pleasure is obtained by hurting another person.

- Substance-related disorders: these disorders involve personal and social impairment caused by the excessive use of drugs or alcohol.

- Eating disorders: these involve potentially dangerous abnormal eating patterns; examples are bulimia nervosa (binge eating usually followed by vomiting or purging) and anorexia nervosa (excessive weight loss produced by a preoccupation with thinness).

Some more general features of DSM-IV should be mentioned before providing an overall evaluation of its value. First, as mentioned before, the disorders identified in DSM-IV are defined by descriptive and observable symptoms rather than by those features that are believed to cause each disorder. Second, each diagnostic category used in DSM-IV is based on *prototypes* (a set of features characteristic of the category). It is assumed that some symptoms are essential, but that others may or may not be present. For example, the diagnosis of generalised anxiety disorder requires the presence of excessive worry and anxiety. However, it requires only three of the following symptoms: restlessness; being easily fatigued; difficulty concentrating; irritability; muscle tension; and sleep disturbance.

Third, DSM-IV (in common with DSM-III and DSM-III-R) was based in part on the findings of *field trials,* in which diagnostic issues were studied by means of programmes of research. Spitzer et al. (1989) carried out a field trial to decide whether to introduce "self-defeating personality disorder" into DSM-IV. This proposed personality disorder consisted of symptoms such as behaving in a self-sacrificing way, and choosing situations that are likely to lead to disappointment. The field trial produced clear findings: the symptoms of self-defeating personality disorder were so similar to those of existing personality disorders that there was no need to add it to DSM-IV.

Discussion points

1. DSM-IV was based on much research and on experience with earlier versions of DSM. How successful does it seem to be? (See Evaluation)

2. DSM-IV is often regarded as the best classificatory system that we have for mental disorders. Is it worthwhile to develop such classificatory systems?

Evaluation of DSM-IV

Any classificatory system needs to be both reliable and valid. Reliability is high if different psychiatrists agree on patients' diagnoses; this is known as **inter-judge reliability**.

Validity is concerned with the extent to which the classificatory system measures what it claims to measure. It is much harder to assess than reliability. There are at least three kinds of validity of relevance to DSM-IV:

- Aetiological validity: this is high when the aetiology or cause of a disorder is the same for most patients suffering from it.
- Descriptive validity: this concerns the extent to which patients in the various diagnostic categories differ from each other.
- Predictive validity: this concerns the extent to which the diagnostic categories allow us to predict the course and the outcome of treatment.

It should be noted that reliability and validity are not entirely independent. A classificatory system that is unreliable cannot be valid.

Fairly detailed evidence on the reliability of DSM-III is available. Inter-judge reliability on some of the major diagnostic categories in DSM-III is as follows (a correlation of about +0.7 or above indicates high reliability):

- Psychosexual disorders: +0.92
- Schizophrenic disorders: +0.81
- Anxiety disorders: +0.63
- Personality disorders: +0.56

As can be seen, the reliability of DSM-III varies considerably from category to category. The reliability of diagnosing personality disorders may be low because there are several different personality disorders and they have overlapping symptoms. The reliability of DSM-IV is almost certainly higher than that of DSM-III. Many of the leading experts in the various mental disorders had an active involvement in the construction of DSM-IV, and there was detailed field testing over a period of years.

There is little evidence on validity. The aetiological validity is probably fairly low for most of the categories of mental disorder, because the causes of any given disorder vary considerably from person to person (see Chapter 25). The descriptive validity of DSM-IV is reduced by **comorbidity**, which is the presence of two or more disorders in the same person at any given time. For example, up to two-thirds of patients with an anxiety disorder have also been diagnosed with one or more additional anxiety disorders (Eysenck, 1997). Such extensive comorbidity blurs the distinctions among categories. The predictive validity of DSM-IV is unknown. However, the facts that the precise form of treatment increasingly depends on the diagnosis, and that treatment is becoming more effective, suggest that its predictive validity may be fairly good.

International Classification of Diseases and Health Related Problems (ICD)

Mental disorders were first included by the World Health Organisation in the sixth edition of ICD in 1948. However, this and some of the following editions of ICD had little impact, because of their low reliability and their reliance on unproven theories. The situation was improved in 1993, with the publication of ICD-10. According to ICD-10, there are 11 major categories of mental disorder:

* Organic, including symptomatic, disorders.
* Schizophrenia, schizotypal, and delusional disorders.
* Mental and behavioural disorders due to psychoactive substance use.
* Mood (affective) disorders.
* Neurotic, stress-related, and somatoform disorders.
* Behavioural and emotional disorders with onset usually occurring in childhood and adolescence.
* Disorders of psychological development.
* Mental retardation.
* Disorders of adult personality and behaviour.
* Behavioural syndromes associated with physiological disturbances and physical factors.
* Unspecified mental disorder.

Early versions of ICD and DSM were very different from each other, but that is no longer the case with ICD-10 and DSM-IV. For example, there are close resemblances between schizophrenia, schizotypal, and delusional disorders in ICD-10 and schizophrenia and other psychotic disorders in DSM-IV; between mental and behavioural disorders due to psychoactive substance use in ICD-10 and substance-related disorders in DSM-IV; and between mood (affective) disorders in ICD-10 and mood disorders in DSM-IV. In more general terms, ICD-10 and DSM-IV are both based on a set of categories of mental disorder, each of which has its own set of symptoms.

In spite of the similarities between ICD-10 and DSM-IV, there are some important differences. There are 16 major categories of mental disorder in DSM-IV compared to only 11 in ICD-10, mainly because the categories in ICD-10 tend to be more general. In addition, some of the major categories in DSM-IV (e.g. sexual and gender identity; eating disorders) are not represented directly in ICD-10.

Evaluation of ICD-10

The situation with respect to the reliability and validity of ICD-10 is similar to that with respect to DSM-IV. That is to say, it has reasonable reliability, but there is little detailed

How would you explain the tendency for the correlation of reliability to be higher for psychosexual disorders than for personality disorders? Which disorders appear to have a greater chance of aetiological validity?

KEY TERM
Comorbidity: the presence of two or more disorders in a given individual at the same time.

How would you explain the increased category-specificity of the DSM-IV and its more precise descriptions of symptoms, in comparison to the ICD? Why would this lead to greater reliability?

information on its validity. According to Costello, Costello, and Holmes (1995), ICD-10 seems to be more reliable than either ICD-9 or DSM-III-R. However, there must be doubts as to whether it is more reliable than DSM-IV. The categories in DSM-IV tend to be more specific, and the defining symptoms are more precise. In general terms, increased category specificity and symptom precision are associated with higher reliability.

As with DSM-IV, the aetiological validity of ICD-10 is low. Its descriptive validity is also likely to be low, given the prevalence of comorbidity in diagnoses based on ICD-10. Finally, the usefulness of ICD-10 diagnoses as the basis for deciding on the appropriate treatment suggests that its predictive validity may be reasonable.

General issues with DSM-IV and ICD-10

DSM-IV and ICD-10 both possess reasonable reliability, and there is no doubt that reliability is important. However, it is possible that this emphasis on reliability carries dangers with it. According to Barlow and Durand (1995, p.112), this emphasis "is understandable, since reliability has been so difficult to achieve. But it is not hard to achieve reliability if you are willing to sacrifice validity." You can achieve high reliability by using very precise criteria for each disorder. For example, the key criterion for generalised anxiety disorder in DSM-IV is as follows: "Excessive anxiety and worry (apprehensive expectation), occurring more days than not for at least six months, about a number of events or activities." This is fairly precise, but has the obvious disadvantage that the time period of six months is arbitrary: someone who suffers from excessive worry for six months is unlikely to differ much from someone who only suffers for five months.

Classificatory systems such as DSM-IV and ICD-10 are based on the assumption that we can assign individuals neatly to certain categories. However, many of the symptoms defining their categories are found in much of the population. For example, the key symptom of panic disorder is the existence of recurring panic attacks. However, Norton, Dorward, and Cox (1986) found that 35% of college students had experienced one or more DSM-III defined panic attacks over the preceding year. In similar fashion, Rachman and de Silva (1978) found that the obsessions and compulsions found in patients with obsessive-compulsive disorder are also found in over half the "normal" population. Such findings make it hard to justify the notion of neat categories.

■ Research activity: An exercise in categorisation

Most people can recall an occasion when they have felt compelled to return home to check that the gas has been turned off or the front door locked. Today, more people than ever before buy disinfecting products to combat germs. These are behaviours that can be taken to extremes in obsessive-compulsive disorder.

Using DSM-IV, ascertain how you might distinguish between behaviours that apply to most people sometimes, and behaviours that are symptomatic of obsessive-compulsive disorder.

Models of Abnormality

Several models of abnormality have been put forward over the years. These models are designed to explain *why* and *how* mental disorders occur. These models have been very influential, because the form of treatment for any given mental disorder is based in part on our understanding of the causes of that disorder. Each of the models of abnormality discussed here is associated with certain kinds of therapy, and the effectiveness of these forms of therapy is discussed in detail in Chapter 26.

The dominant model, at least until fairly recently, was the medical model. According to the medical model, mental disorders are regarded as illnesses. Most psychiatrists accept the medical model, whereas most clinical psychologists reject it in favour of psychological models. There are several psychologically based models of abnormality, but we will focus on the four most important ones here: the behavioural, cognitive, humanistic, and psychodynamic models.

Why are there several different models of abnormality? Mental disorders are caused by numerous factors, and each of the models emphasises some of these factors at the expense of others. It is probable that each of the models is partially correct, and that a full understanding of the origins of mental disorders requires us to combine information from all of them.

Medical model

The essence of the medical model is "the view that abnormal behaviours result from physical problems and should be treated medically" (Halgin & Whitbourne, 1997). In other words, mental disorders resemble physical diseases, in that they are both illnesses of the body. As a result, we should approach mental disorders from the perspective of medicine.

According to the medical model, the causes of mental disorders resemble those of physical illnesses. One possible cause of abnormality is a germ or micro-organism producing disease. Another possible cause lies in genetic factors, and can be tested by looking at patterns of mental disorder within families or within twin pairs. A third possible cause of abnormality lies in the patient's biochemistry. For example, several theorists have argued that one of the factors involved in schizophrenia is an excessive amount of dopamine in the brain (see Chapter 25). A fourth possible cause lies in neuroanatomy, that is, the structure of the nervous system. For example, amnesia may occur because the part of the brain in which long-term memories are stored is easily damaged.

The medical model has had an enormous influence on the terms used to refer to mental disorders and their treatment. As Maher (1966, p.22) pointed out, deviant behaviour

> is termed pathological *and is classified on the basis of symptoms, classification being called* diagnosis. *Processes designed to change behaviour are called* therapies, *and are [sometimes] applied to patients in mental* hospitals. *If the deviant behaviour ceases, the patient is described as* cured.

The medical model approach can be seen clearly in the case of phenylketonuria (PKU), which is a form of mental retardation (see Chapter 25). Medical research showed that PKU is caused by a genetically determined enzyme deficiency that makes the body unable to metabolise phenylalanine into tyrosine. As a result, treatment in the form of a special diet low in phenylalanine has proved very successful in preventing the development of PKU.

Treatment implications

The medical model has clear implications for treatment. If mental illnesses are basically illnesses of the body, then treatment should involve direct manipulation of bodily processes. For example, if a mental disorder (e.g. schizophrenia) involves biochemical abnormalities, then drugs can be used to correct these abnormalities. Drugs have been used with some success to treat various disorders such as schizophrenia, anxiety, and depression (see page 618). However, it should be noted that the success of drug therapy in treating a mental disorder does not prove that the disorder was caused by biological factors.

Other forms of treatment based on the medical model are discussed in detail in Chapter 26. They include fairly drastic methods such as electroconvulsive shock therapy and brain surgery.

Ethical implications

The notion that individuals with mental disorders are suffering from an illness could be regarded as ethically desirable, because it suggests that they are not responsible for their condition. However, when someone is labelled as suffering from a mental illness, this may cause other people to be frightened or wary of that person, and that is clearly ethically undesirable. In addition, it may be undesirable to encourage individuals with mental disorders to hand over complete responsibility for their recovery to experts trained in treating "mental illness".

Ethical issues: What are the ethical implications of a situation in which a person diagnosed as schizophrenic decides to refuse to take his or her drug treatment?

The notion that genetic factors often play a significant role in the development of mental disorders poses some ethical issues. The relatives of someone diagnosed as suffering from such a disorder may well become very anxious, and greatly exaggerate their chances of developing the disorder.

Many of the forms of treatment based on the medical model raise important ethical issues. Drugs can have serious side-effects and lead to drug dependence. More direct

What are the psychological factors that may be neglected by psychiatric medicine in the case of (a) personality disorder, (b) post-traumatic stress disorder, and (c) anorexia nervosa?

interventions such as electroconvulsive shock therapy and brain surgery can make the lives of patients worse rather than better.

Finally, there are ethical issues raised by the relative neglect of psychological factors within the medical model. For example, therapy may take much longer than necessary if the therapist ignores such factors when providing treatment.

Evaluation

How useful is the medical model approach to mental disorders? On the positive side, it has the merit of being based on well-established sciences such as medicine and biochemistry. Some forms of mental disorder (e.g. phenylketonuria; schizophrenia) can be understood from the perspective of the medical model, and numerous mental disorders are caused in part by genetic factors (see Chapter 25). Drug therapies based on the medical model have often proved effective, at least in the sense of reducing the symptoms of those suffering from mental disorder (see Chapter 26).

Genetic and environmental factors are difficult to disentangle in the case of mental disorders. What methodological and ethical problems make this issue hard to clarify?

On the negative side, there is generally only a loose analogy between physical and mental illness. It is easier to establish the causes of most physical illnesses than mental ones, and symptoms of mental disorders are often more subjective than those of physical illnesses. The medical model seems to apply much better to some mental disorders than others. For example, it tells us rather little about the origins of eating disorders (see Chapter 25). The biological differences between individuals with mental disorders and other people may be by-products of the disorder, and may not play a role in causing it. The focus within the medical model is too much on symptoms, and not enough on the patient's experiences and internal processes. The role of psychological factors (e.g. life events; personal difficulties) in explaining mental disorders is ignored.

Behavioural model

The behavioural model of abnormality developed out of the behaviourist approach to psychology that was put forward mainly by John Watson and B.F. Skinner. According to this model, individuals with mental disorders possess maladaptive forms of behaviour, which have been learned. Most of the learning takes the form of classical conditioning or operant conditioning, which are discussed at length in Chapter 10. Bandura (1986) argued that observational learning or modelling is also important. This is a form of learning in which individuals learn by imitating the behaviour of someone else. Observational learning is especially likely to influence behaviour when the other person's behaviour is rewarded or reinforced. The assumption is that all of these forms of learning produce significant changes in people's behaviour.

If the winner of this race is praised or rewarded, he or she is likely to be willing to race again. However, if the losers are ridiculed, they are likely to avoid taking part in future.

Classical conditioning is a basic form of learning that was first demonstrated by Pavlov. In essence, a neutral stimulus is paired repeatedly with a second stimulus. After a while, the natural response to the second stimulus comes to be made to the neutral stimulus when presented on its own. The fear response can be conditioned to neutral stimuli in this way. It has been claimed that specific phobias or extreme fears of certain stimuli (e.g. snakes) develop through classical conditioning.

Operant conditioning involves learning to produce responses that are followed by reward or reinforcement, and to avoid making responses that are followed by unpleasant consequences. For example, Lewinsohn (1974) argued that depression occurs as a result of a low level of reinforcement. When people receive less reinforcement, they produce fewer responses. As a result, they receive even less reinforcement, and this causes them to experience depression.

Observational learning or modelling may be relevant to several mental disorders. In essence, observing a family member or some other person showing the symptoms of a disorder can increase the chances of developing that disorder by imitating their behaviour.

> ■ Research activity: The behavioural model and phobias
>
> Which of the following phobias are most likely to be the consequence of classical conditioning?
>
> - Claustrophobia (fear of enclosed spaces).
> - Agoraphobia (fear of open spaces).
> - Arachnophobia (fear of spiders).
>
> Are there any problems with this approach? What are the weaknesses of the behavioural model as an explanation for mental disorders?

Treatment implications

As we have seen, it is assumed within the behavioural model that mental disorders arise as a result of maladaptive forms of learning based on conditioning or observational learning. It follows fairly logically that an appropriate form of treatment involves further conditioning or observational learning designed to eliminate the maladaptive forms of behaviour that have been learned.

The starting point for treatment based on the behavioural model is to identify those aspects of behaviour that are maladaptive and require changing. After that, conditioning or observational learning techniques are used to reduce or eliminate those maladaptive responses. In contrast to the psychodynamic approach, the focus is very much on the patient's behavioural symptoms rather than on the underlying cause of his or her disorder.

Ethical implications

The behavioural model has some advantages from the ethical perspective. First, it is assumed that mental disorders result from maladaptive learning and thus should not be regarded as "illnesses". Second, the focus on each individual's particular experiences and conditioning history means that the behavioural model is sensitive to cultural and social factors.

Third, the behavioural approach tends to be non-judgemental, in the sense that treatment is recommended only when an individual's behaviour causes severe problems to that person or to other people. Fourth, it is assumed within the behavioural model that abnormal behaviour is determined mainly by environmental factors. As a result, individuals who develop mental disorders should not be held responsible for those disorders.

There are ethical problems with some of the forms of treatment based on the behavioural model. Aversion therapy involves giving very unpleasant stimuli (e.g. electric shocks; nausea-inducing drugs) to patients in order to stop some undesirable form of behaviour, such as drinking in alcoholics. There has been much controversy about the morality of causing high levels of pain and discomfort. Most forms of treatment focus mainly on changing behaviour, and it could be argued that it is dehumanising to neglect the patient's internal experiences and feelings.

In psychotic disorders, behaviour is likely to be chaotic and thoughts disordered. It is unlikely that behavioural approaches could be employed to intervene in such situations. In what way might this model be harmful to such individuals?

Evaluation

Those who favour the behavioural model are correct in assuming that the experiences that people have in life, including the forms of conditioning to which they have been exposed, play a part in the development of mental disorders. However, conditioning is generally less important in humans than in the animal species studied in the laboratory by behaviourists (see Chapter 10). For example, operant conditioning and extinction in humans depend importantly on conscious awareness of the relationship between responding and the provision of reward, whereas this is presumably not the case in other species (Brewin, 1988).

The behavioural model exaggerates the importance of environmental factors in causing disorders, and minimises the role played by genetic factors (see Chapter 27). As a result, it is of little value in explaining disorders such as schizophrenia or bipolar disorder (also known as manic-depressive disorder). The behavioural model emphasises behaviour rather than internal processes (e.g. thinking; feeling). That makes it more applicable to disorders with easily identifiable behavioural symptoms (e.g. the avoidance of phobic stimuli shown by individuals with specific phobias for spiders or snakes) than to disorders having few clear behavioural symptoms (e.g. generalised anxiety disorder).

In general terms, the behavioural model is oversimplified and rather narrow in scope. On the basis of the available evidence, it seems that only a small fraction of mental disorders depend to a large extent on the individual patient's conditioning history.

Cognitive model

The cognitive model was developed mainly by Albert Ellis (1962) and Aaron Beck (1976). Some of the key ideas underlying the cognitive model were expressed by Kovacs and Beck (1978), who argued that psychological problems

may result from commonplace processes such as faulty learning, making incorrect inferences on the basis of inadequate or incorrect information, not distinguishing adequately between imagination and reality.

> ■ Research activity: Beliefs or symptoms?
>
> Are the following best viewed as examples of irrational beliefs in an otherwise normal person, or as symptoms of a mental disorder?
>
> • Athletes approach a competition from the point of view that winning outright is the only acceptable outcome.
> • Divorced people believe that they are a failure because they cannot attract another partner instantly.

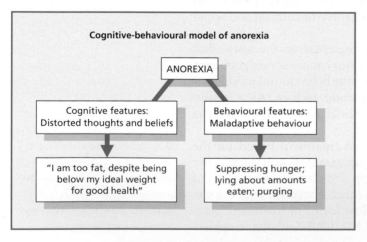

The central notion in the cognitive model is that many of the thoughts of individuals suffering from mental disorders are distorted and irrational. Warren and Zgourides (1991) pointed out that many of these thoughts have a "must" quality about them. Examples are as follows: "I *must* perform well and/or win the approval of others, or else it's awful"; "You *must* treat me fairly and considerately and not unduly frustrate me, or it's awful"; "My life conditions *must* give me the things I want easily and with little frustration ... or else life is unbearable." These distorted thoughts and beliefs influence feelings and behaviour, and can play an important role in the development of mental disorders.

Meichenbaum (1977) argued that an important aspect in many mental disorders is the patient's internal dialogue. Many patients say very negative and unhelpful things to themselves when problems are encountered, and this helps to maintain the disorder.

In recent years, there have been increasing signs of an integration between the behavioural and cognitive models. According to this cognitive-behavioural model, mental disorders involve maladaptive behaviour as well as distorted thoughts and beliefs.

Treatment implications

The main implication for treatment is that active steps should be taken to replace the patient's irrational and distorted thoughts and beliefs with ones that are rational and undistorted. The term **cognitive restructuring** is used to refer to the techniques used to make the patient's thoughts more positive and rational. The therapist may question or challenge patients' beliefs. Alternatively, he or she may persuade patients to test their beliefs in real-world settings to demonstrate how irrational those beliefs are. For example, socially anxious patients who believe that their work colleagues dislike them may be persuaded to ask them out for a drink to put this belief to the test.

Beck et al. (1979) argued that "Acting against an assumption is the most powerful way to change it." This can be done in various ways with patients whose thinking is very negative. One example is "activity raising", in which they are rewarded for becoming involved in more activities. Another example is "graded work assignment", in which patients are rewarded for behaving in a progressively more positive way.

How would you devise a programme of cognitive restructuring for a person with anorexia?

KEY TERM
Cognitive restructuring: the techniques used by cognitive therapists to make distorted and irrational beliefs more rational.

Ethical implications

According to the cognitive model, individuals with mental disorders have distorted thoughts and beliefs, and so it is mainly their own fault. That notion raises a number of ethical issues. First, patients may find it stressful to accept responsibility for their mental disorder. Second, it may be unfair to blame individuals for their mental disorder, because others around them may be mainly responsible. Third, the negative thoughts and beliefs of those with mental disorders are often entirely rational, and reflect accurately the unfortunate circumstances in which they are living. Attempts to put the blame on to the patients may inhibit efforts to produce desirable changes in society.

What situations might be expected to produce negative thoughts and beliefs that could be ameliorated by changes in society? Would social support of a person who is depressed in such a situation be of more or less value than a label of "mental disorder"?

Evaluation

The cognitive model of abnormality has become very influential in recent years. There is no doubt that distorted and irrational beliefs are very common among patients with mental disorders. Such beliefs seem to be of central importance in anxiety disorders and depression (Beck & Clark, 1988), but their importance has not been shown for most other disorders.

On the negative side, the cognitive approach to abnormality is rather limited. Genetic factors are ignored, and little attention is paid to the role of social and interpersonal factors, or of individuals' life experiences, in producing mental disorders. Distorted beliefs are prevalent in those with mental disorders. However, it is generally not clear whether these beliefs help to cause the disorder, or whether they are merely a byproduct of the disorder.

Another problem with the cognitive approach to abnormality is that some of the arguments put forward are circular and tell us little. Davison and Neale (1996, p.57) gave an example of such circularity:

> To say that depression results from a negative schema [organised knowledge in long-term memory] tells us that depressives think gloomy thoughts. But everyone knows that such a pattern of thinking is actually part of the diagnosis of depression.

Humanistic model

The humanist approach to psychology was developed by Carl Rogers and Abraham Maslow in the United States during the 1950s. This approach focuses on personal responsibility, free will, and the striving towards personal growth and fulfilment. It was assumed that people have a need for **self-actualisation**, which involves individuals discovering and fulfilling their own potential in all areas of functioning. The humanistic model is an optimistic one. It was based on the assumption that most people are naturally good and have the potential for personal growth in the appropriate circumstances.

Rogers (1959) focused more than Maslow on mental disorder. However, it should be emphasised that he did not draw a distinction between normality and abnormality. As a

Self-concept   Self-actualisation   Ideal self

result, the humanistic model applies to individuals with serious problems, but should not be regarded as a model of abnormality.

Rogers drew an important distinction between the self-concept and the ideal self. The **self-concept** is the self as it is currently experienced, whereas the **ideal self** is the self-concept that an individual would most like to possess. The relevance of this distinction to clinical psychology is that the incongruence or discrepancy between the self-concept and the ideal self tends to be much greater in individuals suffering from mental disorder than in other people.

Problems can arise when there is a discrepancy between an individual's actual experiences and his or her self-perceptions. For example, a child who believes herself to be unaggressive finds herself behaving aggressively. Two possible reactions are distortion (e.g. the child decides she was behaving assertively rather than aggressively) and denial (e.g. denying the existence of the experience). In either case, there is incongruence, because the experience is not incorporated into the self-concept.

How is incongruence to be avoided in the course of development? According to Rogers (1959), many problems arise because parents and others set conditions of worth (e.g. "I will love you if you do your homework"). Many children react by adopting the standards of others. This can lead them to adopt very high standards that they cannot fulfil, causing them to have low self-esteem. The ideal is for children to be offered unconditional positive regard from parents and others at an early age. This allows them to experience life without their self-concept being distorted by the needs and values of others.

According to Rogers, young children should receive unconditional positive regard from their parents. Parents should not withhold love as a punishment, or make it conditional on specific behaviour or achievements.

Treatment implications

According to the humanistic approach, people possess free will and are generally capable of making sensible decisions about their own lives. As a result, the therapist should provide a supportive environment in which the client can develop increased self-esteem and become more self-actualised. This is achieved by the therapist showing unconditional positive regard for his or her clients, which is the key feature of Rogers' client-centred therapy (later known as person-centred therapy).

In more general terms, the emphasis within the humanistic approach is on the importance of individuals' conscious experience of themselves and of the world around them. As a result, therapy focuses on the clients' conscious experiences rather than on their behaviour. The humanistic approach to treatment is discussed in more detail in Chapter 26.

Ethical implications

The humanistic model could be regarded as ethically desirable because of its focus on the individual, and its refusal to stigmatise individuals by labelling them or giving them a diagnosis. However, this refusal to categorise may slow down the rate of recovery, and there are ethical concerns about prolonging the patient's suffering unnecessarily.

A key aspect of the humanistic model is that individuals should accept responsibility for their own lives. This can cause ethical problems when therapists treat individuals whose problems are so severe that they are simply unable to accept personal responsibility. According to the humanistic model, an important reason why individuals fail to be self-actualised is because of the actions of other people. As a result, friends and relatives of an individual seeking person-centred therapy may be made to feel guilty because they have thwarted his or her efforts at self-development.

Evaluation

The humanistic model is much less influential within clinical psychology than it used to be. Why is this so? One reason is because it ignores important genetic and psychological factors involved in the development of mental disorders. Another reason for this is that Rogers was opposed to diagnosis or labelling. This approach made sense in the 1950s (when diagnostic systems were very primitive), but seems less reasonable in the light of great improvements in our ability to diagnose and categorise mental disorders.

Rogers argued that similar forms of therapy based on unconditional positive regard were suitable for most patients. That argument seems inconsistent with the fact that the most successful current forms of therapy tend to be *specific* to given disorders (Barlow & Durand, 1995). The evidence indicates that therapy based on the humanistic model is often not very effective. According to Halgin and Whitbourne (1997, p.130)

> *the humanistic approach seems best suited for a relatively narrow range of clients, who are motivated to focus on their subjective experience and who are able to discuss their emotional concerns in detail.*

The humanistic model is limited because its emphasis is very much on individuals' reports of their own subjective experience. As Rogers himself admitted, clients are often unaware of their true feelings, and this reduces the value of their reports. In addition, this approach is limited because it ignores the potential importance of focusing on individuals' behaviour as well as on their reported experiences.

How would you define Halgin and Whitbourne's "narrow range of clients" in terms of social and cultural backgrounds? Do you think the use of unconditional positive regard would be beneficial for clients who are (a) bereaved, (b) substance abusers, or (c) suffering from depression associated with ageing?

Psychodynamic model

Sigmund Freud (1856–1939) was the founder of psychoanalysis, and has probably been the most influential person in clinical psychology. He argued that the mind is divided into three parts. First, there is the id. This consists mainly of unconscious sexual and aggressive instincts, with the sexual instinct being called libido. Second, there is the ego, which is the rational and conscious part of the mind. Third, there is the superego or conscience. The three parts of the mind are often in conflict with each other. Conflicts occur most often between the id and the superego, because the id wants immediate gratification, whereas the superego takes account of moral standards.

The psychodynamic model put forward by Freud was based in part on his theory of psychosexual development (see Chapter 2). In essence, the child passes through a series of stages (oral; anal; phallic; latency; and genital). Major conflicts or excessive gratification at any of these stages can mean that the child spends an unusually long time at that stage of development (this process is known as fixation). If an adult experiences great personal problems, he or she will tend to show regression (going backwards through the stages of psychosexual development) to the stage at which he or she had previously been fixated.

Conflicts cause anxiety, and the ego defends itself against anxiety by using several defence mechanisms to prevent traumatic thoughts and feelings reaching consciousness. The major defence mechanism is repression, which forces memories of conflicts and traumas into the unconscious mind. Other defence mechanisms include displacement and projection. Displacement occurs when aggressive or other impulses are transferred away from a threatening person to someone non-threatening, as when someone who has been bullied by their boss kicks the cat.

Freud suggested that conflicts between parents and children during one stage of development could lead to fixation at that stage.

> **Defence mechanisms**
>
> Another example of a defence mechanism is reaction formation, e.g. in an adult who has developed a fear of close, intimate relationships due to a disappointment or hurt experienced during childhood. As a consequence, when this adult meets someone to whom they feel a strong attraction, they may consciously experience the opposite emotion of dislike, or even hatred.

Projection occurs when someone who possesses an undesirable characteristic attributes it to other people. For example, someone who is very hostile may claim that other people are hostile to him or her.

According to Freud, mental disorders can arise when an individual has unresolved conflicts and traumas from childhood. Defence mechanisms may be used to reduce the anxiety caused by such unresolved conflicts, but they act more as sticking plaster than as a way of sorting out an individual's problems.

Treatment implications

What might be some of the barriers to offering treatment by psychodynamic therapy routinely, for example by the National Health Service? Does this limit the kinds of people who might seek this form of treatment?

The implications for treatment are fairly clear (see Chapter 26). A prime goal of therapy is to allow patients to gain access to their repressed ideas and conflicts, and to encourage them to face up to whatever emerges from the unconscious. Freud used the term "insight" to refer to the processes involved. He assumed that insight would permit the repressed memories to be integrated into the ego or conscious self, after which the patient would be better able to cope with life.

Treatment based on the psychodynamic model is generally very time-consuming, because of the patient's reluctance to face up to his or her past. In the words of Freud (1917, p.289):

> *The patient attempts to escape by every possible means. First he says nothing comes into his head, then that so much comes into his head that he can't grasp any of it ... At last he admits that he really cannot say anything, he is ashamed to ... So it goes on, with untold variations.*

Ethical implications

One of the implications of the psychodynamic model is that individuals are not really responsible for their own mental disorders. This is so, because these disorders depend on unconscious processes over which individuals have no control. However, the notion that adult mental disorders have their basis in childhood experiences suggests that parents or other caregivers are at least partially to blame. This can easily cause them distress, if they are led to believe that they are responsible for their child's disorder.

Very serious ethical issues are raised by numerous recent cases of false memory syndrome. In these cases, patients undergoing psychotherapy have made allegations about childhood physical or sexual abuse that have turned out to have no basis in fact. It is often very hard to know whether such allegations are true. However, Brewin, Andrews, and Gotlib (1993) have shown that the childhood memories retrieved by adults are most likely to be accurate when structured interviews are used which focus on eliciting *specific* personal memories rather than more *general* or global judgements about childhood experiences.

Psychodynamic therapy

Which of the following disorders do you think could be treated effectively using the psychodynamic approach?

- Agoraphobia
- Schizophrenia
- Generalised anxiety disorder
- Alcoholism
- Anti-social personality disorder
- Kleptomania
- Anorexia nervosa

If psychodynamic therapy is not the best approach for any of these, which approach do you think would be better suited?

Freud argued that males and females have their own biologically determined sexual natures, and anxiety disorders or depression can develop when the natural course of their sexual development is thwarted. This approach is dubious, in that it ignores the importance of cultural differences in sexual attitudes and behaviour. It is also very sexist in its emphasis that behavioural differences between men and women stem from biology rather than from social and cultural factors.

Evaluation

The psychodynamic model proposed by Freud was the first systematic model of abnormality that focused specifically on psychological factors as the cause of mental disorder and on psychological forms of treatment. As such, it paved the way for later psychological models, especially the humanistic and the cognitive. Another advantage of the psychodynamic model is that it identified traumatic childhood experiences as a factor in the development of adult disorders, an assumption for which there is good evidence (Barlow & Durand, 1995).

A great weakness of the psychoanalytic model as put forward by Freud was the relative lack of interest in the current problems his patients were facing. Even if childhood experiences stored in the unconscious play a part in the development of mental disorders, that does not mean that adult experiences can safely be ignored. Current psychodynamic therapy has evolved out of Freud's approach, but it has more of an emphasis on current problems as well as on childhood experiences.

Another weakness of Freud's approach was that he tended to focus too much on sexual factors as the cause of mental disorders, while de-emphasising the importance of interpersonal and social factors in causing and maintaining mental disorders. These factors are generally regarded as important by most psychodynamic therapists nowadays. Most psychodynamic therapists now believe that most of the sexual problems experienced by patients are a result of poor relationships with others rather than a cause of disorder.

The psychodynamic model is not based on a solid foundation of scientific research. Freud's theoretical views emerged mainly from his interactions with patients in the therapeutic situation. However, this was a weak form of evidence that was probably contaminated by Freud's biases and preconceptions. In practice, the psychodynamic model has been applied mainly to patients suffering from anxiety disorders or depression rather than from severe disorders such as schizophrenia.

Positive aspects of the Freudian approach

Freud's work is often criticised, and it is true that it is difficult to verify the workings of the subconscious mind through scientific investigations. However, post-Freudian study of the importance of subjective feelings and experience has been a major undertaking in both psychology and other dissociated fields such as creative writing, literary theory, and art history. Freud's ideas about the importance of the subconscious mind have been one of the most profound influences on human thought of the twentieth century, leading to in-depth questioning of human motives and intentions. It is hard for us to think about the world without employing Freudian concepts.

In sum, the psychodynamic approach is limited because it tends to ignore genetic factors involved in the development of mental disorders. In its original form, the patient's current concerns and interpersonal relationships were de-emphasised, and there was undue focus on childhood experiences and sexual problems.

Cultural and Subcultural Differences

Are the same mental disorders found in every culture? There are two extreme positions that have been taken in answer to this question. First, there is the notion of **cultural universality**. This involves the assumptions that all mental disorders are found worldwide, and that their origins and symptoms are very similar everywhere. Second, there is the notion of **cultural relativism**. According to this view, mental disorders and their symptoms are determined at least in part by the values, social norms, and lifestyle found within any given culture. There is no need to accept either of these extreme positions. Indeed, it is likely that some forms of mental disorder are found worldwide, whereas others may depend more on cultural factors.

There is also evidence for subcultural differences, that is, differences existing *within* any given culture. For example, the incidence of some mental disorders differs between men and women, or between social classes. Such differences will be considered after we have dealt with cultural differences.

Culture-based syndromes

Traditionally, most classificatory systems for mental disorder (e.g. DSM; ICD) have been based on the notion of cultural universality. For example, DSM-III contained only one cultural reference in its coverage of schizophrenia, the affective disorders, and the

KEY TERMS
Cultural universality: the notion that the same mental disorders are found worldwide, having essentially the same symptoms in each culture.
Cultural relativism: the notion that cultural factors play a significant part in determining the risk of different mental disorders and the symptoms associated with them.

personality disorders. However, an attempt was made in DSM-IV (1994) to take account of cultural factors. DSM-IV (p.844) refers to **culture-bound syndromes**, which are "locality-specific patterns of aberrant behaviour and troubling experience that may or may not be linked to a particular DSM-IV diagnostic category".

In the main body of the manual, there is information about cultural and ethnic factors associated with each disorder. In addition, various culture-bound syndromes are described in an appendix. Here are three examples of such culture-specific disorders:

Cross-cultural issues: Can you think of three disorders that are specific to your own culture? Are these unique, or variations on disorders contained within DSM-IV?

- Ghost sickness: the main symptom is an excessive focus on death and on those who have died: this disorder is relatively common in Native American tribes.
- Koro: this disorder involves extreme anxiety that the penis or nipples will recede into the body, and possibly cause death; it is found in south and east Asia.
- Amok: this disorder involves a period of time spent brooding, followed by a violent outburst; it is found mainly in men, and was originally discovered in Malaysia.

The focus in previous editions of DSM was on mental disorders that are found in the Western world. It is a step forward to admit that people living in other cultures may develop different disorders. However, Kleinman and Cohen (1997, p.76) dismissed the appendix of DSM-IV as "little more than a sop thrown to cultural psychiatrists and psychiatric anthropologists." In addition, many Western experts argue that most culture-bound syndromes are simply *variations* on disorders contained within DSM-IV. This may be correct, or it may be that at least some culture-bound disorders are really unique to a specific culture.

As Cardwell et al. (1996) pointed out, classificatory systems being produced in non-Western cultures often include mental disorders that are not found in DSM or other Western systems. For example, *shenjing shuairuo* is included only in the Chinese Classification of Mental Disorders. It is a very common condition in China, accounting for over half of all psychiatric outpatients. According to Cardwell et al., *shenjing shuairuo* is a complex disorder that seems to include elements of anxiety disorders as well as depression or mood disorder.

Which mental disorders are found worldwide? According to Kendall and Hammen (1995), schizophrenia, depression, manic depression, some anxiety disorders, and dementia or mental deterioration are found in all cultures. There is probably more cross-cultural evidence about schizophrenia than about any other mental disorder, and so we will now consider that evidence.

Universal syndromes? Schizophrenia

The World Health Organisation carried out a large-scale, cross-cultural study of schizophrenia (Sartorius et al., 1986). In most countries, there was about a 1% risk of developing schizophrenia at some point between the ages of 15 and 54. As might be expected, the figure varied somewhat from country to country. For example, it was almost 25% in rural India, compared to only 0.55% in Denmark and Honolulu. Within the United States, the risk of schizophrenia was about the same for different cultural groups. These findings suggest that schizophrenia depends only modestly on cultural factors.

To what extent does the World Health Organisation evidence suggest that schizophrenia is a universal illness? How can we account for the variation in the rates of diagnoses and the symptoms observed in sufferers?

In an earlier study, the World Health Organisation (1981) considered the symptoms of schizophrenia in nine countries: England, China, India, Colombia, the United States, Denmark, the Soviet Union, Nigeria, and Czechoslovakia. There were several symptoms that were commonly found across these countries. Some of the most common symptoms were as follows (the percentage of schizophrenics having each symptom is in brackets): lack of insight (97%); auditory hallucinations (74%); verbal hallucinations (70%); suspiciousness (66%); lack of emotion (66%). It would seem from this evidence that the symptoms that are regarded as central to schizophrenia are much the same across cultures.

In spite of the findings discussed so far, there are some differences in the incidence of type of schizophrenia from one country to another. Three types of schizophrenia are: paranoid

KEY TERM
Culture-bound syndromes: mental disorders that are found in only a few cultures.

Psychology • A Student's Handbook   663

schizophrenia (involving delusions of persecution); catatonic schizophrenia (involving immobility); and hebephrenic schizophrenia (involving disorganised speech and behaviour). Catatonic and hebephrenic schizophrenia are much more common in developing countries than in developed ones, whereas the opposite is the case for paranoid schizophrenia (Kleinman & Cohen, 1997).

The way in which schizophrenia is diagnosed varies somewhat from country to country. Sartorius et al. (1986) found that 40% of schizophrenic patients in developed countries (e.g. England; the United States) had the disorder in a severe and long-lasting form, compared to only 24% in developing countries (e.g. Nigeria; India). There are a number of ways of interpreting these findings. However, Stevens (1987) argued convincingly that the main reason for the difference is misdiagnosis in the developing countries. The fact that 36% of Nigerian patients and 27% of Indian patients recovered in under a month suggests that they had not really been suffering from schizophrenia in the first place.

There are also some cultural differences in the symptoms of schizophrenia. Alaskan Inuit have a concept of "being crazy". It resembles our notion of schizophrenia, in that the symptoms include talking to oneself, screaming at people who do not exist, and making odd facial expressions. However, the Inuit concept also includes thinking one is an animal, drinking urine, killing dogs, and believing that a loved one was murdered by witchcraft.

Suppression–facilitation model

In most of the cross-cultural studies on the frequency of various mental disorders, the emphasis has been on identifying and providing a description of the differences among cultures. What is usually lacking is an explanation of these differences. Weisz et al. (1987) tried to do this in their suppression–facilitation model. According to this model, forms of behaviour that are discouraged within a culture will be suppressed and so observed only rarely. In contrast, forms of behaviour that are rewarded within a culture will be facilitated, and so produced to excess.

Weisz et al. applied their model to Thailand and the United States. In Thailand, parents strongly dislike under-controlled or aggressive behaviour. In the United States, on the other hand, under-controlled behaviour in the form of independence or assertiveness is encouraged. Weisz et al. studied about 400 children in each country who had been referred to a clinic with behaviour problems. As predicted, more of the Thai children than of the American children showed over-controlled behaviour, whereas under-controlled behaviour was more common in the American than in the Thai children.

Some of these cultural differences may be more apparent than real. Weisz et al. (1995) observed children's behaviour in schools in the United States and Thailand. The American children were twice as disruptive as the Thai children in terms of talking and being out of their seats. In spite of this, the Thai children were perceived by their teachers as having significantly more behaviour problems than were the American children by theirs.

Behaviour regarded as naughty in Thai children is more likely to be accepted as a sign of independence or assertiveness by American parents.

> ### KEY STUDY EVALUATION — Weisz et al.
>
> The greatest advantage of the approach taken by Weisz is that it provides evidence showing some of the ways in which cultural factors can influence the development of disorders. This evidence is especially striking because two very different cultures (i.e. American and Thai) were compared. The main limitation of this research is that it is very hard to be confident that categories of behaviour (e.g. aggressive; disruptive) have the same meaning and are applied in the same ways in different cultures.

Discussion points

1. How useful is Weisz's approach as a way of understanding cultural differences in the incidence of various disorders?
2. Why do cultures vary in the types of behaviour they encourage and discourage?

Cultural bias

Kleinman and Cohen (1997, p.74) argued that there are various myths or cultural biases that are making it harder for patients in developing countries to receive adequate treatment. The first myth is that "the forms of mental illness everywhere display similar degrees of prevalence." In other words, any given mental disorder is equally common or rare in every country. The second myth is the notion that "biology is responsible for the underlying structure of a malaise, whereas cultural beliefs shape the specific ways in which a personal experiences it." Thus, the central core of any mental disorder is the same everywhere, but the precise form it takes depends on cultural factors. The third myth is that "various unusual, culture-specific disorders whose biological bases are uncertain only occur in exotic places outside the West." In other words, there are some rare mental disorders that depend on unusual cultural factors, and are found only in non-Western cultures. An example of this is koro, which was discussed on page 662. In this disorder, the individual is very anxious that the penis or nipples will disappear into the body.

In the UK, a person of African-Caribbean descent is more likely than a white person to be diagnosed with schizophrenia, and this is likely to be due to cultural bias.

Some of the most worrying evidence that there may be important cultural biases in the diagnosis of mental disorders has been obtained in the United Kingdom. Cochrane and Sashidharan (1995; cited in Cardwell et al., 1996) discussed studies in which black African-Caribbean immigrants were up to seven times more likely than white people to receive a diagnosis of schizophrenia. This difference does not seem to be due to the stresses of being a recent arrival in a new country, because it tends to be slightly larger among second-generation African-Caribbeans. As Cardwell et al. (1996) pointed out, these findings are puzzling because similar findings for African-Caribbean immigrants have not been found in other countries. Furthermore, the rate of diagnosis of schizophrenia in the United Kingdom for South Asians is about the same as for the white population (Cochrane, 1983).

Cardwell et al. (1996) discuss other apparent examples of cultural bias in the United Kingdom. For example, African-Caribbean patients are more likely than other groups of patients to be compulsorily admitted to secure hospitals. In addition, such patients are more likely than others to be transferred to locked wards (see Fernando, 1988). There are other disturbing findings, such as the over-diagnosis of schizophrenia in West Indian and Asian in-patients (Cochrane, 1977). There are various possible interpretations of these disturbing findings, one of which is that British psychiatry is "shot through with Eurocentric bias". In other words, there is little sensitivity to cultural differences in normal and expected patterns of behaviour.

Fairly good evidence of cultural bias was reported by Blake (1973). He found that clinicians were more likely to use a diagnosis of schizophrenia if the case study described the patient as African-American rather than as white. In similar fashion, Luepnitz, Randolph, and Gutsch (1982) found that a given set of symptoms was much more likely to produce a diagnosis of alcoholism for a lower-class African-American than for a middle-class white person.

There are many different reasons why rates of diagnosis vary across cultures. One is that the symptoms associated with a disorder may vary from culture to culture in ways that are not catered for in diagnostic systems such as DSM-IV or ICD-10. For example, people in the United Kingdom or the United States who are suffering from depression typically complain of feelings of worthlessness and hopelessness, and loss of interest in most activities. In contrast, Nigerians who are depressed often complain of burning sensations in the body, crawling sensations in the head or legs, and a feeling that the stomach is bloated with water (Ebigno, 1986).

Another reason for cultural bias concerns cultural differences in reacting to stress. For example, Puerto Ricans in the United States tend to have more mental disorders than other disadvantaged groups (Guarnaccia, Good, & Kleinman, 1990). It is not known exactly why this happens. However, Guarnaccia et al. pointed out that Puerto Ricans generally react to very stressful events with faintness, brief seizures, and heart palpitations. Therapists who are unaware of this may misinterpret the symptoms of Puerto Rican patients as indicating a severe disorder.

Another reason for cultural differences in rates of diagnosis is because there are cultural differences in the ways in which individuals are expected to deal with mental disorder. For example, there are very low rates of diagnosed depression in most Asian cultures, in spite of the fact that depression seems to be about as common in those cultures as most Western ones (Rack, 1982). In Asia, patients consult their doctors if they are suffering from physical illness, but are very reluctant to do the same if they have a mental illness. However, what they often do is to report to their doctors some of the physical symptoms of depression, such as tiredness or sleep disturbance (Rack, 1982).

Reducing cultural bias

What can be done to reduce cultural bias in diagnosis? Some interesting answers to that question are provided in DSM-IV. One possibility is to take account of language differences between the therapist and the patient. A second possibility is for the therapist to become familiar with the ways in which the members of each cultural group discuss their own distress. A third possibility is to find out the extent to which each patient identifies with different cultural groups, and then to make use of that information before deciding on a diagnosis.

Other measures are also possible. If therapists and clinicians are made aware that their diagnoses may be biased because of stereotypes or other distorted attitudes, this may reduce the extent of any such bias. Another measure is for the therapist and the patient to be of the same cultural background, so that the therapist is more likely to appreciate the real significance of the patient's reported symptoms. In addition, patients may be more forthcoming when discussing their problems with someone from the same culture. Levine and Padilla (1980) found in an American study that Hispanics generally disclosed relatively little about themselves to non-Hispanic white therapists.

Gender bias

There are clear gender differences with respect to several mental disorders. Two of the most striking examples are the eating disorders anorexia nervosa and bulimia nervosa, where over 90% of those diagnosed as having either disorder are female. Robins et al. (1984) considered gender differences in the lifetime occurrence of various disorders across three American cities. Men had a higher rate of alcohol abuse than women (27% vs. 4%, respectively), and they also had more anti-social conduct (5% vs. 1%, respectively). In contrast, women were more likely to have major depression (8% vs. 2%) or specific phobia (9% vs. 4%).

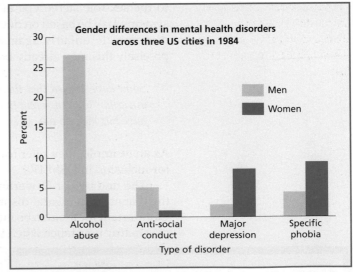

Why do these gender differences occur? The answer varies across disorders, with some gender differences being genuine, whereas others reflect various gender biases. The gender differences for alcohol-related disorders and for eating disorders seem to be almost entirely genuine. On the other hand, there is evidence that gender bias may be a factor with several other mental disorders. Such bias can occur for various reasons, four of which were identified by Worell and Remer (1992) and discussed by Cardwell et al. (1996):

- Disregarding environmental context: the focus in most classificatory systems is on the individual's symptoms rather than on his or her circumstances; this may produce gender bias if female patients are having to cope with more difficult circumstances than male patients.

Gender bias

With reference to the reasons given by Worrell and Remer for gender bias in the diagnosis of mental disorder:

• What "difficult circumstances" arise more frequently for women than for men?
• Which disorders are doctors (medical or psychological) more likely to identify with being female?
• Which approaches make distinctions between the sexes, e.g. psychodynamic notions of sexuality?

• Differential diagnosis on the basis of gender: this can occur when the patient's symptoms are interpreted in terms of traditional sex-role stereotypes, leading the therapist to exaggerate the numbers of women having so-called "women's disorders" and the numbers of men having "men's disorders".
• Therapist misjudgement: traditional sex-role stereotyping may increase the chances that the therapist will detect symptoms of submissiveness or dependence in female patients and of aggressiveness in male patients.
• Theoretical orientation: the therapist may have various theoretical biases related to gender, and these theoretical biases may distort the process of assessment and diagnosis.

Why were therapists reluctant to diagnose male patients as suffering from histrionic personality disorder, and female patients as suffering from anti-social personality disorder?

Evidence of the existence of gender biases in diagnosis was reported by Ford and Widiger (1989). They presented therapists with written case studies of one patient with anti-social personality disorder (irresponsible and reckless behaviour) and of another patient with histrionic personality disorder (excessive emotionality and attention seeking). Each patient was sometimes identified as male and sometimes as female, and the therapists had to decide on the appropriate diagnosis. Anti-social personality disorder was correctly diagnosed over 40% of the time when the patient was male, but under 20% of the time when the patient was female. In contrast, histrionic personality disorder was correctly diagnosed much more often when the patient was female: nearly 80% vs. just over 30%.

The findings of Ford and Widiger indicate a strong bias from traditional sex-role stereotypes. Evidence on these stereotypes was obtained by Broverman et al. (1981). They asked clinicians to identify the characteristics of the healthy adult, the healthy man, and the healthy woman. The characteristics of the healthy adult and the healthy man were rather similar, including adjectives such as independent, decisive, and assertive. In contrast, the adjectives used to describe the healthy woman included adjectives such as dependent, submissive, and emotional.

The findings of Broverman et al. (1981) suggest that there may be other forms of gender bias in the diagnosis of mental disorders. If health and normality are defined with respect to the sex-role stereotype of men, then the symptoms of abnormality in classificatory systems may be based on deviations from this stereotype. If this were to happen, it would discriminate unfairly against women. Kendall and Hammen (1995, p.23) argued that precisely this may already be happening:

> *Some have argued that the DSM includes, or is being pressed to include, diagnoses that are unfair to women and that it labels as a disorder certain kinds of symptoms that women have but men do not.*

As an example, they refer to a severe form of premenstrual distress that was considered for inclusion in DSM-IV.

The findings of Broverman et al. (1981) suggest a further reason for gender bias in the diagnosis of mental disorders. If we assume that men in Western cultures believe it is important for them to be independent, then they may be less likely than women to seek psychiatric assistance when it is needed.

■ Research activity: Sex stereotyping

List the characteristics thought to be indicative of a healthy male and those for a healthy female. Now reverse the characteristics and make an assessment of their usefulness in determining mental health, e.g. emotionality in a man may be considered a sign of weakness or instability.

Discuss in small groups notions of normality that would avoid the use of sex stereotyping. Devise a new list of sex-neutral characteristics indicating mental health.

About twice as many women as men are diagnosed as suffering from depression. There are various possible reasons for this gender difference. First, women often have to cope with sex discrimination and with relative powerlessness, and depression may be one of the results of such stressful circumstances. Second, some of the difference may stem from therapists making use of the traditional sex-role stereotype for women. This stereotype includes submissiveness and emotionality, both of which are associated to some extent with depression. Third, physiological processes in women (including the menstrual cycle and the menopause) may make them more vulnerable than men to depression. Fourth, Nolen-Hoeksma (1990) argued that men respond to depression with distracting activities (e.g. watching television; playing sport), whereas women tend to ruminate or ponder on life and to blame themselves. She reported evidence showing that the male coping style is more effective than the female coping style in reducing the level of depression.

Social class bias

There are variations across social classes in the likelihood of receiving various diagnoses, with social class generally being assessed on the basis of occupation. In general terms, what is usually found is that people belonging to the lower classes are more likely than those belonging to the middle class to be diagnosed with severe disorders. However, the opposite has sometimes been reported for the various neuroses (Cardwell et al., 1996). An individual's financial position is closely related to social class, and powerful evidence of its impact was reported by Bruce, Tadeuchi, and Leaf (1991). People above and below the poverty line who had no mental illness at first assessment were assessed again six months later. Those living below the poverty line were more than twice as likely to have developed alcohol abuse or dependence, bipolar disorder, or major depression during that period, and a staggering 80 times more likely to have developed schizophrenia.

There are various reasons for apparent social class bias in diagnosing mental illness. Mental health professionals have been found to make less encouraging clinical decisions with patients from the lower classes (Umbenhauer & DeWitte, 1978). Mental health professionals are also more likely to offer lower-class patients physical treatments (e.g. drugs) and less likely to offer them psychotherapy. Another possibility is that those from higher social classes have more coping strategies at their disposal. For example, the fact that they tend to have more money means that they are more likely to be able to afford to go to a health farm or on holiday when feeling highly stressed.

The relationship between social class and mental disorder has been explored more thoroughly with schizophrenia than with any other disorder. As a result, we will focus on schizophrenia in this section.

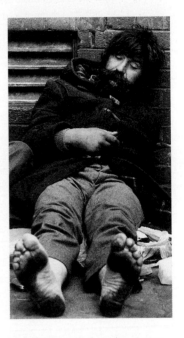

People living below the poverty line are more likely to develop some mental disorders than those in comfortable financial circumstances.

Schizophrenia

Members of the lower social classes are much more likely than those of the higher social classes to be diagnosed as suffering from schizophrenia (Barlow & Durand, 1995). There are several possible explanations of this finding, three of which are considered next.

First, it is possible that there is a bias, with clinicians being more willing to use the diagnosis of schizophrenia when considering the symptoms of individuals from lower social classes. Johnstone (1989) reviewed several studies which showed that lower-class patients were more likely than middle-class patients to be given serious diagnoses (such as schizophrenia), even when there were few if any differences in symptoms.

Second, there is the social causation hypothesis. According to this hypothesis, members of the lowest classes in society tend to experience more stressful lives, because of poverty, unemployment, poorer physical health, and so on. Stress is also likely through discrimination, because ethnic and racial minorities in many cultures tend to belong to the lower social classes. The high level of stress makes them more vulnerable than members of the middle class to schizophrenia. This hypothesis is a reasonable one, but there is little evidence providing direct support for it.

Third, there is the social drift hypothesis. According to this hypothesis, individuals who develop schizophrenia are likely to lose their jobs and so their social status is reduced. In other words, schizophrenia causes reduced social status, rather than low social status causing schizophrenia. If that is the case, then schizophrenics should tend to belong to a lower social class than their parents. Turner and Wagonfeld (1967) found this when he compared schizophrenics and their fathers. However, the fathers also tended to belong to the lower social classes themselves, which is in line with the social causation hypothesis.

Dohrenwend et al. (1992) tested the social causation and social drift hypotheses. They compared two immigrant groups in Israel: (1) European Jews who had settled in Israel

How does the social causation hypothesis conflict with the medical model argument that severe psychotic illnesses can be approached in the same way as a physical illness?

for some time; and (2) more recent immigrants from North Africa and the Middle East. The latter group experiences much prejudice and discrimination, and so should have higher rates of schizophrenia according to the social causation hypothesis. In fact, the advantaged group had a higher rate of schizophrenia, especially among those in the lowest social class. According to the social drift hypothesis, the reason why members of an advantaged group are likely to find themselves in the lowest social class is because they have developed schizophrenia. In contrast, members of a disadvantaged group may well be in the lowest social class because of discrimination rather than mental illness.

What conclusions can we come to regarding the explanation of the relationship between schizophrenia and social class? According to Halgin and Whitbourne (1997, p.361), "far too little research has been done ... to resolve the contrasting viewpoints of the social causation and social drift hypotheses." However, there is one key finding that is hard to account for on the social causation hypothesis. As we saw earlier, the rates of schizophrenia are fairly similar across numerous cultures (Sartorius et al., 1986). This happens in spite of the fact that these cultures vary enormously in some of the factors (e.g. poverty; physical health) claimed by the social causation hypothesis to be important determinants of schizophrenia.

PERSONAL REFLECTIONS

* I am a cognitive psychologist, which perhaps makes me biased. However, it seems to me that the model of abnormality that is becoming dominant in many countries is a model that combines elements of the cognitive and behavioural models. According to this cognitive-behavioural model, it is important to consider the cognitive processes and behaviour of patients, and therapy involves changing *both* cognition and behaviour rather than just one of these. Some of the other models, especially the humanistic and psychodynamic, are in decline as their limitations have become increasingly apparent.

SUMMARY

What is abnormality?

According to the statistical approach, the abnormal is that which is statistically rare in the population. This approach is limited, because it takes no account of whether deviations from the average are desirable or undesirable. Clinical abnormality should not be equated with social deviance, in part because what is socially deviant varies across cultures. Seven key features associated with abnormality are as follows: suffering; maladaptiveness; vividness and unconventionality; observer discomfort; unpredictability and loss of control; irrationality and incomprehensibility; and violation of moral and ideal standards. All of these features require subjective judgements to be made. DSM-IV and ICD-10 both emphasise the importance of distress as central to the definition of mental disorder.

Should we classify?

The diagnosis of mental disorders is generally harder than that of physical illnesses because the symptoms are subjective and the aetiology is only partially known. Rosenhan argued against the value of classifying mental disorders, but his study was flawed. As labelling theory predicts, the ways in which someone is treated are influenced by the psychiatric label of diagnosis they have been given. Labels can be used to exclude non-conformists from society. It would be hard to understand the causes of mental disorders without using some form of classification or diagnosis.

Classification systems

Most classificatory systems focus on syndromes or sets of symptoms that are generally found together. The most used system is DSM-IV, which uses a descriptive approach based on observable symptoms. It is a multi-axial system in which the patient is evaluated on five axes or scales. There are over 200 mental disorders in 16 main categories in DSM-IV, and most disorders are based on prototypes. DSM-IV has generally good reliability, but its validity is hard to assess. ICD-10 has 11 major categories of mental disorders, some of which resemble categories in DSM-IV. ICD-10 seems to be fairly reliable, but its validity is unclear. Both systems seem to emphasise reliability rather than validity, they use categories in spite of the fact that "normal" people often possess many of the symptoms of disorders, and their usefulness is reduced by comorbidity.

There are five major models of abnormality, each of which provides explanations of the origins of mental disorders, and each of which has implications for treatment. These models are not mutually exclusive, and all of them have contributed to our understanding. According to the medical model, the causes of mental disorders resemble those of physical diseases, and treatment should involve direct manipulation of bodily processes. This model ignores the role of psychological factors in explaining mental disorders, and is of little relevance to some disorders (e.g. eating disorders). According to the behavioural model, mental disorders involve maladaptive behaviour which has been learned via conditioning or observational learning. Treatment should be based on conditioning. According to the cognitive model, distorted and irrational beliefs are crucially involved in most mental disorders, and treatment should involve cognitive restructuring. According to the humanistic model, individuals seek therapy when there is incongruence between their self-concept and ideal self, or between their actual experiences and their self-perceptions. Treatment involves a rather passive therapist providing unconditional positive regard to encourage the patient to show personal growth. According to the psychodynamic model, the roots of mental disorder are to be found in unresolved conflicts and traumas from childhood. Treatment is based on various techniques designed to permit the patient to retrieve repressed memories and to gain insight into their meaning.

Models of abnormality

There are several culture-bound syndromes, which are found in only a few cultures. Some mental disorders (e.g. schizophrenia; depression; some anxiety disorders) are probably found in all cultures. Some cultural differences may occur because cultures vary in the forms of behaviour that are encouraged and discouraged. There are cultural differences in rates of diagnosis, some of which involve bias. Biases can occur because the symptoms of a disorder vary across cultures, because of cultural differences in response to disorder, or because the therapist and patient come from different cultures. Some gender differences in rates of diagnosis reflect reality, whereas others indicate biases. Gender bias can occur because the patient's environmental context is ignored, because of sex-role stereotypes, or because of therapist misjudgement or theoretical orientation. There is social class bias, with serious disorders being diagnosed more often in lower-class patients. The higher incidence of schizophrenia in the lower classes may be due to social causation or to social drift.

Cultural and subcultural differences

FURTHER READING

The various models of abnormality are discussed fully in P.C. Kendall and C. Hammen (1998), *Abnormal psychology (2nd Edn.)*, Boston: Houghton Mifflin. The other topics in this chapter are covered in an accessible way in D.H. Barlow and V.M. Durand (1995), *Abnormal psychology: An integrative approach*, New York: Brooks/Cole, and in R.P. Halgin and S.K. Whitbourne (1997), *Abnormal psychology: The human experience of psychological disorders*, Madison, WI: Brown & Benchmark.

REVISION QUESTIONS

1   Compare and contrast the DSM and ICD as alternative approaches to classifying normal and abnormal behaviour. (24 marks)
2a Outline the assumptions of the medical and humanistic models of abnormal behaviour. (12 marks)
2b Analyse the implications of these *two* models for treatment. (12 marks)
3   "Anthropologists are constantly reminding us that 'normal' and 'abnormal' are culturally relative terms; what is unquestioningly seen as normal in one culture may be regarded as definitely abnormal in another ... If Christ were alive today and began turning over the tables of the 'money-lenders', his feet would hardly touch the ground on the way to the nearest mental hospital. So, the criteria [used] in judging what is abnormal behaviour are [always] taken from the prevailing norms of the time" (Heather, 1976). With reference to the above statement, discuss cultural differences in the definition of abnormality. (24 marks)

- **Causal factors**
  Are mental disorders caused by
  internal or external factors, or both?

  The diathesis-stress model

- **Schizophrenia**
  The various approaches to diagnosing
  and treating this disorder.

  DSM-IV five main types of schizophrenia
  Gottesman's concordance theory
  Kety et al.'s adoption study
  The dopamine hypothesis
  Structural studies of the brain
  Psychodynamic and behavioural
  * approaches*
  Social factors

- **Depression**
  How clinical depression differs from
  just feeling down and sad.

  Genetic factors: twin studies
  Kety's biochemical approach
  Psychodynamic approach
  Seligman's learned helplessness theory
  Abramson's et al.'s cognitive approach
  Beck and Clark's schema theory
  Life event studies

- **Phobias**
  The overpowering fear that some
  people experience about all sorts of
  different objects or situations.

  Genetic factors and neurophysiology
  Freud's study of Little Hans
  Bowlby's separation anxiety theory
  Watson and Rayner's study
  Bandura's modelling theory
  Beck and Emery's cognitive bias theory
  Social factors and life events

- **Post-traumatic stress disorder**
  The psychological response to an
  extremely traumatic experience.

  Genetic and biochemical factors
  Horowitz's psychodynamic theory
  Conditioning approach
  Foa et al.'s cognitive theory
  Solomon et al.'s study of social factors

- **Eating disorders**
  How distorted beliefs about body size
  can lead to anorexia or bulimia.

  Genetic factors: twin studies
  Fava et al.'s serotonin hypothesis
  Psychodynamic and behavioural
  * approaches*
  Social and cultural studies
  Cognitive factors

25

Psychopathology

hat is **psychopathology**? According to Davison and Neale (1996), it is "the field concerned with the nature and development of mental disorders" (p.G-20). Psychopathology is the subject matter of this chapter.

One of the key issues in abnormal psychology is to understand *why* some people suffer from psychological disorders such as depression or schizophrenia. This is a very complex task. However, we can make a start by distinguishing between one-dimensional and multidimensional causal models (Barlow & Durand, 1995). According to one-dimensional models, the origins of a psychological disorder can be traced to a single underlying cause. For example, it might be argued that severe depression is caused by a major loss (e.g. death of a loved one), or that schizophrenia is caused by genetic factors. One-dimensional models are now regarded as greatly oversimplified. They have been replaced by multidimensional models, in which it is recognised that abnormal behaviour is typically caused by several different factors.

Causal Factors

What are the factors that play a part in producing psychological disorders? In general terms, we can distinguish between two categories of factors: genetic/neurological factors and social/psychological factors. The medical model focuses on genetic/neurological factors, whereas the behavioural, cognitive, humanistic, and psychodynamic models all focus on social/psychological factors. The main factors influencing the development of psychological disorders (with the category to which they belong) are:

- Genetic factors: twin studies, family studies, and adoption studies may indicate that some people are genetically more vulnerable than others to developing a disorder (genetic/neurological factor).
- Brain chemicals: individuals with unusually high or low levels of certain brain chemicals may be vulnerable to psychological disorders (genetic/neurological factor).
- Cultural factors: cultural values and expectations may be important in causing some disorders; for example, most Western cultures emphasise the desirability of thinness in women, and this may help to trigger eating disorders (social/psychological factor).
- Social factors: individuals who experience severe life events (e.g. divorce; unemployment) may be at risk for various psychological disorders, as may those who lack social support or belong to poorly functioning families (social/psychological factor).

Death of a loved one rates as one of the most stressful events we experience, and may have long-term psychological repercussions.

What life events do you think might be likely to lead to mental disorder?

These factors *interact*. For example, someone may have a very high or a very low level of a given brain chemical because of genetic factors or because he or she has recently experienced a severe life event. Another example concerns the impact of cultural expectations on eating disorders. This is clearly not the *only* factor causing eating disorders, because the overwhelming majority of women in Western societies do not suffer from eating disorders. Eating disorders occur in individuals who are exposed to cultural expectations of thinness *and* who are vulnerable (e.g. because of genetic factors).

The multi-dimensional approach

The multi-dimensional approach to psychopathology is often expressed in the form of the **diathesis-stress model**. According to this model, the occurrence of psychological disorders depends on two factors:

1. Diathesis: a genetic vulnerability or predisposition to disease or disorder.
2. Stress: some severe or disturbing environmental event.

The key notion in the diathesis-stress model is that both diathesis or genetic vulnerability *and* stress are necessary for a psychological disorder to occur.

Types of Disorder

We will be focusing on the factors responsible for the development of several psychological disorders. The main disorders considered are schizophrenia; depression; two of the anxiety disorders (phobias and post-traumatic stress disorder); and eating disorders. You may be surprised to discover how many different kinds of explanations have been put forward. This is due in part to the fact that several different factors are all involved in their development. It is also due to the difficulties of carrying out research in this area. For example, it is likely that life events may help to cause mental disorder. However, evidence about life events is usually obtained several months or years after they have happened, and people's memories for them may be faulty. Even if life events are remembered accurately, there are issues of interpretation. The fact that someone experiences a serious life event six months before becoming severely depressed does not prove that the life event was causally involved in producing the depression.

In what follows, schizophrenia, depression, anxiety disorders such as phobias and post-traumatic stress disorder, and eating disorders will each be examined from the perspective of major approaches such as the biological, behavioural, psychodynamic, social, and cognitive.

Schizophrenia

Schizophrenia is a very serious condition. The term schizophrenia comes from two Greek words: *schizo* meaning "split" and *phren* meaning "mind". About 1% of the population in the United Kingdom suffer from schizophrenia during their lives. The symptoms they exhibit vary somewhat, but typically include problems with attention, thinking, social relationships, motivation, and emotion. According to DSM-IV (the *Diagnostic and Statistical Manual, 4th edition*), the criteria for schizophrenia include:

1. Two or more of the following symptoms, each of which must have been present for a significant period of time over a one-month period: delusions; hallucinations; disorganised speech; grossly disorganised or catatonic (rigid) behaviour; and negative symptoms (lack of emotion; lack of motivation; speaking very little or uninformatively); only one symptom is needed if the delusions are bizarre, or if the hallucinations consist of a voice commenting on the individual's behaviour.
2. Continuous signs of disturbance over a period of at least six months.
3. Social and/or occupational dysfunction or poor functioning.

Schizophrenics generally have confused thinking, and often suffer from delusions. Many of these delusions involve what are known as "ideas of reference", in which the schizophrenic patient attaches great personal significance to external objects or events. Thus, for example, a schizophrenic seeing his neighbours talking may be convinced that they are plotting to kill him.

Schizophrenics often suffer from hallucinations. Delusions arise from mistaken interpretations of actual objects and events, but hallucinations occur in the absence of any external stimulus. Most schizophrenic hallucinations consist of voices, usually saying something of personal relevance to the patient. McGuigan (1966) suggested that these auditory hallucinations occur because patients mistake their own inner speech for someone else's voice. He found that the patient's larynx was often active during the time that the auditory hallucination was being experienced. More recent studies have confirmed this explanation of hallucinations (Frith, 1992).

Finally, there are some schizophrenics whose behaviour is even more bizarre. One of the most common behavioural abnormalities is to remain almost motionless for hours at a time. Some patients make strange grimaces or repeat an odd gesture over and over again.

There are positive and negative symptoms. Positive symptoms include delusions, hallucinations, and bizarre forms of behaviour. Negative symptoms include an absence of emotion and motivation, language deficits, general apathy, and an avoidance of social activity.

Schizophrenics often suffer from delusions, misinterpreting ordinary events, such as conversations between other people, as being about themselves.

Types of schizophrenia

According to DSM-IV, there are five main types of schizophrenia:

1. Disorganised schizophrenia: this type involves great disorganisation, including delusions, hallucinations, incoherent speech, and large mood swings.
2. Catatonic schizophrenia: the main feature is almost total immobility for hours at a time, with the patient simply staring blankly.
3. Paranoid schizophrenia: this type involves delusions of various kinds.
4. Undifferentiated schizophrenia: this is a broad category which includes patients who do not clearly belong within any other category.
5. Residual schizophrenia: this type consists of patients who are only experiencing mild symptoms.

Biological approach: Genetic factors

CASE STUDY: *A Schizophrenic Disorder*

A young man of 19 (WG) was admitted to the psychiatric services on the grounds of a dramatic change in character. His parents described him as always being extremely shy with no close friends, but in the last few months he had gone from being an average-performing student to failing his studies and leaving college. Having excelled in non-team sports such as swimming and athletics, he was now taking no exercise at all. WG had seldom mentioned health matters, but now complained of problems with his head and chest. After being admitted, WG spent most of his time staring out of the window, and uncharacteristically not taking care over his appearance. Staff found it difficult to converse with him and he offered no information about himself, making an ordinary diagnostic interview impossible. WG would usually answer direct questions, but in a flat emotionless tone. Sometimes his answers were not even connected to the question, and staff would find themselves wondering what the conversation had been about. There were also occasions when there was a complete mismatch between WG's emotional expression and the words he spoke. For example, he giggled continuously when speaking about a serious illness that had left his mother bedridden. On one occasion, WG became very agitated and spoke of "electrical sensations" in his brain. At other times he spoke of being influenced by a force outside himself, which took the form of a voice urging him to commit acts of violence against his parents. He claimed that the voice repeated the command "You'll have to do it". (Adapted from Hofling, 1974.)

Schizophrenia depends in part on genetic factors. Much of the relevant evidence comes from the study of twins, one of whom is known to be schizophrenic. What is the probability that the other twin is also schizophrenic?—a state of affairs known as **concordance**. Gottesman (1991) summarised about 40 studies. The concordance rate is about 48% if you have a monozygotic or identical twin with schizophrenia, but only 17% if you have a dizygotic or fraternal twin with schizophrenia.

Monozygotic twins tend to be treated more similarly than dizygotic twins (Loehlin & Nichols, 1976), and this greater environmental similarity for monozygotic twins might help to account for their higher level of concordance. There are two arguments against that view. First, monozygotic twins *elicit* more similar treatment from their parents than do dizygotic twins (Lytton, 1977). This suggests that the greater concordance of identical twins may be a cause, rather than an effect, of their more similar parental treatment. Second, schizophrenia concordance rates for monozygotic twins brought up apart are similar to those for monozygotic twins brought up together (Shields, 1962). The high concordance rate for monozygotic twins brought up apart is presumably not due to a high level of environmental similarity.

KEY TERM

Concordance: the extent to which the fact that one twin has a given disorder predicts that the other twin will have the same disorder.

Gottesman (1991) reviewed other concordance rates. If both your parents have schizophrenia, then you have a 46% chance of developing schizophrenia as well. The concordance rate is 16% if one of your parents has schizophrenia, and it is 8% if a sibling has schizophrenia. These concordance rates should be compared against the 1% probability of someone selected at random suffering from schizophrenia.

The evidence reported by Gottesman indicates clearly that schizophrenia runs in families. Furthermore, as predicted by the genetic hypothesis, the concordance rate is much higher between relatives having high genetic similarity. However, the fact that family members who are more similar genetically tend to spend more time together means that environmental factors may be of importance.

Discussion points

1. Does this research provide strong evidence for the importance of genetic factors in schizophrenia?

2. What are the limitations of twin and family studies of schizophrenia?

Research by Gottesman (1991) indicates that schizophrenia tends to run in families.

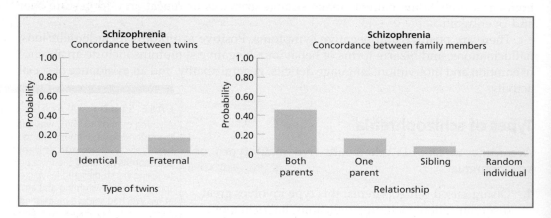

Some of the most striking support for genetic factors was reported by Rosenthal (1963). He studied quadruplets, in which all four girls were identical to each other. Amazingly, all four of them developed schizophrenia, although they did differ somewhat in age of onset and the precise symptoms. They were known as the Genain (dreadful genes) quadruplets.

Finally, Gottesman and Bertelsen (1989) reported some convincing findings on the importance of genetic factors. One of their findings was that their participants had a 17% chance of being schizophrenic if they had a parent who was an identical twin with schizophrenia. This could be due to either heredity or environment. However, they also studied participants having a parent who was an identical twin who did not have schizophrenia, but whose identical twin did. These participants also had a 17% chance of being schizophrenic. In other words, what is of most importance are the genes that are handed on by the parents.

Adoption studies

The notion that genetic factors are important in producing schizophrenia is supported by adoption studies. One approach is to look at adopted children, one of whose parents has schizophrenia. Tienari (1991) did this in Finland. He managed to find 155 schizophrenic mothers who had given up their children for adoption, and they were compared against 155 adopted children not having a schizophrenic parent. There was a large difference in the incidence of schizophrenia in these two groups when they were adults: 10.3% of those with schizophrenic mothers had developed schizophrenia compared to only 1.1% of those without schizophrenic mothers.

Kety et al. (1978) considered adults who had been adopted at an early age between 1924 and 1947. Half had been diagnosed as suffering from schizophrenia and the other half had not. The two groups were matched on

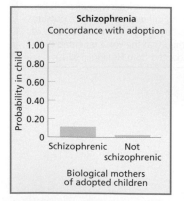

EVALUATION — Kety et al.

Although Kety et al.'s findings appear to support the importance of genetic factors in the incidence of schizophrenia, it is worth noting that these statistics were gathered from a time-span of over 70 years. Earlier interpretations of symptoms and diagnoses were less uniform than would be expected nowadays.

variables such as sex and age. The rate of schizophrenia was greater among the *biological* relatives of those with schizophrenia than those without, which is as expected if genetic factors are important. The rate of schizophrenia did not differ for *adoptive* families that had adopted a child who became, or did not become, schizophrenic. This suggests that environmental factors had little impact on the development of schizophrenia.

Biological approach: Biochemical factors

Biochemical abnormalities may be important in the development and maintenance of schizophrenia. For example, schizophrenia may result in part from excess levels of the neurotransmitter dopamine (see Chapter 3) (Seidman, 1983). A slightly different view is that neurons in the brains of schizophrenic patients are over-sensitive to dopamine.

Identical (monozygotic) twins are not only genetically identical; they are also more likely to be treated identically by their family.

The dopamine hypothesis

Various kinds of evidence suggest that dopamine plays a role in schizophrenia. For example, neuroleptic drugs that block dopamine seem to reduce the symptoms of schizophrenia. The **phenothiazines** are neuroleptic drugs that block dopamine at the synapse (i.e. the juncture between the axon of one neuron and the dendrite of another neuron). The phenothiazines typically reduce many of the symptoms of schizophrenia (Davison & Neale, 1996). However, they have more effect on positive symptoms such as delusions and hallucinations than on negative symptoms such as apathy and immobility.

Other evidence supports the notion that dopamine is involved in schizophrenia. For example, the drug L-dopa, which increases dopamine levels, can produce many of the symptoms of schizophrenia (Davidson et al., 1987). In similar fashion, the symptoms of schizophrenic patients often become worse when they are given amphetamine, which activates dopamine (van Kammen, Docherty, & Bunney, 1982).

Findings from patients suffering from Parkinson's disease are of relevance. Low levels of dopamine are found in Parkinson's patients, and the symptoms of the disease include uncontrolled movements of the limbs (see Cardwell, Clark, & Meldrum, 1996). Similar uncontrolled movements are found in schizophrenics given neuroleptic drugs, presumably because these drugs reduce dopamine levels.

Problems with the dopamine hypothesis

As Barlow and Durand (1995) pointed out, there are some problems with the dopamine hypothesis. Neuroleptic drugs block dopamine fairly rapidly, but generally fail to reduce the symptoms of schizophrenia for days or weeks thereafter. This is puzzling if high levels of dopamine are responsible for maintaining the symptoms. What is also puzzling from the perspective of the dopamine hypothesis is the frequent greater effectiveness of the fairly new drug clozapine than the neuroleptics in reducing schizophrenic symptoms (Kane et al., 1988). Clozapine blocks dopamine activity less than the neuroleptics, and so it should be less effective according to the dopamine hypothesis.

How can we explain the effectiveness of clozapine? According to Barlow and Durand (1995), there is growing support for the view that two neurotransmitters, dopamine and serotonin, both play a role in producing the symptoms of schizophrenia. Clozapine blocks both of these neurotransmitters, which is not the case with the neuroleptics.

The evidence on the relationship between schizophrenia and dopamine levels is mostly correlational in nature. As a result, we do not know whether the changed dopamine activity in schizophrenics occurs *before* or *after* the onset of the disorder. If it occurs after, then clearly dopamine plays no part in causing schizophrenic symptoms.

KEY TERM
Phenothiazines: neuroleptic drugs that reduce dopamine activity.

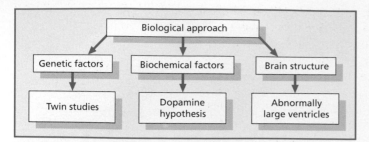

Biological approach: Brain structure

There are several sophisticated techniques for studying the brain (see Chapter 4), some of which have been used to study brain structure in schizophrenics. Pahl, Swayze, and Andreasen (1990) reviewed almost 50 studies, the great majority of which found abnormally large lateral ventricles (liquid-filled cavities) in the brains of schizophrenics. Further evidence of the involvement of the ventricles was reported by Suddath et al. (1990). They used magnetic resonance imaging (MRI) to obtain pictures of brain structure from monozygotic or identical twin pairs in which only one twin had schizophrenia. The schizophrenic twin generally had more enlarged ventricles and reduced anterior hypothalamus. Indeed, the differences were so large that the schizophrenic twin could be identified readily from the brain images in 12 out of 15 twin pairs.

Other parts of the brain may also be involved. Buchsbaum et al. (1984) used PET scans with schizophrenics and normals. The schizophrenics had lower metabolic rates than the normals in the prefrontal cortex while performing psychological tests.

The extent to which the brain abnormalities in schizophrenic patients are due to genetic factors is not clear. However, Suddath et al.'s (1990) finding that there were clear differences in brain structure between schizophrenics and their non-schizophrenic identical twins suggests that environmental factors must be of importance.

Psychodynamic approach

Freud was mainly interested in the neuroses, such as anxiety and depression. He assumed that neuroses occurred as a result of severe conflicts and traumatic experiences. Information about these conflicts and traumas is stored in the unconscious mind, and treatment involves trying to resolve these internal conflicts.

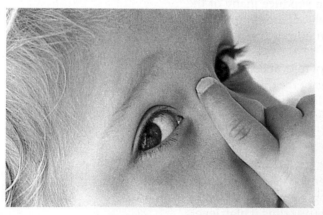

Freud argued that conflicts and traumas are also of importance in schizophrenia. However, an important difference is that schizophrenics have regressed or returned to an earlier stage of psychosexual development than anxious or depressed patients. More specifically, they have regressed to a state of primary narcissism (or great self-interest) which occurs early in the oral stage. In this state, the ego or rational part of the mind has not separated from the id or sexual instinct. The importance of this is that the ego is involved in reality testing and responding appropriately to the external world. Schizophrenics have a loss of contact with reality because their ego is no longer functioning properly.

Freud argued that schizophrenics were driven by strong sexual impulses. That helps to explain why schizophrenia often develops in late adolescence. Later psychodynamic theorists tended to be unconvinced about the involvement of sexual impulses, preferring to emphasise the role of aggression in schizophrenia.

The psychodynamic approach to schizophrenia is limited for several reasons. First, it is very speculative, and is not supported by much evidence. Second, the notion that adult schizophrenics resemble infants in many ways is not very sensible. Third, the psychodynamic approach ignores the role of genetic factors in the development of schizophrenia.

Behavioural approach

According to the behavioural approach, learning plays a key role in causing schizophrenia. Early experience of punishment may lead children to retreat into a rewarding inner world. This causes others to label them as "odd" or "peculiar", and later on they may be

What are the limitations of each of these theories?

diagnosed as suffering from "schizophrenia". According to Scheff's (1966) labelling theory, individuals who have been labelled in this way may continue to act in ways that conform to the label. Their bizarre behaviour may be rewarded with attention and sympathy for behaving bizarrely; this is known as secondary gain.

The fact that schizophrenics often respond to reinforcement provides modest support for the behavioural approach. For example, schizophrenics have learned to make their own beds and to comb their hair when rewarded for doing so (Ayllon & Azrin, 1968). However, labelling theory is not adequate for various reasons. First, it only provides an account of how schizophrenic symptoms are maintained, and does not explain where these symptoms came from initially. Second, the behavioural approach ignores the genetic evidence. Third, it trivialises a very serious disorder, as is shown in the following anecdote. The schizophrenia expert Paul Meehl was giving a lecture, when a member of the audience interrupted and argued in favour of labelling theory. Meehl states: "I was thinking of a patient ... who kept his finger up his arse to 'keep his thoughts from running out', while with his other hand he tried to tear out his hair because it really 'belonged to his father'. And here was this man telling me that he was doing these things because someone had called him a schizophrenic" (Kimble et al., 1980, p.453).

Social factors

If schizophrenia was determined entirely by genetic factors, then the concordance rate for monozygotic or identical twins would be close to 100%. As it is actually under 50%, it is probable that several social or environmental factors contribute to the development of schizophrenia.

Interpersonal communication

Some theorists have argued that there are abnormal and inadequate patterns of communication within the families of schizophrenic patients. Bateson et al. (1956) put forward a double-bind theory, according to which the members of families of schizophrenics communicate in a destructively ambiguous fashion. For example, the mother will tell her child that she loves him, but in a tone of voice that does not indicate love. The double-bind theory accounts in part for the confused thinking of schizophrenic patients. However, it suffers from the serious problem that there is very little evidence supporting it.

The families of schizophrenics tend to have inadequate interpersonal communication. Mischler and Waxler (1968) found that mothers talking to their schizophrenic daughters were rather aloof and unresponsive. However, the same mothers behaved in a much more normal and responsive way when talking to their normal daughters. Thus, the presence of a schizophrenic patient in the family may cause poor communication patterns rather than the other way around.

Expressed emotion. In spite of the lack of support for double-bind theory, there is evidence that the interactions within families can play a key role in maintaining the symptoms of individuals who are already suffering from schizophrenia. What seems to be important is the extent to which a family engages in **expressed emotion**, which involves criticism, hostility, and emotional over-involvement. Individuals who have suffered from schizophrenia and who live in families with high expressed emotion are nearly four times as likely to relapse compared to those who live in families with low expressed emotion (Kavanagh, 1992).

The direction of causality is not clear in studies of expressed emotion. One possibility is that expressed emotion within the family causes relapse. Another possibility is that individuals who are in poor psychological shape are more likely to provoke expressed emotion from members of their family.

Other social factors

Other social factors may be important. Mednick and Schulsinger (1968) studied individuals between the ages of 15 and 25 with a schizophrenic mother. Those individuals

Constant reinforcement for odd or bizarre behaviour may cause a continuous cycle.

were more likely to develop the negative symptoms of schizophrenia if there had been pregnancy and birth complications, and they were more likely to develop the positive symptoms if there was instability within the family.

The social causation hypothesis. Social factors are emphasised by the social causation hypothesis (see Chapter 24). This hypothesis was designed to explain why it is that schizophrenics tend to belong to the lower social classes. According to the hypothesis, members of the lower social classes have more stressful lives than middle-class people, and this makes them more vulnerable to schizophrenia. The key issue here is whether belonging to the lower social classes makes individuals likely to develop schizophrenia, or whether developing schizophrenia leads to reduced social status. There is some evidence that being in the lower social classes can precede the onset of schizophrenia. Turner and Wagonfeld (1967) found that the fathers of schizophrenics tended to belong to the lower social classes.

Stress. Finally, stressful life events sometimes help to trigger the onset of schizophrenia. Day et al. (1987) carried out a study in several countries. They found that schizophrenics tended to have experienced a high number of stressful life events in the few weeks before the onset of schizophrenia.

Theories of schizophrenia: Strengths and weaknesses.

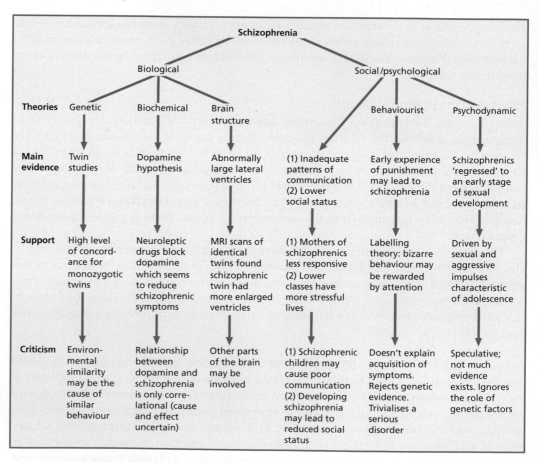

Depression

There is a key distinction between *major depression* (sometimes called unipolar depression) and *bipolar disorder* (also known as manic-depressive disorder). According to DSM-IV, the diagnosis of a major depressive episode requires that five symptoms occur nearly every day for a minimum of two weeks. These symptoms are as follows: sad, depressed mood; loss of interest and pleasure in usual activities; difficulties in sleeping; changes in activity level; weight loss or gain; loss of energy and tiredness; negative self-concept, self-blame, and self-reproach; problems with concentration; recurring thoughts of suicide or death.

Patients with bipolar depression experience both depression and mania (a mood state involving elation, talkativeness, and unjustified high self-esteem). About 10% of men and 20% of women become clinically depressed at some time in their lives. Over 90% of them suffer from unipolar rather than bipolar depression.

Family studies also suggest the involvement of genetic factors. Gershon (1990) presented the findings from numerous family studies in which depression was assessed in the first-degree relatives of patients with depression. For both major depression and bipolar disorder, the rates of depression were about two to three times the rates in the general population.

Additional evidence supporting the notion that genetic factors are of importance comes from adoption studies. Wender et al. (1986) found that the biological relatives of adopted sufferers from major depression were about eight times more likely than adoptive relatives to have had major depression themselves. In similar fashion, it has been found with adopted children who later developed depression that their biological parents were eight times as likely as their adoptive parents to have suffered from clinical depression (Wender et al., 1986).

Why do you think twice as many reported cases of depression involve women rather than men?

Biological approach: Genetic factors

The clearest evidence about the role of genetic factors in the development of major depression and bipolar depression comes from studies on monozygotic and dizygotic twins. Allen (1976) reviewed the relevant studies. For major depression, the mean concordance rate was 40% for monozygotic or identical twins, whereas it was only 11% for dizygotic twins. For bipolar disorder, the mean concordance rate was 72% for monozygotic twins, compared to 14% for dizygotic twins. Similar findings were reported in a large study by Bertelsen, Harvald, and Hauge (1977). They found a concordance rate for major depression of 59% for monozygotic twins and of 30% for dizygotic twins. For bipolar disorder, the concordance rate was 80% for identical twins and 16% for fraternal twins. In the population at large, about 5% have been diagnosed with major depression and 1% with bipolar disorder, and all of the figures for monozygotic and dizygotic twins are much higher.

These findings suggest that genetic factors are involved in both types of depression, and that their involvement is greater for bipolar than for major depression. However, it is not known whether the monozygotic and dizygotic twin pairs experienced equally similar environments. As a result, it is possible that some of the higher concordance rate for monozygotic than for dizygotic twins reflects environmental rather than genetic influences.

Marilyn Monroe suffered with unipolar depression. Famous people who suffered with bipolar depression include Sir Winston Churchill, Abraham Lincoln and Virginia Woolf.

Discussion points

1. Is the evidence of genetic factors in depression stronger or weaker than in schizophrenia?
2. To what extent is the evidence from twin studies supported by family and adoption studies?

CASE STUDY: *Manic Behaviour in Manic Depression*

Robert B had been a successful dentist for 25 years, providing well for his wife and family. One morning he woke up with the idea that he was the best dental surgeon in the world, and that he should try to treat as many people as possible. As a result, he set about enlarging his practice from 2 chairs to 20, planning to treat patients simultaneously. He phoned builders and ordered the necessary equipment. After a day of feeling irritable that there had been delays, he decided to do the work himself and began to knock down the walls. When this proved difficult, he became frustrated and began to smash his X-ray equipment and washbasins. Robert B's family were unaware of his behaviour until patients began to phone his wife after being turned away from the dental surgery. When she mentioned the phone calls to him, Robert B "ranted and raved" at her for 15 minutes. She described her husband as looking "haggard, wild-eyed and run down", and his speech was "over-excited". After several days of this behaviour, Mrs B phoned her daughters and asked them to come over with their husbands to help. On the evening of their visit Robert B began to "brag about his sexual prowess and make aggressive advances towards his daughters". When one of his sons-in-law tried to intervene he was attacked with a chair. Robert B was admitted to hospital, and subsequently it was found that he had had a history of such behaviour.

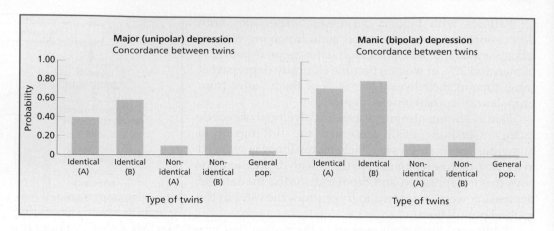

Biological approach: Biochemical factors

There has been much interest in the possibility that depressed patients might have elevated or reduced levels of various neurotransmitters or other substances. Numerous theories have been put forward in this area, many of them based on the notion that low levels of the neurotransmitters noradrenaline and serotonin may play a role in the development of depression. It has also been suggested that there may be increased levels of these neurotransmitters when bipolar disorder patients are in their manic phase. Kety (1975) put forward a permissive amine theory. According to this theory, the level of noradrenaline is generally controlled by the level of serotonin. When the level of serotonin is low, however, noradrenaline levels are less controlled, and so they can become much higher or lower than usual.

Drug studies

These hypotheses receive some support from drug studies. Teuting, Rosen, and Hirschfeld (1981) compared the substances found in the urine of depressed patients and normals. Compounds that are produced as a byproduct of the action of enzymes on noradrenaline and serotonin were present in smaller amounts in the urine of depressed patients. This finding suggests that depressed patients have lower levels of noradrenaline and serotonin. Kety (1975) found very high levels of compounds derived from noradrenaline in the urine of patients suffering from mania. It is hard to know whether the high or low levels of noradrenaline and serotonin helped to cause the depression, or whether the depression altered the levels of those neurotransmitters.

Anti-depressants. Anti-depressant drugs such as the monoamine oxidase inhibitors (MAOIs) increase the active levels of noradrenaline and serotonin in depressed patients, and typically reduce the symptoms of depression (see Chapter 26). Lithium carbonate, which is very effective in reducing manic symptoms in bipolar disorder, is thought to decrease the availability of noradrenaline and serotonin. These drug effects suggest the potential importance of altered levels of serotonin and noradrenaline. However, the drugs rapidly affect neurotransmitter levels, but take much longer to reduce the symptoms of depression or mania. It is possible that the MAOIs reduce depression by increasing the sensitivity of receiving neurons, and it takes time for this increased sensitivity to occur (see Gross & McIlveen, 1996). It is important to note that these drug effects do not provide *direct* evidence of what causes depression in the first place. For example, aspirin can cure a headache, but that does not mean that it was an absence of aspirin that produced the headache!

Cortisol

The levels of the stress hormone cortisol tend to be elevated in depressed patients (Barlow & Durand, 1995). The notion that cortisol may be relevant to depression has been examined by using the dexamethasone suppression test. Dexamethasone suppresses cortisol secretion in normal people, but about 50% of depressed patients show very little suppression (Carroll et al., 1980). Presumably this happens because the levels of cortisol are so high in these patients that they cannot be easily suppressed.

There are two limitations with the cortisol research. First, reduced suppression on the dexamethasone suppression test is also found in anxiety disorders and other mental disorders, and so high levels of cortisol are not specific to depression. Second, high cortisol levels may be a result of depression rather than forming part of the cause.

Psychodynamic approach

Freud argued that depression is like grief, in that it often occurs as a reaction to the loss of an important relationship. However, there is an important difference, because depressed people regard themselves as worthless. What happens is that the individual identifies with the lost person, so that repressed anger towards the lost person is directed inwards towards the self. This inner-directed anger reduces the individual's self-esteem, and makes him or her vulnerable to experiencing depression in the future.

Freud distinguished between actual losses (e.g. death of a loved one) and symbolic losses (e.g. loss of a job). Both kinds of losses can produce depression by causing the individual to re-experience childhood occurrences relating to loss of affection from some significant person (e.g. parent).

What about bipolar disorder? According to Freud, the depressive phase occurs when the individual's superego or conscience is dominant. In contrast, the manic phase occurs when the individual's ego or rational mind asserts itself, and he or she feels in control.

Job loss may cause depression affecting the person's belief in his or her abilities and future prospects.

In order to avoid loss turning into depression, the individual needs to engage in a period of mourning work, during which he or she recalls memories of the lost one. This allows the individual to separate himself or herself from the lost person, and so reduce the inner-directed anger. However, individuals who are very dependent on others for their sense of self-esteem may be unable to do this, and so remain extremely depressed.

Evaluation

There is good evidence that depression is caused in part by loss events. For example, Finlay-Jones and Brown (1981) found that depressed patients experienced more stressful life events than normal controls in the year before onset of the depression, and most of these were loss events. However, the details of the psychodynamic approach are incorrect. Freud would predict that the repressed anger and hostility of depressed people would emerge in dreams, but Beck and Ward (1961) found no evidence of this. Freud would also predict that depressed people should express anger and hostility mainly towards themselves. In fact, they express considerable anger and hostility towards those close to them (Weissman, Klerman, & Paykel, 1971).

Finally, it follows from Freud's theory that individuals who experienced some major loss early in their lives should be more vulnerable than others to developing clinical depression in adult life. The evidence is inconsistent, but often suggests that early loss does not predict adult depression (Crook & Eliot, 1980).

Behavioural approach

Lewinsohn (1974) put forward a behavioural theory based on the notion that depression occurs as a result of a reduction in the level of reinforcement or reward. This relates to the psychodynamic view that depression is caused by the loss of an

EVALUATION — Seligman

Seligman used dogs to illustrate how lack of control over one's experiences might contribute to feeling helpless. In his experiments each dog was "yoked" with another dog. The first dog learned to escape from electric shocks, whereas whether the second dog received a shock or not depended on the expertise of its pair. Later in the experiment the dogs were separated and put into a "shuttle box" where they could escape an electrified floor by jumping over a partition. The dogs that had previously learned to avoid shocks soon learned to jump the partition. However, the dogs who had been yoked behaved passively and gave up trying to escape soon after being put in the shuttle box.

From this research it appears that the most important factor in the animals' behaviour was not the electric shocks, but the failure to learn avoidance. The dogs had learned that they were helpless, so they displayed inappropriate behaviour in the shuttle box and didn't try to escape. Seligman went on to propose that depression in humans may be due to learned helplessness. For example, stressful situations may be experienced as unavoidable and not under the control of the individual.

Although symptoms of learned helplessness in Seligman's dogs and symptoms of depression in humans do appear to be similar, there are problems with these conclusions. The experiments were carried out on dogs in controlled conditions, but do the findings apply to humans in society? Later research indicated that what may be important is not so much the learned helplessness that a person feels, but the way in which the individual might perceive and react to the stressful situation.

Ethical issues: Why might these experiments be considered unethical today?

What is wrong with applying the results of a laboratory experiment on dogs to humans in society?

How might the idea of learned helplessness be applied to battered wife syndrome?

KEY TERM

Learned helplessness: the passive behaviour produced by the perception that punishment is unavoidable.

important relationship, because important relationships are a major source of positive reinforcement. There is also a reduction in reinforcement with other losses, such as being made redundant. People who become depressed because of a major loss may be reinforced in being depressed by the sympathy and understanding shown by other people.

Lewinsohn's behavioural theory clearly presents an oversimplified view of the causes of depression. For example, many people experience major losses without becoming depressed, and the theory does not explain how this happens. The theory also omits any consideration of other causes of depression such as genetic factors.

Learned helplessness

Seligman's (1975) theory and research on learned helplessness have probably been more influential than any other behavioural approach to depression (see Chapter 10). **Learned helplessness** refers to the passive behaviour shown when animals or humans perceive mistakenly that punishment is unavoidable. In his original studies, Seligman exposed dogs to electric shocks they could not avoid. After that, they were put in a box with a barrier in the middle. The dogs were given shocks after a warning signal, but they could escape by jumping over the barrier into the other part of the box. However, most of the dogs passively accepted the shocks, and did not learn to escape. Seligman described this as learned helplessness, and argued that it was very similar to the behaviour shown by depressed people.

This learned helplessness theory was later turned into a cognitive theory by Abramson, Seligman, and Teasdale (1978; see next). One of the problems with the original theory was that it was intended to model the behaviour of patients with major depression. In fact, however, the symptoms of learned helplessness are more like those of patients with bipolar disorder during a depressive episode (Depue & Monroe, 1978).

Cognitive approach

Abramson et al. (1978) developed Seligman's learned helplessness theory by focusing on the thoughts of people experiencing learned helplessness. They started by arguing that people respond to failure in various ways:

- They attribute the failure to an *internal* cause (themselves) or to an *external* cause (other people; circumstances).
- They attribute the failure to a *stable* cause (likely to continue in future) or to an *unstable* cause (might easily change in future).
- They attribute the failure to a *global* cause (applying to a wide range of situations) or to a *specific* cause (applying to only one situation).

People with learned helplessness attribute failure to internal, stable, and global causes. In other words, they feel personally responsible for failure, they think the factors causing that failure will persist, and they think that those factors will influence most situations in future. In view of these negative and pessimistic thoughts, it is no wonder that sufferers from learned helplessness are depressed.

This cognitive theory was modified by Abramson, Metalski, and Alloy (1989). They attached less importance than Abramson et al. (1978) to specific attributions, and more importance to the notion that depressed individuals develop a general sense of hopelessness.

Depressive schemas

Beck and Clark (1988) also argued that cognitive factors may play an important role in the development of depression. They referred to depressive schemas, which consist of organised information stored in long-term memory. Beck and Clark's (1988, p.26) cognitive theory is as follows:

> The schematic organisation of the clinically depressed individual is dominated by an overwhelming negativity. A negative cognitive trait is evident in the depressed person's view of the self, world, and future ... As a result of these negative maladaptive schemas, the depressed person views himself as inadequate, deprived and worthless, the world as presenting insurmountable obstacles, and the future as utterly bleak and hopeless.

The term **cognitive triad** is used to refer to the depressed person's negative views of himself or herself, the world, and the future.

Individuals suffering from depression see themselves as failures, and often attribute this to faults within themselves that cannot be changed.

Evaluation

Depressed people undoubtedly have the kinds of negative thoughts described by Abramson et al. (1978) and by Beck and Clark (1988). Do these negative thoughts help to cause depression, or do they merely occur as a result of being depressed? Lewinsohn et al. (1981, p.218) carried out a prospective study in which negative attitudes and thoughts were assessed *before* any of the participants became depressed. Here are their conclusions:

> Future depressives did not subscribe to irrational beliefs, they did not have lower expectancies for positive outcomes or higher expectancies for negative outcomes, they did not attribute success experiences to external causes and failure experiences to internal causes ... People who are vulnerable to depression are not characterised by stable patterns of negative cognitions.

Most of the evidence suggests that negative thoughts and attitudes are caused by depression rather than the opposite direction of causality. However, Nolen-Hoeksma, Girgus, and Seligman (1992) found that a negative attributional style in older children predicted the development of depressive symptoms in response to stressful life events. It thus remains possible that negative thoughts may make people vulnerable to depression.

Social factors: Life events

Patients suffering from major depression typically experience an above average number of stressful life events in the period before the onset of depression. For example, Brown and Harris (1978) carried out an interview study on women in London. They found that 61% of the depressed women had experienced at least one very stressful life event in the eight months before interview, compared with 19% of non-depressed women. However, many women manage to cope with major life events without becoming clinically depressed. Of those women who experienced

> **KEY TERM**
> **Cognitive triad**: the depressed person's negative views of the self, the world, and the future.

■ Research activity: Compile a set of everyday situations or problems (e.g. not doing well in a particular subject, being late for school, not handing in homework). Ask each other about these problems and decide from the participants' answers which factors are involved. Draw up a table of responses like the examples here.

EXAMPLE:

Question 1 Are there any subjects that you are not doing well in, and if so, why do you think this is?

Participant A: I'm hopeless at maths, it's my own fault. (Internal factor)

	Internal	External	Stable	Unstable	Global	Specific
Q1	✓					
Q2						

Participant B: I'm doing badly in maths, because the teacher is awful. (External factor)

	Internal	External	Stable	Unstable	Global	Specific
Q1		✓				
Q2						

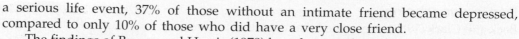

a serious life event, 37% of those without an intimate friend became depressed, compared to only 10% of those who did have a very close friend.

The findings of Brown and Harris (1978) have been replicated several times. Brown (1989) reviewed the various studies. On average, about 55% of depressed patients had at least one severe life event in the months before onset, compared to only about 17% of controls.

There are two main limitations of most life-event studies. First, the information is obtained retrospectively several months afterwards, and so there may be problems in remembering clearly what has happened. Second, the meaning of a life event depends on the context in which it happens. For example, losing your job is very serious if you have a large family to support, but may be much less serious if you are nearing the normal retirement age and have a large pension. This second limitation does not apply to the research of Brown and Harris (1978), because they took full account of the context in which the life events occurred.

LIFE EVENTS

Rank	Life Event	Stress Value
1	Death of a spouse	100
2	Divorce	73
3	Marital separation	65
13	Sex difficulties	39
23	Son or daughter leaving	29
38	Change in sleeping habits	16
41	Vacation	13

Adapted from T. Holmes, & R. Rahe (1967). The social readjustment rating scale. *Journal of Psychosomatic Research, 11*, 213–218.

Phobias

Several anxiety disorders are included in DSM-IV. They include phobias, post-traumatic stress disorder, panic disorder, generalised anxiety disorder, and obsessive-compulsive disorder. In this section, we will focus on the various phobias, with post-traumatic stress disorder being discussed in the next section. Some of the other anxiety disorders will be referred to as and when appropriate.

Phobias involve a high level of fear of some object or situation, with the level of fear being so strong that the object or situation is avoided whenever possible. There are various different categories of phobia: specific phobia; social phobia; and agoraphobia. We will describe each type of phobia in turn.

Specific phobia

Specific phobia involves strong and irrational fear of some specific object or situation. Specific phobias include fear of spiders and fear of snakes, but there are hundreds of different specific phobias. DSM-IV identified four major sub-types of specific phobia:

- Animal type.
- Natural environment type: this includes fear of heights, fear of water, and fear of storms.
- Blood–injection–injury type.
- Situational type: this includes fears about being in various situations, such as in a plane, a lift, or an enclosed space (claustrophobia).

In addition, there is a fifth category labelled "other type". This covers all specific phobias that do not fit any of the four major sub-types.

According to DSM-IV, these are the major diagnostic criteria for specific phobia:

- Marked and persistent fear of a specific object or situation.
- Exposure to the phobic stimulus nearly always produces a rapid anxiety response.
- The individual recognises that his or her fear of the phobic object or situation is excessive.
- The phobic stimulus is either avoided or responded to with great anxiety.
- The phobic reactions interfere significantly with the individual's working or social life, or he or she is very distressed about the phobia.
- In individuals under the age of 18, the phobia has lasted for at least six months.

Social phobia

Social phobia involves extreme concern about one's own behaviour and the reactions of others. Social phobia can be either generalised or specific. As the terms imply, individuals with social phobia generalised type are very shy in nearly all situations, whereas those with social phobia specific type mainly become extremely shy in only a few situations (e.g. public speaking). The main diagnostic criteria for social phobia given in DSM-IV include the following:

- Marked and persistent fear of one or more situations in which the individual will be exposed to unfamiliar people or to the scrutiny of others.
- Exposure to the feared social situation nearly always produces a high level of anxiety.
- The individual recognises that the fear experienced is excessive.
- The feared situations are either avoided or responded to with great anxiety.
- The phobic reactions interfere significantly with the individual's working or social life, or there is marked distress about the phobia.

Social phobia is more common in females than in males, with about 70% of sufferers being female. According to Barlow and Durand (1995, p.186), social phobia "tends to be more prevalent in people who are younger (aged 18–29 years), less educated, single, and of lower socioeconomic class."

CASE STUDY: *A Phobia*

A young student in his first year at university was referred to a therapist after seeking help at the student health centre. During initial interviews he spoke of feeling frightened and often panicking when heading for his classes. He claimed he felt comfortable in his room, but was unable to concentrate on his work or to face other people. He admitted to fears of catching syphilis and of going bald. These fears were so intense that at times he would compulsively scrub his hands, head, and genitals so hard that they would bleed. He was reluctant to touch door handles and would never use public toilets. The student admitted that he knew his fears were irrational, but felt that he would be in even more "mental anguish" if he did not take these precautions.

In later sessions with the therapist, the student's history revealed previous concerns about his sexual identity. As a child he harboured feelings of inferiority because he had not been as fast or as strong as his peers. These feelings were reinforced by his mother who had not encouraged him to play rough games in case he got hurt. At puberty the student had also worried that he might be sexually deficient. At a summer camp he had discovered that he was underdeveloped sexually compared to the other boys. He had even wondered if he was developing into a girl. Although he did in fact mature into a young man, he constantly worried about his masculine identity, even fantasising that he was a girl. The student admitted that at times his anxiety was so great that he considered suicide. (Adapted from Kleinmuntz, 1974.)

Stage-fright: an example of fear when facing the scrutiny of others.

Agoraphobia

Agoraphobia involves great fear of open or public places. Agoraphobia on its own is rather rare, as was pointed out in DSM-IV (1994). In most cases, the panic disorder starts before the agoraphobia. Individuals who are very frightened of having panic attacks feel less secure when away from familiar surroundings and people, and know that they would be very embarrassed if they had a panic attack in public. These

Unusual phobias:
Triskaidekaphobia: fear of the number 13.
Siderophobia: fear of railways.
Monophobia: fear of being alone.

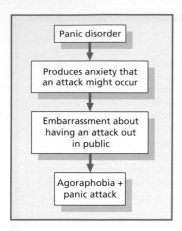

concerns lead them to avoid open or public places, and so agoraphobia is added to the panic disorder.

Panic disorder with agoraphobia is defined by the following criteria in DSM-IV:

*   Recurrent unexpected panic attacks.
*   At least one panic attack has been followed by at least one month of worry about the attack, concern about having more panic attacks, or changes in behaviour resulting from the attack.
*   Agoraphobia, in which there is anxiety about being in situations from which escape might be hard or embarrassing in the event of a panic attack.
*   The panic attacks are not due to use of some substance.

What is the definition of a panic attack? According to DSM-IV, a panic attack involves intense fear or discomfort, with four or more bodily symptoms suddenly appearing. These symptoms include palpitations, shortness of breath, accelerated heart rate, feeling of choking, nausea, sweating, chest pain, feeling dizzy, and fear of dying.

People between the ages of about 25 and 29 are most likely to develop panic disorder. About 75% of those who suffer from agoraphobia are female. One reason why men show less agoraphobic avoidance than women is because they are more likely to drink heavily so that they can go out in public (Barlow & Durand, 1995).

Can you suggest other reasons why more women than men are agoraphobic?

Comparisons

About 6% or 7% of the population suffer from phobias. Some phobias are more disruptive of everyday life than are others. Agoraphobia and social phobia are usually very disabling, whereas specific phobias such as snake or spider phobias generally have less impact on the phobic's enjoyment of life. About 50% of all phobics seen clinically are suffering from agoraphobia with panic disorder.

Biological approach: Genetic factors

The main evidence on genetic factors in the development of the phobias comes from twin studies, although some family studies have also been carried out. Genetic factors are most relevant for agoraphobia and least relevant for specific phobias, with social phobia intermediate.

Panic disorder with agoraphobia

So far as panic disorder with agoraphobia is concerned, Torgersen (1983) considered pairs of monozygotic or identical twins and dizygotic or fraternal twins, at least one of whom had panic disorder. The concordance rate was 31% for identical twins against 0% for fraternal twins. Harris et al. (1983) found that the close relatives of agoraphobic patients were more likely to be suffering from agoraphobia than were the close relatives of non-anxious individuals. Noyes et al. (1986) found that 12% of the relatives of agoraphobics

Torgersen (1983) and Noyes et al. (1986) studied twins and families of people suffering from panic disorder with agoraphobia.

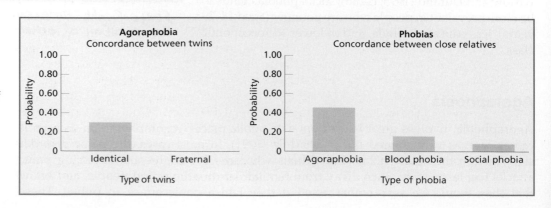

also had agoraphobia, and 17% suffered from panic disorder. Both of these percentage figures are greater than those of controls.

More unusual phobias:
Anthrophobia: fear of men.
Hippophobia: fear of horses.

Genetics or imitation? These findings are consistent with the view that genetic factors play a part in the development of agoraphobia. However, there are some problems with interpreting these findings, especially those of Harris et al. (1983). The close relative of an agoraphobic patient may tend to become agoraphobic because he or she imitates the behaviour displayed by the patient, rather than because of genetic inheritance.

Specific phobia

So far as specific phobia is concerned, Fyer et al. (1990) found that 31% of close relatives of individuals with specific phobias also had a phobia. More striking findings were reported by Ost (1989) in a study on blood phobics. In 64% of the cases, these blood phobics had at least one close relative who also suffered from blood phobia. The findings from these two studies are consistent with the notion that genetic factors are involved. However, the experience of having a close relative with a specific phobia may help to trigger a phobia in close relatives.

Social phobia

So far as social phobia is concerned, Fyer et al. (1993) discovered that 16% of the close relatives of social phobics developed the same disorder, against only 5% of the relatives of individuals without social phobia. However, Skre et al. (1993) found that the concordance rate for social phobia was similar in identical and fraternal twin pairs, leading them to conclude that social phobia is caused mainly by environmental influences.

In spite of the findings of Skre et al. (1993), there is indirect evidence that genetic factors may play a part in the development of social phobia. Individual differences in personality depend to some extent on genetic factors (see Chapter 24), and there are substantial differences in personality between social phobics and normals. Stemberger, Turner, and Beidel (1995) found that social phobics are extremely introverted. Why might introversion be of relevance to social phobia? Introverted people generally have poor social skills and are not well liked, which could lead to the excessive concern about the opinions of others shown by social phobics.

Biological approach: Neurophysiology

It is possible that individuals who generally have a high level of physiological arousal are more vulnerable to the development of phobias. There is some evidence that patients suffering from panic disorder with agoraphobia or with social phobia have high levels of arousal (Lader & Mathews, 1968). However, it is not clear from such evidence whether the high levels of arousal helped to cause the phobia, or whether the phobia led to the increased arousal.

Other evidence suggests that panic disorder with agoraphobia is often *not* associated with increased physiological activity. There have been several studies in which panic patients have been exposed to biological challenges such as inhalation of a mixture of carbon dioxide and oxygen. These biological challenges often produce panic attacks in patients suffering from panic disorder with agoraphobia, but rarely do so in normal controls. The typical finding is that the effects of biological challenge on heart rate, respiratory rate, blood pressure, and other physiological measures are comparable in patients and in normal controls (see Eysenck, 1997, for a review). Thus, patients suffering from panic disorder with agoraphobia differ from normal controls in the way they interpret their bodily symptoms rather than in terms of their actual physiological responsiveness. In other words, these findings support a cognitive rather than a physiological account of panic disorder with agoraphobia.

Little Hans only showed his fear of horses when he saw them pulling a cart at speed—he was not frightened of horses without carts, or of horses pulling carts at a walking pace.

Psychodynamic theory

According to Freud, phobias are a defence against the anxiety that is produced when the impulses of the id or sexual instinct are repressed or forced into the unconscious. This theory developed out of Freud's case study of Little Hans, who developed a phobia of horses. According to Freud, Little Hans was sexually attracted to his mother, but was very frightened that he would be punished for this by his father. Horses resembled his father in that their black muzzles and blinkers looked like his moustache and glasses, and so Little Hans transferred or displaced his fear of his father on to horses.

It would be predicted from this account that Hans would have showed a phobic reaction every time he saw a horse. In fact, he *only* showed his phobia when he saw a horse pulling a cart at high speed. The horse phobia originally developed after Hans had seen a serious accident involving a horse and cart moving at high speed, and this may have produced a conditioned fear response (see below).

Separation anxiety

According to the psychodynamic approach (e.g. Bowlby, 1973), separation anxiety in children may make them more likely to develop panic disorder with agoraphobia as a result. Separation anxiety occurs when a child experiences the threat of separation from an important caregiver such as its mother or father. However, there is little evidence that patients suffering from panic disorder with agoraphobia experienced more childhood separation anxiety than other people.

It follows in a general way from the psychodynamic approach that phobias would be found most often in cultures in which children are brought up in a very strict way and punished for poor behaviour. Whiting and Whiting (1975) reported evidence consistent with that prediction. However, the psychodynamic approach has not received much support, and it ignores many factors associated with phobias (e.g. genetic and social).

Behavioural approach

Albert is shown the rat at the same time as he hears a loud noise.

According to the behaviourists, specific phobias develop through two kinds of conditioning. First, a neutral or conditioned stimulus can come to produce fear if, on several occasions, it is presented at the same time as an unpleasant or unconditioned stimulus. For example, Watson and Rayner (1920) studied an 11-month-old boy called Albert. He was a calm child, but the loud noise produced by striking a steel bar made him cry. He became frightened of a rat when the sight of the rat was paired seven times with a loud noise. This involved classical conditioning.

What happened after that was that the fear produced by the previously neutral stimulus (i.e. the rat) was reduced by avoiding it thereafter. "Albert not only became greatly disturbed at the sight of a rat, but this fear had spread to include a white rabbit, cotton wool, a fur coat and the experimenter's (white) hair" (Jones, 1925). However, it has often proved hard to condition people to fear neutral stimuli by pairing them with unpleasant ones in the laboratory (Davison & Neale, 1996).

The development of phobias can be explained by Mowrer's (1947) two-process theory. The first stage involves classical conditioning (e.g. linking the white rat and the loud noise). Then the second stage involves operant conditioning, because avoidance of the phobic stimulus reduces fear and is thus reinforcing.

Some of the evidence supports the conditioning account. According to Barlow and Durand (1995), about 50% of those with specific phobia of driving remember a traumatic experience while driving (e.g. a car accident) as having caused the onset of the phobia. Barlow and Durand also noted that nearly everyone they have treated for choking phobia has had some very unpleasant choking experience in the past.

Discussion points

1. How convincing is the behavioural or conditioning account of specific phobia in the light of the evidence (see Evaluation section)?

2. Can a conditioning account explain the relative frequency of different phobias (see Evaluation section)?

*Yet more unusual phobias:
Nyctophobia: fear of darkness.
Taphophobia: fear of being buried alive.
Cynophobia: fear of dogs.*

Evaluation

In order to obtain support for the conditioning account of specific phobias, we need to show that phobic patients are much more likely than other people to have had a frightening experience with the phobic object. However, the crucial normal control group is often missing. Consider, for example, a study by DiNardo et al. (1988). They found that about 50% of dog phobics had become very anxious during an encounter with a dog, which seems to support conditioning theory. However, they also found that about 50% of normal controls without dog phobia had also had an anxious encounter with a dog! Thus, these findings suggest that dog phobia does *not* depend on having had a frightening encounter with a dog.

How might a fear response in a child be rewarded or reinforced?

Keuthen (1980) reported that half of all phobics could not remember any highly unpleasant experiences relating to the phobic object. Those who favour a conditioning account have argued that phobics often forget conditioning experiences that happened many years previously. In order to reduce this problem, Menzies and Clarke (1993) carried out a study on child participants suffering from water phobia. Only 2% of them reported a direct conditioning experience involving water.

Evolution. If phobias develop because of accidental pairings of a neutral and a fearful or aversive stimulus, then people could become phobic to almost anything. In fact, many more people have phobias about spiders and snakes than about cars, even though we see cars much more often and they are considerably more dangerous. Seligman (1971) argued that the objects and situations forming the basis of most phobias were real sources of danger hundreds or thousands of years ago, and only those individuals who were sensitive to such objects and situations were favoured by evolution. Thus, there is a "preparedness" or biological predisposition to be sensitive to, and to become phobic about, certain stimuli rather than others.

Modelling and information transmission

Bandura (1986) developed conditioning theory by showing the importance of modelling or observational learning. Individuals learn to imitate the behaviour of others, especially those whose behaviour is seen to be rewarded or reinforced. Mineka et al. (1984) found that monkeys could develop snake phobia simply by watching another monkey experience fear in the presence of a snake. Another possible way in which phobias could be acquired is through information transmission. What happens is that fear-producing information about the phobic object leads to the development of a phobia. Ost (1985) described the case of a severe snake phobic. She had been told repeatedly about the dangers of snakes, and had been strongly encouraged to wear rubber boots to protect herself against snakes. She finally reached the point where she wore rubber boots even when going to the local shops.

Phobia summary
Overall prevalence of phobias in
population studies:
Agoraphobia   2–3%
Social phobia   1–2%
Specific phobia   4–7%
Other phobia   1–2%

Some phobias can be acquired through modelling or information transmission. However, modelling or observational learning seems to be of less importance in producing specific phobias in humans than in other species (Menzies & Clarke, 1994), and there are only a few well documented cases in which information transmission has led to phobias (see Eysenck, 1997). Merckelbach et al. (1996) argued on the basis of the evidence that claustrophobia or fear of enclosed spaces rarely occurs as a result of modelling or information transmission. In contrast, "in small-animal phobias, but also blood–injection–injury phobia, the predominant pathways to fear are modelling and negative information transmission" (Merckelbach et al., 1996, p.354).

Cognitive approach

According to cognitive therapists such as Beck and Emery (1985), anxious patients have various **cognitive biases** which cause them to exaggerate the threateningness of external and internal stimuli. There is good evidence for cognitive biases in phobics. So far as specific phobics are concerned, Tomarken et al. (1989) presented individuals high and low in fears of snakes or spiders with a series of fear-relevant and fear-irrelevant slides. Each slide was followed by electric shock, a tone, or nothing. The high-fear or phobic participants greatly overestimated the number of times fear-relevant slides were followed by shock. This is known as covariation bias, and could help to account for the high level of anxiety produced by phobic stimuli.

Social phobia
Social phobics have a cognitive bias, in that they perceive their behaviour in social situations to be more negative than it appears to observers (Stopa & Clark, 1993). This cognitive bias may help to explain social phobics' fears of being evaluated by others.

Panic disorder
Clark et al. (1988) assessed the ways in which patients suffering from panic disorder or panic disorder with agoraphobia interpret a range of ambiguous events. These patients showed a cognitive bias for their own bodily sensations. For example, they tended to interpret an increase in heart rate as indicating that there was something wrong with their heart. These findings fit well with Clark's (1986) cognitive theory of panic disorder, according to which panic disorder patients tend to interpret their bodily sensations in a catastrophic or life-threatening way. This makes them more anxious, and this in turn increases the tendency to have catastrophic thoughts about their bodily sensations.

Why do agoraphobics with panic disorder misinterpret their bodily sensations? One possibility is that some previous physical illness has made them more concerned than most people about their bodily well-being. Relevant evidence was reported by Verburg et al. (1995). Of their panic disorder patients, 43% had suffered from at least one respiratory disease, compared to only 16% of patients with other anxiety disorders.

Cause or result? There is clear evidence that phobic patients have a range of cognitive biases which lead them to misinterpret their phobic stimuli. However, it has proved very hard to show that these cognitive biases play a part in *causing* phobias rather than simply being a result of having a phobia. The strongest evidence that cognitive biases may be causally involved in phobias was obtained in an unpublished study by Schmidt (discussed in Eysenck, 1997). He assessed the cognitive tendency to respond anxiously to one's own bodily sensations among recruits to the US Air Force Academy who went through stressful basic training. Those with the greatest sensitivity to their own bodily sensations at the start of training were most likely to experience panic attacks thereafter.

Social factors

It is possible that parental rearing styles have an important impact on the development of phobias. This hypothesis was considered by Gerlsman, Emmelkamp, and Arrindell (1990). They reviewed the literature on parental rearing practices in anxious patients,

Misinterpretation of bodily sensations → Anxiety

Research at the US Air Force Academy showed that those recruits who were aware of, and anxious about, their own bodily sensations, such as increased sweating, raised heart rate, or shortness of breath, were more likely to suffer panic attacks as their training progressed.

focusing on the dimension of affection and control or over-protection. They found that phobics (especially social phobics and agoraphobics) were lower than normal controls on parental affection and higher on parental control or over-protection.

Studies on parental rearing practices have the limitation that they are based on information obtained years after the event. Another limitation is that all we have are correlations between rearing practices and anxiety disorders, and correlations cannot prove causes.

Life events

There is evidence that phobic patients tend to experience more serious life events than normal controls in the year or so before the onset of the phobia. In a study by Kleiner and Marshall (1987), 84% of agoraphobics reported having experienced family problems in the months before they had their first panic attack. In similar fashion, Barrett (1979) found that panic disorder patients reported significantly more undesirable life events in the six months prior to onset of their anxiety disorder than did controls over a six-month period.

Finlay-Jones and Brown (1981) found a difference between anxious and depressed patients in terms of the kinds of life events they had experienced in the 12 months prior to onset of their disorder. Both groups had experienced an above-average number of life events, but those of anxious patients tended to be danger events (involving future threats), whereas those of depressed patients tended to be loss events (involving past losses).

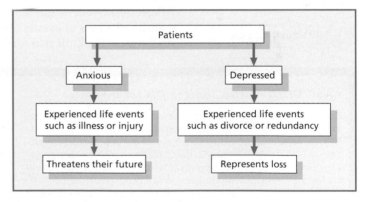

The main problem with most studies is that the information about life events is obtained some time after the events in question. As a result, some events may have been forgotten, or are remembered in a distorted form.

What other life events fit into Finlay-Jones and Brown's categories of "threatens the future" and "represents loss"?

Post-traumatic Stress Disorder

Post-traumatic stress disorder (PTSD) first received official recognition in DSM-III (1980), although related notions such as "shell shock" and "combat fatigue" had been put forward much earlier. According to DSM-III-R (1987), a key factor in producing PTSD is "an event which is outside the range of usual human experience and which would be markedly distressing to almost anybody." The victim's response to such an event is described as being one of "intense fear, terror, and helplessness" (p.248). In DSM-IV (1994),

■ Research activity: Make a list of disasters that have been associated with PTSD.

a distinction was drawn between PTSD and acute stress disorder. The category of acute stress disorder is used when there is fairly rapid recovery from the stress of a traumatic event. If recovery is not rapid, then the diagnosis becomes PTSD.

There are three main categories of symptoms for PTSD, with the diagnosis requiring that symptoms in each category last for more than one month:

1. Re-experiencing the traumatic event: the event is often recalled and nightmares about it are common. Any stimuli that trigger memories of the traumatic event are likely to cause intense emotional upset.
2. Avoidance of stimuli associated with the event or alternatively reduced responsiveness to such stimuli: what often happens is that the individual tries to avoid trauma-related stimuli or thoughts, and there is fluctuation between re-experiencing the traumatic event and a numbing of response to stimuli associated with the event.
3. Increased arousal: as a result, there may be problems with falling asleep or remaining asleep, difficulties with concentration, and an increased startle response.

While those are the three main categories of symptoms, there are several others. For example, patients with PTSD may suffer from various emotions such as anger, anxiety, depression, and guilt. In addition, there may be marital problems, headaches, suicidal thoughts, and explosive violence (Davison & Neale, 1996).

In the United States, about 1% of the population are diagnosed as suffering from PTSD. In a study in Detroit (discussed by Davison & Neale, 1996), 39% of adults had experienced a traumatic event, and 24% of them had developed PTSD.

Traumatic event

By definition, PTSD is triggered by a specific event such as war or a natural disaster (e.g. a flash flood or earthquake), and so the disorder would not develop in the absence of the event. Examples of events causing PTSD are the capsize of the *Herald of Free Enterprise* in Zeebrugge, the Gulf war and the 1999 earthquake in Turkey.

CASE STUDY: *The Jupiter Disaster*

On 21 October 1988, 391 British schoolchildren and 84 adults boarded the cruise liner *Jupiter* in the Greek port of Piraeus for the trip of a lifetime. Disaster struck within 15 minutes of the ship leaving harbour when a freight ship collided with the cruise liner, making a hole in the side of the ship. Within 40 minutes of the collision the ship had sunk in the Mediterranean Sea. Miraculously, only 4 people lost their lives in the disaster, with approximately 70 passengers and crew sustaining injuries. However, for the survivors of the disaster the ordeal of coming to terms with what had happened was the greatest challenge of all.

When the disaster occurred all on board were in danger of being drowned, electrocuted, or crushed to death. However, as most of the passengers were young teenagers who were used to being in a crowd and being guided by adults, the expected crushing, fighting, and trampling in terror did not happen. The teenagers had to play an active role in trying to contain the panic that was rising, and many were successful at calming and helping some of the younger children on the ship. It was partly due to their efforts to minimise panic and cope with the situation that the disaster claimed so few lives.

When the survivors returned to England they were encouraged to write about their experiences as part of their rehabilitation. These testimonies have provided psychologists with an insight into the disaster through the eyes of the victims, and the stories told reveal not only concern for their own well-being, but a deep anxiety for the others caught in the desperate plight. Chloe Warrington, aged 13, described her reaction when the impact occurred:

Half-crying, half-laughing, we stood or sat nervously waiting. Inside I felt panic. A choke of screams in my throat emerged as

silence. The deck was now slanting. The wooden lines of the deck are embedded in my memory, as that is when I began to realise that what was happening was real. I felt not terror, not shock, just confusion; disbelief about what was happening. Questions floated in my mind to which I could find no answers.

Another survivor, Carole Gardner, aged 14 at the time of the disaster remembers how as the ship slanted "other people started sliding down into the chairs ... I felt the air being squeezed out of me by bodies on top of me. To my left was an elderly woman sitting above the chairs. She looked dazed, with blood pouring from her right temple. I wanted so much to help her, but I could not move."

Such testimonies made it apparent that the psychological impact of the disaster was overwhelming. Many of the children found that they suffered waves of total exhaustion, lack of sleep, difficulty concentrating, grief, and even guilt for surviving when others had perished. According to a recent report published by the Institute of Psychiatry, since the disaster in 1988 over half the survivors have been diagnosed as suffering from post-traumatic stress disorder (PTSD). The symptoms of PTSD include nightmares, flashbacks, depression, anxiety, guilt, excessive jumpiness, and constant thoughts of the trauma.

One of the survivors has committed suicide, and 15 of the 158 survivors interviewed by Institute psychologists said they had attempted to do likewise. Many are still haunted today by what happened to them in their early teens, but some have enrolled for counselling that has taught them various coping techniques to combat the psychological side-effects of living through such a frightening experience.

(From Tester 1998.)

March (1991) reviewed evidence on the most common characteristics of events leading to PTSD. They included physical injury, bereavement, participation in atrocities, exposure to grotesque death, and witnessing or hearing about death. As would be expected, the chances of developing PTSD are much greater if the traumatic event is life-threatening than when it is not.

In spite of the obvious importance of a traumatic event in causing PTSD, other factors need to be taken into account. If numerous people are exposed to the same traumatic event (e.g. a sinking ship), what typically happens is that some develop post-traumatic stress disorder, whereas others do not. In order to understand such findings, we need to consider the factors making some people more vulnerable than others to PTSD.

Biological approach: Genetic factors

The hypothesis that genetic factors are involved in PTSD has been investigated in twin studies. Skre et al. (1993) found greater concordance for PTSD in monozygotic or identical twins than in dizygotic twins. They concluded as follows: "The results support the hypothesis of a genetic contribution in aetiology [causation] of ... post-traumatic stress disorder" (p.85).

True et al. (1993) reached the same conclusion in a large twin study focusing on the effects of combat exposure. They also found that the concordance rate was greater for monozygotic than for dizygotic twins. The correlations of symptoms of PTSD ranged between +0.28 and +0.41 in monozygotic twins, compared to a range of +0.11 and +0.24 in dizygotic twins.

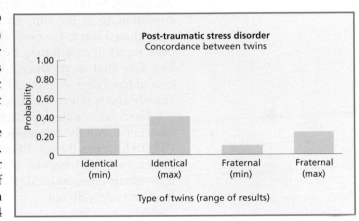

Exposure to combat

Evidence that may be relevant to the genetic hypothesis was reported by Foy et al. (1987). A low level of combat exposure was much more likely to lead to PTSD in those who had family members with other disorders, perhaps because of a genetic vulnerability. However, a high level of combat exposure led to PTSD in about two-thirds of people, and this was the case regardless of whether family members had other disorders. What do these findings mean? They suggest that mildly traumatic events mainly cause PTSD in those who are already vulnerable, whereas strongly traumatic events can cause PTSD in vulnerable *and* non-vulnerable individuals.

Biological approach: Biochemical factors

Several theorists (e.g. Krystal et al., 1989) have argued that exposure to a traumatic event can damage the adrenergic system. This leads to increased levels of noradrenaline and dopamine, and generally increased physiological arousal. As a result of these changes, the individual shows the startle response more readily.

Some evidence supports this biological theory. Kosten et al. (1987) found that patients with PTSD had high levels of adrenaline and noradrenaline. Increased levels of dopamine and noradrenaline were found in the brains of PTSD sufferers by van der Kolk et al. (1985).

How adequate is this biological theory of PTSD? It is certainly true that patients with PTSD do differ from normal controls on a range of physiological and biochemical measures. However, it has not been shown that these biological changes help to cause PTSD. In addition, the biological approach would need to be extended to account for individual differences in susceptibility to PTSD.

Psychodynamic approach

One of the puzzling aspects of PTSD is that its onset can occur months or years after the individual has been exposed to the traumatic event. Horowitz (1986) tried to explain this delayed onset in a psychodynamic theory of PTSD. The traumatic event can make the individual feel overwhelmed, causing panic or exhaustion. These reactions are often so painful that the individual either represses or deliberately suppresses thoughts of the traumatic event. This state of denial does not resolve matters, because the individual is unable to integrate information from the traumatic event into his or her sense of self.

The main strength of Horowitz's psychodynamic approach is that it provides a way of understanding some of the main symptoms of PTSD. However, the theory does not indicate why there are considerable individual differences in vulnerability to PTSD in the face of a traumatic event.

Behavioural approach

According to the conditioning approach to PTSD (e.g. Keane et al., 1985), classical conditioning at the time of the traumatic event causes the individual to acquire a conditioned fear to the neutral stimuli that were present. For example, a woman who has been raped in a park may experience great fear when approaching that park in future. The fear that is produced when stimuli associated with the traumatic event are encountered or even thought about leads to avoidance learning. This avoidance reduces anxiety and is thus rewarding or reinforcing.

The conditioning approach predicts the high level of anxiety produced by any stimuli associated with the traumatic event, and the avoidance of such stimuli by sufferers from PTSD. However, the conditioning approach does not provide a detailed account of what is happening. Moreover, it is not clear from the conditioning approach why some individuals develop PTSD in response to a traumatic event, whereas others exposed to the same event do not.

Cognitive approach

Foa, Skeketee, and Olasov-Rothbaum (1989) put forward a cognitive theory of PTSD. According to this theory, traumatic events violate our normal assumptions about what is safe. For example, a woman who is raped may feel insecure in the presence of every man she meets thereafter. As a result, "the boundaries between safety and danger become blurred" (p.167). This leads to the formation of a large fear structure in long-term memory. Individuals with this fear structure experience a lack of predictability and controllability in their lives.

Unpredictability and uncontrollability of events both cause high levels of anxiety (Mineka & Kihlstrom, 1978), and so it follows that sufferers from PTSD experience a considerable amount of anxiety.

The cognitive approach of Foa et al. (1989) provides a reasonable description of some of the cognitive changes associated with the development of PTSD. However, it leaves much out of the account. For example, it is not clear from the theory why some individuals are more vulnerable than others to PTSD, nor why genetic factors are involved. In other words, it attaches too much importance to the traumatic event itself and not enough to the other factors involved.

Discussion points

1. How does the cognitive approach help to explain PTSD?
2. In what ways does the cognitive approach provide only a limited account of PTSD?

Why does the cognitive theory account for the fact that some individuals do not experience PTSD?

Social factors

One of the factors that help to determine whether someone exposed to a traumatic event will develop PTSD is that person's level of social support. Solomon, Mikulincer, and Avitzur (1988) found that Israeli soldiers involved in the Lebanon war who had good levels of social support had fewer symptoms of PTSD. Over a three-year period, those soldiers who showed the greatest reduction in PTSD symptoms tended to have the largest increase in social support. Similar findings have been reported in other studies.

There is a problem in interpreting findings such as those of Solomon et al. (1988). It is possible that a high level of social support makes it easier for people to deal with a traumatic event, but it is also possible that coping well with a traumatic event increases the social support provided by other people.

Coping strategies and personality

It seems likely that the severity of PTSD may depend in part on the kinds of coping strategies that are used by those suffering from PTSD. Solomon et al. assessed three coping strategies in Israeli soldiers: distancing or denial of the symptoms; emotion-focused coping, based on trying to reduce the feelings of distress; and problem-focused coping, based on active efforts to resolve the symptoms. Severe PTSD was associated with the use of distancing and emotion-focused coping, whereas problem-focused coping was associated with less severe PTSD.

Solomon et al. also found that life events produced a greater increase in the symptoms of PTSD for those soldiers who used distancing and emotion-focused coping. The soldiers using problem-focused coping made more constructive attempts to respond to life events, and these attempts allowed them to control the situation more effectively.

Israeli soldiers involved in the Lebanon war showed fewer symptoms of post-traumatic stress disorder if they had good social support.

Eating Disorders

There are several eating disorders. The most common eating disorders (and the ones discussed in detail here) are anorexia nervosa and bulimia nervosa. However, there are other rare eating disorders, such as the following:

- Binge-eating disorder: a disorder in which there are distress-produced binges.
- Rumination disorder: a disorder in which partially digested food is regurgitated and then swallowed for a second time.
- Pica: a disorder in which non-food substances such as sand, leaves, or string are eaten.

As we will see, there has been a large increase in the number of people suffering from eating disorders over the past 20 years or so. The increase has been so great that Barlow and Durand (1995) described it as an epidemic.

Anorexia nervosa

One of the two main eating disorders identified by DSM-IV is **anorexia nervosa**. According to DSM-IV, there are four criteria for anorexia nervosa:

- The individual has a body weight that is less than 85% of that expected.
- There is an intense fear of becoming fat in spite of being considerably underweight.
- The individual's thinking about his or her body weight is distorted, either by exaggerating its importance to self-evaluation or by minimising the dangers of being considerably underweight.
- In females, the absence of three or more consecutive menstrual cycles; this is known as amenorrhoea.

Over 90% of patients with anorexia nervosa are female, and the age of onset is typically during adolescence. There has been an increase in the frequency of anorexia nervosa in Western societies in recent decades (Cooper, 1994). This probably reflects the growing media emphasis on the attractiveness of slimness in young women. More strikingly,

> **CASE STUDY:** *An Eating Disorder*
>
> At the age of 12, JC had weighed 115 pounds and had been teased by friends and family for being "podgy". At first JC had started to restrict her food intake by eating less at meal times, becoming selective about what she ate, and cutting out snacks between meals. Initially, JC's progressive weight loss was supported by her family and friends. However, as she began to lose pounds she would set herself new targets, ignoring feelings of hunger by focusing on each new target. In her first year of dieting JC's weight dropped from 115 pounds to 88 pounds. Her initial goal had been to lose 10 pounds. JC's periods stopped shortly after she started her regime, her appearance changed dramatically, and in the second year of her regime her weight loss was considered to be out of control. Her personality had also changed, and she was not the active, spontaneous, and cheerful girl she had been before dieting. Her girlfriends were less enthusiastic about coming over to her house, because JC would be stubborn and argumentative, designing strict programmes of activities for them to carry out.
>
> JC's family had asked their GP for help. He had been alarmed at JC's appearance and designed a high calorific diet for her. However, JC believed that there was something inside her that would not let her gain weight. She would pretend to eat, often listing food she claimed to have eaten which had in fact been flushed down the toilet, or would not swallow food she put in her mouth. JC admitted that when she felt down over the past two years she would still feel driven to lose weight, and as a result would go on walks, run errands, or spend long periods of time keeping her room immaculate. (Adapted from Leon, 1984.)

> **KEY TERM**
> **Anorexia nervosa**: an eating disorder in which the individual is seriously underweight.

In the eating disorder bulimia nervosa, sufferers consume much more food over a short period than most people would and compensate by making themselves vomit or by taking laxatives.

anorexia nervosa used to be very rare among blacks in the United States, but has recently shown signs of a marked increase (Hsu, 1990).

Anorexia nervosa is much more common in Western cultures than in other cultures (Barlow & Durand, 1995). Within Western cultures, it is more common in middle-class than working-class individuals. It is potentially a very serious disorder. The near-starvation that anorexics impose on themselves can produce physiological changes, causing about 5% of sufferers to die.

Bulimia nervosa

The other main eating disorder discussed in DSM-IV is **bulimia nervosa**. According to DSM-IV, bulimia nervosa is defined by the following five criteria:

- There are numerous episodes of binge eating, in which much more food is eaten within a two-hour period than most people would consume, and the eater experiences a lack of control over his or her eating behaviour.
- There is frequent inappropriate compensatory behaviour to prevent weight from being gained; examples include self-induced vomiting, excessive exercise, going without meals, and misuse of laxatives.
- Binge eating and inappropriate compensatory behaviour occur at a rate of twice a week or more over a three-month period.
- The individual's self-evaluation depends excessively on his or her shape and weight.
- Binge eating and compensatory behaviour do not occur only during episodes of anorexia nervosa.

There has been a dramatic increase in the number of patients suffering from bulimia nervosa since the late 1970s. Garner and Fairburn (1988) reported some relevant figures from an eating disorder centre in Canada. The number of patients treated for bulimia nervosa increased from 15 in 1979 to over 140 in 1986. As with anorexia nervosa, bulimia nervosa is mostly confined to women, with under 5% of cases presenting for treatment being men. Most patients with bulimia nervosa are in their 20s, and so are somewhat older than sufferers from anorexia. Bulimia nervosa resembles anorexia nervosa in that both disorders are far more common in Western societies than elsewhere in the world, and they occur more often in middle-class than working-class families.

Cross-cultural issues: Why do you think eating disorders occur more in some cultures than in others?

The self-induced vomiting found in most bulimics can produce a variety of medical effects. For example, it can damage the teeth by eroding dental enamel. It can also change the levels of sodium and potassium in bodily fluids, and these changes can be life-threatening.

What could be the reasons for increased incidence of eating disorders in recent years?

There is some overlap between bulimia nervosa and anorexia nervosa, with many bulimic patients also having a history of anorexia. However, bulimia nervosa is far more common than anorexia nervosa. Another key difference is that nearly all patients with bulimia nervosa are within about 10% of their normal weight, whereas anorexic patients by definition are at least 15% below their normal weight.

Biological approach: Genetic factors

There is increasing evidence that genetic factors play a part in the development of eating disorders. For example, relatives of patients with eating disorders are about four or five times more likely than other members of society to suffer from an eating disorder (e.g. Strober & Humphrey, 1987). Most twin studies have used only a few sets of twins, and so have produced only limited findings. However, the general findings are fairly consistent. The concordance rates for monozygotic or identical twins are typically about 40%, compared to 10% or less for dizygotic twins. As monozygotic twins are genetically more similar to each other than dizygotic twins, these findings suggest that eating disorders are partly determined by genetic factors.

> **KEY TERM**
> **Bulimia nervosa**: an eating disorder in which excessive or binge eating is followed by compensatory behaviour such as self-induced vomiting or misuse of laxatives.

A few researchers have carried out twin studies specifically on anorexia nervosa or on bulimia nervosa. Holland, Sicotte, and Treasure (1988) studied anorexia in monozygotic and dizygotic twins. The concordance rate for monozygotic or identical twins was 56% compared to 5% for dizygotic twins. Kendler et al. (1991) carried out a similar study on bulimia in 2163 female twins. They reported a concordance rate of 23% for monozygotic twins compared to 9% for dizygotic twins.

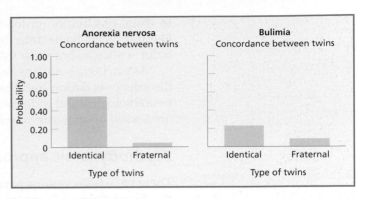

On the face of it, these findings suggest that genetic factors play a part in the development of eating disorders, especially anorexia nervosa. However, it is likely that the family environment experienced by the twins within monozygotic twin pairs is more similar than that experienced by the twins within dizygotic twin pairs (Loehlin & Nichols, 1976). Thus, it is not possible to exclude the possibility that environmental factors contribute towards the higher concordance rates for monozygotic twins.

Holland et al. (1988) and Kendler et al. (1991) studied anorexia and bulimia in twins.

Genetic accounts of eating disorders are clearly limited in various ways. First, it is not clear exactly *what* is inherited that increases vulnerability to eating disorders. Second, the fact that the concordance rate for identical twins is considerably below 100% means that non-genetic factors must also be important. Third, the recent dramatic increase in the number of people suffering from eating disorders cannot be explained in genetic terms, because it is utterly improbable that there have been major genetic changes over the past 20–30 years.

Biological approach: Biochemical factors

Brain function

Some of the factors involved in the development of anorexia nervosa may be biological ones. For example, the parts of the hypothalamus that control eating, sexual activity, and menstruation may function abnormally in anorexics. There is convincing evidence that the hypothalamus plays a central role in hunger regulation (see Chapter 6), and anorexics may have disturbed hypothalamic functioning (Garfinkel & Garner, 1982). However, altered hypothalamic activity may well not be a cause of anorexia nervosa. It is more likely to occur as a result of the weight loss or the anorexic's emotional distress.

Even when sufferers from anorexia nervosa are significantly underweight, they continue to fear becoming fat.

Disease

Evidence that the homeostatic systems involved in hunger regulation may be affected in at least some patients suffering from anorexia nervosa was reported by Park, Lawrie, and Freeman (1995). They studied four females suffering from anorexia nervosa, all of whom had had glandular fever or a similar disease shortly before the onset of the eating disorder. Park et al. (1995) argued rather speculatively that the physical disease may have influenced the functioning of the hypothalamus by affecting the levels of corticotrophin-releasing hormone.

Neurochemistry

Serotonin, which is a neurotransmitter, may be involved in some cases of eating disorder. For example, Fava et al. (1989) reported links between anorexic behaviour and changes in the levels of serotonin and noradrenaline. Eating large amounts of starchy foods containing carbohydrates can increase serotonin levels in the brain, and this may improve mood in individuals who have low serotonin levels. However, patients with bulimia nervosa do not seem to focus specifically on foods containing carbohydrates when they binge (Barlow & Durand, 1995). Some drug treatments involve the use of drugs that increase the level of brain serotonin, but these treatments are no more effective than other drug treatments.

As yet, there is no convincing evidence in support of biological explanations of eating disorders. As Barlow and Durand (1995, p.319) concluded, "The consensus is that some neurobiological and endocrinological abnormalities do exist in eating disorders, but they are a *result* of semi-starvation or a binge–purge cycle, rather than a cause."

Psychodynamic approach

There have been various psychodynamic approaches to anorexia nervosa. The fact that the disorder generally emerges in adolescent girls has suggested to some psychodynamic theorists that anorexia is due to fear of increasing sexual desires or even of oral impregnation. Within that context, semi-starvation may reflect the desire to avoid becoming pregnant, because one of the symptoms of anorexia nervosa is the elimination of periods.

A somewhat different psychodynamic account is based on the notion that anorexia nervosa occurs in females who have an unconscious desire to remain pre-pubescent. Their weight loss prevents them from developing the body shape associated with adult females, and thus allows them to preserve the illusion that they are still children.

Another psychodynamic approach is based on the notion that anorexia nervosa arises because of a disturbed relationship with the mother. As a result, anorexics do not develop any sense of owning their bodies, and refusing to eat provides them with the illusion that they can control their own bodies.

Family dynamics

Minuchin, Roseman, and Baker (1978) developed the notion that the family may play a key role in the development of anorexia nervosa. The family of an anorexic is characterised by **enmeshment**, meaning that none of the members of the family has a clear identity because everything is done together. Such families impose great constraints on children, because they are not allowed to become independent. A child growing up in an enmeshed family may rebel against its constraints by refusing to eat. Minuchin et al. (1978) also argued that enmeshed families find it hard to resolve conflicts. Parental conflicts are reduced by the need to attend to the symptoms of their anorexic child. It is difficult to evaluate this theory. However, there is some evidence for high levels of parental conflict within the families of anorexics (Kalucy, Crisp, & Harding, 1977). Hsu (1990) reported that families with an anorexic child tend to be ambitious, to deny or ignore conflicts, and to blame other people for their problems. These parental conflicts may be more a result of having an anorexic child than a cause of anorexia.

Family conflicts have also been identified in families with a child who shows signs of bulimia as well as anorexia. Such families have more negative and fewer positive interactions than families with a normal adolescent (Humphrey, Apple, & Kirschenbaum, 1986). As with the family studies on anorexics, it is not clear whether the poor family interactions help to cause the disorder or are simply a reaction to it.

Males and females

There is little evidence to support the various psychodynamic accounts discussed in this section. All the accounts seem to be based on the incorrect assumption that eating disorders only develop in adolescent females. As a result, they cannot explain the development of eating disorders in males or in adults.

Behavioural approach

It is possible to think of the development of anorexia nervosa in behaviourist or conditioning terms. According to Leitenberg, Agras, and Thomson (1968), anorexics may have learned to associate eating with anxiety, because eating too much makes people overweight and unattractive. As well as reducing anxiety, food avoidance can be rewarding or

Cross-cultural issues: Could the behavioural approach apply to all cultures?

reinforcing, because it is a good way of gaining attention. It can also be rewarding or reinforcing in that those who are slim are more likely to be admired by other people.

A behaviourist approach can also be applied to bulimia nervosa. According to Rosen and Leitenberg (1985), bingeing causes anxiety, and the subsequent vomiting or other compensatory behaviour reduces that anxiety. This reduction in anxiety is reinforcing and helps to maintain the cycle of bingeing followed by vomiting.

The behaviourist approach helps to provide some of the reasons why anorexics and bulimics maintain their disorders. However, it does not really explain how these disorders start in the first place, nor does it account for individual differences in vulnerability to eating disorders.

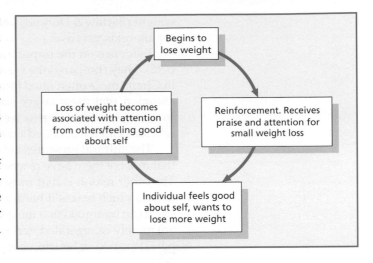

Begins to lose weight

Reinforcement. Receives praise and attention for small weight loss

Individual feels good about self, wants to lose more weight

Loss of weight becomes associated with attention from others/feeling good about self

Social and cultural factors

One of the most striking facts about the eating disorders is that they are considerably more common in Western than in non-Western societies (Cooper, 1994). Indeed, eating disorders may well be more strongly specific to certain cultures than any other psychological disorders. This is most obviously explained by the pressures on young women within Western societies to have a thin body shape. These pressures have increased considerably in recent decades. The emphasis on slimness as desirable is illustrated by the finding that more than half of Miss America contestants are 15% or more below their expected body

Fashions in body shapes have changed dramatically over recent decades; from the flat-chested "flapper" of the 1920s (left), through the curvaceous "hour-glass" figure of Marilyn Monroe (centre) to the currently popular "waif-like" shape epitomised by the model Kate Moss (right).

weight (Barlow & Durand, 1995). Being underweight by that amount is one of the criteria for anorexia nervosa!

Evidence on the importance of cultural factors was reported by Cogan et al. (1996, p.98). They compared the views of students in Ghana and in the United States: "Students in Ghana more often rated larger body sizes as ideal for both males and females, and also assumed that these larger sizes were held as ideal in society, than did US students." In addition, thin females were rated by the American sample as being the happiest, whereas Ghanaians rated fat and thin males and females as equally happy.

The cultural pressures are greatest on adolescent girls for two reasons. One reason is that most of them have reached the stage at which they want to appear attractive to boys. The other reason is that most of the weight girls gain after puberty is in the form of fat tissue, which makes it harder for them to match the ideal shape.

It can be argued that most of the distorted beliefs held by anorexic and bulimic patients are merely exaggerated versions of the beliefs held by society at large. As Cooper (1994, p.942) argued in his discussion of patients with eating disorders

> their self-worth is seen as being evaluated largely in terms of their shape and weight: they view fatness as odious and reprehensible, they see slimness as attractive and desirable, and the maintenance of self-control is of prime importance. In addition, some attach extreme importance to weight loss. It is clear that such beliefs are not radically different from views that are widely held.

Evidence that cultural pressures are involved in the development of eating disorders was reported by Nasser (1986), who compared Egyptian women studying in Cairo and in London. None of the women studying in Cairo developed an eating disorder, in contrast to 12% of those studying in London.

Cultural factors cannot be the only reason for the occurrence of eating disorders. The great majority of young women who are exposed to cultural pressures towards slimness do not develop eating disorders. It is only young women who are already vulnerable who are likely to be greatly affected by such pressures.

Why do you think 1 in 100 girls in private schools suffer with eating disorders, compared to 1 in 300 in state schools?

Perfectionism

Cultural pressures within Western society for slimness in young women are probably more important than any other single factor in producing eating disorders, with genetic factors and episodes of anxiety and/or depression also playing a part. Another factor that has perhaps received less attention than it deserves is the personality characteristic of **perfectionism**, which involves a strong desire to achieve excellence. Individuals high in perfectionism might be more likely than others to strive to achieve an unrealistically slim body shape.

There is some evidence that perfectionism may be relevant to the development of eating disorders. Pike and Rodin (1991) reported evidence that the mothers of girls with disordered eating had perfectionist tendencies. They were very keen that their daughters should be thin, they were likely to be dieting themselves, and they expressed low levels of satisfaction with their family and its level of cohesion. Steinhausen (1994) found that females with eating disorders showed signs of perfectionism, as well as of compliance and dependence.

■ Research activity: Make a list of famous people with different body shapes from different periods in history.

Cognitive approach

As has already been mentioned, sufferers from eating disorders typically have distorted views about body shape and weight; these are known as *cognitive biases*. In order to assess anorexics' perception of their own body size, they can be exposed to an image-distorting technique designed to provide information about their perception of their whole body. Anorexic patients typically overestimate their body size (Garfinkel & Garner, 1982). It has also been shown that this overestimation is greater than that found in controls.

Bulimic patients also have distorted beliefs. In spite of the fact that they are typically not overweight, patients with bulimia typically have a substantial discrepancy between their estimation of their actual body size and their desired body size (Cooper & Taylor, 1988). This discrepancy arises because they overestimate their actual body size more than other people, and because their desired body size is smaller than that of most people.

Distorted beliefs about body size are found even among those not suffering from an eating disorder. Fallon and Rozin (1985) asked males and females to indicate their ideal body size and the body size that would be most attractive to the opposite sex. Females rated their ideal body weight as significantly *lower* than the weight males thought most attractive, whereas males rate their ideal body weight as higher than the weight women found most attractive. These differences place extra pressure on females to be slim.

We know that most patients with anorexia nervosa and bulimia nervosa have strong cognitive biases that, for example, lead them to overestimate their own body size. What is unclear is whether these cognitive biases exist *before* the onset of eating disorders and thus may play a part in their development. The alternative is that these cognitive biases only develop *after* the onset of eating disorders, in which case they cannot form a causal factor.

Depression and anxiety

There is a considerable amount of evidence that patients with eating disorders tend to be depressed. For example, Ben-Tovim and Crisp (1979) found that all twelve of their bulimic patients had clinical levels of depression, as did one-third of their nine anorexic patients. Which is the cause and which is the effect? It could be that depression plays a part in producing eating disorders, or perhaps a serious eating disorder causes depression.

One way of approaching this causality issue is to work out the order in which the various symptoms appear. This was done by Piran et al. (1985) in a study on anorexic patients who had also suffered from major depression. The symptoms of depression occurred before those of anorexia nervosa in 44% of the patients, with the reverse order occurring in 34% of them. In the remaining 22%, the depression and the eating disorder started within the same year. Similar findings were reported by Walsh et al. (1985). Cooper (1994, p.941) drew the following conclusion from the findings by Piran et al. (1985) and Walsh et al. (1985): "it appears that a vulnerability to depression may increase the predisposition to eating disorders, and an episode of depression may contribute to the initiation of its symptoms."

Depression is only one among several factors leading to eating disorders. Most people who become depressed do not go on to develop an eating disorder, and many patients suffering from eating disorders are not depressed.

Anxiety also seems to be associated with eating disorders. Individuals suffering from eating disorders often have an anxiety disorder as well (Barlow & Durand, 1995). In addition, anxiety disorders are much more common in the families of individuals with eating disorders than in the families of individuals who do not have an eating disorder (Schwalberg et al., 1992). It is thus possible that a vulnerability to anxiety may increase the likelihood that an individual will develop an eating disorder.

■ Research activity: Draw a flow chart to show the influence of depression and anxiety on eating disorders.

PERSONAL REFLECTIONS

- It has proved surprisingly hard to identify the factors causing most mental disorders, even though some progress has been made. In my opinion, there are two main reasons for this. First, there are several factors that combine to produce the great majority of mental disorders. Second, there are large differences from one patient to another having the same disorder in terms of the relative importance of different factors in producing that disorder. We now have a general understanding of the factors involved, but I am somewhat pessimistic about the possibility of moving to a detailed grasp of the complex interactions of factors that underlie mental disorders. I also feel that it will prove hard to identify the causal factors involved in producing disorder in any *specific* individual.

SUMMARY

Schizophrenia

There are five main types of schizophrenia: disorganised; catatonic; paranoid; undifferentiated; and residual. Twin studies and adoption studies indicate that genetic factors are of importance in the development of schizophrenia. There may be biochemical abnormalities involving excessive levels of dopamine or an over-sensitivity to dopamine. Psychodynamic and behavioural models have contributed very little to our understanding of the causes of depression. Expressed emotion within the family is of some importance in maintaining schizophrenic symptoms.

Depression

It is important to distinguish between major depression and bipolar depression or manic-depressive disorder. Twin studies and adoption studies have shown that genetic factors are involved in the development of depression, but more so for bipolar depression. The psychodynamic approach has not proved of much value, but there is evidence from the behavioural approach showing that depression in humans resembles learned helplessness in animals. According to one cognitive approach, individuals with depression or learned helplessness attribute failure to internal, stable, and global causes. It is not clear that the negative thoughts emphasised within the cognitive approach help to cause depression, or whether they occur only as a result of being depressed. Stressful life events play a role, especially among those without a very close friend.

Phobias

Specific phobia involves a strong and irrational fear of some specific object or situation, and social phobia involves extreme concern about one's own behaviour and the reactions of others. Agoraphobia, which involves great fear of open or public places, nearly always occurs as a byproduct of panic disorder. Genetic factors are found to be most relevant for agoraphobia and least relevant for specific phobia, with social phobia intermediate. According to psychodynamic theory, phobias are a defence against the anxiety that is produced when the sexual impulses of the id are repressed. There is little support for this theory. According to conditioning theory, phobias develop through a combination of classical and operant conditioning. However, most phobic patients cannot recall any relevant conditioning experience. Phobic patients possess various cognitive biases that exaggerate the threateningness of external and internal stimuli, but it is not clear that these biases play a part in the development of phobias. Some phobic patients have a high level of physiological arousal, but this may be a result of their disorder rather than a cause. Parental rearing practices and life events may also play a part.

Post-traumatic stress disorder

Post-traumatic stress disorder (PTSD) occurs in response to a traumatic event. The symptoms include re-experiencing the event, avoidance of trauma-related stimuli, and increased arousal. The severity of the traumatic event is the main predictor of PTSD, but genetic factors are also involved. There is also the biological view that exposure to a traumatic event can damage the adrenergic system, the behaviourist view that classical and operant conditioning are involved, and the cognitive view that several schemas are altered. People exposed to a traumatic event are less likely to develop PTSD if they have a good level of social support and if they use appropriate coping strategies.

Eating disorders

The criteria for anorexia nervosa include a body weight less than 85% of that expected, intense fear of becoming overweight, and distorted thinking about body weight. The criteria for bulimia nervosa include repeated binge eating, inappropriate compensatory

These ethnic Albanian women and children from Kosovo survived the attack on their village by Serbian forces, but will probably re-live the terrifying experience for the rest of their lives.

behaviour (e.g. vomiting; excessive exercise), and self-evaluation depending too much on body shape and weight. Most of those suffering from anorexia nervosa and bulimia nervosa are young females living in Western societies. Twin studies suggest that genetic factors play a part in the development of eating disorders. However, the most important factor is probably the emphasis in Western societies on slimness as a desirable attribute in young females. There is also evidence to show that depression and anxiety can make individuals more susceptible to developing eating disorders. Finally, the personality characteristic of perfectionism may form part of a vulnerability factor for eating disorders.

FURTHER READING

There is reader-friendly coverage of the mental disorders discussed in this chapter in P.C. Kendall and C. Hammen (1998), *Abnormal psychology (2nd Edn.)*, Boston: Houghton Mifflin. The evidence on causal factors in mental disorders is discussed fully in D.H. Barlow and V.M. Durand (1995), *Abnormal psychology: An integrative approach*, New York: Brooks/Cole; Chapter 5 on anxiety disorders is especially good, because David Barlow is one of the world's leading authorities on anxiety. Another textbook with good coverage of most mental disorders is the well-established G.C. Davison and J.M. Neale (1996), *Abnormal psychology (revised 6th Edn.)*, New York: Wiley.

REVISION QUESTIONS

1   Critically consider the contribution of genetic/neurological factors to schizophrenia.   (24 marks)

2a   Describe the symptoms of depression.   (6 marks)
2b   Discuss the influence of social/psychological factors on depression.   (18 marks)

3   "Anorexia and bulimia nervosa are two of the most common 'disorders' at this time in our culture ... The central point is not one of sickness or pathology but of unrealistic ideas of how women should look ... the current unrealistic cultural images of female beauty and other pressures on women to be slim and to be judged mainly as an object in terms of one's appearance" (Petkova, 1997). Discuss.   (24 marks)

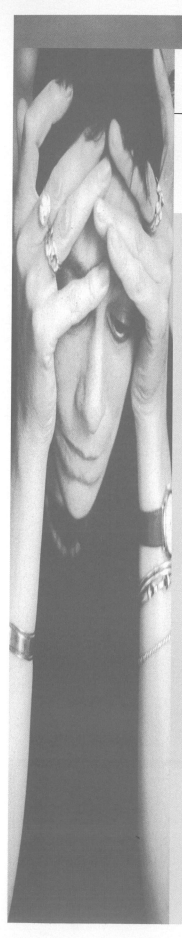

- **Psychodynamic therapy**
  How Freud's theories have developed into a "talkative cure".

  Freud's ideas on insight
  Freud and Breuer's study of Anna O
  Free association
  Dream analysis
  Ego analysis, e.g. Honey, Erikson

- **Somatic therapy**
  An approach to mental illness that treats the systems within the body.

  Moniz and psychosurgery
  ECT
  Drug treatments for depression, anxiety, schizophrenia

- **Humanistic therapy**
  Therapy that involves looking at a person's ideas about his or her self.

  Rogers' client-centred therapy

- **Behaviour therapy**
  Using theories of conditioning to change a person's behaviour.

  Flooding
  Wolpe's systematic desensitisation approach
  Aversion therapy
  Operant conditioning therapy
  Studies of token economies

- **Cognitive therapy**
  Changing a person's thoughts and beliefs to help their mental state.

  Ellis's A-B-C model
  Beck's cognitive triad
  Cognitive-behavioural therapy

- **Effectiveness of therapy**
  How psychologists try to decide if therapy really works.

  Smith et al.'s meta-analysis
  Matt and Navarro's study
  Eysenck's evaluation of psychoanalysis
  Evaluations of other approaches

- **Ethical issues in therapy**
  How the law and ethical guidelines protect the rights of patients undergoing therapy.

  Informed consent
  The UK Mental Health Act
  Confidentiality
  Alexander and Luborsky's therapeutic alliance
  Dual relationships
  Sue et al.'s cross-cultural study

26

Therapeutic Approaches

Individuals suffering from mental disorders exhibit a wide range of symptoms. There may be problems associated with thinking and the mind (e.g. the hallucinations of the schizophrenic), with behaviour (e.g. the avoidance behaviour of the phobic), or with physiology and bodily processes (e.g. the highly activated physiological system of someone with post-traumatic stress disorder). However, all thinking and behaviour finally depend on physiological processes within the body. Thus, thinking, behaviour, and bodily processes are highly interdependent.

Therapeutic approaches to mental disorder might therefore focus on producing changes in thinking, in behaviour, or in physiological functioning within the body. At the risk of over-simplification, this is precisely what has happened. The psychodynamic or psychoanalytic approach was designed to change the functioning of the mind, and the same is true of humanistic therapy. Behaviour therapy, as its name implies, emphasises the importance of changing behaviour. Somatic therapy focuses on manipulations of the body by various means including drugs and surgery. Finally, cognitive-behavioural therapy falls somewhere between behaviour therapy and psychodynamic therapy, in that it attempts to produce changes in clients' thought processes and behaviour.

In this chapter, we will be considering all these forms of therapy, looking at them in roughly the same order in which they appeared historically. We will also consider their appropriateness and effectiveness. Finally, we will discuss some of the key ethical issues that are involved in therapy.

It is important when reading this chapter to avoid making the **treatment aetiology fallacy** (MacLeod, 1998). This is the mistaken notion that the success of a given form of treatment reveals the cause of the disorder. This fallacy is perhaps most common when explaining the effectiveness of drug therapy. For example, aspirin is an effective cure for headache, but no-one believes that a lack of aspirin is the cause of headaches.

Psychodynamic Therapy

Psychodynamic therapy is based on psychoanalysis, and was introduced by Sigmund Freud at the start of the twentieth century. Some of the principles of psychoanalysis were developed in various ways by Freud's followers such as Carl Jung and Alfred Adler.

Psychoanalysis

According to Freud, neuroses such as the anxiety disorders occur as a result of conflicts among the three parts of the mind: the ego (rational mind); the id (sexual and other instincts); and the superego (conscience). These conflicts, many of which go back to early childhood, cause the ego to use various defence mechanisms to protect itself (see Chapters

Why do you think someone who seeks psychodynamic and other forms of therapy is now often referred to as a client, rather than a patient?

2 and 24). The key defence mechanism is repression. **Repression** consists of forcing painful, threatening, or unacceptable thoughts and memories out of consciousness into the unconscious mind. The forces of repression then prevent these thoughts and memories from reappearing in consciousness. The repressed ideas concern impulses or memories that the client could not think about without feeling intense anxiety. Repressed memories mostly refer to childhood, and to the conflicts between the instinctive (e.g. sexual) motives of the child and the restraints imposed by his or her parents. Repression serves the function of reducing the level of anxiety experienced by the client.

According to Freud, adults who experience great personal problems tend to show regression (not repression!). Regression involves going backwards through the stages of psychosexual development they went through in childhood (see Chapter 2). Children often fixate or spend an unusually long time at a given stage of psychosexual development if it is associated with conflicts or excessive gratification, and regression typically occurs back to a stage at which the person had previously fixated.

Freud argued that the way to cure neurosis was to allow the client to gain access to his or her repressed ideas and conflicts, and to encourage him or her to face up to whatever emerged from the unconscious. He insisted the client should focus on the feelings associated with the repressed ideas, and should not simply regard them unemotionally. Freud used the term **insight** to refer to these processes. The ultimate goal of psychoanalysis is to provide the client with insight. There are great obstacles in the way, because the emergence of very painful ideas and memories into consciousness produces an extremely high level of anxiety. As a result, the attempt to uncover repressed ideas meets much resistance from the client.

Freud (1917, p.289) described some of the forms that resistance can take:

> *The patient attempts to escape by every possible means. First he says nothing comes into his head, then that so much comes into his head that he can't grasp any of it ... At last he admits that he really cannot say something, he is ashamed to ... So it goes on, with untold variations.*

Sigmund Freud, 1856–1939.

Freud and the other psychoanalysts used various methods to uncover repressed ideas, and to permit the client to gain insight into his or her unresolved problems. The three main methods are as follows: hypnosis; free association; and dream analysis.

Hypnosis

Ethical issues: Given the suggestibility of people under hypnosis and the possibility that they might then falsely recall things that did not really happen, what are the ethical dangers involved in using hypnosis as a form of therapy?

The use of hypnosis came first in the history of psychoanalysis. Freud and Breuer (1895) treated a 21-year-old woman called Anna O, who suffered from several neurotic symptoms such as paralysis and nervous coughs. Hypnosis uncovered a repressed memory of Anna hearing the sound of dance music coming from a nearby house as she was nursing her dying father, and her guilty feeling that she would rather be dancing than looking after her father. Her nervous coughing stopped after that repressed memory came to light.

Freud gradually lost interest in hypnosis, partly because many clients were hard or impossible to hypnotise. Another problem is that people under hypnosis become very suggestible (see Chapter 5). As a result, little reliance can be placed on the accuracy of what they claim to remember when in the hypnotised state.

Free association

The method of free association is very simple. The client is encouraged to say the first thing that comes into his or her mind. It is hoped that fragments of repressed memories will emerge in the course of free association. However, as we have seen, free association may not prove useful if the client shows resistance, and is reluctant to say what he or she is thinking. On the other hand, the presence of resistance (e.g. an excessively long pause) often provides a strong clue that the client is getting close to some important repressed idea in his or her thinking, and that further probing by the therapist is called for.

KEY TERMS
Repression: the process of forcing very threatening thoughts and memories out of the conscious mind in Freudian theory; motivated forgetting.
Insight: a conscious understanding of important thoughts and feelings that have been subject to repression.

Dream analysis

According to Freud, the analysis of dreams provides "the *via regia* [royal road] to the unconscious". He argued that there is a censor in the mind which keeps repressed material out of conscious awareness; this censor is less vigilant during sleep. As a result, repressed ideas from the unconscious are more likely to appear in dreams than in waking thought. These ideas usually emerge in disguised form because of their unacceptable nature. For example, the ideas may be altered by the process of condensation (combining various ideas into a smaller number) or by displacement (shifting emotion from the appropriate object to another one). The best-known examples of displacement involve sexual symbolism, such as someone dreaming about riding a horse rather than having sex.

Freud distinguished between the actual dream (called the **manifest dream**) and the underlying repressed ideas (called the **latent dream**: see Chapter 5). The unacceptable content of the latent dream is changed into the more acceptable content of the manifest dream. Why do people dream? According to Freud, the main purpose is wish fulfilment: we dream about things that we would like to see happen. Thus, dream analysis can prove useful in making sense of the neurotic client's basic motives.

How plausible is Freud's theory of dreams? A dreamer's major concerns are often expressed in a symbolic fashion rather than directly. For example, patients who are due to have major surgery sometimes dream about standing on an unsteady bridge or falling from a tall ladder, rather than about having an operation (Breger, Hunter, & Lane 1971). The notion that dream symbols are used to disguise unacceptable ideas has been challenged. Hall (1953) suggested that thinking is simpler and more concrete when we are asleep than when we are awake, and that dream symbols are a useful shorthand way of expressing underlying ideas.

The client is reluctant to say what he or she is really thinking.

Dream analysis

There are various schools of thought on the significance of dreams and their possible biological function. Freud and Jung believed that dreams signified the thoughts and feelings of the unconscious mind and are therefore necessary to allow the mind exploration of them. Others have suggested that dreams perform no concrete function, but this view has been contested by referring to examples of sleep deprivation. Sleep-deprived participants tend to experience an increase in dreaming sleep when they are finally permitted to sleep.

What is your view on the role of dreams? How might psychologists test your views scientifically?

Interpretation

Psychoanalysis depends heavily on the therapist's interpretation of what the client says. How, for example, does the therapist know that a girl dreaming about riding a horse is actually thinking about having sex rather than simply about horse-riding? Freud argued that the acid test was the client's reaction to the therapist's proposed interpretation. If the client accepts the accuracy of the interpretation, then it is probably correct. If the client vehemently rejects the therapist's interpretation of a dream, that may simply be resistance by the client's conscious mind to an unacceptable but entirely accurate interpretation.

There is a problem here. The therapist can use either the client's acceptance or denial of the reasonableness of a dream interpretation as supporting evidence that the interpretation is correct! Freud argued that we can regard psychoanalysis as similar to solving a jigsaw puzzle. It may be hard to decide whether a given interpretation is correct, or to decide where to place a particular piece of the puzzle. However, the interpretations of dozens of a client's free associations and dreams should form a coherent picture, just as the pieces of a jigsaw puzzle can only be arranged in one way.

A factor that complicates the interpretation of what clients say and do is what Freud referred to as reaction formation. The basic idea is that the ego may transform unacceptable desires into acceptable ones to protect itself. For example, a person who has homosexual

Freud developed his theory in the early part of the twentieth century when attitudes to sex and sexuality were very different from today. What effect do you think this might have had on the development of psychodynamic therapy?

tendencies but feels uncomfortable about this may claim to be strongly opposed to homosexuality.

Transference

Freud emphasised the notion that the client should gain access not only to repressed information but also to the feelings that accompanied it. A major factor in ensuring adequate emotional involvement on the client's part is provided by **transference**, which involves the client transferring onto the therapist powerful emotional reactions that were previously directed at his or her own parents (or other highly significant individuals). As Gleitman (1986, p.696) pointed out, transference provides "a kind of emotional reliving of the unresolved problems of the patient's childhood."

A crucial aspect of transference is that the therapist responds in a neutral way to the client's emotional outpourings. The fact that the therapist will not retaliate in any way allows the client freedom to express long-repressed anger or hostility to his or her parents. The neutrality of the therapist helps to make it clear to the client that his or her emotional outbursts stem from repressed memories rather than from the therapeutic situation itself. Transference may also occur simply because the person becomes very frustrated at the neutral reactions and lack of feedback provided by the therapist!

> **Ethical issues: Therapist–client relationship**
>
> The therapist–client relationship must be a professional one because it can involve the disclosure of very personal information on the part of the client. All trained counsellors have to abide by a set of ethical guidelines, which are designed to protect both themselves and their clients. What issues might arise in the course of therapy that would justify the existence of such a code of ethics?

Ego analysis

How might a therapist help a client strengthen their rational mind by: (a) changing a negative behaviour pattern when relating to others; (b) fulfilling a personal ambition?

Karen Horney, Anna Freud, Erik Erikson, and others modified the traditional psychoanalytic approach to therapy in the 1940s and 1950s. Their approach is known as ego analysis. **Ego analysis** is based on the notion that the ego or rational mind is important, and that therapy should focus on strengthening the ego so that it can achieve more gratification. This contrasts with Freud's emphasis on gratification of the wishes of the id or sexual instinct.

Ego analysis makes use of free association and most of the other techniques associated with psychoanalysis. However, it focuses much more on the patient's current social and interpersonal problems than on their childhood experiences. Another difference is that ego analysts regard society as being a positive force in most people's lives, whereas Freud emphasised the ways in which society inhibits individuals.

Somatic Therapy

Medical doctors have claimed that mental illness resembles physical illness. According to this medical model (see Chapter 25), so-called mental illness depends on some underlying organic problem, and the best form of treatment involves direct manipulations

> **EARLY SOMATIC THERAPY**
>
> There have been many bizarre treatments for mental illness over the course of history, from blood-letting and purging (use of laxatives) to ice baths. In 1810, Dr Benjamin Rush invented the restraining chair illustrated here. Herman and Green (1991) quote his description of its effectiveness:
>
> *I have contrived a chair and introduced it to our Hospital to assist in curing madness. It binds and confines every part of the body. By keeping the trunk erect, it lessens the impetus of blood toward the brain ... It acts as a sedative to the tongue and temper as well as to the blood vessels.*
>
> Rush coined the word *Tranquilliser* as a name for his apparatus and patients were confined in it for up to 24 hours at a time. No-one today would be surprised that this would subdue anyone, regardless of their mental state.

of the physiological system within the body. **Somatic therapy** (a major part of which is drug therapy) is the term for this method of treatment.

The early history of somatic therapy was not very encouraging. As far back as the Middle Ages, those suffering from mental illness had holes cut in their skulls to allow the devils allegedly causing the illness to escape. This practice, which is known as **trepanning**, cannot be recommended. It did not produce any cures, and many of those subjected to trepanning did not survive the operation.

Psychosurgery

The use of brain surgery to reduce psychological or behavioural disorders is known as psychosurgery. Pioneering work was carried out by Antonio Egas Moniz. He used the surgical method of prefrontal lobotomy, in which fibres running from the frontal lobes to other parts of the brain were cut. In the film, *One Flew Over the Cuckoo's Nest*, a lobotomy operation ends Randle Patrick McMurphy's rebellion against the hospital authorities. Moniz and others claimed that this operation made schizophrenic and other patients less violent and agitated, and much easier to manage. This form of psychosurgery caught on to such an extent that about 70,000 lobotomies were carried out between 1935 and 1955.

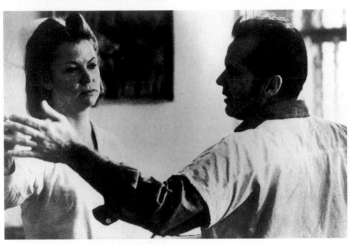

In the film *One Flew Over the Cuckoo's Nest*, Jack Nicholson played Randle Patrick McMurphy, who inspired and awakened his fellow patients, whilst falling out with the authorities. Eventually, the character is lobotomised, and becomes calmer and easier to handle, but loses all his intellectual spark and energy.

Lobotomies typically make patients calmer. However, the side-effects are so serious that they are very rarely performed any more. The side-effects include apathy, diminished intellectual powers, impaired judgements, and even coma and death. In view of the dangers of lobotomies, it is ironic that Moniz was shot in the spine by one of his own lobotomised patients.

Another form of psychosurgery is the amygdalotomy. It involves directing fine wire electrodes at the amygdala through a small hole drilled in the skull. Strong currents are then passed through the electrode, destroying the tissue around its tip. The reason for carrying out amygdalotomies is that the amygdala is a part of the brain centrally involved in anger.

Amygdalotomies were carried out on violent criminals, especially in the United States during the 1950s and 1960s. The operations were usually a success, in that those operated on became less aggressive. However, there were very serious side-effects. Patients often became confused, lacking in motivation, and unable to work (Eysenck & Eysenck, 1989). As a result, this form of psychosurgery is almost never carried out any more.

> ### Ethical issues: Psychosurgery
>
> Consider the following moral objections to psychosurgery as a means to alleviate psychotic symptoms:
>
> - Damage to cognitive capacities, e.g. memory, reasoning.
> - Interference in an individual's exercise of his or her own free will.
> - Irreversible alteration of the person's thought processes.

Electroconvulsive shock treatment

Electroconvulsive shock treatment (ECT) was originally used in the treatment of schizophrenia. As Gross and McIlveen (1996) have described, it was noticed that schizophrenia and epilepsy were rarely found in the same person. It was also found that those schizophrenics who did suffer from epilepsy tended to have reduced schizophrenic symptoms after an epileptic fit. This suggested that using ECT to create fits in schizophrenics might be a useful form of treatment. Unfortunately, it did not work.

ECT is sometimes used in cases of severe depression. What used to happen in ECT was that a strong electric current was passed for about half a second between two electrodes attached to each side of the depressed patient's forehead. This current caused almost immediate loss of consciousness and a convulsive seizure. Nowadays, the current is generally passed through only the non-dominant brain hemisphere, and an anaesthetic and muscle relaxants are given before the treatment itself. As a result, the patient is unconscious during ECT and there are fewer muscular spasms than before.

Why is ECT sometimes used rather than drugs in the treatment of depression? The main reason is that some severely depressed patients fail to respond to drugs, but do respond to ECT. Indeed, about 50–70% of those not responding to drugs benefit from ECT. This is not because the equipment used is impressive, because patients undergoing a "sham" ECT procedure in which no shocks are presented show much less improvement than those receiving ECT (Barlow & Durand, 1995). A useful feature of ECT is that it typically reduces depression more rapidly than do anti-depressant drugs. This is of special value when there are concerns that a depressed patient may commit suicide.

Ethical issues: Given that the full implications of ECT are poorly understood, do you think it is ever right to administer such a treatment to vulnerable patients?

On the negative side, we have little idea of precisely why ECT is so effective. Part of its effectiveness is probably due to the fact that it increases the level of noradrenaline, a hormone that activates the autonomic nervous system. As ECT is so imprecise, it is not surprising that it produces several unwanted side-effects. It can cause a general memory impairment lasting for many months, coupled with a more specific loss of memory for the events preceding the onset of treatment. It can also produce impaired speech. However, this side-effect is much less common if ECT is given only to the right side of the brain, because the speech centre is usually in the left side of the brain.

Drug therapy

Drug therapy has been used in the treatment of several disorders. In this section, we will focus on drug therapy as applied to depression, anxiety disorders, and schizophrenia.

Depression

Drug therapy has been used in the treatment of patients suffering from major depression and from bipolar disorder (see Chapter 25). It has been argued that depression involves a shortage of **monoamines**, which are a type of neurotransmitter including dopamine, serotonin, and noradrenaline. It follows that an effective drug therapy for depression might involve using drugs that increase the supply of these neurotransmitters. Two groups of such drugs are the monoamine oxidase inhibitors (MAOIs) and the tricyclics. The MAOIs work by inhibiting monoamine oxidase, which leads to increased levels of neurotransmitters such as noradrenaline and serotonin. Prozac is a tetracyclic that acts in a similar way to the tricyclics, but mainly affects the level of serotonin rather than any other neurotransmitter. Both groups of drugs decrease the symptoms of depression in most depressed patients, although Prozac sometimes produces a preoccupation with suicide and other violent acts (Barlow & Durand, 1995).

The tricyclics are generally more effective than the MAOIs, and produce fewer side-effects. However, the tricyclics can produce dizziness, blurred vision, and dryness of the mouth. It is not very clear why the various drugs are ineffective with some patients.

KEY TERM
Monoamines: neurotransmitters including dopamine, serotonin, and noradrenaline which seem to be involved in clinical depression.

CASE STUDY: *Virginia Woolf*

The author Virginia Woolf, who committed suicide in 1941 at the age of 59, was plagued by an intermittent form of depression. This affliction appears to have been bipolar depression, but was accompanied by extreme physical symptoms and psychotic delusions. In her biography of Woolf, Hermione Lee (1997) unravels the series of treatments administered to Woolf between 1895, when she experienced her first breakdown, and the 1930s. Later, Woolf's husband Leonard made detailed notes on her breakdowns (Lee, 1997, pp.178–179):

In the manic stage she was extremely excited; the mind raced; she talked volubly and, at the height of the attack, incoherently; she had delusions and heard voices ... During the depressive stage all her thoughts and emotions were the exact opposite ... she was in the depths of melancholia and despair; she scarcely spoke; refused

to eat; refused to believe that she was ill and insisted that her condition was due to her own guilt.

During the period from 1890 to 1930, Woolf consulted more than 12 different doctors, but the treatments barely altered during this time. They tended to consist of milk and meat diets to redress her weight loss; rest to alleviate her agitation; sleep and fresh air to help her regain her energy. Lithium had not yet been discovered as a treatment for manic depression. Instead, bromide, veronal, and chloral, most of which are sedatives, were prescribed. Lee points out that there is great uncertainty about the neuropsychiatric effects of some of these drugs, and Woolf's manic episodes may well have been the result of taking these chemicals.

However, the tricyclics tend to be more effective with fairly severe forms of depression (Stern, Rush, & Mendels, 1980), perhaps because abnormalities in the level of the monoamines are most likely to be found in severely depressed patients.

It could be argued that the tricyclics and the MAOIs are simply stimulants producing physiological activation, rather than drugs that correct depressed patients' biochemical deficits. However, most of the evidence is inconsistent with that notion. Neither the tricyclics nor the MAOIs have much effect on the mood of normal individuals who do not have biochemical deficits (Cole & Davis, 1975).

Drug treatment for the manic phase of bipolar disorder has lagged behind that for major depression. However, lithium carbonate produces rapid improvement in most manic patients, and can delay the onset of depression in patients suffering from bipolar disorder. Lithium carbonate reduces the occurrence of manic and depressed episodes in about 80% of patients with bipolar disorder (Gerbino, Oleshansky, & Gershon, 1978). About 15% of bipolar disorder patients committed suicide before lithium carbonate was introduced, whereas the suicide rate is now much lower.

Lithium carbonate can have serious side-effects on the central nervous system, on the cardiovascular system, and on the digestive system, and an overdose can be fatal. Discontinuation of lithium carbonate increases the chances that the symptoms of bipolar disorder will recur, so it tends to be used on a continuous basis.

In sum, various drugs (especially Prozac) are very effective at reducing patients' level of depression. However, the drugs affect the symptoms rather than the underlying problems causing the depression. Thus, it is desirable for other forms of therapy to be used alongside drug therapy to produce rapid recovery.

It has sometimes been suggested that manic depression is higher among very creative people, and that the manic phase of the disorder can particularly heighten creativity. How might this affect some sufferers' decisions about whether or not to take drug treatment such as lithium carbonate?

Anxiety disorders

Patients suffering from anxiety (e.g. those with generalised anxiety disorder) are often given minor tranquillisers to reduce anxiety and permit normal functioning. At one time, **barbiturates** were the most used form of anti-anxiety drug. They are depressants of the central nervous system, and long-acting barbiturates are effective in reducing anxiety. However, they have various side-effects. These include problems of concentration, lack of co-ordination, and slurred speech. In addition, the barbiturates tend to be addictive. Anxious patients who stop taking barbiturates report numerous symptoms such as delirium, irritability, and increased sweating.

The problems with the barbiturates led to their replacement by the benzodiazepines (e.g. Valium; Librium) in the 1960s. The benzodiazepines are more precise than the barbiturates in their functioning, and so typically produce fewer side-effects. However, they often have sedative effects, with patients reporting drowsiness and lethargy. They can also impair long-term memory. There can be unfortunate withdrawal symptoms when patients stop taking them, and there are potential problems of addiction.

Although it is clear that the benzodiazepines are much safer than the barbiturates, the search has continued for other anti-anxiety drugs that will reduce anxiety without producing the side-effects of previous drugs. One such drug is Buspirone, which does not seem to have the potentially dangerous sedative effects of the benzodiazepines. However, more research is needed to establish whether or not it has any unwanted side-effects.

Drug therapy can be useful in providing rapid reduction of anxiety in patients who are very distressed. However, anti-anxiety drugs are only designed to reduce the symptoms of anxiety, and do not address the underlying problems. Anti-anxiety drugs should generally only be used over fairly short periods of time, and should be used in combination with other forms of therapy.

In what instances might a GP feel justified in prescribing drugs such as valium or librium? What does "tolerance" to drugs mean and what are the problems associated with this and the treatment of anxiety disorders? What other forms of treatment would benefit an anxious patient, together with or instead of drugs?

Schizophrenia

Neuroleptic drugs (drugs that reduce psychotic symptoms but can also produce some of the symptoms of neurological diseases) are often used in the treatment of schizophrenia. Common neuroleptic drugs include the phenothiazines, the butyrophenones, and the thioxanthenes. They reduce the positive symptoms of schizophrenia (e.g. delusions;

Ethical issues: Informed consent
There is a proven link between use of neuroleptic drugs and the onset of Parkinson's disease, in which the mid-brain fails to produce enough dopamine, a chemical that helps to control movement. What ethical issues with regard to informed consent are raised by this fact?

hallucinations) but have little effect on the negative symptoms (e.g. lack of motivation and emotion; social withdrawal).

Another commonly used drug is clozapine, which is a neuroleptic drug that seems to have fewer side-effects than some others. However, as Kendall and Hammen (1998) have pointed out, it has two important limitations. First, it is much more expensive than most other drugs for schizophrenia, and this restricts its availability. Second, it can produce a potentially fatal blood disease in 1–2% of schizophrenic patients.

In spite of the usefulness of neuroleptic drugs, they have serious limitations. Windgassen (1992) found that about half of schizophrenic patients taking neuroleptics reported grogginess or sedation, 18% reported problems with concentration, 16% had problems with salivation, and 16% had blurred vision. In view of these side-effects, neuroleptic drugs are generally given in the smallest possible doses, and there are "drug holidays" during which no drugs are given. Schizophrenic patients are often reluctant to take neuroleptic drugs. As a result, they are sometimes given injections of long-lasting neuroleptics, thus removing the decision whether or not to take a tablet.

The drugs used to treat schizophrenia have the great advantage that schizophrenic patients no longer need to be restrained in straitjackets. However, they have significant disadvantages. First, as we have seen, they have several unfortunate side-effects. Second, the drugs basically reduce symptoms, and cannot be regarded as providing a cure for schizophrenia.

Disorder	Drug/group of drugs	How they work	Drawbacks
Depression (major)	Monoamine oxidase inhibitors (MAOIs)	Inhibit oxidation of monoamines (neurotransmitters, including dopamine, serotonin, and nor-adrenaline), so that levels increase	A range of side-effects
	Tricyclics	As MAOI's	Dizziness, blurred vision, dry mouth
	Tetracyclics (e.g. Prozac)	As MAOI's, but mainly affects levels of serotonin	Preoccupation with suicide and violence
Depression (bipolar)	Lithium carbonate	Anti-mania, but mechanism is imperfectly understood	Side-effects on CNS, cardiovascular, and digestive systems. Overdose can be fatal
Anxiety disorders	Barbiturates	Treat symptoms of anxiety: palpitations, shortness of breath, accelerated heart rate, feeling of choking, nausea, dizziness, etc.	Problems of concentration, lack of co-ordination, slurred speech. Addictive. Withdrawal symptoms include delirium, irritability.
	Benzodiazepines (e.g. valium, librium)	Have a sedative effect on the CNS	Drowsiness, lethargy, impairments of long-term memory. Withdrawal symptoms and possible addiction
	Buspirone	Stimulate serotonin receptors in the brain	Does not appear to have sedative effect, but other side-effects not yet established
Schizophrenia	Neuroleptic drugs (e.g. phenothiazines butyrophenones, thioxanthenes)	Reduce delusions, hallucinations	Little effect on lack of motivation and emotion, social withdrawal. Some patients report grogginess, sedation, difficulty concentrating, dry mouth, blurred vision
	Clozapine	As neuroleptics, but with fewer side-effects	Expensive. May produce fatal blood disease in 1–2% of patients

Overall evaluation of somatic therapy

There are various problems with somatic therapy. First, it tends to take responsibility away from the patient and give it directly to the therapist or psychiatrist. Second, there is the problem of compliance with treatment. Patients often dislike taking drugs that have serious side-effects, and it is hard for therapists to make sure that the drugs are being taken as and when they should be. Third, there is the problem that somatic therapy involves treating the symptoms rather than the underlying reasons. As a result, there is a real danger that the symptoms will reappear when somatic therapy comes to an end, or that different symptoms will appear.

Humanistic Therapy

The main form of humanistic therapy is **client-centred therapy** (Rogers, 1951, 1959), also known as person-centred therapy. Rogers' starting point for this form of therapy was the concept of self, with our self-concept being based on our conscious experiences of ourselves and of our position in society (see Chapter 20) . Individuals often experience problems and seek therapy when there is **incongruence** (or major discrepancies) between the self-concept and the ideal self. In other words, incongruence is perceived when there is a large difference between the way someone is and the way he or she would like to be—between the ideal self and the actual self.

Client-centred therapy involves the discussion of the client's self-concept and life goals with the therapist, who tries to help the client make sense of his or her experiences.

Rogers (1986) identified the major assumptions lying behind client-centred or person-centred therapy. According to him:

> *The individual has within him or herself, vast resources of self-understanding, for altering his or her self-concept, attitudes and self-directing behaviour, and … these resources can be tapped if only a definable climate of facilitative psychological attitudes can be provided.*

Why do you think Rogers preferred the term "facilitator" to "therapist"?

Client-centred therapy involves the client discussing his or her self-concept and life goals with the therapist (called the facilitator by Rogers). The aim is to create a comfortable atmosphere in which the client will share his or her experiences with the facilitator. The facilitator invites the client to interpret or make sense of his or her experience. It is expected that therapy will allow the client to develop increased self-esteem, and so reduce the discrepancy between his or her self-concept and ideal self. An important part of the reason why client-centred therapy increases the self-esteem of the client is because it allows him or her to develop a greater sense of being in control of his or her destiny. Client-centred therapy differs from psychodynamic therapy in that the focus is very much on current concerns and hopes for the future, whereas the emphasis in psychodynamic therapy is on childhood experiences.

According to Rogers (1951), the way in which the therapist or facilitator behaves towards the client is of key importance in determining the success of treatment. Rogers argued that therapists should be:

Is there a potential conflict between a facilitator being non-judgemental and also allowing his or her true feelings to emerge?

- Unconditional in positive regard: this involves the therapist accepting and valuing the client, and avoiding being critical or judgemental.
- Genuine, in the sense of allowing their true feelings and thoughts to emerge.
- Empathic (i.e. understanding the other person's feelings).

These therapists should be more effective in treating clients than therapists lacking some or all of those characteristics. Part of the reason for this is that therapists having these characteristics really listen to what their clients are telling them, rather than being too influenced by their own beliefs.

> **KEY TERMS**
> **Client-centred therapy**: a form of humanistic therapy introduced by Rogers and designed to increase the client's self-esteem and reduce incongruence.
> **Incongruence**: in Rogers' approach, the discrepancies between an individual's self-concept and his or her ideal self.

Rogers suggested that the therapist should often focus on clarifying what the client is saying, but should not express approval or disapproval of what he or she is saying. Rogers (1947, pp.138–139) showed this approach at work in the following exchanges with a female client called Mary Jane Tildon:

Read the exchange between Rogers and Mary Jane Tildon. In what respect does the therapist take on the role of a facilitator, rather than that of a doctor or adviser? Why might this approach be more effective in changing a client's negative self-concept into a more positive one?

> Tildon: *"I don't know what I'm looking for. It's just that I wonder if I'm insane sometimes. I think I'm nuts."*
>
> Rogers: *"It just gives you concern that you're as far from normal as you feel you are."*
>
> Tildon: *"That's right. It's silly to tell me not to worry because I do worry. It's my life … Well, I don't know how I can change my concept of myself."*
>
> Rogers: *"You feel very different from others and you don't see how you can fix that."*

This short exchange reveals some aspects of client-centred therapy. One aspect is *reflection*, in which the therapist repeats the gist of what the client has just said. Another aspect is *active interpretation*, in which the therapist tries to express the client's real feelings.

Evaluation of humanistic therapy

MacLeod (1998, p.570) provided an evaluation of the humanistic approach to therapy. According to him:

> *The humanistic approach is useful in that it reminds us of the importance of choice, the sense of self, and personal responsibility in human experience. Its influence has been fairly pervasive and has altered the way we think about our lives, emphasising personal fulfilment rather than duty. However, if taken in a one-sided way this can provide an alibi for self-indulgence, which itself creates problems.*

What do you think MacLeod means when he uses the phrase "an alibi for self-indulgence"? Could this also apply to other forms of therapy?

Rogers originally believed that his client-centred therapy was non-directive, in the sense that the therapist did not provide the client with solutions but expected that the client would find his or her own answers. However, Truax (1966) recorded some therapy sessions between Rogers and his clients. What emerged was that Rogers was much more likely to reward or encourage his clients when they produced positive statements and seemed to be making progress. In other words, Rogers was directing the thoughts of his clients much more than he had intended.

Behaviour Therapy

Behaviour therapy developed during the late 1950s and 1960s. The underlying notions are that most forms of mental illness occur through maladaptive learning, and that the best treatment consists of appropriate new learning or re-education. Behaviour therapists believe that abnormal behaviour develops through conditioning (see Chapter 10), and that it is through the use of the principles of conditioning that clients can recover. In other words, behaviour therapy is based on the assumption that classical and operant conditioning can change unwanted behaviour into a more desirable pattern. An important feature of behaviour therapy is its focus on *current* problems and behaviour, and on attempts to remove any symptoms that the patient finds troublesome. This contrasts greatly with psychodynamic therapy, where the focus is much more on trying to uncover unresolved conflicts from childhood.

One of the distinguishing features of behaviour therapy is that more than other forms of therapy it is based on the scientific approach. As MacLeod (1998, p.571) pointed out:

> *The behavioural model of disorders and behaviour was a direct application of behavioural principles from experimental psychology, and was closely related to laboratory-based studies of learning (conditioning) which were often carried out on rats. As such, behaviour*

KEY TERM
Behaviour therapy: a form of treatment involving the application of conditioning principles to produce recovery.

therapy has been ... closely connected with scientific methodology, both in elaborating the principles of therapy and in evaluating the success of therapy.

The key ingredients in classical and operant conditioning are discussed in Chapter 10, and will not be repeated here. What will be done here is to discuss some of the main forms of treatment used by behaviour therapists. After a brief general evaluation, we will deal with three forms of treatment based mainly on classical conditioning, and then consider treatment based on operant conditioning. It has sometimes been argued that the term "behaviour therapy" should be restricted to forms of therapy based on classical conditioning, with the term "behaviour modification" being used to apply to forms of therapy involving operant conditioning. What is done here is to use the term "behaviour therapy" in a general way to cover any therapy based on conditioning principles.

How would you use behaviour therapy to address the maladaptive behaviour of compulsive lying?

General evaluation of behaviour therapy

There are three persistent criticisms of behaviour therapy. First, as Kendall and Hammen (1998, p.75) pointed out:

Critics have described behaviour therapy as mechanical in its application and as limiting the benefits of treatment to changes in observable behaviour.

Second, it has been argued that the focus of behaviour therapists on eliminating symptoms is very limited. In particular, it has been claimed by psychodynamic therapists that the failure to consider the underlying causes of mental illness leads to the danger of **symptom substitution**. In other words, one symptom may be eliminated, but the underlying problems lead to its replacement with another symptom. Third, there is what is known as the problem of generalisation. The application of behaviour therapy may serve to produce the desired behaviour by the patient in the therapist's room. However, it does not necessarily follow that the same behaviour will be produced in other situations.

Flooding or exposure

According to behaviour therapists, phobic fears (e.g. of spiders) are acquired by means of classical conditioning, in which the phobic stimulus is associated with a painful or aversive stimulus which creates fear. This fear can be reduced by avoiding the phobic stimulus.

One way of breaking the link between the conditioned stimulus (e.g. spider) and fear is by experimental extinction. This can be achieved by a technique known as **flooding** or exposure, in which the client is exposed to an extremely fear-provoking situation. In the case of a spider-phobic, the client could either be put in a room full of spiders or asked to imagine being surrounded by dozens of spiders. The client is initially flooded or overwhelmed by fear and anxiety. However, the fear typically starts to subside after some time. If the client can be persuaded to remain in the situation for long enough, there is often a marked reduction in fear.

Why is flooding or exposure effective? It teaches the patient that there is no objective basis to his or her fears (e.g. the spiders do not actually cause any bodily harm). In everyday life, the phobic person would avoid those stimuli relevant to the phobia, and so would have no chance to learn this.

The main problem with the flooding technique is that it is deliberately designed to produce very high levels of fear. It can, therefore, have a very disturbing effect on the client. If the client feels compelled to bring the session to a premature end, this may teach him or her that avoidance of the phobic stimulus is rewarding, in the sense that it leads to reduced fear. This can make later treatment of the phobic harder.

This 18cm poisonous spider is perhaps more terrifying than the type that would be used in flooding!

Systematic desensitisation

Do you think the approach of systematic desensitisation relies more on biological factors or on the sense of power and control gained by the clients?

Joseph Wolpe (1958) developed an alternative form of behaviour therapy for phobic patients known as **systematic desensitisation**. It is based on **counterconditioning**, and involves the attempt to replace the fear response to phobic stimuli with a new response that is incompatible with fear. This new response is usually muscle relaxation. Clients are initially given special training in deep relaxation until they can rapidly achieve muscle relaxation when instructed to do so.

What happens next is that the client and the therapist together construct what is known as an "anxiety hierarchy", in which the client's feared situations are ordered from the least to the most anxiety-provoking. Thus, for example, a spider phobic might regard one small, stationary spider five metres away as only modestly threatening, but a large, rapidly moving spider one metre away as highly threatening. The client reaches a state of deep relaxation, and is then asked to imagine (or is confronted by) the least threatening situation in the anxiety hierarchy. The client repeatedly imagines (or is confronted by) this situation until it fails to evoke any anxiety at all, indicating that the counterconditioning has been successful. This process is repeated while working through all of the situations in the anxiety hierarchy until the most anxiety-provoking situation of all is reached.

Aversion therapy

Aversion therapy is used when there are stimulus situations and associated behaviour patterns that are attractive to the client, but which the therapist and the client both regard as undesirable. For example, alcoholics enjoy going to pubs and consuming large amounts of alcohol. **Aversion therapy** involves associating such stimuli and behaviour with a very unpleasant unconditioned stimulus, such as an electric shock. In the case of alcoholism, what is often done is to require the client to take a sip of alcohol while under the effect of a nausea-inducing drug. Sipping the drink is followed almost at once by vomiting.

Apart from ethical considerations (discussed on pages 728–733), there are two other issues relating to the use of aversion therapy. First, it is not very clear how the shocks or drugs have their effects. It may be that they make the previously attractive *stimulus* (e.g. sight of alcohol) aversive, or it may be that they inhibit the *behaviour* of drinking. Second, there are doubts about the long-term effectiveness of aversion therapy. It can have dramatic effects in the therapist's office. However, it is often much less effective in the outside world, where no nausea-inducing drug has been taken and it is obvious that no shocks will be given (Barlow & Durand, 1995).

> **KEY TERMS**
> **Systematic desensitisation**: a form of treatment for phobias, in which the fear response to threatening stimuli is replaced by a different response such as muscle relaxation.
> **Counterconditioning**: the substitution of a relaxation response for the fear response to threatening stimuli in systematic desensitisation.
> **Aversion therapy**: a form of treatment in which undesirable behaviour is eliminated by associating it with severe punishment.

Therapy based on operant conditioning

So far we have focused on forms of behaviour therapy based on classical conditioning. However, much behaviour involves the use of operant conditioning (see Chapter 10).

> Consider the application of aversion therapy to treat:
> • Compulsive gambling.
> • Sexual perversion (e.g. "flashing").
> Assess the probable degree of success in treating either of these forms of maladaptive behaviour. How important is it for the client to want their behaviour to change?

Therapy using operant conditioning is based on a careful analysis of the maladaptive behaviour of the client, and on the reinforcers or rewards which maintain that behaviour. When the therapist has a clear idea of the current patterns of behaviour and their causes, he or she will try to produce environmental changes to increase the rewards for adaptive behaviour and decrease the rewards for maladaptive behaviour.

There are various techniques open to the behaviour therapist using operant conditioning:

- Extinction: if a maladaptive behaviour is performed by a patient because it is followed by positive reinforcement, then the incidence of that behaviour can be reduced or extinguished by ensuring that the behaviour is no longer followed by reward. Crooks and Stein (1991) discussed an example of extinction involving a 20-year-old woman who picked away at any small spot or blemish on her face until it started bleeding. This compulsive behaviour seemed to be rewarded by the attention she received from her fiancé and from her family. When this behaviour was ignored, but her desirable forms of behaviour received attention, she rapidly stopped exhibiting her compulsive behaviour.
- Selective punishment: a specific maladaptive behaviour is punished by means of an aversive stimulus (e.g. electric shock) whenever it occurs; this is part of what is involved in aversion therapy
- Selective positive reinforcement: a specific adaptive behaviour (or "target behaviour") is selected, and positive reinforcement is provided whenever this target behaviour is produced by the patient. This form of therapy is discussed next.

Token economies

One important form of therapy based on selective positive reinforcement or reward is the **token economy**. This is used with institutionalised patients, who are given tokens (e.g. coloured counters) for behaving in appropriate ways. These tokens can later be used to obtain various privileges (e.g. playing snooker; cigarettes). Ayllon and Azrin (1968) carried out a classic study. Female patients who had been hospitalised for an average of 16 years were rewarded with plastic tokens for actions such as making their beds or combing their hair. The tokens were exchanged for pleasant activities such as seeing a film or having an additional visit to the canteen. This token economy was very successful. The number of chores the patients performed each day increased from about 5 to over 40 when this was rewarded with tokens.

Paul and Lentz (1977) used a token economy with long-term hospitalised schizophrenic patients. As a result, the patients developed various social and work-related skills, they became better able to look after themselves, and their symptoms were reduced. These findings are all the more impressive in that they were achieved at the same time as there was a substantial reduction in the number of drugs being given to the patients.

The main problem with token economies is that the beneficial effects they produce are often greatly reduced when good behaviour is no longer followed by the rewards that the patients have grown used to receiving. Thus, there is a danger that token economies may produce only token (i.e. minimal) learning. There is no easy answer to this problem. Token economies work because the environment is carefully structured so that good behaviour is consistently rewarded and bad behaviour is not. The outside world is very different, and patients find it hard to *transfer* what they have learned in a token economy to the much less structured environment outside the institution.

KEY STUDY EVALUATION — Token economies

Token economies reward patients for socially acceptable behaviour, but they do not allow for variations in patients' capabilities. These may result in fewer tokens being given to the more maladapted individuals because they are more unstable and less able to learn new skills. This might have the undesirable effect of creating a hierarchy in which self-esteem becomes weakened among the more vulnerable people.

The use of incentives to reward good behaviour may not only eradicate undesirable behaviour but may also fail to build a patient's personal autonomy. This will be essential when he or she is faced with choices about how to behave in a given setting. Rewarding people for the absence of negative behaviour, rather than when positive behaviour actually occurs, may not effect change in the person, because they are not making a moral decision based on the protection of their own self-esteem, but rather for an external reward.

Ethical issues: All three forms of therapy based on operant conditioning are limited by ethical considerations. Which of the three presents the most ethical problems? Why do you think this is the case?

> **KEY TERM**
> **Token economy**: institution-based use of operant conditioning to alter the behaviour of mental patients by selective positive reinforcement.

Discussion points

1. Do token economies resemble the approach that might well be taken by non-psychologists trying to change someone's behaviour?
2. What could be done to increase transfer of learning to the outside world?

Cognitive Therapy

Behaviour therapy focuses on external stimuli and responses, and ignores the cognitive processes (e.g. thoughts; beliefs) happening between stimulus and response. This omission was dealt with in the early 1960s with the introduction of **cognitive therapy**, based on the assumption that successful treatment can involve changing or restructuring clients' cognitions or thinking.

Albert Ellis

Albert Ellis (1962) was one of the first therapists to put forward a version of cognitive therapy. He argued that anxiety and depression occur as the end points in a three-point sequence:

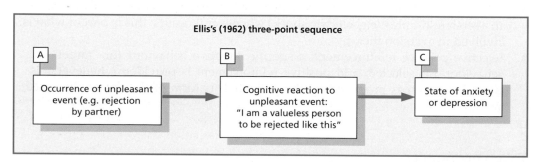

According to this A-B-C model, anxiety and depression do not occur as a direct result of unpleasant events. More precisely, these negative mood states are produced by the irrational thoughts that follow from the occurrence of unpleasant events. The interpretations that are produced at point B depend on the individual's belief system.

Ellis (1962) developed rational-emotive therapy as a way of removing irrational and self-defeating thoughts and replacing them with more rational and positive ones. As Ellis (1978) pointed out:

> If he [the individual] wants to be minimally disturbable and maximally sane, he'd better substitute for all his absolutistic "It's terribles" two other words which he does not parrot or give lip-service to but which he incisively thinks through and accepts—namely, "Too bad!" or "Tough shit!".

In more technical terms, Ellis argued that individuals who are anxious or depressed should create a point D. This is a dispute belief system that allows them to interpret life's events in ways that do not cause them emotional distress.

Rational-emotive therapy starts with the therapist making patients aware of the self-defeating nature of many of their beliefs. Patients are then encouraged to ask themselves searching questions about these beliefs in order to discover whether these

KEY TERM
Cognitive therapy: a form of treatment involving attempts to change or restructure the client's thoughts and beliefs.

beliefs are rational and logical. For example, patients may be told to ask themselves questions such as the following: "Why do I have to be liked by everybody?"; "Why is it so terrible if I can't have my own way all the time?"; "Does it really matter if I am not competent in every way?". After that, patients are taught to replace their faulty and irrational beliefs with more realistic ones (e.g. "It is impossible to be liked by everybody, but most people like me"; "My life can be happy even if I sometimes can't do what I want"; "I will strive to be fairly competent, and accept that perfection cannot be achieved"). The crucial final step is for patients to have *full acceptance* of these new, rational beliefs.

Convincing evidence that anxious patients are much more likely than normals to have irrational beliefs was reported by Newmark et al. (1973). They found that 65% of anxious patients (but only 2% of normals) agreed with the statement, "It is essential that one be loved or approved of by virtually everyone in his community." The statement, "One must be perfectly competent, adequate, and achieving to consider oneself worthwhile", was agreed to by 80% of anxious patients compared with 25% of normals.

Evaluation

Therapists using rational-emotive therapy tend to be much more argumentative than those using client-centred therapy, and they show less concern for the sensitivities of their clients. It may well be that which form of therapy is preferable depends on the individual client. For example, there is evidence that rational-emotive therapy is especially effective with clients who feel guilty because of their own perceived inadequacies and who generally impose high demands on themselves (Brandsma, Maultsby, & Welsh, 1978). Rational-emotive therapy seems more suitable for individuals suffering from anxiety or depression than for those with severe thought disorders (Barlow & Durand, 1995).

Why does rational-emotive therapy appear to be more effective with individuals suffering from anxiety or depression than with those who have severe thought disorders?

Aaron Beck

Probably the most influential cognitive therapist is Aaron Beck. He has developed forms of cognitive therapy for anxiety, but is better known for his work on depression. Beck (1976) argued that therapy for depression should involve uncovering and challenging the negative and unrealistic beliefs of depressed clients. Of great importance is the **cognitive triad**. This consists of negative thoughts that depressed individuals have about themselves, about the world, and about the future. Depressed clients typically regard themselves as helpless, worthless, and inadequate. They interpret events in the world in an unrealistically negative and defeatist way, and they see the world as posing obstacles that cannot be handled. The final part of the cognitive triad involves depressed individuals seeing the future as totally hopeless, because their worthlessness will prevent any improvement occurring in their situation.

According to Beck et al. (1979), the first stage of cognitive therapy involves the therapist and the client agreeing on the nature of the problem and on the goals for therapy. This stage is called collaborative empiricism. The client's negative thoughts are then tested out by the therapist challenging them or by the client engaging in certain forms of behaviour between therapy sessions. It is hoped that the client will come to accept that many of his or her negative thoughts are irrational and unrealistic. For example, a depressed client who argues that people are always avoiding him or her can be asked to keep a diary of specific occasions on which this happens. It is very likely that it happens much less often than the patient imagines.

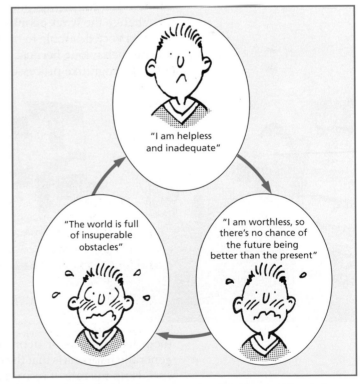

Aaron Beck's cognitive triad.

> **KEY TERM**
> **Cognitive triad**: negative thoughts about the self, the world, and the future, found in depressed clients.

Cognitive therapy: A summary

Cognitive therapists differ among themselves in terms of the approaches they adopt towards their clients. However, the common features were identified by Beck and Weishaar (1989, p.308):

> Cognitive therapy consists of highly specific learning experiences designed to teach patients (1) to monitor their negative, automatic thoughts (cognitions); (2) to recognise the connections between cognition, affect, and behaviour; (3) to examine the evidence for and against distorted automatic thoughts; (4) to substitute more reality-oriented interpretations for these biased cognitions; and (5) to learn to identify and alter the beliefs that predispose them to distort their experiences.

Cognitive-behavioural Therapy

In what way might a person's thoughts about themself influence the way they react in a particular situation, e.g. a job interview?

In recent years, there have been increasing efforts to add some of the more successful features of behaviour therapy to cognitive therapy. This combination is referred to as **cognitive-behavioural therapy**. According to Kendall and Hammen (1998), the four basic assumptions underlying cognitive-behavioural therapy are as follows:

1. Patients typically respond on the basis of their *interpretations* of themselves and the world around them rather than on the basis of what is *actually* the case.
2. Thoughts, behaviour, and feelings are all interrelated, and they all influence each other. Thus, it would be wrong to identify one of these factors (e.g. behaviour) as being more important than the others.
3. In order for therapeutic interventions to be successful, they need to clarify and to change the ways people think about themselves and about the world around them.
4. It is very desirable to try to change both the client's cognitive processes and his or her behaviour, because the benefits of therapy are likely to be greater than when only cognitive processes or behaviour are changed.

We have already considered some of the ways in which cognitive therapists such as Ellis (1962) and Beck (1976) try to restructure the thoughts and beliefs of their clients. They also try to change the behaviour of their clients in a fairly direct fashion, and so can be regarded as cognitive-behavioural therapists. Beck (1976) instructs his clients to monitor and log their thought processes between therapy sessions. He also emphasises the use of homework assignments that require clients to behave in ways in which they were previously unable to behave. A client suffering from a high level of social anxiety might be told to initiate conversations with everyone in his or her office over the following few days. A crucial ingredient in such homework assignments is *hypothesis testing*. Clients typically predict that carrying out their homework assignments will make them feel anxious or depressed, and so they are told to test these predictions. What generally happens is that the clients' hypotheses are shown to be too pessimistic, and this speeds up the rate of recovery.

Effectiveness of Therapy

In order to assess the effectiveness of a given form of therapy, it is usual to compare the percentage of clients receiving that therapy who recover against the recovery percentage among clients receiving either no therapy or a different form of therapy. There are various problems associated with assessing the effectiveness of therapy. Some of the main ones are as follows:

- There are numerous different ways of defining and assessing recovery (e.g. in terms of behaviour or in terms of self-report measures); for example, the goal of therapy for psychodynamic therapists is to resolve internal conflicts, whereas for behaviour therapists it is to change overt behaviour. The ideal approach would be to obtain a wide range of self-report, behavioural, and physiological measures.

- Therapy that is effective in producing recovery may or may not be effective in preventing relapse (return of the disorder); thus, therapy that seems effective in the short term may or may not be so in the long term.

- It is generally unethical to compare the effects of a given form of therapy against those found in a control group of patients who are denied treatment.

- It is often hard to tell whether any beneficial effects of therapy are due to **specific factors** (features that are unique to that form of therapy) or to **common factors** (e.g. patient expectations; personal qualities of the therapist).

- Clients with the same diagnosis often differ considerably in terms of the severity of their symptoms and in the precise pattern of symptoms they exhibit.

- Any given form of therapy tends to be given in a different way by different therapists. As Lazarus and Davison (1971, p.203) pointed out, "The clinician ... approaches his work with ... a framework for ordering the complex data that are his domain. But frameworks are insufficient. The clinician ... must fill out the theoretical skeleton. Individual cases present problems that always call for knowledge beyond basic psychological principles."

- The effectiveness of therapy depends in part on the skills and personal qualities of the therapist as well as on the content of the therapy itself.

- It cannot be assumed that patients are allocated *randomly* to different forms of therapy; there is some *self-selection*, with patients often having some say over the therapy they will receive. This complicates the issue of comparing different forms of therapy.

- Some forms of therapy may work much better with some kinds of patients than with others. For example, there is evidence that psychodynamic therapy works best with patients who are young, attractive, verbally skilled, intelligent, and successful (Garfield, 1980). (If you take the first letters of young, attractive, and so on, you arrive at YAVIS, which may assist your memory for this list!)

Ethical issues: What are the possible reasons why it may be unethical to compare effects between a treated group of depressives (using drugs) and an untreated control group (using a placebo)?

Individual cases

The diagnosis and treatment of a person suffering from, for example, an eating disorder is likely to vary from one individual to another, depending on the person's symptoms, their severity, and the individual case history. The effectiveness of the treatment may therefore hinge on the extent of the therapist's knowledge and understanding of each individual case, rather than on a specific psychological approach to eating disorders.

Strupp (1996) argued that the effectiveness of any given form of therapy should be considered from three different perspectives. First, there is the perspective of society. This includes the individual's ability to function in society and the individual's adherence to social norms. Second, there is the client's own perspective. This includes the client's overall subjective well-being. Third, there is the therapist's perspective. This includes relating the client's thinking and behaviour to the theoretical framework of mental disorder underlying the form of therapy used by the therapist. The extent to which a client has recovered may vary considerably from one perspective to another.

Control groups

Suppose we find that clients receiving a given form of therapy are no more likely to recover than those in a control group not receiving any systematic therapy. Does this prove that the therapy is totally ineffective? It does not, because of the **placebo effect**. This effect has been found in drug research, where it refers to the finding that patients who are given a

KEY TERMS
Specific factors: features unique to a given form of therapy that help the client to recover.
Common factors: general factors found in most forms of therapy (e.g. patient expectations; therapist's personal qualities) that help the client to recover.
Placebo effect: positive responses to a drug or form of therapy based on the patient's beliefs that the drug or therapy will be effective, rather than on the actual make-up of the drug or therapy.

Do you think that by seeking help in the form of any kind of therapy, clients are in fact expressing hope for the future? Might this contribute to the placebo effect?

neutral substance (e.g. a salt tablet), but told they have been given a strong drug, will often show signs of medical improvement. Thus, the mistaken belief that one has received an effective form of treatment can produce strong beneficial effects. In similar fashion, according to Mair (1992), control clients who are led to expect that they will show improvement may do so:

> *As a symbolic communication that combats demoralisation by inspiring the patient's hopes for relief, administration of a placebo is a form of psychotherapy. It is therefore not surprising that placebos can provide marked relief in patients who seek psychotherapy.*

General studies of therapy

Smith, Glass, and Miller (1980) reviewed 475 studies in which the effectiveness of therapy had been evaluated. In order to be included in the review, each study had to include a comparison group drawn from the same population, who were treated differently (e.g. untreated). Smith et al. carried out a **meta-analysis**, which involves combining the data from numerous studies so that an accurate estimate can be made of the effectiveness of each form of treatment. The studies varied considerably. Some involved comparisons between different forms of therapy, whereas others involved comparisons between therapy and no treatment. Several different outcome measures were used in many of the studies, ranging from self-report measures to behavioural and physiological measures of various kinds. Altogether, there were 1776 outcome measures from the 475 studies. The studies considered by Smith et al. were unrepresentative of most clinical outcome studies in that more than 50% of the patients receiving treatment in the 475 studies were students (Gross & McIlveen, 1996).

Smith et al. (1980) concluded: "Different types of psychotherapy (verbal or behavioural), psychodynamic, client-centred, or systematic desensitisation) do not produce different types or degrees of benefit." On average, their analyses indicated that a client receiving any systematic form of psychotherapy was better off than 80% of controls in terms of recovery. They reported that the effectiveness of therapy did not depend on its length. As behaviour therapy typically takes much less time than psychodynamic therapy, that is an argument for preferring behaviour therapy.

The approach adopted by Smith et al. was limited in a number of ways. They failed to include all the existing studies in their review. In addition, they gave equal weight to all studies, regardless of quality. This is serious, because it has been argued (Prioleau, Murdock, & Brody, 1983) that only 32 of the studies considered by Smith et al. were based on sound methods.

Would it be possible to offer effective therapy if one did not believe in that particular approach?

Smith et al. found that the beliefs and preferences of therapists were important in determining the effectiveness of therapy. Any form of therapy was more effective when it was provided by therapists who believed strongly in that therapy. However, it is important to note that recovery in most of the studies was assessed by experts who did not know which form of therapy any patient had received.

Smith et al. also found that some forms of therapy were especially effective with certain disorders. Cognitive therapy and cognitive-behaviour therapy were most effective with specific phobias, fear, and anxiety. Client-centred therapy worked best with clients having low self-esteem.

Rosenhan and Seligman (1995) considered the issue of the most effective forms of therapy for different disorders. Some of their conclusions were as follows:

- Anxieties, fears, phobias, and panic: systematic desensitisation, cognitive therapy, and drugs (benzodiazepines) are among the best forms of therapy.
- Depression: cognitive therapy, electroconvulsive treatment, and drugs (e.g. Prozac) are all very effective.
- Schizophrenia: drugs (neuroleptics such as chlorpromazine) and family intervention (involving communication skills) are effective.

KEY TERM
Meta-analysis: a form of analysis in which the data from several related studies are combined to obtain an overall estimate (e.g. of the effectiveness of therapy).

Matt and Navarro

Matt and Navarro (1997) considered evidence from 63 meta-analyses of the effects of therapy. Across the 28 meta-analyses providing relevant data, the mean effect size was 0.67, meaning that 75% of patients improved more than untreated controls. This is somewhat lower than the figure reported by Smith et al. (1980).

Matt and Navarro also addressed the issue of whether the effects of therapy are due to specific effects or to common effects (e.g. placebo effects). They did this by focusing on 10 meta-analyses in which three types of group were compared:

1. Specific therapy groups, for whom any benefits may depend on specific effects or common effects.
2. Placebo control groups (involving general encouragement but no specific therapy), for whom any benefits are likely to depend on common effects.
3. Waiting list control groups, for whom no benefits are expected.

The evidence indicated that 57% of placebo control patients did better than the average waiting list control patient, indicating that common or placebo effects exist. However, 75% of the patients receiving specific therapy did better than the average placebo control patient, indicating that specific effects are almost four times more powerful than common or placebo effects.

Do different forms of therapy vary in their general effectiveness? Matt and Navarro (1997, p.22) considered the relevant meta-analyses, and concluded as follows: "Typically, differences favoured behavioural and cognitive therapy approaches over psychodynamic and client-centred approaches." However, they accepted that it was hard to interpret such differences because there was no standardisation of disorder severity, outcome measures, and so on.

Discussion points

1. What are the strengths and weaknesses of meta-analyses as a way of discovering the effectiveness of therapy?
2. How impressed are you by the apparent effectiveness of most forms of therapy revealed by Matt and Navarro?

Wampold et al. (1997, p.211) carried out a meta-analysis on studies in which two or more forms of therapy had been compared directly, and in which the same outcome measures had been applied to patients receiving different forms of therapy. Their findings suggested that the beneficial effects of all forms of therapy are essentially the same. They concluded as follows:

Why is it that researchers persist in attempts to find treatment differences, when they know that these effects are small in comparison to other effects, such as therapists' effects ... or effects of treatment versus no-treatment comparisons?

Evaluation of meta-analyses of therapy

We need to be cautious about interpreting the evidence from meta-analyses, because most of them are limited in various ways. According to Matt and Navarro (1997, p.20)

psychotherapy outcome studies do not adequately represent patient populations, settings, interventions, and outcomes commonly found in clinical practice ... [They] overrepresent anxiety disorders ... younger age groups and student patients ... recruited rather than referred patients ... and difficult to treat patients ... Settings were found to overrepresent outpatient settings, universities, highly

■ Research activity: The treatment of more complex cases is under-researched, according to Matt and Navarro. Explore some of the practical difficulties involved in accessing information on patients whose mental health problems do not fall into a neat category and whose therapeutic needs are therefore complicated, e.g. chronic alcoholics.

controlled environments and to underrepresent clinical practice and psychiatric setting. As for types of interventions, meta-analysts note the overrepresentation of cognitive and behavioural interventions, therapists in training or with little experience ... and interventions targeting fairly circumscribed [limited] and behavioural problems ... With respect to outcomes, several meta-analysts have argued ... there is overreliance on self-report measures, therapist ratings, and behavioural measures.

Effectiveness of psychodynamic therapy

The first systematic attempt to evaluate the effectiveness of psychoanalysis was reported by Eysenck (1952), who reviewed studies in which clients either received psychoanalysis or did not receive any systematic treatment. The figures were striking: 72% of clients with no proper treatment recovered over a period of two years (this is known as spontaneous remission), compared to only 44% of those receiving psychoanalysis. These findings imply that psychoanalysis is actually bad for you!

The findings reported by Eysenck cannot be accepted at face value. He counted clients who dropped out of psychoanalysis as clients for whom therapy had failed. If these clients are excluded, then the recovery rate was 66% for patients receiving psychoanalysis. In addition, there are great doubts as to whether the studies on psychoanalysis and on spontaneous remission were comparable in the severity of the initial disorders and the criteria for recovery. Bergin (1971) considered the same information used by Eysenck (1952), but used different criteria for recovery. According to his analyses, psychoanalysis produced a 83% success rate, whereas the spontaneous remission rate was only 30%.

Sloane et al. (1975) carried out a detailed study mainly on patients with anxiety disorder. Behaviour therapy and ego analysis both produced an 80% improvement rate, which was greater than the 48% found in the wait-list control group. However, the three groups did not differ at the eight-month follow-up, because the control patients had improved considerably. Thus, psychodynamic therapy in the form of ego analysis was as effective as behaviour therapy, and produced more rapid recovery than no treatment.

Psychodynamic therapy is more appropriate for the treatment of some disorders than others. It has proved of value in the treatment of anxiety disorders, depression, and some sexual disorders, but is considerably less effective in the treatment of schizophrenia (Luborsky & Spence, 1978). The central focus of psychodynamic therapy is to permit the client to gain insight into himself or herself. Patients (such as schizophrenics who are not taking drug therapies) who cannot do this are unsuitable for this form of therapy.

Psychodynamic therapy is most appropriate for some types of individuals. Some of the relevant evidence was discussed by Luborsky and Spence (1978): patients who are better educated benefit more from psychodynamic therapy, perhaps because language skills are so important in therapy. Psychodynamic therapy may not be very appropriate for adults who genuinely had very happy and contented childhoods. If they have very few repressed childhood memories, there is little opportunity for them to gain insight into the meaning of their childhood suffering.

Effectiveness of somatic therapy

Most forms of somatic therapy (with the exception of psychosurgery) have proved fairly effective. There are common themes running through drug therapy for anxiety, depression, and schizophrenia. First, drugs are usually effective in producing a rapid reduction in symptoms. This can be very valuable, because drugs reduce distress, and may stop patients from attempting suicide. Another reason why drugs are useful with schizophrenia is because they may permit schizophrenic patients to benefit from therapy based on the attainment of insight (e.g. psychodynamic therapy).

Second, nearly all drugs used in therapy have side-effects, and these side-effects can be serious and even dangerous. Third, many drugs can be addictive, and there can be problems of withdrawal when they are no longer given to a patient. Fourth, most drugs reduce the symptoms of a disorder, but do not provide a cure. However, they can form part of a combined therapeutic approach designed to produce a cure.

Somatic therapy emphasises changes in the physiological and biochemical systems, and so it seems especially appropriate to the treatment of disorders involving physiological and/or biochemical abnormalities. A clear example is schizophrenia. Drug therapy is also appropriate when patients are in state of great distress (e.g. anxiety disorders; depression). However, it is generally not sufficient on its own. For example, consider panic disorder. As we saw in Chapter 25, patients with panic disorder greatly exaggerate the seriousness of their own physiological symptoms. As a result, cognitive-behavioural therapy designed to reduce these exaggerated cognitions is more effective than drug therapy in producing recovery from panic disorder (Eysenck, 1997).

In general terms, somatic therapy is inappropriate for disorders that are not clearly based on physiological or biochemical abnormalities. For example, cultural values and expectations play an important role in producing eating disorders (see Chapter 25), and so somatic therapy is unlikely to be of much relevance.

Effectiveness of humanistic therapy

There is some evidence that Rogers was right to emphasise the importance of the therapist being genuine, empathic, and unconditional in positive regard. Truax and Mitchell (1971) reviewed several studies involving various methods of psychotherapy. The most successful therapists tended to have these three characteristics. However, some more recent evidence indicates that these characteristics are less important than was claimed by Rogers (e.g. Beutler, Cargo, & Arizmendi, 1986).

Rogers (1951) emphasised the importance of the therapist's personal qualities in determining the success of therapy. However, the actual situation is rather more complicated. The therapist and the client interact with each other, and it is easier for the therapist to be unconditional in positive regard, empathic, and genuine with some clients than with others. Fiske, Cartwright, and Kirtner (1964) found that the behaviour and attitudes of the client do matter. Those patients who discussed their feelings and problems concerning personal relationships at the first interview recovered much more in therapy than did those who discussed their problems as if they were someone else's.

Rogers was one of the first therapists to provide detailed information about therapy sessions to other interested therapists and researchers. This often took the form of tape recordings. Such information is of great value if there is to be a proper understanding of changes in the client's thoughts and behaviour. It also helps in the task of evaluating the success of therapy. Rogers' contributions in this area were so great that Davison and Neale (1990, p.527) argued that, "Rogers can be credited with originating the whole field of psychotherapy research."

Encounter groups developed out of client-centred therapy. Participants in encounter groups are encouraged to examine their own feelings with great honesty, and to discuss them freely with the rest of the group. Encounter groups have often proved of benefit. However, individuals who are rather disturbed or low in self-esteem may suffer adverse effects from participating in encounter groups (Kaul & Bednar, 1986).

It is hard to assess the effectiveness of client-centred therapy. Part of the reason for this is that there is no attempt to diagnose or classify the client's symptoms, and so it is not easy to compare his or her state before and after therapy. Humanistic therapists tend to rely on clients' self-reports when deciding whether they have recovered, paying little attention to their clients' behaviour. These self-reports can be distorted, as even humanistic therapists accept that people are often unaware of their true feelings. However, the Q-sort

Participants in encounter groups examine and discuss their feelings with great honesty, but disturbed individuals or those with low self-esteem may be worse off after an experience like this.

method can be used to assess recovery (see Chapter 2). This method was devised by Rogers (1959), and involves the client deciding which personal statements on cards (e.g. "I am a friendly person") best describe him or her. This is then repeated for the ideal self. Recovery is indicated by a reduced discrepancy between the self-concept and the ideal self on this Q-sort method.

When is client-centred therapy most appropriate? Halgin and Whitbourne (1997, p.130) concluded as follows:

> With regard to therapy, the humanistic approach seems best suited for a relatively narrow range of clients, who are motivated to focus on their subjective experience and who are able to discuss their emotional concerns in detail.

Client-centred therapy is also limited in the kinds of disorder for which it is appropriate. According to Davison and Neale (1996):

> As a way to help unhappy but not severely disturbed people understand themselves better (and perhaps even to help them behave differently), client-centred therapy may very well be appropriate and effective.

This would explain why there is considerable use of client-centred therapy in counselling, and why it is hardly used any more in the treatment of severe mental disorders such as schizophrenia.

Effectiveness of behaviour therapy

Behaviour therapy is a moderately effective form of therapy. As we have seen, Smith et al. (1980) found that behaviour therapy was as effective as other major forms of therapy. Subsequent reviews of the literature have suggested that behaviour therapy and cognitive-behavioural therapy are usually more effective than psychodynamic therapy (see the next section).

Behaviour therapy, especially exposure, is often very effective with anxiety disorders. Ost (1989) used one-session exposure on patients with specific phobias, and reported that "90% of the patients obtained a clinically significant improvement ... which was maintained after an average of 4 yr." One of the few anxiety disorders for which exposure is not very effective is obsessive-compulsive disorder. Van Oppen et al. (1995) found that 17% of patients with obsessive-compulsive disorder recovered after exposure therapy, compared to 39% who received cognitive therapy.

The success of some forms of behaviour therapy does not depend on the factors claimed by behaviour therapists to be responsible. For example, Wolpe (1958) assumed that systematic desensitisation works because clients learn to link a relaxation response to phobic stimuli. Lick (1975) obtained evidence that this is not the whole story. He told his clients that he was presenting them with subliminal phobic stimuli (i.e. below the level of conscious awareness) and that repetition of these stimuli reduced their physiological fear reactions. In fact, he did not present any stimuli, and the feedback about physiological responses was fake! In view of Lick's (1975) total failure to follow the "correct" procedures, it would be expected by behaviour therapists that the therapy should have been ineffective. In fact, Lick's "make-believe" procedure was as successful in reducing the clients' fear responses to phobic stimuli. Presumably the "make-believe" procedure made the clients think they could control their fear, even though the counterconditioning emphasised by behaviour therapists did not occur.

Behaviour therapy is most appropriate in the treatment of disorders in which behavioural symptoms are central, and is least appropriate when the key symptoms are internal. For example, specific phobics have the behavioural symptom of avoidance of the phobic stimulus, and behaviour therapy works well with that disorder (Ost, 1989). In contrast, many of the key symptoms of obsessive-compulsive disorder are in the form of internal thoughts and obsessions, and behaviour therapy is no more than modestly effective (van Oppen et al., 1995).

Ethical issues: Does the fact that clients in Lick's study experienced a positive outcome override the ethical problems of the deception he used?

What therapeutic approach or approaches might be most effective in treating obsessive-compulsive disorder?

Behaviour therapy is also not very appropriate when dealing with serious disorders having a substantial genetic component. The prime example here is schizophrenia. Token economies have been successful in modifying the behaviour of schizophrenics in desirable ways, but no form of behaviour therapy has removed the main symptoms of schizophrenia.

Effectiveness of cognitive and cognitive-behavioural therapy

Cognitive therapy and cognitive-behavioural therapy both involve taking full account of the client's own views of the world, no matter how distorted those views might be. If one is trying to produce beneficial change, then it is of value to have clear evidence of the client's present state. There are some advantages of cognitive-behavioural therapy over cognitive therapy, in that many of the symptoms about which clients are concerned are related to their behaviour. As a result, it is reasonable to try to change behaviour *directly*, as well as *indirectly* by changing some of their thoughts and beliefs.

Beck's approach is more developed and sophisticated than that of Ellis. Ellis tends to assume that rather similar irrational beliefs underlie most mental disorders, whereas Beck argues that specific irrational beliefs tend to be associated with each disorder. In spite of the limitations of Ellis's rational-emotive therapy, it is reasonably effective. Engels, Garnefski, and Diekstra (1993) found, across 28 studies, that rational-emotive therapy was as effective as systematic desensitisation and markedly superior to no treatment.

Cognitive-behavioural therapy has proved successful in the treatment of depression and anxiety disorders, and Meichenbaum (1985) has shown its effectiveness in stress reduction (see Chapter 6). However, it is of little value in the treatment of disorders that do not involve irrational beliefs. Dobson (1989) reviewed 28 studies of therapy for depression. He concluded that cognitive therapy compared favourably to other forms of psychotherapy in most of the studies. Cognitive-behavioural therapy works well with nearly all anxiety disorders (Eysenck, 1997), but is especially effective with panic disorder. According to Rachman (1993, p.279), "As far as anxiety disorders are concerned, the greatest theoretical and clinical progress has been made in applying cognitive-behaviour therapy (CBT) to the ... treatment of panic." It is also more effective than behaviour therapy in the treatment of obsessive-compulsive disorder (van Oppen et al., 1995).

Cognitive-behavioural therapy combines the advantages of cognitive therapy and behaviour therapy, and so provides appropriate forms of treatment for a wide range of disorders. As it is also a very inexpensive and cost-effective form of treatment, it is being used increasingly in Britain and the United States as the preferred form of therapy. Cognitive-behavioural therapy has limited appropriateness for the treatment of schizophrenia. However, schizophrenia is a very serious disorder that has proved extremely hard to treat successfully.

Ethical issues: Are there any ethical problems involved in using cost-effectiveness as a criterion for choice of preferred form of therapy?

Processes involved in therapy

The effectiveness of any form of therapy depends on specific factors unique to that therapy, and common factors such as warmth, acceptance, and empathy on the part of the therapist.

Common factors
The fact that different therapies are of roughly equal effectiveness suggests that common factors are important. Indeed, it has been argued that about 85% of the variation in the effectiveness of therapy depends on common rather than specific factors (Strupp, 1996).

Positive common factors. Sloane et al. (1975) conducted a study on patients who had derived benefit from either behaviour therapy or from insight-oriented therapy. The

...warmth, acceptance and empathy on the part of the therapist.

two groups were asked to indicate those aspects of therapy that they had found useful. In spite of the large differences in the treatment received, the two groups identified very much the same factors. The helpful factors included the therapist's personality, being able to talk to a sympathetic person, and the therapist's encouragement to handle issues that the patients found hard to deal with. Thus, the same common factors are of major importance in both forms of therapy.

Negative outcomes. Mohr (1995) focused on some of the common factors in therapy that seem to produce negative outcomes, in which therapy actually makes the patient's condition worse rather than better. Therapists who show a lack of empathy, who underestimate the severity of the patient's problems, or who disagree with the patient about the process of therapy are most likely to provide unsuccessful treatment. On the other side, patients who are poorly motivated, who expect that therapy will be easy, or who have very poor interpersonal skills are most likely to experience negative outcomes.

Specific factors

In spite of the importance of common factors, it is important not to ignore the role of specific factors. Consider, for example, treatment for depression. Drug therapy and cognitive therapy are both equally effective in producing recovery from depression (e.g. Barber & DeRubeis, 1989). However, drug therapy is only designed to reduce the symptoms of depression, whereas cognitive therapy or cognitive-behaviour therapy is intended to equip clients with more realistic and positive beliefs about themselves and their situation. As might be expected, patients who have been treated for depression with drug therapy are more likely to relapse into depression in the year following recovery than are patients who received cognitive-behaviour therapy (Barber & DeRubeis, 1989). Thus, some of the specific factors involved in cognitive-behaviour therapy for depression have greater long-term effectiveness than those involved in drug therapy.

Ethical issues: If a depressed person is likely to try to commit suicide, should long-term effectiveness be a major consideration in choice of appropriate therapy?

Ethical Issues in Therapy

There is general agreement that there are important ethical issues relating to therapy. However, few people would go as far as Masson (1989) in his condemnation of the therapeutic process. He was concerned about the fact that the therapist is in a much more powerful position than the client. This led him to the conclusion (1989, p.24) that

> *the very idea of psychotherapy is wrong. The structure of psychotherapy is such that no matter how kindly a person is, when that person becomes a therapist, he or she is engaged in acts that are bound to diminish the dignity, autonomy, and freedom of the person who comes for help.*

Masson's attack on therapy is exaggerated, but there are important ethical issues, which will be considered next:

1. Informed consent.
2. Confidentiality.
3. Choice of therapeutic goals.
4. Dual relationships.
5. Cultural and subcultural factors.

Informed consent

With the following types of clients, might it be justifiable to proceed with therapy in the absence of informed consent: a schizophrenic patient; a child who has witnessed a murder; a paedophile?

It may seem obvious that therapy should only be carried out with the full informed consent of the client. To achieve that, the patient should be fully informed about the various forms of treatment that are available, about the probability of success of each treatment, about any possible dangers or side-effects, about the right to terminate treatment at any time, and about the likely cost of treatment. Evidence of the value of informed consent was reported by Devine and Fernald (1973). Snake phobics were shown four films of different forms of treatment. Those who were given their preferred form of treatment showed more recovery than those who were not.

There are strong ethical and practical reasons in favour of informed consent. In practice, as is discussed below, there are several reasons why full informed consent is not achieved.

First, the therapist may not have detailed information about the respective benefits and costs of different forms of treatment. In addition, some forms of treatment are very successful with some patients, but cause serious problems with others. These considerations mean that the therapist may be unable to provide the patient with enough information to come to a clear decision.

Second, the client or patient may find it hard to remember the information that he or she has been given by the therapist. Evidence on this issue was obtained by Irwin et al. (1985). They engaged in detailed questioning of patients who had said they understood the benefits and possible side-effects of a form of treatment. In fact, about 75% of them were mistaken, because they had forgotten important information.

Third, many clients are not in a position to provide full informed consent. Examples include young children, those with severe learning difficulties, and schizophrenic patients. So far as schizophrenics are concerned, however, there is evidence (discussed by Davison & Neale, 1996) that they vary considerably in their ability to give informed consent. What typically happens when clients are unable to give informed consent is that a guardian or close relative provides it.

Fourth, clients may agree to a form of treatment because of their exaggerated respect for the expertise of the therapist, rather than because of information about the likely benefits and costs of that treatment. This is perhaps especially likely to occur when the client has little or no prior knowledge of different forms of treatment.

Fifth, some clients may not be in a position to provide informed consent because of social and cultural pressures on them. For example, Silverstein (1972, p.4) expressed clearly the difficulties that some homosexuals may have:

> *To suggest that a person comes voluntarily to change his sexual orientation is to ignore the powerful environmental stress ... that has been telling him for years that he should change. To grow up in a family where the word "homosexual" was whispered, to play in a playground and hear the words "faggot" and "queer", to go to church and hear of "sin" and then to college and hear of "illness", and finally to the counselling centre that promises to "cure", makes it hard [to live in] an environment of freedom and voluntary choice. The homosexual is expected to want to be changed and his application for treatment is implicitly praised as the first step toward "normal" behaviour.*

> **Informed consent**
>
> Consider the five instances given as possible barriers to obtaining informed consent. In each case there is evidence that the client has a role subservient to that of the therapist. How does this relate to Masson's description of the power-balance in a client–therapist relationship?

Ethical issues: Are there separate ethical issues involved in allowing relatives to give informed consent on behalf of a client?

Removal of informed consent

A key question regarding the issue of informed consent was posed by Barlow and Durand (1995, p.675): "Are people with mental illness in need of help and protection from society, or is society in need of protection from them?" According to Barlow and Durand, the emphasis in the United States until about 1980 was on the rights and needs of the individual. Since about 1980, however, there has been an increasing emphasis on the needs of society. As a result, individuals in the United States have increasingly been required to have treatment and/or to be committed to mental hospitals against their will. In other words, some patients are not allowed to give their informed consent to treatment.

In the United Kingdom, the key provisions are currently contained in the Mental Health Act for England and Wales (1983). As MacLeod (1998) pointed out, Section 2 of this Act allows for compulsory admission and detention of patients for a period of up to 28 days, provided that this is recommended by an approved social worker and two doctors. The grounds for such detention are as follows:

• The patient is suffering from a mental illness that requires treatment.
• Detention is needed for the health and/or safety of the patient.
• Detention is needed for the protection of others.

Section 3 of the Mental Health Act of 1983 is concerned with renewable orders for compulsory treatment for up to six months. These orders can be obtained in the following circumstances:

• The patient is in need of treatment.
• The proposed treatment will probably be effective.
• The proposed treatment is necessary for the health and/or safety of the patient, or to protect others.
• The proposed treatment can only be provided if the patient is detained.

■ Research activity: Consider the case of a young man who has approached the police claiming that he is hearing voices which are instructing him to attack women. He is detained, following an examination by two doctors and the recommendation of a social worker. Consider some of the possible ways he might be assessed, under the Mental Health Act of 1983, in order to grant his release after 28 days?

Finally, Section 4 of this Act allows for emergency compulsory admission for 72 hours. This requires the recommendation of one approved social worker and one doctor.

Some of the criteria used in the various Sections of the Mental Health Act can be hard to use in practice. Account is supposed to be taken of the risks to the individual and to others if there is no detention, but it is not usually possible to assess these risks with any precision. This means that mistakes will inevitably be made, with some patients being detained unnecessarily and others not being detained when they should have been.

Confidentiality

Confidentiality is of basic importance in therapy. It is essential if the client is to trust the therapist, and so feel free to disclose intimate details or his or her life. The law ensures confidentiality in most circumstances. For example, the Police and Criminal Evidence Act (1984) contains within it the requirement that there must be an order signed by a judge before the authorities can consider trying to gain access to a client's confidential records.

MacLeod (1998) pointed out that absolute confidentiality is unusual. For example, cases are discussed with other therapists working in the same place (e.g. a National Health Service Trust). This is done to ensure that clients obtain the best possible treatment, and is not a matter for great concern. However, sensitive information about a patient is sometimes revealed to others *outside* the organisation for which the therapist works. Some examples are considered next.

Suppose that it emerges during therapy that the client is thinking of killing someone against whom he or she has a grudge. If the therapist believes this is a serious threat, then he or she is under an obligation to tell the relevant authorities, to ensure that the threat is not carried out. There are two sets of circumstances in which therapists in the United Kingdom have a legal obligation to disclose information about their clients to the relevant authorities. First, when the information is relevant to acts of terrorism. Second, when the information is of relevance to the welfare of children.

The situation is similar in the United States. The ethical position with respect to confidentiality was spelled out by the American Psychological Association (1991): "Psychologists disclose confidential information only as required by law, or where permitted by law, for a valid purpose such as: (1) to provide needed professional services to the patient or client, (2) to obtain appropriate professional consultations, (3) to protect the patient or client or others from harm, or (4) to obtain payment for services."

Ethical issues are raised by the existence of all these exceptions to the general rule of confidentiality. Wise (1978) surveyed therapists in California after legislation was passed requiring them to notify the authorities if their clients seemed to pose a danger to society. About 20% of the therapists indicated that this had led them to stop asking their clients about violence. This has the potential disadvantage that it might reduce the effectiveness of therapy.

> **Confidentiality and anonymity**
>
> Anonymity is an important part of confidentiality. The discussion of case notes at a public lecture or in a published article or book must not involve identifying the client. A breach of this aspect of confidentiality could result in the client or client's relatives taking legal action against the therapist concerned. In situations like these, and with the permission of those involved, clients are usually identified by pseudonyms or initials only.

Most clients initially expect that everything they disclose during the course of therapy will remain confidential. In fact, as we have seen, there are various circumstances in which confidential information from clients is revealed to other people. Clients should be told before the outset of treatment that confidentiality does not extend to everything they might say. In addition, the kinds of information that therapists would have to disclose to others should be made clear to them.

Choice of therapeutic goals

It is clearly desirable that the client should set the goals for therapy. At the very least, he or she should be fully involved with the therapist in determining suitable goals. Alexander and Luborsky (1984) argued that there should be a "therapeutic alliance", in which the therapist and the client co-operate in determining the goals of therapy and the ways in which those goals can best be achieved. Their evidence indicates that this leads to more effective treatment.

What are the essential requirements for a successful therapist–client relationship according to the psychodynamic approach? In what ways might these militate against the imposition of the therapist's values on his or her client?

In practice, there are various reasons why the client is often not fully involved in setting therapeutic goals. For example, young children or severely disturbed patients such as schizophrenics may be unable to become fully involved in the decision-making process. In such cases, a close relative should be consulted to ensure that the goals set for treatment are in the best interests of the client. Another example concerns many token economies within institutions. What often happens is that the institution decides what the therapeutic goals are going to be, and the individual patients have little or no choice in the matter.

The dangers associated with certain therapeutic goals need to be spelled out clearly to patients. For example, psychodynamic therapy is designed to provide patients with insight into the childhood experiences that underlie their current distress. However, such insight may involve bringing to light very disturbing memories (e.g. of physical or sexual abuse). There are also dangers if the retrieved memories are false (this is known as false memory syndrome). If the memories are false, then the parents of clients may be unjustly accused of having abused their children. Clients need to be aware of these potential dangers before accepting insight as a primary goal of therapy.

Davison and Neale (1996) pointed out that there are special problems in the case of therapy for couples or families. A form of therapy that benefits one person within a couple or family may have negative effects on their partner or other family members. For example, an individual may benefit from becoming more assertive, but this may disrupt the communication patterns within his or her family. In such cases, it may be very hard or impossible to choose goals for therapy that satisfy everyone involved.

Clients may be more influenced than they realise by the values and beliefs of their therapist. As a result, they may not be in a position to make up their own minds about the goals of therapy. This point was expressed forcefully by Halleck (1971, p.19):

> *A model of psychiatric practice based on the contention that people should just be helped to learn to do the things they want to do seems uncomplicated and desirable. But it is an unobtainable model. Unlike a technician, a psychiatrist cannot avoid communicating and at times imposing his own values upon his patients. The patient usually has considerable difficulty in finding the way in which he would wish to change his behaviour, but as he talks to the psychiatrist his wants and needs become clearer ... He ends up wanting some of the things the psychiatrist thinks he should want.*

Ethical issues: The use of medication to treat children who have been diagnosed with ADHD may be undertaken by obtaining parental consent. What ethical problems arise from this practice?

The behaviour of some patients is so disruptive or poses such dangers to others that therapeutic goals have to be set without obtaining their consent. How far should this go? Paul and Lentz (1977) argued that a distinction should be drawn between minimal goals (e.g. eating meals; not being violent) and optimal goals (e.g. acquiring work-related skills). It is sometimes ethically sound to set minimal goals of therapy without the consent of the client, but it is less defensible to set optimal goals in that way.

A final problem is that it may not be possible to achieve the goals that the therapist and client have set. Consider, for example, the use of aversion therapy to cure alcoholism. Most clients will agree to its use if they are convinced that it will not be too unpleasant and that it has a high probability of success. In fact, however, neither the therapist nor the client can predict accurately whether aversion therapy will succeed or whether the process of treatment will be unduly painful. This makes it hard to decide on the suitability of certain forms of treatment.

Dual relationships

Pope and Vetter (1992) asked therapists to identify ethical and other challenging issues they had had to deal with over the past year or two. Of the issues raised, 18% related to confidentiality, 17% to dual relationships, and 14% to payment. We will focus on the issue of dual relationships, which relates to the need for therapists not to have a personal relationship as well as a professional relationship with any of their clients.

The most damaging form of personal relationship involves sexual intimacy. It is far more common between male therapists and female clients than between female therapists and male clients. It is totally unacceptable, because clients with mental disorders can often be exploited by therapists who have more status than they have. Sexual contact between therapist and client is explicitly forbidden by nearly all professional therapy organisations, and it is a crime in many states in the USA. The 1993 Ethical Standards of Psychologists strongly recommend that therapists should not develop a personal or sexual relationship with their former clients. At the very least, they should not consider becoming romantically involved with any former client until at least two years after the end of treatment.

Cultural and subcultural factors

Sue et al. found that therapy sessions such as this might have greater effect if the therapist and client were from the same ethnic background.

Most therapists in Western societies are white and middle-class. As a result, white, middle-class clients may be in the best position to profit from therapy. Sue et al. (1991) argued that therapy might be more effective when there is ethnic and language matching, i.e. the therapist and the client are from the same ethnic background and have the same native language. They found in the United States that ethnic matching led to Asian Americans and Mexican Americans having lower dropout rates and attending more treatment sessions, but there were no effects of ethnic matching for African Americans. Clients may find self-disclosure harder with therapists from a different ethnic background.

Sue et al. also found that language matching was associated with better treatment outcome for all groups of non-English native speakers. The simplest explanation of this finding is obvious: communication is easier between people having the same native language.

In general terms, Sue et al. argued that treatment is most likely to be effective when therapists are sensitive to the values and expectations of their clients. Some of the relevant considerations they identified were summarised as follows by Davison and Neale (1996, pp.619–620):

Asians respect structure and formality in interpersonal relationships, whereas a Western therapist is likely to favour informality and a less authoritarian attitude ... the very acceptability of psychotherapy as a way to handle stress is likely to be much lower among Asian-Americans, who tend to see emotional distress as something to be handled on one's own and through willpower ... Asian-Americans may consider some areas off-limits for discussion with a therapist, for example, the nature of the marital relationship, and especially sex.

Discussion points

1. How important is it for therapists to be sensitive to cultural differences?
2. Is ethnic matching needed in order that all clients have the best chance of benefiting from therapy?

There is some evidence that the type of treatment that is given is affected by the cultural background of the clients. Bond, Dicandia, and MacKinnon (1988) compared white and black schizophrenic patients with similar symptoms in the USA. The white patients were less likely than the black patients to be physically restrained, and they were also less likely to receive high drug doses. There are various possible explanations of these findings, but they clearly raise ethical issues about the ways in which ethnic minorities are treated.

Evidence of cultural bias was reported by Nazroo (1997) in a study based on over 8000 Caribbeans, Asians, and whites in the UK. The rate of psychoses such as schizophrenia among Caribbean men was found to be no greater than among white men, even though they are about five times more likely to be hospitalised with such conditions. According to Nazroo, this happens because Caribbean men are assumed to be at higher risk of severe mental illness, and so are denied non-hospital options such as therapy.

Grant (1994) argued that special ethical issues are raised when white therapists treat black clients. The therapists may mistakenly believe that there are "black problems", or that they have a good understanding of the ways in which black people think. In either case, they may fail to respond to the particular problems and ways of thinking of the individual black patient they are treating.

What can be done to ensure that no group is disadvantaged in the treatment it receives? First, therapists need to be more sensitive to cultural issues, and to ensure that they develop the skills to provide effective treatment to all ethnic groups. Second, steps should be taken to increase the number of therapists from various minority ethnic groups. Third, there is **role preparation**, which involves using brief discussions or audiotaped information to ensure that clients have realistic expectations about therapy before it starts. Lambert and Lambert (1984) found that role preparation improved attendance at therapy sessions, and satisfaction with therapy, and led to more favourable outcomes.

KEY STUDY EVALUATION — Sue et al.

The abilities of therapists to empathise in a non-judgemental fashion and to offer unconditional support to their clients would appear to be compromised by a significant difference in cultural background between client and therapist. Sue et al.'s research demonstrates that this is likely to be attributable to the predominance of white middle-class therapists. The class element would appear to be more significant, as racial origin is not in itself a determinant of cultural values.

It seems obvious that for any therapist to be effective they must have the ability to communicate well with their client. This involves much more than the ability to converse in the same language. They must also have a thorough knowledge and understanding of their client's world view, which includes understanding of their cultural and class background.

One possible alternative to role preparation might be a provision for therapists to be counselled themselves by people from a variety of social and cultural backgrounds. As counselling is an important part of training in psychotherapy, this would be a good opportunity to develop the experience of new therapists, whatever their cultural background.

PERSONAL REFLECTIONS

- It is easy to get the impression that every therapist focuses narrowly on his or her preferred form of therapy. In fact, this is not at all the case. Most therapists believe in (and practise) **eclectism**, in which techniques taken from various forms of therapy are used as and when they seem to be appropriate.
- There have been major therapeutic advances in recent years, and so older meta-analyses like the one by Smith et al. (1980) have limited relevance now. For example, no effective forms of cognitive-behavioural therapy for the anxiety disorder of obsessive-compulsive disorder were developed until the early 1990s. This changed very rapidly, so that van Oppen et al. (1995) found that 39% of obsessive-compulsives recovered with cognitive-behaviour therapy, against only 17% with behaviour therapy in the form of exposure or flooding.

KEY TERMS
Role preparation: information given to clients to provide them with realistic expectations about the course and outcome of therapy.
Eclectism: an approach in which therapists make use of techniques drawn from various forms of therapy.

SUMMARY

Psychodynamic therapy

Psychodynamic forms of therapy are based on Freud's psychoanalysis. Freud argued that individuals with mental disorders have repressed threatening thoughts and feelings. Techniques such as hypnosis, free association, and dream analysis need to be used to produce insight into the client's problems and past experiences. Therapy often involves transference, with the client transferring strong emotions towards someone of major significance in his life onto the therapist. Psychoanalysis relies very much on the therapist's interpretations of what the client says, and these interpretations may be wrong. There has been controversy about the effectiveness of psychoanalysis, but it is generally accepted as reasonably effective.

Somatic therapy

This form of therapy involves direct manipulations of the client's physiological system. Electroconvulsive shock treatment (ECT) is often effective in the treatment of severe depression. However, it is not known how it works, and there can be side-effects (e.g. memory loss). Drugs such as monoamine oxidase inhibitors and tricyclics increase the supply of various neurotransmitters, and reduce depression in most depressed patients. Lithium reduces the occurrence of manic and depressed episodes in bipolar depressives. Anxiety disorders used to be treated by barbiturates until they were replaced by the benzodiazepines. The benzodiazepines are effective, but often have sedative effects. Drugs typically reduce the client's symptoms without resolving the underlying problems.

Humanistic therapy

Client-centred therapy was introduced by Rogers. It involves the therapist being unconditional in positive regard, genuine, and empathic in order to increase the client's self-esteem and to reduce the incongruence or discrepancy between his or her self-concept and ideal self. This form of therapy is used mostly with mild disorders.

Behaviour therapy

Behaviour therapy involves the use of classical and operant conditioning to change unwanted behaviour into something more desirable. Some of the main techniques are flooding, systematic desensitisation, aversion therapy, and the token economy. This form of therapy underestimates the importance of cognitive processes and structures.

Freud's original couch in his London house, which is now a museum.

Cognitive therapy involves changing or restructuring negative irrational beliefs and thoughts into more positive and rational ones. Its development owes much to the work of Ellis and Beck. Recently, cognitive therapy has evolved into cognitive-behavioural therapy, which includes elements of behaviour therapy. The central assumption is that the client's thinking and behaviour both need to change in order to produce the most beneficial effects.

Cognitive therapy

Problems arise from differences between therapists, from the difficulty of defining recovery, and from the existence of placebo effects. It is important to work out not only whether any given form of therapy is effective, but also why it is effective. One large-scale meta-analysis suggested that most forms of therapy are about equally effective, with clients being better off than 80% of controls in terms of recovery. However, other evidence indicates that each form of therapy is more effective with some disorders than with others. Many of the beneficial effects of therapy are due to common factors rather than specific factors.

Effectiveness of therapy

Therapy raises a number of ethical issues. Therapy is normally only carried out with the full informed consent of the client. However, the need to protect society means that there are numerous exceptions. Confidentiality and the avoidance of dual relationships are of great importance in therapy. The client should be fully involved in the choice of therapeutic goals, but their thinking may be unduly influenced by their therapist.

Ethical issues in therapy

FURTHER READING

There are several good textbooks in abnormal psychology that cover the main therapeutic approaches. They include P.C. Kendall and C. Hammen (1998), *Abnormal psychology: Understanding human problems (2nd Edn.)*, Boston: Houghton Mifflin; D.H. Barlow and V.M. Durand (1995), *Abnormal psychology: An integrative approach*, New York: Brooks/Cole; and R.P. Halgin and S.K. Whitbourne (1997), *Abnormal psychology: The human experience of psychological disorders*, Madison, WI: Brown & Benchmark.

REVISION QUESTIONS

1   Discuss the relative effectiveness of behaviour therapies and humanistic therapies.   (24 marks)

2   Critically consider how psychologists assess the appropriateness of alternative types of treatment therapies for psychological disorders.   (24 marks)

3   Critically consider ethical issues involved in alternative types of therapies/treatments for psychological disorders.   (24 marks)

27

Individual Differences

In our everyday lives, we immediately notice that people are very different from each other. Some are nearly always lively and cheerful, whereas others tend to be gloomy and pessimistic. In addition, some people seem to be very quick thinkers, whereas others think more slowly. There are important individual differences in intelligence and personality, both of which are discussed in this chapter.

We can approach intelligence and personality from a number of perspectives. The main perspective considered here focuses on how we should assess intelligence and personality. **Psychometrics** has been defined as "the field of psychology that is concerned with mental testing and measurement" (Zimbardo et al., 1995), and so we will be focusing on psychometric testing. It is useful to consider psychometric testing from the perspective of the theoretical approaches that have led to the development of specific psychometric tests. Accordingly, some relevant theories will be discussed.

Intelligence Testing

In the 1920s, it was argued that intelligence is what is measured by intelligence tests. However, that is a superficial definition. A more contemporary definition was offered by Sternberg (1985, p.45):

Mental activity directed toward purposive adaptation to, and selection and shaping of, real-world environments relevant to one's life.

The first proper intelligence test was devised by the Frenchman Alfred Binet. At the start of the twentieth century, he devised an intelligence test to allow mentally retarded children to be identified, so they could be given special educational facilities. In 1905, Binet and his associate Simon produced a wide range of tests measuring comprehension, memory, and other cognitive processes. This led to numerous later tests. Among the best known of such tests are the Stanford–Binet test produced at Stanford University in 1916, the Wechsler Intelligence Scale for Children, and, in the 1970s, the British Ability Scales.

These, and other, tests measure several aspects of intelligence. Many contain vocabulary tests in which individuals are asked to define the meanings of words. Tests often also include problems based on analogies (e.g. "Hat is to head as shoe is to ___"), and tests of spatial ability (e.g. "If I start walking northwards, then turn left, and then turn left again, what direction will I be facing?"). They also include vocabulary tests to assess an individual's level of verbal ability.

All the major intelligence tests share key similarities. They have manuals that spell out how the test should be administered. This is important, because the wording of the instructions often affects the tested person's score. The major tests are also alike in that they

KEY TERM
Psychometrics: measurement of psychological characteristics (e.g. personality; intelligence) by means of tests.

737

are **standardised tests**. Standardisation of a test involves giving it to large, representative samples of the age groups for which the test is intended. The meaning of an individual's score can then be evaluated by comparing it against the scores of other people.

It is possible with most standardised tests to obtain several measures of an individual's performance. These measures are mostly of a fairly specific nature (e.g. arithmetic ability or spatial ability). However, the best-known measure is the very general IQ or **intelligence quotient**. This reflects performance on all of the sub-tests contained in an intelligence test, and is thus regarded as an overall measure of intellectual ability.

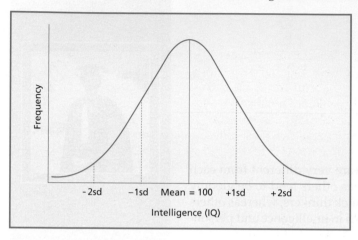

How is the IQ calculated? An individual's test performance is compared against the scores obtained by other children of his or her age or by other adults in the standardisation sample. Most intelligence tests are devised so that the overall scores are normally distributed: we do not know what the "real" distribution of intelligence looks like. The normal distribution is a bell-shaped curve in which there are as many scores above the mean as below it. Most scores cluster fairly close to the mean, and there are fewer and fewer scores as you move away from it. The spread of scores in a normal distribution is usually indicated by a statistic known as the standard deviation. In a normal distribution, 68% of the scores fall within one standard deviation of the mean or average, and 95% fall within two standard deviations.

Intelligence tests have a mean of 100 and a standard deviation of about 16. Thus, an IQ of 116 is one standard deviation above the mean, and indicates that the individual is more intelligent than 84% of the population. That is because 50% fall below the mean, and a further 34% between the mean and one standard deviation above it.

Those with high IQs do not usually perform well on all of the tests within an intelligence-test battery, nor do those with low IQs perform poorly on every test. As a result, tests are usually constructed to obtain measures of various abilities (e.g. numerical; spatial; reasoning; perceptual speed). We can obtain a more accurate assessment of an individual's intelligence by considering the profile of his or her performance across these abilities than by focusing only on IQ.

Reliability and validity

Good intelligence tests have high reliability and validity. **Reliability** refers to the extent to which a test provides consistent findings, and **validity** refers to the extent to which a test measures what it is supposed to be measuring. These two requirements will be considered in turn.

Reliability

Suppose that someone obtained an IQ of 125 when taking an intelligence test on one occasion, but an IQ of 95 when re-taking the same test a short time later. If that happened, the test would clearly be unreliable, and could not be an adequate measure of something as relatively unchanging as intelligence.

Reliability is generally assessed by means of the test–retest method. A group of people take the same test on two separate occasions. Their scores on the two occasions are then correlated with each other. The higher the correlation (a measure of the relationship between the two scores), the greater is the reliability of the test. This method has the drawback that when participants are given the test for the second time, they may remember some of the answers they gave on the first administration. This can produce a high reliability coefficient for the wrong reason. In addition, there can be practice effects from taking an intelligence test with which the participants are already familiar.

Most standard intelligence tests have good reliability. Reliability correlation coefficients tend to be about +0.85 to +0.90. This is not far short of perfect reliability, which would be represented by a correlation coefficient of +1.0.

How might you overcome practice effects when people take the same test on two separate occasions?

Validity

There are three main ways of trying to assess the validity of an intelligence test:

1. Content validity:
   - Face.
   - Factorial.
2. Empirical validity.
   - Predictive.
   - Concurrent.
3. Test validity.

Content validity involves considering the types of items contained in a test. There are two kinds of content validity, known as face validity and factorial validity. Face validity simply concerns whether or not the content of the test seems to be relevant. For example, a test of mathematical ability that included a vocabulary test would have rather low face validity. Factorial validity is more complex. First, a statistical technique known as factor analysis (described on page 750) is used to work out the number and nature of the different abilities or factors contained within a test. If all of the items dealing with mathematics form a factor that differs from the factors formed from the other items in the test, then it is argued that these items measure mathematical ability.

The most direct approach to validity is known as **empirical validity**. The basic idea is that we would expect highly intelligent people to be more likely than less intelligent ones to achieve certain criteria, such as doing well at school. Performance on an intelligence test is correlated with whatever criterion has been selected. Predictive validity is involved if the criterion measure is obtained after the test has been given, whereas concurrent validity is involved if information about the criterion is available at the time the test is given. Nearly all the criteria that have been used are influenced by other factors apart from intelligence. For example, academic success at school depends in part on intellectual ability. However, it also depends on motivation, amount of parental encouragement, and so on. In practice, intelligence test scores usually correlate about +0.5 with school or college performance, indicating that there is a fairly good relationship between the two measures.

In what circumstances might it be useful to use predictive validity?

Test validity involves correlating scores on a new intelligence test with one or more well-established tests. If a well-established test has good reliability and validity, then a new test which correlates highly with that test is also likely to be a valid measuring instrument.

In sum, intelligence tests possess reasonable validity. For example, intelligence has consistently been found to correlate about +0.3 with job success (Ghiselli, 1966). However, the validity of intelligence tests is considerably lower than their reliability.

Controversies in intelligence testing

Several million intelligence tests have been completed by individuals all round the world. Intelligence tests were used many years ago in the United Kingdom as part of the selection process for entry into grammar school at the age of 11. This was controversial. Those children who did not gain entry into grammar school often regarded themselves as "failures". They went to secondary modern schools, where there was less emphasis on academic abilities. Intelligence tests have also been used to select students at some British universities.

Nowadays, the main use of intelligence tests is in personnel selection, which involves trying to select the best person for a job. Intelligence tests are often used in combination with other tests, biographical data, and interviews in the selection process. There are several controversies associated with the use of intelligence tests. Some of the main ones are discussed next.

Breadth of measurement

The first controversy is whether intelligence tests actually measure intelligence. Most intelligence tests only measure limited aspects of intelligence. They usually measure

Gardner's seven intelligences

Logical-mathematical

Spatial

Musical

Bodily-kinaesthetic

Linguistic

Intrapersonal

Interpersonal

thinking, reasoning, and problem-solving ability, but do not assess practical intelligence, such as the skills associated with being "street-wise".

Multiple intelligences

Howard Gardner (1983) argued strongly in favour of a broader assessment of intelligence. He argued that there are seven separate intelligences. An intelligence in Gardner's terms was defined as "an ability or set of abilities that permits an individual to solve problems or fashion products that are of consequence in a particular cultural setting" (Walters & Gardner, 1986, p.165). Gardner's seven intelligences were as follows:

1. Logical-mathematical intelligence: this is of special value in handling abstract problems of a logical or mathematical nature.

2. Spatial intelligence: this is used when deciding how to go from one place to another, how to arrange suitcases in the boot of a car, and so on.

3. Musical intelligence: this is used both for active musical processes such as playing an instrument or singing, and for more passive processes such as appreciating the music one hears.

4. Bodily-kinaesthetic intelligence: this is involved in the fine control of bodily movements in activities such as sport, ballet, and dancing.

5. Linguistic intelligence: this is involved in language activities on both the input (reading and listening) and the output (writing and speaking) sides.

6. Intrapersonal intelligence: this is concerned with sensitivity to one's own abilities and emotional states.

7. Interpersonal intelligence: this is involved in interacting with other people; it includes communication with, and understanding of, others.

Gardner's theory of multiple intelligences seems to have major implications for intelligence testing. Most standard intelligence tests contain items relating to linguistic, logical-mathematical, and spatial intelligence. However, they do not assess musical, bodily-kinaesthetic, interpersonal, or intrapersonal intelligence. If one accepts Gardner's theoretical position, then nearly all existing intelligence tests are woefully inadequate. However, the seven intelligences are not equally important. Deficiencies in linguistic, logical-mathematical, spatial, or interpersonal intelligence all have serious consequences for everyday life, but it is less clear that the same is true of musical or bodily-kinaesthetic intelligence. Someone can have very low musical and bodily-kinaesthetic intelligence (i.e. be tone-deaf and poorly co-ordinated) without it having any great effects on his or her ability to function effectively in most societies.

Discussion points

1. Do you agree with Gardner that there are seven intelligences?

2. Which of his seven intelligences do you think are the most and the least important?

Value of the concept of "intelligence"

The second controversial issue concerns the concept of "intelligence". According to Howe (1990, p.599):

> For the important task of helping to discover the underlying causes of differing levels of performance, there is no convincing evidence that the concept of intelligence can play a major role.

Howe argued that statements such as "Tom is better at solving most kinds of problems than John because he is more intelligent", merely describe a state of affairs without explaining it.

Kline (1991) pointed out that tests of intelligence are fairly successful in predicting how well different individuals will do in their future study of subjects about which they know nothing at the time of testing. Such successful predictions do not simply provide redundant descriptions of behaviour, as Howe argued.

The value of the concept of intelligence can also be seen if we consider an imaginary situation in which two new companies are set up. One company recruits only those with IQs of 130 and above, and the other company recruits only those with IQs of 70 and below. If intelligence does not exist, then presumably the two companies would be equally likely to succeed. In fact, the evidence from occupational psychology makes it clear that the prospects would be much brighter for the former company, because intelligence is a factor in real-world success.

Heredity versus environment

The third controversial issue concerns the relative importance of heredity and environment in determining individual differences in intelligence.

Some psychologists argue that the issue is meaningless. Donald Hebb argued that asking whether intelligence is determined more by heredity or by environment is like asking whether the area of a field is determined more by its length or by its width: both are absolutely crucial. However, we can still ask whether the differences in the areas of several fields are due more to their different lengths or their different widths. For example, if 10 fields have very similar widths but widely varying lengths, then clearly the differences in their areas depend much more on length than on width. If we apply that logic to intelligence, it makes sense to ask whether individual differences in intelligence occur mainly because these individuals differ in heredity or because they differ in their experiences or environment.

One of the initial problems is that experimental control is lacking. We cannot ethically manipulate heredity by a breeding programme, nor can we achieve much control over the environment in which children develop (however, see Chapter 23). In addition, we cannot assess accurately an individual's genetic potential (known as the **genotype**). All that we can measure directly are the observable characteristics (known as the **phenotype**). There is also no agreement regarding which aspects of the environment are most important for the development of intelligence. Finally, intelligence or IQ is assessed from standard intelligence tests, but they may not be good measures of intelligence.

With reference to child development, what factors have been put forward that could enhance a child's cognitive development? Could these factors influence a child's intelligence-test performance?

Studies of families

In spite of the problems, much useful information has been obtained from studying twins. Identical or **monozygotic twins** derive from the same fertilised ovum, and so have essentially identical genotypes. In contrast, fraternal or **dizygotic twins** derive from two different fertilised ova, and so their genotypes are no more similar than those of two ordinary siblings. If heredity influences intelligence, then we would expect to find that identical twins are more alike in intelligence than are fraternal twins.

In their review of 111 studies, Bouchard and McGue (1981) reported that the mean correlation for identical twins was +0.86, and it was +0.60 for fraternal twins. Thus, identical twins are more similar in intelligence than are fraternal twins, and this suggests that heredity plays a part in determining individual differences in intelligence. However, the environment is generally more similar for identical twins than for fraternal twins (Loehlin & Nichols, 1976; see Chapter 16).

KEY TERMS

Genotype: an individual's genetic potential.

Phenotype: an individual's observable characteristics, which depend on his or her genotype plus experiences.

Monozygotic twins: identical twins derived from the same fertilised ovum.

Dizygotic twins: fraternal twins derived from two fertilised ova.

742 Chapter 27 • Individual Differences

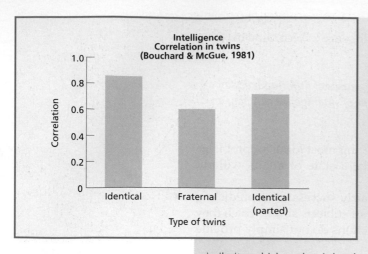

Additional evidence is available from identical twins reared apart. Such twins are very important, because (at least in principle) we have a clear distinction between very similar heredity within each pair, but a relatively dissimilar environment. According to Bouchard and McGue (1981), the mean correlation for identical twins brought up apart was +0.72. This also suggests that heredity is involved in producing individual differences in intelligence. However, at least some of the pairs of identical twins were brought up in fairly similar environments, so some of their similarity in intelligence may be due to the environment rather than to heredity.

Below are the correlations indicating the similarity of IQ between different groups of relatives. In general terms, relatives who have greater genetic similarity tend to be more similar in IQ. However, relatives having greater genetic similarity tend to live in more similar environments than those with less genetic similarity, which makes it hard to interpret the findings. As Bouchard and McGue (1981) concluded, "Most of the results of studies of family resemblance ... can be interpreted as either supporting the genetic or the environmentalist theory."

Relationship	Mean correlation
Siblings reared apart	+0.24
Siblings reared together	+0.47
Single parent—offspring reared apart	+0.22
Single parent—offspring reared together	+0.42
Half-siblings	+0.31
Cousins	+0.15
Adopted parent—offspring	+0.19

Discussion points

1. How convincing is the evidence reviewed by Bouchard and McGue for the notion that heredity plays an important role in determining individual differences in intelligence?

2. Most of the correlations reported by Bouchard and McGue were based on studies in a small number of Western cultures. Would the same findings be obtained in other cultures (see below)?

Why might a family's financial status make a difference to a child's intelligence-test performance?

Adoption studies provide another way of assessing the relative importance of heredity and environment in determining individual differences in intelligence. If heredity is more important than environment, then the correlation of the children's IQs with those of their biological parents will be greater than that with their adoptive parents. However, the opposite pattern will be found if environment is more important. Capron and Duyne (1989) reported a study on adopted children. The socio-economic status of the biological parents had a substantial impact on the adopted children's IQs, and the same was true of the socio-economic status of the adoptive parents. Favourable heredity or favourable environment both led to significant increases in the children's level of intelligence, and the effects of heredity and environment were of about the same importance.

In sum, heredity and environment both play a major role in determining intelligence. About 50% of individual differences in intelligence are due to heredity, and about 50% to environmental influences. However, these percentages have emerged from research in the United States and Western Europe. There is probably greater uniformity of environment in such societies than in some other, non-Western societies. If that is true, then the role of environment in determining intelligence would be greater in those non-Western societies. The role of heredity in producing individual differences in intelligence is greater when individuals experience similar environments than when they experience dissimilar ones. If everyone experienced exactly the same environment, then all *individual differences* in intelligence would have to be due to heredity!

Group differences

The fourth controversial issue relates to group differences in intelligence-test performance. There has been great political controversy about the fact that the mean difference in IQ between white people and black people in the United States is about 15 points. This is an average figure, and it should be noted that about 20% of black people have a higher IQ than that of the average white person. Most psychologists have assumed that the difference between white people and black people is due to the environmental deprivation suffered by black people. However, Jensen (1969) and H.J. Eysenck (1981) argued that genetic differences might be involved, which led to accusations of racism.

The first point to make about this controversial issue is that it is of very little scientific interest, in that it is unlikely to tell us anything about the processes involved in human intelligence. This makes it strange that so much time and money have been spent in studying this issue.

When groups of white and West Indian children were matched for levels of environmental deprivation, only very small differences in intelligence were found.

The second point is that the issue is meaningless in some ways, because it is based on the incorrect assumption that whites and blacks form separate biological groups. Indeed, the whole notion of "race" has been questioned, and seems to have no precise scientific definition.

The third point is that we cannot carry out definitive research on this issue. We cannot measure accurately the levels of deprivation experienced by black people, nor can we compare the genetic endowment of white people and black people. Even H.J. Eysenck (1981, p.79) admitted that the issue cannot be resolved by experimental evidence: "Can we ... argue that genetic studies ... give direct support to the hereditarian position? The answer must, I think, be in the negative. The two populations (black and white) are separate populations, and none of the studies carried out on whites alone, such as twin studies are feasible."

A major reason why black people perform less well than white people on intelligence tests is because of environmental deprivation. Mackintosh (1986) compared white and West Indian children in England. Some of the children were matched for father's job, number of brothers and sisters, family income, and other measures relevant to deprivation, whereas the others were unmatched. In one study, there was a 9-point difference between unmatched groups, but only a 2.6-point difference in the matched groups. Thus, there were very small differences in intelligence between the two groups when the two groups were equated for the level of deprivation.

In sum, deprivation accounts for most (or all) of the differences in measured intelligence between black people and white people. However, the issue is in some ways a meaningless one. In addition, such research poses major ethical issues. Extreme groups, such as the National Front, have used the findings to promote racial disharmony, which is totally unacceptable. Many working in this area have been insensitive to the dangerous political uses to which their research was likely to be put, and it is an issue that would have been better left unexplored.

Racial and cultural bias

Nearly all intelligence tests have been devised by white, middle-class psychologists. We might assume that black people brought up in a very different culture would be disadvantaged by this cultural divide when taking an intelligence test. In similar fashion, members of minority groups might also be disadvantaged when confronted by standard intelligence tests. This issue is important. Legislation designed to ensure equal opportunities for everyone has been passed in Britain, the United States, and numerous other countries. If intelligence tests are biased against certain groups, then there is a real danger that people's rights to have equal opportunities are being infringed.

How should we proceed? According to Sternberg (1994, p.595):

> We need to take into account culture in considering both the nature and the assessment of intelligence. Simply translating a test from one language to another scarcely constitutes doing so. Rather, we need to be sensitive to cultural differences that may artificially inflate the scores of one group over another due to the kinds of materials or tasks used to measure intelligence.

■ Research activity: Design a sample of an IQ test that is not biased towards or against any race, culture, or group (e.g. using shapes).

One way to do this is to construct what are known as "culture-fair" tests, which consist mainly of abstract and non-verbal items that should not be more familiar to members of one group than another. However, such culture-fair tests tend to produce larger differences in intelligence across cultural groups than are found when conventional verbal tests of intelligence are used (Sternberg, 1994)!

There is only limited support for the notion that intelligence tests show racial and cultural bias. The Stanford–Binet intelligence test was translated into what is known as "Black English" (the English dialect spoken by many black Americans). It was then given to black children by black testers. The tested intelligence of the black children was about the same as when the test was given in its standard form (Quay, 1971). However, rather different findings were obtained with the Black Intelligence Test of Cultural Homogeneity (BITCH), which was designed for black Americans. White American children did no better than black American children on this test, and sometimes performed worse (Williams, 1972).

Personality Testing

A definition that captures much of what psychologists mean by **personality** was provided by Child (1968, p.83). He described it as

> more or less stable, internal factors that make one person's behaviour consistent from one time to another, and different from the behaviour other people would manifest in comparable situations.

As Hampson (1988) pointed out, the four key words in Child's definition are "stable", "internal", "consistent", and "different". According to Child's perspective, personality is relatively stable or unchanging over time; moods or emotional states may change dramatically over shortish periods of time, but personality does not; personality is internal, and must not be equated with external behaviour; behaviour (e.g. restlessness; lack of eye contact) is relevant, but only because it allows us to draw inferences about someone's underlying personality. If personality is moderately stable over time, and if personality determines behaviour, then it should follow that individuals will behave in a reasonably consistent fashion on different occasions. Finally, there are individual differences in personality, and these differences are revealed by different ways of behaving in a given situation. For example, extraverted people will talk more than introverted ones in a social group.

Types of test

Four major kinds of tests have been developed for the task of assessing personality:

KEY TERM

Personality: semi-permanent internal predispositions that make people behave consistently, but in ways that differ from those of other people.

1. Questionnaires.
2. Ratings.
3. Objective tests.
4. Projective tests.

Questionnaires

The most common way of assessing personality is by means of **self-report questionnaires**. This method requires people to decide whether various statements about their thoughts, feelings, and behaviour are true. Sample questions are as follows: Do you tend to be moody? Do you have many friends? Do you like to be involved in numerous social activities? The questionnaire approach is easy to administer. It also has the advantage that the individual presumably knows more about himself or herself than do other people. Self-report questionnaires are used by trait theorists such as Cattell and H.J. Eysenck.

Ratings

The second form of personality assessment is by **ratings**, in which observers produce ratings of other people's behaviour. Typically, the raters are given a list of different kinds of behaviour (e.g. "initiates conversations"), and they then rate their ratees (i.e. those being rated) on those aspects of behaviour. The more different situations in which the raters observe the ratees, the more accurate their ratings are likely to be.

Objective tests

The third form of personality assessment involves the use of **objective tests**. More than 400 objective tests exist. They measure behaviour under laboratory conditions so that the participants do not know what the experimenter is looking for. For example, asking participants to blow up a balloon until it bursts is a measure of timidity, and the extent to which people sway when standing on tiptoe is a measure of anxiety.

Projective tests

The fourth form of personality assessment is by **projective tests**. Participants are given a rather unstructured task to perform, such as making up a story to fit a picture or describing what can be seen in an inkblot. The underlying rationale of projective tests is that people confronted by such unstructured tasks will reveal their innermost selves. Many of those who use projective tests favour the psychodynamic psychological approach.

Reliability and validity

Any useful method of personality assessment needs to be standardised on large representative samples. It also needs to have high reliability (consistency of measurement) and validity (measuring what it claims to measure).

Reliability

As with intelligence tests, the most common way of assessing reliability is by the test–retest method, in which a personality test is given to the same people on two occasions, and the scores are correlated. The test–retest reliability for major questionnaires such as Cattell's 16PF (Personality Factor) test and the Eysenck Personality Questionnaire is about +0.80 or +0.85, provided that there is a short interval between test and retest. Reliability is much lower when there is an interval of several years between successive administrations of a personality test.

What about the reliability of other forms of personality assessment? The reliability of ratings is generally about as high as for questionnaires. However, the reliability of projective tests and objective tests is low (Eysenck, 1994a). The best-known projective tests are the Rorschach Inkblot Test, introduced by the Swiss psychologist Hermann Rorschach in 1921, and the Thematic Apperception Test developed by Henry Murray (Morgan & Murray, 1935). The standard form of the Rorschach test involves presenting 10 inkblots. The participants are asked to suggest what each inkblot might represent, and to indicate which part of the inkblot formed the basis of their response. The main emphasis with the Thematic Apperception Test is on content. The participants are presented with various pictures, and asked to say what is happening, what led up to the situation depicted, and what will happen next. These stories are interpreted in a flexible way, taking the individual's case history into account. The goal is to identify the participant's underlying motives and conflicts.

An example of a Rorschach inkblot.

Why are the Rorschach test and the Thematic Apperception Test unreliable? The unstructured nature of these tests encourages the participants to respond to them rather differently on each occasion. In addition, the participants' responses are interpreted subjectively.

Validity

Only tests that are reliable can be valid. Thus, we would not expect projective or objective tests to be valid, and that is what the evidence indicates (Eysenck, 1994a). That leaves questionnaires and ratings. One way of deciding whether they are measuring what they are claimed to measure is by assessing **consensual validity**. We need to have self-report questionnaire responses for a given aspect of personality, together with ratings on those individuals from observers (e.g. friends) for the same aspect of personality. This approach is based on the assumption that the inadequacies of self-report questionnaires and of ratings are different. Self-report questionnaires have the disadvantage that people may provide too favourable an impression of themselves, whereas ratings have the disadvantage that the rater may have limited information about the person being rated.

McCrae (1982) looked at consensual validity. Self-reported extraversion and ratings of extraversion correlated +0.72, and self-reported neuroticism (a measure of anxiety and tension) correlated +0.47 with ratings. The correlation was probably higher for extraversion than for neuroticism because it is a more observable personality characteristic.

Another form of validity is empirical validity (described on page 739), which involves relating the scores on a test to some relevant external criterion. For example, Spielberger's State–Trait Anxiety Inventory measures trait anxiety, which is the tendency to experience considerable anxiety. Eysenck et al. (1991) showed that the test has empirical validity when they found that patients diagnosed with generalised anxiety disorder had much higher trait-anxiety scores than most other people.

People diagnosed with generalised anxiety disorder often score highly on Spielberger's State–Trait Anxiety Inventory

Controversies in personality testing

The most widely used forms of personality assessment are self-report questionnaires such as Cattell's 16PF (Personality Factor) and the Eysenck Personality Questionnaire. Some of the major controversies associated with this form of personality testing will be considered next.

Personality dimensions

Personality dimensions such as extraversion are at one end of a continuum, with their opposite at the other end. Personality testing does not simply determine that a person is either extraverted or introverted, but places them at the relevant point on the continuum, showing their degree of extraversion/ introversion, as in the diagram below. This person is more extraverted than introverted.

```
       1  2  3  4  5  6  7  8  9  10
EXTRAVERSION....................●.................INTROVERSION
(Social, outgoing, active)          (Unsocial, quiet, passive)
```

Nomothetic or idiographic?

Psychologists who make use of self-report questionnaires claim that everyone can be placed at some point on each of a set of personality dimensions (e.g. extraversion). This is an example of the **nomothetic approach**, according to which psychology is a science that seeks general laws of human behaviour. Allport (1937) argued that each individual is absolutely unique, and that this uniqueness is ignored when the same personality test is given to large groups of people. He favoured what he called the **idiographic approach**, within which the uniqueness of every individual is emphasised. The way to understand an individual and his or her personality is to study that person in detail over a longish period of time.

A case study reported by Allport (1965) illustrates the idiographic approach. He made use of about 300 letters written by a woman called "Jenny" over a period of several years. Detailed examination of these letters revealed the existence of various recurrent major themes, and allowed Allport to form an impression of Jenny's personality.

Idiographic psychologists may have drawn the wrong conclusion from the uniqueness of human personality. If everyone is unique, then people differ from each other in several ways. However, the existence of differences implies similarities. For example, two people may be similar in terms of how extraverted they are, but differ a lot in their anxiety levels. As Guilford (1936, p.675) pointed out, many psychologists "seem unable to see that one individual can differ quantitatively [in amount] from another in many variables, common variables though they may be, and still have a unique personality." In other words, uniqueness can be handled within a scientific approach to individual differences based on psychometric testing.

A strict application of the idiographic approach implies that each person has his or her own unique personality characteristics or traits. As Brody (1988, p.110) pointed out, this leads to a ludicrous position:

> If the trait applies to only one person, then it cannot be described in terms that apply to more than one person. This would require one to invent a new language to describe each person.

Distorted responding

Various problems beset most personality tests. For example, someone completing a personality test can fake his or her responses. Faking most often takes the form of social desirability response set, which is the tendency to respond to questionnaire items in the socially desirable way. Thus, for example, the socially desirable answer to the question "Do you tend to be moody?" is clearly "no" rather than "yes".

One way of dealing with social desirability effects is to try to detect their existence by means of a lie scale. Lie scales usually consist of items where the socially desirable answer is rather unlikely to be the true answer (e.g. "Do you ever gossip?"; "Do you always keep your promises?"). If someone answers most of the questions in the socially desirable direction, it is assumed they are faking their responses. Of course, this is unfair on the small minority of genuinely saintly people in the population!

In what situations might people be inclined to fake their responses?

Another problem with questionnaire assessment of personality is known as acquiescence response set. This is the tendency to answer "yes" to all items regardless of their content. Acquiescence response set can be assessed by selecting the items carefully. If, for example, we want to measure trait anxiety, then half the items can be written so that a "yes" answer indicates high anxiety, with the rest being written so that a "no" answer indicates high anxiety. Anyone who consistently answers "yes" to both sets of items is showing acquiescence response set.

How many personality traits?

If you were to look through some of the hundreds of personality tests that have been developed, you might be surprised at the differences among them. The most obvious difference is in the number of personality traits that are measured. At one extreme, the Eysenck Personality Questionnaire assesses only three personality dimensions, whereas Cattell's 16PF test assesses sixteen dimensions. The fact that personality theorists could not agree on the number or the nature of the main personality traits used to be a source of controversy. It suggested that psychometric testing could not be used to identify the structure of personality in a clear way.

In recent years, there has been much progress in personality testing. There is now fairly general agreement that there are five major personality traits (known as the Big Five). The names of the factors differ from one personality theorist to another, but generally resemble the following factors identified by McCrae and Costa (1985):

1. Extraversion.
2. Agreeableness.
3. Conscientiousness.
4. Neuroticism.
5. Openness.

This issue is discussed in more detail later on pages 753–754.

Importance of personality?

Those who use personality tests assume that the scores obtained can be used to *predict* how individuals will behave in numerous situations. For example, it is assumed that someone who has an extraverted personality will behave in an extraverted way in numerous situations. In other words, it is assumed that there is **cross-situational consistency**, i.e. any given individual will behave in a consistent way in different situations. Mischel (1968) argued that people exhibit little cross-situational consistency. He reviewed studies in which people's personality scores were correlated with their behaviour. Such correlations rarely exceeded about +0.30, indicating that we cannot predict someone's behaviour very well from their scores on a personality test. Mischel drew the conclusion that the ways in which people behave are determined by the situation and by their specific experiences, rather than by their personality.

If Mischel (1968) is right, then personality tests are of limited value. However, cross-situational consistency is not always low. For example, Small, Zeldin, and Savin-Williams (1983) obtained various measures of dominance and pro-social or co-operative behaviour from four groups of adolescents in various situations on camping trips. Correlations were worked out across pairs of situations separately for dominance and pro-social behaviour for each group. Every correlation was greater than +0.30, and the great majority exceeded +0.70.

The issue of cross-situational consistency is closely related to the *person–situation controversy*. This concerns the relative importance of the individual (and his or her personality) and the situation in determining how he or she will respond in any given situation. If behaviour is determined by the individual (as is assumed by those who use personality tests), then high cross-situational consistency is to be expected. On the other hand, if behaviour is determined mainly by the situation, then the expectation is that cross-situational consistency will be low. Buss (1989a) argued that the relative importance of the situation and of personality depends on key aspects of the situation. Behaviour is largely determined by the situation when the situation is novel, formal, and public, when individuals have little choice of behaviour, and when the situation is short-lived. Examples are stopping your car at a red light and behaving respectfully in church. On the other hand, personality largely determines behaviour when the situation is familiar, informal, and private, when there is much choice of behaviour, and when the situation is long-lasting.

Novel, formal, and public situations

Familiar, informal, and private situations

Sarason, Smith, and Diener (1975) reviewed evidence on the person–situation controversy from 138 experiments. They worked out the average impact of personality and of the situation on participants' behaviour. Personality and the situation were both important factors, but the situation had slightly more impact on behaviour. These findings indicate that personality tests can help to predict how individuals will behave.

Predicting job performance

Blinkhorn and Johnson (1990) were interested in the issue of whether personality tests can predict job performance. They focused on three of the main personality tests used in occupational settings: the California Psychological Inventory; Cattell's 16PF; and the Occupational Personality Questionnaire. They found that these tests were not very effective at predicting job performance. This led Blinkhorn and Johnson (1990, p.672) to the following conclusion: "We see precious little evidence that even the best personality tests predict job performance, and a good deal of evidence of poorly understood statistical methods being pressed into service to buttress shaky claims. If this is so for the most reputable tests in the hands of specialists, one may imagine what travesties are committed further down market."

More promising findings have been reported by others. Hough et al. (1990) gave a personality inventory called the Assessment of Background and Life Experiences to soldiers. Hough et al. (1990, p.594) argued on the basis of their findings that personality tests can be very useful in predicting job performance, provided that the following steps are taken: "(a) use response validity scales [such as lie scales] to detect potentially inaccurate self-descriptions; (b) warn applicants that inaccurate descriptions will be detected; and (c) use additional or other information to make employment decisions about those persons who are identified as providing inaccurate self-descriptions."

The findings of Hough et al. are encouraging. However, the concerns raised by Blinkhorn and Johnson do apply to many uses of personality tests at work. Of particular concern, personality tests are increasingly used in personnel selection, that is, deciding who is the most suitable applicant for a job. At present, most of the tests that are used are not adequate. There is a real danger that highly suitable applicants are failing to obtain jobs they deserve because they are mistakenly thought to have the "wrong" personality. There is an urgent need to ensure that only the most reliable and valid tests are used in personnel selection.

Discussion points

1. Many personality tests seem to provide good measures of personality, but they often fail to predict job performance very well. Why do you think that is so?

2. How much does it matter if personality tests having low reliability and validity are used in personnel selection?

Conclusions

First, even though the predictive power of personality tests tends to be rather low, there are consistent findings. In particular, personality dimensions relating to motivation (e.g. achievement motivation; conscientiousness) are reliably related to job success. Second, it is very much in the interests of companies to select the best job applicants. Personality testing can play an important role in that selection process, as mistakes can be very costly. Third, numerous personality tests have proved successful at predicting job satisfaction. Job satisfaction is important both to the individual worker and to the cohesiveness of the work groups to which workers belong. For example, there is generally a correlation of about –0.3 to –0.4 between neuroticism or trait anxiety and job satisfaction (Brief et al., 1991). However, this is only correlational evidence, and it is possible that those high in trait anxiety or neuroticism have more stressful or demanding jobs. Fourth, inadequate tests are often used in personnel selection, and this is probably depriving excellent applicants of jobs they deserve.

Different jobs suit different people. In the highly stressful work atmosphere of the stock exchange an introverted, nervous person with low confidence in his or her judgement and decision making would be unlikely to succeed or to be happy.

Trait Theories of Personality

Personality theorists argue that personality consists of a number of **traits**, which are broad, semi-permanent, and stable internal characteristics used to explain behaviour. For example, smiling, talkativeness, participation in social events, and so on, could together underlie a personality trait such as "sociability". Most traits are normally distributed, with most people being close to the average on sociability, trait anxiety, extraversion, and so on.

Factor analysis

Factor analysis, which has been used by most trait theorists, uses information about the inter-correlations of items from questionnaires, ratings, or other measures of personality. If two items correlate highly with each other, it can be assumed that they measure the same factor or aspect of intelligence. If the two items do not correlate, then it is likely they are measuring different factors. For example, items such as openness, ease in social situations, and wanting to take part in group activities would be correlated highly under the factor of extraversion.

Factor analysis has a number of limitations. First, factor analysis can only reveal the factors contained within the items that are included in it. If, for example, no items dealing with sociability are included in the factor analysis, then a factor of sociability will not emerge from the factor analysis.

Second, factor analysis is merely a statistical technique, and so can only suggest guidelines for theory and research. What is also needed is evidence that that trait is of significance in everyday life.

Third, factor analysis involves making a number of rather arbitrary decisions. The number and nature of the factors or traits extracted from any given set of data depend on decisions concerning the precise form of factor analysis to be carried out on the data.

Factor theorists have to decide whether to allow two factors or traits to be correlated with each other. With *orthogonal factors*, all of the factors must be uncorrelated with each other. In other words, knowing an individual's score on one trait provides no basis for predicting his or her score on a second trait. In contrast, *oblique factors* are correlated with each other. Orthogonal factors are found in the approaches of Eysenck and the Big Five model, but Cattell prefers to make use of oblique factors. Both approaches have their limitations. Reliance on orthogonal or independent factors is arbitrary, as there is no obvious reason why important personality traits should be uncorrelated with each other. Reliance on oblique factors allows numerous personality traits to be identified, but some of these traits tend to be very similar to each other.

Cattell's trait theory

How can trait theorists ensure that all of the important personality traits are included in their measuring instruments (e.g. questionnaires)? Raymond Cattell adopted an ingenious approach to that problem. He made use of the **fundamental lexical hypothesis**, according to which the language contains words describing all of the main personality traits.

Cattell's use of this hypothesis led him to the work of Allport and Odbert (1936). They found a total of 18,000 words in the dictionary that are of relevance to personality, 4500 of which are used for personality description. These 4500 words were reduced to 160 trait words, in part by eliminating synonyms and removing unfamiliar words. Cattell (1946) then added 11 traits from the personality literature, producing a total of 171 trait names which were claimed to cover almost everything of importance in the personality sphere.

Cattell was still left with an unwieldy number of potential traits. As a result, he made use of the findings from several previous rating studies to identify traits that correlated highly. It was argued that such traits were basically similar to each other, and reflected a single underlying trait. By this means, Cattell was left with 35 traits. He called them *surface traits*, because they were readily observable. These surface traits were investigated in rating studies. The findings from these rating studies suggested to Cattell that there are about 16 *source traits*, which are basic traits underlying the surface traits.

Having found 16 traits in rating data, or life (L) data in his terms, the unflagging Cattell decided to study personality traits with questionnaire (Q) and objective test (T) data. Q data were obtained by asking multiple choice questions, such as: "Do your moods sometimes make you seem unreasonable, even to yourself? Yes/No". T data were obtained by objective means, such as using the amount of body sway to measure anxiety or slowness to blow up a balloon until it bursts to measure timidity. He assumed initially that L, Q, and T data would all give rise to the same personality traits. In fact, he found reasonable similarity between the traits emerging from L and Q data, but T data produced rather different traits.

The factors of Cattell's 16PF	
Remember that each pair represents a continuum.	
Reserved	Outgoing
Less intelligent	More intelligent
Affected by feelings	More emotionally stable
Humble	Assertive
Sober	Happy-go-lucky
Expedient	Conscientious
Shy	Venturesome
Tough-minded	Tender-minded
Trusting	Suspicious
Practical	Imaginative
Forthright	Shrewd
Placid	Apprehensive
Conservative	Experimenting
Group-dependent	Self-sufficient
Casual	Controlled
Relaxed	Tense

Evidence

The best-known measuring instrument devised by Cattell is his Sixteen Personality Factor Questionnaire, generally known as the 16PF. It was intended to assess 16 personality factors, some of which relate to intelligence and social attitudes rather than to personality in the narrow sense. In spite of the massive popularity of the 16PF, it is inadequate. Systematic factor analyses of this test have shown that it does not actually measure anything like 16 different personality traits. For example, Barrett and Kline (1982) gave the 16PF to almost 500 participants. They then carried out five different factor analyses on their data, some of which were precisely in line with Cattell's recommendations. They obtained between seven and nine factors in each factor analysis, and these factors generally did not relate closely to the factors proposed by Cattell.

Evaluation

Cattell's approach was very thorough in two ways. First, his use of the fundamental lexical hypothesis helped to ensure that no important personality traits were ignored. Second, he carried out large-scale investigations of personality traits in rating, questionnaire, and objective-test data. His assumption that major personality traits should emerge in all three kinds of data is convincing, even though in practice the data obtained from objective tests were disappointing.

Many of the weaknesses of Cattell's approach stem from his emphasis on oblique or correlated personality factors, which tend to be smaller and harder to find consistently than are orthogonal or independent factors. Precisely this was the case with the 16PF.

Eysenck's trait theory

Eysenck (e.g. 1947) agreed with Cattell that factor analysis is a useful tool to discover the structure of human personality. However, they disagreed over the use of orthogonal or independent factors versus oblique factors. Cattell has always emphasised oblique or correlated factors, because he argues that it is at this level that the most informative description of personality is possible. In contrast, Eysenck (1947) argued that orthogonal or independent factors are preferable, because oblique factors are often so weak that they cannot be found consistently.

Eysenck's (1944) initial attempt to use factor analysis to identify the main orthogonal factors involved a sample of 700 patients suffering from neurotic disorders. Psychiatrists' ratings on 39 scales were accounted for fairly well by the two factors or traits of *neuroticism* and *extraversion*. Those high in neuroticism are more tense and anxious than those low in neuroticism, and extraverts are more sociable and impulsive than introverts.

Most later research on normal and abnormal groups has confirmed the importance of the factors of neuroticism and extraversion. The Eysenck Personality Inventory was devised to measure these two factors. Of importance, these two factors are also contained within Cattell's 16PF. The oblique or correlated factors identified by Cattell are known as first-order factors. When a factor analysis is performed on these first-order factors, it is

Eysenck's three personality factors

NEUROTICISM

UNSTABLE	STABLE
Tense, anxious	Relaxed

←——————→

EXTRAVERSION

HIGH	LOW
Sociable, impulsive	Unsocial, cautious (introversion)

←——————→

PSYCHOTICISM

HIGH	LOW
Egocentric, aggressive, impersonal, cold	Warm, aware of others, non-aggressive

←——————→

possible to obtain orthogonal, second-order factors from the 16PF. Saville and Blinkhorn (1981) did precisely this, and found that second-order factors resembling extraversion and neuroticism emerged from the 16PF.

Eysenck (1978) added a third personality factor, which he called *psychoticism*. High scorers on psychoticism are "egocentric, aggressive, impulsive, impersonal, cold, lacking in empathy and concern for others, and generally unconcerned about the rights and welfare of other people" (Eysenck, 1982, p.11).

Neuroticism, extraversion, and psychoticism are measured by the Eysenck Personality Questionnaire (EPQ). As assessed by the EPQ, these three factors are all almost uncorrelated or orthogonal.

Where do the personality dimensions of extraversion, neuroticism, and psychoticism come from? According to Eysenck (1982, p.28), "genetic factors contribute something like two-thirds of the variance in major personality dimensions."

Evidence

The prediction that neuroticism is strongly influenced by genetic factors has been tested in several twin studies. Across eight twin studies on neuroticism, the mean correlation for monozygotic or identical twins was +0.52, compared to +0.24 for dizygotic or fraternal twins (Zuckerman, 1987). These findings indicate that only about 40% of individual differences in neuroticism are due to genetic influences.

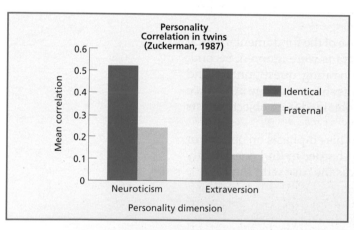

The prediction that individual differences in extraversion depend strongly on genetic influences has also been tested. The mean correlation for identical twins across several studies was +0.51, compared to +0.12 for fraternal twins (Zuckerman, 1987), indicating that about 40% of individual differences in extraversion are due to genetic influences.

The most thorough twin study on neuroticism and extraversion was reported by Pedersen et al. (1988). Identical twins brought up apart had a correlation of +0.25 for neuroticism; identical twins brought up together had a correlation of +0.41; fraternal twins brought up apart had a correlation of +0.28; and fraternal twins brought up together had a correlation of +0.24. These findings suggested that 31% of individual differences in neuroticism are due to heredity. For extraversion, the correlations were +0.30 and +0.54 for identical twins brought up apart and together, respectively, and they were +0.04 and +0.06 for fraternal twins brought up apart and together. These findings suggested that 41% of individual differences in psychoticism are due to genetic factors.

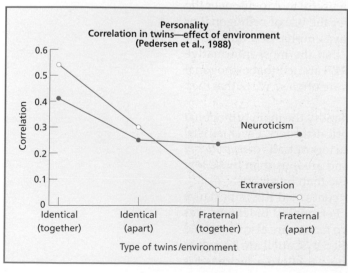

Zuckerman (1989) reviewed four twin studies in which psychoticism was assessed. There was a median correlation of +0.52 for identical twins, compared to +0.21 for fraternal twins. These findings suggest that about 40% of individual differences in extraversion stem from heredity.

About 30% or 40% of individual differences in extraversion, neuroticism, and psychoticism are due to genetic factors, which is considerably less than the 67% claimed by Eysenck (1982). There are two reasons why the reported figure of 30–40% may be inflated. First, monozygotic twins are generally treated more alike than dizygotic twins. Their parents are more likely to try to treat them alike, they spend more time together, they play together more, and they are more likely to have the same teachers at school (Loehlin & Nichols, 1976). Second, monozygotic twins brought up apart are often brought up in two branches of the same family, and some of them go to the same school (e.g. Shields, 1962). As a result, they probably experience more similar environments than is generally assumed to be the case.

Evaluation

Eysenck's main contribution has been the research he devoted to the personality dimensions of extraversion and neuroticism. There is recent evidence that these are two of the major personality traits. Eysenck's third factor, psychoticism, is less important. Recent research reported in the next section has failed to confirm that it is a major personality trait. According to Eysenck (1978), psychoticism measures vulnerability to psychosis, in which there is a loss of contact with reality. In fact, there is less of an association between psychoticism and psychosis than he assumed. Psychotic individuals such as schizophrenics typically score lower on psychoticism than do juvenile delinquents and prisoners (Zuckerman, 1989). According to Zuckerman (1989), the psychoticism scale is actually a psychopathy scale, because psychopaths are aggressive criminals having an anti-social personality.

Eysenck's emphasis on the important contribution made by heredity to individual differences in personality has received some support. However, Eysenck (e.g. 1982) exaggerated the role played by heredity in determining individual differences in personality.

Eysenck typically showed a lack of scientific objectivity in his writings. Pervin (1993, p.290) referred to "Eysenck's tendency to dismiss the contributions of others and exaggerate the empirical support for his own point of view ... frequently he ignores contradictory findings and overstates the strength of positive results."

Big Five model

In recent years, several theorists have argued that there are five major personality traits. Their approach is generally known as the Big Five model or the five-factor model of personality. There are minor differences of opinion about the exact nature of these five traits.

Norman (1963) used small groups of students to study Cattell's rating scales.

Important research in the move towards the Big Five model was reported by Norman (1963). Small groups of students all rated each other on several of Cattell's rating scales. The rating data were then submitted to a factor analysis, and the following five unrelated factors emerged:

1. Extraversion (e.g. talkative; sociable).
2. Agreeableness (e.g. good-natured; co-operative).
3. Conscientiousness (e.g. responsible; tidy).
4. Emotional stability (e.g. calm; composed).
5. Culture (e.g. artistically sensitive; imaginative).

Costa and McCrae's NEO-PI Five Factors

Openness to experience
Conscientiousness
Extraversion
Agreeableness
Neuroticism

Subsequent research has usually confirmed the importance of these five personality traits, with the possible exception of culture. For example, Costa and McCrae (1992) produced the NEO-PI Five-Factor Inventory to measure neuroticism, extraversion, agreeableness, conscientiousness, and openness to experience. The last factor replaces culture, and is defined by curiosity, broad interests, creativity, and imagination. If you want to remember the names of Costa and McCrae's five factors, it is useful to note that their initial letters can be rearranged to form the word OCEAN.

Evidence

The Big Five model of personality has been supported by numerous factor analyses identifying the same (or nearly the same) five traits (see Digman, 1990). Comparison of self-report measures on each of the five personality traits with ratings on those traits made by others (i.e. consensual validity) has produced good agreement. For example, McCrae and Costa (1990) reported the following moderately high correlations between self-reports and ratings by spouses: +0.53 for neuroticism; +0.53 for extraversion; +0.59 for agreeableness; +0.57 for conscientiousness; and +0.59 for openness.

Advocates of the Big Five model (e.g. McCrae & Costa, 1985) have argued that all five personality traits are much influenced by genetic factors. Jang, Livesley, and Vernon (1996) reported that there are moderately strong genetic influences on all five traits, but especially on openness to experience. It is probable that the greater impact on openness to experience occurs because it relates to intelligence, and intelligence is known to be strongly influenced by heredity (see Chapter 16).

Evaluation

The Big Five or five-factor model of personality (and the questionnaires associated with it) provide a good description of the structure of personality. The notion that there are five independent personality traits is a sensible compromise between the sixteen identified by Cattell and the three identified by Eysenck. Numerous factor analyses support the contention that there are five major personality factors approximately as described by Costa and McCrae's (1992) NEO-PI Five-Factor Inventory.

The Big Five model does not provide an account of the processes underlying the five factors or traits. Another weakness is that it is based on the assumption that the five factors are independent of each other. There are many exceptions to this assumption. Costa and McCrae (1992) reported in the manual of the NEO-PI that the factors of neuroticism and conscientiousness correlated –0.53 with each other, and that extraversion and openness correlated +0.40. In other words, the various factors are not nearly as separate from one another as they should be.

Evaluation of trait theories

The trait approach to personality possesses several strengths. It is fairly scientific, and so has shown progress over time. A second strength is that the trait approach has now produced an approximate description of the structure of human personality. Several different lines of research converge on the conclusion that openness to experience, conscientiousness, extraversion, agreeableness, and neuroticism are the five major personality traits. A third strength is the emphasis within the trait approach on the

People who experienced the flooding of autumn 1998 are more likely to be anxious about the permanence of their homes.

importance of genetic factors in producing individual differences in personality. There is good evidence indicating that genetic factors have a definite influence on individual differences in personality.

One of the greatest weaknesses of the trait approach is its assumption of cross-situational consistency, i.e. the assumption that any given individual will behave in a consistent way in different situations. Some theorists (e.g. Bowers, 1973) have argued for what is known as an **interactionist approach**, according to which the person, the situation, and their interaction are all important determinants of behaviour. The interactionist approach can be understood by considering an example. Suppose we ask the question, "When do people experience a high level of anxiety?". Trait theorists might argue that individuals high in trait anxiety (i.e. with anxious personalities) will experience much anxiety. Theorists who emphasise the importance of the situation might argue that it is exposure to a stressful situation that creates a high level of anxiety. According to an interactionist approach, what may be important is the joint impact of personality and environmental stress. As predicted by this approach, the *combination* of high trait anxiety and a stressful situation is needed for really high levels of anxiety to be experienced (Hodges, 1968).

Atkinson et al. (1993) argued that interactions between personality and situation can take three different forms. First, there is reactive interaction, in which individuals differ in their behaviour in a given situation because they interpret the situation in different ways. Second, there is evocative interaction, in which the social situation in which we find ourselves depends on the effects of our behaviour on the behaviour of others. Third, there is proactive interaction, in which the situations in which we spend most of our time are determined in part by our own active choices. For example, Furnham (1981) found that extraverts are much more inclined than introverts to spend a lot of time in social situations.

PERSONAL REFLECTIONS

- My views on intelligence may be regarded by some as controversial, although hardly as controversial as those of my father! I agree with Cooper (1998) who wrote

> **KEY TERM**
> **Interactionist approach**: the notion that the person, the situation, and their interaction help to determine behaviour.

as follows: "If you were allowed to gather one piece of psychological data in order to predict how individuals would behave in *any* situation, then I would have no hesitation in recommending a test of general ability. Intelligence tests have many weaknesses, but the fact remains that job performance can generally be predicted better by an intelligence test than by interviews, biographical information, and so on. Of course, psychologists should try to improve intelligence tests, but they have already proved their usefulness."

SUMMARY

Intelligence testing

Good intelligence tests are standardised and possess high reliability and validity. Reliability is generally assessed by the test–retest method. There are three main forms of validity: content; empirical; and test. The most direct of them is empirical validity. Most intelligence tests have high reliability and moderate validity.

Most intelligence tests only measure limited aspects of intelligence, and do not assess practical, musical, bodily-kinaesthetic, interpersonal, or intrapersonal intelligence. It has been argued that the concept of intelligence is descriptive rather than explanatory. The role of heredity in determining individual differences in intelligence is controversial. However, twin and adoption studies indicate that about 50% of individual differences in intelligence in Western societies depend on genetic factors. Group differences in intelligence seem to depend largely or entirely on environmental factors (e.g. deprivation).

Personality testing

Personality is relatively unchanging over time. It can be assessed by questionnaires, ratings, objective tests, and projective tests. All useful measures of personality are standardised, and have good reliability and validity. Questionnaires and ratings often possess good reliability and moderate validity. This has been shown in measures of consensual validity, in which questionnaire and rating data are correlated with each other. In contrast, objective and projective tests generally have low reliability and validity.

Psychometric testing of personality is based on the nomothetic approach. Those who favour the idiographic approach emphasise the uniqueness of the individual and reject the use of personality tests. The responses given on questionnaires can be distorted by

How good are personality tests at predicting performance and satisfaction in a work situation?

social desirability effects and by acquiescence response set. Lie scales are used to detect the presence of social desirability effects. There used to be controversy about the number of personality traits, but there is now general agreement that there are five major traits. Mischel argued that personality testing is of limited value, because people exhibit poor cross-situational consistency. However, there is often reasonable cross-situational consistency. This issue is related to the person–situation controversy. The evidence indicates that the person and the situation are about equally important in determining behaviour. Personality tests typically only have a modest ability to predict job performance, but are more successful at predicting job satisfaction. Inadequate personality tests are often used in personnel selection.

Factor analysis is generally used to decide on the number and nature of the traits or factors contained in a questionnaire. It can be carried out so as to extract either orthogonal or oblique factors. Cattell made use of the fundamental lexical hypothesis to assess human personality as fully as possible. His 16PF test only contains about half of the 16 factors it is claimed to contain. H.J. Eysenck identified only the three personality traits of extraversion, neuroticism, and psychoticism. Genetic factors account for about 40% of individual differences in each of these traits. Extraversion and neuroticism are major personality dimensions, but psychoticism is not. There is good support for the Big Five model. It consists of five personality traits, with individual differences in all of them depending in part on heredity. There is less cross-situational consistency than is assumed by trait theorists, and an interactionist approach is preferable.

Trait theories of personality

FURTHER READING

Intelligence and personality are both discussed at length by M.W. Eysenck (1994), *Individual differences: Normal and abnormal*, Hove, UK: Psychology Press. Major approaches to intelligence are dealt with by R.J. Sternberg (1994), "Intelligence and cognitive styles", in A.M. Colman (Ed.), *Companion encyclopedia of psychology, Vol. 1*, London: Routledge. L.A. Pervin (1996) covers all of the main issues in personality research very thoroughly in *The science of personality*, New York: Wiley.

REVISION QUESTIONS

1 Discuss the controversial use of *either* intelligence tests *or* personality tests.   (24 marks)
2 Critically consider issues relating to psychometric testing.   (24 marks)

- **Advertising, propaganda, and psychological warfare**
  Is it right to use psychology to control or change people's attitudes and behaviour?

  Pratkanis and Aronson's definition of propaganda
  Subliminal perception
  Inferences
  Issues for psychologists
  McGuire's five factors of persuasion
  Message manipulation
  Petty et al.'s receiver characteristics study
  AIDS and propaganda
  Cults and brainwashing
  Sensory deprivation and interrogation

- **Is psychology a science?**
  Changing views about science, and their relevance to studying human behaviour.

  Features and goals of science
  Popper's views on objectivity and falsifiability
  Kuhn's paradigm approach
  Replicability
  Ecological validity in laboratory experiments
  Phenomenology, e.g. Maslow and Rogers

- **Cultural diversity and bias**
  What is true of people in one culture is often not true of those in another.

  Hofstede's multi-national study of work values
  Berry's etic and emic constructs
  Howitt and Owusu-Bempah's analysis of racial bias

- **Gender and bias**
  Does psychology include too many stereotypes about differences between men and women?

  Hare-Mustin and Maracek's alpha and beta biases
  Constructionism, e.g. Gergen, Burns

758

28

Controversies in Psychology

This chapter is concerned with some of the major controversies within psychology. For example, psychologists have studied persuasion, and identified several processes that change people's attitudes and behaviour. Some of this knowledge has been applied in a controversial way in advertising, in propaganda, and in psychological warfare, all of which are discussed in detail in this chapter.

Psychologists have developed tests to measure individual differences in intelligence and personality. There are various doubts about the validity and general usefulness of these tests. In spite of this, they are used widely, especially in connection with personnel selection. Issues relating to intelligence and personality are discussed in Chapter 27.

One of the most important issues in psychology is whether it qualifies as a science. As we will see, psychology is well on the way to becoming a science, but has probably not achieved that status as yet. One problem is that it may be harder to make objective observations in psychology than in sciences such as physics or chemistry. Another problem is that the findings obtained under laboratory conditions often do not apply in everyday life.

There are biases in theory and research that psychologists are becoming increasingly aware of, and starting to eliminate. Most textbooks focus on studies carried out in the United States and in Europe, which is an example of cultural bias. It is an important bias, because there is strong evidence for large cross-cultural differences. Gender bias is also important. The most common form of gender bias is to assume that there are larger differences between males and females than is actually the case. Another aspect of gender bias is to exaggerate the extent to which any gender differences depend on biological factors rather than on cultural ones.

Advertising, Propaganda, and Psychological Warfare

Many psychologists are interested in **persuasion**, which involves deliberate efforts to change people's attitudes and behaviour. We are all exposed to attempts at persuasion every day, perhaps most obviously from advertisers. Most people encounter hundreds or even thousands of advertisements every week on television, on radio, in the cinema, on billboards, and in newspapers. Companies spend millions of pounds on advertisements because they want to persuade us to buy their products.

Many people are unhappy about the ways in which advertisers use their knowledge of the processes of persuasion to manipulate consumers into buying products they do not really need. However, persuasion is used in other ways, which are even more

How would you define "attitude"? Is it possible to change a person's attitude, but not their behaviour?

KEY TERM

Persuasion: deliberate attempts to change others' attitudes and behaviour.

759

controversial and alarming. One way is through **propaganda**. This was defined by Pratkanis and Aronson (1992) as

> *mass suggestion or influence, through the manipulation of symbols and the psychology of the individual. Propaganda is the communication of a point of view with the ultimate goal of having the recipient of the appeal come to "voluntarily" accept this position as if it were his or her own.*

How easy is it to distinguish between "persuasion" and "propaganda"? What are the similarities and differences between the two?

However, another definition of propaganda was rather more specific: "the dissemination of biased ideas and opinions, often through the use of lies and deception" (Pratkanis & Aronson, 1992, p.9).

One of the best-known examples of mass propaganda occurred in Nazi Germany. The superiority of the German nation to all others and the inferiority of the Jewish race were emphasised repeatedly in a very emotional way. The Nazi regime tried to maximise the impact of these obnoxious messages by forbidding anyone from expressing a different point of view, and by relying on obedience to authority (see Chapter 21). Some of this propaganda involved implying that Jews were like rats coming out of sewers. This was done so that Jews would be regarded as vermin rather than as human beings, and led on to the mass killings of about six million Jews.

Persuasion is also involved in **psychological warfare**. Psychological warfare is used in conflict situations. It takes many forms, including propaganda, brainwashing, sensory and perceptual deprivation, various interrogation techniques, and battle-proofing. Battle-proofing involves making soldiers less concerned about killing the enemy by, for example, repeatedly showing them films of mass slaughter.

We will first of all consider some of the approaches used by advertisers to influence cognitive processes. After that, the techniques of persuasion found in advertising and propaganda will be discussed. Finally, the issue of psychological warfare will be addressed.

Dazzling lights, sleeplessness, hunger, and humiliation are all used as weapons of intimidation.

Advertising: Cognitive processes

When we see or hear an advertisement, we make use of the various cognitive processes discussed in Chapters 11 to 14. Thus, we attend to the advertisement, we perceive it, and we may draw inferences from the information it contains. As a result of these processing activities, we may or may not remember the advertisement in the future. These processes are of interest to advertisers. If an advertisement is to succeed in producing increased sales for the product being advertised, it must be remembered. Some of the effects of advertisements on cognitive processes are considered in this section.

Subliminal perception

Subliminal perception is perception that occurs although the stimulus is presented so briefly or at such low intensity that it is below the threshold of conscious awareness. There is a widespread belief that subliminal perception can be effective in selling products. In one study (Zanot, Pincus, & Lamp, 1983), it was found that 70% of Americans who knew something about subliminal advertising believed that it influenced consumer buying habits.

Interest in subliminal advertising was started by James Vicary, who was running a failing marketing business. He claimed to have flashed the words EAT POPCORN and DRINK COCA-COLA for 1/3000th of a second numerous times during the showing of a film in a cinema in 1957. This subliminal advertising continued over a six-week period. It was supposed to have led to an 18% increase in the cinema sales of Coca-Cola, and a 58% increase in the sales of popcorn. However, the film that was showing (*Picnic*) contained scenes of eating and drinking, and so it is unclear whether it was the subliminal advertising or the film itself that caused the increased sales. More worryingly, there are strong indications that James Vicary made up the whole study in order to prop up his business (Weir, 1984).

Pratkanis and Aronson (1992) considered more than 200 studies on subliminal advertising. They concluded that there was little or no convincing evidence that it is effective. However, many laboratory studies have shown the existence of subliminal perception. For example, consider a study by Mogg et al. (1993). They asked anxious patients to name colours. At the same time, they presented threatening or neutral words at a subliminal level. Mogg et al. found that the anxious patients took significantly longer to name the colours when paired with threatening words than with neutral words. This indicates that the patients were processing the threat value of the words, even though they were not consciously aware of what was being presented to them.

If subliminal perception exists, why is subliminal advertising so ineffective? Very limited processing of subliminal stimuli is needed to produce the small and immediate effects on behaviour (e.g. increased time to name colours) that are found in the laboratory. In contrast, fairly thorough processing of subliminal stimuli is needed to persuade people to buy products they would not normally buy.

> **Subliminal advertising**
> Despite the fact that there is no evidence that subliminal advertising is at all effective, it is illegal in the UK. The subject of subliminal advertising and messages has provided rich material for conspiracy theorists, who argue that people could be being influenced without their knowledge. However, suggesting that a subliminal message exists when in fact it does not could be regarded as an equally effective way to control people's behaviour. After all, if you can detect the message then it is not a subliminal one!

How might retailers use subliminal perception to encourage purchasers to spend more?

Inferences

Advertisers who make false assertions about a product can find themselves in trouble. To get round this problem, they often avoid making direct assertions, but instead try to persuade people to draw certain inferences (see page 354). For example, advertisers do not normally say "X washes whiter than any other washing powder". What they do is to say, "X washes whiter", hoping that people will draw the inference that X washes whiter than other washing powders. If challenged, however, the advertisers could claim that they meant only that X washes whiter than coal dust!

Another common way of persuading consumers to draw false inferences is found in car advertisements reporting several pieces of information (e.g. "The new Z has more front-seat room than an A, more rear-seat hiproom than a B, and a larger boot than a C"). This suggests that the Z is amazingly roomy. However, it is entirely possible that the new Z is actually more cramped overall than cars A, B, and C.

Do people distinguish between assertions and implications? Harris et al. (1980) asked people to watch the evening news on a major American television channel. During the news programme there were commercials for several products, including Old Spice after-shave, Mazola margarine, Ever-ready batteries, Miller High Life beer, and Ford cars. When asked questions about the advertisements, the participants were as confident of the truth of implied claims as they were of asserted claims.

> **Ethical issues: Language in advertising**
> Language used in advertising must be as accurate as possible and must not set out to deceive. Consumer television programmes and organisations have given rise to a more discriminating public, and legal implications must be considered by manufacturers when making claims about their products. One lager brewing company famously got round this problem by inserting the word "probably" into their slogan.

> ■ Research activity: Make a list of ways in which advertisers can convey a desired message about their product without the use of language. Television advertisements for alcohol and confectionery offer good examples.
> Looking back at your list of language-free advertising methods, how much did their memorability depend on depth or distinctiveness of processing?

Memory

In order for advertisements to be effective, it is obvious that they need to be memorable. There are several ways in which that can be achieved, some of which were discussed in Chapter 13. For example, if information is processed in a distinctive or unusual way, then it is usually well remembered (Eysenck & Eysenck, 1980). As a result, many advertisers try to make their advertisements distinctive. A good example is the series of advertisements for Benson & Hedges, showing a cigarette packet in landscapes and other unlikely settings.

Jacoby (1978) carried out a study in which the participants were presented with pairs of related words (e.g. foot–shoe). In one condition, they simply read all the pairs of words.

In the other condition (the problem-solving condition), they had to work out what the second word in each pair was intended to be (e.g. foot – s _ _ e). Memory for the second word in each pair was much better (57% vs. 27%) when the participants had to put effort into deciding what that word was. This idea was used in an advertising campaign for the *Financial Times* based on the slogan, "No FT, no comment". Some of the advertisements contained the following: A B C D E G H I J K L M N O P Q R S U V W X Y Z. The intention was that people reading the advertisement would spend some time working out that the missing letters were F and T, and this would lead them to remember it better.

Controversial issues

As we have seen, advertisers use the knowledge obtained by psychologists to sell various products. Is this controversial? It probably depends on the nature of the product being sold. Advertisements for particular brands of soft drinks are usually regarded as harmless. However, there is general disapproval of advertisements designed to persuade people to smoke cigarettes, and many people are uncomfortable about advertisements for "alcopops" aimed at adolescents. If the findings of psychologists have led (even indirectly) to deaths from smoking and to excessive consumption of alcohol in the young, then this is clearly very disturbing.

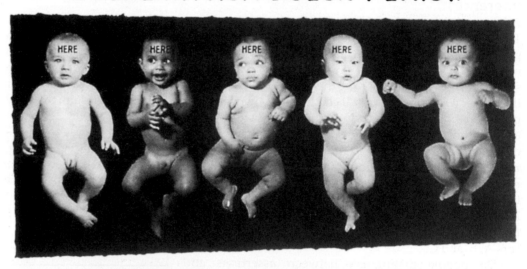

This poster produced by the Commission for Racial Equality is an example of an advertising campaign that attempts to change people's attitudes by persuasion.

Ethical issues: How could the idea of freedom of choice be satisfied at the same time as certain forms of advertising are banned?

What should be done? In principle, there are two major possibilities. First, psychologists could stop doing research that increases the effectiveness of advertising. Second, laws can be passed to prevent undesirable products from being advertised. In practice, only the second approach is used. Governments in Britain and many other countries have passed laws to limit or forbid the advertising of cigarettes, and attempts have been made to prevent advertising of alcohol being directed at adolescents.

Persuasion

McGuire (1969) pointed out that there are five different kinds of factors involved in persuasion:

1. Source: sources differ greatly in terms of attractiveness, power, credibility, and so on.
2. Message: the information presented may appeal to reason or to emotion, it may or may not contain many facts, and so on.
3. Channel: the message may be presented visually or aurally, and may be most effective when it is both (e.g. television advertisements).

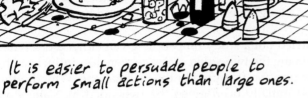

It is easier to persuade people to perform small actions than large ones.

4. Receiver: the effectiveness of a persuasive message depends in part on the amount of attention paid to it by the receiver, and by his or her personality, pre-existing attitudes, and level of intelligence.

5. Target behaviour: it is easier to persuade people to perform small actions (e.g. voting for a given political party) than large ones (e.g. spending weeks canvassing for that party); note that behaviour can be changed without changing attitudes, and vice versa.

Source

What characteristics should the source of a communication have in order for him or her to be persuasive? Communicators who are trustworthy, attractive, who have expertise and credibility, and who are similar to the receiver of the message usually produce more attitude change than communicators lacking these characteristics (Petty & Cacioppo, 1981). The importance of the source's characteristics was shown by Hovland and Weiss (1951). Their participants were given information about drug-taking, and were led to believe that the source was either a prestigeful medical journal or a newspaper. The amount of attitude change produced by the communication was more than twice as great when the source was thought to be the medical journal.

As Deaux and Wrightsman (1988) pointed out, there are two biases that may lead us to disregard the source's message. First, there is **reporting bias**, which occurs when we think that the source is unwilling to tell the truth. For example, a politician seeking re-election may well be motivated to argue that the economy is performing better than is actually the case. Second, there is **knowledge bias**, which occurs when we think that the source's knowledge is likely to be inaccurate. For example, someone who is very wealthy may know little about the problems experienced by homeless people.

Message

Balance.   When trying to persuade other people of a given point of view, we may decide to present only one side of the argument. This is especially common with propaganda. According to Hitler, "As soon as our propaganda admits so much as a glimmer of right on the other side, the foundation of doubt in our own right has been laid." An alternative approach is to present both sides of the argument, but to try to identify weaknesses in the opposing side. Which approach is more effective? As we will see, presenting both sides of the argument is generally (but by no means always) more effective.

Towards the end of the Second World War, the American army did not want its soldiers to think that Japan could be defeated quickly and easily. Accordingly, two radio broadcasts were prepared, in both of which it was claimed that the war against the Japanese would last for more than two years. One broadcast was one-sided and the other was two-sided.

Hovland, Lumsdaine, and Sheffield (1949) found that the broadcast presenting both sides of the argument produced more attitude change than the one-sided broadcast among soldiers who initially believed that the war would last for less than two years. They were already familiar with some of the arguments in favour of a rapid end to the war, and so found the one-sided broadcast biased and limited. In contrast, those soldiers who initially believed that the war would last for a long time were more influenced by the one-sided message.

Lumsdaine and Janis (1953) carried out a study on people given either a one-sided or a two-sided message. Those receiving the two-sided message were less influenced by a later message arguing against the position favoured in the original one. Why did this happen? The participants who had initially been given the two-sided message were already aware of the counter-arguments contained in the second message, and they also knew about weaknesses in those counter-arguments.

What link might there be between Janis and Feshbach's findings and Seligman's (1975) work on learned helplessness (see Chapter 10)?

Fear. It is often assumed that emotional messages are more effective than non-emotional ones. The evidence is mixed. Janis and Feshbach (1953) tried to change their participants' tooth-brushing and dentist-visiting habits by showing them films. Those who were exposed to a film producing mild fear began to take more care of their teeth. However, there was no behaviour change among those exposed to a film producing strong fear, in which the emphasis was on the pain and discomfort that would result from neglecting their teeth.

Leventhal, Singer, and Jones (1965) showed films about tetanus. The participants shown the high-fear film had a greater change in their attitudes towards tetanus and the value of having tetanus inoculations than did those shown the low-fear film. However, the two groups did not differ in terms of actually going to have a tetanus inoculation. This illustrates a very important point: communications often have rather different effects on attitudes than on behaviour.

How can we ensure that high-fear communications influence behaviour as well as attitudes? Leventhal (1970) found that this happened when a high-fear communication was accompanied by specific instructions on what to do in order to avoid the feared outcome. Smokers were exposed to a film showing a young man whose X-rays showed that he was suffering from lung cancer, followed by a film showing an operation for lung cancer. The film was much more effective in reducing smoking behaviour when the

This emotionally charged advertisement aimed to alter people's attitudes towards drink-driving, and to change their behaviour.

smokers were also instructed to buy magazines instead of cigarettes and to drink water when they felt the urge to smoke.

Rogers (1983) put forward a protection-motivation theory to account for the varying effects of fear on attitude and behaviour change. According to this theory, fear is effective under these conditions:

■ Research activity: Apply Rogers' protection-motivation theory to the task of devising a campaign about the risk of HIV infection. How effective would it be in changing behaviour? How do previous campaigns compare with this theoretical approach?

- The receiver accepts that the dangers are serious.
- The receiver accepts that the dangers are likely to happen.
- The receiver believes that the recommended ways of avoiding the dangers will be effective.
- The receiver believes that he or she has the skills needed to perform the recommended actions.

Receiver

According to Petty, Cacioppo, and Goldman (1981), the impact of a persuasive message on attitude change depends on characteristics of the receiver. People can be persuaded in two rather different ways involving two distinct routes. Receivers who are motivated to think carefully about the content of the message follow the *central route* to persuasion. This involves detailed consideration of the persuasive message. Those who have less motivation follow the *peripheral route*. This involves being influenced more by non-content aspects of the message (e.g. the number of arguments produced) and by the context (e.g. the attractiveness of the communicator) than by message content. Thus, those who use the peripheral route pay relatively little attention to the persuasive message.

Petty et al. tested these ideas. Students at the University of Missouri read a message strongly supporting the notion that a new large-scale examination should be introduced. All students would need to pass this examination in order to graduate. Some of the participants were told that this examination might be introduced the following year, in order to provide them with strong motivation to use the central route. The other participants were told that there would be no changes for 10 years, and thus any changes would not affect them personally. This was designed to produce low motivation to process the essay thoroughly, so that they would use the peripheral route.

Petty et al. prepared several versions of the message. The message was either attributed to a source high in expertise (the Carnegie Commission on Higher Education) or to a source low in expertise (a local high school class). The quality of the arguments in the message was also varied. There were either strong arguments based on statistics and other data, or there were only weak arguments based on personal opinions and anecdotes.

What did Petty et al. find? For students expected to use the central route, the quality of the arguments was the main factor determining how persuaded they were. In contrast, for those students expected to use the peripheral route, the source of the message was the main factor influencing its persuasiveness. Thus, they obtained good evidence that there are two separate routes to persuasion.

KEY STUDY EVALUATION — Petty et al.

A possible problem with Petty et al.'s study could be that the groups of participants were not balanced; factors relating to all levels of cognitive processing could be so different between the two groups that their responses could not reasonably be compared. The manipulation of the key variables, i.e. quality and source of message, does demonstrate the significance of these factors in determining the response to the message received, but the possibility of intervening variables such as low attention levels and/or low recall levels in the case of the second, peripheral-route group would suggest that direct comparison between the groups would be questionable. The feelings of the participants towards assessments would need to be measured before the study so that later comparisons could be made. Students who perform badly in exams in general may respond negatively towards the message, irrespective of its content or context or whether it will affect them directly.

Discussion points

1. Do most persuasive messages influence you via the central or the peripheral route?
2. What kinds of motivational factors might lead someone to pay close attention to a persuasive message?

Eagly and Chaiken (1993) described the processes involved in the peripheral route to persuasion in a slightly different way from Petty et al. (1981). They argued that people who are not very interested in a persuasive message make use of simple rules of thumb or heuristics. Here are three examples of the kinds of heuristics they might use: "Messages containing many arguments are more persuasive than those containing only a few";

"Messages communicated by an expert are more persuasive than those communicated by a non-expert"; "Statistics don't lie".

AIDS awareness and safer sex

The knowledge that psychologists have obtained about techniques of persuasion has been applied to the issue of AIDS. About 1.5 million Americans are infected with the human immunodeficiency virus (HIV) that causes AIDS, and HIV is also common throughout western Europe and many other parts of the world. It was initially referred to as the "gay plague". However, this is very misleading, because about 75% of HIV-positive people in the world are heterosexual. As a result, it is extremely important for everyone to behave in ways that minimise the risks of contracting HIV and AIDS. The most effective approach is to use condoms (apart from avoiding all sexual contact!). Persuasive messages have emphasised the importance of using condoms (so-called safer sex), and have stressed the life-threatening consequences of not doing so. In spite of the importance of these messages, they are generally disregarded. For example, a recent study in the United States reported that only 17% of heterosexuals use condoms on a regular basis (Miller, Turner, & Moses, 1990).

Kimble et al. (1992) shed light on the mystery of why persuasive messages about safer sex and AIDS have had little impact. They studied college students, and found that most of them regarded relative strangers and those over-anxious for sex as potentially risky sexual partners. College students believed that the risk was very small when they were in a caring relationship with their partner. In the words of one student (Kimble et al., 1992, p.926), "When you get to know the person ... as soon as you begin trusting the person ... you don't really have to use a condom." Unfortunately, there is no evidence to support these views on which sexual partners are risky and safe, and it is dangerous to use these views to support the continuing practice of unsafe sex.

Despite prominent public health campaigns to encourage safer sexual practices, a study in the USA found that only 17% of heterosexuals use condoms regularly.

Propaganda

Propaganda is defined in the following way by *Collins English Dictionary*: "the organised dissemination of information, allegations, etc., to assist or damage the cause of a government, movement, etc." As was mentioned earlier, some of the most infamous propaganda was produced during the 1930s and 1940s by the Nazis in Germany. They used allegedly documentary films, radio messages, posters, and mass rallies to argue that the Jews were sub-human beings who were largely responsible for the economic and other problems confronting Germany. Nazi propaganda was typical of most propaganda in that it consisted of incredibly distorted and totally inaccurate information. For example, there was the film *The Eternal Jew*, which was made in 1940. According to this film, Jews are money-grabbing criminals who carry diseases and engage in ritual animal slaughter.

> **Ethical issues: Propaganda**
>
> The media have considerable power over the information available to the public. It has been suggested that propaganda can be described in many ways, other than simply blatant use of lies, for example the introduction of censorship. To what extent should the media be given free rein by governments during times of war, so that journalists could report whatever they see fit to include?

Goebbels, the Nazi minister of propaganda, believed in "the big lie". He argued that if big lies were told often enough, people would come to believe them. The underlying logic was expressed in the 1920s by Hitler. He argued that propaganda "must be aimed at the emotions and only to a very limited degree at the so-called intellect ... all effective propaganda must be limited to a very few points and must harp on these slogans until the last member of the public understands what you want him to understand by your slogan."

Another example of propaganda was that used by the Americans during the war in Vietnam. An analysis of their propaganda leaflets revealed that 69% of them emphasised differences based on ethnic group or political grouping, and so were intended to increase inter-group conflict (Cardwell et al., 1996). About 30 of the leaflets focused on emotions, especially fear.

Propaganda can be considered in terms of the five factors involved in persuasion that were identified by McGuire (1969):

1. Source: the source is often a government or ruling class that is likely to be perceived as powerful and credible.

2. Message: this tends to be emotional, and (as in the case of Nazi propaganda) is designed to produce hatred and/or fear of some other group. In dictatorships, great efforts are usually made to ensure that the recipients of propaganda do not have access to other, more accurate, information.

3. Channel: with the enormous increase in the number of television sets in the world, propaganda is typically seen and heard at the same time.

4. Receiver: propaganda is most effective when it is consistent with the receivers' ideology ("a set of beliefs and values held by the members of a social group, which explains its culture both to itself and to other groups", Franzoi, 1996, p.16). In the case of Nazi Germany, there was already fairly widespread anti-Semitism or prejudice against the Jews, and this helped to make the obnoxious Nazi propaganda more readily acceptable to Germans. Propaganda often consists of short, emotional messages. This may lead receivers to process the messages via the peripheral route only; if they used the central route, then the absurdity of the message would be much more apparent to them.

> **CASE STUDY:** *The Vietnam War*
>
> Changes in ideology affect the effectiveness of propaganda. In 1954 when war began between north and south Vietnam, the north was largely communist and the south was backed by money and armaments from America. There was already widespread anti-communist hysteria in America, fuelled by Senator Joseph McCarthy's "witch-hunts" of suspected communist party members in government and the arts. Against this background, anti-communist propaganda led to strong support for greater US involvement in Vietnam, leading to American troops becoming active there in the early 1960s. After Senator McCarthy's death, it was found that evidence against people accused of being communists had been falsified, and in the more open social climate of the 1960s public attitudes to people's political affiliations began to change. Support for the US involvement in the Vietnam war waned, and anti-war propaganda began to appear, until 1973 when the American troops began to withdraw.

5. Target behaviour: those who produce propaganda do not generally expect the receivers to show large changes in their behaviour. The goals of propagandists are often served if receivers alter their attitudes towards some other group (e.g. enemy during a war). For example, a key goal of Nazi propaganda was to increase fear and hatred of the Jews, so that the population would not protest when the Nazi government treated the Jews in an increasingly harsh and murderous way. However, propaganda is sometimes designed to change behaviour. For example, propaganda issued by the British government at the start of the First World War successfully persuaded hundreds of thousands of young men to volunteer for the army.

Cults

Propaganda plays an important role in the development of cults or fanatical groups. Members of cults often behave in bizarre ways. For example, the Reverend Jim Jones set up a cult in Guyana known as Jones's People's Temple. On 18 November 1978, he ordered his followers to drink fruit punch containing sedatives and the poison cyanide. He claimed that they were about to be attacked by the Central Intelligence Agency (CIA), and that they should commit suicide as revolutionaries before that happened. As a result, 914 members of this cult committed suicide.

Another example involved Korean industrialist Sun Myung Moon who established a Unification Church in 1954. On several occasions, Moon arranged mass marriages, in which cult members were required to marry complete strangers who had been selected by him and his associates.

How are cults set up and maintained? According to Pratkanis and Aronson (1992), there are seven key factors:

1. The members of a cult construct their own social reality by making sure they are isolated, and are not exposed to information from the outside world. The leader of the cult tries to convince the group members of the correctness of his or her views. For example, Jim Jones argued that the world was evil, and that the group members must be ready to die.

Using your knowledge of theories of personality, which types of personality would be likely to be most attracted to cults?

2. The group creates its own social identity, which may include new names, distinctive clothing, and ways of behaving. Other groups are regarded as inferior.

3. Strong commitment to the group is created by requiring group members to obey the leader's orders. These orders become more extreme, but explanations are provided (e.g. having sex with the leader is explained as a necessary self-sacrificing discipline).

4. Myths are created about the leader, who may be regarded as the son of God or an individual who has been given a divine purpose.

5. Members of the cult are sent out to convert other people. This forces them to express the advantages of belonging to the cult, and can make them more convinced that they were right to join the cult in the first place.

6. Attempts are made to stop cult members from thinking negative thoughts about the cult. For example, new recruits may never be left alone, and they may be told that doubts about the leader are evil and come from the devil.

7. In order to encourage the cult members, the leader keeps telling them that the future will be wonderful. For example, Jim Jones told his followers (who came from poor backgrounds) that they would have the chance "to live comfortably— you'll have your own home, get a good school, college, swim, fish."

Psychological warfare

Brainwashing

One of the most powerful and sinister forms of psychological warfare is brainwashing, in which an attempt is made to change an individual's thoughts and beliefs. Lifton (1961) carried out detailed interviews in Hong Kong with 25 Westerners and 15 Chinese people who had been victims of Chinese thought-reform programmes. The goal of these programmes was to convince those involved of the superiority of the communist ideology or set of ideas. There were numerous ingredients in these programmes, some of which are discussed in what follows.

After the victim had been arrested, he or she was put in a cell with others who were also victims of the thought-reform programme. These cellmates were under much pressure to assist in the reform of the new arrival, because this could reduce the amount of time they spent in prison. Lifton used the term "struggle" to refer to the discussions between the new arrival and his or her cellmates. After several hours of struggle, the new arrival was taken to an official interrogation, at which the judge conveyed the following message: "The government knows all about your crime. That is why we arrested you. It is now up to you to confess everything to us and in this way your case can be quickly solved and you will soon be released."

If the victim refused to confess, he or she was denied sleep for several days while there were alternations between struggle and interrogation. When the victim finally confessed to a range of crimes, he or she was rewarded or reinforced by being allowed to sleep and by a general reduction in the pressure that was applied. The victim was then required to make more and more confessions, with each confession sounding more plausible and convincing than the one before. After that, the victim was provided with better living conditions.

It is often believed that the effects of such brainwashing cannot be reversed, and this was the case for a few victims. However, Lifton found that most of his sample did not accept the superiority of Chinese communism. Indeed, they were more opposed to it than they had been before imprisonment.

There were several psychological processes at work in these thought-reform programmes. First, there was the reliance on reward and punishment to produce the changes in attitude and behaviour desired by the Chinese authorities. Second, there were the strong group pressures applied by the victim's cellmates. Third, there was the use of sleep deprivation so that the victim started to confuse real and imaginary events. Fourth, the victim was not allowed contact with anyone who

KEY STUDY EVALUATION — Brainwashing

The term "brainwashing" suggests a clearing-out of old beliefs and attitudes, and their replacement with a completely new set of ideas. Lifton's study shows that the use of group pressure to conform, conditioning in the form of reward and punishment, and disorientation by sleep deprivation left the victims in a very vulnerable state, where resistance must have come to seem quite pointless. The research of Milgram in the 1960s, Sherif in the 1930s, and Asch in the 1950s has shown that people have a tendency to conform in far less stressful circumstances than these. Those in power in China would probably have argued that it was important for everyone to support the communist ideology in the interests of social stability. However, the fact that most people's views were not changed, but were actually reinforced, by their imprisonment suggests that thought-reform by such brutal means can be counterproductive.

might criticise the communist ideology or point out that the victim had not committed any crimes. This is known to increase pressures to conform (see Chapter 21).

Discussion points

1. What are likely to be the key factors that allow brainwashing to work?

2. How could the world's community try to prevent victims being brainwashed?

Sensory deprivation

Another technique that has been used in psychological warfare is sensory deprivation. The essence of sensory deprivation is that the individual is put in a situation in which there is much less visual, auditory, social, and other forms of stimulation than normal. For example, Lilly (1956) produced extreme sensory deprivation by suspending his blindfolded participants on their own in water at body temperature. Sensory deprivation has often been used in psychological warfare. For example, IRA suspects interned in Northern Ireland in the eary 1970s were often forced to wear hoods to eliminate visual stimulation.

We can distinguish between *sensory* deprivation, involving a relative absence of sensory stimulation, and *perceptual* deprivation, involving an absence of *patterned* stimulation. Someone kept in darkness experiences sensory deprivation, whereas someone wearing semi-transparent goggles which allow unpatterned light to reach the eyes experiences perceptual deprivation. In general, perceptual deprivation is more likely than sensory deprivation to lead to confusion, mood swings, and hallucinations (Zubek, 1969).

Ethical issues: What ethical problems are involved in research such as Lilly's, in which blindfolded participants were suspended in water?

Sensory and perceptual deprivation are both uncomfortable. When poor university students are offered fairly large sums of money to spend several days in a deprivation situation, substantial numbers are unable to remain there. It is thus reasonable to assume that forcibly exposing captured enemy soldiers to sensory or perceptual deprivation could be an effective way of making them feel vulnerable and persuading them to reveal information.

Interrogation

Efforts are often made to extract military secrets from captured enemy troops, and various interrogation techniques have been used for that purpose. In one study (Biderman, 1960), the focus was on members of the American Air Force who had been captured by the Chinese communists during the Korean War. Their interrogations often lasted for more than a day, and sometimes for much longer. Interrogation techniques that did not involve administering pain were more effective than those that did. As would be expected from work on operant conditioning (see Chapter 10), providing the person being interrogated with reward or reinforcement (such as food or the chance to sleep) in return for giving useful information was often effective.

What were the other features of successful interrogation according to Biderman's (1960) account? Cardwell et al. (1996) discussed some of these features:

- Asking a series of short questions in rapid succession; the interrogator made it clear that he already knew the answers, so the prisoner simply sat there silently.
- The prisoner would often start to defend himself, feeling that silence would be regarded as incriminating.
- The interrogator would ask dozens or hundreds of complex questions which the prisoner could not answer; when eventually he was asked a simple question, the prisoner usually gave the correct answer with relief.
- The interrogator never responded in a hostile way to the prisoner; the intention was that the prisoner would displace his hostility onto fellow prisoners, thus undermining their group solidarity.
- The interrogator made vague threats, which upset the prisoner more than threats that were specific and detailed.

Is Psychology a Science?

The appropriate starting point for a discussion of whether psychology is a science is to consider the definition of science. This is hard to do, because views on the nature of science changed during the course of the twentieth century. According to the traditional view, science has the following features (Eysenck & Keane, 1990):

1. It is objective.
2. This objectivity is ensured by careful observation and experimentation.
3. The knowledge obtained by scientists is turned into law-like generalisations.

The behaviourists were much influenced by a version of this traditional view known as logical positivism. Logical positivists such as Ayer and Carnap argued that the theoretical constructs used in science are meaningful only to the extent that they can be observed. This was very much the position adopted by behaviourists such as Watson and Skinner. As a result, some important concepts within psychology were discarded. For example, Skinner argued as follows: "There is no place in a scientific analysis of behaviour for a mind or self."

Law-like generalisations are not always true.

It is now generally accepted that there are major problems with the traditional view of science held by the behaviourists and others. As is discussed in more detail shortly, the notion that behaviour can be observed objectively has been vigorously attacked. Authorities such as Kuhn (1970) have argued that the scientific enterprise has important social and subjective aspects to it. This view was taken to extremes by Feyerabend (1975). He argued that science progresses by a sort of "who-shouts-the-loudest" strategy, in which publicity and visibility count for more than the quality of the research. According to this position, objectivity is essentially irrelevant to the conduct of science.

What about the view that science involves forming law-like generalisations? Suppose we test a given hypothesis several times, and the findings consistently support the hypothesis. Does that prove that the hypothesis is correct? Popper (1969) argued that it does not. Generalisations based on what has been found to be in the past may not hold true in the future. Consider Bertrand Russell's example of a turkey forming the generalisation, "Each day I am fed", because for all of its life that has been true. This generalisation provides no certainty that the turkey will be fed tomorrow, and if tomorrow is Christmas Eve it is likely to be proved false!

In view of the fact that the traditional definition of science is inadequate, it is clear that a new definition is needed. This is easier said than done. As Eysenck and Keane (1990, p.5) pointed out, the views of Feyerabend and other twentieth-century philosophers of science "have established the point that the division between science and non-science is by no means as clear cut as used to be believed." However, there is probably reasonable agreement that the following are key features of science:

1. Objectivity: even if total objectivity is impossible, it is still important for data to be collected in a way as close to objectivity as possible.
2. Falsifiability: the notion that scientific theories can potentially be disproved by evidence.
3. Paradigm: there is a generally accepted theoretical orientation within a science.
4. Replicability: the findings obtained by researchers need to be replicable or repeatable; it would be hard (or impossible) to base a science on inconsistent findings.

Goals of science

What are the goals of science? According to Allport (1947), science has the aims of "understanding, prediction and control above the levels achieved by unaided common sense." Thus, three of the main goals of science are as follows:

1. Understanding.
2. Prediction.
3. Control.

As we will see shortly, psychologists differ among themselves as to the relative importance of these three goals.

Scientists put forward theories, which are general explanations or accounts of certain findings or data. These theories can then be used to generate various hypotheses, which are predictions or expectations of what will happen in given situations (see Chapter 31). One of the best-known theories in psychology is Thorndike's (1911) law of effect, according to which acts that are rewarded or reinforced are "stamped in", whereas those that are punished are "stamped out". This theory has generated numerous hypotheses including, for example, the predicted behaviour of rats who are rewarded for lever pressing or the behaviour of pigeons rewarded for pecking at a disc. The success or otherwise of predictions stemming from a theory is of great importance. Any theory that generates numerous incorrect predictions is seriously flawed.

Even if a theory generates a number of accurate predictions, it does not necessarily follow that this will give us a good understanding of what is happening. For example, Craik and Lockhart's (1972) levels-of-processing theory led to the prediction that memory will be better for material that has been processed in terms of its meaning than for material that has not. This prediction has been confirmed experimentally numerous times (see Chapter 13). However, the precise reasons why it is beneficial to process meaning still remain unclear.

After prediction and understanding have been achieved, it is sometimes possible to move on to control. For example, Thorndike, Skinner, and others predicted (and found) that people tend to repeat behaviour that is followed by reward or positive reinforcement, and the principles of operant conditioning were put forward in an attempt to understand what is going on. It is possible to use reinforcement to control human behaviour, as when parents persuade their children to behave well in return for sweets. Skinner (1948), in his utopian novel *Walden Two*, went further, and argued that it would be possible to create an ideal society by arranging matters so that only socially desirable behaviour was rewarded or reinforced.

If Skinner and Thorndike's theories are correct, then punishment should always be a deterrent, but this is not always true. What could be the reason for this?

Objectivity

We have already referred to the importance of data collection or scientific observation as a way of testing hypotheses. According to the traditional view of science, scientific observations are entirely **objective**. However, Popper (1969, 1972) argued that scientific observations are theory-driven rather than objective. His famous lecture demonstration involved telling the audience, "Observe!" Their obvious and immediate retort was, "Observe what?" This demonstration makes the point that no-one ever observes without some idea of what they are looking for. In other words, scientific observation is always driven by hypotheses and theories, and what you observe depends in part on what you expect to see.

We can make this argument more concrete by taking a specific example. There have been thousands of experiments carried out in the Skinner box, in which the number of lever presses produced by a rat in a given period of time is the key behavioural measure. In most studies, the equipment is designed so that each lever press is recorded automatically. This procedure is less objective than might be thought. Lever presses with the rat's right paw, with its left paw, and even with its nose or tail are all recorded as a single lever press, even though the rat's actual behaviour differs considerably.

Popper argues that we all see the world from our own particular viewpoints or biases. This influences the topic that we choose to look at. How can scientists try to avoid bias in their work?

Furthermore, the rat sometimes presses the lever too gently to activate the mechanism, and this is not counted as a lever press at all.

A more sweeping attack on the notion that data in psychology are objective has been made by social constructionists such as Gergen (1985) and Harré and Secord (1972). Semin (1995, p.545) described their key assumptions as follows:

> In their view, there are no such things as pure observations. All observations require a prior viewpoint, irrespective of whether these stem from a theoretical perspective, or are due to learning ... Thus data are socially "manufactured", irrespective of which form these data take.

Wallach and Wallach (1994) agreed that perfect objectivity cannot be achieved, and that it is not possible to be certain that the interpretation of someone's behaviour is correct. However, they pointed out that we can be more confident in our interpretation of behaviour if it is supported by other evidence. According to Wallach and Wallach (1994, p.234):

> When a subject presses a lever that ostensibly [apparently] delivers shocks to another subject, it may be far from certain that he or she intends to harm this other subject. If the subject also asserts that this was his or her intention, or it happens that on the experimenter's declaration that the experiment is over, the subject proceeds to punch the other subject in the nose, then, all else being equal, it seems likely that harm was intended.

Falsifiability

An extremely influential view of what distinguishes science from non-science was put forward by Popper (1969). He argued that the hallmark of science is **falsifiability** rather than generalisation from positive instances or findings. Scientists should form theories and hypotheses that can potentially be shown to be untrue by experimental tests. According to Popper, the possibility of falsification is what separates science from religions and pseudo-sciences such as psychoanalysis and Marxism.

Some theories in psychology are falsifiable, whereas others are not. For example, H.J. Eysenck (1967) put forward a theory, according to which those high in neuroticism (anxiety and depression) should be more physiologically responsive than those low in neuroticism (see Chapter 27). Numerous studies have tested this theory, with the great majority failing to support it (Fahrenberg, 1992). In other words, the theory has been falsified.

Another example of a theory that is falsifiable is Broadbent's (1958) filter theory of attention. If two messages are presented at the same time, the filter only allows one of them to be processed thoroughly. As a result, the other message receives only minimal processing. This clear prediction of the theory has been disproved or falsified several times (see Chapter 12).

In contrast, Freud's notion that the mind consists of three parts (ego, superego, and id) is unfalsifiable. It is not possible to imagine any findings that would disprove such a vague and poorly specified theoretical position. In similar fashion, it is hard to test or to falsify Maslow's (1954) theory of motivation based on a hierarchy of needs. This theory assumes that there are five types of needs arranged in a hierarchical way, from need for survival at the bottom to need for self-actualisation at the top (see Chapter 2). The problems associated with falsifying this theory may explain why relatively few studies have tested it.

Paradigm: Kuhn's approach

According to Thomas Kuhn (1962, 1970, 1977), the most essential ingredient in a science is what he called a **paradigm**. This is a general theoretical orientation that is accepted by the great majority of workers in that field of study. With the advance of knowledge, the

KEY TERMS

Falsifiability: the notion that scientific theories can potentially be disproved by evidence; the hallmark of science, according to Popper.

Paradigm: according to Kuhn, a general theoretical orientation that is accepted by most scientists in a given discipline.

dominant paradigm in any science will gradually become less adequate. When there is very strong evidence against the current paradigm, it is eventually replaced by another paradigm.

These considerations led Kuhn (1970) to argue that there are three distinct stages in the development of a science:

1. Pre-science: there is no generally accepted paradigm, and there is a wide range of opinion about the best theoretical approach to adopt.

2. Normal science: there is a generally accepted paradigm, and it accounts for the phenomena that are regarded as being central to the field. This paradigm influences the experiments that are carried out, and how the findings are explained. A classic example of normal science is the use of Newtonian mechanics by physicists until the emergence of relativity theory.

3. Revolutionary science: when the evidence against the old paradigm reaches a certain point, there is what is known as a paradigm shift. This involves the old paradigm being replaced by a new one. An example of a paradigm shift is the Copernican revolution, in which the old view that the planets and the sun revolve around the earth was replaced by our present view that the earth and the other planets revolve around the sun.

> ■ Research activity: Causes of schizophrenia
>
> The competing theories that exist for the causes of schizophrenia could be indicative of a pre-scientific stage in the psychology of mental disorders. Using other sources, research the dominant paradigms that exist in this area, and compare them to other less adequate explanations for schizophrenia. Can we say that psychologists have established a generally accepted explanation for the causes of certain forms of schizophrenia? If so, are these explanations proof of a scientific approach? What do you think are the chances of a competing explanation resulting in a paradigm shift, for example to environmental and/or social causes?

The replacement of an old paradigm by a new one does not usually happen in an orderly way. Scientists who support the old paradigm often ignore disconfirming evidence, or dismiss it as of little importance. Adherents of the old paradigm resist change for as long as possible, until they can no longer hold out against the onslaught. In other words, social and other pressures lead scientists to stick with paradigms that are clearly inadequate. Which scientists are most likely to favour the new paradigm? Sulloway (1994) considered the views of hundreds of scientists writing during periods of scientific revolution. Scientists who were first-born children were much less likely to adopt the new scientific paradigm than were those who were later-born. Presumably later-born children have had more experience of rebellion through their childhood experiences with older siblings, and this helps them to reject the previous paradigm.

It is time to return to Kuhn's three stages to consider where psychology fits in. Kuhn (1962) argued that psychology has failed to develop a paradigm, and so remains at the pre-science stage. Various arguments support this point of view. First, there are several general theoretical approaches within psychology (e.g. psychodynamic; behaviourist; humanist; cognitive). As a result, it cannot really be argued that most psychologists support the same paradigm.

Second, psychology is an unusually fragmented discipline. It has connections with several other disciplines, including biology, physiology, biochemistry, neurology, and sociology. Psychologists studying, for example, biochemistry have very little in common with those studying social factors within society. The fragmentation and diversity make it unlikely that agreement can be reached on a common paradigm or general theoretical orientation.

Valentine (1982, 1992) argued for a different position. She claimed that behaviourism can be regarded as at least coming close to being a paradigm. As she pointed out, behaviourism has had a massive influence on psychology through its insistence that psychology is the study of behaviour, and that behaviour should be observed in controlled experiments. It also had a great influence (but one that has declined considerably in recent decades) through its theoretical assumptions that the study of learning is of fundamental importance to psychology, and that learning can be understood in terms of conditioning principles.

Before Copernicus showed that the planets, including the earth, revolved around the sun, all astronomical theories had been based on the paradigm that the earth was the centre of the universe. The complete change in science post-Copernicus is an example of a paradigm shift.

It is not clear that behaviourism is a paradigm. Behaviourism's greatest impact on psychology has been at the methodological level, with its emphasis on studying behaviour. However, a paradigm in Kuhn's sense is more concerned with a general theoretical orientation rather than with methodological issues. Thus, behaviourism does not seem to be a paradigm, and Kuhn (1962) was probably correct to place psychology at the pre-science stage. This may not make psychology as different from other sciences as is often assumed. Kuhn's view of normal science, in which nearly all scientists within a discipline are working in harmony using the same paradigm, seems to exaggerate the similarity of perspective found among researchers in physics, chemistry, biology, and so on.

Replicability

What are the main obstacles to replicability in human psychology?

It was indicated earlier that **replicability** or repeatability of findings is an important requirement for a subject to be considered as a science. Replicability of findings in psychology varies enormously as a function of the area and type of study being carried out. Replicability tends to be greatest when experiments are conducted in a carefully controlled way, and it tends to be lowest when the experimenter is unable to manipulate the variable or variables of interest.

Clear evidence of replicability is available from studies of operant conditioning. There are characteristic patterns of responding that are found when animals are put into a Skinner box and rewarded on various schedules of reinforcement (see Chapter 10). For example, there is the fixed interval schedule, in which the animal is rewarded with food for the first response after a given interval of time (e.g. 30 seconds). What nearly always happens is that the animal stops responding immediately after receiving food, because it has learned that no additional food is available at that time. The animal starts to respond again more and more rapidly as the time at which reward will be available approaches.

Replicability tends to be lower when studies are carried out in social psychology, but often remains high when the situation is under good experimental control. For example, there is the Asch situation (see Chapter 21), in which there is one genuine participant and several participants who are confederates of the experimenter. They are given the task of deciding which of three lines is the same length as another line. The key condition is one in which all the confederates of the experimenter provide the same incorrect decision. Convincing evidence of conformity by the genuine participant has been found in numerous studies in several countries.

Laboratory experiments

Most experiments in psychology are carried out in the laboratory. Some of the issues that need to be considered when designing such experiments are dealt with in Chapter 31. In order for psychology to be regarded as a science, we must have confidence in laboratory (and other) experiments as a way of obtaining valid information about human behaviour. As we will see, psychologists differ enormously in their evaluation of the value of experiments in psychology.

At one extreme, Boring (1957) argued as follows: "The application of the experimental method to the problem of mind is the great outstanding event in the history of the study of mind, an event to which no other is comparable." In contrast, Nick Heather (1976) was very dismissive of laboratory experiments. He argued that they are very artificial, and that all that can be learned from them is how strangers interact in an unusual situation.

Some of the strengths and weaknesses of laboratory research can be made clearer by looking at two kinds of validity (see also Chapter 31). **Internal validity** refers to the validity of research within the context in which it is carried out. For example, if the same experiment is carried out time after time, and the same findings are obtained each time, this would indicate high internal validity. Experiments that can be repeated in this way are said to be high in replicability. **External validity** refers to the validity of the research outside the research situation. Many laboratory experiments are rather low in external validity, meaning that we cannot be confident that what is true in the laboratory is also true of everyday life. The term **ecological validity** is often used to refer to the extent to which experimental findings can be generalised to everyday settings.

Much psychological research on humans lacks external validity or ecological validity to a greater or lesser extent. We spend most of our time actively dealing with our environment, deciding in which situations to put ourselves, and then responding to those situations as seems appropriate. Much of that dynamic interaction is lacking in laboratory research. The experimenter (rather than the participant) determines the situation in which the participant is placed, and what is of interest is the participant's response to that situation. This led Silverman (1977) to argue that the findings obtained from laboratory studies are only likely to generalise to institutions such as prisons, hospitals, or schools.

Non-scientific approaches to psychology

As we have seen, the behaviourists firmly believed that psychology should be a science, and they tried hard to achieve this. However, there are other approaches to psychology in which there is much less emphasis on the notion of psychology as a science (see Chapter 2). The humanistic psychologists and social constructionists agreed strongly that psychology should not be a science, and the social constructionists went further and argued that it cannot be a science. The humanistic psychologists such as Maslow and Rogers favoured the use of **phenomenology**, in which individuals report their conscious experiences in as pure and undistorted way as possible. This approach was justified in the following way by Rogers (1959):

> *This personal, phenomenological type of study—especially when one reads all of the responses—is far more valuable than the traditional "hard-headed" empirical approach. This kind of study, often scorned by psychologists as being "merely self-reports", actually gives the deepest insight into what the experience has meant.*

It will be remembered that three of the major aims of science are understanding, prediction, and control. The humanistic psychologists emphasised the goal of understanding. However, their approach failed to be scientific in part because they attached much less importance to the other two aims of prediction and control.

Those psychologists who favour **social constructionism** argue that there are no objective data, and that our "knowledge" of ourselves and of the world is based on social constructions. In other words, "What we call facts are simply versions of events which, for various reasons, are presently enjoying wide currency" (Burr, 1997, p.8). Social constructionists have attacked the "so-called objectivity of the 'scientist', disengaged from the cultural and historical circumstances" (Semin, 1995, p.545). According to them, the observations made by psychologists, and the ways in which those observations are interpreted, are determined in large measure by the cultural and historical forces influencing them. Thus, for example, teachers beating disruptive schoolchildren are now regarded as behaving violently and unacceptably, but the same behaviour was generally tolerated 20 or 30 years ago.

The importance of historical forces was emphasised by Gergen (1973, p.318). According to him, "We must think in terms of a *continuum of historical durability*, with phenomena highly susceptible to historical influence at one extreme and the more stable processes at the other." Behaviourists

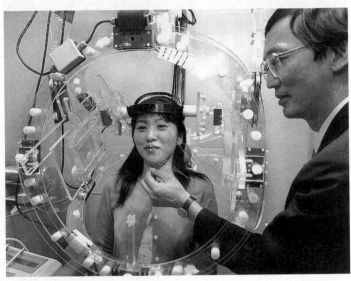

Many laboratory-based experiments in psychology show low external validity—that is, their findings do not translate reliably to behaviour outside the laboratory.

Phenomenology vs. empiricism

A simplistic example of the difference between the phenomenological school of thought and that of the empiricists might be approaches to the personality changes that tend to take place during adolescence. Whereas the empiricists would observe and record the reactions (verbal and non-verbal) to a given stimulus such as a list of questions, a phenomenological approach would make observations within the context of the individual adolescent's personal profile, e.g. early childhood memories. The humanist would concentrate on the changes occurring against a backdrop of the whole self. The empiricist would concentrate on the stage of development reached.

SCHOOL IN THE LAST CENTURY.   "TAKE DOWN HIS BREECHES."

In the past, physical punishment of disobedient children was generally accepted as appropriate. Psychologists today would view it differently, as the social view of physical punishment has undergone drastic changes.

and other psychologists who favour the scientific approach tend to assume that the historical durability of phenomena is high, whereas social constructionists assume that it is often very low.

It follows from what has been said so far that social constructionists believe that psychology cannot be a science. How do they think that psychologists should proceed? According to Burr (1997, p.8), "Since there is no ultimate knowledge of human beings that we can call a final truth, what we must do instead is to try to understand where our current ways of understanding have come from." One of the ways in which that can be done is by means of **discourse analysis**, which involves focuses on analysing people's use of language in order to understand how they perceive the world (see Chapter 30).

Wetherell and Potter (1988) carried out discourse analysis on interviews conducted with white New Zealanders. These interviews dealt with the issue of the teaching of Maori culture in schools. What emerged from this discourse analysis was that many white New Zealanders had racist views, even though they claimed not be racist. They argued in favour of encouraging Maori culture, but emphasised the importance of togetherness (all New Zealanders working co-operatively) and of pragmatic realism (being in touch with the modern world). The hidden message was that fostering Maori culture would have adverse effects on togetherness and pragmatic realism, and so should not be done.

There is some validity in the social constructionist position. However, many psychologists regard it as making exaggerated claims. For example, suppose that several people saw a policeman hitting a student hard with a long stick. Regardless of their beliefs, they would probably be able to agree on the basic facts of what had happened. However, there would be much disagreement as to whether the policeman's action was justified or unjustified (see Chapter 22). In other words, our beliefs may colour our *interpretation* of an action, but they are less likely to influence our *description* of that action.

Summary and conclusions

It is hard to decide whether psychology should be regarded as a science. In general terms, psychology possesses many of the features of a science. However, it tends to possess them less clearly and less strongly than other sciences such as physics or chemistry.

On the positive side, some theoretical approaches in psychology have been successful in achieving the goals of prediction, understanding, and control. Many psychological theories fulfil Popper's criterion of falsifiability, as they have been disproved by experimental studies. The findings of numerous experiments in psychology have been replicated successfully, which is another criterion of a science. However, psychology is very variable with respect to falsifiability and replicability. As we have seen, some theories in psychology are not sufficiently precisely expressed to be falsifiable, and many findings are not replicable.

On the negative side, there are some doubts about the objectivity of the data collected by psychologists. At least some of the data obtained seem to be influenced by the experimenter's biases, which are determined by his or her social and cultural background. Many of the findings obtained from psychological research lack external or ecological validity, because they have been obtained under the artificial conditions of the laboratory. Finally, Kuhn (1970) is probably correct in arguing that psychology is a pre-science, because it lacks a generally accepted paradigm.

The issue of whether psychology is or is not a science can have important implications for research funding. The reason is that subjects regarded as sciences generally receive more research funding than those not so regarded. At the end of the 1970s, the main provider of research funding for psychology in Britain was the Social Science Research Council. However, the Conservative government under Mrs Thatcher was not convinced that psychology, economics, and the other disciplines funded by the Social Science Research Council were really sciences, and it was nearly closed down altogether. What actually happened was that it was re-named the Economic and Social Research Council, and it received less money than before.

In sum, there are good reasons for arguing that psychology is on the way to becoming a science. At present, however, it should probably be regarded as having only some of the features of a science rather than being a fully fledged science.

Cultural Diversity and Bias

Research in psychology has for very many years been dominated by the United States. According to Rosenzweig (1992), 64% of the world's 56,000 researchers in psychology are Americans. Their impact on textbooks in psychology is often even greater. For example, consider Baron and Byrne's (1991) textbook on social psychology. In that book, 94% of the studies referred to were from North America, compared to 2% from Europe, 1% from Australasia, and 3% from the rest of the world.

The Japanese work culture includes the requirement to socialise outside working hours with colleagues.

Facts like those just mentioned are of relevance to *cross-cultural psychology*, in which different cultures are studied and compared. What is a culture? According to Smith and Bond (1993, p.36), a culture "is a *relatively organised* system of shared meanings." For example, the word "work" has a rather different meaning in the Japanese culture than in others. In Japan, it typically includes going drinking after normal working hours, and sharing in other recreational activities with one's work colleagues. Most cross-cultural psychology has involved comparisons between different nations or countries. This suffers from the problem that a country is generally not the same as a culture. For example, there are several cultures within a single country such as the United States.

Cultural differences

It is often assumed that what is true of our culture or country is also true of most other cultures or countries. Many psychologists who carry out studies in the United States or in the United Kingdom make that assumption. However, the assumption is wrong. For example, an attempt was made to repeat the findings of six American studies on an Israeli population similar to that used in the American studies (Amir, 1989). There were 64 significant findings in the American studies, only 24 of which were repeated among the Israeli participants. The other 40 findings were not repeated. In addition, there were six new findings in the Israeli sample that had not been obtained in the American studies.

Consider evidence for the view that Westerners shun laziness, passivity, and low productivity. Where do these attitudes come from?

What are the main differences between cultures? Westen (1996, p.679) expressed some of them in vivid terms:

> *By twentieth century Western standards, nearly every human who has ever lived outside the contemporary West is lazy, passive, and lacking in industriousness. In contrast, by the standards of most cultures in human history, most Westerners are self-centred and frenetic.*

Our culture also differs from many others in more fundamental ways, including the ways in which we think of ourselves. As Westen (1996, p.693) pointed out:

> *The prefix "self-", as in "self-esteem" or "self-representation", did not evolve in the English language until around the time of the Industrial Revolution ... The contemporary Western view of the person is of a bounded individual, distinct from others, who is defined by more*

or less idiosyncratic attributes. In contrast, most cultures, particularly the nonliterate tribal societies ... view the person in her social and familial context, so that the self-concept is far less distinctly bounded.

Hofstede

Evidence consistent with Westen's position was reported by Hofstede (1980). He carried out a survey of work-related values among workers in a large multi-national company. These workers came from 40 different countries. One of the main dimensions that emerged from the survey was that of individualism–collectivism. Individualism involves an emphasis on individual needs and self-development rather than on group needs, whereas collectivism is based on group needs taking precedence over individual ones. The United States had the highest score for individualism of any country, the United Kingdom was third, and France was tenth. Of special interest was Hofstede's finding that individualism correlated +0.82 with modernity as measured by national wealth. This indicates that there is a strong tendency for wealthier countries to be individualistic and self-centred.

Discussion points

1. Why are the people in wealthier countries more individualistic than those in poorer countries?
2. What are the advantages and disadvantages of the individualistic and collectivistic approaches?

The general insensitivity to cultural differences reveals itself clearly in the personality area. Most studies of personality in non-Western cultures have assessed personality by means of translated versions of Western tests rather than by devising new, culture-relevant tests. Evidence that personality structure may vary from one culture to another was reported by Kuo-shu Yang and Bond (1990). They asked students in Taiwan to describe several people they knew using two sets of adjectives. One set of adjectives was drawn from Cattell's 16PF test, whereas the other set was taken from Chinese newspapers. The Big Five personality factors (extraversion, agreeableness, emotional stability, culture, and conscientiousness), which have been found repeatedly in Western studies, emerged from the analysis of Cattell's adjectives. Kuo-shu Yang and Bond also found that five factors emerged from an analysis of the adjectives taken from the Chinese newspapers: social orientation; expressiveness; competence; self-control; and optimism. There was some agreement between the two sets of factors. For example, the Big Five factor of agreeableness correlated +0.66 with social orientation, and emotional stability correlated +0.55 with competence. However, the overall similarity between the two sets of personality factors was fairly low, suggesting that personality structure in Taiwanese culture differs from that in Western cultures.

What social psychological explanations can you give for the results of Kuo-shu Yang and Bond's study?

Etic and emic constructs

Berry (1969) drew a distinction between emic constructs and etic constructs. **Emic constructs** are specific to a given culture, and so vary from one culture to another. In contrast, **etic constructs** refer to universal factors that hold across all cultures. The notion of the "family" is an example of an etic construct. According to Berry, what has happened fairly often in the history of psychology is that what are actually emic constructs are assumed to be etic constructs. The study of intelligence (discussed next) can be used to illustrate this point.

It has often been argued that the same abilities of problem solving, reasoning, memory, and so on define intelligence in every culture. Berry (1974) disagreed strongly with that view. He favoured a viewpoint known as cultural relativism. According to this viewpoint, the meaning of intelligence is rather different in each culture. For example, as Sternberg (1985, p.53) pointed out

KEY TERMS
Emic constructs: those that vary from one culture to another.
Etic constructs: universal factors that hold across cultures.

coordination skills that may be essential to life in a preliterate society (e.g., those motor skills required for shooting a bow and arrow) may be all but irrelevant to intelligent behaviour for most people in a literate and more "developed" society.

Cole et al. (1971) provided evidence of the advantage of emic constructs over etic ones. They asked adult members of the Kpelle tribe in Africa to sort familiar objects into groups. In most Western societies, people would sort the objects into categories (e.g. foods; tools). What the Kpelle tribespeople did was to sort them into functional groups (e.g. a knife with an orange, because an orange can be cut by a knife). Thus, what is regarded as intelligent behaviour can differ from one culture to another. By the way, the Kpelle tribespeople showed that they could sort the objects into categories when asked to do so —they did not naturally do this, because they thought it was a stupid way of sorting.

Racial bias

Racial bias is a particularly unpleasant form of cultural bias. Some of the ways in which it manifests itself were discussed by Howitt and Owusu-Bempah (1990). They considered every issue of the *British Journal of Social and Clinical Psychology* between 1962 and 1980. They were dismayed at the way in which Western personality tests such as the 16PF were used inappropriately in non-Western cultures. As they pointed out (p.399), "There were no studies which attempted to explore, for example, the Ghanaian or Chinese personality structures in their own terms rather than through Western eyes."

Owusu-Bempah and Howitt (1994) claimed to have found evidence of racism in the well-known textbook by Atkinson, Atkinson, Smith, and Bem (1993). They pointed out that Atkinson et al. tended to categorise Western cultures together, and to do the same for non-Western ones. This included referring to work on African tribes without bothering to specify which tribe or tribes had been studied. Owusu-Bempah and Howitt (1994, p.165) argued as follows: "The *cumulative* effect of this is the 'naturalness' of white people and their ways of life, and the resultant exclusion ... of black people and their cultures."

The central point made by Owusu-Bempah and Howitt (1994) was that Atkinson et al. (1993) evaluated other cultures in relation to the technological and cultural achievements of the United States and Europe. In their own words (p.163):

> *Cultures which fall short of this arbitrary Euro-centric standard are frequently described as "primitive", "undeveloped" or, at best, "developing". Religion, morality, community spirit, etc., are ignored in this racist ideological league table.*

In sum, many Western psychologists have written in insensitive ways about cross-cultural differences. Sometimes the mistaken impression may have been given that some cultures are "better" than others rather than simply different. There are certainly grounds for concern, but thankfully any explicit or implicit racism is very much in decline.

Cross-cultural issues: What do you think is meant by the phrase "in their own terms" when applied to personality structures in different cultures?

Gender and Bias

There are many popular (and misleading) stereotypes about the differences between the sexes. For example, it has often been claimed that women are more emotional than men. This was expressed poetically by Alfred, Lord Tennyson:

> *Man for the sword and for the needle she:*
> *Man with the head and woman with the heart.*

Stereotypes about gender have been fairly common in psychology as well as in society at large. One of the worst offenders was Sigmund Freud. He argued that anatomy is destiny, meaning that there are great psychological differences between men and women because of their anatomical differences. For example, Freud claimed that young girls suffer from "penis envy" when they find out that boys have a penis but they do not.

Alpha bias and beta bias

Hare-Mustin and Maracek (1988) considered the issue of gender bias in psychology in detail. Their starting point was that there are two basic forms of gender bias: **alpha bias**

KEY TERM

Alpha bias: the tendency to exaggerate differences between the sexes.

and **beta bias**. According to Hare-Mustin and Maracek (1988, p.457), "Alpha bias is the tendency to exaggerate differences; beta bias is the tendency to minimise or ignore differences." They used the term "bias" to refer to an inclination to focus on certain aspects of experience rather than on others.

Within Western cultures, alpha bias has been more common than beta bias. For example, Freud claimed that children's superego or conscience develops when they identify with the same-sexed parent. Girls do not identify with their mother as strongly as boys identify with their father. As a result, Freud argued that girls develop weaker superegos than boys (see Chapter 17). However, Freud did admit that "the majority of men are far behind the masculine ideal [in terms of strength of superego]." The evidence does not support Freud. Hoffman (1975) discussed studies in which the tendency of children to do what they had been told not to do was assessed. The behaviour of boys and girls did not differ in most of the studies. When there was a sex difference, it was the girls (rather than the boys) who were better at resisting temptation.

Maccoby and Jacklin (1974) reviewed research on sex differences. They concluded that there were only four differences between boys and girls for which there was strong evidence. This is a much smaller number of sex differences than would have been predicted by most psychologists, and suggests that they show alpha bias. The four differences identified by Maccoby and Jacklin were as follows:

- Girls have greater verbal ability than boys.
- Boys have greater visual and spatial abilities than girls (e.g. arranging blocks in specified patterns).
- Boys have greater arithmetical ability than girls, but this difference only appears at adolescence.
- Girls are less aggressive than boys: this is found in nearly all cultures, and is usually present from about two years of age.

Maccoby and Jacklin (1974) found strong evidence for only four differences between boys' and girls' behaviour.

Most of these differences are fairly small, and there is much overlap in behaviour between boys and girls. Sex differences in abilities (verbal, visual, spatial, and mathematical) are even smaller now than they were in the early 1970s (Hyde & Linn, 1988). However, as Shaffer (1993) pointed out, there are some differences in behaviour that were not identified by Maccoby and Jacklin (1974). First, girls show more emotional sensitivity (e.g. they respond more attentively to babies). Second, girls are less vulnerable developmentally than boys, and they are less likely to suffer from learning disabilities, various language disorders, or hyperactivity. Third, boys tend to be more physically active than girls. Fourth, girls tend to be more timid than boys in unfamiliar situations.

Hare-Mustin and Maracek (1988) argued that beta bias or the tendency to minimise or ignore sex differences is less common than alpha bias. They suggested that Bem's (1974) theory of psychological androgyny is an example of beta bias. According to that theory, it is better to be androgynous (having a mixture of positive masculine and feminine characteristics) than to have only masculine or only feminine characteristics. Masculine characteristics are those fitting an instrumental role (e.g. dominance; competitiveness; and assertiveness). In contrast, feminine characteristics are those fitting an expressive role (e.g. sensitivity to others and co-operativeness). Bem (1985) implied that masculine and feminine characteristics are of equal value. However, Hare-Mustin and Maracek (1988) argued that society tends to value the masculine qualities more than the feminine ones.

There is evidence of beta bias in experimental research. Male and female participants are used in most studies, but there is typically no attempt to analyse the data to see whether there are significant sex differences. Sex differences have often been found when they have been looked for (e.g. Rosenthal, 1966). However, sex differences are sometimes found simply because male experimenters treat their female participants differently from their male ones. Rosenthal (1966) reported that they were more pleasant, friendly, honest, and encouraging with female than with male participants. Such findings led Rosenthal (1966) to conclude: "Male and female subjects may, psychologically, simply not be in the same experiment at all."

It has been claimed that some psychological theories show evidence of beta bias. Kohlberg (1963) put forward a theory of moral development based mainly on studies of moral dilemmas with males as the main actors and with males as participants. He claimed that men tended to be at a higher level of moral development than women (see Chapter 17). This claim was disputed by Gilligan (1977). She argued that Kohlberg had focused too much on the morality of justice and too little on the morality of care. According to her, boys develop the morality of justice, whereas girls develop the morality of care.

Gilligan (1982) reported evidence that supported her position. However, most of the evidence indicates that there are small or non-existent differences in moral reasoning between males and females. For example, Walker et al. (1987) reported a meta-analysis, in which only 8 out of 54 studies revealed significant evidence of sex differences in moral development. That confirms Gilligan's view that Kohlberg had unfairly concluded that female moral development was less advanced than male moral development. In addition, as Durkin (1995, p.493) pointed out, Gilligan's "critical perspective opened up the study of moral development in important ways by broadening conceptions of what morality is and how it should be measured."

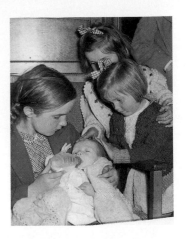

Girls are more likely than boys to respond attentively to babies.

Facts and values

According to the traditional view, science involves the discovery of facts, and these facts can be distinguished from values. A different view is favoured by constructionists such as Gergen (1985). They argue that values determine what are regarded as facts. In other words, "scientific knowledge, like all other knowledge, cannot be disinterested or politically neutral" (Hare-Mustin & Maracek, 1988, p.456).

> How would you measure moral development in a way that is not gender-specific? Make direct reference to the work of Kohlberg and Gilligan in order to arrive at a non-gender-specific scale.

Burns (1993, p.103) provided an example of how society's values can influence the approach taken to women. She pointed out that a major focus of research on women with learning disabilities is on "sexuality and the issues and concerns surrounding women with learning disabilities becoming pregnant, having babies, being sterilised, using contraception, managing periods and being sexually abused." In other words, such women are seen in a negative way in terms of the possible problems they may cause. As Burns (1993, p.103) pointed out, "the consequence of this position is to deny women with learning disabilities a positive identity and role as a woman."

If values help to determine the focus of research and the "facts" that are discussed, then it is very important to adopt a suitable approach. This issue was raised by Griffin (1995, p.120), who put forward a feminist approach. According to this approach, the criteria for useful research, "include the extent to which women's perspectives are considered in research outcomes; the accountability of researchers; and the potential contribution of research to the empowerment of women and to progressive social change."

As well as influencing the focus of research, values also determine in part the ways in which findings are interpreted. In most cultures, achievement and self-reliance are regarded as more important for boys than for girls, whereas nurturance or being supportive is thought to be more important for girls than for boys (Barry et al., 1957). These sex differences have sometimes been interpreted as being "natural" or biologically determined. As Hare-Mustin and Maracek (1988, p.459) pointed out, these sex differences probably depend in large measure on the fact that men tend to be in more powerful positions than women: "women's concern with relationships can be understood as the need to please others that arises from a lack of power ... those in power advocate rules, discipline, control, and rationality, whereas those without power espouse relatedness and compassion."

> ■ Research activity: Make a list of value-free factual points about the experience of studying psychology. Now make a second list of value-free factual points about female psychology students. How difficult was it to construct non-judgemental views for either list? To what extent did gender appear to be an issue?

In sum, there is evidence of gender bias within psychology. However, most of the clearest examples of such bias occurred a long time ago. This suggests that psychologists have become more concerned to avoid gender bias.

PERSONAL REFLECTIONS

- In my view, one of the greatest problems that psychology has to face is the following: those issues that lend themselves to precise, well-controlled experimentation tend to be fairly trivial, whereas important issues are difficult or impossible to submit to proper experimental tests. For example, we can study the motivational effects of hunger in the rat on its lever-pressing behaviour in the laboratory. However, we have no scientific way of exploring the motivational forces that lead some people to work exceptionally hard at their careers for several decades. One partial answer to this problem (which I have tried to apply in my own research) is to study moderately important issues in as scientific and controlled way as is possible.

SUMMARY

Advertising, propaganda, and psychological warfare

Subliminal advertising does not seem to be effective. Advertisements are more likely to be memorable if they are distinctive in some way, or if they require effort to understand them. Advertisements and propaganda are more persuasive if the communicator is trustworthy, attractive, and similar to the receivers, and if he or she has expertise and credibility. Presenting both sides of the argument is usually more effective than presenting only one, especially among receivers who already know some of the counter-arguments. Motivated receivers are influenced mainly by the content of a message, whereas those who are less motivated are influenced by non-content aspects of the message and by the context. Propaganda is often produced by a powerful government in the form of short, emotional messages that are seen and heard at the same time. Propaganda is most effective when it is consistent with the receivers' ideology, and when they process it by the peripheral route. Propaganda is usually intended to change beliefs about other groups, but may also be intended to change behaviour. The techniques used in

During the Second World War the British government used posters to encourage women to replace men in factories and on farms, which required a major shift in behaviour and attitudes towards women and work. After the war, when men were once more available for such work, there were attempts to persuade women to revert to pre-war attitudes and behaviour, which were not always successful.

psychological warfare include brainwashing, sensory and perceptual deprivation, propaganda, and interrogation.

According to the traditional view, science involves the collection of objective data and the drawing of generalisations. This view has been challenged. Four features generally associated with science are as follows: falsifiability; use of a paradigm; replicable findings; and relatively objective data. Three of the main goals of science are prediction, understanding, and control. According to social constructionists, the observations made by psychologists, and their interpretations of those observations, are determined by cultural forces. Kuhn claimed psychology has failed to develop a paradigm. Laboratory studies in psychology are often well controlled and possess internal validity. However, they often lack external validity or ecological validity. Humanistic psychologists and social constructionists argue that psychology should not be a science, and social constructionists argue further that it cannot be a science. Psychology has some features of a science (falsifiability; replicability) but does not fully possess other features (paradigm; objectivity).

Is psychology a science?

Many psychologists in the Western world have ignored important cross-cultural differences. It is important to distinguish between emic constructs, which are specific to a given culture, and etic constructs, which are universal. Racial bias often takes the form of evaluating other cultures against the technological and cultural achievements of the United States and Europe, and concluding that other cultures are primitive or undeveloped.

Cultural diversity and bias

One form of gender bias is alpha bias, which is the tendency to exaggerate gender differences. The other form of gender bias is beta bias, which is the tendency to minimise or ignore gender differences. In the Western world, alpha bias has been more common than beta bias. A key issue with respect to gender bias is the extent to which values determine facts.

Gender and bias

FURTHER READING

Some of the issues discussed in this chapter are discussed in M.W. Eysenck (1994), *Perspectives on psychology*, Hove, UK: Psychology Press. There is good coverage of cross-cultural research and the issues it raises in P. Smith and M.H. Bond (1993), *Social psychology across cultures: Analysis and perspectives*, New York: Harvester Wheatsheaf. There is broad coverage of controversial issues in A. Wadeley, A. Birch, and A. Malim (1997), *Perspectives in psychology (2nd Edn.)*, London: Macmillan.

REVISION QUESTIONS

1a Describe how psychologists have studied personality and intelligence through psychometric testing.

(12 marks)

1b Assess how such work might be considered controversial.

(12 marks)

2   Critically consider arguments for and against psychology being regarded as a science.

(24 marks)

3   "When psychologists began to study women in their own right, they found that many of women's experiences ... had simply been left out of psychology altogether: experiences like female sexuality, pregnancy, childbirth and breastfeeding; the experience of bringing up small children, or being a woman in a male-dominated workplace, or trying to juggle motherhood and paid work. Those experiences are still not covered in most of the mainstream psychology textbooks" (Kitzinger, 1998). Critically consider examples of gender bias in psychological theory or research.

(24 marks)

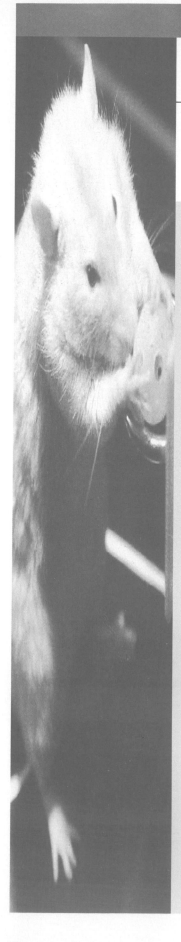

- **Use of human participants**
  Deception, confidentiality, and the acceptable use of data from psychological studies.

  Berkun et al.'s study of fear in soldiers
  Views of Milgram and Zimbardo's work
  Gamson et al.'s market research study
  Ethical committees and guidelines
  Kimmel's cross-cultural meta-analysis

- **Use of participants**
  Why use animals in research? Do animals have "rights"?

  Animals in research vs. psychology
  Specieism and racism
  Absolute and relative morality
  BPS guidelines (1985)
  Cuthill's meta-analysis of animal studies

- **Socially sensitive research**
  Psychologists must consider the social consequences of their research.

  Sieber and Stanley's definition
  Interpretation and application of results (e.g. racial theories, eyewitness testimony)
  Scarr's defence of socially sensitive research

- **Socially sensitive research areas**
  Research relating to race, sexual orientation, or ethnic background needs special care.

  Race-related studies
  Kitzinger and Coyle's phases of studies into "alternative" sexuality
  Cultural diversity: Berry's theory of acculturation

29

Ethical Issues

S cientists often confront important ethical questions in the course of their work. For example, was it morally defensible for physicists to develop the atomic bomb during the 1940s? Can research on human embryos be justified? Should scientists participate in the development of chemical weapons that could potentially kill millions of people? All these questions about the ethics of scientific research are hard to answer, because there are good arguments for and against each programme of research.

There are probably more major ethical issues associated with research in psychology than in any other scientific discipline. There are various reasons for this. First, all psychological experiments involve the study of living creatures (whether human or the members of some other species), and their right to be treated in a caring and respectful way can be infringed by an unprincipled or careless experimenter.

Second, the findings of psychological research may reveal what seem to be unpleasant or unacceptable facts about human nature, or about certain groups within society. No matter how morally upright the experimenter may be, there is always the danger that extreme political organisations will use the findings to further their political aims.

Third, psychological research may lead to the discovery of powerful techniques that can be used for purposes of social control. There is the danger that such techniques might be exploited by dictators or others seeking to exert unjustifiable influence on society or to inflame people's prejudices.

Use of Human Participants

The human participant in a psychological experiment is in a rather vulnerable and exploitable position. As Kelman (1972, p.993) pointed out, "most ethical problems arising in social research can be traced to the subject's power deficiency."

The power of the experimenter

The experimenter is often a person of fairly high status (such as a university researcher or professor), and he or she has expertise and knowledge about the experimental situation which are not shared by the participant. When an experiment takes place in the laboratory, the experimenter has the advantage of operating on "home ground", and the setting is almost entirely under his or her control. In addition, the acceptance of scientific research as an activity that is valued by society also enhances the position of power enjoyed by the experimenter.

The power of the participant

The position of the participant is typically very different. He or she may have lower academic status than the experimenter, and may have only a partial understanding of the purpose of the experiment. As a result, the participant assumes the experimenter knows what he or she is doing, and so surrenders control of the experimental situation to him or her. This makes it unlikely that the participant will question what is being done, or refuse to continue further with an experiment, even if he or she finds that what is involved is distasteful.

The lengths to which participants will go to fulfil what they regard as their obligations to the experimenter were shown most strikingly by Milgram (1974; see Chapter 21). About half of his participants were prepared to give very severe electric shocks to another participant in a learning experiment when the experimenter told them they must. This shows a very high degree of obedience to the power and authority of the experimenter. It should be noted, however, that most of the participants did not totally surrender responsibility to the experimenter in an unthinking way. Many of those who obeyed the experimenter became very tense and uneasy as the experiment progressed, and were acutely aware of the moral dilemma in which they had been placed.

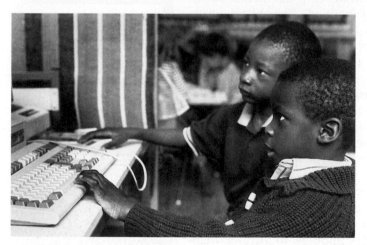

If research were to suggest that the main reason why black children fail to achieve equality with their white peers is to do with factors within the black community, it might be easier for politicians to ignore poor provision of educational resources.

Use of data

Ethical problems can occur while participants are actually taking part in an experiment. They can also arise from the ways in which information gathered from an experiment is later used. Those who plan and carry out research tend to come from the more powerful and influential groups within society, whereas those who act as participants often come from weak and low-status groups. There is a danger that the knowledge obtained from an experiment might be used to the disadvantage of those who supplied the data.

For example, consider the Moynihan Report (Rainwater & Yancey, 1967). This report identified the disintegration of the black family as the most important barrier to black people's ability to achieve equality. The ethical problem here is that the findings could have been used to discourage politicians from taking action on other fronts, such as reducing inequalities in the distribution of resources.

Changing views

Society's views on ethically acceptable and unacceptable treatment of human participants in research have changed considerably in recent decades. Research carried out by Berkun et al. (1962) did not cause an outcry at the time, but would certainly be regarded as totally unacceptable nowadays. In one of their experiments, the participants were flying in a military plane when one of the engines failed. They were told to fill in an "emergency procedure" form for insurance purposes before the plane ditched in the sea. As you may have guessed, there was nothing actually wrong with the plane—the situation was set up on purpose by the experimenters to observe the effects of fear on behaviour.

Berkun et al. carried out another study in which soldiers were on their own out in the field, and could only communicate with base by using a radio transmitter. Some of the soldiers were exposed to explosions sounding like artillery shells, others were told that there had been an accident causing dangerous radioactive fall-out in the area, and still others were enveloped

KEY STUDY EVALUATION — Berkun

Berkun's studies using soldiers as participants confront us with a slightly different set of ethical issues from studies that use ordinary members of the public as participants. It could be argued that soldiers are trained to follow orders without knowing the full reasoning behind those orders, and thus they are often "deceived". However, does this justify the use of deceit in psychological experiments using soldiers? The fact that military personnel are trained to cope with high levels of stress and fear could explain some of Berkun's findings, as well as offering a rationale for such studies to be undertaken—to test the effectiveness of military training techniques.

in smoke so that they thought a forest fire had broken out. When they tried to contact base, they discovered that their radio transmitters would not work.

Berkun et al. found from blood and urine samples that all three groups of soldiers differed biochemically from control soldiers who were not exposed to stress. They assessed the effects of stress on performance by seeing how rapidly the soldiers repaired the radio. Surprisingly, only soldiers exposed to the artillery shells showed worse performance on this task than the control soldiers.

Ethical issues: Berkun's participants were not told the true nature of the studies, and were therefore deceived. Is deception ever acceptable within research studies?

Discussion points

1. Why would research such as that of Berkun et al. be regarded as ethically unacceptable nowadays?
2. Why do you think that views about the kinds of research that are ethically unacceptable have changed over the years?

Milgram

Milgram's (1974) research on obedience to authority was carried out in the days before most institutions had ethical committees responsible for ensuring the ethical acceptability of all research. He asked his participants to administer very strong (and possibly lethal) electric shocks to someone who was said to suffer from a heart condition. It is very unlikely that an ethical committee would permit the type of research done by Milgram, which explains why very few such studies have been carried out in recent years. Milgram's research failed to fulfil some criteria that are now regarded as very important. The participants were deceived about key aspects of the study, such as the fact that the other person did not actually receive any shocks. When any of the participants said they wanted to leave the experiment or to stop giving electric shocks, they were told that they had to continue with the experiment. Nowadays it is standard practice to make it clear to participants that they have the right to withdraw from the experiment at any time without providing an explanation. However, Milgram's research did provide us with important insights into obedience to authority.

With hindsight, the work of Milgram can be regarded as ethically unacceptable. However, it has been invaluable in extending knowledge, and led psychologists to become more aware of their social responsibilities towards individual research participants.

Zimbardo

Zimbardo's (1973) Stanford prison experiment is another study from many years ago that raises considerable ethical issues (see Chapter 21). In this study, a mock prison was set up with mock guards and mock prisoners. Some of the mock guards behaved very aggressively, causing four of the mock prisoners to be released because of "extreme depression, disorganised thinking, uncontrollable crying and fits of rage" (Zimbardo, 1973). Savin (1973) compared Zimbardo to used-car salesmen and others "whose roles tempt them to be as obnoxious as the law allows." He concluded that:

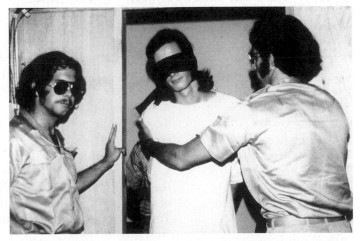

Professors who ... deceive, humiliate, and otherwise mistreat their students, are subverting the atmosphere of mutual trust and intellectual honesty without which, as we are fond of telling outsiders who want to meddle in our affairs, neither education nor free inquiry can flourish.

Zimbardo tried to minimise the after-effects of participation in his Stanford prison experiment by asking the participants to sign an informed consent form before the experiment began. Even so, some of the mock guards became very aggressive during the experiment, and four of the mock prisoners had to be released early.

Zimbardo pointed out that all of his participants had signed a formal informed consent form, which indicated that there would be an invasion of privacy, loss of some civil rights, and harassment. He also noted that day-long debriefing sessions were held with the participants, so that they could understand the moral conflicts being studied. However, Zimbardo failed to protect his participants from physical and mental harm. It was entirely predictable that the mock guards would attack the mock prisoners, because that is exactly what had happened in a pilot study that Zimbardo carried out before the main study.

General principles

Most ethical problems in human research stem from the participant being typically in a much less powerful position than the experimenter. It follows that steps need to be taken to ensure that the participant is not placed in a powerless and vulnerable position.

Consent and deception

In general, the easiest method to empower the participant is to make sure he or she is told precisely what will happen in the course of the experiment. After that, he or she is asked to give **voluntary informed consent** to take part. However, small children are unable to provide informed consent, and there are some types of experiments in which deception is an essential feature of the research. Deception is certainly widespread. Menges (1973) considered about 1000 experimental studies that had been carried out in the United States. Full information about what was going to happen was provided in only 3% of cases.

Even the most independent of individuals can feel the need to conform under social pressure from peers.

A well-known example of research involving deception is the work of Asch (1956; see Chapter 21). He gave participants the task of deciding which one of three lines was equal in length to a standard line. This task was done in groups of between four and eleven people, all but one of whom were "stooge" participants working under instructions from the experimenter. The participants gave their judgements one at a time, and the seating was arranged so that the genuine participant gave his or her opinion last. On key trials, all the stooge participants gave the same wrong answer. The aim of the experiment was to see whether the genuine participants would conform to group pressure, which happened on about one-third of the trials. If the participants had been told the experiment was designed to study conformity to group pressure, and that all the other participants were stooges of the experimenter, then this important study would have been pointless.

One possible reaction is to argue that there should never be any deception in psychological experiments, even if that means that some lines of research have to stop. However, this ignores the fact that many forms of deception are entirely harmless. For example, some memory researchers are interested in incidental learning, which involves people's ability to remember information they were not asked to remember. This can only be done by deceiving the participants as to the true purpose of the experiment until the memory test is presented.

When is deception justified? There is no simple answer. Various relevant factors need to be taken into consideration. First, the less potentially damaging the consequences of the deception, the more likely it is to be acceptable. Second, it is easier to justify the use of deception in studies that are important in scientific terms than in those that are trivial. Third, deception is more justifiable when there are no alternative, deception-free ways of studying an issue.

Handling the deception issue

One way of avoiding the ethical problems associated with deception is the use of **role-playing experiments**. The participants are asked to play the role of participants in a deception experiment, but they are told beforehand about the experimental manipulations. This approach eliminates the ethical problems of deception studies, but it is not clear that it is a satisfactory way of studying behaviour. As Freedman (1969) pointed out, what we are likely to obtain from role-playing studies are "people's guesses as to how they would behave if they were in a particular situation."

■ Research activity: Imagine that you are one of twelve participants role-playing a jury, after viewing a video of a simulated event. Consider whether you would be more or less likely to find the accused guilty or innocent because:

(a) This is a pretend situation.

(b) You are:
  (i)   emotionally committed to the decision.
  (ii) motivated to put forward personal views.
  (iii) in a position to empathise with the accused and/or victim.
  (iv) able to recall all the events.
  (v)   able to believe the situation to be real.
  (vi) able to feel the decision matters.

After considering these factors, do you think role play is a valuable research technique or an effective way to measure human behaviour?

Gamson, Fireman, and Rytina

Another way of handling the deception issue was used by Gamson, Fireman, and Rytina (1982). Their participants were told that they were taking part in market research. They were videotaped while they discussed in groups what was described as a forthcoming court case concerning the manager of a filling station who had lost his franchise because he was living with someone to whom he was not married. The man had decided to sue the company for breach of contract and for invasion of privacy.

The experimenters made repeated efforts to persuade the participants to argue for a point of view different from their own. What was of major interest to Gamson et al. was the extent to which the participants would be willing to go along with these attempts at persuasion. In fact, nearly all the groups refused to continue at some point, because they resented being manipulated by the experimenter.

The participants clearly needed to be deceived for the experiment to be carried out. Gamson et al. addressed this ethical issue by arranging for all the potential participants to be telephoned beforehand. They were asked whether they would be willing to take part in research in which they would be misled about its purpose until after it was over. Only those who indicated that they were willing to do this were later recruited for the actual experiment.

How could a role-playing experiment be used in this teacher's meeting without deceiving the participants?

Discussion points

1. Could the approach adopted by Gamson et al. be adapted to handle the deception issue in most kinds of research?
2. Are there any ethical problems with the approach used by Gamson et al.?

Right to withdraw

Whether or not an experiment involves deception, there are other important safeguards that should be built into nearly all experiments on humans. It should be made clear to the participants at the outset of the experiment that they have the **right to withdraw** from the experiment at any time. Furthermore, they do not have to say why they are withdrawing from the experiment if they choose not to do so. If the participants wish, they can also insist that the data they have provided during the experiment should be destroyed. The right to withdraw, when coupled with voluntary informed consent, helps to ensure that those taking part in research are not powerless and vulnerable.

Debriefing

Another important safeguard in experimental research is **debriefing**. There are two main aspects to debriefing:

1. Provision of information about the experiment.
2. Attempts to reduce any distress that may have been caused by the experiment.

However, as is pointed out in *Ethical principles for conducting research with human participants* (published by the BPS in 1993; reproduced on pp.810–811), the fact that participants are debriefed does not justify carrying out any unethical procedures.

Milgram

What other reasons could there be for the fact that so many of Milgram's participants said they were glad to have taken part in the experiments? Would the fact that they were paid volunteers have any effect on how they felt afterwards, or on what they told the experimenters?

Milgram's (1974) research on obedience provides a good example of how debriefing often works. At the end of the experiment, the participants were reassured that they had not actually given any electric shocks to the learner. They then had a lengthy discussion with the experimenter and with the person who had apparently received the electric shocks. Those participants who had obeyed the experimenter by being willing to give severe shocks were told that their behaviour was normal, and that many others who had taken part in the experiment had also experienced feelings of conflict and tension. All the participants later received a detailed report on the study.

The debriefing and other procedures used by Milgram seem to have been successful. Over 80% of the participants said they were glad to have taken part in the experiment, and only 1% expressed negative feelings about the experiment. Further questioning revealed that four-fifths of the participants felt that more experiments of this sort should be carried out, and 74% said they had learned something of personal importance as a result of taking part.

Discussion points

1. Milgram's research on obedience to authority is often regarded as ethically unacceptable. Do the debriefing procedures used by Milgram make his research more acceptable?

2. Is there anything else Milgram could have done to reassure his participants?

When setting up observational research it is important to consider whether the participants would normally expect to be observed by strangers in the situation. For example, making observations of the people in this picture would be acceptable, but observing them in a changing room would not.

Confidentiality and stress

Another safeguard that is increasingly built into experimental research is that of **confidentiality**. The convention in psychology is for published accounts of research to refer to group means, but to withhold information about the names and the performance of individuals. If the experimenter cannot guarantee anonymity, then this should be made clear to potential participants beforehand. There are very exceptional cases in which it is appropriate to ignore confidentiality. Suppose, for example, that the behaviour of a severely depressed patient in an experiment leads the researcher to suspect that he or she may commit suicide. It may then be necessary for the well-being of the patient to break the confidentiality rule.

At a more general level, it is essential that investigators ensure that they protect those who participate in their studies. Of particular importance is the need to protect them from stress, however this might be created.

Outside the laboratory

Finally, there are issues that arise with observational research or field experiments, in which people are observed in real-life settings rather than in the laboratory. According to the ethical principles of the British Psychological Society, such observations should not be made when the participants would not normally expect to be observed by strangers, unless informed consent is given beforehand.

Ethical committees

One way of trying to ensure that psychological research is ethically acceptable is by setting up *ethical committees*. Most institutions (e.g. universities; research units) in which research is carried out now have their own ethical committee, which considers all research proposals from the perspective of the rights and dignity of the participants. The existence of such committees helps to correct the power imbalance between experimenter and participant. However, if all the members of an ethical committee are researchers in psychology, they may be disinclined to turn down proposals from professional colleagues. For this and other reasons, it is desirable for every ethical committee to include some non-psychologists and at least one non-expert member of the public.

Ethical guidelines

In many countries, professional bodies of psychologists maintain an active involvement in ensuring that all psychological research conforms to ethical principles. For example,

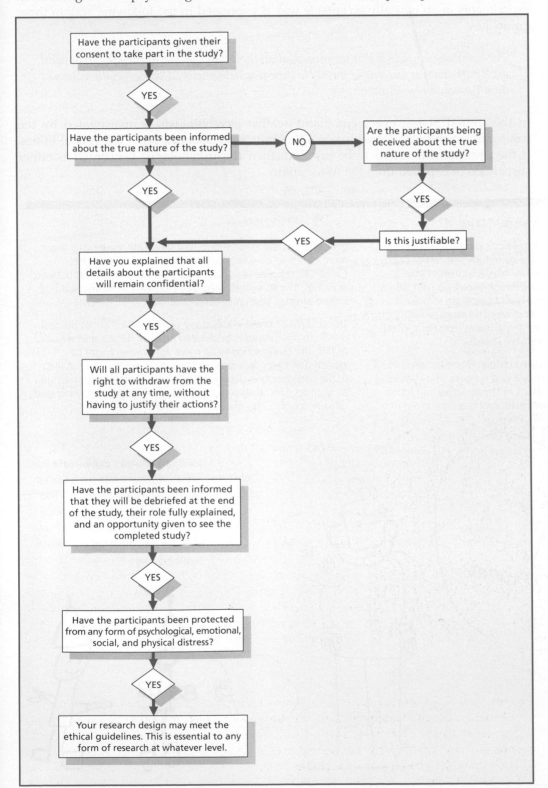

Without ethical guidelines, how difficult would it be to express misgivings about questionable research methods?

the British Psychological Society and the American Psychological Association have published detailed guidelines for the ethical conduct of research in Britain and the United States, respectively. These guidelines include several conditions designed to protect human participants, including voluntary participation, informed consent, right to withdraw, privacy, and freedom from harm.

The *Ethical principles for conducting research with human participants* issued by the British Psychological Society should be followed by all researchers in the United Kingdom, including students carrying out experiments as part of their course. The key to conducting experiments in an ethically acceptable way is expressed in the following way in these guidelines:

> *The essential principle is that the investigation should be considered from the standpoint of all participants; foreseeable threats to their psychological well-being, health, values or dignity should be eliminated.*

In the United States, every complaint against psychologists is investigated by the American Psychological Association's Committee on Scientific and Professional Ethics. If the complaint is found to be justified, then the psychologist concerned is either suspended or expelled from the Association.

CASE STUDY: *Drawing Santa Claus*

Some studies that involve deception of participants can still be regarded as ethically acceptable. One such study was carried out by Solley and Haigh in 1957 (described in Solley & Murphy, 1960). It involved a study on children focusing on a phenomenon resembling "perceptual set". Perceptual set is a bias to perceive a stimulus in a particular way as opposed to any other way, and can arise from external cues (the environment) or internal forces (emotions) which make the individual more sensitive to the stimuli.

In their study, Solley and Haigh asked children aged between 4 and 8 to draw pictures of Santa Claus and his gifts. The children drew their pictures before and after Christmas. Solley and Haigh suggested that emotional set (anticipation of the excitement of

Christmas) would lead to increased sensitivity resulting in larger, more elaborate drawings before Christmas, whereas after Christmas, reduced sensitivity would lead to smaller, less detailed drawings. The study indicated that increased sensitivity had indeed affected perceptual organisation.

The children involved in this study were deceived about the real reason for the research. In order to produce natural and realistic results, the children had to be naive about what might be expected of them. However, in this case deception did not lead to the participants experiencing any form of stress and so could be justified. This study was also ecologically valid, as it generated valuable insights into the effect of perceptual set.

Solley and Haigh's experiment was recently replicated with some Cornish children, with these results. The two larger, more elaborate versions were drawn just before Christmas, but after Christmas they produced the smaller, simple drawings.

Cross-cultural issues

Kimmel (1996) compared the ethical codes produced by 11 different countries. An ethical code in psychology was first published in the United States in 1953. Several other countries (Australia, France, Germany, and The Netherlands) followed in the 1960s. The United Kingdom had its first ethical code in psychology in 1978, followed by Slovenia (1982), Canada (1986), and Scandinavia (1989). Finally, Spain and Switzerland produced ethical codes in the early 1990s.

There are important similarities among the ethical codes produced by the various countries. Most focus on three basic principles:

1. Protection of individuals from physical harm.
2. Protection of individuals from psychological harm.
3. Confidentiality of the data obtained from individual participants.

It is argued in nearly all of the ethical codes that informed consent and avoidance of deception are important in ensuring that the first two principles are achieved.

There are some differences in the ethical codes adopted by different countries. The French ethical code emphasises the fundamental rights of individuals, but has little to say about the ways in which research should be conducted, or on the importance of informed consent. The British ethical code differs from many others in that it is mainly concerned with research rather than the ethical issues posed by the professional activities of clinical psychologists. The ethical code in the Netherlands contains many very general statements, and so is hard to use in practice. One example is as follows: "The psychologist shall not employ methods that are in any way detrimental to the client's dignity or that penetrate into the client's private life deeper than is necessary for the objectives set." Another example is: "The psychologist shall do everything within his power to ensure that the client is entirely free to decide in a responsible manner whether to enter into the professional relationship."

Ethical issues: Do we need to create a universal code of ethics that incorporates the best features from all the national codes?

There is a valuable feature of the American and Canadian ethical codes that is absent from the other nine. These two codes made use of an empirical approach, in which professional psychologists were asked to indicate how they personally resolved ethical issues. As a result, the American and Canadian codes contain case examples and applications of key research principles. These concrete examples make it easier for psychologists to follow ethical principles in the ways intended.

Use of Animals

Animals and medicines

Animal work has been very useful in the medical field, and has led to the saving of millions of human lives. For example, Alexander Fleming discovered penicillin in 1928. However, it was only in 1940 that research on mice showed that penicillin was a very effective antibiotic. Another example concerns kidney dialysis, which is required by about 200,000 people every year in the United States if they are to stay alive. The drug heparin is essential for dialysis, and it has to be extracted from animal tissues, and then tested for safety on anaesthetised animals.

Animals and psychological research

The benefits of animal research are less clear in psychology than in medicine. However, there are several reasons why psychologists use non-human animals in so many of their experiments. It is possible (although there are major ethical considerations) to carry out surgical procedures on animals that simply would not be permissible with humans. Gray (1985) discussed animal research designed to identify those parts of the brain associated with anxiety. This animal research stemmed from work on humans, in which it was found that anti-anxiety drugs such as the benzodiazepines and alcohol had 19 separate effects. These findings were compared against those of animal studies in which the effects of

Monkeys reared in isolation react very aggressively when they are brought together (Harlow & Mears, 1979). This sort of social deprivation would be unacceptable in an experiment on human beings.

septo-hippocampal lesions or cuts were observed. The effects of these lesions were very similar to those of anti-anxiety drugs in humans in 18 out of 19 cases. It is probable that the septo-hippocampal system is involved in anxiety, and so lesions or cuts in it produce the same non-anxious behaviour as anti-anxiety drugs.

Social deprivation

It is possible to expose non-human animals to prolonged periods of social or other forms of deprivation. For example, studies have been carried out on monkeys who were not allowed to interact with other monkeys for the first few months of life. When monkeys who had been brought up in isolation were brought together, they reacted very aggressively (Harlow & Mears, 1979). Early isolation also produced a virtual absence of a sex life in adulthood. These findings indicate the potentially severe effects of social isolation.

Heredity and early experiences

The members of many species develop and reproduce over much shorter time periods than do members of the human species. As a result, it is much more feasible to carry out studies focusing on the effects of either heredity or early experience on behaviour in such species. For example, in one study a breeding programme was used to produce rats who were either reactive or non-reactive to loud noise and bright lights (Eysenck & Broadhurst, 1964). The reactive rats were found to be much more anxious than the non-reactive ones in a wide range of situations. These findings suggest that individual differences in anxiety depend in part on genetic factors.

Instead of using poison to deter birds from eating crops, a recent programme of research into animal behaviour has led to the development of more effective scarecrows.

Behaviour

It is generally accepted that the human species is more complex than other species. It may thus be easier to understand the behaviour of other species than that of humans. This makes animal research very useful, provided we assume that other species are broadly similar to our own. This line of argument was used by the behaviourists to justify the fact that rats (rather than humans) were used in most of their experiments.

Much animal research is acceptable to nearly everyone. Malim, Birch, and Wadeley (1992) discussed examples of such animal research. One programme of research was designed to provide us with a better understanding of the behaviour of animals that damage crops. This research led to the development of more effective scarecrows, so that more unpleasant methods of preventing crop damage (e.g. poison) were no longer needed. In this case, animal research actually served to produce a large reduction in animal suffering.

Another example of animal research that was almost entirely beneficial in its effects was reported by Simmons (1981). Pigeons were carefully trained by means of operant conditioning to detect life rafts floating on the sea. Pigeons have excellent vision, and so their detection performance was much better than that of helicopter crews: 85% detection compared to only 50%. In this case, animal research has enabled many human lives to be saved.

Psychological examinations of animals can produce benefits for the animals themselves as well as for humans. Examples include wildlife management programmes, efforts to preserve endangered species, and conservation programmes (Cardwell et al., 1996).

Numbers of animals used

How many animals are used in psychological research? Thomas and Blackman (1991) answered that question for psychology departments in the United Kingdom in 1977 and 1989. The figure for the earlier year was 8694 animals, whereas it was only 3708 animals in 1989. This dramatic reduction over a 12-year period has almost certainly continued since 1989. Several species were used in psychological research, but about 95% of the total was accounted for by just three species: the mouse, the rat, and the pigeon.

The total figures for animal research of all kinds are declining year by year, but are still very high. According to Mukerjee (1997), about 1.5 million primates, dogs, cats, guinea pigs, rabbits, hamsters, and other similar species are used in laboratories in the United States each year. In addition, however, about 17 million rats, mice, and birds are used in American research every year.

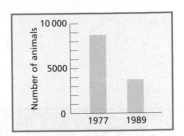

Between 1977 and 1989 the numbers of animals used in experiments in the UK reduced considerably.

Society's views

In the long run, the ethical principles applied to animal research depend on the views of society at large. However, there are enormous differences of opinion among members of the public. Some people are totally opposed to all animal experiments, whereas others are in favour of animal experiments so long as unnecessary suffering is avoided. In order to obtain some factual information, Furnham and Pinder (1990) gave a questionnaire examining attitudes to animal experimentation to 247 young adults. Their average views were not extremely for or against animal research. For example, they agreed on average with the statements that "Research from animal labs produces great benefits in the lives of both animals and people", and "There should be more animal experimentation in areas of medicine where cures are not yet known (AIDS etc.)", and they disagreed with the statement, "I believe in total abolition of animal experiments". On the other hand, they agreed that "All lethal experiments on animals of all sorts should be banned", and "There is no justification for the use of animal experimentation in the testing of cosmetics", and they disagreed with the statement that "Fundamental (for no specific purpose) research using animals is valid".

Furnham and Pinder found that different groups varied in terms of how much they were opposed to animal experimentation. Females were more opposed than males, left-wing people were more opposed than right-wing people, and vegetarians were more opposed than non-vegetarians. Other studies have indicated that people who are older or less educated tend to be more in favour of animal experiments than those who are younger or better educated (Mukerjee, 1997). Thus, no set of ethical principles for animal experimentation could possibly satisfy all of these different groups of people.

Dogs that are trained to sniff out drugs and explosives act as if they enjoy their work which is useful to human society.

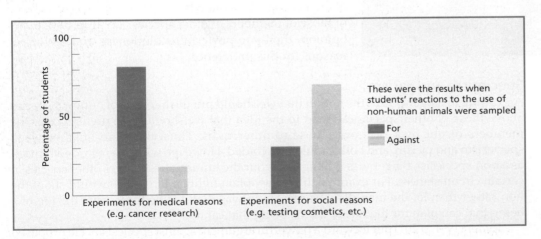

These were the results when students' reactions to the use of non-human animals were sampled

■ For
□ Against

What factors might account for these results?

Cross-cultural differences

There are also important cultural differences in attitudes towards animal research. Mukerjee pointed out that there is a higher level of public support for animal research in

Is the rise of vegetarianism, anti-hunting lobbies, and conservation groups responsible for changing attitudes to the use of animals in research?

the United States than in Europe. However, even in the United States, there has been a decline in support. In 1985, 63% of Americans agreed with the statement that "scientists should be allowed to do research that causes pain and injury to animals like dogs and chimpanzees *if* it produces new information about human health problems". Ten years later, that figure had dropped to 53%.

Change over time

It is not surprising that the views of society have changed over the years. As Herzog (1988) pointed out, our moral codes depend on what he referred to as "human psychology". In other words, our particular values, emotions, and beliefs determine our position on ethical issues. Herzog argued that an alternative approach would be one based on "pure reason", but ethical issues do not lend themselves to any simple logical resolution.

Speciesism

Human participants in experiments must have their rights and feelings protected by requiring experimenters to follow strict ethical guidelines. However, a key issue is whether non-human participants deserve (as far as possible) to be as fully protected as humans by ethical guidelines. This issue relates to the notion of **speciesism**, which is "discrimination and exploitation based upon a difference in species" (Ryder, 1990). As we will see, some experts (e.g. Gray, 1991) are in favour of speciesism, whereas others (e.g. Ryder, 1990, 1991; Singer, 1991) are strongly opposed to it.

We are more willing to inflict suffering on species other than our own, and on species for which we feel fear or disgust. Rats are among the most commonly used laboratory animals, but the pet owner in the picture would be as unhappy about inflicting pain on one as he would be about inflicting pain on a puppy or kitten.

Gray accepted that it is ethically wrong to inflict unnecessary pain on the members of any species. However, he also argued that, "we owe a special duty to members of our own species" (1991, p.197). It is thus acceptable to inflict a fairly high level of suffering on animals to avoid a smaller level of suffering by humans, as is often the case in medical research. However, Gray accepted that there comes a point at which the level of suffering inflicted on animals becomes unacceptable. Gray's major reason for believing in speciesism is that, "It is likely ... to be better for lions, tigers, mice and men if they each put the interests of their conspecifics [members of their own species] ahead of those of members of other species" (1991, p.198). In his opinion, there are powerful evolutionary and biological reasons for this preference.

Speciesism and racism

According to Singer (1991), the notion that we should put the interests of our own species above those of other species can lead to the idea that we should give preference to the members of our own race over those of other races. Thus, there are links between speciesism and racism, and both should be avoided. However, while he regarded himself as a non-speciesist, Singer was willing to favour the human species over other species in certain circumstances. For example, if he saw a lion fighting a man, he would shoot the lion rather than let the man die. His reasoning was that it is better to save the life of a being that can plan for the future than a being that cannot.

Ryder (1991, p.201) put forward a powerful argument against speciesism. He proposed that speciesism, racism, and sexism all

discriminate unjustly against individuals on irrelevant grounds such as skin colour, physical sexual characteristics and quadrupedality [having four legs]. The infliction of pain or distress upon others without consent is wrong—regardless of their race, sex, or species.

Ryder also rejected Gray's argument that speciesism is acceptable because it has biological origins. According to him, what is ethically right should not be based on biology. As Ryder pointed out, "Presumably, Gray would also defend rape, pillage, and murder ... where these behaviours have 'biological origins'" (1991, p.201).

Ethical issues

The position that is taken on the issue of using animals in research depends on how similar to humans other species are seen to be. It is much less reasonable to use animals in a wide range of experiments if they are rather similar to us than if they are very different. Views on the similarity of our species to others have changed very much over the centuries. At one extreme is the seventeenth-century philosopher René Descartes. He argued that animals are very much like machines, and that they lack the soul (with its powers of thinking) that is the supreme human characteristic. It follows from this position that animals are inferior to humans.

The views of Charles Darwin (1859) stand in stark contrast to those of Descartes. According to Darwin, the human species has evolved out of other species. As a result, we are all members of the animal kingdom. It is hard from the evolutionary perspective to cling to the notion that we are radically different from other species. We may be more intelligent, of course, but this is simply a matter of degree. In support of Darwin's argument is the fact that the basic physiology and nervous system of nearly all mammalian species are very similar.

Darwin's (1872) work on emotions is of particular importance to the use of animals in research. He was impressed by the similarities in the expression of emotional states between humans and other species. His findings suggest that it might be unwise to assume that animals experience emotions in very different ways from humans. We cannot be certain, however, because there is no way of knowing the emotional experiences of members of other species.

Many psychologists do not believe that the human species is rather similar to other species. Humanistic psychologists argued that a key feature of humans is our need for self-actualisation, which involves full realisation of our potential in all ways. Other species lack this need, focusing instead on much more basic needs such as those for food, drink, and sex. Within the context of the humanistic approach, members of the human species are very different and much more complex than the members of any other species.

There are ethical problems for animal research regardless of the position one adopts on the issue of the relationship between the human and other species. If other species are very different from us, then studies on them cannot tell us about human behaviour. On the other hand, as Mukerjee (1997, p.77) pointed out:

If animals are close enough to humans that their bodies, brains, and even psyches [minds] are good models for the human condition, then ethical dilemmas must surely arise in using them.

Washoe the chimpanzee was taught to communicate with humans using some American Sign Language signs. She still enjoys the company of humans after being part of a study that began in 1966. Have we as humans a responsibility to care for Washoe for the rest of her life, even though she is now 33 years old and has a life expectancy of 60 years?

Types of morality

It is important to distinguish between **absolute morality** and **relative morality**. Immanuel Kant and other philosophers argued in favour of an absolute morality in which the ends cannot justify the means. In contrast, most people probably agree with the notion of relative morality, according to which the acceptability of actions is judged in terms of the benefits that accrue.

Absolute morality. The notion of an absolute morality may have some appeal, but it tends to be inflexible and unrealistic in practice. For example, the moral principle "Always tell the truth" sounds very reasonable. However, if a madman with a gun demands to know where your mother is, it would make very little sense to adhere to the principle.

Relative morality. The alternative view that the ends can justify the means is favoured by most psychologists. It was expressed in the following terms by the American Psychological Association Committee on Ethical Standards in Psychological Research: "The general ethical question is whether there is a negative effect upon the dignity and welfare of the participants that the importance of the research does not warrant." Animal research of high quality, with minimal animal suffering, and with a high probability of benefit is the most justifiable. In contrast, animal research of poor quality, with considerable animal suffering, and with a low probability of benefit is hard to justify.

Ethical issues: When do the ends justify the means? If we cannot ask an animal directly how much pain it is suffering, is it safe to guess how they feel from their behaviour? Do you know for certain how a cat will behave when in distress?

Costs and benefits. The notion that decisions about the use of animals in research should be based on an analysis of the benefits and costs involved is sensible. Suppose, for example, a proposed experiment will inflict considerable pain on several animals. This would surely seem less acceptable if the experiment were designed to produce improved cosmetics than if it were intended to lead to the development of treatment for a dreadful disease affecting humans.

In practice, however, there can be problems. First, it is often impossible to know what the benefits and costs of a piece of research are going to be until after the experiment has been carried out. Second, one person's assessment of the benefits and costs of a piece of research may not agree with someone else's.

Is it possible to empathise with the suffering experienced by another species? Is the creation of pain scales therefore an impossible task?

Levels of suffering. There is the difficult matter of deciding how much suffering a given experimental procedure inflicts on an animal. As we cannot ask an animal directly what it is experiencing, we have to rely on its behaviour. However, this may be a misleading guide to its feelings. What needs to be done is to find out as much as possible about each species. In spite of the problems involved in assessing animal distress, attempts have been made in several countries such as Australia, Canada, and The Netherlands to develop pain scales. According to this form of assessment, 54% of the animals used in The Netherlands in 1995 suffered minor discomfort, 26% had moderate discomfort, and the remaining 20% suffered severe discomfort.

There is growing concern about the ways in which animals are treated—such as these hens living in battery cages.

When a species becomes endangered because of low numbers, is it ethically acceptable to keep representatives of the species in a zoo environment and try to encourage breeding?

Other uses of animals

Finally, we will broaden our discussion to consider the ways in which humans (other than psychologists) treat animals. There are three main areas of concern: meat production; ill-treatment of pets; and animals kept in captivity in zoos and circuses. There is increasing criticism in all three areas. So far as meat production is concerned, it seems cruel and immoral to many people that animals such as calves and chickens are kept in severely restricted conditions so that they can scarcely move. There is also growing concern that the methods of slaughtering used in abattoirs may involve much more suffering than is generally admitted by those involved in meat production.

The UK's Royal Society for the Prevention of Cruelty to Animals is one of the main organisations concerned with ill-treatment of animals. Every year it deals with many thousands of cases of animals that have been starved, beaten, or ill-treated in other ways. Battersea Dogs Home in London receives many dogs every week that have simply been abandoned by their owners. There are indications that public concern at the ill-treatment of pets is growing, at least in terms of the amount of media coverage it commands.

Zoos and circuses have attracted more adverse publicity in recent years. It is argued that animals kept in captivity in relatively restricted and alien environments may suffer stress. There is also disquiet that many circus animals are degraded by being forced to perform unnatural tricks.

In sum, there is growing unease about the ways in which animals are treated. The increased focus on ethical issues in animal experimentation is part of a more general re-evaluation of our relationship with other species. Much remains to be done. However, there are encouraging signs that the rights of animals to humane treatment (whether inside or outside the laboratory) are being increasingly recognised.

Ethical principles

In general terms, most animal researchers subscribe to what are sometimes known as the "three Rs":

- Replacement of animals by other research methods.
- Reduction in the number of animals used by means of more advanced statistical techniques.
- Refinement of experimental procedures to reduce animal suffering.

Use of the three Rs has proved very fruitful. For example, 5000 monkeys a year were used in the Netherlands in the 1970s to produce polio vaccines. During the 1990s, the number was reduced to only 10 monkeys.

The most obvious problem with the use of animals in research is that many of the ethical principles guiding research on human participants cannot be applied. For example, it is impossible for animals to give voluntary informed consent to take part in an experiment, and they cannot be debriefed at the end. Bateson (1986) argued that there are three main criteria that should be taken into account when deciding whether a study on animals is justifiable (this is often known as Bateson's decision cube):

1. The quality of the research: this can be assessed by the funding agency.
2. The amount of animal suffering: this can be assessed from the animal's behaviour and any signs of stress.
3. Likelihood of benefit: this is important, but can be hard to judge ahead of time.

Animal research of high quality, involving minimal suffering, and with a high probability of benefit is the most justifiable. In contrast, animal research of poor quality, involving considerable suffering, and offering a low probability of benefit is hard to justify.

UK guidelines

It is very important for psychologists to develop ethical guidelines to protect animals' rights, and to prevent the animals from suffering or being exploited. Most institutions regard the use of animals in research as being such a sensitive matter that it is normal practice for all proposed animal experiments to be carefully considered by an ethical committee. In the United Kingdom, the Home Office has overall control. Anyone who wants to carry out animal research must have a licence, and inspectors from the Home Office regularly inspect all animal facilities. All research on vertebrates in the United Kingdom is governed by the Animals (Scientific Procedures) Act of 1986. This Act contains numerous safeguards to ensure that vertebrate research is ethically sound.

Investigators in most countries who are planning studies on animals are required to make use of ethical guidelines. Within the United Kingdom, the most important guidelines are those that were issued by the British Psychological Society in 1985. These guidelines state that researchers should "avoid, or at least minimise discomfort to living animals". They represent a systematic attempt to provide a comprehensive set of rules and recommendations to guide the behaviour of any investigators who wish to carry out experiments on non-human participants. Here are the main points of these guidelines:

- First, investigators must be aware of all relevant current legislation. They must comply with all of the laws protecting animals.
- Second, any investigator who intends to harm or stress animals in any way "must consider whether the knowledge to be gained justifies the procedure". Thus, trivial

Cross-cultural issues: Do you think the things that are considered benefits to human society are fixed qualities, or do they vary across cultures and over time? Do the needs of human societies change over time? How might this affect how we decide whether research is ethically acceptable or not?

experiments should not be carried out on animals even if it is possible that they will suffer only low levels of harm or stress.

- Third, account needs to be taken of the differences between species in terms of the pain or discomfort they are likely to experience from a given procedure. If there is any choice, then the members of whichever species will suffer the least should be selected.

- Fourth, experiments should be carefully designed in order to minimise the number of animals that are required for a given experiment. It is recommended that statistical tests allowing several factors to be considered together should be used.

- Fifth, experiments should not be carried out on the members of any endangered species. The only exception is if the experiment is part of a conservation programme.

- Sixth, investigators need to ensure that they obtain animals from reputable suppliers, and that they are provided with detailed information about their history, including any previous laboratory studies in which they have participated. In addition, investigators should confirm that animals are handled appropriately and with minimal stress on the way to the laboratory. If any animals were trapped in the wild, then the investigators should confirm that this was done as painlessly as possible.

Ethical issues: Field experiments can disrupt the animal's natural environment. This can continue to be stressful to the animal long after the experiment has finished.

- Seventh, care should be taken with respect to caging conditions. There are clear differences among species in reactions to caging in isolation and in the effects of high density or crowding. Information on the recommended requirements for the members of the species being caged should be obtained and followed.

- Eighth, investigators engaged in fieldwork should disturb the animals being studied as little as possible. It needs to be remembered that breeding and even survival can be markedly affected by simple observations. Marking animals for identification or attaching radio transmitters may stress them, as may their capture and recapture.

Consider the normal eating and drinking habits of the animals being studied.

- Ninth, animal aggression or predation should preferably be studied in the field rather than by means of staged encounters. If it is necessary to make use of staged encounters, then efforts should be made to use models or animals behind glass.

- Tenth, care should be taken with studies in which animals are deprived of food or water. The key requirement is to consider the normal eating and drinking habits of the animals being studied, and also to pay attention to their metabolic requirements.

- Eleventh, investigators should only use procedures causing pain or distress if there are no other ways in which the experiment can be carried out. In such cases, it is illegal for investigators in the United Kingdom to cause pain or distress unless they hold a Home Office licence together with the relevant certificates.

- Twelfth, no surgical or pharmacological procedures can be carried out on vertebrate animals in the United Kingdom unless the investigators have a Home Office licence plus the relevant certificate. Further safeguards are that only experienced staff should perform these procedures, that the investigators should take steps to prevent post-operative infection, and that they know about the technical aspects of anaesthesia.

- Thirteenth, it is essential that animals receive adequate care following an operation; this may involve the use of local anaesthetics and/or nursing. It is also essential that there is frequent monitoring of each animal's condition. If an animal suffers severe and enduring pain, then it must be killed using recommended procedures for euthanasia.

- Fourteenth, the investigator should obtain a second opinion if he or she is unsure about the condition of any animals involved in an experiment. This second opinion must come from someone who has no direct involvement in the experiment, and is best provided by a qualified veterinarian.
- Fifteenth, there are two organisations that can be contacted if investigators are unclear about any issues relating to animal experimentation. These are the Committee of the Experimental Psychology Society and the Standing Advisory Committee on Standards for Psychological Research and Teaching Involving Animals.

Types of animal research

Most psychological investigations of animals consist of laboratory studies. However, Cuthill (1991) considered over 900 research papers, and found that 46% of them were field studies carried out in the wild. About one-third of the field studies were field experiments, meaning that they involved some kind of experimental manipulation. The four most common types of manipulation used in these studies were as follows:

1. Dummies: these were mainly stuffed dummy predators; in order to be effective, they need to be realistic, and this means that they cause much distress to animals who encounter them.
2. Non-trivial handling: tagging or marking of animals so they can be identified subsequently is an example of this; as mentioned already, this can be a stressful procedure.
3. Playback of recorded signals: these recorded signals are generally realistic; if they are alarm calls, then this can lead to high levels of distress.
4. Food addition: when the experimenter artificially introduces food into an area, it can cause territorial disputes and fights; it can also lead to undesirable changes in the availability of the animals' normal sources of food supply. Thus, food addition can have serious consequences for the animals affected.

Animals are often marked for identification, or have radio transmitters attached to them, to track and observe them in the wild. This may cause significant stress to the animal being observed and might affect their behaviour and possibly even survival.

In order to film wildlife programmes for television, experimental manipulation techniques like the ones listed are sometimes necessary. What are the ethical implications of this?

Socially Sensitive Research

As we have seen, ethical guidelines focus mainly on the well-being and protection of those who participate in experiments. However, much research raises issues of relevance to society as a whole. As a result, psychologists need to be concerned about broader ethical issues. This is true of nearly all psychological research, but is especially true of socially sensitive research. This was defined by Sieber and Stanley (1988, p.49) as

> *studies in which there are potential social consequences or implications either directly for the participants in research or the class of individuals represented by the research.*

Socially sensitive research can produce risks for many people other than those directly involved as participants. Among the non-participants at risk, according to Sieber and Stanley, are the following:

- Members of the groups (e.g. racial; religious) to which the participants belong.
- People closely associated with the participants (e.g. family; friends).
- The experimenter or experimenters.
- The research institution to which the experimenter or experimenters belong.

Ethical issues: Which are more important, the interests of the individual or the interests of society as a whole?

In their thorough discussion of socially sensitive research, Sieber and Stanley argued that important ethical concerns can arise with respect to four major aspects of such research:

1. Deciding on the research question or hypothesis to be tested.
2. The conduct of research and the treatment of participants.
3. The institutional context (e.g. the organisation in which the research is carried out may make unjustified use of the findings).
4. Interpretation and application of research findings, especially the application of findings in ways far removed from the intentions of the experimenter.

What are the kinds of problems that can occur in each of these aspects of research? We have already discussed at some length issues relating to the conduct of research and the treatment of participants. Accordingly, we will focus on the other three aspects here.

Research into sleep deprivation has shown that people are easily confused when under stress from lack of sleep. This apparently innocent finding may have been incorporated into the indoctrination procedures of cults, such as the People's Temple—the followers of Jim Jones who committed mass suicide in Guyana in 1978.

The research question

The first part of the research process involves deciding on the question or questions that the research is designed to answer. Simply asking certain questions can pose ethical issues. For example, suppose that a researcher asks the question, "Are there racial differences in intelligence?", and decides to answer it in a study. It is likely (but not certain) that he or she assumes that there are racial differences in intelligence, and that this assumption is motivating the research. In similar fashion, most researchers who carry out twin studies to decide the extent to which criminality is inherited probably assume that genetic factors are important. The very fact that this issue is being investigated may cause concern to the relatives of criminals.

The institutional context

The institutional context can pose ethical issues in at least two ways. First, if the institutional context is perceived to be prestigious or intimidating, it may make the participants feel powerless and thus affect their behaviour. This happened in the work of Milgram (1974), in which he studied obedience to authority in the form of a willingness to administer very strong electric shocks (see Chapter 21). When the research setting was Yale University, 65% of the participants were fully obedient. This figure dropped to 48% when the setting was a run-down office building. Second, when research is carried out in a company, there can be various ethical problems with respect to the ways in which those running the company use the findings. For example, suppose that a researcher finds that the average stress levels in a company are only moderate. This may lead the company to abandon plans to offer stress counselling to their workers.

Interpretation and application

Application of findings

The research carried out by psychologists such as John Bowlby and Sir Cyril Burt, among others, had a profound effect on social policy. These studies examined the role of the mother in childcare, and the development of IQ, and resulted in policies such as encouraging mothers to stay at home rather than going out to work, and the introduction of the 11-plus examination. The studies posed ethical dilemmas for the researchers because their findings could be used to manipulate human behaviour and life choices, as well as adding to the knowledge-base of science.

No-one doubts that researchers should be concerned about the ways in which their findings are interpreted and applied. However, we need to distinguish between those uses of research findings that are predictable and those that are not. For example, it was predictable that the National Front and other organisations of the extreme right would use findings of racial differences in intelligence for their own ends. However, researchers studying the effects of sleep deprivation could not reasonably have expected that their findings would be used in brainwashing and cult indoctrination.

Eyewitness testimony

By now, you may have decided that socially sensitive research should be avoided altogether. However, some socially sensitive research is wholly desirable and of real benefit to society. Consider, for example, research on eyewitness testimony (see Chapter 13). This research has shown convincingly that the memories of eyewitnesses for events are fragile and easily distorted. An implication is that defendants should not be found guilty solely on the basis of eyewitness identification. However, in the United States in 1973, there were nearly 350 cases in which eyewitness identification was the only evidence of guilt. In 74% of these cases, the defendant was convicted.

As a result of psychological research, courts and juries are less impressed by eyewitness testimony than used to be the case. However, there was a time when such research was ignored. The Devlin Report on Evidence of Identification in Criminal Cases was published in the United Kingdom in 1976. One of its main conclusions was as follows: "The stage seems not yet to have been reached at which the conclusions of psychological research are sufficiently widely accepted or tailored to the needs of the judicial process to become the basis for procedural change."

Evaluation

There is some evidence that socially sensitive research (at least in the United States) is more likely than non-sensitive research to be rejected by institutional ethical committees. Ceci et al. (1985) found that the rejection rate was about twice as great. There are some valid reasons for doing this. The very fact that certain socially sensitive issues are being studied by psychologists can suggest to society at large that these issues are real and important. For example, the fact that psychologists have compared the intelligence of different races implies that there are racial differences, and that intelligence exists and can be measured.

Socially sensitive research can be used to justify various forms of discrimination against individuals or groups. In the most extreme cases, the findings of psychological studies have even been used to produce discriminatory changes in the laws and regulations within a given society. Thus, the findings of socially sensitive research can be used to justify new (and often unwarranted) forms of social control.

A case in point occurred in the United States when intelligence tests were developed in the early years of the twentieth century. Between 1910 and 1920, several American states passed laws designed to prevent certain categories of people (including those of low intelligence) from having children. Psychologists often exerted pressure to have these laws passed. For example, the prominent Californian psychologist Lewis Terman argued as follows: "If we would preserve our state for a class of people worthy to possess it, we must prevent, as far as possible, the propagation of mental degenerates."

As a result of Terman's views, and those of other psychologists, a Californian law of 1918 required all compulsory sterilisations to be approved by a board including "a clinical psychologist holding the degree of PhD". In similar fashion, pressure by psychologists helped to persuade the state of Iowa to legislate in 1913 for "the prevention of the procreation of criminals, rapists, idiots, feeble-minded, imbeciles, lunatics, drunkards, drug fiends, epileptics, syphilitics, moral and sexual perverts, and diseased and degenerate persons."

No psychologists nowadays would agree with the introduction of such harsh measures. However, some psychologists in the second half of the twentieth century have argued that psychological principles should be used for purposes of social control. For example, B.F. Skinner claimed that we can determine and control people's behaviour by providing the appropriate rewards at the appropriate times: "Operant conditioning shapes behaviour as a sculptor shapes a lump of clay." Skinner (1948), in his novel *Walden Two*, described the use of operant conditioning to create an ideal society. He envisaged a high degree of external control in this society, with children being reared mainly by child-rearing professionals, and government being by self-perpetuating committees rather than by elected representatives.

Which different groups of people do you think might face prejudice and discrimination because of findings of socially sensitive research?

Who controls what is acceptable behaviour? Should an individual's behaviour be modified to conform to cultural standards?

The case in favour of socially sensitive research was made by Scarr (1988, p.56). She argued as follows:

> *Science is in desperate need of good studies that highlight race and gender variables ... to inform us of what we need to do to help underrepresented people to succeed in this society. Unlike the ostrich, we cannot afford to hide our heads for fear of socially uncomfortable discoveries.*

Scarr made another important point, arguing that there are very good reasons why most ethical guidelines focus much more on the protection of the participants in experiments than on the protection of the groups to which they belong. In essence, researchers can usually predict fairly accurately the direct effects of their experiment on the participants. However, they are unlikely to be able to predict the indirect effects on the groups to which the participants belong until the outcomes of the experiment are known.

We have considered several advantages and disadvantages of socially sensitive research. It is important to strike a balance. The American Psychological Association tried to do this in its *Ethical principles in the conduct of research with human participants* (1982, p.74):

> *On one side is an obligation to research participants who may not wish to see derogatory information ... published about their valued groups. On the other side is an obligation to publish findings one believes relevant to scientific progress, an objective that in the investigator's views will contribute to the eventual understanding and amelioration of social and personal problems.*

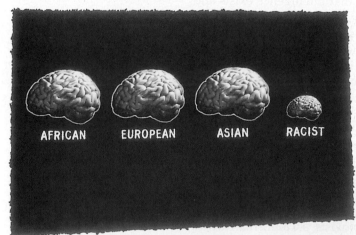

This poster was produced by the European Youth Campaign Against Racism and the Commission for Racial Equality.

Socially Sensitive Research Areas

Race-related research

The best-known (or most notorious) race-related research in psychology has focused on racial differences in intelligence, especially between blacks and whites in the United States (see Chapter 27). Our concern here is with the ethical issues associated with this research. First we will consider the arguments in favour of carrying out such research, followed by the arguments against permitting such research to be done.

One of the main arguments in favour of race-related research is that researchers should be free to carry out whatever research seems important to them. If governments start passing laws to prohibit certain kinds of research, then there is a real danger that research will be stopped for political rather than for ethical reasons. What about the ethics of publishing the findings of race-related research that may be used by racists for their own unacceptable purposes? H.J. Eysenck (1981, pp.167–168) argued that

> *it should not be assumed that those who feel that they have a duty to society to make known the results of empirical work are guided by less lofty ethical aspirations than those who hold the opposite view ... the obvious social problem produced by the existence of racial and class differences in ability can only be solved, alleviated or attenuated by greater knowledge ... it is ethically indefensible to refrain from acquiring such knowledge and making it available to society.*

One of the strongest arguments against race-related research into intelligence is that the findings are often used in unacceptable ways. For example, Goddard (1913) gave intelligence tests to immigrants arriving in New York. He claimed that his findings demonstrated that 87% of Russians, 83% of Jews, 80% of Hungarians, and 79% of Italians were "feeble-minded". Goddard reached this ludicrous conclusion by ignoring the obvious fact that most of these immigrants had a very limited command of the English language.

Subsequent work on immigrant soldiers in the United States seemed to confirm Goddard's findings, while also showing that immigrants from Great Britain and Scandinavia performed better. These various findings were used by the American government in 1924 to introduce national origin quotas to reduce the level of immigration from southern and eastern Europe.

A second argument against much race-related research is that it is almost meaningless given the fact that blacks and whites in the United States do not form biological groups. It is also fairly pointless, because it is impossible to discover for certain precisely why there are race differences in intelligence. Another argument is that such research does not possess any particular scientific interest, in that it offers no prospect of shedding much light on the processes and mechanisms involved in intelligence. If it could be shown that all racial differences in intelligence are due to environmental factors, this would tell us nothing about the different problem-solving strategies used by those high and low in intelligence. Finally, such research has no obvious policy implications. It should be the goal of every society to provide good opportunities for everyone regardless of race, and this is true irrespective of the factors producing racial differences in intelligence.

Is knowing how intelligent you are important to having a happy life?

A major focus of race-related research in psychology has been on racial differences in intelligence. One of the arguments against permitting such research is that it moves society no nearer the goal of providing good opportunities for all.

"Alternative" sexuality

According to Kitzinger and Coyle (1995), research on gays and lesbians has gone through three distinct phases:

1. **Heterosexual bias**: the notion that heterosexuality is more natural than, and superior to, homosexuality.
2. **Liberal humanism**: this is based on the assumption that homosexual and heterosexual couples have an underlying similarity in their relationships.
3. **Liberal humanism plus**: what is added to the liberal humanistic view is an increased recognition of the specific characteristics of gay and lesbian relationships.

Heterosexual bias

Morin (1977) obtained convincing evidence of heterosexual bias in his review of studies on gays and lesbians published between 1967 and 1974. He found that about 70% of these studies addressed issues such as whether homosexuals are sick, ways in which homosexuality can be identified, and the causes of homosexuality. Focusing on such issues suggests that being homosexual was regarded almost like a disease that needed to be "cured".

This biased approach to research, with its clear implication that gays and lesbians are inferior to heterosexuals, poses serious ethical issues relating to discrimination against gays and lesbians. The American Psychological Association in 1975 took steps to prevent such discrimination by adopting the following resolution:

Homosexuality per se implies no impairment in judgement, stability, reliability, or general social or vocational capabilities. Further, the American Psychological Association urges all mental health professionals to take the lead in removing the stigma of mental illness that has long been associated with homosexual orientations.

Another feature of the research reviewed by Morin (1977) was that 82% of the studies compared gays and/or lesbians against heterosexual individuals. This poses ethical problems, because it misleadingly implies that all gays and lesbians possess the same characteristics that distinguish them from heterosexuals. In fact, of course, gays, lesbians, and heterosexuals are all

The decision to remove homosexuality from the DSM (Diagnostic and Statistical Manual) was taken in the 1970s, and it was finally removed from the DSM in 1980. Before that, homosexuality was seen as abnormal behaviour that needed to be "cured" like other forms of illness.

KEY TERM
Heterosexual bias: the notion that heterosexuality is more natural than, and preferable to, homosexuality.

individuals. Knowing about someone's sexual orientations tells us little or nothing about that person's attitudes, personality, and behaviour.

Discussion points

1. How can alternative sexuality be studied in an ethically acceptable way?
2. Can psychological research change some of the unfortunate and misleading stereotypes that prevail in this area?

Liberal humanism

The next phase of research was based on the liberal humanistic approach. This approach rejected the notion that gays and lesbians are inferior to heterosexuals, and accepted that they should be regarded as individuals rather than as members of a group defined by sexual orientation. It was accepted within this approach that homosexuality is as natural and normal as heterosexuality.

Kurdek and Schmitt (1986) carried out a typical study within the liberal humanistic perspective. They compared gay, lesbian, married heterosexual, and heterosexual-cohabiting couples. These couples were assessed for relationship quality based on love for partner, liking of partner, and relationship satisfaction. The gay, lesbian, and married heterosexual couples all had very similar levels of relationship quality, with heterosexual-cohabiting couples being significantly lower. These findings support the view of an underlying similarity between homosexuals and heterosexuals.

The Kurdek and Schmitt study assessed relationship quality in gay, lesbian, married heterosexual, and cohabiting heterosexual couples. The findings supported the liberal humanistic view of an underlying similarity between homosexual and heterosexual relationships.

The liberal humanist approach is limited rather than ethically dubious, but it does raise ethical issues. It has two major limitations. First, there is an assumption that gays and lesbians conform to heterosexual norms in their attitudes and behaviour. As a result, according to Kitzinger and Coyle (1995, p.67), "Researchers ... have tended to ignore, distort or pathologise [regard as a disease] those aspects of lesbian and gay relationships which cannot easily be assimilated into heterosexual models." There is an ethical problem here, because it is implicitly assumed that differences between homosexuals and heterosexuals reflect badly on homosexuals.

Second, the approach tends to ignore the difficulties with which gays and lesbians have to contend in terms of the prejudices of society. Some of these difficulties were identified by Kitzinger and Coyle:

Lesbian and gay couples are struggling to build and to maintain relationships in the context of a society which often denies their existence, condemns their sexuality, penalises their partnerships and derides their love for each other.

Liberal humanism plus. The third phase of research on gays and lesbians (liberal humanism plus) is gradually becoming more prominent. This approach accepts the equality of homosexuals and heterosexuals. However, it also recognises that there are some important differences between the relationships of gays and lesbians on the one hand and heterosexuals on the other, based in part on the negative views of gay and lesbian relationships adopted by large sections of society. It is the only approach that manages to avoid most ethical problems.

Social and cultural diversity

We have discussed the importance of ensuring that psychological research is sensitive to ethical issues relating to race and sexuality. Similar issues are raised by research that is concerned with social and/or cultural diversity. Here we will consider research on

ethnic groups; that is, cultural groups living within a larger society. These ethnic groups can be defined in racial, religious, or other terms. The ethical issues raised by research on ethnic groups will be discussed after their position in society has been covered.

One of the key issues that members of an ethnic group have to address is that of **acculturation strategy**. This has two main aspects:

1. The extent to which they want to retain their original cultural identity and customs.
2. The extent to which they seek contact with other groups in society.

As Berry (1997) pointed out, the fact that people have two choices to make (each of which can be for or against) means that there are four major acculturation strategies (see also pages 500–501):

- Integration: retaining one's own cultural identity while also seeking contact with other groups.
- Separation: retaining one's own cultural identity and avoiding contact with other groups.
- Assimilation: losing one's own cultural identity and moving into the larger society.
- Marginalisation: relatively little contact with one's own culture or with other cultures.

It can be difficult for members of ethnic groups to integrate into a larger society without compromising religious or ethnic beliefs when those beliefs call for them to dress in a way that makes them look different from the majority.

How might schools encourage integration of different cultures into the curriculum (e.g. by celebrating different cultural festivals)?

Cross-cultural issues: By learning to value different cultures and beliefs, children can develop a positive self-image, and so increase the likelihood of tolerance within the wider society.

Most of the research has indicated that members of ethnic groups experience stress as they strive to find the most suitable acculturation strategy. However, the typical finding is that acculturative stress is lowest among those adopting the integration option, and is highest among those who are marginalised (Berry, 1997). As might be expected, acculturative stress is lower when there is a high level of tolerance for diverse ethnic attitudes and behaviour within the larger society.

Why are acculturation strategy and acculturative stress relevant to ethical issues? There are three main reasons. First, the fact that many members of ethnic groups experience acculturative stress means that they are on average more vulnerable psychologically than members of the dominant cultural group. Second, research findings that seem to indicate that members of an ethnic group are inferior to the dominant cultural group may make members of the dominant cultural group less willing to have contact with them. This makes it harder for members of an ethnic group to adopt the integration or assimilation strategies.

Third, research findings that cast an unfavourable light on the members of an ethnic group may make them question their own cultural values. In extreme cases, this can lead to marginalisation and to the stress caused by lacking any stable sense of cultural identity.

In sum, it is important for all investigators to have an awareness of the pressures experienced by many ethnic groups. Investigators then need to ensure that their research (and the findings resulting from it) does not increase those pressures.

PERSONAL REFLECTIONS

- I am impressed by the progress that has been made over the years in developing more ethical approaches to psychological research. In a nutshell, there is now much more recognition of the fact that we need to take full account of the needs and sensitivities of all those involved in experiments, as well as the broader society or culture in which experiments are carried out.

KEY TERMS

Ethnic groups: cultural groups (e.g. those defined by race or religion) living within a larger society.

Acculturation strategy: the approach adopted by members of ethnic groups, involving decisions about preserving their own cultural identity and about contact with other cultural groups.

- What is regarded as acceptable or unacceptable for psychologists to do depends very much on the prevailing cultural values and standards. Some psychologists used to treat their participants in ways that are now unthinkable. They did this not because they were wicked, but because their ethical standards resembled those of the culture in which they lived and worked.

SUMMARY

Use of human participants

The participants in experiments are usually in a less powerful position than the experimenter, and this produces ethical problems. The participants should give their voluntary informed consent before taking part in an experiment. They should also be told that they have the right to withdraw from the experiment at any time without giving a reason. At the end of the experiment, there should be a debriefing period in which the experiment is discussed fully. Another safeguard is confidentiality, with no information about individual participants being divulged. Professional organisations such as the British Psychological Society publish detailed ethical guidelines, and most research institutions have ethical committees.

Use of animals

Animals are used in experiments because some procedures would not be permissible with humans, because they reproduce over much shorter time periods than humans, and because it is easier to understand their behaviour. Females, left-wing people, and vegetarians are more opposed to animal experimentation than males, right-wing people, and non-vegetarians, respectively. Speciesism can be defended on the grounds that we owe a special duty to our own species, but it can be opposed on the basis that it resembles racism and sexism. Darwin argued that there are important similarities between the human species and other species, whereas the humanistic psychologists emphasised the differences. The views of most people on animal experimentation are based on relative morality. Animal experiments should be considered in the context of meat production, ill-treatment of pets, and zoos and circuses. The BPS Ethical Guidelines emphasise the necessity to comply with current legislation; the importance of the knowledge to be gained from a study; differences among species in pain sensitivity; minimising the number of animals used; not using the members of any endangered species; ensuring that reputable suppliers are used; providing suitable caging conditions; and disturbing animals as little as possible in fieldwork.

Socially sensitive research

Ethical guidelines focus mainly on protection of the participants. However, it is important with socially sensitive research to consider the protection of groups to which the participants belong and those closely associated with the participants. These broader social issues need to be considered with respect to the research question selected, the conduct of the research, the institutional context, and the interpretation and application of research findings. The institutional context may make the participants feel powerless, or those running the organisation in which the research takes place may misuse the findings. The findings of socially sensitive research may be applied in dubious ways not anticipated by the researcher, or the research may be used to justify new forms of social control. On the positive side, socially sensitive research may provide useful information to help minority groups. In addition, researchers cannot generally be expected to foresee what they will find or how such findings will be used by others.

Socially sensitive research areas

Race-related research has been defended on the grounds that researchers should be free to carry out whatever research seems important to them. An important counter-argument is that the findings of such research have sometimes been used in unacceptable ways. Race-related research on intelligence in the United States is almost meaningless, because blacks and whites do not form distinct biological groups. In addition, it is not possible to discover for certain why race differences occur. Early research on "alternative" sexuality suffered from heterosexual bias. This was replaced by a liberal humanistic approach that assumed that gays and lesbians conform to heterosexual norms in their attitudes and behaviour, and that minimised the specific problems encountered by gays and lesbians. More recently, an ethically acceptable approach (which may be called liberal humanism plus) has evolved. Ethnic groups often experience acculturative stress. Investigators need to ensure that their research does not interfere with the attempts to members of ethnic minorities to use a suitable acculturation strategy.

FURTHER READING

Many of the issues discussed in this chapter are also dealt with in M.W. Eysenck (1994a), *Perspectives on psychology*, Hove, UK: Psychology Press. Another textbook in this area is A. Wadeley, A. Birch, and A. Malim (1997), *Perspectives in psychology (2nd Edn.)*, London: MacMillan. Anyone who is considering carrying out any kind of study on human participants is strongly urged to consult the following before proceeding: British Psychological Society (1993), Ethical principles for conducting research with human participants, *The Psychologist, 6*, 33–35 (reproduced on the following pages).

REVISION QUESTIONS

1   Discuss the role of ethical guidelines in psychological investigations with humans.   (24 marks)

2   Discuss the case for and against using non-human animals in psychological investigations.   (24 marks)

3   "Although carrying out research in socially sensitive areas may raise difficult ethical issues ... refusing to carry out this type of research does not seem to be the answer. Whilst we cannot ignore the ethical issues in such research, neither can we shy away from controversial issues." (Cardwell, 1997). Discuss.   (24 marks)

Ethical Principles for Conducting Research with Human Participants

Reproduced from *The Psychologist* (January 1993, 6, 33–35)

1 Introduction

1.1 The principles given below are intended to apply to research with human participants. Principles of conduct in professional practice are to be found in the Society's Code of Conduct and in the advisory documents prepared by the Divisions, Sections and Special Groups of the Society.

1.2 Participants in psychological research should have confidence in the investigators. Good psychological research is possible only if there is mutual respect and confidence between investigators and participants. Psychological investigators are potentially interested in all aspects of human behaviour and conscious experience. However, for ethical reasons, some areas of human experience and behaviour may be beyond the reach of experiment, observation or other form of psychological investigation. Ethical guidelines are necessary to clarify the conditions under which psychological research is acceptable.

1.3 The principles given below supplement for researchers with human participants the general ethical principles of members of the Society as stated in the British Psychological Society's Code of Conduct (1985) and any subsequent amendments to this Code. Members of the British Psychological Society are expected to abide by both the Code of Conduct and the fuller principles expressed here. Members should also draw the principles to the attention of research colleagues who are not members of the Society. Members should encourage colleagues to adopt them and ensure that they are followed by all researchers whom they supervise (e.g. research assistants, postgraduate, undergraduate, A-Level and GCSE students).

1.4 In recent years, there has been an increase in legal actions by members of the general public against professionals for alleged misconduct. Researchers must recognise the possibility of such legal action, if they infringe the rights and dignity of participants in their research.

2 General

2.1 In all circumstances, investigators must consider the ethical implications and psychological consequences for the participants in their research. The essential principle is that the investigation should be considered from the standpoint of all participants; foreseeable threats to their psychological well-being, health, values or dignity should be eliminated. Investigators should recognise that, in our multi-cultural and multi-ethnic society and where investigations involve individuals of different ages, gender and social background, the investigators may not have sufficient knowledge of the implications of an investigation for the participants. It should be borne in mind that the best judges of whether an investigation will cause offence may be members of the population from which the participants in the research are to be drawn.

3 Consent

3.1 Whenever possible, the investigator should inform all participants of the objectives of the investigation. The investigator should inform the participants of all aspects of the research or intervention that might reasonably be expected to influence willingness to participate. The investigator should, normally, explain all other aspects of the research or intervention about which the participants enquire. Failure to make full disclosure prior to obtaining informed consent require additional safeguards to protect the welfare and dignity of th participants (see Section 4).

3.2 Research with children or with participants who hav impairments that will limit understanding and/or communicatio such that they are unable to give their real consent requires specia safeguarding procedures.

3.3 Where possible, the real consent of children and of adults wit impairments in understanding or communication should be obtained In addition, where research involves any persons under sixteen year of age, consent should be obtained from parents or from those in *loc parentis*. If the nature of the research precludes consent being obtained from parents or permission being obtained from teachers, befor proceeding with the research, the investigator must obtain approva from an Ethics Committee.

3.4 Where real consent cannot be obtained from adults wit impairments in understanding or communication, wherever possibl the investigator should consult a person well-placed to appreciate th participant's reaction, such as a member of the person's family, anc must obtain the disinterested approval of the research from independent advisors.

3.5 When research is being conducted with detained persons particular care should be taken over informed consent, payin attention to the special circumstances which may affect the person' ability to give free informed consent.

3.6 Investigators should realise that they are often in a position o authority or influence over participants who may be their students employees or clients. This relationship must not be allowed tc pressurise the participants to take part in, or remain in, ar investigation.

3.7 The payment of participants must not be used to induce them tc risk harm beyond that which they risk without payment in their normal lifestyle.

3.8 If harm, unusual discomfort, or other negative consequences for the individual's future life might occur, the investigator must obtain the disinterested approval of independent advisors, inform the participants, and obtain informed, real consent from each of them.

3.9 In longitudinal research, consent may need to be obtained on more than one occasion.

4 Deception

4.1 The withholding of information or the misleading of participants is unacceptable if the participants are typically likely to object or show unease once debriefed. Where this is in any doubt, appropriate consultation must precede the investigation. Consultation is best carried out with individuals who share the social and cultural background of the participants in the research, but the advice of ethics committees or experienced and disinterested colleagues may be sufficient.

4.2 Intentional deception of the participants over the purpose and general nature of the investigation should be avoided whenever possible. Participants should never be deliberately misled without extremely strong scientific or medical justification. Even then there hould be strict controls and the disinterested approval of ndependent advisors.

3 It may be impossible to study some psychological processes without withholding information about the true object of the study or deliberately misleading the participants. Before conducting such a study, the investigator has a special responsibility to (a) determine that alternative procedures avoiding concealment or deception are not available; (b) ensure that the participants are provided with sufficient information at the earliest stage; and (c) consult appropriately upon the way that the withholding of information or deliberate deception will be received.

Debriefing

.1 In studies where the participants are aware that they have taken part in an investigation, when the data have been collected, the investigator should provide the participants with any necessary information to complete their understanding of the nature of the research. The investigator should discuss with the participants their experience of the research in order to monitor any unforeseen negative effects or misconceptions.

.2 Debriefing does not provide a justification for unethical aspects of an investigation.

.3 Some effects which may be produced by an experiment will not be negated by a verbal description following the research. Investigators have a responsibility to ensure that participants receive any necessary debriefing in the form of active intervention before they leave the research setting.

Withdrawal from the Investigation

.1 At the onset of the investigation investigators should make plain to participants their right to withdraw from the research at any time, irrespective of whether or not payment or other inducement has been offered. It is recognised that this may be difficult in certain observational or organisational settings, but nevertheless the investigator must attempt to ensure that participants (including children) know of their right to withdraw. When testing children, avoidance of the testing situation may be taken as evidence of failure to consent to the procedure and should be acknowledged.

.2 In the light of experience of the investigation, or as a result of debriefing, the participant has the right to withdraw retrospectively any consent given, and to require that their own data, including recordings, be destroyed.

7 Confidentiality

7.1 Subject to the requirements of legislation, including the Data Protection Act, information obtained about a participant during an investigation is confidential unless otherwise agreed in advance. Investigators who are put under pressure to disclose confidential information should draw this point to the attention of those exerting such pressure. Participants in psychological research have a right to expect that information they provide will be treated confidentially and, if published, will not be identifiable as theirs. In the event that confidentiality and/or anonymity cannot be guaranteed, the participant must be warned of this in advance of agreeing to participate.

8 Protection of Participants

8.1 Investigators have a primary responsibility to protect participants from physical and mental harm during the investigation. Normally, the risk of harm must be no greater than in ordinary life, i.e. participants should not be exposed to risks greater than or additional to those encountered in their normal lifestyle. Where the risk of harm is greater than in ordinary life the provisions of 3.8 should apply. Participants must be asked about any factors in the procedure that might create a risk, such as pre-existing medical conditions, and must be advised of any special action they should take to avoid risk.

8.2 Participants should be informed of procedures for contacting the investigator within a reasonable time period following participation should stress, potential harm, or related questions or concern arise despite the precautions required by these Principles. Where research procedures might result in undesirable consequences for participants, the investigator has the responsibility to detect and remove or correct these consequences.

8.3 Where research may involve behaviour or experiences that participants may regard as personal and private the participants must be protected from stress by all appropriate measures, including the assurances that answers to personal questions need not be given. There should be no concealment or deception when seeking information that might encroach on privacy.

8.4 In research involving children, great caution should be exercised when discussing the results with parents, teachers or others in *loco parentis*, since evaluative statements may carry unintended weight.

9 Observational Research

9.1 Studies based upon observation must respect the privacy and pyschological well-being of the individuals studied. Unless those observed give their consent to being observed, observational research is only acceptable in situations where those observed would expect to be observed by strangers. Additionally, particular account should be taken of local cultural values and of the possibility of intruding upon the privacy of individuals who, even while in a normal public space, may believe they are unobserved.

10 Giving Advice

10.1 During research, an investigator may obtain evidence of psychological or physical problems of which a participant is, apparently, unaware. In such a case, the investigator has a responsibility to inform the participant if the investigator believes that by not doing so the participant's future well-being may be endangered.

10.2 If, in the normal course of psychological research, or as a result of problems detected as in 10.1, a participant solicits advice concerning educational, personality, behavioural or health issues, caution should be exercised. If the issue is serious and the investigator is not qualified to offer assistance, the appropriate source of professional advice should be recommended. Further details on the giving of advice will be found in the Society's Code of Conduct.

10.3 In some kinds of investigation the giving of advice is appropriate if this forms an intrinsic part of the research and has been agreed in advance.

11 Colleagues

11.1 Investigators share responsibility for the ethical treatment of research participants with their collaborators, assistants, students and employees. A psychologist who believes that another psychologist or investigator may be conducting research that is not in accordance with the principles above should encourage that investigator to re-evaluate the research.

Reference

The British Psychological Society. (1985). A Code of Conduct for Psychologists. *Bulletin of The British Psychological Society, 38*, 41–43.

See also proposed revisions to this code in The Psychologist, 5, 562–563.

Copies of this article may be obtained from The British Psychological Society, St. Andrews House, 48 Princess Road East, Leicester LE1 7DR.

**Questionnaire:
Lifestyle**

Do you drink more than 21 units of alcohol per week?

yes ✓   no

Do you take recreational drugs?

yes   ✓

Do you eat fruit regularly?

yes ✓   no

Do you eat vegetables daily?

yes ✓   no

Do you have a hobby?

yes ✓   no

Do you go to the theatre?

yes   no

Do you sleep for 8 hours per day?

yes   no

Do you find your job stressful?

yes ✓   no

- **Experimental method**
  The factors to bear in mind when designing and running a psychology experiment.

  Dependent, independent, and confounding variables
  Choosing participants and settings
  Cause and effect, replication
  Laboratory vs. field experiments
  Carlsmith et al.'s mundane and experimental realisms

- **Quasi-experiments**
  Studies that use the experimental method with pre-existing groups or natural situations.

  Williams' study of Canadian children
  Adams and Adams' Mount St Helens study

- **Correlational studies**
  Looking for links between various factors.

  Twin studies and the nature/nurture question
  Issues of causality and ethics

- **Naturalistic observation**
  Examining behaviour by watching it take place naturally, without influencing it experimentally.

  Brown et al.'s study of child language development
  Bales' interaction process analysis

- **Case studies**
  Studying one individual over a period of time, e.g. a person who has suffered brain damage.

  Allport's and Skinner's arguments
  Freud's case study of Dr Schreber

- **Interviews**
  Obtaining data from participants by asking them questions.

  Coolican's types of interview
  Piaget's clinical interviews

- **Discourse analysis**
  What people say is influenced by the context in which they say it.

  Potter and Wetherell's definition
  Curtis's list of seven features

30

Psychological Enquiry

In common with other sciences, psychology is concerned with theories and with data. A **theory** provides a general explanation or account of certain findings or data. It also generates a number of **experimental hypotheses**, which are predictions or expectations about behaviour based on the theory. For example, someone might propose a theory in which it is argued that some people are more hostile than others. This theory could be used to produce various hypotheses or predictions, such as the following: hostile people will express anger more often than non-hostile ones; hostile people will react more strongly than non-hostile ones to frustrating situations; hostile people will be more sarcastic than non-hostile people.

Psychologists spend a lot of their time collecting data in the form of measures of behaviour. Data are collected in order to test various hypotheses. Most people assume that this data collection involves proper or true experiments carried out under laboratory conditions, and it is true that literally millions of laboratory experiments have been carried out in psychology. However, psychologists make use of several methods of investigation, each of which has provided useful information about human behaviour.

As you read through the various methods of investigation, it is natural to wonder which methods are the best and the worst. In some ways, it may be more useful to compare the methods used by psychologists to the clubs used by the golf professional. The driver is not a better or worse club than the putter, it is simply used for a different purpose. In similar fashion, each method of investigation used by psychologists is very useful for testing some hypotheses, but is of little or no use for testing other hypotheses. However, as we will see, the experimental method provides the best way of being able to make inferences about cause and effect.

Experimental Method

The method of investigation used most often by psychologists is the experimental method. In order to understand what is involved in the experimental method, we will consider a concrete example.

Dependent and independent variables

Suppose that a psychologist wants to test the experimental hypothesis that loud noise will have a disruptive effect on the performance of a task. As with most hypotheses, this one refers to a **dependent variable**, which is some aspect of behaviour that is going to be measured. In this case, the dependent variable is some measure of task performance.

Most experimental hypotheses state that the dependent variable will be affected systematically by some specified factor, which is known as the **independent variable**. In

KEY TERMS
Theory: a general explanation of a set of findings; it is used to produce experimental hypotheses.
Experimental hypotheses: the testable predictions generated by a theory.
Dependent variable: some aspect of the participant's behaviour that is measured in a study.
Independent variable: some aspect of the experimental situation that is manipulated by the experimenter.

Participants in a psychological experiment should be tested under constant controlled conditions (e.g. consistent lighting, temperature, and sound levels).

the case we are considering, the independent variable is the intensity of noise. More generally, the independent variable is some aspect of the experimental situation that is manipulated by the experimenter.

We come now to the most important principle involved in the use of the experimental method: the independent variable of interest is manipulated, but all other variables are *controlled*. It is assumed that, with all other variables controlled, the one and only variable that is being manipulated is the cause of any subsequent change in the dependent variable. In terms of our example, we might expose one group of participants to very intense noise, and a second group to mild noise. What would we need to do to ensure that any difference in the performance of the two groups was due to the noise rather than any other factor? We would control all other aspects of the situation by, for example, always using the same room for the experiment, keeping the temperature the same, and having the same lighting.

Confounding variables

Another way of expressing the essence of the experimental method is that it is of fundamental importance to avoid any **confounding variables**. These are variables that are manipulated or allowed to vary systematically along with the independent variable. The presence of any confounding variables has grave consequences, because it prevents us from being able to interpret our findings. For example, suppose that the participants exposed to intense noise performed the task in poor lighting conditions so that they could hardly see what they were doing, whereas those exposed to mild noise enjoyed good lighting conditions. If the former group performed much worse than the latter group, we would not know whether this was due to the intense noise, the poor lighting, or some combination of the two.

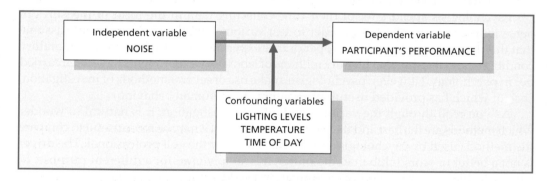

You might think that it would be easy to ensure that there were no confounding variables in an experiment. However, there are many well-known published experiments containing confounding variables. Consider, for example, a study by Jenkins and Dallenbach (1924). They gave a learning task to a group of participants in the morning, and then tested their memory for the material later in the day. The same learning task was given to a second group of participants in the evening, and their memory was tested the following morning after a night's sleep.

What did Jenkins and Dallenbach find? Memory performance was much higher for the second group than for the first. They argued that this was due to there being less interference with memory when people are asleep than when they are awake. Can you see the flaw in this argument? The two groups learned the material at different times of day, and so time of day was a confounding variable. Hockey, Davies, and Gray (1972) discovered many years later that the time of day at which learning occurs is much more important than whether or not the participants sleep between learning and the memory test.

Participants and settings

Proper use of the experimental method requires careful consideration of the ways in which the participants are allocated to the various conditions. A detailed account is given in

Chapter 31, so we will focus here only on experiments in which there are different participants in each condition. Suppose that the participants exposed to intense noise were on average much less intelligent than those exposed to mild noise. We would then be unable to tell whether poorer performance by the former participants was due to the intense noise or to their low intelligence. The main way of guarding against this possibility is by means of **randomisation**, in which the participants are allocated at random to the two conditions.

Numerous studies are carried out using students as participants. This raises the issue of whether students are representative of society as a whole. For example, it is possible that students would be less distracted than other people by intense noise because they are used to studying over long periods of time in conditions that can be noisy, such as halls of residence.

The experimental method is used mainly in laboratory experiments. However, it is also used in **field experiments**, which are experiments carried out in natural settings such as in the street, in a school, or at work. Some of the advantages of the experimental method are common to both laboratory and field experiments, whereas other advantages and limitations are specific to one type of experiment. We will consider the common advantages next, with more specific advantages and limitations being discussed after that.

In many studies, use is made of pre-existing groups of people. For example, we might compare the performance of males and females, or that of young and middle-aged individuals. Do such studies qualify as genuine experiments? The answer is "No". Use of the experimental method requires that the independent variable is *manipulated* by the experimenter, but clearly the experimenter cannot decide whether a given person is going to be male or female for the purposes of the study!

Common advantages

Causal relationships

What is generally regarded as the greatest advantage of the experimental method is that it allows us to establish cause and effect relationships. In the terms we have been using, the independent variable in an experiment is often regarded as a cause, and the dependent variable is the effect. Philosophers of science have argued about whether or not causality can be established by experimentation. However, the general opinion is that causality can only be inferred. If y (e.g. poor performance) follows x (e.g. intense noise), then it is reasonable to infer that x caused y.

We can see why findings from studies based on the experimental method do not necessarily establish causality from the following imaginary example. An experiment on malaria is carried out in a hot country. Half of the participants sleep in bedrooms with the windows open, and the other half sleep in bedrooms with the windows closed. Those sleeping in bedrooms with the windows open are found to be more likely to catch malaria. It would obviously be wrong to argue that having the window open caused malaria. Having the window open or closed is relevant to catching the disease, but it tells us nothing directly about the major causal factor in malaria (infected mosquitoes).

Replication

The other major advantage of the experimental method concerns what is known as **replication**. If an experiment has been conducted in a carefully controlled way, it should be possible for other researchers to repeat or replicate the findings obtained from that experiment. There have been numerous failures to replicate using the experimental method, but the essential point is that the chances of replication are greater when the experimental method is used than when it is not.

Ideally, psychological **experiments** should select a random sample of the population, although true randomness can be hard to achieve.

Can you think of examples of situations in which a wrong causal inference could be made, i.e. y followed x, but x did not cause y?

When bystanders saw a staged fight in an experiment by Shotland and Straw (1976) they were more likely to help when they thought two strangers were involved than if they thought the couple were married.

Laboratory vs. field experiments

Laboratory and field experiments both involve use of the experimental method, but they differ in that field experiments are carried out in more natural settings. As an example of a field experiment, let us consider a study by Shotland and Straw (1976; see page 594). They arranged for a man and a woman to stage an argument and a fight fairly close to a number of bystanders. In one condition, the woman screamed, "I don't know you". In a second condition, she screamed, "I don't know why I ever married you!". When the bystanders thought the fight involved strangers, 65% of them intervened, against only 19% when they thought it involved a married couple. Thus, people were less likely to lend a helping hand when it was a "lovers' quarrel" than when it was not. The bystanders were convinced that the fight was genuine, as was shown by the fact that 30% of the women were so alarmed that they shut the doors of their rooms, turned off the lights, and locked their doors.

The greatest advantage of laboratory experiments over field experiments is that it is generally easier to eliminate confounding variables in the laboratory than in the field. The experimenter is unlikely to be able to control every aspect of a natural situation.

Another clear advantage of laboratory experiments over field experiments is that it is much easier to obtain large amounts of very detailed information from participants in the laboratory. For example, it is hard to see how information about participants' physiological activity or speed of performing a range of complex cognitive tasks could be obtained in a field experiment carried out in a natural setting. There are two main reasons why field experiments are limited in this way. First, it is not generally possible to introduce bulky equipment into a natural setting. Second, the participants in a field experiment are likely to realise they are taking part in an experiment if attempts are made to obtain a lot of information from them.

One of the advantages of field experiments over laboratory experiments is that the behaviour of the participants is often more *typical* of their normal behaviour. However, the greatest advantage of field experiments over laboratory experiments is that they are less artificial. The artificiality of laboratory experimentation was emphasised by Heather (1976, pp.31–33):

> Psychologists have attempted to squeeze the study of human life into a laboratory situation where it becomes unrecognisably different from its naturally occurring form ... Experiments in psychology ... are social situations involving strangers, and it might be suggested that the main kind of knowledge gleaned from years of experimentation with human subjects is information about how strangers interact in the highly artificial and unusual setting of the psychological experiment.

The effects of being observed

In what type of investigations might participants act in an unnatural way?

An important reason why laboratory experiments are more artificial than field experiments is because the participants in laboratory experiments are aware that their behaviour is being observed. As Silverman (1977) pointed out, "Virtually the only condition in which a subject [participant] in a psychological study will not behave as a subject [participant] is if he does not know he is in one." One consequence of being observed is that the participants try to work out the experimenter's hypothesis, and then act accordingly. In this connection, Orne (1962) emphasised the importance of **demand characteristics**, which are "the totality of cues which convey an experimental hypothesis to the subjects." Orne found that the participants in one of his studies were willing to spend several hours adding numbers on random number sheets and then tearing up each

KEY TERM
Demand characteristics: cues that allow participants to guess the nature of the study.

completed sheet. Presumably the participants interpreted the experiment as a test of endurance, and this motivated them to keep going.

Another consequence of the participants in laboratory experiments knowing they are being observed is **evaluation apprehension**. Rosenberg (1965) defined this as "an active anxiety-toned concern that he [the participant] win a positive evaluation from the experimenter or at least that he provide no grounds for a negative one."

Sigall et al. (1970) contrasted the effects of demand characteristics and evaluation apprehension on the task of copying telephone numbers. The experimenter told participants doing the task for the second time that he expected them to perform it at a rate that was actually slower than their previous performance. Adherence to the demand characteristics would have led to slow performance, whereas evaluation apprehension and the need to be capable would have produced fast times. The participants actually performed more quickly than they had done before, indicating the greater importance of evaluation apprehension.

Participants in psychological experiments usually try to perform the task set by the experimenter as well as they can, in order to gain his or her approval.

This conclusion was strengthened by the findings from a second condition, in which the experimenter not only said that he expected the participants to perform at a slower rate, but also told them that those who rush are probably obsessive-compulsive. The participants in this condition performed the task slowly, because they wanted to be evaluated positively.

What examples can you give for an experiment that has involved an Implacable experimenter?

Another way in which laboratory experiments tend to be more artificial than field experiments was identified by Wachtel (1973). He used the term **implacable experimenter** to describe the typical laboratory situation, in which the experimenter's behaviour (e.g. instructions) affects the participant's behaviour, but the participant's behaviour does not influence the experimenter's behaviour. There are two serious problems with experiments using an implacable or unyielding experimenter. First, because the situation (including the experimenter) is allowed to influence the participant but the participant isn't allowed to affect the situation, it is likely that the effects of situations on our behaviour are over-estimated. Second, because much of the richness of the dynamic interactions between individual and situation has been omitted, there is a real danger that seriously over-simplified accounts of human behaviour will emerge.

> **KEY TERMS**
> **Evaluation apprehension**: anxiety-toned concern felt by participants to perform well and please the experimenter.
> **Implacable experimenter**: the typical laboratory situation in which the experimenter's behaviour is uninfluenced by the participant's behaviour.

Artificiality

How much does it matter that laboratory experiments are artificial? As Coolican (1998) pointed out, "In scientific investigation, it is often *necessary* to create artificial circumstances in order to *isolate* a hypothesised effect." If we are interested in studying basic cognitive processes such as those involved in perception or attention, then the artificiality of the laboratory is unlikely to affect the results. On the other hand, if we are interested in studying social behaviour, then the issue of artificiality does matter. For example, Zegoib et al. (1975) found that mothers behaved in a warmer and more patient way with their children when they knew they were being observed than when they did not.

Right: When trying to observe the behaviour of mothers with their children, Zegoib et al. (1975) found that the mothers were warmer and more patient when they knew they were being observed.

If Milgram's study is an example of experimental realism, can you suggest an example for mundane realism?

Carlsmith, Ellsworth, and Aronson (1976) drew a distinction between **mundane realism** and **experimental realism**. Mundane realism refers to experiments in which the situation is set up to resemble situations often found in everyday life. In contrast, experimental realism refers to experiments in which the situation may be rather artificial, but is sufficiently interesting to produce full involvement from the participants. Milgram's (1974) research on obedience to authority is a good example of experimental realism (see Chapter 21). The key point is that experimental realism may be more important than mundane realism in producing findings that generalise to real-life situations.

Ethical issues

Ethical issues in psychological research were discussed in detail in Chapter 29. What we will do here is to discuss a few ethical issues that are of special relevance to laboratory or field experiments. So far as laboratory experiments are concerned, there is a danger that the participants will be willing to behave in a laboratory in ways they would not behave elsewhere. For example, Milgram (1974) found in his work on obedience to authority that 65% of his participants were prepared to give very intense electric shocks to someone else when the experiment took place in a laboratory at Yale University. In contrast, the figure was only 48% when the same study was carried out in a run-down office building. Thus, participants are often willing to do what they would not normally do in the setting of a prestigeful laboratory.

Why is it that participants care about causing disruption to an experimenter's work?

Another ethical issue that applies especially to laboratory experiments concerns the participant's right to withdraw from the experiment at any time. It is general practice to inform participants of this right at the start of the experiment. However, participants may feel reluctant to exercise this right if they think it will cause serious disruption to the experimenter's research.

So far as field experiments are concerned, the main ethical issue relates to the principle of voluntary informed consent, which is regarded as central to ethical human research (see Chapter 29). By their very nature, most field experiments do not lend themselves to obtaining informed consent from the participants. For example, the study by Shotland and Straw (1976) would have been rendered almost meaningless if the participants had been asked beforehand to give their consent to witnessing a staged quarrel! The participants in that study could reasonably have complained about being exposed to a violent quarrel.

Another ethical issue with field experiments is that it is not possible in most field experiments to tell the participants that they have the right to withdraw at any time without offering a reason.

> **KEY TERMS**
> **Mundane realism**: the use of an artificial situation that closely resembles a natural situation.
> **Experimental realism**: the use of an artificial situation in which the participants become fully involved.
> **Internal validity**: the validity of an experiment in terms of the context in which it is carried out.
> **External validity**: the validity of research findings outside the research situation.
> **Quasi-experiment**: a type of experiment resembling a "true" experiment, but with some aspects of the experimental method omitted.

Summary

The respective strengths and weaknesses of laboratory experiments and field experiments can be summed up with reference to two different kinds of validity: internal validity and external validity (see Chapter 27). **Internal validity** refers to the validity of an experiment within the confines of the context in which it is carried out, whereas **external validity** refers to the validity of an experiment outside the research situation itself. Laboratory experiments tend to be high in internal validity but low in external validity, whereas field experiments are high in external validity but low in internal validity.

> ■ Research activity: In small groups, devise a table to summarise the advantages and limitations of the two different approaches: laboratory experiments and field experiments. Choose a selection of topics that psychologists might wish to investigate. Which approach would most suit each example?

Quasi-experiments

"True" experiments based on the experimental method provide the best way of being able to draw causal inferences with confidence. However, it is often the case that there are practical or ethical reasons why it is simply not possible to carry out a true experiment. In such circumstances, investigators often carry out what is known as a **quasi-experiment**. Quasi-experimental designs "resemble experiments but are weak on some of the characteristics" (Raulin & Graziano, 1994). There are two main ways in which quasi-experiments tend to fall short of being true experiments. First, the manipulation of the independent variable is often not under the control of the experimenter. Second, it is usually not possible to allocate the participants randomly to groups.

There are numerous hypotheses in psychology that can only be studied by means of quasi-experiments rather than true experiments. For example, suppose that we are interested in studying the effects of divorce on young children. We could do this by comparing children whose parents had divorced with those whose parents were still married. There would, of course, be no possibility of allocating children at random to the divorced or non-divorced parent groups! Studies in which pre-existing groups are compared often qualify as quasi-experiments. Examples of such quasi-experiments would be comparing the learning performance of males and females, or comparing the social behaviour of introverted and extraverted individuals.

Why would a study comparing the learning performance of males and females be a quasi-experiment and not a true experiment?

Natural experiments

The **natural experiment** is a type of quasi-experiment in which a researcher makes use of some naturally occurring event for research purposes. An example of a natural experiment is a study by Williams (1986) on the effects of television on aggressive behaviour in Canadian children aged between 6 and 11 years. Three communities were compared: one in which television had just been introduced, one in which there was only one television channel, and one in which there were several channels. The children in the first community showed a significant increase in verbal and physical aggression during the first two years after television was introduced, whereas those in the other two communities did not. This was not a true experiment, because the children were not allocated randomly to the three conditions or communities.

Adams and Adams (1984) carried out a natural experiment following the eruption of the Mount St Helens volcano in 1980. As the volcanic eruption had been predicted, they were able to assess the inhabitants of the small town of Othello before and after it happened. There was a 50% increase in mental health appointments, a 198% increase in stress-aggravated illness, and a 235% increase in diagnoses of mental illness.

Adams and Adams (1984) designed a natural experiment around the eruption of the Mount St Helens volcano in which they assessed the effects of stress on the population of a small town threatened by the eruption.

Advantages and limitations

What are the advantages of natural experiments? The main one is that the participants in natural experiments are often not aware that they are taking part in an experiment, even though they are likely to know that their behaviour is being observed. Another advantage of natural experiments is that they allow us to study the effects on behaviour of independent variables that it would be unethical for the experimenter to manipulate. For example, Adams and Adams (1984) were interested in observing the effects of a major stressor on physical and mental illness. No ethical committee would have allowed them to expose their participants deliberately to stressors that might cause mental illness, but they were able to take advantage of a natural disaster to conduct a natural experiment.

What are the limitations of natural experiments? The greatest limitation occurs because the participants have not been assigned at random to conditions. As a result, observed differences in behaviour between groups may be due to differences in the types of participants in the groups rather than to the effects of the independent variable. Consider, for example, the study by Williams (1986) on television and aggression. The children in the community that had just been exposed to television might have been naturally more aggressive than the children in the other two communities. However, the children in the three communities did not differ in their level of aggression at the start of the study.

It is usually possible to check whether the participants in the various conditions are comparable. For example, they can be compared with respect to variables such as age, sex, socio-economic status, and so on. If the groups do differ significantly in some respects irrelevant to the independent variable, then this greatly complicates the task of interpreting the findings of a natural experiment.

The other major limitation of natural experiments involves the independent variable. In some natural experiments, it is hard to know exactly what aspects of the independent

> **QUASI-EXPERIMENTS**
>
> **Advantages**
> - Participants behave naturally
> - Investigates the effects of independent variables that it would be unethical to manipulate
>
> **Limitations**
> - Participants not allocated at random to conditions
> - Difficult to identify what aspects of the independent variable have caused the effects on behaviour
>
> Add these points to your summary table of advantages and limitations of laboratory and field experiments for revision purposes (page 818).

variable have caused any effects on behaviour. For example, there is no doubt that the eruption of Mount St Helens was a major stressor. It caused stress in part because of the possibility that it might erupt again and produce more physical devastation. However, social factors were also probably involved. If people in Othello observed that one of their neighbours was highly anxious because of the eruption, this may have heightened their level of anxiety.

Ethical issues

What might be the practical uses of results such as those from the Mount St Helens study?

It can be argued that there are fewer ethical issues with natural experiments than with many other kinds of research. The reason is that the experimenter is not responsible for the fact that the participants have been exposed to the independent variable. However, natural experiments can raise various ethical issues. First, there can be the issue of informed voluntary consent, in view of the fact that the participants are often not aware that they are taking part in an experiment. Second, experimenters carrying out natural experiments need to be sensitive to the situation in which the participants find themselves. People who have been exposed to a natural disaster such as a volcanic eruption may resent it if experimenters start asking them detailed questions about their mental health or psychological well-being.

■ Research activity: In groups of three, design a summary table to illustrate the ethical issues involved in laboratory, field, and natural experiments, with each group member taking one type of experiment then reporting back to the group.

The issue of whether or not there is a correlation between violence on television and aggressive behaviour is frequently debated in the media.

Correlational Studies

Suppose that we were interested in the hypothesis that watching violence on television leads to aggressive behaviour. One way of testing this hypothesis would be to obtain two kinds of information from a large number of people: (1) the amount of violent television they watched; and (2) the extent to which they behaved aggressively in various situations. If the hypothesis is correct, then we would expect that those who have seen the most violence on television would tend to be the most aggressive. In technical terms, this study would be looking for a **correlation**, or association, between watching violent programmes and being aggressive. Thus, the closer the link between them, the greater would be the correlation or association.

One of the best-known uses of the correlational approach is in the study of the role of nature and nurture in intelligence (see Chapter 27). What is done is to assess the intelligence of pairs of identical or monozygotic and fraternal or dizygotic twins. After that the degree of similarity in intelligence within pairs is worked out by means of a correlation. Identical twins are more alike genetically than fraternal twins. As a result, their levels of intelligence should be more similar than those of fraternal twins if heredity plays an important role in determining intelligence. As predicted, the correlation indicating the degree of similarity in intelligence is nearly always higher for identical twins than for fraternal twins. However, it has proved hard to provide a detailed interpretation of the findings (see Chapter 27).

Advantages and limitations

Correlational designs are generally regarded as inferior to experimental designs, because it is hard (or impossible) to establish cause and effect. In our example, the

---

CORRELATIONAL STUDIES

Advantages	Limitations
• Allows study of hypotheses that cannot be examined directly	• Interpretation of results is difficult
• More data on more variables can be collected more quickly than in an experimental set-up	• Cause and effect cannot be established
• Problems of interpretation are reduced when no association is found	• Direction of causality is uncertain
• Even when strong correlations are found it may be obvious that no causal relationship exists	• Variables other than the one of interest may be operating

---

existence of an association between the amount of television violence watched and aggressive behaviour would certainly be consistent with the hypothesis that watching violent programmes can cause aggressive behaviour. However, there are other possible interpretations of the data. The causality may actually operate in the opposite direction. In other words, aggressive individuals may choose to watch more violent programmes than those who are less aggressive. There may be a third variable which accounts for the association between the variables of interest, i.e. watching violent programmes and aggressive behaviour. For example, people in disadvantaged families may watch more television programmes of all kinds than those in non-disadvantaged families, and their deprived circumstances may also cause them to behave aggressively. If that were the case, then the number of violent television programmes watched might have no direct effect at all on aggressive behaviour.

In spite of the interpretive problems posed by the findings of correlational studies, there are several reasons why psychologists continue to use this method.

First, many hypotheses cannot be examined directly by means of experimental designs. For example, the hypothesis that smoking causes a number of physical diseases cannot be tested by forcing some people to smoke and forcing others not to smoke! All that can be done is to examine correlations or associations between the number of cigarettes smoked and the probability of suffering from various diseases.

Second, it is often possible to obtain large amounts of data on a number of variables in a correlational study much more rapidly and efficiently than would be possible using experimental designs. Use of a questionnaire, for example, would permit a researcher to investigate the associations between aggressive behaviour and a wide range of activities (such as watching violent films in the cinema; reading violent books; being frustrated at work or at home).

Third, interpretive problems are much reduced if there is no association between two variables. For example, if it were found that there was no association at all between the amount of violent television watched and aggressive behaviour, this would provide fairly strong evidence that aggressive behaviour is not caused by watching violent programmes on television.

Fourth, the interpretive problems with associations or correlations between two variables are often not as great as in the example of violent programmes and aggression. Suppose, for example, we discover a correlation between age and happiness, in which older people are generally less happy than younger people. Although it would not be possible to offer a definitive interpretation of this finding, we could be entirely confident that unhappiness does not cause old age!

Ethical issues

Correlational analyses are used very widely. As a result, it is not possible to identify any particular ethical issues that apply to most studies in which such analyses are carried out. However, correlational analyses are often used in socially sensitive research, which raises political and/or social issues. For example, consider the correlational evidence suggesting that individual differences in intelligence depend in part on genetic factors. Some people have argued mistakenly that this implies that race differences in intelligence also depend on genetic factors. The key ethical issue here (and in many other correlational studies) is for the researcher to be fully aware of the social sensitivity of the findings that he or she has obtained.

Another ethical issue is raised by the real possibility that the public at large will misinterpret the findings from correlational studies. For example, the finding that there was a correlation between the amount of television violence watched by children and their level of aggression led many influential people to argue that television violence was having a damaging effect. In other words, they mistakenly supposed that correlational evidence can demonstrate a causal relation. Television companies may have suffered from such over-interpretation of findings.

Naturalistic Observation

Naturalistic observation involves methods designed to examine behaviour without the experimenter interfering with it in any way. This approach was originally developed by the ethologists such as Lorenz and Tinbergen. They studied animals in their natural habitat rather than in the laboratory, and discovered much about their behaviour (see Chapter 9). An example of the use of naturalistic observation in human research is the work of Brown, Fraser, and Bellugi (1964). They studied the language development of three children (Adam, Eve, and Sarah) by visiting them at home about 35 times a year.

One of the key requirements of the method of naturalistic observation is to avoid *intrusion*. Dane (1994, p.1149) defined this as "anything that lessens the participants' perception of an event as natural." There are various ways in which intrusion can occur. For example, there will be intrusion if observations are made in an environment that the participants regard as a research setting. There will also be intrusion if the participants are aware that they are being observed. In many studies, the experimenter is in the same room as the participants, and so they are almost certain to realise they are being observed. When this is the case, the experimenter may try to become a familiar and predictable part of the situation before any observations are recorded.

■ Research activity: Choose an event to observe. This could be a video recording of a scene from a television drama. Alternatively a group could role-play a job interview or a heated debate. Observe the event and individually record what you see, comparing notes afterwards. Have you all recorded the same observations?

The participants in naturalistic observation often display a wide range of verbal and non-verbal behaviour. How can observers avoid being overloaded in their attempts to record this behaviour? One approach is to focus only on actions or events that are of particular interest to the researcher; this is known as event sampling. Another approach is known as time sampling, in which observations are only made during specified time periods (e.g. the first 10 minutes of each hour). A third approach is point sampling, in which one individual is observed in order to categorise their current behaviour, after which a second individual is observed.

In considering the data obtained from naturalistic observation, it is important to distinguish between recording and interpretation or coding. For example, an observer may record that the participant has moved forwards, and interpret that movement as an aggressive action. In practice, however, observers typically only focus on interpreting or coding the participants' behaviour. For example, Bales (1950) developed the interaction process analysis, which allows observers to record inferred meanings for the forms of behaviour shown by members of a group (e.g. "offers suggestion").

There have been various attempts to develop ways of categorising people's behaviour in naturalistic observation without interpreting it. For example, McGrew (1972)

In order to categorise children's behaviour in a nursery school, McGrew (1972) used a recording system consisting of 110 different categories.

devised a detailed and comprehensive recording system to place the social interactions of children at nursery school into 110 categories.

Advantages and limitations

What are the advantages of naturalistic observation? First, if the participants are unaware that they are being observed, then it provides a way of observing people behaving naturally. When this happens, there are no problems from demand characteristics, evaluation apprehension, the implacable experimenter, and so on. Second, many studies based on naturalistic observation provide richer and fuller information than typical laboratory experiments. For example, participants' behaviour may be observed in a range of different social contexts rather than on their own in the laboratory. Third, it is sometimes possible to use naturalistic observation when other methods cannot be used. For example, the participants may be unwilling to be interviewed or to complete a questionnaire. In the case of participants being observed at work, it may be impossible to obtain permission to disrupt their work in order to carry out an experiment.

NATURALISTIC OBSERVATION

Advantages	Limitations
• People tend to behave naturally • Information that is gathered is rich and full • Can be used where other methods are not possible	• Experimenter has no control over the situation • Participants can be aware of being watched and this can affect behaviour • Problems of reliability due to bias or imprecise categorisation of behaviour • Problems of validity due to observers' or coders' assumptions • Replication is not usually possible

---

What are the limitations of naturalistic observation? These are some of the major ones:

- The experimenter has essentially no control over the situation; this can make it very hard or impossible to decide what caused the participants to behave as they did.
- The participants are often aware that they are being observed, with the result that their behaviour is not natural.
- There can be problems of reliability with the observational measures taken, because of bias on the part of the observer or because the categories into which behaviour is coded are imprecise. Attempts to produce good reliability often involve the use of very precise but narrow categories, leading to much of the participants' behaviour simply being ignored. Reliability can be assessed by correlating the observational records of two different observers. This produces a measure of inter-rater reliability.
- The fact that observations are typically interpreted or coded prior to analysis can cause problems with the validity of measurement. For example, it may be assumed invalidly that all instances of one child striking another child represent aggressive acts, when in fact many of them are only playful gestures. Thus, great care needs to be taken in **operationalisation**, which is a procedure in which a variable (e.g. aggressive act) is defined by the operations taken to measure it.
- There are often problems of replication with studies of naturalistic observation. For example, the observed behaviour of children in a school may depend in part on the fact that most of the teachers are very lenient and fail to impose discipline. The findings might be very different at another school in which the teachers are strict.

Ethical issues

Naturalistic observation poses ethical problems if the participants do not realise that their behaviour is being observed. In those circumstances, they obviously cannot give their

Is this aggression or play? What happened just before this action was observed could be vital to a correct interpretation.

KEY TERM
Operationalisation: a procedure in which variables of interest are defined by the operations taken to measure them.

voluntary informed consent to be involved in the study. There can also be problems about confidentiality. Suppose, for example, that naturalistic observation takes place in a particular school, and the published results indicate that many of the children are badly behaved. Even if the name of the school is not mentioned in the report, many people reading it will probably be able to identify the school because they know that the researchers made detailed observations there.

Case Studies

The great majority of studies in psychology have involved the use of experimental or correlational methods on groups of participants. These approaches permit the use of statistical techniques providing information about the extent to which the results obtained from a given sample can be generalised to some larger population.

There are often good reasons why it is not feasible to use numerous participants in a study. For example, a brain-damaged patient may have a very unusual pattern of impaired performance, and there may not be other patients having the same pattern. Another example might be a therapist who has a patient with a rare mental disorder, but there is no possibility of him or her collecting data from other patients with the same disorder. In such circumstances, it can be very useful to carry out a **case study**, in which one individual is investigated thoroughly and over a period of time.

Some researchers have argued that the study of individual cases can be more fruitful than the study of groups of participants. One of the most convincing statements of that argument was put forward by Gordon Allport (1962):

> Why should we not start with individual behaviour as a source of hunches ... and then seek our generalisations but finally come back to the individual not for the mechanical application of laws but for a fuller and more accurate assessment than we are now able to give? ... We stop with our wobbly laws of generality and seldom confront them with the concrete person.

Some of those who have favoured single-case studies have been of an anti-scientific persuasion. However, a prominent experimentalist who advocated the use of single-case studies was the behaviourist B.F. Skinner. In a discussion of research on operant conditioning, Skinner (1966) argued, "instead of studying a thousand rats for one hour each, or a hundred rats for ten hours each, the investigator is likely to study one rat for a thousand hours."

There are several types of case studies, and they are carried out for various reasons, some of which will be considered here. One reason is to test a current theory. For example, Atkinson and Shiffrin (1968) argued that information only enters the long-term memory store via the short-term memory store (see Chapter 13). As a result, a brain-damaged individual with impaired short-term memory should also have impaired long-term memory. Evidence that seemed to be inconsistent with this theory was reported in a case study on KF, who was involved in a motorcycle accident (Shallice & Warrington, 1970). He had very poor short-term memory for words and digits, but his long-term learning and recall were unaffected.

Can psychologists learn as much from the detailed study of the behaviour of a single rat as they can from a more superficial study of a large number of rats?

Case studies can also be used to refine theories. Baddeley and Hitch (1974) argued that people possess an articulatory loop which is used in the rehearsal of verbal information (see Chapter 13). It used to be assumed that rehearsal within the articulatory loop requires use of the speech muscles. However, Baddeley and Wilson (1985) carried out a case study on a student, GB. He suffered from anarthria, which meant that he could not use his speech muscles and was unable to speak. In spite of this disorder, GB was able to make use of the articulatory loop.

Developing new theories

Case studies are also of value in the development of new theories. For example, Sigmund Freud carried out a case study on Dr Schreber, a lawyer who suffered from paranoia (a mental disorder involving delusions). Freud was puzzled by the fact that Dr Schreber and other paranoid patients had a number of apparently unrelated delusions. These included a jealous feeling that their spouses or lovers had been unfaithful to them, the belief that others were plotting against them, the belief that several members of the opposite sex were in love with them, and delusions of grandeur.

Freud's discussions with Dr Schreber led him to an analysis of paranoia. According to Freud, homosexual desires underlie paranoia. However, because homosexuality was viewed with disfavour by society at that time, Freud felt that these desires remain unconscious and become distorted in various ways. One such distortion is for a male paranoiac to think his wife or lover loves another man, which produces jealousy. Delusions of grandeur were accounted for by assuming that the male paranoid individual's thought "I love a man", turns into "I love no-one", and then into "I love no-one but myself". This analysis led Freud to develop a new (but implausible) theory of paranoia.

Discussion points

1. Can you spot any problems with the case study on Dr Schreber?
2. Is there any way in which we could test Freud's proposed interpretation of the case study?

Some case studies are based on very unusual individuals. For example, there was Chris Sizemore, who was the central character in the film *The Three Faces of Eve* (see page 115). Some of the time she was Eve White, a well-behaved and inhibited woman. At other times, she was Eve Black, who was promiscuous and impulsive. At still other times, she was Jane, who was more stable than either of the other two personalities. The existence of individuals with multiple personalities raises issues about our usual assumption that everyone has one personality and one self.

Why use case studies?

- To test current theories
- To refine existing theories
- To develop new theories
- To test usual assumptions

Advantages and limitations

What are the advantages of case studies? First, as we have seen, a single-case study can provide good evidence that a particular theory is in error. Of course, it is then desirable to find and test other individuals to check the findings from the first case study. Second, a case study can help to refine our theoretical understanding. Third, case studies can provide rich information that is used by the researcher or therapist to develop new theoretical ideas. An example of this is the case of Dr Schreber, which was discussed earlier. Fourth, case studies can provide information about exceptional types of behaviour or performance that had been thought to be impossible.

What are the limitations of case studies? The greatest limitation is their typically low reliability. The findings that are obtained from one unusual or exceptional individual are unlikely to be repeated in detail from another individual. Thus, it is often very hard to generalise from a single-case study. Second, many case studies involve the use of lengthy, fairly unstructured, interviews. Such case studies share the limitations that are identified for interviews in the next section. Third, researchers generally only report some of the data they obtained from their interviews with the participant. They may be unduly selective in terms of what they choose to report or to omit.

Ethical issues

Case studies with clinical patients can pose important issues about confidentiality. A therapist such as Sigmund Freud may want to publish details of his case studies because they seem to support his theoretical position. However, the patient may be very unwilling for personal information about him or her to be published. Case studies with brain-damaged patients can pose ethical issues about voluntary informed consent. For example, patients with severe language impairments may find it hard to understand what will be involved in a case study, and so they cannot give proper informed consent.

Interviews

As Coolican (1994) pointed out, there are various kinds of interview which vary enormously in terms of the amount of structure they contain. In what follows, we will make use of his categorisation of different types of interview.

Non-directive interviews

Non-directive interviews possess the least structure, with the person being interviewed (the interviewee) being free to discuss almost anything he or she wants. The role of the interviewer in non-directive interviews is to guide the discussion and to encourage the interviewee to be more forthcoming. This type of interview is used very often in psychotherapy, but has little relevance to research.

There are various types of interviews used for psychological experimentation, from non-directive interviews to fully structured designs that have a standard set of questions with restricted-choice answers.

Informal interviews

Informal interviews resemble non-directive interviews, in that the interviewer listens patiently and focuses mainly on encouraging the interviewee to discuss issues in more depth or detail. However, informal interviews differ in that there are certain general topics that the interviewer wishes to explore. One of the best-known examples involving informal interviews was a large-scale study of workers at the Hawthorne works of Western Electric. The aim of this study was to explore industrial relations via a series of interviews. What emerged from informal interviews was that the relatively minor issues initially raised by the workers generally reflected deeper and more serious worries (Roethlisberger & Dickson, 1939; see page 851).

Guided interviews

Informal but guided interviews possess a little more structure than informal interviews. The interviewer identifies beforehand the issues to be addressed, but how and when to raise those issues is decided during the course of the interview. Structured but open-ended interviews use a formal procedure in which all interviewees are asked precisely the same questions in the same order. Such a procedure prevents the interviewee from side-tracking the interview and taking control of it away from the interviewer. The interviews are open-ended, in the sense that the questions that are asked allow plenty of scope for various kinds of answers (e.g. "How do you see your career developing?").

Clinical interviews

The clinical interview or clinical method resembles the structured but open-ended interview. In essence, all of the interviewees or participants are asked the same questions, but the choice of follow-up questions depends on the answers that are given. Piaget made much use of the clinical method in his research on cognitive development in children (see Chapter 16). Piaget understood that children might perform poorly on a task because they did not understand fully what the experimenter wanted them to do. One way of trying to avoid this problem was by giving the experimenter the flexibility to ask questions in various ways. In spite of this, critics of Piaget have argued that the children he studied often failed to solve problems because of the complex language used by the experimenter.

Fully structured interviews

Finally, there is the fully structured interview. In this type of interview, a standard set of questions is asked in the same fixed order to all of the interviewees, and they are only allowed to choose their answers from a restricted set of possibilities (e.g. "Yes"; "No"; "Don't know"). As Coolican (1994, pp.121–122) pointed out, "this approach is hardly an interview worth the name at all. It is a face-to-face data-gathering technique, but could be conducted by telephone or by post."

Advantages and limitations

What are the advantages of the interview method? As might be expected, the precise advantages depend on the type of interview. Relatively unstructured interviews have the advantage that they are responsive to the personality, interests, and motivations of the interviewee. In principle, they can perhaps reveal more about the interviewee than is likely to be the case with more structured interviews. One of the advantages of fairly structured interviews is that it is easy to compare the responses of different interviewees, all of whom have been asked the same questions. Another advantage is good reliability, in that two different interviewers are likely to obtain similar responses from an interviewee when they ask exactly the same questions in the same order. A further advantage is that there is a reasonable probability of being able to replicate or repeat the findings from a study using structured interviews. Finally, structured interviews have the advantage that it is usually fairly easy to analyse the data obtained from them.

> ■ Research activity: Using one of the types of interviews listed, design a scenario and role-play the interview with a partner, recording their responses. What changes would you make if you were able to try the activity again?
> • Non-directive interview
> • Informal interview
> • Guided interview
> • Clinical interview
> • Fully structured interview

What are the limitations of the interview method? So far as unstructured interviews are concerned, there is the problem that the kinds of information obtained from different interviewees vary in an unsystematic way. As a result, the data from unstructured interviews tend to be hard to analyse. A further limitation with unstructured interviews is that what the interviewee says is determined in a complex way by the interaction between him or her and the interviewer. In other words, the personality and other characteristics of the interviewer typically influence the course of the interview, and make it hard to work out which of the interviewee's contributions are and are not affected by the interviewer. Finally, the fact that the information obtained from interviewees in unstructured interviews is influenced by the interviewer means that the data obtained can be viewed as unreliable.

One of the main limitations with structured interviews is that what the interviewee says may be somewhat constrained and artificial because of the high level of structure built into the interview. Another limitation is that there is little or none of the flexibility associated with unstructured interviews.

Finally, we need to consider three limitations that are common to all types of interview. First, there is the issue of social desirability bias. Most people want to present a favourable impression of themselves to other people, and this may lead them to distort their answers to personal questions. For example, people are much more willing to admit that they are unhappy when filling in a questionnaire anonymously than when being interviewed (Eysenck, 1990). Second, interviews can only extract information of which the interviewee is consciously aware. This is a significant limitation, because people are often unaware of the reasons why they behave in certain ways (Nisbett & Wilson, 1977). Third, there is the limitation that

People are more willing to answer embarrassing or personal questions on an anonymous written questionnaire than in a face-to-face interview.

■ Research activity: Using the list of interview types given on pages 826–827, in small groups decide which areas of psychological investigation are best suited to each approach. What advantages and limitations of each type have affected your choices?

many interviewers lack some of the skills necessary to conduct interviews successfully. Good interviewers are able to make an interview seem natural, they are sensitive to non-verbal cues, and they have well-developed listening skills (Coolican, 1994).

Ethical issues

Interviews (especially clinical interviews) are often concerned with personal issues about which the interviewee is sensitive. This clearly raises the issue of confidentiality. There are various ways in which confidentiality can be broken. For example, Coolican (1994) discussed a study by Vidich and Bensman (1958) in which direct quotations from interviewees in Springdale in the United States were published. Made-up names were used, but the people of Springdale were able to identify the actual individuals on the basis of what they said.

Confidentiality can also be broken if a detailed written account or video recording of an interview falls into the wrong hands. Finally, of course, the interviewer himself or herself may disclose sensitive personal information about the interviewee to other people.

There is another ethical issue that is of particular importance with structured interviews. Interviewees may be aware that several other interviewees are being asked the same questions, and that their answers will be compared. As a result, some interviewees may feel that they must answer embarrassing questions in order not to spoil the experiment.

Discourse Analysis

According to Potter and Wetherell (1987), **discourse analysis** is concerned with "all forms of spoken interaction, formal and informal, and written texts of all kinds." The basic underlying assumption is that the ways in which we use language are greatly affected by the social context. Thus, for example, when politicians give speeches, it would be naive to assume that what they say simply reflects their genuine beliefs and views. It is generally accepted that what they say is designed to have certain effects on their audience, on other politicians, and on the public.

There is much evidence to indicate that people do adjust what they say or write to fit the circumstances. For example, consider studies using the bogus pipeline. The participants are wired up to an impressive-looking machine (the bogus pipeline), and informed that it can detect any lies they produce. Most white participants express more negative attitudes towards black people when wired up to the bogus pipeline than under standard conditions. The implication is that the attitudes that people express normally are constructed so as to be socially acceptable to other people.

KEY TERM

Discourse analysis: a qualitative form of analysis applied to language productions in spoken or written form.

People adjust what they say to fit the circumstances.

Gilbert and Mulkay (1984) carried out a discourse analysis based on interviews with 34 scientists. The importance of social factors in discourse was revealed by comparing what these scientists said during the interviews with their academic publications. The general pattern was for scientists to be much more confident about the meaning of their findings when interviewed than they were in their writings.

As Curtis (1997, p.24) pointed out, "The idea that there is one way to perform discourse analysis is both naive and illusory." Nevertheless, he identified seven features that are often found in discourse analysis:

1. Select some written or spoken material that is relevant to the issues you want to study.
2. Read or listen to the discourse several times, trying to decide how it has been constructed. Account needs to be taken of the social context in which it was produced.
3. Develop a qualitative coding system focusing on the functions or purposes that seem to be served by the discourse.
4. Produce some tentative hypotheses about the purposes served by the discourse, but be willing to modify these hypotheses if subsequent analysis indicates that they are inadequate.
5. How has the person producing the discourse tried to legitimise or make persuasive his or her version of events?
6. Examine the discourse for evidence of extreme case formulations. People often use extreme terms (e.g. always; never) to make their preferred interpretation seem more persuasive.
7. Examine the discourse carefully to see whether the purposes or functions it serves vary from one part to another.

> ■ Research activity: Choose either a role-played conversation, a newspaper interview, or a clip from a popular television programme. Using the seven features that are often found in discourse analysis, try to highlight the most important features of your chosen text.

Advantages and limitations

One of the advantages of discourse analysis is that it is based on the correct assumption that our use of language is often much influenced by the social context. This is true of how we remember events in our lives as well as our expressed attitudes and beliefs. As Coolican (1994, p.178) pointed out:

> *When we remember and attribute in real life, as opposed to the psychology experiment, our accounts attend to blame, defence, accountability, explanation and so on. What we often do is to present rememberings as facts when they are really constructions.*

For example, the way you describe events in your life is likely to vary depending on whether you are talking to your parents, to your best friend, or to an acquaintance.

If Coolican is correct in saying that rememberings are more like constructions than facts, what impact could this have on the testimony of an eye-witness?

Another advantage is that discourse analysis focuses on the ways in which language is used in real-life settings. As such, it avoids much of the artificiality of most experiments. In addition, the claims of those who favour discourse analysis that language is the primary mode of communication among human beings are correct.

There are several limitations of discourse analysis, many of which were discussed by Burman and Parker (1993). A major limitation is that the validity of discourse analysis is open to considerable doubt, and that procedures for assessing validity are lacking. For example, if two researchers interpret a given piece of discourse in very different ways, we cannot be sure which of them has produced the more valid interpretation.

A further limitation is that we often have little information about the reliability or consistency with which the discourse analysis has been carried out. When such information is available, it frequently indicates that reliability is low (Coolican, 1994).

Another limitation is that what emerges from discourse analysis may be unduly influenced by the views and beliefs of the researcher. As Human (1992) expressed it, discourse analysis is sometimes simply "a researcher's ideas with examples." A key reason why this can happen is because there are so few constraints on the researcher as he or she tries to make sense of any given written or spoken discourse.

A final limitation is that discourse analysis is based solely on the analysis of language in its various forms. However, language is by no means the only means of communication open to people. Account needs to be taken of non-verbal communication of various kinds (e.g. body language).

Ethical issues

It is often important for the researcher to make sure that anyone whose discourse is to be analysed has given their permission for it to be used for that purpose. However, that ethical issue may not arise if the discourse is in the public domain (e.g. a speech or television interview given by a politician).

There can also be ethical issues if the researcher's proposed interpretation is likely to offend those who provided the discourse. For example, Wetherell and Potter (1988) carried out discourse analysis on interviews with white New Zealanders. They concluded that those interviewed had racist attitudes towards the Maoris, although they did not directly say so in the interviews (see Chapter 28). In such circumstances, it is important for the researcher to discuss his or her proposed interpretation with the participants before the results of the study are published or made generally available.

A final ethical issue stems from the fact that discourse analysis often involves detailed analysis of an individual's discourse. As a result, it is sometimes impossible to adhere to the ethical principles that the information provided by participants should be confidential and that individuals should not be identifiable (see Chapter 29).

■ Research activity: Which method would you choose to investigate the following?

- The relationship between hours spent watching violent television programmes and aggressive behaviour
- Attitudes towards racial issues
- The effect of caffeine on memory
- The differences in personality of identical twins separated at birth
- Gender-typed play in young children

PERSONAL REFLECTIONS

- One of the key developments in psychology over the past 50 years has been the gradual increase in the range of research methods used by psychologists. Indeed, the change has been so marked that it is hard to believe that much research used to consist of studying rats in mazes and Skinner boxes! Some psychologists have tried to start a controversy between "traditional" researchers and those who favour the newer methods such as discourse analysis. My view is that *both* approaches have significant advantages: the key issue is to use whatever research method is best suited in the particular circumstances.

SUMMARY

Experimental method

The key principle of the experimental method is that the independent variable is manipulated (with all other variables controlled) in order to observe its effect on some dependent variable. In other words, it is important to avoid confounding variables. The experimental method is used in laboratory and field experiments. Use of the experimental method allows us to infer causality, and it often permits replication. Laboratory experiments have various advantages over field experiments: it is usually easier to eliminate confounding variables, and to obtain detailed behavioural and physiological information. The greatest advantage of field experiments over laboratory experiments is that they are less artificial, and suffer less from factors such as demand characteristics, evaluation apprehension, and the implacable experimenter.

Quasi-experiments

Quasi-experiments fall short of true experiments either because the experimenter has not manipulated the independent variable or because the participants are not allocated at random to conditions. Natural experiments are quasi-experiments involving some naturally occurring event. Advantages of natural experiments include the possibility that the participants will not be aware they are taking part in an experiment and the opportunity to study the effects of very stressful events. Limitations include problems of interpreting the findings due to a lack of randomisation or to the use of complex independent variables.

Correlational designs are inferior to experimental designs, because they do not permit inferences about causality. However, many issues can only be studied by assessing correlations or associations between variables. It is often possible to obtain large amounts of data very rapidly in correlational studies. The problems of interpretation are much reduced if there is no correlation or association between two variables.

Correlational studies

Naturalistic observation involves the use of methods designed to assess behaviour without the experimenter interfering in any way. Methods of data collection include event sampling, time sampling, and point sampling. We should distinguish between data recording and interpretation or coding. Naturalistic observation can provide rich and full information from people who are unaware that they are being observed. However, the experimenter has essentially no control over the situation, the participants are often aware they are being observed, and there can be problems with the reliability and validity of measurement.

Naturalistic observation

A single individual is investigated thoroughly in a case study. Case studies can be carried out to test a current theory, to refine a theory, to permit the development of new theoretical ideas, and to reveal the exceptional characteristics of certain individuals. Case studies generally have very low reliability, and this makes it hard to generalise from a single-case study. Case studies based on interviews often suffer from the limitation that what the participant says is determined in part by the interviewer or researcher, who may then be too selective in what he or she reports of the interview.

Case studies

There are several types of interview ranging from the unstructured to the totally structured. Unstructured interviews are responsive to the personality, interests, and motivations of the interviewee, but the data obtained tend to be unreliable. In contrast, structured interviews permit comparisons among interviewees, and they tend to be fairly reliable, but what the interviewee says can be constrained and artificial. All types of interviews can produce problems due to social desirability bias, and interviewees can only provide information of which they are consciously aware.

Interviews

Discourse analysis is based on the assumption that our use of language is much affected by the social context. It involves a careful analysis to identify the underlying purposes of the person who produced the discourse, using a qualitative coding system. Limitations of discourse analysis include low validity and reliability, and the danger that the views of the researcher will influence the findings too much. Ethical issues arise unless the permission of anyone providing discourse for analysis is obtained, and it can be hard to maintain confidentiality of the data.

Discourse analysis

FURTHER READING

A book that covers most research methods in an accessible way is H. Coolican (1994), *Research methods and statistics in psychology*, London: Hodder & Stoughton. Another useful textbook is J.J. Foster and J. Parker (1995), *Carrying out investigations in psychology: Methods and statistics*, Leicester, UK: BPS Books.

REVISION QUESTIONS

Sample questions on research methods are given at the end of Chapter 32 on page 887.

- **Aims and hypotheses**
  Why studies are carried out and what
  they are designed to test.

  Independent and dependent variables
  One- and two-tailed hypotheses
  Null hypotheses
  Manipulating and measuring the variables

- **Selecting participants**
  Different ways of selecting the people
  to take part in a study.

  Random and systematic sampling
  Stratified and quota sampling
  Opportunity sampling
  Sample size

- **Good practice in
  experimentation**
  Using standardised procedures and
  avoiding unwanted variables.

  Standardised procedures
  Confounding and controlled variables
  Random error
  Operationalisation

- **Experimental designs**
  The three types of design available to
  experimenters.

  Independent design
  Matched participants design
  *Repeated measures design and
    counterbalancing*

- **Good practice in
  non-experimental designs**
  How to design interview, survey, and
  case studies, and some pitfalls to
  avoid.

  *Evaluation apprehension and demand
    characteristics*
  *Participant and non-participant
    observation*
  *Survey, questionnaire, and attitude scale
    design*
  Correlational studies

- **Problems with experimental
  research**
  Experimenters can influence the
  outcome of their studies in unexpected
  ways.

  Experimenter's effects, e.g. "Clever Hans"
  Rosenthal's flatworm study
  Barber's list of nine effects
  *Demand characteristics and evaluation
    comprehension*

- **General issues in investigations**
  Other things that can and sometimes
  do affect the results of psychological
  studies.

  *The Hawthorne effect (Roethlisberger and
    Dickson's Western Electric study)*
  Validity and generalisability
  Meta-analyses
  Reliability and replication

31

Design of Investigations

In order to carry out a study successfully, care and attention must be devoted to each stage in its design and implementation. This chapter is concerned with these issues mostly with respect to experimental designs. However, there is also full consideration of the factors involved in producing good non-experimental designs.

As we will see, several decisions need to be made when designing an experimental study:

1. The investigator must decide what he or she hopes to achieve by carrying out the study. This involves generating appropriate aims and hypotheses.
2. The investigator has to work out how the variables specified in the hypotheses are to be manipulated and/or measured.
3. Appropriate procedures need to be used when selecting participants for the study.
4. Attention needs to be paid in the experimental design to ensuring that the effects of any situational variables on the participants' behaviour are minimised.
5. If the investigator is using an experimental design, then he or she has to select an appropriate one. This includes a decision as to whether each participant will be included in only one condition or in both conditions.
6. Care has to be paid to the relationship between the participants and the investigator in order to prevent systematic biases in the data obtained.

The success or otherwise of the investigator's study can be evaluated in terms of various criteria. If the design and its implementation are appropriate, then the reliability of the findings and their replicability will tend to be high. In addition, use of an appropriate design maximises the validity of the findings.

Is it possible to obtain useful psychological data from a single individual?

Aims and Hypotheses

The first step that needs to be taken when designing an experimental or non-experimental study is to decide on the aims and hypotheses of the study. The aims are usually more general than the hypotheses, and they help to explain the reasons for the investigator deciding to test some specific hypothesis or hypotheses. In other words, the aims tell us *why* a given study is being carried out, whereas the hypotheses tell us *what* the study is designed to test.

Experimental studies

The distinction between aims and hypotheses can be seen more clearly if we consider an example. Suppose that we

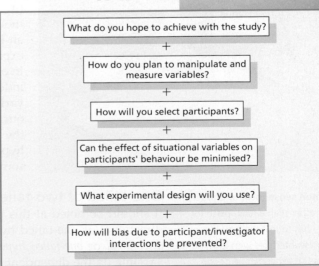

What do you hope to achieve with the study?
+
How do you plan to manipulate and measure variables?
+
How will you select participants?
+
Can the effect of situational variables on participants' behaviour be minimised?
+
What experimental design will you use?
+
How will bias due to participant/investigator interactions be prevented?

decide to test the levels-of-processing theory put forward by Craik and Lockhart (1972), which states that information that has been processed for meaning will be remembered better than information that has not. In order to do this, we might present all of our participants with the same list of nouns and then ask them to provide free recall 30 minutes later. Half of them might be asked to think of adjectives to go with the nouns (processing of meaning or semantic processing), whereas the other half are asked to think of rhyming words (non-semantic processing). In such a study, the main aim is to investigate levels-of-processing theory. In more general terms, the aim is to see whether long-term memory is influenced by the kind of processing that occurs at the time of learning. The experimental hypothesis is more specific: free recall from long-term memory is higher when there is semantic processing at the time of learning than when there is non-semantic processing.

Non-experimental studies

The situation with regard to the aims and hypotheses is somewhat different in qualitative research, in which the data are *not* in numerical form. Qualitative research is often based on interviews, observations, or case studies. Qualitative researchers frequently have no specific hypotheses at the outset of the study; rather, the hypotheses to be tested emerge from a detailed consideration of the data. The aims of qualitative research tend to be more general and wide-ranging than those of traditional research.

An example of qualitative research is the work of Marsh, Rosser, and Harré (1978) with football fans. Marsh's original aim was to try to understand the aggressive behaviour that they often display, but he had few if any preconceptions or hypotheses in mind at the outset of the study. During the course of the study, Marsh et al. (1978) began to realise that there were complex rules or social norms that were shared by football fans, and which played an important role in determining their behaviour (see Chapter 21).

Hypotheses

Most experimental research starts with someone thinking of an **experimental hypothesis** (also known as the alternative hypothesis). This is simply a prediction or expectation of what will happen in a given situation. For example, you might think of the experimental hypothesis that loud noise will have an effect on people's ability to carry out a task, such as learning the information in a chapter of an introductory psychology textbook.

Variables

As with most experimental hypotheses, the one just mentioned predicts that some aspect of the situation (in this case, the presence of loud noise) will have an effect on the participants' behaviour (in this case, their learning of the information in the chapter). In more technical language, the experimental hypothesis refers to an **independent variable**, which is usually some aspect of the experimental situation that is manipulated by the experimenter. In our example, the presence versus absence of loud noise is the independent variable. The hypothesis also refers to a **dependent variable**, which is some aspect of the participants' behaviour. In our example, some measure of learning would be used to assess the dependent variable. In a nutshell, most experimental hypotheses predict that a given independent variable will have some specified effect on a given dependent variable.

Do you consider that a scientist's views and explanations are any better than our own "commonsense" views? If so, why might this be the case?

Common sense recommends a quiet rather than a noisy place for study—but to test the hypothesis that noise interferes with learning requires an experimental design.

One-tailed or two-tailed?

It should be noted at this point that there are two types of experimental hypothesis: directional or one-tailed hypotheses, and non-directional or two-tailed hypotheses. A *directional* or *one-tailed hypothesis* predicts the *nature* of the effect of the independent variable on the dependent variable. In terms of our example, a directional hypothesis might be as follows: loud noise will reduce people's ability to learn the information contained in the chapter of a textbook. A *non-directional* or *two-tailed hypothesis* predicts that the independent variable will have an effect on the dependent variable, but the *direction* of the effect is not specified. In terms of our example, a non-directional hypothesis would be as follows: loud noise will have an effect on people's ability to learn the information contained in the chapter of a textbook. This hypothesis allows for the possibility that loud noise might actually improve learning.

Null hypothesis

The experimental hypothesis consists of the predicted effect of the independent variable on the dependent variable. This can be contrasted with the null hypothesis. The **null hypothesis** simply states that the independent variable will have no effect on the dependent variable. In terms of our example, a suitable null hypothesis would be as follows: loud noise will have no effect on people's ability to learn the information contained in the chapter of the textbook. In a sense, the purpose of most studies using the experimental method is to decide between the merits of the experimental hypothesis and those of the null hypothesis.

Why do we need a null hypothesis when what we are interested in is the experimental hypothesis? The key reasons are because the null hypothesis is much more precise than the experimental hypothesis, and we need precise hypotheses in order to use statistical tests properly. For example, the null hypothesis that loud noise will have no effect on people's learning ability is precise because it leads to the prediction that the single most likely outcome is that performance will be equal in the loud noise and no noise conditions. Failing that, there will probably only be a small difference between the two conditions, with the difference being equally likely to go in either direction. In contrast, consider the experimental hypothesis that loud noise will reduce people's learning ability. This hypothesis is very imprecise, because it does not indicate how much learning ability will be impaired. This lack of precision makes it impossible to decide the *exact* extent to which the findings support or fail to support the experimental hypothesis.

> ■ Research activity: Generating a hypothesis
>
> 1 Generate a hypothesis for each of these questions:
>   • What are "football hooligans" really like?
>   • Do children play differently at different ages?
>   • What are the effects of caffeine on attention and concentration?
>
> 2 Identify the independent variable (IV) and dependable variable (DV) from each hypothesis.
>
> 3 Identify whether your hypotheses are one-tailed or two-tailed (remember, a one-tailed hypothesis predicts the direction of the effect of the IV on the DV, whereas a two-tailed hypothesis does not).
>
> 4 Write a null hypothesis for each of the experimental hypotheses.

Manipulating the independent variable

It might seem easy to do a study to test the experimental hypothesis that loud noise disrupts learning. However, there are various pitfalls that need to be avoided. The first issue that needs to be considered is how to manipulate the independent variable. In our example, we want to compare loud noise with no noise, so we have to decide exactly how loud we want the noise to be. If it is very loud, then it might damage the hearing of our participants, and so would be totally unacceptable. If it is fairly soft, then it is unlikely to have any effect on the learning ability of our participants. It is also likely to make a difference whether the noise is meaningful (e.g. music or speech) or meaningless (e.g. the noise of a road drill).

Measuring the dependent variable

The second issue is how to measure the dependent variable or aspect of the participants' behaviour. We could ask the participants various questions to measure their understanding of the material in the textbook chapter. However, selecting the questions so that they are not too easy or too hard requires careful thought.

KEY TERM
Null hypothesis: prediction that the independent variable will have no effect on the dependent variable.

Ethical issues: Questions that are too complex, negative, ambiguous, or highly socially sensitive must be avoided, so that they do not offend the participants or cause distress.

Selecting Participants

Studies in psychology rarely involve more than about 100 participants. However, researchers generally want their findings to apply to a much larger group of people than those acting as participants. In technical terms, the participants selected for a study form a *sample*. This sample is taken from some larger *population*, which consists of all the members of the group from which the sample has been drawn. For example, we might select a sample of 20 children aged 5, for a study, in which case the population might consist of all the 5-year-olds living in England.

When we carry out a study, we want the findings obtained from our sample to be true of the population from which they were drawn. In order to achieve this, we must use a *representative sample*, i.e. participants who are representative or typical of the population in question. However, numerous studies have been carried out with non-representative samples; the term *sampling bias* is used to refer to this state of affairs. Coolican (1994, p.36) was pessimistic about the chances of selecting a representative sample:

> ■ Research activity: Representative samples
>
> Identify a representative sample for each of these research aims:
> * To discover whether there are enough youth facilities in your community.
> * To discover whether cats like dried or tinned cat food.
> * To discover whether children aged between 5 and 11 watch too much violent television.
> * To discover the causes of anxiety experienced by participants in research studies.

The simple truth is that a truly representative sample is an abstract ideal unachievable in practice. The practical goal we can set ourselves is to remove as much sampling bias as possible.

Random samples

To return to our earlier example, we might study the effects of loud noise on learning in students preparing for a psychology exam. The best way of obtaining a representative sample from that population would be to make use of **random sampling**. We could obtain lists of names of all the students due to sit the psychology exam in a given year. After that we could use some random method to select our sample. This could be done by picking names out of a hat, or by sticking a pin repeatedly into the lists.

Another approach is to assign a number to everyone in the population from which the sample is to be selected. After that, a computer can be used to generate a series of random numbers that can be used to select the sample. Alternatively, random number tables can be used in a similar way to produce the sample.

If we wanted to have a representative sample of the entire adult population, then we could apply one of the methods of random selection just described to the electoral roll. However, even that would be an imperfect procedure. Several groups of people, including the homeless, illegal immigrants, and prisoners, are not included in the electoral roll.

As Cardwell et al. (1996) pointed out, there is a modified version of random sampling which is easier to use. This is **systematic sampling**. It involves selecting the participants by a quasi-random procedure. For example, if we have a list of all the members of the population, we could select every hundredth name from that list as participants. This procedure is not as effective as random sampling because it cannot be claimed that every member of the population is equally likely to be selected.

> Systematic sampling is not as effective as random sampling, but it does help to overcome the biases of the researcher. If we select every hundredth name on the list, we avoid missing out names that we cannot pronounce, or do not like the look of.

Random sampling typically fails to produce a truly representative sample, because it is actually very hard for an experimenter to obtain a random sample. There are various reasons for this. First, it may not be possible to identify all of the members of the larger population from which the sample is to be selected. Second, it may not be possible to contact all those who have been selected randomly to appear in the sample.

Third, some of those who are selected to be in the sample are likely to refuse to take part in the study. This might not matter if those who agreed to take part in research were very similar in every way to those who did not. However, there is considerable evidence that volunteers differ in various ways from non-volunteers. Manstead and Semin (1996, p.93) discussed some of the evidence, and concluded, "there *are* systematic personality

KEY TERMS
Random sampling: selecting participants on some random basis (e.g. coin tossing).
Systematic sampling: a modified version of random sampling in which the participants are selected in a quasi-random way (e.g. every hundredth name from a population list).

differences between volunteers and non-volunteers." Volunteers tend to be more sensitive to the demand characteristics (cues used by participants to work out what a study is about), and they are also more likely to comply with those demand characteristics.

Why do you think volunteers are more likely than non-volunteers to be sensitive to the design characteristics of a study?

In sum, it is worth bearing in mind what Coolican (1998, p.720) had to say about random samples: "Many students write that their sample was 'randomly selected'. In fact, research samples are very rarely selected at random."

Stratified and quota samples

Another way of obtaining a representative sample is by using what is known as **stratified sampling**. The first step is to decide which characteristics of the population might be relevant for the study we want to carry out. These characteristics might include gender and the part of the country in which they live. This allows us to think in terms of sub-groups. After that, we select participants at random from within each of the sub-groups.

> Stratified sampling is time-consuming and difficult to carry out effectively. Pressures on time and tight budgets may make this sampling technique impossible.

Suppose that we want to carry out a study on A level psychology students. We know that 75% of A level psychology students are female, and that 40% of all A level psychology students live in the north of England. We could then ensure that the participants used in our experiment were selected in a random way so that 75% of them were female, and 40% of them lived in the north of England. If we make use of enough criteria, then stratified sampling can be an effective way of finding a representative sample.

There is a modified version of stratified sampling which is known as **quota sampling**. It resembles stratified sampling in that participants are selected in proportion to their representation in the population. However, it differs in that the researcher decides who to include in each sub-group, rather than the decision being made at random. Quota sampling is often used in market research. It tends to be faster than stratified sampling. However, it has the disadvantage that people who are readily available (e.g. the unemployed) are more likely to be included than those who are not.

The problem with stratified and quota sampling is that it is often hard to know which sub-groups to identify. It is a waste of time and effort if we use characteristics (e.g. gender) that are of no relevance to the study. What is more troublesome is if we fail to identify sub-groups on the basis of some characteristic (e.g. GCSE performance) which is actually highly relevant.

Your quota sample is to come from 30 individuals who work for a large chain of superstores. Would you simply collect your information from the first 30 workers to leave the building?

Opportunity sampling

Random sampling, stratified sampling, and quota sampling are often expensive and time-consuming. As a result, many researchers use **opportunity sampling**. This involves selecting participants on the basis of their availability rather than by any other method. Opportunity sampling is often used by students carrying out experiments, and it is also very common in natural experiments (see Chapter 30).

Opportunity sampling is the easiest way to proceed. However, it has the severe disadvantage that the participants may be nothing like a representative sample. For example, students who are friends of the student carrying out a study may be more willing to take part than students who are not.

KEY TERMS

Stratified sampling: a modified version of quota sampling, in which the selection of participants according to certain characteristics is decided by the researcher, rather than in a random way.
Quota sampling: selecting participants at random from a population so that they are similar to it in certain respects (e.g. proportion of females; proportion of teenagers).
Opportunity sampling: selecting participants only on the basis of their availability.

Sample size

One of the issues that anyone carrying out a piece of research has to consider is the total number of participants to be included. What is the ideal number of participants in each condition? There is no definite answer to that question, but here are some of the relevant factors:

These people might provide the perfect sample for a psychologist wanting to get answers to a questionnaire, conduct a survey, or observe behaviour—that is, until their train arrives!

Consider the total number of participants to be included...

- It is generally expensive and time-consuming to make use of large samples running into hundreds of participants.
- If it requires very large samples to obtain a statistically significant effect of some independent variable on some dependent variable, then this suggests that the effect is small and of little practical importance.
- If we use very small samples (fewer than 10 participants in each condition), then this reduces the chances of obtaining a significant effect.
- In general terms, sampling bias is likely to be greater with small samples than with large ones.

If there is a golden rule that applies to deciding on sample size, it is the following:

The smaller the likely effect being studied, the larger the sample size needed to demonstrate it.

For most purposes, however, having about 15 participants in each condition is a reasonable number.

Good Practice in Experimentation

In order for an experiment to be designed and carried out successfully, there are several considerations that the researcher needs to bear in mind. Some of the main considerations are discussed in detail in this section.

Standardised procedures

If an experimenter used different wording in the instructions to different participants, how might this affect the results of the study?

In order to carry out an experiment successfully, it is very important that every participant in a given condition is treated in the same way. In other words, it is necessary to use standardised procedures. For example, consider the instructions that are given to the participants. In order to ensure that all of the participants get precisely the same instructions, the experimenter should write them down. He or she should then either read them to the participants, or ask the participants to read them to themselves.

In similar fashion, standardised procedures should be used for the collection of data. Suppose we want to assess the effects of loud noise on learning from a book chapter. We might ask the participants to write down everything they could remember about the chapter. However, it would be very hard to compare the recalls of different participants with any precision. A standardised procedure would be to ask all of the participants the same set of, say, 20 questions relating to the chapter. Each participant then obtains a score between 0 and 20 as a measure of what he or she has learned.

Is it easy to make sure that standardised procedures are being used? No, it is not. Most experiments can be thought of as social encounters between the experimenter and the participant, and it is customary to behave in different ways towards different people. Robert Rosenthal (1966) studied some of the ways in which experimenters fall short of standardised procedures. He found, for example, that male experimenters were more pleasant, friendly, honest, encouraging, and relaxed when their participants were female than when they were male. This led him to conclude as follows: "Male and female subjects [participants] may, psychologically, simply not be in the same experiment at all."

Confounding variables

> **KEY TERM**
> **Confounding variable**: a variable that is mistakenly manipulated along with the independent variable.

Another issue to consider is whether or not our experiment contains any **confounding variables**. These are variables that are mistakenly manipulated along with the independent variable. Suppose there is a study in which one group of participants receives no noise and reads a chapter at midday, whereas the other group of participants receives loud noise and reads the same chapter at midnight. If we find that the latter group learns less well than the former group, we would not know whether this was because of the loud noise or because they did their learning late at night when they were very tired. In this example, time of day is a confounding variable.

Confounding variables are especially likely to be found in non-experimental investigations in which the researcher has no control over the independent variable. One of the classic examples concerns the work on maternal deprivation that was carried out on institutionalised children (see Chapter 15). Bowlby (1951) argued that these children had poorer social and intellectual development than other children because of the absence of the mother. However, these children also had to cope with the unstimulating environment of the institutions of those days, and this was a confounding variable that Bowlby tended to ignore.

Confounding variables are a form of constant error. **Constant error** is present when the effects of any unwanted variable on the dependent variable differ between conditions. There are numerous types of constant error. The participants in one condition may be more tired than those in another condition, or they may be more intelligent, or they may be more motivated.

The type of experimenter could act as a confounding variable. Some participants may feel more comfortable than others in the study situation...

Controlled variables

How do we avoid having any confounding variables? One useful approach is to turn them into **controlled variables**, which are variables that are held constant or controlled. Suppose that we want to study the effects of noise on learning, and we are concerned that the time of day may have an effect. We could make time of day into a controlled variable by testing all of our participants at a given time of day, such as late morning or early evening. If we did this, we would know that time of day could not distort our findings.

Any study of the effects of maternal deprivation on these orphans would have to consider the confounding variable of the unstimulating environment of the orphanage itself.

Random error

Random error occurs when variables that are totally irrelevant to the experiment influence the behaviour of the participants. The key difference between random error and constant error is that random error generally affects both conditions equally and so has *unsystematic effects*, whereas constant error has *systematic effects* on one condition but not on the other. Constant error is more serious than random error, because it can lead us to misinterpret our findings. However, random error is also of concern, because it introduces unwanted variation in the dependent variable.

There are almost limitless types of random error. For example, suppose we are interested in comparing learning performance under noise and no-noise conditions. Participants in either condition may learn poorly because they have a splitting headache, because they have just argued with a close friend, because a relationship broke up last week, because the weather is bad, or because they are worried about an important examination they have to take next week. The experimenter cannot control most forms of random error, but should try to control those that can be controlled. For example, he or she should ensure that the lighting conditions, the heating conditions, the experimenter's tone of voice, and so on remain constant for all participants.

Operationalisation

Psychologists carry out studies to test experimental hypotheses, such as "anxiety impairs performance" or "maternal deprivation leads to maladjustment". There is an immediate problem with designing a study to test such hypotheses: there is little or no agreement on the best way to measure psychological concepts or variables such as "anxiety", "performance", "maternal deprivation", or "maladjustment". The most common approach to this problem is to make use of **operationalisation**. This involves defining each variable of interest in terms of the operations taken to measure it. Such a definition is referred to as an operational definition. For example, anxiety might be defined as the score on the trait anxiety scale of Spielberger's State–Trait Anxiety Inventory, and performance might be defined as the number of five-letter anagrams that can be solved in five minutes.

Operationalisation has the great advantage that it generally provides a clear and objective definition of even complex variables. However, there are various limitations associated with the use of operational definitions. First, operational definitions are entirely circular. As Stretch (1994, p.1076) pointed out:

> A psychological construct is defined in terms of the operations necessary to measure it, and the measurements are defined to be measures of the psychological construct.

Second, an operational definition typically only covers part of the meaning of the variable or concept. For example, defining anxiety in terms of the score on a self-report questionnaire largely ignores physiological and behavioural aspects of anxiety, and no-one believes that performance can *only* be assessed in terms of rate of anagram solution.

In spite of these important limitations with operational definitions, it is hard to carry out research without using them. Stretch (1994, p.1076) argued that operational definitions should be used in a careful fashion:

> A useful rule of thumb is to consider many different ways of measuring the psychological construct of interest and determine the extent to which each method could yield different experimental results. If you find that the measurement techniques radically affect the results that emerge, this should indicate that more work is needed on developing the underlying psychological and measurement models to explain these effects.

Experimental Designs

If we wish to compare two groups with respect to a given independent variable, it is essential to make sure that the two groups do not differ in any other important way. This general rule is important when it comes to selecting participants to take part in an experiment. Suppose all the least able participants received the loud noise, and all the most able participants received no noise. We would not know whether it was the loud noise or the low ability level of the participants causing poor learning performance.

How should we select our participants so as to avoid this problem? There are three main types of experimental design:

- Independent design: each participant is selected for only one group.
- Matched participants design: each participant is selected for only one group, but the participants in the two groups are matched for some relevant factor or factors (e.g. ability; sex; age).
- Repeated measures design: each participant appears in both groups, so that there are exactly the same participants in each group.

Independent design

With the independent design, the most common way of deciding which participants go into which group is by means of randomisation. In our example, this could involve using a random process such as coin tossing to decide whether each participant is exposed to loud noise or to no noise. It is possible with randomisation for all the most able participants to be selected for the same group. However, what happens in the great majority of cases is that the participants in the two groups are similar in ability, age, and so on.

Matched participants design

With the matched participants design, we make use of information about the participants to decide which group each participant should join. In our example, we might have information about the participants' ability levels. We could then use this information to make sure that the two groups were matched in terms of range of ability.

Repeated measures design

With the repeated measures design, every participant is in both groups. In our example, that would mean that each participant learns the chapter in loud noise and that they also learn the chapter in no noise. The great advantage of the repeated measures design is that we do not need to worry about the participants in one group being cleverer than those in the other group: as the same participants appear in both groups, the ability level (and all other individual characteristics) must be identical in the two groups!

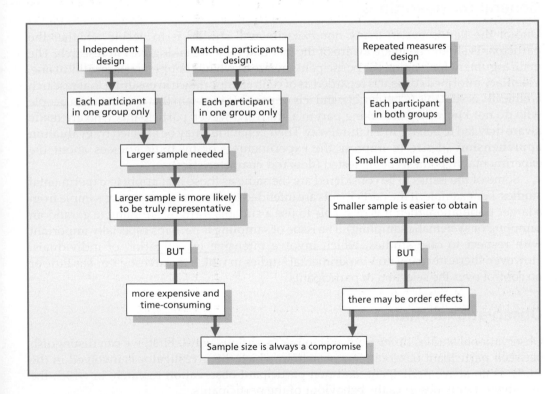

The main problem with the repeated measures design is that there may well be order effects. Their experiences during the experiment may change the participants in various ways. They may perform better when they appear in the second group because they have gained useful information about the experiment or about the task. On the other hand, they may perform less well on the second occasion because of tiredness or boredom. It would be hard to use a repeated measures design in our example: participants are almost certain to show better learning of the chapter the second time they read it, regardless of whether they are exposed to loud noise.

Counterbalancing

Suppose we used a repeated measures design in which all of the participants first learned the chapter in loud noise and then learned it in no noise. We would expect

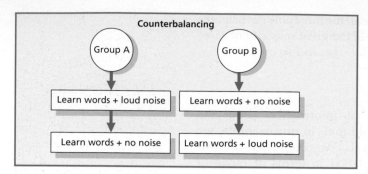

Counterbalancing

the participants to show better learning in no noise simply because of order effects. A better procedure would be to have half the participants learn the chapter first in loud noise and then in no noise, while the other half learn the chapter first in no noise and then in loud noise. In that way, any order effects would be balanced out. This approach is known as **counterbalancing**. It is the best way of preventing order effects from disrupting the findings from an experiment.

Good Practice in Non-experimental Designs

There are several kinds of non-experimental studies (see Chapter 30). They include naturalistic observation, participant observation, studies based on correlational analysis, interviews and surveys, and case studies. Case studies involve the collection of detailed information from individuals rather than from groups of participants. We will begin by considering some general points that need to be taken into account when designing and implementing a non-experimental study.

General considerations

One of the key issues in many non-experimental studies is to decide whether the participants should be made aware of the fact that they are taking part in research. The main argument for making the participants aware of what is happening is an ethical one. Voluntary informed consent is regarded as of central importance in ensuring that research is ethically acceptable (Chapter 29), and it is impossible to obtain that consent from people who do not know they are taking part in a study. However, participants who are made aware may fail to behave in a natural way. Their behaviour may be affected by **evaluation apprehension** (desire to impress the experimenter) or by their guesses about the experimental hypothesis being tested (**demand characteristics**).

Some of the issues to be considered are the same as those that apply to experimental studies. For example, if the participants are intended to form a representative sample from a larger population, then it is desirable to use a suitable form of sampling (e.g. random sampling or systematic sampling). The issue of sampling is perhaps especially important with respect to case studies, which involve intensive investigation of individuals. However, there are many non-experimental studies in which the investigator has little or no control over the selection of participants.

Observational studies

Observational studies differ from each other in various ways. First, we can distinguish between participant observation research, in which the investigator is involved in the study as an active participant, and non-participant observation research, in which the investigator only observes the behaviour of the participants.

Second, there is a distinction between unstructured observation and structured observation. According to Dyer (1995, p.153), unstructured observation is research "where the aim is simply to ensure that everything which appears to be of relevance to the research at a given moment is recorded." In contrast, an investigator using structured observation makes prior decisions about what to observe, and this "renders the research process relatively inflexible and incapable of responding to unpredictable situations" (1995, p.154).

Participant observation

The key factor in participant observation is that the researcher has to do his or her best to become accepted by the social group being studied. The goal is to develop a good understanding of what it is like to be a member of that group, and this can only be done

Psychology students often use other psychology students as their sample. However well-intentioned students are as participants, they are seldom naive as to the nature of the research. Bearing in mind the effects of evaluation apprehension and demand characteristics, what do you think are the advantages and disadvantages of using fellow students as a sample?

when its members accept and trust the researcher. It follows that participant observation research is very time-consuming, because it can take weeks or months for the researcher to gain the confidence of group members.

Dyer (1995) discussed three stages that are involved in carrying out a participant observation study:

1. Entering the field: an important early step is to be accepted by the "gatekeeper" who controls access to the group to be studied; in a school, it is likely to be the headteacher. It is usually desirable to let the fact that you are doing research emerge gradually over time. However, there are major ethical issues to be considered, and it is important to have the informed consent of those responsible for the running of the school or other organisation.
2. Being in the field: for the duration of the study, you have the hard task of trying to fit in as a member of the group and of remaining detached as an observer. You should take field notes, which are an extensive record of what members say and do. These field notes should be condensed into a field diary that is written up every day, and which should identify key themes. Finally, the field diary is used as the basis for the research report. The initial field notes might include information in the following categories suggested by Lovland (1976): acts (short actions); activities (actions taking up at least several days); meanings (participants' explanations for their actions); participation (the various roles participants play); relationships among the group members; and settings (the situations in which the group members find themselves)
3. Leaving the field: there are major ethical issues in participant observation research, because it tends to deal with personal and sensitive issues. It is thus very important to make sure that the group members have the chance to read and comment on your research, and that you take their comments seriously.

To carry out an observational study at a school, you have to convince the teachers that your research is harmless and worthwhile, and that it will not hamper them or the children, or expose them to criticism or ridicule.

Non-participant observation

Most non-participant observation research starts with the researcher thinking of an experimental hypothesis. If structured observations are to be made, it is then necessary to devise the behavioural categories that are going to be used by the observers. The categories should possess the following features:

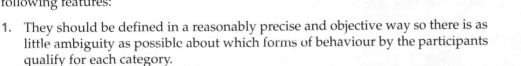
Try to fit in as a member of the group and remain detached as an observer.

1. They should be defined in a reasonably precise and objective way so there is as little ambiguity as possible about which forms of behaviour by the participants qualify for each category.
2. The system of categories needs to be comprehensive, in the sense that all aspects of behaviour that are relevant to the experimental hypothesis should be included.
3. The categories should be usable in the context of the study. For example, a researcher studying the reactions of drivers stuck in traffic jams might include various categories of facial expression. This is only sensible provided that the observer is going to be able to see drivers' facial expressions clearly from his or her viewing position.

Sometimes it is not possible to write field notes as events are happening. What aspects of human memory have a bearing on the accuracy and usefulness of notes written after the event?

Another key decision concerns the way in which the participants' behaviour is to be sampled. Dyer (1995) identified four possible sampling procedures:

1. Continuous observation: the observer records behaviour falling into the various categories non-stop over a fairly lengthy period of time (e.g. 60 minutes).
2. Time-interval sampling: the sampling period is divided into a series of short time intervals (e.g. 60 seconds), and the observer decides whether any given participant produces each category of behaviour during each period. Any

behaviour is simply recorded as absent or present, so that no distinction is drawn between a given behaviour exhibited once versus more than once during a single time interval.

3. Time-point sampling: the sampling period is divided into a series of short time intervals, and the observer decides whether the various categories of behaviour are present at the end of each sampling period.

4. Random sampling: this is like time-point sampling, except that the points in time at which behaviour is sampled are selected at random.

Survey studies

The survey method involves collecting information from a large group of individuals. This information is often gathered using questionnaires, but can include interviews or phone contacts. It is important in any survey study to ensure that the sample selected is as representative as possible (see earlier). A problem that applies to nearly all sampling methods is that of non-responding. Some individuals who are selected to form part of the sample are likely to refuse to participate. Others agree to participate, but then fail to provide all of the information requested. Persuasion and persistence should be used to minimise the problem of non-responding, but it is very rare for the response rate to be 100% in a survey study.

What could you do to encourage participants to respond satisfactorily to your study?

Survey designs

According to Dyer (1995), there are four main types of survey: one-shot survey; before–after design; two-groups controlled comparison design; and the two-groups before–after design.

If the respondents' answers in a one-shot survey were then divided into those given by males and females, would this be a valid basis for creating comparison groups?

One-shot surveys. The one-shot survey is the simplest, but also generally the least informative type of survey. Information is obtained from a single sample at a given point in time. The reason why it is fairly uninformative is that we cannot compare the findings from our sample against those of other groups. As a result, we can only describe what we have found to be the case in the sample we tested.

Before–after surveys. The before–after design is an advance on the one-shot survey, in that data are collected from a single sample on two occasions. The design is most likely to produce interesting findings if some major event or experience intervenes between the first and second data collections. For example, attitudes towards the Labour party could have been obtained shortly before and after the general election of 1997. Suppose (as seems to have been the case) that attitudes were more positive after the election than before. This might have been due to the election victory, but there are other possibilities. Attitudes to the Labour party might have become more positive even if there had not been an election, or it may be that people tend to respond differently on the second occasion that an attitude questionnaire is completed than on the first. In general, it is hard to interpret the findings based on the before–after design.

Do events such as a general election victory affect attitudes towards a political standpoint, or vice versa?

Two-groups controlled comparison surveys. The two-groups controlled comparison design is potentially more informative than the designs discussed so far. In essence, there are two similar groups of participants, one of which is exposed to some treatment before data collection, whereas the other is not. For example, attitudes towards the opposite sex could be assessed in those who have (or have not) recently experienced the breakdown of a heterosexual relationship. If the former group was more negative in their attitudes, it could be argued that this was due to the breakdown of the relationship. However, this requires the assumption that the two groups had the same attitudes before the breakdown occurred, and we cannot be sure that that assumption is justified.

Two-groups before–after surveys. The two-groups before–after design is an advance on the two-groups controlled comparisons design. Two samples or groups are tested for the first time, then one group is exposed to some treatment, and finally both groups are tested for a second time. Dyer (1995) gave as an imaginary example a study in which the participants are allocated at random to two groups. The attitudes of all of them towards Third World issues are assessed. One group is then exposed to several presentations of a television commercial focusing on the need to provide economic aid to Third World countries. Finally, the attitudes of both groups towards Third World countries are assessed. This survey method is the most complicated one to use, but the findings are easier to interpret than those from other survey methods.

The two-groups before–after design is more reliable and easier to interpret, but there is still an assumption that individual differences are controlled for. Is this justified?

Questionnaire construction

In order to address the specific issues that interest them, researchers using the survey method often construct their own questionnaire. The first step is to generate as many ideas as possible that might be relevant to the questionnaire. Then those ideas that seem of little relevance are discarded, working on the basis (Dyer, 1995, p.114) that:

> *It is better to ask carefully designed and quite detailed questions about a few precisely defined issues than the same number on a very wide range of topics.*

Question styles: A survey on chocolate

Closed question: Do you like chocolate? (tick one)

[YES] [NO] [NOT SURE]

Open question: Why do you like or dislike chocolate?

Ambiguous question: Is chocolate likely to do you more harm than a diet that consists mainly of junk food?

Biased question: Plain chocolate is a more sophisticated taste

---

Closed and open questions. There is an important distinction between closed and open questions. Closed questions invite the respondent to select from various possible answers (e.g. yes or no; yes, unsure, or no; putting different answers in rank order), whereas open questions allow respondents to answer in whatever way they prefer. Most questionnaires use closed questions, because the answers are easy to score and to analyse. Open questions have the disadvantage of being much harder to analyse, but they can be more informative than closed questions.

Ambiguity and bias. Questions that are ambiguous or are likely to be interpreted in various ways should be avoided. Questions that are very long or complicated should also be avoided, because they are likely to be misunderstood. Finally, questions that are biased should be avoided. Here is an example of a biased question: "In view of the superiority of Britain, why should we consider further political integration with the rest of Europe?".

Reliability and validity. Good questionnaires need to have high reliability or consistency of measurement. They also need reasonable validity, meaning that they should measure what they claim to measure. Issues of reliability and validity are discussed in Chapter 27. Reliability can be assessed by means of the test–retest method, in which the questionnaire is given to the same individuals on two different occasions. The scores can then be correlated by means of a test such as Spearman's rho (see Chapter 32). If the correlation is fairly high (about +0.7 or +0.8), then the questionnaire can be regarded as reliable.

There are several ways of assessing the validity of a test. For example, there is empirical validity, in which the scores on a questionnaire are compared against some external criterion. For example, suppose that someone devised a questionnaire to measure conscientiousness. It seems reasonable to assume that conscientious people will perform better on examinations, and so we could use examination performance as the external criterion. Conscientiousness scores on the questionnaire could be correlated with examination performance using Spearman's rho, with the assumption being that there would be a significant positive correlation.

Attitude scale construction

Many of the points made about questionnaire construction also apply to the construction of attitude scales. However, there are some differences.

Likert scales. One of the most common ways to construct an attitude scale is to use the Likert procedure. Initially various statements are collected together, and the participants' task is to indicate their level of agreement on a five-point scale running from "strongly disagree" at one end to "strongly agree" at the other end. For positive statements (e.g. "Most Hollywood stars are outstanding actors"), strongly disagree is scored as 1 and strongly agree as 5, with intermediate points being scored 2, 3, or 4. For negative statements (e.g. "Most Hollywood stars are not outstanding actors"), the scoring is reversed so that strongly disagree is scored as 5 and strongly agree as 1.

Most attitude scales based on the Likert method contain some unsatisfactory items. One way of finding out which items are unsuitable is by correlating each item separately with the total score on the scale. Only items that correlate positively at a moderate level with the total score (+0.3 and above) are retained for the scale.

Reliability and validity. The reliability of an attitude scale can be assessed by the test–retest method. Its validity can generally be assessed by some measure of empirical validity. For example, we could obtain evidence about the validity of a scale concerned with attitudes towards religion by correlating the scores with a measure such as regularity of attendance at church, by using Spearman's rho. However, it is important to note that the correlation may be low either because an attitude scale lacks validity or because there is often a large difference between people's attitudes and their behaviour (see Chapter 19).

How would results be affected by the possibility that people might decide to give the socially acceptable response to statements such as: "Smacking children is an appropriate method of punishment"?

Correlational studies

Correlational studies typically involve obtaining two different measures from a group of participants, and then assessing the degree of association between the measures by using a test of correlation such as Spearman's rho. For example, participants' level of extraversion could be correlated with their number of friends, based on the prediction that extraverts are likely to have more friends than introverts.

Correlational studies are easy to carry out. For example, there are thousands of questionnaires for measuring personality or attitudes, and it is possible to take any two at random and administer them to a large group of people. After that, the scores on the two questionnaires can be correlated. However, the fact that correlational studies are easy to perform does *not* mean that good correlational studies are easily carried out. What features characterise good correlational studies?

An underlying theory

First, the study should be based on some underlying theory. The two variables that are measured in the study should both be of clear relevance to the theory. In addition, the predicted direction of the correlation (positive or negative) should follow from the theory. For example, there is the matching hypothesis, according to which we are attracted to those who are about as physically attractive as we are. This was tested in a correlational study by Murstein (1972; see Chapter 20). The physical attractiveness of couples was judged from photographs. There was a strong positive correlation, with the most physically attractive individuals tending to have someone very attractive as their partner, whereas those who were physically unattractive had unattractive partners.

If you were conducting a study using photographs of attractive people, how would you decide which pictures to include? How would you avoid accusations of subjectivity?

In many correlational studies, one of the variables can be regarded as the predictor variable with the other one as the outcome variable. The predictor variable can be seen as occurring before the outcome variable in some sense. It is called the predictor variable, because it forms the basis for predicting the value of the outcome variable. For example, there is a positive correlation between the Type A Behaviour Pattern (hostility, impatience, tension) and coronary heart disease (Miller et al., 1991; see Chapter 6). Here the Type A Behaviour Pattern is the predictor variable and coronary heart disease is the outcome variable. This approach may suggest the existence of a causal relationship. However, it is very important to remember that "correlations cannot prove causes". There could be a third factor (e.g. genetic vulnerability) that leads to the Type A Behaviour Pattern and to susceptibility to heart disease.

Careful measurement

Another feature of good correlational studies is that the variables are carefully measured. Let us consider an example. Martin et al. (1989) argued that Type A individuals are much more highly motivated than Type B individuals, who are relaxed, patient, and calm. This suggests that Type A individuals might have better job performance than Type Bs; thus, there should be a positive correlation between Type A and job performance. How can job performance be measured? In the case of managers whose jobs involve forward planning, motivating their staff, monitoring the performance of their staff, and so on, it may be very hard to assess their work performance in a single measure. It would be preferable to study a group such as insurance salespeople. Their main work goal is to sell as much insurance as possible, and so the amount of insurance sold over a given period of time (e.g. three months) would provide a reasonable measure of job performance.

Correlation or causation?

Wide range

A final feature of good correlational studies is that the scores on both variables vary considerably from individual to individual. For example, IQ is supposed to reflect general intellectual ability, and so one might predict that there would be a positive correlation between IQ and job performance. This has been found numerous times (Eysenck, 1994a). Suppose, however, that we correlated IQ and job performance among chartered accountants. The great majority of chartered accountants have high IQs, and so we have what is known as restriction of range. This restriction of range would reduce the strength of the association between IQ and job performance, and so it should be avoided.

Why is a wide range important? If a strong positive correlation is found between two factors when a wide range of different participants take part in a study, what does this suggest about the conclusions to be drawn from the results?

Problems with Experimental Research

In most experimental research (and some non-experimental research), the experimenter and the participants interact with each other. This can produce various kinds of problems. The ways in which experimenters behave and talk may influence the behaviour of the participants in ways that have nothing to do with the independent variable or variables being manipulated. In addition, the participants may form mistaken ideas of what the experiment is about, and these mistaken ideas may affect their behaviour. Some of the main problems stemming from the relationship between the researcher and the participants are discussed in this section.

Experimenter effects

The ideal experimenter is someone who behaves in exactly the same mildly positive way with every participant, and who does not allow his or her expectations and experimental hypotheses to influence the conduct of a study. In reality, the experimenter's expectations, personal

The way in which experimenters behave and talk may influence the behaviour of the participant.

Clever Hans, the "counting" horse.

characteristics, and so on often have an effect on the participants' behaviour; these are known as **experimenter effects**.

Experimenter expectancy

One of the most important experimenter effects is experimenter expectancy, in which the experimenter's expectations have a systematic effect on the performance of the participants. Perhaps the first systematic demonstration of experimenter expectancy involved a horse known as Clever Hans. The horse was apparently able to count, tapping its hoof the right number of times when asked a simple mathematical question (e.g. 8 + 6). Pfungst (1911) studied Clever Hans. He found that Clever Hans could not produce the correct answer when the horse was blindfolded. What happened normally was that the experimenter made slight movements when the horse had tapped out the correct number, and Clever Hans was simply using these movements as the cue to stop tapping.

Rosenthal

KEY STUDY EVALUATION — Rosenthal

Psychological experiments like Rosenthal's are carried out by humans on humans. As such they are unique social situations in which social interactions play an important part. Inevitably, problems can arise in the form of experimenter effects. According to Rosenthal, the participants could be influenced to expect certain results to occur within the experiment. However, it is possible that the experimenter could have given clues as to how the participants were expected to behave, either verbal or non-verbal in nature. Rosenthal suggested that the perceived competence and authority of the research could also produce experimenter effects. This would be influenced by the participant's own personal characteristics such as a need for approval.

One of the best-known studies on experimenter effects was reported by Rosenthal (1966). He asked student experimenters to count the number of head turns and body contractions made by flatworms. Before the experiment started, the students were told that they should expect a lot of activity from half of the worms, but very little activity from the others. In fact, worms were assigned at random to the two groups, so there was no reason for assuming that they would actually differ in activity level.

What do you think Rosenthal found? Somewhat surprisingly, the experimenters reported *twice* as many head turns and *three* times as many body contractions in the worms that were allegedly "highly active" as in the "inactive" ones! Rosenthal

How could the results obtained by Rosenthal be due to the participants deviating from the standardised procedure, rather than to the experimenter expectancy effect?

argued that this was an experimenter expectancy effect, but it is more likely that it was due to the experimenters failing to follow the proper procedures and/or misrecording of the data. As Coolican (1994) pointed out, there was no evidence of expectancy effect in at least 40 experiments specifically designed to find it. There is evidence that the behaviour of human participants, especially those high in need for approval, can be influenced by the experimenter's behaviour. However, it seems less likely that flatworms would respond to a smile or a frown from the experimenter!

Discussion points

1. Are you surprised that it has proved hard to replicate Rosenthal's findings on flatworms?
2. In what circumstances would you expect to find experimenter effects (see later)?

Other effects

Barber (1976) argued that there are numerous ways in which the experimenter can influence the findings obtained. In addition to experimenter expectancy, he identified several other kinds of experimenter effects (summarised in Coolican, 1994). These effects are listed here. In this list, a distinction is drawn between the investigator (the person *directing* the research) and the experimenter (the person actually *carrying out* the experiment). For example, an academic psychologist will often be the investigator, whereas an undergraduate or postgraduate student is the experimenter. So far as the studies carried out by undergraduate studies are concerned, the investigator and the experimenter will typically be the same person.

KEY TERM
Experimenter effects: the various ways in which the experimenters' expectancies, personal characteristics, misrecordings of data, and so on can influence the findings of a study.

1. Investigator paradigm effect: the entire approach adopted by the investigator can make it harder or easier to obtain certain findings.
2. Investigator experimental design effect: for example, if an investigator wanted to show that a learning programme for disadvantaged children was not effective, he or she could arrange for the programme to last for a very short period of time to reduce the chances that there would be any noticeable effects.
3. Investigator loose procedure effect: if the instructions and other aspects of the procedure are not clearly specified, there is more scope for the results to be influenced by the investigator.
4. Investigator data analysis effect: the investigator can decide to carry out several unplanned analyses of the data *after* seeing what patterns seem to be present.
5. Investigator fudging effect: there is evidence that Burt, who believed strongly that intelligence depends on heredity, fudged some of his twin data.
6. Experimenter personal attributes effect: for example, an experimenter who liked women but not men might treat male and female participants differently, and so produce a spurious gender effect in the data.
7. Experimenter failure to follow the procedure effect: if this happens, then the independent variable may not be manipulated as it should be, which makes it hard to interpret the findings.
8. Experimenter misrecording effect: experimenters are most likely to misrecord data if the information provided by participants is ambiguous (e.g. did the participant give a little smile?).
9. Experimenter fudging effect: the experimenter may fudge the data to please the investigator or to obtain good marks for his or her study.

Using computers to give instructions, present experimental material, and record results in psychology studies helps to reduce the problem of many of Barber's experimenter effects.

Reducing experimenter effects

What steps can be taken to minimise experimenter effects? One approach is to use a **double blind** procedure, in which neither the experimenter working with the participants nor the participants know the experimental hypothesis (or hypotheses) being tested. The double blind procedure reduces the possibility of experimenter bias, but it is often too expensive and impractical to use. However, the incidence of experimenter effects is probably less than it used to be, for the simple reason that more and more experiments involve participants interacting with computers rather than with human experimenters. In addition, data are increasingly stored directly in computers, making it harder to misrecord the information obtained from participants.

What do you think is the difference between single blind and double blind procedures?

Demand characteristics

A common criticism of laboratory research is that the situation is so artificial that participants behave very differently from the way they do normally. Guy Claxton (1980) discussed an amusing example of this. He considered a laboratory task, in which participants have to decide as rapidly as possible whether sentences such as "Can canaries fly?" are true or false. Under laboratory conditions, people perform this task uncomplainingly. However, as Claxton pointed out, "If someone asks me 'Can canaries fly?' in the pub, I will suspect either that he is an idiot or that he is about to tell me a joke."

Why do people behave in unusual ways under laboratory conditions? The American psychologist Orne (1962) emphasised the importance of what he termed *demand characteristics*, which are "the totality of cues which convey an experimental hypothesis to the subjects [participants]." Demand characteristics include "the rumours or campus scuttle-butt about the research, the information conveyed during the original situation, the person of the experimenter, and the setting of the laboratory, as well as all explicit and implicit communications during the experiment proper." (In case you are wondering,

Ethical issues: Is honesty the best policy? If both the experimenter and the participants are armed with the aims and goals of the study, would this reduce the problem of demand characteristics?

the word "scuttle-butt" means gossip.) Orne's basic idea is that most participants do their best to comply with what they perceive to be the demands of the experimental situation, but their perception will often be inaccurate.

As Orne showed, the demand characteristics in an experiment are so powerful that the participants can often be persuaded to do some very strange things. He discussed one study in which the participants spent several hours adding numbers on random number sheets, then tearing up each completed sheet into at least 32 pieces. Many of the participants treated the situation as a test of endurance, and this motivated them to keep going.

There is another problem with demand characteristics, which applies to participants who have previously taken part in an experiment in which they were deceived about the experimental purpose. As a result of being deceived, some participants tend thereafter to respond in the opposite direction to the one suggested by an experiment's demand characteristics. Why should this be so? Silverman, Shulman, and Wiesenthal (1970) explained this effect in the following way:

> Deceived subjects [participants] may have become so alerted to possible further deceptions that they tend to respond counter to any cues regarding the experimenter's hypothesis. An element of gamesmanship may enter the experimental situation in that subjects [participants] become wary of "tricks" underlying the obvious, and do not want to be caught in them.

Reducing demand characteristics

Information about the demand characteristics in any given experimental setting can be obtained by asking the participants afterwards to describe in detail what they felt the experiment was about. Armed with this information, the experimenter can take steps to make sure that the results of future experiments are not adversely affected by demand characteristics.

Some (but not all) of the problems of demand characteristics can be reduced by the double blind procedure described earlier. Another possibility in some studies is the **single blind** procedure, in which the participants are not informed of the condition in which they have been placed. However, this raises ethical issues, because full informed consent cannot be obtained in such circumstances.

Evaluation apprehension

Rosenberg (1965) pointed out that an important aspect of most participants' behaviour in the experimental or laboratory situation is what he called *evaluation apprehension*. He defined this as "an active anxiety-toned concern that he [the participant] win a positive evaluation from the experimenter or at least that he provide no grounds for a negative one." It could be argued that the main reason why participants comply with the demand characteristics of experimental situations is because of their evaluation apprehension. However, evidence that the need for favourable personal evaluation can be more important than the need to comply with demand characteristics was reported by Sigall, Aronson, and Van Hoose (1970).

Sigall et al. carried out an experiment on copying telephone numbers. The experimenter told the participants doing the test for the second time that he expected them to perform it at a rate that was actually slower than their previous performance. Adherence to the demand characteristics would have led to slow performance, whereas evaluation apprehension and the need to be capable would have produced fast times. In fact, the participants performed faster than they had done before, indicating the greater importance of evaluation apprehension than of demand characteristics.

General Issues in Investigations

So far in this chapter, we have considered several specific issues that are important to ensure that the design of a study is appropriate. In this section, we will address some important general criteria that can (and should) be used to evaluate how successfully a study has been designed and carried out. The criteria to be discussed are participant reactivity; validity; generalisability; and reliability.

Participant reactivity

A weakness that is found in many studies is what is known as **participant reactivity**. This refers to a situation in which an independent variable has an effect on behaviour simply because the participants know that they are being observed or studied. Any measure of the participants' behaviour which could suffer from this effect is called a reactive measure, and reactivity is the term used to refer to the changes in behaviour produced in this way.

The Hawthorne effect

In order to clarify the meaning of participant reactivity, we will consider a series of studies carried out at the Hawthorne Western Electric plant in Chicago (Roethlisberger & Dickson, 1939). They found that the workers became more productive when the amount of lighting was increased, suggesting that work rate increases when the working conditions become easier. However, they also found that *decreasing* the amount of lighting also led to increased productivity! In general, it was found that productivity increased when *any* changes were made to the working conditions, whether these changes were to wages, length of the working day, or to rest. Productivity even improved when there was a return to the original working conditions. Presumably what was happening was that the workers responded to the interest being shown in them, rather than to the specific changes in their working environment.

The term Hawthorne effect came to be used to refer to changes produced because people know they are being studied, although the same phenomenon is now generally referred to as participant reactivity. There are several published findings that may have been influenced by participant reactivity. For example, Klaus and Kennell (1976) reported that mothers who were allowed to interact for several hours a day with their newborn babies developed a closer relationship with them than did mothers who spent less time with their babies (see Chapter 15). The extra-contact mothers were mostly unmarried teenagers, and it has been argued that this effect was due to the interest shown in them by the hospital workers rather than to the extra contact itself. This interpretation is supported by the fact that this finding has generally not been replicated in studies of mothers who are less likely to be flattered at being the centre of attention (Durkin, 1995).

> ### KEY STUDY EVALUATION — The Hawthorne effect
>
> Examining human relations in the workplace grew out of Roethlisberger and Dickson's (1939) study, which aimed to consider the relationship between working conditions and productivity. The initial emphasis was on the extrinsic rewards the worker received, and it was found that there was no relationship between extrinsic rewards and productivity. What became apparent was that intrinsic rewards had a greater effect. These intrinsic rewards derived from the workers' own attitudes towards their work both individually and as part of an informal group. The human need to be part of a social group and to be accepted within it determines attitudes to work and the motivation needed to perform successfully far more than financial rewards. From the Hawthorne study new research was stimulated, which examined the range of needs experienced by the workforce. To increase productivity it was found that social needs had to be met, such as friendship, group support, acceptance, approval, recognition, status, and the need for "self-actualisation", which involves the development of an individual's talents, creativity, and personality to the full.

Participant reactivity or the Hawthorne effect is a serious problem, because it can lead us to misinterpret our findings. How can we decide whether some effect is due to participant reactivity? In essence, we need to make sure that participant reactivity is the same in both conditions, by making it equally clear to both groups that they are being studied and that their behaviour is of interest. If the effect is still found, then it cannot have been due to participant reactivity. For example, if extra contact of mothers and babies was still associated with a closer relationship even when equal interest was shown in the mothers given only routine contact, then it would be reasonable to conclude that it was the contact itself that produced the effect.

Discussion points

1. How much of a problem is participant reactivity in research?
2. When would you *not* expect to find evidence of participant reactivity?

Validity and generalisability

One of the key requirements of a study or experiment is that any findings obtained are valid, in the sense that they are genuine and provide us with useful information about

How would you define the difference between "validity" and "reliability"?

the phenomenon being studied. Campbell and Stanley (1966) drew a distinction between internal validity and external validity, which is of most relevance to experiments and quasi-experiments. **Internal validity** refers to the issue of whether the effects observed are genuine and are caused by the independent variable. In contrast, **external validity** refers to the extent to which the findings of a study can be generalised to situations and samples other than those used in the study. This distinction between two kinds of validity is an important one: many experiments possess internal validity while lacking external validity (see Chapter 30).

Internal validity

We will shortly consider some of the reasons why an experiment may lack external validity, but what are some of the main threats to the internal validity of an experiment? Coolican (1994) pointed out that there are many such threats, most of which were discussed earlier in the chapter. For example, the existence of any confounding factors threatens internal validity, as does the use of unreliable or inconsistent measures. Problems with internal validity can also arise if an experiment is designed without careful attention being paid to issues such as standardisation, counterbalancing, and randomisation. Other threats to internal validity include experimenter effects, demand characteristics, participant reactivity, and the use of inappropriate statistical tests. In a nutshell, virtually all of the principles of experimental design are intended to enhance internal validity, and failures to apply these principles threaten internal validity. If internal validity is high, then there are good prospects for being able to replicate the findings. If it is low, then replication is likely to be difficult or impossible.

External validity and generalisability

What about external validity? There are close links between external validity and **generalisability**, because both are concerned with the issue of whether the findings of an experiment or study are applicable to other situations. More specifically, Coolican (1994) argued that there are four main aspects to external validity or generalisability, which we consider in turn:

- Populations: do the findings obtained from a given sample of individuals generalise to a larger population from which the sample was selected?
- Locations: do the findings of the study generalise to other settings or situations? If the findings generalise to various real-life settings, then the study is said to possess ecological validity. Silverman (1977, p.108) was sceptical about the ecological validity of laboratory experiments: "the conclusions we draw from our laboratory studies pertain to the behaviour of organisms in conditions of their own confinement and control and are probably generalisable only to similar situations (institutions, perhaps, such as schools or prisons or hospitals)."
- Measures or constructs: do the findings of the experiment or study generalise to other measures of the variables used? For example, suppose we find that people who are high on the personality dimension of trait anxiety as assessed by Spielberger's State–Trait Anxiety Inventory have worse long-term memory measured by recall than those low in trait anxiety. Would we obtain the same findings if trait anxiety were assessed by a different questionnaire or if we used a recognition test of long-term memory?
- Times: do the findings generalise to the past and to the future? For example, it could be argued that the sweeping changes in many cultures in recent decades have affected conformity behaviour as studied by Asch, and obedience to authority as studied by Milgram (see Chapter 21).

What can we do to maximise the external validity of an experiment? Unfortunately, there is no easy answer to that question. What usually happens is that the external validity of an experiment only becomes clear when other researchers try to generalise the findings to other samples or populations, locations, measures, and times. It might

Surveys of women's daily activities and attitudes towards domestic work carried out even a few decades ago bear little relevance to conditions and attitudes current today.

Validity: Social changes need to be considered when using data from different timespans, where changing roles can give invalid test comparisons.

be thought that the findings of field experiments are more likely than those of laboratory experiments to generalise to other real-life locations or settings, but that is not necessarily so.

Meta-analyses. One way of trying to determine whether certain findings generalise is to carry out what is known as a **meta-analysis**. What is done in a meta-analysis is to combine all of the findings from many studies designed to test a given hypothesis into a single analysis. If the meta-analysis indicates that some finding has been obtained consistently, this suggests that it generalises across populations, locations, measures, and times. For example, Smith et al. (1980) discussed a meta-analysis on over 400 studies concerned with the effectiveness of psychotherapy (see Chapter 26). They concluded that psychotherapy was reasonably effective, because patients receiving psychotherapy improved more than did 75% of the patients not receiving any therapy.

The greatest limitation of meta-analyses is that differences in the quality of individual studies are often ignored. This can lead to the situation in which a finding is accepted as genuine when it has been obtained in several poorly designed studies but not in a smaller number of well-designed studies. Another problem is that it is often hard to know which studies to include and which to exclude. For example, Smith et al. considered all forms of non-behavioural therapy together. However, some forms of non-behavioural therapy were more effective than others (Barlow & Durand, 1995), so it was perhaps undesirable to put them together into a single meta-analysis.

KEY TERM
Meta-analysis: an analysis in which all of the findings from many studies relating to a given hypothesis are combined for statistical testing.

Reliability

One of the main goals of experimental research is to design and carry out studies in such a way that *replication* or repetition of its findings is possible. In order to achieve that goal, it is important that the measures we use should possess good *reliability* or consistency. As Coolican (1994, p.50) pointed out:

> *Any measure we use in life should be reliable, otherwise it's useless. You wouldn't want your car speedometer or a thermometer to give you different readings for the same values on different occasions. This applies to psychological measures as much as any other.*

Problems relating to reliability are likely to arise when the experimenter is trying to code the complex

Reliability

Internal reliability = consistency within the method of measurement. For instance, a ruler should be measuring the same distance between 0 and 5 centimetres as between 5 and 10 centimetres.

External reliability = consistency between uses of the method of measurement. For instance, the ruler should measure the same on a Monday as it does on a Friday.

- Reliability = consistent and stable
- Validity = measuring what is intended
- Standardisation = comparisons can be made between studies and samples

behaviour of participants using a manageable number of categories. For example, it is common in studies of naturalistic observation to record certain events (e.g. performing an aggressive act). However, it may be hard to define those events with enough precision to produce reliable results. One way of assessing this is by asking two (or more) judges to provide ratings in the observational situation. The ratings can then be compared to provide a measure of inter-judge reliability.

PERSONAL REFLECTIONS

- As you were reading this chapter, you may have thought that the various recommendations for designing experimental and non-experimental studies seemed fairly obvious and easy to follow in practice. In fact, it is very hard to design a study that has no flaws. Three of the greatest problems with experimental designs occur with respect to operationalisation, experimenter effects, and external validity. Thus, it is usually difficult to find ways of operationalising key variables; to avoid the experimenter influencing the participants' behaviour in unwanted ways; and to ensure that the findings will apply to other situations and participants.

SUMMARY

Aims and hypotheses

The first stage in designing a study is to decide on its aims and hypotheses. There will generally be an experimental or alternative hypothesis and a null hypothesis. The experimental hypothesis may be directional or one-tailed, or it may be non-directional and two-tailed.

Selecting participants

The participants selected for a study represent a sample from some population. They should form a representative sample; in other words, sampling bias should be avoided. The best approach is random sampling, but other reasonable methods are systematic sampling, stratified sampling, and quota sampling. Opportunity sampling is the easiest but least satisfactory method. The sample size depends on the likely size of the effect being studied.

Good practice in experimentation

It is important to use standardised procedures. It is also important to avoid confounding variables and other forms of constant error, and to keep random error to a minimum. Operationalisation is useful, but operational definitions typically cover only part of the meaning of the independent or dependent variable in question.

Experimental designs

There are three main types of experimental design: independent design; matched participants design; and repeated measures design. With an independent design, randomisation is generally used to allocate the participants to groups. Counterbalancing is often used with the repeated measures design in order to balance out any order effects and prevent them from disrupting the findings.

Good practice in non-experimental designs

We can distinguish between participant observation and non-participant observation research. Participant research involves the three stages of entering the field; being in the field; and leaving the field. Non-participant observation research involves devising precise, comprehensive, and usable behavioural categories. The sampling of behaviour can be continuous; based on time intervals; based on time points; or random. Survey studies can use various designs: one-shot; before–after; two-groups controlled comparison; two-groups before–after. When questionnaires or attitude scales are constructed, the items need to be short, unambiguous, and unbiased, and the tests need to be reliable and valid. Correlational studies should be based on an underlying theory, the variables should be carefully measured, and the scores on both variables should vary considerably from individual to individual.

Most research involves interactions between the experimenter and the participants. This can introduce various systematic biases, which can be divided into experimenter effects and demand characteristics. Experimenter effects include experimenter expectancy, experimenter misrecording, and experimenter fudging. Demand characteristics involve the participants responding on the basis of their beliefs about the experimental hypothesis or hypotheses. In addition, the behaviour of participants is sometimes influenced by evaluation apprehension.

Problems with experimental research

In some studies, the independent variable has an effect on behaviour simply because the participants know they are being observed. This is known as participant reactivity or the Hawthorne effect. It is a serious problem, because it can lead us to misinterpret our findings. It is important for a study to have internal validity, meaning that the findings are genuine and caused by the independent variable. External validity, which refers to the extent to which the findings of a study can be generalised, is also important. Issues of generalisability apply to populations, locations, measures, and times. Information about the generalisability of any particular findings can be obtained by means of a meta-analysis. The measures used in a study should possess good reliability or consistency. If they do not, then they are inadequate measures of the variables in question, and it will be hard to replicate or repeat any findings obtained.

General issues in investigations

FURTHER READING

The various forms of non-experimental study are discussed in a very accessible way by C. Dyer (1995), *Beginning research in psychology*, Oxford: Blackwell. Most of the topics discussed in this chapter are dealt with in a clear fashion by H. Coolican (1994), *Research methods and statistics in psychology (2nd Edn.)*, London: Hodder & Stoughton.

REVISION QUESTIONS

Sample questions on research methods are given at the end of Chapter 32 on page 887.

32
Data Analysis

The data obtained from a study may or may not be in numerical or quantitative form, that is, in the form of numbers. If they are not in numerical form, then we can still carry out qualitative analyses based on the experiences of the individual participants. If they are in numerical form, then we typically start by working out some descriptive statistics to summarise the pattern of findings. These descriptive statistics include measures of central tendency within a sample (e.g. mean) and measures of the spread of scores within a sample (e.g. range). Another useful way of summarising the findings is by means of graphs and figures. Several such ways of summarising the data are discussed later on in this chapter.

In any study, two things might be true: (1) there is a difference (the experimental hypothesis), or (2) there is no difference (the null hypothesis). Various statistical tests have been devised to permit a decision between the experimental and null hypotheses on the basis of the data. Decision making based on a statistical test is open to error, in that we can never be sure whether we have made the correct decision. However, certain standard procedures are generally followed, and these are discussed in this chapter.

Finally, there are important issues relating to the validity of the findings obtained from a study. One reason why the validity of the findings may be limited is that the study itself was not carried out in a properly controlled and scientific fashion. Another reason why the findings may be partially lacking in validity is that they cannot readily be applied to everyday life, a state of affairs that occurs most often with laboratory studies. Issues relating to these two kinds of validity are discussed towards the end of the chapter.

How would you define "validity"? How does it differ from "reliability"?

Qualitative Analysis of Data

There is an important distinction between quantitative research and qualitative research. In quantitative research, the information obtained from the participants is expressed in numerical form. Studies in which we record the number of items recalled, reaction times, or the number of aggressive acts are all examples of quantitative research. In qualitative research, on the other hand, the information obtained from participants is *not* expressed in numerical form. The emphasis is on the stated experiences of the participants and on the stated meanings they attach to themselves, to other people, and to their environment. Those carrying out qualitative research sometimes make use of direct quotations from their participants, arguing that such quotations are often very revealing.

There has been rapid growth in the use of qualitative methods since the mid-1980s. This is due in part to increased dissatisfaction with the quantitative or scientific approach that has dominated psychology for the past 100 years. Coolican (1994) discussed a quotation from Reason and Rowan (1981), which expresses that dissatisfaction very clearly:

Quantitative research would measure the number of aggressive acts witnessed. Qualitative research may help to explain why the aggressive acts occurred.

857

There is too much measurement going on. Some things which are numerically precise are not true; and some things which are not numerical are true. Orthodox research produces results which are statistically significant but humanly insignificant; in human inquiry it is much better to be deeply interesting than accurately boring.

Many experimental psychologists would regard this statement as being clearly an exaggeration. "Orthodox research" with its use of the experimental method has transformed our understanding of attention, perception, learning, memory, reasoning, and so on. However, qualitative research is of clear usefulness within some areas of social psychology, and it can shed much light on the motivations and values of individuals. As a result, investigators using interviews, case studies, or observations often make use of qualitative data, although they do not always do so.

Why do people behave in this way when on holiday? What motivates them to risk their health in the sun?

Investigators who collect qualitative data use several different kinds of analysis, and so only general indications of what can be done with such data will be presented here. However, there would be general agreement among such investigators with the following statement by Patton (1980; cited in Coolican, 1994):

The cardinal principle of qualitative analysis is that causal relationships and theoretical statements be clearly emergent from and grounded in the phenomena studied. The theory emerges from the data; it is not imposed on the data.

How do investigators use this principle? One important way is by considering fully the categories spontaneously used by the participants *before* the investigators develop their own categories. An investigator first of all gathers together all the information obtained from the participants. This stage is not always entirely straightforward. For example, if we simply transcribe tape recordings of what our participants have said, we may be losing valuable information. Details about which words are emphasised, where the speaker pauses, and when the speaker speeds up or slows down should also be recorded, so that we can understand fully what he or she is trying to communicate.

The investigator then arranges the items of information (e.g. statements) into various groups in a preliminary way. If a given item seems of relevance to several groups, then it is included in all of them. Frequently, the next step is to take account of the categories or groupings suggested by the participants themselves. The final step is for the investigator to form a set of categories based on the information obtained from the previous steps. However, the investigator is likely to change some of the categories if additional information comes to light.

Cross-cultural issues: How might your own learned cultural experiences determine how you view others' behaviour?

Qualitative investigators are not only interested in the number of items or statements falling into each category. Their major concern is usually in the variety of meanings, attitudes, and interpretations found within each category. For example, an investigator might study attitudes towards A-level psychology by carrying out interviews with several A-level students. One of the categories into which their statements were then placed might be "negative attitudes towards statistics". A consideration of the various statements in this category might reveal numerous reasons why A-level psychology students dislike statistics!

When qualitative researchers report their findings, they will often include some raw data (e.g. direct quotations from participants) as well as analyses of the data based on categories. In addition, they often indicate how their hypotheses changed during the course of the investigation.

Cross-cultural issues: Investigators must take care that cultural bias does not lead to their own values, norms, and beliefs distorting the data they collect.

Evaluation

Qualitative analysis is often less influenced than is quantitative analysis by the biases and theoretical assumptions of the investigator. In addition, it offers the prospect of understanding the participants in a study as rounded individuals in a social context. This contrasts with quantitative analysis, in which the focus is often on rather narrow aspects of behaviour.

The greatest limitation of the qualitative approach is that the findings that are reported tend to be unreliable and hard to replicate. Why is this so? The qualitative approach is subjective and impressionistic, and so the ways in which the information is categorised and then interpreted often differ considerably from one investigator to another.

> ■ Research activity: Categorising television programmes
>
> In small groups of three or four people, consider how you might conduct a study to analyse the number of aggressive acts witnessed by children when they watch television cartoon programmes designed for a child audience. Would quantitative methods be most appropriate? How would you ensure that your results were as reliable as possible?

There are various ways in which qualitative researchers try to show that their findings are reliable (Coolican, 1994). Probably the most satisfactory approach is to see whether the findings obtained from a qualitative analysis can be replicated. This can be done by comparing the findings from an interview study with those from an observational study. Alternatively, two different qualitative researchers can conduct independent analyses of the same qualitative data, and then compare their findings.

Qualitative researchers argue that the fact that they typically go through the "research cycle" more than once helps to increase reliability. Thus, for example, the initial assumptions and categories of the researcher are checked against the data, and may then be changed. After that, the new assumptions and categories are checked against the data. Repeating the research cycle is of value in some ways, but it does not ensure that the findings will have high reliability.

Interpretation of Interviews, Case Studies, and Observations

Qualitative analyses as discussed in the previous section are carried out in several different kinds of studies. They are especially common in interviews, case studies, and observational studies, although quantitative analyses have often been used in all three types of studies. Some of the advantages and limitations of these types of studies were discussed in Chapter 30. What we will do in this section is to consider the interpretation of interviews, case studies, and observations.

Interviews

As was discussed in Chapter 30, interviews vary considerably in terms of their degree of structure. In general terms, unstructured interviews (e.g. non-directive or informal) lend themselves to qualitative analyses, whereas structured interviews lend themselves to

Reicher and Potter argued that the St Paul's crowd saw themselves as a legitimate presence and the police as an illegitimate presence. Each group attached a different meaning to their actions. Does that make interpretation of discourse problematic?

quantitative analysis. As Coolican (1994) pointed out, there are various skills that interviewers need in order to obtain valuable data. These skills involve establishing a good understanding with the person being interviewed, adopting a non-judgemental approach, and developing effective listening skills.

Cardwell et al. (1996) illustrated the value of the interview approach by discussing the work of Reicher and Potter (1985) on a riot in the St Paul's area of Bristol in April 1980. Many of the media reports on the riot were based on the assumption that those involved in the riot were behaving in a primitive and excessively emotional way. Unstructured interviews with many of those involved indicated that in fact they had good reasons for their actions. They argued that they were defending their area against the police, and they experienced strong feelings of solidarity and community spirit. This interpretation was supported by the fact that very little of the damage affected private homes in the area.

Evaluation

There are various problems involved in interpreting interview information.

First, there is the problem of **social desirability bias**. Most people want to present themselves in the best possible light, so they may provide socially desirable rather than honest answers to personal questions. This problem can be handled by the interviewer asking additional questions to establish the truth.

Second, the data obtained from an interviewer may reveal more about the social interaction processes between the interviewer and the person being interviewed (the interviewee) than about the interviewee's thought processes and attitudes.

Third, account needs to be taken of the **self-fulfilling prophecy**. This is the tendency for someone's expectations about another person to lead to the fulfilment of those expectations. For example, suppose that a therapist expects his or her patient to behave very anxiously. This expectation may cause the therapist to treat the patient in such a way that the patient starts to behave in the expected fashion.

Case studies

Case studies (intensive investigations of individuals) come in all shapes and sizes. Probably the best-known case studies are those of Freud and others in the field of clinical psychology. However, detailed case studies have also been carried out in personality research and in studies of cognitive functioning in brain-damaged patients.

One way in which case studies have been used to study personality involves an approach known as **psychobiography**. This was defined by McAdams (1988, p.2) as "the systematic use of psychological (especially personality) theory to transform a life into a coherent and illuminating story." A key feature of psychobiography is identification of the most important events in an individual's account of his or her own life story. How can this be done? According to McAdams (1988, pp.12–13), we should look for

clues about primacy (what comes first in a story), uniqueness (what stands out in the story), omission (what seems to be missing from the story), distortion and isolation (what doesn't follow logically in the story), and incompletion (when the story fails to end in a satisfying way.

Weiskrantz (1986) reported a very different kind of case study. He studied DB, who had had an operation designed to reduce the number of severe migraines from which he suffered. As a result of this operation, DB exhibited what is known as "blindsight". He was able to tell whether a visual stimulus had been presented, and he could point at it, even though he had no conscious awareness of having seen it. These findings are

---

CASE STUDY: *The Effects of Extreme Deprivation*

Freud and Dann (1951) studied six preschool children who had lost their parents during the Second World War. It is not known how long each child had spent with their parents before being taken to Nazi concentration camp nurseries. The children remained together, despite moving camp several times, and appeared to have received only the most basic forms of care and attention. In the absence of a caring adult, they had formed close and loving bonds with each other. These strong bonds provided a protective and stable influence in their lives.

The children were rescued at the end of the war and brought to England for medical and psychological treatment. Their mental and physical development had been restricted, so that they had very poor speech skills. They feared adults and clung to each other for reassurance. Gradually they began to form bonds with the adults who cared for them, and their social and language skills improved. Despite all the problems they had experienced, the children did not show the

levels of extreme disturbance that were once expected when there is a complete lack of "mothering" (Bowlby, 1951). Freud and Dann's study highlights the fundamental importance of having someone to bond with, even if it is not the mother, as well as the reversibility of the effects of extreme deprivation.

Case studies are often seen as rather unscientific and unreliable. The sample is not representative of the wider population, the study cannot be repeated, and interpretation of the findings is very subjective. However, case studies can be of great interest because they highlight unique and unexpected behaviour, and can stimulate research that may contradict established theories such as Bowlby's. Freud and Dann's work offers insights into human experience that would otherwise be impossible to gain: ethical considerations prevent the deliberate separation of children and parents in order to study the effects of deprivation.

---

important, because they suggest that many perceptual processes can occur in the absence of conscious awareness.

Evaluation

We need to be very careful when interpreting the evidence from a case study. The greatest danger is that very general conclusions may be drawn on the basis of a single atypical individual. For this reason, it is important to have supporting evidence from other sources before drawing such conclusions.

It is often hard to interpret the evidence from case studies. For example, Freud claimed that the various case studies he reported served to show the validity of his theoretical ideas. However, such evidence is suspect, because there was a real chance of contamination in the data Freud obtained from his patients. What any patient said to Freud may have been influenced by what Freud had said to him or her previously, and Freud may have used his theoretical views to interpret what the patient said in ways that distorted it.

How, then, should the findings from a case study be interpreted? Probably the greatest value of a case study is that it can suggest hypotheses which can then be tested under more controlled conditions with larger numbers of participants. In other words, case studies usually provide suggestive rather than definitive evidence. In addition, case studies can indicate that there are limitations in current theories. The discovery of blindsight in DB suggested that visual perception depends much less on conscious awareness than was thought to be the case by most theorists.

Jourard's (1966) survey of how many times one person touched another during an hour spent sitting in a cafe is an example of quantitative data collected from an observational study.

Observations

As was discussed in Chapter 30, there are numerous kinds of observational studies, and the data obtained may be either quantitative or qualitative. We will consider issues relating to interpreting the data from observational studies by focusing on a concrete example. Jourard (1966) watched pairs of people talking in cafes, and noted down the number of times one person touched another at one table during one hour. In San Juan, the capital of Puerto Rico, the total number of touches was 180. In contrast, the total in Paris was 110, and in London it was 0. One problem with interpreting these data is that the kinds of people who go to cafes in San Juan, Paris, and London may be quite

different. It is also entirely possible that those who spend much of their time in cafes are not representative of the general population. These issues of representativeness apply to many observational studies.

How would you interpret this behaviour? Are these people dedicated supporters of an important cause, or hooligans?

Evaluation

Jourard's (1966) findings do not really tell us *why* there is (or was, in 1966) much more touching in San Juan than in London. It is possible that Londoners are simply less friendly and open, but there are several other possibilities (e.g. Londoners are more likely to go to cafes with business colleagues). The general issue here is that it is often very hard to interpret or make sense of the data obtained from observational studies, because we can only speculate on the reasons why the participants are behaving in the ways that we observe.

Another issue was raised by Coolican (1994) in his discussion of the work of Whyte (1943). Whyte joined an Italian street gang in Chicago, and became a participant observer. The problem he encountered in interpreting his observations was that his presence in the gang influenced their behaviour. A member of the gang expressed this point as follows: "You've slowed me down plenty since you've been down here. Now, when I do something, I have to think what Bill Whyte would want me to know about it and how I can explain it."

Content Analysis

Content analysis of advertising can tell us a great deal about society's attitudes to men and women.

Content analysis is used when originally qualitative information is reduced to numerical terms. **Content analysis** started off as a method for analysing messages in the media, including articles published in newspapers, speeches made by politicians on radio and television, various forms of propaganda, and health records. More recently, the method of content analysis has been applied more widely to almost any form of communication. As Coolican (1994, p.108) pointed out:

> *The communications concerned were originally those already published, but some researchers conduct content analysis on materials which they ask people to produce, such as essays, answers to interview questions, diaries, and verbal protocols [detailed records].*

One of the types of communication that has often been studied by content analysis is television advertising. For example, McArthur and Resko (1975) carried out a content analysis of American television commercials. They found that 70% of the men in these commercials were shown as experts who knew a lot about the products being sold. In contrast, 86% of the women in the commercials were shown only as product users. There was another interesting gender difference: men who used the products were typically promised improved social and career prospects, whereas women were promised that their family would like them more.

More recent studies of American television commercials (e.g. Brett & Cantor, 1988) indicate that the differences in the ways in which men and women are presented have been reduced. However, it remains the case that the men are far more likely than women to be presented as the product expert.

The first stage in content analysis is that of sampling, or deciding what to select from what may be an enormous amount of material. For example, when Cumberbatch (1990) carried out a study on over 500 advertisements shown on British television, there were two television channels showing advertisements. Between them, these two channels were broadcasting for about 15,000 hours a year, and showing over 250,000 advertisements. Accordingly, Cumberbatch decided to select only a sample of advertisements taken from prime-time television over a two-week period.

The issue of sampling is an important one. For example, television advertisers target their advertisements at particular sections of the population, and so arrange for the advertisements to be shown when the relevant groups are most likely to be watching television. As a result, advertisements for beer are more likely to be shown during a football match than a programme about fashion. By focusing on prime-time television, Cumberbatch (1990) tried to ensure that he was studying advertisements designed to have general appeal.

The other key ingredient in content analysis is the construction of the **coding units** into which the information is to be categorised. In order to form appropriate coding units, the researcher needs to have considerable knowledge of the kinds of material to be used in the content analysis. He or she also needs to have one or more clear hypotheses, because the selection of coding units must be such as to permit these hypotheses to be tested effectively.

The coding can take many forms. The categories used can be very specific (e.g. use of a given word) or general (e.g. theme of the communication). Instead of using categories, the coders may be asked to provide *ratings*. For example, the apparent expertise of those appearing in television advertisements might be rated on a 7-point scale. Another form of coding involves *ranking* items, or putting them in order. For example, the statements of politicians could be ranked in terms of the extent to which they agreed with the facts.

> ### Gender and advertising
>
> Cumberbatch (1990) found that men outnumbered women in advertisements by 2:1. In addition, 75% of the men in ads were aged over 30, whereas 75% of women in ads were aged under 30. Male voices were used where the information in the soundtrack concerned technical expertise, whereas women's voices were used in sexy and sensuous ways. What does this say about the way we view men and women in society? Comparing the results of studies such as Cumberbatch's with earlier ones (e.g. McArthur & Resko, 1975) can begin to provide answers to questions such as this.

Evaluation

One of the greatest strengths of content analysis is that it provides a way of extracting information from a wealth of real-world settings. The media influence the ways we think and feel about issues, and so it is important to analyse media communications in detail. Content analysis can reveal issues of concern. For example, Cumberbatch (1990) found in his study of advertisements on British television that only about 25% of the women appearing in these advertisements seemed to be over 30 years old, compared to about 75% of the men. On the face of it, this would seem to reflect a sexist bias.

> **KEY TERM**
> **Coding units**: the categories into which observations are placed prior to analysis.

Food Diary – Week 1

Time	What eaten	B	V	L	Antecedents & Consequences
8.00	All-bran				A: Still full from yesterday. C: Must make an effort not to binge today.
12.00	1 apple				A: Hungry. C: Still hungry, mustn't eat more in case it starts me off on a binge.
3.00	1 lb grapes, 2 choc. bars		!		A: Had phone call from John, he will be home late. C: Disgusted with myself. I am the most hopeless person in the world.
6.00	peanuts + chocs, picked from shopping	!!			A: No food in flat. Had to go shopping. Couldn't stop myself putting loads of sweets in the trolley. Ate loads of stuff in the car. Had to go on eating once at home.
			!!		
7.00	2 portions of curry, 3 choc. bars	!! !!			C: Very angry with myself. I feel so lonely. Totally exhausted, went to bed early.

B = Binge, V = Vomited, L = Laxatives

Food Diary – Week 4

Time	What eaten	B	V	L	Antecedents & Consequences
8.00	Cottage cheese, 2 sl. toast with honey				Enjoyed this.
11.00	apple				
12.30	baked potato, tuna fish				Eaten in the canteen at work. Tina said "You haven't been here for ages". Could have run away, felt everybody was looking at me.
3.00	yoghurt, crunch bar				
6.00	1 sl. toast				
7.00	fish + vegetables, 1 portion ice cream				Had not planned dessert. John suggested ice cream. My initial response was to say no, but I knew I would then finish the packet off whilst washing up. So I had a portion and enjoyed it sitting with John. John put it away and made coffee, which we drank relaxing on the sofa. Washing up left.

Diary studies are often used in clinical psychology, such as in this example from the diary of a bulimia sufferer. Diaries may be used to record actions, thoughts, and feelings, but may not be totally accurate, particularly if the diarist is embarrassed to reveal the truth about himself or herself.

The greatest limitation of content analysis is that it is often very hard to interpret the findings. Consider, for example, the difference in the ages of men and women appearing in advertisements found by Cumberbatch (1990). One interpretation is that this difference occurred because most television viewers prefer to see older men and younger women in advertisements. However, it is also possible that those making the advertisements thought mistakenly that this is what the viewers wanted to see. There are other possible interpretations, but the available data do not allow us to discriminate among them.

There are also problems of interpretation with other communications such as personal diaries or essays. Diaries or essays may contain accurate accounts of what an individual does, thinks, and feels. On the other hand, individuals may provide deliberately distorted accounts in order to protect their self-esteem, to make it appear that their lives are more exciting than is actually the case, and so on.

Another problem is that the selection and scoring of coding units can be rather subjective. The coding categories that are used need to reflect accurately the content of the communication, and each of the categories must be defined as precisely as possible.

Quantitative Analysis: Descriptive Statistics

Suppose that we have carried out an experiment on the effects of noise on learning with three groups of nine participants each. One group was exposed to very loud noise, another group to moderately loud noise, and the third group was not exposed to noise at all. What they had learned from a book chapter was assessed by giving them a set of questions, producing a score between 0 and 20.

What is to be done with the raw scores? There are two key types of measures that can be taken whenever we have a set of scores from participants in a given condition. First, there are measures of central tendency, which provide some indication of the size of average or typical scores. Second, there are measures of dispersion, which indicate the extent to which the scores cluster around the average or are spread out. Various measures of central tendency and of dispersion are considered next.

Measures of central tendency

Measures of central tendency describe how the data cluster together around a central point. There are three main measures of central tendency: the mean; the median; and the mode.

Mean

The **mean** in each group or condition is calculated by adding up all the scores in a given condition, and then dividing by the number of participants in that condition. Suppose that the scores of the nine participants in the no-noise condition are as follows: 1, 2, 4, 5, 7, 9, 9, 9, 17. The mean is given by the total, which is 63, divided by the number of participants, which is 9. Thus, the mean is 7.

The main advantage of the mean is the fact that it takes all the scores into account. This generally makes it a sensitive measure of central tendency, especially if the scores resemble the **normal distribution**, which is a bell-shaped distribution in which most scores cluster fairly close to the mean. However, the mean can be very misleading if the distribution differs markedly from the normal and there are one or two extreme scores in one direction. Suppose that eight people complete one lap of a track in go-karts. For seven of them, the times taken (in seconds) are as follows: 25, 28, 29, 29, 34, 36, and 42. The eighth person's go-kart breaks down, and so the driver has to push it around the track. This person takes 288 seconds to complete the lap. This produces an overall mean of 64 seconds. This is clearly misleading, because no-one else took even close to 64 seconds to complete one lap.

Median

Another way of describing the general level of performance in each condition is known as the **median**. If there is an odd number of scores, then the median is simply the middle

---

Coding units might include time, space, words, themes, roles, items, actions, etc. How would you use these to analyse the content of television programmes such as "soaps"?

Mean	
Scores	Number
1	1
2	2
4	3
5	4
7	5
9	6
9	7
9	8
17	9
63	9 Total
63 ÷ 9	= 7

KEY TERMS
Mean: an average worked out by dividing the total of all participants' scores by the number of participants.
Normal distribution: a bell-shaped distribution in which most scores cluster fairly close to the mean.
Median: the middle score out of all participants' scores in a given condition.

score, having an equal number of scores higher and lower than it. In the example with nine scores in the no-noise condition (1, 2, 4, 5, 7, 9, 9, 9, 17), the median is 7. Matters are slightly more complex if there is an even number of scores. In that case, we work out the mean of the two central values. For example, suppose that we have the following scores in size order: 2, 5, 5, 7, 8, 9. The two central values are 5 and 7, and so the median is

$$\frac{5+7}{2} = 6$$

Scores	
1	
2	
4	
5	
7	= Median
9	
9	
9	
17	

The main advantage of the median is that it is unaffected by a few extreme scores, because it focuses only on scores in the middle of the distribution. It also has the advantage that it tends to be easier than the mean to work out. The main limitation of the median is that it ignores most of the scores, and so it is often less sensitive than the mean. In addition, it is not always representative of the scores obtained, especially if there are only a few scores.

Mode

The final measure of central tendency is the **mode**. This is simply the most frequently occurring score. In the example of the nine scores in the no-noise condition, this is 9. The main advantages of the mode are that it is unaffected by one or two extreme scores, and that it is the easiest measure of central tendency to work out. In addition, it can still be worked out even when some of the extreme scores are not known. However, its limitations generally outweigh these advantages. The greatest limitation is that the mode tends to be unreliable. For example, suppose we have the following scores: 4, 4, 6, 7, 8, 8, 12, 12, 12. The mode of these scores is 12. If just one score changed (a 12 becoming a 4), the mode would change to 4! Another limitation is that information about the exact values of the scores obtained is ignored in working out the mode. This makes it a less sensitive measure than the mean. A final limitation is that it is possible for there to be more than one mode.

Scores	
1	
2	
4	
5	
7	
9	
9	= Mode
9	
17	

The mode is useful where other measures of central tendency are meaningless, for example when calculating the number of children in the average family. It would be unusual to have 0.4 or 0.6 of a child!

Levels of measurement

From what has been said so far, we have seen that the mean is the most generally useful measure of central tendency, whereas the mode is the least useful. However, we need to take account of the level of measurement when deciding which measure of central tendency to use (the various levels are discussed further on page 871). At the interval and ratio levels of measurement, each added unit represents an equal increase. For example, someone who hits a target four times out of ten has done twice as well as someone who hits it twice out of ten. Below this is the ordinal level of measurement, in which we can only order, or rank, the scores from highest to lowest. At the lowest level, there is the nominal level, in which the scores consist of the numbers of participants falling into various categories. The mean should only be used when the scores are at the interval level of measurement. The median can be used when the data are at the interval or ordinal level. The mode can be used when the data are at any of the three levels. It is the only one of the three measures of central tendency that can be used with nominal data.

Measures of dispersion

The mean, median, and mode are all measures of central tendency. It is also useful to work out what are known as measures of dispersion, such as the range, interquartile range, variation ratio, and standard deviation. These measures indicate whether the scores in a given condition are similar to each other or whether they are spread out.

Range

The simplest of these measures is the **range**, which can be defined as the difference between the highest and the lowest score in any condition. In the case of the no-noise group (1, 2, 4, 5, 7, 9, 9, 9, 17), the range is 17 − 1 = 16.

In fact, it is preferable to calculate the range in a slightly different way (Coolican, 1994). The revised formula (when we are dealing with whole numbers) is as follows: (highest score – lowest score) + 1. Thus, in our example, the range is (17 – 1) + 1 = 17. This formula is preferable because it takes account of the fact that the scores we recorded were rounded to whole numbers. In our sample data, a score of 17 stands for all values between 16.5 and 17.5, and a score of 1 represents a value between 0.5 and 1.5. If we take the range as the interval between the highest possible value (17.5) and the lowest possible value (0.5), this gives us a range of 17, which is precisely the figure produced by the formula.

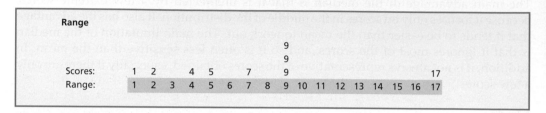

Range

Suppose that the scores obtained in a study were as follows:

Group A: 5, 10, 15, 20, 25, 30, 35, 40, 45, 50   total = 275
Mean = 27.5
Median = 27.5

Group B: 15, 20, 20, 25, 25, 30, 35, 35, 35, 35   total = 275
Mean = 27.5
Median = 27.5

Although the means and medians are the same for both sets of scores, the spread of scores is quite different. This becomes highly relevant if we are assessing something like the range of abilities in children in a class.

What has been said so far about the range applies only to whole numbers. Suppose that we measure the time taken to perform a task to the nearest one-tenth of a second, with the fastest time being 21.3 seconds and the slowest time being 36.8 seconds. The figure of 21.3 represents a value between 21.25 and 21.35, and 36.8 represents a value between 36.75 and 36.85. As a result, the range is 36.85 – 21.25, which is 15.6 seconds.

The main advantages of the range as a measure of dispersion are that it is easy to calculate and that it takes full account of extreme values. The main weakness of the range is that it can be greatly influenced by one score which is very different from all of the others. In the example, the inclusion of the participant scoring 17 increases the range from 9 to 17. The other important weakness of the range is that it ignores all but two of the scores, and so is likely to provide an inadequate measure of the general spread or dispersion of the scores around the mean or median.

Interquartile range

The **interquartile range** is defined as the spread of the middle 50% of scores. For example, suppose that we have the following set of scores: 4, 5, 6, 6, 7, 8, 8, 9, 11, 11, 14, 15, 17, 18, 18, 19. There are 16 scores, which can be divided into the bottom 25% (4), the middle 50% (8), and the top 25% (4). The middle 50% of scores start with 7 and run through to 15. The upper boundary of the interquartile range lies between 15 and 17, and is given by the mean of these two values, i.e. 16. The lower boundary of the interquartile range lies between 6 and 7, and is their mean, i.e. 6.5. The interquartile range is the difference between the upper and lower boundaires, i.e. 16 – 6.5 = 9.5.

The interquartile range has the advantage over the range that it is not influenced by a single extreme score. As a result, it is more likely to provide an accurate reflection of the spread or dispersion of the scores. It has the disadvantage that it ignores information

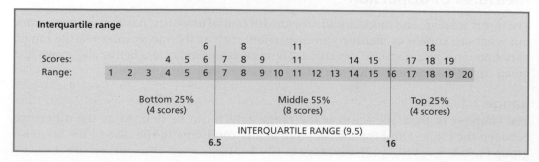

from the top and the bottom 25% of scores. For example, we could have two sets of scores with the same interquartile range, but with more extreme scores in one set than in the other. The difference in spread or dispersion between the two sets of scores would not be detected by the interquartile range.

Variation ratio

Another simple measure of dispersal is the **variation ratio**. This can be used when the mode is the chosen measure of central tendency. The variation ratio is defined simply as the proportion of the scores obtained which are not at the modal value (i.e. the value of the mode). The variation ratio for the no-noise condition discussed earlier (scores of 1, 2, 4, 5, 7, 9, 9, 9, 17), where the mode is 9, is as follows:

$$\frac{\text{number of non-modal scores}}{\text{total number of scores}} = \frac{6}{9} = 0.67$$

The advantages of the variation ratio are that it is not affected by extreme values, and that it is very easy to calculate. However, it is a very limited measure of dispersal, because it ignores most of the data. In particular, it takes no account of whether the non-modal scores are close to, or far removed from, the modal value. Thus, the variation ratio can only provide a very approximate measure of dispersal.

Standard deviation

The most generally useful measure of dispersion is the **standard deviation**. It is harder to calculate than the range or variation ratio, but generally provides a more accurate measure of the spread of scores. However, you will be pleased to learn that many calculators allow the standard deviation to be worked out rapidly and effortlessly, as in the worked example.

Standard deviation: A worked example

Participant	Score X	Mean M	Score – Mean X – M	(Score – Mean)^2 (X – M)^2
1	13	10	3	9
2	6	10	–4	16
3	10	10	0	0
4	15	10	5	25
5	10	10	0	0
6	15	10	5	25
7	5	10	–5	25
8	9	10	–1	1
9	10	10	0	0
10	13	10	3	9
11	6	10	–4	16
12	11	10	1	1
13	7	10	–3	9
13	130	10		136

Total of scores = ΣX = 130

Number of participants = N = 13

Mean = $\frac{\Sigma X}{N} = \frac{130}{13} = 10$

Variance = $\frac{136}{13 - 1} = 11.33$

Standard deviation = $\sqrt{11.3} = 3.37$

The first step is to work out the mean of the sample. This is given by the total of all of the participants' scores (ΣX = 130; the symbol Σ means the sum of) divided by the number of participants (N = 13). Thus, the mean is 10.

The second step is to subtract the mean in turn from each score (X – M). The calculations are shown in the fourth column. The third step is to square each of the

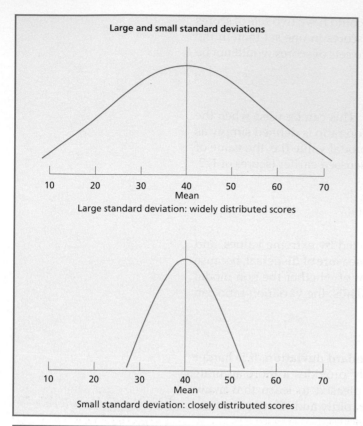

Large and small standard deviations

10 20 30 40 50 60 70
          Mean

Large standard deviation: widely distributed scores

10 20 30 40 50 60 70
          Mean

Small standard deviation: closely distributed scores

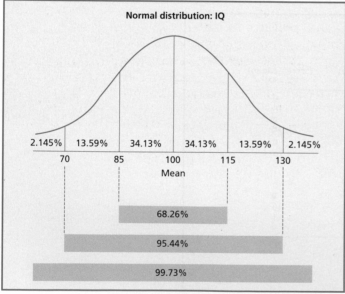

Normal distribution: IQ

2.145% | 13.59% | 34.13% | 34.13% | 13.59% | 2.145%

70   85   100   115   130
               Mean

68.26%

95.44%

99.73%

scores in the fourth column $(X - M)^2$. The fourth step is to work out the total of all the squared scores, $\Sigma (X - M)^2$. This comes to 136. The fifth step is to divide the result of the fourth step by one less than the number of participants, $N - 1 = 12$. This gives us 136 divided by 12, which equals 11.33. This is known as the **variance**, which is in squared units. Finally, we use a calculator to take the square root of the variance. This produces a figure of 3.37; this is the standard deviation.

The method for calculating the standard deviation that has just been described is used when we want to estimate the standard deviation of the population. If we want merely to describe the spread of scores in our sample, then the fifth step involves dividing the result of the fourth step by N.

What is the meaning of this figure for the standard deviation? We expect about two-thirds of the scores in a sample to lie within one standard deviation of the mean. In our example, the mean is 10.0, one standard deviation above the mean is 13.366 and one standard deviation below the mean is 6.634. In fact, 61.5% of the scores lie between those two limits, which is only slightly below the expected percentage.

The standard deviation has special relevance in relation to the so-called normal distribution. As was mentioned earlier, the normal distribution is a bell-shaped curve in which there are as many scores above the mean as below it. Intelligence (or IQ) scores in the general population provide an example of a normal distribution. Other characteristics such as height and weight also form roughly a normal distribution (see page 738). Most of the scores in a normal distribution cluster fairly close to the mean, and there are fewer and fewer scores as you move away from the mean in either direction. In a normal distribution, 68.26% of the scores fall within one standard deviation of the mean, 95.44% fall within two standard deviations, and 99.73% fall within three standard deviations.

The standard deviation takes account of all of the scores and provides a sensitive measure of dispersion. As we have seen, it also has the advantage that it describes the spread of scores in a normal distribution with great precision. The most obvious disadvantage of the standard deviation is that it is much harder to work out than the other measures of dispersion.

Data Presentation

Information about the scores in a sample can be presented in several ways. If it is presented in a graph or chart, this may make it easier for people to understand what has been found, compared to simply presenting information about the central tendency and dispersion. We will shortly consider some examples. The key point to remember is that all graphs and charts should be clearly labelled and presented so that the reader can rapidly make sense of the information contained in them.

Suppose that we ask 25 male athletes to run 400 metres as rapidly as possible, and record their times (in seconds). Having worked out a table of frequencies (see the boxed example), there are several ways to present these data.

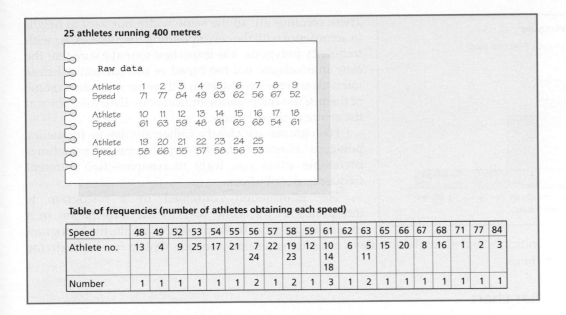

25 athletes running 400 metres

Raw data

Athlete	1	2	3	4	5	6	7	8	9
Speed	71	77	84	49	63	62	56	67	52

Athlete	10	11	12	13	14	15	16	17	18
Speed	61	63	59	48	61	65	68	54	61

Athlete	19	20	21	22	23	24	25
Speed	58	66	55	57	58	56	53

Table of frequencies (number of athletes obtaining each speed)

Speed	48	49	52	53	54	55	56	57	58	59	61	62	63	65	66	67	68	71	77	84
Athlete no.	13	4	9	25	17	21	7 24	22	19 23	12	10 14 18	6	5 11	15	20	8	16	1	2	3
Number	1	1	1	1	1	1	2	1	2	1	3	1	2	1	1	1	1	1	1	1

Frequency polygon

One way of summarising these data is in the form of a **frequency polygon**. This is a simple form of chart in which the scores from low to high are indicated on the x or horizontal axis and the frequencies of the various scores (in terms of the numbers of individuals obtaining each score) are indicated on the y or vertical axis. The points on a frequency polygon should only be joined up when the scores can be ordered from low to high. In order for a frequency polygon to be most useful, it should be constructed so that most of the frequencies are neither very high nor very low. The frequencies will be very high if the width of each class interval (the categories used to summarise frequencies) on the x axis is too broad (e.g. covering 20 seconds), and the frequencies will be very low if each class interval is too narrow (e.g. covering only 1 or 2 seconds).

Each point in a frequency polygon should be placed in the middle of its class interval. There is a technical point that needs to be made here (Coolican, 1994). Suppose that we include all times between 53 and 57 seconds in the same class interval. As we have only measured running times to the nearest second, this class interval will cover actual times between 52.5 and 57.5 seconds. In this case, the mid-point of the class interval (55 seconds) is the same whether we take account of the actual measurement interval (52.5–57.5 seconds) or adopt the simpler approach of focusing on the lowest and highest recorded times in the class interval (53–57 seconds, respectively). When the two differ, it is important to use the actual measurement interval.

How should we interpret the findings shown in the frequency polygon? It is clear that most of the participants were able to run 400 metres in between about 53 and 67 seconds. Only a few of the athletes were able to better a time of 53 seconds, and there was a small number who took longer than 67 seconds.

Histogram

A similar way of describing these data is by means of a **histogram**. In a histogram, the scores are indicated on the horizontal axis and the frequencies are shown on the vertical axis. In contrast to a frequency polygon, however, the frequencies are indicated by rectangular columns.

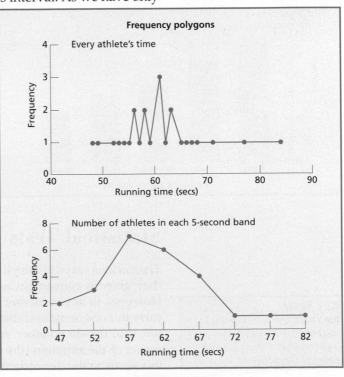

Frequency polygons

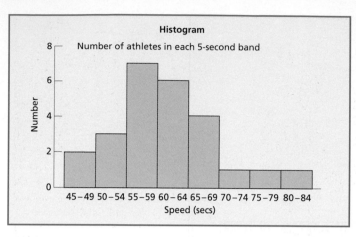

These columns are all the same width but vary in height in accordance with the corresponding frequencies. As with frequency polygons, it is important to make sure that the class intervals are not too broad or too narrow. All class intervals are represented, even if there are no scores in some of them. Class intervals are indicated by their mid-point at the centre of the columns.

Histograms are clearly rather similar to frequency polygons. However, frequency polygons are sometimes preferable when you want to compare two different frequency distributions.

The information contained in a histogram is interpreted in the same way as the information in a frequency polygon. In the present example, the histogram indicates that most of the athletes ran 400 metres fairly quickly. Only a few had extreme times.

Bar chart

Frequency polygons and histograms are suitable when the scores obtained by the participants can be ordered from low to high. In more technical terms, the data should be either interval or ratio (see next section). However, there are many studies in which the scores are in the form of categories rather than ordered scores; in other words, the data are nominal. For example, 50 people might be asked to indicate their favourite leisure activity. Suppose that 15 said going to a party, 12 said going to the pub, 9 said watching television, 8 said playing sport, and 6 said reading a good book.

These data can be displayed in the form of a **bar chart**. In a bar chart, the categories are shown along the horizontal axis, and the frequencies are indicated on the vertical axis. In contrast to the data contained in histograms, the categories in bar charts cannot be ordered numerically in a meaningful way. However, they can be arranged in ascending (or descending) order of popularity. Another difference from histograms is that the rectangles in a bar chart do not usually touch each other.

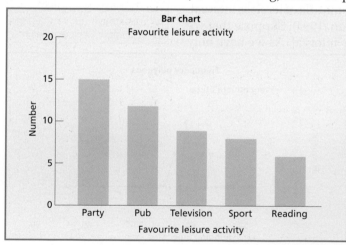

The scale on the vertical axis of a bar chart normally starts at zero. However, it is sometimes convenient for presentational purposes to have it start at some higher value. If that is done, then it should be made clear in the bar chart that the lower part of the vertical scale is missing. The columns in a bar chart often represent frequencies. However, they can also represent means or percentages for different groups (Coolican, 1994).

How should we interpret the information in a bar chart? In the present example, a bar chart makes it easy to compare the popularity of different leisure activities. We can see at a glance that going to a party was the most popular leisure activity, whereas reading a good book was the least popular.

Statistical Tests

The various ways in which the data from a study can be presented are all useful in that they give us convenient and easily understood summaries of what we have found. However, to have a clearer idea of what our findings mean, it is generally necessary to carry out one or more statistical tests. The first step in choosing an appropriate statistical test is to decide whether your data were obtained from an experiment in which some aspect of the situation (the independent variable) was manipulated in order to observe its effects on the dependent variables (i.e. the scores). If so, you need a test of difference (see pages 873–879). On the other hand, if you simply have two observations from each of your participants in a non-experimental design, then you need a test of association or correlation (see pages 879–881).

In using a statistical test, you need to take account of the experimental hypothesis. If you predicted the direction of any effects (e.g. loud noise will disrupt learning and memory), then you have a directional hypothesis, which should be evaluated by a one-tailed test. If you did not predict the direction of any effects (e.g. loud noise will affect learning and memory), then you have a non-directional hypothesis, which should be evaluated by a two-tailed test (see Chapter 31).

Another factor to consider when deciding which statistical test to use is the type of data you have obtained. There are four types of data of increasing levels of precision:

Interval

Nominal

- **Nominal**: the data consist of the numbers of participants falling into various categories (e.g. fat, thin; men, women).
- **Ordinal**: the data can be ordered from lowest to highest (e.g. the finishing positions of athletes in a race).
- **Interval**: the data differ from ordinal data, because the units of measurement are fixed throughout the range; for example, there is the same "distance" between a height of 1.82 metres and 1.70 metres as between a height of 1.70 metres and one of 1.58 metres.
- **Ratio**: the data have the same characteristics as interval data, with the exception that they have a meaningful zero point; for example, time measurements provide ratio data because the notion of zero time is meaningful, and 10 seconds is twice as long as 5 seconds. The similarities between interval and ratio data are so great that they are sometimes combined and referred to as interval/ratio data.

Ordinal

Ratio

Statistical tests can be divided into **parametric tests** and **non-parametric tests**. Parametric tests should only be used when the data obtained from a study satisfy various requirements. More specifically, there should be interval or ratio data, the data should be normally distributed, and the variances in the two conditions should be reasonably similar. In contrast, non-parametric tests can nearly always continue to be used, even when the requirements of parametric tests are satisfied. In this chapter, we will confine ourselves to a discussion of some of the most useful non-parametric tests.

Statistical significance

So far we have discussed some of the issues that influence the choice of statistical test. What happens after we have chosen a statistical test, and analysed our data, and want to interpret our findings? We use the results of the test to choose between the following:

- Experimental hypothesis (e.g. loud noise disrupts learning).
- Null hypothesis, which asserts that there is no difference between conditions (e.g. loud noise has no effect on learning).

If the statistical test indicates that there is only a small probability of the difference between conditions (e.g. loud noise vs. no noise) having occurred if the null hypothesis

■ Research activity: Devising hypotheses

Devise suitable null and experimental hypotheses for the following:

- An investigator considers the effect of noise on students' ability to concentrate and complete a word-grid. One group only is subjected to the noise in the form of a distractor, i.e. a television programme.
- An investigator explores the view that there might be a link between the amount of television children watch and their behaviour at school.

From percentage to decimal

10%	=	0.10
5%	=	0.05
1%	=	0.01
2.5%	=	?

To go from decimal to percentage, multiply by 100: move the decimal point two places to the right.

To go from percentage to decimal, divide by 100: move the decimal point two places to the left.

were true, then we reject the null hypothesis in favour of the experimental hypothesis.

Why do we focus initially on the null hypothesis rather than the experimental hypothesis? The reason is that the experimental hypothesis is rather imprecise. It may state that loud noise will disrupt learning, but it does not indicate the *extent* of the disruption. This imprecision makes it hard to evaluate an experimental hypothesis directly. In contrast, a null hypothesis such as loud noise has no effect on learning *is* precise, and this precision allows us to use statistical tests to decide the probability that it is correct.

Psychologists generally use the 5% (0.05) level of **statistical significance**. What this means is that the null hypothesis is rejected (and the experimental hypothesis is accepted) if the probability that the results were due to chance alone is 5% or less. This is often expressed as $p = 0.05$, where p = the probability of the result if the null hypothesis is true. If the statistical test indicates that the findings do not reach the 5% (or $p = 0.05$) level of statistical significance, then we retain the null hypothesis, and reject the experimental hypothesis. The key decision is whether or not to reject the null hypothesis and that is why the 0.05 level of statistical significance is so important. However, our data sometimes indicate that the null hypothesis can be rejected with greater confidence, say, at the 1% (0.01) level. If the null hypothesis can be rejected at the 1% level, it is customary to state that the findings are highly significant. In general terms, you should state the precise level of statistical significance of your findings, whether it is the 5% level, the 1% level, or whatever.

These procedures may seem easy. In fact, there are two errors that may occur when reaching a conclusion on the basis of the results of a statistical test:

- **Type I error**: we may reject the null hypothesis in favour of the experimental hypothesis even though the findings are actually due to chance; the probability of this happening is given by the level of statistical significance that is selected.
- **Type II error**: we may retain the null hypothesis even though the experimental hypothesis is actually correct.

It would be possible to reduce the likelihood of a Type I error by using a more stringent level of significance. For example, if we used the 1% ($p = 0.01$) level of significance, this would greatly reduce the probability of a Type I error. However, use of a more stringent level of significance increases the probability of a Type II error. We could reduce the probability of a Type II error by using a less stringent level of significance, such as the 10% ($p = 0.10$) level. However, this would increase the probability of a Type I error. These considerations help to make it clear why most psychologists favour the 5% (or $p = 0.05$) level of significance: it allows the probabilities of both Type I and Type II errors to remain reasonably low.

KEY TERMS
Statistical significance: the level at which the decision is made to reject the null hypothesis in favour of the experimental hypothesis.
Type I error: mistakenly rejecting the null hypothesis in favour of the experimental hypothesis when the results are actually due to chance.
Type II error: mistakenly retaining the null hypothesis when the experimental hypothesis is actually correct.

Psychologists generally use the 5% level of significance. However, they would use the 1% or even the 0.1% level of significance if it were very important to avoid making a Type I error. For example, clinical psychologists might require very strong evidence that a new form of therapy was more effective than existing forms of therapy before starting to use it on a regular basis. The 1% or 0.1% ($p = 0.001$) level of statistical significance is also used when the experimental hypothesis seems improbable. For example, very few people would accept that telepathy had been proved to exist on the basis of a single study in which the results were only just significant at the 5% level!

Tests of difference

In this section, we will consider those statistical tests that are applicable when we are interested in deciding whether the differences between two conditions or groups are significant. As was discussed in Chapter 31, there are three kinds of design that can be used when we want to compare two conditions. First, there is the independent design, in which each participant is allocated at random to one and only one condition. Second, there is the repeated measures design, in which the same participants are used in both conditions. Third, there is the matched participants design, in which the participants in the two conditions are matched in terms of some variable or variables that might be relevant (e.g. intelligence; age).

When deciding which statistical test to use, it is very important to take account of the particular kind of experimental design that was used. If the independent design has been used, then the Mann-Whitney U test is likely to be an appropriate test to use. If the repeated measures or matched participants design has been used, then the sign test or the Wilcoxon matched pairs signed ranks test is likely to be appropriate. Each of these tests is discussed in turn next.

Mann-Whitney U test

The Mann-Whitney U test can be used when an independent design has been used, and the data are either ordinal or interval. The worked example in the box shows how this test is calculated.

Mann-Whitney U test: A worked example

Experimental hypothesis: extensive training improves performance

Null hypothesis: training has no effect on performance

Participant	Condition A	Rank	Participant	Condition B	Rank
1	4	2	1	21	15
2	10	9	2	26	18
3	12	11	3	20	14
4	28	20	4	22	16
5	7	5	5	32	22
6	13	13	6	5	3
7	12	11	7	12	11
8	2	1	8	6	4
9	9	7.5	9	8	6
10	27	19	10	24	17
			11	29	21
			12	9	7.5

Smaller sample = condition A
Sum of ranks in smaller sample (T) = 98.5
Number of participants in smaller sample (N_A) = 10
Number of participants in larger sample (N_B) = 12

Formula: $U = N_A N_B + \left(\dfrac{N_A(N_A + 1)}{2} \right) - T$

Example: $U = (10 \times 12) + \left(\dfrac{10(10 + 1)}{2} \right) - 98.5 = 76.5$

Formula for calculating U': $U' = N_A N_B - U$

Example: $U' = (10 \times 12) - 76.5 = 43.5$

Comparing U and U', U' is the smaller value. The calculated value of U' (43.5) is checked against the tabled value for a one-tailed test at 5%.

Table values

	$N_A = 10$
$N_B = 12$	34

Conclusion: as 43.5 is greater than 34, the null hypothesis should be retained—i.e. training has no effect on performance in this task.

Suppose that we have two conditions. In both conditions, the participants have to fire arrows at a board, and the score obtained is recorded. There are 10 participants in Condition A, in which no training is provided before their performance is assessed. There are 12 participants in Condition B, and they receive extensive training before their performance is assessed. The experimental hypothesis was that extensive training would improve performance; in other words, the scores in Condition B should be significantly higher than those in Condition A.

The first step is to rank all of the scores from both groups together, with a rank of 1 being given to the smallest score, a rank of 2 to the second smallest score, and so on. If there are tied scores, then the mean of the ranks involved is given to each of the tied participants. For example, two participants were tied for the 7th and 8th ranks, and so they both received a rank of 7.5.

The second step is to work out the sum of the ranks in the smaller sample, which is Condition A in our example. This value is known as T, and it is 98.5 in the example.

The third step is to calculate U from the formula

$$U = N_A N_B + \left(\frac{N_A(N_A + 1)}{2}\right) - T,$$

in which N_A is the number of participants in the smaller sample and N_B is the number in the larger sample.

The fourth step is to calculate U′ from the formula $U' = N_A N_B - U$.

The fifth step is to compare U and U′, selecting whichever is the smaller value provided that the results are in the correct direction. The smaller value (i.e. 43.5) is then looked up in Appendix 1. The observed value must be equal to, or smaller than, the tabled value in order to be significant. In this case, we have a one-tailed test, because the experimental hypothesis stated that extensive training would improve performance and the statistical significance is the standard 5% (0.05). With 10 participants in our first condition and 12 in our second condition, the tabled value for significance is 34 (value obtained from the table at the bottom of page 893). As our value of 43.5 is greater than 34, the conclusion is that we retain the null hypothesis. It should be noted that the presence of ties reduces the accuracy of the tables, but the effect is small unless there are several ties.

Sign test

The sign test can be used when a repeated measures or matched participants design has been used, and the data are ordinal. If the data are interval or ratio, then it would be more appropriate to use the Wilcoxon matched pairs signed ranks test. The worked example in the box illustrates the way in which the sign test is calculated.

> The sign test is ideal to use if the data are ordinal as it analyses at a very basic level, e.g. in a race it can tell you that "John beat Peter". It can also be used with interval or ratio data, but as it only gives a crude analysis, this data would be better applied to the Wilcoxon test, which can give a more sophisticated analysis, e.g. "John beat Peter by 2 seconds".

Suppose that there were 12 participants in an experiment. In Condition A these participants were presented with 20 words to learn in a situation with no noise; learning was followed five minutes later by a test of free recall in which they wrote down as many words as they could remember in any order. Condition B involved presenting 20 different words to learn in a situation of loud noise, again followed by a test of free recall. The experimenter predicted that free recall would be higher in the no-noise condition. Thus, there was a directional hypothesis.

In order to calculate the sign test it is necessary first of all to draw up a table like the one in the example, in which each participant's scores in Condition A and in Condition B are recorded. Each participant whose score in Condition A is greater than his or her score in Condition B is given a plus sign (+) in the sign column, and each participant whose score in Condition B is greater than his or her score in Condition A is given a minus sign (–) in the sign column. Each participant whose scores in both conditions are the same receives a 0 sign in the sign column, and are ignored in the subsequent calculations—they do not contribute to N (the number of paired scores), as they provide no evidence about effect direction.

Sign test: A worked example

Experimental hypothesis: free recall is better when learning takes place in the absence of noise than in its presence

Null hypothesis: free recall is not affected by whether or not noise is present during learning

Participant	Condition A (no noise)	Condition B (loud noise)	Sign
1	12	8	+
2	10	10	0
3	7	8	–
4	12	11	+
5	8	3	+
6	10	10	0
7	13	7	+
8	8	9	–
9	14	10	+
10	11	9	+
11	15	12	+
12	11	10	+

Number of + signs = 8
Number of – signs = 2
Number of 0 signs = 2

Number of participants with differing scores (N) = 8 + 2 = 10
Number of participants with less-frequent sign (S) = 2

Question: Is the value of S in this example the same as or lower than the tabled value for S?

Table values

	5%
N = 10	S = 1

Conclusion: in this experiment the value of S is higher than the tabled value, when N = 10. The null hypothesis (that noise has no effect on learning and memory) cannot be rejected.

In the example, there are eight plus signs, two minus signs, and two participants had the same scores in both conditions. If we ignore the two participants with the same scores in both conditions, this gives us N = 10. Now all we need to do is to work out the number of these 10 participants having the less frequently occurring sign; this value is known as S. In terms of our example, S = 2. We can refer to the relevant table (Appendix 2) with N = 10 and S = 2 and the statistical significance is the standard 5%. The obtained value for S must be the same as or lower than the value for S given in the table. The tabled value for a one-tailed test is 1. Thus, our obtained S value of 2 is not significant at the 5% level on a one-tailed test. We therefore conclude that we cannot reject the null hypothesis that noise has no effect on learning and memory.

Wilcoxon matched pairs signed ranks test

The Wilcoxon matched pairs signed ranks test can be used when a repeated measures or matched participants design has been used, and the data are at least ordinal. This test or the sign test can be used if the data are ordinal, interval, or ratio. However, the Wilcoxon matched pairs signed ranks test uses more of the information obtained from a study, and so is usually a more sensitive and useful test than the sign test.

The worked example uses the data from the sign test. The first step is to place all the data in a table in which each participant's two scores are in the same row. The second step is to subtract the Condition B score from the Condition A score for each participant to give the difference (d). The third step is to omit all the participants whose two scores are the same, i.e. d = 0. The fourth step is to rank all the difference scores obtained in the second step from 1 for the smallest difference, 2 for the second smallest difference, and so on. For this purpose, ignore the + and – signs, thus taking the absolute size of the difference. The fifth step is to add up the sum of the positive ranks (50 in the example) and separately to add up the sum of the negative ranks (5 in the example). The smaller of these values is T, which in this case is 5. The sixth step is to work out the number of participants whose two scores are not the same, i.e. d ≠ 0. In the example, N = 10.

Use the sign test if your data are ordinal, and the Wilcoxon test if your data are interval or ratio to get the best results from your analysis.

A positive correlation:
The taller the player,
the higher the score.

A negative correlation:
The more time spent
playing computer games,
the less time spent
studying.

No correlation:
Where there is no
relationship, variables
are uncorrelated.

Wilcoxon matched pairs signed ranks test: A worked example

Experimental hypothesis: free recall is better when learning takes place in the absence of noise than in its presence

Null hypothesis: free recall is not affected by whether or not noise is present during learning

Participant	Condition A (no noise)	Condition B (loud noise)	Difference (d) (A – B)	Rank
1	12	8	4	7.5
2	10	10	0	–
3	7	8	−1	2.5
4	12	11	1	2.5
5	8	3	5	9
6	10	10	0	–
7	13	7	6	10
8	8	9	−1	2.5
9	14	10	4	7.5
10	11	9	2	5
11	15	12	3	6
12	11	10	1	2.5

Sum of positive ranks (7.5 + 2.5 + 9 + 10 + 7.5 + 5 + 6 + 2.5) = 50

Sum of negative ranks (2.5 + 2.5) = 5

Smaller value (5) = T

Number of participants who scored differently in condition A and B (N) = 10

Question: For the results to be significant, the value of T must be the same as, or less than, the tabled value.

Table values

	5%	1%
N = 10	11	5

Conclusion: in this experiment T is less than the tabled value at the 5% level and the same as the tabled value at the 1% level of significance, so the null hypothesis is rejected in favour of the experimental hypothesis.

The obtained value of T must be the same as, or less than, the tabled value (see Appendix 3) in order for the results to be significant. The tabled value for a one-tailed test and N = 10 is 11 at the 5% level of statistical significance, and it is 5 at the 1% level. Thus, the findings are significant at the 1% level on a one-tailed test. The null hypothesis is rejected in favour of the experimental hypothesis that free recall is better when learning takes place in the absence of noise than in its presence ($p = 0.01$). The presence of ties means that the tables are not completely accurate, but this does not matter provided that there are only a few ties.

You may be wondering how it is possible for the same data to produce a significant finding on a Wilcoxon matched pairs signed ranks test but not on a sign test. Does this indicate that statistics are useless? Not at all. The sign test is insensitive (or lacking in power) because it takes no account of the *size* of each individual's difference in free recall in the two conditions. It is because this information is made use of in the Wilcoxon matched pairs signed ranks test that a significant result was obtained using that test. Thus, the Wilcoxon matched pairs signed ranks test has more power than the sign test to detect differences between two conditions.

Correlational studies

In the case of correlational studies, the data are in the form of two measures of behaviour from each member of a single group of participants. What is often done is to present the data in the form of a **scattergraph** (also known as a scattergram). It is given this name, because it shows the ways in which the scores of individuals are scattered.

Scattergraphs

Suppose that we have carried out a study on the relationship between the amount of television violence seen and the amount of aggressive behaviour displayed. We could have a scale of the amount of television violence seen on the horizontal axis, and a scale of the amount of aggressive behaviour on the vertical axis. We could then put a dot for each participant indicating where he or she falls on these two dimensions. For example, suppose that one individual watched 17 hours of television and obtained a score of 8 for aggressive behaviour. We would put a cross at the point where the invisible vertical line from the 17 meets the invisible horizontal line from the 8.

How do we interpret the information contained in a scattergraph? If there is a positive relationship between watching violence and aggression, then the dots should tend to form a pattern going from the bottom left of the scattergraph to the top right. If there is no relationship between the two variables, then the dots should be distributed in a fairly random way within the scattergraph. If there is a negative relationship between the two variables, then the dots will form a pattern going from the top left to the bottom right. In the present example, this would mean that watching a lot of television violence was associated with a *low* level of aggression.

As we will see shortly, the strength of a correlation between two variables can be assessed statistically by Spearman's rho. What, then, is the value of a scattergraph? Spearman's rho is limited in that it sometimes indicates that there is no relationship between two variables even when there is. For example, Spearman's rho would not reveal the existence of a strong curvilinear relationship between two variables, but this would be immediately obvious in a scattergraph.

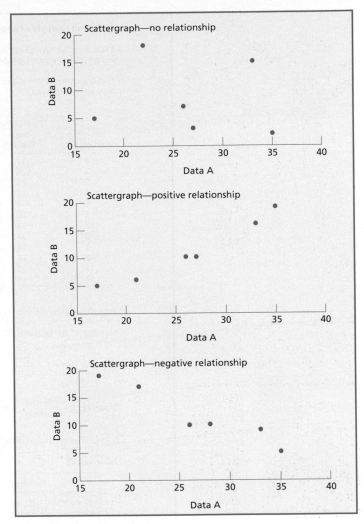

Spearman's rho

Suppose that we have scores on two variables from each of our participants, and we want to see whether there is an association or correlation between the two sets of scores. This can be done by using a test known as Spearman's rho, provided that the data are at least ordinal. Spearman's rho or r_s indicates the strength of the association. If r_s is +1.0, then there is a perfect positive correlation between the two variables. If r_s is –1.0, then there is a perfect negative correlation between the two variables. If r_s is 0.0, then there is generally no relationship between the two variables. The working of this test is shown in the worked example.

An experimenter collects information about the amount of television violence seen in the past month and about the amount of aggressive behaviour exhibited in the past month from 12 participants. She predicts that there will be a positive association between these two variables, i.e. those participants who have seen the most television violence (variable A) will tend to be the most aggressive (variable B). In other words, there is a directional hypothesis.

The first step is to draw up a table in which each participant's scores for the two variables are placed in the same row.

The second step is to rank all the scores for variable A. A rank of 1 is assigned to the smallest score, a rank of 2 to the second smallest score, and so on up to 12. What do we do if there are tied scores? In the example, participants 9 and 12 had the same score for variable A. The ranks that they are competing for are ranks 5 and 6. What is done is to take the average or mean of the ranks at issue: $(5 + 6)/2 = 5.5$.

A worked example of a test for correlation between two variables using Spearman's rho

Experimental hypothesis: there is a positive association between amount of television violence watched and aggressive behaviour

Null hypothesis: there is no association between amount of television violence watched and aggressive behaviour

Participants	TV violence seen (hours)	Aggressive behaviour (out of 10)	Rank A	Rank B	Difference d	d²
1	17	8	7.5	9	−1.50	2.25
2	6	3	2	2	0.00	0.00
3	23	9	10	10.5	−0.50	0.25
4	17	7	7.5	8	−0.50	0.25
5	2	2	1	1	0.00	0.00
6	20	6	9	5.5	+3.50	12.25
7	12	6	4	5.5	0.00	2.25
8	31	10	12	12	0.00	0.00
9	14	6	5.5	5.5	+0.50	0.00
10	26	9	10.5	10.5	+0.50	0.25
11	9	6	5.5	5.5	−2.50	6.25
12	14	4	3	3	+2.50	6.25

Sum of squared difference scores (Σd^2) = 30

Number of participants (N) = 12

Formula: $\text{rho} = 1 - \frac{(\Sigma d^2 \times 6)}{N(N^2 - 1)}$

Example: $1 - \frac{(30 \times 6)}{12(143)} = 1 - 0.105 = +0.895$

Is the value of rho (+0.895) as great as, or greater than the tabled value?

Table values

	0.05 level	0.01 level	0.005 level
N = 12	+0.503	+0.671	+0.727

Conclusion: null hypothesis rejected in favour of experimental hypothesis, i.e. there is a positive correlation between the amount of television violence watched and aggressive behaviour ($p = 0.005$).

The third step is to rank all the scores for variable B, with a rank of 1 being assigned to the smallest score. Participants 6, 7, 9, and 11 are all tied, with the ranks at issue being ranks 4, 5, 6, and 7. The mean rank at issue is $(4 + 5 + 6 + 7)/4 = 5.5$.

The fourth step is to calculate the difference between the two ranks obtained by each individual, with the rank for variable B being subtracted from the rank for variable A. This produces 12 difference (d) scores.

The fifth step is to square all of the d scores obtained in the fourth step. This produces 12 squared difference (d²) scores.

The sixth step is to add up all of the d² scores in order to obtain the sum of the squared difference scores. This is known as Σd^2, and comes to 30 in the example.

The seventh step is to work out the number of participants. In the example, the number of participants (N) is 12.

The eighth step is to calculate rho from the following formula:

$$\text{rho} = 1 - \frac{(\Sigma d^2 \times 6)}{N(N^2 - 1)}$$

The "6" in the equation is always present, and is a feature of the Spearman's rho formula.

In the example, this becomes $1 - \frac{(30 \times 6)}{12(143)} = 1 - 0.105 = +0.895$.

The ninth and final step is to work out the significance of the value of rho by referring the result to the table (see Appendix 4). The obtained value must be as great as, or greater than, the tabled value. The tabled value for a one-tailed test with N = 12 is +0.503 at the 0.05 level, it is +0.671 at the 0.01 level, and it is +0.727 at the 0.005 level. Thus, it can be concluded that the null hypothesis should be rejected in favour of the experimental hypothesis that there is a positive correlation between the amount of television violence watched and aggressive behaviour ($p = 0.005$).

An important point about Spearman's rho is that the statistical significance of the obtained value of rho depends very heavily on the number of participants. For example, the tabled value for significance at the 0.05 level on a one-tailed test is +0.564 if there are 10 participants. However, it is only +0.306 if there are 30 participants. In practical terms, this means that it is very hard to obtain a significant correlation with Spearman's rho if the number of participants is low.

According to APA convention, numbers that cannot be greater than 1, e.g. correlations and probabilities, should be presented without a zero before the decimal point. However, this convention has not been used throughout this text.

Test of association

The **chi-squared test** is a test of association. It is used when we have nominal data in the form of frequencies, and when each and every observation is independent of all the other observations. For example, suppose that we are interested in the association between eating patterns and cholesterol level. We could divide people into those having a healthy diet with relatively little fat and those having an unhealthy diet. We could also divide them into those having a fairly high level of cholesterol and those having a low level of cholesterol. In essence, the chi-squared test tells us whether membership of a given category on one dimension (e.g. unhealthy diet) is associated with membership of a given category on the other dimension (e.g. high cholesterol level).

In the worked example, we will assume that we have data from 186 individuals with an unhealthy diet, and from 128 individuals with a healthy diet. Of those with an unhealthy diet, 116 have a high cholesterol level and 70 have a low cholesterol level. Of those with a healthy diet, 41 have a high cholesterol level and 87 have a low cholesterol level. Our experimental hypothesis is that there is an association between healthiness of diet and low cholesterol level.

The first step is to arrange the frequency data in a 2 × 2 "contingency table" as in the worked example, with the row and column totals included. The second step is to work out what the four frequencies would be if there were no association at all between diet and cholesterol levels. The expected frequency (by chance alone) in each case is given by the following formula:

$$\text{expected frequency} = \frac{\text{row total} \times \text{column total}}{\text{overall total}}$$

For example, the expected frequency for the number of participants having a healthy diet and high cholesterol is 157 × 128 divided by 314, which comes to 64. The four expected frequencies (those expected by chance alone) are also shown in the table.

The third step is to apply the following formula to the observed (O) and expected (E) frequencies in each of the four categories:

$$\frac{(|O - E| - 1/2)^2}{E}$$

In the formula, $|O - E|$ means that the difference between the observed and the expected frequency should be taken, and it should then have a + sign put in front of it regardless of the direction of the difference. The correction factor (i.e. $-1/2$) is only used when there are two rows and two columns.

The fourth step is to add together the four values obtained in the third step in order to provide the chi-squared statistic or X^2. This is $7.91 + 5.44 + 7.91 + 5.44 = 26.70$.

The fifth step is to calculate the number of "degrees of freedom" (df). This is given by (the number of rows − 1) × (the number of columns − 1). For this we need to refer back to the contingency table. In the example, this is 1 × 1 = 1. Why is there

As vertical lines denote absolute values, "|O − E|" is the difference between these values. Whether it is say, 5–3 or 3–5, the difference between the values is always a positive number, i.e. 2 in this case.

Test of association: Chi-squared test, a worked example

Experimental hypothesis: there is an association between healthiness of diet and low cholesterol level

Null hypothesis: there is no association between healthiness of diet and low cholesterol level

Contingency table:

	Healthy diet	Unhealthy diet	Row total
High cholesterol	41	116	157
Low cholesterol	87	70	157
Column total	128	186	314

Expected frequency if there were no association:

Formula: $\dfrac{\text{row total} \times \text{column total}}{\text{expected frequency}}$ = overall total

	Healthy diet	Unhealthy diet	Row total
High cholesterol	64	93	157
Low cholesterol	64	93	157
Column total	128	186	314

Calculating chi-squared statistic (χ^2):

Formula: $\chi^2 = \sum \dfrac{(|O - E| - 1/2)^2}{E} = 26.7$

Note: Correction factor ($-1/2$) is only used where there are two rows and two columns

Category	Observed	Expected	$|O - E|$	$\dfrac{(|O - E| - 1/2)^2}{E}$
Healthy, high cholesterol	41	64	23	7.91
Unhealthy, high cholesterol	116	93	23	5.44
Healthy, low cholesterol	87	64	23	7.91
Unhealthy, low cholesterol	70	93	23	5.44
				26.70

Calculating degrees of freedom:

Formula: (no. of rows − 1) × (no. of columns −1) = degrees of freedom (2 − 1) × (2 − 1) = 1

Compare chi-squared statistic with tabled values:

Table values

	0.025 level	0.005 level	0.0005 level
df = 1	3.84	6.64	10.83

Question: is the observed chi-square value of 26.70 and one degree of freedom the same as or greater than the tabled value?

Conclusion: the chi-square value is greater than the tabled value, so the null hypothesis can be rejected, and the experimental hypothesis, that there is an association between healthiness of diet and cholesterol level, accepted.

1 degree of freedom? Once we know the row and column totals, then only one of the four observed values is free to vary. Thus, for example, knowing that the row totals are 157 and 157, the column totals are 128 and 186, and the number of participants having a healthy diet and high cholesterol is 41, we can complete the entire table. In other words, the number of degrees of freedom corresponds to the number of values that are free to vary.

The sixth step is to compare the tabled values in Appendix 5 with chi-square = 26.70 and one degree of freedom. The observed value needs to be the same as, or greater than, the tabled value for a one-tailed test in order for the results to be significant.

The tabled value for a one-tailed test with df = 1 is 3.84 at the 0.025 level, 6.64 at the 0.005 level, and 10.83 at the 0.0005 level. Thus, we can reject the null hypothesis, and conclude that there is an association between healthiness of diet and cholesterol level ($p = 0.0005$).

It is easy to use the chi-squared test wrongly. According to Robson (1994), "There are probably more inappropriate and incorrect uses of the chi-square test than of all the other statistical tests put together." In order to avoid using the chi-squared test wrongly, it is important to make use of the following rules:

- Ensure that every observation is independent of every other observation; in other words, each individual should be counted once and in only *one* category.
- Make sure that each observation is included in the appropriate category; it is not permitted to omit some of the observations (e.g. those from individuals with intermediate levels of cholesterol).
- The total sample should exceed 20; otherwise, the chi-squared test as described here is not applicable. More precisely, the minimum expected frequency should be at least 5 in every use.
- The significance level of a chi-squared test is assessed by consulting the one-tailed values in the Appendix table if a specific form of association has been predicted and that form was obtained. However, the two-tailed values should always be consulted if there are more than two categories on either dimension.
- Remember that showing that there is an association is not the same as showing that there is a causal effect; for example, the association between a healthy diet and low cholesterol does not demonstrate that a healthy diet *causes* low cholesterol.

Issues of Experimental and Ecological Validity

Assume that you have carried out a study, and then analysed it using a statistical test. The results were statistically significant, so you are able to reject the null hypothesis in favour of the experimental hypothesis. When deciding how to interpret your findings, you need to take account of issues relating to experimental and ecological validity. **Experimental validity** is based on the extent to which a given finding is genuine, and is due to the independent variable that was manipulated. In other words, it is essentially the same as internal validity, which was discussed in Chapter 31. In contrast, **ecological validity** refers to the extent to which research findings can be generalised to a range of real-world settings. It is clearly desirable for a study to possess both of these forms of validity.

Experimental validity

How can we assess the experimental or internal validity of the findings from a study? The key point was made in Chapter 31: we can only have confidence that the independent variable produced the observed effects on behaviour or the dependent variable provided that all of the principles of experimental design were followed. These principles include the standardisation of instructions and procedures; counterbalancing; randomisation; and the avoidance of confounding variables, experimenter effects, demand characteristics, and participant reactivity.

We can check these by asking various questions about a study, including the following:

- Were there any variables (other than the independent variable) that varied systematically between conditions?
- Did all the participants receive the same standardised instructions?
- Were the participants allocated at random to the conditions?

- Did the experimenter influence the performance of the participants by his or her expectations or biases?
- Were the participants influenced by any demand characteristics of the situation?
- If the participants knew they were being observed, did this influence their behaviour?

Probably the most convincing evidence that a study possesses good experimental validity is if its findings can be repeated or replicated in other studies. Why is that so? Suppose, for example, that we obtain significant findings in one study because we failed to allocate our participants at random to conditions. Anyone else carrying out the same study, but allocating the participants at random, would be very unlikely to repeat the findings of our study.

Ecological validity

As Coolican (1994) pointed out, the term ecological validity has been used in various ways. It is sometimes used to refer to the extent to which a given study was carried out in a naturalistic or real-world setting rather than an artificial one. However, as was mentioned earlier, it is probably more useful to regard ecological validity as referring to the extent to which a study generalises to various real-world settings. Bracht and Glass (1968) put forward a definition of ecological validity along those lines. According to them, the findings of ecologically valid studies generalise to other locations or places, to other times, and to other measures. Thus, the notion of ecological validity closely resembles that of external validity (see Chapter 31), except that external validity also includes generalisation to other populations.

How do we know whether the findings of a study possess ecological validity? The only conclusive way of answering that question is by carrying out a series of studies in different locations, at different times, and using different measures. Following that approach is generally very costly in terms of time and effort.

It is often possible to obtain some idea of the ecological validity of a study by asking yourself whether there are important differences between the way in which a study has been conducted and what happens in the real world. For example, consider research on eyewitness testimony (see Chapter 13). The participants in most laboratory studies of eyewitness testimony have been asked to pay close attention to a series of slides or a video depicting some incident, after which they are asked various questions. The ecological validity of such studies is put in danger for a number of reasons. The participants have their attention directed to the incident, whereas eyewitnesses to a crime or other incident may fail to pay much attention to it. In addition, eyewitnesses are often very frightened and concerned about their own safety, whereas the participants in a laboratory study are not.

It may seem reasonable to argue that we could ensure ecological validity by taking research out of the laboratory and into the real world. However, powerful arguments against doing that with memory research were put forward by Banaji and Crowder (1989):

CASE STUDY: Criticism of Intelligence Testing

Gould's (1982) study included criticism of intelligence testing based on the methodological and theoretical problems experienced when these tests are used. Gould suggested that many IQ tests contain errors of validity. They have design flaws in relation to the wording used, which is often based on cultural definitions of meaning. Lack of access to the relevant cultural interpretations would disadvantage certain groups and individuals. For example, the Yerkes Tests of Intelligence were based on American culture and cultural knowledge, so that immigrants' performance was almost always poorer than that of the native groups. Gould also emphasised the fact that the procedures used were flawed, especially during the testing of black participants.

Interpretation of findings from the use of Yerkes tests ignored the role of experience and education in IQ, and focused on the role of heredity. The research evidence was used to support racist social policy, which restricted work opportunities for ethnic groups within society and denied many the right to seek political refuge in America.

Imagine astronomy being conducted with only the naked eye, biology without tissue cultures ... or chemistry without test tubes! The everyday world is full of principles from these sciences in action, but do we really think their data bases should have been those of everyday applications? Of course not. Should the psychology of memory be any different? We think not.

In sum, investigators should consider the issue of ecological validity seriously when interpreting their findings. They should try to identify the main ways in which the situation or situations in which their participants were placed differ from those of everyday life. They should also take account of the desirability of measuring behaviour that is representative of behaviours that occur naturally. At the very least, they should interpret their findings cautiously if there are several major differences. Finally, they should discuss relevant published research that indicates the likely impact of these differences on participants' behaviour.

Ecological validity

The term ecological validity refers to the extent to which any study's findings can be generalised to other settings. Although many laboratory studies may lack ecological validity, so do some of those conducted in natural settings.

Consider Skinner's work on pigeons pecking at a disc to receive food pellets. Could the results of his study be generalised to explain how dog handlers train their dogs to seek out illegal drugs and explosives? Do the procedures for operant conditioning remain the same, i.e. the use of reinforcement to shape behaviour?

Imagine you are an observer watching birds in their natural environment, collecting data on how the parents are caring for their offspring. You disturb the parent birds by making too much noise, and they abandon their nesting site. Would your research have ecological validity because it was carried out in the natural environment? Could you generalise your findings to other settings?

Writing up a Practical

Practicals in psychology are written up in a standard way. Thus, your write-ups need to be organised in a certain fashion. Initially, this may seem difficult. However, it has the great advantage that this organisation makes it easy for someone reading your write-ups to know where to look to find information about the type of participants used, the statistical analyses, and so on. The details of how to produce a write-up differ slightly depending on whether it is based on an experimental or a non-experimental design. However, the general approach is exactly the same, and the essence of that approach is given later. The sections are arranged in the order they should appear in your write-ups. It is essential to refer to coursework assessment criteria issued by the relevant examination board.

Finally, be sure to write in a formal way. For example, write "It was decided to study the effects of attention on learning" rather than, "I decided to study the effects of attention on learning."

Title
This should give a short indication of the nature of your study. In the case of an experimental study, it might well refer to the independent and dependent variables. A non-experimental study would include reference to the qualitative nature of the investigation.

Abstract
This should provide a brief account of the purpose of the study, the key aspects of the design, the use of statistics, and the key findings and their interpretation.

Introduction
This should start with an account of the main concepts and background literature relevant to your study. It should then move on to a consideration of previous work that is of *direct* relevance to your study. Avoid describing several studies that are only loosely related to your study.

Aim
This resembles the experimental hypothesis, but is more general in that it indicates the background to the hypothesis.

Method

Design. Here you should indicate the number of groups, the use of an independent samples or repeated measures design (if applicable), the nature of the independent and dependent variables (if any), the experimental hypothesis, and the null hypothesis. You should also indicate any attempts made to control the situation effectively so as to produce an effective design.

Participants. The number of participants should be given together with relevant information about them (e.g. age, gender, educational background). You should indicate how they were selected for your study and, in the case of an experiment, refer to the way in which they were allocated to conditions.

Apparatus and materials. There should be a brief description of any apparatus used in the study, together with an account of any stimuli presented to the participants (e.g. 20 common 5-letter nouns). The stimuli should be referred to in a numbered section in the appendix where they can be examined in detail.

Procedure. The sequence of events experienced by the participants, including any instructions given to them, should be indicated here. Standardised instructions may be given in detail in an appendix.

Results

It is generally useful to restate the aims of the study and to indicate the independent and dependent variables in the case of an experiment.

Also, it is desirable to provide a summary table of the performance of participants. Tables of central tendency and standard deviation are usually informative ways of getting an overall "picture" of results. A bar chart or some other suitable figure may provide ready visual access to a large body of information.

- Make sure that tables and figures are clearly labelled.
- Make sure that raw data appear in a numbered section of the appendix.

Statistical test and level of significance. The test that has been applied to the data should be indicated, together with the justification for the selection of the test. Also there should be reference to the level of statistical significance that was achieved with respect to the test statistic chosen. Make sure you indicate whether a one-tailed or a two-tailed test was used, and relate your findings to the experimental and null hypotheses.

Discussion

The discussion should start by considering your findings, especially with respect to the results of the statistical test or tests. Be as precise as possible in terms of what your findings show (and do not show!). You may wish to comment on individual results that were inconsistent with the rest of the participants' data.

The next part of this section should consist of how your findings relate to previous findings referred to in the introduction. Ask yourself if they support or refute existing theories or approaches and how you might account for the behaviour of the participants.

Next, identify any weaknesses in your study, and indicate how they could be eliminated in a subsequent study. For example, there may have been ethical issues which arose during the investigation which only became apparent after you had started.

Finally, consider whether there are interesting ways in which your study could be extended to provide more information about the phenomenon you have been investigating. This is a very satisfactory section to deal with because your imagination can take over producing ideal studies unencumbered by the necessity to go and find participants! Always remember, though, that possible extension studies should be relevant and the likely outcome to them should be mentioned.

References

Full information about any references you have referred to in the write-up should be provided here. Textbooks (including this one) typically have a reference section set out in conventional style and you should refer to it.

PERSONAL REFLECTIONS

- Data analysis is very important. In its absence, all we could do is to interpret our data in an entirely subjective way. Data analysis has the great advantage that it allows us to be as precise as possible in our interpretations of the findings we have obtained. Data analysis sometimes seems difficult, but it is a crucial ingredient in psychological research.

SUMMARY

Qualitative research is concerned with the experiences of the participants, and with the meanings they attach to themselves and their lives. Investigators using interviews, case studies, or observations often (but not always) make use of qualitative data. A key principle of qualitative analysis is that theoretical understanding emerges from the data, and is not imposed by the researcher. Qualitative researchers typically categorise the data after taking account of all of the data and of the participants' own categories. Findings based on qualitative data tend to be unreliable and hard to replicate.

Qualitative analysis of data

It can be hard to interpret the information obtained from interviews because of social desirability bias, complex interactional processes, and the self-fulfilling prophecy. The greatest danger with case studies is drawing very general conclusions from a single atypical individual. Case studies can suggest hypotheses, which can then be tested with larger groups. The findings of observational studies are often difficult to interpret, because it is not clear *why* the participants are behaving as they are. In addition, the participants in observational studies may not be representative.

Interpretation of interviews, case studies, and observations

Content analysis has been used as a method for analysing messages in the media as well as communications that participants have been asked to produce, such as diaries. The first step is the construction of coding units into which the selected information can be categorised. Coders may be asked to provide ratings or rankings as well as to categorise.

Content analysis

When we have obtained scores from a group of participants, we can summarise our data by working out a measure of central tendency and a measure of dispersion or spread of scores around the central tendency. The mean is the most generally useful measure of central tendency, but other measures include the median and mode. The standard deviation is the most useful measure of dispersion. Other measures include the range and the variation ratio.

Quantitative analysis: Descriptive statistics

Summary data from a study can be presented in the form of a figure, so that it is easy to observe general trends. Among the possible ways of presenting the data in a figure are the following: frequency polygon; histogram; and bar chart. Frequency polygons and histograms are used when the scores can be ordered from low to high, whereas bar charts are used when the scores are in the form of categories.

Data presentation

If the experimental hypothesis predicts the direction of effects, then a one-tailed test should be used. Otherwise, a two-tailed test should be used. There are four types of data of increasing levels of precision as follows: nominal; ordinal; interval; and ratio. Psychologists generally use the 5% level of statistical significance. This produces fairly

Statistical tests

small probabilities of incorrectly rejecting the null hypothesis in favour of the experimental hypothesis (Type I error) or of incorrectly retaining the null hypothesis (Type II error).

A test of difference is used when data are obtained from a study in which an independent variable was manipulated to observe its effects. The Mann-Whitney U test is the appropriate test of difference if an independent design was used. The sign test can be used when a repeated measures or matched participants design was used and the data are nominal or ordinal. The same is true of the Wilcoxon matched pairs signed ranks test, except that the data must be at least ordinal.

The data from correlational studies are in the form of scores on two response variables from every participant. These data can be presented in the form of a scattergraph or scattergram. The correlation between two sets of scores can be calculated by means of Spearman's rho test, provided that the data are at least ordinal.

The chi-squared test is a test of association. It is used when we have nominal data in the form of frequencies, and when each and every observation is independent of all the other observations. The test is nearly always one-tailed. All the expected frequencies should be five or more. Finding an association is not the same as showing the existence of a causal effect.

Issues of experimental and ecological validity

Experimental validity is based on the extent to which a given finding is genuine, and is due to the independent variable that was manipulated. A study is most likely to be high in experimental validity when all the principles of experimental design (e.g. randomisation; standardisation) have been followed. Replication provides some assurance that experimental validity is high. Ecological validity refers to the extent to which the findings of a study generalise to other locations, times, and measures. The ecological validity of a study is best assessed by carrying out a range of further studies using different locations, times, and measures.

FURTHER READING

There is detailed but user-friendly coverage of the topics discussed in this chapter in H. Coolican (1994), *Research methods and statistics in psychology (2nd Edn.)*, London: Hodder & Stoughton. A shorter version of the Coolican (1994) textbook is H. Coolican (1995), *Introduction to research methods and statistics in psychology*, London: Hodder & Stoughton. There is extensive coverage of the main types of qualitative analysis in P. Banister, E. Burman, I. Parker, M. Taylor, and C. Tindall (1994), *Qualitative methods in psychology: A research guide*, Buckingham, UK: Open University Press.

REVISION QUESTIONS

1a	What are *two* advantages of laboratory experiments over field experiments?	(6 marks)
1b	What are *two* advantages of field experiments over laboratory experiments?	(6 marks)
1c	What is a natural experiment?	(6 marks)
1d	Identify *two* strengths and *two* weaknesses of natural experiments.	(6 marks)

2 An experimenter was interested in testing the experimental hypothesis that there is an association between cigarette smoking and physical health. Accordingly, she obtained a sample of 700 people, and placed them in the following four categories: non-smoker; light smoker; moderate smoker; and heavy smoker. Their physical health was assessed as either good or poor.

2a	Indicate which statistical test would be appropriate to test the experimental hypothesis, and provide reasons for your choice.	(9 marks)
2b	Describe a suitable method for obtaining the sample for the study.	(6 marks)
2c	What is a two-tailed test?	(3 marks)
2d	If the findings were statistically significant on a two-tailed test, what conclusions would you draw?	(6 marks)

3 A researcher predicted that eight-year-old children would be better than six-year-old children at solving 15 simple arithmetic problems. The mean number of problems solved by the eight-year-olds was 10.8 out of 15, compared to 8.2 by the six-year-olds.

3a	What is meant by the term *mean*?	(3 marks)
3b	When is it preferable to use the median rather than the mean as a measure of central tendency?	(6 marks)
3c	Which statistical test would you use to test the prediction? Give reasons for your choice.	(9 marks)
3d	Would you use a one-tailed or a two-tailed test, and why?	(6 marks)

4 Research was conducted into the relationship between the amount of television violence that children watched and their level of aggression. The investigator predicted that there would be a positive relationship between the two variables. The findings from 12 children were as follows:

Participant	Television violence seen per week (minutes)	Level of aggression (maximum = 20)
1	15	8
2	24	11
3	156	18
4	29	11
5	121	10
6	84	9
7	63	7
8	68	17
9	0	5
10	58	8
11	99	12
12	112	15

The researcher used Spearman's rho to analyse the data. She obtained a value of r_S of +0.64, which is significant at $p = 0.025$ on a one-tailed test. Accordingly, she rejected the null hypothesis in favour of the experimental hypothesis that there is a positive relationship between the amount of television violence watched and the level of aggression.

4a	How may the data be represented?	(3 marks)
4b	Draw a figure to represent these data.	(9 marks)
4c	What conclusions may be drawn from your figure?	(6 marks)
4d	Identify *two* reasons why Spearman's rho was used to analyse the data.	(12 marks)
4e	What is a one-tailed test?	(6 marks)
4f	What is the meaning of $p = 0.025$?	(6 marks)
4g	What was the null hypothesis for this study?	(6 marks)

Appendices

In order to use the statistical tables on the following pages, you first need to decide whether:

1. Your data is in numerical form, in which case it is suitable for quantitative analysis; otherwise, use qualitative analysis.
2. You have obtained nominal, ordinal, interval or ratio data.
3. Your data shows a difference between the two conditions (the experimental hypothesis) or not (the null hypothesis).
4. You can use parametric tests (i.e. if data is interval or ratio, normally distributed, and the variances in the two conditions are similar); otherwise non-parametric tests can be used. Non-parametric tests can be used in nearly all cases, and it is the most useful of these that are described in this book.

Once you have obtained your results, you can construct a table of frequencies, and decide which type of chart or graph you wish to use in order to present your data graphically in the clearest way possible.

The next step to take is to analyse your data, as follows:

1. Calculate measures of central tendency: mean, median and mode.
2. Calculate measures of dispersion: range, interquartile range, variation ratio and standard deviation.

You will then need to apply further statistical analysis using the statistical tests described in Chapter 32. Please refer to the worked examples for each of these and follow the step-by-step instructions in the main text.

How to Decide Which Test to Use

The main purpose of these tests is to decide the probability of the null hypothesis being correct, and to evaluate its significance. Each test involves calculating your observed value from your results, and then looking up the critical value in a table of values, to see whether your value is greater than, equal to, or less than the critical value. Use the appropriate column or table, depending on (a) whether you used a one- or two-tailed test and (b) which level of significance, or probability (p) you wish to check. If p is less than or equal to 0.05 or 5%, which is the standard probability of significance used by psychologists, the null hypothesis is rejected in favour of the experimental hypothesis. To see whether the findings are highly significant, look at whether the null hypothesis still holds true at $p = 0.01$, or 1%, or even $p = 0.001$, or 0.1%.

If your experimental hypothesis is directional (i.e. you predicted the direction of any effects), you need to use a one-tailed test; otherwise you have a non-directional hypothesis, in which case you need to use a two-tailed test.

If the design of your test of difference is independent, as long as the data are ordinal or interval, the Mann-Whitney U test can be used. If you have used a repeated measures or matched participants design, the sign test can be used, as long as the data are ordinal; or if the data are interval or ratio, the Wilcoxon matched pairs signed ranks test can be used. The latter is more sensitive than the signed test. The sign test provides us with a crude analysis, which is sufficient when data are ordinal, but when actual values are obtained (interval or ratio data) the Wilcoxon test will provide a more sophisticated analysis. Therefore, although it is possible to use the sign test for interval or ratio data, it would be best to limit its use to analysis of ordinal data.

If you manipulated the independent variable (some aspect of the situation), you need to use a test of difference (such as the Mann-Whitney U test, the sign test or the Wilcoxon matched pairs signed ranks test); otherwise, you need to use a test of correlation (such as Spearman's rho test, as long as the data are ordinal, interval or ratio) or a test of association (such as the chi-squared test, as long as the data are nominal).

How to Use the Tables

Mann-Whitney U test
Appendix 1, pages 892–893

In the Mann-Whitney U test, use the smaller value of U and U' to look up the critical value of U for a one- or two-tailed test, as appropriate, at 0.05, initially (bottom table, page 893). If the tabled value is equal to or less than your value at that level, the null hypothesis is retained; if it is greater than your value, it is rejected and your experimental hypothesis is proved.

Sign test
Appendix 2, page 894

In the sign test, look up the critical value of S for a one- or two-tailed test, as appropriate, for N, the number of participants with differing scores, at 0.05, initially. If the tabled value is equal to or less than your value at that level, the null hypothesis is retained; if it is greater than your value, it is rejected and your experimental hypothesis is proved.

Wilcoxon test
Appendix 3, page 894

In the Wilcoxon test, look up the critical value of T for a one- or two-tailed test, as appropriate, for N, the number of participants with differing scores, at 0.05, initially. If the tabled value is equal to or less than your value at that level, the null hypothesis is retained; if it is greater than your value, it is rejected and your experimental hypothesis is proved.

Spearman's rho test
Appendix 4, page 895

In the Spearman's rho test, look up the critical value of r_s for a one- or two-tailed test, as appropriate, for N, the number of participants, at 0.05, initially. If the tabled value is greater than or equal to your value at that level, the null hypothesis is retained; if it is less than your value, it is rejected and your experimental hypothesis is proved.

Chi-squared test
Appendix 5, page 896

In the chi-squared test, look up the critical value of chi-squared (also shown as χ^2) for a one- or two-tailed test, as appropriate, for df, the degrees of freedom, at 0.05, initially. If the tabled value is greater than or equal to your value at that level, the null hypothesis is retained; if it is less than your value, it is rejected and your experimental hypothesis is proved.

Tips

Remember that decisions based on statistical tests are open to error, but if you follow the standard procedures outlined in Chapter 32 the potential for errors can be minimised. Try to be as unbiased as possible, and try not to assume too much about the results in advance.

Ensure that you have not made errors of either Type I, which can be reduced by using a greater level of significance (e.g. $p = 0.01$, or 1%, or even $p = 0.001$, or 0.1%), or Type II, which can be reduced by using a lesser level of significance (e.g. $p = 0.10$, or 10%).

In the Mann-Whitney U test, remember that ties are possible—this reduces the accuracy, but has only a small effect unless there are several ties.

In the chi-squared test, do follow the rules on page 881 to avoid incorrect use of this test.

The tests described in Chapter 32 provide different levels of analysis, and they require a particular type of data. The following chart outlines the tests that can be used for different data types and experimental designs. Please note that this chart deals only with the statistical tests described in Chapter 32, even though other tests do exist.

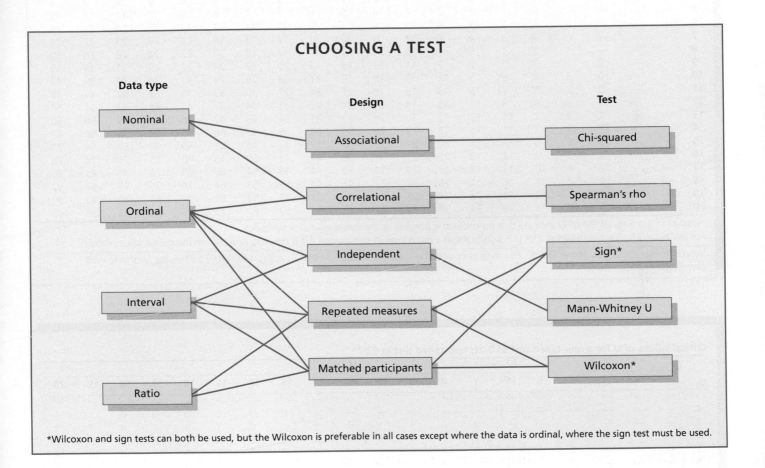

CHOOSING A TEST

Data type

Nominal

Ordinal

Interval

Ratio

Design

Associational

Correlational

Independent

Repeated measures

Matched participants

Test

Chi-squared

Spearman's rho

Sign*

Mann-Whitney U

Wilcoxon*

*Wilcoxon and sign tests can both be used, but the Wilcoxon is preferable in all cases except where the data is ordinal, where the sign test must be used.

Appendix 1: Mann–Whitney U test

Critical values of U for a one-tailed test at 0.005; two-tailed test at 0.01*

										N_A										
N_B	1	2	3	4	5	6	7	8	9	10	11	12	13	14	15	16	17	18	19	20
1	—	—	—	—	—	—	—	—	—	—	—	—	—	—	—	—	—	—	—	—
2	—	—	—	—	—	—	—	—	—	—	—	—	—	—	—	—	—	—	0	0
3	—	—	—	—	—	—	—	—	0	0	0	1	1	1	2	2	2	2	3	3
4	—	—	—	—	—	0	0	1	1	2	2	3	3	4	5	5	6	6	7	8
5	—	—	—	—	0	1	1	2	3	4	5	6	7	7	8	9	10	11	12	13
6	—	—	—	0	1	2	3	4	5	6	7	9	10	11	12	13	15	16	17	18
7	—	—	—	0	1	3	4	6	7	9	10	12	13	15	16	18	19	21	22	24
8	—	—	—	1	2	4	6	7	9	11	13	15	17	18	20	22	24	26	28	30
9	—	—	0	1	3	5	7	9	11	13	16	18	20	22	24	27	29	31	33	36
10	—	—	0	2	4	6	9	11	13	16	18	21	24	26	29	31	34	37	39	42
11	—	—	0	2	5	7	10	13	16	18	21	24	27	30	33	36	39	42	45	48
12	—	—	1	3	6	9	12	15	18	21	24	27	31	34	37	41	44	47	51	54
13	—	—	1	3	7	10	13	17	20	24	27	31	34	38	42	45	49	53	56	60
14	—	—	1	4	7	11	15	18	22	26	30	34	38	42	46	50	54	58	63	67
15	—	—	2	5	8	12	16	20	24	29	33	37	42	46	51	55	60	64	69	73
16	—	—	2	5	9	13	18	22	27	31	36	41	45	50	55	60	65	70	74	79
17	—	—	2	6	10	15	19	24	29	34	39	44	49	54	60	65	70	75	81	86
18	—	—	2	6	11	16	21	26	31	37	42	47	53	58	64	70	75	81	87	92
19	—	0	3	7	12	17	22	28	33	39	45	51	56	63	69	74	81	87	93	99
20	—	0	3	8	13	18	24	30	36	42	48	54	60	67	73	79	86	92	99	105

*Dashes in the body of the table indicate that no decision is possible at the stated level of significance.
For any N_A and N_B the observed value of U is significant at a given level of significance if it is *equal* to or *less* than the critical values shown.

Source: R. Runyon and A. Haber (1976), *Fundamentals of behavioural statistics (3rd Edn.)*, Reading, MA: McGraw Hill, Inc. With the kind permission of the publisher.

Critical values of U for a one-tailed test at 0.01; two-tailed test at 0.02*

										N_A										
N_B	1	2	3	4	5	6	7	8	9	10	11	12	13	14	15	16	17	18	19	20
1	—	—	—	—	—	—	—	—	—	—	—	—	—	—	—	—	—	—	—	—
2	—	—	—	—	—	—	—	—	—	—	—	—	0	0	0	0	0	0	1	1
3	—	—	—	—	—	—	0	0	1	1	1	2	2	2	3	3	4	4	4	5
4	—	—	—	—	0	1	1	2	3	3	4	5	5	6	7	7	8	9	9	10
5	—	—	—	0	1	2	3	4	5	6	7	8	9	10	11	12	13	14	15	16
6	—	—	—	1	2	3	4	6	7	8	9	11	12	13	15	16	18	19	20	22
7	—	—	0	1	3	4	6	7	9	11	12	14	16	17	19	21	23	24	26	28
8	—	—	0	2	4	6	7	9	11	13	15	17	20	22	24	26	28	30	32	34
9	—	—	1	3	5	7	9	11	14	16	18	21	23	26	28	31	33	36	38	40
10	—	—	1	3	6	8	11	13	16	19	22	24	27	30	33	36	38	41	44	47
11	—	—	1	4	7	9	12	15	18	22	25	28	31	34	37	41	44	47	50	53
12	—	—	2	5	8	11	14	17	21	24	28	31	35	38	42	46	49	53	56	60
13	—	0	2	5	9	12	16	20	23	27	31	35	39	43	47	51	55	59	63	67
14	—	0	2	6	10	13	17	22	26	30	34	38	43	47	51	56	60	65	69	73
15	—	0	3	7	11	15	19	24	28	33	37	42	47	51	56	61	66	70	75	80
16	—	0	3	7	12	16	21	26	31	36	41	46	51	56	61	66	71	76	82	87
17	—	0	4	8	13	18	23	28	33	38	44	49	55	60	66	71	77	82	88	93
18	—	0	4	9	14	19	24	30	36	41	47	53	59	65	70	76	82	88	94	100
19	—	1	4	9	15	20	26	32	38	44	50	56	63	69	75	82	88	94	101	107
20	—	1	5	10	16	22	28	34	40	47	53	60	67	73	80	87	93	100	107	114

*Dashes in the body of the table indicate that no decision is possible at the stated level of significance.
For any N_A and N_B the observed value of U is significant at a given level of significance if it is *equal* to or *less* than the critical values shown.

Source: R. Runyon and A. Haber (1976), *Fundamentals of behavioural statistics (3rd Edn.)*, Reading, MA: McGraw Hill, Inc. With the kind permission of the publisher.

Critical values of U for a one-tailed test at 0.025; two-tailed test at 0.05*

N_B \ N_A	1	2	3	4	5	6	7	8	9	10	11	12	13	14	15	16	17	18	19	20
1	—	—	—	—	—	—	—	—	—	—	—	—	—	—	—	—	—	—	—	—
2	—	—	—	—	—	—	—	0	0	0	0	1	1	1	1	1	2	2	2	2
3	—	—	—	—	0	1	1	2	2	3	3	4	4	5	5	6	6	7	7	8
4	—	—	—	0	1	2	3	4	4	5	6	7	8	9	10	11	11	12	13	13
5	—	—	0	1	2	3	5	6	7	8	9	11	12	13	14	15	17	18	19	20
6	—	—	1	2	3	5	6	8	10	11	13	14	16	17	19	21	22	24	25	27
7	—	—	1	3	5	6	8	10	12	14	16	18	20	22	24	26	28	30	32	34
8	—	0	2	4	6	8	10	13	15	17	19	22	24	26	29	31	34	36	38	41
9	—	0	2	4	7	10	12	15	17	20	23	26	28	31	34	37	39	42	45	48
10	—	0	3	5	8	11	14	17	20	23	26	29	33	36	39	42	45	48	52	55
11	—	0	3	6	9	13	16	19	23	26	30	33	37	40	44	47	51	55	58	62
12	—	1	4	7	11	14	18	22	26	29	33	37	41	45	49	53	57	61	65	69
13	—	1	4	8	12	16	20	24	28	33	37	41	45	50	54	59	63	67	72	76
14	—	1	5	9	13	17	22	26	31	36	40	45	50	55	59	64	67	74	78	83
15	—	1	5	10	14	19	24	29	34	39	44	49	54	59	64	70	75	80	85	90
16	—	1	6	11	15	21	26	31	37	42	47	53	59	64	70	75	81	86	92	98
17	—	2	6	11	17	22	28	34	39	45	51	57	63	67	75	81	87	93	99	105
18	—	2	7	12	18	24	30	36	42	48	55	61	67	74	80	86	93	99	106	112
19	—	2	7	13	19	25	32	38	45	52	58	65	72	78	85	92	99	106	113	119
20	—	2	8	13	20	27	34	41	48	55	62	69	76	83	90	98	105	112	119	127

*Dashes in the body of the table indicate that no decision is possible at the stated level of significance.
For any N_A and N_B the observed value of U is significant at a given level of significance if it is *equal* to or *less* than the critical values shown.

Source: R. Runyon and A. Haber (1976), *Fundamentals of behavioural statistics (3rd Edn.)*, Reading, MA: McGraw Hill, Inc. With the kind permission of the publisher.

Critical values of U for a one-tailed test at 0.05; two-tailed test at 0.10*

N_B \ N_A	1	2	3	4	5	6	7	8	9	10	11	12	13	14	15	16	17	18	19	20
1	—	—	—	—	—	—	—	—	—	—	—	—	—	—	—	—	—	—	0	0
2	—	—	—	—	0	0	0	1	1	1	1	2	2	2	3	3	3	4	4	4
3	—	—	0	0	1	2	2	3	3	4	5	5	6	7	7	8	9	9	10	11
4	—	—	0	1	2	3	4	5	6	7	8	9	10	11	12	14	15	16	17	18
5	—	0	1	2	4	5	6	8	9	11	12	13	15	16	18	19	20	22	23	25
6	—	0	2	3	5	7	8	10	12	14	16	17	19	21	23	25	26	28	30	32
7	—	0	2	4	6	8	11	13	15	17	19	21	24	26	28	30	33	35	37	39
8	—	1	3	5	8	10	13	15	18	20	23	26	28	31	33	36	39	41	44	47
9	—	1	3	6	9	12	15	18	21	24	27	30	33	36	39	42	45	48	51	54
10	—	1	4	7	11	14	17	20	24	27	31	34	37	41	44	48	51	55	58	62
11	—	1	5	8	12	16	19	23	27	31	34	38	42	46	50	54	57	61	65	69
12	—	2	5	9	13	17	21	26	30	34	38	42	47	51	55	60	64	68	72	77
13	—	2	6	10	15	19	24	28	33	37	42	47	51	56	61	65	70	75	80	84
14	—	2	7	11	16	21	26	31	36	41	46	51	56	61	66	71	77	82	87	92
15	—	3	7	12	18	23	28	33	39	44	50	55	61	66	72	77	83	88	94	100
16	—	3	8	14	19	25	30	36	42	48	54	60	65	71	77	83	89	95	101	107
17	—	3	9	15	20	26	33	39	45	51	57	64	70	77	83	89	96	102	109	115
18	—	4	9	16	22	28	35	41	48	55	61	68	75	82	88	95	102	109	116	123
19	0	4	10	17	23	30	37	44	51	58	65	72	80	87	94	101	109	116	123	130
20	0	4	11	18	25	32	39	47	54	62	69	77	84	92	100	107	115	123	130	138

*Dashes in the body of the table indicate that no decision is possible at the stated level of significance.
For any N_A and N_B the observed value of U is significant at a given level of significance if it is *equal* to or *less* than the critical values shown.

Source: R. Runyon and A. Haber (1976), *Fundamentals of behavioural statistics (3rd Edn.)*, Reading, MA: McGraw Hill, Inc. With the kind permission of the publisher.

Appendix 2: Sign test

N	Level of significance for one-tailed test				
	0.05	0.025	0.01	0.005	0.0005
	Level of significance for two-tailed test				
	0.10	0.05	0.02	0.01	0.001
5	0	—	—	—	—
6	0	0	—	—	—
7	0	0	0	—	—
8	1	0	0	0	—
9	1	1	0	0	—
10	1	1	0	0	—
11	2	1	1	0	0
12	2	2	1	1	0
13	3	2	1	1	0
14	3	2	2	1	0
15	3	3	2	2	1
16	4	3	2	2	1
17	4	4	3	2	1
18	5	4	3	3	1
19	5	4	4	3	2
20	5	5	4	3	2
25	7	7	6	5	4
30	10	9	8	7	5
35	12	11	10	9	7

Calculated S must be *equal* to or *less* than the table (critical) value for significance at the level shown.

Source: F. Clegg (1982), *Simple statistics*, Cambridge University Press. With the kind permission of the publisher.

Appendix 3: Wilcoxon signed ranks test

Sample size	Levels of significance			
	One-tailed test			
	0.05	0.025	0.01	0.001
	Two-tailed test			
	0.1	0.05	0.02	0.002
N = 5	T ≤ 0			
6	2	0		
7	3	2	0	
8	5	3	1	
9	8	5	3	
10	11	8	5	0
11	13	10	7	1
12	17	13	9	2
13	21	17	12	4
14	25	21	15	6
15	30	25	19	8
16	35	29	23	11
17	41	34	27	14
18	47	40	32	18
19	53	46	37	21
20	60	52	43	26
21	67	58	49	30
22	75	65	55	35
23	83	73	62	40
24	91	81	69	45
25	100	89	76	51
26	110	98	84	58
27	119	107	92	64
28	130	116	101	71
29	141	125	111	78
30	151	137	120	86
31	163	147	130	94
32	175	159	140	103
33	187	170	151	112

Calculated T must be *equal* to or *less* than the table (critical) value for significance at the level shown.

Source: From R. Meddis (1975), *Statistical handbook for non-statisticians*, London: McGraw-Hill. With the kind permission of the publisher.

Appendix 4: Spearman's rho test

	Level of significance for two-tailed test			
	0.10	0.05	0.02	0.01
	Level of significance for one-tailed test			
	0.05	0.025	0.01	0.005
N = 4	1.000			
5	0.900	1.000	1.000	
6	0.829	0.886	0.943	1.000
7	0.714	0.786	0.893	0.929
8	0.643	0.738	0.833	0.881
9	0.600	0.700	0.783	0.833
10	0.564	0.648	0.745	0.794
11	0.536	0.618	0.709	0.755
12	0.503	0.587	0.671	0.727
13	0.484	0.560	0.648	0.703
14	0.464	0.538	0.566	0.675
15	0.443	0.521	0.604	0.654
16	0.429	0.503	0.582	0.635
17	0.414	0.485	0.566	0.615
18	0.401	0.472	0.550	0.600
19	0.391	0.460	0.535	0.584
20	0.380	0.447	0.520	0.570
21	0.370	0.435	0.508	0.556
22	0.361	0.425	0.496	0.544
23	0.353	0.415	0.486	0.532
24	0.344	0.406	0.476	0.521
25	0.337	0.398	0.466	0.511
26	0.331	0.390	0.457	0.501
27	0.324	0.382	0.448	0.491
28	0.317	0.375	0.440	0.483
29	0.312	0.368	0.433	0.475
30	0.306	0.362	0.425	0.467

For n > 30, the significance of r_s can be tested by using the formula:

$$t = r_s \sqrt{\frac{n-2}{1-r_s^2}} \quad df = n - 2$$

and checking the value of t.

Calculated r_s must *equal* or *exceed* the table (critical) value for significance at the level shown.

Source: J.H. Zhar (1972), Significance testing of the Spearman Rank Correlation Coefficient, *Journal of the American Statistical Association, 67,* 578–80. With the kind permission of the publisher.

Appendix 5: Chi-squared test

	Level of significance for one-tailed test					
	0.10	0.05	0.025	0.01	0.005	0.0005
	Level of significance for two-tailed test					
df	0.20	0.10	0.05	0.02	0.01	0.001
1	1.64	2.71	3.84	5.41	6.64	10.83
2	3.22	4.60	5.99	7.82	9.21	13.82
3	4.64	6.25	7.82	9.84	11.34	16.27
4	5.99	7.78	9.49	11.67	13.28	18.46
5	7.29	9.24	11.07	13.39	15.09	20.52
6	8.56	10.64	12.59	15.03	16.81	22.46
7	9.80	12.02	14.07	16.62	18.48	24.32
8	11.03	13.36	15.51	18.17	20.09	26.12
9	12.24	14.68	16.92	19.68	21.67	27.88
10	13.44	15.99	18.31	21.16	23.21	29.59
11	14.63	17.28	19.68	22.62	24.72	31.26
12	15.81	18.55	21.03	24.05	26.22	32.91
13	16.98	19.81	22.36	25.47	27.69	34.53
14	18.15	21.06	23.68	26.87	29.14	36.12
15	19.31	22.31	25.00	28.26	30.58	37.70
16	20.46	23.54	26.30	29.63	32.00	39.29
17	21.62	24.77	27.59	31.00	33.41	40.75
18	22.76	25.99	28.87	32.35	34.80	42.31
19	23.90	27.20	30.14	33.69	36.19	43.82
20	25.04	28.41	31.41	35.02	37.57	45.32
21	26.17	29.62	32.67	36.34	38.93	46.80
22	27.30	30.81	33.92	37.66	40.29	48.27
23	28.43	32.01	35.17	38.97	41.64	49.73
24	29.55	33.20	36.42	40.27	42.98	51.18
25	30.68	34.38	37.65	41.57	44.31	52.62
26	31.80	35.56	38.88	42.86	45.64	54.05
27	32.91	36.74	40.11	44.14	46.96	55.48
28	34.03	37.92	41.34	45.42	48.28	56.89
29	35.14	39.09	42.69	46.69	49.59	58.30
30	36.25	40.26	43.77	43.49	50.89	59.70
32	38.47	42.59	46.19	50.49	53.49	62.49
34	40.68	44.90	48.60	53.00	56.06	65.25
36	42.88	47.21	51.00	55.49	58.62	67.99
38	45.08	49.51	53.38	57.97	61.16	70.70
40	47.27	51.81	55.76	60.44	63.69	73.40
44	51.64	56.37	60.48	65.34	68.71	78.75
48	55.99	60.91	65.17	70.20	73.68	84.04
52	60.33	65.42	69.83	75.02	78.62	89.27
56	64.66	69.92	74.47	79.82	83.51	94.46
60	68.97	74.40	79.08	84.58	88.38	99.61

Calculated value of χ^2 must *equal* or *exceed* the table (critical) value for significance at the level shown.

Abridged from R.A. Fisher and F. Yates (1974), *Statistical tables for biological, agricultural and medical research (6th Edn.)*, Harlow, UK: Addison Wesley Longman.

References

Abele, L.G., & Gilchrist, S. (1977). Homosexual rape and sexual selection in acanthocephalan worms. *Science, 197,* 81–83.

Abeles, R.P. (1976). Relative deprivation, rising expectations and black militancy. *Journal of Social Issues, 32,* 119–137.

Aboud, F.E. (1988). *Children and prejudice.* Oxford: Blackwell.

Aboud, F.E. (1989). Disagreements between friends. *International Journal of Behavioral Development, 12,* 495–508.

Abramson, L.Y., Metalsky, G.I., & Alloy, L.B. (1989). Hopelessness depression: A theory-based subtype of depression. *Psychological Review, 96,* 358–372.

Abramson, L.Y., Seligman, M.E., & Teasdale, J. (1978). Learned helplessness in humans: Critique and reformulation. *Journal of Abnormal Psychology, 87,* 49–74.

Adams, E.S., & Caldwell, R.L. (1990). Deceptive communications in asymmetric fights of the stomatopod crustacean, *Gonodactylus bredini. Animal Behaviour, 39,* 706–716.

Adams, P.R., & Adams, G.R. (1984). Mount Saint Helen's ashfall: Evidence for a disaster stress reaction. *American Psychologist, 39,* 252–260.

Adorno, T.W., Frenkel-Brunswik, E., Levinson, D., & Sanford, R. (1950). *The authoritarian personality.* New York: Harper.

Ainsworth, M.D.S. (1979). Attachment as related to mother–infant interaction. In J.G. Rosenblatt, R.A. Hinde, C. Beer, & M. Busnel (Eds.), *Advances in the study of behaviour, Vol. 9.* Orlando, FL: Academic Press.

Ainsworth, M.D.S. (1982). Infant-mother attachment. *American Psychologist, 34,* 932–937.

Ainsworth, M.D.S., & Bell, S.M. (1970). Attachment, exploration and separation: Illustrated by the behaviour of one-year-olds in a strange situation. *Child Development, 41,* 49–67.

Ainsworth, M.D.S., Bell, S.M., & Stayton, D.J. (1971). Individual differences in strange situation behaviour of one-year-olds. In H.R. Schaffer (Ed.), *The origins of human social relations.* London: Academic Press.

Akerstedt, T. (1977). Inversion of the sleep wakefulness pattern: Effects on circadian variations in psychophysiological activation. *Ergonomics, 20,* 459–474.

Alatalo, R.V., Carlson, A., Lundberg, A., & Ulfstrand, S. (1981). The conflict between male polygyny and female monogamy: The case of the pied flycatcher, *Ficedula hypoleuca. American Naturalist, 117,* 738–753.

Alatalo, R.V., Lundberg, A., & Råtti, O. (1990). Male polyterritoriality, and imperfect female choice in the pied flycatcher, *Ficedula hypoleuca. Behavioural Ecology, 1,* 171–177.

Alexander, L., & Luborsky, L. (1984). Research on the helping alliance. In L. Greenberg & S. Pinsof (Eds.), *The psychotherapeutic process: A research handbook.* New York: Guilford Press.

Alexander, R.D. (1974). The evolution of social behaviour. *Annual Review of Ecology and Systematics, 5,* 325–383.

Alexander, R.D., & Borgia, G. (1979). On the origin and basis of the male–female phenomenon. In M.S. Blum & N.A. Blum (Eds.), *Sexual selection and reproductive competition in insects.* Cambridge: Cambridge University Press.

Allen, M.G. (1976). Twin studies of affective illness. *Archives of General Psychiatry, 33,* 1476–1478.

Allen, V.L., & Levine, J.M. (1971). Social support and conformity: The role of independent assessment of reality. *Journal of Experimental Social Psychology, 7,* 48–58.

Allison, T., & Cicchetti, D.V. (1976). Sleep in mammals: Ecological and constitutional correlates. *Science, 194,* 732–734.

Allport, D.A. (1989). Visual attention. In M.I. Posner (Ed.), *Foundations of cognitive science.* Cambridge, MA: MIT Press.

Allport, D.A. (1993). Attention and control: Have we been asking the wrong questions? A critical review of twenty-five years. In D.E. Meyer & S.M. Kornblum (Eds.), *Attention and performance, Vol. XIV.* London: MIT Press.

Allport, D.A., Antonis, B., & Reynolds, P. (1972). On the division of attention: A disproof of the single channel hypothesis. *Quarterly Journal of Experimental Psychology, 24,* 225–235.

Allport, G.W. (1937). *Personality.* London: Constable.

Allport, G.W. (1947). *The use of personal documents in psychological science.* London: Holt, Rinehart, & Winston.

Allport, G.W. (1954). *The nature of prejudice.* Reading, MA: Addison-Wesley.

Allport, G.W. (1962). The general and the unique in psychological science. *Journal of Personality, 30,* 405–422.

Allport, G.W. (1965). *Letters from Jenny.* New York: Harcourt, Brace & World.

Allport, G.W., & Odbert, H.S. (1936). Trait-names: A psycho-lexical study. *Psychological Monographs, 47,* No. 211.

Allport, G.W., & Pettigrew, T.F. (1957). Cultural influences on the perception of movement: The trapezoidal illusion among Zulus. *Journal of Abnormal and Social Psychology*, 55, 104–113.

Altman, I., & Taylor, D.A. (1973). *Social penetration theory: The development of interpersonal relationships*. New York: Holt, Rinehart, & Winston.

American Psychological Association (1991). Draft of APA ethics code. *APA Monitor*, 22, 30–35.

Ames, G.J., & Murray, F.B. (1982). When two wrongs make a right: Promoting cognitive change by social conflict. *Developmental Psychology*, 18, 894–897.

Amir, T. (1989). The Asch conformity effect: A study in Kuwait. *Social Behavior and Personality*, 12, 187–190.

Amir, Y. (1969). Contact hypothesis in ethnic relations. *Psychological Bulletin*, 71, 319–342.

Anand, B.K., & Brobeck, J.R. (1951). Hypothalamic control of food intake in rats and cats. *Yale Journal of Biological Medicine*, 24, 123–140.

Anderson, C.A. (1989). Temperature and aggression: Unbiquitous effects of heat on occurrence of human violence. *Psychological Bulletin*, 106, 74–96.

Anderson, J.C., Williams, S., McGee, R., & Silva, P.A. (1987). DSM-III: Disorders in preadolescent children. *Archives of General Psychiatry*, 44, 69–76.

Anderson, J.L., Crawford, C.B., Nadeau, J., & Lindberg, T. (1992). Was the Duchess of Windsor right? A cross-cultural review of the socioecology of ideals of female body shape. *Ethology and Sociobiology*, 13, 197–227.

Andersson, B., Grant, R., & Larsson, S. (1956). Central control of heat loss mechanisms in the goat. *Acta Physiologica Scandinavica*, 37, 261–280.

Andersson, M. (1982). Female choice selects for extreme tail length in a widow-bird. *Nature*, 299, 818–820.

Andersson, M., & Wicklund, C.G. (1978). Clumping versus spacing out: Experiments on nest predation in fieldfares (*Turdus pilaris*). *Animal Behaviour*, 26, 1207–1212.

Andreeva, G. (1984). Cognitive processes in developing groups. In L.H. Strickland (Ed.), *Directions in Soviet social psychology*. New York: Springer.

Annis, R.C., & Frost, B. (1973). Human visual ecology and orientation anisotropies in acuity. *Science*, 182, 729–741.

Archer, J. (1992). Childhood gender roles: Social context and organisation. In H. McGurk (Ed.), *Childhood social development: Contemporary perspectives*. Hove, UK: Psychology Press.

Archer, R.L. (1979). Role of personality and the social situation. In G.J. Chelune (Ed.), *Self-disclosure*. San Francisco: Jossey-Bass.

Archer, S. (1982). The lower age boundaries of identity development. *Child Development*, 53, 1551–1556.

Argyle, M. (1988). Social relationships. In M. Hewstone, W. Stroebe, J.-P. Codol, & G.M. Stephenson (Eds.), *Introduction to social psychology*. Oxford: Blackwell.

Argyle, M. (1994). *The psychology of interpersonal behaviour (5th Edn.)*. London: Penguin.

Argyle, M., & Furnham, A. (1983). Sources of satisfaction and conflict in long-term relationships. *Journal of Marriage and the Family*, 45, 481–493.

Argyle, M., Furnham, A., & Graham, J.A. (1981). *Social situations*. Cambridge: Cambridge University Press.

Argyle, M., & Henderson, M. (1984). The rules of friendship. *Journal of Social and Personal Relationships*, 1, 211–237.

Argyle, M., Henderson, M., Bond, M., Iizuka, Y., & Contarello, A. (1986). Cross-cultural variations in relationship rules. *International Journal of Psychology*, 21, 287–315.

Argyle, M., Henderson, M., & Furnham, A. (1985). The rules of social relationships. *British Journal of Social Psychology*, 24, 125–139.

Arnetz, B.B., Wasserman, J., & Petrini, B. (1987). Immune function in unemployed women. *Psychosomatic Medicine*, 49, 3–12.

Arnold, J., Cooper, C.L., & Robertson, I.T. (1995). *Work psychology: Understanding human behaviour in the workplace (2nd Edn.)*. London: Pitman Publishing.

Aronoff, J. (1967). *Psychological needs and cultural systems: A case study*. Princeton, NJ: Van Nostrand.

Aronson, E., Blaney, N., Stephan, C., Sikes, J., & Snapp, M. (1978). *The jigsaw classroom*. Beverly Hills, CA: Sage.

Aronson, E., & Osherow, N. (1980). Co-operation, prosocial behaviour, and academic performance: Experiments in the desegregated classroom. In L. Bickerman (Ed.), *Applied social psychology annual*. Beverley Hills, CA: Sage.

Arterberry, M., Yonas, A., & Bensen, A.S. (1989). Self-produced locomotion and the development of responsiveness to linear perspective and texture gradients. *Developmental Psychology*, 25, 976–982.

Asch, S.E. (1951). Effects of group pressure on the modification and distortion of judgements. In H. Guetzkow (Ed.), *Groups, leadership and men*. Pittsburgh: Carnegie.

Asch, S.E. (1956). Studies of independence and conformity: A minority of one against a unanimous majority. *Psychological Monographs*, 70 (Whole no. 416).

Aserinsky, E., & Kleitman, N. (1955). Two types of ocular motility occurring in sleep. *Journal of Applied Physiology*, 8, 1–10.

Ashley, W.R., Harper, R.S., & Runyon, D.L. (1951). The perceived size of coins in normal and hypnotically induced economic states. *American Journal of Psychology*, 64, 564–572.

Ashton, H. (1997). Benzodiazepine dependency. In A. Baum, S. Newman, J. Weinman, R. West, & C. McManus (Eds.), *Cambridge handbook of psychology, health and medicine*. Cambridge: Cambridge University Press.

Atchley, R. (1977). *The sociology of retirement*. Cambridge, MA: Schenkman.

Atkinson, R.C., & Raugh, M.R. (1975). An application of the mnemonic keyword method to the acquisition of a Russian vocabulary. *Journal of Experimental Psychology: Human Learning and Memory*, 104, 126–133.

Atkinson, R.C., & Shiffrin, R.M. (1968). Human memory: A proposed system and its control processes. In K.W. Spence and J.T. Spence (Eds.), *The psychology of learning and motivation, Vol. 2*. London: Academic Press.

Atkinson, R.L., Atkinson, R.C., Smith, E.E., & Bem, D.J. (1993). *Introduction to psychology (11th Edn.)*. New York: Harcourt Brace College Publishers.

Aubry, T., Tefft, B., & Kingsbury, N. (1990). Behavioural and psychological consequences of unemployment in blue-collar couples. *Journal of Community Psychology*, 18, 99–109.

Ax, A.F. (1953). The physiological differentiation between fear and anger in humans. *Psychosomatic Medicine*, 15, 433–442.

Axelrod, R. (1984). *The evolution of cooperation*. New York: Basic Books.

Axelrod, R., & Hamilton, W.D. (1981). The evolution of cooperation. *Science*, 211, 1390–1396.

Axline, V. (1971). *Dibs: In search of self.* Harmondsworth, UK: Penguin.

Ayllon, T., & Azrin, N.H. (1968). *The token economy: A motivational system for therapy and rehabilitation.* New York: Appleton-Century-Crofts.

Ayman, R., & Chemers, M.M. (1983). The relationship of supervisory behaviour ratings to work group effectiveness and subordinate satisfaction among Iranian managers. *Journal of Applied Psychology, 68,* 338–341.

Baars, B.J. (1997). Consciousness versus attention, perception, and working memory. *Consciousness and Cognition, 5,* 363–371.

Bachen, E., Cohen, S., & Marsland, A.L. (1997). Psychoimmunology. In A. Baum, S. Newman, J. Weinman, R. West, & C. McManus (Eds.), *Cambridge handbook of psychology, health, and medicine.* Cambridge: Cambridge University Press.

Baddeley, A.D. (1990). *Human memory: Theory and practice.* Hove, UK: Psychology Press.

Baddeley, A.D., & Hitch, G.J. (1974). Working memory. In G. H. Bower (Ed.), *The psychology of learning and motivation, Vol. 8.* London: Academic Press.

Baddeley, A.D., & Lewis, V.J. (1981). Inner active processes in reading: The inner voice, the inner ear and the inner eye. In A.M. Lesgold & C.A. Perfetti (Eds.), *Interactive processes in reading.* Hillsdale, NJ: Lawrence Erlbaum Associates Inc.

Baddeley, A.D., Thomson, N., & Buchanan, M. (1975). Word length and the structure of short-term memory. *Journal of Verbal Learning and Verbal Behavior, 14,* 575–589.

Baddeley, A.D., & Warrington, E.K. (1970). Amnesia and the distinction between long- and short-term memory. *Journal of Verbal Learning and Verbal Behavior, 9,* 176–189.

Baddeley, A.D., & Wilson, B. (1985). Phonological coding and short-term memory in patients without speech. *Journal of Memory and Language, 24,* 490–502.

Baillargeon, R., & Graber, M. (1988). Evidence of location memory in 8-month-old infants in a nonsearch AB task. *Developmental Psychology, 24,* 502–511.

Bakeman, R., & Brownlee, J. (1980). The strategic use of parallel play: A sequential analysis. *Child Development, 51,* 873–878.

Bales, R.F. (1950). *Interaction process analysis: A method for the study of small groups.* Reading, MA: Addison-Wesley.

Bales, R.F., & Slater, P.E. (1955). Role differentiation in small decision-making groups. In T. Parsons & R.F Bales (Eds.), *Family, socialisation and interaction process.* Glencoe: Free Press.

Banaji, M.R., & Crowder, R.G. (1989). The bankruptcy of everyday memory. *American Psychologist, 44,* 1185–1193.

Bandura, A. (1965). Influences of models' reinforcement contingencies on the acquisition of initiative responses. *Journal of Personality and Social Psychology, 1,* 589–593.

Bandura, A. (1973). *Aggression: A social learning analysis.* Englewood Cliffs, NJ: Prentice-Hall.

Bandura, A. (1977). Self-efficacy: Toward a unifying theory of behavioural change. *Psychological Review, 84,* 191–215.

Bandura, A. (1986). *Social foundations of thought and action: A social cognitive theory.* Englewood Cliffs, NJ: Prentice-Hall.

Bandura, A., & Cervone, D. (1983). Self-evaluation and self-efficacy mechanisms governing the motivational effect of goal systems. *Journal of Personality and Social Psychology, 45,* 1017–1028.

Bandura, A., & McDonald, F.J. (1963). The influence of social reinforcement and the behaviour of models in shaping children's moral judgements. *Journal of Abnormal and Social Psychology, 67,* 274–281.

Bandura, A., Ross, D., & Ross, S.A. (1963). Transmission of aggression through imitation of aggressive models. *Journal of Abnormal and Social Psychology, 66,* 3–11.

Banuazizi, A., & Mohavedi, S. (1973). Interpersonal dynamics in a simulated prison: A methodological analysis. *American Psychologist, 30,* 152–160.

Baran, S.J. (1979). Television drama as a facilitator of pro-social behaviour. *Journal of Broadcasting, 23,* 277–285.

Barber, J.P., & DeRubeis, R.J. (1989). On second thought: Where the action is in cognitive therapy for depression. *Cognitive Therapy and Research, 13,* 441–457.

Barber, T.X. (1976). *Pitfalls in human research.* Oxford: Pergamon.

Barkley, R.A., DuPaul, G.J., & McMurray, M.B. (1990a). A comprehensive evaluation of attention deficit disorder with and without hyperactivity defined by research criteria. *Journal of Consulting and Clinical Psychology, 58,* 775–789.

Barkley, R.A., Fischer, M., Edelbrock, C.S., & Smallish, L. (1990b). The adolescent outcome of hyperactive children diagnosed by research criteria: 1. An 8 year prospective follow-up study. *Journal of the American Academy of Child and Adolescent Psychiatry, 29,* 546–557.

Barkley, R.A., Karlsson, J., Pollard, S., & Murphy, J.U. (1985). Developmental changes in the mother–child interactions of hyperactive boys: Effects of two dose levels of Ritalin. *Journal of Child Psychology and Psychiatry, 26,* 705–715.

Barkley, R.A., Ullman, D.G., Otto, L., & Brecht, J.M. (1977). The effects of sex typing and sex appropriateness of modelled behaviour on children's imitation. *Child Development, 48,* 721–725.

Barlow, D.H., & Durand, V.M. (1995). *Abnormal psychology: An integrative approach.* New York: Brooks/Cole.

Barnard, C.J. (1980). *Animal behaviour: Ecology and evolution.* London: Croom Helm.

Barnier, G. (1989). L'effet-tuteur dans des situations mettant en jeu des rapports spatiaux chez des enfants de 7–8 ans en interactions dyadiques avec des pairs de 6–7 ans. *European Journal of Psychology of Education, 4,* 385–399.

Baron, R.A. (1973). Threatened retaliation from the victim as an inhibitor of physical aggression. *Journal of Research in Personality, 7,* 103–115.

Baron, R.A. (1977). *Human aggression.* New York: Plenum.

Baron, R.A., & Bell, P.A. (1976). Aggression and heat: The influence of ambient temperature, negative affect, and a cooling drink on physical aggression. *Journal of Personality and Social Psychology, 33,* 245–255.

Baron, R.A., & Byrne, D. (1991). *Social psychology: Understanding human interaction (6th Edn.).* Boston: Allyn & Bacon.

Baron, R.A., & Kepner, C.R. (1970). Model's behaviour and attraction toward the model as determinants of adult aggressive behaviour. *Journal of Personality and Social Psychology, 14,* 335–344.

Baron, R.A., & Richardson, D.R. (1993). *Human aggression (2nd Edn.).* New York: Plenum.

Baron-Cohen, S. (1994). Infantile autism. In A.M. Colman (Ed.), *Companion encyclopedia of psychology, Vol. 2.* London: Routledge.

Baron-Cohen, S., Leslie, A.M., & Frith, U. (1985). Does the autistic child have a "theory of mind"? *Cognition, 21,* 37–46.

Barrett, J.E. (1979). The relationship of life events to the onset of neurotic disorders. In J.E. Barrett (Ed.), *Stress and mental disorder*. New York: Raven Press.

Barrett, M., & Short, J. (1992). Images of European people in a group of 5–10 year old English school children. *British Journal of Developmental Psychology, 10*, 339–363.

Barrett, P.T., & Kline, P. (1982). An item and radial parcel analysis of the 16PF questionnaire. *Personality and Individual Differences, 3*, 259–270.

Barry, H., Bacon, M.K., & Child, I.L. (1957). A cross-cultural survey of some sex differences in socialisation. *Journal of Abnormal and Social Psychology, 55*, 327–332.

Bartlett, F.C. (1932). *Remembering: A study in experimental and social psychology*. Cambridge: Cambridge University Press.

Bates, J. E., Maslin, C.A., & Frankel, K.A. (1985). Attachment security, mother–child interaction, and temperament as predictors of behaviour-problem ratings at age three years. In I. Bretherton & E. Waters (Eds.), *Growing points of attachment theory and research*. Monographs of the Society for Research in Child Development, 50, No. 209.

Bateson, G., Jackson, D.D., Haley, J., & Weakland, J. (1956). Toward a theory of schizophrenia. *Behavioral Science, 1*, 251–264.

Bateson, P. (1986). When to experiment on animals. *New Scientist, 109*, 30–32.

Batson, C.D. (1987). Prosocial motivation: Is it ever truly altruistic? In L. Berkowitz (Ed.), *Advances in experimental social psychology, Vol. 20*. New York: Academic Press.

Batson, C.D., Batson, J.G., Slingsby, J.K., Harrell, K.L., Peekna, H.M., & Todd, R.M. (1991). Empathic joy and the empathy-altruism hypothesis. *Journal of Personality and Social Psychology, 61*, 413–426.

Batson, C.D., et al. (1978). Failure to help when in a hurry: Callousness or conflict? *Personality and Social Psychology Bulletin, 4*, 97–101.

Batson, C.D., Duncan, B.D., Ackerman, P., Buckley, T., & Birch, K. (1981). Is empathic emotion a source of altruistic motivation? *Journal of Personality and Social Psychology, 40*, 290–302.

Batson, C.D., Dyck, J.L., Brandt, J.R., Batson, J.G., Powell, A.L., McMaster, M.R., & Griffit, C. (1988). Five studies testing new egotistic alternativies to the empathy-altruism hypothesis. *Journal of Personality and Social Psychology, 55*, 52–77.

Batson, C.D., & Oleson, K.C. (1991). Current status of the empathy-altruism hypothesis. In M.S. Clark (Ed.), *Prosocial behaviour: Review of personality and social psychology, Vol. 12*. Newbury Park, CA: Sage.

Batson, C.D., O'Quinn, K., Fultz, J., Vanderplas, N., & Isen, A.M. (1983). Influence of self-reported distress and empathy on egoistic versus altruistic motivation to help. *Journal of Personality and Social Psychology, 45*, 706–718.

Baumrind, D. (1980). New directions in socialisation research. *American Psychologist, 35*, 639–652.

Beaman, A.L., Klentz, B., Diener, E., & Svanum, S. (1979). Self-awareness and transgression in children: Two field studies. *Journal of Personality and Social Psychology, 37*, 1835–1846.

Beck, A.T. (1976). *Cognitive therapy of the emotional disorders*. New York: New American Library.

Beck, A.T., & Clark, D.A. (1988). Anxiety and depression: An information processing perspective. *Anxiety Research, 1*, 23–36.

Beck, A.T., & Emery, G. (1985). *Anxiety disorders and phobias*. New York: Basic Books.

Beck, A.T., Rush, A.J., Shaw, B.F., & Emery, G. (1979). *Cognitive therapy of depression*. New York: Guilford Press.

Beck, A.T., & Ward, C.H. (1961). Dreams of depressed patients: Characteristic themes in manifest content. *Archives of General Psychiatry, 5*, 462–467.

Beck, A.T., & Weishaar, M.E. (1989). Cognitive therapy. In R.J. Corsini & D. Wedding (Eds.), *Current psychotherapies*. Itacca, IL: Peacock.

Beck, I.L., & Carpenter, P.A. (1986). Cognitive approaches to understanding reading. *American Psychologist, 41*, 1088–1105.

Becker, J.M.T. (1977). A learning analysis of the development of peer-oriented behaviour in nine-month-old infants. *Developmental Psychology, 13*, 481–491.

Bee, H. (1994). *Lifespan development*. New York: HarperCollins.

Bee, H.L., & Mitchell, S.K. (1984). *The developing person: A life-span approach (2nd Edn.)*. New York: Harper & Row.

Beehler, B.M., & Foster, M.S. (1988). Hotshots, hotspots, and female preference in the organisation of lek mating systems. *American Naturalist, 14*, 203–219.

Behrend, D.A., Harris, L.L., & Cartwright, K.B. (1992). Morphological cues to verb meaning: Verb inflections and the initial mapping of verb meanings. *Journal of Child Language, 22*, 89–106.

Bellrose, F.C. (1958). Celestial orientation in wild mallards. *Bird Banding, 29*, 75–90.

Belsky, J., & Rovine, M. (1987). Temperament and attachment security in the Strange Situation: A rapprochement. *Child Development, 58*, 787–795.

Bem, S.L. (1974). The measurement of psychological androgyny. *Journal of Consulting and Clinical Psychology, 42*, 155–162.

Bem, S.L. (1985). Androgyny and gender schema theory: A conceptual and empirical integration. In T.B. Snodegegger (Ed.), *Nebraska symposium on motivation: Psychology and gender*. Lincoln, NE: University of Nebraska Press.

Benderly, B.L. (1980). The great ape debate. *Science, 174*, 1139–1141.

Benson, D.F. (1985). Aphasia. In K.M. Heilman & E. Valenstein (Eds.), *Clinical neuropsychology*. Oxford: Oxford University Press.

Ben-Tovim, M.V., & Crisp, A.H. (1979). Personality and mental state within anorexia nervosa. *Journal of Psychosomatic Research, 23*, 321–325.

Bereiter, C., Burtis, P.J., & Scardamalia, M. (1988). Cognitive operations in constructing main points in written composition. *Journal of Memory and Language, 27*, 261–278.

Bereiter, C., & Scardamalia, M. (1987). *The psychology of written composition*. Hillsdale, NJ: Lawrence Erlbaum Associates Inc.

Bergen, D.J., & Williams, J.E. (1991). Sex stereotypes in the United States revisited. *Sex Roles, 24*, 413–423.

Berger, J. (1983). Induced abortion and social factors in wild horses. *Nature, 303*, 59–61.

Bergin, A.E. (1971). The evaluation of therapeutic outcomes. In A.E. Bergin & S.L. Garfield (Eds.), *Handbook of psychotherapy and behaviour change*. New York: Wiley.

Berk, L.E. (1994). Why children talk to themselves. *Scientific American, November*, 60–65.

Berkman, L.F., & Syme, S.L. (1979). Social networks, host resistance, and mortality: A nine year follow-up study of

Alameda County residents. *American Journal of Epidemiology, 109,* 186–204.

Berko, J. (1958). The child's learning of English morphology. *Word, 14,* 150–177.

Berkowitz, L. (1968). Impulse, aggression and the gun. *Psychology Today, September,* 18–22.

Berkowitz, L. (1989). Frustration-aggression hypothesis: Examination and reformulation. *Psychological Bulletin, 106,* 59–73.

Berkowitz, L., & LePage, A. (1967). Weapons as aggression-eliciting stimuli. *Journal of Personality and Social Psychology, 7,* 202–207.

Berkun, M.M., Bialek, H.M., Kern, R.P., & Yagi, K. (1962). Experimental studies of psychological stress in man. *Psychological Monographs, 76,* No. 15.

Bermond, B., Nieuwenhuyse, B., Fasotti, L., & Schwerman, J. (1991). Spinal cord lesions, peripheral feedback, and intensities of emotional feelings. *Cognition and Emotion, 5,* 201–220.

Berndt, R., & Sternberg, H. (1969). Alters und Geschlechtsunterschiede in der dispersion des Trauerschnappers *(Ficedula hypoleuca). Journal Ornithologie, 110,* 22–26.

Bernstein, B. (1961). Social class and linguistic development. In A.H. Halsey, J. Flaud, & C.A. Anderson (Eds.), *Education, economy and society.* London: Collier-Macmillan.

Bernstein, B. (1973). *Class, codes and control.* London: Paladin.

Berry, D.C., & Broadbent, D.E. (1984). On the relationship between task performance and associated verbalisable knowledge. *Quarterly Journal of Experimental Psychology, 36A,* 209–231.

Berry, D.T.R., & Webb, W.B. (1983). State measures and sleep stages. *Psychological Reports, 52,* 807–812.

Berry, J.W. (1969). On cross-cultural comparability. *International Journal of Psychology, 4,* 119–128.

Berry, J.W. (1974). Radical cultural relativism and the concept of intelligence. In J.W. Berry & P.R. Dasen (Eds.), *Culture and cognition: Readings in cross-cultural psychology.* London: Methuen.

Berry, J.W. (1997). Acculturation strategies. In A. Baum, S. Newman, J. Weinman, R. West, & C. McManus (Eds.), *Cambridge handbook of psychology, health, and medicine.* Cambridge: Cambridge University Press.

Berryman, J.C., Hargreaves, D., Herbert, M., & Taylor, A. (1991). *Developmental psychology and you.* Leicester: BPS Books.

Bertelsen, B., Harvald, B., & Hauge, M. (1977). A Danish twin study of manic-depressive disorders. *British Journal of Psychiatry, 130,* 330–351.

Berthold, P., Wiltschko, W., Miltenberger, H., & Querner, W. (1990). Genetic transmission of migratory behaviour into a non-migrating population. *Experientia, 46,* 107–108.

Bertram, B.C.R. (1980). Vigilance and group size in ostriches. *Animal Behaviour, 28,* 278–286.

Bettelheim, B. (1973). Bringing up children. *Ladies Home Journal, 90,* 28.

Beutler, L.E., Cargo, M., & Arizmendi, T.G. (1986). Therapist variables in psychotherapy process and outcome. In S.L. Garfield & A.E. Bergin (Eds.), *Handbook of psychotherapy and behaviour change (3rd Edn.).* Chichester: Wiley.

Biderman, A.D. (1960). Social psychological needs and "involuntary" behaviour as illustrated by compliance in interrogation. *Sociometry, 23,* 120–147.

Biederman, I. (1987). Recognition-by-components: A theory of human image understanding. *Psychological Review, 94,* 115–147.

Biederman, I., & Cooper, E. (1991). Priming contour-deleted images: Evidence for intermediate representations in visual object recognition. *Cognitive Psychology, 23,* 393–419.

Biederman, I., Glass, A.L., & Stacy, E.W. (1973). Searching for objects in real-world scenes. *Journal of Experimental Psychology, 97,* 22–27.

Biederman, I., Ju, G., & Clapper, J. (1985). *The perception of partial objects.* Unpublished manuscript, State University of New York at Buffalo.

Binet, A., & Simon, T. (1916). *The development of intelligence in children.* Baltimore: Williams & Wilkins.

Birch, H.G. (1945). The relationship of previous experience to insightful problem solving. *Journal of Comparative Psychology, 38,* 267–283.

Birkhead, T.R., & Moller, A.P. (1992). *Sperm competition in birds: Evolutionary causes and consequences.* London: Academic Press.

Bjorklund, A., & Lindvall, O. (1986). Catecholaminergic brainstem regulatory systems. In V. B. Mountcastle, F.E. Bloom, & S.R. Geiger (Eds.), *Handbook of physiology: The nervous system, Vol. 4.* Bethesda, MD: American Psychological Society.

Bjorkqvist, K., Lagerspetz, K.M.J., & Kaukiainen, A. (1992). Do girls manipulate and boys fight? Developmental trends regarding direct and indirect aggression. *Aggressive Behavior, 18,* 157–166.

Blake, M.J.F. (1967). Time of day effects on performance on a range of tasks. *Psychonomic Science, 9,* 349–350.

Blake, W. (1973). The influence of race on diagnosis. *Smith College Studies in Social Work, 43,* 184–192.

Blakemore, C. (1988). *The mind machine.* London: BBC Publications.

Blasdel, G.G. (1992). Orientation selectivity, preference, and continuity in monkey striate cortex. *Journal of Neuroscience, 12,* 3139–3161.

Blasi, A. (1980). Bridging moral cognition and moral action: A critical review of the literature. *Psychological Bulletin, 88,* 1–45.

Blinkhorn, S., & Johnson, C. (1990). The insignificance of personality testing. *Nature, 348,* 671–672.

Blumenthal, M., Kahn, R.L., Andrews, F.M., & Head, K.B. (1972). *Justifying violence: The attitudes of American men.* Ann Arbor: Institute for Social Research.

Blumstein, P., & Schwartz, P. (1983). *American couples: Money, work, sex.* New York: Morrow.

Bock, K., & Levelt, W. (1994). Language production: Grammatical encoding. In M.A. Gernsbacher (Ed.), *Handbook of psycholinguistics.* London: Academic Press.

Bodenhausen, G.V. (1988). Stereotypic biases in social decision making: Testing process models of stereotype use. *Journal of Personality and Social Psychology, 55,* 726–737.

Bogdonoff, M.D., Klein, E.J., Shaw, D.M., & Back, K.W. (1961). The modifying effect of conforming behaviour upon lipi responses accompanying CNS arousal. *Clinical Research, 9,* 135.

Bohannon, J.N., & Warren-Leubecker, A. (1989). Theoretical approaches to language acquisition. In J.B. Gleason (Ed.), *The development of language.* Columbus, OH: Merrill.

Bohannon, P. (1970). *Divorce and after.* New York: Doubleday.

Bokert, E. (1970) *The effects of thirst and related auditory stimulation on dream reports.* Paper presented to the Association for the Physiological Study of Sleep, Washington, DC.

Bond, C.F., DiCandia, C.G., & MacKinnon, J.R. (1988). Responses to violence in a psychiatric setting: The role of the patient's race. *Personality and Social Psychology Bulletin, 14,* 448–458.

Bond, R., & Smith, P. B. (1993). Culture and conformity: A meta-analysis of studies using Asch's (1952b, 1956) line judgment task. *Psychological Bulletin, 119,* 111–137.

Bond, S., & Cash, T.F. (1992). Black beauty: Skin colour and body images among African-American college women. *Journal of Applied Social Psychology, 22,* 874–888.

Boring, E.G. (1957). *A history of experimental psychology (2nd Edn.).* New York: Appleton-Century-Crofts.

Bornstein, M.H., Toda, S., Azuma, H., Tamis-Lemonda, C., & Ogino, M. (1990). Mother and infant activity and interaction in Japan and in the United States: II. A comparative microanalysis of naturalistic exchanges focused on the organisation of infant attention. *International Journal of Behavioral Development, 13,* 289–308.

Bossard, J. (1932). Residential propinquity as a factor in marriage selection. *American Journal of Sociology, 38,* 219–224.

Bouchard, T.J., Lykken, D.T., McGue, M., Segal, N.L., & Tellegen, A. (1990). Sources of human psychological differences: The Minnesota study of twins reared apart. *Science, 250,* 223–228.

Bouchard, T.J., & McGue, M. (1981). Familial studies of intelligence: A review. *Science, 212,* 1055–1059.

Bourke, P.A., Duncan, J., & Nimmo-Smith, I. (1996). A general factor involved in dual-task performance decrement. *Quarterly Journal of Experimental Psychology, 49A,* 525–545.

Bower, G.H., Black, J.B., & Turner, T.J. (1979). Scripts in memory for text. *Cognitive Psychology, 11,* 177–220.

Bower, G.H., Clark, M.C., Lesgold, A.M., & Winzenz, D. (1969). Hierarchical retrieval schemes in recall of categorised word lists. *Journal of Verbal Learning and Verbal Behavior, 8,* 323–343.

Bower, T.G.R. (1966). The visual world of infants. *Scientific American, 215,* 80–92.

Bower, T.G.R. (1971). The object in the world of the infant. *Scientific American, 225,* 31–38.

Bower, T.G.R. (1979). *Human development.* San Francisco: W.H. Freeman

Bower, T.G.R. (1982). *Development in infancy (2nd Edn.).* San Francisco: W.H. Freeman.

Bower, T.G.R., Broughton, J.M., & Moore, M.K. (1970). The co-ordination of visual and tactual input in infants. *Perception & Psychophysics, 8,* 51–53.

Bower, T.G.R., & Wishart, J.G. (1972). The effects of motor skill on object permanence. *Cognition, 1,* 165–172.

Bowers, K.S. (1973). Situationism in psychology: An analysis and a critique. *Psychological Review, 80,* 307–336.

Bowers, K.S. (1983). *Hypnosis for the seriously curious.* New York: Norton.

Bowlby, J. (1946). *Forty-four juvenile thieves.* London: Balliere, Tindall & Cox.

Bowlby, J. (1951). *Maternal care and mental health.* Geneva: World Health Organisation.

Bowlby, J. (1958). The nature of the child's tie to his mother. *International Journal of Psycho-Analysis, 39,* 350–373.

Bowlby, J. (1969). *Attachment and love, Vol. 1: Attachment.* London: Hogarth.

Bowlby, J. (1973). *Attachment and loss, Vol. 3.* Harmondsworth: Penguin.

Boycott, B.B. (1965). Learning in the octopus. *Scientific American, 212,* 42–50.

Bozarth, M.A., & Wise, R.A. (1985). Toxicity associated with long-term intravenous heroin and cocaine self-administration in the rat. *Journal of the American Medical Association, 254,* 81–83.

Bracht, G.H., & Glass, G.V. (1968). The external validity of experiments. *American Educational Research Journal, 5,* 437–474.

Bradbard, M.R., Martin, C.L., Endsley, R.C., & Halverson, C.F. (1986). Influence of sex stereotypes on children's exploration and memory: A competence versus performance distinction. *Developmental Psychology, 22,* 481–486.

Bradburn, N. (1969). *The structure of psychological well-being.* Chicago: Aldine.

Bradshaw, J.L., & Sherlock, D. (1982). Bugs and faces in the two visual fields: The analytic/holistic processing dichotomy and task sequencing. *Cortex, 18,* 211–226.

Bradshaw, P.W., Ley, P., Kincey, J.A., & Bradshaw, J. (1975). Recall of medical advice: Comprehensibility and specificity. *British Journal of Social and Clinical Psychology, 14,* 55–62.

Braine, M.D.S. (1963). The ontogeny of English phrase structure: The first phase. *Language, 39,* 1–13.

Braine, M.D.S., Reiser, B.J., & Rumain, B. (1984). Some empirical justification for a theory of natural propositional logic. In G. H. Bower (Ed.), *The psychology of learning and motivation, Vol. 18.* New York: Academic Press.

Brainerd, C.J. (1983). Modifiability of cognitive development. In S. Meadows (Ed), *Developing thinking: Approaches to children's cognitive development.* London: Methuen.

Brandsma, J.M., Maultsby, M.C., & Welsh, R. (1978). Self-help techniques in the treatment of alcoholism. Cited in G.T. Wilson & K.D. O'Leary, *Principles of behaviour therapy.* Englewood Cliffs, NJ: Prentice-Hall.

Bransford, J.D. (1979). *Human cognition: Learning, understanding and remembering.* Belmont, CA: Wadsworth.

Bransford, J.D., Barclay, J.R., & Franks, J.J. (1972). Sentence memory: A constructive versus interpretive approach. *Cognitive Psychology, 3,* 193–209.

Bransford, J.D., Franks, J.J., Morris, C.D., & Stein, B.S. (1979). Some general constraints on learning and memory research. In L.S. Cermak & F.I.M. Craik (Eds.), *Levels of processing in human memory.* Hillsdale, NJ: Lawrence Erlbaum Associates Inc.

Bransford, J.D., & Johnson, M.K. (1972). Contextual prerequisites for understanding: Some investigations of comprehension and recall. *Journal of Verbal Learning and Verbal Behavior, 11,* 717–726.

Breger, L., Hunter, I., & Lane, R.W. (1971). The effect of stress on dreams. *Psychological Issues, 7,* 1–213.

Brehm, S.S. (1992). *Intimate relationships (2nd Edn.).* New York: McGraw-Hill.

Breland, K., & Breland, M. (1961). The misbehaviour of organisms. *American Psychologist, 61,* 681–684.

Brennan, S.E. (1990). *Seeking and providing evidence for mutual understanding.* Unpublished PhD thesis. Stanford University, Stanford, CA.

Brett, D.J., & Cantor, J. (1988). The portrayal of men and women in US television commercials: A recent content analysis and trends over 15 years. *Sex Roles, 18*, 595–609.

Brewer, M.B., & Miller, N. (1984). Beyond the contact hypothesis: Theoretical perspectives on desegregation. In N. Miller & M.B. Brewer (Eds.), *Groups in contact: The psychology of desegregation*. Orlando, FL: Academic Press.

Brewin, C.R. (1988). *Cognitive foundations of clinical psychology*. Hove, UK: Psychology Press.

Brewin, C.R., Andrews, B., & Gotlib, I.H. (1993). Psychopathology and early experience: A reappraisal of retrospective reports. *Psychological Bulletin, 113*, 82–98.

Brickman, P., Rabinowitz, V.C., Karuza, J., Coates, D., Cohn, E., & Kidder, L. (1982). Models of helping and coping. *American Psychologist, 37*, 368–384.

Brief, A.P., Burke, M.J., George, J.M., Robinson, B.S., & Webster, J. (1991). Should negative affectivity remain an unmeasured variable in the study of job stress? *Journal of Applied Psychology, 73*, 193–198.

Brien, D. (Ed.) (1992). *Dictionary of British Sign Language/English*. London: Faber & Faber.

Brigham, J.C. (1971). Ethnic stereotypes. *Psychological Bulletin, 76*, 15–38.

Bright, M. (1984). *Animal language*. London: BBC Publications.

Brill, N.Q., & Christie, R.L. (1974). A theory of visual stability across saccadic eye movements. *Behavioral and Brain Sciences, 17*, 247–292.

Brinkman, C. (1984). Supplementary motor area of the monkey's cerebral cortex: Short- and long-term deficits after unilateral ablation and the effects of subsequent callosal section. *Journal of Neuroscience, 4*, 918–929.

British Psychological Society (1993). *Code of conduct, ethical principles and guidelines*. Leicester: British Psychological Society.

Broadbent, D.E. (1958). *Perception and communication*. Oxford: Pergamon.

Broadbent, D.E. (1982). Task combination and selective intake of information. *Acta Psychologica, 50*, 253–290.

Broca, P. (1861). Remarques sur le siège de la faculté du langage articulé suivées d'une observation d'aphémie. *Bulletin de la Société Anatomique, 6*, 330–357.

Brody, G.H., & Shaffer, D.R. (1982). Contributions of parents and peers to children's moral socialisation. *Developmental Review, 2*, 31–75.

Brody, N. (1988). *Personality: In search of individuality*. London: Academic Press.

Bronfenbrenner, U. (1970). *Two worlds of childhood: US and USSR*. New York: Russell Sage Foundation.

Bronfenbrenner, U. (1979). *The ecology of human development: Experiments by nature and design*. Cambridge, MA: Cambridge University Press.

Broverman, I.K., Broverman, D.M., Clarkson, F.E., Rosencrantz, P.S., & Vogel, S.R. (1981). Sex role stereotypes and clinical judgements of mental health. In E. Howell & M. Bayes (Eds.), *Women and mental health*. New York: Basic Books.

Brown, C.R., & Brown, M.B. (1986). Ectoparasitism as a cost of coloniality in cliff swallows (*Hirundo pyrrhonota*). *Ecology, 67*, 1206–1218.

Brown, G.W. (1989). Depression. In G.W. Brown & T.O. Harris (Eds.), *Life events and illness*. New York: Guilford Press.

Brown, G.W., & Harris, T. (1978). *Social origins of depression*. London: Tavistock.

Brown, G.W., & Harris, T. (1982). Fall-off in the reporting of life events. *Social Psychiatry, 17*, 23.

Brown, J. (1991). Staying fit and staying well: Physical fitness as a moderator of life stress. *Journal of Personality and Social Psychology, 60*, 555–561.

Brown, J.L. (1964). The evolution of diversity in avian territorial systems. *Wilson Bulletin, 76*, 160–169.

Brown, J.S., & Burton, R.D. (1978). Diagnostic model for procedural bugs in basic mathematical skills. *Cognitive Science, 2*, 155–192.

Brown, M. (1993). Sequential and simultaneous choice processes in the radial arm maze. In T. Zentall (Ed.), *Animal cognition: A tribute to Donald A. Riley*. Hillsdale, NJ: Lawrence Elrbaum Associates Inc.

Brown, R. (1965). *Social psychology*. New York: Free Press.

Brown, R. (1973). *A first language: The early stages*. London: George Allen & Unwin.

Brown, R. (1978). Divided we fall: An analysis of relations between sections of a factory work-force. In H. Tajfel (Ed.), *Differentiation between social groups: Studies in the social psychlogy of intergroup relations*. London: Academic Press.

Brown, R. (1988). Intergroup relations. In M. Hewstone, W. Stroebe, J.P. Codol, & G.M. Stephenson (Eds.), *Introduction to social psychology*. Oxford: Blackwell.

Brown, R. (1996). Intergroup relations. In M. Hewstone, W. Stroebe, & G.M. Stephenson (Eds.), *Introduction to social psychology (2nd edn.)*. Oxford: Blackwell.

Brown, R., Cazden, C., & Bellugi, U. (1969). The child's grammar from I to III. In J.P. Hill (Ed.), *Minnesota symposium on child psychology, Vol. 2*. Minneapolis, MI: University of Minnesota Press.

Brown, R., Fraser, C., & Bellugi, U. (1964). The acquisition of language. *Monographs of the Society for Research in Child Development, 29*, 92.

Brown, R., & Kulik, J. (1977). Flashbulb memories. *Cognition, 5*, 73–99.

Brown, R.C., & Tedeschi, J.T. (1976). Determinants of perceived aggression. *Journal of Social Psychology, 100*, 77–87.

Brown, R.J., & Wade, G.S. (1987). Superordinate goals and intergroup behaviour. In J.C. Turner & H. Giles (Eds.), *Intergroup behaviour*. Oxford: Blackwell.

Brown, V., & Geis, F.L. (1984). Turning lead into gold: Evaluations of men and women leaders and the alchemy of social consensus. *Journal of Personality and Social Psychology, 46*, 811–824.

Brownell, C.A. (1990). Peer social skills in toddlers: Competencies and constraints illustrated by same-age and mixed-age interaction. *Child Development, 61*, 838–848.

Brownell, C.A., & Carriger, M.S. (1990). Changes in cooperation and self–other differentiation during the second year. *Child Development, 61*, 1164–1174.

Bruce, M.L., Takeuchi, D.T., & Leaf, P.J. (1991). Poverty and psychiatric status: Longitudinal evidence from the New Haven Epidemiologic Catchment Area Study. *Archives of General Psychiatry, 48*, 470–474.

Bruce, V., & Green, P.R. (1990). *Visual perception: Physiology, psychology, and ecology (2nd Edn.)*. Hove, UK: Psychology Press.

Bruce, V., Green, P.R., & Georgeson, M.A. (1996). *Visual perception: Physiology, psychology, and ecology (3rd Edn.)*. Hove, UK: Psychology Press.

Bruner, J.S., & Goodman, C.D. (1947). Value and need as organising factors in perception. *Journal of Abnormal and Social Psychology, 42*, 33–44.

Bruner, J.S., Olver, R.R., & Greenfield, P.M. (1966). *Studies in cognitive growth*. New York: Wiley.

Bruner, J.S., Postman, L., & Rodrigues, J. (1951). Expectations and the perception of colour. *American Journal of Psychology, 64*, 216–227.

Bruno, N., & Cutting, J.E. (1988). Mini-modularity and the perception of layout. *Journal of Experimental Psychology: General, 117*, 161–170.

Bryant, P.E., & Bradley, L. (1985). *Children's reading problems*. Oxford: Blackwell.

Buchsbaum, M.S., Kessler, R., King, A., Johnson, J., & Cappelletti, J. (1984). Simultaneous cerebral glucography with positron emission tomography and topographic electroencephalography. In G. Pfurtscheller, E.J. Jonkman, & F. H. Lopes da Silva (Eds.), *Brain ischemia: Quantitative EEG and imaging techniques*. Amsterdam: Elsevier.

Buehler, R., Griffin, D., & Ross, M. (1994). Exploring the "planning fallacy": Why people underestimate their task completion times. *Journal of Personality and Social Psychology, 67*, 366–381.

Bunker-Rohrbaugh, J. (1980). *Women: Psychology's puzzle*. Brighton: Harvester Press.

Burgess, R.L., & Wallin, P. (1953). Marital happiness of parents and their children's attitudes to them. *American Sociological Review, 18*, 424–431.

Burghardt, G.M. (1970). Defining "communication." In J.W. Johnston, D.G. Moulton, & A. turk (Eds.), *Communication by chemical signals*. New York: Appleton-Century-Crofts.

Burk, T. (1984). Male–male interactions in Caribbean fruit flies, *Anastrepha suspensa* (Loew) (Diptera: Tephritidae): Territorial fights and signalling stimulation. *Florida Entomologist, 67*, 542–547.

Burman, E., & Parker, I. (1993). *Discourse analytic research: Repertoires and readings of texts in action*. London: Routledge.

Burns, J. (1993). Invisible women — Women who have learning disabilities. *The Psychologist, 6*, 102–105.

Burr, V. (1997). Social constructionism and psychology. *The New Psychologist, April*, 7–12.

Burt, C. (1955). The evidence for the concept of intelligence. *British Journal of Psychology, 25*, 158–177.

Burton, R.V. (1976). Honesty and dishonesty. In T. Lickona (Ed.), *Moral development and behaviour*. New York: Holt, Rinehart & Winston.

Bury, M., & Holme, A. (1991). *Life after ninety*. London: Routledge.

Bushman, B.J., & Cooper, H.M. (1990). Effects of alcohol on human aggression: An integrative research review. *Psychological Bulletin, 107*, 341–354.

Bushnell, I.W.R., Sai, F., & Mullin, J.T. (1989). Neonatal recognition of the mother's face. *British Journal of Developmental Psychology, 7*, 3–13.

Buss, A.H. (1989a). Personality as traits. *American Psychologist, 44*, 1378–1388.

Buss, D.M. (1989b). Sex differences in human mate preferences: Evolutionary hypotheses tested in 37 cultures. *Behavioral and Brain Sciences, 12*, 1–49.

Buss, D.M., Larsen, R.J., Westen, D., & Semmelroth, J. (1992). Sex differences in jealousy: Evolution, physiology and psychology. *Psychological Science, 3*, 251–255.

Butterworth, G.E. (1974). *The development of the object concept in human infants*. Unpublished PhD thesis, University of Oxford.

Butterworth, G.E., & Cicchetti, D. (1978). Visual calibration of posture in normal and Down's syndrome infants. *Perception, 5*, 155–160.

Butterworth, G.E. & Jarrett, N. (1991). What minds have in common is space: Spatial mechanisms serving joint attention in infancy. *British Journal of Developmental Psychology, 9*, 55–72.

Buunk, B.P. (1996). Affiliation, attraction and close relationships. In M. Hewstone, W. Stroebe, & G.M. Stephenson (Eds.), *Introduction to social psychology (2nd Edn.)*. Oxford: Blackwell.

Buunk, B.P., & VanYperen, N.W. (1991). Referential comparisons, relational comparisons and exchange orientation: Their relation to marital satisfaction. *Personality and Social Psychology Bulletin, 17*, 710–718.

Byrne, D. (1971). *The attraction paradigm*. New York: Academic Press.

Byrne, D., London, O., & Griffit, W. (1968). The effect of topic importance and attitude similarity–dissimilarity on attraction in an intrastranger design. *Psychonomic Science, 11*, 303–313.

Cahoun, J.B. (1962). Population density and social pathology. *Scientific American, February*, 206.

Calvert, W.H., Hedrick, L.E., & Brower, L.P. (1979). Mortality of the monarch butterfly (*Danaus plexippus L.*): Avian predation at five overwintering sites in Mexico. *Science, 204*, 847–851.

Campbell, D.T., & Stanley, J.C. (1966). *Experimental and quasi-experimental designs for research*. Chicago: Rand McNally.

Campbell, F.A., & Ramey, C.T. (1994). Effects of early intervention on intellectual and academic achievement: A follow-up study of children from low-income families. *Child Development, 65*, 684–698.

Campfield, L.A., & Smith, F.J. (1990). Systemic factors in the control of food intake: Evidence for patterns as signals. In E.M. Stricker (Ed.), *Handbook of behavioral neurobiology, Vol. 10: Neurobiology of food and fluid intake*. New York: Plenum.

Campos, J.J., Hiatt, S., Ramsay, D., Henderson, C., & Svejda, M. (1978). The emergence of fear on the visual cliff. In M. Lewis & L.A. Rosenblum (Eds.), *The development of affect*. New York: Plenum Press.

Cannon, T.D., Barr, C.E., & Mednick, S.A. (1991). Genetic and perinatal factors in the aetiology of schizophrenia. In E.F. Walker (Ed.), *Schizophrenia: A life-course developmental perspective*. New York: Academic Press.

Cannon, W.B. (1929). *Bodily changes in pain, hunger, fear and rage*. New York: Appleton-Century-Crofts.

Cantwell, D.P., Baker, L., & Rutter, M. (1978). Family factors. In S.B. Cruze, I.J. Baris, & J.E. Barrett (Eds.), *Childhood psychopathology and development*. New York: Raven.

Capron, C., & Duyne, M. (1989). Assessment of effects of socio-economic status on IQ in a full cross-fostering study. *Nature, 340*, 552–554.

Caraco, T., Martindale, S., & Pulliam, H.R. (1980). Flocking: Advantages and disadvantages. *Nature, 285*, 400–401.

Carayon, J. (1974). Insémination traumatique heterosexuelle et homosexuelle chez *Xylocoris maculipennis* (Hem. Anthocoridae). *C.R. Academy of Science Paris, D. 278*, 2803–2806.

Cardon, L.R., Smith, S.D., Fulker, D.W., & Kimbverling, W.J. (1994). Quantitative trait locus for reading disability on chromosome 6. *Science, 266,* 276–279.

Cardwell, M., Clark, L., & Meldrum, C. (1996). *Psychology for A level.* London: Collins Educational.

Carey, M.P., Kalra, D.L., Carey, K.B., Halperin, S., & Richard, C.S. (1993). Stress and unaided smoking cessation: A prospective investigation. *Journal of Consulting and Clinical Psychology, 61,* 831–838.

Carlsmith, H., Ellsworth, P., & Aronson, E. (1976). *Methods of research in social psychology.* Reading, MA: Addison-Wesley.

Carlsmith, J.M., & Anderson, C.A. (1979). Ambient temperature and the occurrence of collective violence: A new analysis. *Journal of Personality and Social Psychology, 37,* 337–344.

Carlson, C.L., Lahey, B.B., & Neeper, R. (1984). Peer assessment of the social behaviour of accepted, rejected, and neglected children. *Journal of Abnormal Child Psychology, 12,* 189–198.

Carlson, N.R. (1994). *Physiology of behavior (5th Edn.).* Boston: Allyn & Bacon.

Carmichael, L.C., Hogan, H.P., & Walters, A.A. (1932). An experimental study of the effect of language on the reproduction of visually perceived form. *Journal of Experimental Psychology, 15,* 73–86.

Caron, A.J., Caron, R.F., & Carlson, V.R. (1979). Infant perception of the invariant shape of objects varying in slant. *Child Development, 50,* 716–721.

Carpenter, F.L., Paton, D.C., & Hixon, M.A. (1983). Weight gain and adjustment of feeding territory size in migrant hummingbirds. *Proceedings of the National Academy of Science, USA, 80,* 7259–7263.

Carpenter, G. (1975). Mother's face and the newborn. In R. Lewin (Ed.), *Child alive.* London: Temple Smith.

Carroll, B.J., Feinberg, M., Greden, J.F., Haskett, R.F., James, N.M., Steiner, M., & Tarika, J. (1980). Diagnosis of endogenous depression: Comparison of clinical, research, and neuroendocrine criteria. *Journal of Affective Disorders, 2,* 177–194.

Carroll, J.B., & Casagrande, J.B. (1958). The function of language classifications in behaviour. In E.E. Maccoby, T.M. Newcombe, & E. L. Hartley (Eds.), *Readings in social psychology (3rd Edn.).* Boston: Allyn & Bacon.

Cartwright, D.S. (1979). *Theories and models of personality.* Dubuque, IO: Brown Company.

Carugati, F. (1990). Everyday ideas, theoretical models and social representations: The case of intelligence and its development. In G.R. Semin & K.J. Gergen (Eds.), *Everyday understanding: Social and scientific implications.* London: Sage.

Case, R. (1974). Structures and strictures: Some functional limitations on the course of cognitive growth. *Cognitive Psychology, 6,* 544–573.

Case, R. (1985). *Intellectual development.* Orlando, FL: Academic Press.

Case, R. (1992). Neo-Piagetian theories of intellectual development. In H. Beilin & P.B. Pufall (Eds.), *Piaget's theory: Prospects and possiblities.* Hillsdale, NJ: Erlbaum.

Catchpole, C. (1984). Song is a serenade for the warblers. In G. Ferry (Ed.), *The understanding of animals.* Oxford: Blackwell.

Catchpole, C., Dittami, J., & Leisler, B. (1984). Differential response to male song repertoires in female songbirds implanted with oestradiol. *Nature, 312,* 563–564.

Cattell, R.B. (1946). *Description and measurement of personality.* London: Harrap.

Ceci, S.J. (1991). How much does schooling influence general intelligence and its cognitive components? A reassessment of the evidence. *Developmental Psychology, 27,* 703–722.

Ceci, S.J., Peters, D., & Plotkin, J. (1985). Human subjects review, personal values and the regulation of social science research. *American Psychologist, 40,* 994–1002.

Central Statistical Office. (1996). *Social trends.* London: Central Statistical Office.

Challis, B.H., & Brodbeck, D.R. (1992). Level of processing affects priming in word fragment completion. *Journal of Experimental Psychology: Learning, Memory, and Cognition, 18,* 595–607.

Charlton, A. (1998). TV violence has little impact on children, study finds. *The Times,* 12 January, p. 5.

Chemers, M.M., Hays, R.B., Rhodewalt, F., & Wysocki, J. (1985). A person–environment analysis of job stress: A contingency model explanation. *Journal of Personality and Social Psychology, 24,* 172–177.

Cheney, D.L., & Seyfarth, R.M. (1990). *How monkeys see the world.* Chicago: University of Chicago Press.

Cheng, P., & Holyoak, K.J. (1985). Pragmatic reasoning schemas. *Cognitive Psychology, 17,* 391–416.

Cheng, P.W. (1985). Restructuring versus automaticity: Alternative accounts of skills acquisition. *Psychological Review, 92,* 414–423.

Cherry, E.C. (1953). Some experiments on the recognition of speech with one and two ears. *Journal of the Acoustical Society of America, 25,* 975–979.

Chi, M.T. (1978). Knowledge, structure and memory development. In R.S. Siegler (Ed.), *Children's thinking. What develops?* Hillsdale, NJ: Erbaum.

Child, I.L. (1968). Personality in culture. In E.F. Borgatta & W.W. Lambert (Eds.), *Handbook of personality theory and research.* Chicago: Rand McNally.

Chodorow, N. (1978). *The reproduction of mothering.* Berkeley, CA: University of California Press.

Chomsky, N. (1959). Review of Skinner's "Verbal behaviour". *Language, 35,* 26–58.

Chomsky, N. (1965). *Aspects of the theory of syntax.* Cambridge, MA: MIT Press.

Chomsky, N. (1986). *Knowledge of language: Its nature, origin, and use.* New York: Praeger.

Christensen-Szalanski, J.J., & Bushyhead, J.B. (1981). Physicians' use of probabilistic information in a real clinical setting. *Journal of Experimental Psychology: Human Perception and Performance, 7,* 928–935.

Churchland, P.S., & Sejnowski, T.J. (1991). Perspectives on cognitive neuroscience. In R.G. Lister & H.J. Weingartner (Eds.), *Perspectives on cognitive neuroscience.* Oxford: Oxford University Press.

Cialdini, R.B., Borden, R.J., Thorne, A., Walker, M.R., Freeman, S., & Sloan, L.R. (1976). Basking in reflected glory: Three (football) field studies. *Journal of Personality and Social Psychology, 34,* 366–375.

Cialdini, R.B., Schaller, M., Houlihan, D., Arps, K., Fultz, J., & Beaman, A.L. (1987). Empathy-based helping: Is it selflessly or selfishly motivated? *Journal of Personality and Social Psychology, 52,* 749–758.

Claparède, E. (1911). Recognition et moitié. *Archives de Psychologie, 11,* 75–90.

Clark, D.M. (1986). A cognitive approach to panic. *Behaviour Research and Therapy, 24,* 461–470.

Clark, D.M., Salkovskis, P.M., Gelder, M., Koehler, K., Martin, M., Anastasiades, P., Hackman, A., Middleton, H., & Jeavons, A. (1988). Tests of a cognitive theory of panic. In I. Hand & H.-U. Wittchen (Eds.), *Panic and phobias, Vol. 2*. Berlin: Springer.

Clark, H.H., & Carlson, T.B. (1981). Context for comprehension. In J. Long & A. Baddeley (Eds.), *Attention and performance, Vol. IX*. Hillsdale, NJ: Lawrence Erlbaum Associates Inc.

Clark, M.S. (1984). Record keeping in two types of relationships. *Journal of Personality and Social Psychology, 47*, 549–557.

Clark, M.S., & Mills, J. (1979). Interpersonal attraction in exchange and communal relationships. *Journal of Personality and Social Psychology, 37*, 12–24.

Clark, M.S., & Pataki, S.P. (1995). Interpersonal processes influencing attraction and relationships. In A. Tesser (Ed.), *Advanced social psychology*. New York: McGraw-Hill.

Clark, R.D., & Hatfield, E. (1989). Gender differences in receptivity to sexual offers. *Journal of Psychology and Human Sexuality, 2*, 39–55.

Claxton, G. (1980). Cognitive psychology: A suitable case for what sort of treatment? In G. Claxton (Ed.), *Cognitive psychology: New directions*. London: Routledge & Kegan Paul.

Cloninger, C.R. (1987). Neurogenetic adaptive mechanisms in alcoholism. *Science, 236*, 410–416.

Cloninger, C.R., Bohmann, M., Sigvardsson, S., & von Knorring, A.-L. (1985). Psychopathology in adopted-out children of alcoholics. The Stockholm Adoption Study. *Recent Developments in Alcoholism, 3*, 37–51.

Clutton-Brock, T.H., & Albon, S.D. (1979). The roaring of red deer and the evolution of honest advertisement. *Behaviour, 69*, 145–170.

Clutton-Brock, T.H., & Harvey, P.H. (1977). Primate ecology and social organisation. *Journal of Zoology London, 183*, 1–39.

Clutton-Brock, T.H., & Vincent, A.C.J. (1991). Sexual selection and the potential reproductive rates of male and females. *Nature, 351*, 58–60.

Cochrane, R. (1977). Mental illness in immigrants to England and Wales: An analysis of mental hospital admissions, 1971. *Social Psychology, 12*, 25–35.

Cochrane, R. (1983). *The social creation of mental illness*. London: Longman.

Cochrane, R. (1988). Marriage, separation and divorce. In S. Fisher & J. Reason (Eds.), *Handbook of life stress, cognition and health*. Chichester: Wiley.

Cochrane, R., & Sashidharan, S.P. (1995). *Mental health and ethnic minorities: A review of the literature and implications for services*. Paper presented to the Birmingham and Northern Birmingham Health Trust.

Cocker, J. (1998). Where Monarchs spend the winter. *Journal of the Association for Teaching Psychology, 7*, 2–20.

Coe, W.C. (1989). Post-hypnotic amnesia: Theory and research. In N.P. Spanos & J. F. Chaves (Eds.), *Hypnosis: The cognitive-behavioural perspective*. Buffalo, NY: Prometheus.

Cogan, J.C., Bhalla, S.K., Sefa-Dedeh, A., & Rathblum, E.D. (1996). A comparison study of United States and African students on perceptions of obesity and thinness. *Journal of Cross-Cultural Psychology, 27*, 98–113.

Cohen, G. (1983). *The psychology of cognition (2nd Edn.)*. London: Academic Press.

Cohen, N.J., & Squire, L.R. (1980). Preserved learning and retention of patter-analysing skill in amnesia using perceptual learning. *Cortex, 17*, 273–278.

Cohen, S., & Hoberman, H.M. (1983). Positive events and social supports as buffers of life change stress. *Journal of Applied Social Psychology, 13*, 99–125.

Cohen, S., Tyrrell, D.A.J., & Smith, A.P. (1991). Psychological stress and susceptibility to the common cold. *New England Journal of Medicine, 325*, 606–612.

Cohen, S., & Williamson, G.M. (1991). Stress and infectious disease in humans. *Psychological Bulletin, 109*, 5–24.

Colby, A., Kohlberg, L., Gibbs, J., & Lieberman, M. (1983). A longitudinal study of moral judgement. *Monographs of the Society for Research in Child Development, 48* (Nos. 1–2, serial No. 200).

Cole, J.O., & Davis, J.M. (1975). Antidepressant drugs. In A.M. Freedman, H.I. Kaplan, & B.J. Saddock (Eds.), *Comprehensive textbook of psychiatry, Vol. 2*. Baltimore: Williams & Williams.

Cole, M., & Cole, S.R. (1993). *The development of children (2nd Edn.)*. New York: Scientific American Books.

Cole, M., Gay, J., Glick, J., & Sharp, D.W. (1971). *The cultural context of learning and thinking*. New York: Basic Books.

Colebatch, J.G., Deiber, M.-P., Passingham, R.E., Friston, K.J., & Frackowiak, R.S.J. (1991). Regional cerebral blood flow during voluntary arm and hand movements in human subjects. *Journal of Neurophysiology, 65*, 1392–1401.

Collins, A.M., & Loftus, E.F. (1975). A spreading-activation theory of semantic processing. *Psychological Review, 82*, 407–428.

Collins, A.M., & Quillian, M.R. (1969). Retrieval time from semantic memory. *Journal of Verbal Learning and Verbal Behavior, 8*, 240–248.

Collins, B.E. (1970). *Social psychology*. Reading, MA: Addison-Wesley.

Collins, B.E., & Raven, B.H. (1969). Group structure: Attraction, coalitions, communication and power. In G. Lindzey & E. Aronson (Eds.), *The handbook of social psychology, Vol. 4 (2nd Edn.)*. Reading, MA: Addison-Wesley.

Collis, G.M., & Lewis, V. (1997). Reflections on blind children and developmental psychology. In V. Lewis & G.M. Collis (Eds.), *Blindness and psychological development in young children*. Leicester: BPS Books.

Comstock, G., & Paik, H. (1991). *Television and the American child*. San Diego: Academic Press.

Condry, J., & Condry, S. (1976). Sex differences: A study in the eye of the beholder. *Child Development, 47*, 812–819.

Conley, J.J. (1984). The hierarchy of consistency: A review and model of longitudinal findings on adult individual differences in intelligence, personality and self-opinion. *Personality and Individual Differences, 5*, 11–25.

Conner, D.B., Knight, D.K., & Cross, D.R. (1997). Mothers' and fathers' scaffolding of their 2–year-olds during problem-solving and literary interactions. *British Journal of Developmental Psychology, 15*, 323–338.

Connolly, J.A., & Doyle, A. (1984). Relation of social fantasy play to social competence in preschoolers. *Developmental Psychology, 20*, 797–806.

Conrad, C. (1972). Cognitive economy in semantic memory. *Journal of Experimental Psychology, 92*, 148–154.

Conrad, R. (1979). *The deaf schoolchild*. New York: Harper & Row.

Conway, M.A., Anderson, S.J., Larsen, S.F., Donnelly, C.M., McDaniel, M.A., McClelland, A.G.R., & Rawles, R.E.

(1994). The formation of flashbulb memories. *Memory and Cognition, 22*, 326–343.

Cooley, C.H. (1902). *Human nature and the social order.* New York: Scribner.

Coolican, H. (1994). *Research methods and statistics in psychology (2nd Edn.).* London: Hodder & Stoughton.

Coolican, H. (1998). Research methods. In M.W. Eysenck (Ed.), *Psychology: An integrated approach.* London: Addison-Wesley Longman.

Cooper, C. (1998). *Individual differences.* London: Arnold.

Cooper, P.J. (1994). Eating disorders. In A.M. Colman (Ed.), *Companion encyclopaedia of psychology, Vol. 2.* London: Routledge.

Cooper, P.J., & Taylor, M.J. (1988). Body image disturbance in bulimia nervosa. *British Journal of Psychiatry, 153*, 32–36.

Coopersmith, S. (1967). *The antecedents of self-esteem.* San Francisco: W.H. Freeman.

Coren, S., & Girgus, J.S. (1972). Visual spatial illusions: Many explanations. *Science, 179*, 503–504.

Costa, P.T., & McCrae, R.R. (1980). Influence of extraversion and neuroticism on subjective well-being: Happy and unhappy people. *Journal of Personality and Social Psychology, 38*, 668–678.

Costa, P.T., & McCrae, R.R. (1992). *NEO-PI-R, Professional manual.* Odessa, FL: Psychological Assessment Resources.

Costanzo, P.R., Coie, J.D., Grumet, J., & Famill, D. (1973). A re-examination of the effects of intent and consequence on the quality of child rearing. *Child Development, 57*, 362–374.

Costello, T.W., Costello, J.T., & Holmes, D.A. (1995). *Abnormal psychology.* London: HarperCollins.

Council, J.R., & Kenny, D.A. (1992). Expert judgements of hypnosis from subjective state reports. *Journal of Abnormal Psychology, 101*, 657–662.

Courchesne, E., Yeung-Courchesne, R., Press, G., Hesselink, J., & Jernigan, T. (1988). Hypoplasia of cerebellar vernal lobules VI and VII in infantile autism. *New England Journal of Medicine, 318*, 1349–1354.

Cox, M.J., Owen, M.T., Lewis, J.M., & Henderson, K.V. (1989). Marriage, adult adjustment, and early parenting. *Child Development, 60*, 1015–1024.

Cox, T. (1978). *Stress.* London: Macmillan Press.

Craik, F.I.M. (1973). A "levels of analysis" view of memory. In P. Pliner, L. Krames, & T.M. Alloway (Eds.), *Communication and affect: Language and thought.* London: Academic Press.

Craik, F.I.M., & Lockhart, R.S. (1972). Levels of processing: A framework for memory research. *Journal of Verbal Learning and Verbal Behavior, 11*, 671–684.

Craik, F.I.M., & Tulving, E. (1975). Depth of processing and the retention of words in episodic memory. *Journal of Experimental Psychology, 104*, 268–294.

Crews, F. (1996). The verdict on Freud. *Psychological Science, 7*, 63–68.

Crick, F., & Mitchison, G. (1983). The function of dream sleep. *Nature, 304*, 111–114.

Cronbach, L.J. (1957). The two disciplines of scientific psychology. *American Psychologist, 12*, 671–684.

Crook, T., & Eliot, J. (1980). Parental death during childhood and adult depression: A critical review of the literature. *Psychological Bulletin, 87*, 252–259.

Crooks, R.L., & Stein, J. (1991). *Psychology: Science, behaviour and life (2nd Edn.),* London: Harcourt Brace Jovanovich.

Crowne, D.P., & Marlowe, D. (1964). *The approval motive: Studies in evaluative dependence.* New York: Wiley.

Crutchfield, R.S. (1955). Conformity and character. *American Psychologist, 10*, 191–198.

Cullen, E. (1957). Adaptations in the kittiwake to cliff-nesting. *Ibis, 99*, 275–302.

Cumberbatch, G. (1990). *Television advertising and sex role stereotyping: A content analysis* (working paper IV for the Broadcasting Standards Council), Communications Research Group, Aston University.

Cumming, E. (1975). Engagement with an old theory. *International Journal of Ageing and Human Development, 6*, 187–191.

Cumming, E., & Henry, W.H. (1961). *Growing old.* New York: Basic Books.

Cunningham, J.D., & Antrill, J.K. (1995). Current trends in non-marital cohabitation: In search of the POSSLQ. In J.T. Wood & S. Duck (Eds.), *Understudied relationships: Off the beaten track.* Thousand Oaks, CA: Sage.

Cunningham, M.R. (1986). Measuring the physical in physical attractiveness: Quasi experiments on the sociobiology of female facial beauty. *Journal of Personality and Social Psychology, 50*, 925–935.

Curtis, A. (1997). Discourse analysis — The search for meanings. *Psychology Review, 4*, 23–25.

Curtiss, S. (1977). *Genie: A psycholinguistic study of a modern-day 'wild child'.* London: Academic Press.

Curtiss, S. (1989). The independence and task-specificity of language. In M.H. Bornstein & J.S. Bruner (Eds.), *Interaction in human development.* Hillsdale, NJ: Lawrence Erlbaum Associates Inc.

Cuthill, I. (1991). Field experiments in animal behaviour. *Animal Behaviour, 42*, 1007–1014.

Cutting, J.E., & Kozlowski, L.T. (1977). A biomechanical invariant for gait perception. *Journal of Experimental Psychology: Human Perception and Performance, 4*, 357–372.

Dalton, K. (1964). *The premenstrual syndrome.* London: Heinemann.

Damasio, A.R., Brandt, J.P., Tranel, D., & Damasio, H. (1991). Name dropping: Retrieval of proper or common noun depends on different systems in left temporal cortex. *Society for Neuroscience Abstracts, 17*, 4.

Damasio, H. (1989). Neuroimaging contributions to the understanding of aphasia. In F. Boller & J. Grafman (Eds.), *Handbook of neuropsychology, Vol. 2.* New York: Elsevier.

Damasio, H., Eslinger, P., & Adams, H.P. (1984). Aphasia following basal ganglia lesions: New evidence. *Seminars in Neurology, 4*, 151–161.

Dammann, E.J. (1997). "The myth of mental illness": Continuing controversies and their implications for mental health professionals. *Clinical Psychology Review, 17*, 733–756.

Damon, W., & Hart, D. (1988). *Self-understanding in childhood and adolescence.* Cambridge: Cambridge University Press.

Dane, F.C. (1994). Survey methods, naturalistic observations, and case-studies. In A.M. Colman (Ed.), *Companion encyclopaedia of psychology, Vol. 2.* London: Routledge.

Daneman, M., & Carpenter, P. (1980). Individual differences in working memory and reading. *Journal of Verbal Learning and Verbal Behavior, 19*, 450–466.

Daniels, D., & Plomin, R. (1985). Origins of individual differences in infant shyness. *Developmental Psychology, 21*, 118–121.

Dannemiller, J.L., & Stephens, B.R. (1988). A critical test of infant pattern preference models. *Child Development, 59*, 210–216.

Dansky, J. (1980). Make-believe: A mediator of the relationship between play and associative fluency. *Child Development*, *51*, 576–579.

Darley, J.M. (1991). Altruism and prosocial behaviour research: Reflections and prospects. In M.S. Clark (Ed.), *Prosocial behaviour: Review of personality and social psychology, Vol. 12*. Newbury Park, CA: Sage.

Darley, J.M., & Latané, B. (1968). Bystander intervention in emergencies: Diffusion of responsibility. *Journal of Personality and Social Psychology*, *8*, 377–383.

Darling, F.F. (1938). *Bird flocks and the breeding cycle*. Cambridge, UK: Cambridge University Press.

Dartnall, H.J.A., Bowmaker, J.K., & Mollon, J.D. (1983). Microspectrophotometry of human photoreceptors. In J.D. Mollon & L. T. Sharpe (Eds.), *Colour vision: Physiology and psychophysics*. New York: Academic Press.

Darwin, C. (1859). *The origin of species*. London: Macmillan.

Darwin, C. (1871). *The descent of man and selection in relation to sex*. London: Murray.

Darwin, C. (1872). *The expression of the emotions in man and animals*. London: John Murray.

Darwin, C.J., Turvey, M.T., & Crowder, R.G. (1972). An auditory analogue of the Sperling partial report procedure: Evidence for brief auditory storage. *Cognitive Psychology*, *3*, 255–267.

Davey, G.C.L. (1983). An associative view of human classical conditioning. In G.C.L. Davey (Ed.), *Animal models of human behaviour: Conceptual, evolutionary, and neurobiological perspectives*. Chichester: Wiley.

Davidson, M., Keefe, R.S.E., Mohs, R.C., Siever, L.J., Losonczy, M.F., Horvath, T.B., & Davis, K.L. (1987). L-Dopa challenge and relapse in schizophrenia. *American Journal of Psychiatry*, *144*, 934–938.

Davidson, R., Ekman, P., Saron, C.D., Senulis, J.A., & Friesen, W.V. (1990). Approach–withdrawal and cerebral asymmetry. *Journal of Personality and Social Psychology*, *58*, 330–341.

Davies, N.B., & Brooke, M. de L. (1988). Cuckoos versus reed warblers: Adaptations and counter-adaptations. *Animal Behaviour*, *36*, 262–284.

Davies, N.B., & Houston, A.I. (1981). Owners and satellites: The economics of territory defence in the pied wagtail, *Motacilla alba*. *Journal of Animal Ecology*, *50*, 157–180.

Davies, N.B., & Lundberg, A. (1984). Food distribution and a variable mating system in the dunnock, *Prunella modularis*. *Journal of Animal Ecology*, *53*, 895–913.

Davis, M.H. (1983). Empathic concern and the muscular dystrophy telethon: Empathy as a multidimensional construct. *Personality and Social Psychology Bulletin*, *9*, 223–229.

Davis, S. (1990). Men as success objects and women as sex objects: A study of personal advertisements. *Sex Roles*, *23*, 43–50.

Davison, G.C., & Neale, J.M. (1986). *Abnormal psychology (4th Edn.)*. New York: Wiley.

Davison, G.C., & Neale, J.M. (1990). *Abnormal psychology (5th Edn.)*. New York: Wiley.

Davison, G.C., & Neale, J.M. (1996). *Abnormal psychology (revised 6th Edn.)*. New York: Wiley.

Dawkins, M. (1971). Perceptual change in chicks: Another look at the "search image" concept. *Animal Behaviour*, *19*, 566–574.

Dawkins, R. (1976). *The selfish gene*. Oxford: Oxford University Press.

Dawkins, R., & Krebs, J.R. (1979). Arms races within and between species. *Proceedings of the Royal Society of London*, *B205*, 489–511.

Deaux, K., & Wrightsman, L.S. (1988). *Social psychology (5th Edn.)*. Pacific Grove, CA: Brooks/Cole.

De Boysson-Bardies, B., Sagart, L., & Durand, C. (1984). Discernible differences in the babbling of infants according to target language. *Journal of Child Language*, *11*, 1–16.

DeGroot, H.P., & Gwynn, M.I. (1989). Trance logic, duality, and hidden-observer responding. In N.P. Spanos & J.F. Chaves (Eds.), *Hypnosis: The cognitive-behavioural perspective*. Buffalo, NY: Prometheus.

DeGroot, P. (1980). Information transfer in a socially roosting weaver bird (*Quelea quelea; Plocinae*): An experimental study. *Animal Behaviour*, *28*, 1249–1254.

Dell, G.S. (1986). A spreading-activation theory of retrieval in sentence production. *Psychological Review*, *93*, 283–321.

DeLucia, P.R., & Hochberg, J. (1991). Geometrical illusions in solid objects under ordinary viewing conditions. *Perception & Psychophysics*, *50*, 547–554.

Dement, W.C. (1960). The effects of dream deprivation. *Science*, *131*, 1705–1707.

Dement, W.C., & Kleitman, N.(1957). The relation of eye movements during sleep to dream activity: An objective method for the study of dreaming. *Journal of Experimental Psychology*, *53*, 339–346.

Dement, W.C., & Wolpert, E.A. (1958). The relation of eye movements, body motility, and external stimuli to dream content. *Journal of Experimental Psychology*, *55*, 543–553.

Depue, R.A., & Monroe, S.M. (1978). Learned helplessness in the perspective of the depressive disorders: Conceptual and definitional issues. *Journal of Abnormal Psychology*, *87*, 3–20.

Derakshan, N., & Eysenck, M.W. (1997). Interpretive biases for one's own behaviour in high-anxious individuals and repressors. *Journal of Personality and Social Psychology*, *73*, 816–825.

Deregowski, J., Muldrow, E.S., & Muldrow, W.F. (1972). Pictorial recognition in a remote Ethiopian population. *Perception*, *1*, 417–425.

De Renzi, E. (1986). Current issues in prosopagnosia. In H.D. Ellis, M.A. Jeeves, F. Newcombe, & A. Young (Eds.), *Aspects of face processing*. Dordrecht: Martinus Nijhoff.

Deutsch, J.A., & Deutsch, D. (1963). Attention: Some theoretical considerations. *Psychological Review*, *70*, 80–90.

Deutsch, J.A., & Deutsch, D. (1967). Comments on "Selective attention: Perception or response?" *Quarterly Journal of Experimental Psychology*, *19*, 362–363.

Deutsch, J.A., & Gonzalez, M.F. (1980). Gastic nutrient content signals satiety. *Behavioral and Neural Biology*, *30*, 113–116.

Deutsch, M., & Collins, M.E. (1951). *Inter-racial housing: A psychological evaluation of a social experiment*. Minneapolis, MN: University of Minneapolis Press.

Deutsch, M., & Gerard, H.B. (1955). A study of normative and informational influence upon individual judgement. *Journal of Abnormal and Social Psychology*, *51*, 629–636.

DeValois, R.L., & DeValois, K.K. (1975). Neural coding of colour. In E. C. Carterette & M.P. Friedman (Eds.), *Handbook of perception, Vol. 5*. New York: Academic Press.

DeValois, R.L., & DeValois, K.K. (1988). *Spatial vision*. Oxford: Oxford University Press.

de Villiers, J.G., & de Villiers, P.A. (1973). A cross-sectional study of the acquisition of grammatical morphemes in child speech. *Journal of Psycholinguistic Research, 2,* 267–278.

Devine, P.A., & Fernald, P.S. (1973). Outcome effects of receiving a preferred, randomly assigned or non-preferred therapy. *Journal of Consulting and Clinical Psychology, 41,* 104–107.

Devine, P.G. (1995). Prejudice and out-group perception. In A. Tesser (Ed.), *Advanced social psychology.* New York: McGraw-Hill.

Diamond, M. (1982). Sexual identity, monozygotic twins reared in discordant sex roles and a BBC follow-up. *Archives of Sexual Behavior, 11,* 181–186.

Diener, E. (1980). Deindividuation: The absence of self-awareness and self-regulation in group members. In P.B. Paulus (Ed.), *Psychology of group influence.* Hillsdale, NJ: Lawrence Erlbaum.

Diener, E., Fraser, S.C., Beaman, A.L., & Kelem, R.T. (1976). Effects of deindividuation variables on stealing among Halloween trick-or-treaters. *Journal of Personality and Social Psychology, 33,* 178–183.

Digman, J.M. (1990). Personality structure: Emergence of the five-factor model. *Annual Review of Psychology, 41,* 417–440.

DiNardo, P.A., Guzy, L.T., Jenkins, J.A., Bak, R.M., Tomasi, S.F., & Copland, M. (1988). Aetiology and maintenance of dog fears. *Behaviour Research and Therapy, 26,* 241–244.

Dindia, K., & Allen, M. (1992). Sex differences in self-disclosure: A meta-analysis. *Psychological Bulletin, 112,* 106–124.

Dindia, K., & Baxter, L.A. (1987). Maintenance and repair strategies in marital relationships. *Journal of Social and Personal Relationships, 4,* 143–158.

DiPietro, J.A. (1981). Rough and tumble play: A function of gender. *Developmental Psychology, 17,* 50–58.

Di Vesta, F.J. (1959). Effects of confidence and motivation on susceptibility to informational social influence. *Journal of Abnormal and Social Psychology, 59,* 204–209.

Dobelle, W.H., Mladejovsky, M.G., & Girvin, J.P. (1974). Artificial vision for the blind: Electrical stimulation of visual cortex offers hope for a functional prosthesis. *Science, 183,* 440–444.

Dobson, K.S. (1989). A meta-analysis of the efficacy of cognitive therapy for depression. *Journal of Consulting and Clinical Psychology, 57,* 414–419.

Dohrenwend, B.P., Levav, P.E., Schwartz, S., Naveh, G., Link, B.G., Skodol, A.E., & Stueve, A. (1992). Socioeconomic status and psychiatric disorders: The causation-selection issue. *Science, 255,* 946–952.

Doise, W. (1976). *L'articulation psychosociologique et les relations entre groupes.* Brussels: de Boeck.

Doise, W., & Mugny, G. (1984). *The social development of the intellect.* Oxford: Pergamon.

Doise, W., Rijsman, J.B., van Meel, J., Bressers, I., & Pinxten, L. (1981). Sociale markering en cognitieve ontwikkeling. *Pedagogische Studien, 58,* 241–248.

Dollard, J., Doob, L.W., Miller, N.E., Mowrer, O.H., & Sears, R.R. (1939). *Frustration and aggression.* New Haven, CT: Yale University Press.

Dollard, J., & Miller, N.E. (1950). *Personality and psychotherapy.* New York: McGraw-Hill.

Donaldson, M. (1978). *Children's minds.* London: Fontana.

Doob, L.W., & Sears, R.R. (1939). Factors determining substitute behaviour and the overt expression of aggression. *Journal of Abnormal and Social Psychology, 34,* 293–313.

Dosher, B.A., & Corbett, A.T. (1982). Instrument inferences and verb schemata. *Memory and Cognition, 10,* 531–539.

Douvan, E., & Adelson, J. (1966). *The adolescent experience.* New York: Wiley.

Dovidio, J.F., Piliavin, J.A., & Clark, R.D. (1991). The arousal-cost reward model and the process of intervention: A review of the evidence. In M.S. Clark (Ed.), *Review of personality and social psychology, Vol. 12. Prosocial behaviour.* New York: Academic Press.

Drever, J. (1964). *A dictionary of psychology.* Harmondsworth: Penguin.

Drew, M.A., Colquhoun, W.P., & Long, M.A. (1958). Effect of small doses of alcohol on a task resembling driving. *British Medical Journal, 1,* 993–998.

Driver, J., & Tipper, S.P. (1989). On the nonselectivity of "selective seeing": Contrast between interference and priming in selective attention. *Journal of Experimental Psychology: Human Perception and Performance, 15,* 448–456.

DSM (updated regularly). *Diagnostic and Statistical Manual of Mental Disorders.*

Duck, S. (1982). *Personal relationships 4: Dissolving personal relationships.* London: Academic Press.

Duck, S. (1992). *Human relationships (2nd Edn.).* London: Sage.

Duncan, J. (1979). Divided attention: The whole is more than the sum of its parts. *Journal of Experimental Psychology: Human Perception and Performance, 5,* 216–228.

Dunlea, A. (1989). *Vision and the emergence of meaning: Blind and sighted children's early language.* Cambridge: Cambridge University Press.

Dunn, J., & Plomin, R. (1990). *Separate lives: Why siblings are so different.* New York: Basic Books.

Durkin, K. (1995). *Developmental social psychology: From infancy to old age.* Oxford: Blackwell.

Durrett, M.E., Otaki, M., & Richards, P. (1984). Attachment and the mother's perception of support for the father. *International Journal of Behavioral Development, 7,* 167–176.

Dworetzsky, J.P. (1996). *Introduction to child development (6th Edn.).* New York: West Publishing Co.

Dyer, C. (1995). *Beginning research in psychology.* Oxford: Blackwell.

Eagly, A.H., & Chaiken, S. (1993). *The psychology of attitudes.* Fort Worth, TX: Harcourt Brace Jovanovich.

Eagly, A.H., & Crowley, M. (1986). Gender and helping behaviour: A meta-analytic review of the social psychological literature. *Psychological Bulletin, 100,* 283–308.

Eagly, A.H., & Johnson, B.T. (1990). Gender and leadership style: A meta-analysis. *Psychological Bulletin, 108,* 233–256.

Eagly, A.H., & Steffen, V.J. (1986). Gender and aggressive behaviour: A meta-analytic review of the social psychological literature. *Psychological Bulletin, 90,* 1–20.

Ebbesen, E.B., Kjos, G.L., & Konecni, V.J. (1976). Spatial ecology: Its effects on the choice of friends and enemies. *Journal of Experimental Social Psychology, 12,* 505–518.

Ebbinghaus, H. (1885/1913). *Uber das Gedachtnis.* Leipzig: Dunker. [Translated by H. Ruyer & C.E. Bussenius, 1913, *Memory.* New York: Teachers College, Columbia University.]

Ebigno, P.O. (1986). A cross-sectional study of somatic complaints of Nigerian females using the Enugu Somatization Scale. *Culture, Medicine, and Psychiatry, 10,* 167–186.

Edwards, J. (1994). *The scars of dyslexia.* London: Cassell.

Eisdorfer, C., & Wilkie, F. (1977). Stress, disease, aging and behaviour. In J.E. Birren & K.W. Schaie (Eds.), *Handbook of the psychology of aging (3rd Edn.)*. San Diego: Academic Press.

Eisenberg, N., Lennon, R., & Roth, K. (1983). Prosocial development: A longitudinal study. *Developmental Psychology, 19,* 846–855.

Eisenberg, N., Miller, P.A., Shell, R., McNalley, S., & Shea, C. (1991). Prosocial development in adolescence: A longitudinal study. *Developmental Psychology, 27,* 849–857.

Eisenberg, N., & Mussen, P.H. (1989). *The roots of prosocial behaviour in children*. Cambridge: Cambridge University Press.

Eisenberg-Berg, N., & Hand, M. (1979). The relationship of preschoolers' reasoning about prosocial moral conflicts to prosocial behaviour. *Child Development, 50,* 356–363.

Elgar, M.A. (1986). House sparrows establish foraging flocks by giving chirrup calls if the resources are divisible. *Animal Behaviour, 29,* 868–872.

Elicker, J., Englund, M., & Sroufe, L.A. (1992). Predicting peer competence and peer relationships in childhood from early parent–child relationships. In R.D. Parke & G.W. Ladd (Eds.), *Family–peer relationships: Modes of linkage*. Hillsdale, NJ: Lawrence Erlbaum Associates Inc.

Elkin, I., Parloff, M. B., Hadley, S.W., & Autry, J.H. (1985). NIMH Treatment of Depression Collaborative Research Program. *Archives of General Psychiatry, 42,* 305–316.

Ellis, A. (1962). *Reason and emotion in psychotherapy*. Secaucus, NJ: Prentice-Hall.

Ellis, A. (1978). The basic clinical theory of rational emotive therapy. In A. Ellis & R. Grieger (Eds.), *Handbook of rational emotive therapy*. New York: Springer.

Ellis, A.W. (1993). *Reading, writing and dyslexia (2nd Edn.)*. Hove, UK: Psychology Press.

Ellis, A.W., & Young, A.W. (1988). *Human cognitive neuropsychology*. Hove, UK: Psychology Press.

Ellis, S., & Gauvain, M. (1992). Social and cultural influences on children's collaborative interactions. In L.T. Winegar & J. Valsiner (Eds.), *Children's development within social context, Vol. 2. Research and methodology*. Hillsdale, NJ: Erlbaum.

Emlen, J.M. (1966). The role of time and energy in food preference. *American Naturalist, 100,* 611–617.

Empson, J.A.C. (1989). *Sleep and dreaming*. London: Faber & Faber.

Endler, N.S., & Parker, J.D.A. (1990). Multidimensional assessment of coping: A critical evaluation. *Journal of Personality and Social Psychology, 58,* 844–854.

Engels, G.I., Garnefski, N., & Diekstra, R.F.W. (1993). Efficacy of rational-emotive therapy: A quantitative analysis. *Journal of Consulting and Clinical Psychology, 61,* 1083–1090.

Enquist, M. (1985). Communication during aggressive interactions with particular reference to variation in choice of behaviour. *Animal Behaviour, 33,* 1152–1161.

Erhardt, D., & Hinshaw, S.P. (1994). Initial sociometric impressions of ADHD and comparison boys: Predictions from social behaviours and from nonbehavioural variables. *Journal of Consulting and Clinical Psychology, 62,* 833–842.

Erichsen, J.T., Krebs, J.R., & Houston, A.I. (1980). Optimal foraging and cryptic prey. *Journal of Animal Ecology, 49,* 271–276.

Ericsson, K.A. (1988). Analysis of memory performance in terms of memory skill. In R.J. Sternberg (Ed.), *Advances in the psychology of human intelligence, Vol. 4*. Hillsdale, NJ: Lawrence Erlbaum Associates Inc.

Eriksen, C.W. (1990). Attentional search of the visual field. In D. Brogan (Ed.), *Visual search*. London: Taylor & Francis.

Erikson, E.H. (1950). *Childhood and society*. New York: Norton.

Erikson, E.H. (1959). *Identity and life styles: Selected papers*. New York: International Universities Press.

Erikson, E.H. (1963). *Childhood and society (2nd Edn.)*. New York: Norton.

Erikson, E.H. (1968). *Identity: Youth and crisis*. New York: Norton.

Erikson, E.H. (1969). *Gandhi's truth: On the origin of militant nonviolence*. New York: W. W. Norton.

Erlenmeyer-Kimling, L., & Jarvik, L.F. (1963). Genetics and intelligence: A review. *Science, 142,* 1477–1479.

Eron, L.D. (1982). Parent–child interaction, television violence, and aggression of children. *American Psychologist, 37,* 197–211.

Ervin-Tripp, S. (1964). An analysis of the interaction of language, topic and listener. *American Anthropologist, 66,* 94–100.

Estes, W.K. (1944). An experimental study of punishment. *Psychological Monographs: General & Applied, 54,* No. 263.

Etcoff, N.L., Ekman, P., Frank, M., Magee, J., & Torreano, L. (1992). *Detecting deception: Do aphasics have an advantage?* Paper presented at the Conference of International Society for Research on Emotions. Carnegie Mellon University, Pittsburgh, PA.

Evans, J.St.B.T. (1989). *Bias in human reasoning*. Hove, UK: Psychology Press.

Evans, J.St.B.T. (1994). Thinking and reasoning. In A.M. Colman (Ed.), *Companion encyclopedia of psychology, Vol. 1*. London: Routledge.

Evans, J.St.B.T., Clibbens, J., & Rood, B. (1995). Bias in conditional inference: Implications for mental models and mental logic. *Quarterly Journal of Experimental Psychology, 48A,* 644–670.

Evans, J.St.B.T., Over, D.E., & Manktelow, K.I. (1994). Reasoning, decision making and rationality. In P.N. Johnson-Laird & E. Shafir (Eds.), *Reasoning and decision making*. Oxford: Blackwell.

Eysenck, H.J. (1944). Types of personality: A factorial study of 700 neurotic soldiers. *Journal of Mental Science, 90,* 851–861.

Eysenck, H.J. (1947). *Dimensions of personality*. London: Routledge & Kegan Paul.

Eysenck, H.J. (1952). The effects of psychotherapy: An evaluation. *Journal of Consulting Psychology, 16,* 319–324.

Eysenck, H.J. (1967). *The biological basis of personality*. Springfield, IL: C.C. Thomas.

Eysenck, H.J. (1978). Superfactors P, E, and N in a comprehensive factor space. *Multivariate Behavioral Research, 13,* 475–482.

Eysenck H.J. (1981). *The intelligence controversy: H. J. Eysenck vs. Leon Kamin*. New York: Wiley.

Eysenck, H.J. (1982). *Personality, genetics and behaviour*. New York: Praeger.

Eysenck, H.J., & Broadhurst, P.L. (1964). Experiments with animals. In H.J. Eysenck (Ed.), *Experiments in motivation*. London: Pergamon Press.

Eysenck, H.J., & Eysenck, M.W. (1981). *Mindwatching*. London: Michael Joseph.

Eysenck, H.J., & Eysenck, M.W. (1985). *Personality and individual differences*. New York: Plenum.

Eysenck, H.J., & Eysenck, M.W. (1989). *Mindwatching: Why we behave the way we do*. London: Prion.

Eysenck, M.W. (1977). *Human memory: Theory, research and individual differences*. New York: Pergamon Press.

Eysenck, M.W. (1978). Verbal remembering. In B.M. Foss (Ed.), *Psychology survey, No. 1*. London: Allen & Unwin.

Eysenck, M.W. (1979). Depth, elaboration, and distinctiveness. In L.S. Cermak & F.I.M. Craik (Eds.), *Levels of processing in human memory*. Hillsdale, NJ: Lawrence Erlbaum Associates Inc.

Eysenck, M.W. (1982). *Attention and arousal: Cognition and performance*. Berlin: Springer.

Eysenck, M.W. (1984). *A handbook of cognitive psychology*. Hove, UK: Psychology Press.

Eysenck, M.W. (1990). *Happiness: Facts and myths*. Hove, UK: Psychology Press.

Eysenck, M.W. (1993). *Principles of cognitive psychology*. Hove, UK: Psychology Press.

Eysenck, M.W. (1994a). *Individual differences: Normal and abnormal*. Hove, UK: Psychology Press.

Eysenck, M.W. (1994b). *Perspectives on psychology*. Hove, UK: Psychology Press.

Eysenck, M.W. (1997). *Anxiety and cognition: A unified theory*. Hove, UK: Psychology Press.

Eysenck, M.W. (1998). *Psychology: An integrated approach*. Harlow, UK: Addison Wesley Longman.

Eysenck, M.W., & Eysenck, M.C. (1980). Effects of processing depth, distinctiveness, and word frequency on retention. *British Journal of Psychology, 71*, 263–274.

Eysenck, M.W., & Keane, M.T. (1990). *Cognitive psychology: A student's handbook (2nd Edn.)*. Hove, UK: Psychology Press.

Eysenck, M.W., & Keane, M.T. (1995). *Cognitive psychology: A student's handbook (3rd Edn.)*. Hove, UK: Psychology Press.

Eysenck, M.W., Mogg, K., May, J., Richards, A., & Mathews, A. (1991). Bias in interpretation of ambiguous sentences related to threat in anxiety. *Journal of Abnormal Psychology, 100*, 144–150.

Ezaki, Y. (1990). Female choice and the causes and adaptiveness of polygyny in great reed warblers. *Journal of Animal Ecology, 59*, 103–119.

Fabes, R.A., Fultz, J., Eisenberg, N., May-Plumlee, T., & Christopher, F.S. (1989). Effects of rewards on children's prosocial motivation: A socialisation study. *Developmental Psychology, 25*, 509–515.

Fagot, B.I. (1985). Beyond the reinforcement principle: Another step toward understanding sex-role development. *Developmental Psychology, 21*, 1097–1104.

Fagot, B.I., & Leinbach, M.D. (1989). The young child's gender schema: Environmental input, internal organisation. *Child Development, 60*, 663–672.

Fahrenberg, J. (1992). Psychophysiology of neuroticism and emotionality. In A. Gale & M.W. Eysenck (Eds.), *Handbook of individual differences: Biological perspectives*. Chichester: Wiley.

Faigley, L., & Witte, S. (1983). Analysing revision. *College Composition and Communication, 32*, 400–414.

Fairbank, J.A., & Brown, T.A. (1987). Current behavioural approaches to the treatment of posttraumatic stress disorder. *The Behavior Therapist, 3*, 57–64.

Falek, A., & Moser, H.M. (1975). Classification on schizophrenia. *Archives of General Psychiatry, 32*, 59–67.

Fallon, A.E., & Rozin, P. (1985). Sex differences in perceptions of desirable body shape. *Journal of Abnormal Psychology, 94*, 102–105.

Fantz, R.L. (1961). The origin of form perception. *Scientific American, 204*, 66–72.

Fantz, R.L. (1966). Pattern discrimination and selective attention as determinants of perceptual development from birth. In A.H. Kidd & J.F. Rivoire (Eds.), *Perceptual development in children*. New York: International Universities Press.

Farr, J.L. (1976). Task characteristics, reward contingency, and intrinsic motivation. *Organizational Behavior and Human Performance, 16*, 294–307.

Fava, M., Copeland, P.M., Schweiger, U., & Herzog, D.B. (1989). Neurochemical abnormalities of anorexia and bulimia nervosa. *American Journal of Psychiatry, 47*, 213–219.

Fein, S., Hilton, J.L., & Miller, D.T. (1990). Suspicion of ulterior motivation and the correspondence bias. *Journal of Personality and Social Psychology, 58*, 753–764.

Feingold, B.F. (1975). *Why your child is hyperactive*. New York: Random House.

Felipe, N.J., & Sommer, R. (1966). Invasion of personal space. *Social Problems, 14*, 206–214.

Fellner, C.H., & Marshall, J.R. (1981). Kidney donors revisited. In J.P. Rushton & R.M. Sorrentino (Eds.), *Altruism and helping behaviour*. Hillsdale, NJ: Erlbaum.

Ferguson, T.J., & Rule, B.G. (1983). An attributional perspective on anger and aggression. In R. Green & E. Donnerstein (Eds.), *Aggression: Theoretical and empirical reviews, Vol. 1: Method and theory*. New York: Academic Press.

Fernando, S. (1988). *Race and culture in psychiatry*. London: Croom Helm.

Ferris, C., & Branston, P. (1994). Quality of life in the elderly: A contribution to its understanding. *American Journal of Ageing, 13*, 120–123.

Festinger, L., Schachter, S., & Back, K. (1950). *Social pressures in informal groups: A study of a housing community*. New York: Harper.

Feyerabend, P. (1975). *Against method: Outline of an anarchist theory of knowledge*. London: New Left Books.

Fiedler, F.E. (1967). *A theory of leader effectiveness*. New York: McGraw-Hill.

Fiedler, F.E. (1978). The contingency model and the dynamics of the leadership process. In L. Berkowitz (Ed.), *Advances in experimental social psychology, Vol. 12*. New York: Academic Press.

Fiedler, F.E., & Potter, E.H. (1983). Dynamics of leadership effectiveness. In H.H. Blumberg, A.P. Hare, V. Kent, and M. Davies (Eds.), *Small groups and social interaction, Vol. 1*. Chichester: Wiley.

Fiedler, K. (1988). The dependence of conjunction fallacy on subtle linguistic factors. *Psychological Research, 50*, 123–129.

Field, D. (1981). Can preschool children really learn to conserve? *Child Development, 52*, 326–334.

Field, D., & Minkler, M. (1988). Continuity and change in social support between young-old and old-old or very-old age. *Journal of Gerontology, 43*, 100–107.

Fijneman, Y.A., Willemsen, M.E., & Poortinga, Y.H. (1996). Individualism-collectivism: An empirical study of a conceptual issue. *Journal of Cross-Cultural Psychology, 27*, 381–402.

Fincham, F.D., & Bradbury, T.N. (1993). Marital satisfaction, depression, and attributions: A longitudinal analysis. *Journal of Personality and Social Psychology, 64*, 442–452.

Finlay-Jones, R.A., & Brown, G.W. (1981). Types of stressful life events and the onset of anxiety and depressive disorders. *Psychological Medicine, 11*, 803–815.

Fischer, E.A. (1980). The relationship between mating system and simultaneous hermaphroditism in the coral reef fish, *Hypoplectrus nigricans. Animal Behaviour, 28*, 620–633.

Fischhoff, B. (1977). Perceived informativeness of facts. *Journal of Experimental Psychology: Human Perception and Performance, 3*, 349–358.

Fischhoff, B., & Beyth, R. (1975). 'I knew it would happen' — Remembered probabilities of once-future things. *Organizational Behaviour and Human Performance, 13*, 1–16.

Fisher, R.A. (1930). *The genetical theory of natural selection.* Oxford: Clarendon Press.

Fisher, R.P., Geiselman, R.E., Raymond, D.S., Jurkevich, L.M., & Warhaftig, M.L. (1987). Enhancing enhanced eyewitness memory: Refining the cognitive interview. *Journal of Police Science and Administration, 15*, 291–297.

Fiske, D.W., Cartwright, D.S., & Kirtner, W.L. (1964). Are psychotherapeutic changes predictable? *Journal of Abnormal and Social Psychology, 69*, 418–426.

Fiske, S.T. (1993). Social cognition and social perception. *Annual Review of Psychology, 44*, 155–194.

Fitts, P.M., & Posner, M.I. (1967). *Human performance.* Englewood Cliffs, NJ: Prentice-Hall.

Fitzgibbon, C.D., & Fanshaw, J.H. (1988). Stotting in Thompson's gazelles: An honest signal of condition. *Behavioral Ecology and Sociobiology, 23*, 69–74.

Flynn, J.P. (1976). Neural basis of threat and attack. In R.G. Grenell & S. Gabay (Eds.), *Biological foundations of psychiatry.* New York: Raven.

Flynn, J.R. (1987). Massive IQ gains in 14 nations: What IQ tests really measure. *Psychological Bulletin, 101*, 271–291.

Foa, E.B., Skeketee, G., & Olasov-Rothbaum, B. (1989). Behavioural/cognitive conceptualisations of post-traumatic stress disorder. *Behavior Therapy, 20*, 155–176.

Foa, U.G., & Foa, E.B. (1975). *Resource theory of social exchange.* Morristown, NJ: General Learning Press.

Fodor, J.A. (1983). *The modularity of mind.* Cambridge, MA: MIT Press.

Fodor, J.A., & Pylyshyn, Z.W. (1981). How direct is visual perception? Some reflections on Gibson's "ecological approach". *Cognition, 9*, 139–196.

Folstein, S., & Rutter, M. (1978). A twin study of individuals with infantile autism. In M. Rutter & E. Schopler (Eds.), *Autism: A reappraisal of concepts and treatment.* New York: Plenum.

Ford, M. (1995). Two modes of mental representation and problem solution in syllogistic reasoning. *Cognition, 54*, 1–71.

Ford, M.R., & Widiger, T.A. (1989). Sex bias in the diagnosis of histrionic and antisocial personality disorders. *Journal of Consulting and Clinical Psychology, 57*, 301–305.

Forman, E.A., & Cazden, C.B. (1985). Exploring Vygotskyin perspectives in education: The cognitive value of peer interaction. In J.V. Wertsch (Ed.), *Culture, communication, and cognition: Vygotskyian perspectives.* Cambridge: Cambridge University Press.

Fortenberry, J.C., Brown, D.B., & Shevlin, L.T. (1986). Analysis of drug involvement in traffic fatalities in Alabama. *American Journal of Drug and Alcohol Abuse, 12*, 257–267.

Foulkes, D. (1985). *Dreaming: A cognitive-psychological analysis.* Hillsdale, NJ: Lawrence Erbaum Associates Ltd.

Foy, D.W., Resnick, H.S., Sipprelle, R.C., & Carroll, E.M. (1987). Premilitary, military, and postmilitary factors in the development of combat-related post-traumatic stress disorder. *The Behavior Therapist, 10*, 3–9.

Francolini, C.N., & Egeth, H.E.(1980). On the non-automaticity of automatic activation: Evidence of selective seeing. *Perception & Psychophysics, 27*, 331–342.

Frank, A. (1997). *The diary of a young girl* (Eds. O. Frank & M. Pressler). London: Viking.

Franzoi, S.L. (1996). *Social psychology.* Madison: Brown & Benchmark.

Freedman, J.L. (1969). Role playing: Psychology by consensus. *Journal of Personality and Social Psychology, 13*, 107–114.

Freud, A., & Dann, S. (1951). An experiment in group upbringing. *Psychoanalytic Study of the Child, 6*, 127–168.

Freud, S. (1885). The effects of cocaine on thought processes. In *Collected Papers, Vol. V* (1950). London: Hogarth.

Freud, S. (1900). *The interpretation of dreams* [translated by J. Strachey]. London: Allen & Unwin.

Freud, S. (1915). Repression. In Freud's *Collected papers, Vol. IV*. London: Hogarth.

Freud, S. (1917). Introductory lectures on psychoanalysis. In J. Strachey (Ed.), *The complete psychological works, Vol. 16.* New York: Norton.

Freud, S. (1924). *A general introduction to psychoanalysis.* New York: Washington Square Press.

Freud, S. (1930). *Civilisation and its discontents.* London: Hogarth Press.

Freud, S. (1933). *New introductory lectures in psychoanalysis.* New York: Norton.

Freud, S. (1971). *The psychopathology of everyday life* [translated by A. Tyson]. New York: W.W. Norton.

Freud, S., & Breuer, J. (1895). Studies on hysteria. In J. Strachey (Ed.), *The complete psychological works, Vol. 2.* New York: Norton.

Friedman, A. (1979). Framing pictures: The role of knowledge in automatised encoding and memory for gist. *Journal of Experimental Psychology: General, 108*, 316–355.

Friedman, M., & Rosenman, R.H. (1959). Association of specific overt behaviour pattern with blood and cardiovascular findings. *Journal of the American Medical Association, 96*, 1286–1296.

Friedman, M.I., Tordoff, M.G., & Ramirez, I. (1986). Integrated metabolic control of food intake. *Brain Research Bulletin, 17*, 855–859.

Friedrich, L.K., & Stein, A.H. (1973). Aggressive and pro-social television programmes and the natural behaviour of pre-school children. *Monographs of the Society for Research in Child Development, 38*, 1–64.

Frijda, N.H., Kuipers, P., & ter Schure, E. (1989). Relations among emotion, appraisal, and emotional action readiness. *Journal of Personality and Social Psychology, 57*, 212–228.

Frisby, J.P. (1986). The computational approach to vision. In I. Roth & J.P. Frisby (Eds.), *Perception and representation: A cognitive approach.* Milton Keynes: Open University Press.

Frith, C.D. (1992). *The cognitive neuropsychology of schizophrenia.* Hove, UK: Psychology Press.

Frith, C.D., & Cahill, C. (1994). Psychotic disorders: Schizophrenia, affective psychoses, and paranoia. In A.M. Colman (Ed.), *Companion encyclopedia of psychology, Vol. 2.* London: Routledge.

Frueh, T., & McGhee, P.E. (1975). Traditional sex-role development and the amount of time spent watching television. *Developmental Psychology, 11*, 109.

Fruzzetti, A.E., Toland, K., Teller, S.A., & Loftus, E.F. (1992). Memory and eyewitness testimony. In M. Gruneberg & P. Morris (Eds.), *Aspects of memory: The practical aspects*. London: Routledge.

Furnham, A. (1981). Personality and activity preference. *British Journal of Social and Clinical Psychology, 20*, 57–68.

Furnham, A., & Pinder, A. (1990). Young people's attitudes to experimentation on animals. *The Psychologist, 3*, 444–448.

Fyer, A.J., Mannuzza, S., Chapman, T.F., Liebowitz, M.R., & Klein, D.F. (1993). A direct-interview family study of social phobia. *Archives of General Psychiatry, 50*, 286–293.

Gabrieli, J.D.E., Cohen, N.J., & Corkin, S. (1988). The impaired learning of semantic knowledge following bilateral medial temporal-lobe resection. *Brain, 7*, 157–177.

Gabrieli, J.D.E., Desmond, J.E., Demb, J.B., Wagner, A.D., Stone, M.V., Vaidyla, C.J., & Glover, G.H. (1996). Functional magnetic resonance imaging of semantic memory processes in the frontal lobes. *Psychological Science, 7*, 278–283.

Gaertner, S.L., & Dovidio, J.F. (1977). The subtlety of white racism, arousal, and helping behaviour. *Journal of Personality and Social Psychology, 35*, 691–707.

Gainotti, G. (1972). Emotional behaviour and hemispheric side of lesion. *Cortex, 8*, 41–55.

Gale, A. (1983). Electroencephalographic studies of extraversion-introversion: A case study in the psychophysiology of individual differences. *Personality and Individual Differences, 4*, 371–380.

Galli, I., & Nigro, G. (1987). The social representation of radioactivity among Italian children. *Social Science Information, 26*, 535–549.

Gallup, G.G. (1979). Self-recognition in chimpanzees and man: A developmental and comparative perspective. In M. Lewis & L.A. Rosenblum (Eds.), *Genesis of behaviour, Vol. 2: The child and its family*. New York: Plenum.

Gamson, W.B., Fireman, B., & Rytina, S. (1982). *Encounters with unjust authority*. Homewood, IL: Dorsey Press.

Ganster, D.C., Schaubroeck, J., Sime, W.E., & Mayes, B.T. (1991). The nomological validity of the Type A personality among employed adults. *Journal of Applied Psychology, 76*, 143–168.

Garcia, J., Ervin, F.R., & Koelling, R. (1966). Learning with prolonged delay of reinforcement. *Psychonomic Science, 5*, 121–122.

Gardner, H. (1983). *Frames of mind: The theory of multiple intelligences*. New York: Basic Books.

Gardner, R.A., & Gardner, B.T. (1969). Teaching sign language to a chimpanzee. *Science, 165*, 664–672.

Garfield, S.L. (1980). *Psychotherapy: An eclectic approach*. New York: Wiley.

Garfinkel, P.E., & Garner, D.M. (1982). *Anorexia nervosa: A multidimensional perspective*. New York: Basic Books.

Garner, D.M., & Fairburn, C.G. (1988). Relationship between anorexia nervosa and bulimia nervosa: Diagnostic implications. In D.M. Garner & P.E. Garfinkel (Eds.), *Diagnostic issues in anorexia nervosa and bulimia nervosa*. New York: Brunner/Mazel.

Garrett, M.F. (1975). The analysis of sentence production. In G.H. Bower (Ed.), *The psychology of learning and motivation, Vol. 9*. San Diego, CA: Academic Press.

Garrett, M.F. (1976). Syntactic processes in sentence production. In R.W. Wales & E. Walker (Eds.), *New approaches to language mechanisms*. Amsterdam: North-Holland.

Garrett, M.F. (1984). The organisation of processing structures for language production: Applications to aphasic speech. In D. Caplan, A.R. Lecours, & A. Smith (Eds.), *Biological perspectives on language*. Cambridge, MA: MIT Press.

Gatchel, R. (1997). Biofeedback. In A. Baum, S. Newman, J. Weinman, R. West, & C. McManus (Eds.), *Cambridge handbook of psychology, health, and medicine*. Cambridge: Cambridge University Press.

Gauld, A., & Stephenson, G.M. (1967). Some experiments relating to Bartlett's theory of remembering. *British Journal of Psychology, 58*, 39–50.

Gavey, N. (1992). Technologies and effects of heterosexual coercion. *Feminism and Psychology, 2*, 325–351.

Geis, M., & Zwicky, A.M. (1971). On invited inferences. *Linguistic Inquiry, 2*, 561–566.

Geiselman, R.E., Fisher, R.P., MacKinnon, D.P., & Holland, H.L. (1985). Eyewitness memory enhancement in police interview: Cognitive retrieval mnemonics versus hypnosis. *Journal of Applied Psychology, 70*, 401–412.

Gelder, M., Gath, D., & Mayon, R. (1989). *Oxford textbook of psychiatry (2nd Edn.)*. Oxford: Oxford University Press.

Gerbino, L., Oleshansky, M., & Gershon, S. (1978). Clinical use and mode of action of lithium. In M.A. Lipton, A. DiMascio, & F.K. Killam (Eds.), *Psychopharmacology: A generation of progress*. New York: Raven Press.

Gergen, K.J. (1973). Social psychology as history. *Journal of Personality and Social Psychology, 26*, 309–320.

Gergen, K.J. (1985). Social constructionist inquiry: Context and implications. In K.J. Gergen & K.E. Davis (Eds.), *The social construction of the person*. New York: Springer-Verlag.

Gergen, K.J. (1997). Social psychology as social construction: The emerging vision. In C. McGarty & A. Haslam (Eds.), *The message of social psychology*. Oxford: Blackwell.

Gergen, K.J., & Gergen, M.M. (1991). Toward reflexive methodologies. In F. Steier (Ed.), *Research and reflexivity*. London: Sage.

Gergen, K.J., Morse, S.J., & Gergen, M.M. (1980). Behaviour exchange in cross-cultural perspective. In H.C. Triandis & W.W. Lambert (Eds.), *Handbook of cross-cultural psychology, Vol. 5: Social psychology*. Boston: Allyn & Bacon.

Gerlsman, C., Emmelkamp, P.M.G., & Arrindell, W.A. (1990). Anxiety, depression, and perception of early parenting: A meta-analysis. *Clinical Psychology Review, 10*, 251–277.

Gershon, E.S. (1990). Genetics. In F.K. Goodwin & K.R. Jamison (Eds.), *Manic-depressive illness*. Oxford: Oxford University Press.

Geschwind, N. (1979). *The brain*. San Francisco: Freeman.

Ghiselli, E.E. (1966). *The validity of occupational aptitude tests*. New York: Wiley.

Gibbs, J., Young, R.C., & Smith, G.P. (1973). Cholecystokinin decreases food intake in rats. *Journal of Comparative and Physiological Psychology, 84*, 488–495.

Gibson, E.J. (1969). *Principles of perceptual learning and development*. New York: Appleton-Century-Crofts.

Gibson, E.J., & Spelke, E.S. (1983). The development of perception. In J.H. Flavell & E.M. Markman (Eds.), *Cognitive development. Vol. III: Handbook of child psychology*. Chichester: Wiley.

Gibson, E.J., & Walk, R.D. (1960). The visual cliff. *Scientific American, 202,* 64–71.

Gibson, J.J. (1950). *The perception of the visual world.* Boston: Houghton Mifflin.

Gibson, J.J. (1966). *The senses considered as perceptual systems.* Boston: Houghton Mifflin.

Gibson, J.J. (1979). *The ecological approach to visual perception.* Boston: Houghton Mifflin.

Gilbert, D.T. (1995). Attribution and interpersonal perception. In A. Tesser (Ed.), *Advanced social psychology.* New York: McGraw-Hill.

Gilbert, D.T., Pelham, B.W., & Krull, D.S. (1988). On cognitive busyness: When person perceivers meet persons perceived. *Journal of Personality and Social Psychology, 54,* 733–740.

Gilbert, G.N., & Mulkay, M. (1984). *Opening Pandora's box: A sociological analysis of scientists' discourse.* Cambridge: Cambridge University Press.

Gill, F.B., & Wolf, L.L. (1975). Economics of feeding territoriality in the golden-winged sunbird. *Ecology, 56,* 333–345.

Gilligan, C. (1977). In a different voice: Women's conceptions of the self and of morality. *Harvard Educational Review, 47,* 481–517.

Gilligan, C. (1982). *In a different voice: Psychological theory and women's development.* Cambridge, MA: Harvard University Press.

Ginsburg, H.J., & Miller, S.M. (1982). Sex differences in children's risk taking behaviour. *Child Development, 53,* 426–428.

Gittleman, J.L., & Harvey, P.H. (1980). Why are distasteful prey not cryptic? *Nature, 286,* 149–150.

Glanzer, M., & Cunitz, A.R. (1966). Two storage mechanisms in free recall. *Journal of Verbal Learning and Verbal Behavior, 5,* 351–360.

Gleitman, H. (1986). *Psychology (2nd Edn.).* London: Norton.

Glenn, N.D., & McLanahan, S. (1982). Children and marital happiness: A further specification of the relationship. *Journal of Marriage and the Family, 44,* 63–72.

Goa, K.L., & Ward, A.(1986). Buspirone: A preliminary review of its pharmacological properties and therapeutic efficacy as an anxiolytic. *Drugs, 32,* 114–129.

Goddard, H.H. (1913). *Feeble-mindedness: Its causes and consequences.* New York: Macmillan.

Goldberg, L.R. (1990). An alternative "description of personality": The big-five factor structure. *Journal of Personality and Social Psychology, 59,* 1216–1229.

Goldfarb, W. (1947). Variations in adolescent adjustment of institutionally reared children. *American Journal of Orthopsychiatry, 17,* 499–557.

Goldman, R.J., & Goldman, J.D.G. (1981). How children view old people and ageing: A developmental study of children in four countries. *Australian Journal of Psychology, 3,* 405–418.

Goldwyn, E. (1979). The fight to be male. *Listener, 24 May,* 709–712.

Gomulicki, B.R. (1956). Recall as an abstractive process. *Acta Psychologica, 12,* 77–94.

Goodkin, K., Blaney, T., Feaster, D., Fletcher, M., Baum, M.K., Mantero-Atienza, E., Klimas, N.G., Millon, C., Szapocznik, J., & Eisdorfer, C. (1992). Active coping style is associated with natural killer cell cytotoxicity in asymptomatic HIV-1 seropositive homosexual men. *Journal of Psychosomatic Research, 36,* 635–650.

Goodman, R., & Stevenson, J. (1989). A twin study of hyperactivity: II. The aetiological role of genes, family relationships, and perinatal adversity. *Journal of Child Psychology and Psychiatry, 30,* 691–709.

Goodwin, R. (1995). Personal relationships across cultures. *The Psychologist, 8,* 73–75.

Gopher, D. (1993). The skill of attentional control: Acquisition and execution of attentional strategies. In S. Kornblum & D.E. Meyer (Eds.), *Attention and performance, Vol. XIV.* Cambridge, MA: MIT Press.

Gordon, I.E. (1989). *Theories of visual perception.* Chichester: Wiley.

Gorer, G. (1968). Man has no "killer" instinct. In M.F.A. Montague (Ed.), *Man and aggression.* Oxford: Oxford University Press.

Goss-Custard, J.D. (1977a). Feeding dispersion in some overwintering wading birds. In J.H. Crook (Ed.), *Social behaviour in birds and mammals.* London: Academic Press.

Goss-Custard, J.D. (1977b). Variation in the dispersion of redshank (*Tringa totanus*) on their winter feeding grounds. *Ibis, 118,* 257–263.

Gottesman, I.I. (1991). *Schizophrenia genesis: The origins of madness.* New York: W.H. Freeman.

Gottesman, I.I., & Bertelsen, A. (1989). Dual mating studies in psychiatry: Offspring of inpatients with examples from reactive (psychogenic) psychoses. *International Review of Psychiatry, 1,* 287–296.

Gottfried, A.W. (1984). Home environment and early cognitive development: Integration, meta-analyses, and conclusions. In A.W. Gottfried (Ed.), *Home environment and early cognitive development: Longitudinal research.* Orlando, FL: Academic Press.

Gould, J.L. (1992). Honey bee cognition. In C.R. Gallistel (Ed.), *Animal cognition.* Cambridge, CA: MIT Press.

Gould, S.J. (1981). *The mismeasure of man.* New York: Norton.

Gove, W.R. (1979). The relationship between sex roles, marital status and mental illness. *Social Forces, 51,* 34–44.

Graesser, A.C., Singer, M., & Trabasso, T. (1994). Constructing inferences during narrative text comprehension. *Psychological Review, 101,* 371–395.

Graf, P., & Schacter, D.L. (1985). Implicit and explicit memory for new associations in normal and amnesic subjects. *Journal of Experimental Psychology: Learning, Memory, and Cognition, 11,* 501–518.

Graf, P., Squire, L.R., & Mandler, G. (1984). The information that amnesic patients do not forget. *Journal of Experimental Psychology: Learning, Memory, and Cognition, 10,* 164–178.

Graham, I.D., & Baker, P.M. (1989). Status, age and gender: Perceptions of old and young adults. *Psychology and Aging, 8,* 10–17.

Grant, P. (1994). Psychotherapy and race. In P. Clarkson & M. Pokorny (Eds.), *The handbook of psychotherapy.* London: Routledge.

Gray, J.A. (1985). A whole and its parts: Behaviour, the brain, cognition and emotion. *Bulletin of the British Psychological Society, 38,* 99–112.

Gray, J.A. (1991). On the morality of speciesism. *The Psychologist, 14,* 196–198.

Gray, J.A., & Wedderburn, A.A. (1960). Grouping strategies with simultaneous stimuli. *Quarterly Journal of Experimental Psychology, 12,* 180–184.

Green, S. (1994). *Principles of biopsychology.* Hove, UK: Psychology Press.

Greenberg, J.H. (1963). Some universals of grammar with particular reference to the order of meaningful elements.

In J.H. Greenberg (Ed.), *Universals of language.* Cambridge, MA: MIT Press.

Greenberg, M., Calderon, R., & Kusché, C. (1984). Early intervention using simultaneous communication with deaf infants: The effect on communication development. *Child Development, 55,* 607–616.

Greene, J. (1975). *Thinking and language.* London: Methuen.

Gregor, A.J., & McPherson, D.A. (1965). A study of susceptibility to geometrical illusion among cultural subgroups of Australian aborigines. *Psychology in Africa, 11,* 1–13.

Gregory, R. (Ed.) (1987). *The Oxford companion to the mind.* Oxford: Oxford University Press.

Gregory, R.L. (1970). *The intelligent eye.* New York: McGraw-Hill.

Gregory, R.L. (1972). Seeing as thinking. *Times Literary Supplement,* 23 June.

Gregory, R.L. (1973). The confounded eye. In R.L. Gregory & E.H. Gombrich (Eds.), *Illusion in nature and art.* London: Duckworth.

Gregory, R.L. (1980). Perceptions as hypotheses. *Philosophical Transactions of the Royal Society of London, Series B, 290,* 181–197.

Gregory, S., & Barlow, S. (1989). Interaction between deaf babies and hearing mothers. In B. Woll (Ed.), *Language development and sign language.* Monograph 1, International Sign Linguistics Association, University of Bristol.

Grice, H.P. (1967). Logic and conversation. In P. Cole & J.L. Morgan (Eds.), *Studies in syntax, Vol. III.* New York: Seminar Press.

Grier, J.W., & Burk, T. (1992). *Biology of animal behaviour.* Dubuque, IO: W.C. Brown.

Griffin, C. (1995). Feminism, social psychology and qualitative research. *The Psychologist, 8,* 119–121.

Griffin, D.R. (1955). Bird navigation. In A. Wolfson (Ed.), *Recent studies in avian biology.* Urbana, IL: University of Illinois Press.

Griggs, R.A., & Cox, J.R. (1982). The elusive thematic-material effect in Wason's selection task. *British Journal of Psychology, 73,* 407–420.

Griggs, R.A., & Cox, J.R. (1983). The effects of problem content and negation on Wason's selection task. *Quarterly Journal of Experimental Psychology, 35A,* 519–533.

Groeger, J.A. (1997). *Memory and remembering: Everyday memory in context.* Harlow, Essex: Addison Wesley Longman.

Gross, M.R., & MacMillan, A.M. (1981). Predation and the evolution of colonial nesting in bluegill sunfish (*Lepomis macrochirus*). *Behavioral Ecology and Sociobiology, 8,* 163–174.

Gross, M.R., & Shine, R. (1981). Parental care and mode of fertilisation in ectothermic vertebrates. *Evolution, 35,* 775–793.

Gross, R. (1996). *Psychology: The science of mind and behaviour (3rd Edn.).* London: Hodder & Stoughton.

Gross, R., & McIlveen, R. (1996). *Abnormal psychology.* London: Hodder & Stoughton.

Grossman, K., Grossman, K.E., Spangler, S., Suess, G., & Uzner, L. (1985). Maternal sensitivity and newborn responses as related to quality of attachment in Northern Germany. In J. Bretherton & E. Waters (Eds.), *Growing points of attachment theory. Monographs of the Society for Research in Child Development, 50,* No. 209.

Grubb, T.C. (1977). Why ospreys hover. *Wilson Bulletin, 89,* 149–150.

Grudin, J.T. (1983). Error patterns in novice and skilled transcription typing. In W.E. Cooper (Ed.), *Cognitive aspects of skilled typewriting.* New York: Springer.

Gruzelier, J. (1988). The neuropsychology of hypnosis. In M. Heap (Ed.), *Hypnosis: Current clinical, experimental and forensic practices.* London: Croom Helm.

Guarnaccia, P.J., Good, B.J., & Kleinman, A. (1990). A critical review of epidemiological studies of Puerto Rican mental health. *American Journal of Psychiatry, 147,* 1449–1456.

Guerra, N.G., & Slaby, R.G. (1990). Cognitive mediators of aggression in adolescent offenders: 2. Intervention. *Developmental Psychology, 26,* 269–277.

Guilford, J.P. (1936). Unitary traits of personality and factor theory. *American Journal of Psychology, 48,* 673–680.

Guimond, S., Begin, G., & Palmer, D.L. (1989). Education and causal attributions: The development of "person-blame" and "system-blame" ideology. *Social Psychology Quarterly, 52,* 126–140.

Gunter, B., & McAleer, J.L. (1990). *Children and television: The one-eyed monster?* London: Routledge.

Gurr, T.R. (1970). *Why men rebel.* Princeton, NJ: Princeton University Press.

Guterman, L. (1998). Trail of dung spells disaster for roaches. *New Scientist, 2160,* 12.

Gwynne, D.T. (1981). Sexual difference theory: Mormon crickets show role reversal in mate choice. *Science, 213,* 779–780.

Hagedorn, M., & Heiligenberg, W. (1985). Court and spark: Electric signals in the courtship and mating of gymnotoid fish. *Animal Behaviour, 33,* 254–265.

Hailman, J. (1992). The necessity of a "show-me" attitude in science. In J. W. Grier & T. Burk, *Biology of animal behaviour (2nd Edn.).* Dubuque, IO: W.C. Brown.

Hajek, P., & Belcher, M. (1991). Dreams of absent-minded transgression: An empirical study of a cognitive withdrawal symptom. *Journal of Abnormal Psychology, 100,* 487–491.

Halgin, R.P., & Whitbourne, S.K. (1997). *Abnormal psychology: The human experience of psychological disorders.* Madison, WI: Brown & Benchmark.

Hall, C.S. (1953). A cognitive theory of dream symbols. *Journal of General Psychology, 48,* 169–186.

Hall, C.S. (1966a). *The meaning of dreams.* New York: McGraw-Hill.

Hall, E.T. (1966b). *The hidden dimension.* New York: Doubleday.

Hall, J.A. (1990). *Nonverbal sex differences: Accuracy of communication and expressive style.* Baltimore, MD: Johns Hopkins University Press.

Halleck, S.L. (1971). *The politics of therapy.* New York: Science House.

Halliday, T. (1980). *Sexual strategy.* Oxford: Oxford University Press.

Halliday, T., & Arnold, S.J. (1987). Multiple mating by females: A perspective from quantitative genetics. *Animal Behaviour, 35,* 939–941.

Hamilton, L.W., & Timmons, C.R. (1995). Psycho-pharmacology. In D. Kimble & A. M. Colman (Eds.), *Biological aspects of behaviour.* London: Longman.

Hamilton, W.D. (1964). The genetical evolution of social behaviour. I and II. *Journal of Theoretical Biology, 7,* 1–52.

Hamilton, W.D., & Zuk, M. (1982). Heritable true fitness and bright birds: A role for parasites? *Science, 218,* 384–387.

Hammen, C.L. (1991). The generation of stress in the course of unipolar depression. *Journal of Abnormal Psychology, 100,* 555–561.

Hampson, P.J. (1989). Aspects of attention and cognitive science. *Irish Journal of Psychology, 10,* 261–275.

Hampson, S.E. (1988). *The construction of personality: An introduction (2nd Edn.).* London: Routledge.

Han, P.J., Feng, L.Y., & Kuo, P.T. (1972). Insulin sensitivity of pair-fed, hyperlipemic, hyperinsulinemic, obese hypothalamic rats. *American Journal of Physiology, 223,* 1206–1209.

Hanley, J.R., Hastie, K., & Kay, J. (1991). Developmental surface dyslexia and dysgraphia: An orthographic processing impairment. *Quarterly Journal of Experimental Psychology, 43A,* 285–310.

Hardyck, C.D., & Petrinovich, L.F. (1970). Subvocal speech and comprehension level as a function of the difficulty level of reading material. *Journal of Verbal Learning and Verbal Behavior, 9,* 647–652.

Hare-Mustin, R.T., & Maracek, J. (1988). The meaning of difference: Gender theory, post-modernism and psychology. *American Psychologist, 43,* 455–464.

Harley, T.A. (1995). *The psychology of language: From data to theory.* Hove, UK: Psychology Press.

Harlow, H.F. (1958). The nature of love. *American Psychologist, 13,* 673–685.

Harlow, H.F. (1959). Love in infant monkeys. *Scientific American, 200,* 68–74.

Harlow, H.F., & Mears, C. (1979). *The human model: Primate perspectives.* Washington, DC: Winston.

Harré, R., & Secord, P. (1972). *The explanation of social behaviour.* Oxford: Basil Blackwell.

Harris, E.L., Noyes, R., Crowe, R.R., & Chaudhry, D.R. (1983). Family study of agoraphobia: Report of a pilot study. *Archives of General Psychiatry, 40,* 1061–1064.

Harris, M. (1990). Language and thought. In M.W. Eysenck (Ed.), *The Blackwell dictionary of cognitive psychology.* Oxford: Blackwell.

Harris, M., & Barlow-Brown, F. (1997). Learning to read in blind and sighted children. In V. Lewis & G.M. Collis (Eds.), *Blindness and psychological development in young children.* Leicester: BPS Books.

Harris, M., Jones, D., Brookes, S., & Grant, J. (1986). Relations between the non-verbal context of maternal speech and rate of language development. *British Journal of Developmental Psychology, 4,* 261–268.

Harris, R.J., et al. (1980). Remembering implied advertising claims as facts: Extensions to the "real world". *Bulletin of the Psychonomic Society, 16,* 317–320.

Harris, T. O. (1997). Adult attachment processes and psychotherapy: A commentary on Bartholomew and Birtschnell. *British Journal of Medical Psychology, 70,* 281–290.

Harris, W.H. (1995). *The opportunity for romantic love among hunter-gatherers.* Paper presented at the annual convention of the Human Behavior and Evolution Society, June, Santa Barbara, California.

Hart, B., & Risley, T. (1995). *Meaningful differences in everyday parenting and intellectual development in young American children.* Baltimore: Brookes.

Harter, S. (1982). The perceived competence scale for children. *Child Development, 53,* 87–97.

Harter, S. (1987). The determinants and mediational role of global self-worth in children. In N. Eisenberg (Ed.),

Contemporary topics in developmental psychology. New York: Wiley.

Harter, S., & Monsour, A. (1992). Developmental analysis of conflict caused by opposing attributes in the adolescent self-portrait. *Developmental Psychology, 28,* 251–260.

Harter, S., & Pike, R. (1984). The pictorial scale of perceived competence and social acceptance for young children. *Child Development, 55,* 1969–1982.

Hartshorne, H., & May, M.S. (1928). *Studies in the nature of character, Vol. 1: Studies in deceit.* New York: Macmillan.

Harvey, L.O., Roberts, J.O., & Gervais, M.J. (1983). The spatial frequency basis of internal representations. In H.-G. Geissler, H.F.J.M. Buffart, E.L.J. Leeuwenberg, & V. Sarris (Eds.), *Modern issues in perception.* Rotterdam: North-Holland.

Harwood, R.L., & Miller, J.G. (1991). Perceptions of attachment behaviour: A comparison of Anglo and Puerto Rican mothers. *Merrill-Palmer Quarterly, 37,* 583–599.

Hasler, A.D. (1986). Review of R.J.F. Smith (1985). *Zeitschrift für Tierpsychologie, 70,* 168–169.

Hatfield, E., Utne, M.K., & Traupmann, J. (1979). Equity theory and intimate relationships. In R.L. Burgess & T.L. Huston (Eds.), *Exchange theory in developing relationships.* New York: Academic Press.

Havighurst, R.J. (1964). Stages of vocational development. In H. Borrow (Ed.), *Man in a world of work.* Boston: Houghton Mifflin.

Havighurst, R.J., Neugarten, B.L.A., & Tobin, S.S.C. (1968). Disengagement and patterns of aging. In B.L. Neugarten (Ed.), *Middle age and aging.* Chicago: University of Chicago Press.

Hawke, C. (1950). Castration and sex crimes. *American Journal of Mental Deficiency, 55,* 220–226.

Hawkes, N. (1998). Clue to season depression. *The Times,* 26 May, p.9.

Hay, D.F., & Vespo, J.E. (1988). Social learning perspectives on the development of the mother–child relationship. In B. Birns & D.F. Hay (Eds.), *The different faces of motherhood.* New York: Plenum Press.

Hay, J.F., & Jacoby, L.L. (1996). Separating habit and recollection: Memory slips, process dissociations, and probability matching. *Journal of Experimental Psychology: Learning, Memory, and Cognition, 22,* 1323–1335.

Hayes, C. (1951). *The ape in our house.* New York: Harper.

Hayes, J.R., & Flower, L.S. (1980). Identifying the organisation of writing processes. In L.W. Gregg & E.R. Sternberg (Eds.), *Cognitive processes in writing.* Hillsdale, NJ: Lawrence Erlbaum Associates Inc.

Hayes, J.R., & Flower, L.S. (1986). Writing research and the writer. *American Psychologist, 41,* 1106–1113.

Hayes, J.R., Flower, L.S., Schriver, K., Stratman, J., & Carey, L. (1985). *Cognitive processes in revision* (Technical Report No. 12). Pittsburgh, PA: Carnegie Mellon University.

Hayes, N. (1993). *Principles of social psychology.* Hove, UK: Psychology Press.

Hearnshaw, L. (1987). *The shaping of modern psychology: An historical introduction.* London: Routledge & Kegan Paul.

Hearold, S. (1986). A synthesis of 1043 effects of television on social behaviour. In G. Comstock (Ed.), *Public communication and behaviour, Vol. 1.* Orlando, FL: Academic Press.

Heather, N. (1976). *Radical perspectives in psychology.* London: Methuen.

Heber, R., Garber, H., Harrington, S., Hoffman, C., & Falender, C. (1972). *Rehabilitation of families at risk for mental retardation: Progress report*. University of Wisconsin: Rehabilitation Research and Training Center in Mental Retardation.

Heckhausen, J. (1997). Developmental regulation across adulthood: Primary and secondary control of age-related challenges. *Developmental Psychology, 33*, 176–187.

Hedricks, C., Piccinino, L.J., Udry, J.R., & Chimbia, T.H. (1987). Peak coital rate coincides with onset of luteinising hormone surge. *Fertility and Sterility, 48*, 234–238.

Heider, E.R. (1972). Universals in colour naming and memory. *Journal of Experimental Psychology, 93*, 10–20.

Heider, F. (1958). *The psychology of interpersonal relations*. New York: Wiley.

Heinicke, C.H., & Guthrie, D. (1992). Stability and change in husband-wife adaptation and the development of the positive parent-child relationship. *Infant Behavior and Development, 15*, 109–127.

Henggeler, S. W., Watson, S.M., & Cooper, P.F. (1984). Verbal and nonverbal maternal controls in hearing mother–deaf child interaction. *Journal of Applied Developmental Psychology, 5*, 319–329.

Hennigan, K.M., Del Rosario, M.L., Cook, T.D., & Calder, B.J. (1982). Impact of the introduction of television on crime in the United States: Empirical findings and theoretical implications. *Journal of Personality and Social Psychology, 42*, 461–477.

Hering, E. (1878). *Outlines of a theory of the light sense* [translated by L.M. Hurvich & D. Jameson]. Cambridge, MA: Harvard University Press.

Herman, D., & Green, J. (1991). *Madness: A study guide*. London: BBC Education.

Herman, J.L., & Schatzow, E. (1987). Recovery and verification of memories of childhood sexual trauma. *Psychoanalytic Psychology, 4*, 1–14.

Herman, L.M., Richards, D.G., & Wolz, J.P. (1984). Comprehension of sentences by bottlenosed dolphins. *Cognition, 16*, 129–219.

Herzlich, C. (1973). *Health and illness: A social-psychological analysis*. London: Academic Press.

Herzog, H.A. (1988). The moral status of mice. *American Psychologist, 43*, 473–474.

Heslin, R. (1964). Predicting group task effectiveness from member characteristics. *Psychological Bulletin, 62*, 248–256.

Hess, R.D., & Shipman, V. (1965). Early experience and the socialisation of cognitive modes in children. *Child Development, 36*, 860–886.

Hetherington, A.W., & Ranson, S.W. (1942). The relation of various hypothalamic lesions to adiposity in the rat. *Journal of Comparative Neurology, 76*, 475–499.

Hewstone, M., & Antaki, C. (1988). Attribution theory and social explanations. In M. Hewstone, W. Stroebe, J.-P. Codol, & G.M. Stephenson (Eds.), *Introduction to social psychology*. Oxford: Blackwell.

Hewstone, M.R.C., & Brown, R.J. (1986). Contact is not enough: An intergroup perspective on the contact hypothesis. In M.R.C. Hewstone & R.J. Brown (Eds.), *Contact and conflict in intergroup encounters*. Oxford: Blackwell.

Heylighen, F. (1992). Evolution, selfishness and co-operation. *Journal of Ideas, 2*, 70–76.

Hilgard, E.R. (1977). *Divided consciousness: Multiple controls in human thought and action*. New York: Wiley.

Hilgard, E.R. (1986). *Divided consciousness: Multiple controls in human thought and action* (expanded edition). New York: Wiley.

Hilgard, E.R., & Hilgard, J.R. (1983). *Hypnosis in the relief of pain*. Los Altos, CA: William Kaufmann.

Hilgard, E.R., & Marquis, D.G. (1961). *Conditioning and learning*. London: Methuen.

Hinde, R.A. (1977). Mother-infant separation and the nature of inter-individual relationships: Experiments with rhesus monkeys. *Proceedings of the Royal Society of London B, 196*, 29–50.

Hirt, E.R., Zillmann, D., Erickson, G.A., & Kennedy, C. (1992). Costs and benefits of allegiance: Changes in fans' self-ascribed competencies after team victory versus defeat. *Journal of Personality and Social Psychology, 63*, 724–738.

Hitch, G., & Baddeley, A.D. (1976). Verbal reasoning and working memory. *Quarterly Journal of Experimental Psychology, 28*, 603–621.

Hobfoll, S.E., & London, P. (1986). The relationship of self-concept and social support to emotional distress among women during the war. *Journal of Social and Clinical Psychology, 4*, 189–203.

Hobson, J.A. (1988). *The dreaming brain*. New York: Basic Books.

Hobson, J.A. (1994). Sleep and dreaming. In A.M. Colman (Ed.), *Companion encyclopedia of psychology, Vol. 1*. London: Routledge.

Hobson, J.A., & McCarley, R.W. (1977). The brain as a dream state generator: An activation-synthesis hypothesis of the dream process. *American Journal of Psychiatry, 134*, 1335 1348.

Hockett, C.F. (1960). The origin of speech. *Scientific American, 203*, 89–96.

Hockey, G.R.J. (1983). Current issues and new directions. In R. Hockey (Ed.), *Stress and fatigue in human performance*. Chichester: Wiley.

Hockey, G.R.J., Davies, S., & Gray, M.M. (1972). Forgetting as a function of sleep at different times of day. *Quarterly Journal of Experimental Psychology, 24*, 386–393.

Hodges, J., & Tizard, B. (1989). Social and family relationships of ex-institutional adolescents. *Journal of Child Psychology and Psychiatry, 30*, 77–97.

Hodges, W.F. (1968). Effects of ego threat and threat of pain on state anxiety. *Journal of Personality and Social Psychology, 8*, 364–372.

Hoebel, B.G., & Teitelbaum, P. (1966). Weight regulation in normal and hypothalamic hyperphagic rats. *Journal of Comparative and Physiological Psychology, 61*, 189–193.

Hoffman, C., Lau, I., & Johnson, D.R. (1986). The linguistic relativity of person cognition. *Journal of Personality and Social Psychology, 51*, 1097–1105.

Hoffman, D.D., & Richards, W.A. (1984). Parts of recognition. *Cognition, 18*, 65–96.

Hoffman, M.L. (1970). Moral development. In P.H. Mussen (Ed.), *Carmichael's manual of child psychology, Vol. 2*. New York: Wiley.

Hoffman, M.L. (1975). Altruistic behaviour and the parent–child relationship. *Journal of Personality and Social Psychology, 31*, 937–943.

Hoffman, M.L. (1988). Moral development. In M.H. Bornstein & M. E. Lamb (Eds.), *Developmental psychology: An advanced textbook*. Hillsdale, NJ: Erlbaum.

Hofling, C.K. (1974). *Textbook of psychiatry for medical practice*.

Hofling, K.C., Brotzman, E., Dalrymple, S., Graves, N., & Pierce, C.M. (1966). An experimental study in the nurse–physician relationship. *Journal of Nervous and Mental Disorders, 143*, 171–180.

Hofstede, G. (1980). *Culture's consequences: International differences in work-related values*. Beverly Hills, CA: Sage.

Hohmann, G.W. (1966). Some effects of spinal cord lesions on experienced emotional feelings. *Psychophysiology, 3*, 143–156.

Holland, A.J., Sicotte, N., & Treasure, J. (1988). Anorexia nervosa: Evidence for a genetic basis. *Journal of Psychosomatic Research, 32*, 561–572.

Hollander, E.P. (1993). Legitimacy, power, and influence: A perspective on relational features of leadership. In M.M. Chemers & R. Ayman (Eds.), *Leadership theory and research: Perspectives and directions*. San Diego, CA: Academic Press.

Holldobler, B. (1971). Communication between ants and their guests. *Scientific American, 224*, 85–93.

Holmes, D.S. (1990). The evidence for repression: An examination of sixty years of research. In J. Singer (Ed.), *Repression and dissociation: Implications for personality theory, psychopathology, and health*. Chicago: University of Chicago Press.

Holmes, T.H., & Rahe, R.H. (1967). The social readjustment rating scale. *Journal of Psychosomatic Research, 11*, 213–218.

Holmes, W.G., & Sherman, P.W. (1982). The ontogeny of kin recognition in two species of ground squirrels. *American Zoologist, 22*, 491–517.

Holt, R.R. (1967). Individuality and generalisation in the psychology of personality. In R.L. Lazarus & J.R. Opton (Eds.), *Personality*. Harmondsworth: Penguin.

Holway, A.F., & Boring, E.G. (1941). Determinants of apparent visual size with distance variant. *American Journal of Psychology, 54*, 21–37.

Hoogland, J.L. (1979). Aggression, ectoparasitism, and other possible costs of prairie dog (*Sciuridae, Cynomys spp.*) coloniality. *Behaviour, 69*, 1–35.

Hoogland, J.L. (1983). Nepotism and alarm calling in the black-tailed prairie dog (*Cynomys ludovicianus*). *Animal Behaviour, 31*, 472–479.

Hooley, J.M., Orley, J., & Teasdale, J.D. (1986). Levels of expressed emotion and relapse in depressed patients. *British Journal of Psychiatry, 148*, 642–647.

Horn, J.M. (1983). The Texas adoption project: Adopted children and their intellectual resemblance to biological and adoptive parents. *Child Development, 54*, 268–275.

Horne, J. (1988). *Why we sleep? The functions of sleep in humans and other mammals*. Oxford: Oxford University Press.

Horowitz, M.J. (1986). *Stress-response syndromes (2nd Edn.)*. New Jersey: Jason Aronson.

Hough, L.M., Eaton, N.K., Dunnette, M.D., Kamp, J.D., & McCloy, R.A. (1990). Criterion-related validities of personality constructs and the effect of response distortion on those validities. *Journal of Applied Psychology, 75*, 581–595.

Hovland, C.I., Lumsdaine, A.A., & Sheffield, R.D. (1949). *Experiments in mass communication*. Princeton, NJ: Princeton University Press.

Hovland, C., & Sears, R. (1940). Minor studies in aggression: VI. Correlation of lynchings with economic indices. *Journal of Personality, 9*, 301–310.

Hovland, C.I., & Weiss, W. (1951). The influence of source credibility on communication effectiveness. *Public Opinion Quarterly, 151*, 635–650.

Howard, J.A., Blumstein, P., & Schwartz, P. (1987). Social evolutionary theories? Some observations on preferences in human mate selection. *Journal of Personality and Social Psychology, 53*, 194–200.

Howard, J.W., & Dawes, R.M. (1976). Linear prediction of marital happiness. *Personality and Social Psychology Bulletin, 2*, 478–480.

Howard, R.D. (1978). The evolution of mating strategies in bullfrogs, *Rana catesbeiana*. *Evolution, 32*, 850–871.

Howarth, E., & Browne, J.A. (1971). An item-factor-analysis of the 16PF. *Personality, 2*, 117–139.

Howe, C., Tolmie, A., & Rodgers, C. (1992). The acquisition of conceptual knowledge in science by primary school children: Group interaction and the understanding of motion down an incline. *British Journal of Developmental Psychology, 10*, 113–130.

Howe, M. (1990). Useful word but obsolete construct. *The Psychologist, 3*, 498–499.

Howe, M.J.A. (1988). "Hot house" children. *The Psychologist, 1*, 356–358.

Howitt, D., & Owusu-Bempah (1990). Racism in a British journal? *The Psychologist, 3*, 396–400.

Hrdy, S.B. (1977). Infanticide as a primate reproductive strategy. *American Scientist, 65*, 40–49.

Hsu, F. (1981). *Americans and Chinese: Passage to difference (3rd Edn.)*. Honolulu: University Press of Honolulu.

Hsu, L.K. (1990). *Eating disorders*. New York: Guilford.

Hubel, D.H., & Wiesel, T.N. (1962). Receptive fields, binocular interaction and functional architecture in the cat's visual cortex. *Journal of Physiology, 160*, 106–154.

Hubel, D.H., & Wiesel, T.N. (1979). Brain mechanisms of vision. *Scientific American, 249*, 150–162.

Huber-Weidman, H. (1976). *Sleep, sleep disturbances and sleep deprivation*. Cologne: Kiepenheuser & Witsch.

Hudson, W. (1960). Pictorial depth perception in subcultural groups in Africa. *Journal of Social Psychology, 52*, 183–208.

Huesmann, L.R., & Eron, L.D. (1986). *Television and the aggressive child: A cross-national comparison*. Hillsdale, NJ: Erlbaum.

Huesmann, L.R., Lagerspitz, K., & Eron, L.D. (1984). Intervening variables in the TV violence–aggression relation: Evidence from two countries. *Developmental Psychology, 20*, 746–775.

Hughes, M. (1975). *Egocentrism in preschool children*. Unpublished PhD thesis, University of Edinburgh.

Hull, C.L. (1943). *Principles of behaviour*. New York: Appleton-Century-Crofts.

Hull, J.G., & Bond, C.F. (1986). Social and behavioural consequences of alcohol consumption and expectancy: A meta-analysis. *Psychological Bulletin, 99*, 347–360.

Human, I.E. (1992). Multiple approaches to remembering. *The Psychologist, 5*, 450–451.

Humphrey, L.L., Apple, R.F., & Kirschenbaum, D.S. (1986). Differentiating bulimic-anorexic from normal families using interpersonal and behavioural observational systems. *Journal of Consulting and Clinical Psychology, 54*, 190–195.

Humphrey, N. (1993). *The inner eye*. London: Vintage.

Hunt, E., & Agnoli, F. (1991). The Whorfian hypothesis: A cognitive psychological perspective. *Psychological Review, 98*, 377–389.

Hunter, M.L., & Krebs, J.R. (1979). Geographical variation in the song of the great tit (*Parus major*) in relation to ecological factors. *Journal of Animal Ecology, 48*, 759–785.

Huntingford, F. A. (1976). The relationship between anti-predator behaviour and aggression among conspecifics in the three-spined stickleback, *Gasterosteus aculeatus*. *Animal Behaviour, 24*, 245–260.

Huntingford, F.A., & Turner, A. (1987). *Animal conflict*. London: Chapman & Hall.

Huston, A.C. (1985). The development of sex typing: Themes from recent research. *Developmental Review, 5*, 1–17.

Huston, T.L., Ruggiero, M., Conner, R., & Geis, G. (1981). Bystander intervention into crime: A study based on naturally-occurring episodes. *Social Psychology Quarterly, 44*, 14–23.

Huttenlocher, P.R. (1974). Dendritic development in neocortex of children with mental defect and infantile spasms. *Neurology, 24*, 203–210.

Hyde, J.S., & Linn, M.C. (1988). Gender differences in verbal ability: A meta-analysis. *Psychological Bulletin, 104*, 53–69.

Hyde, T.S., & Jenkins, J.J. (1973). Recall for words as a function of semantic, graphic, and syntactic orienting tasks. *Journal of Verbal Learning and Verbal Behavior, 12*, 471–480.

Imperato-McGinley, J., Guerro, L., Gautier, T., & Peterson, R.E. (1974). Steroid 5–reductase deficiency in man: An inherited form of male pseudohermaphroditism. *Science, 186*, 1213–1216.

Inglis, I.R., & Ferguson, N.J.K. (1986). Starlings search for food rather than eat freely-available, identical food. *Animal Behaviour, 34*, 614–617.

Inhelder, B., & Piaget, J. (1958). *The growth of logical thinking from childhood to adolescence*. New York: Basic Books.

International Classification of Diseases (1992). *The ICD-10 classification of mental and behavioural disorders: Clinical descriptions and diagnostic guidelines*. Geneva. WHO.

Irwin, M., Lovitz, A., Marder, S.R., Mintz, J., Winslade, W.J., Van Putten, T., & Mills, M.J. (1985). 'Psychotic patients' understanding of informed consent. *American Journal of Psychiatry, 142*, 1351–1354.

Isack, H.A., & Reyer, H.U. (1989). Honeyguides and honey gatherers: Interspecific communication in a symbiotic relationship. *Science, 243*, 1343–1346.

Ittelson, W.H. (1951). Size as a cue to distance: Static localisation. *American Journal of Psychology, 64*, 54–67.

Ittelson, W.H. (1952). *The Ames demonstrations in perception*. New York: Hafner.

Jacobs, K.C., & Campbell, D.T. (1961). The perpetuation of an arbitrary tradition through several generations of a laboratory microculture. *Journal of Abnormal and Social Psychology, 62*, 649–658.

Jacobsen, C.F., Wolfe, J.B., & Jackson, T.A. (1935). An experimental analysis of the functions of the frontal association areas in primates. *Journal of Nervous and Mental Disorders, 82*, 1–14.

Jacoby, L.L. (1978). On interpreting the effects of repetition: Solving a problem versus remembering a solution. *Journal of Verbal Learning and Verbal Behavior, 17*, 649–667.

Jacoby, L.L. (1983). Remembering the data: Analysing interactive processing in reading. *Journal of Verbal Learning and Verbal Behavior, 22*, 485–508.

James, W. (1890). *Principles of psychology*. New York: Holt.

Jang, K.L., Livesley, W.J., & Vernon, P.A. (1996). Heritability of the Big Five personality dimensions and their facets: A twin study. *Journal of Personality, 64*, 577–591.

Janis, I.L., & Feshbach, S. (1953). Effects of fear-arousing communications. *Journal of Abnormal and Social Psychology, 48*, 78–92.

Jenkins, C.D., Hurst, M.W., & Rose, R.M. (1979). Life changes: Do people really remember? *Archives of General Psychiatry, 36*, 379–384.

Jenkins, J.G., & Dallenbach, K.M. (1924). Obliviscence during sleep and waking. *American Journal of Psychology, 35*, 605–612.

Jensen, A.R. (1969). How much can we boost IQ and scholastic achievement? *Harvard Educational Review, 39*, 1–123.

Jodelet, D. (1991). Représentation sociale: Phénomenes, concept et théorie. In S. Moscovici (Ed.), *Psychologie sociale*. Pairs: Presses Universitaires de France.

Johansson, G. (1973). Visual perception of biological motion and a model for its analysis. *Perception & Psychophysics, 14*, 201–211.

Johnson, C., & Blinkhorn, S. (1994). Desperate measures: Job performance and personality test validities. *The Psychologist, 7*, 167–170.

Johnson, R.D., & Downing, L.L. (1979). Deindividuation and valence of cues: Effects on prosocial and antisocial behaviour. *Journal of Personality and Social Psychology, 39*, 1532–1538.

Johnson-Laird, P.N. (1980). Mental models in cognitive science. *Cognitive Science, 4*, 71–115.

Johnson-Laird, P.N. (1983). *Mental models*. Cambridge: Cambridge University Press.

Johnston, J., & Ettema, J.S. (1982). *Positive image: Breaking stereotypes with children's television*. Beverly Hills: Sage.

Johnston, W.A., & Dark, V.J. (1986). Selective attention. *Annual Review of Psychology, 37*, 43–75.

Johnston, W.A., & Heinz, S.P. (1978). Flexibility and capacity demands of attention. *Journal of Experimental Psychology: General, 107*, 420–435.

Johnston, W.A., & Wilson, J. (1980). Perceptual processing of non-targets in an attention task. *Memory & Cognition, 8*, 372–377.

Johnstone, L. (1989). *Users and abusers of psychiatry: A critical look at traditional psychiatric practice*. London: Routledge.

Jones, E.E., & Davis, K.E. (1965). From acts to dispositions: The attribution process in person perception. In L. Berkowitz (Ed.), *Advances in Experimental Social Psychology, Vol. 2*. New York: Academic Press.

Jones, E.E., & Harris, V.A. (1967). The attribution of attitudes. *Journal of Experimental Social Psychology, 3*, 1–24.

Jones, E.E., & Nisbett, R.E. (1972). The actor and the observer: Divergent perceptions of the causes of behaviour. In E.E. Jones, D.E. Kanouse, H.H. Kelley, R.E. Nisbett, S. Valins, & B. Weiner (Eds.), *Attribution: Perceiving the causes of behaviour*. Morristown, NJ: General Learning Press.

Jones, E.E., & Sigall, H. (1971). The bogus pipeline: A new paradigm for measuring affect and attitude. *Psychological Bulletin, 76*, 349–364.

Jones, M.C. (1925). A laboratory study of fear: The case of Peter. *Pedagogical Seminary, 31*, 308–315.

Jordan, I.K., & Karchmer, M.A. (1986). Patterns of sign use among hearing impaired students. In A.N. Schildroth & M.A. Karchmer (Eds.), *Deaf children in America*. San Diego, CA: College-Hill Press.

Josephson, W.L. (1987). Television violence and children's aggression: Testing the priming, social script, and disinhibition predictions. *Journal of Personality and Social Psychology, 53*, 882–890.

Jourard, S.M. (1966). An exploratory study of body-accessibility. *British Journal of Social and Clinical Psychology, 5,* 221–231.

Julesz, B. (1971). *Foundations of cylopean perception.* Chicago: University of Chicago Press.

Juola, J.F., Bowhuis, D.G., Cooper, E.E., & Warner, C.B. (1991). Control of attention around the fovea. *Journal of Experimental Psychology: Human Perception and Performance, 15,* 315–330.

Kaas, J.H., Nelson, R.J., Sur, M., & Merzenich, M.M. (1981). Organisation of somatosensory cortex in primates. In F.O. Schmitt, F.G. Worden, G. Adelman, & S. G. Dennis (Eds.), *The organisation of the cerebral cortex.* Cambridge, MA: MIT Press.

Kacelnik, A. (1984). Central place foraging in Starlings *(Sturnus vulgaris).* I. Patch residence time. *Journal of Animal Ecology, 53,* 283–299.

Kagan, J. (1984). *The nature of the child.* New York: Basic Books.

Kagan, J., & Klein, R.E. (1973). Cross-cultural perspectives on early development. *American Psychologist, 28,* 947–961.

Kahneman, D., & Henik, A. (1979). Perceptual organisation and attention. In M. Kubovy & J.R. Pomerantz (Eds.), *Perceptual organisation.* Hillsdale, NJ: Lawrence Erlbaum Associates Inc.

Kahneman, D., & Tversky, A. (1972). Subjective probability: A judgment of representativeness. *Cognitive Psychology, 3,* 430–454.

Kahneman, D., & Tversky, A. (1973). On the psychology of prediction. *Psychological Review, 80,* 237–251.

Kahneman, D., & Tversky, A. (1979). Intuitive prediction: Biases and corrective procedures. *TIMS Studies in Management Science, 12,* 313–327.

Kahneman, D., & Tversky, A. (1984). Choices, values and frames. *American Psychologist, 39,* 341–350.

Kalucy, R.S., Crisp, A.H., & Harding, B. (1977). A study of 56 families with anorexia nervosa. *British Journal of Medical Psychology, 50,* 381–395.

Kamin, L. (1981). *The intelligence controversy: H.J. Eysenck vs. Leon Kamin.* New York: Wiley.

Kamin, L.J. (1969). Predictability, surprise, attention and conditioning. In R. Campbell & R. Church (Eds.), *Punishment and aversive behaviour.* New York: Appleton-Century-Crofts.

Kandel, D.B. (1978). Similarity in real-life adolescent friendship pairs. *Journal of Personality and Social Psychology, 36,* 306–312.

Kane, J., Honigfeld, G., Singer, J., & Meltzer, H.Y. (1988). Clozapine for the treatment resistant schizophrenic. *Archives of General Psychiatry, 45,* 789–796.

Kanizsa, G. (1976). Subjective contours. *Scientific American, 234,* 48–52.

Kanner, L. (1943). Autistic disturbances of affective contact. *Nervous child, 2,* 217–250.

Kanner, L. (1973). Follow-up of eleven autistic children originally reported in 1943. In L. Kanner (Ed.), *Childhood psychosis: Initial studies and new insights.* Washington, DC: Winston-Wiley.

Karney, B.R., & Bradbury, T.N. (1995). The longitudinal course of marital quality and stability: A review of theory, method, and research. *Psychological Bulletin, 118,* 3–34.

Kashima, Y., & Triandis, H.C. (1986). The self-serving bias in attributions as a coping strategy: A cross-cultural study. *Journal of Cross-Cultural Psychology, 17,* 83–97.

Kassin, S.M., Ellsworth, P.C., & Smith, U.L. (1989). The "general acceptance" of psychological research on eyewitness testimony. *American Psychologist, 44,* 1089–1098.

Katz, D., & Braly, K.W. (1933). Racial stereotypes of one hundred college students. *Journal of Abnormal and Social Psychology, 28,* 280–290.

Kaufer, D., Hayes, J.R., & Flower, L.S. (1986). Composing written sentences. *Research in the Teaching of English, 20,* 121–140.

Kaul, T.J., & Bednar, R.L. (1986). Experiential group research: Results, questions, and suggestions. In S.L. Garfield & A.E. Bergin (Eds.), *Handbook of psychotherapy and behaviour change (3rd Edn.),* Chichester: Wiley.

Kavanagh, D.J. (1992). Recent developments in expressed emotion and schizophrenia. *British Journal of Psychiatry, 160,* 601–620.

Kay, P., & Kempton, W. (1984). What is the Sapir-Whorf hypothesis? *American Anthropologist, 86,* 65–79.

Keane, T.M., Fairbank, J.A., Caddell, J.M., Zimmering, R.T., & Gender, M. (1985). A behavioural approach to assessing and treating posttraumatic stress disorder in Vietnam veterans. In C.R. Figley (Ed.), *Trauma and its wake: The study and treatment of post-traumatic stress disorder.* New York: Brunner/Mazel.

Keeton, W.T. (1974). The mystery of pigeon homing. *Scientific American, 231,* 96–107.

Keller, H., Scholmerich, A., & Eibl-Eibesfeldt, I. (1988). Communication patterns in adult–infant interactions in Western and non-Western cultures. *Journal of Cross-cultural Psychology, 19,* 427–445.

Kelley, H.H. (1967). Attribution theory in social psychology. In D. Levine (Ed.), *Nebraska symposium on motivation.* Lincoln, NE: University of Nebraska Press.

Kelley, H.H. (1973). The processes of causal attribution. *American Psychologist, 28,* 107–128.

Kellogg, R.T. (1988). Attentional overload and writing performance: Effects of rough draft and outline strategies. *Journal of Experimental Psychology: Learning, Memory, and Cognition, 14,* 355–365.

Kellogg, R.T. (1990). Writing. In M.W. Eysenck (Ed.), *The Blackwell dictionary of cognitive psychology.* Oxford: Blackwell.

Kelman, H.C. (1958). Compliance, identification and internalisation: Three processes of attitude change. *Journal of Conflict Resolution, 2,* 51–60.

Kelman, H.C. (1972). The rights of the subject in social research: An analysis in terms of relative power and legitimacy. *American Psychologist, 27,* 989–1016.

Kendall, P.C., & Hammen, C. (1995). *Abnormal psychology.* Boston: Houghton Mifflin.

Kendall, P.C., & Hammen, C. (1998). *Abnormal psychology (2nd Edn.).* Boston: Houghton Mifflin.

Kendler, K.S., Maclean, C., Neale, M., Kessler, R., Heath, A., & Eaves, L. (1991). The genetic epidemiology of bulimia nervosa. *American Journal of Psychiatry, 148,* 1627–1637.

Kenny, D.A., & Zaccaro, S.J. (1983). An estimate of variance due to traits of leadership. *Journal of Applied Psychology, 68,* 678–685.

Kenward, R.E. (1978). Hawks and doves: Factors affecting success and selection in goshawk attacks on wood-pigeons. *Journal of Animal Ecology, 47,* 449–460.

Kerckhoff, A.C., & Davis, K.E. (1962). Value consensus and need complementarity in mate selection. *American Sociological Review, 27,* 295–303.

Kessel, E.L. (1955). Mating activities of balloon flies. *Systematic Zoology, 4*, 97–104.

Kety, S.S. (1974). From rationalisation to reason. *American Journal of Psychiatry, 131*, 957–963.

Kety, S.S. (1975). Biochemistry of the major psychoses. In A. Freedman, H. Kaplan, & B. Sadock (Eds.), *Comprehensive textbook of psychiatry*. Baltimore: Williams & Wilkins.

Kety, S.S., Rosenthal, D., Wender, P.H., Schulsinger, F., & Jacobsen, B. (1978). The biological and adoptive families of adoptive individuals who become schizophrenic. In L.C. Wynne, R.L. Cromwell, & S. Matthysse (Eds.), *The nature of schizophrenia*. New York: John Wiley.

Keuthen, N. (1980). *Subjective probability estimation and somatic structures in phobic individuals*. Unpublished manuscript, State University of New York at Stony Brook.

Kimble, D.L., Covell, N.H., Weiss, L.H., Newton, K.J., & Fisher, J.D. (1992). College students use implicit personality theory instead of safer sex. *Journal of Applied Social Psychology, 22*, 921–933.

Kimble, D.P., Robinson, T.S., & Moon, S. (1980). *Biological psychology*. New York: Holt, Reinhart, & Winston.

Kimmel, A.J. (1996). *Ethical issues in behavioural research*. Oxford: Blackwell.

Kimura, D. (1964). Left–right differences in the perception of melodies. *Quarterly Journal of Experimental Psychology, 16*, 355–358.

Kimura, D. (1979). Neuromotor mechanisms in the evolution of human communication. In H.E. Steklis & M.J. Raleigh (Eds.), *Neurobiology of social communication in primates*. New York: Academic Press.

Kimura, D., & Watson, N. (1989). The relation between oral movement control and speech. *Brain and Language, 37*, 565–590.

Kinchla, R.A., & Wolf, J.M. (1979). The order of visual processing: "Top-down," "bottom-up," or "middle-out." *Perception & Psychophysics, 25*, 225–231.

Kinnunen, T., Zamanky, H.S., & Block, M.L. (1995). Is the hypnotised subject lying? *Journal of Abnormal Psychology, 103*, 184–191.

Kitzinger, C., & Coyle, A. (1995). Lesbian and gay couples: Speaking of difference. *The Psychologist, 8*, 64–69.

Klaus, M.H., & Kennell, J.H. (1976). *Parent–infant bonding*. St. Louis: Mosby.

Klein, D.F., & Gittelman-Klein, R. (1975). Are behavioural and psychometric changes related in methyphenidate treated, hyperactive children? *International Journal of Mental Health, 14*, 182–198.

Klein, K.E., Wegman, H.M., & Hunt, B.I. (1972). Desynchronisation of body temperature and performance circadian rhythm as a result of outgoing and homegoing transmeridian flights. *Aerospace Medicine, 43*, 119–132.

Kleiner, L., & Marshall, W.L. (1987). The role of interpersonal problems in the development of agoraphobia with panic attacks. *Journal of Anxiety Disorders, 1*, 313–323.

Kleinman, A., & Cohen, A. (1997). Psychiatry's global challenge. *Scientific American, March*, 74–77.

Kleinmuntz, B. (1974). *Essentials of abnormal psychology*.

Kline, P. (1981). *Fact and fantasy in Freudian theory*. London: Methuen.

Kline, P. (1991). *Intelligence: The psychometric view*. London: Routledge.

Kline, P., & Storey, R. (1977). A factor analytic study of the oral character. *British Journal of Social and Clinical Psychology, 16*, 317–328.

Kluver, H., & Bucy, P. (1939). Preliminary analysis of functions of the temporal lobes in monkeys. *Archives of Neurology and Psychiatry, 42*, 979–1000.

Knight, J. (1998). 1 in 3 thinks disabled are less intelligent. *The Times*, 26 May, p. 9.

Knox, J.V., Morgan, A.H., & Hilgard, E.R. (1974). Pain and suffering in ischemia: The paradox of hypnotically suggested anaesthesia as contradicted by reports from the "hidden-observer". *Archives of General Psychiatry, 30*, 840–847.

Koegel, R.L., O'Dell, M.C., & Koegel, L.K. (1987). A natural language paradigm for teaching non-verbal autistic children. *Journal of Autism and Developmental Disorders, 9*, 383–397.

Koehler, J.J. (1996). The base rate fallacy reconsidered: Descriptive, normative, and methological challenges. *Behavioral and Brain Sciences, 19*, 1–53.

Koestner, R., & McClelland, D.C. (1990). Perspectives on competence motivation. In L.A. Pervin (Ed.), *Handbook of personality: Theory and Research*. New York: Guilford.

Koffka, K. (1935). *Principles of Gestalt psychology*. New York: Harcourt Brace.

Kohlberg, L. (1963). Development of children's orientations toward a moral order. *Vita Humana, 6*, 11–36.

Kohlberg, L. (1966). A cognitive-development analysis of children's sex-role concepts and attitudes. In E.E. Maccoby (Ed.), *The development of sex differences*. Stanford: Stanford University Press.

Kohlberg, L. (1975). The cognitive-developmental approach to moral education. *Phi Delta Kappan, June*, 670–677.

Kohlberg, L. (1981). *Essays on moral development, Vol. 1: The philosophy of moral development*. San Francisco: Harper & Row.

Kohler, W. (1925). *The mentality of apes*. New York: Harcourt Brace & World.

Kolb, B., & Whishaw, I.Q. (1990). *Fundamentals of human neuropsychology (3rd Edn.)*. New York: Freeman.

Koluchova, J. (1976). The further development of twins after severe and prolonged deprivation: A second report. *Journal of Child Psychology and Psychiatry, 17*, 181–188.

Korsakoff, S.S. (1889). Uber eine besonderes Form psychischer Storung, kombiniert mit multiplen Neuritis. *Archiv für Psychiatrie und Nervenkrankheiten, 21*, 669–704.

Kosslyn, S.M. (1988). Aspects of cognitive neuroscience of mental imagery. *Science, 240*, 1621–1626.

Kosten, T.R., Mason, J.W., Giller, E.L., Ostroff, R., & Harkness, I. (1987). Sustained urinary norepinephrine and epinephrine elevation in posttraumatic stress disorder. *Psychoneuroendocrinology, 12*, 13–20.

Kovacs, M., & Beck, A.T. (1978). Maladaptive cognitive structures in depression. *American Journal of Psychiatry, 135*, 525–533.

Kozlowski, L.T., & Cutting, J.E. (1978). Recognising the gender of walkers from point-lights mounted on ankles: Some second thoughts. *Perception & Psychophysics, 23*, 459.

Kramer, A.F., & Hahn, S. (1995). Splitting the beam: Distribution of attention over noncontiguous regions of the visual field. *Psychological Science, 6*, 381–386.

Kramer, G. (1953). Die Sonnenorientiering der Vogel. *Verh. Deut. Zool. Ges. Freiburg, 1952*, 72–84.

Krause, N., Jay, G., & Liang, J. (1991). Financial strain and psychological well-being among the American and Japanese elderly. *Psychology and Aging, 6*, 170–181.

Krebs, J.R. (1971). Territory and breeding density in the great tit, *Parus major L. Ecology, 52*, 2–22.

Krebs, J.R. (1984). The song of the great tit says "Keep Out". In G. Ferry (Ed.), *The understanding of animals*. Oxford: Blackwell.

Krebs, J.R., & Davies, N.B. (1993). *An introduction to behavioural ecology (3rd Edn.)*. Oxford: Blackwell.

Kruuk, H. (1964). Predators and anti-predator behaviour of the black headed gull, *Larus ridibundus. Behaviour Supplement, 11*, 1–129.

Kruuk, H. (1971). *The spotted hyena*. Chicago: University of Chicago Press.

Krystal, J.H., Kosten, T.R., Southwick, S., Mason, J.W., Perry, B.D., & Giller, E.L. (1989). Neurobiological aspects of PTSD: Review of clinical and preclinical studies. *Behavior Therapy, 20*, 177–198.

Kuhn, T.S. (1962). *The structure of scientific revolutions*. Chicago: Chicago University Press.

Kuhn, T.S. (1970). *The structure of scientific revolutions (2nd Edn.)*. Chicago: Chicago University Press.

Kuhn, T.S. (1977). *The essential tension: Selected studies in scientific tradition and change*. Chicago: Chicago University Press.

Kunnapas, T.M. (1968). Distance perception as a function of available visual cues. *Journal of Experimental Psychology, 77*, 523–529.

Kuo-shu, Yang, & Bond, M.H. (1990). Exploring implicit personality theories with indigenous or imported constructs: The Chinese case. *Journal of Personality and Social Psychology, 58*, 1087–1095.

Kurdek, L.A., & Schmitt, J.P. (1986). Relationship quality of partners in heterosexual married, heterosexual cohabiting, and gay and lesbian relationships. *Journal of Personality and Social Psychology, 51*, 711–720.

LaBerge, D. (1983). Spatial extent of attention to letters and words. *Journal of Experimental Psychology: Human Perception and Performance, 9*, 371–379.

LaBerge, S., Greenleaf, W., & Kedzierski, B. (1983). Physiological responses to dreamed sexual activity during lucid REM sleep. *Psychophysiology, 20*, 454–455.

Lachiewicz, A.M., Spiridigliozzi, G.A., Gullion, C.M., Ransford, S.N., & Rao, K. (1994). Aberrant behaviours of young boys with fragile X syndrome. *American Journal of Mental Retardation, 98*, 567–579.

Lack, D. (1968). *Ecological adaptations for breeding in birds*. London: Methuen.

Lader, M.H., & Mathews, A. (1968). A physiological model of phobic anxiety and desensitisation. *Behaviour Research and Therapy, 6*, 411–421.

Laing, R.D. (1967). *The politics of experience*. New York: Ballantine.

Lalljee, M. (1981). Attribution theory and the analysis of explanations. In C. Antaki (Ed.), *The psychology of ordinary explanations of social behaviour*. London: Academic Press.

Lambert, R.G., & Lambert, M.J. (1984). The effects of role preparation for psychotherapy on immigrant clients seeking mental health services in Hawaii. *Journal of Community Psychology, 12*, 263–275.

Land, E.H. (1977). The retinex theory of colour vision. *Scientific American, 237*, 108–128.

Landau, B. (1997). Language and experience in blind children: Retrospective and prospective. In V. Lewis & G.M. Collis (Eds.), *Blindness and psychological development in young children*. Leicester: BPS Books.

Langer, E.J., & Rodin, J. (1976). The effects of choice and enhanced personal responsibility for the aged. *Journal of Personality and Social Psychology, 34*, 191–198.

Lank, D.B., Oring, L.W., & Maxson, S.J. (1985). Mate and nutrient limitation of egg laying in a polyandrous shorebird. *Ecology, 66*, 1513–1524.

LaPiere, R.T. (1934). Attitudes vs. actions. *Social Forces, 13*, 230–237.

Larson, R.W., & Lampman-Petraitis, C. (1989). Daily emotional states as reported by children and adolescents. *Child Development, 60*, 1250–1260.

Larson, R.W., Richards, M.H., Moneta, G., Holmbeck, G., & Duckett, E. (1996). Changes in adolescents' daily interactions with their families from ages 10 to 18: Disengagment and transformation. *Developmental Psychology, 32*, 744–754.

Lashley, K. (1931). Mass action in cerebral function. *Science, 73*, 245–254.

Lassonde, M., Sauerwein, H., Chicoine, A.-J., & Geoffroy, G. (1991). Absence of disconnexion syndrome in callosal agenesis and early callosotomy: Brain reorganisation or lack of structural specificity during ontogeny? *Neuropsychologia, 29*, 481–495.

Latané, B., & Darley, J.M. (1970). *The unresponsive bystander: Why doesn't he help?* Englewood Cliffs, NJ: Prentice-Hall.

Latham, G.P., & Yukl, G.A. (1975). Assigned versus participative goal setting with educated and uneducated woods workers. *Journal of Applied Psychology, 60*, 299–302.

Lazar, I., & Darlington, R. (1982). Lasting effects of early education: A report from the Consortium for Longitudinal Studies. *Monographs of the Society for Research in Child Development, 47*, No. 195.

Lazarus, A.A., & Davison, G.C. (1971). Clinical innovation in research and practice. In A.E. Bergin & S.L. Garfield (Eds.), *Handbook of psychotherapy and behaviour change: An empirical analysis*. Chichester: Wiley.

Lazarus, R.S. (1966). *Psychological stress and the coping process*. New York: McGraw-Hill.

Lazarus, R.S. (1982). Thoughts on the relations between emotion and cognition. *American Psychologist, 37*, 1019–1024.

Lazarus, R.S. (1991). *Emotion and adapatation*. Oxford: Oxford University Press.

Le Bon, G. (1895). *The crowd*. London: Ernest Benn.

Lednore, A.J., & Walcott, C. (1983). Homing pigeons in navigation: The effects of in-flight exposure to a varying magnetic field. *Comparative Biochemistry and Physiology, 76*, 665–671.

LeDoux, J.E. (1989). Cognitive-emotional interactions in the brain. *Cognition and Emotion, 3*, 267–289.

LeDoux, J.E. (1995). Emotion: Clues from the brain. *Annual Review of Psychology, 46*, 209–235.

Lee, H. (1997). *Virginia Woolf*. London: Vintage.

Lee, L. (1984). Sequences in separation: A framework for investigating endings of the personal (romantic) relationship. *Journal of Social and Personal Relationships, 1*, 49–74.

Lee, V.E., Brooks-Gunn, J., Schnur, E., & Liaw, F. (1990). Are Head Start effects sustained? A longitudinal follow-up comparison of disadvantaged children attending Head Start, no preschool, and other preschool programmes. *Child Development, 61*, 495–507.

Leibowitz, H., Brislin, R., Permutter, L., & Hennessy, R. (1969). Ponzo perspective illusions as a manifestation of space perception. *Science, 166*, 1174–1176.

Leitenberg, H., Agras, W.S., & Thomson, L.E. (1968). A sequential analysis of the effect of selective positive reinforcement in modifying anorexia nervosa. *Behaviour Research and Therapy, 6,* 211–218.

Lemyre, L., & Smith, P.M. (1985). Intergroup discrimination and self-esteem in the minimal group paradigm. *Journal of Personality and Social Psychology, 49,* 660–670.

Lenneberg, E.H. (1967). *The biological foundations of language.* New York: Wiley.

Lenneberg, E.H., & Roberts, J.M. (1956). *The language of experience Memoir 13.* University of Indiana, Publications in Anthropology and Linguistics.

Leon, G.R. (1984). *Case histories of deviant behaviour (3rd Edn.).* Boston: Allyn & Bacon.

Lerner, R.M., & Galambos, N.L. (1985). The adolescent experience: A view of the issues. In R.M. Lerner & N.L. Galambos (Eds.), *Experiencing adolescents: A sourcebook for parents, teachers, and teens.* New York: Garland.

Leslie, A.M. (1987). Pretence and representation: The origins of "theory of mind". *Psychological Review, 94,* 412–426.

Leventhal, H.R. (1970). Findings and theory in the study of fear communications. In L. Berkowitz (Ed.), *Advances in experimental social psychology, Vol. 5.* New York: Academic Press.

Leventhal, H.R., Singer, P., & Jones, S. (1965). Effects of fear and specificity of recommendations upon attitudes and behaviour. *Journal of Personality and Social Psychology, 2,* 20–29.

Levine, E.S., & Padilla, A.M. (1980). *Crossing cultures in therapy: Counselling for the Hispanic.* Monterey, CA: Brooks/Cole.

Levine, J.M., & Moreland, R.L. (1995). Group processes. In A. Tesser (Ed.), *Advanced social psychology.* New York: McGraw-Hill.

Levine, R., Sato, S., Hashimoto, T., & Verma, J. (1995). Love and marriage in eleven cultures. *Journal of Cross-Cultural Psychology, 26,* 554–571.

Levinger, G. (1976). A social psychological perspective on marital dissolution. *Journal of Social Issues, 32,* 21–47.

Levinger, G. (1980). Toward the analysis of close relationships. *Journal of Experimental Social Psychology, 16,* 510–544.

Levinson, D.J. (1978). *The seasons of a man's life.* New York: Ballantine.

Levinson, D.J. (1986). A conception of adult development. *American Psychologist, 41,* 3–13.

Levy, J., Trevarthen, C., & Sperry, R.W. (1972). Perception of bilateral chimeric figures following hemispheric deconnection. *Brain, 95,* 61–78.

Lewin, K., Lippitt, R., & White, R. (1939). Patterns of aggressive behaviour in experimentally created 'social climates'. *Journal of Social Psychology, 10,* 271–299.

Lewinsohn, P.M. (1974). A behavioural approach to depression. In R.J. Friedman & M.M. Katz (Eds.), *The psychology of depression: Contemporary theory and research.* Washington, DC: Winston-Wiley.

Lewinsohn, P.M., Steimetz, J.L., Larsen, D.W., & Franklin, J. (1981). Depression related cognitions: Antecedent or consequences? *Journal of Abnormal Psychology, 90,* 213–219.

Lewis, M. (1990). Social knowledge and social development. *Merrill-Palmer Quarterly, 36,* 93–116.

Lewis, M., & Brooks-Gunn, J. (1979). *Social cognition and the acquisition of self.* New York: Plenum.

Lewis, M., Sullivan, M.W., Stanger, C., & Weiss, M. (1989). Self-development and self-conscious emotions. *Child Development, 60,* 146–156.

Lewis, V. (1987). *Development and handicap.* Oxford: Blackwell.

Ley, P. (1978). Memory for medical information. In M.M. Gruneberg, P.E. Morris, & R.N. Sykes (Eds.), *Practical aspects of memory.* London: Academic Press.

Ley, P. (1988). *Communicating with patients: Improving communication, satisfaction and compliance.* London: Chapman Hall.

Ley, P. (1997). Recall by patients. In A. Baum, S. Newman, J. Weinman, R. West, & C. McManus (Eds.), *Cambridge handbook of psychology, health, and medicine.* Cambridge: Cambridge University Press.

Leyens, J.-P., Camino, L., Parke, R.D., & Berkowitz, L. (1975). Effects of movie violence on aggression in a field setting as a function of group dominance and cohesion. *Journal of Personality and Social Psychology, 32,* 346–360.

Lichtenstein, S., Slovic, P., Fischhoff, B., Layman, M., & Combs, B. (1978). Judged frequency of lethal events. *Journal of Experimental Psychology: Human Learning and Memory, 4,* 551–578.

Lick, J. (1975). Expectancy, false galvanic skin response feedback and systematic desensitisation in the modification of phobic behaviour. *Journal of Consulting and Clinical Psychology, 43,* 557–567.

Lick, J., & Bootzin, R. (1975). Expectancy factors in the treatment of fear: Methodological and theoretical issues. *Psychological Bulletin, 82,* 917–931.

Lieberman, M., & Coplan, A. (1970). Distance from death as a variable in the study of aging. *Developmental Psychology, 2,* 71–84.

Lifton, R.J. (1961). *Thought reform and the psychology of totalism: A study of "brain-washing" in China.* London: Gollancz.

Light, P., Buckingham, N., & Robbins, A.H. (1979). The conservation task as an interactional setting. *British Journal of Educational Psychology, 49,* 304–310.

Light, P., Littleton, K., Messer, D., & Joiner, R. (1994). Social and communicative processes in computer-based problem solving. *European Journal of Psychology of Education, 9,* 93–109.

Likert, R. (1967). *The human organisation.* New York: McGraw-Hill.

Lilly, J.C. (1956). Mental effects of reduction of ordinary levels of physical stimuli on intact, healthy persons. *Psychiatric Research Reports, 5,* 1–9.

Lindsay, D.S. (1990). Misleading suggestions can impair eyewitnesses' ability to remember event details. *Journal of Experimental Psychology: Learning, Memory, and Cognition, 16,* 1077–1083.

Locke, E.A. (1968). Toward a theory of task motivation and incentives. *Organizational Behavior and Human Performance, 3,* 157–189.

Locke, E.A., Bryan, J.F., & Kendall, L.M. (1968). Goals and intention as mediators of the effects of monetary incentives on behaviour. *Journal of Applied Psychology, 52,* 104–121.

Locke, E.A., & Latham, G.P. (1990). *A theory of goal setting and task performance.* Englewood Cliffs, NJ: Prentice Hall.

Locke, E.A., Shaw, K.N., Saari, L.M., & Latham, G.P. (1981). Goal setting and task performance: 1969–1980. *Psychological Bulletin, 90,* 125–152.

Loehlin, J.C., Horn, J.M., & Willerman, L. (1989). Modeling IQ change: Evidence from the Texas Adoption Project. *Child Development*, 60, 893–904.

Loehlin, J.C., & Nichols, R.C. (1976). *Heredity, environment and personality*. Austin, TX: University of Texas Press.

Loftus, E.F., & Burns, H.J. (1982). Mental shock can produce retrograde amnesia. *Memory & Cognition*, 10, 318–323.

Loftus, E.F., & Loftus, G.R. (1980). On the permanence of stored information in the human brain. *American Psychologist*, 35, 409–420.

Loftus, E.F., & Palmer, J.C. (1974). Reconstruction of automobile destruction: An example of the interaction between language and memory. *Journal of Verbal Learning and Verbal Behavior*, 13, 585–589.

Loftus, E.F., & Zanni, G. (1975). Eyewitness testimony: The influence of the wording of a question. *Bulletin of the Psychonomic Society*, 5, 86–88.

Logan, G.D. (1988). Toward an instance theory of automatisation. *Psychological Review*, 95, 492–527.

Logvinenko, A.D., & Belopolskii, V.I. (1994). Convergence as a cue for distance. *Perception*, 23, 207–217.

Loo, C.M. (1979). The effects of spatial density on the social behaviour of children. *Journal of Applied Social Research*, 2, 372–381.

Lopata, H.Z. (1979). Widowhood and husband sanctification. In L.A. Bugen (Ed.), *Death and dying: Theory, research, practice*. Dubuque, IA: WC Brown.

Lord, R.G. (1977). Functional leadership behaviour: Measurement and relation to social power and leadership perceptions. *Administrative Science Quarterly*, 22, 114–133.

Lord, R.G., De Vader, C.L., & Alliger, G.M. (1986). A meta-analysis of the relation between personality traits and leadership perception: An application of validity generalisation procedures. *Journal of Applied Psychology*, 71, 402–410.

Lorenz, K.Z. (1935). The companion in the bird's world. *Auk*, 54, 245–273.

Lott, A.J., & Lott, B.E. (1974). The role of reward in the formation of positive interpersonal attitudes. In T. Huston (Ed.), *Foundations of interpersonal attraction*. New York: Academic Press.

Lott, B.E. (1994). *Women's lives: Theories and variations in gender learning*. Pacific Grove, CA: Brooks Cole.

Lotter, V. (1978). Follow-up studies. In M. Rutter & E. Schopler (Eds.), *Autism: A reappraisal of concepts and treatment*. New York: Plenum.

Lou, H., Hendriksen, L., Bruhn, P., Bourner, H., & Nielsen, J. (1989). Striatal dysfunction in attention deficit and hyperkinetic disorder. *Archives of Neurology*, 46, 48–52.

Lovaas, O.I. (1987). Behavioural treatment and normal educational and intellectual functioning in young autistic children. *Journal of Consulting and Clinical Psychology*, 55, 3–9.

Loveless, N.E. (1983). Event-related brain potentials and human performance. In A. Gale & J.A. Edwards (Eds.), *Physiological correlates of human behaviour: Vol. II. Attention and performance*. London: Academic Press.

Lovland, J. (1976). *Doing social life: The qualitative study of human interaction in natural settings*. New York: Wiley.

Lozoff, B. (1983). Birth and "bonding" in non-industrial societies. *Developmental Medicine & Child Neurology*, 25, 595–600.

Luborsky, L., & Spence, D.P. (1978). Quantitative research on psychoanalytic therapy. In S.L. Garfield & A.E. Bergin (Eds.), *Handbook of psychotherapy and behaviour change: An empirical analysis (2nd Edn.)*. New York: Wiley.

Lucy, J., & Schweder, R. (1979). Whorf and his critics: Linguistic and non-linguistic influences on colour memory. *American Anthropologist*, 81, 581–615.

Luepnitz, R.R., Randolph, D.L., & Gutsch, K.U. (1982). Race and socioeconomic status as confounding variables in the accurate diagnosis of alcoholism. *Journal of Clinical Psychology*, 38, 665–669.

Lugaressi, E., Medori, R., Montagna, P., Baruzzi, A., Cortelli, P., Lugaressi, A., Tinuper, A., Zucconi, M., & Gambetti, P. (1986). Fatal familial insomnia and dysautonomia in the selective degeneration of thalamic nuclei. *New England Journal of Medicine*, 315, 997–1003.

Lumsdaine, A., & Janis, I. (1953). Resistance to counterpropaganda produced by a one-sided versus a two-sided propaganda presentation. *Public Opinion Quarterly*, 17, 311–318.

Lund, M. (1985). The development of investment and commitment scales for predicting continuity of personal relationships. *Journal of Social and Personal Relationships*, 2, 3–23.

Luthans, F., & Kreitner, R. (1975). *Organisational behaviour modification*. Glenview, IL: Scott-Foresman.

Lynch, J.J. (1977). *The broken heart: The medical consequences of loneliness*. New York: Basic Books.

Lytton, H. (1977). Do parents create, or respond to, differences in twins? *Developmental Psychology*, 13, 456–459.

Lytton, H., & Romney, D.M. (1991). Parents' differential socialisation of boys and girls: A meta-analysis. *Psychological Bulletin*, 109, 267–296.

MacArthur, R.H., & Pianka, E.R. (1966). On optimal use of a patchy environment. *American Naturalist*, 100, 603–609.

Maccoby, E.E. (1992). The role of parents in the socialisation of children: An historical review. *Developmental Psychology*, 28, 1006–1017.

Maccoby, E.E., & Jacklin, C.N. (1974). *The psychology of sex differences*. Stanford, CA: Stanford University Press.

MacDonald, K., & Parke, R.D. (1984). Bridging the gap: Parent–child play interaction and peer interactive competence. *Child Development*, 55, 1265–1277.

MacKay, D. (1987). Divided brains — divided minds. In C. Blakemore & S. Greenfield (Eds.), *Mindwaves: Thoughts on intelligence, identity and consciousness*. Oxford: Blackwell.

Mackintosh, N.J. (1986). The biology of intelligence? *British Journal of Psychology*, 77, 1–18.

Mackintosh, N. J. (1994). Classical and operant conditioning. In A.M. Colman (Ed.), *Companion encyclopedia of psychology, Vol. 1*. London: Routledge.

MacLean, P.D. (1949). Psychosomatic disease and the "visceral brain": Recent developments bearing on the Papez theory of emotion. *Psychosomatic Medicine*, 11, 338–353.

MacLeod, A. (1998). Abnormal psychology. In M.W. Eysenck (Ed.), *Psychology: An integrated approach*. Harlow, UK: Addison Wesley Longman.

Macrae, C.N., Milne, A.B., & Bodenhausen, G.V. (1994). Stereotypes as energy-saving devices: A peek inside the cognitive toolbox. *Journal of Personality and Social Psychology*, 66, 37–47.

Maddox, G.L. (1970). Persistence of life style among the elderly. In E. Palmore (Ed.), *Normal aging*. Durham: Duke University Press.

Magoun, H.W., Harrison, F., Brobeck, J.R., & Ranson, S.W. (1938). Activation of heat loss mechanisms by local heating of the brain. *Journal of Neurophysiology, 1,* 101–114.

Maher, B.A. (1966). *Principles of psychopathology: An experimental approach.* New York: McGraw-Hill.

Main, M., & Solomon, J. (1986). Discovery of a disorganised disoriented attachment pattern. In T.B. Brazelton & M.W. Yogman (Eds.), *Affective development in infancy.* Borwood, NJ: Ablex.

Main, M., & Weston, D.R. (1981). The quality of the toddler's relationship to mother and father: Related to conflict behaviour and the readiness to establish new relationships. *Child Development, 52,* 932–940.

Mair, K. (1992). The myth of therapist expertise. In W. Dryden & C. Feltham (Eds.), *Psychotherapy and its discontents.* Buckingham: Open University Press.

Major, P.F. (1978). Predator-prey interactions in two schooling fishes, *Caranx ignobilis* and *Stolephorus purpureus. Animal Behaviour, 26,* 760–777.

Malim, T., Birch, A., & Wadeley, A. (1992). *Perspectives in psychology.* London: Macmillan.

Mallick, S.K., & McCandless, B.R. (1966). A study of cartharsis of aggression. *Journal of Personality and Social Psychology, 4,* 591–596.

Malott, R.W., Malott, M.K., & Pokrzywinski, J. (1967). The effects of outward pointing arrowheads on the Muller-Lyer illusion in pigeons. *Psychonomic Science, 9,* 55–56.

Malthus, T.R. (1798). *An essay on the principle of population.* Harmondsworth: Penguin Books.

Mandler, G. (1967). Organisation and memory. In K.W. Spence & J.T. Spence (Eds.), *The psychology of learning and motivation: Advances in research and theory, Vol. 1.* London: Academic Press.

Mann, L. (1981). The baiting crowd in episodes of threatened suicide. *Journal of Personality and Social Psychology, 41,* 703–709.

Mann, L., Newton, J.W., & Innes, J.M. (1982). A test between deindividuation and emergent norm theories of crowd aggression. *Journal of Personality and Social Psychology, 42,* 260–272.

Mann, R.D. (1959). A review of the relationships between personality and performance in small groups. *Psychological Bulletin, 56,* 241–270.

Manstead, A.S.R., & Semin, G.R. (1996). Methodology in social psychology: Putting ideas to the test. In M. Hewstone, W. Stroebe, & G.M. Stephenson (Eds.), *Introduction to social psychology (2nd Edn.).* Oxford: Blackwell.

Maranon, G. (1924). Contribution a l'étude de l'action emotive de l'adrenaline. *Révue Française d'Endocrinologie, 2,* 301–325.

March, J.S. (1991). The nosology of posttraumatic stress disorder. *Journal of Anxiety Disorders, 4,* 61–81.

Marcia, J. (1966). Development and validation of ego-identity status. *Journal of Personality and Social Psychology, 3,* 551–558.

Marcia, J. (1967). The case history of a construct: Ego identity status. *Journal of Personality and Social Psychology, 3,* 551–558.

Marcia, J. (1976). Identity six years after: A follow-up study. *Journal of Youth and Adolescence, 5,* 145–160.

Marcia, J. (1980). Identity in adolescence. In J. Adelson (Ed.), *Handbook of adolescent psychology.* New York: Wiley.

Markus, H.R., & Kitayama, S. (1991). Culture and the self: Implications for cognition, emotion, and motivation. *Psychological Review, 98,* 224–253.

Marr, D. (1982). *Vision: A computational investigation into the human representation and processing of visual information.* San Francisco: W.H. Freeman.

Marr, D., & Nishihara, K. (1978). Representation and recognition of the spatial organisation of three-dimensional shapes. *Philosophical Transactions of the Royal Society (London), B200,* 269–294.

Marr, D., & Poggio, T. (1976). Co-operation computation of stereo disparity. *Science, 194,* 283–287.

Marschark, M. (1993). *Psychological development of deaf children.* Oxford: Oxford University Press.

Marsh, H.W. (1989). Age and sex effects in multiple dimensions of self-concept: A replication and extension. *Australian Journal of Psychology, 37,* 197–204.

Marsh, P., Rosser, E., & Harré, R. (1978). *The rules of disorder.* London: Routledge & Kegan Paul.

Marshall, G.D., & Zimbardo, P.G. (1979). Affective consequences of inadequately explained physiological arousal. *Journal of Personality and Social Psychology, 37,* 970–988.

Martin, C.L., & Halverson, C.F. (1981). A schematic processing model of sex typing and stereotyping in children. *Child Development, 52,* 1119–1134.

Martin, C.L., & Halverson, C.F. (1983). The effects of sex-typing schemas on young children's memory. *Child Development, 54,* 563–574.

Martin, C.L., & Halverson, C.F. (1987). The roles of cognition in sex role acquisition. In D.B. Carter (Ed.), *Current conceptions of sex roles and sex typing: Theory and research.* New York: Praeger.

Martin, R.A. (1989). Techniques for data acquisition and analysis in field investigations of stress. In R.W.J. Neufeld (Ed.), *Advances in the investigation of psychological stress.* New York: Wiley.

Martin, R.A., Kulper, N.A., & Westra, H.A. (1989). Cognitive and affective components of the Type A behaviour pattern: Preliminary evidence for a self-worth contingency model. *Personality and Individual Differences, 10,* 771–784.

Martone, M., Butters, N., Payne, M., Becker, J.T., & Sax, D.S. (1984). Dissociations between skill learning and verbal recognition in amnesia and dementia. *Archives of Neurology, 41,* 965–970.

Marzloff, J.M., Heinrich, B., & Marzloff, C.S. (1996). Raven roosts are mobile information centres. *British Journal of Animal Behaviour, 51*(1), 89.

Maslow, A.H. (1954). *Motivation and personality.* New York: Harper.

Maslow, A.H. (1962). *Toward a psychology of being.* Princeton, NJ: Van Nostrand.

Maslow, A.H. (1968). *Toward a psychology of being (2nd Edn.).* New York: Van Nostrand.

Maslow, A.H. (1970). *Toward a psychology of being (3rd Edn.).* New York: Van Nostrand.

Mason, J.W. (1975). A historical view of the stress field. *Journal of Human Stress, 1,* 22–36.

Masson, J. (1989). *Against therapy.* Glasgow: Collins.

Masters, J.C., Ford, M.E., Arend, R., Grotevant, H.D., & Clark, L.V. (1979). Modelling and labelling as integrated determinants of children's sex-typed imitative behaviour. *Child Development, 50,* 364–371.

Matheny, A.P. (1983). A longitudinal twin study of the stability of components from Bayley's Infant Behaviour Record. *Child Development, 54,* 356–360.

Mathes, E.W., Adams, H.E., & Davies, R.M. (1985). Jealousy: Loss of relationship rewards, loss of self-esteem, depression, anxiety, and anger. *Journal of Personality and Social Psychology, 48,* 1552–1561.

Matlin, M.W., & Foley, H.J. (1997). *Sensation and perception (4th Edn.).* Bostyn: Allyn & Bacon.

Matsuda, L.A., Lolait, S.J., Brownstein, M.J., Young, A.C., & Bonner, T.I. (1990). Structure of a cannabinoid receptor and functional expression of the cloned DNA. *Nature, 346,* 561–564.

Matt, G.E., & Navarro, A.M. (1997). What meta-analyses have and have not taught us about psychotherapy effects: A review and future directions. *Clinical Psychology Review, 17,* 1–32.

Matthews, G.V.T. (1953). Navigation in the Manx shearwater. *Journal of Experimental Biology, 28,* 508–536.

Matthews, K.A. (1988). Coronary heart disease and Type A behaviour: Update on and alternative to the Booth-Kewley and Friedman (1987) quantitative review. *Psychological Bulletin, 104,* 373–380.

Matthews, K.A., Glass, D.C., Rosenman, R.H., & Bortner, R.W. (1977). Competitive drive, Pattern A, and coronary heart disease: A further analysis of some data from the Western Collaborative Group. *Journal of Chronic Diseases, 30,* 489–498.

Matthews, R.T., & German, D.C. (1984). Electrophysiological evidence for excitation of rat ventral tegmental area dopaminergic neurons by morphine. *Neuroscience, 11,* 617–626.

Maurer, D., & Salapatek, P. (1976). Developmental changes in the scanning of faces by young infants. *Child Development, 47,* 523–527.

May, R. (1998). Timebomb threatens thousands of species. *Evening Standard,* 6 July, p.19.

Mayer, J. (1955). Regulation of energy intake and the body weight: The glucostatic theory and the lipostatic hypothesis. *Annals of the New York Academy of Sciences, 63,* 15–43.

Maynard Smith, J. (1964). Group selection and kin selection. *Nature, 201,* 1145–1147.

Maynard Smith, J. (1976). Group selection. *Quarterly Review of Biology, 51,* 277–283.

Maynard Smith, J. (1977). Parental investment: A prospective analysis. *Animal Behaviour, 25,* 1–9.

Maynard Smith, J., & Ridpath, M.G. (1972). Wife sharing in the Tasmanian native hen *Tribonyx mortierii*: A case of kin selection? *American Naturist, 106,* 447–452.

McAdams, D.P. (1988). *Intimacy, power, and the life history.* New York: Guilford.

McArthur, L.Z., & Post, D.L. (1977). Figural emphasis and person perception. *Journal of Experimental Social Psychology, 13,* 520–535.

McArthur, L.Z., & Resko, B.G. (1975). The portrayal of men and women in American TV commercials. *Journal of Social Psychology, 97,* 209–220.

McCain, B., Gabrielli, W.F., Bentler, P.M., & Mednick, S.A. (1980). Rearing, social class, education, and criminality: A multiple indicator model. *Journal of Abnormal Psychology, 90,* 354–364.

McCauley, C., & Stitt, C.L. (1978). An individual and quantitative measure of stereotypes. *Journal of Personality and Social Psychology, 36,* 929–940.

McClelland, D.C., Atkinson, J.W., Clark, R.A., & Lowell, E.L. (1953). *The achievement motive.* New York: Appleton-Century-Crofts.

McConaghy, M.J. (1979). Gender permanence and the genital basis of gender: Stages in the development of constancy of gender identity. *Child Development, 50,* 1223–1226.

McCracken, G.F. (1984). Communal nursing in Mexican free-tailed bat maternity colonies. *Science, 223,* 1090–1091.

McCrae, R.R. (1982). Consensual validation of personality traits: Evidence from self-ratings and ratings. *Journal of Personality and Social Psychology, 43,* 293–303.

McCrae, R.R., & Costa, P.T. (1982). Aging, the life course, and models of personality. In T.M. Field, A. Huston, H.C. Quay, L. Troll, & G.E. Finley (Eds.), *Review of human development.* New York: Wiley.

McCrae, R.R., & Costa, P.T. (1985). Updating Norman's "adequate taxonomy": Intelligence and personality dimensions in natural language and in questionnaires. *Journal of Personality and Social Psychology, 49,* 710–721.

McCrae, R.R., & Costa, P.T. (1990). *Personality in adulthood.* New York: Guilford.

McDougall, W. (1912). *Psychology: The study of behaviour.* London: Williams & Norgate.

McFarland, D. (1985). *Animal behaviour.* Harlow, Essex: Longman.

McFarland, S.G., Ageyev, V.S., & Abalakina-Paap, M.A. (1992). Authoritarianism in the former Soviet Union. *Journal of Personality and Social Psychology, 63,* 1004–1010.

McGarrigle, J., & Donaldson, M. (1974). Conservation accidents. *Cognition, 3,* 341–350.

McGrew, W.C. (1972). *An ethological study of children's behaviour.* New York: Academic Press.

McGue, M., Brown, S., & Lykken, D.T. (1992). Personality stability and change in early adulthood: A behavioural genetic analysis. *Developmental Psychology, 29,* 96–109.

McGuigan, F.J. (1966). Covert oral behaviour and auditory hallucinations. *Psychophysiology, 3,* 421–428.

McGuire, W.J. (1969). The nature of attitudes and attitude change. In G. Lindzey & E. Aronson (Eds.), *Handbook of social psychology, Vol. 3 (2nd Edn.).* Reading, MA: Addison-Wesley.

McIlveen, R. (1995). Hypnosis. *Psychology Review, 2,* 8–12.

McIlveen, R. (1996). Applications of hypnosis. *Psychology Review, 2,* 24–27.

McIlveen, R., & Gross, R. (1996). *Biopsychology.* London: Hodder & Stoughton.

McKoon, G., & Ratcliff, R. (1992). Inference during reading. *Psychological Review, 99,* 440–466.

McLeod, P. (1977). A dual-task response modality effect: Support for multiprocessor models of attention. *Quarterly Journal of Experimental Psychology, 29,* 651–667.

McNeill, D. (1970). *The acquisition of language: The study of developmental psycholinguistics.* New York: Harper & Row.

Mead, G.H. (1934). *Mind, self, and society: From the standpoint of a social behaviourist.* Chicago: University of Chicago Press.

Mead, M. (1935). *Sex and temperament in three primitive societies.* New York: Morrow.

Meadows, S. (1986). *Understanding child development.* London: Routledge.

Meadows, S. (1994). Cognitive development. In A.M. Colman (Ed.), *Companion encyclopedia of psychology, Vol. 2.* London: Routledge.

Meddis, R. (1979). The evolution and function of sleep. In D.A. Oakley & H.C. Plotkin (Eds.), *Brain, behaviour and evolution*. London: Methuen.

Meddis, R., Pearson, A.J.D., & Langford, G. (1973). An extreme case of healthy insomnia. *Electroencephalography and Clinical Neurophysiology, 35*, 213–224.

Mednick, S.A., & Schulsinger, F. (1968). Some premorbid characteristics related to breakdown in children with schizophrenic mothers. *Journal of Psychiatric Research, 6*, 267–291.

Meehl, P.E. (1954). *Clinical versus statistical prediction: A theoretical analysis and a review of the evidence*. Minneapolis: University of Minneapolis.

Meichenbaum, D. (1977). *Cognitive-behaviour modification: An integrative approach*. New York: Plenum Press.

Meichenbaum, D. (1985). *Stress inoculation training*. New York: Pergamon.

Meilman, P.W. (1979). Cross-sectional age changes in ego identity status during adolescence. *Developmental Psychology, 15*, 230–231.

Meltzoff, A.N. (1988). Imitation of televised models by infants. *Child Development, 59*, 1221–1229.

Menges, R.J. (1973). Openness and honesty versus coercion and deception in psychological research. *American Psychologist, 28*, 1030–1034.

Menzel, E.W. (1978). Cognitive mapping in chimpanzees. In S.H. Hulse, F. Fowler, & W.K. Honig (Eds.), *Cognitive processes in animal behaviour*. Hillsdale, NJ: Lawrence Erlbaum Associates Inc.

Menzies, R.G., & Clarke, J.C. (1993). The aetiology of childhood water phobia. *Behaviour Research and Therapy, 31*, 499–501.

Menzies, R.G., & Clarke, J.C. (1994). Retrospective studies of the origins of phobias: A review. *Anxiety, Stress, and Coping, 7*, 305–318.

Merckelbach, H., de Jong, P.J., Muris, P., & van den Hout, M.A. (1996). The etiology of specific phobias: A review. *Clinical Psychology Review, 16*, 337–361.

Merriman, A. (1984). Social customs affecting the role of elderly women in Indian society. In D.B. Bromley (Ed.), *Gerontology: Social and behavioural perspectives*. London: Croom Helm.

Metter, E.J. (1991). Brain–behaviour relationships in aphasia studied by positron emission tomography. *Annals of the New York Academy of Sciences, 620*, 153–164.

Meudell, P., & Mayes, A. (1981). The Claparede phenomenon: A further example in amnesics, a demonstration of a similar effect in normal people with attenuated memory, and a reinterpretation. *Current Psychological Research, 1*, 75–88.

Meudell, P., & Mayes, A. (1982). Normal and abnormal forgetting: Some comments on the human amnesic syndrome. In A. Ellis (Ed.), *Normality and pathology in cognitive function*. London: Academic Press.

Meyer, D.E., & Schvaneveldt, R.W. (1971). Facilitation in recognising pairs of words: Evidence of a dependence between retrieval operations. *Journal of Experimental Psychology, 90*, 227–234.

Michaels, J.W., Acock, A.C., & Edwards, J.N. (1986). Social exchange and equity determinants of relationship commitment. *Journal of Social and Personal Relationships, 3*, 161–175.

Midlarsky, E., & Bryan, J.H. (1972). Affect expressions and children's imitative altruism. *Journal of Experimental Research in Personality, 6*, 195–203.

Miles, T.R. (1990). Developmental dyslexia. In M.W. Eysenck (Ed.), *The Blackwell dictionary of cognitive psychology*. Oxford: Blackwell.

Milgram, S. (1974). *Obedience to authority: An experimental view*. New York: Harper & Row.

Milinski, M. (1979). An evolutionarily stable feeding strategy in sticklebacks. *Zeitschrift für Tierpsychologie, 51*, 36–40.

Miller, D.T. (1976). Ego involvement and attributions for success and failure. *Journal of Personality and Social Psychology, 34*, 901–906.

Miller, D.T., & Ross, M. (1975). Self-serving bias in the attribution of causality: Fact or fiction? *Psychological Bulletin, 82*, 213–225.

Miller, G.A. (1956). The magic number seven, plus or minus two: Some limits on our capacity for processing information. *Psychological Review, 63*, 81–93.

Miller, G.A., & McNeill, D. (1969). Psycholinguistics. In G. Lindzey & E. Aronson (Eds.), *The handbook of social psychology, Vol. III*. Reading, MA: Addison-Wesley.

Miller, H.G., Turner, C.F., & Moses, L.E. (1990). *AIDS: The second decade*. Washington, DC: National Academy

Miller, J.G. (1984). Culture and the development of everyday social explanation. *Journal of Personality and Social Psychology, 46*, 961–978.

Miller, L.B., & Bizzell, R.P. (1983). Long-term effects of four preschool programs: Sixth, seventh, and eighth grades. *Child Development, 54*, 727–741.

Miller, N.E. (1941). The frustration-aggression hypothesis. *Psychological Review, 48*, 337–342.

Miller, P.H. (1993). *Theories of developmental psychology (3rd Edn.)*. New York: Freeman.

Miller, R.J., Hennessy, R.T., & Leibowitz, H.W. (1973). The effect of hypnotic ablation of the background on the magnitude of the Ponzo perspective illusion. *International Journal of Clinical and Experimental Hypnosis, 21*, 180–191.

Miller, T.Q., Turner, C.W., Tindale, R.S., Posavac, E.J., & Dugoni, B.L. (1991). Reasons for the trend toward null findings in research on Type A behaviour. *Psychological Bulletin, 110*, 469–485.

Milner, D., & Goodale, M.A. (1993). Visual pathways to perception and action. *Progress in Brain Research, 95*, 317–337.

Minard, R.D. (1952). Race relations in the Pocohontas coalfield. *Journal of Social Issues, 8*, 29–44.

Mineka, S., Davidson, M., Cook, M., & Kuir, R. (1984). Observational conditioning of snake fear in rhesus monkeys. *Journal of Abnormal Psychology, 93*, 355–372.

Mineka, S., & Kihlstrom, J. (1978). Unpredictable and uncontrollable aversive events. *Journal of Abnormal Psychology, 87*, 256–271.

Minuchin, S., Roseman, B.L., & Baker, L. (1978). *Psychosomatic families: Anorexia nervosa in context*. Cambridge, MA: Harvard University Press.

Miranda, P.L., Donnelflan, A.M., & Yoder, D.E. (1983). Gaze behaviour: A new look at an old problem. *Journal of Autism and Developmental Disorders, 13*, 397–409.

Mischel, W. (1968). *Personality and assessment*. New York: Wiley.

Mischel, W. (1970). Sex-typing and socialisation. In P.H. Mussen (Ed.), *Carmichael's manual of child psychology, Vol. 2*. New York: Wiley.

Mischler, E.G., & Waxler, N.E. (1968). Interaction in families: An experimental study of family processes and schizophrenia. In A. Smith (Ed.), *Childhood schizophrenia.* New York: Wiley.

Mock, D.W., & Parker, G.A. (1986). Advantages and disadvantages of egret and heron brood reduction. *Evolution, 40,* 459–470.

Mogford, B. (1993). Play assessment for play-based intervention: A first step with young children with communication difficulties. In J. Hellendoorn & R. van der Kooij (Eds.), *Play and intervention.* Albany, NY: State University of New York Press.

Mogg, K., Bradley, B.P., Williams, R., & Mathews, A. (1993). Attentional bias in anxiety and depression: The role of awareness. *Journal of Abnormal Psychology, 102,* 304–311.

Moghaddam, F.M., Taylor, D.M., & Wright, S.C. (1993). *Social psychology in cross-cultural perspective.* New York: W.H. Freeman.

Mohr, D.C. (1995). Negative outcome in psychotherapy: A critical review. *Clinical Psychology: Science and Practice, 2,* 1–27.

Moller, A.P. (1990). Effects of a haematophagous mite on the barn swallow *Hirundo rustica*: A test of the Hamilton and Zuk hypothesis. *Evolution, 44,* 771–784.

Money, J., & Ehrhardt, A.A. (1972). *Man and woman, boy and girl.* Baltimore: John Hopkins University Press.

Monk, T.H., & Folkard, S. (1983). Circadian rhythms and shiftwork. In R. Hockey (Ed.), *Stress and fatigue in human performance.* Chichester: Wiley.

Monteith, M.J. (1993). Self-regulation of prejudiced responses: Implications for progress in prejudice-reduction efforts. *Journal of Personality and Social Psychology, 65,* 469–485.

Moore, B.R. (1973). The form of the auto-shaped response with food or water reinforcers. *Journal of the Experimental Analysis of Behavior, 20,* 163–181.

Moray, N. (1959). Attention in dichotic listening: Affective cues and the influence of instructions. *Quarterly Journal of Experimental Psychology, 11,* 56–60.

Morgan, C.D., & Murray, H.A. (1935). A method of investigating fantasies: The thematic apperception test. *Archives of Neurological Psychiatry, 34,* 289–306.

Morin, S.F. (1977). Heterosexual bias in psychological research on lesbianism and male homosexuality. *American Psychologist, 32,* 629–637.

Morris, C.D., Bransford, J.D., & Franks, J.J. (1977). Levels of processing versus transfer appropriate processing. *Journal of Verbal Learning and Verbal Behavior, 16,* 519–533.

Morris, P.E. (1979). Strategies for learning and recall. In M.M. Gruneberg & P.E. Morris (Eds.), *Applied problems in memory.* London: Academic Press.

Morris, P.E., & Reid, R.L. (1970). The repeated use of mnemonic imagery. *Psychonomic Science, 20,* 337–338.

Moscovici, S. (1961). *La psychoanalyse: Son image et son public.* Paris: Presses Universitaires de France.

Moscovici, S. (1976). *Social influence and social change.* London: Academic Press.

Moscovici, S. (1980). Toward a theory of conversion behaviour. In L. Berkowitz (Ed.), *Advances in experimental social psychology, Vol. 13.* New York: Academic Press.

Moscovici, S. (1981). On social representations. In J.P. Forgas (Ed.), *Social cognition: Perspectives on everyday understanding.* London: Academic Press.

Moscovici, S. (1985). Social influence and conformity. In G. Lindzey & E. Aronson (Eds.), *Handbook of social psychology, Vol. 2.* New York: Random House.

Moscovici, S. (1988). Notes towards a description of social representations. *European Journal of Social Psychology, 18,* 211–250.

Moscovici, S., & Hewstone, M. (1983). Social representations and social explanations: From the 'naive' to the 'amateur' scientist. In M. Hewstone (Ed.), *Attribution theory: Social and functional extensions.* Oxford: Basil Blackwell.

Moscovici, S., Lage, E., & Naffrenchoux, M. (1969). Influence of a consistent minority on the responses of a majority in a colour perception task. *Sociometry, 32,* 365–380.

Moscovitz, S. (1983). *Love despite hate: Child survivors of the Holocaust and their adult lives.* New York: Schocken.

Moser, K.A., Fox, A.J., & Jones, D.R. (1984). Unemployment and mortality in the OPCS longitudinal study. *Lancet, 2,* 1324–1329.

Moskowitz, H., Hulbert, S., & McGlothin, W.H. (1976). Marihuana: Effects on simulated driving performance. *Accident Analysis and Prevention, 8,* 45–50.

Moss, E. (1992). The socioaffective context of joint cognitive activity. In L.T. Winegar & J. Valsiner (Eds.), *Children's development within social context, Vol. 2: Research and methodology.* Hillsdale, NJ: Erlbaum.

Motluck, A. (1999). When too much sex is exhausting. *New Scientist, 2181,* 8.

Mowrer, O.H. (1947). On the dual nature of learning: A re-interpretation of "conditioning" and "problem-solving." *Harvard Educational Review, 17,* 102–148.

Moynihan, M.H. (1970). Control, suppression, decay, disappearance and replacement of displays. *Journal of Theoretical Biology, 29,* 85–112.

Mueller, E., & Lucas, T. (1975). A developmental analysis of peer interaction among toddlers. In M. Lewis & L. Rosenblum (Eds.), *Friendship and peer relations.* New York: Wiley.

Mukerjee, M. (1997). Trends in animal research. *Scientific American, February,* 70–77.

Mulford, R.C. (1987). First words of the blind child. In M.D. Smith & J.L. Locke (Eds.), *The emergent lexicon: The child's development of a linguistic vocabulary.* London: Academic Press.

Mullen, B., Brown, R., & Smith, C. (1992). Ingroup bias as a function of salience, relevance and status: An integration. *European Journal of Social Psychology, 22,* 103–122.

Mumme, R.L. (1992). Do helpers increase reproductive success: An experimental analysis in the Florida scrub jay. *Behavioural Ecology and Sociobiology, 31,* 319–328.

Munro, G., & Adams, G.R. (1977). Mothers, infants and pointing: A study of gesture. In H.R. Schaffer (Ed.), *Studies in mother–infant interaction.* London: Academic Press.

Munroe, R.H., Shimmin, H.S., & Munroe, R.L. (1984). Gender understanding and sex-role preferences in four cultures. *Developmental Psychology, 20,* 673–682.

Murphy, G., & Kovach, J.K. (1972). *Historical introduction to modern psychology.* London: Routledge & Kegan Paul.

Murray, H.A. (1938). *Explorations in personality.* Oxford: Oxford University Press.

Murray, S.L., & Holmes, J.G. (1993). Seeing virtues in faults: Negativity and the transformation of interpersonal narratives in close relationships. *Journal of Personality and Social Psychology, 65,* 707–722.

Murstein, B.I. (1972). Physical attractiveness and marital choice. *Journal of Personality and Social Psychology, 22,* 8–12.

Murstein, B.I., & Christy, P. (1976). Physical attractiveness and marriage adjustment in middle-aged couples. *Journal of Personality and Social Psychology, 34*, 537–542.

Murstein, B.I., MacDonald, M.G., & Cerreto, M. (1977). A theory and investigation of the effects of exchange-orientation on marriage and friendship. *Journal of Marriage and the Family, 39*, 543–548.

Mussen, P.H., & Rutherford, E. (1963). Parent–child relations and parental personality in relation to young children's sex-role preferences. *Child Development, 34*, 589–607.

Myers, L.B., & Brewin, C.R. (1994). Recall of early experiences and the repressive coping style. *Journal of Abnormal Psychology, 103*, 288–292.

Naitoh, P. (1975). Sleep stage deprivation and total sleep loss: Effects on sleep behaviour. *Psychophysiology, 12*, 141–146.

Nash, A. (1988). Ontogeny, phylogeny, and relationships. In S. Duck (Ed.), *Handbook of personal relationships: Research and interventions*. Chichester: Wiley.

Nash, E.H., Hoehn-Saric, R., Battle, C.C., Stone, A.R., Imber, S.D., & Frank, J.D. (1965). Systematic preparation of patients for short-term psychotherapy. II. Relation to characteristics of patient, therapist and the psychotherapeutic process. *Journal of Nervous and Mental Disorders, 140*, 374–383.

Nasser, M. (1986). Eating disorders: The cultural dimension. *Social Psychiatry and Psychiatric Epidemiology, 23*, 184–187.

National Commission on Marijuana and Drug Abuse (1972). *Marijuana: A signal of misunderstanding*. New York: New American Library.

Navon, D. (1977). Forest before trees: The precedence of global features in visual perception. *Cognitive Psychology, 9*, 353–383.

Nazroo, J. (1997). Research scotches racial myth. *The Independent*, 30 September, p. 2.

Neisser, U. (1964). Visual search. *Scientific American, 210*, 94–102.

Neisser, U. (1967). *Cognitive psychology*. New York: Appleton-Century-Crofts.

Neisser, U. (1976). *Cognition and reality*. San Francisco: W.H. Freeman.

Neisser, U., & Becklen, P. (1975). Selective looking: Attending to visually superimposed events. *Cognitive Psychology, 7*, 480–494.

Nelson, K. (1973). Structure and strategy in learning to talk. *Monographs of the Society for Research in Child Development, 38* (serial no. 149).

Nemeth, C., Swedlund, M., & Kanki, G. (1974). Patterning of the minority's responses and their influence on the majority. *European Journal of Social Psychology, 4*, 53–64.

Neufeld, R.W.J. (1979). *Advances in the investigation of psychological stress*. New York: Wiley.

Neugarten, B.L. (1975). Personality and aging. In J.E. Birren & K.W. Schaie (Eds.), *Handbook of the psychology of aging*. New York: Reinhold.

Newcomb, T.M. (1961). *The acquaintance process*. New York: Holt, Rinehart & Winston.

Newmark, C.S., Frerking, R.A., Cook, L., & Newmark, L. (1973). Endorsement of Ellis' irrational beliefs as a function of psychopathology. *Journal of Clinical Psychology, 29*, 300–302.

Newport, E.L. (1994). Maturational constraints on language learning. *Cognitive Science, 14*, 11–28.

Newstead, S.E., Pollard, P., Evans, J.St.B.T., & Allen, J.L. (1992). The source of belief bias effects in syllogistic reasoning. *Cognition, 45*, 257–284.

Nisbett, R.E. (1972). Hunger, obesity and the ventromedial hypothalamus. *Psychological Review, 79*, 433–453.

Nisbett, R.E., Caputo, C., Legant, P., & Maracek, J. (1973). Behaviour as seen by the actor and as seen by the observer. *Journal of Personality and Social Psychology, 27*, 154–164.

Nisbett, R.E., & Wilson, T.D. (1977). Telling more than we can know: Verbal reports on mental processes. *Psychological Review, 84*, 231–259.

Nolen-Hoeksma, S. (1990). *Sex differences in depression*. Stanford, CA: Stanford University Press.

Nolen-Hoeksma, S., Girgus, J.S., & Seligman, M.E.P. (1992). Predictors and consequences of childhood depressive symptoms: A 5-year longitudinal study. *Journal of Abnormal Psychology, 101*, 405–422.

Norman, D.A., & Bobrow, D.G. (1975). On data-limited and resource-limited processes. *Cognitive Psychology, 7*, 44–64.

Norman, W.T. (1963). Toward an adequate taxonomy of personality attributes: Replicated factor structure in peer nomination personality ratings. *Journal of Abnormal and Social Psychology, 66*, 574–583.

Norton, G.R., Dorward, J., & Cox, B.J. (1986). Factors associated with panic attacks in nonclinical subjects. *Behavior Therapy, 17*, 239–252.

Norton-Griffiths, M.N. (1969). The organisation, control and development of parental feeding in the oystercatcher (*Haemataopus ostralegus*). *Behaviour, 34*, 55–114.

Noyes, R., Crowe, R.R., Harris, E.L., Hamra, B.J., McChesney, C.M., & Chandry, D.R. (1986). Relationship between panic disorder and agoraphobia: A family study. *Archives of General Psychiatry, 43*, 227–232.

Nuckolls, K.B., Cassel, J., & Kaplan, B.H. (1972). Psychological assets, life crisis and the prognosis of pregnancy. *American Journal of Epidemiology, 95*, 431–441.

Nystedt, L. (1996). Who should rule? Does personality matter? *Reports from the Department of Psychology, Stockholm University*, No. 812.

Oaker, G., & Brown, R.J. (1986). Intergroup relations in a hospital setting: A further test of social identity theory. *Human Relations, 39*, 767–778.

Oakley, D.A. (1985). The plurality of consciousness. In D.A. Oakley (Ed.), *Brain and mind*. London: Methuen.

O'Connor, J. (1980). Intermediate-size transposition and children's operational level. *Developmental Psychology, 16*, 588–596.

Ogden, J. (1996). *Health psychology: A textbook*. Buckingham: Open University Press.

Ohbuchi, K., & Kambara, T. (1985). Attacker's intent and awareness of outcome, impression management, and retaliation. *Journal of Experimental Social Psychology, 21*, 321–330.

Ohman, A. (1986). Face the beast and fear the face: Animal and social fears as prototypes for evolutionary analyses of emotion. *Psychophysiology, 23*, 123–145.

Ojemann, G.A. (1979). Individual variability in cortical localisation of language. *Journal of Neurosurgery, 50*, 164–169.

Olds, J., & Milner, P. (1954). Positive reinforcement produced by electrical stimulation of septal area and other regions of rat brain. *Journal of Comparative and Physiological Psychology, 47*, 419–427.

Olds, M.E., & Forbes, J.L. (1981). The central basis of motivation: Intracranial self-stimulation studies. *Annual Review of Psychology, 32,* 523–574.

Olson, D.R. (1970). Language and thought: Aspects of a cognitive theory of semantics. *Psychological Review, 77,* 257–273.

Olson, D.R. (1980). *The social foundation of language and thought.* New York: W.W. Norton.

Olson, R.K., Wise, B., Conners, F.A., & Rack, J.P. (1990). Specific deficits in component reading and language skills: Genetic and environmental influences. *Journal of Learning Disabilities, 22,* 339–348.

Olweus, D. (1985). Aggression and hormones. Behavioural relationships with testosterone and adrenalin. In D. Olweus, J. Block, & M. Radke-Yarrow (Ed.), *The development of antisocial and prosocial behaviour: Research, theories and issues.* New York: Academic Press.

Oring, L.W. (1986). Avian polyandry. *Current Ornithology, 3,* 309–351.

Orne, M.T. (1959). The nature of hypnosis: Artifact and essence. *Journal of Abnormal and Social Psychology, 58,* 277–299.

Orne, M.T. (1962). On the social psychology of the psychological experiment: With particular reference to demand characteristics and their implications. *American Psychologist, 17,* 776–783.

Ost, L.G. (1985). Mode of acquisition of phobias. *Acta Universitatis Uppsaliensis, 529,* 1–45.

Ost, L.G. (1989). *Blood phobia: A specific phobia subtype in DSM-IV.* Paper requested by the Simple Phobia subcommittee of the DSM-IV Anxiety Disorders Work Group.

Oswald, I. (1980). *Sleep (4th Edn.).* Harmondsworth: Penguin Books.

Owusu-Bempah, & Howitt, D. (1994). Racism and the psychological textbook. *The Psychologist, 7,* 163–166.

Packer, C. (1977). Reciprocal altruism in *Papio anubis. Nature, 265,* 441–443.

Packer, C. (1986). The ecology of sociality in felids. In D.J. Rubenstein & R.W. Wrangham (Eds.), *Ecological aspects of social evolution.* Princeton, NJ: Princeton University Press.

Packer, C., Gilbert, D.A., Pusey, A.E., & O'Brien, S.J. (1991). A molecular genetic analysis of kinship and cooperation in African lions. *Nature, 351,* 562–565.

Padden, C., & Humphries, T. (1988). *Deaf in America: Voices from a culture.* Cambridge, MA: Harvard University Press.

Pahl, J.J., Swayze, V.W., & Andreasen, N.C. (1990). Diagnostic advances in anatomical and functional brain imaging in schizophrenia. In A. Kales, C.N. Stefanis, & J.A. Talbot (Eds.), *Recent advances in schizophrenia.* New York: Springer-Verlag.

Palincsar, A.S., & Brown, A.L. (1984). Reciprocal teaching of comprehension-fostering and comprehension-monitoring activities. *Cognition and Instruction, 1,* 117–175.

Papez, J.W. (1937). A proposed mechanism of emotion. *Archives of Neurology and Psychiatry, 38,* 725–743.

Papi, F. (1982). Olfaction and homing in pigeons: Ten years of experiments. In F.P. Wallraff & H. G. Wallraff (Eds.), *Avian navigation.* Berlin: Springer-Verlag.

Park, R.J., Lawrie, J.M., & Freeman, C.P. (1995). Post-viral onset of anorexia nervosa. *British Journal of Psychology, 166,* 386–389.

Parke, R.D. (1977). Some effects of punishment on children's behaviour: Revisited. In E.M. Hetherington & R.D. Parke (Eds.), *Contemporary readings in child psychology.* New York: McGraw-Hill.

Parker, G.A. (1978). Evolution of competitive mate searching. *Annual Review of Entomology, 23,* 173–196.

Parkes, C.M. (1986). *Bereavement: Studies in grief in adult life.* London: Tavistock.

Parkinson, B. (1994). Emotion. In A.M. Colman (Ed.), *Companion encyclopaedia of psychology, Vol. 2.* London: Routledge.

Parten, M. (1932). Social participation among preschool children. *Journal of Abnormal and Social Psychology, 27,* 243–269.

Pascual-Leone, J. (1984). Attentional, dialectic, and mental effort. In M.L. Commons, F.A. Richards, & C. Armon (Eds.), *Beyond formal operations.* New York: Plenum.

Pastore, N. (1952). The role of arbitrariness in the frustration-aggression hypothesis. *Journal of Abnormal and Social Psychology, 47,* 728–731.

Patterson, F.G. (1979). Conversations with a gorilla. *National Geographic, 154,* 438–465.

Patterson, G.R. (1982). *Coercive family processes.* Eugene, OR: Castiia Press.

Pattie, F.A. (1937). The genuineness of hypnotically produced anaesthesia of the skin. *American Journal of Psychology, 49,* 435–443.

Patton, M.Q. (1980). *Qualitative evaluation methods.* London: Sage.

Paul, G.L., & Lentz, R.J. (1977). *Psychosocial treatment of chronic mental patients: Milieu versus social learning programs.* Cambridge, MA: Harvard University Press.

Paykel, E.S. (1974). Life stress and psychiatric disorder: Applications of the clinical approach. In B.S. Dohrenwend & B.P. Dohrenwend (Eds.), *Stressful life events: Their nature and effects.* New York: Wiley.

Payne, J. (1976). Task complexity and contingent processing in decision making: An information search and protocol analysis. *Organizational Behavior and Human Performance, 16,* 366–387.

Payne, K., & Payne, R. (1985). Large scale changes over 19 years in songs of humpback whales in Bermuda. *Zeitschrift für Tierpsychologie, 68,* 89–114.

Pedersen, N.L., Plomin, R., McClearn, G.E., & Friberg, I. (1988). Neuroticism, extraversion, and related traits in adult twins reared apart and reared together. *Journal of Personality and Social Psychology, 55,* 950–957.

Peek, F. (1972). An experimental study of the territorial function of vocal and visual display in the male red-winged blackbirds (*Ageliaus phoenicens*). *Animal Behaviour, 20,* 112–118.

Penfield, W. (1969). Consciousness, memory, and man's conditioned reflexes. In K. Pribram (Ed.), *On the biology of learning.* New York: Harcourt, Brace, & World.

Penfield, W., & Boldrey, E. (1937). Somatic motor and sensory representations in cerebral cortex of man as studied by electrical stimulation. *Brain, 60,* 389–443.

Pengelley, E.T., & Fisher, K.C. (1957). Onset and cessation of hibernation under constant temperature and light in the golden-mantled ground squirrel. *Nature, 180,* 1371–1372.

Peplau, L.A. (1991). Lesbian and gay relationships. In J.C. Gonsiorek & J. Dweinrich (Eds.), *Homosexuality: Research implications for public policy.* Newbury Park, NJ: Sage.

Perdeck, A.C. (1958). Two types of orientation in migrating starlings, *Sturnus vulgaris L.,* and chaffinches, *Fringilla coelbs L.,* as revealed by displacement experiments. *Ardea, 46,* 1–37.

Perez, S., Taylor, O., & Jander, R. (1977). A sun compass in Monarch butterflies. *Nature, 387,* 29.

Perrin, S., & Spencer, C. (1980). The Asch effect: A child of its time. *Bulletin of the British Psychological Society, 33,* 405–406.

Perrin, S., & Spencer, C. (1981). The Asch effect and cultural factors: Further observations and evidence. *Bulletin of the British Psychological Society, 34,* 385–386.

Perry, D.G., & Bussey, K. (1979). The social learning theory of sex differences: Imitation is alive and well. *Journal of Personality and Social Psychology, 37,* 1699–1712.

Pervin, L.A. (1993). *Personality: Theory and research (6th Edn.).* Chichester: Wiley.

Petersen, S.E., Fox, P.T., Mintun, M.A., Posner, M.I., & Raichle, M.E. (1989). Studies of the processing of single words using averaged positron emission tomographic measurements of cerebral blood flow change. *Journal of Cognitive Neuroscience, 1,* 153–170.

Pettigrew, T.F. (1959). Regional difference in anti-Negro prejudice. *Journal of Abnormal and Social Psychology, 59,* 28–56.

Petty, R.E., & Cacioppo, J.T. (1981). *Attitudes and persuasion: Classic and contemporary approaches.* Dubuque: W.C. Brown.

Petty, R.E., Cacioppo, J.T., & Goldman, R. (1981). Personal involvement as a determinant of argument-based persuasion. *Journal of Personality and Social Psychology, 41,* 847–855.

Pfungst, O. (1911). *Clever Hans, the horse of Mr. von Osten.* New York: Holt, Rinehart, & Winston.

Phinney, J. (1993). A three-stage model of ethnic identity development. In M. Bernal & G. Knight (Eds.), *Ethnic identity: Formation and transmission among Hispanics and other minorities.* Albany, NY: State University of New York Press.

Piaget, J. (1932). *The moral judgement of the child.* Harmondsworth: Penguin.

Piaget, J. (1967). *The child's conception of the world.* Totowa, NJ: Littlefield, Adams.

Piaget, J. (1970). Piaget's theory. In J. Mussen (Ed.), *Carmichael's manual of child psychology, Vol. 1.* New York: Basic Books.

Piaget, J., & Inhelder, B. (1969). *The psychology of the child.* London: Routledge & Kegan Paul.

Piaget, J., & Szeminska, A. (1952). *The child's conception of number.* London: Routledge & Kegan Paul.

Pietrewicz, A.T., & Kamil, A.C. (1981). Search images and the detection of cryptic prey: An operant approach. In A.C. Kamil & T.D. Sargent (Eds.), *Foraging behaviour: Ecological, ethological and psychological approaches.* New York: Garland STPM Press.

Pietsch, T.W., & Grobecker, D.B. (1978). The compleat angler: Aggressive mimicry in an antennariid anglefish. *Science, 201,* 369–370.

Pike, K.M., & Rodin, J. (1991). Mothers, daughters, and disordered eating. *Journal of Abnormal Psychology, 100,* 198–204.

Piliavin, I.M., Rodin, J., & Piliavin, J.A. (1969). Good samaritarianism: An underground phenomenon? *Journal of Personality and Social Psychology, 13,* 289–299.

Piliavin, J.A., Dovidio, J.F., Gaertner, S.L., & Clark, R.D. (1981). *Emergency intervention.* New York: Academic Press.

Pilleri, G. (1979). The blind Indus dolphin. *Platanista indi. Endeavour, 3,* 48–56.

Pinel, J.P.J. (1997). *Biopsychology (3rd Edn.).* Boston: Allyn & Bacon.

Piran, N., Kennedy, S. Garfinkel, P.E., & Owens, M. (1985). Affective disturbance in eating disorders. *Journal of Nervous and Mental Disease, 173,* 395–400.

Plomin, R. (1988). The nature and nurture of cognitive abilities. In R.J. Sternberg (Ed.), *Advances in the psychology of human intelligence, Vol. 4.* Hillsdale, NJ: Erlbaum.

Plomin, R. (1990). The role of inheritance in behaviour. *Science, 248,* 183–188.

Plomin, R. (1997). DNA: Implications. *The Psychologist, 11,* 61–62.

Plomin, R., Chipuer, H.M., & Loehlin, J.C. (1990a). Behavioural genetics and personality. In L.A. Robson, C. (1994). *Experimental design and statistics in psychology (3rd. Ed).* Harmondsworth, Middlesex: Penguin.

Plomin, R., Chipuer, H.M., & Loehlin, J.C. (1990b). Behavioural genetics and personality. In L.A. Pervin (Ed.), *Handbook of personality: Theory and research.* New York: Guilford.

Pollack, J.M. (1979). Obsessive-compulsive personality: A review. *Psychological Review, 86,* 225–241.

Pomerantz, J., & Garner, W.R. (1973). Stimulus configuration in selective attention tasks. *Perception & Psychophysics, 14,* 565–569.

Pope, K.S., & Vetter, V.A. (1992). Ethical dilemmas encountered by members of the American Psychological Association. *American Psychologist, 47,* 397–411.

Popper, K.R. (1969). *Conjectures and refutations.* London: Routledge & Kegan Paul.

Popper, K.R. (1972). *Objective knowledge.* Oxford: Oxford University Press.

Posner, M.I., & Petersen, S.E. (1990). The attention system of the human brain. *Annual Review of Neuroscience, 13,* 25–42.

Postmes, T., & Spears, R. (1998). Deindividuation and anti-normative behaviour: A meta-analysis. *Psychological Bulletin, 123,* 238–259.

Potter, J., & Wetherell, D. (1987). *Discourse and social psychology: Beyond attitudes and behaviour.* London: Sage.

Pottiez, J-M. (1986). *A walk with a white Bushman.* London: Chatto & Windus.

Power, M.E. (1984). Habitat quality and the distribution of algae-grazing catfish in a Panamanian stream. *Journal of Animal Ecology, 53,* 357–374.

Pratkanis, A.R., & Aronson, E. (1992). *Age of propaganda: The everyday use and abuse of persuasion.* New York: W.H. Freeman.

Preisler, G. (1997). Social and emotional development of blind children: A longitudinal study. In V. Lewis & G.M. Collis (Eds.), *Blindness and psychological development in young children.* Leicester: BPS Books.

Preston, J.L. (1978). Communication systems and social interactions in a goby-shrimp symbiosis. *Animal Behaviour, 26,* 791–802.

Pring, L. (1997). Blindness. In A. Baum, S. Newman, J. Weinman, R. West, & C. McManus (Eds.), *Cambridge handbook of psychology, health, and medicine.* Cambridge: Cambridge University Press.

Prioleau, L., Murdock, M., & Brody, N. (1983). An analysis of psychotherapy versus placebo studies. *Behavior and Brain Sciences, 6,* 273–310.

Pritchard, S. (1998). Triumph of mind over matter. *The Independent,* 16 October.

Profet, M. (1992). Pregnancy sickness as adaptation: A deterrent to maternal ingestion of teratogens. In J.H.

Barlow, I. Cosmides, & J. Tooby (Eds.), *The adapted mind: Evolutionary psychology and the generation of culture.* Oxford: Oxford University Press.

Putnam, B. (1979). Hypnosis and distortions in eyewitness memory. *International Journal of Clinical and Experimental Hypnosis, 27,* 437–448.

Putnam, F.W. (1991). Dissociative disorders in children and adolescents: A developmental perspective. *Psychiatric Clinics of North America, 14,* 519–531.

Putnam, H. (1973). Reductionism and the nature of psychology. *Cognition, 2,* 131–146.

Quattrone, G.A., & Jones, E.E. (1980). The perception of variability within ingroups and outgroups. *Journal of Personality and Social Psychology, 38,* 141–152.

Quay, L.C. (1971). Language, dialect, reinforcement, and the intelligence test performance of Negro children. *Child Development, 42,* 5–15.

Rabain-Jamin, J. (1989). Culture and early social interactions. The example of mother–infant object play in African and native French families. *European Journal of Psychology of Education, 4,* 295–305.

Rabbie, J.M., Schot, J.C., & Visser, L. (1989). Social identity theory: A conceptual and empirical critique from the perspective of a behavioural interaction model. *European Journal of Social Psychology, 19,* 171–202.

Rachman, S.J. (1993). A critique of cognitive therapy for anxiety disorders. *Behaviour Research and Therapy, 24,* 274–288.

Rachman, S.J., & de Silva, P. (1978). Abnormal and normal obsessions. *Behaviour Research and Therapy, 16,* 233–238.

Rack, P. (1982). *Race, culture and mental disorder.* London: Routledge.

Raichle, M.E. (1994). Images of the mind: Studies with modern imaging techniques. *Annual Review of Psychology, 45,* 333–356.

Rainwater, L., & Yancey, W.L. (1967). *The Moynihan Report and the politics of controversy.* Cambridge, MA: MIT Press.

Ramsey, C.T., Bryant, D.M., & Suarez, T.M. (1985). Preschool compensatory education and the modifiability of intelligence: A critical review. In D.K. Detterman (Ed.), *Current topics in human intelligence, Vol. 1: Research methodology.* Norwood, NJ: Ablex.

Ramsay, R., & de Groot, W. (1977). A further look at bereavement: Paper presented at EATI conference, Uppsala. [Cited in Hodgkinson, P.E. (1980, 17 January). Treating abnormal grief in the bereaved. *Nursing Times,* 126–128.]

Rasmussen, T., & Milner, B. (1975). Excision of Broca's area without persistent aphasia. In K.J. Zulch, O. Creutzfeldt, & G.C. Galbraith (Eds.), *Cerebral localisation.* New York: Springer.

Raulin, M.L., & Graziano, A.M. (1994). Quasi-experiments and correlational studies. In A.M. Colman (Ed.), *Companion encyclopaedia of psychology, Vol. 2.* London: Routledge.

Raven, B., & Haley, R.W. (1980). Social influence in a medical context. In L. Bickman (Ed.), *Applied social psychology annual, Vol. 1.* Beverley Hills, CA: Sage.

Raven, J. (1980). *Parents, teachers and children: A study of an educational home visiting scheme.* London: Hodder & Stoughton.

Rayner, K., Carlson, M., & Frazier, L. (1983). The interaction of syntax and semantics during sentence processing: Eye movements in the analysis of semantically biased sentences. *Journal of Verbal Learning and Verbal Behavior, 22,* 358–374.

Rayner, K., & Sereno, S.C. (1994). Eye movements in reading: Psycholinguistic studies. In M.A. Gernsbacher (Ed.), *Handbook of psycholinguistics.* New York: Academic Press.

Reason, J.T. (1979). Actions not as planned: The price of automatisation. In G. Underwood & R. Stevens (Eds.), *Aspects of consciousness, Vol. 1: Psychological issues.* London: Academic Press.

Reason, J.T. (1992). Cognitive underspecification: Its variety and consequences. In B.J. Baars (Ed.), *Experimental slips and human error: Exploring the architecture of volition.* New York: Plenum Press.

Reason, J.T., & Rowan, J. (Eds.) (1981). *Human enquiry: A sourcebook in new paradigm research.* Chichester: Wiley.

Reber, A.S. (1993). *Implicit learning and tacit knowledge.* Oxford: Oxford University Press.

Rechtschaffen, A., Gilliland, M., Bergmann, B., & Winter, J. (1983). Physiological correlates of prolonged sleep deprivation in rats. *Science, 221,* 182–184.

Reibstein, J., & Richards, M. (1992). *Sexual arrangements: Marriage and affairs.* London: Heinemann.

Reichard, S., Livson, F., & Peterson, P.G. (1962). *Aging and personality: A study of 87 older men.* New York: Wiley.

Reicher, S.D. (1984). The St. Pauls' riot: An explanation of the limits of crowd action in terms of a social identity model. *European Journal of Social Psychology, 14,* 1–21.

Reicher, S.D., & Potter, J. (1985). Psychological theory as intergroup perspective: A comparative analysis of 'scientific' and 'lay' accounts of crowd events. *Human Relations, 38,* 167–189.

Reichert, S.E. (1985). Why do some spiders cooperate? *Agelena consociata,* a case study. *Florida Entomologist, 68,* 105–116.

Reinberg, R. (1967). *Eclairement et cycle menstruel de la femme.* Rapport au Colloque International du CRNS, la photorégulation de la reproduction chez les oiseaux et les mammifères. Montpelier, France.

Reisenzein, R. (1983). The Schachter theory of emotion: Two decades later. *Psychological Bulletin, 94,* 239–264.

Reitman, J.S. (1971). Mechanisms of forgetting in short-term memory. *Cognitive Psychology, 2,* 185–195.

Rescorla, R.A., & Wagner, A.R. (1972). A theory of Pavlovian conditioning: Variations in the effectiveness of reinforcement and nonreinforcement. In A.H. Black & W.F. Prokasy (Eds.), *Classical conditioning II: Current research and theory.* New York: Appleton-Century-Crofts.

Richards, W. (1975). Visual space perception. In E.C. Carterette & M.P. Friedman (Eds.), *Handbook of perception.* New York: Academic Press.

Ridley, M. (1983). *The explanation of organic diversity.* Oxford: Clarendon Press.

Ridley, M. (1995). *Animal behaviour (2nd Edn.).* Oxford: Blackwell.

Ritter, S., & Taylor, J.S. (1990). Vagal sensory neurons are required for lipoprivic but not glucoprivic feeding in rats. *American Journal of Physiology, 258,* R1395–R1401.

Roberts, P., & Newton, P.M. (1987). Levinsonian studies of women's adult development. *Psychology and Aging, 2,* 154–163.

Robertson, J., & Bowlby, J. (1952). Responses of young children to separation from their mothers. *Courier Centre International de l'Enfance, 2,* 131–142.

Robertson, J., & Robertson, J. (1971). Young children in brief separation. *Psychoanalytic Study of the Child, 26,* 264–315.

Robins, L.N., Helzer, J.E., Weissman, M.M., Orvaschel, H., Gruenberg, E., Burke, J.K., & Regier, D.A. (1984). Lifetime prevalence of specific psychiatric disorders in three cities. *Archives of General Psychiatry, 41*, 949–958.

Robinson, T.E., & Berridge, K.C. (1993). The neural basis of drug craving: An incentive-sensitisation theory of addiction. *Brain Research Reviews, 18*, 247–291.

Robson, C. (1994). *Experimental design and statistics in psychology (3rd Edn.)*. Harmondsworth, Middlesex: Penguin.

Roeder, K.D., & Treat, A.E. (1961). The detection and evasion of bats by moths. *American Scientist, 49*, 135–148.

Roediger, H.L. (1990). Implicit memory: Retention without remembering. *American Psychologist, 45*, 1043–1056.

Roethlisberger, F.J., & Dickson, W.J. (1939). *Management and the worker*. Cambridge, MA: Harvard University Press.

Rogers, C.R. (1947). The case of Mary Jane Tilden. In W.U. Snyder (Ed.), *Casebook of non-directive counseling*. Cambridge, MA: Houghton Mifflin.

Rogers, C.R. (1951). *Client-centred therapy*. Boston: Houghton Mifflin.

Rogers, C.R. (1959). A theory of therapy, personality, and interpersonal relationships as developed in the client-centred framework. In S. Koch (Ed.), *Psychology: A study of a science*. New York: McGraw-Hill.

Rogers, C.R. (1986). Client-centred therapy. In I. Kutash & A. Wolf (Eds.), *Psychotherapist's casebook*. San Francisco: Jossey-Bass.

Rogers, P.J., & Blundell, J.E. (1980). Investigation of food selection and meal parameters during the development of dietary induced obesity. *Appetite, 1*, 85–88.

Rogers, R.W. (1983). Cognitive and psychological processes in fear appeals and attitude change: A revised theory of protection motivation. In J. Cacioppo & R. Petty (Eds.), *Social psychophysiology: A sourcebook*. New York: Guilford.

Rohner, R.P. (1975). Parental acceptance–rejection and personality development: A universalist approach to behavioural science. In R.W. Brislin et al. (Eds.), *Cross-cultural perspectives on learning*. New York: Sage.

Rohner, R.P. (1986). *The warmth dimension: Foundations of parental acceptance–rejection theory*. Beverly Hills, CA: Sage.

Rohner, R.P., & Pettengill, S.M. (1985). Perceived parental acceptance–rejection and parental control among Korean adolescents. *Child Development, 56*, 524–528.

Rohner, R.P., & Rohner, E.C. (1981). Parental acceptance–rejection and parental control: Cross-cultural codes. *Ethnology, 20*, 245–260.

Rokeach, M. (1960). *The open and closed mind*. New York: Basic Books.

Roland, P.E. (1993). *Brain activation*. New York: Wiley–Liss.

Rolls, B.J., & Rolls, E.T. (1982). *Thirst*. Cambridge: Cambridge University Press.

Rolls, B.J., Wood, R.J., & Rolls, R.M. (1980). Thirst: The initiation, maintenance, and termination of drinking. In J.M. Sprague & A.N. Epstein (Eds.), *Progress in psychology and physiological psychology*. New York: Academic Press.

Rosekrans, M.A., & Hartup, W.W. (1967). Imitative influences of consistent and inconsistent response consequences to a model on aggressive behaviour in children. *Journal of Personality and Social Psychology, 7*, 429–434.

Rosen, J.C., & Leitenberg, H. (1985). Exposure plus response prevention treatment of bulimia. In D.M. Garner & P.E. Garfinkel (Eds.), *Handbook of psychotherapy for anorexia nervosa and bulimia*. New York: Guilford Press.

Rosenberg, M.J. (1965). When dissonance fails: On eliminating evaluation apprehension from attitude measurement. *Journal of Personality and Social Psychology, 1*, 28–42.

Rosenbloom, S., Campbell, M., George, A.E., Kricheff, I.I., Taleporos, E., Anderson, L., Reuben, R.N., & Korein, J. (1984). High resolution CT scanning in infantile autism: A quantitative approach. *Journal of the American Academy of Child Psychiatry, 23*, 72–77.

Rosenfield, D., Stephan, W.G., & Lucker, G.W. (1981). Attraction to competent and incompetent members of cooperative and competitive groups. *Journal of Applied Social Psychology, 11*, 416–433.

Rosenhan, D.L. (1970). The natural socialisation of altruistic autonomy. In J. Macaulay & L. Berkowitz (Eds.), *The uncommon child*. New York: Plenum Press.

Rosenhan, D.L. (1973). On being sane in insane places. *Science, 179*, 250–258.

Rosenhan, D.L., & Seligman, M.E.P. (1989). *Abnormal psychology (2nd Edn.)*. New York: Norton.

Rosenhan, D.L., & Seligman, M.E.P. (1995). *Abnormal psychology (3rd Edn.)*. New York: Norton.

Rosenman, R.H., Brand, R.J., Jenkins, C.D., Friedman, M., Straus, R., & Wurm, M. (1975). Coronary heart disease in the Western Collaborative Group Study: Final follow-up experience of $8^{1}/_{2}$ years. *Journal of the American Medical Association, 233*, 872–877.

Rosenthal, D. (1963). *The Genain quadruplets: A case study and theoretical analysis of heredity and environment in schizophrenia*. New York: Basic Books.

Rosenthal, D. (1970). *Genetic theory and abnormal behaviour*. New York: McGraw-Hill.

Rosenthal, R. (1966). *Experimenter effects in behavioural research*. New York: Appleton-Century-Crofts.

Rosenzweig, M.R. (1992). Psychological science around the world. *American Psychologist, 47*, 718–722.

Ross, C.A., Miller, S.D., Reagor, P., Bjornson, L., Fraser, G., & Anderson, G. (1990). Structured interview data on 102 cases of multiple personality disorder from four centres. *American Journal of Psychiatry, 147*, 596–601.

Roth, I. (1986). An introduction to object perception. In I. Roth & J.P. Frisby (Eds.), *Perception and representation: A cognitive approach*. Milton Keynes, UK: Open University Press.

Rowe, M.P., Coss, R.G., & Owings, D.H. (1986). Rattlesnake rattles and burrowing owl hisses: A case of acoustic batesian mimicry. *Ethology, 72*, 53–71.

Rowland, C. (1983). Patterns of interaction between three blind infants and their mothers. In A.E. Mills (Ed.), *Language acquisition in the blind child: Normal and deficient*. London: Croom Helm.

Roy, D.F. (1991). Improving recall by eyewitnesses through the cognitive interview: Practical applications and implications for the police service. *The Psychologist: Bulletin of the British Psychological Society, 4*, 398–400.

Rubin, K.H., & Trotter, K.T. (1977). Kohlberg's moral judgement scale: Some methodological considerations. *Developmental Psychology, 13*, 535–536.

Rubin, Z. (1970). Measurement of romantic love. *Journal of Personality and Social Psychology, 16*, 265–273.

Rubin, Z. (1973). *Liking and loving: An invitation to social psychology*. New York: Holt, Rinehart & Winston.

Ruble, D.N., Balaban, T., & Cooper, J. (1981). Gender constancy and the effects of sex-typed televised toy commercials. *Child Development, 52,* 667–673.

Ruble, D.N., Boggiano, A.K., Feldman, N.S., & Loebl, J.H. (1980). A developmental analysis of the role of social comparison in self-evaluation. *Developmental Psychology, 16,* 105–115.

Ruble, D.N., Fleming, A.S., Hackel, L.S., & Stangor, C. (1988). Changes in the marital relationship during the transition to first time motherhood: The effects of violated expectations concerning division of household labour. *Journal of Personality and Social Psychology, 55,* 78–87.

Rumelhart, D.E., & Norman, D.A. (1981). Analogical processes in learning. In J.R. Anderson (Ed.), *Cognitive skills and their acquisition.* Hillsdale, NJ: Lawrence Erlbaum Associates Inc.

Rumelhart, D.E., & Ortony, A. (1977). The representation of knowledge in memory. In R.C. Anderson, R.J. Spiro, & W.E. Montague (Eds.), *Schooling and the acquisition of knowledge.* Hillsdale, NJ: Lawrence Erlbaum Associates Inc.

Runciman, W.G. (1966). *Relative deprivation and social justice.* London: Routledge & Kegan Paul.

Rundus, D., & Atkinson, R.C. (1970). Rehearsal processes in free recall, a procedure for direct observation. *Journal of Verbal Learning and Verbal Behavior, 9,* 99–105.

Rusbult, C.E. (1980). Commitment and satisfaction in romantic associations: A test of the investment model. *Journal of Experimental Social Psychology, 16,* 172–186.

Rusbult, C.E., Zembrodt, I., & Iwaniszek, J. (1986). The impact of gender and sex-role orientation on responses to dissatisfaction in close relationships. *Sex Roles, 15,* 1–20.

Russek, M. (1971). Hepatic receptors and the neurophysiological mechanisms controlling feeding behaviour. In S. Ehrenpreis (Ed.), *Neurosciences Research, Vol. 4.* New York: Academic Press.

Russell, C.S. (1974). Transition to parenthood: Problems and gratifications. *Journal of Marriage and the Family, 36,* 294–302.

Russell, D.W., & Catrona, C.E. (1991). Social support, stress, and depressive symptoms among the elderly: Test of a process model. *Psychology and Aging, 6,* 190–201.

Russell, G.W., & Goldstein, J.H. (1995). Personality differences between Dutch football fans and non-fans. *Social Behavior and Personality, 23,* 199–204.

Rutter, M. (1981). *Maternal deprivation reassessed (2nd Edn.).* Harmondsworth: Penguin.

Rutter, M., & Rutter, M. (1992). *Developing minds: Challenge and continuity across the life-span.* Harmondsworth: Penguin.

Rutter, M., & The ERA Study Team. (1998). Developmental catch-up and deficit following adoption after severe early privation. *Journal of Child Psychology and Psychiatry, 39,* 465–476.

Ryder, R. (1990). *Animal revolution: Changing attitudes towards speciesism.* Oxford: Blackwell.

Ryder, R. (1991). Sentientism: A comment on Gray and Singer. *The Psychologist, 14,* 201.

Ryle, G. (1949). *The concept of mind.* London: Hutchinson.

Sabey, B.E., & Codling, P.J. (1975). Alcohol and road accidents in Great Britain. In S. Israelstam & S. Lambert (Eds.), *Alcohol, drugs and traffic safety.* Ontario: Liquor Control Board.

Sacks, O. (1991). *Seeing voices.* London: Picador.

Sagi, A., & Lewkowicz, K.S. (1987). A cross-cultural evaluation of attachment research. In L.W.C. Tavecchio & M.H. van IJzendoorn (Eds.), *Attachment in social networks: Contributions to the Bowlby-Ainsworth attachment theory.* Amsterdam: North-Holland.

Sagi, A., van IJzendoorn, M.H., & Koren-Karie, N. (1991). Primary appraisal of the Strange Situation: A cross-cultural analysis of the pre-separation episodes. *Developmental Psychology, 27,* 587–596.

Sagotsky, G., Wood-Schneider, M., & Konop, M. (1981). Learning to co-operate: Effects of modelling and direct instructions. *Child Development, 52,* 1037–1042.

Salamon, S. (1977). Family bonds and friendship bonds: Japan and West Germany. *Journal of Marriage and the Family, 39,* 807–820.

Salomon, G., & Globerson, T. (1989). When groups do not function the way they ought to. *International Journal of Educational Research, 13,* 89–99.

Salovey, P. (Ed.) (1991). *The psychology of jealousy and envy.* New York: Guilford Press.

Sameroff, A.J., Seifer, R., Baldwin, A., & Baldwin, C. (1993). Stability of intelligence from preschool to adolescence: The influence of social and family risk factors. *Child Development, 64,* 80–97.

Sandford, R.N. (1936). The effects of abstinence from food on imaginal process. *Journal of Psychology, 2,* 129–136.

Sanford, F.H. (1950). *Authoritarianism and leadership.* Philadelphia: Institute for Research in Human Relations.

Santrock, J.W. (1975). Moral structure: The interrelations of moral behaviour, moral judgement, and moral affect. *Journal of Genetic Psychology, 127,* 201–213.

Sarason, I.G., Smith, R.E., & Diener, E. (1975). Personality research: Components of variance attributable to the person and the situation. *Journal of Personality and Social Psychology, 32,* 199–204.

Sarbin, T.R., & Slayle, R.W. (1972). Hypnosis and psychophysiological outcomes. In E. Fromm & R.E. Shor (Eds.), *Hypnosis: Research, developments and perspectives.* Chicago: Aldine-Atherton.

Sartorius, N., Jablensky, A., Korten, A., Ernberg, G., Anker, M., Cooper, J.E., & Day, R. (1986). Early manifestations and first-contact incidence of schizophrenia in different cultures. *Psychological Medicine, 16,* 909–928.

Savage-Rumbaugh, E.S. (1986). *Ape language: From conditioned responses to symbols.* New York: Columbia University Press.

Savage-Rumbaugh, E.S., & Hopkins, D. (1986). Awareness, intentionality and acquired communicative behaviours: Dimensions of intelligence. In R.J. Schusterman, J.A. Thomas, & F.G. Wood (Eds.), *Dolphin cognition and behaviour: A comparative approach.* Hillsdale, NJ: Erlbaum.

Savage-Rumbaugh, E.S., McDonald, K., Sevcik, R.A., Hopkins, W.D., & Rupert, E. (1986). Spontaneous symbol acquisition and communicative use by pygmy chimpanzees *(Pan paniscus). Journal of Experimental Psychology: General, 115,* 211–235.

Saville, P., & Blinkhorn, S. (1981). Reliability, homogeneity and the construct validity of Cattell's 16PF. *Personality and Individual Differences, 2,* 325–333.

Savin, H.B. (1973). Professors and psychological researchers: Conflicting values in conflicting roles. *Cognition, 2,* 147–149.

Scarr, S. (1988). Race and gender as psychological variables. *American Psychologist, 43,* 56–59.

Scarr, S., & Weinberg, R.A. (1976). IQ test performance of black children adopted by white families. *American Psychologist, 31*, 726–739.

Schachter, S., & Singer, J.E. (1962). Cognitive, social, and physiological determinants of an emotional state. *Psychological Review, 69*, 379–399.

Schachter, S., & Wheeler, L. (1962). Epinephrine, chlorpromazine and amusement. *Journal of Abnormal and Social Psychology, 65*, 121–128.

Schacter, D.L. (1987). Implicit memory: History and current status. *Journal of Experimental Psychology: Learning, Memory, and Cognition, 13*, 501–518.

Schaefer, C., Coyne, J.C., & Lazarus, R.S. (1981). The health-related functions of social support. *Journal of Behavioral Medicine, 4*, 381–406.

Schafer, R., & Murphy, G. (1943). The role of autism in visual figure–ground relationship. *Journal of Experimental Psychology, 32*, 335–343.

Schaffer, H.R., & Emerson, P.E. (1964). *The development of social attachments in infancy*. Monographs of the Society for Research on Child Development, No. 29.

Schaller, G.B. (1972). *The Serengeti lion*. Chicago: University of Chicago Press.

Scheff, T.J. (1966). *Being mentally ill: A sociological theory*. Chicago: Aldine.

Scheper-Hughes, N. (1992). *Death without weeping: The violence of everyday life in Brazil*. Berkeley, CA: University of California Press.

Schiff, M., Duyne, M., Dumaret, A., & Tomkiewicz, S. (1982). How much could we boost scholastic achievement and IQ scores? A direct answer from a French adoption study. *Cognition, 12*, 165–196.

Schiffman, H.R. (1967). Size estimation of familiar objects under informative and reduced conditions of viewing. *American Journal of Psychology, 80*, 229–235.

Schlenoff, D.H. (1985). The startle responses of blue jays to *Catocala* (Lepidoptera: Noctuidae) prey models. *Animal Behaviour, 33*, 1057–1067.

Schliefer, S.J., Keller, S.E., Camerino, M., Thornton, J.C., & Stein, M. (1983). Suppression of lymphocyte stimulation following bereavement. *Journal of the American Medical Association, 250*, 374–377.

Schmid-Hempel, P., Kacelnik, A., & Houston, A.I. (1985). Honeybees maximise efficiency by not filling their crop. *Behavioural Ecology and Sociobiology, 17*, 61–66.

Schneider, W., & Shiffrin, R.M. (1977). Controlled and automatic human information processing: I. Detection, search and attention. *Psychological Review, 84*, 1–66.

Schochat, T., Luboshitzky, R., & Lavie, P. (1997). Nocturnal melatonin onset is phase locked to the primary sleep gate. *American Journal of Physiology, 273*, R364–R370.

Schriesham, C.A., Hinkin, T.R., & Podsakoss, P.M. (1991). Can ipsative and single item measures produce erroneous results in the field studies of French and Raven's five bases of power? An empirical investigation. *Journal of Applied Psychology, 76*, 106–114.

Schroeder, D.H., & Costa, D.T. (1984). Influence of life event stress on physical illness: Substantive effects or methodological flaws? *Journal of Personality and Social Psychology, 46*, 853–863.

Schuz, E. (1971). *Grundriss der Vogelzugskunde*. Berlin: Paul Parey.

Schwalberg, M.D., Barlow, D.H., Alger, S.A., & Howard, L.J. (1992). Comparison of bulimics, obese binge eaters, social phobics, and individuals with panic disorder or comorbidity across DSM-III-R anxiety. *Journal of Abnormal Psychology, 101*, 675–681.

Schwartz, G.E. (1973). Biofeedback as therapy: Some theoretical and practical issues. *American Psychologist, 28*, 666–673.

Schwartz, S.H. (1977). Normative influences on altruism. In L. Berkowitz (Ed.), *Advances in experimental social psychology, Vol. 10*. New York: Academic Press.

Schwarzer, R., & Leppin, A. (1992). Social support and mental health: A conceptual and empirical overview. In L. Montada, S.H. Filipp, & M.J. Lerner (Eds.), *Life crises and experience of loss in adulthood*. Hillsdale, NJ: Lawrence Erlbaum.

Schweinhart, L.J., & Weikart, D.P. (1985). Evidence that good early childhood programs work. *Phi Delta Kappa, 66*, 545–551.

Scott, S. (1994). Mental retardation. In M. Rutter, E. Taylor, & L. Hersov (Eds.), *Child and adolescent psychiatry*. Oxford: Blackwell.

Seeley, T.D. (1985). *Honeybee ecology: A study of adaptation in social life*. Princeton, NJ: Princeton University Press.

Seer, P. (1979). Psychological control of essential hypertension: Review of the literature and methodological critique. *Psychological Bulletin, 86*, 1015–1043.

Segal, S.J., & Fusella, V. (1970). Influence of imaged pictures and sounds on detection of visual and auditory signals. *Journal of Experimental Psychology, 83*, 458–464.

Segall, M.H., Campbell, D.T., & Herskovits, M.J. (1963). Cultural differences in the perception of geometrical illusions. *Science, 139*, 769–771.

Seger, C.A. (1994). Implicit learning. *Psychological Bulletin, 115*, 163–196.

Seghers, B.H. (1974). Schooling behaviour in the guppy *Poecilia reticulata*: An evolutionary response to predation. *Evolution, 28*, 486–489.

Seidman, L.J. (1983). Schizophrenia and brain dysfunction: An integration of recent neurodiagnostic findings. *Psychological Bulletin, 94*, 195–238.

Seifer, R., Schiller, M., Sameroff, A.J., Resnick, S., & Riordan, K. (1996). Attachment, maternal sensitivity, and infant temperament during the first year of life. *Developmental Psychology, 32*, 12–25.

Sekuler, R., & Blake, R. (1994). *Perception (3rd Edn.)*. New York: McGraw-Hill.

Selfe, L. (1976). An autistic child with exceptional drawing ability. In G.E. Butterworth (Ed.), *The child's representation of the world*. New York: Plenum.

Selfe, L. (1983). *Normal and anomalous representational drawing ability in children*. London: Academic Press.

Seligman, M.E.P. (1970). On the generality of the laws of learning. *Psychological Review, 77*, 406–418.

Seligman, M.E.P. (1971). Phobias and preparedness. *Behavior Therapy, 2*, 307–320.

Seligman, M.E.P. (1975). *Helplessness: On depression, development and death*. San Francisco: W.H. Freeman.

Sellen, A.J., & Norman, D.A. (1992). The psychology of slips. In B.J. Baars (Ed.), *Experimental slips and human error: Exploring the architecture of volition*. New York: Plenum Press.

Selye, H. (1950). *Stress*. Montreal: Acta.

Semenza, C., Cipolotti, L., & Denes, G. (1992). Reading aloud in jargonaphasia: An unusual dissociation in speech output. *Journal of Neurology, Neurosurgery, and Psychiatry, 55*, 205–208.

Semin, G.R. (1995). Social constructionism. In A.S.R. Manstead, M. Hewstone, S.T. Fiske, M.A. Hogg, H.T. Reis, & G.R. Semin (Eds.), *The Blackwell encyclopaedia of social psychology*. Oxford: Blackwell.

Sergent, J., Ohta, S., & MacDonald, B. (1992). Functional neuroanatomy of face and object processing. *Brain, 115*, 15–36.

Serpell, R.S. (1979). How specific are perceptual skills? A cross-cultural study of pattern reproduction. *British Journal of Psychology, 70*, 365–380.

Shaffer, D.R. (1993). *Developmental psychology: Childhood and adolescence (3rd Edn.)*. Pacific Grove, CA: Brooks/Cole.

Shaffer, L.H. (1975). Multiple attention in continuous verbal tasks. In P.M.A. Rabbitt & S. Dornic (Eds.), *Attention and performance, Vol. V*. London: Academic Press.

Shallice, T. (1982). Specific impairments of planning. *Philosophical Transactions of the Royal Society of London, B298*, 199–209.

Shallice, T., & Warrington, E.K. (1970). Independent functioning of verbal memory stores: A neuropsychological study. *Quarterly Journal of Experimental Psychology, 22*, 261–273.

Shallice, T., & Warrington, E.K. (1974). The dissociation between long-term retention of meaningful sounds and verbal material. *Neuropsychologia, 12*, 553–555.

Shapiro, C.M., Bortz, R., Mitchell, D., Bartel, P., & Jooste, P. (1981). Slow-wave sleep: A recovery period after exercise. *Science, 214*, 1253–1254.

Shapiro, D., Tursky, B., & Schwartz, G.E. (1970). Control of blood pressure in man by operant conditioning. *Circulation Research, 26*, 127–132.

Shatz, M., & Gelman, R. (1973). *The development of communication skills: Modifications in the speech of young children as a function of the listener*. Monographs of the Society for Research in Child Development, Np. 38.

Shaver, J.P., & Strong, W. (1976). *Facing value decisions: Rationale-building for teachers*. Belmont, CA: Wadsworth.

Shaver, P.R., Wu, S., & Schwartz, J.C. (1991). Cross-cultural similarities and differences in emotion and its representation: A prototype approach. In M.S. Clark (Ed.), *Review of personality and social psychology, Vol. 13*. Beverly Hills, CA: Sage.

Shaywitz, S.E. (1996). Dyslexia. *Scientific American, 276*, 78–84.

Shea, J.D.C. (1981). Changes in interpersonal distances and categories of play behaviour in the early weeks of preschool. *Developmental Psychology, 17*, 417–425.

Sherif, M. (1935). A study of some factors in perception. *Archives of Psychology, 27*, No. 187.

Sherif, M. (1966). *Group conflict and co-operation: Their social psychology*. London: Routledge & Kegan Paul.

Sherif, M., Harvey, O.J., White, B.J., Hood, W.R., & Sherif, C.W. (1961). *Intergroup conflict and co-operation: The robber's cave experiment*. Norman, OK: University of Oklahoma.

Shields, J. (1962). *Monozygotic twins*. Oxford: Oxford University Press.

Sherman, P.W. (1977). Nepotism and the evolution of alarm calls. *Science, 197*, 1246–1253.

Shiffrin, R.M., & Schneider, W. (1977). Controlled and automatic human information processing: II. Perceptual learning, automatic attending, and a general theory. *Psychological Review, 84*, 127–190.

Shotland, R.L., & Straw, M.K. (1976). Bystander response to an assault: When a man attacks a woman. *Journal of Personality and Social Psychology, 34*, 990–999.

Sieber, J.E., & Stanley, B. (1988). Ethical and professional dimensions of socially sensitive research. *American Psychologist, 43*, 49–55.

Sigall, H., Aronson, E., & Van Hoose, T. (1970). The co-operative subject: Myth or reality? *Journal of Experimental Social Psychology, 6*, 1–10.

Silverman, I. (1977). *The human subject in the psychological laboratory*. Oxford: Pergamon.

Silverman, I., Shulman, A.D., & Wiesenthal, D. (1970). Effects of deceiving and debriefing psychological subjects on performance in later experiments. *Journal of Personality and Social Psychology, 21*, 219–227.

Silverstein, C. (1972). *Behaviour modification and the gay community*. Paper presented at the annual convention of the Association for Advancement of Behaviour Therapy, New York.

Simmons, J.V. (1981). *Project Sea Hunt: A report on prototype development and tests*. Technical Report, No. 746. San Diego: Naval Ocean System Center.

Simmons, R.G., Burgeson, R., Carlton-Ford, S., & Blyth, D.A. (1987). The impact of cumulative changes in early adolescence. *Child Development, 58*, 1220–1234.

Simon, H.A. (1974). How big is a chunk? *Science, 183*, 482–488.

Simon, H.A. (1978). Rationality as process and product of thought. *American Economic Association, 68*, 1–16.

Sinclair-de-Zwart, H. (1969). Developmental psycholinguistics. In D. Elkind & J. Flavell (Eds.), *Studies in cognitive development*. Oxford: Oxford University Press.

Singer, P. (1991). Speciesism, morality and biology: A response to Jeffrey Gray. *The Psychologist, 14*, 199–200.

Siqueland, E.R., & DeLucia, C.A. (1969). Visual reinforcement of non-nutritive sucking in human infants. *Science, 165*, 1144–1146.

Sivinski, J. (1984). Effect of sexual experience on male mating success in a lek forming tephritid *Anastrepha suspensa* (Loew). *Florida Entolomologist, 67*, 126–130.

Skinner, B.F. (1938). *The behaviour of organisms*. New York: Appleton-Century-Crofts.

Skinner, B.F. (1948). *Walden Two*. New York: Macmillan.

Skinner, B.F. (1957). *Verbal behaviour*. New York: Appleton-Century-Crofts.

Skinner, B.F. (1966). Operant behaviour. In W.K. Honig (Ed.), *Operant behaviour: Areas of research and application*. New York: Appleton-Century-Crofts.

Skinner, B.F. (1971). *Beyond freedom and dignity*. New York: Knopf.

Skinner, B.F. (1980). *The shaping of a behaviourist*. Oxford: Holdan Books.

Skre, I., Onstad, S., Torgersen, S., Lygren, S., & Kringlen, E. (1993). A twin study of DSM-III-R anxiety disorders. *Acta Psychiatrica Scandinavica, 88*, 85–92.

Slaby, R.G., & Frey, K.S. (1975). Development of gender constancy and selective attention to same-sex models. *Child Development, 46*, 849–856.

Slamecka, N.J. (1966). Differentiation versus unlearning of verbal associations. *Journal of Experimental Psychology, 71*, 822–828.

Slater, A.M. (1990). Perceptual development. In M.W. Eysenck (Ed.), *The Blackwell dictionary of cognitive psychology*. Oxford: Blackwell.

Slavin, R.E. (1983). When does cooperative learning increase student achievement? *Psychological Bulletin, 94,* 429–445.

Sloane, R.B., Staples, F.R., Cristol, A.H., Yorkston, N.J., & Whipple, K. (1975). *Psychotherapy versus behaviour therapy.* Cambridge, MA: Harvard University Press.

Slovic, P., & Fischhoff, B. (1977). On the psychology of experimental surprises. *Journal of Experimental Psychology: Human Perception and Performance, 3,* 544–551.

Sluckin, W. (1965). *Imprinting and early experiences.* London: Methuen.

Small, S.A., Zeldin, R.S., & Savin-Williams, R.C. (1983). In search of personality traits: A multi-method analysis of naturally occurring prosocial and dominance behaviour. *Journal of Personality, 51,* 1–16.

Smith, J.N.M., Yom-Tov, Y., & Moses, R. (1982). Polygyny, male parental care and sex ratios in song sparrows: An experimental study. *Auk, 99,* 555–564.

Smith, K.D., Keating, J.P., & Stotland, E. (1989). Altruism reconsidered: The effect of denying feedback on a victim's status to empathic witnesses. *Journal of Personality and Social Psychology, 57,* 641–650.

Smith, M.L., Glass, G.V., & Miller, T.I. (1980). *The benefits of psychotherapy.* Baltimore: John Hopkins Press.

Smith, N.V., & Tsimpli, I.-M. (1991). Linguistic modularity? A case-study of a "savant" linguist. *Lingua, 84,* 315–351.

Smith, P., & Bond, M.H. (1993). *Social psychology across cultures: Analysis and perspectives.* New York: Harvester Wheatsheaf.

Smith, P.K. (1983). Human sociobiology. In J. Nicholson & B. Foss (Eds.), *Psychology survey, No. 4.* Leicester: British Psychological Society.

Smith, S.M., Brown, H.O., Toman, J.E.P., & Goodman, L.S. (1947). Lack of cerebral effects of D-tubocurarine. *Anaesthesiology, 8,* 1–14.

Snarey, J.R. (1985). Cross-cultural universality of social-moral development: A critical review of Kohlbergian research. *Psychological Bulletin, 97,* 202–232.

Snow, C.E., & Hoefnagel-Hohle, M. (1978). The critical period for language acquisition: Evidence from second language learning. *Child Development, 49,* 1114–1128.

Solley, C.M., & Murphy, G. (1960). *Development of the perceptual world.* New York: Basic Books.

Solomon, R.L., & Wynne, L.C. (1953). Traumatic avoidance learning: Acquisition in normal dogs. *Psychological Monographs, 67,* 1–19.

Solomon, Z., Mikulincer, M., & Avitzur, E. (1988). Coping, locus of control, social support, and combat-related posttraumatic stress disorder: A prospective study. *Journal of Personality and Social Psychology, 55,* 279–285.

Sommer, R. (1969). *Personal space: The behavioural basis of design.* Englewood Cliffs, NJ: Prentice Hall.

Spangler, G. (1990). Mother, child, and situational correlates of toddlers' social competence. *Infant Behavior and Development, 13,* 405–419.

Spanos, N.P. (1982). A social psychological approach to hypnotic behaviour. In G. Weary & H.L. Mirels (Eds.), *Integrations of clinical and social psychology.* New York: Oxford University Press.

Spanos, N.P. (1989). Experimental research on hypnotic analgesia. In N.P. Spanos & J.F. Cahves (Eds.), *Hypnosis: The cognitive-behavioural perspective.* Buffalo, NY: Prometheus.

Spanos, N.P., Perlini, A.H., Patrick, L., Bell, S., & Gwynn, M.I. (1990). The role of compliance in hypnotic and nonhypnotic analgesia. *Journal of Research in Personality, 24,* 433–453.

Speisman, J.C., Lazarus, R.S., Mordkoff, A., & Davison, L. (1964). Experimental reduction of stress based on ego-defence theory. *Journal of Abnormal and Social Psychology, 68,* 367–380.

Spelke, E.S., Hirst, W.C., & Neisser, U. (1976). Skills of divided attention. *Cognition, 4,* 215–230.

Sperling, G. (1960). The information available in brief visual presentations. *Psychological Monographs, 74* (Whole No. 498), 1–29.

Sperry, R.W. (1985). Consciousness, personal identity, and the divided brain. In D.F. Benson & E. Zaidel (Eds.), *The dual brain: Hemispheric specialisation in humans.* New York: Guilford Press.

Sperry, R.W., Zaidel, E., & Zaidel, D. (1979). Self recognition and social awareness in the deconnected minor hemisphere. *Neuropsychologia, 17,* 153–166.

Spitz, R.A. (1945). Hospitalism: An inquiry into the genesis of psychiatric conditions in early childhood. *Psychoanalytic Study of the Child, 1,* 113–117.

Spitzer, R.L., & Fleiss, J.L. (1974). A re-analysis of the reliability of psychiatric diagnosis. *British Journal of Psychiatry, 125,* 341–347.

Spitzer, R.L., Williams, J.B.W., Kass, F., & Davies, M. (1989). National field trial of the DSM-III-R diagnostic criteria for self-defeating personality disorder. *American Journal of Psychiatry, 146,* 1561–1567.

Sprafkin, J.N., Liebert, R.M., & Poulos, R.W. (1975). Effects of a pro-social televised example on children's helping. *Journal of Experimental Child Psychology, 20,* 119–126.

Spriggs, W.A. (1998). *Evolutionary psychology and the male criminal mind.* http://www.evoyage.com/criminal.html

Springett, B.P. (1968). Aspects of the relationship between burying beetles, *Necrophorus* spp. and the mite *Poecilochirus necrophori* (Vitz). *Journal of Animal Ecology, 37,* 417–424.

Squire, L.R. (1987). *Memory and brain.* Oxford: Oxford University Press.

Squire, L.R., Knowlton, B., & Musen, G. (1993). The structure and organisation of memory. *Annual Review of Psychology, 44,* 453–495.

Squire, L.R., Ojemann, J.G., Miezin, F.M., Petersen, S.E., Videen, T.O., & Raichle, M.E. (1992). Activation of the hippocampus in normal humans: A functional anatomical study of memory. *Proceedings of the National Academy of Science, USA, 89,* 1837–1841.

Sroufe, L.A., Bennett, C., Englund, M., & Urban, J. (1993). The significance of gender boundaries in preadolescence: Contemporary correlates and antecedents of boundary violation and maintenance. *Child Development, 64,* 455–466.

Stang, D.J. (1972). Conformity, ability, and self-esteem. *Representative Research in Social Psychology, 3,* 97–103.

Steffenburg, S., Gillberg, C., Hellgren, L., Andersson, L., Gillberg, I.C., Jakobsson, G., & Bohman, M. (1989). A twin study of autism in Denmark, Finland, Iceland, Norway, and Sweden. *Journal of Child Psychology and Psychiatry, 30,* 405–416.

Steinhausen, H.C. (1994). Anorexia and bulimia nervosa. In M. Rutter, E. Taylor, & L. Hersov (Eds.), *Child and adolescent psychiatry.* Oxford: Blackwell.

Stemberger, R.T., Turner, S.M., & Beidel, D.C. (1995). Social phobia: An analysis of possible developmental factors. *Journal of Abnormal Psychology, 104,* 526–531.

Stephan, W.G. (1987). The contact hypothesis in intergroup relations. In C. Hendrick (Ed.), *Group processes in intergroup relations: Review of personality and social psychology, Vol. 9*. Newbury Park, CA: Sage.

Stephan, W.G., & Stephan, C.W. (1989). Antecedents of intergroup anxiety in Oriental-Americans and Hispanics. *International Journal of Intercultural Communication, 13*, 203–219.

Steptoe, A. (1997). Stress management. In A. Baum, S. Newman, J. Weinman, R. West, & C. McManus (Eds.), *Cambridge handbook of psychology, health, and medicine*. Cambridge: Cambridge University Press.

Stern, S.L., Rush, J., & Mendels, J. (1980). Toward a rational pharmacotherapy of depression. *American Journal of Psychiatry, 137*, 545–552.

Sternberg, R.J. (1985). *Beyond IQ: A triarchic theory of human intelligence*. Cambridge: Cambridge University Press.

Sternberg, R.J. (1986). A triangular theory of love. *Psychological Review, 93*, 119–135.

Sternberg, R.J. (1994). Intelligence and cognitive styles. In A. M. Colman (Ed.), *Companion encyclopedia of psychology, Vol. 1*. London: Routledge.

Sternberg, R.J. (1995). *In search of the human mind*. New York: Harcourt Brace.

Sternberg, R.J., & Grajek, S. (1984). The nature of love. *Journal of Personality and Social Psychology, 47*, 312–329.

Stevens, J. (1987). Brief psychoses: Do they contribute to the good prognosis and equal prevalence of schizophrenia in developing countries? *British Journal of Psychiatry, 151*, 393–396.

Stevens, R. (1989). *Freud and psychoanalysis*. Milton Keynes: Open University Press.

Stevenson, H.W., & Stigler, J.W. (1992). *The learning gap*. New York: Summit Books.

Stevenson, M.R., & Black, K.N. (1988). Paternal absence and sex-role development: A meta-analysis. *Child Development, 59*, 793–814.

Stogdill, R.M. (1974). *Handbook of leadership: A survey of theory and research*. New York: Free Press.

Stopa, L., & Clark, D.M. (1993). Cognitive processes in social phobia. *Behaviour Research and Therapy, 31*, 255–267.

Storms, M.D. (1973). Videotape and the attribution process: Reversing actors' and observers' points of view. *Journal of Personality and Social Psychology, 27*, 165–175.

Strack, F., Martin, L.L., & Stepper, S. (1988). Inhibiting and facilitating conditions of facial expressions: A non-obtrusive test of the facial feedback hypothesis. *Journal of Personality and Social Psychology, 54*, 768–776.

Streissguth, A.P. (1994). A long-term perspective of FAS. *Alcohol Health and Research World, 18*, 74–81.

Stretch, D.D. (1994). Experimental design. In A.M. Colman (Ed.), *Companion encyclopedia of psychology, Vol. 2*. London: Routledge.

Strober, M., & Humphrey, L.L. (1987). Familial contributions to the aetiology and course of anorexia nervosa and bulimia. Special issue: Eating disorders. *Journal of Consulting and Clinical Psychology, 55*, 654–659.

Stroebe, M.S., Stroebe, W., & Hansson, R.O. (1993). Contemporary themes and controversies in bereavement research. In M.S. Stroebe, W. Stroebe, & R.O. Hansson (Eds.), *Handbook of bereavement: Theory, research and intervention*. New York: Cambridge University Press.

Strupp, H.H. (1996). The tripartite model and the Consumer Reports study. *American Psychologist, 51*, 1017–1024.

Stuart-Hamilton, I. (1994). *The psychology of ageing: An introduction (2nd Edn.)*. London: Jessica Kingsley.

Styles, E.A. (1997). *The psychology of attention*. Hove, UK: Psychology Press.

Suddath, R.L., Christison, G.W., Torrey, E.F., Casanova, M.F., & Weinberger, D.R. (1990). Anatomical abnormalities in the brains of monozygotic twins discordant for schizophrenia. *New England Journal of Medicine, 322*, 789–794.

Sue, S., Fujino, D.C., Hu, L., Takeuchi, D.T., & Zane, N.S.W. (1991). Community mental health services for ethnic minority groups: A test of the cultural responsiveness hypothesis. *Journal of Consulting and Clinical Psychology, 59*, 533–540.

Sulin, R.A., & Dooling, D.J. (1974). Intrusion of a thematic idea in retention of prose. *Journal of Experimental Psychology, 103*, 255–262.

Sullivan, L. (1976). Selective attention and secondary message analysis: A reconsideration of Broadbent's filter model of selective attention. *Quarterly Journal of Experimental Psychology, 28*, 167–178.

Sulloway, E. (1994). *Born to rebel: Radical thinking in science and social thought*. Unpublished MS, Cambridge, MA: MIT Press.

Symington, T., Currie, A.R., Curran, R.S., & Davidson, J. (1955). The reaction of the adrenal cortex in conditions of stress. In *Ciba Foundations Colloquia on Endocrinology, 20*, 156–164.

Szasz, T.S. (1962). *The myth of mental illness: Foundation of a theory of personal conduct*. New York: Hoeber-Harper.

Szasz, T.S. (1974). *The age of madness: The history of involuntary hospitalisation*. New York: Jason Aronson.

Tache, J., Selye, H., & Day, S. (1979). *Cancer, stress, and death*. New York: Plenum Press.

Taguiri, R. (1969). Person perception. In G. Lindzey & E. Aronson (Eds.), *Handbook of social psychology, Vol. 3*. Reading, MA: Addison-Wesley.

Tajfel, H. (1978). Intergroup behaviour. 1: Individualistic perspectives. In H. Tajfel, & C. Fraser (Eds.), *Introducing social psychology*. Harmondsworth: Penguin.

Tajfel, H. (1981). *Human groups and social categories: Studies in social psychology*. Cambridge: Cambridge University Press.

Tajfel, H., Flament, C., Billig, M.G., & Bundy, R.P. (1971). Social categorisation and intergroup behaviour. *European Journal of Social Psychology, 1*, 149–178.

Tajfel, H., & Turner, J.C. (1979). An integrative theory of intergroup conflict. In W.C. Austin & S. Worchel (Eds.), *The social psychology of intergroup relations*. Monterey, CA: Brooks/Cole.

Tallamy, D.W. (1984). Insect parental care. *Bioscience, 34*, 20–24.

Taraban, R., & McClelland, J.L. (1988). Constituent attachment and thematic role assignment in sentence processing: Influences of content-based expectations. *Journal of Memory and Language, 27*, 597–632.

Taylor, A., Sluckin, W., Davies, D.R., Reason, J.T., Thomson, R., & Colman, A.M. (1982). *Introducing psychology (2nd Edn.)*. Harmondsworth: Penguin.

Taylor, H. (1964). Programmed instruction in industry: A review of the literature. *Personnel Practice Bulletin, 20*, 14–27.

Teitelbaum, P. (1957). Random and food-directed activity in hyperphagic and normal rats. *Journal of Comparative and Physiological Psychology, 50*, 486–490.

Temple, C., & Marshall, J.C. (1983). A case study of developmental phonological dyslexia. *British Journal of Psychology, 74,* 517–533.

Terman, M. (1988). On the question of mechanism in phototherapy for seasonal affective disorder: Considerations of clinical efficacy and epidemiology. *Journal of Biological Rhythms, 3,* 155–172.

Terrace, H.S. (1979). *Nim.* New York: Alfred Knopf.

Terrace, H.S., Petitto, L.A., Sanders, D.J., & Bever, T.G. (1979). On the grammatical capacities of apes. In K. Nelson (Ed.), *Children's language, Vol. 2.* New York: Gardner Press.

Tester, N. (1998). Forty minutes that changed everything. The Independent Magazine, 10th October, 1998.

Teuting, P., Rosen, S., & Hirschfeld, R. (1981). *Special report on depression research.* NIMH-DHHS Publication No. 81–1085: Washington, DC.

Thibaut, J.W., & Kelley, H.H. (1959). *The social psychology of groups.* New York: Wiley.

Thigpen, C.H., & Cleckley, H.M. (1957). *The three faces of Eve.* New York: Fawcett.

Thoits, P.A. (1982). Direct, indirect, and moderating effects of social support on psychological distress and associated conditions. In H.B. Kaplan (Ed.), *Psychosocial stress: Trends in theory and research.* New York: Academic Press.

Thomas, J., & Blackman, D. (1991). Are animal experiments on the way out? *The Psychologist, 4,* 208–212.

Thomas, M.H., Horton, R.W., Lippincott, E.C., & Drabman, R.S. (1977). Desensitisation to portrayals of real-life aggression as a function of exposure to television violence. *Journal of Personality and Social Psychology, 35,* 450–458.

Thompson, J.N. (1982). *Interaction and coevolution.* New York: Wiley.

Thompson, L.W., Gallagher-Thompson, D.G., & Futterman, A. (1991). The effects of late-life spousal bereavement over a 30-month internal. *Psychology and Aging, 6,* 434–441.

Thompson, W.C., Cowan, C.L., & Rosenhan, D.L. (1980). Focus of attention mediates the impact of negative affect on altruism. *Journal of Personality and Social Psychology, 38,* 291–300.

Thorndike, E.L. (1911). *Animal intelligence: Experimental studies.* New York: MacMillan.

Thornhill, R. (1980). Rape in *Panorpa* scorpionflies and a general rape hypothesis. *Animal Behaviour, 28,* 52–59.

Tieger, T. (1980). On the biological basis of sex differences in aggression. *Child Development, 51,* 943–963.

Tienari, P. (1991). Interaction between genetic vulnerability and family environment: The Finnish adoptive family study of schizophrenia. *Acta Psychiatrica Scandinavica, 84,* 460–465.

Tinbergen, N. (1951). *The study of instinct.* Oxford: Oxford University Press.

Tinbergen, N. (1959). Comparative studies of the behaviour of gulls (Laridae): A progress report. *Behaviour, 15,* 1–70.

Tinbergen, N. (1963). On aims and methods of ethology. *Zeitschrift für Tierpsychologie, 20,* 410–433.

Tizard, B. (1977). *Adoption: A second chance.* London: Open Books.

Tizard, B. (1986). *The care of young children.* London: Institute of Education.

Tizard, B., & Hodges, J. (1978). The effect of early institutional rearing on the development of eight-year-old children. *Journal of Child Psychology and Psychiatry, 19,* 99–118.

Tolman, E.C., & Honzik, C.H. (1930). Introduction and removal of reward and maze learning in rats. *University of California Publications in Psychology, 4,* 257–275.

Tolstedt, B.E., & Stokes, J.P. (1984). Self-disclosure, intimacy, and the depenetration process. *Journal of Personality and Social Psychology, 46,* 84–90.

Tomarken, A.J., Mineka, S., & Cook, M. (1989). Fear-relevant associations and covariation bias. *Journal of Abnormal Psychology, 98,* 381–394.

Tomlinson-Keasey, C., & Keasey, C.B. (1974). The mediating role of cognitive development in moral judgement. *Child Development, 45,* 291–298.

Tomlinson-Keasey, C., Eisert, D.C., Kahle, L.R., Hardy-Brown, K., & Keasey, B. (1979). The structure of concrete-operational thought. *Child Development, 57,* 1454–1463.

Tompkins, C.A., & Mateer, C.A. (1985). Right hemisphere appreciation of intonational and linguistic indications of affect. *Brain and Language, 24,* 185–203.

Torgersen, S. (1983). Genetic factors in anxiety disorders. *Archives of General Psychiatry, 40,* 1085–1089.

Tout, K. (1989). *Ageing in developing countries.* Oxford: Oxford University Press.

Towhey, J.C. (1979). Sex-role stereotyping and individual differences in liking for the physically attractive. *Social Psychology Quarterly, 42,* 285–289.

Townsend, P., & Davidson, N. (1982). *Inequalities in health: The Black report.* Harmondsworth: Penguin.

Treisman, A.M. (1964). Verbal cues, language, and meaning in selective attention. *American Journal of Psychology, 77,* 206–219.

Treisman, A.M. (1988). Features and objects: The fourteenth Bartlett memorial lecture. *Quarterly Journal of Experimental Psychology, 40A,* 201–237.

Treisman, A.M., & Geffen, G. (1967). Selective attention: Perception or response? *Quarterly Journal of Experimental Psychology, 19,* 1–18.

Treisman, A.M., & Gelade, G. (1980). A feature integration theory of attention. *Cognitive Psychology, 12,* 97–136.

Treisman, A.M., & Riley, J.G.A. (1969). Is selective attention selective perception or selective response: A further test. *Journal of Experimental Psychology, 79,* 27–34.

Treisman, A.M., & Sato, S. (1990). Conjunction search revisited. *Journal of Experimental Psychology: Human Perception and Performance, 16,* 459–478.

Treisman, A.M., & Schmidt, H. (1982). Illusory conjunctions in the perception of objects. *Cognitive Psychology, 14,* 107–141.

Tresilian, J.R. (1994). Two straw men stay silent when asked about the "direct" versus "inferential" controversy. *Behavioral and Brain Sciences, 17,* 335–336.

Triandis, H.C. (1993). The contingency model in cross-cultural perspective. In M.M. Chemers & R. Ayman (Eds.), *Leadership theory and research: Perspectives and directions.* San Diego, CA: Academic Press.

Triandis, H.C. (1994). *Culture and social behaviour.* New York: McGraw-Hill.

Triandis, H.C., & Vassiliou, V. (1967). A comparative analysis of subjective culture. In H.C. Triandis (Ed.), *The analysis of subjective culture.* New York: Wiley.

Trivers, R. (1985). *Social evolution.* Menlo Park, CA: Benjamin/Cummings.

Trivers, R.L. (1971). The evolution of reciprocal altruism. *Quarterly Review of Biology, 46*, 35–57.

Trivers, R.L. (1972). Parental investment and sexual selection. In B. Campbell (Ed.), *Sexual selection and the descent of man, 1871–1971*. Chicago: Aldine.

Trivers, R.L. (1974). Parent–offspring conflict. *American Zoologist, 14*, 249–264.

Trivers, R.L., & Hare, H. (1976). Haplodiploidy and the evolution of the social insects. *Science, 191*, 249–263.

Truax, C.B. (1966). Therapist empathy, genuineness, and warmth and patient therapeutic outcome. *Journal of Consulting Psychology, 30*, 395–401.

Truax, C.B., & Mitchell, K.M. (1971). Research on certain therapist interpersonal skills in relation to process and outcome. In A.E. Bergin & S.L. Garfield (Eds.), *Handbook of psychotherapy and behaviour change*. Chichester: Wiley.

True, W.R., Rice, J., Eisen, S.A., Heath, A.C., Goldberg, J., Lyons, M.J., & Nowak, J. (1993). A twin study of genetic and environmental contributions to liability for posttraumatic stress symptoms. *Archives of General Psychiatry, 50*, 257–264.

Tulving, E. (1972). Episodic and semantic memory. In E. Tulving & W. Donaldson (Eds.), *Organisation of memory*. Hillsdale, NJ: Lawrence Erlbaum Associates Inc.

Tulving, E. (1974). Cue-dependent forgetting. *American Scientist, 62*, 74–82.

Tulving, E. (1979). Relation between encoding specificity and levels of processing. In L.S. Cermak & F.I.M. Craik (Eds.), *Levels of processing in human memory*. Hillsdale, NJ: Lawrence Erlbaum Associates Inc.

Tulving, E. (1989). Memory: Performance, knowledge, and experience. *European Journal of Cognitive Psychology, 1*, 3–26.

Tulving, E., & Pearlstone, Z. (1966). Availability versus accessibility of information in memory for words. *Journal of Verbal Learning and Verbal Behavior, 5*, 381–391.

Tulving, E., & Psotka, J. (1971). Retroactive inhibition in free recall: Inaccessibility of information available in the memory store. *Journal of Experimental Psychology, 87*, 1–8.

Tulving, E., Schachter, D.L., & Stark, H.A. (1982). Priming effects in word-fragment completion are independent of recognition memory. *Journal of Experimental Psychology: Learning, Memory, and Cognition, 17*, 595–617.

Turnbull, C.M. (1961). *The forest people*. New York: Simon & Schuster.

Turnbull, C.M. (1989). *The mountain people*. London: Paladin.

Turner, J.S., & Helms, D.B. (1983). *Lifespan development (2nd Edn.)*. New York: Holt, Rinehart and Winston.

Turner, R.H., & Killian, L.M. (1972). *Collective behaviour (2nd Edn.)*. Englewood Cliffs, NJ: Prentice-Hall.

Turner, R.J., & Wagonfeld, M.O. (1967). Occupational mobility and schizophrenia. *American Sociological Review, 32*, 104–113.

Tversky, A. (1972). Elimination by aspects: A theory of choice. *Psychological Review, 79*, 281–299.

Tversky, A., & Kahneman, D. (1973). Availability: A heuristic for judging frequency and probability. *Cognitive Psychology, 5*, 207–232.

Tversky, A., & Kahneman, D. (1980). Causal schemas in judgements under uncertainty. In M. Fishbein (Ed.), *Progress in social psychology*. Hillsdale, NJ: Erlbaum.

Tversky, A., & Kahneman, D. (1983). Extensional versus intuitive reasoning: The conjunction fallacy in probability judgement. *Psychological Review, 90*, 293–315.

Tversky, A., & Kahneman, D. (1987). Rational choice and the framing of decisions. In R. Hogarth & M. Reder (Eds.), *Rational choice: The contrast between economics and psychology*. Chicago: University of Chicago Press.

Tversky, A., & Shafir, E. (1992). The disjunction effect in choice under uncertainty. *Psychological Science, 3*, 305–309.

Tweney, R.D., Doherty, M.E., Worner, W.J., Pliske, D.B., Mynatt, C.R., Gross, K.A., & Arkelin, D.L. (1980). Strategies for rule discovery in an inference task. *Quarterly Journal of Experimental Psychology, 32*, 109–123.

Tyerman, A., & Spencer, C. (1983). A critical test of the Sherifs' Robbers' Cave experiment: Intergroup competition and co-operation between groups of well-acquainted individuals. *Small Group Behaviour, 14*, 515–531.

Tyrell, J.B., & Baxter, J.D. (1981). Glucocorticoid therapy. In P. Felig, J.D. Baxter, A.E. Broadus, & L.A. Frohman (Eds.), *Endocrinology and metabolism*. New York: McGraw-Hill.

Ucros, C.G. (1989). Mood state-dependent memory: A meta-analysis. *Cognition and Emotion, 3*, 139–167.

Umbenhauer, S.L., & DeWitte, L.L. (1978). Patient race and social class: Attitudes and decisions among three groups of mental health professionals. *Comprehensive Psychiatry, 19*, 509–515.

Underwood, B.J., & Postman, L. (1960). Extra-experimental sources of interference in forgetting. *Psychological Review, 67*, 73–95.

Underwood, G. (1974). Moray vs. the rest: The effects of extended shadowing practice. *Quarterly Journal of Experimental Psychology, 26*, 368–372.

Ungerleider, L.G., & Haxby, J.V. (1994). "What" and "where" in the human brain. *Current Opinion in Neurobiology, 4*, 157–165.

Ungerleider, L.G., & Mishkin, M. (1982). Two cortical visual systems. In D.J. Ingle, M.A. Goodale, & R.J.W. Mansfield (Eds.), *Analysis of visual behaviour*. Cambridge, MA: MIT Press.

Vaillant, C.O., & Vaillant, G.E. (1993). Is the U-curve of marital satisfaction an illusion? A 40-year study of marriage. *Journal of Marriage and the Family, 55*, 230–239.

Vaillant, G.E. (1977). *Adaptation to life: How the best and brightest come of age*. Boston: Little, Brown.

Valentine, E.R. (1982). *Conceptual issues in psychology*. London: Routledge.

Valentine, E.R. (1992). *Conceptual issues in psychology (2nd Edn.)*. London: Routledge.

van Avermaet, E. (1988). Social influence in small groups. In Hewstone, W. Stroebe, J.-P. Codol, & G.M. Stephenson (Eds.), *Introduction to social psychology: A European perspective*. Oxford: Blackwell.

van Avermaet, E. (1996). Social influence in small groups. In M. Hewstone, W. Stroebe, & G.M. Stephenson (Eds.), *Introduction to social psychology (2nd Edn.)*. Oxford: Blackwell.

Vandell, D.L., & Mueller, E.C. (1980). Peer play and friendships during the first two years. In H.C. Foot, A.J. Chapman, & J.R. Smith (Eds.), *Friendship and social relations in children*. Chichester: Wiley.

Vandell, D.L., & Wilson, K.S. (1987). Infants' interactions with mother, sibling, and peer: Contrasts and relations between interaction systems. *Child Development, 59*, 1286–1292.

Van der Kolk, B., Greenberg, M., Boyd, H., & Krystal, J.H. (1985). Inescapable shock, neurotransmitters, and addiction to trauma: Toward a psychobiology of posttraumatic stress. *Biological Psychiatry, 20*, 314–325.

van Dijk, T.A., & Kintsch, W. (1983). *Strategies of discourse comprehension.* London: Academic Press.

Van IJzendoorn, M.H., & Kroonenberg, P.M. (1988). Cross-cultural patterns of attachment: A meta-analysis of the Strange Situation. *Child Development, 59*, 147–156.

Van Kammen, D.P., Docherty, J.P., & Bunney, W.E. (1982). Prediction of early relapse after pimozide discontinuation by response to d-amphetamine during pimozide treatment. *Biological Psychiatry, 17*, 223–242.

Vanneman, R.D., & Pettigrew, T.F. (1972). Race and relative deprivation in the urban United States. *Race, 13*, 461–486.

van Oppen, P., de Haan, E., van Balkom, A.J.L.M., Spinhoven, P., Hoogduin, K., & van Dyck, R.(1995). Cognitive therapy and exposure in vivo in the treatment of obsessive-compulsive disorder. *Behaviour Research and Therapy, 33*, 379–390.

Verburg, K., Griez, E., Meijer, J., & Pols, H. (1995). Respiratory disorders as a possible predisposing factor for panic disorder. *Journal of Affective Disorders, 33*, 129–134.

Verner, J., & Willson, M.F. (1966). The influence of habitats on mating systems of North American passerine birds. *Ecology, 47*, 143–147.

Vernon, P.E. (1972). The distinctiveness of field independence. *Journal of Personality, 40*, 366–391.

Vidich, A.J., & Bensman, J. (1958). *Small town in mass society.* Princeton, NJ: Princeton University Press.

Vivian, J., & Brown, R. (1994). Prejudice and intergroup conflict. In A.M. Colman (Ed.), *Companion encyclopaedia of psychology, Vol. 2.* London: Routledge.

Von Wright, J.M., Anderson, K., & Stenman, U. (1975). Generalisation of conditioned GSRs in dichotic listening. In P.M.A. Rabbitt & S. Dornic (Eds), *Attention and performance, Vol. V.* London: Academic Press.

Vygotsky, L.S. (1962). *Thought and language.* Cambridge, MA: MIT Press.

Vygotsky, L.S. (1976). Play and its role in the mental development of the child. In J.S. Bruner, A. Jolly, & K. Sylva (Eds)., *Play.* Harmondsworth: Penguin.

Vygotsky, L.S. (1978). *Mind in society: The development of higher psychological processes.* Cambridge, MA: MIT Press.

Vygotsky, L.S. (1981). The genesis of higher mental functions. In J.V. Wertsch (Ed.), *The concept of activity in Soviet psychology.* Armonk, NY: Sharpe.

Wachtel, P.L. (1973). Psychodynamics, behaviour therapy and the implacable experimenter: An inquiry into the consistency of personality. *Journal of Abnormal Psychology, 82*, 324–334.

Waddington, D., Jones, K., & Critcher, C. (1987). Flashpoints of public disorder. In G. Gaskell & R. Benewick (Eds.), *The crowd in contemporary Britain.* London: Sage.

Wadeley, A.E., Birch, A., & Malim, A. (1997). *Perspectives in psychology (2nd Edn.).* Basingstoke: MacMillan.

Wagstaff, G.F. (1977). An experimental study of compliance and post-hypnotic amnesia. *British Journal of Social and Clinical Psychology, 16*, 225–228.

Wagstaff, G.F. (1991). Compliance, belief and semantics in hypnosis: A non-state sociocognitive perspective. In S.J. Lynn & J.W. Rhue (Eds.), *Theories of hypnosis: Current models and perspectives.* New York: Guilford.

Wagstaff, G.F. (1994). Hypnosis. In A.M. Colman (Ed.), *Companion Encyclopedia of psychology, Vol. 2.* London: Routledge.

Walcott, C., & Green, R.P. (1974). Orientation of homing pigeons altered by a change in the direction of an applied magnetic field. *Science, 184*, 180–182.

Walcott, C., & Schmidt-Koenig, K. (1971). The effect of anaesthesia during displacement on the homing performance of pigeons. *Auk, 90*, 281–286.

Walker, L.J. (1984). Sex differences in the development of moral reasoning: A critical review. *Child Development, 55*, 677–691.

Walker, L.J. (1999). Seedy world: Sexual scandal is rife in the grain store. *New Scientist, 2181*, 12.

Walker, L.J., de Vries, B., & Trevethan, S.D. (1987). Moral stages and moral orientations in real-life and hypothetical dilemmas. *Child Development, 58*, 842–858.

Walker, M. (1999). Seedy world: Sexual scandal is rife in the grain store. *New Scientist, 2181*, 12.

Wallach, L., & Wallach, M.A. (1994). Gergen versus the mainstream: Are hypotheses in social psychology subject to empirical test? *Journal of Personality and Social Psychology, 67*, 233–242.

Walmsley, J., & Margolis, J. (1987). *Hot house people: Can we create super human beings?* London: Pan Books.

Walsh, B.T., Roose, S.P., Glassman, A.H., Gladis, M.A., & Sadik, C. (1985). Depression and bulimia. *Psychosomatic Medicine, 47*, 123–131.

Walster, E., Aronson, V., Abrahams, D., & Rottman, L. (1966). The importance of physical attractiveness in dating behaviour. *Journal of Personality and Social Psychology, 4*, 508–516.

Walster, E., & Walster, G.W. (1969). *A new look at love.* Reading, MA: Addison Wesley.

Walster, E., Walster, G.W., & Berscheid, E. (1978). *Equity: Theory and research.* Boston: Allyn & Bacon.

Walters, J., & Gardner, H. (1986). The crystallizing experience: Discovering an intellectual gift. In R.J. Sternberg & J.E.. Davidson (Eds.), *Conceptions of giftedness.* New York: Cambridge University Press.

Walters, R.H., & Brown, M. (1963). Studies of reinforcement of aggression. III. Transfer of responses to an interpersonal situation. *Child Development, 34*, 536–571.

Wampold, B.E., Mondin, G.W., Moody, M., Stich, F., Benson, K., & Ahn, H. (1997). A meta-analysis of outcome studies comparing bona fide psychotherapies: Empirically, "All must have prizes". *Psychological Bulletin, 122*, 203–215.

Ward, P., & Zahavi, A. (1973). The importance of certain assemblages of birds as "information-centres" for food-finding. *Ibis, 115*, 517–534.

Warr, P.B. (1987). *Work, unemployment and mental health.* Oxford: Clarendon Press.

Warren, R., & Zgourides, G.D. (1991). *Anxiety disorders: A rational-emotive perspective.* New York: Pergamon Press.

Warren, R.M., & Warren, R.P. (1970). Auditory illusions and confusions. *Scientific American, 223*, 30–36.

Warrington, E.K., & Shallice, T. (1972). Neuropsychological evidence of visual storage in short-term memory tasks. *Quarterly Journal of Experimental Psychology, 24*, 30–40.

Wason, P.C. (1960). On the failure to eliminate hypotheses in a conceptual task. *Quarterly Journal of Experimental Psychology, 12*, 129–140.

Wason, P.C. (1968). Reasoning about a rule. *Quarterly Journal of Experimental Psychology, 20*, 273–281.

Wason, P.C., & Shapiro, D. (1971). Natural and contrived experience in reasoning problems. *Quarterly Journal of Experimental Psychology, 23*, 63–71.

Waterman, A.S. (1982). Identity development from adolescence to adulthood: An extension of theory and review of research. *Developmental Psychology, 18,* 341–348.

Waterman, A.S. (1985). Identity in the context of adolescent psychology. *New directions for child development, 30,* 5–24.

Waters, E., Wippman, J., & Sroufe, L.A. (1979). Attachment, positive affect, and competence in the peer group: Two studies in construct validation. *Child Development, 50,* 821–829.

Watkins, M.J., Watkins, O.C., Craik, F.I.M., & Mazauryk, G. (1973). Effect of nonverbal distraction on short-term storage. *Journal of Experimental Psychology, 101,* 296–300.

Watson, J.B. (1913). Psychology as the behaviourist views it. *Psychological Review, 20,* 158–177.

Watson, J.B. (1924). *Psychology from the standpoint of a behaviourist (2nd Edn.).* Philadelphia: Lippincott.

Watson, J.B., & Rayner, R. (1920). Conditioned emotional reactions. *Journal of Experimental Psychology, 3,* 1–14.

Watson, O.M., & Graves, T.D. (1966). Quantitative research in proxemic behaviour. *American Anthropology, 68,* 971–985.

Webb, W.B. (1968). *Sleep: An experimental approach.* New York: Macmillan.

Weinberger, D.A., Schwartz, G.E., & Davidson, J.R. (1979). Low-anxious, high-anxious, and repressive coping styles: Psychometric patterns and behavioural and physiological responses to stress. *Journal of Abnormal Psychology, 88,* 369–380.

Weiner, M.J., & Wright, F.E. (1973). Effects of underlying arbitrary discrimination upon subsequent attitudes toward a minority group. *Journal of Experimental Social Psychology, 3,* 94–102.

Weingarten, H.P., & Kulikovsky, O.T. (1989). Taste-to-postingestive consequence conditioning: Is the rise in sham feeding with repeated experience a learning phenomenon? *Physiology & Behavior, 45,* 471–476.

Weinreich, P. (1979). Ethnicity and adolescent identity conflicts. In S. Khan (Ed.), *Minority families in Britain.* London: Macmillan.

Weir, W. (1984). Another look at subliminal "facts". *Advertising Age,* 15 October, 46.

Weiskrantz, L. (1986). *Blindsight: A case study and its implications.* Oxford: Oxford University Press.

Weiskrantz, L., Warrington, E.K., Sanders, M.D., & Marshall, J. (1974). Visual capacity in the hemianopic field following a restricted occipital ablation. *Brain, 97,* 709–728.

Weissman, M.M., Klerman, G.L., & Paykel, E.S. (1971). Clinical evaluation of hostility in depression. *American Journal of Psychiatry, 39,* 1397–1403.

Weisstein, N., & Harris, C.S. (1974). Visual detection of line segments: An object-superiority effect. *Science, 186,* 752–755.

Weist, R.M. (1972). The role of rehearsal: Recopy or reconstruct? *Journal of Verbal Learning and Verbal Behavior, 11,* 440–445.

Weisz, J.R., Chaiyasit, W., Weiss, B., Eastman, K., & Jackson, E. (1995). A multimethod study of problem behaviour among Thai and American children in school: Teacher reports versus direct observations. *Child Development, 66,* 402–415.

Weisz, J.R., Suwanlert, S., Chaiyasit, W., & Walter, B.R. (1987). Over- and undercontrolled referral problems among children and adolescents from Thailand and the United States: The wat and wai of cultural differences. *Journal of Consulting and Clinical Psychology, 55,* 719–726.

Weltman, G., Smith, J.E., & Egstrom, G.H. (1971). Perceptual narrowing during simulated pressure-chamber exposure. *Human Factors, 13,* 99–107.

Wender, P.H., Kety, S.S., Rosenthal, D., Schulsinger, F., Ortmann, J., & Lunde, I. (1986). Psychiatric disorders in the biological and adoptive families of adopted individuals with affective disorders. *Archives of General Psychiatry, 43,* 923–929.

Werner, C., & Parmalee, P. (1979). Similarity of activity preferences among friends: Those who play together, stay together. *Social Psychology Quarterly, 42,* 62–66.

Wertheimer, M. (1912). Experimental studies on the seeing of motion [translated by T. Shipley]. In *Classics in perception.* Princeton, NJ: Van Nostrand.

Wertsch, J.V., McNamee, G.D., Mclane, J.B., & Budwig, N.A. (1980). The adult–child dyad as a problem-solving system. *Child Development, 51,* 1215–1221.

Westcott, M.R. (1982). Quantitative and qualitative aspects of experienced freedom. *Journal of Mind and Behavior, 3,* 99–126.

Westen, D. (1996). *Psychology: Mind, brain, and culture.* New York: Wiley.

Weston, D.R., & Main, M. (1981). The quality of the toddler's relationship to mother and to father: Related to conflict behaviour and the readiness to establish new relationships. *Child Development, 52,* 932–940.

Wetherell, M. (1982). Cross-cultural studies of minimal groups: Implications for the social identity theory of intergroup relations. In H. Tajfel (Ed.), *Social identity and intergroup relations.* Cambridge: Cambridge University Press.

Wetherell, M., & Potter, J. (1988). Discourse analysis and the identification of interpretive repertoires. In C. Antaki (Ed.), *Analysing everyday explanation: A casebook of methods.* London: Sage.

Wever, R. (1979). *Circadian rhythms system of man: Results of experiments under temporal isolation.* New York: Springer.

Wheatstone, C. (1838). Contributions to the physiology of vision. Part I: On some remarkable and hitherto unobserved phenomena of binocular vision. *Philosophical Transactions of the Royal Society of London, 128,* 371–394.

Wheeler, L.R. (1932). The intelligence of East Tennessee children. *Journal of Educational Psychology, 23,* 351–370.

Wheeler, L.R. (1942). A comparative study of the intelligence of East Tennessee mountain children. *Journal of Educational Psychology, 33,* 321–334.

Wheldall, K., & Poborca, B. (1980). Conservation without conversation: An alternative, non-verbal paradigm for assessing conservation of liquid quantity. *British Journal of Psychology, 71,* 117–134.

White, M.J., Kruczek, T.A., Brown, M.T., & White, G.B. (1989). Occupational sex stereotypes among college students. *Journal of Occupational Behavior, 34,* 289–298.

Whitham, T.G. (1980). The theory of habitat selection examined and extended using Pemphigus aphids. *American Naturalist, 115,* 449–466.

Whiting, B.B., & Whiting, J.W. (1975). *Children of six countries: A psychological analysis.* Cambridge, MA: Harvard University Press.

Whorf, B.L. (1956). *Language, thought, and reality: Selected writings of Benajmain Lee Whorf.* New York: Wiley.

Whyte, W.F. (1943). *Street corner society: The social structure of an Italian slum.* Chicago: University of Chicago Press.

Wickens, C.D. (1984). Processing resources in attention. In R. Parasuraman & D.R. Davies (Eds.), *Varieties of attention*. London: Academic Press.

Wider, E., Johnsen, S., & Balser, E. (1999). Light show. *New Scientist, 2177*, 11.

Wiesenthal, D.L., Endler, N.S., Coward, T.R., & Edwards, J. (1976). Reversibility of relative competence as a determinant of conformity across different perceptual tasks. *Representative Research in Social Psychology, 7*, 35–43.

Wiggins, D.A., & Morris, R.D. (1986). Criteria for female choice of mates: Courtship feeding and paternal care in the common tern. *American Naturalist, 128*, 126–129.

Wilder, D.A. (1984). Intergroup contact: The typical member and the exception to the rule. *Journal of Experimental Social Psychology, 20*, 177–194.

Wilkinson, G.S. (1984). Reciprocal food sharing in the vampire bat. *Nature, 308*, 181–184.

Wilkinson, R.T. (1969). Sleep deprivation: Performance tests for partial and selective sleep deprivation. In L.A. Abt & J.R. Reiss (Eds.), *Progress in clinical psychology*. New York: Grune & Stratton.

Williams, J.E., & Best, D.L. (1990). *Measuring sex stereotypes: A multination study*. Newbury Park, CA: Sage.

Williams, R.L. (1972). *The BITCH Test (Black Intelligence Test of Cultural Homogeneity)*. St. Louis, MI: Washington University.

Williams, T.M. (Ed.) (1986). *The impact of television: A national experiment in three communities*. New York: Academic Press.

Williams, T.P., & Sogon, S. (1984). Group composition and conforming behaviour in Japanese students. *Japanese Psychological Research, 26*, 231–234.

Wills, T.A. (1985). Supportive function of interpersonal relationships. In S. Cohen & S.L. Syme (Eds.), *Social support and health*. Orlando, FL: Academic Press.

Wilson, E.O. (1975). *Sociobiology: The new synthesis*. Harvard: Harvard University Press.

Wilson, E.O. (1978). *On human nature*. Cambridge, MA: Harvard University Press.

Wiltschko, W. (1972). The influence of magnetic total intensity and inclination on directions preferred by migrating European robins (*Erithacus rubecula*). In S.R. Galler (Ed.), *Animal orientation and navigation*. Science and Technical Information Office, NASA Special Publications, Washington, DC.

Winch, R.F. (1958). *Mate selections: A study of complementary needs*. New York: Harper.

Windgassen, K. (1992). Treatment with neuroleptics: The patient's perspective. *Acta Psychiatrica Scandinavica, 86*, 405–410.

Winson, H. (1997). The relationship of dissociative conditions to sleep and dreaming. In S. Krispner & S.M. Powers (Eds.), *Broken images, broken selves: Dissociative narratives in clinical practice*. Bristol, PA: Brunner/Mazel.

Wise, T. (1978). Where the public peril begins: A survey of psychotherapists to determine the effects of Tarasoff. *Stanford Law Review, 31*, 165–190.

Wish, M., Deutsch, M., & Kaplan, S.J. (1976). Perceived dimensions of interpersonal relations. *Journal of Personality and Social Psychology, 33*, 409–420.

Witkin, H.A. (1967). A cognitive style approach to cross-cultural research. *International Journal of Psychology, 2*, 233–250.

Witkin, H.A., & Berry, J.W. (1975). Psychological differentiation in cross-cultural perspective. *Journal of Cross-Cultural Psychology, 6*, 4–87.

Witkin, H.A., Dyke, R.B., Faterson, H.F., Goodenough, D.R., & Karp, S.A. (1962). *Psychological differentiation*. New York: Wiley.

Wittgenstein, L. (1953). *Philosophical investigations*. New York: Macmillan.

Wolpe, J. (1958). *Psychotherapy by reciprocal inhibition*. New York: Pergamon Press.

Wood, D.J., Bruner, J.S., & Ross, G. (1976). The role of tutoring in problem solving. *Journal of Child Psychology and Psychiatry, 17*, 89–100.

Wood, J.T., Dendy, L.L., Dordek, E., Germany, M., & Varallo, S. (1994a). The dialectic of difference: A thematic analysis of intimates' meanings for differences. In K. Carter & M Presnell (Eds.), *Interpretive approaches to interpersonal communication*. New York: SUNY Press.

Wood, J.T., & Duck, S. (1995) (Eds). *Understanding relationships: Off the beaten track*. Thousand Oaks: Sage.

Wood, R.E., Mento, A.J., & Locke, E.A. (1987). Task complexity as a moderator of goal effects: A meta-analysis. *Journal of Applied Psychology, 72*, 416–425.

Wood, W., Lundgren, S., Ouellette, J.A., Busceme, S., & Blackstone, T. (1994b). Minority influence: A meta-analytic review of social influence processes. *Psychological Bulletin, 115*, 323–345.

Wood, W., Wong, F.Y., & Chachere, J.G. (1991). Effects of media violence on viewers' aggression in unconstrained social interaction. *Psychological Bulletin, 109*, 371–383.

Woods, S.C., Lotter, E.C., McKay, L.D., & Porte, D. (1979). Chronic intracerebroventricular infusion of insulin reduces food intake and body weight of baboons. *Nature, 282*, 503–505.

Woodworth, R.S. (1918). *Dynamic psychology*. New York: Columbia University Press.

Woodworth, R.S., & Schlosberg, H. (1954). *Experimental psychology (2nd Edn.)*. New York: Holt, Rinehart, & Winston.

Worell, J., & Remer, P. (1992). *Feminist perspectives in therapy*. Chichester: Wiley.

World Health Organisation (1981). *International classification of diseases and related health problems*. Geneva: WHO.

Wrangham, R.W., & Rubenstein, D.I. (1986). Social evolution in birds and mammals. In D.I. Rubenstein & R.W. Wrangham (Eds.), *Ecological aspects of social evolution*. Princeton, NJ: Princeton University Press.

Yaguchi, K., Otsuka, T., Fujita, T., & Hatano, S. (1987). The relationships between the emotional status and physical activities of the Japanese elderly. *Journal of Human Development, 23*, 42–47.

Yarrow, M.R., Scott, P.M., & Waxler, C.Z. (1973). Learning concern for others. *Developmental Psychology, 8*, 240–260.

Yeates, K.O., MacPhee, D., Campbell, F.A., & Ramey, C.T. (1983). Maternal IQ and home environment as determinants of early childhood intellectual competence: A developmental analysis. *Developmental Psychology, 19*, 731–739.

Yelsma, P., & Athappily, K. (1988). Marital satisfaction and communication practices: Comparisons among Indian and American couples. *Journal of Comparative Family Studies, 19*, 37–54.

Young, W.C., Goy, R.W., & Phoenix, C.H. (1964). Hormones and sexual behaviour. *Science, 143*, 212–219.

Zach, R. (1979). Shell dropping: Decision making and optimal foraging in Northwestern crows. *Behaviour, 68,* 106–117.

Zahavi, A. (1977). The cost of honesty (further remarks on the handicap principle). *Journal of Theoretical Biology, 67,* 603–605.

Zahavi, A. (1987). The theory of signal selection and some of its implications. In V.P. Delfino (Ed.), *International symposium of biological evolution.* Bari, Italy: Adriatica Editrice.

Zahavi, S., & Asher, S.R. (1978). Aggressive behaviour in adolescents. *Journal of School Psychology, 16,* 146–153.

Zahn-Waxler, C., Radke-Yarrow, M., & King, R.A. (1979). Child rearing and children's prosocial initiations toward victims of distress. *Child Development, 50,* 319–330.

Zaidel, E. (1983). A response to Gazzaniga. *American Psychologist, 38,* 542–546.

Zajonc, R.B. (1980). Feeling and thinking: Preferences need no inferences. *American Psychologist, 35,* 151–175.

Zajonc, R.B. (1984). On the primacy of affect. *American Psychologist, 39,* 117–123.

Zametkin, A.J., Nordahl, T.E., Gross, M., King, A.C., Semple, W.E., Rumsey, J., Hamburger, S., & Cohen, R.M. (1990). Cerebral glucose metabolism in adults with hyperactivity of childhood onset. *The New England Journal of Medicine, 20,* 1361–1366.

Zanot, E.J., Pincus, J.D., & Lamp, E.J. (1983). Public perceptions of subliminal advertising. *Journal of Advertising, 12,* 37–45.

Zegoib, L.E., Arnold, S., & Forehand, R. (1975). An examination of observer effects in parent–child interactions. *Child Development, 46,* 509–512.

Zeki, S. (1992). The visual image in mind and brain. *Scientific American, 267,* 43–50.

Zeki, S. (1993). *A vision of the brain.* Oxford: Blackwell.

Zigler, E.F., Abelson, W.D., & Seitz, V. (1973). Motivational factors in the performance of economically disadvantaged children on the Peabody Picture Vocabulary Test. *Child Development, 44,* 294–303.

Zigler, E.F., & Cascione, R. (1984). Mental retardation: An overview. In E.S. Gollin (Ed.), *Malformations of development: Biological and psychological sources and consequences.* New York: Academic Press.

Zihl, J., von Cramon, D., & Mai, N. (1983). Selective disturbance of movement vision after bilateral brain damage. *Brain, 106,* 313–340.

Zillmann, D. (1979). *Hostility and aggression.* Hillsdale, NJ: Erlbaum.

Zillmann, D., Johnson, R.C., & Day, K.D. (1974). Attribution of apparent arousal and proficiency of recovery from sympathetic activation affecting excitation transfer to aggressive behaviour. *Journal of Experimental Social Psychology, 10,* 503–515.

Zimbardo, P. (1969). The human choice: Individuation, reason, and order versus deindividuation, impulse, and chaos. In W.J. Arnold & D. Levine (Eds.), *Nebraska Symposium on Motivation, 17.* Lincoln, NE: University of Nebraska Press.

Zimbardo, P.G. (1973). On the ethics of intervention in human psychological research: With special reference to the Stanford prison experiment. *Cognition, 2,* 243–256.

Zubek, J.P. (1969). *Sensory deprivation: Fifteen years of research.* New York: Appleton-Century-Crofts.

Zubin, J., Eron, L.D., & Shumer, F. (1965). *An experimental approach to projective techniques.* New York: Wiley.

Zuckerman, M. (1987). All parents are environmentalists until they have their second child. *Behavioral and Brain Sciences, 10,* 42–43.

Zuckerman, M. (1989). Personality in the third dimension: A psychobiological approach. *Personality and Individual Differences, 10,* 391–418.

Author Index

Subject Index

moral development, 446, 447
phobia development, 689–690
Observer discomfort, 643
Occipital lobes, 45, 77–78
Octopus
adaptation by, 162
operant conditioning, 236
Odour and navigation, 244
Oedipus complex, **17**, 17, **440**, 440
Oestrogen, 455
Off-centre cells, 88
Old age, 480–485, 492
On-centre cells, 88
"One is a bun", 340–341
One-trial learning, 231–232
Open words, 347–348
Operant conditioning, **23**, 23, 232–237, 256, **350**, 350
Operationalisation, **823**, 823, **840**, 840
Operative schemes, 424
Opiates, 60–62
Opponent-process theory, 92–93
Opportunity sampling, **837**, 837
Optic array, **277**, 277
Optic chiasma, 87
Optic flow patterns, **277**, 277
Optical dye techniques, 76
Optimal foraging theory, 238–240
Ordinal data, **871**, 871
Organisational behaviour modification, **24**, 24, 26–27
Orthetrum cancellatum, 187
Osmosis, 131
Osprey foraging behaviour, 239
Ostrich group living, 212, 213
Outgroups, **509**, 509
Ovaries, 50
Overcrowding, 578
Over-extension, **347**, 347
Over-regularisation, **348**, 348
Oxygen deprivation at birth, 619
Oxytocin, 50
Oystercatchers, parental care, 192

Pancreas, 51
Panic attacks, 685–686
Panic disorder with agoraphobia, **686**, 686–687, 690, 691
Panting, 53
Papez circuit, **138**, 138
Papez–McLean limbic model, 138–139
Parachlorophenylalanine, 57
Paradigm, **772**, 772–774
Parametric tests, **871**, 871
Paranoia, 825
Paranoid schizophrenia, 673
Parasympathetic nervous system, 48–49
Parathyroid gland, 51
Parent-offspring conflict, 196–201, 203, 250–252
Parental care, 192–193, 202, 206
Parental investment, **183**, 183, 184, 201–202
Parental rejection, 402
Parental stress, 486–487

Parental style, 402
attention-deficit hyperactivity disorder, 630
autism, 633
cross-cultural differences, 402
field dependency, 285
moral development, 448
phobia development, 690–691
self-esteem development, 402, 465
sociability, 384
Parietal lobes, 45, 77
Parkinson's disease, 56, 675, 711
Parsing, **352**, 352–353
Parthenogenesis, **181**, 181
Participants in research, 785–793, 808, 810–811
confidentiality, **790**, 790
debriefing, **789**, 789–790
informed consent, **788**, 788
reactivity, **851**, 851
right to withdraw, **789**, 789
selection, 814–815, 836–838
Parvocellular pathway, 87
Passerine mating behaviour, 196
Past tense acquisition, 348
Pathogens, **150**, 150
Pattern recognition, **272**, 272–276, 288
computational theory, 274–275
feature theories, 273
recognition-by-components, 275–276
structural descriptions, 274
template theories, 272
Pavlov, Ivan, 23, 230
PCP (phencyclidine), 63, 64
PCPA (parachlorophenylalanine), 57
Peacock tail length, 167
Peak experiences, **28**, 28
Peer tutoring, **427**, 427–428
Penguins, parental care, 192
Peppered moth, 164–165
Peptides and eating behaviour, 130
Perception, **259**, 259–289, *see also* Visual perception
cross-cultural variations, 285–286, 289
development, 259–264, 287
and emotion, 280
factors affecting, 280, 284–287, 289
individual variations, 284, 286–287, 289
and language, 373–374
and motivation, 280
organisation, 264–268, 288
social variations, 285, 289
subliminal, **760**, 760–761
theories, 276–284, 288–289
Perceptual cycle, 282–283
Perceptual deprivation, 769
Perceptual segregation, 265
Perfectionism, **700**, 700
Performance patterns
sleep-deprivation, 104–105
time of day, 101

Performance versus competence, 417–418
Periaqueductal grey matter, 46
Peripheral nervous system, 44, 46–49
Permissive amine theory, 680
Perseverative search, **411**, 411, 412
Person-centred therapy, *see* Client-centred therapy
Person-situation controversy, 748
Personal space, **578**, 578–579
Personalities, multiple, 115
Personality, **744**, 744
authoritarian, **512**, 512–513
Big Five model, 747, 753–754
and bystander intervention, 595
changes in adulthood, 475–480, 492
Freudian theory, 18, 19, 22
genetic factors, 752–753
and happiness, 485
and leadership, 572
relationship formation, 533
trait theories, 747, 750–755, 757
Personality testing, 744–749, 756–757
faking, 747
job performance prediction, 748–749
job satisfaction prediction, 749
reliability, 745–746
validity, 746
Personnel selection, 748–749
Persuasion, **759**, 759–760, 762–766
PET scans, **72**, 72–73
Phencyclidine (PCP), 63, 64
Phenomenology, **27**, 27, 30, **775**, 775
Phenothiazines, **675**, 675
Phenotype, **432**, 432, **741**, 741
Phenylketonuria, 618, 653
Pheromones, 220
Phobias, 684–691, 702
agoraphobia, 685–687, 690
anthrophobia, 687
arousal level, 687
behavioural theory, 688–690
cognitive biases, 690
cynophobia, 689
desensitisation therapy, 26, 716
exposure/flooding therapy, **715**, 715
genetic factors, 686–687
hippophobia, 687
life events, 691
monophobia, 685
nyctophobia, 689
observational learning, 689–690
parental style, 690–691
prevalence, 690
psychodynamic theory, 688
siderophobia, 685
social, 685, 687, 690
specific, 684–685, 687, 690
taphophobia, 689
therapy for, 26, 715–716
triskaidekaphobia, 685
Phonological loop, **319**, 319, 320
Phonology, 346
Phototherapy, 102

Illustration Credits

Brian Rogers/Biofotos. Page 222 (bottom): Heather Angel/Biofotos. Page 225: TRIP.

Chapter 10
Page 228: Popperfoto/Reuters. Page 229: Popperfoto/Reuters. Page 231: Heather Angel/Biofotos. Page 234: Popperfoto. Page 237: Reproduced with kind permission of Professor Albert Bandura. Page 239: TRIP. Page 247: Photograph by Mike Nichols. Page 248: From E.S. Savage-Rumbaugh and R. Lewin (1994), *Kanzi: At the brink of the human mind.* New York: Wiley. Copyright © 1994, reprinted by permission of John Wiley & Sons, Inc. Page 251: TRIP. Page 252: Popperfoto/Reuters. Page 253: Popperfoto. Page 256: TRIP.

Chapter 11
Page 258: Popperfoto. Page 259: Popperfoto. Page 261: Photograph by David Linton, in *Scientific American.* Reproduced with permission. Page 268: Popperfoto. Page 275: Photographed and supplied by Bipinchandra J. Mistry. Page 275: Photographed and supplied by Bipinchandra J. Mistry. Page 277: TRIP. Page 282: Photographed and supplied by Bipinchandra J. Mistry. Page 283: Photographed and supplied by Bipinchandra J. Mistry. Page 284: Popperfoto. Page 286: TRIP. Page 288: Lupe Cunha Photographer and Photo Library.

Chapter 12
Page 290: Popperfoto. Page 291: Popperfoto. Page 292: Eliza Armstrong/Impact. Page 299: Photofusion/Louis Quail. Page 301: Popperfoto. Page 304: TRIP. Page 311: TRIP.

Chapter 13
Page 314: Photofusion/Wayne Tippetts. Page 315: Photofusion/Wayne Tippetts. Page 318: Photofusion/David Montford. Page 326: TRIP. Page 332: TRIP. Page 334 (top): VinMag Archive. Page 334 (bottom): TRIP. Page 340: Photofusion/Crispin Hughes.

Chapter 14
Page 344: Popperfoto. Page 345: Homer Sykes/Impact. Page 346: Photos by C. Trevarthen. From C. Trevarthen (1980), Development of interpersonal cooperative understanding in infants. In D.R. Olson (Ed.), *The social foundations of language and thought: Essays in honor of Jerome J. Bruner.* New York: W.W. Norton. Copyright © 1980 by David R. Olson. Reprinted by permission of W.W. Norton & Company, Inc. Page 354: TRIP. Page 357: Popperfoto. Page 372: Archives of the History of American Psychology/The University of Akron. Page 378: Steve Benbow/Impact.

Chapter 15
Page 380: Penny Tweedie/Panos Pictures. Page 381: TRIP. Page 382: Popperfoto. Page 382: Popperfoto. Page 383: Sally and Richard Greenhill. Page 386: Reproduced with kind permission of Harlow Primate Laboratory, University of Wisconsin. Page 388: Sean Sprague/Panos Pictures. Page 389: Ben Edwards/Impact. Page 391: Popperfoto. Page 392: Mark Hakansson/Panos Pictures. Page 394: Popperfoto/Reuters. Page 396: Penny Tweedie/Panos Pictures. Page 398: Popperfoto. Page 400: Heldur Netocny/Panos Pictures. Page 405: Penny Tweedie/Panos Pictures.

Chapter 16
Page 408: Photofusion/Bob Watkins. Page 409: Photofusion/Bob Watkins. Page 410 (top): Popperfoto. Page 410 (bottom): From J.J. Ducret (1990), *Jean Piaget: Biographie et parcours intellectuel.* Lausanne, Switzerland: Editions Delachaux et Niestlé. Page 411: Photos by Peter Willatts. Reproduced with permission. Page 421: Photofusion/Bob Watkins. Page 423: Popperfoto. Page 426: Photofusion/Christa Stadtler. Page 427: Lupe Cunha Photographer and Photo Library. Page 428: Photofusion/Ewa Ohlsson. Page 429: Photographed and supplied by Bipinchandra J. Mistry. Page 431: Popperfoto/Reuters. Page 433: Popperfoto.

Chapter 17
Page 438: Popperfoto. Page 439: Popperfoto. Page 444: Photographed and supplied by Bipinchandra J. Mistry. Page 447: Popperfoto. Page 450: Popperfoto. Page 454 (top): TRIP. Page 454 (left): Photofusion/Helen Stone. Page 454 (right): Photofusion/David Montford. Page 457: Photofusion/Crispin Hughes. Page 459: Photos by Donna Bierschwale, courtesy of the University of Southwestern Louisiana. Reproduced with permission. Page 463 (left): Photofusion/David Trainer. Page 463 (right): Photofusion/David Trainer. Page 467: Lupe Cunha Photographer and Photo Library.

Chapter 18
Page 468: Popperfoto/Reuters. Page 469: Popperfoto/Reuters. Page 475: Popperfoto. Page 477: TRIP. Page 480: Popperfoto. Page 481 (top): Photofusion/Paul Baldesare. Page 481 (bottom): Photofusion/Sam Tanner. Page 484 (top): Photofusion/Mark Campbell. Page 484 (bottom): Popperfoto. Page 485: TRIP. Page 487: Photofusion/Reen Pilkington. Page 488: TRIP. Page 489: Popperfoto/Reuters. Page 490: Sally and Richard Greenhill. Page 492: Photofusion/Sam Tanner.

Chapter 19
Page 494: Photofusion/Steve Eason. Page 495: Photofusion/Steve Eason. Page 496: Mark Cator/Impact. Page 500: Photofusion/Bob Watkins. Page 504: Photofusion/John Southworth. Page 505: Photofusion/Steve Eason. Page 508: Popperfoto. Page 509 (top): TRIP. Page 509 (bottom left): Bruce Paton/Panos Pictures. Page 509 (bottom centre): Sean Sprague/Panos Pictures. Page 509 (bottom right): Börje Tobiasson/Panos Pictures. Page 511: Popperfoto. Page 513: Popperfoto. Page 514 (top): Popperfoto/Reuters. Page 514 (bottom): Popperfoto. Page 515: Jeremy Hartley/Panos Pictures. Page 520: Photofusion/Emily Barney.

Chapter 20
Page 522: Gisele Wulfsohn/Panos Pictures. Page 523: Gisele Wulfsohn/Panos Pictures. Page 526: Popperfoto. Page 527: TRIP. Page 531 (top left): Popperfoto. Page 531 (top right): Photofusion/David Montford. Page 531 (bottom left): Popperfoto. Page 531 (bottom right): Photofusion/Jane Austin. Page 532: TRIP. Page 534: Popperfoto. Page 535: Popperfoto. Page 539: Photofusion/Debbie Humphry. Page 540: Photofusion/Debbie Humphry. Page 543: Popperfoto. Page 545: Popperfoto/Reuters. Page 546: Popperfoto/Reuters. Page 547: Photofusion/Sarah Wyld. Page 550: Photofusion/Paul Doyle. Page 556: Popperfoto/Reuters.

Chapter 21
Page 554: TRIP. Page 555: TRIP. Page 560: Hulton Getty. Page 561 (left): Popperfoto. Page 561 (right): Popperfoto/Reuters. Page 566: From the film *Obedience.* Copyright © 1965 by Stanley Milgram and distributed by Penn State Media Sales. Permission granted by Alexandra Milgram. Page 568: TRIP. Page 570 (top): Photofusion/Steve Eason. Page 570 (centre): Popperfoto. Page 570 (bottom): TRIP. Page 576: Popperfoto. Page 577: Photofusion/Tomas Carter. Page 579: Popperfoto. Page 580: Popperfoto/Reuters. Page 581: TRIP. Page 582: Popperfoto.

Chapter 22
Page 584: Popperfoto/Reuters. Page 585: Popperfoto/Reuters. Page 586: Photofusion/Paul Doyle. Page 587: Photofusion/Gina Glover. Page 588: Photofusion/Vicky White. Page 589: Popperfoto/Reuters. Page 591: Photofusion/Sam Tanner. Page 594: Popperfoto. Page 597 (top): Photofusion/G. Montgomery. Page 597 (bottom): Photographed by Tom Hunt, supplied by Bipinchandra J. Mistry. Page 600: TRIP. Page 601: Sally and Richard Greenhill.

Page 603: Reproduced by kind permission of Professor Albert Bandura. Page 604: Popperfoto. Page 605: Steve Parry/Impact. Page 606: Photofusion/Sam Scott Hunter. Page 607: Alex MacNaughton/Impact. Page 609: VinMag Archive. Page 610: TRIP. Page 611: TRIP.

Chapter 23
Page 614: Popperfoto. Page 615: Popperfoto. Page 618: Photofusion/David Montford. Page 620: Photofusion/David Tothill. Page 623: TRIP. Page 624: Popperfoto/Reuters. Page 628: TRIP. Page 630: Photographed and supplied by Bipinchandra J. Mistry. Page 632: VinMag Archive. Page 634: From L. Selfe (1976), *An autistic child with exceptional drawing ability*. New York, Plenum Press. Reproduced with permission. Page 635: Photofusion/Emily Barney. Page 637: Popperfoto/Reuters. Page 639: Popperfoto/Reuters.

Chapter 24
Page 642: Alex MacNaughton/Impact. Page 643: Photofusion/Peter Marshall. Page 644: Photofusion/David Montford. Page 654: TRIP. Page 658: Photofusion/David Montford. Page 659: Lupe Cunha Photographer and Photo Library. Page 663: Photofusion/Bob Watkins. Page 664: Photofusion/Louis Quail. Page 667: Photofusion/Ingrid Gavshon.

Chapter 25
Page 670: Sally and Richard Greenhill. Page 671: Sally and Richard Greenhill. Page 672: Photofusion/Paul Baldesare. Page 673: Photofusion/Debbie Humphry. Page 675: Photofusion/Linda Sole. Page 676: Popperfoto. Page 681: Photofusion/Steve Eason. Page 683: Photofusion/Crispin Hughes. Page 684: Popperfoto. Page 688 (top): TRIP. Page 688 (bottom): Reproduced with the kind permission of Benjamin Harris, University of Wisconsin. Page 689: Popperfoto. Page 695: TRIP. Page 696: Sally and Richard Greenhill. Page 697: Sally and Richard Greenhill. Page 699 (left): Popperfoto. Page 699 (centre): Popperfoto. Page 699 (right): Popperfoto/Reuters. Page 703: Popperfoto.

Chapter 26
Page 704: Sally and Richard Greenhill. Page 705: Sally and Richard Greenhill. Page 706: Popperfoto. Page 709: VinMag Archive. Page 713: TRIP. Page 715: Popperfoto. Page 720: Photofusion/Bob Watkins. Page 725 (top): Photofusion/Sarah Saunders. Page 725 (bottom): Photofusion/Debbie Humphry. Page 729: Photofusion/Steve Eason. Page 732: Photofusion/Helen Stone. Page 734 (top): Photofusion/Sarah Saunders. Page 734 (bottom): Popperfoto/Reuters.

Chapter 27
Page 736: TRIP. Page 737: TRIP. Page 743 (top): Photofusion/Crispin Hughes. Page 743 (bottom): Photofusion/Paul Mattsson. Page 746: Photofusion/Debbie Humphry. Page 749: Popperfoto. Page 753: Photofusion/Crispin Hughes. Page 755: Popperfoto/Reuters. Page 756: Popperfoto. Page 766: Photofusion/Crispin Hughes.

Chapter 28
Page 758: Popperfoto. Page 759: Popperfoto. Page 760: Popperfoto. Page 762: Image supplied by the Commission for Racial Equality. Reproduced with permission. Page 764: VinMag Archive. Page 767: Popperfoto. Page 773: Science Photo Library. Page 775: Popperfoto. Page 776: Popperfoto. Page 777: TRIP. Page 780: Anita Corbin/Impact. Page 781: Popperfoto. Page 782: Popperfoto.

Chapter 29
Page 784: Popperfoto/Reuters. Page 785: Popperfoto/Reuters. Page 786: Photofusion/ Janis Austin. Page 787: Reproduced with permission of P.G. Zimbardo Inc. Page 789: Photofusion/Crispin Hughes. Page 790: Photofusion/Steve Eason. Page 794 (top): Popperfoto/Reuters. Page 794 (bottom): TRIP. Page 795: TRIP. Page 796: Photographed and supplied by Bipinchandra J. Mistry. Page 797: Photo by April Ottey. Reproduced with permission of the Chimpanzee and Human Communication Institute, Central Washington University. Page 798: Photofusion/Rob Scott. Page 801: Richard Day/Biofotos. Page 802: Popperfoto. Page 804: Image supplied by the Commission for Racial Equality. Reproduced with permission. Page 805: TRIP. Page 806: Photofusion/David Montford. Page 807: Photofusion/George Montgomery. Pages 810-811: *Ethical principles for conducting research with human participants* are Society guidelines and have been reproduced by kind permission of The British Psychological Society.

Chapter 30
Page 812 (top part of montage): Photofusion/Ingrid Gavshon. Page 813: Photographed and supplied by Bipinchandra J. Mistry. Page 814: Photographed and supplied by Bipinchandra J. Mistry. Page 815: Popperfoto/Reuters. Page 816: Jorn Stjerneklar/Impact. Page 817 (top): Popperfoto/Reuters. Page 817 (bottom): Photographed and supplied by Bipinchandra J. Mistry. Page 819: TRIP. Page 820: TRIP. Page 822: Lupe Cunha Photographer and Photo Library. Page 823: Popperfoto. Page 824: Photographed and supplied by Bipinchandra J. Mistry. Page 826: Photofusion/Crispin Hughes. Page 827: Photographed and supplied by Bipinchandra J. Mistry.

Chapter 31
Page 832: Popperfoto/Reuters. Page 833: Popperfoto/Reuters. Page 834: Photofusion/Bob Watkins. Page 837: Photofusion/Peter Marshall. Page 839: Lieba Taylor/Panos Pictures. Page 843: Photofusion/Julia Martin. Page 844 (top): TRIP. Page 844 (bottom): Photofusion/Steve Eason. Page 848: From O. Pfungst (1965), *Clever Hans: The horse of Mr Van Osten*. New York: Holt. (German original, 1908). Page 849: Photofusion/Giles Barnard. Page 852: Popperfoto. Page 854: TRIP.

Chapter 32
Page 856: Popperfoto/Reuters. Page 857: Popperfoto/Reuters. Page 858: Photofusion/Sally Lancaster. Page 860: Popperfoto. Page 861: Popperfoto/Reuters. Page 862 (top): Photofusion/Nick Cobbing. Page 862 (bottom): VinMag Archive. Page 863: Food diaries reproduced from U. Schmidt and J. Treasure (1993), *Getting better bit(e) by bit(e): A survival kit for sufferers of bulimia nervosa and binge eating disorders*. Hove, UK: Psychology Press Ltd. Reproduced with permission.

Appendices
Pages 892–893: Critical values of U for the Mann-Whitney U test from R. Runyon and A. Haber (1976), *Fundamentals of behavioural statistics (3rd edition)*. Reading, MA: McGraw-Hill. Reproduced with permission. Page 894 (top): Sign test values from F. Clegg (1982), *Simple statistics*. Cambridge, UK: Cambridge University Press. Reproduced with permission. Page 894 (bottom): Wilcoxon signed ranks test values from R. Meddis (1975), *Statistical handbook for non-statisticians*. London: McGraw-Hill. Reproduced with permission of the publisher. Page 895: Critical values of Spearman's r from J.H. Zhar (1972), Significance testing of the Spearman Rank Correlation Coefficient. *Journal of the American Statistical Association, 67,* 578-580. Reprinted with permission. Copyright © by the American Statistical Association. All rights reserved. Page 896: Critical values of chi-square abridged from R.A. Fisher and F. Yates (1974), *Statistical tables for biological, agricultural and medical research (6th edition)*. Harlow, UK: Addison Wesley Longman. Reprinted by permission of Pearson Education Ltd.